KV-215-036

WITHDRAWN
RSA LIBRARY
05347

A DIRECTORY OF RARE BOOK AND SPECIAL COLLECTIONS

A DIRECTORY OF
RARE BOOK
AND
SPECIAL COLLECTIONS
IN THE
UNITED KINGDOM
AND THE
REPUBLIC OF IRELAND

Edited by
MOELWYN I WILLIAMS
for the Rare Books Group
of the Library Association

LA
LIBRARY ASSOCIATION
LONDON

 Published by Library Association Publishing Limited, 7 Ridgmount Street, London WC1E 7AE and printed and bound in Great Britain at the University Press, Cambridge.

First published 1985

British Library Cataloguing in Publication Data

A Directory of rare book and special collections
in the United Kingdom and the Republic of Ireland
1. Libraries, Special——Great Britain——Directories
I. Williams, Moelwyn I.
027'.0025'41 Z675.2

ISBN 0 85365 646 0

Designed by Geoff Green
Photoset in Paladium by Library Association Publishing

123458887868584

Contents

Foreword

In the Introduction Moelwyn Williams makes acknowledgement to those who have helped him to bring the *Directory* to the point of publication. My function as Chairman is to add the thanks of the Group to the host of voluntary contributors, to those employing institutions who afforded forms of time off and secondment to some of the contributors, to the British Library Board for its financial support, and, of prime importance, to offer the heartfelt appreciation of the Group to Moelwyn Williams himself.

When the first editor, Stanley Roberts, died, only about 50 of the approximately 1,300 reports that now go to make up the *Directory* had been completed, and it fell to his successor, Moelwyn Williams, until his retirement Keeper of Printed Books in the National Library of Wales, to receive and organize the bulk of the contents of the book, combining this task with that of Chairman of the Rare Books Group (1979–82). To say that the Group is in his debt is an understatement.

The Group is also indebted to those responsible for the care of rare book collections—owners, trustees, committees, curators and library staffs—at the very least for granting access to the Group's organizers and other representatives, but often for much more positive co-operation, for example, in answering questions, completing forms and checking entries. Nor must the Group omit to thank those officials of the British Library and the Library Association who have been generous in the amount of time and attention that they have devoted to advising on and administering applications for grants and matters relating to printing and publication.

The Rare Books Group has for long regarded the compilation of the *Directory* as one of its major objectives, and many members and non-members have been involved, to a greater or lesser extent, in creating it. It is 17 years since the Group instructed its Committee 'to formulate a project' for the recording of rare book collections. If, over the next 17 years, which takes us past the end of the century, even as many people benefit from the *Directory* as have participated in its production, its compilers will have reason for satisfaction.

National Library of Scotland, Edinburgh
October 1984

Robert Donaldson
Chairman, Rare Books Group

Introduction

Background

The publication of the *Directory of Rare Book and Special Collections* marks the culmination of an ambitious project set in train some six years ago by the Rare Books Group of the Library Association. The idea that the Group should aim at producing a *Directory* was first mooted in 1967 by the late Stanley Roberts, MA, formerly Deputy Librarian of the University of Manchester, who eventually undertook its editorship until his untimely death in January 1979. Before his death, Roberts had almost completed the setting up of a network of voluntary regional organizers who accepted the responsibility for gathering information about local collections, and for recruiting local helpers, where necessary, to expedite their work. Since then, however, on account of unforeseen difficulties, many of the organizers have not been able to cover the ground as quickly nor as thoroughly as was originally planned. Any deficiency which may have resulted from these limitations will be made up either by means of a supplementary volume, or in a second edition. Nevertheless, the coverage of libraries in general has been quite substantial, while the work embodied in the *Directory* is surely a unique tribute to the combined voluntary effort of all those who have contributed in different ways to its compilation. In this connection, special mention must be made of the generous grant which the Rare Books Group received from the British Library Board in 1977 toward the expenses involved in collecting and editing the material. The grant not only provided the necessary financial support for the project, but was also an endorsement of the importance which the Group had attached to it, and an expression of the British Library's confidence in our ability to carry it through to a successful conclusion. Without the grant the compilation of the *Directory* would have been considerably more protracted. The *Directory* is further indebted to the British Library for allowing staff time to be devoted to the organization and completion of the formidable section relating to the libraries within the Greater London region. In this context a special debt is owed to Mr J E C Palmer, for his unsparing labour. In addition to his own entry for the British Library itself, his unrivalled knowledge of the libraries in the Greater London area ensured that many of this region's reports were enriched with details that would otherwise have been overlooked.

When I was invited to succeed Stanley Roberts as the editor of the *Directory* in March 1979, the first essential was to translate the relevant files and documents from Manchester University Library to Aberystwyth. The transfer was greatly facilitated by the friendly and enthusiastic co-operation of Mr William Dieneman, the Librarian at the University College of Wales, Aberystwyth, who provided me with the necessary accommodation and other facilities to enable me to carry out my editorial duties in the Hugh Owen Library. This kindness was complemented by the readiness of the University Registrar to allow the University College of Wales to act as the host institution to administer the residue of the British Library grant which was transferred from the University of Manchester, where it had been administered previously under the supervision of its former Librarian and Director, Dr F W Ratcliffe, now Librarian of Cambridge University Library.

Aim

The basic aim of the *Directory* is to bring to the notice of scholars and researchers the location of rare book collections in libraries in the United Kingdom and the Republic of Ireland, and to provide such information about their nature, size and importance as will enable them to assess whether or not further investigation is likely to be to their benefit. It is not possible to offer a generally acceptable definition of 'rare', but in the context of the *Directory* it will signify all printed matter before 1851, as well as later collections of rare material such as first editions, limited editions, and ephemera. It may be argued, too, that 'special collections' in libraries of whatever date imply rarity, and on this basis, these collections also have been included where they have been adjudged to be relevant and appropriate. It was originally intended to include all collections of manuscripts in libraries, but in general it will be found that only those manuscript collections in libraries which relate to their rare book collections (and which enrich the total information about them) have been included in the *Directory*.

Scope

Despite many organizational difficulties, every effort has been made to make the *Directory* as comprehensive as possible. It contains descriptions of rare book collections (and their complementary mss collections) as well as 'special' collections wherever they have been located, in public and national libraries, in libraries of universities, colleges and schools, cathedrals and churches, societies and institutes, and in a limited number of private libraries where there is likely to be some continuity or permanence, and which can be made available to bona fide research workers. It should be mentioned that several private libraries have not been included in the *Directory* because their respective owners, for security reasons, do not wish to publicize their rare collections. (For similar reasons some librarians have also declined to provide descriptions of rare collections in their custody.) However, access to most of the privately-owned libraries will be through an institutional library such as a university or national library, and to those libraries in National Trust Houses in England and Wales, on application to the Libraries Adviser, National Trust, 42 Queen Anne's Gate, London SW1H 9AS. Application for admission to libraries in National Trust for Scotland properties should be made to the Curatorial Department, National Trust for Scotland, 5 Charlotte Square, Edinburgh EH2 4DU.

Arrangement

The names of libraries and institutions have been arranged in alphabetical order within the respective regions. Each library is given its address, telephone number, hours of opening, conditions of admission, research facilities, and a brief history (where provided) with published references. Then follows a description of each collection, giving its origin and history, its size, a chronological summary of its contents and subject fields. Details of catalogues and published references have been included whenever possible.

Acknowledgements

In the process of compiling this *Directory* I have incurred many debts which I would like gratefully to acknowledge here. First of all my warmest thanks must go to the several regional organizers (see Appendix) and their helpers for the kind and friendly co-operation I have had in bringing the work to fruition. In the nature of the case, many reports were submitted earlier than others, and I am grateful to those contributors who have waited patiently for so long before seeing their reports in print. I would also like to express my deep appreciation for the support and encouragement given to me by the officers and members of the Rare Books Group Committee, and in particular by members of its Directory Management Committee. Finally, the lack of uniformity in the way reports were submitted made it necessary to transcribe and rearrange a vast number of entries. In this connection my typist made my work considerably lighter by undertaking the formidable task of converting what was, unavoidably, a mass of untidy manuscripts, into a neat typescript, for which valuable contribution I am immeasurably grateful.

Aberystwyth
October 1984

Moelwyn I Williams
Editor

Abbreviations and Acronyms

Abbott	*Catalogue of 15th century books in the library of Trinity College Dublin in Marsh's Library, Dublin...* by T K Abbott; Dublin: Hodges Figgis; London: Longmans Green, 1905. (Repr New York, B Franklin, 1970, Burt Franklin bibliography and reference series).
Allison and Rogers	A R Allison and D M Rogers, *Biographical Studies, 1534–1829. Materials towards a biographical dictionary of Catholic History in the British Isles from the breach with Rome to Catholic emancipation.* Bognor Regis, 1951–6.
BL	British Library
Black	*A catalogue of pamphlets on economic subjects published between 1750 and 1900...in Irish libraries* by R D Collison Black. Belfast: Queen's University Library, 1969.
BLAISE	British Library Automated Information Service
BLR	*Bodleian Library Record*
BQR	*Bodleian Quarterly Record*
BUCEM	*British union catalogue of early music printed before the year 1801; a record of over one hundred libraries throughout the British Isles*: editor Edith B Schnapper, 2 vols. London, 1957.
BUCoP	British Union Catalogue of Periodicals
c	*circa*
Cat(s)	Catalogue(s)
Cent	Century(ies)
CLW	College of Librarianship, Wales
COM	Computer-Output Microfilm(ing)
Comp	Compiled
Craig 1954	Maurice Craig, *Irish book bindings 1600–1800.* London: Cassell & Co., 1954.
Craig 1976	Maurice Craig, *Irish book bindings* (Irish heritage series 6) Dublin: Eason & Son, 1976.
Craster	Sir E Craster, *History of the Bodleian Library, 1845–1945*, Oxford 1952.
CUI	Catholic University of Ireland
Dict	Dictionary
Don	Donation
EEC	European Economic Community
Esp	Especially
ESTC	Eighteenth Century Short-title Catalogue
FAO	Food and Agriculture Organization
Gen	General
GLC	Greater London Council

Goff	Frederick Richmond Goff (1916–) ed. *Incunabula in American libraries; a third census of fifteenth century books recorded in North American collections.* Reproduced from the annotated copy maintained by F R Goff, compiler and editor. New York, 1973.
GUL	Glasgow University Library
Hain	Ludwig Friedrich Theodor Hain, *Repertorium bibliographicum in quo libri omnes ab arte typographia inventa usque ad annum MD typis expressi...* Milano Görlick, [1948].
Hayes	*Manuscript sources for the history of Irish civilisation* edited by Richard J Hayes. 11 vols. Boston (Mass): G K Hall, 1965. (First supplement 1965–1975. 3 v. Boston...1979).
HMC	Historical Manuscripts Commission
INPADOC	International Patent Documentation Centre (Vienna)
Incl	Including
Ker	Neil Kepley Ker, *Medieval libraries of Great Britain: a list of surviving books.* 2nd ed. London: Royal Historical Society, 1964.
LAR	*Library Association Record*
LC	Library of Congress
LCC	London County Council
LOC	(Project LOC) refers to the pilot project (directed by John Jolliffe) on a union catalogue of early books to (1801) in the British Library, the Bodleian Library and the University of Cambridge Library. The symbols LOC represent the three libraries covered in the catalogue.
Macray	W D Macray, *Annals of the Bodleian Library*, Oxford, 2nd edition Oxford 1890.
Ms(s)	Manuscript(s)
NLS	National Library of Scotland
NLW	National Library of Wales
NRA	National Register of Archives
Obit	Obituary
OCLC	Ohio College Library Center, Inc (USA)
op	Out of print
PLA	Private Libraries Association
Priv pr	Privately printed
Ramage	David Ramage, *A finding list of English books to 1640 in libraries in the British Isles (excluding the national libraries and the libraries of Oxford and Cambridge): based on the numbers in Pollard and Redgrave's Short-title catalogue... 1475–1640*, Durham: Council of the Durham Colleges, 1958.
RBG	Rare Books Group of the Library Association
RIA	Royal Irish Academy
RILM	Répertoire International de Littérature Musicale
RISM	Research Institute for the Study of Man
SCICAT	Science Reference Library Catalogue (BL)
STC	*A short-title catalogue of books printed in England, Scotland and Ireland, and of English books printed abroad 1475–1640.* Compiled by A W Pollard and G R Redgrave...and others. London 1926. (2nd ed rev and enlarged 1976).

TCD	Trinity College Dublin
TLS	*Times Literary Supplement*
tp	Title-page
UCW	University College of Wales, Aberystwyth
UDC	Universal Decimal Classification
v	Volume(s)
Vac	Vacation
WAC	Welsh Agricultural College
Wing	*Short Title Catalogue of books printed in England, Scotland, Ireland, Wales and British America, and of English books printed in other countries 1641–1700.* Compiled by Donald Wing. Columbia University Press, NY (3v) 1945–51. 2nd ed rev. (Vol 1 1972, Vol 2 1982).

THE DIRECTORY

ENGLAND

Avon

Bath

Bath Reference Library (Avon County Library), 18 Queen Square, Bath BA1 2HP. Tel (0225) 28144. Open Mon-Fri 9.30 am-7.30 pm, Sat 9.30 am-5 pm. Admission unrestricted; rare material may be consulted only on prior application. 40 seats in the main reference library; periodicals reading room; photocopying facilities.

Abbey Collection Begun by Bishop Arthur Lake, and added to by local benefactors and visitors, until 1730. In 1895 the library was transferred to the care of Bath Corporation. It comprises 323 v, the bulk of which is 17th cent. It includes four incunabula and 58 v 16th cent.

Ms (author) cat.

Broome Collection Christopher Edmund Broome, one of the leading botanists of his time, bequeathed his library to the Royal Literary and Scientific Institution in 1886. A botanical library, it contains 340 v, many of which are rare items.

Card cat.

Buxton Collection Given to the library in 1950. It contains 200 pamphlets of the Civil War period, most of them with some Somerset interest.

Early Printed Books Built up from various bequests, it consists of 781 v, (160 v presented by Capt F H Huth in 1903) and includes 18 incunabula; rare items on horsemanship; set of Curtis's Botanical Magazine; first editions 18th and 19th cent.

Printed books 1476-1640; cat of incunabula.

French Revolution and Napoleonic newspapers Donated 1924 by Cedric Chivers, who had bought the collection in 1913. It was formed by Hughon & Co of Versailles, and consists of 799 items of contemporary newspapers, mainly French, but other European papers represented.

Sheaf cat.

Jenyns Collection In 1869 the Rev Leonard Jenyns presented the scientific portion of his library to the Royal Literary and Scientific Institution whose collections are now in the care of Avon County Library (Bath Reference Library). The collection contains 1,200 items, mainly works on natural history, including voyages and travels, transactions of societies, eg Geological, Linnaean, Ray, Zoological Society; meteorological records kept by Jenyns and others over long periods. Autograph letters addressed to Jenyns from other naturalists, including Darwin.

Card cat.

Juvenile Collection A collection of c1,385 early children's books given by various donors, containing a number of chapbooks and pre-1851 titles, but most are late 19th cent.

Subject cat (sheaf cat).

Local Collection (Bath) Built up over the years through purchases and donations, it contains 7,753 items and includes various valuable scrapbooks, first editions of Bath books, collections of pamphlets, etc. Particularly rich in prints, engravings and photographs of the City of Bath.

Subject cat (as sheaf cat).

Miles Collection The library of Col S B Miles of Hinton Charterhouse, given by his widow in 1920. It contains 341 v, mainly books of travel of the Middle East, together with some Middle Eastern literature, a number of them in fine bindings.

Napoleon Collection Made up of part of Col Miles's Library (given 1920), and part of Oppenheim's collection (given 1919), it consists of 948 books on Napoleon and the Napoleonic period, with many first editions.

Subject cat (as sheaf cat).

Private Press Books A collection of 520 v bequeathed by Mrs G Molony in 1948, it includes some of the best productions of the Golden Cockerel Press.

Collection of Early Music Given by Alfred Jones, a local secondhand book dealer, between 1915 and 1920, the collection totals 308 v consisting of sheet music, much of it of the 18th cent, including music by Bath composers.

Card cat.

The collection is listed in *The British union catalogue of early music*, ed by E B Schnapper. Butterworth, 1957.

Kingswood School, Lansdown, Bath. Tel (0225) 311627. Open by appointment on application to the headmaster's office. Photocopying facilities available.

The Wesleyana Collection The nucleus of the collection

was donated by John Wesley (1703-91) when he founded the school in 1748. It contains works from his personal library, and extracts and summary versions of various works which he prepared for use in the school. There are *c*500 v, predominantly 18th cent works showing Wesley's interest in science, physics etc, also early hymn books of the Wesley brothers, and some works on Kingswood School; seven autographed letters of John Wesley. Many of Wesley's books are annotated by him. Some earlier works may have belonged to Wesley's father. It is interesting to note that two cartloads of books were lost on the journey from Old Kingswood, Bristol to Bath in 1851.

Ms cat of 1782.

Author subject card cat 1978.

Typescript cat (with briefer description) 1981.

A G Ives, *Kingswood School in Wesley's day and since*, London, 1970.

Royal Photographic Society, The Octagon, Milsom Street, Bath. Tel (0225) 62841. Open 10 am-5.15 pm. The library is open to members and to others on application to the secretary. Photocopying facilities.

The library of the Royal Photographic Society, the Du Mont Collection of books illustrated with early photographs, and the Special Collection of 19th cent books on photography, have been assembled by the Society since its foundation in 1853, and is the oldest photographic library in Britain, if not the world. It holds 10,500 books, of which 1,500 are uncatalogued. The Du Mont Collection and the Special Collection contain 2,000 books relating to photography and photographic processes, and historical works. Apart from these two collections, the library contains predominantly 20th cent material.

Author cat, 1939, with *Supplements* 1952 and 1953.

Periodicals cat, 1952.

Subject cat, 1952, with *Supplement*, 1953.

The Directory of British Photographic Collections, compiled by J Wall, Heinemann, 1977.

University of Bath, Claverton Down, Bath BA2 7AY. Tel (0225) 61233. Open (Term) Mon-Fri 9 am-8.45 pm, Sat 10 am-4.45 pm, Sun 10 am-5.45 pm; (Vacation) Mon-Fri 9 am-5 pm. Admission on written application to the librarian. Microform readers and photocopying facilities.

Library of the Royal Bath and West and Southern Counties Society Assembled by the Society, principally in the 18th and 19th cent, the total stock consists of *c*1,800 items spanning the period from the Society's foundation in 1777 by Edmund Rack (1735-87), with some earlier materials. The books include 4 STC and 6 Wing items; 210 ESTC, 230 19th cent. The periodicals comprise the transactions and journals of this and similar societies, with some agricultural periodicals. With the books they reflect the Society's aim of 'the encouragement of agriculture, arts, manufactures and commerce', with some emphasis on the first. Of exceptional rarity is Vial de St Bel, *Plan for establishing an institution to cultivate and teach veterinary medicine*, 1790 (30p).

Printed cat of 1864 superseded by printed cat of 1964 and Addenda of 1973.

P Bryant, 'The "Bath and West" and its library', *Lib Assoc Record* 72 (1970), p194-6.

Library of the Holburne and Menstrie Museum Assembled by Sir Thomas William Holburne (1793-1874), with about 30 later additions from the library of Sir Frederick Henry Huth (1844-1918), the collection totals 800 books, and includes 1 STC item; 9 English; 2 French 17th cent; 40 English, 116 French, 18th cent; 500 English, 58 French, 51 Italian 19th cent works. Subject coverage is mainly history, topography, travel, antiquities, exploration, with some literature, and a section of *c*30 books on field sports, hippology and the martial arts, added at the beginning of this cent.

Printed cat of 1887.

*c*30 later additions remain uncatalogued.

Bath Chronicle, 18th May, 1918.

Antiquarian Collection Assembled by the University Library, the collection totals *c*250 v, including 3 16th cent, 1 17th cent, 41 18th cent, 92 19th cent, 95 20th cent items, being historical material on architecture, building and related crafts.

The books in this collection appear in the University Library's microfiche cat with the prefix AQ. A select print-out can be produced.

The Pitman Collection Assembled by Sir Isaac Pitman (1813-97), subsequently passed to Pitman Printing Ltd and housed at the company's offices. Now in Bath University Library. The collection contains 4,000 items re-catalogued (as at July 1982) which include 3 STC and 14 Wing items; 1 16th cent; 18 17th cent; 56 18th cent; 1,473 19th cent items. These contain historical material on shorthand dictionaries and handbooks adapted to individual professions etc. Also works of Sir Isaac Pitman and his correspondence with G B Shaw; ephemera, eg menus, greetings cards in shorthand. The material is predominantly in the English language, but there is some foreign material, and material in foreign shorthand systems (European and Asian).

The original card cat is incomplete and unreliable.

The collection is at present being re-catalogued to appear in the University Library's microfiche cat. A print-out can be produced of the Pitman Collection material.

Bristol

Avon County Reference Library, County Central Library, College Green, Bristol BS1 5TL. Tel (0272) 276121. Open Mon-Fri 9.30 am-8 pm, Sat 9.30 am-5 pm. Admission unrestricted; rare material may be consulted only on prior application. Photocopying and microform facilities. Photographic service available.

Bristol Local Studies Collection The collection was begun in 1855 by the then City Librarian, George Pryce, who was a local antiquary of some note. It is thought to have been the first specifically local collection in a public library. There are *c*25,000 printed works in addition to ephemera, maps, illustrations and cuttings, and include all printed material and literary manuscripts likely to be of significance for the study of Bristol history. It also includes the Braikenridge collections (*c*1830-40) of engravings, prints and extracts of Bristol interest, and is rich in 18th cent material. STC and Wing items are separately catalogued in the three published catalogues of early printed books (see General Collections). There are some medieval mss, but the bulk of record material is in Bristol Record Office.

Printed catalogue (*The Bristol Bibliography*) lists accessions to the end of 1916, with supplementary card cat thence to date. Separate indexes or cats of mss, photographs, cuttings.

Chatterton Collection A collection of *c*2,100 items acquired by gift and purchase from about 1855 onwards, and comprising Thomas Chatterton's mss and editions of his works, together with material written about him, which includes books, articles, newspaper cuttings, letters etc and Chattertoniana, 1769 to date. It comprises (a) Richard Smith's collection of volumes, cuttings and ms material, which includes much of George Symes Catcott's collection of Chattertoniana, and his transcripts of Chatterton's works (*c*22 bound v); (b) Michael Lort's collection of volumes, cuttings and ms material (9 bound v); (c) Dean Milles's collection (26 items).

Printed catalogue (1916), supplementary card cat.

Emanuel Green Collection Amassed in connection with the compilation of *Bibliotheca Somersetensis* (3 v, 1902) by Emanuel Green (1832-1919), the collection was received as a bequest in 1920 to the then Bristol City Libraries. It contains over 10,000 items—books, pamphlets and single sheets relating to the history of Somerset and the City of Bath. Strong in early topographical and biographical material. STC and Wing titles from this collection are included (but not identified as such) in the printed catalogues of early books produced by Bristol Reference Library (see note under General Collections).

Marked copies of *Bibliotheca Somersetensis*, supplemented by card cat.

General Collections These date from the founding of Bristol City Library in 1613 and include the stock of the Bristol Library Society and of the Bristol Museum and Library (1773-1893) which total 266,000 v. This grand total includes the special collections itemized separately, and also the stock of three subject libraries dealing with music, fine art and commerce, and contains 15 medieval mss (listed in Ker); 26 incunabula; 440 STC; about 2,300 Wing; *c*1,000 pre-1700 foreign works. The number of books printed between 1700 and 1851 cannot be established with certainty, but is very considerable; especially strong in travel and topography.

Printed cats: Early printed English books 1499-1640; Early printed books 1641-1700; Early printed foreign books 1473-1700. Remainder on card cats.

Charles Tovey, *The Bristol City Library*. Bristol, 1853.

Geoffrey Langley, 'A place to put books'. *LAR*, Nov 1963.

Paul Kaufman, *Borrowings from the Bristol Library 1773-1784*. Charlottesville, 1960.

Private Press Collection Acquired by gift and purchase, principally after *c*1950, the collection consists of *c*880 items, many of which are pamphlets. It is strong in Cuala (14 titles), Golden Cockerel (32 titles), High House (40 titles), Nonesuch (40 titles), Pear Tree (12 titles), Temple Sheen (23 titles).

'Catalogue of Private Press and other finely printed books in Bristol Reference and Fine Art Libraries', compiled by Anthony Baker, 1972 (unpublished)

Anthony Baker, 'The quest for Guido'. *Private Library*, 2, Winter 1969.

Vincent Stuckey Lean Collection A collection of *c*5,000 books, pamphlets and some music built up by Vincent Stuckey Lean (1820-1899), chiefly during travels abroad; bequeathed to Bristol Reference Library. Basic subject fields are philology, proverbs and folklore. Some material of considerable rarity; some pre-1700 works which are included (but not identified as such) in the printed catalogues of early books in Bristol Reference Library (for details see General Collections). About 300 v lost during the war; some works peripheral to the main subjects of the collection have been taken into the General Collections.

Printed cat.

Memoir of Lean included as preface to *Collectanea: collections by V S L of proverbs (etc)*, edited by T W Williams, Bristol, 1902-4, 4 v in 5.

Music Library Not acquired as a collection, but by miscellaneous donation and purchase. It contains 44 v containing 71 items of music printed 1732-99, and listed in the *International Inventory of Musical Sources, Series A: Music printed before 1800*. Included in the collection are works by Handel, Corelli, Stanley and minor 18th-cent composers.

Bristol Baptist College, Woodland Road, Bristol BS8 1UN. Tel (0272) 20248. Admission by arrangement, preferably on written application.

The College has a few books bearing the name of Edward Terrill whose trust, made in 1679, is regarded as the foundation date. The Library began in 1720, and the College later received all the books of Andrew Gifford (*d*1783), and subsequently developed as the working library of a theological college preparing men and women for ministry in the Baptist Church. The library has a particularly strong collection of early printed English Bibles from Tyndale's Testament (1520) to the 'He' and 'She' AV 1611 edition; a large collection of Bibles from early years of Serampore Press, and a complete run of Baptist hymn books from *c*1700; also a good collection of other hymn books; works of 18th and early 19th cent Baptist writers—papers, letters etc of some, including letters of John Newton to Dr Ryland; a fair selection of 17th cent pamphlets and books written on religious-political controversy; long detailed mss (in English) by Joshua Thomas, 'Materials for a history of the Baptist Churches in Wales', *c*1782, 'History of the Baptist Churches in Wales', *c*1796; and 2 v 'Ecclesiastical History of Wales'. The notebooks and commonplace books of Andrew Gifford compiled when a student at Tewkesbury Academy (1719) and mss notes of some lectures by Foskett of Bristol shed light on education in early 18th cent Dissenting. The library contains a few medieval mss.

During the 1960s and 1970s specialist books which were in use when the College was a Dissenting Academy—dealing with natural philosophy etc—were sold to universities and libraries of professions. Also part of the Bible collection has been sold through Sotheby's, and some Caxtons.

Bristol City Museum and Art Gallery, Department of Geology, Queens Road, Bristol BS8 1RL. Tel (0272) 299771. The library is a working library for museum staff; outside users only allowed access under special circumstances.

Department of Geology The library was originally part of the Bristol Institution for the Advancement of Science, Literature and the Arts, founded in 1823 which amalgamated, in 1871, with the Bristol Library Society (founded early in the 1770s) to form the Bristol Museum and Library. The City and County of Bristol assumed control in the 1890s, subsequent to which major reorganization took place. The library covers geology, and is particularly rich in early 19th cent works on palaeontology, many of which have been annotated by museum staff.

Card index.

W R Barker, *The Bristol museum and art gallery ...* Printed for the Museum and Art Gallery Committee, Bristol, 1906.

Natural History Collection The majority of the rare books in this collection belonged to the Bristol Philosophical and Literary Society and the older Bristol Library Society. The books, *c*3,000, were obtained by purchase and by donations from wealthy benefactors, and range from *c*1733 to the 20th cent. About half the collection is 19th cent, and has a particularly good representation of early works on conchology, entomology and mammals, with some finely illustrated folios, first editions (eg Darwin and Wallace), and limited editions.

Older books are in printed cat of Museum library.

Natural History collection being recatalogued (1982).

Bristol Record Office, The Council House, College Green, Bristol BS1 5TR. Tel (0272) 26031. Ext 441. Open Mon-Thurs 8.45 am-4.45 pm, Fri 8.45 am-4.15 pm, Sat 9 am-12 noon (by appointment). Microfilm and photocopy facilities.

All Saints' Church, City Eight v traditionally regarded as survivors of the Guild of Kalendars' Library, established by John Carpenter, Bishop of Worcester, in 1464. Four are mss dating from the 14th and 15th cent, the remainder are printed works from between 1481 and 1503. Seven are Latin works of theology and the eighth is the *Catholicon* of John of Genoa, the standard Latin dictionary of the later Middle Ages.

T W Williams, 'Gloucestershire Medieval Libraries'. *Trans of the Bristol and Gloucestershire Arch Soc* v 31 (1908) p87-90.

N R Ker, *Medieval Libraries of Great Britain*, 2nd ed, 1964, p13.

N Orme, 'The Guild of Kalendars, Bristol'. *Trans of the Bristol and Gloucestershire Arch Soc* v 96 (1978), p42-3.

Harvey's Wine Museum, John Harvey and Sons Ltd, 12 Denmark Street, Bristol BS1. Tel (0272) 298011. Open Mon-Fri by appointment only. Admission by appointment. Reference on premises only.

Jack Harvey Library Collected by Jack Harvey, former chairman of the company, and given to the museum by his son, the library contains some 250 v, of which 90 are pre-1850, 25 of these pre-1750. Basically books on wine—120 items in French, 20 Portuguese, 11 Italian, 9 Spanish and 5 Latin.

Handlist only.

Imperial Tobacco Company Ltd, Commercial and Marketing Intelligence Department, Lombard Street, Bedminster, Bristol BS3. Tel (0272) 666961. Open office hours Mon-Fri. Admission by appointment for reference only.

Thornton Wills Collection Collected by T Thornton Wills, a member of the Wills tobacco family, the collection consists of *c*200 v, including books and pamphlets relating to tobacco (mainly late-Victorian), of which 30 items are pre-1860.

Handlist only.

New Room, John Wesley's Chapel, 36 The Horsefair, Bristol BS1 3JE. Tel (0272) 24740. Open weekdays (except Wed) 10 am-1 pm, 2-4 pm. Admission for reference to any bona fide enquirer seeking material not readily available elsewhere. Enquiries which may involve some preliminary searching and the assembling of selected material,

would be welcomed in writing about a week before the date of the proposed visit.

The New Room Bristol Collection The major part of the present collection has been assembled since 1932 when the Methodist Church took over the maintenance of the New Room from the Welsh Calvinistic Methodists. It has been built up by both gifts and purchase. A major gift was that of the Rev Maldwyn Edwards (1903-74), President of the Methodist Conference in 1961. The collection is made up of 685 titles in 922 v, as well as 230 pamphlets and 380 bound periodicals. There are 5 Wing items; 163 ESTC v covering 77 titles and 636 v published later than 1851, incorporating 559 titles. The pamphlets include 1 Wing item; 12 published between 1701 and 1800; and 10 issued from the press during the first half of the 19th cent. The particular strength of the collection lies in its early Bibles and Methodist hymn books, biographies and autobiographies and annals of Methodism in particular areas (usefully complemented by the volumes of 'Hall's Arrangement' and 'Hill's Arrangement' also on the shelves) and church and chapel histories, including a special section on Bristol and the adjacent areas. There is a collection of early editions of John Wesley's own works and excellent runs of minutes of conference for Wesleyan Methodism, the United Free Methodist Church, and the early years of the Bible Christian Movement. There are only six monthly issues lacking from a run of the *Wesleyan Methodist Magazine* (initially upon its inception in 1778 the *Arminian Magazine*) otherwise complete, and a run of *The Watchman* from 1837-1878.

A subject cat under broad headings is gradually being replaced by a dictionary cat.

The Society of Merchant Venturers, Merchants' Hall, The Promenade, Clifton, Bristol BS8 3NH. Tel (0272) 38058. Open Mon-Fri 10 am-4 pm. Admission by recommendation of a university tutor. Research facilities only on certain Thurs and Fri.

The Society of Merchant-Venturers Private Collection The Collection consists mainly of books on the history of Bristol, including some early guides and 18th cent poll books. There are also some 18th-cent sermons preached at the Society's annual commemoration services. *c*30 books deal with the history of livery companies in both London and Bristol. There are 2 ms v, one in a 19th cent hand gives an account of John Guy (*d*1629), the first governor of Newfoundland, and the other is a mid-17th cent treatise on navigation. Six items are of Wing date, 38 v were published between 1701 and 1800, 50 v 1801-1850 and the rest are modern. All bound v and pamphlets total 48 titles.

Typed handlist available.

University of Bristol, Spelaeological Society, University Road, Bristol BS8 1SP. (Access via main entrance to the Department of Geography.) Open by arrangement, and admission to non-members on written application to the librarian.

Spelaeological Society Library The precursor of the present day Society was the Bristol Spelaeological Research Society founded in 1912. The outbreak of World War I put an end to its activities, but in 1919 some former members reunited to form the University of Bristol Spelaeological Society, adding to their objective of cave exploration the establishment of a museum, the enlargement of the work of the Society to include prehistory, and the publication of proceedings. The first library and museum were destroyed by fire in an air raid on Bristol during the night of 24-25 Nov 1940. About half the prewar book stock has now been replenished, and in 1978 the collections were greatly augmented by the acquisition of the personal library of Professor Edgar Kingsley Tratman (1899-1978), one of the leading figures in British spelaeological research. The library now contains 950 v (910 titles); 450 bound v of serials; *c*1,850 pamphlets (unbound); and 4 v of the period 1801-50. In addition there are *c*450 maps, 4,100 photographs, 5,350 slides, 2,500 negatives, and 2 cine films shot in 1933 and 1937, the first and third ever made of subterranean exploration. Subjects covered are the geology, topography, physiography and hydrology of carboniferous limestone areas. World-wide exchanges for the Society's proceedings bring in a good collection of current caving and prehistory serials which are difficult to obtain elsewhere. The prehistory collections relate especially to Avon, Gloucestershire, Wiltshire, and Somerset. The Savory Collection of slides showing Mendip caving in the early 20th cent has now been transferred to the Wells Museum.

Card cat of books, slides and maps.

University of Bristol, University Library, Tyndall Avenue, Bristol BS8 1TJ. Tel (0272) 24161. Telex: 449174. Open weekdays 9.30 am-4.30 pm. Admission to non-members on written application to the librarian. Microform readers, photocopying and photographic services.

Architecture Library Originally established in 1851 as the library of the old Bristol Society of Architects, it has, in consequence, one of the best collections of old and rare books on architecture in the provinces. It includes 3 Wing items; 28 1701-1800; 250 1801-50.

Card cat.

Botany Rare Book Collection Built up by bequest, gift and purchase. Major bequests include those from Hiatt Baker, Agnes Fry, S H Vines and James Walter White. The collection contains 340 books and 210 v of serials. There are 2 STC; 5 other pre-1640; 11 Wing; 4 other pre-1700; and 79 18th cent items. There are also ms notes for the revision of J W White's *Flora of the Bristol Coalfield*, and volumes of paintings of British plants by J Steuart-Powell and F E Cundall.

Card cat.

Business History Collection The core of the collection is made up of books and pamphlets collected over many years by A C Langford, Officer of Customs and Excise at Bristol Airport, and donated by him to the University. The original collection has been much augmented by purchase. It contains *c*24,000 v, a further 5,000 pamphlets are accessible but still await cataloguing. Much of the material is ephemeral: published by firms for limited circulation among their employees. It is added to regularly by purchase.

Card cat.

Courtesy Books Collection Built up by purchase, it contains 367 v which include 21 STC items; 7 other 16th cent; 50 Wing; 14 other 17th cent; 168 18th cent; 107 other (mainly pre-1800).

Card cat.

Early Novel Collection Built up by W L Cooper, Librarian of the University of Bristol (1923-46) it contains 1,854 v, including 15 STC; 72 Wing; 927 ESTC; 840 other pre-1850 items. The collection is of English novels before Dickens, together with early English translations of foreign novels. Most are first editions.

Card cat with ms handlist.

Early Science and Philosophy Collection Built up by gift and purchase, it includes an important recent gift of early and rare books on geology from the library of V A and J M Eyles. It contains 1,352 v with 5 incunabula; 50 STC, 63 other 16th cent; 395 Wing, 64 other 17th cent; 647 ESTC, and 128 other mainly pre-1850 items. Added to regularly by donation.

Card cat.

Garden History Collection Built up by gift and purchase: part of the University Library's substantial holdings in horticultural and agricultural history. It totals 159 v, including 1 Wing; 49 18th cent; 92 other (mainly fine limited eds). Accompanied by a small ms collection of Repton letters, notes and sketches. It is added to regularly.

Card cat.

Garner Collection At least half the volumes were donated by Professor William Edward Garner (1889-1960), who was on the staff of the University of Bristol 1926-54. Many of the remainder were also donated by members of the teaching staff. Further material held in the stackrooms complements the Garner Collection proper. It totals *c*740 v, including 1 STC; 14 other pre-1640; 45 Wing, 42 other pre-1700 items; the remainder mainly pre-1850. The majority are mainly chemical and alchemical history, with some of more general interest.

Card cat.

Gladstone Library Formerly in the possession of the National Liberal Club, Whitehall Place, London, it was founded in 1883. Purchased by the University of Bristol in 1976, the Gladstone Library incorporates the libraries of the daughters of Richard Cobden and T Fisher Unwin, and a large pamphlet collection started by Charles Bradlaugh. At the time of purchase there were *c*30,000 v of monographs and serials, and 45,000 pamphlets, together with much ms and other archival material. It is intended to keep the pamphlet collection, which contains much rare and early material, together. At present it consists of 974 boxes and wallets and 1,061 bound volumes, and covers subjects such as slavery and the slave trade, English liberalism, socialism, railways, bimetallism, etc. The Gladstone collection has already been recatalogued, and is housed separately. Of particular interest is the collection of election addresses of parliamentary candidates of all parties and general elections from 1892 to the present. This is being kept up to date. There are several collections of ms letters, together with what survives of the archives of the National Liberal Club. It does not, however, contain the archives of the Liberal Party as such. Duplicates have been disposed of, and the remainder of the books and serials dispersed among the general and restricted collections of the University Library.

The existing guard book and card cat are being kept intact as a record of what the Gladstone Library held in 1976. As items are recatalogued, they will appear in the card cat of the University Library.

A W Hutton, 'A political Club Library', *The Library*, 2, 1890. *The Gladstone Library: a unique service.* London: National Liberal Club (196?). *Early Railway Pamphlets 1825-1900*, London, Ibid 1938.

Law Library Rare Books Collection Built up by bequest, gift and purchase, it contains 694 v, and incorporates 256 v deposited on permanent loan by the Bristol Law Society in 1934, the arrangement being renewed in 1969. There are 1 incunabulum; 43 STC, 3 other pre-1640; 103 Wing, 1 other pre-1700; 250 18th cent; 293 1800-50 items. The collection is available to members of the Bristol Law Society and to accredited readers.

Card cat.

Long Ashton Research Station Library The Library has been built up by purchase, bequest and donation. Many of the older works came as a gift from A D Turner of North Petherton, 1963. Its rare book section consists of 118 v, including 1 STC, 4 Wing, 19 ESTC and 34 before 1850.

Card cat with typescript list of books of antiquarian interest.

See: Fruit and Cider: a list of horticultural and cider classics and works of antiquarian interest in the Library of the Long Ashton Research Station, 1963.

Maria Mercer Physics Library. Rare Books Collection Built up from gifts and from a section of the Exley Bequest (see: Queen's Building Library, Exley Collection, *infra*), the collection has 86 monograph titles (and 295 v of serials) which include 2 Wing; 21 ESTC; 63 1801-50 items, together with 4 v 18th cent and 291 v 1801-50 of serials.

Card cat.

Medical Library

(Open to members of the University of Bristol, the Bristol Medico-Chirurgical Society and to other bona fide students at the discretion of the librarian.)

(a) *General Collections* The library was founded in 1893 as joint library of the Medical School (f1833) and Bristol Medico-Chirurgical Society (f1874), Library (f1890). Incorporated are collections originally forming the libraries of Bristol Royal Infirmary (f1735; library, acquired 1894, established 1826 with gifts of books from Richard Smith (1722-1843) and Richard Lowe (d1850), the Bristol General Hospital (f1831, library acquired 1894), the Bristol Medical Library, later the Bristol Museum and Library (f1832), and the Royal United Hospital Bath. The early collections which cover most aspects of contemporary medicine, including basic sciences, dentistry and veterinary science are:

i *Strongroom Collection* (1478-1799) contains 1,900 18th cent and 300 earlier volumes, including 2 incunabula (*Cyrurgia Guidonis*, 1498 (Hain 4811), *Dioscorides* 1478 (Hain 6258); 29 STC and 77 Wing items.

ii *Nineteenth Century Collection* (1800-99) 7,640 books and 6,240 periodical volumes; 4,750 pamphlets, of which 4,000 bound in 159 v.

iii *Mineral Waters and Spas Collection* 285 v, the majority 18th cent, almost all 1600-1850. 3 STC; 21 Wing. Varied origin, assembled by Library.

Card cat, author and classified subject.

(b) *Parry Collection* The library of Caleb Hillier Parry (1755-1822). A Bath physician, agriculturalist and geologist, Parry was a friend of Sir Joseph Banks, Lord Sommerville, Sir William Herschel, William Heberden, Mrs Barbauld and, in particular, of Edward Jenner. He wrote on exophthalmic goitre, rabies and angina pectoris, and has been credited with the first descriptions of congenital magacolon, facial hemiatrophy and histaminic cephalgia. His library was presented by his son to the Royal United Hospital, Bath, and passed to Bath City Reference Library in 1933, together with the library (estimated in 1948 at 220 items) of John Smith Soden (1780-1863), an original member of the BMA, and Surgeon to the Royal United Hospital. Both collections were donated to Bristol University by Bath City Council in 1950. The Parry part has a separate ms sheaf catalogue, and these books are kept together as 'The Parry Collection', while the others have been absorbed into the general arrangement of the Medical Library. It contains 900 early medical works, including 16 STC and 27 Wing items.

J Apley, 'Caleb Parry of Bath', *Medical Journ of the South West*, 71:259 (Jan 1956) p30-2.

L M Griffiths, 'The Bristol Medical Library', *Bristol Medico-Chirurgical Journ* 29:114 (Dec 1911), p335-44.

A E S Roberts, 'The Medical Library of the University of Bristol', *Medical Journ of the South West*, 73:267 (Jan 1958), p12-14.

——'An exhibition of important anatomical books'. Ibid 73:270 (Oct 1958), p104-7.

——'On the history and growth of the Bristol Medical School Library'. *Bristol Medico-Chirurgical Journ* 85:316, (Oct 1970), p93-100.

Sir H Rolleston, 'Caleb Hillier Parry, MD, FRS'. *Annals of Medical History* 7:3 (Autumn 1925), p205-15.

R W M Wright, 'Bath Hospital Medical Library', *The Record: Bull Victoria Art Gallery and Municipal Library, Bath*, 1:7 (1948), p225-34.

Moravian Collection Formerly the archive and parish library of the Maudlin Street Bristol congregation of the Moravian Church, deposited on permanent loan in the University of Bristol Library in 1966. The Danckerts atlas had already been deposited in 1951. The deposits were accompanied by a gift of books from Bishop Macleavy, formerly part of the library of Bishop Benjamin Latrobe. Books total 175, which include 1 17th cent and 104 ESTC books. Included also is a rare early edition of the atlas of Justus Danckerts (26 maps *c*1670-90, augmented by J P Homann and other 18th cent maps, all hand-coloured and extensively indexed; formerly the property of Dr H O Stephens). The collection is accompanied by extensive ms holdings: diaries, minutes, sermons, etc of the Bristol congregation.

Typescript cat (1966).

Penguin Books Collection Originally the gift of Sir Allen Lane in 1960 to mark his completion of 25 years as chairman of Penguin Books Ltd, it was supplemented by him in 1965 and 1966, and rounded off in 1969. In 1975 Penguin Books Ltd undertook to supply a copy of each new or reprinted title, and this arrangement continues. The collection contains *c*9,615 v. With few exceptions, each volume is signed by its author, editor or translator, and there are also many signed letters, photographs and other memorabilia. Most volumes are first editions, many of the early ones complete with wrappers.

Publisher's printed cat of 1966, manually updated to 1975; now regularly updated by publisher's microfiche.

Queen's Building Library

(i) *Engineering Rare Books Collection* Built up by gift and purchase, the collection totals 157 v (127 titles), mainly of the collected works of famous engineers of the 19th and early 20th cent, together with some of the more important single works. Includes: Besson, Jacques, *Theatrum instrumentorum et machinarum* 1582 (imperfect), and 4 18th cent works.

Card cat with separate listing.

(ii) *Exley Collection* This collection was formed by two Bristol teachers, Thomas Exley (1775-1855), co-editor of the *Imperial Encyclopaedia: a Dictionary of Science and the Arts*. . . and his son John Thompson Exley (1815-99), and contains 262 v (230 titles). The bulk of the library was presented to University College, Bristol, in 1899. There are 62 18th cent works. Amongst the English mathematicians represented are Isaac Barrow, Roger Cotes, Colin Maclaurin, Benjamin Martin, Isaac Newton (including a

2nd edition of *Philosophiae Naturalis Principia Mathematica*), Nicholas Saunderson, Thomas Simpson, Robert Simson, Brook Taylor and Matthew Young. This part of the Exley Collection also includes 18 early 18th cent Italian tracts on hydraulics, and a copy of the very rare second edition of the *Universal Measurer and Mechanic* by Abraham Fletcher (1714-93). Other books of early date, later added to the original Exley Collection, came in part from the library of the Bristol Education Society established in 1770. The 19th cent books added by John Thompson Exley are, perhaps, less worthy of remark. They are chiefly text-books in elementary applied mathematics. There are also runs of many major English, German and French mathematical journals. The original Exley Bequest was divided between the Physics, Mathematics and Engineering Libraries.

Card cat with separate listing.

(iii) *History of Geology Collection* The collection has been assembled mainly as a result of the personal enthusiasm of two Professors of Geology at the University of Bristol—Sidney Hugh Reynolds, who held the Channing-Wills Chair from 1901-33, and Professor Walter Frederick Whittard who held the same Chair from 1937-66. Other donors include Herbert Leader Hawkins, 1887-1968, of the University of Reading (earlier University College of Reading), and Henry Woods (1868-1952), Lecturer in Palaeozoology at the University of Cambridge, and Stanley Smith (1883-1955) of the University of Bristol. Stanley Smith's work on the Tortworth Inlier in Gloucestershire established a link between the University Department of Geology and the Ducie family of Tortworth Court, from which further gifts were received. Henry John Morton, 3rd Earl of Ducie (1827-1921) built up an excellent collection, mainly of local fossils, and possessed a library containing interesting early works. He was at one time a member of the Cotteswold Naturalists' Field Club, as was another vicarious benefactor Edward Bestbridge Wethered, whose donation reached the collection through his son Ernest Handel Cossham Wethered (1878-1975), a county court judge. Other volumes came to the collection from the estate of another judge of the high court, and thereafter Lord Justice of Appeal, Sir Edward Fry (1827-1918). Books acquired from the Bristol Baptist College include former possessions of Andrew Gifford (1700-84), a Baptist Minister who became an Assistant Librarian at the British Museum. The collection includes works from the mid-17th cent onwards important in the historical developments of geology. There are books on the local geology of the Bristol and Bath areas, as well as all the chief publications of William Smith (1769-1839), the 'father of British geology', who made his first investigations in the Bristol area. There are also first editions of James Hutton's 'Theory of the Earth' and William Phillip's 'Selection of Facts...'. In stratigraphy there is a first edition of Murchison's 'Silurian System' (1839) and of J L Giraud-Soulavie's *Histoire naturelle de la France meridionale*, 8 v..., (1780-1784). Early mineralogy books include the treatises of Buffon, Geinitz, Hauy, Jameson, Kirwan, and Schlotheim. The palaeontological items include a set of monographs on fossil fish compiled by Louis Agassiz, the second edition of Lluyd *Lithophylacii Brittanica Ichnographia* (1760) and Martin Lister's *Historiae Animalium Angliae...* (1678). There are other interesting early works on gemmology, volcanology, palaeobotany, conchology and evolutionary theory. There are 2 STC, 8 Wing and 19 ESTC items.

Card cat with separate listing.

(iv) *Nelson Collection* The collection of mathematical tables made by Edward Milles Nelson (1851-1938), and given to the University of Bristol in 1933 represents only one aspect of his many interests, which included meteorology, oceanography, archaeology and microscopy. He was three times president of the Quekett Microscopical Club between 1893 and 1895, and served the Royal Microscopical Society in a similar capacity between 1897 and 1899. Of the total of 196 v (191 titles), 91 v (85 titles) of these appear to have been added to the original collection after its receipt, some having been transferred from the Exley Collection (qv). There are 8 ESTC items, the remainder being predominantly 19th cent works. The mathematical tables include a ms v compiled by Nelson.

Card cat. A subject approach is possible via Fletcher, Miller and Rosenhead, *An index of mathematical tables*, 1946.

See also R C Archibald, *Mathematical table makers*, 1948.

Restricted Collections Built up by gift, bequest and purchase, the collections incorporate early and rare material from the libraries of Nicholas Pocock (1814-97), Oskar Teichman (1880-1959) and Thomas Exley (1775-1855), and from collections donated by members of the Wills and Fry families, and others connected with the life of the University of Bristol. It contains 10,618 v of books, pamphlets and serials, and includes 9 incunabula; 147 STC, 274 other 1501-1640; 611 Wing, 318 other 1641-1700; 5,313 18th cent, 3,946 other pre-1850 limited eds, private press, etc. The majority fall into the subject areas of classics, theology, history and agricultural history. There is a useful cartographical section containing early maps and atlases. The Fry bequests include many extra-illustrated books, and are accompanied by a fine collection of prints known as the Fry Portrait Collection. Twelve hand-coloured prints showing views of St Petersburg in 1799, formerly in the Paschkof Palace, Moscow, came with the Teichman Bequest. The collections are frequently augmented by gifts and special purchase.

Card cat.

Veterinary Science Library The general collection includes six monographs and three v of serials 1801-50.

Card cat.

Wiglesworth Ornithological Collection Bequeathed to the University of Bristol by Dr Joseph Wiglesworth (1853-1919), an amateur ornithologist who had moved to

Somerset five years before his death. The collection contains c1,750 v books, 1,200 v serials, and includes 4 STC; 2 Wing; 88 18th cent; 298 other rare works (mainly fine editions with hand-tinted litho plates).

Card cat.

Wesley College, Henbury Road, Westbury on Trym, Bristol BS10 7QD. Tel (0272) 501700. The library is open during College terms to non-members by appointment with the librarian. Photocopying facilities are available.

General Collection Forms part of the general undergraduate and research collections, and includes books from Didsbury College, Manchester (founded 1842, moved to Bristol 1949), Wesley College, Headingley (founded 1868, amalgamated with Bristol 1968), Richmond College, London (founded 1843, closed 1972), and Hartley Victoria College, Manchester (still in existence). The collections have undergone many changes before and since arriving in Bristol. Chief sources of the Didsbury collections, which form the bulk of the material, were the Rev James Everett, schismatic Wesleyan minister (1784-1872), J D Fernley, a Manchester Wesleyan businessman of the 19th cent, and Rev William Burt Pope (1822-1903), Wesleyan minister and tutor at Disbury from 1867. A recent donor, S G Woodall (d1972), Methodist surgeon and trades union benefactor, bequeathed the library c1,000 v of literature in English and German, mostly c1850-c1940.

The stock totals c20,000 v, including 58 STC books, 27 foreign published pre-1640, and c3,000 published pre-1851. The overwhelming emphasis is on theology and church history, with particular strengths in Methodist history, the writings of the Wesley family and hymnody. Three items, one 15th cent ms and two 16th cent books have been sold at Sotheby's (9 and 24 June 1980).

Card cat.

Associated Manuscript Materials The surviving college archives of Didsbury College, Manchester, and Wesley College, Headingley, together with antiquarian collections (sermons, correspondence, etc) relative to the history of Methodism in the 18th and 19th cent, mainly collected by the Rev George Morley (d1843), Wesleyan minister, and his son George Morley, surgeon of Leeds, were presented by Mrs Morley junior to Wesley College, Headingley in 1880. The collection contains c2,000 antiquarian items.

Typescript cat.

Printed Ephemera Includes 69 items on Methodist controversy, 1783-1888, mainly collected by the Morleys.

Shapland Collection Rev C R B Shapland, Methodist minister (d1952). 168 books on patristics, including 2 foreign 16th cent books; 7 17th cent; 6 18th cent; and 32 1800-51.

Wesley College, Headingley, Tract and Pamphlet Collections Two series relating to Methodist and other church controversies, c1730-1850, one in uniform binding (24 v). Second series, 40 bound v, and one unbound item.

Provenance unknown.

Didsbury College, Hall Collection of Tracts and Pamphlets Rev Samuel Romilly Hall (d1876), Wesleyan minister and antiquarian, compiled this series on 18th and 19th cent Methodist and other church controversies. It contains 54 v, but v 14, 23, 28, 39 missing for many years.

Cat in progress.

Didsbury College, Tract and Pamphlet Collection Methodist and other church controversies, c1730-c1850. 44 v and 124 unbound items.

Partially cat.

Bedfordshire

Bedford

Bedford College of Higher Education, Polhill Avenue, Bedford. Tel (0234) 51671. Open Mon-Fri 9 am-5 pm. Admission free by appointment to bona fide students. Study accommodation, modern education library, photocopying facilities.

The Hockliffe Collection of Early Children's Books The collection of Frederick Hockliffe (1833-1914) printer and bookseller of Bedford, was presented to the Bedford Training College in 1927, and in 1966 the ownership was made over to its successor, the Bedford College of Education which merged into the present college in 1975. The collection is made up of 1,200 v covering fables, fairy tales, nursery stories, stories before 1850, annuals, games, history, natural sciences, etc. A large portion of the collection dates from the first half of the 19th cent, with a few items going back to the 18th cent, eg N L Du Fresnoy, *Geography for children...*, London, J Johnson and E Newbury, 1787. The bindings are mostly original and in fair condition.

Doreen H Boggis, *Catalogue of the Hockliffe Collection of early children's books*, 1969. L Salway, *Special collections of children's literature*. Library Association Youth Libraries Group, 1972.

Bedford Museum, The Embankment, Bedford. Tel (0234) 53323. Open Tues-Sat 11 am-5 pm; Sun 2-5 pm. Admission to rare books collection to bona fide researchers. Limited study accommodation.

Bedford Museum (formerly Bedford Modern School Museum) The School Museum was established in 1884 and handed over to Bedford Borough Council in 1961. The library contains *c*200 v with historical emphasis on Bedfordshire connections; eg *State of the prisons in England and Wales* by John Howard, 1784; Lucan's *Pharsalia*, ed by Nicholas Rowe, published by Tonson, 1718. Included in the collection is an edition of *Monachi Albanensis* (Matthew Paris), published (Guiliemi Pele) 1649, and *Historical collections of private passages of state*... by John Rushworth, 1680.

No printed cat available but accessions register kept.

The Museum also has a collection of early national and provincial newspapers, some from the 18th cent and earlier, but mostly in single or ranging from 2-8 issues.

Bedfordshire County Library, Central Library, Harpur Street, Bedford MK40 1PG. Tel (0234) 50931. Open Mon-Fri 10 am-8 pm; Sat 10 am-5 pm. Admission free to bona fide students. Study accommodation in quiet room. Access to Central Library lending and reference collections. Photocopying facilities available subject to the permission of the librarian.

The Old Library, Bedford Founded in 1700, the library was originally housed in the vestry of St Paul's Church until 1830 when it was placed in the newly founded Bedford General Library, later Bedford Public Library. The present collection was transferred to the new Central Library in 1973. It contains 725 v plus *c*100 Bedfordshire sermons and charges, unbound. Subject content mainly theology. Earliest traced volume: *Hieronymi Opera cum Indice*. London, 1516. The collection also includes, *Acta Eruditorum* No 1 MDCLXXXII—No 80 MDCCXLV; 53 bound v of tracts and sermons. Numerous editions contained in this collection are listed in STC.

Catalogue of the Circulating and Reference Libraries of the Old Library founded in 1700. (The Bedford Literary and Scientific Institute 1892.) A duplicated list of the present collection has been compiled.

T A Blyth, *History of Bedford*, 1873, p166-7. (op)

Gentleman's magazine, May 1817, Pt 2, p135-6. (op)

Bedfordshire notes and queries, Vol 3, 1891. (op)

A Baker, *The library story*, *c*1958. (op)

Quaritch sale, *c*1901.

Private sale, 1911.

Bedfordshire County Library, County Hall, Bedford MK42 9AP. Tel (0234) 56181. Telex 82244. Open Mon-Thurs 9 am-6 pm; Fri 9 am-7 pm; Sat 9 am-4 pm. Admission free to bona fide students and researchers. Closed access. Student accommodation, library services, photocopying facilities available.

The Offor Bunyan Collection The Collection derives from two gifts, one of 304 v donated by the British Museum in 1959, and the other of 382 v from the late Dr Richard Offor in 1964. It now comprises *c*700 v which include several English first editions of books by John Bunyan, as well as editions of *Pilgrim's Progress* in more than 20 languages. These have not been included in STC. Many items show signs of damage, being the result of a fire at Sotheby's previous to a sale, in 1865, at which they were offered.

No printed cat, but separate mss cats for the British Museum and Offor items are available for users.

Richard Offor, 'The Offor Bunyan Books at Elstow'. *Library Assoc Record* Vol 62, No 4, April 1960.

H G Tibbutt, 'Bunyan Libraries', *Bedfordshire Magazine*, Vol 15, 1975.

Frank Mott Harrison, John Bunyan Collection Donated in 1938 by Frank Mott Harrison of Hove, Sussex, to the Borough of Bedford, the collection consists of *c*1,200 books, pamphlets and ephemera; *c*400 items are pre-1851. The collection is made up of individual, collected and selected works of John Bunyan, of which many are first editions, including the first edition of Bunyan's first book published, *viz Some Gospel truths opened*, London, J Wright, 1656. The collection also includes criticism, commentaries, works by contemporaries, imitative works, biography of Bunyan, local history and topography relating to the 17th cent.

Catalogue of John Bunyan Library (Frank Mott Harrison Collection), Bedford, 1938.

V Brittain, *In the steps of John Bunyan*, 1950.

Bromham Parish Library The library was founded by Thomas, 2nd Baron Trevor, in 1740 and added to later by members of the Trevor family. It consists of *c*800 v including a copy of the poetical works of Robert Hampden-Trevor, 4th Baron Trevor, printed at the Bodoni Press, Parma, 1792. The greater part of the library dates from the 17th and 18th cent, with emphasis on theological, literary and historical subjects. It was housed in a room over the church porch until 1978 when it was removed for safe custody to the County Library, Bedford.

A 'Catalogue of Books in the Library of the Parish Church of St Owen, Bromham, Bedfordshire...compiled by E C Cooper, 1959' is available. The catalogue refers to the sale, in 1809, of Walton's *Polyglot* and Castelli's *Lexicon* from the proceeds of which a further 13 titles were purchased.

Bedfordshire notes and queries, Vol 2, 1889, p18-20; Harvey, *The Hundred of Willey*, 1872-78, (op); *The parochial libraries of the Church of England*, 1959.

The Yielden Parish Library A collection of *c*400 v, the bequest of E S Buntin, rector, *d*1849. It contains 20 volumes published pre-1700, including several of the works of Cicero from J Blaeu of Amsterdam in 1656 and 1659. The subject coverage is largely theological, with various other items on education, medicine and mechanics. The ownership of the library remains with the parish of Yielden while it remains deposited with the County Library.

Alphabetical author/title card cat.
Notes and queries, 5th Series, Vol 8, 1877, p325.

The Bunyan Meeting Library and Museum, c/o The County Record Office, County Hall, Bedford. Tel (0234) 63222. Ext 178. Open by appointment to bona fide students. Books required for study will be transferred to the County Record Office for use. (Mon-Fri 9 am-1 pm, 2 pm-5 pm). CRO collections and services available.

The Bunyan Library It began with books donated by church members, and grew considerably during the ministry of Dr John Brown (1864-1903), Bunyan biographer and scholar. The Library is particularly strong in foreign language editions and earlier editions of John Bunyan's works which total *c*1,550 v, and several first editions. The earliest edition of *Pilgrim's Progress* is third 1679 (STC B5559). The collection also includes works by writers contemporary with Bunyan, biographical and topographical works associated with Bunyan and Bedfordshire. Also some criticism and explanatory works devoted to Bunyan, and printed before 1851. Numerous items are listed in STC. Bound volumes of sermons date mainly from the 18th and 19th cent, but some earlier, eg 1636.

Catalogue of the Bunyan Meeting Library and Museum, Bedford. Published by the Trustees of the Bunyan Meeting, 1955.

Cecil Higgins Art Gallery, Castle Close, Bedford MK40 3NY. Tel (0234) 211222. Open Tues-Sat 11 am-5 pm; Sun 2 pm-5 pm; Bank Holiday Mon 11 am-1 pm, 2-5 pm. Limited study accommodation by arrangement; photographs can be supplied.

Cecil Higgins Art Gallery Library The Library derives from the book collection of Cecil Higgins (1855-1941), and consists of 1,200 v, of which 35 titles are pre-1851. The Library is devoted mainly to works concerning the visual arts and topography; the decorative arts are well represented. Many of the earliest books are about religion and ethics.

No cat available, but an accessions register is maintained.

County Record Office, Bedfordshire County Hall, Bedford MK42 9AP. Tel (0234) 63222. Open Mon-Fri 9 am-1 pm, 2 pm-5 pm. Admission free to bona fide students. Research room, microfilm reader, photocopying facilities.

The book collection consists of *c*2,000 v, of which *c*250 are pre-1850, with special emphasis on the legal system, land ownership and church history. An apparently unique item is *The Lutes Apology for Her Excellency* by Richard Mathew, 1652. A note in the book dated 9.6.1933 states that it seems to be the only known copy!

Typescript cat only.

Cardington

Cardington Parochial Library. All enquiries to be addressed to the County Librarian, County Hall, Bedford MK42 9AP. Open by special arrangement for bona fide research.

The Library consists of *c*157 v contained in a bookcase which bears the following inscription: 'This bookcase with books for parochial use the gift of Samuel Whitbread and John Howard, the philanthropist, stood from 1788 in the vestry of Cardington Church...'. The collection contains mainly theological works of the 18th and 19th cent. It is not noted in *The parochial libraries of the Church of England* published 1959 by the Central Council for the Care of Churches.

Luton

Luton Museum and Art Gallery, Wardown Park, Luton, Beds. LU2 7HA. Tel (0582) 36941. Open Mon-Fri 10 am-5 pm. Admission free by appointment to bona fide students. Students' room available; photocopying services.

The Bagshawe Collection The Collection was acquired as a gift from Mr T W Bagshawe in 1957. It contains *c*9,500 items, of which *c*2,000 were published before 1851. The subject areas cover agricultural history, rural crafts, general British topography, Bedfordshire topography and folklore. Much of the pre-1851 part of the collection dates from the first half of the 19th cent, with 24 titles from the 18th cent and 6 from the 17th cent.

Card cat on microfiche.

Sandy

Royal Society for the Protection of Birds, The Lodge, Sandy, Bedfordshire SE19 2DL. Tel (0767) 80551. Library Ext 254. Open Mon-Fri 9 am-12.45 pm, 1.30-5.15 pm. Not open to the general public, but telephone enquiries will be dealt with; bona fide scholars should apply in writing for an appointment. Photocopier; microfiche reader available.

The library of the Society specializes in ornithological and related topics, and also contains the special collection of W H Hudson (1841—1922)—complete printed works, letters and other papers.

Berkshire

Bracknell

ICI Plant Protection Division, Jealott's Hill Research Station, Bracknell, Berks. RG12 6EY. Tel (0344) 24701 Ext 3313 or 3475. Open Mon-Fri 8.45 am-5 pm. Admission to serious enquirers by prior arrangement. Photocopying facilities, microfilm and fiche reader/printers.

Nuptown House Collection Acquired by purchase *c*1946-58. Originally housed in Nuptown House and, on the disposal of that property, moved to its present location in the Old Library, Jealott's Hill. Comprises some 165 works, including two periodicals, in 250 v, the bulk of it pre-1851, relating to agriculture, overwhelmingly English, very strong on 18th cent and Board of Agriculture county reports.

Sheaf cat, with author, title and some subject entries in one sequence. Handlist available.

National Meteorological Library, Meteorological Office, London Road, Bracknell, Berks RG12 2SZ. Tel (0344) 20242; Information Ext 2712. Open Mon-Thurs 8.30 am-4.45 pm, Fri 8.30 am-4.15 pm. Admission to anyone with genuine interest; advanced notice preferred. Photocopier, microfiche readers and copier, fiche and film reader/printer.

The rare book collection has been built up, partly by presentation, since the establishment of the Meteorological Office Library in 1870, and comprises *c*500 pre-1851 v, including some 100 16th-18th cent printed books (one-third foreign) on meteorology and associated subjects, plus mss weather diaries, in the separate rare books section; general meteorology, voyages and explorations in the library's main collection. The collection is only rarely added to now, and no disposals are known.

In author cat of whole library.

Shelf list of separate rare books section.

Union cat of rare meteorological books held in the National Meteorological Library and the Royal Meteorological Society, Bracknell, available.

Hurley

The Grassland Research Institute, Hurley, Maidenhead, Berks SL6 5LR. Tel (062 882) 3631. Open Mon-Thurs 8.30 am-5 pm; Fri to 4.30 pm. Non-members admitted after written application. Microfilm and microfiche reading and photocopying facilities available.

The library maintains a separately shelved historical or rare book collection built up by purchases made from time to time since the foundation of the Institute (1948). It presently consists of *c*70 titles, virtually all rare, most of which are 18th or 19th cent standard English works on agriculture, more particularly grasslands and meadows, and include reports of the Board of Agriculture and works by Arthur Young. Other pre-1850 material exists in the library, mainly in the form of periodicals.

The books are included in the main author and subject cat on cards, but a separate list of the rare book collection is available at the library and could be photocopied for bona fide enquirers.

Langley

The Kederminster (or Kedermister) Library, St Mary's Church, Langley Marish, St Mary's Road, Langley, Slough, Berks SL3 6BZ. Tel (0753) 42068. Library open by prior arrangement after written application to Mrs M Kemp, 15 Springgate Field, Langley, Slough, Berks.

Bequeathed (1623) by Sir John Kederminster (*d*1639) of Langley Park, for the benefit of the local clergy and others. Purpose-built library room by 1631, a remarkable survival in near original state. Administered by a trust. Rouse (1941) describes subsequent history, period of serious neglect and deterioration of books and building, reorganization of trust in 1911, and restoration (by Zaensdorf), with grant from Pilgrim Trust 1939/40. Since Rouse wrote, the volumes transferred to Aylesbury have been returned to Langley and all surviving books are there now, with the sole exception of the Gospels at BL (see below). The library room is now air-conditioned.

The library comprises *c*270 works, mainly patristic writings in Latin, printed on the Continent in the late 16th and early 17th cent; also English and Latin works of the early 16th cent, and theology and ecclesiastical history of the early 17th cent. Two medieval mss (a) 11th cent English Kederminster Gospels, deposited at the BL (see *British Museum Quarterly* v 6 (1932), p93). (b) 13th cent French *Aurora* of Peter de Riga; 17th cent ms *Pharmacopolium* of John and Mary Kedermister. Of the two incunabula named by Rouse, the St Ambrose is now missing. The missal by Renchen, *c*1480-90, remains. Rouse names many other individual items, including lost books, to which must also be added Gower's *Confessio amantis* 1532. A number of interesting blind-stamped bindings are included.

Original vellum cat, 1638, hangs in the library. Also a detailed typewritten cat, 1953, in shelf order with author index.

E C Rouse, 'The Kederminster Library', (*Records of Buckinghamshire* v 14 (1941), p50-66). The most detailed account of the history, content and restoration of the library, with many references to earlier notices. Basis of the entry in *The parochial libraries of the Church of England*, 1959, p85.

J Harris, 'A rare and precious room', *Country Life* v 159, (1977), p1576-79. col illus.

Note Rouse (p57) describes the furnishing of the library as an 'unrivalled example of an early 17th cent library interior almost in its original condition'. It is also 'the most complete and untouched survival of seventeenth century colour decoration' (M Jourdain, *English interior decoration 1500-1830* (1950), p12).

This aspect of the Kederminster Library is at least as important as the surviving volumes. A satisfactory and comprehensive description must take account of both, and of the adjoining Kederminster family pew and other memorials in the church.

Reading

Royal County of Berkshire, County Library, Central Library, Belgrave Street, Reading RG1 1QL. Tel (0734) 55911. Telex 849421. Open Mon and Sat 9.30 am-5 pm; Tues-Fri 9.30 am-7 pm. Admission free for all. Material required for consultation in Reference Library available on application. Photocopying by arrangement.

Berkshire Local History Collection Built up by the Reading Public Library since its foundation in 1883, and in 1924 it was augmented by a donation from A E O Slocock of Newbury of the bulk of his important personal collection. It consists of *c*6,000 books and pamphlets (of which 1,200-1,500 books may be considered rare); 3,000 illustrations, and 560 bound v of local newspapers and maps. (A 12th cent ms from Reading Abbey is now in the custody of Reading Museum.) The collection covers all aspects of the history of Berkshire (ie the pre-1974 county), one-third relating specifically to the Borough of Reading. Special strengths include books, mss, and als of, and concerning, Mary Russell Mitford, and T N Talfourd; printed pamphlets relating to Archbishop Laud, and the Civil War; books from the Golden Cockerel Press during the time it was at Waltham Saint Lawrence; local newspapers printed in Reading, 1723 onwards. It includes *c*100 STC and Wing items.

Printed cat; *Reading Public Libraries. Local collection catalogue of books and maps relating to Berkshire* (1955) and *Supplement* (1967). Card and microfiche author cat, and sheaf classified cat available in the library.

Note The Public Library also houses the library of the Berkshire Archeological Society which consists of a small collection (*c*40 v) of pre-1851 books, largely duplicating material in the local collection proper.

Local studies collections exist at other Berkshire County Library locations, but containing little pre-1851 material. Probably the most important is at Newbury Library, Carnegie Road, Newbury. Part of the stock was inherited from the 19th cent Newbury Literary and Scientific Institute, and relates specifically to Newbury and its environs, and to West Berkshire in general. There are strong collections of local and associated pre-1914 authors.

The local collection at Maidenhead Public Library, St Ives Road, Maidenhead, contains mss and unpublished material relating to the history of Maidenhead and Cookham. Other local study collections in the county include Bracknell and Slough, where the area of interest includes what was formerly part of Buckinghamshire.

Douai Abbey, Upper Woolhampton, Reading, Berks RG7 5TH. Tel (073 521) 3163. Admission to general monastic library given freely to bona fide scholars; to rare books section only on application to librarian. Women cannot be admitted, but books can be brought to them for use in non-monastic buildings. Accommodation available in monastery (for women in school during vacations). Reference only. Photocopying. Card cats, author and chronological, in process of revision. Provenance cat in progress.

The Abbey of St Edmund, Douai, was founded as a community of English Benedictines, Paris, in 1615; moved to Douai in 1817, and returned to England in 1903. Books collected in England and France, especially from old Catholic mission stations in England, including recently the library of St Mary's Convent, Haslemere. Purchases are still regularly made. Some books lost *c*1793 during the French Revolution; others, including some early books, left at Douai and sold by the town (copy of sale catalogue in library).

General Monastic Library Contains over 100 v of early 19th cent pamphlets, plus periodicals, on Catholic emancipation and after; some modern private press books, particularly Stanbrook Abbey Press (printers to the English Benedictine Community).

Rare Books Section *c*3,900 v (including pamphlets). Include *c*40 v of mss, of which the medieval ones are in Ker; 6 incunabula; 150 STC, 250 Wing, *c*425 foreign books of the 16th-17th cent. Most subjects are represented, but of particular interest are English Catholic books of 16th-19th cent, especially recusant books published abroad; Benedictine collection, especially English; catechisms; early patristic, scriptural, liturgical and spiritual material; small collection on the town of Douai; over 100 v of first editions of modern Catholic authors, eg Francis Thompson, the Meynells, Belloc, Chesterton, publications of St Dominic's Press, Ditchling (incl *The Game*), some with association interest. The Turner Collection of French Revolution pamphlets was placed on permanent loan in 1966 in Reading University Library (qv). Most books are in early bindings, usually plain, but a few deserve attention.

The monastic archives, dealing with the refoundation of English Benedictines in the 17th cent, are housed separately from the library.

Reading Pathological Society, c/o The Bryn Thomas Memorial Library, Royal Berkshire

Hospital, Reading, Berks RG1 5AN. Tel (0734) 85111 Ext 248. Open Mon-Thurs 9 am-5 pm, Fri 4.30 pm. Admission to medical practitioners and hospital staff; others on application to the librarian, for reference only. Full range of library services, photocopying.

Reading Pathological Society Library Reading Pathological Society was founded in 1841. In 1899, it amalgamated with the Reading Medico-Chirurgical Society, founded in 1824 to maintain a medical library and diffuse medical literature. The combined collections, including museum exhibits, were housed in the Pathological Society's handsome library and meeting room, provided by the hospital in 1883, and substantially remain there today. Now part of the District Medical Library Service, run from the Postgraduate Centre, the old library holds all pre-1960 material, mainly about medicine and related subjects. Collection includes ms, 'Day Book of the Court Apothecary, time of William and Mary, date 1691' (*see* L G Matthews *Medical History* 22 (1978), p161-73); autograph letters; estimated 230 pre-1851 monographs, dating from 17th cent, but the bulk of them post-1800, plus some 20 periodical runs beginning in the same period.

Local classification into broad subject groups. Author and title card cat and accession shelflist. Work in progress on revised cat with eventual publication envisaged.

J B Hurry, *A history of the Reading Pathological Society*, London, Bale, Sons and Danielsson, 1909, p154-6 (lists some titles).

Reading School, Reading, Berks RG1 5LW. Tel (0734) 61406. Open by appointment to bona fide enquirers, after written application. Photocopying facilities.

The Reading School Collection dates from at least the middle of the 18th cent but much is thought to have disappeared in the period 1866-70 when the old school closed and the new was established. Since 1870 the collection has been built up, partly through presentation and purchase, to the present *c*250 items, the bulk of it within the RBG's definition.

It comprises printed books and ephemera relating in some way to Reading School history, including 1 STC and 2 Wing books, but the bulk is 18th and early 19th cent. A strength is the collection of ephemera relating to school drama and other functions especially from the last quarter of the 18th cent and early 19th cent. Reading printing is naturally a significant feature of the whole collection.

A card cat is in progress. Additions continue to be made when the opportunity presents itself.

Reading University, Department of Botany, Plant Science Laboratories, Whiteknights, Reading, Berks RG6 2AS. Tel (0734) 875123. Open: weekdays, normal working hours. Admission to bona fide enquirers; application in writing or by telephone. Photocopying facilities.

Herbarium Library Mainly books numbering *c*450 presented by the executors of Norman Douglas Simpson in 1974, of which about half are rare by RBG's definition. Main emphasis is on botany, especially plant taxonomy, some British floras, including almost a complete set of editions of Philip Miller's *Gardener's Dictionary* and its abridgements; works by Ray, Dillenius and others. The collection includes 13 Wing, 72 ESTC, and 18 16th-18th cent continental items.

Author and subject cat on cards. Also included in Reading University Library's main author and subject cat.

Simpson was the author of *A bibliographical index of the British flora* (1960), based largely on his own collection. The major part of the collection went to the Botany School, Cambridge, some also to the British Museum (Natural History) and the Royal Botanic Gardens, Kew. His herbarium passed to the Royal Horticultural Society at Wisley. Some of the portion presented to Reading's Botany Department have since been transferred to the main University Library.

W T Stearn, 'Norman Douglas Simpson (1890-1974)', *Watsonia* 10 (1974-5), p403-10.

University Library, Whiteknights, Reading, Berks RG6 2AE. Tel (0734) 874331. Telex 847813. Open: (Term) Mon-Thurs 9 am-10.15 pm; Fri 9 am-7 pm; Sat 9 am-6 pm; Sun 2-6 pm; (Vacation) Mon-Fri 9 am-5 pm; Sat 9 am-1 pm. Books from closed access can normally only be fetched and used on Mon-Fri 9 am-5 pm. Admission to non-members by permission of the librarian. Written application is necessary to use special collections. Microform reader/printers and photocopying facilities. Photographic department. On-line information service.

The main collection dates from the foundation of the University Extension College, Reading, in 1892, and is made up of several thousands of pre-1851 printed books. Early donations included over 400 v of 17th and 18th cent books of Edward Cobb of Banbury in 1918-19, and early books from Sir Charles Firth in the late 1920s and '30s. The collection, together with outlier libraries (music and education), and other collections specified below, totals over 535,000 printed books, 80,000 pamphlets, and 1,750 collections of mss plus microforms, sound recordings and Reading University theses. Subject areas well represented in the general stock (excluding collections specified below) include: (i) early agriculture and horticulture—an estimated 1,200 pre-1851 works, English and foreign, including books on bees and beekeeping presented by Dr H Malcolm Fraser, and early gardening books from Leonard Sutton; (ii) early mathematics, including *c*300 pre-1851 works from the library of E H Neville; (iii) The

Great Exhibition of 1851, including exhibitors' prospectuses, prints and ephemera; (iv) over 600 v of political and other pamphlets, especially *c*2,000 political pamphlets of the period 1780-1850, including *c*90 v apparently from the library of William Wyndham, Baron Grenville; (v) English literature of the 1890s; (vi) W B Yeats and the Cuala Press; (vii) Robert Gibbings and the Golden Cockerel Press, including wood blocks (see *Four aspects of the work of Robert Gibbings* (1975)). Modern literary first editions are among the Samuel Beckett, John Wain, Hale White (Mark Rutherford) and Robert Sherard collections, and in the Finzi Book Room (poets of the 20th cent).

Including the collections specified below, there are 11 incunabula; 320 STC; 1,500 Wing; 6,000 ESTC items; 550 16th cent and 865 17th cent continental works.

Author cat on cards.

Subject cat (Library of Congress headings).

Separate card cats of pre-1701 books, 18th cent English books (recently begun), printers (pre-1701, private and famous presses, Reading printing).

Chronological cat of political pamphlets are available.

R Vosper, 'Rare books in redbrick cases', *Book Collector*, 11 (1962), p25-6.

'University of Reading Library', *Library Assoc Record*, 66 (1964), p575-80.

J C Holt, *The University of Reading: the first fifty years*, Reading UP (1977), p257-60.

'Appendix 4. The library: by Doris Mary Stenton', p343-6.

The Finzi Book Room at the University of Reading: a catalogue, by Pauline Dingley, 1981.

Abingdon Parish Library The chained library from the Church of St Helen, Abingdon. Founded about 1618, possibly the gift of Laurence Stevenson Esq, (*d*1623-4). Transferred to Reading University Library, via the Bodleian, on permanent deposit, June 1962. Many in poor condition, and most imperfect to some extent. W Blades noted their bad condition in *Books in chains*, 1892, pp29-30, having been placed in an aisle beneath a defective roof, and listed 11 items. B H Streeter recorded 11 volumes in glass cases, in poor condition in *The chained library*, 1931, p290. The books have now been cleaned and treated, but no comprehensive restoration has been undertaken. Some chains remain. The contents are usually reckoned as 35 works in 12 v, but Abingdon 6 and 7, two volumes containing 25 quarto pamphlets are almost certainly an edition of *A collection of cases and other discourses, lately written to recover dissenters*, lacking the general title-pages. All are 17th cent English theological and ecclesiastical, and there are 7 STC and 28 Wing items.

Not catalogued. The library has the Bodleian's original list identifying, with one exception, the contents of the library.

Two Bibles, one with chains, remain in the church.

Buckland (All Saints) Parish Library Early history not known. Listed by T Kelly in *Early public libraries*, 1966, p245 as an endowed library, probably founded in the 17th cent, but 3 volumes have the plate of the Bray trustees, and at least one other is uniformly bound. Other volumes were donated at various times. It was transferred to the Old Manor House, Buckland in 1951, and to Reading University Library in 1969 on permanent deposit. It contains *c*70 works in 58 v, virtually all pre-1851 and is overwhelmingly theological and ecclesiastical in emphasis, and mainly English and 18th cent, *not* 'mainly 17th cent and in Latin' (N Ker, *The parochial libraries of the Church of England*, 1959, p112). They include a copy of 'Breeches Bible', Geneva, 1560, and various editions of the works of John Rogers, DD, sometime curate of Buckland. Also included is an Oxford binding, probably by John Westall, on Casaubon *De sacris*, 1614, 2 STC, 10+ Wing, 35+ ESTC items, 5 16th cent and 9 17th cent continental works.

Not catalogued. Typescript list available.

The Children's Collection Founded as a separate collection in 1961, from children's books distributed throughout the main library collections, and the gift of some 70 early 19th cent children's books from Sir Frank and Lady Stenton, it numbers *c*4,000 v, including runs of periodicals which comprise children's literature primarily up to 1939, intended to illustrate the bibliographical evolution of genre. It includes *c*800 pre-1851 titles, predominantly English and 19th cent, among which are *The history of Little Fanny*, 1810, and good collections of Mrs Hofland and Mrs Sherwood.

Classified arrangement by Dewey. In University Library's main author and subject cats, with separate author card cat. A published cat, probably classified with author/title index is contemplated.

Additions are made as a matter of policy, primarily by donation.

The Cole Library The private library of F J Cole, Professor of Zoology in the University of Reading, 1907-39, and author of *Early theories of sexual generation* (1930), and *A history of comparative anatomy* (1944), both of which were written largely from his own collection. (*See* K J Franklin, 'Francis Joseph Cole, 1872-1959', *Biographical memoirs of Fellows of the Royal Society*, 5 (1960), p37-47, and N B Eales, 'Francis Joseph Cole, 1872-1959', *Journal of the history of medicine*, 14 (1959), p267-72.) His library was bequeathed to Dr Nellie B Eales, and acquired from her by the University in 1960. It is housed in a separate room on the fifth floor of the University Library, Whiteknights. It includes *c*8,000 v of printed books and scientific papers, a few mss and some papers of Professor Cole. Early medicine and zoology in general, more particularly, comparative anatomy and reproductive physiology, with an estimated 1,700 or more pre-1851 works, especially strong in continental books, 2 incunabula; 13 STC; 106 Wing; 260 ESTC; 53 16th cent; 242 17th cent and 392 18th cent continental works.

The Cole Library of early medicine and zoology: catalogue... by Nellie B Eales, pt 1, 1472-1800; pt 2, 1800 to the present day, and supplement. The Library, University of Reading, 1969-75. Cole's analytical card catalogue is housed with the books. Some Cole Library books have temporary cards in the University Library's main author catalogue.

N B Eales, 'The Cole Library of zoology and early medicine', *Nature*, 188 (1960), p1148-51.

An endowment allows some additions to be made from time to time. Duplicates were disposed of by Professor Cole. The Cole Museum of Zoology is housed in the Zoology Department.

The Hawkins Collection Made by H L Hawkins, Professor of Geology in the University of Reading 1920-52, and passed to the University Library under the provisions of his will in 1969. Housed separately in the Cole Library, it comprises *c*235 works (over half of them 'rare'), plus a collection of papers and pamphlets concerning geology, paleontology and echinoderms, with emphasis on continental works; first and early editions of many classics in the field, including *Rondelet Libri de piscibus marinus*, Lugduni, 1554; Gesner *De rerum fosilium*, Tiguri, 1565; Agricola *De re metallica* Basileae 1621, and works by T Burnet, J T Klein, Linnaeus, Lhuyd, Murchison, J Phillips, etc. There are 12 Wing; 14 ESTC; 2 16th cent; 4 17th cent and 31 18th cent continental works.

Temporary author cat on cards with books.

Not in University Library cat.

P Allen, 'Herbert Leader Hawkins 1887-1968', *Biographical memoirs of the Fellows of the Royal Society*, 16 (1970), p315-29, notes Hawkins's activities as a collector.

Henley-on-Thames Parish Library Founded 1737, under the will of Dr Charles Aldrich (1681-1737), Rector of Henley, 1709-1737, who bequeathed his own books to the parish. Miscellaneous additions were made thereafter. A period of neglect in the second half of the 19th cent led to some 250 works being transferred to Christ Church, Oxford, in 1909 for safe keeping, and a further 9 in 1942. Many of Aldrich's books were originally Christ Church 'duplicates' obtained under the provisions of the will of his uncle Dean Henry Aldrich (*see* P Morgan, *Oxford libraries outside the Bodleian*, 1972, p30-1). The residue of about 475 v, many in poor condition, was transferred to Reading University Library in 1957 on permanent deposit. The collection has been extensively restored with the help of a grant from an anonymous donor. It comprises *c*400 works in 475 v, all but three pre-1851—some imperfect and unidentified. Less than half the collection consists of theological, history and voyages (*c*60 v including Dr Bry *India orientalis*, 1598-1612), science and mathematics (*c*45 v including Archimedes, Basle 1544; Copernicus, Basle 1566; Flamsteed, *Atlas coelestis* 1729), classics (*c*40 v), philosophy, law, literature, art and architecture are also represented. There are 38 STC, 127 Wing, 34 ESTC items, and 20 16th cent and 118 17th and 18th cent continental works. Binding is represented by William Seale of Oxford on Epictetus and Theophrastus 1707 (ed Charles Aldrich, dedicated to Henry Aldrich).

'A catalogue of books left to the rectory of Henley by the late Dr Aldrich' *c*1780 (RUL MS 411/1/1) (*see* J A Edwards, 'Manuscript catalogue of Henley parish library', *Library History*, 1, No 6 (Autumn 1969), pp216-7); *A catalogue of the old library at Henley-on-Thames*, 1852 (RUL Microfilm P109); Catalogue of books in the parochial lending library in the parish of [Henley-on-Thames, co Oxon], *c*1860 (RUL MS 1172/1/1), records books presented to the library by the SPCK and includes a loan record. Temporary cards in University Library author cat.

N Ker, *The parochial libraries of the Church of England*, 1959, p82, and further references therein.

The Overstone Library Collected by John Ramsay McCulloch (1789-1864), the political economist, from at least 1821, when he purchased pamphlets formerly belonging to Rogers Ruding. On his death his library was purchased by his friend and collaborator Samuel Jones Loyd, Baron Overstone (1796-1883), banker, who added to it (see *The correspondence of Lord Overstone*, ed D P O'Brien (1971), volume 3, 1063, 1065, 1068-70). Overstone's daughter, Lady Wantage, bequeathed the collection remaining at Overstone Park, Northants, to Reading University College in 1920, and it is now housed in a separate room on the fifth floor of the University Library, Whiteknights. Comprising *c*5,200 titles in 7,860 v, it is a handsome example of a 19th cent private library, with emphasis on good copies and the best editions, of which over 90 per cent are rare. The collection is strong in economics, including early pamphlets (eg two editions of *An advice*... (1627) by John Reynolds 'of the Mint'), also travel, history, literature and classics, political and religious philosophy, with French a strong second to the predominantly English 18th cent emphasis. There are 20 STC, 110 Wing, 1,440 ESTC, 7 16th cent continental and 720 17th and 18th cent continental works, many good specimens of Elzevirs, Barbou, Baskerville, Foulis, Strawberry Hill Press, 18th and early 19th cent English and French bindings (including signed bindings by C Kalthoeber, Hering, C Smith, Mackenzie, Derome, Bozerian, Simier and others)—a few exceptional ones; illustrated books, including 'Illustrations of Northamptonshire' *c*1820—a collection of nearly 1,000 prints, drawings and water-colours of Northants interest. (A microfilm copy at Delapre Abbey and at Northampton Public Library—checklist available). Entered in University Library's main author catalogue. The entire collection remains substantially as it was recorded in *Catalogue of the library, Overstone Park* (1867).

The progress of McCulloch's collection is recorded in *A catalogue of books, the property of the author of the commercial dictionary* (1856) and *A catalogue of books, the property of a political economist* (1862), in the preface to which he describes his attitude to book-collecting. Much of this was reprinted by James Bonar in *Contributions towards a dictionary of English book collectors*, ed by Bernard Quaritch, pt VI (1895). See also D P O'Brien, *J R McCulloch* (1970), p80-1, and D H

Knott, 'Note 365' (*Book Collector*, 22 (1973), p384-8).

No deliberate disposals are known, but not everything in McCulloch's 1862 *Catalogue* is in the Overstone Library. Furthermore, some items in the Overstone Park *Catalogue* of 1867, mainly collections of autograph letters, did not go to Reading in 1920. They were retained by the Loyd family at Lockinge, Berks, and have since been disposed of.

The Stenton Library The working libraries of Sir F M Stenton and Doris Lady Stenton. He was Professor of Modern History in the University of Reading 1912-46, Vice-Chancellor 1946-50, and author of *Anglo-Saxon England*, 1943. Lady Stenton was Lecturer, later Reader, in History 1920-59, General Editor of the Pipe Roll Society, 1925-62, and author of *The English woman in history*, 1957. Their collection was bequeathed to the University under the will of Lady Stenton in 1972, and is housed on the fifth floor of the University Library at Whiteknights, in a room furnished with some of the pieces from the Stenton's home at Shitley Park Farm. It includes *c*4,700 printed v, plus mss, correspondence and Stenton family papers. As both were mediaevalists, English mediaeval history is strongly represented in the collection. There are also over 1,100 pre-1851 English and continental works, including 57 STC; 251 Wing; 397 ESTC; 20 16th cent; 48 17th cent; and 22 18th cent continental works. They are arranged in broad subject groups. Mss include 'Court roll for the view of frankpledge of the court baron of Sonning, co Berks: 25 Oct 1615-24 (Oct 1636) (RUL MS 1264), some 30 deeds and charters and collections of original documents (RUL MS 1148/13/1-31), and a notebook recording the provenance and prices of books acquired by the Stentons 1926-66 (MS 1148/20/9).

The Stenton's ms card catalogue with University Library's additions accompanies the books. Not in University Library cat.

D M Stenton, 'Frank Merry Stenton, 1880-1967', *Proceedings of the British Academy*, 54 (1968), p315-423.

K Major, 'Doris Mary Stenton, 1894-1971', *Proceedings of the British Academy*, 58 (1972), p525-35.

The Turner Collection Collected by Father John Turner (1765-1844), a member of the Community of English Benedictines in France during the Revolution. He was personally involved in events in Paris, taking the civil oath, and suffering imprisonment in St Pégalie 1793-5. The collection was preserved in the community's monastery at Douai, despite efforts by Turner, who had returned to England to have it sold, until the community's return to England in 1903, when it was transferred to Douai Abbey, Woolhampton (qv). Placed on permanent deposit in the University Library by the Abbot and Community of Douai in July 1966.

The collection is made up of 275 v containing an estimated 2,500 separate pamphlets, plus newspaper cuttings, extracts, ms notes and transcripts amounting to some 8,000 items in all, and concerning, mainly, the events of 1787-1806. The collection remains largely as Turner originally arranged it, in contemporary paper-covered bindings and portfolios, and recorded in his ms catalogue (RUL MS 1723). This catalogue is in three parts: 'Ouvrages politiques', arranged chronologically, and later designated Catalogue A; 'Affaires ecclésiastiques', arranged by subject, designated Catalogue C; Catalogue B, which overlaps with both A and C but is not entirely superseded by them. There is a modern, temporary ms author catalogue of the pamphlets on cards, and a chronological and subject index to the entire collection, on slips with the collection.

Manuscripts and archives 1,750 collections of historical and literary mss, and large body of University archives. The mss collection is divided into six main groups:

(1) Records of British publishing and printing, including (i) Bailliere, Tindall and Cox Ltd (MS 1570), 21 v of out-letters, 1875-1910, (ii) George Bell and Sons Ltd (MS 1640), accounts and correspondence 1832-1977, including Charles Whittingham and Co and the Chiswick Press 1880-1920, (iii) De La Rue and Co Ltd (MS 937), correspondence, designs, specimens, inventories, etc 1837-1965, (iv) Otto and Marie Neurath Isotype collection (MS 1091), comprising correspondence 1941-67, subject files, specimens, books, charts, diagrams, etc (see *Graphic communication through ISOTYPE* (1975), (v) London Typographical Designers Ltd (MS 1643), 10,000 job packets and specimens, 1945-70, (vi) Longman Group Ltd (MS 1393), ledgers, registers and bound records referring to the publishing business 1794-1963; miscellaneous papers and documents relating to publishing and the Longman family, Sir Richard Phillips 1798-1864, A J Valpy 1815-1838, Thomas Cadell 1747-1846, J W Parker, Son & Bourn 1863, Thomas Moore 1818-1846, correspondence with authors; *c*350 printed books, plus runs of periodicals. The archives, 1794-1914, are available on microfilm from Chadwyck-Healey Ltd, Cambridge (Archives of British publishers), (vii) Macmillan and Company (MS 1089), 50,000 in-letters 1875-1940 (the residue of the collection of which the British Library holds the more important part) are art-work specimens 1950 onwards, (viii) Charles Elkin Mathews (MS 392), correspondence, etc 1811-1938 (see *Charles Elkin Mathews: poets' publisher*, 1967 [op]). This collection is available on microfilm from Chadwyck-Healey Ltd, Cambridge (Archives of British publishers), (ix) Phoenix Houst Ltd (MS 1255), art-work and publicity 1945-65, (x) Routledge and Kegan Paul Ltd (MS 1489) correspondence files 1935-70 (other records at University College, London).

(2) Historical farm records Over 400 groups of records, 16th to 20th-cent, representing every English county (see *Historical farm records: a summary guide* (1973)).

(3) Records of contemporary writing, representing over 170 authors, especially Samuel Beckett (see *Samuel Beckett: an exhibition* (1971), *The Samuel Beckett collection: a catalogue* (1978)), also W B Yeates, Peter Fleming, Peter Porter. (See also Sound-writing: *George Bernard Shaw and a modern alphabet* (1972), *The Group:*

an exhibition of poetry (1974), *John Wain: poet, novelist, critic* (1977).)

(4) Modern political papers, especially the papers of Nancy, Viscountess Astor (1879-1964) (MS 1416) and Waldorf, 2nd Viscount Astor (1879-1952) (MS 1066).

(5) Illuminated and other mss, 12 specimens, held on behalf of the Guild of St George, 11th-17th cent (seen by Ker).

J S Dearden, 'John Ruskin, the collector, with a catalogue of the illuminated and other manuscripts formerly in his collection', *The Library* 5th ser, 21 (1966), pp124-54). See also separate description of Ruskin Museum.

(6) Other historical and literary manuscripts, including Aubrey Beardsley (MS 160), Huntley and Palmers Ltd (MS 1490), Peek Frean and Co Ltd, (MS 1216), John Ruskin letters, held on behalf of the Guild of St George, William Edward Tate's papers (Mss 1093 and 1234) on enclosures and schools (see M E Turner (ed), *A Doomsday of English enclosure acts and awards*, The Library, University of Reading, 1978). The University archives contain both formal archives of the University and miscellaneous historical material, and the papers of ex-members of staff, including Sir Frank and Lady Stenton (see *Making a university: an exhibition* (1968)). Loose-leaf typescript summary catalogue, plus personal and place-name indexes for fully catalogued collections, and handlists and inventories, for uncatalogued collections, available in the Department.

J A Edwards, *Archives and manuscripts in the Library, University of Reading: a brief guide* (1980).

University of Reading, Institute of Agricultural History and Museum of English Rural Life, Whiteknights, Reading, Berks RG6 2AG. Tel (0734) 875123. Open Mon-Fri 9.15 am-1 pm, 2.15-5 pm. Admission to non-members of University by appointment, and for reference only. Microfilm reader; photographic and photocopying service through University Library.

Institute of Agricultural History Library and Archive Collections Materials collected since the establishment of the Museum in 1952. General area of interest—English agricultural history, rural life and industries, history of UK food and agricultural engineering industries.

Library collections include *c*400 v printed books and journals pre-1851, predominantly post 1750, and including the county reports of the Board of Agriculture and the *Annals of agriculture.*

Archival collections include manufacturers' catalogues in the Trade Records Collection, and ephemera, including the Soulby and Kitchen collections of printed ephemera. (*See* M Twyman, *John Soulby, printer, Ulverston*, Reading, Museum of English Rural Life (1966); *The Kitchen Collection*, Museum of English Rural Life and Typography Unit (1974).

Author and classified subject cat on cards. Library collections also filed in University Library's main catalogue.

Museum procedure: Library, by J S Creasey, 2nd ed, Institute of Agricultural History and Museum of English Rural Life (1978).

Collections are added to as a matter of policy, and complemented by the object and photographic collections, and by the Bibliographical Unit. Historical farm records are held by the University Library (qv).

Windsor

The Chapter Library, St George's Chapel, Windsor Castle, Windsor, Berks SL4 1NJ. No telephone, but librarian can be reached via the Chapter clerk on Windsor (07535) 65538. Admission to bona fide scholars after initial written application to the librarian.

The origins of the Chapter Library go back to the establishment of the Royal Free Chapel in 1348. There were 17th cent bequests from Dean Henry Beaumont (1627, 80 v) and Dean Anthony Maxey (1648, 80 v), 18th cent acquisitions from Canon John Hartcliffe, Canon William Cave (purchased in 1714) and by bequest from Lord Ranelagh in 1712 (mainly 17th cent books). In 1947 it was decided to maintain only a 'museum library', substantially the collection as it was in 1692, and it is not added to. This chronological distinction was not strictly observed, however, as some earlier books, especially literature, were disposed of (Sotheby 25-6 October 1948, lots 312-337), while some later material was retained. In March 1950, several hundred miscellaneous post-1692 books were disposed of through booksellers. In 1612 70 mss were surrendered to the Bodleian. A broad programme of restoration and cataloguing was initiated in 1947.

The collection comprises 5,728 books printed before 1751 (described by Callard) plus *c*50 v of local topography. There are 9 incunabula, 380 STC, 2,353 Wing and 2,553 continental books of the 16th and 17th cent. Predominant subjects are theology and ecclesiastical history, classics, history and geography, with particular strength in 17th cent pamphlets. In the 19th cent the library received 1,150 sermons and pamphlets of the late 17th and early 18th cent, bound in 127 v, many of which had belonged to the 4th Duke of Bedford. There are also 79 disbound tracts of the same centuries in the Aerary. There is a separately published catalogue of the music mss. 17 Oxford bindings are listed by Ker (*Fragments of medieval mss used as pastedowns*. . . 1954) and there are a few other interesting blind-stamped bindings.

Sheaf author cat.

J Callard, *A catalogue of printed books (pre-1751) in the library of St George's Chapel, Windsor Castle*. . . Windsor, 1976. (Includes additional published references and an account of the surviving historic catalogues.)

C Mould, *The musical MSS of St George's Chapel*. . . *a*

descriptive catalogue, Windsor, 1973.

Note For all other mss and archives of the Chapel, application must be made to the Custodian of the Muniments, The Aerary, Dean's Cloister, Windsor Castle. They are described in: J N Dalton, *The manuscripts of St George's Chapel*, Windsor, 1957.

The Royal Library, Windsor Castle, Windsor, Berks. Tel (07535) 68286. Applications for access to this material should be made to the Librarian, Royal Library, Windsor Castle, Berkshire.

The Royal Library at Windsor Castle is the personal library of Her Majesty the Queen, and is not in principle open for research. Applications to see unique material are, however, considered. Applicants must be qualified researchers, and must hold a British Library reader's ticket. In the field of printed books, material that is possibly unique may be found under the following heads: privately printed works, notably on genealogy and regimental history; F Madan's collection of the Eikon Basilike; incunabula. The library contains 236 incunabula, 110 from Italian presses and 81 from German presses. One group was presented to King George III by the notable antiquary and bibliophile Jacob Bryant (1715-1804). Others had at one time belonged to the library of Dr J G F B Kloss of Frankfurt-am-Main, which was sold at Sotheby's in 1835.

One of the rarest incunabula in the Royal Library is Rodericus Zamorensis, *Speculum Vitae*, printed by Helias Heliae at Beromünster, Switzerland, 7 December 1472 (Goff F 217) and inscribed with the name of Dawson Turner (1775-1858), the well-known antiquary, who acquired it in Paris in 1815. There is also a copy in beautiful condition, but lacking six leaves, of the Mainz Psalter, 14 August 1457, printed by Fust and Schoeffer. In addition, the Royal Library has the only known perfect copy of William Caxton's edition of the *Fables of Aesop*, printed at Westminster on 26 March 1484, and presented to King George III by Mr Hewett of Ipswich.

Eton College Library, Penzance, Eton College, Windsor, Berks SL4 6DB. Tel (07535) 69991, Ext 38 (for information of other librarians. *Not* for intending readers). Open, Mon-Fri 8 am-12.30 pm, 1.30-5.30 pm. Closed Sat and for ten days at Christmas and Easter. Admission to graduate scholars after initial written application; undergraduates and others are asked to provide references. Microfilm-fiche reader, and ultra-violet lamp available. Quick copying subject to discretion; no pre-1800 book and no mss can be copied. Competent photographers accompanying readers welcomed. For commissioning photographs or microfilm, enquire. (Arrangements with Bodleian Library and University Microfilms.)

Eton College Library is an integral part of the College, founded 1440, and is the Provost and Fellows' Library (cf Eton College School Library). Donations and bequests, more especially from R Topham, J Reynolds, N Mann and A Storer, have been particularly important in building up the library which contains *c*30,000 titles in 25,000 v, almost all of which are rare (by RBG definition). A general collegiate library to 1800, later additions have been mainly in theology, history, literature, bibliography and 'Etoniana' (author/subject association); 17th-19th cent school texts printed at Eton. There are 192 incunabula, 820 STC, *c*3-4,000 Wing; Aldines; Elzeviers; fine bindings (including Roger Payne); modern presses (including complete Kelmscott set) from Major Abbey; 17th cent pamphlets, etc; pre-Restoration plays.

Cat.

Robert Birley, *The history of Eton College Library* (Eton, CUP 1970); *One hundred books in Eton College Library* (Eton, CUP 1970).

Note Birley's *History* in 'Notes' (there is no proper bibliography) refers to many books and articles in which individual Eton books, groups of bindings etc are described in detail.

Eton College School Library, Eton College, Windsor, Berks SL4 6DB. Tel (07535) 68987. Not open to the general public, but to bona fide scholars after written application.

School Library, Eton College, Rare Book Collection Founded in the 1820s, the main school borrowing library, rare books, and mss deposited since that time. There are *c*5,000 v (total school library *c*30,000 v). Most of the collection is 20th cent and late 19th cent, with a representative collection (*c*1,200 v) of earlier books, including one incunabulum. The remainder modern firsts—strengths are Thomas Hardy, 20th cent Eton authors and fore-edge paintings (about 200 representing the best collection outside the British Library). The school library also has the Macnaghten collection of First World War material (5,000 items)—fine editions, association copies, some mss.

No cat of rare book collection.

Buckinghamshire

Aylesbury

Buckinghamshire Archaeological Society, County Museum, Church Street, Aylesbury, Bucks HP20 2QP. Tel (02406) 2909. Open Wed 10 am-4 pm.

Books may not be borrowed. Photocopies can be made.

Buckinghamshire Archaeological Society Collection Built up since the end of the 19th cent by donations and purchases, it contains 900 books (160 pre-1851) and 650 pamphlets (200 pre-1851). With the exception of *c*90 books, the collection is concerned with the topography and history of Buckinghamshire, including its archaeology, buildings and people. No printed works before the 17th cent.

Author and classified cat for printed books.

Classified cat only for pamphlets.

Buckinghamshire County Library, County Reference Library, County Library HQ, Walton Street, Aylesbury, Bucks HP20 1UU. Tel (0296) 5000. Open Mon 9 am-5 pm; Tues-Fri 9 am-8 pm; Sat 9 am-1 pm. Open to general public. Study carrels plus additional seating capacity. Photocopy service; microfilm reader/printer.

County Reference Stock
Acquired by the County Library through purchase and donation in General Collection Building; the pre-1851 collection is made up of 33 single-volume works and 11 multi-volume works dealing with British topography.

Buckingham Collection Acquired gradually by County Library since the beginning of the county service from a variety of sources. A collection of *c*6,500 works (including rare and modern items), pamphlets, newspapers, magazines, maps and ephemera relating to the history, topography, families etc of Buckinghamshire dating from the 17th cent to the present day. Local newspapers and census of the 19th cent are available on microfilm. There are also local topographical collections at branch libraries, notably High Wycombe and Milton Keynes, containing rare items on their particular locality. The collection is added to regularly.

For further information apply to the Reference Library.

Loose-leaf bibliography (unpublished) available for consultation at most branch libraries.

County Reserve Stock
The Basden Collection (Thomas Gray). Part of the collection of material relating to Buckinghamshire consisting of 48 items, including 29 editions of the poems or poems and letters of the poet Thomas Gray dating from 1783 to 1953 (mostly 19th cent); 11 editions of Gray's Elegy (dating from 1869-1955); 18 miscellaneous items relating to Gray.

List available on application to librarian.

Early Children's Book Collection
Most of the collection has been purchased from local booksellers, and added to through donations. It contains *c*1,100 literary items (including 120 chapbooks/magazines) written for children, and dating from 1711 to 1940s, including several first editions. For further information apply to the School Library Service.

Buckinghamshire County Record Office, County Offices, Walton Street, Aylesbury, Bucks HP20 1UU. Tel (0296) 5000. Open Tues-Thurs 9 am-5.15 pm; Fri 9.45 am-4.30 pm. Admission on application to the archivist.

Thomas Wright Collection Acquired by a collector and purchased by the County Library, the collection contains 85 v, plus mss from the personal library of Thomas Wright (1859–1936), writer, poet and biographer, born and lived in Olney, Buckinghamshire. Most of the volumes are first editions of Wright's works. Quite a number of the items relate to John Payne, the poet and translator, and the collection includes some of his works. There is also a considerable amount of ms material. For further details apply to the archivist.

Carreras Rothmans Ltd, Oxford Road, Aylesbury, Bucks. Tel (0296) 26111. Open Mon-Thurs 9 am-5 pm; Fri 9 am-3.45 pm. Not open to the general public; bona fide scholars should apply in writing. Photocopier available.

Carreras Rothmans Company Library The main subject areas of the library centre on tobacco. There are important ephemera on the subject of tobacco from the 1880s onwards, including cigarettes, cigars and tobacco packs, advertising material, books on tobacco.

High Wycombe

Hughenden Manor (National Trust), High Wycombe, Bucks. The house is open at the advertised times. Access to the library is by written application, in advance, stating the precise reason for requiring admission. Requests must be addressed to The Libraries Adviser, The National Trust, 42 Queen Anne's Gate, London SW1H 9AS.

The house contains such parts of the library of Benjamin Disraeli as were not sold after his death. It incorporates many books from the library of his father Isaac D'Israeli, including works with manuscript corrections prepared for later editions. Some of Isaac's books are curiosities of literature. The collection is strong in history and literature, with some 16th cent foreign books, though none of them is especially uncommon. There are a number of books presented to Benjamin Disraeli and, of course, copies of his own works. Some books have been taken from the collection since Disraeli's death. There are in all *c*2,500 v. The Disraeli papers have been deposited in the Bodleian Library, Oxford.

Shelflists only for the printed books.

Lists of papers are in the Bodleian Library, Oxford.

Watson Hawksley, Consulting Engineers, Terriers House, Amersham Road, High Wycombe, Bucks. Tel (0494) 26240. Ext 244 and 245. Not open to the general public; bona fide scholars should apply in writing. Photocopier; microfilm/microfiche readers available.

The Library, Watson Hawksley Contains *c*1,000 books and 2,000 reports and pamphlets, plus journals, British and Overseas Standards, Acts of Parliament, and manufacturers' catalogues. Subjects covered are water and water engineering, and related subjects. The library also contains (1) a collection of early works on sewerage and sewage treatment, formerly owned by D Watson, FICE; (2) a unique collection of Water Acts, 18th cent-1974, formerly owned by Thomas Hawksley, FRS.

Milton Keynes

Milton Keynes College, Wolverton Campus, Stratford Road, Wolverton, Milton Keynes MK12 5NU. Tel (0908) 313042. Ext 6. Open (Term times) Mon-Thurs 9.30 am-6 pm; Fri 9.30 am-4.30 pm. Admission to general public.

Milton Keynes College Library The library has a general subject coverage, but with some emphasis on engineering. It contains the Ernest George Coker collection of antiquarian and classic engineering of *c*150 titles ranging from the 19th cent to *c*1930.

Olney

Cowper and Newton Museum, Orchard Side, Market Place, Olney, Buckinghamshire MK46 4AJ. Tel (0234) 711516. Open by appointment.

The museum is a memorial to the two compilers of *Olney hymns*, William Cowper (1731—1800) the poet, and his friend the Rev John Newton (1725—1807). It originated with the collection of Cowper and Newton books, mss, and memorabilia collected by the Rev Thomas Wright (1859—1936) headmaster of the Cowper School at Olney, partly inherited from his father William Samuel Wright (1831—18??) of Olney. He exhibited it in Olney at a meeting of the Buckinghamshire Archaeological Society in 1890, hoping that a permanent home would be offered for it. He persuaded William Henry Collingridge (*c*1826—1905) the printer and proprietor of the *City Press*, who owned Cowper's home Orchard Side, to donate it to a trust, and at the centenary in 1900 of Cowper's death, it was opened to the public as a museum incorporating Collingridge's own Cowper mss and printed collections in addition to Wright's. The Cowper Society was founded at the same time, with its headquarters there. There are over 1,000 v of printed books, in addition to ephemera and mss. There are some 18th cent editions, but the main strength of the collection lies in its 19th cent holdings, especially locally printed material, much of it containing specific reference to Cowper, and much to the Wright family and others who were interested in Cowper and Newton.

There is no cat, other than an out of date shelflist.

Guide to Cowper and Newton Museum, 2nd ed 1918.

Thomas Wright, *Autobiography*, London, 1936, p53, 71-5, 248-9.

E V Lucas, *A rover I would be*, London, 1928, p21-6.

Slough

Cement and Concrete Association, Wexham Springs, Slough, Bucks SL3 6PL. Tel (02816) 2727. Ext 326. Open Mon-Fri 9 am-5 pm. Open to general public, but visits by appointment only. Microfilm/microfiche reader available.

The library of the Association contains an important historical collection of *c*350 v on concrete—19th cent English and foreign.

Cat of concrete (available free).

Waddesdon

Waddesdon Manor (National Trust), Waddesdon, Nr Aylesbury, Bucks. Tel (029665) 1211. Admission to the library by prior application, in writing, for appointment (giving detailed reasons for visit) to the Libraries Adviser, National Trust, 42 Queen Anne's Gate, London SW1H 9AS.

Waddesdon Manor Library Founded by Baron Ferdinand de Rothschild (*d*1898), the library is made up of *c*800 printed items, mainly devoted to French 17th and 18th cent illustrated books and fine bindings. There are also *c*30 early mss.

Cat of books and bindings in preparation.

The S A de Rothschild collection at Waddesdon Manor, illuminated manuscripts by L M J Delarssé (and others), Fribourg, 1977.

A R A Hobson, 'Waddesdon Manor' (unfamiliar libraries, 5), *The Book Collector*, VIII (1959), p131-9.

Cambridgeshire

Cambridge

Anatomy School Library, University of Cambridge, Downing Street, Cambridge. Tel (0223) 68665. Ext 48. Open 9.15 am-1 pm, 2-6 pm (5.30 outside full term; 5 pm Fri), Sat 9.15 am-1 pm (closed Sat outside full term), to members of the

University; others on application to the librarian. Photocopying, microform reader/printer available.

Formed in 1887 by the then University Professor of Comparative Anatomy, A Macalister, who also bequeathed his fine collection of the works of such pioneers of anatomy as Vesalius and Owen. The library contains 9,000 v of printed books, 5,500 bound v of periodicals and 16,000 offprints. The library also has a small collection (14 v) of various works of Darwin; 90 v of 19th cent palaeontology and 120 v of 19th cent anthropology. Pre-1850 holdings include 2 STC; 22 European 1500–1640; 9 Wing; 28 European 1641–99; 33 18th cent British; 34 18th cent European; 115 British 1800–50; 124 European 1800–50. It also contains, on loan, a collection of *c*300 early 19th cent books from West Suffolk General Hospital: a copy of the catalogue of this is in the University Library.

Cat author/title and subject. Dewey classification.

Applied Biology Library, Department of Applied Biology, University of Cambridge, Pembroke Street, Cambridge. Tel (0223) 358381 Ext 225. Open Term, 9 am-5.30 pm, Sat 9 am-12.30 pm; Vacation, 9 am-1 pm, 2-5.30 pm, closed Sat. Free admission to members of the University; others on application.

Biffin Collection Collected by Sir Rowland Biffin (1874–1949), Professor of Agricultural Botany in the University. Given to the then University Department of Agriculture after his death in October 1949. The collection contains *c*1,100 reprints and offprints bound together, and includes many pamphlets. The collection is a world-wide coverage of plant breeding and plant genetics reprints, mainly late 19th-early 20th cent.

Card author cat.

Marshall Collection Collected by F H A Marshall (1878–1949), University Reader in Agricultural Physiology and given to the then University Department of Agriculture on his death in 1949. It contains *c*1,750 reprints in bound volumes, including many pamphlets dealing with the physiology of reproduction giving a world-wide coverage. Mainly 20th cent.

Card author cat.

Yule Collection Collected by G V Yule (1871–1951), University Lecturer in Statistics, and presented to the University Department of Agriculture after his death. Transferred, on permanent loan, to the University Library.

Botany School, Downing Street, Cambridge. Tel (0223) 61414. Open Mon-Fri 8.30 am-5.15 pm, Sat 9 am-12.15 pm. Closed vacation. Members of the University admitted freely; others on application to the librarian. Photocopying; microform reader.

Botany School Library Founded in 1762 as part of the Botanic Garden. In 1765 John Martyn (1699–1768) presented 200 v; 1895 Charles Babington (1808–95) bequeathed 1,600 v; in 1903 the library moved into its present building. Its stock totals *c*20,000 v, and includes general botanical and ecological textbooks and monographs. Particularly strong in floras (world-wide collection) and early herbals. There are 1 incunabulum; 80 books printed 1501–1640 (10 from Britain, 70 from Europe); 80 books printed 1641–1700 (34 from Britain, 46 from Europe); 337 18th cent works (178 from Britain, 159 from Europe); 350 works printed 1801–50 (189 from Britain, 161 from Europe). The most notable collection is the N D Simpson collection of local flora (*c*1,200 v). The library also holds the botanical correspondence of Babington, J S Henslow (1796–1861) and William Borrer (1781–1862).

Modified Bliss classification scheme; author cat.

Cambridge University Library, West Road, Cambridge CB3 9DR. Tel (0223) 61441. Open Mon-Fri 9 am-7.05 pm, (Easter Term) 9 am-9.45 pm; Sat 9 am-1 pm. Admission to members of Cambridge University; others on application to the librarian. Full photographic service, Hinman collator, U/V lamps, microform readers, microfilm reader/printer.

The University owned books by the mid-14th cent, but the earliest mention of a library is found in 1416. By 1473 it contained 330 v. Early major benefactors include Walter Crome (*d*1453), Thomas Rotherham (Archbishop of York, *d*1500) and Cuthbert Tunstall (Bishop of London, *d*1559). Despite neglect, the library survived throughout the Reformation and its aftermath, and in the late 16th cent was properly established once again through the gifts of Matthew Parker (Archbishop of Canterbury, who gave 25 mss and 75 printed books in 1574), Sir Nicholas Bacon (Lord Keeper of the Great Seal), Robert Horne (Bishop of Winchester) and James Pilkington (Bishop of Durham). Theodorus Beza gave the so-called Codex Bezae, a 5th cent copy of the Gospels and Acts of the Apostles in Greek and Latin, in 1581. In 1632 the library laid the foundations of its oriental collections in acquiring 87 v from the widow of the Duke of Buckingham, all but one of them mss, from the library of Thomas Erpenius. Shortly afterwards the library was transformed by three major donations: of Richard Holdsworth (Master of Emmanuel College, *d*1649: 10,095 printed books and 186 mss) and Henry Lucas (MP for the University), both in 1664, and of John Hacket, Bishop of Coventry, in 1670.

By 1715 the library contained *c*15,000 books. In that year it was trebled by the gift (of George I) of the library of John Moore, Bishop of Ely (1646–1714), comprising some 30,000 books, including 1,790 mss. This included a ms of Bede (written *c*737), the 9th cent Book of Cerne, the 9th-10th cent Book of Deer, an early 12th cent Winchester Pontifical and a 13th cent Life of Edward the Confessor, and (in printed books) an outstanding collection of

Caxtons. Further, but lesser, 18th cent donations included the oriental collections of George Lewis (mostly Persian, and given in 1726), and many of Thomas Baker's volumes of transcripts relating to University history (the remainder are in the British Library). Most later collections are described separately below.

Under the Licensing Acts of 1662–79 and 1685–95, the library was established as a copyright deposit library, a right confirmed by the Copyright Act of 1710, and has continued in subsequent legislation ever since. Until the early 19th cent the library selected books registered at Stationers' Hall only sparingly, but since the mid-19th cent it has sought to be comprehensive.

General

Note: In addition to the references cited under individual collections described below, the following union catalogues and more general works provide essential guides to the holdings of libraries in the University.

A N L Munby, *Cambridge college libraries: aids for research students*. 2nd ed Cambridge, 1962.

Guide to libraries of the University of Cambridge. Cambridge 1969. (repr from *Cambridge University Reporter*, v99, 1969.

Printed Books

H M Adams, *Catalogue of books printed on the Continent of Europe, 1501–1600 in Cambridge libraries*. 2 vols, Cambridge 1967.

No union cat exists of early printed books in Cambridge, but the Rare Books Department of the University Library maintains copies of STC and Wing annotated with locations of copies of English books 1475–1700 in college and departmental libraries. An incomplete card cat with details of incunabula is also available.

Union catalogue of scientific (departmental) libraries in the University of Cambridge: books published before 1801. Compiled at the Scientific Periodicals Library, University of Cambridge. 9 microfiches. London, 1977.

E P Tyrrell and J S G Simmons, 'Slavonic books before 1700 in Cambridge libraries' *Trans Cambridge Bibliographical Soc*, III (1963), p382-400.

For serials, see under section C 'Periodicals' below.

Bindings

G D Hobson, *Bindings in Cambridge libraries*. Cambridge 1929.

Music (copies of each of the following are kept in xerographic form in the University Library):

C Hogwood, *Summary catalogue of books on theoretical music printed before 1801 in the libraries of Cambridge University*, 1964.

R M Andrewes, *Source inventory of manuscripts of attributed music up to 1800 in Cambridge libraries*, 1969.

Manuscripts

P E Easterling, 'Greek manuscripts at Cambridge: recent acquisitions by college libraries, the Fitzwilliam Museum, and private collectors'. *Trans Cambridge Bibliographical Soc*, 4 (1966), p179-91.

E G Browne, *A supplementary handlist of the Muhammadan manuscripts preserved in the libraries of the University and colleges of Cambridge*. Cambridge 1922.

A J Arbery, *A second supplementary handlist*. Cambridge 1952.

The Principal Special Collections (apart from earlier collections mentioned above) include:

A Printed Books

(i) *Western*

The library of Lord Acton (1834–1902): *c*60,000 v, mainly European history, with excellent holdings on French, German and Italian history;

Books from the library of John Couch Adams (1819–92): *c*1,500 v early printed books on astronomy;

Early books on agriculture, formerly in the Dept of Applied Biology. Includes books from the Royal Library at Windsor and important donations by G Udney Yule;

Atlases and early books on cartography: *c*1,500 atlases pre-1850;

Auction and sale catalogues. Registered in A N L Munby and L Coral *British book sale catalogues 1676–1800*, 1977 and in an annotated copy of the British Museum *List of catalogues of English book sales*, 1915, in the Rare Books Room;

Bassingbourn (Hunts) Parish Library: 412 v bought in 1969, the remainder of the library going to Essex University Library;

Collection of Bibles: presented by A W Young, includes 42-line Bible;

Sir Frederic Madden's (1801–73) collection of broadside ballads: *c*1,600 sheets, mostly 18th-early 19th cent;

Broughton (Hunts) Parish Library. Bought 1958.

Sir Geoffrey Keynes's collection (formerly in the Royal College of Physicians) of Sir Thomas Browne.

Broxbourne type specimens and books of typographical interest. Presented by J Ehrman, 1978 (see A Fern 'Typographical specimen books in the Broxbourne Library' (*Book Collector*, Autumn 1956, p256-72, and J G Dreyfus and D McKitterick *French eighteenth century type specimens*, Roxburghe Club, 1982).

T E Buckley collection, mostly 19th cent books on central and southern Africa, bequeathed to the University in 1903 and formerly in the Balfour Library.

Bury St Edmunds Grammar School (See A T Bartholomew and C Gordon 'The Library of King Edward VI School, Bury St Edmund's', *The Library*, Jan 1910.

Part of the Marquess of Bute's collection of 16th cent Italian literature. 902 v purchased 1949.

Cambridge collection. Centred on the bequest of J W Clark (1833–1910). (See A T Bartholomew, *Catalogue of the books and papers for the most part relating to the*

University, town and county of Cambridge. Cambridge 1912.)

Cambridge imprints collection, supplemented by the pre-1801 portion of the collection formerly at the University Press (see H S Bennett 'The Syndics Library at the University Press', *Trans Cambridge Bibliographical Soc*, IV (1966), p253-6.

Chapbooks, mainly from the collection of J W L Glaisher (1928).

Darwin and Darwiniana. Most of Charles Darwin's (1809–82) library. (For a part of the collection see H W Rutherford, *Catalogue of the library of Charles Darwin now in the Botany School, Cambridge.* Cambridge 1908.)

de Laszlo collection on phytotherapy. Bequeathed to the University by H G de Laszlo in 1968. (See *Library of medicinal plants collected by Henry G de Laszlo*, 1958.)

Early economics books from the library of George Pryme (1781–1868), Alfred Marshall (1842–1924), and J M Keynes (1883–1946), formerly in the Marshall Library of Economics.

Εικων Βασιλικε Collection made by F Madan and others.

Ely Cathedral Library. Transferred to Cambridge in 1970, with the exception of those books sold at Sotheby's 9–10 March 1972.

Erasmus. Mainly from the collection of Frederic Seebohm (1833–1912), presented by his family in 1925.

Fairy Chess. Given by A S M Dickins in 1972–3 etc (see *A catalogue of fairy chess books and opuscules donated to Cambridge University Library by A Dickins*, 2nd ed Kew Gardens, 1973).

Geology books from the Woodwardian Museum, later the Dept of Geology.

The library of William Gerhardie (1895–1977).

G W F Hegel. From the library of John McTaggart, presented by Mrs McTaggart, 1925.

Heraldry and Genealogy. Bequeathed by Gavin Macfarlane-Grieve, 1974.

The Richard Hunter collection on the history of psychiatry and psychiatric treatment.

Huntingdon Archdeaconry Library.

Incunabula c4,600 items (see J C T Oates *A catalogue of the fifteenth-century printed books in the University Library, Cambridge.* Cambridge, 1954).

Irish books. Irish imprints and books about Ireland. Founded on the collection of Henry Bradshaw (1831–86). (See C E Sayle, *A catalogue of the Bradshaw collection of Irish books in the University Library, Cambridge.* 3 v, Cambridge 1916.)

Sir Geoffrey Keynes's (1887–1982) library. For a partial cat see his *Bibliotheca Bibliographici* (privately printed, 1964). The collection is particularly strong in Jane Austen, George Berkeley, Thomas Bewick, William Blake, Robert Boyle, Timothy Bright, Rupert Brooke, John Donne, John Evelyn, Edward Gibbon, William Harvey, Martin Lister, Siegfried Sassoon, and the history of medicine and science generally. For Sir Thomas Browne, see above.

G E Moore (1873–1958). c200 books from his library, mainly of philosophy and by members of the Bloomsbury Group. Bought with his papers, 1980.

Stanley Morison's (1889–1967) library. c6,000 v on typography, palaeography, church history, etc. Presented by Sir Allen Lane, 1968.

Munby collection. Books relating to the history of the book trade, including booksellers' and auctioneers' catalogues, from the library of A N L Munby (*d*1974). (See D McKitterick 'The Munby collection in the University Library', *Trans Cambridge Bibliographical Soc*, VI (1975), p205-10.)

Mathematical and early scientific books from the library of F P White (*d*1969). *c*1,250 v.

Nazi literature and propaganda.

Orwell (Cambs) School Library. Presented by Francis Jenkinson, 1911.

Early medical books, transferred from the Dept of Pathology. Includes 17th-18th cent collections of the Hunterian Society of London.

Peterborough Cathedral Library. c5,000 pre-1800 titles. (The mss are also deposited in the University Library.)

Petronius. Bequeathed by Sir Stephen Gaselee, 1943.

Restif de la Bretonne. Bequeathed by L C G Clarke, 1960.

Ridley Hall. Early printed books from Ridley Hall, presented 1962.

Salt collection of private Acts of Parliament from the collection of William Salt (1805–63).

Samuel Sandars' library, including the First Folio, bequeathed 1894.

Early Spanish books (see *Catalogue of the MacColl collection and other Spanish books*, Cambridge 1910, and A J C Bainton, *Comedias sueltas in Cambridge University Library; a descriptive catalogue*, Cambridge 1977.

Laurence Sterne, including 18th cent imitations.

Jonathan Swift and his circle. Bequeathed by Sir Harold Williams, 1964.

Venn collection of books on logic. Given by J Venn (1834–1923). (See *Catalogue of a collection of books on logic, presented to the library by John Venn.* Cambridge, 1889.)

Wane collection on ornithology, on deposit from Clare College. *c*200 v.

War of 1914–1918. (See H F Stewart, *Francis Jenkinson . . . a memoir*, Cambridge 1926, p140-2.) Includes collection of posters and ephemera.

Library of James Yorke, Bishop of Ely 1781–1808. Deposited 1952.

Yule collection on applied biology, founded by G U Yule (1871–1951). On permanent loan from the Dept of Applied Biology.

(ii) *Oriental*

The library of Sir Thomas Wade (*d*1895). 4,304 v (see H A Giles, *A catalogue of the Wade collection of Chinese and Manchu books in the library of the University of Cambridge.* Cambridge, 1898, and H A Giles,

Supplementary catalogue of the Wade collection. Cambridge 1915).

W G Aston (1841–1911) collection. c9,500 books in Japanese, including many rare blockprints.

W J Gibb (1857–1901) collection of Turkish books. 422 v (see E G Browne *A handlist of the Turkish and other books presented by Mrs E J W Gibb.* Cambridge 1906).

Charles Taylor (1840–1908) collection of Tibetan block books. 103 v.

B Adversaria

See (H R Luard and C Babington) *A catalogue of adversaria and printed books containing ms notes preserved in the library of the University of Cambridge.* Cambridge, 1864.

C Periodicals

See (B E Eaden and M P Curtis) *Non-current serials: a select list of holdings in the University Library.* Cambridge, 1978; *Supplement.* Cambridge, 1980.

For a list of current serials, see *Current serials available in the University Library and in other libraries connected with the University.* 2 v. Cambridge, 1980.

List of serials available in the University: supplement (to both the above). Three microfiches, 1982.

D Manuscripts

(i) *Western*

See *A catalogue of the manuscripts preserved in the Library of the University of Cambridge.* 6 v. Cambridge 1856–67.

A E B Owen, *Summary guide to accessions of western manuscripts—other than medieval—since 1867.* Cambridge 1966.

Index to the Baker manuscripts (in the British Library and Cambridge University Library). Cambridge, 1848.

P E Easterling 'Handlist of the additional Greek manuscripts in the University Library'. *Scriptorium,* 16 (1962), p302-23.

The manuscripts of Peterhouse, Pembroke College, Sidney Sussex College, Corpus Christi College (oriental collection), Kings' (Pote), St John's (Assyriology), Queens' (college archives) and Peterborough Cathedral are on deposit in the University Library.

N.B. Collections of papers of an archival nature have been ignored for the purposes of this survey.

(ii) *Oriental*

See E G Browne 'Catalogue and description of 27 Babi manuscripts' (in Cambridge University Library). *Journ of the Royal Asiatic Soc,* 1892.

T Preston, *Catalogus bibliothecae Burckhardtianae cum appendice librorum aliorum orientalium in bibliotheca Academiae Cantabrigiensis asservatorum.* Cambridge, 1853.

E Ullendorff and S G Wright. *Catalogue of Ethiopian manuscripts in the Cambridge University Library.* Cambridge, 1961.

R P Blake 'Catalogue of the Georgian manuscripts in the Cambridge University Library'. *Harvard Theological Review,* 25 (1932).

S M Schiller-Szinessy, *Catalogue of the Hebrew manuscripts preserved in the University Library Cambridge.* Cambridge, 1876 (not completed).

P Voorhoeve, *List of Indonesian manuscripts in the University Library, Cambridge followed by notes about certain college manuscripts.* Cambridge 1950–4. Photocopy of typescript available in University Library.

P S van Ronkel, *Bericht aangaande de jongste aanwinst van Maleische handschriften in het buitenland, Cambridge.* (Mededeelingen der k. Akad. van Wet, Afd letterkunde, 59, Serie A, no 8). Amsterdam, 1925.

E G Browne, *A handlist of the Muhammadan manuscripts, including all those written in the Arabic character, preserved in the library of the University of Cambridge.* Cambridge, 1900. See also above, under general works on Cambridge libraries.

C R Bawden, 'A first description of a collection of Mongol manuscripts in the University Library, Cambridge'. *Journ of the Royal Asiatic Soc,* 1957.

T W Rhys Davids 'List of Pali manuscripts in the Cambridge University Library'. *Journ of the Pali Text Soc,* 1883, p145-6.

E G Browne, *A catalogue of the Persian manuscripts in the Library of the University of Cambridge.* Cambridge, 1896.

C Bendall, *Catalogue of the Buddhist Sanskrit mss in the University Library Cambridge.* Cambridge, 1883.

William Wright, *A catalogue of the Syriac manuscripts preserved in the Library of the University of Cambridge.* 2 v, Cambridge, 1901.

A E Goodman, 'The Jenks collection of Syriac mss in the University Library, Cambridge'. *Journ of the Royal Asiatic Soc,* 1939.

S C Reif, *A guide to the Taylor-Schechter Genizah collection.* Cambridge, 1973. (The collection, from the Cairo Genizah, contains an estimated 140,000 fragments of the 7th cent onwards.)

The Cheshunt Foundation, Westminster College, Cambridge. Tel (0223) 353997. Admission by prior arrangement with the librarian.

Cheshunt College, now the Cheshunt Foundation, and sharing buildings with Westminster College, was founded originally by the Countess of Huntingdon in 1768. It is a training college for clergy, with no restrictions as to denominations.

The library contains c1,000 v of rare books, including much of the Countess of Huntingdon's personal library, with her 1536 Tyndale *New Testament* and her Baskerville *Bible.* It is a general theological library ranging from the 16th cent onwards. Ms material includes papers relating to the early history of Methodism; memorabilia and papers of the Countess of Huntingdon; also a ms of Charles Wesley's hymns, in his own hand.

Christ's College, Cambridge. Tel (0223) 67641. Open to members of the College; visiting scholars are received by appointment.

The College was founded in 1506. The printed books total is now *c*30,000 v, of which *c*6,000 are pre-1850 titles which include 52 incunabula. The most notable collections are: the *Milton Collection* of over 100 items (described by S W Grose in *Christ's College Magazine*, 33, 1921); the *Charles Lesingham Smith Collection* of *c*900 items of early mathematical and other scientific subjects; the *William Robertson Smith* oriental library received in 1894.

The medieval mss have been described by M R James, *A descriptive catalogue of the western manuscripts in the library of Christ's College, Cambridge*, Cambridge, 1905. The Oriental mss, in turn, have been described by E G Browne, *Supplementary handlist*, p310-5.

A N L Munby, *Cambridge College Libraries*, 2nd ed 1962, p2-4.

Early printed books to the year 1500 in the library of Christ's College, Cambridge, Cambridge, 1912.

S W G(rose), 'Early editions of Milton's works in Christ's College library', *Christ's College Magazine*, 33, (1921).

R Auty and E P Tyrrell, 'A H Wratislaw's Slavonic books in the library of Christ's College, Cambridge'. *Trans Cambridge Bibliographical Soc*, 5 (1969).

Some of the muniments are described in *HMC*, 1 (1874).

Churchill College, Storey's Way, Cambridge CB3 0DS. Tel (0223) 61200. Open Mon-Fri 9 am-1 pm, 1.30-5.30 pm. Admission on written application to the librarian. 35 mm microfilm reader available.

The College was founded in 1960. Its stock of pre-1850 books totals *c*400, of which few are early printed books. The most notable collection is the Napoleon Collection (*c*150 titles) accumulated by Sir Winston Churchill, and presented by Lady Spencer Churchill in 1965.

Clare College, Cambridge. Tel (0223) 358681. Open to members of the College; others should apply to the Fellows' Librarian. Visiting scholars are received by appointment. The Fellows' Library is separate from the modern college library.

Clare College Library The College was founded in 1326, but nothing remains in the library of the original collection. The present collection consists of *c*7,500 pre-1850 titles, which include *c*35 incunabula; *c*400 STC and several hundred Wing items; several hundred 16th cent foreign titles. In 1620 George Ruggle, author of *Ignoramus*, presented 284 books, including a notable group of French, Spanish and Italian plays. The library also includes *c*300 Hebrew books given by Humphrey Prideaux (1648–1724); considerable collection on the Deists, given by Gilbert Bouchery (Fellow 1736–46); the Wane collection of bird books, given in 1954, is on deposit in the University Library. Besides 31 medieval mss, the library holds Cecil Sharp's (1859–1924) collections relating to folk songs etc.

A N L Munby, *Cambridge College Libraries*, 2nd ed, 1962, p5-6.

M R James, *A descriptive catalogue of the Western Manuscripts in the library of Clare College, Cambridge*, Cambridge, 1905.

C G(ordon) and A H C(ook), *Early printed books to the year 1500 in the library of Clare College, Cambridge*, Cambridge, 1919.

M Forbes (ed), *Clare College 1326–1926*, Cambridge 1928–30. Vol II, p301-53.

Corpus Christi College Library, Cambridge. Tel (0223) 59418. Open by appointment with the librarian.

The College was founded in 1352. The Parker Library (distinct from the rest of the college library) houses *c*5,000 printed books, the most important part of which is the library of Matthew Parker, Archbishop of Canterbury (*d*1575) comprising over 600 printed books (including *c*142 incunabula) and the renowned collection of medieval mss—*c*500 in number. These include 38 containing Anglo-Saxon (bequeathed by Parker) and 21 of miscellaneous papers dealing with the Reformation. Perhaps the most notable mss are the 'A text' of the Anglo-Saxon Chronicle and the sixth-cent Italian 'Gospels of St Augustine'. The oriental mss given by E G Browne in 1883–4 are housed in the University Library: see E G Browne, *A supplementary hand-list of the Muhammadan manuscripts preserved in... Cambridge* (1922).

A N L Munby, *Cambridge College Libraries*, 2nd ed, 1962, p7-9.

Stephen Gaselee (Sir), *The early printed books in the library of Corpus Christi College* (—Additions 1922), Cambridge 1921–2. (op).

R I Page and G H S Bushnell, *Matthew Parker's legacy: books and plate.* Cambridge, 1975.

Bruce Dickins, 'The making of the Parker Library'. *Trans Cambridge Bibliographical Soc*, 6 (1972).

M R James, 'The sources of Archbishop Parker's collection of manuscripts at Corpus Christi College Cambridge, with a reprint of the catalogue of Thomas Markaunt's Library'. *Cambridge Antiquarian Soc*, 1899 (op).

——*A descriptive catalogue of the manuscripts in the library of Corpus Christi College Cambridge.* Cambridge 1912 (op).

R Vaughan and J Fines, 'A handlist of manuscripts in the library of Corpus Christi College Cambridge not described by M R James'. *Trans Cambridge Bibliographical Soc*, 3 (1960).

James Nasmith, *Catalogus librorum manuscriptorum quos Collegio Corporis Christi legavit Matthaeus Parker, Archiepiscopus Cantuariensis*. Cambridge, 1777 (op).

Sheila Strongman, 'John Parker's manuscripts: an edition of the lists in Lambeth Palace Ms 737'. *Trans Cambridge Bibliographical Soc*, 7 (1977), p1-27.

R I Page, 'The Parker Register and Matthew Parker's Anglo-Saxon manuscripts'. *Ibid*. 8 (1981), p1-28.

Cory Library, University Botanic Garden, 1 Brookside, Cambridge. Tel (0223) 350101. Open 9 am-1 pm, 2.15-5.15 pm to staff and student gardeners; others on application. Photocopying.

Cory Library Origins of the library are obscure. The Botanic Garden was founded in 1831 and a few books existed then, but it was not officially recognized until 1885 when the University gave a grant towards the purchase of books. In 1947 it was re-named 'Cory Library' after a Welsh businessman, Reginald Cory, the Botanic Garden's greatest benefactor. Its stock totals *c*6,000 v which are strong on the practical aspects of gardens, practical manuals on all the aspects of horticulture, gardening monographs. There is a fine collection of floras, including many dealing with the Far East and India. Most of the early works are catalogues of famous gardens. There are 4 books printed before 1640 (3 British, 1 European); 18 items 1641–1700 (12 British, 6 European); *c*150 18th cent v (130 British, 20 European); 250 items published 1801–50 (220 British, 30 European). It contains an annotated copy of Thomas Martyn's *Catalogus horti botanici Cantabrigiensis.*

Own classification scheme. Author cat.

Subject index to pamphlets.

Department of Zoology, University of Cambridge, Downing Street, Cambridge. Tel (0223) 358717. Open Mon-Fri 8.30 am-5.30 pm; Sat 9 am-12.30 pm; closed vacation. Open to members of the University; others on application. Photocopying; microform reader.

Balfour and Newton Library Named after Francis Maitland Balfour (1851–82), Professor of Animal Morphology, and Alfred Newton (1829–1907), Professor of Zoology. Balfour's books, given in 1883, formed the nucleus, and Newton's outstanding collection of ornithological works was bequeathed in 1907. From 1883 to 1933 it was housed in the University Cavendish Laboratory but moved to its present site in 1933. Its stock totals *c*32,500 v, including general zoological textbooks and monographs, especially strong in entomology and ornithology. It holds an almost complete set of the many editions of Gilbert White's *Natural History of Selborne* (many collected by Newton). There are one incunabulum; *c*80 books printed 1501–1640 (3 in Britain, 75 in Europe); 480 18th cent items (120 English, 360 in Europe); *c*520 items printed 1801–50 (*c*75 printed in Britain, *c*445 in Europe). The library also holds the mss correspondence of Newton (*c*35 bundles) as well as his notebooks; William Swainson's ornithological and entomological correspondence; 'Notes and sketches' by John Gould (1804–81) for his *Birds of Australia.*

Modified Bliss classification scheme; author/subject cat on cards.

The Divinity School, St John's Street, Cambridge. Tel (0223) 358933. Open (Term) Mon-Fri 9 am-12.55 pm, 2-5.10 pm; (Vacation) Mon-Thurs 9 am-12.55 pm, 2-4.40 pm; Fri 9 am-12.55 pm, 2-4.30 pm. Closed on Sats. Admission to members of the University; others should apply to the librarian.

Divinity School Library Includes the collection of *c*3,500 v from the library of J B Lightfoot, Bishop of Durham (*d*1890).

Downing College, Cambridge. Tel (0223) 59491. Open to members of the College; others should apply to the librarian.

The College was founded in 1800. Among its special printed books collections is a bequest by Admiral Sir Herbert Richmond (1871–1946) of *c*500 v on navigation and naval history. The mss collections include John Bowtell's bequest (1813) consisting mainly of mss relating to the history of Cambridge (and includes the town accounts for 1510–1787), and the mss of F W Maitland (1850–1906), the legal historian, most of which are published.

A N L Munby, *Cambridge College Libraries*, 2nd ed, 1962, p10-11.

Emmanuel College Library, Emmanuel College, Cambridge. Tel (0223) 65411. Open 9 am-1 pm; 2.15-5.15 pm. Open to members of the College. Visiting scholars should apply in writing to the librarian. Photographic reproduction can usually be arranged, though the library has no photographic service of its own.

Emmanuel College Library The College was founded in 1584, and the pre-1800 books of *c*18,000 v form the working library of the College which has survived from past centuries. This collection includes 5,750 v which now constitute the *Sancroft Library*—the personal library of Archbishop William Sancroft (1617–1693), and given to the College (of which he was Master 1662–65) shortly before his death—and is housed in a separate room, classified and shelved in the order given to it after its accession. The whole library contains *c*2,600 STC items and 101 incunabula (30 being in the Sancroft Library). The Sancroft Library includes a large proportion of works on theology, liturgy and church history, with classical literature, law, natural science, history and antiquities well represented. A considerable number of books are in French, Italian and Spanish.

The library also houses (a) the *Liturgical Collection of the Rev William Chatterly Bishop* (*d*1922), Fellow of the College (1876–89), made of up *c*638 v, of which *c*200 are pre-1850; (b) 100 Hebrew books bequeathed by *Edmund Castell, 1685*; (c) the *Graham Watson Library* given to Emmanuel in 1975 by W Graham Watson of Bradford, Yorks, a graduate of the College. It comprises *c*2,000-3,000 v with coloured plates, almost all before 1850. The collection is not limited by subject matter. It includes many rarities, and is notable for the fine bindings. Of particular interest are the Georgian break-front glazed mahogany bookcases which house it and form part of the gift.

The College Library has *c*400 mss from 12th-20th cent. Of the modern mss mention should be made of those of the composer and writer on musical history, Edward Woodall Naylor (1867–1934, Hon Fellow of the College).

A N L Munby, *Cambridge College Libraries*, 2nd ed, 1962, p12-13.

P W Wood, *A hand-list of English books... in Emmanuel College printed before 1641.* (CUP, 1915).

——*Early printed books to the year 1500 in... Emmanuel College* (Addenda). (CUP, 1911, 1913).

J B Pearson, *An index to the English books and pamphlets in the Library of Emmanuel College, printed before 1700. (Cambridge, 1869). (op).*

Brief historical articles in Emmanuel College Magazine, XXXVIII (1955/6) p37-41; XLV (1962/3) p32-6; LVII (1974/5) p22-4; LVIII (1975/6) p15-17.

Faculty of Education Library, 17-19 Brookside, Cambridge. Tel (0223) 55271. Open: Michaelmas and Easter terms, 8.45 am-7 pm; Lent term, Mon & Thurs 8.45 am-7 pm, Tues, Wed & Fri 8.45 am-5 pm. Free admission to members of the University; others by arrangement. Copycat photocopying machine.

W H D Rouse Collection Given to the Department of Education in 1940 by W H D Rouse. The collection contains *c*150 v of teaching manuals, grammars, school textbooks and books dealing with philosophy of education, including six editions of Comenius and several works by Roger Ascham. It includes 1 STC; 24 Wing; 40 18th cent and 50 pre-1851 items.

Card author cat.

Fitzwilliam Museum, Department of Manuscripts and Printed Books, Trumpington Street, Cambridge CB2 1RB. Tel (0223) 69501. Open Tues-Fri 10 am-1 pm, 2.15-4.45 pm. Admission on application, in writing, supported by letter of recommendation. Full photographic service, microfilm/fiche reader-printer.

The Museum was founded on the death of Richard, 7th Viscount Fitzwilliam of Merrion in 1816, who bequeathed his books (*c*10,000), music, illuminated mss and fine art collection to the University of Cambridge. The total collection of books in the Department of Manuscripts and Printed Books numbers *c*15,000, which include *c*350 incunabula; *c*200 STC; *c*400 Wing; *c*1,000 Adams, together with *c*500 Private Press books, and *c*1,000 fine bindings. Mss and printed music comprise *c*10,000 individual compositions, including the Fitzwilliam Virginal Book, and an outstanding collection of Handel. Other mss include 1,000 illuminated mss, *c*20,000 autograph letters and *c*1,000 historical, literary and other mss. The department incorporates, *inter alia*, the following collections:

Lord Fitzwilliam (1745–1816) books, illum mss, music.
F McClean (1837–1904) illum mss, rare books.
C B Marlay (1831–1912) illum mss, rare books.
R E Kerrich (–1872) rare books, mss.
Jane Alice Morris (–1935) Kelmscott Press books.
Loan collection, National Trust Books from Anglesey Abbey.

Card cat for most printed books.

A N L Munby, *Cambridge College Libraries*, 2nd ed, 1962, p14-16.

M R James, *Descriptive catalogue of the McClean collection of manuscripts in the Fitzwilliam Museum.* Cambridge, 1912. (op).

——*Descriptive catalogue of the manuscripts in the Fitzwilliam Museum.* Cambridge, 1895. (op).

C E Sayle, *Catalogue of the early printed books bequeathed to the Museum by Frank McClean.* Cambridge, 1916. (op).

J A Fuller-Maitland and A H Mann, *Catalogue of the music in the Fitzwilliam Museum...* London, 1893. (op).

F Wormald and P Giles, *A descriptive catalogue of the additional illuminated manuscripts in the Fitzwilliam Museum.* 2 v, Cambridge, 1982.

——*Illuminated manuscripts in the Fitzwilliam Museum: an exhibition.* Cambridge, 1966.

Handel and the Fitzwilliam: a collection of essays and a catalogue of an exhibition. Cambridge, 1974.

French music and the Fitzwilliam: a collection of essays and a catalogue of an exhibition. Cambridge, 1975.

Italian music and the Fitzwilliam: a collection of essays and a catalogue of an exhibition. Cambridge, 1976.

Geography Library, Department of Geography, University of Cambridge, Downing Place, Cambridge. Tel (0223) 64416 or 64417, Ext 33. Open Term: Mon-Fri 8.45 am-6 pm, Sat 8.45 am-12.45 pm; Vacation: 9 am-5 pm, Closed Sat. Admission by arrangement, excepting for members of the Department. Photocopying; microform reader.

J W Clark Collection Collected by John Willis Clark (1833–1910) Registrary of Cambridge University, and bequeathed to the University Department of Geography in 1912. The Collection consists of *c*450 works mainly on travel, and exploration, covering all regions of the globe: the New World, 101 titles; the Pacific 59; Asia 58; Polar 43 and Africa 38. The rest are European travel, both English and continental. There are 13 Wing items; 3 17th cent European; 153 18th cent (mainly British); the rest are 19th cent.

Card cat arranged by author.

Girton College, Cambridge. Tel (0223) 76219. Open to members of the College; others should write to the librarian.

The College was founded in 1869, and its library contains *c*60,000 v including a small collection of early books, and the bequest of Jane Catherine Gamble (1885); 400 v from the library of Barbara Bodichon (1827—91) and a collection on women's suffrage bequeathed by Helen Blackburn. There are also 41 Hebrew mss in the Mary Frere Hebrew Library, as well as some printed material.

A N L Munby, *op cit* p17.

H M J Loewe, *Catalogue of the printed books and of the Semitic and Jewish mss in the Mary Frere Hebrew Library at Girton College, Cambridge*. London, 1915.

Gonville and Caius College, Cambridge CB2 1TA. Tel (0223) 312211. Open to members of the College; others should write to the librarian. Ultra-violet light; illuminated magnifier available.

The College was founded in 1349, and since then the library has received numerous bequests from former Masters and Fellows, in addition to purchases. The largest and most notable of the early gifts was that of William Branthwaite, Master of the College from 1607 until his death in 1620, and the College still possesses most of the books left to it by Walter Crome in 1452 and John Beverley in 1462. John Caius's own library is described in the article by Grierson, listed below. The library's stock now totals *c*49,000 v, of which *c*13,000 are pre-1850, including *c*100 incunabula. Also *c*810 medieval mss.

Guard book cat.

A N L Munby, *op cit.* p18-19.

W R Collett, *An index of English books printed before the year 1600, now in the library of Gonville and Caius College, Cambridge*. London, 1850 (op).

——*A list of the early printed books in the library of Gonville and Caius College, Cambridge*. Cambridge, 1850 (op).

M R James, *A descriptive catalogue of the manuscripts in the library of Gonville and Caius College*. 3 v, Cambridge, 1907-14 (op).

G A S Schneider, *A descriptive catalogue of the incunabula in the library of Gonville and Caius College Cambridge*. Cambridge, 1928 (op).

J Venn, *Biographical history of Gonville and Caius College* III. Cambridge, 1901, p188-95.

P Grierson, 'John Caius' Library'. Venn *op cit* vol VII, Cambridge, 1978, p509-25.

E Leedham-Green, 'A catalogue of Caius College Library, 1569'. *Trans Cambridge Bibliographical Soc*, VIII (1981), p29-41.

Haddon Library, Faculty of Archaeology and Anthropology, Downing Street, Cambridge CB2 3DZ. Tel (0223) 59714. Ext 59/24. Open 9 am-7.30 pm (5 pm outside term), 9 am-5.30 pm, Sat, (closed Sat out of term), to faculty members and students; others on application to the librarian. Open to members of Cambridge Antiquarian Society. Photocopying, microfiche reader available.

Named in 1936 after the University of Cambridge's first Reader of Anthropology, Alfred Haddon; the modern collections are geared towards faculty teaching. Printed books total 32,600 v and 16,700 v periodicals. Pre-1850 holdings are: 2 STC; 19 Wing; 16 European 1640—99; 123 18th cent British; 61 18th cent European; 268 British 1800—1850; 89 European 1800—1850; and 6 extra-European 1800—1850. Particular strengths include antiquities of Britain, Europe, New World and Third World; travel books and handbooks; ethnography and archaeological excavation reports. Notable gifts and collections have been received from Alfred Haddon, J G D Clark, Sir James Frazer and William Ridgway. Professor Charles McBurney presented *c*4,000 offprints, and Dr Miles Burkitt *c*2,000 offprints. The library also houses the collection of the Cambridge Antiquarian Society.

Cats author/title; classified (Bliss classification scheme).

Institute of Astronomy, The Observatories, Madingley Road, Cambridge. Tel (0223) 362204. Open Mon-Fri 9 am-1 pm, 2-5 pm. Closed Sat. Open to members of the University; visiting scholars and qualified members of the public admitted on application. Photocopying; microform reader.

Institute of Astronomy Library The Observatory was opened in 1824, and the library was gradually built up by a series of small donations. In 1892 John Couch Adams (1819-92) bequeathed a valuable collection (*c*150 v) of 17th and 18th cent books on astronomy. In 1946 the Solar Physics Observatory Library was amalgamated. The stock totals 10,500 v and includes books on observational rather than theoretical astronomy, of which 11 items were printed before 1640 (2 from Britain, 9 from Europe); 20 items printed 1641—1700 (14 from Britain, 12 from Europe); 113 18th cent items (52 from Britain, 61 from Europe); *c*200 items printed 1801—50 (80 from Britain, 112 from Europe). The papers of Sir Arthur Eddington are held in the library.

Own classification scheme. Author/subject card cat. Periodical title cat.

Jesus College, Cambridge. Tel (0223) 68611. Open to members of the College; others should apply to the librarian. Visiting scholars are received by appointment.

The College was founded in 1496. The old library totals *c*10,500 v (ie excluding the undergraduate library) which include *c*40 incunabula; *c*750 STC; *c*1,800 Wing and *c*700 16th cent foreign items. Also included are the library of T R Malthus (*c*2,300 v), and the Parish Library of Graveley, Cambs (*c*1,000 v, mainly 17th and early 18th cent), and *c*130 v on military science assembled in 18th cent. Mss collection includes *c*80 medieval mss; 17 oriental mss described in E G Browne, *Supplementary handlist*, p308-9.

A N L Munby, *Cambridge College Libraries*, 2nd ed, 1962, p20-1.

M R James, *A descriptive catalogue of the manuscripts in the library of Jesus College, Cambridge.* London, 1895.

J Harrison, R Miniami, P James, W Peterson and J Pullen, *The Malthus library catalogue: the personal collection of Thomas Robert Malthus at Jesus College, Cambridge.* New York: Pergamon, 1983.

King's College Library, Cambridge. Tel (0223) 50411. Open to members of the College, but visiting scholars are received by appointment with the librarian.

The College was founded in 1441, and its library now holds over 100,000 v which include over 240 incunabula, *c*1,500 STC, *c*1,650 Wing items. Some of the more notable special collections include the (a) *Keynes Collection*—bequeathed by Lord Keynes (John Maynard Keynes) in 1946 and contains *c*6,000 v on the history of thought, with especially important holdings in Locke, Hobbes, Gibbon, Bentham, Berkeley, Hume, Descartes, Kant, Mallebranche, J S Mill, Newton, Pascal, Rousseau, Voltaire; *c*200 17th cent English plays and a fine collection of books printed by Baskerville; (b) *Rowe Music Library*—strong in 18th cent music, especially Handel. Contains mss and papers of E J Dent (1876—1957). (See *Music Review* XII, 1951.)

John Hayward bequest (1965). Strong in 20th cent literature, especially T S Eliot.

Thackeray bequest—from Provost George Thackeray (1777—1850)—of 16th-cent Protestant literature and natural history books.

M R James (1862—1936) Collection—strong in literature on the Apocalypse in art.

D H Beves Collection—of French literature and history of the 16th cent.

The library has a large collection of mss and printed books relating to Rupert Brooke, E M Forster and the Bloomsbury Group; and the journals and papers of C R Ashbee.

A N L Munby, *Cambridge College Libraries*, 2nd ed 1962, p22-4.

——A catalogue of first and early editions of the works of Thomas Hobbes, forming part of the library bequeathed by John Maynard, Baron Keynes, 1949. Typescript in Cambridge University Library.

——A catalogue of the mss and printed books in the Sir Isaac Newton collection bequeathed by...Baron Keynes of Tilton, 1949. Part typewritten. Copy in Cambridge University Library.

——A catalogue of the works of George Berkeley forming part of the library bequeathed by John Maynard, Baron Keynes, 1951. Typescript in Cambridge University Library.

——Donors' lables printed for King's College Library, Cambridge. Privately pr Cambridge, 1950.

E H Palmer, Catalogue of the oriental manuscripts in the library of King's College, Cambridge. London 1867. (These mss were given by Edward Pote in 1788 and are deposited in the University Library; the rest of his collection is at Eton.)

M R James, *A descriptive catalogue of the manuscripts other than oriental in the library of King's College, Cambridge.* Cambridge, 1895.

A R Benten, *A handlist of books connected with Aeschylus, principally from the library of...Walter Headlam, now in the library of King's College.* Cambridge, 1910.

Handlist of the literary manuscripts in the T S Eliot collection bequeathed to King's College, Cambridge by J D Hayward in 1965. Cambridge, 1973.

G Chawner, *A list of the incunabula in the library of King's College, Cambridge.* Cambridge, 1908.

Modern literary manuscripts from King's College, Cambridge. An exhibition in memory of A N L Munby, Fitzwilliam Museum. Cambridge, 1976.

Some of the muniments are described in *HMC* 1 (1874).

Magdalene College Library, Cambridge CB3 0AG. Tel (0223) 61543. Open by prior arrangement. Microfilm and photographic facilities (no microfilm reader).

Old Library The College was founded in 1542. The library, which includes many volumes from the library of Daniel Waterland (Master 1713—40), contains *c*6,000 v on various subjects, and mss and typescripts of Rudyard Kipling, Thomas Hardy and T S Eliot.

M R James, *A descriptive catalogue of the manuscripts in the College Library of Magdalene College Cambridge.* (CUP, 1909).

A N L Munby, *Cambridge College Libraries*, 2nd ed, 1962, p28-9.

Pepys Library Consists of the personal collection of Samuel Pepys (1633—1703) bequeathed to the College. It totals *c*3,000 v and includes 27 incunabula. It is particularly strong in naval and maritime history, broadside ballads and chapbooks, fine bindings, and topographical prints. The mss include Pepys diary; the Anthony Roll of Ships; music; medieval English and Scottish poetry.

Bibliotheca Pepysiana. A descriptive catalogue of the library of Samuel Pepys. Pt I *Sea Mss* J R Tanner, 1914; Pt II *General Introduction* by F Sidgwick and *Early Printed Books to 1558* by E Gordon Duff, 1914; *Medieval manuscripts* by M R James, 1923; *Shorthand books* by W J Carlton, 1940.

Cat of the Pepys Library, Magdalene College, Cambridge. I *Printed Books* by N A Smith (1978); III *Prints and Drawings, general* by A W Aspital (1980); VII *Modern Manuscripts* by C S Knighton (1981). Other v in preparation. This lists 27 incunabula, including fragments.

S Gaselee, *Spanish Books in the Library of Samuel Pepys*, 1921.

E M Wilson, 'Samuel Pepys's Spanish chap-books'. *Trans Cambridge Bibliographical Soc* 2 (1955, 1956, 1957).

F M C Turner, *The Pepys Library*, Cambridge, 1951.

J R Tanner, *A descriptive catalogue of the Naval Manuscripts in the Pepysian Library at Magdalene College.* London, 1903-.

(E K Purnell), *Report on the Pepys manuscripts preserved at Magdalene College.* (Hist Mss Comm). London, 1911.

Mineralogy and Petrology Departmental Library, Downing Place, Cambridge. Tel (0223) 64131. Open Mon-Fri 8.45 am-5.30 pm; Sat 8.45 am-1 pm. Admission to staff, research and third year students of the Department. Photocopying facilities.

The library was formed by W H Miller, Professor of Mineralogy. On his death in 1880 *c*300 v were left to the University. The library contains *c*1,700 v of books and 2,300 v of periodicals. Early works on mineralogy and crystallography includes 1 16th cent and 1 17th cent item; 12 18th cent and 63 pre-1850 items. The library represents Prof Miller's working collection rather than a specific rare book collection.

Classified and author cat.

Newnham College, Cambridge. Tel (0223) 62273. Visiting scholars are received by appointment. Free admission to members of the College.

The College was founded in 1871; the present library dates from 1897, and was established principally through the generosity of Henry Yates Thompson (1838–1928) and his wife. Other major benefactors have included J W Cross, who gave books in memory of George Eliot; H E Young (1931) and the Hon Mrs Wood. A new extension to house the rare books and other special collections was built in 1981. The rare books collection includes 14 incunabula; *c*100 STC; and *c*100 Wing items, as well as *c*40 16th cent foreign books. There is also a good collection of works printed by John Baskerville.

A N L Munby, *Cambridge College Libraries*, 2nd ed (1962), p30-1.

Nuttall Library, Molteno Institute, Downing Street, Cambridge. Tel (0223) 350577. Open Mon-Fri 8.45 am-5.15 pm. Closed Sat. Admission by application, excepting University graduate workers in Biology. Photocopying.

Shipley Collection Collected by Sir Arthur Shipley (1861–1927), Vice-Chancellor of Cambridge University (1917–19). By his will, Shipley left the Library 30 v of pamphlets. The rest of the collection was purchased with the help of a grant of £100 from P A Molteno in 1928. It comprises *c*260 v—83 are bound volumes of pamphlets. The offprint/pamphlet volumes cover parasitology, in particular helminthology, and are mainly late 19th-early 20th cent. The monographs deal with different parasites and their effects; mainly European, but some American volumes. 7 pre-1800 v, including one British item; 2 v 1800–1850. One volume from the library of Charles Darwin.

Card cat arranged by author.

Pembroke College, Cambridge. Tel (0223) 52241. Open to members of the College; others should apply to the librarian.

The College was founded in 1343. The library's holdings total *c*30,000 v, of which *c*15,000 are pre-1850, including 106 incunabula. It possesses good collections of Lancelot Andrewes, Thomas Gray, Christopher Smart, Edmund Spenser and Aristophanes; and *c*2,000 v on Napoleonic history. Also over 300 mss, about half from its medieval library, and including over 100 from Bury St Edmunds Abbey; six ms part books for liturgical music, mostly by Elizabethan composers (*c*1650); ms compositions by John Dunstable; mss of Thomas Gray, including a ms of the *Elegy*. The medieval mss are on deposit in the University Library.

A N L Munby, *op cit* p32-3.

M R James, *A descriptive catalogue of the manuscripts in the library of Pembroke College, Cambridge, with a handlist of the printed books to the year 1500 by E H Minns.* Cambridge, 1905.

G E Corrie, 'A list of books presented to Pembroke College, Cambridge, by different donors during the 14th and 15th cent'. *Camb Antiq Soc Communications*, II (1860).

Some of the muniments are described in *HMC* 1 (1874) and 5 (1876).

Pendlebury Library of Music, University Music School, West Road, Cambridge CB3 9DP. Tel (0223) 61661. Ext 47. Open Mon-Fri 9.30 am-1.15 pm, 2.30-5.30 pm; Sat 9.30 am-1 pm. In vacation, admission is by appointment only. Will supply microfilms.

Primarily the library is for the Faculty of Music. It contains *c*1,600 pre-1800 printed music; *c*100 18th cent mss; 80 19th cent mss; 30 boxes of unbound 20th cent mss; over 1,000 microfilms of primary sources; diaries of R J S Stevens (1757–1837); mss of C B Rootham and Sir W Herschel; early printed editions and microfilms of mss of J S Bach (presented by L E R Picken and W Emery).

Peterhouse, Cambridge. Tel (0223) 350256. Visiting scholars are admitted by previous appointment with the librarian.

The College was founded in 1284, and still owns much of its medieval library. The mss are on deposit in the University Library. It contains *c*5,500 pre-1800 v which include much of the library of Andrew Perne, University Registrary (1519?–89). There are *c*65 incunabula.

A N L Munby, *Cambridge College Libraries*, 2nd ed, 1962, p34-5.

Anselm Hughes, *Catalogue of the musical manuscripts at Peterhouse, Cambridge*. Cambridge, 1953.

M R James, *A descriptive catalogue of the manuscripts in the Library of Peterhouse.* Cambridge, 1899.

C G(ordon), *Early printed books to the year 1500 in the Library of Peterhouse, Cambridge.* Cambridge, 1914.

Some of the muniments are described in *HMC* 1 (1874).

Queens' College, Cambridge. Tel (0223) 65511. Open to members of the College; visiting scholars are received by appointment.

The College was founded in 1448. The library contains *c*30,000 pre-1850 titles, including *c*25 incunabula; of special interest is the bequest by Isaac Milner in 1820 of 3,000 books on the Reformation and on 18th and early 19th-cent science and mathematics, 22 Western mss and 13 oriental mss.

A N L Munby, *op cit* p36-7.

T H Horne, *A catalogue of the Library of the College of St Margaret and St Bernard commonly called Queens' College.* 2 v, London, 1827.

M R James, *A descriptive catalogue of the western manuscripts in the Library of Queens' College Cambridge.* Cambridge, 1905.

F G Plaistowe, *Early printed books to the year 1500 in the Library of Queens' College Cambridge.* Cambridge, 1910.

Some of the muniments are described in *HMC* 1 (1874).

Ridley Hall, Cambridge. Tel (0223) 350747. Admission on previous application to the librarian.

Ridley Hall is a theological college, founded in 1881. Its library contains (a) 1 incunabulum; (b) papers of Charles Simeon (1759–1836); (c) the library of Richard Cecil (1748–1810), a prominent member of the Evangelical revival in the Church of England; *c*200 v theology and general English literature, 16th-19th cent; *c*350 theological pamphlets, mostly late 18th cent; (d) *c*150 miscellaneous early theological books.

A N L Munby, *op cit* p38.

F W B Bullock, *The history of Ridley Hall*, 2v, (1941–53) 2, p248-54.

St Catharine's College Library, Cambridge CB2 1RL. Tel (0223) 59445, Ext 60. Admission by written appointment.

The College was founded in 1473. The Library has grown over the years through various donations, especially from donors such as Bishop Thomas Sherlock (1678–1761), Dr John Addenbrooke (1680–1719), Thomas Neale etc, and now contains *c*10,000 v of mixed antiquarian interest. There are *c*77 books printed before 1521, the bulk of the collection belonging to the 17th and 18th cent with emphasis on politics and religion. The *Addenbrooke Collection* (given in 1719) consists mainly of medical books; the *Neale Collection* is strong in law and medicine. There are good holdings of first editions of works by the dramatist James Shirley and by John Ray—an old member of the College.

Card cat available at the library. Separately typed list of books up to 1600.

J B Bilderbeck, *Early printed books in the Library of St Catharine's College, Cambridge.* CUP, 1911 (op).

C Prescot, *Catalogus librorum in bibliotheca Aulae Divae Catharinae* (Cambridge, 1771).

A N L Munby, *op cit* p39-40.

M R James, *A descriptive catalogue of the manuscripts in the library of St Catharine's College Cambridge.* Cambridge, 1925.

St John's College Library, Cambridge. Tel (0223) 61621. Open: Term, Mon-Fri 9 am-1 pm, 2-7.30 pm; Sat 9 am-1 pm. Other, Mon-Fri 9 am-1 pm, 2.30-5 pm. Closed September. Open to members of the college; others by appointment with the librarian.

The College was founded in 1511. In 1624 a new library building was erected at the instance of Bishop John Williams, to house the gift of Henry Wriothesley, Earl of Southampton: this collection included many books from the library of William Crashawe. Other notable collections included gifts from the poet Edward Bendlowes, Thomas Baker (historian of the College, *d*1740), John Newcome (Master, *d*1765)— includes a number of incunabula from the Harleian Library, Domenico Antonio Ferrari and Thomas Gisborne (Fellow, 1753). The Library now has *c*40,000 pre-1850 v, which include *c*275 incunabula; *c*2,800 STC; 7,800 Wing; *c*1,700 Adams. There are also the special collections of William Wordsworth; Samuel ('Erewhon') Butler; early mathematical books (from John Couch Adams); Rabelais; *The Imitation of Christ*, and early 20th cent press books.

Handlist to the Rabelais collection given by the late W F Smith to St John's College Library, Cambridge. Cambridge, 1920.

E W Lockhart and C E Sayle, *Incunabula in the library of St John's College Cambridge*. Cambridge, 1911. (Repr from *The Eagle* v32. (op).

H F Jones and A T Bartholomew, *The Samuel Butler collection at St John's College Cambridge: a catalogue and a commentary*. Cambridge, 1921. (op).

J C T Oates, 'The G U Yule collection of the Imitatio Christi'. *Trans Cambridge Bibliographical Soc*, 1 (1949), p88-90.

P J Wallis, 'The library of William Crashawe'. *Ibid*. 2 (1956), p213-28.

D McKitterick, 'Two sixteenth-century catalogues of St John's College Library'. *Ibid*. 7 (1978), p135-55.

M R James, *A descriptive catalogue of the manuscripts in the library of St John's College Cambridge*. Cambridge, 1913.

B M Cowie, *A descriptive catalogue of the manuscripts and scarce books in the library of St John's College Cambridge*. 3 pts. Cambridge, 1842–3.

School of Architecture and History of Art, 1-3 Scroope Terrace, Cambridge. Tel (0223) 69501. Open (Term) Mon-Fri 9.15 am-5.45 pm, (Vacation) Mon-Fri 9.15 am-1.15 pm, 1.45-5.45 pm. Closed Sat and Sun. Admission to members of the Faculty and students reading the subject; others by arrangement with the librarian.

Fine Arts Faculty Library Founded in 1920, it contains *c*1,000 v pre-1850 on architecture and art history, and includes the Maurice Webb collection of rare architectural books of 16th-18th cent.

Scientific Periodicals Library, Bene't Street, Cambridge. Tel (0223) 358381, Ext 252. Open: Mon-Fri in full term 9 am-9.50 pm; outside full term 9 am-6 pm; Sat 9 am-1 pm. Free admission to members of the University and members of Cambridge Philosophical Society; others by arrangement. Photocopying; microform reader/printers; translation service; some borrowing for members of University.

Cambridge Philosophical Society Collection The Philosophical Society was founded in 1819, and its library grew gradually from that date. The library became associated with the University in 1881, and a department of the University Library in 1976. The collection, containing *c*6,000 v, covers all branches of science, and is particularly strong in mathematics and physics. It has a large collection of 19th cent memoirs and monographs, and contains the Philosophical Society archive and some mss material by Babbage. It owns long runs of journals annotated by Darwin, and long runs of proceedings of learned societies (eg Linnean and Royal Societies). The early scientific works include *c*25 STC; *c*40 Wing and *c*80 16th cent foreign items.

Author/subject card cat.

Scott Polar Research Institute Library, Lensfield Road, Cambridge. Tel (0223) 66499. Ext 454. Open 9 am-1 pm; 2.15-5.30 pm to members of the University; others by arrangement. Photocopying, microform readers; no borrowing.

The library was founded by Prof Frank Debenham in 1920 as an integral part of the previously founded Institute. The Institute eventually became a sub-department of the Department of Geography in 1957 and the Department of Earth Sciences from 1980. The Library contains *c*15,000 v printed books; 2,500 v of periodicals; 19,000 maps and 3,000 pictures besides a large collection of pamphlets and offprints, covering all sciences and arts relating to polar and sub-polar regions. There are *c*12 pre-1700 and *c*150 pre-1800 items. The special collections include: (a) The *Lefroy bequest* of books relating to Sir John Franklin; (b) *Dr Vaino Tanner Library* of Scandinavian books; (c) *The Brown Roberts* collection of Polar books, including rare works on ornithology; (d) Administrative documents relating to the Falkland Islands; (e) Collections of exploration expeditions which include first Antarctic printed volume (Scott's expedition had its own printing press); (f) Major mss collections relating to polar exploration, including *Sir George Back* collection; *Cherry-Garrard* collection; *Edward Wilson* watercolours.

Author, subject and regional cat; classification UDC.

G K Hall published catalogue in 19 v in 1976.

A Savours, 'The manuscript collection of the Scott Polar Research Institute Cambridge', *Archives*, v 4, p102-8.

Seeley Historical Library, History Faculty, West Road, Cambridge. Tel (0223) 61661. Open (Full Term) Mon-Fri 8.45 am-7.15 pm, Sat 8.45 am-12 noon, 2-6 pm; (Other times) 9 am-5 pm; closed Sat and Sun. Open to members of the University; others should apply in writing.

The library was established in 1807 by John Symonds, Regius Professor of Modern History 1771–1807. Further books were added by his successor, Professor Smyth, but the collection was revitalized and made generally available to history undergraduates as the result of an appeal by Oscar Browning in 1884. It was renamed after Sir John Seeley (*d*1895), the greater part of whose memorial fund was made into an endowment for the library. There are *c*500 pre-1850 books.

Card cat.

Selwyn College Library, Cambridge. Tel (0223) 62381. Admission on application to the librarian.

The College Library was founded in 1882, and now holds *c*6,000 pre-1850 printed books. These include 37 incunabula, *c*100 STC, *c*250 Wing and *c*250 Adams. The library also holds the diaries and papers of G A Selwyn

(1809–78), Primate of New Zealand, and the papers of Brooks Foss Westcott (1825–1901), Bishop of Durham.

C W Phillips, *List of incunabula, Selwyn College, Cambridge.* Cambridge, 1934. (op)

Sidney Sussex College, Cambridge. Tel (0223) 61501. Visiting scholars are received by appointment. The Old Library is housed in the Muniment Room, and is separate from the modern library.

The College was founded in 1596. The Old Library has *c*7,300 v, with *c*50 incunabula. It includes a collection of 18th and early 19th cent mathematics books in the Taylor Mathematical library named after Samuel Taylor (*d*1732), and the library of F S Parris, University Librarian (*d*1759).

A N L Munby, *op cit* p45.

M R James, *A descriptive catalogue of the manuscripts in the library of Sidney Sussex College Cambridge.* Cambridge, 1895.

A H Cook, *Early printed books to the year 1500 in the library of Sidney Sussex College Cambridge.* Cambridge, 1922.

Some of the muniments are described in *HMC* 3 (1872).

Squire Law Library, The Old Schools, Cambridge. Tel (0223) 358933. Open (Term) Mon-Fri 9 am-8 pm, Sat 9 am-5.45 pm; (Vacation) 9 am-5 pm, Sat 9 am-1 pm. Closed Sun. Admission to members of the University; others on application to the librarian.

The library is named after Miss Rebecca Flower Squire (*d*1898), whose bequest enabled the University to erect a library. It was opened in 1906, and was moved from its first site in Downing Street to the Old Schools in 1935. In 1982 it became part of the University Library. It contains *c*1,500 v, pre-1850, including two incunabula.

Law Catalogue, compiled by M A Lekner under the direction of W A F P Steiner, 14 v. Dobbs Ferry, NY 1974–5.

Trinity College Library, Cambridge CB2 1TQ. Tel (0223) 58201. Open Mon-Fri 9 am-5 pm. Closed briefly at Easter and Christmas. Admission by appointment. Accommodation for four readers of early printed books and mss.

The Wren Library The College was founded in 1546, and the Wren Library (built to the design of Sir Christopher Wren in 1676–90), now contains 60,000 pre-1820 printed books which include 750 incunabula; *c*6,000 STC; *c*15,000 Wing; *c*4,100 Adams. There are also *c*1,000 medieval mss. Collections of printed books within the Library include the *Capell Collection* of Shakespeariana; The *Rothschild Collection* of 18th cent books; and the *Library of Sir Isaac Newton.* The mss collection includes the mss of Roger Gale (*d*1744), a large group of mss from monastic houses at Canterbury, and important autograph collections of Milton, Thackeray (including *Henry Esmond*), Tennyson, Edward Fitzgerald, Macaulay and Wittgenstein.

Card cat of printed books.

Card cat of 'Additional Mss'.

A N L Munby, *Cambridge College Libraries*, 2nd ed, 1962, p46-50.

J P W Gaskell and W W Robson, *The library of Trinity College, Cambridge: a short history*, Cambridge, 1971.

——*Trinity College Library, the first 150 years*, Cambridge, 1980.

A catalogue of the books bequeathed to the library of Trinity College, Cambridge by C W King, Cambridge, 1889. (op)

W W Greg, *Catalogue of the books presented by Edward Capell to the library of Trinity College.* Cambridge, 1900. (op)

R Sinker, *A catalogue of the English books printed before 1601 now in the library of Trinity College.* Cambridge, 1885. (op)

——*A catalogue of the fifteenth century printed books in the library of Trinity College.* Cambridge, 1876. (op)

——'Biographical notes on the libraries of Trinity College Cambridge'. *Cambridge Antiquarian Soc*, 1897. (op)

John Hayward, *The Rothschild Library*, 2 v. Cambridge, 1954. (op)

J R Harrison, *The Library of Isaac Newton.* Cambridge, 1978.

T Aufrecht, *A catalogue of Sanskrit manuscripts in the library of Trinity College, Cambridge.* Cambridge, 1869.

H M J Loewe, *Catalogue of the manuscripts in the Hebrew character collected and bequeathed to Trinity College Library by W A Wright.* Cambridge, 1926.

E H Palmer, *A descriptive catalogue of the Arabic, Persian and Turkish manuscripts in the library of Trinity College, Cambridge. With an appendix containing a catalogue of the Hebrew and Samaritan mss in the same library* (by W A Wright). Cambridge, 1870.

M R James, *The western manuscripts in the library of Trinity College Cambridge.* 4 v, Cambridge, 1900–04.

Trinity Hall, Cambridge. Tel (0223) 51401. Open to members of the College; others should apply to the librarian.

The College was founded in 1350, and has a strong tradition in law. The library holds *c*4,000 pre-1800 items, including 28 incunabula. There are 31 Western mss described by M R James.

A N L Munby, *op cit* p51.

M R James, *A descriptive catalogue of the manuscripts in the Library of Trinity Hall.* Cambridge, 1907.

Early printed books to the year 1500 in the Library of Trinity Hall Cambridge. Cambridge, 1909.

(H L Pink), 'List of Trinity Hall documents to 1600'. Typewritten. Copy in Cambridge University Library.

Westminster College Library, Cambridge. Tel (0223) 53997. Open on application to the librarian. Visiting scholars are received by appointment.

Founded as a post-graduate Presbyterian theological college in 1899, its library now includes 1 incunabulum, *c*160 STC, *c*100 Wing, *c*100 Adams, and *c*2,500 v of hymnology, mostly 19th cent English. Also included is a considerable collection of Hebrew mss, principally fragments from the Cairo Genizah.

Cambridge City Central Library, 7 Lion Yard, Cambridge CB2 3QD. Tel (0223) 65252 Ext 30. Open Mon-Fri 9 am-5.30 pm; Sat 9 am-5 pm. Admission to all without charge or appointment.

The Cambridgeshire Collection Founded in 1855 when Cambridge Free Library was established; it was transferred from the control of Cambridge City to Cambridgeshire County Council after local government reorganization in 1974. The collection is made up of *c*40,000 books/pamphlets relating to Cambridgeshire—pollbooks, election addresses, histories, geologies, directories etc; 600 newspaper vols—*c*40 titles 1770 to date, and virtually complete; *c*10,000 handbills and playbills, including 18th cent notices to present day posters.

Extensive cats.

M J Petty, 'The resources of nostalgia: Local librarianship' in *Library Review*, 28 (Spring 1979), p19-23.

To collect every scrap: local studies in librarianship in Cambridge 1855-1982. Library Association, 1983?

Whipple Science Museum Library, Free School Lane, Cambridge. Tel (0223) 358381. Ext 383. Open Mon-Fri 9.30 am-1 pm, 2-5 pm. Unrestricted admission to members of the University; others strictly on application. Microfilm reader; photocopying facilities.

The library was founded by R S Whipple in 1944, who presented *c*1,000 v plus a selection of early scientific instruments to the University. It totals *c*6,500 v which include 7 incunabula; 30 STC; 180 16th cent foreign; 140 Wing; 180 17th cent foreign; 540 18th cent v.

The library includes the (a) *Whipple Collection* of *c*1,100 v with 155 books by Robert Boyle; (b) *Sleeman Collection* of 24 v on late 19th/early 20th cent chemistry; (c) *Steward Collection* of 50 v on early physics and chemistry; (d) *Cambridge Instrument Company Collection* of trade ephemera, 1870—1950. 51 boxes, *c*1,000 items of trade catalogues. (The Company's archives are in the University Library.)

Author and subject cat.

Huntingdon

Cromwell Museum Library, Grammar School Walk, Huntingdon. Tel (0480) 52181 (Mon-Fri), 52861 (Sat-Sun). Administrator, Cromwell Museum, c/o County Library HQ, Princes Street, Huntingdon PE18 6NS. Open to public Tues-Fri 11 am-1 pm, 2-5 pm; Sat 11 am-1 pm, 2-4 pm; Sun 2-4 pm. Bona fide students should apply by letter (or phone) to the Administrator for access. Photocopying, transcripts of most documents. Catalogue forms part of general guide to Museum.

The library has been built up by gift, purchase and loan since the Museum opened in 1962. It contains 20 books and pamphlets (4 STC, 16 Wing), 34 letters and contemporary documents relating to Cromwell family and Commonwealth.

Guide to the Museum. Latest edition 1978.

Lode

Anglesey Abbey Library, Lode, Cambs CB5 9EJ. (National Trust) Tel (022 020) 257. Open April-Oct except Fri, 2-6 pm. Permission to consult should be sought in writing from the Libraries Adviser, National Trust, 42 Queen Anne's Gate, London SW1H 9AS.

The library was brought together by Hutleston Broughton, 1st Lord Fairhaven, from 1926 (when he bought the house) to his death in 1966, when the house and contents were bequeathed to the National Trust. It contains *c*9,000 v, of which *c*4,000 are pre-1851. Notable for its large collection of colour-plate and other illustrated books, particularly topography and natural history, published between 1770 and 1830. Ackermann and Repton are well represented, also works on Cambridgeshire and the Fens; military history, and Golden Cockerel Press books, as well as many fine modern bindings by Birdsall, Sangorski, Wright and Zaehnsdorf. In 1968, 163 of the more important colour-plate books were placed on loan in the Fitzwilliam Museum, Cambridge.

Author card cat, with shelf marks.

There is also a contents list of the library, arranged by shelf mark, compiled as part of an inventory of the house by Christie's in 1967.

St Ives

Norris Library and Museum, The Broadway, St Ives, Huntingdon. Tel (0480) 65101. All enquiries to be addressed to the curator at the above address. Open Tues-Fri 10 am-1 pm, 2-5 pm. Closed on Bank Holidays, and 4 pm closing during winter months. Admission to the Museum is open to the public, but access to the library subject to the consent of the curator.

The Museum and Library were founded in 1931 by a bequest from Herbert Ellis Norris (1859–1931), a native of St Ives and a local antiquary. He bequeathed to the then Borough Council the bulk of his estate to provide a library and museum to house his collection of Huntingdonshire books, mss and papers. The collection has since grown, principally by gift, and now totals *c*2,400 books. 850 are pre-1851, of which 47 are STC, and 96 Wing items. It includes much local non-book material such as the pamphlets by John Groode against the practices of Matthew Hopkins as Witchfinder-General.

Norris Catalogue (typescript), 2 v arranged by parish and subject.

Herbert E Norris, *Catalogue of the Huntingdonshire Books*, Cirencester, 1895 (printed for private circulation).

Wimpole

Wimpole Hall, Wimpole, Royston, Cambs. Admission by appointment with the Libraries Adviser, National Trust, 42 Queen Anne's Gate, London SW1H 9AS.

The main library room was designed in 1719 by James Gibbs to house part of the Harleian Library. In 1740, however, Edward Harley, 2nd Earl of Oxford, was forced to sell the house; the printed books were dispersed and the manuscripts became one of the foundation collections of the British Museum. Only a handful of Harleian books now remain, mostly collected together within the last 50 years.

The existing library (*c*8,000 v) is largely the collection of Phillip Yorke, 1st Earl of Hardwicke (1690–1764), Lord Chancellor from 1736–62. It is the collection of a book collector, and not simply a country house library. Many of the 18th cent books are on large paper, and there are good collections of mostly foreign 16th and 17th cent books with French, Italian and Spanish especially noticeable. Part of the collection was sold at auction in 1792 by the 3rd Earl. Little was added in the 19th cent, and in 1894 Wimpole was acquired by the 2nd Lord Robartes who, in 1897, moved to Lanhydrock. In 1939 the house was again sold to Captain and Mrs Bambridge. Mrs Bambridge was the only surviving child of Rudyard Kipling, and the library contains an important collection of his works. The Kipling papers, left with the rest of Wimpole to the National Trust on Mrs Bambridge's death in 1976, are housed in the University of Sussex.

Wisbech

Wisbech and Fenland Museum, Museum Square, Wisbech, Cambs PE13 1ES. Tel (0945) 3817. Open, Oct-March (except Mon) 10 am-1 pm, 2-4 pm; April-Sept 10 am-1 pm, 2-5 pm. Closed on Bank Holidays. The library is for reference only, and admission is strictly by appointment through the Museum Curator. Photocopying facilities available at County Branch Library when staffing permits.

The library of the Wisbech and Fenland Museum comprises several major collections which have grown up with the Museum. The original museum, founded in 1835, was later combined with the Wisbech Literary Society founded in 1781, mainly as a book circulating club. In 1847 a new building (in which the library is still housed) was opened and divided between the Literary Society and the Museum. The book collections grew by gift and purchase, but it was with the bequest of the collection of the Rev Chauncy Hare Townsend that the library assumed major importance. Townsend was a friend of Dickens and other Victorian writers, and his collection comprised *c*6,000 books, the literary and historical mss and autographs. (His colour plate books went to the Victoria and Albert Museum.) By 1878, the Literary Society had become insolvent and there was a change of constitution whereby the two bodies were officially united to form the Wisbech Museum and Literary Society. In 1928 the *Peckover Collection* of Bibles and 16th and 17th cent atlases was acquired. The other major collection which forms part of the library is the *Wisbech Town Library* (*c*1,100 printed volumes) begun in 1653–4, and previously housed in St Mary's Church.

Wisbech and Fenland Museum Library Comprises *c*11,000 v and 1,000 literary and historical mss (mainly from the Townsend Library. See *Supra*). The collection is strong in literature, with a fine collection of two-and three-decker novels, mainly pre-1850; a good basic collection of first and early editions of the works of Dickens (including the ms of *Great Expectations*), many inscribed by the author to Townsend, some are the first in book form, others bound from the parts; a good collection of miscellaneous Victorian travel, biography and history; a choice collection of romantic literature—Keats, Shelley, Byron and Coleridge well represented. Other items include the ms of *The Monk* by M G Lewis, a fine copy of Drayton's *Poly-Olbion* (1612), and Chaucer's works (1560).

English blind stamp bindings of the 16th and 17th cent must constitute one of the best collections in the country.

Local material relating to Wisbech and the surrounding areas is strong, and includes all standard works in superb copies, and in several editions. The collection of works illustrated by the local etcher R Farren is larger than that in the British Library.

There are printed and ms material relating to slavery (since Thomas Clarkson was a native of Wisbech), and works by Clarkson and Wilberforce are quite good. In general the collection includes *c*8,000 pre-1850 items, of which *c*2,250 are pre-1700, including *c*1,700 STC items. There are 15 known incunabula in the collection.

Catalogue of the library of the Wisbech Museum comprising the books formerly belonging to the Wisbech Literary Society, and those of the Townsend Bequest. Wisbech. Leach and Son, 1882. (op and unreliable).

Author card cat.

Cheshire

Chester

Cheshire Libraries and Museums. Chester Library, St John Street, Chester CH1 1DH. Tel (0244) 21938 and 43427. Open Mon, Tues, Thurs, Fri 9.30 am-7 pm; Wed 9.30 am-5.30 pm; Sat 9.30 am-1 pm.

Local Collection Originated in the collections of the City Library and the Mechanics' Institute in the early 19th cent. The Free Public Library was opened in 1877 and became part of the Cheshire Libraries and Museums in 1974. The collection includes the Hughes and Vernon Collections. There are *c*10,000 v with many (not estimated) pre-1850 items on a variety of subjects, but principally on Chester and Cheshire, including Civil War pamphlets.

Dict card cat.

Chester Cathedral Library, Cathedral Office, 1 Abbey Square, Chester CH1 2HU. Tel (0244) 24756. Open on application to the Canon Librarian to all bona fide research workers.

Chester Cathedral Library includes the private library of William Jacobson, Bishop of Chester, 1808–84 (bequeathed) and that of the Rev Francis Sanders, Vicar of Hoylake, 1891–1912 (bequeathed). Its main subject area concerns the lives and writings of the Bishops of Chester, *c*1616–1889. It contains *c*1,400 pre-1800 items (the later books forming a working library) which include 3 incunabula, 87 STC, 365 Wing, 361 English of the period 1701–1800, and 104 pre-1600, 313 (1601–1700) and 129 (1701–1800) continental items.

'A catalogue of certain books belonging to Christ Church at Chester' 1768. (A thin folio ms catalogue seen by Botfield, no 13, but now lost.)

Catalogue of the Jacobson Library' *c*1884, ms.

Francis Sanders, 'Catalogue of books relating to, or written by, the Bishops of Chester', *c*1,900 ms (arranged chronologically by Bishops, and alphabetically by author).

A card cat is maintained in the Library.

K M Maltby, 'Notes on the Cathedral Library'. *Newsletter of the Friends of Chester Cathedral* (1975–).

E Anne Read, 'A checklist of books, catalogues and periodical articles relating to the cathedral libraries of England'. *Oxford Bib Soc Occasional Publications*. 6, 1970, p11-12.

——Cathedral libraries: a supplementary checklist. *Library History*. 4(5), p145, 1978.

Knutsford

Tatton Park, Knutsford, Cheshire WA16 6QN. Tel (0565) 3155. Admission restricted to items not readily available elsewhere, on application, in writing, to the Director of Libraries and Museums, 91 Hoole Road, Chester CH2 3NG. Material available at Tatton, or by arrangement at County Record Office, The Castle, Chester. Photographs and photocopies available by arrangement.

Tatton Park Library Collection made by the Egerton family 1598–1958. Bequeathed to the National Trust 1958, and administered by the Cheshire County Council. It totals *c*12,000 v, and includes strong 18th cent collection, mainly in mint condition; 16th and 17th cent English and European books, especially Italian, French and Dutch. There are 45 STC and 324 Wing items. Small collections of Tracts against Papist *c*1685; plays *c*1710; sheet music 1790–1850. It includes the library of Samuel Hill of Shenstone (fl 1700–50)—strong in architecture, art, classics and English law; 18th and 19th cent county histories, genealogy, horticulture, sport, travel, exploration, poetry, novels; 19th and early 20th cent travel and game hunting in limited or presentation copies. There is a ms copy of Purcell, transcribed by Phil Hayes 1781–84 in 4 v.

Author cat.

A catalogue of the library at Tatton Park, compiled by Shirley Pargeter, Cheshire Libraries and Museums, 1977. £18. ISBN 0 904 53240 2 B78-15974.

Library Association Record, May 1976.

Tatton Park Guide. National Trust, 1962, rep 1975.

Some books disposed of by Executors of last Baron Egerton, 1958.

Macclesfield

The King's School, Macclesfield, Cheshire SK10 1DA. Tel (0625) 22271. Open Mon-Sat 9 am-4.30 pm, school terms only. Admission by written application to the librarian.

King's School Collection Accumulated since the foundation of the school, mostly presented, the collection totals *c*200 v, of which 100 v are pre-1850, mainly classics 17th-18th cent, history and local history 18th-19th cent. Included are the *Complete works of George Buchanan* ed. Thomas Ruddiman, Leyden 1725, and a large book of prints of the pictures in the Galerie Du Palais Royale, with notes by L'Abbe de Fontenal, eng. J Couche and J Bouilliard, Paris 1786.

Nantwich

St Mary's Parish Church, Nantwich, Cheshire. Admission by written application to the librarian, or to the Rector, The Rectory, St Mary's Church, Nantwich.

Church Library Founded in 1704 for the benefit of

clergy and students, with books donated by the Rev Samuel Edgley, the then Vicar of Acton, the library was 'active' until the early 19th cent. It contains *c*135 v, including theological and classical works from the 16th and 17th cent, and 18th and 19th cent works of local interest. There are 13 STC and 36 Wing items. Works included are *Expositio hymnorum* and *Expositio Sequentiarum*, London 1502, Wynkyn de Worde (only other known copy in New York which is imperfect), and Purchas *Pilgrammage*, London 1613.

Ms cat of 1712. This catalogue was re-edited by Mr Alan Jeffreys of Keele University. (181 works, of which 85 are lost.) Typed copy at Keele and with librarian.

Northwich

Brunner Library, Witton Street, Northwich, Cheshire. Tel (0606) 44221. Open Mon and Tues 9.30 am-5.30 pm; Wed and Sat 9.30 am-1 pm; Thurs and Fri 9.30 am-7 pm. Admission free, no conditions.

Local History Collection Developed from acquisitions and donations since the founding of the library in 1884, the collection now totals *c*500 v. It includes general works on local history on Cheshire and the Northwich area. Its particular strength is in its coverage of the salt industry, and there are a number of books and mss which are genuinely rare.

Cat.

Cornwall

Bodmin

Lanhydrock (National Trust Property), Bodmin, Cornwall PL30 4DE. Tel (0208) 4281. Admission by appointment with the Libraries Adviser, 42 Queen Anne's Gate, London SW1H 9AS.

Lanhydrock Library The collection has grown up with the house. The house and estate were owned by the Robartes family from the early 17th cent until 1953 when it was given to the National Trust. The library contains 3,100 items in 3,500 v made up of 28 incunabula; 825 16th cent, 2,100 17th cent, 100 18th cent, 50 19th cent books. It is a fine and famous library of early books on all subjects, many of them English, including a notable collection of 17th cent pamphlets, especially of the Commonwealth period, and over 100 rare almanacs.

Two handwritten cats in 3 v. One is a shelflist and the other is arranged alphabetically. There is also a card cat.

St Mary's Abbey Library, Bodmin, Cornwall PL31 1NF. Tel (0208) 2833. Open by special arrangement on application to the Prior. Since this is a men's order, women are not normally able to consult the books. Reading room available.

The library has grown up since the Order (of Canons Regular, Lateran Congregation) returned to England from the Continent in 1881. It consists of *c*10,000 v, located in two main rooms and various other places. The subject field is mainly theological, but includes history and literature; a large number of editions of Thomas á Kempis (who was a member of the Order), and a collection of books about the Order. There is quite a good collection of books on Cornwall. Most of the pre-1700 books are continental, and include 1 incunabulum, 70 16th cent, 170 17th cent, 325 18th cent, *c*750 pre-1851 19th cent.

Card cat. Dewey classification scheme.

Penzance

The Penzance Library, Morrab Gardens, Penzance TR18 4DQ. Tel (0736) 4474. Open Mon-Fri 10 am-5 pm (Summer), 10 am-4 pm (Winter); Sat 10 am-1 pm. Admission on application to the librarian. Reading Room and Newspaper Reading Room.

The library was founded in 1818 and has grown steadily since that time, by gift and purchase. It contains *c*40,000 items in *c*60,000 v covering many subjects, but especially strong in Cornish material, 19th cent biography, history, topography and foreign travel. About 30,000 v are pre-1900 and include *c*25 16th cent, *c*300 17th cent, *c*2,000 18th cent and *c*24,000 19th cent works. The following important donations are worthy of mention; (a) *J O Halliwell*, who presented many of his books in 1862. Much of the rarest material (including all the incunabula and early English plays) was sold in 1964 and is now in Edinburgh University Library (qv). Much of the collection, however, still remains. (b) *Prebendary P Hedgeland* (presented 1911). Mainly theological, but includes other subjects. There are a number of volumes of tracts and some early printed books. (c) *Thomas Dawson* (presented 1869). Two fascinating series of scrapbooks. The first series (10 v) relates to Napoleon, and consists of engravings and ephemera. The second series (25 v) relates mainly to late 18th and 19th cent notable figures, and includes letters as well as engravings and ephemera. (d) *William Borlase* (presented 1905). An important collection of his mss, 9 v of correspondence and 11 other mss. The collection of Cornish material is a very important one and probably ranks second only to the County Library's collection at Redruth. There is also a fine collection of newspapers, 19th and 20th cent, including a full set of the *Cornishman*, which started in 1878. Other significant local interest mss are: Jonathan Couch on the fish of Cornwall, and 20 other various mss by Cornish authors; John Ralfs's *Flora of West Cornwall*

(9 v); 3 v of archaeological sketches and drawings by J T Blight; 3 mss of travel and medicine by Dr John Davy (brother of Sir Humphry Davy).

Card cat. There is a separate card cat of the Halliwell Collection.

Cyril Noall. *The Penzance Library, 1818–1968.* Penzance, 1968.

Redruth

Camborne School of Mines, Trevenson, Pool, Redruth, Cornwall TR15 3SE. Tel (0209) 714866. Open, Term: Mon-Fri 9 am-9 pm; Vacation: 9 am-5 pm. Admission to all scholars. Reading area, microform readers, photocopying.

Rare Books Collection Accumulated by purchase and gift, mainly since the opening of the new library in 1975, it contains 310 v forming a special collection of rare books on mining, mineralogy, geology, and includes 4 18th cent and 75 19th cent books. The remainder are modern works.

Card cat.

Cornwall County Library, Clinton Road, Redruth TR15 2QE. Tel (0209) 216760. Open Tues-Thurs 9.30 am-12.30 pm, 1.30-5 pm, Fri 9.30 am-12.30 pm, 1.30-7 pm, Sat 9.30 am-12.30 pm. Free admission to public. 20 study places. Microform readers, photocopying.

County Local Studies Collection Formed by the amalgamation of the former Redruth Library collection with Cornish material from various other public libraries in Cornwall. It contains 9,000 printed items in 15,000 v and 10,000 non-book items. The printed books include 5 17th cent, 50 18th cent, and 4,500 19th cent books. The remainder are modern. This is probably the best collection of Cornish material in existence, including maps, periodicals, photographs, but excluding manuscript material unless it is given as part of a collection. There are three notable collections within the library: (a) *Hambly and Rowe Collection.* Acquired in 1950 and containing about 2,200 items. It was originally the library of Dr Joseph Hambly Rowe (*d*1937), and this was acquired by Mr Edmund Hambly, who also added to it; (b) *Hamilton Jenkin Collection* on mining (mainly about Cornwall, but not exclusively so), includes a fine run of the *Mining Journal* (1835 to date), *c*1,000 items; (c) *Ashley Rowe Collection.* The library of a local historian, *c*600 items.

Note There are also collections of local material in some of the local libraries, and a number of items in each place are rare and unique to the area. On the whole, however, these collections contain modern material or duplicates of older material which is also at Redruth, the main centre for local studies. The most significant local libraries are: Falmouth (1,500 items); Launceston (1,000 items); Penzance (2,300 items); St Ives (1,000 items); Truro (1,500 items).

Truro

Bishop Phillpotts Library, Quay Street, Truro TR1 2HF. Admission by special arrangement after written application to the librarian. Reading room available.

Bishop Phillpotts Library The nucleus was Bishop Phillpotts' own personal library (presented in 1866; library building completed in 1871), and there were two other major 19th cent bequests, that of the Rev J Ford and that of the Rev Franke Parker. There are 15,000 v, of which 1,475 items (2,500 v) are pre-1800. Mainly theological, the collection includes a 63 v Grangerized version of Macklin's Bible of 1800. Also a fine collection of Bibles, including all the major polyglots (the Complutensian, Plantin, Paris, etc), as well as a good collection of pamphlets, 18th and 19th cent. There are 11 incunabula; 135 16th cent; 610 17th cent and 715 18th cent books. The remainder of the books are mainly 19th cent.

Printed cat: *The Bishop Phillpotts Library, Truro, Catalogue of books published before 1800*, Truro, 1970 (op). Also card cat. The library is arranged in Dewey order.

E B and G E Bentley: 'Bishop Phillpotts' Library, the Franke Parker bequest', in *Book Collector*, Autumn 1980, p363-94.

The Cathedral, Truro, Cornwall. Admission by special arrangement on application to Canon Librarian. Reading space available.

Truro Cathedral Library The library has gradually grown up since the opening of the Cathedral in 1880. It contains 1,500 v, mainly on theological subjects, and includes 3 incunabula; 130 16th and 17th cent; 175 18th cent books, and *c*,200 post-1800, of which half are pre-1900. Part of the collection is kept in the Canon's Vestry at the Cathedral, but much of it is stored in the same building as the Bishop Phillpotts Library (qv).

Card cat, authors only, kept at the Canon's Vestry at the Cathedral.

Cornwall County Library, Old County Hall, Station Road, Truro TR1 3UW. Tel (0872) 74282. Open by appointment only. Books required for study would be temporarily transferred to the Truro Reference Library, or the Schools Library Service.

Rare Books Collection It contains *c*150 v of old books and those of particular bibliographic interest taken from the stores of the old County Library and the formerly independent authorities in 1974. Subject field mainly 19th cent works of natural history with hand-coloured plates; a collection of early Bibles (including 'Breeches' Bible of 1615).

Early Children's Books The collection contains *c*80 v culled from the branch and school library collections, together with bequest from private donor. The books are late 19th cent, early 20th cent juveniles in publishers decorated cloth bindings—works by Mrs Ewing; illustrated books by Walter Crane, Randolph Caldecott and Kate Greenaway.

Royal Institution of Cornwall, Courtney Library, River Street, Truro. Tel (0872) 2205. Open Mon-Sat 9 am-1 pm, 2-5 pm. (Closed Mondays in Winter.) Non-members admitted to the Reading Room on application to the librarian. Reference facilities only. Microfilm and fiche readers. Photocopying service available.

Rare Book Collection/Muniments The library was founded when the RIC was formed in 1818. Rare books and manuscripts were acquired as part of older library stock and by donation/bequest. Some books and newspapers were acquired from the Cornwall County Library (1792–1920). The rare books collection contains *c*200 v plus many pre-1851 items in general stock. Ephemeral material numbers several hundred items. The subject area is mainly Cornish local history and agriculture. The library also includes the *De Pass Collection* of fine bindings and printed books; the *Doble Collection* of hagiography (deposited on long-term loan). Ephemera include handbills and posters printed locally *c*1840. The mss collection includes correspondence of Giddy, Trevithick and Hornblower; Cornish family archives from the 13th cent, including Borlase, Rashleigh, Trelawny; the *Henderson Collection* of family mss including St Aubyn, Bassett, Hawkins and Mohun; the *Hamilton-Jenkin Collection* on mining.

Card cat. Author, title, subject and Cornish Collection sequences. Typed inventory of archives.

Cumbria, Northumberland, North Tyne and Wear

Barrow-in-Furness

Cumbria County Library, Barrow Library, Ramsden Square, Barrow-in-Furness. Tel (0229) 20650. Open Mon, Tues, Wed, Fri 9 am-7 pm, Thurs and Sat 9 am-1 pm. Admission unrestricted. Microfilm reader; photocopying and photographic facilities.

Furness Library Established in the early 1950s as a special collection. It contains *c*10,000 v, 3,500 files of local history material, maps, plans, archives, illustrations, which relate to the North West of England, with a concentration on materials specifically dealing with Furness, Carmel and South Lakeland. The material is arranged as follows:

Soulby Collection A collection of *c*650 handbills covering the period 1790–1815 from the firm of John Soulby, Ulverston. (A microfilm of the other half of the collection at Reading University also held.)

M Twyman, *John Soulby, printer, Ulverston*. Reading University, Dept of Typography, 1966.

Furness Railway Company Collection Maps, plans and miscellaneous materials ranging from 1846 to 1923.

Furness Iron Industry Collection Maps, plans and wide range of printed materials covering the period 1711–20th cent.

Collection of printed Lake District guides 1790–1900

General Local History Collection *c*9,500 v, 1,000 maps and plans, illustrations collection, local newspapers (many on microfilm), *c*3,500 files on local aspects and topics (18th-20th cent).

Card cat, author and classified.

Archives all reported to NRA.

H W Hodgson, *A bibliography of the history and topography of Cumberland and Westmorland*. Joint Archives Committee for Cumberland, Westmorland and Carlisle. 1968. (Most of the Barrow Library material included.)

Carlisle

Carlisle Cathedral, c/o The Canon Librarian, 3 The Abbey, Carlisle CA3 8TZ. Tel (0228) 21834. Open by prior arrangement on written application to the Canon Librarian. Arrangements can be made for mss to be taken and used under supervision at the County Record Office, Carlisle Castle.

Cathedral Library A library was in existence pre-Dissolution, but little survived from this period (lost *c*1644). The present collection was reconstituted in the late 17th cent, and holds *c*4,000 v which include 1 incunabulum and 350 STC items listed in Ramage. Essentially the library is made up of 17th and 18th cent works, the subject content being theology, canon law, philosophy and history. A major section of the library was donated by Thomas Smith (1615–1702), chaplain to Charles II, later Bishop of Carlisle. His library is particularly rich in biblical commentaries, classics and the writings of the humanists. A collection by the local historian Bishop Wm Nicolson (1655–1727), including some of his mss notebooks, are also held.

The mss held include a 13th cent *Lives of the Saints;* 14th cent 'Roman de la Rose' (8 leaves); 15th cent 'Apocalypse' (selections).

Various mss cats and card cats 1707–1900. For details see E A Read, *A checklist of books, catalogues. . . relating to the cathedral libraries of England.* Oxford Bibliog Soc, 1970.

R T Holtby, 'Carlisle Cathedral Library and Records', in *Trans Cumb and West Antiq and Archaeol Soc,* v 66, p201-19.

R W Dixon, 'The Chapter Library of Carlisle', *Ibid,* v 2, 1875, p312-36.

Cumbria County Library, Carlisle Group HQ, Tullie House, Castle Street, Carlisle CA3 8SY. Tel (0228) 24166. Open Mon, Tues, Thurs, Fri 9 am-7 pm; Wed 9 am-5 pm; Sat 9 am-1 pm. Admission by application in person at enquiry desk, or by letter to Group Librarian. Local collection is closed access, card cat on public display. Microfilm readers; xerox facilities; audio and video facilities.

Carlisle Library Local Studies Collection (formerly the Bibliotheca Jacksoniana) The Jackson Library was bequeathed in 1890 by William Jackson of St Bees, and subsequent additions by donation and purchase combine to form the present collection. It houses *c*16,000 v, primarily material on Cumberland, Westmorland and Furness (the present Cumbria), and includes many local imprints from 1740 (particularly from Carlisle); two chapbook collections; collections of election ephemera; and a large collection of Lake District prints. Mss material includes the journals of Bishop Nicolson and James Losh.

Printed cat 1909 (op).

Updated card cat.

'Chapbooks in the Carlisle Library' in *Trans Cumb and West Antiq and Archaeol Soc,* (Old Series) v XIV and XVI.

K Smith, *Lakeland prints: early prints of the Lake District,* Hendon Publishing Co, 1973.

Dixon Collection Brought together from the estate of the late F J Bassett Dixon, it contains 200 v, chiefly 18th cent editions, including some first editions of English and French literature; also some modern private press books.

Card cat.

Wordsworth Collection A collection of 800 v, most first editions and later printings of works, including fine and large paper copies.

H W Hodgson (comp), *Catalogue of the Wordsworth Collection,* Carlisle City Council, 1970 (op).

K Smith, 'Carlisle's Wordsworth Collection' in G Stephenson, *The inward eye.* Midnag, 1970, p12-14.

Cumbria Record Office, The Castle, Carlisle, Cumbria CA3 8UR. Tel (0228) 23456. Ext 314 or 316. Open Mon-Fri 9 am-5 pm. Admission unrestricted. Photocopying facilities; microfilm reader.

Carlisle Law Library *c*150 v of legal textbooks 1773–1950, including 8 v of Local Acts of Parliament 1761–1906; and *c*2,000 v Law reports 1641–1949.

Typescript cat.

Carlisle Society of Friends Monthly Meeting Library *c*200 v of Tracts, papers and pamphlets—late 17th-mid 19th cent.

Lord Lonsdale's pamphlets These amount to *c*1,000 printed pamphlets, sermons etc, 1576–1839. The pamphlets relate mainly to trade, shipping, politics and the Civil War. *c*270 are pre-1700.

Typescript cat for material 1576–1723.

General search room collection Contains all standard local histories for the area of Cumbria and Westmorland.

B G Jones, 'Cumberland, Westmorland and Carlisle Record Offices, 1960–65' in *Trans Cumb and West Antiq and Archaeol Soc.* New Series, v LXV, 1965, p408-18.

——'Cumberland and Westmorland Record Office, 1968' in *Northern History,* v 3, 1968, p162-71.

Northumberland

North Tyneside Libraries, Central Library, Northumberland Square, North Shields, Tyne and Wear NE30 1QU. Tel (0632) 582811. Open Mon, Thurs, Fri 9 am-1 pm, 2-5 pm; Tues 9 am-1 pm, 2-7 pm; Wed 9 am-1 pm. Copying; microfilm reader.

Local Studies Centre, Old Library, Howard Street Little pre-1850 material other than standard local histories. Stock concentrates on Whitley Bay, North Shields and Tynemouth area. A collection of playbills (N Shields and S Shields theatres) however, date from 1821–75.

Card cat.

Wallington Hall, Cambo, Morpeth, Northumberland. Tel (067 074) 283. Access by prior arrangement, on written request, accompanied by two references to either the Libraries Adviser, National Trust, 42 Queen Anne's Gate, London SW1, or the Special Collections Librarian, University Library, Newcastle-upon-Tyne.

The Wallington Hall Library was collected by the Trevelyan family with part of Lord Macaulay's library. A country gentleman's library (primarily late 18th-19th cent), it contains *c*3,700 v covering history, some philosophy, memoirs, Victorian fiction and works on local topography, and includes 5 STC and 25 Wing items; 15 pre-1700 continental works. Many of Lord Macaulay's books contain annotations.

C J Hunt, 'Catalogue of the Library at Wallington Hall, Northumberland'. *Newcastle University Library publication*, no 9, 1968.

A N L Munby, *Macaulay's library*, Glasgow University Press. *David Murray Lecture*, no 28, 1966.

Northumberland County Library, Central Library, Morpeth, Northumberland. Tel (0670) 512385. Open Mon, Wed, Fri 10 am-8 pm; Tues 10 am-5 pm; Sat 9 am-12 noon. Closed Thurs. Copying facilities; microfilm reader.

Local History Collection c5,000 items, including all pre-1850 standard county histories. Most early material on microfilm from Newcastle Central Library and Northumberland County Record Office.

Card cat.

Northumberland County Record Office, Melton Park, North Gosforth, Northumberland. Tel (089 426) 2680. Open Mon 9 am-9 pm; Tues-Thurs 9 am-5 pm; Fri 9 am-4.30 pm. Admission unrestricted. Microfilm readers; photocopying facilities. The following collections have been acquired since 1962 by gift, loan and purchase:

General Reference Collection c1,200 printed books and pamphlets relating to Northumberland local history and national aspects. All standard pre-1850 local histories in stock.

Lockhart Collection (NRO Deposit 95) An archive deposit made in 1963 including a library of legal works. It contains c200 v of the period 1724–1920, of which c20 items are 18th cent; c60 pre-1850. A good example of a working lawyer's library.

Butler (Ewart) Collection (NRO Deposit 229) An archive collection deposited in 1966, it contains 55 Victorian novels. No volume is complete, but various authors represented, eg W H Ainsworth, Frances Trollop, Harry Lorrequer and Charles Dickens.

Coanwood Reading Library (NRO Deposit 1114) Deposit of library papers, accounts and printed materials made in 1974. c60 v, mostly copies of 19th cent magazines, eg *Jerold's Magazine* 1845–7; *Colonial Magazine* 1840–41; *J of Agriculture* 1861–68.

Armstrong Papers (NRO Deposit 309) Deposited 1967. Includes many pamphlets (c35) on 19th cent agriculture, mining and local health matters, covering the period 1794–1900 (mostly 1870s).

Newcastle-upon-Tyne

Literary and Philosophical Society of Newcastle-upon-Tyne, Westgate Road, Newcastle-upon-Tyne NE1 1SE. Tel (0632) 320192. Open Mon, Wed, Thurs, Fri 9.30 am-7 pm; Tues 9.30 am-8 pm; Sat 9.30 am-1 pm. Admission to non-members on written application to the librarian.

The library was founded in 1793 through donation and purchase. It now contains c130,000 v, 50,000 of which are 20th cent. It is particularly rich in 18th and 19th cent material relating to science and technology, history and local history. A collection of c5,000 pamphlets is held covering all subjects (19th-cent primarily), c20 per cent being of local interest. There are 5 incunabula; c60 STC items (35 listed in Ramage); 120 pre-1640 continental works; c225 Wing items; 100 continental works 1641–1700. Wide selection of national and local 19th cent periodicals held.

All items in detailed card cat.

Printed cats issued in 1829, 1836, 1858–1878.

Most comprehensive cat is that issued in 1903. (op)

Checklist of books and pamphlets printed before 1701 in the Society's Library, c1965. Typescript.

R S Watson, *The history of the Literary and Philosophical Society of Newcastle-upon-Tyne, 1793–1896*. 1897. (op)

Natural History Society of Northumbria, Hancock Museum, Barras Bridge, Newcastle-upon-Tyne. Tel (0632) 326386. Open Mon-Fri normally only between 10 am and 1 pm. Admission to non-members on written application.

The library was started with the Society's foundation in 1829, and now houses c10,000 v. It contains few pre-1700 items, but is rich in works on all aspects of natural history from that date onwards. It contains a wide selection of 19th cent periodical literature.

Card cat.

T R Goddard, *History of the Society, 1829–1929*. NHS, 1929. (op)

G Hickling, *The Natural History Society of Northumbria 1929–1979*. NHS, 1980.

Newcastle-upon-Tyne City Libraries, Princess Square, Newcastle-upon-Tyne NE99 1MC. Tel (0632) 610619. Open Mon-Thurs 9 am-9 pm, Fri and Sat 9 am-5 pm. Admission unrestricted. Formal application required for all special collections. Photocopying facilities; microfilm readers; carrels available in reference area.

Bell Collection The collection relates to the Bell family of 19th cent booksellers, surveyors and land agents. The principal collector was John Bell (1785–1860) and Seymour Thomas Bell (1842–1922). Much of the Bell material (which is archival or pseudo-archival, ie annotated printed works, transcripts) is now widely scattered throughout the north of England, and housed at the Record Office, Newcastle University, Gateshead Public Library, Northumberland City Libraries.

Individual volumes have their own indices in some instances.

Bewick Collection Primarily the collection of *c*330 v of local businessman John William Pease, bequeathed to the Library in 1901 (Bewick paintings and watercolours bequeathed to the Hancock Museum). All new materials relating to Bewick and his apprentices are purchased or donated. The collection includes *c*450 v of first and later editions of all Bewick illustrated books, and a further 300 items which include Christmas cards, keepsakes, newspaper cuttings etc, proof copies of some works and blocks. All first editions are in fine bindings. The collection includes all critical and descriptive works relating to Thomas Bewick and his 'school'. It covers the period 1772 to date. Some letters, watercolours and Bewick's tools are also preserved, and many original blocks are also in the possession of the City Libraries.

Cat of the Bewick Collection. Newcastle City Libraries, 1904. (op)

Thomas Hugo, *The Bewick Collections: a descriptive catalogue of the works of Thomas and John Bewick.* Reeve, 1866.

S Roscoe, *Thomas Bewick: a bibliography.* OUP, 1953. (Reprinted Daesons 1973).

S Doncaster, *Some notes on Bewick's trade blocks.* Newcastle Imprint Club. 1980.

I Bain, *Thomas Bewick.* Laing Art Gallery, Newcastle. 1979.

Foster-Harvey Collection A 19th-cent collection made by Charles T Tallent-Bateman, Manchester, and purchased by Newcastle *c*1910. It contains 350 v of illustrated books, periodicals etc, particularly by the artists William Harvey (1796–1866)—Bewick pupil—and Birket Foster (1825–1899). The Harvey material is not very complete, but the Miles Birket Foster items include all major first and later editions.

Card index in library incomplete.

General Collection (early printed books) and *Local collection* (early printed works) They contain 100 STC works (partly covered by Ramage); 485 Wing and 220 pre-1700 continental items. The bulk of the items were purchased in two main collections: (a) *C W Merrifield*, FRS. The library, bought in 1883, contains *c*1,000 scientific works, principally mathematical; 96 pre-1700 items, which include first editions of all the major European mathematicians, including Euclid. (b) *Matthew Mackey Collection*. A local businessman, his collection contains 131 tracts relating to the North East 1640–1680, purchased in 1919.

J C Day, 'Early printed books in the General and Local Collections, Newcastle City Libraries', 1980. (Typescript)

Local Collection Built up by donation, purchase etc, this collection contains 30,000 v; 40,000 illustrations; 5,000 maps, covering Northumberland, Tyne and Wear and Durham, but also much regional material relating to the Borders and Cumbria. There is a unique collection of locally printed works 1639 to date; local newspapers from 1711; local directories from 1780s, and printed election tracts and broadsides for 19th cent elections, especially 1826 election (25 v).

Local cat. Newcastle City Libraries, 1932 (op) (only covers Newcastle and Northumberland material) kept up to date by a card cat which includes other local area coverage.

Short guide to the archives. Newcastle City Libraries, 1961 (op) (most archive materials now transferred to Northumberland Record Office; Tyne and Wear Record Office and Durham County Record Office).

Thomlinson Collection The personal library of Dr Robert Thomlinson (1668–1747), local clergyman, left before his death to the public of Newcastle and housed with the 'Old Library' at St Nicholas's Church (later Cathedral) until 1880 when it was transferred to City Libraries—the Old Library going to the University (qv). It contains 5,593 v, including 4 mss; 2 incunabula; 391 STC and 2,507 Wing items, with 740 pre-1700 continental works. The remainder are of 1700–1880 period (STC works only partly covered by Ramage). Half the collection is primarily theological and philosophical, with some 17th cent travel, mathematical, medical and early histories. Poetry and literature poorly represented.

Five mss cats are incorporated in the collection.

E Charnley, *Complete catalogue of the public library in St Nicholas's Church*, 1829. (op)

J C Day, 'Short title catalogue of the books (English and Continental) printed before 1701 in the Thomlinson Collection' (FLA thesis, 1970, available through University Microfilms).

Author/classified cat on cards completed 1981.

Contents of the collection—particularly of the later period, is best described in J Knott, 'A history of the libraries of Newcastle' (M Litt thesis, Newcastle-upon-Tyne Univ, 1975).

S Jeffery, *The Thomlinson Library.* Newcastle City Libraries, 1981 (a brief introduction to the collection).

North of England Institute of Mining and Mechanical Engineers, Neville Hall, Westgate Road, Newcastle-upon-Tyne NE1 1TD. Tel (0632) 322201. Open Mon-Fri 10 am-4 pm; to non-members of the Society on written application to the librarian.

The library was started on the Society's foundation in 1852, and now contains 30,000 v of which *c*6,000 are 19th cent or earlier, and include many early 19th cent treatises on mining and mining engineering. Special donations are largely of archival material, but include printed material, eg John Buddle; Buddle Atkinson; London Lead Company; Thomas Bell collection on the coal trade (1239–1850) 9v.

Card cat. (BL cataloguing programme in progress.)

Catalogue of the Library to 1883. 1886. (op)

Handlist of archives. Northumberland Record Office 1960–1. Rev 1970. (Typescript)

St Mary's College, Fenham, Newcastle-upon-Tyne NE4 9YH. Tel (0632) 743320. Open: Term, Mon-Thurs 9 am-8 pm, Fri 9 am-6 pm; Vacation, closed all of August, and for variable lengths of time at Easter and Christmas. Prior application to be made to the librarian for use of research facilities.

The Library The main library holds *c*30,000 v, of which *c*350 items make up the special collection acquired by donations from time to time. The special collection contains 2 mss (Dutch Book of Hours—15th cent and an Italian copy of *Meditations of St Bernard, c*1450); 4 incunabula; 9 STC items (not in Ramage); 6 editions of the Bible 1561—1669; 5 pre-1700 continental items; *c*20 Wing items; 300 works of a miscellaneous nature of the 17th-19th cent.

Card cat (not complete).

Society of Antiquaries of Newcastle-upon-Tyne, Black Gate, Newcastle-upon-Tyne. Tel (0632) 27938. Open Wed-Fri 2-4 pm; Sat 10 am-1 pm; to non-members of the Society by formal application.

The library was started with the Society's foundation in 1813, and now contains *c*25,000 v which include 21 STC items located (not covered by Ramage's list); 170 Wing items; 15 pre-1700 continental works. These relate mainly to Civil War activities in northern England. The collection relates particularly to the archaeology and antiquities of the north east, with an emphasis on the Roman remains in Durham, Northumberland, Cumbria. All early and later local histories held. Rich in transactions and proceedings of other British and continental archaeological and antiquarian societies. The collection is largely maintained by donation.

The archives are now transferred to Northumberland County Record Office.

Catalogue of the library belonging to the Society of Antiquaries of Newcastle-upon-Tyne. 1896. (op) (includes drawings, maps etc)

J C Day, 'Early printed books in the Society of Antiquaries of Newcastle-upon-Tyne', 1982. (Typescript)

Society of Friends, Archbold Terrace, Newcastle-upon-Tyne 2. Tel (0632) 812924. Open by arrangement with the librarian on written application.

The formal library began *c*1820, and now houses *c*2,500 v which cover Quakerism, biblical criticism, history and biography. Some 1,100 items are pre-1900, notably *c*60 Wing titles. They include the standard tracts in defence of the Quaker beliefs by Fox, Howgill, Fell, Whitehead, etc, and 300 v of 18th-cent religious controversy and biography.

Card cat.

Catalogue of books in the Friends' Library. 1885 (op)

Catalogue of books and pamphlets in the Friends' Library, 1900. (op) *Supplement to 1915* (op)

J W Steel, *A historical sketch of the Society of Friends in Newcastle and Gateshead, 1653—1898.* (op)

Trinity House, Broad Chare, Newcastle-upon-Tyne 1. Tel (0632) 328226. Open Mon-Fri 9 am-5 pm. Brethren are admitted by right; researchers on written application to the Secretary.

The Guild was founded in 1492 and the library *c*1700. It now contains *c*750 v made up of *c*175 18th cent and 250 19th cent works, while the remainder is primarily 19th cent periodicals. Subject areas include commerce, economics, naval history and travel. *c*30 miscellaneous maps and charts (18th-19th cent). The Guild retains all its own archives.

Cat of books. Rev ed 1971. Typescript. (Handlist of archives produced by Newcastle Record Office.)

Catalogue of books belonging to the Master and Brethren of the Trinity House, Newcastle-upon-Tyne. 1833 (op)

D R Moir, *The birth and history of the Trinity House, Newcastle,* 1958. Official history. (Ch 5 makes a passing reference to the library.)

The Library, University of Newcastle-upon-Tyne NE1 7RU. Tel (0632) 328511. Open Mon-Fri 9 am-9 pm, Sat 9 am-4.30 pm in term; Mon-Fri 9 am-5 pm, Sat 9 am-1 pm in vacation. Admission to non-members by written application only. Photocopying, photography, microfilm readers available. Beta-radiography plate.

Newcastle-upon-Tyne—Special Collections All of the Special Collections are entered in the main card catalogue unless otherwise stated. Those collections not at the moment included in the main catalogue will be incorporated in OCLC by the end of 1983. Card indices of printers; publishers; place of printing; bookplates and provenance; and of special bindings are all in progress.

Chronological

Manuscripts The library has a small collection of mediaeval mss, mostly acquired by gift. They include a 13th cent *Vitae Sanctorum.* The others are service books or missals of various dates. Later mss materials take the form of individual holograph letters of the 19th and 20th cent scientists or literary men.

B C Raw, *Lives of the saints* (description of the *Vitae Sanctorum*). Newcastle University Library publications no 2, 1961.

Incunabula Small collection of about 25 incunabula. For the most part they have been presented, and include such works as the *Epistolae* of St Jerome, Palma, 1480: a tract on the plague printed in Bologna, 1478, and the earliest printed work on architecture *De re aedificatoria,* Florence, 1485, by Alberti.

*STC items c*300 items, mostly covered by Ramage. Collection notable for the number of early Bibles, for several well-known herbals and for a number of dictionaries, medical works and editions of the classics.

W S Mitchell, 'A list of post-incunabula in the University Library, Newcastle-upon-Tyne', 1965. *University Library publication. Extra series no 3.*

Bradshaw Room Collection Includes c1,750 v of English works 1641–1700 and continental items 1601–1700.

Eighteenth-cent Collection c4,220 v comprising items taken from the general stacks which were not already in a special collection. The Collection was formed in 1972.

1800–1851 Collection c12,700 v brought together in 1973 from the general collection.

The Victorian Collection c1,200 v consisting of Victorian editions of major and minor English writers, 'Yellow backs', and other bindings.

Alphabetical

Bainbrigg Library c1,200 v constituting the historical portion of the library of Appleby Grammar School, and named after its 16th cent founder, Richard Bainbrigg, deposited at Newcastle in 1966. Subject areas are mainly classical and later literature and history. A number of early 16th cent English bindings are included.

E Hichcliffe, 'Catalogue of the Bainbrigg Library of the Appleby Grammar School'. 1977 (not published).

Gertrude Bell Collection c2,000 v, being the working library of Miss Gertrude Bell (1868–1926), archaeologist, Oriental scholar, administrator and political adviser, and presented by her sister, Lady Richmond, in 1926. It contains her books on the Arabic and Persian languages, and on the history and antiquities of Arabia, Iraq and the Near East. c6,000 photographs, chiefly of Near East antiquities, taken by Miss Bell have been transferred to the Dept of Antiquities at the University.

W C Donkin, 'Catalogue of the Gertrude Bell Collection', 1960. *University of Newcastle-upon-Tyne Library Publication*, no 1.

——Letters and papers of Gertrude Bell: a list. 1966. *Ibid.* Extra Series, no 4. (op)

Bosanquet Papers The papers of Bernard Bosanquet, philosopher (1848–1923), and his wife Helen Bosanquet (1860–1925), who was a member of the 1909 Poor Law Commission. Deposited in 1965 by the then Vice-Chancellor, Dr C I C Bosanquet.

Bosanquet Papers: a handlist. 1972. Typescript.

Burman Collection c500 items deposited by Alnwick Urban District Council. The Collection, made by the late Dr C Clark Burman, is of books, chapbooks and other material printed in Alnwick, mainly in the 18th and 19th cent.

P G C Isaac, 'The Burman Alnwick Collection, 1973'. *University of Newcastle-upon-Tyne Library Publication*, no 6.

Jack Common Papers Newcastle novelist and journalist, 1903–68. Deposited 1976. Personal papers.

Draft cat in progress.

Joseph Cowen Tracts Most of the books belonging to Joseph Cowen (1831–1900) have been shelved separately in the library with the exception of some 150 v which contain approximately 6,000 political, social and economic tracts, which form the basis of this collection.

A M Blenkinsop, 'The Joseph Cowen Collection of pamphlets and tracts'. (Uncompleted thesis for MA degree, 1969.)

Gilchrist Collection Early works on agriculture formed from the nucleus of the historical library of the late Prof D A Gilchrist, who held the Chair of Agriculture in Armstrong College, Newcastle, from 1902–27. The Collection now totals 350 v. Particularly rich in 18th and 19th cent reports on farming in many part of Great Britain.

Heslop Collection of Dictionaries Some 250 dictionaries bequeathed by R Oliver Heslop, philologist and antiquary, in 1916. It contains such works as Baret's *Alvearie*, 1580, Florio's *World of wordes*, 1598 and 1611, Minsheu's *Ductor in linguas*, 1625 and 1627, the works of the major lexicographers, eg Bullokar, Coles, Holyoake and Johnson, and an almost complete set of the publications of the English Dialect Society.

W S Mitchell, 'Catalogue of the Heslop Collection of Dictionaries', 1955. *King's College Library Publication*, no 2.

Heversham Collection The library of Heversham Grammar School, Westmorland. Transferred to the University in 1964. c450 v of the 600 titles listed in a mss catalogue of 1800 have survived. The library was founded in 1767 by a gift of books from the Assoc of Dr Bray. It was intended for the use of the neighbouring clergy as well as for the masters and boys of the school. Additions were made by donation from local gentry and former pupils. The collection consists mainly of editions of classical or theological authors, and in spite of its comparatively late foundation, approximately half the volumes were printed pre-1700, with a few pre-1600.

Hindson-Reid Collection A collection of 900 engraved woodblocks used by Messrs Hindson and Andrew Reid Ltd. Illustrative of local printing over a period 200 years. It was deposited in 1964, along with 5 v compiled by John Bell, Jnr on the history of local printing. Two further collections of woodblocks have since been added: those used in J C Bruce's *Lapidarium Septentrionale*, 1875, deposited by the Newcastle Society of Antiquaries; and a number used by Alnwick printers which were deposited by the Northumberland and Durham Travel Association.

F M Thomson, 'A Newcastle collection of woodblocks', *The Book Collector*, v 17, 1968, p443-57.

Thomas Hodgkin Collection North East banker and historian (1831–1913). A collection of 25 v of his mss of published and unpublished works, including his travel journals. Copies and offprints of his works (not a complete collection).

L Creighton, *Life and letters of Thomas Hodgkin.* Longmans, 1917.

Kepier Collection A library of *c*750 v from the Kepier Grammar School, Houghton le Spring, Co Durham. The School, founded in 1574, closed in 1933. The collection contains 4 incunabula and *c*30 pre-1640 items. The books consist mainly of 17th and 18th cent classics and theological writings. They form an interesting example of an early school library.

'Books from the Kepier School in the Library of King's College', nd. Typescript.

R W Ramsey, 'Kepier Grammar School, Houghton and its library', *Archaeologia Aeliana*. Ser 3, v 3, 1907, p306-33.

Merz Collection Donated by John Theodore Merz, an electrical engineer and philosopher. His mathematical works were presented to Armstrong College in 1909, and 10 years later his collection of books, on which he based his *History of European thought in the nineteenth century* were added. The collection in all totals *c*4,000 v and contains notable works on science, European history and German literature. Many works have been bound by Zaehnsdorf, and the collection is well known for its fine leather and half-leather bindings.

R A Sampson, 'Personal reminiscences and impressions of Dr J T Merz'. *Proc Univ of Durham Philosophical Soc*, v VI, 1916–23, p233-90.

Pybus Collection A library of books, engravings, prints and busts which illustrates the history of medicine. Collected by Emeritus Professor F C Pybus over a period of 40 years, it was handed over by him in September 1965. It comprises 2,000 v, 2,000 engravings, 50 portraits and busts, and a number of holograph letters. The books are classics of the history of medicine, with particular reference to the history of anatomy, surgery, and of medical illustration. The engravings, oil paintings and busts are of medical men from the 16th-20th cent. (See also below Special Medical Collection.)

J S Emerson, *Catalogue of the Pybus Collection*, Manchester Univ Press, 1981.

Runciman Papers The political papers of Walter Runciman, 1st Viscount Runciman of Doxford, 1870–1949. Deposited 1969, they cover Runciman's career as Liberal MP and Cabinet Minister (Education—1908–11; Trade—1914–16; and Trade—1931–37, and his mission to Czechoslovakia in 1938).

A Elliot and C Williams, *Catalogue of the papers of Walter Runciman, 1st Viscount of Doxford.* 1973. Newcastle Univ Library Publication.

St Bees School Library The historical portion of St Bees School, Cumberland, transferred to the University in 1965. The School was founded in 1583, and the library was built up during the 17th cent by donations from local gentry and clergy, being described by Daniel Defoe as 'very valuable and still increasing'. The collection totals 405 v, mainly of theological and classical literature. It contains 1 ms, 1 incunabulum, and 102 16th cent works. A number of 16th cent blind stamped bindings are also preserved.

Not in main card cat, but items catalogued on slips.

St Nicholas Cathedral Library The theological library of some 3,000 v placed on permanent loan in 1965. It contains 26 incunabula and *c*200 works printed in the 16th and 17th cent. The remainder consist of 19th cent theological works and series.

Not in main card cat, but items catalogued on slips.

Newcastle Cathedral Chapter Library. Preliminary Catalogue, 1888. (op)

Catalogue of the Newcastle Chapter Library and of the churchwardens' or old parish library, 1890. (op)

The Sandes Library The historical portion of Kendal Grammar School Library, consisting of 350 v of classics and theology, including some notable examples of early printing and binding. Deposited 1967.

A Elliot and J Bagnall, 'Short-title list of the Sandes Library', 1969. Typescript.

Newcastle University. Library Publications. Extra Series no 11.

Special Medical Collection This collection of over 3,000 v has its origin in the libraries of the Newcastle Infirmary, founded in 1819, and of the College of Medicine, founded in 1834. The collection covers all branches of medicine, and is rich in the works of the 17th-19th cent.

Catalogue of the Medical Library at the Infirmary, 1834. (op) (lists *c*1,200 v: 16 16th cent continental works; 3 STC; 30 Wing items; 40 17th cent continental works; 600 18th cent English works).

J S Emmerson, 'On the Gallery', *Univ of Durham Medical Gazette*, v 47, 1953, p24-7. (op)

——'Thomas Masterman Winterbottom, MD, 1766–1859'. *Ibid.* v 48, 1955, p23-7. (op)

(Both Emmerson articles are bio-bibliographical accounts with reference to some of the more interesting items.)

The Spence Watson Collection A collection of some 500 v on English literature, consisting largely of the publications of the Shakespeare Society, the Spenser Society, the Ballad Society, the Chaucer Society and similar publications. Presented in 1908 by the Rt Hon R Spence Watson (1837–1911), one of the founders of the Durham College of Physical Science, and President of Armstrong College in 1911.

Trevelyan Papers The family papers of the Trevelyans of Wallington Hall, Northumberland. Deposited in 1967. They contain much unpublished material about Ruskin and the Pre-Raphaelites, and political material of both this and the last century. Two members of the family became Cabinet Ministers, and two have been appointed to the Order of Merit.

Catalogues of the four Trevelyan manuscript collections have been produced.

A J A Morris, *C P Trevelyan, 1870–1958, Portrait of a radical.* Blackstaff Press. 1977.

V Surtees, *ed. Reflections of a friendship: John Ruskin's letters to Pauline Trevelyan, 1848–1866.* Allen & Unwin, 1979.

R Trevelyan, *A Pre-Raphaelite Circle.* Chatto and Windus, 1978.

See also the entry for Wallington Hall, Northumberland.

Ure Collection The books of Peter Ure, Joseph Cowen, Professor of English Language and Literature, 1960–69. Bought and presented to the Library after his death in 1969. The books by and about Yeats were kept together as a valuable and useful group, now called the Ure Collection of *c*200 v.

Robert Whyte Collection A personal library which was built up, distributed and re-assembled. Robert White, born in Roxburghshire in 1802, moved to Newcastle in 1825 where he became a clerk. He was interested in local history and antiquities, and in English literature, particularly in ballads. His knowledge of street literature made him a valuable contributor to F J Child during the preparation of the latter's great work. White's library passed to his sisters in 1874, and re-assembled during World War II. The library consists of *c*4,400 v, and is especially rich in English literature (ballads and chapbooks), ecclesiastical history and the history of the Border country. Besides printed books, the collection contains some prints and engravings of local scenes.

D S Bland, *Chapbooks and garlands in the Robert White Collection,* 1956. King's College Library Publication, no 3.

C J Hunt, 'Scottish ballads and music in the Robert White Collection', *Bibliotheck,* v 5, 1967, p138-41.

F W Ratcliffe, 'Chapbooks with Scottish imprints in the Robert White Collection', *Ibid,* v 4, 1964, p88-174.

F M Thomson, *Newcastle Chapbooks.* Oriel Press, 1969. (op)

Whyte Papers The papers of Frederic Whyte, 1867–1941, publisher and biographer of W T Stead and William Heinemann. Deposited 1972.

Handlist of papers, 1973.

Devon

Barnstaple

North Devon Athenaeum, Barnstaple, Devon EX32 8LN. Tel (0271) 2174. Open Mon-Fri 10 am-1 pm, 2.15-6 pm; Sat 10 am-1 pm. Closed during Spring and Autumn staff holidays. Microfilm reader available.

North Devon Athenaeum Library Founded in 1898 by W F Rock, as a private trust library and museum, it contains *c*40,000 v and several thousands of archival and ms material. A variety of subjects are covered, but the library is particularly strong in biography, travel and topography, art and natural history. There are hundreds of pre-1800 books, but since they are shelved by subject and are not separated from more modern works, it is not possible to be more precise. The particular emphases of the library are on a collection of some 1,500–2,000 v on Devon and North Devon, some prints and maps; the *John Gay Collection* of *c*200 items comprising first and later editions of his works, and books, newspaper cuttings, copies of letters etc about him; a collection of *c*150 Bibles of various dates and languages. The mss collection includes the *Harding Collection* of the 19th cent mss relating to Devon parish history, and papers of W R Lethaby, born in Barnstaple and became consultant architect to Westminster Abbey in the 19th cent.

There is an author and subject card cat available.

A E Blackwell, 'The North Devon Athenaeum at Barnstaple' in *Trans of the Devonshire Assoc,* XCIII (1961), pp174–183.

J R Chanter, 'Report on the Harding Collection of manuscripts, records. . .', *Ibid,* XX (1888), p49-68.

Bideford

Bideford Divisional Library, New Road, Bideford. Tel (023 72) 6075. Open Mon, Tues, Thurs, Fri 9.30 am-7 pm; Wed 9.30 am-1 pm; Sat 9.30 am-5 pm. Admission unrestricted.

The Pearse-Chope Collection Presented to the Bideford Free Library in the 1940s by Mr Pearse-Chope, the collection was his personal library, and reflects his interest in the history of Devon, especially North Devon. In 1974 the Bideford Free Library became part of the Devon Library Services. The Collection consists of *c*1,500 books mainly about Devon, but many are rare items, especially those relating to North Devon area which are not available elsewhere.

A catalogue is being prepared, and when completed will be available through the Devon Library Services.

Buckfastleigh

Buckfast Abbey, Buckfastleigh, Devon TQ11 0EE. Tel (03644) 3301. Admission (men only at present) on written application to the librarian. Reading room and photocopying facilities.

Buckfast Abbey Library was started in 1882. Its holdings comprise 5 incunabula, 70 16th cent, 320 17th cent, 810 18th cent and *c*200 19th cent vols. Two special collections recently acquired are: 500 v from the library of Sir Henry Slessor, consisting almost entirely of modern books on history and biography, and the *Martin Gillet Collection* consisting of 300 books (mainly modern), and a large collection of ms notes, photographs etc on Mariology—possibly one of the most extensive collections on the subject. The library is arranged in Dewey order, and the older books are intermingled with the modern ones on the shelves. Several hundred pre-1800 books remain uncatalogued in the librarian's room, most of which are of continental origin. The range of subjects covers theology, church history (especially monastic) and local Devon and Cornwall material. Only modern books are added to the collection, and only modern books have been dispersed.

Chudleigh

Ugbrooke Park Library, Chudleigh, Devon TQ13 0AD. Tel (0626) 852179. The library is owned by Col the Lord Clifford of Chudleigh, OBE, DL. Admission by special arrangement with Lord Clifford.

The main library was sold in 1964 to the National University Library, Canberra, where it is afforded the status of the foundation collection. The books remaining number *c*6,000, of which *c*2,000 are 19th cent, *c*200 18th cent, and *c*50 earlier books. They cover a wide subject field, with emphasis on Catholic material published in Britain, France and Italy. Some items relate to Ireland. There are many pamphlets and other ephemera of considerable rarity, often in original covers. Several books of local interest relate to the Clifford family and to the house. Family account books, cellar books, etc are kept with the printed books, but the family archives are kept in a special muniments room.

Dartmouth

Britannia Royal Naval College, Dartmouth TQ6 0HJ. Tel (080 43) 2141, Ext 328. Open Mon-Fri 9 am-5 pm. Admission by letter.

The Britannia Royal Naval College Library was started mid-19th cent, and comprises *c*35,000 v which include a small collection of rare books and mss (including Jenkins's Naval Achievements of Great Britain), mainly of naval and travel interest. The books include 4 17th cent, 20 18th cent, with the remainder being 19th and 20th cent. There is a fine run of the *Navy List* from 1805 to date, and of the College magazine.

In the general library stock there is a very good collection of *c*3,000 v on naval and military history, of which approximately 400 are pre-1850.

Sheaf, author, title and subject (UDC) catalogue.

The John Simon Collection Comprising 2,700 v the collection was recently presented by John Simon (who lectured on naval history in Belgium) and covers the naval history of the First and Second World Wars. Some 1,000 v are in French and contain a few pre-20th cent works, many of which are of considerable rarity.

Not fully catalogued, but list available. Special permission must be obtained to consult the Collection.

East Budleigh

Bicton College of Agriculture, East Budleigh, Devon. Tel (0395) 68353. Open Mon-Fri 9 am-5 pm. Admission to anyone, but prior appointment should be made. Reading room.

College Library Started in 1950 with the establishment of the College, the library now holds 8,000 v and pamphlets. The books are mainly modern (20th cent) though there are a small number of 19th cent books. The main interest of the library is confined to agriculture and horticulture, and contains Devon County Library's main collection in these areas. Particularly good are the sections on beekeeping and horses.

Author and subject card cat.

Exeter

Exeter Cathedral Library, Bishop's Palace, Exeter. Tel (0392) 72894. Open Mon-Fri 2 pm-5 pm. Application for admission to be made by letter to the librarian. Reading room available; photocopying by arrangement with the librarian, Exeter University Library, who is also responsible for the administration and staffing of the Cathedral Library.

The library was founded by Bishop Ledfric in the 11th cent, and added to steadily since. It consists of *c*251,000 printed books, *c*40 mss, and some thousands of ms records. The most famous items in the library are the mss Exeter Book and the Exon Domesday. There are two large collections of medical and scientific books which rank among the finest in the country, and a fairly large collection of books ranging from the 16th to the 19th cent on a variety of other subjects. There are also 18 incunabula in the collection as well as several interesting bindings, a catalogue of which is being prepared.

All items appear in a card cat. Cards of holdings are also filed in the University Library cat. There are separate typed cats of the collections of medical and scientific books.

N R Ker, *Medieval libraries of Great Britain: a list of surviving books*, 3rd ed. London, 1964.

L J Lloyd and A M Erskine, *The Library of Exeter Cathedral*, Exeter 1967. (1974 reprint).

M P Crighton, *A catalogue of the medical books and manuscripts, including a selection of scientific works in Exeter Cathedral Library*. Exeter, 1934. (op)

Devon and Exeter Institution Library, 7 Cathedral Close, Exeter. Tel (0392) 74727. Open Mon-Fri 9 am-5 pm. Admission on written application to the librarian. Reading room and photocopying available through the University Library. The Library is administered and staffed by the University Library.

The Devon and Exeter Institution Library was founded in the early 19th cent and is still operating as a private institution, and houses c33,000 v, mainly 18th and 19th cent books on a wide range of subjects, but especially strong on local history. Local newspapers are also well represented.

Card cat available. The cards are also filed in the University Library cat.

Catalogue of the Devon and Exeter Institution Library. Exeter, 1863. (op)

Appendix to the Catalogue of the Devon and Exeter Institution. Exeter, 1880. (op)

Devon Library Services, Exeter Central Library, Castle Street, Exeter EX4 3PQ. Tel (0392) 73047. Open Mon, Tues, Thurs, Fri 9.30 am-8 pm, Wed, Sat 9.30 am-6 pm. Admission free. Study facilities, microfiche, microfilm and cassette readers, and photocopying in reference library.

Rare Books Collection c2,000 pre-1800 v separated from the main stock of Exeter Central Library after World War II and arranged by date of publication. The collection is strong in early legal works, and includes some fine herbals (eg William Turner's *Herbal* 1568 and John Parkinson's *Paradisi in sole*, 1656, presented by Lady Rosalind Northcott). The *Herber Mardon Collection* of material on Napoleon has been absorbed into the general stock, and includes over 400 prints and 185 medals.

A large proportion of the collection is entered in Exeter Central Library's card cat, but much of it is uncatalogued.

Edward Pocknell Collection Assembled by Edward Pocknell, an Exeter journalist, and presented by him to Exeter City Library in 1894, the Collection contains 500 v of manuals of a wide range of shorthand systems, mainly 19th cent, but including 30 pre-1801 items. It is arranged by system of shorthand.

No separate cat, but contents of Collection included in *Catalogue of the Reference Library of the Royal Albert Memorial Museum*. Exeter, 1901.

'The Pocknell Collection at Exeter, England' in *Phonographic Magazine*, v 17, Aug 1903, pp216-18.

West Country Studies Library Originated in 1974 after the amalgamation of the local studies collection run by Devon County and Exeter City Libraries. The Exeter City Library Collection had been built up by purchase and bequest since the opening of the public library service in 1869. The Collection includes, *inter alia*, c25,000 books and pamphlets, and some 100 feet of shelving occupied by cuttings and ephemera. It covers all aspects of West Country (Devon, Cornwall, Somerset and Dorset) history, especially Devon and Exeter. There are c300 STC and Wing items, and 800 pre-1800 items, with c300 local imprints, including many broadsheets. Literary works by local authors and works about notable persons of local origin are well represented. There are some ms items, predominantly compilations of local genealogy and topography, but including literary mss, among them items by R D Blackmore. The Burnet Morris index of over 1,000,000 references to Devon people, places and subjects is housed in the library.

A card cat is in progress. Printed books relating to Devon are listed in Allan Brockett, *The Devon Union List*, Exeter, The University Library, 1977.

Devon Library Services, Administrative Centre, Barley House, Isleworth Road, Exeter EX4 1RQ. Tel (0392) 74142. Admission by arrangement.

Early Children's Books A collection of c2,200 items (fiction and non-fiction) dating from 1692–1940, and built up by the amalgamation of separate collections held by Devon County Library, Exeter Central Library and Torquay Library up to 1974, of which the Exeter collection was the largest and most valuable. It includes c735 books pre-1850, made up of chapbooks, incitements to learning and some locally printed material.

Card cat and a descriptive cat for 1692–1849 only.

Killerton House, Killerton, Broadclyst, Exeter EX5 3 LE. Tel (039 288) 345. The house is owned by the National Trust, and is open to the public from April to October from 11 am-6 pm. Access to the library is very restricted, and application for admission should be made in writing to the Libraries Adviser, National Trust, 42 Queen Anne's Gate, London SW1H 9AS.

Sabine Baring-Gould Collection This was the library of the Rev Sabine Baring-Gould of Lewtrenchard (1834–1924), and is the property of the Baring-Gould family, but is on long loan to the National Trust. It contains c3,150 v and 3,500 items. It may be described as a fine scholar's library. Baring-Gould wrote about 140 books, and of special note is the collection of the author's own writings. Also worthy of mention are the Devon and Cornwall books, the collection of 19th cent literature—an extensive group relating to Iceland. Other important subjects covered are classics, theology, folklore, mythology, witchcraft, ballads, chapbooks, voyages, French and German literature, and history. Most of the books are 19th cent or early 20th cent, but there are several hundred of the 18th cent, and c50 of an earlier date.

Exeter University Library, Prince of Wales Road, Exeter EX4 4PT. Tel (0392) 77911. Open (Term): Mon-Fri 9 am-10 pm, Sat 9 am-1 pm; (Vacation): Mon-Fri 9 am-5.30 pm, Sat 9 am-12 pm. Admission to non-members by written application to the librarian. Photocopying, microfilm and microfiche readers available. Books may be consulted in Rare Books Room.

The University Library Collection of Rare Books and

Manuscripts has been acquired mainly by donation from various sources, and consists of *c*4,500 works in *c*5,200 v covering a variety of subjects. There are *c*600 pre-1700 items, including 7 incunabula, *c*95 works of the 16th cent and *c*500 of the 17th cent. Illustrated 18th cent French books represent a special feature of the Collection. The most outstanding item is a superb copy of Curtis's *North American Indians*. There are also a few mss of R D Blackmore, John Marshall and the Stockdale manuscripts on Devon history.

All books appear in the main library cat.

Exeter University: Manuscript Collections, 1976, and *Exeter University: Special collections in the University Library*, 1976. (Both can be supplied free of charge.)

The Crediton Collection Transferred from Crediton Parish Church to the University Library in 1968 on permanent loan. It comprises *c*1,000 books and 2,000 pamphlets. The books, which include 3 incunabula, are mostly of the 16th and 17th cent, and many are very rare; they cover all subjects. The pamphlet collection is a particularly fine one, consisting mainly of early 18th cent works on theology, politics and history. There are several interesting bindings.

A card cat is available on request.

The Dodderidge Collection The private library of Judge Dodderidge (1555–1628) was moved in 1888 from the Parish Church vestry room, Barnstaple to North Devon Athanaeum, and transferred to Exeter University Library in 1957 on permanent loan. The Collection is made up of *c*250 works in 350 v, which include 2 incunabula, *c*50 16th cent and *c*200 17th cent books. They cover mainly religion and philosophy, but also classics, geography, history and science. A number of interesting old bindings are also included.

A typed cat available on request.

The Ottery St Mary Parish Library Most of the collection appears to have been acquired in the 19th cent. It consists of 103 items in 109 v, among which are 6 incunabula, 17 books of the 16th cent and 50 of the 17th cent, 25 of the 18th cent and 5 of the 19th cent. There are 6 16th-cent bindings, blind-stamped, which command interest. A number of 19th and 20th cent items remain in Ottery St Mary church.

Cat cards in main University Card Cat.

The Totnes Collection The Collection was in Totnes Parish Church from the 17th cent until 1967 when it was transferred on permanent loan to the University Library. It contains 302 items in 293 v which include 37 16th cent, 235 17th cent and 30 18th cent items. There are also a numberof 16th and 17th cent bindings. The Collection is predominantly theological.

Old printed cat available, but all entries appear in the University Library card cat.

Note A cat of all the bindings of interest in the University Library is in preparation.

Ilfracombe

Ilfracombe Museum, Wilder Road, Ilfracombe, Devon EX34 8AF. Tel (0271) 63541. Open 10 am-5 pm daily (mornings only in winter). Admission on written application to the Curator.

The Museum was opened in 1932, and the book collection has grown steadily since then, both by gift and purchase. The books total *c*1,000, of which 250 are about Devon. The newspaper collection amounts to 150 v which include a complete run of the *Ilfracombe Chronicle* (1880–1953) —probably the only set in Devon. The books on Ilfracombe and neighbourhood are very rare.

Cat entries on cards for all the books available.

Kingsbridge

Cookworthy Museum Library, 108 Fore Street, Kingsbridge, Devon. Tel (0548) 3235. Open Mon-Fri 10 am-5 pm, Apr-Oct.

The library has 100 v and pamphlets, and 30 v newspapers on local history, all 19th cent. The newspapers are most valuable, being the best sets available—*Kingsbridge Gazette and South Hams Advertiser*, 1857–99; *South Devon Advertiser and Agricultural Times*, 1857–1900; *South Devon Gazette*, 1883–1902.

Newton Abbot

St Augustine's Priory, Newton Abbot, Devon TQ12 5PP. Admission by arrangement after written application to the Mother Prioress. Room available for study.

St Augustine's Priory Library The Community was founded in 1609 in Louvain. In 1795 it moved to England and has been in Newton Abbot since 1860. The library has grown over the years, but most of the books have been acquired since the move to Newton Abbot. It contains *c*2,000 v which include 5 17th cent, 100 18th cent and *c*300 19th cent books. The library is mainly devotional in its subject content and contains no great rarities. There are some 18th cent dictionaries, English and continental, and some interesting 17th and 18th cent books printed in Belgium and the Netherlands. There are also a number of 19th cent Irish-printed devotional works.

Typed cat list available.

Some books have been sent to the Bodleian Library and some have been sold.

Paignton

The Herbert Whitley Trust, Primley Estate Office, 190 Totnes Road, Paignton, Devon. Tel (0803) 558189. Open Mon-Fri 9.15 am-1 pm, 2.15-5.30 pm. Admission by arrangement with the librarian.

The Herbert Whitley Trust Library The Trust was founded in 1955 and the core of the library of *c*3,600 v is the private collection of Herbert Whitley, founder of Paignton Zoo. Only *c*500 books are pre-1900. The library is devoted almost entirely to biological studies—mainly vertebrates, botany and horticulture. Among the ornithological books is an unusual collection on domestic poultry and pigeons. There are also 100 v of scrapbooks (indexed) compiled under the direction of Herbert Whitley on subjects covered by the books.

Card cat (authors only).

Plymouth

City Museum and Art Gallery, Drake Circus, Plymouth PL4 8AJ. Tel (0752) 68000 Ext 4378. Open Mon-Sat 10 am-6 pm. Application for admission must be made by letter. Limited study accommodation.

Cottonian Collection Library The library forms part of the famous Cottonian Collection of prints and drawings which was left to Plymouth in 1853 by William Cotton, and was housed in the Plymouth Public Library until 1916. Subsequently it has been in the Plymouth Art Gallery. The Collection was mainly built up in the 18th cent by Charles Rogers of London, and after he died in 1784 it was inherited by William Cotton, also of London. Eventually it descended to his son William, and finally to his grandson, also called William. The latter lived at Highland House, Ivybridge (from 1839), and it was he who eventually bequeathed the Collection to Plymouth.

The books total 2,000 and though forming part of the Cottonian art collection, its subject content is not limited to fine art. It includes an excellent collection of literature, classics, history etc, and represents a splendid gentleman's library. The books are in superb condition, and many of them are finely bound. Most of the books are 18th cent, but there are several hundred of the 16th and 17th cent, and some acquired up to the mid-1850s. There are 3 15th cent illuminated mss, 2 French and 1 English. Much of the original collection was sold at Philipe's sale rooms in Warwick Street, Golden Square in March and April 1799, but the library seems to have remained intact.

Card cat.

Devon Library Services, Central Library, Drake Circus, Plymouth PL4 8AL. Tel (0752) 25616. Open Mon-Fri 9 am-9 pm, Sat 9 am-5.30 pm. Admission free, but naval personnel have concessions at the discretion of the librarian. Photocopier, microfilm/fiche reader available.

Local Studies Library Contains *c*20,500 books, of which *c*500 are pre-1851. The history of Plymouth is well emphasised in the collection, which also contains *c*375 pre-1851 playbills.

The Moxon Collection Originating from a bequest by A E Moxon, FRGS, to the City of Plymouth Public Library in the 1920s, the Collection has been in the charge of the Devon Library Service since 1974. It consists of works of the 19th and 20th cents, covering a wide range of subjects. Some items were dispersed into the general library stock, but a number of books, including some limited editions and fine bindings, have been kept together as the Moxon Collection. Of a total of 468 books, 60 are pre-1851 publications dealing mainly with travel, exploration and voyages.

No complete cat.

Naval History Library Developed from the Admiralty Mount Wise Library which was presented to the City of Plymouth in 1962, and has been in the charge of the Devon Library Service since 1974. New and out-of-print items have been added from time to time. The collection comprises *c*11,000 items, of which *c*500 works (multiple volume works are counted as one) are pre-1851. It contains material on foreign navies, as well as the British fleet. All aspects of the history and development of sea-power are covered, including information on ships, personnel, naval life, etc.

Author and classified cat available.

Marine Biological Association of the United Kingdom, The Laboratory, Citadel Hill, Plymouth, Devon PL1 2PB. Tel (0752) 21761. Open Mon-Fri 9 am-5 pm. Admission by prior arrangement with the Head of Library and Information Services. Photocopying facilities. Microtext readers.

Rare Book and Archives Collection Library established 1888. Rare books and archives have been acquired gradually by donation and purchase as part of a comprehensive library on marine biology. There are *c*500 archives, personal papers, laboratory notebooks and letters of marine biologists, particularly scientists connected with the MBA, including Edward T Browne.

Printed works in library cat on cards with sequences for author, subject and subject index. Cat to 1977 was published in 16 v by G K Hall in 1977. Archives uncatalogued but names of relevant scientists are listed briefly for library staff use.

A Varley, 'Library and information services of the Marine Biological Association of the United Kingdom', *Aslib Proceedings*, 30 (7), 1978, p251-9.

The Plymouth Athenaeum (formerly the Plymouth Institution), Derry Cross, Plymouth PL1 2SW. Tel (0752) 266079. Open Mon-Fri (members only) 10.30 am-10 pm. Non-members admitted by advance arrangement with the librarian.

The original Scientific Library of the Plymouth Institution, to which were added the Devon and Cornwall Natural History Society Library (1851) and the Plymouth Mechanics' Institute Library (1899), was destroyed by fire in 1941, with the exception of 109 items forming the nucleus of the modern library which comprises *c*150 printed books and 3 mss (Woollcombe's History of Plymouth *c*1810; James Young's Plymouth memoirs; Allen Diaries 1663, 1671). The collection deals mainly with the local history of Devon and Cornwall, with special emphasis on Plymouth. 14 rare books of non-local material were sold at Sotheby's on 29 September 1980 (lots 87-100).

Author and subject card cat.

N S M Paterson, 'The Athenaeum Library, 1979'. *Plymouth Association Proceedings*, v 24.

Plymouth Health District Medical Library, North Friary House, Greenbank Terrace, Plymouth PL4 8QQ. Tel (0752) 668080 Ext 323. Open Mon-Fri 9 am-5 pm. Admission by prior arrangement with the librarian (who will liaise, where necessary, with the PMS Hon Librarian). Microfilm and fiche readers available.

Plymouth Medical Society Library The formation of a library was an original aim of the PMS, founded 1794, and the collection far exceeded 2,000 v by 1884, when 1,600 v were donated to the Plymouth Free Library which was damaged and the contents ruthlessly reduced during 1939–45. It now contains *c*270 items (of which 200 are pre-1851) relating to medical and surgical subject areas, including anatomical atlases, dating from 1661, but only 18 v are pre-1800.

Card author index. Printed cats 1841 and 1872.

History of PMS Library is currently being researched and is expected to be published in professional journals eventually.

Plymouth Polytechnic Learning and Resources Centre, Drake Circus, Plymouth, Devon PL4 8AA. Tel (0752) 21312. Open Mon-Fri 9 am-5 pm. Admission free to all researchers. Xerox, microform readers, etc available.

Architecture Collection A collection of 50 folio volumes, received as gifts over the years, with emphasis on architecture, mainly of the 19th cent. It contains some costly plate-books as well as some on continental architecture.

Not cat.

Royal Naval Engineering College, Manadon, Plymouth PL5 3AQ. Tel (0752) 553740 Ext Manadon 419. Open Mon-Fri 8 am-4 pm. Admission by appointment with the librarian. Microfilm and microfiche readers.

Naval History Collection Originally part of the Portsmouth Port Library, the collection consists of *c*250 items on naval history. About 30 items are pre-1851, 35 for 1851–99, and 64 for 1900–29. The collection contains copies of works by Burchett (1720), Barrow (1761), Campbell (1779) and Admiralty Regulations...1790. The general library contains 500 works on naval history, including pre-1851 works on steam engineering.

There is a brief author cat of books in the special collection.

Other holdings on naval history (*c*500) are in the general cat.

Royal Naval Hospital, Medical Library, Plymouth PL1 3JY. Tel (0752) 29363 Ext 279. Open Mon-Fri mornings only. Admission by advance arrangement with the librarian who will request the necessary permission for the applicant to enter this Service Establishment. Reference only. Microfiche reader.

The Medical Library was established *c*1832 and maintained by the Medical Department of the Navy. Bequests by Dr Robert McKinnal, 1838, and by Dr Leonard Gillespie, 1842, naval surgeons. The rare books form *c*60 per cent of the historical collection which includes 313 pre-1851 (plus 84 University of Edinburgh MD theses, mainly for the year 1818 but spanning 1814–1823) works, mainly medical including ancient and medieval authors, but chiefly 17th, 18th and early 19th cent writers. Emphasis on naval interests, such as health in different climates. Some classical and scientific literature, particularly in the McKinnal donation. Several works in French published *c*1810–1830.

No cat survives, but a brief entry card shelflist was created in 1963. The surviving items are listed in: M Lattimore, *The Medical Library of the Royal Naval Hospital Plymouth 1825–1900: a checklist...with notes on the early history and organisation of the library.* Plymouth Polytechnic, 1980.

B S Lewis, 'The Medical Library, Royal Naval Hospital, Plymouth' *and* 'A second bite at the cherry'. *J Royal Naval Medical Service*, 49 (1963) p115-18, p218-21.

Note The library is thought to have suffered considerable losses in wartime and through casual borrowing during earlier periods of neglect, but the only items known to have been deliberately disposed of are 5 v on pathology donated to the Royal College of Pathology, London.

Saltram House, Plympton, Plymouth PL7 3UH. Tel (0752) 336546. Admission to bona fide research workers by appointment with the Libraries Adviser, National Trust, 42 Queen Anne's Gate, London SW1H 9AS. The house itself is open to the public daily (except Mondays) 11 am-6 pm, Apr-Oct. Room available for study.

Saltram House Library A good gentleman's country-house library, it was founded in the mid-18th cent and was added to considerably until the mid-19th cent.

Afterwards the growth was slower. It comprises *c*5,000 items and volumes covering a wide range of subjects. Especially interesting are the illustrated books of the 18th and 19th cent. These plate books cover botany, gardening and natural history; costume, art; and travel. There is also a good collection of English, French and Italian literature. Many of the books are in fine contemporary bindings. The collection includes 1 (Nuremberg Chronicle) 15th cent, 17 16th cent, 150 17th cent, 2,370 18th cent, 2,000 19th cent.

Card cat and shelflist.

Note Saltram House is a National Trust property. It was formerly the property of the Parker family, Earls of Morley.

Sidmouth

Norman Lockyer Observatory Library, Salcombe Hill, Sidmouth, Devon. Tel (039 55) 3140. Open most days, but admission by written application to the librarian, University of Exeter, Exeter EX4 4PT.

Norman Lockyer Collection It belonged to Sir Norman Lockyer (*d*1920) who founded the Observatory in 1912, and includes *c*2,200 v, of which *c*500 are monographs, among them Lockyer's own writings, and a number of star atlases and catalogues ranging from the end of the 19th cent to the 1930s. The books all relate to astronomy, astrophysics etc and are mostly modern. Of the *c*2,000 ms items in the collection, the letters are particularly interesting (the correspondents include many famous names in the scientific, political and literary world), and cover the second half of the 19th cent and the first quarter of the 20th cent. The collection of books was at one time much larger, but many were transferred to the Physics Department of the University Library at Exeter.

A typed list is available but it is not complete.

Sidmouth Museum, Church Street, Sidmouth, Devon. Tel (039 55) 6139. Open Mon-Sat (June-Sept) 10.30 am-12.30 pm, 2.30-4.30 pm. For admission apply by letter to the Curator. Research office available.

The library has grown up with the Museum since 1950, and comprises 250 books, 100 v of newspapers, constituting the best collection of local material in Devon. Of the 250 books, *c*150 relate to Sidmouth or East Devon. There is also a small collection (including mss of some of his works) of the local author R F Delderfield. The local newspaper collection consists of almost complete runs of all Sidmouth papers from 1850 to date. The most noteworthy complementary mss are Peter Orlando Hutchinson's 'History of Sidmouth' and Tindall's studies on Sidmouth shingle, 1920–31 (10 v).

Card cat of books.

South Brent

Syon Abbey (Library), South Brent, Devon TQ10 9JX. Tel (036) 472256. Open by arrangement through the Mother Abbess.

Syon Abbey Library The Community of Bridgettine nuns was founded by Henry V in 1415 at Syon Abbey in Isleworth, Middlesex. The Community lived for two centuries abroad, mainly in Lisbon, and returned to Britain in 1861. The library now contains over 5,000 v, nearly all being devotional. They include 50 books of the 16th cent, 150 17th cent and 300 of the 18th cent—of these there are 50 STC and 60 Wing items. Among the foreign books are some 50 Spanish and Portuguese rare works.

The Canon J R Fletcher (1861–1944) spent many years collecting material for Syon Abbey Library, and his mss (35 v) provide a unique source of information on the subject.

There is a ms cat of printed books. *See also* M Bateson, *Catalogue of the library of Syon Monastery Isleworth*, 1898.

For information on the mss *see* N R Ker, *Medieval Libraries of Great Britain*, 1941; Torre Hyberg, 'The Canon Fletcher manuscripts in Syon Abbey', *Nordisk Tidskrift for bok-och biblioteks vasen*, 1960, p56-69; *Salzburger Studien zur Anglistik und Amerikanistik*, (University of Salzburg, 1978–9).

Teignmouth

St Scholastica's Benedictine Abbey (Library), 99 Dawlish Road, Teignmouth, Devon TQ14 8TH. Tel (062 67) 4394. Open by arrangement with the librarian.

St Scholastica's Abbey Library The Community was founded at Dunkirk in 1662. From 1795 to 1863 it was at Hammersmith, and thereafter it has been at Teignmouth. The library has grown up since the Community's foundation and contains over 5,000 v, of which there are 2 incunabula (dated 1484 and 1491), 5 16th cent, *c*250 17th cent (including 40 STC and 40 Wing items), and *c*350 18th cent items. These are mainly devotional works and include some rare 17th cent English Catholic books. There are *c*300 French works among the 17th and 18th cent books.

The library also includes various archives relating to the Abbey and devotional works by former members. Among the individual works of note is Lady Lucy Knatchbull's *Foundation of the Convent Boulogne*.

No full cat available, but the older books are kept apart from the modern ones.

Tiverton

Blundell's School, Tiverton, Devon. Tel (088 42) 2543. Open normally during school hours 9 am-4 pm. Admission by written application to the

Headmaster. Room for study; photocopying by arrangement.

The Blundell's School Muniment Room includes a collection of books and records which has evolved with the school, founded in 1604. The books, *c*300 v include a small number (*c*50 v mostly undistinguished) of pre-1700 editions of the classics. The greater part are 18th and 19th cent with a few later ones containing a number of rare Devon, and especially Tiverton, items; a complete run of the *Blundellian* (School Magazine) 1861– , and a run of the *Tiverton Gazette* (1889–1930).

Private Library of R G Pratt, 'Popes', Shillingford, Tiverton EX16 9BP. Tel (039 83) 553. Admission strictly by application to Mr Pratt.

The library includes 300 v of books and periodicals, 4,000 photographs and 200 postcards relating to steam road vehicles. Although relatively small, it is probably a unique collection of material about all kinds of steam road vehicles—steam carriages, steam cars, traction engines, steam wagons, steam rollers, steam plough engines and fairground equipment. Many of the books and periodicals are rare; the makers' catalogues and drivers' manuals date from 1857.

St Peter's Church, (Newte Library), Tiverton, Devon. Admission on written application to the librarian or the Rector well in advance of visit.

The Newte Library Founded by the Rev Richard Newte in the 17th cent, and continued by his son, the Rev John Newte, it was bequeathed to the church in 1716. The books total *c*250 v, including approximately 300 17th cent pamphlets. They are mainly of theological interest, but the pamphlets cover politics and history. Nearly all the books are pre-1700. Other notable items included in the collection are an illuminated ms Book of Hours, 1438, and Ptolemy's Atlas, 1513, with coloured maps.

Ms cat kept with the collection; also card cat.

Published list may be found in: E S Chalk, *A history of the Church of St Peter, Tiverton*. Tiverton, 1905.

A Welsford, 'Mr Newte's library in St Peter's Church, Tiverton', in *Trans of the Devonshire Association*, v 106 (pp17-31) and 107 (pp11-20).

Torquay

Devon Library Services, Torquay Central Library, Lymington Road, Torquay, Devon TQ1 3DT. Tel (0803) 211251. Open Mon-Fri 9 am-7 pm, Thurs 9 am-6 pm, Sat 9 am-5 pm. Microfilm reader for newspaper research; xerox copying facilities.

Hughan Collection Bequeathed to the original Carnegie Library at Torquay by the late William James Hughan, a collector of, and lecturer on, old Bibles. The collection contains 132 items, including early printed Bibles and Prayer Books, mainly English, but some foreign together with a few volumes of general literature. There are *c*14 STC items.

Ms cat.

The Moyse Collection The library of Dr Charles E Moyse, LlD, (born Torquay 1852, a Professor of English Literature who became Dean of the Faculty of Arts and Vice-Principal of McGill University, Montreal) which he bequeathed, upon his death in 1924, to the Torquay Library on condition that it be maintained as a unit. It contained *c*8,000 v (now *c*10,000 v with recent additions), plus a pamphlet collection of *c*1,000 items and 43 private letters. The emphasis is mainly on English literature with linguistics, travel and history.

A complete cat available.

Torquay Natural History Society, The Museum, Babbacombe Road, Torquay. Tel (0803) 23975. Open Mon-Fri 10 am-5 pm. Admission by written application. Reading room available.

The library of the Torquay Natural History Society was founded in 1844 and now comprises *c*25,000 v, of which *c*200 are pre-1800, but most are 19th and 20th cent. Particularly noteworthy are books relating to local history, especially of Torquay, the local newspaper collection, and works by West Country authors, eg Eden Phillpotts and Jan Stewer. The mss collection includes the papers of William Pengelly and Father John MacEnery, the best known explorers of, and researchers into the history of Kent's Cavern.

An old card cat available.

Totnes

Dartington Hall, Dartington, Totnes, Devon TQ9 6EJ. Tel (0803) 862224. Open Mon-Fri 9.30 am-5.30 pm. (closed for lunch). Admission by letter to the Records Officer.

Dartington Hall Records Mainly the personal archives of Leonard and Dorothy Elmhirst, and the records of the Dartington Trust which they founded. In addition to the documents, plans etc, there is a collection of 170 printed books which relate to Dartington (see also under Dartington College Library).

Typed cat.

Library and Resources Centre, Dartington College of Arts, Dartington, Totnes, Devon TQ9 6EJ. Tel (0803) 862224. Open Mon-Fri 9.30 am-5.30 pm. Admission by application to librarian. Xerox copying and microform readers available.

Dartington College Library Based on the personal library of Dorothy and Leonard Elmhirst, founders of the

Dartington Trust, but now much added to and expanded. The library with c30,000 v is strong on theatre and drama, including costume (c4,000 v), music (c4,000 v, including 30 v of early editions of Handel). It includes two collections of rare books, (a) The Devon Collection of c600 v, mainly of local material, and (b) the miscellaneous collection of c900 v, mainly on architecture, art, literature, horticulture, of which 50 are pre-1700 and c200 18th cent. The collection is being added to (see also under Dartington Hall).

Card cat, but many of the rare books are not yet catalogued.

Totnes Museum, The Elizabethan House, 70 Fore Street, Totnes, Devon. Tel (0803) 863821. Open 10.30 am-5.30 pm, Apr-Sept. Admission on prior application to the Custodian.

The Rutter Library Bequeathed to Totnes in October 1928 by J A Rutter Esq. It comprises c1,000 v, mostly relating to Devon, Cornwall, general history and archaeology, most of which belong to the 19th and 20th cent. The Museum also possesses the library of the Totnes Mechanics' Institute of c300 v which are of no special interest except for the fact that they formed the Mechanics' Institute Library.

Typed cat and card cat of the Rutter Library; the Mechanics' Institute Library is not catalogued, but a sketchy manuscript list available.

Yealmpton

Kitley House, Yealmpton, Nr Plymouth, Devon. Admission strictly by written application to the owner, Capt John Bastard.

Kitley Library This is the Bastard family library. It seems to have originated in the 16th cent, but most of the additions appear to have been made in the 18th and 19th cent. The collection of c2,500 v typifies a gentleman's library covering a general range of subjects. It is in fine condition with many attractive 19th cent bindings. Fewer than 100 books are pre-1700, approximately half of the collection belongs to the 18th cent, and the remainder mostly 19th cent. There are many attractive plate-books, mainly topographical or relating to art and architecture.

Card cat available.

Dorset

Bournemouth

Lansdowne Reference Library, Meyrick Road, Bournemouth BH1 3DJ. Tel (0202) 292021. Open Mon-Fri 9.30 am-7 pm; Sat 9 am-1 pm. Reading desks, microfilm/fiche readers; photocopier.

Bournemouth Local History Collection The collection, which forms part of the general reference collection, contains a wide coverage of material on the Borough of Bournemouth, including books, pamphlets, maps, ephemera, etc.

Author/classified cat with subject index.

Dorchester

Dorchester Reference Library, Colliton Park, Dorchester, Dorset. Tel (0305) 63131 Ext 4442. Open to members of the general public Mon, Tues, Wed, Fri 9.30 am-7 pm, Thurs 9.30 am-5 pm; Sat 9 am-1 pm. Microform readers and photocopying facilities.

Local Studies Collection Built up over the last 20-30 years from a small nucleus already held, the collection, together with the three special collections described below, now consists of c10,594 v, 682 micro-texts and 33 mss. Its subject content relates to the whole of Dorset, with particular emphasis on West Dorset, and includes books, pamphlets, maps (current and historical), photographs and ephemera. Included is Hutchin's *History of Dorset* 1st ed 1774, also an extra-illustrated ed (12 v).

Published cat 1975, updated manually; card cat.

Thomas Hardy Collection Everything by, and about, Thomas Hardy (1840–1928), including first editions of most of his works, bibliographies, biographies, criticisms, foreign language translations, periodical articles, photographs, ephemera, eg play programmes etc. One original mss held by the Dorset County Museum.

Card cat.

Published cat 1973. First section on Hardy's works has recently been updated and will shortly be published. (Original cat still available, 40p.)

Powys Family Collection Most of the Powys family had strong connections with Dorset. The Collection includes material by, and about, several members of the family and their wives, including John Cowper Powys, Littleton C Powys, Theodore F Powys, Albert R Powys and Llewelyn Powys. Books and periodical articles constitute the bulk of the collection which, although by no means complete, is sufficiently comphrehensive to be acknowledged as being of importance.

Cat published in 1972 to coincide with centenary of the birth of John Cowper Powys; it is updated manually and by card cat. (Original still available, 20p.)

William Barnes Collection William Barnes (1801–86), poet in Dorset dialect. The Collection includes works by, and about him, including some first editions. Articles from periodicals and theses also collected.

Typewritten cat produced 1972, updated manually. Card cat.

Weymouth

Weymouth Library, Westwey Road, Weymouth, Dorset DT4 8SU. Tel (0305) 786498. Open Mon, Tues, Thurs, Fri 9.30 am-7 pm; Sat 9 am-1 pm. Closed all day Wednesday. Photocopier available.

Weymouth Library Local Studies Collection Founded when Weymouth and Melcombe Regis Public Library opened in 1944; part of Dorset County Library since 1 April 1974. The collection contains *c*11,000 items, of which many (unspecified) are rare according to RBG definition, and include books, pamphlets, illustrations, maps and local newspaper files. Main emphasis is on Weymouth, Portland and the surrounding area. Includes 'Royal Weymouth' compiled by A M Broadley, 1907, a four-volume collection of items relating to the visits of King George III to Weymouth 1789–1805. It also includes the *Bowles Barrett Collection* of books and pamphlets collected by a local man, William Bowles Barrett (1833–1916), including his ms notes on the history of Weymouth and his botanical notebooks.

Alphabetical card cat, author and subject.

Durham, Cleveland, South Tyne and Wear

Barnard Castle

The Bowes Museum, Barnard Castle, Co Durham DL12 8NP. Tel (833) 37139. Admission by arrangement, on advance written application. Photography, photocopying, ultra-violet light; microfilming by special arrangement.

General Collection Based on the collection of John Davidson of Ridley Hall, Northumberland, a gentleman's library of the late 18th and early 19th cent, bequeathed to the founder of the Museum, John Bowes (1811–85), and augmented by the latter and, to a small extent since, by gifts and purchases, and kept separately, apart from modern reference books for the Museum, especially on Durham and Yorkshire. There are *c*2,200 pre-1851 titles (2,500 v) of printed matter which includes 6 incunabula, *c*24 16th cent foreign books, at least 10 STC, 50 Wing items, mostly 18th and early 19th cent English, notably travel and topography (including many guide books), practical botany, gardening and arboriculture, natural history, sports, humour, epitaphs, costumes, portraits, belles lettres (particularly poetry, including a group of songsters). Also some newspapers and other periodicals. Considerable number of colour-plate books. Presentations from Sir Walter Scott.

The mss (bound and loose) are miscellaneous, with a strong local interest, including two volumes of the Bowes family papers from Streatlam Castle, correspondence between Bishop Trevor and Dean Cowper of Durham, literary compositions of William Hutchinson (1723–1814), autograph letters 15th-19th cent besides correspondence of John Bowes concerning his English estates and his residence in France, and the archives of the Museum.

Modern card author/subject cats; copy on sheaf slips of part of classified cat in the University Library, Palace Green, Durham.

Cat of the Reference Library (Carlisle 1912; Supplementary Cat 1913) has rudimentary alphabetical order within broad subject sections.

French Collection Formed by the founders of the Museum, John Bowes (1811–85) and his first wife, Josephine Coffin-Chevalier (1825–74), during their regular residence in France, for the most part. The collection is made up of 1,045 titles, including 1 incunabulum; 12 16th cent; 93 17th cent; 210 18th cent; 309 1801–50; 9 medieval mss, mostly books of hours and several printed 16th cent. Subject areas are mainly history, travel and topography in French, or concerning France, illustrated, and with fine bindings, 16th-early 19th cent; French literature, mostly minor authors of 19th cent—many items in original wrappers. Also mid-19th cent periodicals.

Card cat alphabetical and classified; slip copies of both at the University Library, Palace Green, Durham.

Ker, *Medieval Manuscripts*, II, p151-62.

Bishop Auckland

Library of the See of Durham, Auckland Castle, Bishop Auckland, Co Durham. Admission by prior appointment after written enquiry (in the first instance advisable via the Chapter Librarian, The College, Durham). Research facilities available through the Dean and Chapter Library of Durham Cathedral.

Auckland Castle Library Formed by Bishops Lightfoot, Westcott, Moule and Henson (1879–1939), at first for the use of the College of Ordinands at Auckland, and later for the personal use of the Bishops. A selection of the older and some modern works were deposited in Durham Cathedral Library in 1966. There are *c*3,000 titles, of which some 300 are deposited at Durham. These include *c*200 v up to 1700, including works by Bishop Cuthbert Tunstall, the *King's Book* of 1543, and a Zurich 1542 German Bible. A predominantly theological collection, with some rare local ephemera.

Modern sheaf slip cat of authors, with copies at Durham Chapter and University Libraries.

B S B(enedikz): Auckland Castle Unicum? (with an account of the library). *The Durham Philobiblon*, v 2 (1955–69), p70-2.

Darlington

Durham County Library, Darlington Branch, Crown Street, Darlington. Tel (0325) 62034 or 69858. Open Mon and Sat 9 am-1 pm, 2.15-5 pm; Tues-Fri 9 am-1 pm, 2.15-7 pm. Microfilm reader and photocopier available.

Local History Collection Started in the 1880s, it now contains over 45,000 items, covering in depth Darlington, South Durham, the northern area of Yorkshire and the North East of England in general. *c*1,300 items printed 1700–1850; none pre-1700. All ms material is now in the adjacent Darlington branch of Durham County Record Office, including that relating to the Allan family of Blackwell Grange, of whose private press products the library has an important collection. Illustrations collection of over 7,000 items including engravings and a large collection of maps.

Cat on cards (dictionary).

Separate cat of newspaper cuttings and photographs.

The library has published a series of brief Local History Guides, available on application. These are based on the library's own resources.

Raby Castle, Staindrop, Darlington, Co Durham. Tel (0833) 36202. Admission by advance arrangement only on written application to the Curator. No research facilities, but arrangements may be made for deposit in the University Library, Palace Green, Durham, subject to costs of insurance being met, and permission for photocopying.

Raby Castle Library The family library of Lord Barnard collected by members of the Vane family in the 18th and 19th cent. There have been past disposals by sale. There are *c*4,000 v, mostly in English, but with some French and Italian, on secular subjects, chiefly from the 18th cent; only a few from pre-1640, rather more for the period 1641–1700. Sets of short-lived newspapers, and longer ones of court calendars, parliamentary reports and general periodicals running on into the mid-19th cent. Writings and memoirs of members of the Vane family. A considerable collection of army and regimental lists from the early 18th cent onwards, and of illustrated works of military history and tactics, in both English and French; some architectural and travel books. Manuscript *Remembrances for the conduct of business in the House of Lords* 1729, 1735, 1763, in contemporary red morocco bindings. The remainder of the collection is almost all in contemporary blind-tooled calf in excellent condition.

Printed cat and supplement on cards.

Durham

Bibliotheca Franciscana: Private library of the Rt Rev Dr J R H Moorman, 22 Springwell Road, Durham DH1 4LR. Tel (0385) 63503. Books can be consulted by advance arrangement, in writing, to the University Library, Palace Green, Durham DH1 3RN. Research facilities and services as for the University Library, Palace Green.

Bibliotheca Franciscana A personal life-long collection of a leading Franciscan scholar, which is to go eventually to St Deiniol's Library, Hawarden, near Chester. It contains 2,000 v (a large number of them pre-1851) of books, periodicals and pamphlets on St Francis of Assisi and the Franciscan Order, probably the largest collection in Great Britain outside the British Library. There are 7 incunabula and 9 medieval mss.

Alphabetical card cat; copy at the University Library, Palace Green, Durham, available on application.

J R H Moorman, 'Bibliotheca Franciscana', *The Book Collector*, v 23 (1974), p19-26.

Durham County Library, Durham City Branch, South Street, Durham. Tel (0385) 64003. Open Mon-Fri 10 am-7 pm; Sat 9.30 am-5 pm. Microfilm readers and photocopier available.

Local History Collection Started in 1936, the collection now totals 5,566 printed items (exclusive of newspaper cuttings, etc), of which *c*300 up to 1850 (pamphlets of 1640s); 2,710 maps, of which 150 up to 1850; 1,000 loose topographical prints, mostly 19th cent; a few mss. The collection covers all the old county of Durham, though now concentrating on the current administrative area.

Dictionary cat on sheaf slips for printed books and pamphlets.

Loose-leaf cat of maps, by date, area and topic.

The Dean and Chapter Library (Durham Cathedral), The College, Durham DH1 3EH. Tel (0385) 62489. Open Mon-Fri 9 am-1 pm, 2.15-5 pm. Closed all August, Christmas Eve–New Year's Day, and from Thurs before to Wed after Easter, inclusive. Admission by written application in advance giving reasons and credentials. Photography and photocopying can be arranged, and microfilm supplied, subject to copyright, physical suitability of material, and service/reproduction fees. Large stock of negatives and transparencies; microfilm reader and ultra-violet lamp available; also beta-radiography.

Dean and Chapter Library Descends directly from the library of the Benedictine monastery and its dependent cells, suppressed 1540, which at its foundation in 1083 succeeded the community originating in the 7th cent at Lindisfarne which had migrated to Chester-le-Street and then Durham, bringing some of its books, to which were added others from Jarrow or Monkwearmouth. Although much was lost in the 16th cent the bulk survived and has been continuously added to since. There are now 360 medieval ms codices, of which 330 are from the monastic library; nearly 1,000 v/portfolios of post-medieval mss and some thousands of loose papers; 11,000 v (23,000? titles) pre-1851; local maps, prints, postcards, photographs. Printed books include 70 incunabula (6 English and 28 from the monastic library); *c*500 foreign 16th cent; 270 STC; *c*2,000 Wing; *c*3,500 ESTC items. The broad range of printed books include a very large collection of 17th-18th cent foreign theses, chiefly, but not wholly, theological.

Medieval mss range from the 7th cent onwards, including Northumbrian, Norman and scholastic material of high textual art and palaeographical importance; 7 codices containing Old English, 4 Middle English, 6 French and 2 Greek; fragments of medieval music; 16th-early 19th cent choral, 17th-18th cent instrumental music, ms and printed, respectively, from the Cathedral choir repertory and 18th cent Canons' collections (Philip Falle (*d*1742), Thomas Sharp (*d*1758) and John Sharp (*d*1792)), (the last two being part of the Bamburgh Library described under Durham University Library); historical collections, of original documents and transcripts, for County Durham and the NE of England, with much of wider interest, formed by local antiquaries, 17th-20th cent; papers and correspondence of 19th-20th cent bishops and other churchmen.

Sheaf author/title slips, with copies in main University Library cat and main entries in Cathedral's Union Cat to 1700 and BL pre-1801 Union Cat.

Indexes of former owners, imprints, bindings etc.

R A Harman, *A catalogue of the printed music at Durham Cathedral*, Oxford, 1968. Still available from Chapter Library.

N R Ker, *Catalogue of manuscripts containing Anglo-Saxon*, Oxford, 1957, p144-9.

H D Hughes, *A history of Durham Cathedral Library*... Durham, 1925.

T Rud, *Codicum Mss Ecclesiae Cathedralis Dunelmensis catalogus classicus*. Durham, 1825.

R A Nynors, *Durham Cathedral manuscripts to the end of the 12th century*, Oxford, 1939.

N R Ker, *Medieval manuscripts in British Libraries*, v 2, Oxford 1967, p483-511.

Durham University Library: Special Collections, Palace Green, Durham DH1 3RN. Tel (0385) 61262/3 or 64466 (University exchange). Telex 537351. Open Mon-Fri 9 am-1 pm, 2-4.45 pm; Sat 9 am-12 noon. Closed Christmas Eve–New Year's Day, Good Friday–Easter Mon, August Bank Holiday; Sats in Christmas and Summer vacations. Open to all registered members of the University, and others on application giving reasons, and credentials. Advance written requests desirable, particularly for ms material, and good evidence of identity essential on arrival. Magnifiers, ultra-violet light, microform reader and printer; xeroxing subject to safety and copyright; photography and microfilming can be arranged with some delay. Also beta-radiographic prints.

General The University Library began in 1833 and, besides donated and deposited collections, kept and listed separately, includes old and rare printed, manuscript and other material acquired by gift and purchase, shelved by type of material, age, place of origin etc, and some not yet segregated from the general stock of the library. The total stands at *c*50,000 v (55,000 titles) up to 1850, and includes 90 medieval ms codices; more than 6,000 later mss; 1,000 topographical and portrait prints; 600 maps; 300 election ephemera. (These figures include all the separately listed collections described below.) There are 204 incunabula, 3,000-4,000 foreign 16th cent; over 2,200 STC; 9,500 Wing. The collections are strongest in 16th and 17th cent books, and in theology and church history, with Latin and English as the predominant languages; but classical and English literature, general history, especially British and European, common and canon law, the natural sciences, early medicine, topography and travel are all well represented by important editions and rare works. The library has participated regularly in the co-operation scheme for acquiring background material in English for the period 1670–89.

Except for the majority of the Bamburgh Library, all the printed books are included (though in varying degrees of detail) in the main library cat (name) and in the regional and BL union cat; many are cited in STC, Wing (2), etc.

A I Doyle, E Rainey and D B Wilson. *Manuscript to print: tradition and innovation in the Renaissance book*. (Illustrated from examples in the University Library.) Durham, 1975. £1 from University Library.

D G R(amage), University Library Mss. *The Durham Philobiblon*, v 1, 1949–55, p48-9.

——'Summary List of the additional manuscripts accessioned and listed between Sept 1945 and Sept 1961'. Durham, 1963. 30p.

D S B(land), 'Chapbooks', *Ibid*. v 2, 1955–69, p25-6.

The Special Collections maintain indexes of former owners, portraits, illustrators, imprints by place and date, which, however, as yet cover only the minority of stock.

Abbott Collection A small collection of 19th and 20th cent mss of literary interest from the collection of Claude Colleer Abbott (1889–1971), Prof of English in the

University of Durham, given by his literary trustees, and personal papers and correspondence deposited by them. There are *c*600 items (more in the deposit), including letters from George Darley, D G Rossetti, G M Hopkins (to Coventry Patmore), Edward Thomas, André Gide, Hugh Walpole in the gift. The deposit contains working papers (including photostats of other Hopkins correspondence) and letters to Abbott.

Typescript handlist.

A D Burnett, *The Abbott Collection of Literary Manuscripts: an Introduction with the Catalogue of an Exhibition.* Durham University Library guides, special ser 2. Durham, 1975. 50p.

Bamburgh Library Based on the collection of John Sharp (1644–1714), Archbishop of York, his sons John (1677–1727), MP for Ripon, Thomas (1693–1758), Archdeacon of Northumberland and Canon of Durham, and the latter's son John (1723–92), also Archdeacon and Canon, (and Thomas, Perpetual Curate of Bamburgh), who gave the collection to the Trustees of Lord Crewe's Charity as a public library at Bamburgh Castle, Northumberland, in 1779, and maintained by them there until 1958, with additions until *c*1860. Select class transferred to Durham in 1938, and deposited with the remainder in University Library in 1958, except for music placed in the Cathedral Library. There are 6,386 v (8,445 titles), 16 incunabula (6 English); 320 foreign 16th cent; 330 STC and 2,461 Wing. Highly miscellaneous but strong in 17th cent controversy and natural science, besides theology, common law, English literature, some French and Italian, atlases and periodicals. Also 3 medieval ms psalters (one Scottish *c*1200, one Slavonic in Moscow binding).

Catalogue of the Library at Bamburgh Castle. 2 v, London, 1859, (superseding *A catalogue*... Durham (1795?) and *Supplement*... Berwick (1834?), which, however, have lists of foreign language items.

A I Doyle, 'Unfamiliar Libraries IV: The Bamburgh Library', *The Book Collector*, v 8, 1959, p14-24.

——'Early printed tracts', *Durham Philobiblon*, 1, 1949–55, p66-9; 2, 1955–69, p7-8, 23.

N R Ker, *Medieval Manuscripts in British Libraries*, II, p46-8.

Bishop Cosin's Library (Bibliotheca Episcopalis Dunelmensis) Predominantly the personal collection of John Cosin (1595–1672) established by him as a public library for the Bishopric of Durham in a specially erected building, 1668, including also gifts from others, especially medieval mss from George Davenport (*d*1677), printed books from Bishop Richard Trevor (1707–71) and post-medieval mss from Bishop Shute Barrington (1734–1826). The University utilized the building from 1834 and became trustee of the library in 1937. No significant additions have been made since the early 19th cent. Stock totals 4,400 printed v (5,137 titles) and 230 ms v. Included are 9 incunabula; over 600 foreign 16th cent titles; 541 STC; 841 Wing items. The collection is strongest in theology, liturgy and canon law, with a good representation of other subjects such as literature, travel and science. Notable treasures are, a fine copy of the Shakespeare First Folio acquired by Cosin before 1644, a Book of Common Prayer 1619, with Cosin's proposals for the 1662 revision, and a 1662 BCP and companion Bible bound by Samuel Mearne for Charles II. There are *c*600 items in French, mostly pamphlets of religious controversy from the period of Cosin's exile in Paris, 1644–60, a considerable number not in the Bibliothèque Nationale.

The medieval mss are almost all of British origin, from the late 11th to early 16th cent, about 20 containing English and 6 French, the majority of the Latin theological or liturgical, a high proportion of the English in verse or on medical and astrological questions. The post-medieval mss include original letters to Durham from Cosin and others, 1593–1686, and a large collection of documents and transcripts made by members of the Mickleton and Spearman families, local lawyers and antiquaries, of great importance for north-eastern history up to *c*1700.

Single entries in main cat of University Library.

Catalogi Veteres Librorum Ecclesiae Cathedralis Dunelm... including the mss preserved in the library of Bishop Cosin (by Thomas Rud). Surtees Soc 7 (1838), p136-91.

C E Whiting, 'Cosin's Library', *Trans Architectural and Archaeol Soc of Durham and Northumberland.* 9, i (1939), p18-32.

D G R(amage), 'Cosin's French Books', *The Durham Philobiblon*, 2, 1955–69, p57-62, 65.

F J W H(arding), 'Mickleton and Spearman Manuscripts', *Ibid.* 1, 1949–55, p40-44.

Collingwood Library Bequeathed by Sir Edward Collingwood (1900–70), FRS, of Lilburn Tower, Northumberland. Most items duplicated in the stock of the University Library of older books and of periodicals were sold to provide an endowment for continuing the collection. The monographs of modern date are housed in the Mathematics Department; periodicals mostly in the Science Section, and older works at Palace Green. There are over 3,000 v, 75 older titles are housed in the Special Collections at the University Library, Palace Green. Subjects covered are mathematics and related subjects such as astronomy. The older items include a few 17th cent editions, but are chiefly 18th and early 19th cent, by English and French authors such as Newton, Hutton, Lagrange, Lacroix and Laplace.

Incorporated in the main cat of the University Library so far as the older books and periodicals are concerned.

I Grattan-Guinness, 'The mathematical papers and library of Sir Edward Collingwood in the University of Durham', *Historia Mathematica*, 2 (1975), p200-2.

Historical Science Collection (Class prefix M) Besides separate Special Collections containing important material, especially the Cosin and Bamburgh Libraries, items from various sources formerly housed in the Science Section, are shelved together now at Palace Green. They include the older books from the Observatory Library and the Collingwood Library, of which the modern stock is elsewhere, and some of the gifts of Miss Alice Edleston, from the collection of the Rev Joseph Edleston (*d*1895). It is strongest in mathematics and astronomy, but with representation of geology, botany, zoology and chemistry. Sir Isaac Newton and William Emerson are the two authors most amply present, besides Thomas Wright of Byers Green, Co Durham (1711–86), of whose manuscripts and publications the library has the most extensive collection. It totals 6,000 v (500 titles), including some Wing and foreign 17th cent items.

Incorporated in the main cat of the University Library and the classified cat of the Science Section.

A D Burnett and D M Knight, 'History of Science in Durham Libraries', *British Journ for the Hist of Sci*, v 8, no 28 (1975), p94-9.

Kellet Collection Part of the library on the history of medicine of Dr C E de M Kellet (1908–78), given by himself and his executors. It contains over 200 items printed up to 1800 and nearly 200 modern works, with a particular emphasis on theory and teaching of medicine, in 16th and 17th cent France and Italy, together with photostats, microfilms, slides and related papers for Dr Kellet's publications and lectures on medical iconography. The older books are mainly foreign (74 of the 16th cent), including Vidius's *Chirurgia* (1544) and Estienne's *De dissectione* (1545). A small but very coherent and rich scholarly collection.

Temporary handlist and author index.

C E Kellet, 'Two medicines', *The Medical World*, 9 Feb 1945 (on the raison d'être of the collection).

Local Collection Built up gradually during the present century from gifts and purchases. Since the creation of the Durham Public Library with its differences of scope and operation, the University Library has continued to be stronger in older material, especially mss, besides those described under Bishop Cosin's Library. The collection contains *c*5,000 books and pamphlets and 1,500 serial volumes, 1,000 topographical and portrait prints and drawings, 600 maps, 300 election ephemera, 100 other single sheets, 4,000 mss, 2,000 photographic negatives and slides, 250 microfilms, 300 photographic prints. Of the books and pamphlets, over 1,000 titles fall within the terms of the survey, together with almost all the prints and drawings, maps, election ephemera, other single sheets and manuscripts. Only a few Wing items and none earlier are included in this collection, though the maps and prints go back to the 16th and 17th cent respectively, and the mss to the 13th. The subject coverage is primarily the old county of Durham, but also the adjoining counties of Northumberland, Cumberland, Westmorland and the North Riding of Yorkshire, with the city of York to a lesser degree, purchasing being confined mainly to County Durham and overlapping publications.

Cat for printed matter, included in the main cat of the library, with a distinct section in the classified cat.

Also cat of items printed within the area up to 1860 arranged by place, printer/publisher and date.

R M Turner, *Maps of Durham 1578–1872 in the University Library, Durham, including some other maps of local interest: a catalogue*. Durham, 1954.

A I Doyle, *Maps of Durham 1607–1872: a supplementary catalogue* (1960) available from the University Library.

H R Klieneberger, *Durham elections: a list of material relating to parliamentary elections in Durham 1675–1874*. Durham, 1956, 50p.

P M Benedikz, *Durham topographical prints up to 1800: an annotated bibliography*. Durham, 1968, £1.

Maltby Library Given by Edward Maltby (1770–1859) on retirement from the See of Durham in 1856. In 1929, under pressure for space, about a third of the collection was discarded as duplicates of items in other collections or editions of supposedly little interest, some being given to what is now the University of Newcastle, and others sold or scrapped. The stock now totals 1,603 v (1,500 titles), all but one printed. Included are 50 foreign 16th cent; 9 STC; 61 Wing. Mostly classical literature and philology, besides theology. Some science and English literature, including Sir Thomas Browne's *Hydriotaphia* (1658) with an inscription and corrections by the author.

Catalogus Librorum Impressorum Quos Legavit Universitati Dunelmensi E Maltby (London 1863)—containing the items subsequently discarded. Still available from the University Library for cost of postage.

Observatory Library The University Observatory was established in 1840, and besides current reference works, books of historical interest were acquired from the collections of Thomas Wright (1711–86), the Durham polymath, *viz* that of Thomas Thurlow, Bishop of Durham, and from Dr T J Hussey, astronomer, 1850. Transferred to the Science Section of the University Library in 1953. The library contains over 600 titles, mostly continuous series of observations from other observatories, and a complete run of the *Nautical Almanac*, but including a number of 17th and 18th cent monographs, some with annotations by Thomas Wright. The older items are now kept at Palace Green (up to *c*1850), and the remainder in the Science Section, South Road, Durham. Included are the first suppressed edition of John Flamsteed's *Historiae coelestis libri duo* (1712) from the Bignon collection, and the author's own copies of Thomas Wright's *Clavis caelestis* (1742) etc. There are a few Wing items. The ms records of the Observatory up to 1953 are also on deposit at Palace Green.

A typescript cat in volume form by Dr W Hall.

Card cat, both alphabetical and classed; not all the contents are yet included in the main and Science Section cat of the library, but all are up to 1800.

A descriptive cat of the ms records is being completed.

A D Burnett and D M Knight, 'History of Science in Durham Libraries', *British Journ for the Hist of Sci*, v 8, no 28 (1975), p94-5.

Plomer Collection The residual library of William Plomer (1903–71), man of letters, together with his literary papers and in-coming correspondence, presented by his executor, Sir Rupert Hart-Davis, together with some outgoing correspondence added by gift and purchase subsequently. There are over 500 printed items, chiefly copies of Plomer's own works, some with corrections, and of those of contemporaries, often with presentation inscriptions, many in first or early editions, with cuttings of relevant reviews. About 2,000 ms items, some drafts of his own writings, but principally correspondence with some 200 friends and acquaintances such as Edmund Blunden, Benjamin Britten, Roy Campbell, E M Forster, Dame Edith and Sir Osbert Sitwell, and Leonard Woolf. There is also much material relating to Plomer's collaboration with Britten, and one of two surviving diaries of Francis Kilvert, which he edited.

Interim typescript handlists.

A I D(oyle), 'Plomer Collection', *Durham University Journ.* 69 (1976), p186-7.

Routh Library The printed books (except for some selected by his family) collected by Martin Joseph Routh (1755–1854), President of Magdalen College, Oxford, bequeathed to the University of Durham. The collection of 14,890 v (16,470 titles), include 146 incunabula (all foreign); 1,189 STC; 4,509 Wing; 305 foreign 1501–36. Strong in scripture, patristics, church history, religious controversy (especially English), liturgy, classical literature and philosophy, archaeology, European and British history (particularly 17th cent), bibliography. More patchy in topography, travel and English literature. Rich in first and important editions, association copies and examples of fine printing and binding. Notable items include Marsiglio Ficino's *Epistolae* (1495) with an autograph epistle and corrections; the only known copy of the first version of Thomas More's *Opus contra Lutherum* (1523); one of the few surviving sets of engravings of Maurist monasteries in the 17th cent made for the *Monasticon Gallicanum.* Apart from a few items bound with printed books, Routh's mss were not bequeathed to Durham and were sold at Sotheby's on 5 July 1855, when 16 were bought by Sir Thomas Phillipps (no 14026-41 in his cat).

Included in main University Library sheaf cat.

Incunabula included in E V Stocks's cat of those in Durham libraries.

Many items cited in STC (9e 1 and 2) and Wing (ed 2) and Munby and Coral.

N R Ker, *Medieval Manuscripts in British Libraries*, II, p517-21.

A I Doyle, 'The Routh Library', *Times Lit Supp*, 24 Dec 1954, p844.

——'Martin Joseph Routh and his books in Durham University Library', *Durham Univ Journ*, 48 (1955–6), p100-7.

Sunderland Society of Friends The majority of the library of the Sunderland Meeting of the Society of Friends deposited in the University Library in 1972. All items within the scope of the published catalogue, ie up to 1856, are kept separately, the remainder of more recent date being dispersed in the general collections of the library. Ms records, from the early 18th cent onwards are in the County Record Office. There are 680 v (600 titles) kept together; about 200 more recent dispersed. Included are 100 Wing items. The collection is entirely by and about Quakers from the foundation of the Society onwards, or some of their special interests (eg pacifism).

Catalogue of books belonging to the Society of Friends, of Sunderland. Sunderland, 1856.

Also incorporated in the main cat of the University Library and BL pre-1801 union cat.

Winterbottom Collection Thomas Winterbottom (1766–1859), physician, of South Shields, bequeathed his medical books to the General Infirmary at Newcastle, whence they have descended to the University Library there, and his other books to the University of Durham. The former were seriously diminished by fire and damp, and the latter drastically reduced in 1926 when some were given to Newcastle. There remain 1,625 v (*c*1,600 titles) including 7 incunabula; 16 STC; 9 Wing, but mostly 18th and 19th cent, strong in travel, especially Africa and Asia, natural science; small but interesting representation of French, German and Italian literature.

Ms cat of the original collection.

Entries in main cat of University Library.

J S Emmerson, 'On the Gallery (Account of medical collection, including Winterbottom's, in Newcastle University Library)', *Univ of Durham Med Gaz*, 47 (1953), p24-7.

——'Thomas Masterman Winterbottom, MD', *Ibid.* 49 (1955), p23-7.

University Library, Oriental Section, Elvet Hill, Durham. Tel (0385) 64371. Open Mon-Fri 9 am-1 pm, 2-5 pm; Sat (not Christmas vacation, nor July-Sept) 9 am-12 noon. Closed Christmas Eve–New Year's Day, Good Friday–Easter Mon, Autumn Bank Holiday. Admission by application in advance to the Keeper, giving reasons, and production of good evidence of identity.

Oriental Section Established separately from the main library in 1950 to serve the expansion of Oriental Studies in Durham resulting from the Scarborough Report, subsequently developed by the Hayter Report for the field of modern as well as ancient Middle-Eastern subjects. There are nearly 400 pre-1850 titles published chiefly abroad, and another 200 with oriental imprints 1851–99, so that early printing in a number of countries such as Iran, Turkey and Soviet Central Asia is significantly represented. There are also a number of specialized collections in Armenian, Aramaic, Sanskrit, Egyptology, Chinese and Japanese, a few 16th cent European editions and a few Wing items.

Included in draft cat of the Section, of which there is a duplicate in the main University Library.

R Collison and B E Moon, *Directory of Libraries and*

Special Collections on Asia and North Africa. London, 1970, p26-8.

St Chad's College, North Bailey, Durham. Admission by application in advance, in writing, to the librarian. Research facilities and services through the University Library.

St Chad's College Library The old and rare books have been given at various times since the foundation of the College in 1904, notably most of the 15th and early 16th cent items by L A Body in 1940. There are several hundred pre-1851 printed items, including 9 incunabula and numerous 16th cent foreign books, chiefly editions of the Latin and Greek classics (including 8 Aldines and 6 Estiennes); 12 STC; 15 Wing items, mostly theological; strong in Eastern and Western rite liturgy 17th-19th cent. There are two medieval mss. The manuscripts, incunabula and a number of the other earlier items are deposited in the University Library, Palace Green, to which application may be made direct, giving due notice and credentials.

Sheaf slips to 1975; duplicate in University Library, Palace Green.

H W Acomb, 'Early printed books', *St Chad's College Magazine*, no 3 (1940), p14-27. (op)

Ushaw College, Durham DH7 9RH. Tel (0385) 731367. Admission by arrangement, on advance written application to the librarian. Microfilm reader; photography by special arrangement.

The Big Library and the Lower Library The library has been built up since 1800 as the research library of the College (descended from the English College, Douai, 1568—1793, but not inheriting its books), embracing earlier Catholic clergy and lay collections, such as those of Bishop Edward Dicconson (1670—1752) and John Lingard (1771—1851). It also serves as a repository of books from northern parishes and religious communities. It houses over 40,000 printed titles, the great majority being pre-1851. In addition there are on deposit (and kept separately), selections of books and pamphlets from the English College, Lisbon (for which see separate report), the diocese of Lancaster, and St Cuthbert's parish, Durham (*c*500 v). There are 138 incunabula; 650 STC; more than 2,000 Wing items; 42 medieval mss (to be described in Ker's *Medieval Manuscripts in British Libraries*, v 4); college archives, including mss from Douai; letters and papers of 19th cent. Roman Catholics (especially Lingard and Cardinal Nicholas Wiseman); miscellaneous mss including letters of Alexander Pope, and J A Comenius (to Antoinette Bourignon); Radcliffe (Earls of Derwentwater) papers and relics. Main subject areas are early, medieval and counter-Reformation theology; devotional literature and liturgy; church history; Roman Catholicism in England; Jansenism; general medieval history, particularly of Italy; 17th-19th cent mathematics, astronomy and natural history; architectural illustrations, topography and travel. Many early blind-tooled bindings and some fine gold-tooled later ones.

Author/subject cat of printed material on cards (copy of former at Durham University Library).

STC items listed by Ramage, and many by Allison and Rogers; Wing items cited in 2nd ed v 2-3 and in Clancy.

Detailed card cat of archive collections, of which copies (on sheets) are available at Durham University Library, the Bodleian Library, National Register of Archives, Westminster Cathedral Archives, and Birmingham Diocesan Archives (RC).

A I Doyle, 'The significance of the Big Library today', *Ushaw Magazine*, v 83, no 240 (Dec 1972), p3-6.

W S Mitchell, 'Ushaw College bindings', *Libri*, v 7 (1957), p156-66, pl 1-8.

The Lisbon Collection On the closure of the English College in Lisbon (1628—1971), the archives of the college and a selection from its library were brought to Ushaw and housed as a collection in a Lisbon Room. It contains *c*2,000 printed books; 300 archive volumes and 5 filing cabinets of loose papers. The great majority of the printed books are pre-1851, and include 10 incunabula, some STC and Wing items; a considerable number of 16th cent foreign printed books (including rare 1st edition of St Ignatius Loyola's *Exercitia Spiritualia*, 1548); many 17th-19th cent Portuguese and Spanish publications, as well as in other languages and from other countries (mainly Italy, France and England). Predominantly theological and historical interest, but including a wider range of subjects, eg travel.

The mss (which include 1 medieval ms), include not only the archives of the college, but also sermons etc of its members, the correspondence of Bishop Richard Russell (1630—93), confessor of Queen Catherine of Braganza, and the papers of two Anglo-Portuguese families, Jorge and Donovan, concerning trade between the two countries in the earlier part of the 19th cent.

Short title author cat on cards for the printed books, of which copies are incorporated in the duplicate Ushaw cat in the University Library.

A detailed card cat of the archives is in progress.

M S S(harratt), 'Marginalia Dunelmensia: Ushaw College', *Durham Univ Journ*, v 69 (1976—77), p187-8.

——'The Lisbon Collection at Ushaw', *Northern Catholic History*, no 8 (Autumn 1978), p30-4.

Gateshead

Gateshead Public Libraries, Central Library, Prince Consort Road, Gateshead, Tyne and Wear NE8 4LN. Tel (0632) 773478. Open to general public Mon, Tues, Thurs, Fri 9.30 am-8 pm; Wed 9.30 am-5 pm; Sat 9.30 am-1 pm. 16/35 mm microfilm readers; xerox copier; access to dyeline copier.

Local Studies Collection Total stock *c*7,000 v, of which

c120 are pre-1801, covering the area of Gateshead Metropolitan Borough. It contains the Bell collection of several hundred ms maps, late 18th-early 19th cent, and the Cotesworth/Ellison mss (family papers of 17th-18th cent) relating mainly to the coal trade.

Author/subject cat.

Middlesbrough

Cleveland County Library, Central Library, Victoria Square, Middlesbrough, Cleveland. Tel (0642) 249440. Open to general public Mon-Fri 9.30 am-7 pm; Sat 9.30 am-5 pm. Photocopier available.

William Kelly Collection Presented by William Kelly, a prominent Plymouth Brother, to the Middlesbrough Public Library in 1904, the collection contains 15,000 v (including periodicals), about one-third pre-1801; over 400 editions of the Christian scriptures and scriptural commentaries from 16th cent onwards; 2 incunabula, *Biblia Latina* (Nuremberg 1478) and M Ficino *Epistolae* (Nuremberg 1497). Subject coverage mainly theological, but also a large number of Greek and Latin classics.

Included in Middlesbrough Reference Library cat.

Essex

Chelmsford

Chelmsford Cathedral Library, The Cathedral, Chelmsford, Essex CM1 1EH. Tel (0245) 352702. Open Tues 6.30-8.30 pm, and by appointment with the librarian. Admission subject to discretion of the librarian.

Knightbridge Library The library of the Rev John Knightbridge, a native of Chelmsford, and given to St Mary's Church, Chelmsford (now the Cathedral) in 1679 in accordance with his wish. It consists of 405 v (581 items). Certain volumes consist of Puritan tracts bound together: these have been counted as individual items. Mainly theological works of the 16th and 17th cent, and also Patristics and other early books, with some volumes of pamphlets and sermons, many of them interesting as illustrating the controversies of that day. The more notable items include *Luther: In Genesin* with rubricated title page and preface by Melancthon, published at Nuremberg in 1552: this bears Dr Knightbridge's signature. Other works with this signature are: *Remains of that reverend and famous postillar John Boys* (1631); and Cartwright's *Confutation of the Rhemists translation* (1618); part of the *Paraphrases* of Erasmus, which was deposited in the church at Chelmsford in accordance with the injunctions of Edward VI in 1547 which ordered that this work was to be placed in every church along with the Bible itself; a copy with beautiful rubricated title page, of Lyndwood's *Provinciale*, published in London about 1505: a book which remains a standard authority on English ecclesiastical law; a dual work, published in Paris in 1554 and bound in vellum, consisting of the Commentary of St Ambrose on the Apocalypse, with preface by Cuthbert Tunstall, Bishop of Durham; and the latter's treatise on Catholic Eucharistic doctrine, of which it is the first edition; the works of St Irenaeus, Bishop of Lyons, published at Basle in 1571; the complete works of St Augustine in 17 v, bound in vellum and published at Lyons, 1563–71; Hooker's *Ecclesiastical politie* (1617) with autograph of Francis Quarles (1592–1644), the Romford-born poet; Paolo Sarpi's *Historie of the Council of Trent* (1629) translated by Nathanael Brent (belonged to 'Fra Quarles' who stayed with the translator at Brent Hall, Finchingfield); St Ignatius's Epistles in Greek, Latin and French (Paris, 1562), with ms note at beginning by A(nthony) G(rant) (1806–83), curate of Chelmsford, afterwards Archdeacon of St Albans.

Index to the Library at Chelmsford Church, Essex, 1815 ms.

A Clark, 'Knightbridge Library, Chelmsford: catalogue, 1903' (Bodleian ms Eng misc c42-3).

Author card cat. Contents also recorded in a short-title cat of the holdings of cathedral libraries up to 1701 which will be published in due course by the Bibliographical Society.

Library History, 4(5), Spring 1978, p159-60.

Dictionary of National Biography, 'John Knightbridge'.

Parochial Libraries of the Church of England (Central Council for the Care of Churches, 1959), p73-4.

Essex Record Office, County Hall, Chelmsford, Essex CM1 1LX. Tel (0245) 67222. Ext 2104. Open Mon 9.15 am-8.45 pm; Tues, Wed, Thurs 9.15 am-5.15 pm; Fri 9.15 am-4.15 pm. Admission preferably by appointment. Search room (30 seats); photographic services.

The Essex Record Office was set up in 1938, and includes the *Avery, Landon* and *Sage* collections. There are 5,000 printed books, 6,000 pamphlets, and other ephemera. Although primarily an archive repository, it contains Civil War pamphlets; Essex sermons; Poll books; Pamphlets and broadsheets printed by Charles Clark (1806–80), with associated letters and papers 1838–53 (DDU 668).

No published cat in its entirety, but see *Victoria County History of Essex*. Bibliography vol (1959)—

indicates rare holdings except sermons and literary works.

Guide to the Essex Record Office. (op)

Colchester

Essex Libraries, Local Studies Department, Central Library, Trinity Square, Colchester. Tel (0206) 62243 Ext 41. Open Mon, Tues, Wed, Fri 9 am-8 pm; Thurs, Sat 9 am-5 pm. Admission to special collections by arrangement. Microfilm, microfiche, photography (by arrangement) facilities.

Castle Collection The collection was founded in mid-summer 1745, by Charles Gray, MP, antiquary and owner of Colchester Castle, as a 'book club' intended for doctors, parsons, etc in and around Colchester. The annual subscription was two guineas (£2.10) per annum. The library remained at the Castle until the late 1920s when it transferred to the Colchester Public Library. While it remained as a subscription library for its members, regular auction sales of books were conducted. Consequently the catalogues now available account for those books available at the time of their compilation. The collection of books now totals 2,493, covering religion, science, literature, history, biography, and includes 1 incunabulum; 20 v 'Tracts against Popery'; 68 v (over 2,000 items) of 17th and 18th cent 'Tracts'; 70 v Commons and Lords Journals (13th, 14th, 17th and 18th cent). The particular interest of the library is that it demonstrates an 18th cent subscription library in its final form before closure.

Printed cats 1816, 1833, 1848, 1856, 1886 (extant).

Card cat author and subject (class no) indexes.

Cunnington Collection Mostly collected by the Cunnington family of Braintree, of the late 19th cent and presented to Essex County Council in the 1930s. It comprises *c*400 v, plus *c*100 pamphlets and ephemera, of which *c*190 are pre-1850 and 210 post-1850. These include 70 general works (eg Newcourt, Grose, etc); 168 Essex volumes, including some 17th and 18th cent printing, but mostly 19th cent; a small number of mss including pencil sketches (A Bennett Banford); compilations of ephemera, particularly 2 v of Charles Clark's printing (squibs, leaflets, parodies, etc).

A cat is available, but inaccurate owing to substantial losses.

Essex Review, v 9, 11, 16, etc. (op)

Harsnett Collection Personal library of Archbishop Samuel Harsnett (1561–1631), Archbishop of York 1628–31. Library left to Colchester Corporation where he was born and was master of the Free School (now the Royal Grammar School), from 1586–8. It was added to the Public Library in 20th cent. It consists of *c*900 v, 15 pre-1500, *c*860 1500–1600 items covering divinity, dogma, polemics, Bibles, psalters etc. Early printing represented by Koberger, Etienne, Kesler, Aldus, Froben, Plantin, De Colines etc. Venetian, Parisian, Swiss early printers. Some items from the libraries of Sir Christopher Hatton, Archbishop Whitgift, Dudley, Earl of Leicester, etc.

G Goodwin, *Catalogue of the Harsnett Library, 1888* (Few copies still available from above, £5).

The Taylor Collection Collected by the Taylor family of Ongar, Lavenham and Colchester, 1759–1901, it includes 200 pre-1850 and 126 1850–1900 items, plus 250 mss including Taylor letters. All are of Taylor significance, either being by members of the family, or part of their studies or contributions by them to other works. Some classics, classical studies, theology, polemics, history, architecture, philosophy, biography, magazines, but the principal and most interesting part is the early 19th cent editions of the children's and youth books by members of the Taylor family.

Card cat (primitive).

G Edward Harris, *Contributions towards a bibliography of the Taylors of Ongar and Stanford Rivers*. Cosby Lockwood, 1965 (limited ed 350 copies). (op)

Nayland Parish Library, St James' Church, Nayland, Colchester, Essex. Tel (0206) 262316. Admission on application to the incumbent, The Vicarage, Nayland.

Nayland Parish Library The library was probably started in the late 18th cent during the incumbency of the Rev William Jones FRS (1777–1800) or his predecessor the Rev John White (1715–55). There are 106 v (*c*40 works), including 1 STC and 3 Wing items.

List of 27 v in a Terrier, 1837, (Suffolk Record Office Bury Branch) 806/1/112.

J A Fitch, 'Some ancient Suffolk parochial libraries' in *Suffolk Arch Proceedings*, XXX (1964), p44-87.

Stoke-by-Nayland Parish Library, St Mary's Church, Stoke-by-Nayland, Colchester, Essex. Tel (0206) 262248. Admission on application to the incumbent, The Vicarage, Stoke-by-Nayland, Colchester, Essex.

Stoke-by-Nayland Parish Library The library was formed *c*1699 during the incumbency of the Rev Thomas Reeve (1685–1719). It remained in a room over the south porch until it was rehoused in new bookcases *c*1975. From inscriptions, copies were intended for loan. There are 142 v containing *c*160 items, which include 12 STC and 75 Wing books; 6 Latin works printed in the 16th cent; a set of Parker Society publications in their original casing.

Typescript cat.

C M Torlesse, *Some account of Stoke-by-Nayland*, 1877, p97-9 (lists 116 v).

Suffolk Parochial Libraries: a catalogue. Mansell, 1977.

J A Fitch, *op cit* XXX (1964), p44-87.

University of Essex Library, P O Box 24, Colchester

C14 3UA. Tel (0206) 062286. Open, Term: Mon-Fri 9 am-10 pm; Sat 9 am-6 pm; Sun 2-7 pm; Vacation: Mon-Fri 9 am-5.30 pm. Admission by prior application, in writing, to the librarian. Photocopying, microfilm, microfiche etc. Photography, slide making. Access to computerized data bases etc. Inter library loan.

Bassingbourn Collection Formerly the Parish Library of Bassingbourn, Cambs, on the Essex border. Purchased and shared jointly by Essex University and Cambridge University with help from the Pilgrim Trust. It is made up of 374 items, mainly on theology, but some history and classical literature, and includes 45 STC, 177 Wing and 68 ESTC items.

Unpublished cats held at Essex and Cambridge.

Bensusan Collection The personal papers, diaries and proof and final versions of the published works of Samuel Levy Bensusan (1872–1958); they include 79 printed volumes and 9 linear feet of typescript and manuscripts.

Friends Collection Deposited by Colchester and Coggeshall Meeting of the Society of Friends. It includes *c*1,400 printed books, 3 pre-1640, 748 1701–1800, 164 1801–50, plus 201 mss.

Copies of cat of printed books at Essex University Library and Friends Meeting House, Colchester; handlist of mss similarly available, also at Essex Record Office.

S H G Fitch, *Colchester Quakers*, (1962).

General 'Special Collection' Made up of acquisitions from various sources since foundation of the library in 1963, it includes 40 STC, 45 Wing and 184 ESTC items, as well as the mss of Henri and Sophie Gaudier-Brzeska, Donald Davie, T E Lawrence, and Henry W Hall (local figure 1891–1980).

Hassall Collection The letters, newspaper cuttings, work ledgers and printed work of John Hassall (1868–1948) artist.

Rowhedge Collection Business archive of the Rowhedge Ironworks, a shipbuilding firm on the river Coln, 1904–64. Deposited by Essex Record Office. 150 linear feet.

Russell Collection The family library of 'Stubbers', Essex, formerly belonging to the Champion, Branfill and Russell families. A general country family library covering several generations. It contains a total of 667 items, including 2 STC, 77 Wing and 488 ESTC.

Separate cat available for consultation in library.

Dedham

Dedham Parochial Library, Parish Church, Dedham, Essex.

The history of the library is uncertain, but it was probably assembled by Canon Rendall who lived at Dedham after his retirement as Headmaster of Charterhouse (1911) and moved the library into its present quarters about 1938. The books total 150, and include *c*9 17th and 12 18th cent items, and the remainder pre-1850. Subject coverage includes theology, Old and New Testament commentaries, collections of Bibles and prayer books. Local material includes Essex books, pamphlets and periodicals. Ms items include transcripts of Dedham Manor rolls; index to the Redpaper book of Colchester; 19th and 20th cent Parish Magazine.

Felsted

Felsted School Library, Felsted, Nr Great Dunmow, Essex. Tel (0371) 820258. Open 8.30 am-10 pm. The library is open to all members of the school, and to members of the public on written application to the librarian.

Felsted School Library It is not known when precisely the school formed a library, but some of its earliest books are dated *c*1600 and several others are gifts of *c*1750 when the first collection was probably formed. There are now *c*10,000 books, of which *c*100 are of exceptional rarity within the subject fields of history, Greek and Roman literature.

The library uses the Cheltenham system of cataloguing.

Hatfield Broad Oak

St Mary's Parish Church, Hatfield Broad Oak, Essex. Admission on written application to the incumbent.

The library was founded by George Stirling, Vicar of Hatfield 1648–1728; Sir Charles Barrington built a small room at the east end of the South chancel to contain them. The room was enlarged in 1843. There are 320 v, predominatly theological, some history, travel, philosophy. Tracts include 2 v of the 'Glorious Revolution', 1 v State Trials, 1678–80. Bindings are undistinguished, but two are 16th cent blind tooled and also plain calf, 17th cent Barrington Arms. The collection includes 2 incunabula (Orosius, 1499, Aristotle, 1498); 27 1500–1600; 155 1600–1700; 124 1700–1800; 5 1800–50. The condition of some books is poor, and the majority are unsafe to be handled without extreme care.

Excursions of Essex, 1819. (op)

A D Jones, *Church Library of Hatfield Regis*. (op)

Essex Arch Soc Trans, ns 1898, v 6, 1898, p339. (op)

Maldon

Dr Thomas Plume's Library, Market Hill, Maldon, Essex. Tel (0621) 55912. Open Tues, Wed, Thurs 2-4 pm; Sat 10 am-12 noon. Admission by appointment on written application to the librarian. Photocopying facilities.

Dr Thomas Plume's Collection The private library of Dr

Plume (1630–1704) was bequeathed to Maldon in 1704 for use as a lending library. It remains almost intact, and consists of 1,500 pamphlets, bills and miscellaneous documents, and 8,000 books. They include 1 pre-1500 item, 6,000 1500–1700 and 2,000 1700– items. Subjects covered include theology, chemistry, astronomy, medicine, history, travel. Strong on theology and politics of the 17th cent.

Pre-1959 cat in mss only. 1959 printed cat, £3 per copy.

Newport

Newport Parish Library, Parish Church, Newport, Essex.

A Bray Library was established about 1710, and was housed above the South porch. It contains 800 v which include 15th, 16th and 17th cent works, as well as 19th cent theology and a collection of Bibles, including Breeches, Vinegar, etc).

Saffron Walden

Victorian Studies Centre—Saffron Walden, 2 King Street, Saffron Walden, Essex. Tel (0799) 23178. Open Mon, Tues, Thurs, Fri 9 am-7 pm; Sat 9 am-5 pm. Admission free, under supervision of a member of staff. Advance notice preferred. Study room, fiche reader, photocopier available.

Saffron Walden Town Library The former Literary and Scientific Institute (1832) benefited from donations of private librarians during the 19th cent. In 1967 the Trusteeship was transferred to Essex County Library. The original collection of the Literary and Scientific Institute has been, since 1970, the basis of a Victorian Studies Centre specializing mainly in Art and Architecture. The library contains *c*20,000 v with special emphasis on botany, topography, Victorian Art and Architecture. There are 5 incunabula and a good number of 18th cent items; with many dozen mss—some monastic.

Single-entry card cat (1978).

Printed dictionary cat (1980) with mss additions to 1950.

Waltham Abbey

Abbey Church of Waltham Holy Cross and St Lawrence, Vestry Library, Church Street, Waltham Abbey, Essex EN9 1DX. Open by appointment only, after written application to the Curator.

A collection of 160 v built up by donation, especially from the parochial clergy and after 1910; they include 53 pre-1851 (4 STC; 6 Wing).

Typescript shelflist.

Service books and Bibles A collection of *c*50 items includes 3 STC Bibles and the *Book of Common Prayer* 1718, rebound in 1817 for William Clark, Churchwarden (the only book in the library definitely known to have been associated with the Abbey before 1910).

Waltham Abbey Books and pamphlets on the history of Waltham Abbey (town and building) and Essex, including Farmer *History of Waltham Abbey* 1735, extra illustrated; and the histories of Essex by Britton 1810 and Ogbourne 1814. Many of the works of William Winters (1835?–93), bookseller at Waltham Abbey. 1 v of pamphlets on the Abbey 1859 onwards collected by J Frances. Books on the Abbey by William Burges, including *Report* 1860.

Books by incumbents of the Abbey, especially Thomas Fuller (1608–61), including his *Worthies* 1662, *Abel redevivus* 1652, and *Holy War* 1640 (Winters copy with contemporary ms poem on the author).

Theology and miscellaneous This collection includes Kellett *Tricoenium Christi* 1641, Hall *Works* 1648 and a few later works of general theology.

Waltham Abbey Historical Society Library, Old Town Hall, Highbridge Street, Waltham Abbey, Essex EN9 1DE. Open by appointment only, after letter of application to the Curator. Photocopying by arrangement.

The Society was founded in 1952. The library has been built up from donations; *c*50 v, including 10 pre-1851.

Waltham Abbey Books on the history of the Abbey and the area, including Farmer (1765) with Scrope Berdmore's bookplate, and some local authors, eg T Fuller (Wing F241).

Buxton Library Eight books from the library of Sir Thomas Fowell Buxton, MP, 1st Bart (1786–1845), brewer and philanthropist, husband of Hannah Gurney, and author of *The African Slave Trade (1839)*; and descendants. Quaker theology and memoirs, including Joseph J Gurney's *Minor works* (1839). (A large collection of anti-slavery pamphlets from this library was sold by the Society in 1980, supplement to Quaritch cat no 1006.)

Card cat (Museum Documentation Assoc format) being compiled.

Gloucestershire

Cheltenham

Cheltenham Divisional Library, Clarence Street, Cheltenham, Glos. GL50 3JT. (Formerly Cheltenham Public Library, now incorporated in

Gloucestershire County Library.) Tel (0242) 22476, 52131 or 55636. Telex 43362. Open Mon-Fri 9.30 am-7 pm; Sat 9.30 am-5 pm.

(a) *Francis Day Collection* c1,200 v on natural history, particularly fish and fish culture, collected by Francis Day (1829–89), the ichthyologist, and presented by his daughters as a memorial to him.

(b) *Gustav Holst Collection* 18 scrapbooks of programmes and press-cuttings connected with his music, collected by Gustav Holst (1874–1934), and dating from the 1890s. They were presented to the library by his daughter Imogen at the outbreak of the 1939–45 war.

Catalogue of Holst's concert programmes and press-cuttings in the Central Library, Cheltenham by Sheila Lumby and Vera Hounsfield, Gloucester, 1974.

(c) *Local History Collection* c10,000 items dealing mainly with Cheltenham and the North Cotswolds.

Cheltenham Ladies' College, Cheltenham, Glos. GL50 3EP. Tel (0452) 20691. Admission by arrangement with the librarian, to whom application should be made in writing.

The Cheltenham Ladies' College Libraries represent the basic literary requirement of the College, but include old and rare volumes donated over the years by such well-known people as John Ruskin, William Morris, Queen Mary, Miss Beale, etc. There are c20,000 v covering a wide subject range, both in the general collections and in the special collection, with a comprehensive coverage of the education of women from c1850. Two rare volumes donated by John Ruskin are deposited for safety at the Bodleian, *viz* the Arras Winter breviary 1284 and an 11th cent Greek testament. There is also a collection of letters and autographs of well-known personages, including Nelson, Emma Hamilton, Byron, Swinburne, Kipling, Barrie, and others.

Cheltenham Ladies' College 2nd ed 1958. (op)

Cirencester

Royal Agricultural College, Cirencester, Gloucestershire. Tel (0285) 2361. Open Mon-Thurs 9 am-7 pm; Fri 9 am-5 pm. Admission to members of the College; others by prior permission of the Principal. Photocopying facilities.

The Royal Agricultural College Collection has been built up by the College since its inception in 1845, and now holds c2,000 v. It constitutes a general historical collection on all aspects of farming, animal and crop husbandry, forestry and estate management.

Cat.

Gloucester

County Library, Brunswick Road, Gloucester GL1 1HT. Tel (0452) 20020. Open Mon, Tues, Thurs 9 am-8 pm; Wed, Fri, Sat 9 am-5 pm. Admission to the Gloucester Collection after signing the Visitors' Book.

Gloucester Collection The nucleus of this collection was a bequest by the late J J Powell, QC, who left to the city several volumes of cuttings from Gloucester newspapers, on condition that should a public library be established, they were to be kept there. On the death of Judge Powell, in 1891, the Misses Powell added to the bequest, and 111 v and 27 pamphlets were transferred to the library when it was opened on 31 May 1900. The collection now comprises 8,083 printed books and 57,564 pamphlets relating mainly to the country, cities, towns and villages of Gloucestershire, and includes (a) *The Dancey Gift* comprising *inter alia* 225 v, 321 pamphlets and 282 prints and portraits relating to Gloucestershire (presented by Councillor C H Dancey, 31 May 1911); (b) *Painswick House Collection* consisting of 1,678 pamphlets and 1,877 single sheets (bound in 110 v), relating to the history of Gloucestershire (presented by Francis Adams Hyett Esq in 1915); (c) *Hockaday Abstracts* consisting of c500 files of abstracts relating to the ecclesiastical affairs of every parish in Gloucestershire. Each file has been catalogued under the respective parishes. Various indexes included. (Presented by the family of the late Mr F S Hockaday of Lydney, in August 1924.)

Published cat up to 1927; card cat to date.

The Hartland (Herbals) Collection An outstanding collection of over 100 herbals containing examples of the major European herbals, including the Grete Herball, the first illustrated herbal in English published in 1526. It forms part of the library of the late Ernest Hartland, containing c9,124 books presented after his death by his widow Mrs A G Hartland. Hartland was also interested in historical bibliography and acquired specimens of early printed books, including Aldus and Elzevier.

See Markwick, E M T. *Hartland Herbals* (Gloucester County Library, 1972).

Hitchings Collection of Bibles and New Testaments A very important collection of Bibles and New Testaments bequeathed to the Gloucester Public Library by Alfred Walter Hitchings of Nottingham in May 1936. It contains over 100 Bibles dating from 1540 to 1906, and these include 2 copies of the translation of Miles Coverdale printed in 1550 by Christopher Froschover; 8 editions of the 'Great Bible' (Thomas Cromwell's, often called Cranmer's); a perfect copy of Mathew's Bible in two v printed in 1551 by Thomas Petyt; editions of the Genevan Bible include those printed by Robert Barker, and the first edition printed by Rouland Hill in 1560. There is also a fine collection of 50 New Testaments, of which the earliest is that of Erasmus, in Latin, printed 1519, and others of various dates to 1926. The Hitchings' bequest also includes a number of rare 16th cent works by Tyndale and John Frith, the martyr and friend of Tyndale.

County Library, Quayside Wing, Gloucester GL1 2HY. Tel (0452) 21444. Telex 43155. Open by arrangement on written application. Microform readers and photocopying facilities.

Hartland Collection 9,124 v on art, archaeology and historical bibliography, including specimens of books issued by early printers. They were collected by Ernest Hartland, Hardwick Court, Chepstow, and presented in 1936 by his widow, Mrs A G Hartland. Particularly noteworthy is a fine set of herbals, English and foreign. The Hartland Collection of Bibles, early printed books and mss in the John Rylands University Library, Manchester (qv) came from the same source.

There is a card cat (alphabetico-classed) of the Collection, and a printed list of the herbals is available on request.

Gloucester Cathedral Library, Gloucester Cathedral, Gloucester. Not open to the public. Application by serious scholars should be made in writing well in advance of the proposed date of visit, and should state which books are required. Reference may be asked for.

History Present collection began in 1648, and has been formed mainly by gifts. Miss Eward is at present writing a history of the library. Only books specially concerned with Gloucester Cathedral are now added to the library. There are *c*7,000 v, of which about two-thirds are pre-1851; 46 mss (medieval ones noted by Ker), 45 incunabula, *c*2,000 books printed before 1700, of which *c*1,000 are English. Only one book is now chained.

Selden Collection On John Selden's death in 1654, most of his books went to the Bodleian Library, but Sir Matthew Hale, one of the executors, persuaded Bodley's Librarian to send duplicates to the newly founded library at Gloucester Cathedral where they were received in 1663. They number about 200, and are preserved as a separate collection. There is a contemporary list of the books at the Bodleian Library.

Wheeler Library Maurice Wheeler, Master of the College School 1684–1712, and also Cathedral Librarian from 1709, encouraged the creation of a school library, mainly by donations. Many books were given by subsequent generations, but following a fire in 1849, only about 300 books remain. Of *c*140 titles recorded as given to the library in Wheeler's day, only 40 are left. They are housed as a separate collection in the Cathedral Library.

Josiah Tucker (1712–99), Dean of Gloucester 1758–99, is recorded as having given *c*50 books, including works on trade and commerce and the Jesuits. In addition a bound collection of *c*200 mid-18th cent pamphlets clearly came from him.

References
A catalogue of Gloucester Cathedral Library. Compiled by Suzanne M Eward. Published by the Dean and Chapter, 1972. It includes a list of the more interesting bindings by H M Nixon.

Gloucestershire County Record Office, Worcester Street, Gloucester. Tel (0452) 21444. Open Mon-Fri 9 am-5 pm.

Hyett Collection of Civil War Pamphlets 1643–1649 Purchased from Sir Francis Hyett's executors in 1942, the Collection consists of *c*50 v of contemporary tracts and pamphlets.

Roland Austin, *A catalogue of Glos. books collected by Sir Francis Hyett of Painswick and placed in the Shire Hall*, 1949. (op)

Hampshire, Wiltshire, Isle of Wight

Aldershot

Prince Consort's Army Library, Knollys Road, Aldershot, Hants GU11 1PS. Tel (0252) 24431 Ext Montgomery 307/382. Open Mon-Thurs 9 am-1 pm, 2-5.30 pm, Fri 9 am-1 pm, 2-5.00 pm. Membership is open to military personnel, serving and retired, their families and MOD staff employed in local army establishments. Historical enquiries are answered by post and telephone as time permits. Reader's tickets (but not borrower's tickets) are available to other users on written application, supported by references. Photocopying, microfilms, etc. Photocopies can be supplied by arrangement.

Prince Consort's Library Original building and books were donated by the Prince Consort in 1860. Now part of the Army Library Service. Historical collection *c*10,000. Total stock 40,000+. Particular strength is late 18th and early 19th cent books of military uniforms. The collection is added to frequently.

Card cat—author and title and classified. Subject index in course of compilation.

Original printed cat, 1860. References in Army Museums Ogilby Trust Index, Index to British Military Costume prints, 1972.

Alton

Jane Austen Memorial Trust, Jane Austen House,

Chawton, Alton, Hants. Tel (0420) 83262 (private number of Curator). Open 11 am-4.30 pm daily (not open Mondays and Tuesdays Nov-March). Admission by appointment only. No facilities, but a room could be set aside.

The library has grown by gifts since the Society was formed in 1940 and the Trust in 1948. It contains 85 pre-1850 items by and about Jane Austen and members of her family.

Card and author cat.

Beaulieu

Private Library of Lord Montagu of Beaulieu, Palace House, Beaulieu, Hants SO4 7ZN. Tel (0590) 612345. Access to bona fide students by arrangement on application in writing to Lord Montagu, to whom all enquiries should be directed. No special facilities.

The library originated in the collection of the Dukes of Montagu (late 17th and early 18th cent) of whose residences Beaulieu was one. Books were added by the Dukes of Buccleuch, to whose family Beaulieu passed at the end of the 18th cent. Lord Henry Scott, 2nd son of the 5th Duke of Buccleuch and later 1st Lord Montagu of Beaulieu, became the owner of Beaulieu in 1867. Further books were added by him, his son, and his grandson, the present Lord Montagu. The library consists of *c*900 works, comprising about 1,700 v, 250 with imprints of 1850 or before. There are 14 STC; 18 Wing items, and 11 16th cent and 60 17th cent works. The collection is varied, covering literature, history, memoirs, travel, natural history and sport. A number of Italian and French works of the 16th-18th cent are included. Some manuscripts relating to the Montagu family, and the 'Montagu of Beaulieu' mss reported on by the Historical Manuscripts Commission (1900).

The books have been listed, but not catalogued in detail. Last inventory taken 1977.

Christchurch

Red House Museum and Art Gallery, Quay Road, Christchurch, Dorset. Tel (0202) 2860. Open Tues-Sat, Sun pm. Photocopying, microfilms, etc. Access can be arranged for serious students.

Druitt Collection Started by Herbert Druitt and added to. It consists of fashion magazines and plates (1786 onwards); books and maps of regional interest and by local authors.

Card and sheaf cat for *Fashion Plates.*

'Fashion Plates at Red House Museum' in *Costume,* 8.

Farnborough

St Michael's Abbey, 280 Farnborough Road, Farnborough, Hants GU14 7NQ. Tel (0252) 46105. Not normally open to the public, but access can usually be made available, for reference use only, by prior arrangement by letter. Microfilm reader and photocopying facilities.

The present community of monks moved to Farnborough as recently as 1947, and the library was started more or less from scratch. A number of the older items have been collected from other foundations, particularly St Augustine's Monastery, Ramsgate. The previous occupants moved to Quarr Abbey (qv), in 1946, and took their library with them. The library has *c*16,000 v, mainly individual titles—printed books and pamphlets on most subjects, mainly theological. It is strong on history of monasticism and church music; *c*300 v on French Second Empire (what is now the abbey church was originally built by the Empress Eugénie as a mausoleum for her husband, Napoleon III and their son the Prince Imperial), and in the archives a number of photographs of the Empress, and of her funeral; also the 'Chevalier letters' from the Prince Imperial's nurse to an emigré family in London, and other family papers. There are *c*7 16th cent and 60 17th cent v (*c*50 titles), mainly continental imprints. The collection includes 2 STC and 5 Wing items; also *c*450 other pre-1851. These are mainly theological works. There is a small museum in the Abbey of likely interest to scholars of the Second Empire.

Card index, rather than cat. Attempts are being made to improve it.

Isle of Wight

County Library, Parkhurst Road, Newport, Isle of Wight PO30 5TX. Tel (0983) 2324. Open Mon-Fri 9 am-5 pm. Photocopying facilities.

The collection representing the development of printing and illustration through the ages, comprises the Brett and Terry Collections, as well as items donated and purchased. It totals *c*100 items of rare books dating from 1512 to modern times, and includes examples of the works of such printers as Robert Estienne, Aldus Manutius, Christopher Plantin, the Elzeviers, and later printers such as William Pikering. It contains some fine examples of hand-coloured illustrations, eg Blackwell's *Herbal*; aquatints, eg 'Dr Syntax' illustrated by Rowlandson; engravings, some by William Blake; and lithographs, eg Morris: British Birds. There are also examples of fine modern printing from various private presses.

Card cat by date of printing.

Quarr Abbey, Ryde, Isle of Wight PO33 4ES. Tel (0983) 882420. Open by arrangement with the librarian.

The whole library is within the monastic enclosure, and is

therefore private. Admission granted to bona fide scholars only on written application to the librarian. *Women cannot be admitted*, but in exceptional cases books could be brought to them to consult in non-monastic areas. Photocopying available if necessary. Accommodation available within guest-house attached to the monastery.

Quarr Abbey Library The community was founded on the Isle of Wight by the exiled Benedictine monks of Solesmes, France in 1901. The nucleus of the present library is what they left behind when they returned to France in 1922. The total stock of the library is estimated to be at least 45,000 v, but only a *nucleus* of the collection, possibly 5 or 6,000, are rare by our definition and these are not kept as a separate section but interspersed throughout the whole collection. There are very few items estimated to be of such exceptional rarity that they would not be found in libraries where the rare book sections are specifically set aside. The collection is predominantly theological, ecclesiastical history, philosophy, scripture, saints, etc.

Author card cat, not complete.

Ruskin Galleries, Bembridge School, Isle of Wight. Tel (098 387) 2101. Open by appointment for research. Prior application accompanied by a reference from a Ruskin scholar known to the Curator, or from another academic of status is vital. If available and necessary, accommodation can be arranged.

Originally founded by J Howard Whitehouse about 1895, the Ruskin Collection at Bembridge is the world's leading centre for the study of Ruskiniana. It consists of *c*3,000 v, including books by and about Ruskin, and *c*500 from his library. The collection contains almost every book and pamphlet ever printed on the subject of John Ruskin, together with copies of all the books by him in almost every edition in which they were published. The mss collection contains 26 v of Ruskin's diaries, 1835–89; 2,500 letters written by Ruskin to his cousin between 1864 and 1895; 900 letters which passed between Ruskin and his parents, as well as several hundred letters to or from Ruskin and his friends or associates. The collection is added to as a regular policy.

Bulletin of John Rylands Library. 51, no 2, p310-47; 55, no 2, p300-23.

Marlborough

Marlborough College, Marlborough, Wilts SN8 1PA. Open strictly by arrangement with the librarian. Xerox facilities available.

St Mary's Vicar's Library Collected by William White, Head of Magdalen College School, Oxford, 1678. It consists of *c*1,000 v which include 3 incunabula; the remainder are 16th and 17th cent works—prior to 1678. There is a vol of pamphlets by Wynkyn de Worde, and many bear annotations by William White. The collection is on permanent loan to the College.

Card cat.

Petersfield

Bedale's Memorial Library, Bedales School, Petersfield, Hants. Tel (0730) 2970. This is a working school library, but visitors can usually be accommodated by prior arrangement by letter.

The library has been built up by purchases and donations since *c*1900. It contains *c*30,000 v, mainly individual titles, of which there is a designated rare books collection of *c*100 v kept separately, although an unrecorded number of first editions of modern authors, and of pre-1851 items are on the open shelves. The rare books collection contains 4 STC items, including a first edition of Raleigh's *History of the World*, and 4 other 16th cent items, all continental editions of classic authors, including a 1544 edition of *Trebellius Pollio* by Robert Etienne; 9 other 16th cent items; 40 18th cent items (57 v) and *c*20 1800–51, including a first edition of the Bronte sisters' poems; a few books illustrated by Rackham, and miscellaneous association volumes.

Card cat.

Portsmouth

City of Portsmouth Museums and Art Gallery, Museum Road, Portsmouth, Hants PO1 2LJ. Tel (0705) 27261. Access to books to bona fide researchers by prior arrangement by telephone or letter.

Guermonprez Collection The museum has a small working collection of books built up for the use of its staff since 1893. The collection, however, was acquired in 1972 and belonged to H L F Guermonprez (*c*1858–1924), a naturalist/collector who lived in Bognor Regis. There is also material from the library of H Overton, *c*1930, sometime president of the Conchological Society, and J G Turner, *c*1942, a geologist. It comprises *c*500 v, mainly individual titles, covering natural history, including geology, mostly dating from *c*1850–*c*1900 (*c*20 pre-1851 items); many notable for their illustrations, including Perry's *Conchology*, 1811; Montagu's *Testacea Britannica*, 1803; Moquin-Tandon's *Histoire naturelle des mollusques*. . ., 1831; Kirby's *European Butterflies and Moths*, 1889.

Hampshire County Library, Portsmouth Central Library, Guildhall Square, Portsmouth, Hants PO1 2DX. Tel (0705) 819311. Open Mon-Fri 10 am-7 pm; Sat 10 am-4 pm. Admission on written application with reference and proof of identity. Microfilm/fiche readers available; reader/printer; photographs reproduced to order.

Dickens Collection In 1903 Portsmouth Town Council purchased Landport House (where Dickens was born 7 Feb 1812) for £1,125, thus saving it from destruction, and opened it as the Charles Dickens Birthplace Museum. The museum was under the control of successive City Librarians who, over the years, had built up and maintained a comprehensive collection of books and other material about Dickens. The books were transferred from the house to the Central Library in 1967 while the house, items of furniture, letters, portraits, illustrations and pictorial material associated with Dickens were transferred to the care of the City Curator, Museums Department. In 1976 the new Central Library, Guildhall Square, was opened with the Dickens Collection housed on its second floor. There are over 1,000 v in the Collection, including first editions, single copies, plays, poems, speeches, letters, bibliographies, scrapbooks etc. Among works in the original edition wrappers are *Our Mutual Friend*, the six part set of the unfinished novel *The Mystery of Edwin Drood*, and odd numbers of *David Copperfield, Dombey and Son*, and *Little Dorritt*. *c*12 v are pre-1851.

Cat included in the Portsmouth Libraries microfiche cat: will be included in the Hampshire Libraries cat.

Naval History Collection Brought together in the 1950s in response to expressed demand, this important collection totals *c*8,000 v mainly about the Royal and other navies. Especially good for Navy Lists (1783 onwards) and naval periodicals. It includes 2 STC; 8 Wing; *c*40 ESTC and *c*12 pre-1851 items. Both new and secondhand material is added as a regular policy.

The cat is included in the Portsmouth microfiche cat. Separate author and class numbers, print-outs at enquiry desk.

Hampshire County Library, Portsmouth District, The Central Library, Guildhall Square, Portsmouth, Hants PO1 2DX. Tel (0705) 21441/2, 27089 Telex 86382. Open Mon-Fri 10 am-7 pm; Sat 10 am-5 pm. Seats/tables and carrels at all times. Coin-operated photocopiers, 'wet-process' copier. Quality reproductions of prints/drawings/photos on application. Facilities for camera. Microfilm/fiche readers and printer. Facilities for tape-recording.

Local History Library Contains *c*5,600 v dealing with Portsmouth and Hampshire in depth.

Naval History Library Contains *c*5,800 v on all aspects of naval history—mainly Britain.

Charles Dickens Collection This consists of first editions, original parts and collected editions, criticism etc. It includes much non-book material.

Genealogical Collection Includes old peerages and heraldic works, visitations, registers.

Note: No figures are available for pre-1850 material in any of the above collections.

Card cat and computer output microfilm or printout.

Portsmouth Polytechnic Central Library, Cambridge Road, Portsmouth, Hants PO1 2ST. Tel (0705) 2768. Open, Term: Mon-Thurs 9 am-10 pm, Fri 9 am-9 pm, Sat 9 am-5.30 pm, Sun 2-5 pm. Vacation: (public holidays excepted) Mon-Fri 9 am-5 pm. Admission to bona fide members of the public for reference purposes on application in writing to the librarian. Photocopiers, microform readers.

Bolton Collection Takes its name from A T Bolton, one time Curator of the RIBA Library, and whose son sold it to the Portsmouth Polytechnic Central Library. It contains *c*300 v, mainly of old architecture books, and includes one 17th cent and several 18th cent items.

Note Most of the collection is located in the School of Architecture, and the hours of access may not be as wide as indicated above.

Cat in the Polytechnic Library's general cat.

Royal Marines Museum Library, Royal Marines Barracks, Eastney, Portsmouth, Hants PO4 9PX. Tel (0705) 22351, Ext 6186. Open (Museum) Mon-Fri 10 am-4.30 pm, Sat, Sun 10 am-12.30 pm. Admission to Library/Archives, by prior appointment by letter or telephone.

Royal Marines Museum Reference Library In 1963 it became necessary to establish a reference library for the use of the Royal Marines Historian and Museum Curator. A certain amount of money was made available for the purchase of books by the Commandant General Royal Marines, supplemented by gifts from individuals. In 1965 a number of military and naval reference books were transferred to the museum from the Royal Marines Officers' Mess Library at Plymouth to be followed by the transfer of similar books from the Depot Royal Marines Library in 1967/8. Meanwhile the Commandant General's grant continued, which, together with the sale of unwanted books, provided the basis for further purchases. More recently the museum has been able to provide funds from its Ministry of Defence grant for the purchase of, in particular, antiquarian books, and additional assistance has been provided from the Education Branch of the Ministry of Defence. Over and above the purchases, books are occasionally received as a direct donation or from bequests. The library contains *c*9,000 v, mainly individual titles by and about Royal Marines; associated naval and military history; particularly strong on biographical works and sources, and on contemporary accounts of campaigns and battles; various other research material, eg Admiralty Orders in Council 1663–; Navy Lists 1805–; *c*300 pre-1851 items (earliest is 1707); special rarities include John Clarke's *An impartial and authentic narrative of the battle fought...on Bunker's Hill...1775; A narrative of the* *operation of a small British force under the command of Brigadier-General Sir Samuel Auchmuty employed in the reduction of Montevideo on the River Plate AD 1807.* 1807.

At the time of writing (1981) sufficient funds are available to obtain nearly all relevant material. The museum also contains the archives of the Royal Marines Corps, and some 10,000 photographs, both collections indexed in the same way as the printed material.

Subject index to home-made classification scheme.

Royal Naval Museum, HM Naval Base, Portsmouth, Hants. Tel (0705) 22351 Ext 23868/9. Open Summer, Mon-Sat 10.30 am-5 pm, Sun 1.30-5 pm. (Seasonal variations). Admission to Library/ Archives by prior appointment by letter or telephone. Photocopier available.

Royal Naval Museum Mostly built up since 1970 by regular purchase and a few substantial private donations. It contains over 4,000 v, mostly individual titles; *c*100 pre-1851 items. The collection is devoted to naval matters; strong on 18th and 19th cent naval history and on 19th cent naval biography. Related research material includes *Illustrated London News* (complete to 1900) and *London Gazette* (complete). An associated collection of archival material strong on social and administrative history of the Royal Navy in the 19th cent.

Card cat.

Romsey

Mottisfort Abbey, Romsey, Hants SO5 OLP. Tel (0794) 278. Admission on personal application. Xerox, photography, study desks available.

Mottisfort Library Formed by its present owners, Mrs B M and Mr J P Cavanagh, and includes *c*25,000 photographs, prints, etc. The emphasis is on the history of the theatre, in all languages and relating to all times and places, including ballet and opera. Not classified, but shelved in broad subject groups. Aimed at the postgraduate researcher.

Card cat. Author index only.

Salisbury

Salisbury Cathedral, Salisbury, Wilts SP1 2EN. Admission by arrangement with the librarian.

Salisbury Cathedral Library Total stock *c*10,000 v which include 35 incunabula. The library includes: *Bishop Seth Ward's Collection* of 17th cent science; *Bishop Guest's Collection* of the works of Protestant reformers; *Izaak Walton's Collection* (34 v); *Dean Hamilton's* bequest of 1880 (*c*1,009 v), and later gifts and bequests.

Printed cat of 1880.

E A Read, 'The Cathedral libraries of England, 1970', *Oxford Bibliog Soc Occasional publication* no 6.

Selborne

Oates Memorial Library and the Gilbert White Museum, The Wakes, Selborne, Alton, Hants GU34 3JH. Tel (042 050) 275. Open 12 noon-5.30 pm. Research facilities, photocopying, microfilms etc.

Natural History Collection This includes the Gilbert White material and consists of *c*3,000 v, mainly 18th and 19th cent material on natural history.

Oates Family Archives and Thomas Holt White Papers Both were collected by Robert Washington Oates 1930–55. There are 750 v, mostly late 19th and early 20th cent, including a few Titus Oates material (Wing items).

Southampton

Hampshire County Library, Southampton Central Library, Civic Centre, Southampton S09 4XP. Tel (0703) 23855. Open Mon-Fri 10 am-7 pm; Sat 10 am-4 pm. The Public Library is open to all, but admission to special collections strictly on application to the librarian. Photocopying facilities available (only under special circumstances in Local History Library). Study facilities available in Reference Library and Local History Library.

Maritime Collection Collected since the establishment of the Public Library in 1888, this collection totals *c*3,000 v. Subject content has main emphasis on merchant ships and shipping, including naval material and items on small boats (ie yachts etc). Strength lies with ships and shipping lines (and shipbuilders) with some connection with Southampton. Special collection on the SS Titanic. Largely printed books, pamphlets and periodicals, but also some unpublished material, plus printed ephemera.

Printed 'Catalogue of the Maritime Collection', 1981.

Pitt Collection A library formed from a combination of the books of three men: William Molyneux (1656–98), Samuel Molyneux (1689–1728), and Nathaniel St Andre (1680–1776). It was given by George Frederick Pitt to the Mayor, Bailiffs and Burgesses of Southampton on 29 September 1831. A substantial part of the original Molyneux/St Andre Library was sold in 1818 to the Royal College of Surgeons (books on medicine and surgery). The Pitt Collection is the remainder. With the library came a large number of William Molyneux's manuscripts, including the *Proceedings of the Dublin Philosophical Society*, and these are now in the hands of the Southampton City Archivist. The library contains 1,100 v and is strong in astronomy, mathematics and physics; it also reflects Molyneux's political and economic interest, especially in Ireland. Gives an insight into the cultural background of a 17th cent scholar. Includes a copy of Basilius Besler *Hortus Eystettensis*, Nuremburg, 1613.

Printed 'Catalogue of the Pitt Collection'.

K T Hoppen, *The common scientist in the seventeenth century*. 1970.

King Edward VI School, Southampton. Tel (0703) 774561. Open by arrangement.

Select Library A late 17th-cent Grammar School Foundation Library containing *c*700 v on various subjects; some classical and local history strength. It includes Isaac Watts collection. There are *c*100 STC and Wing items.

Card and book cat.

La Sainte Union College of Higher Education, The Avenue, Southampton, Hants S09 5HB. Tel (0703) 28761 Ext 246. Open Mon-Fri 8.45 am-8.45 pm. Vacation 9 am-5 pm. *Reference only* for members of the public. Photocopying, microfiche and microfilm reading facilities available.

La Sainte Union College of Higher Education Rare Book Collection The College was founded in 1905 and the library in its present form originated in 1960, and includes several items from the Canon O'Mahoney Collection. The volumes total 24 and relate to Catholic theology and children's literature. A notable item is the first edition of Sir Thomas More's *Workers*, 1557.

Card cat.

Southampton University Library, Highfield, Southampton, Hants. Tel (0703) 559122. Open Mon-Fri 9 am-10 pm; Sat 9 am-5 pm; Sun 3-6 pm. Photocopying, microfilm, tape/slide, calculators.

Main Library The General University Collection comprises *c*480,000 v, which include 5 incunabula, 150+ STC, 500+ Wing; special authors collected include Dante, George Orwell, J B Priestley.

Card cat by author.

Cope Collection Nucleus bequeathed in 1890s by the Rev Sir William Cope, Bart, and includes *c*7,000 v and 2,500 maps and prints which cover almost everything available on Hampshire and the Isle of Wight.

Author cat, classified and subject index. Recently catalogued items in computer and available for print-out.

Card cat.

Hartley Collection Bequeathed by Henry Robinson Hartley in 1850, it contains *c*500 v and represents the surviving volumes of the original Hartley Institution Collection. They are mainly 17th and 18th cent, and early 19th cent items.

In main library card cat. Author, classified and subject index.

Parkes Library Donated by the Rev Dr J W Parkes in 1964, comprising *c*9,000 v, and many transcripts and press cuttings etc, all relating to relationships between Jews and non-Jews at all times and places. It contains 3 incunabula, some early, many rare.

Author, classified and subject index.

Perkins Agricultural Library Bequeathed as a lending collection by Walter Frank Perkins, containing *c*2,100 titles and comprising books by British and Irish authors on British and Irish agriculture from earliest times to 1900.

Main library card cat. Author, classified and subject index.

Sheaf (author and classified).

Printed.

Warminster

Longleat House, Warminster, Wilts BA12 7NN. Tel (09853) 551. Admission by prior arrangement. Microfiche reader and photocopying facilities.

Longleat Library Collected by successive members of the Thynne family since 1500, the library comprises 39,000 v; 10,000 tracts; papers and mss. It includes 150-200 incunabula (including 12 Caxtons). The collection is strong in early heraldry and law; early travels; atlases; medicine; gardening; 17th cent theology; contemporary works on the French Revolution; 18th and 19th cent natural history and county history; late 19th-early 20th cent children's books; Churchilliana and Hitleriana. The library also contains the Botfield Collection of books and mss. Some duplicate copies were sold at Sotheby's in 1979.

Working author cat.

Mss only. HMC, 58.

Winchester

Fellows' Library, Winchester College, Winchester, Hants SO23 9NA. Tel (0962) 64242 Ext 37. Open Mon-Fri by appointment only. Photocopying facilities.

Fellows' Library The collection dates from the founding of the College by William Wykeham and contains *c*25,000 v covering religion, divinity, literature, classics, geography, road-books; many STC items and *c*50 incunabula.

Card cat.

Booklets by W F Oakeshott and J M G Blakiston.

Hampshire County Museum Service, Chilcomb House, Chilcomb Lane, Bar End, Winchester, Hants SO23 8RD. Tel (0962) 66242/3. Admission by appointment only on application to librarian. Photocopying available.

Library of the Hampshire County Museum Service Consists of books brought from Curtis Museum and Allen Gallery, Alton; Willis Museum and Art Gallery,

Basingstoke; Red House Museum and Art Gallery, Christchurch. Total library stock c2,500 v, of which 50 may be classed as rare (incl mss). Subjects covered include natural history, entomology, practical agriculture, husbandry. Of special interest are: (i) F M Halford, *Dry fly entomology*, 2 v, 1897, incl 100 specimens of floating fly. This is no 68 of 100 copies only; (ii) Early eds of Gilbert White's *Natural history of Selborne*; (iii) Early eds of William Cobbett MP, incl *Rural rides*. Autograph letters, press cuttings and portraits written between 1801 and 1832; (iv) William Curtin, FLS, *Flora Londinensis*, 6 v 1777 and mss—6 v of lectures, notes of experiments, drawings, letters.

No cat. (The Library is still (1984) in the process of being sorted and organized.)

Winchester District Library, Jewry Street, Winchester, Hants. Tel (0962) 3909. Open Mon-Fri 9.30 am-7 pm, Sat 9.30 am-5 pm. Photocopying.

The Local History Collection The collection has been run down as part of reorganization, but some items in it date from the 1840s when the Jewry Street building was also Winchester Museum. There are no incunabula but 2 STC and 17 Wing items. Strong on local history.

Card cat.

Hereford and Worcester

Broadway

Snowshill Manor (National Trust), Broadway, Worcestershire WR12 7JU. Tel (0386) 852410. Open April and Oct Sats and Suns 11 am-1 pm, 2-6 pm; May to Sept Wed-Sun (incl) 11 am-1 pm, 2-6 pm. Admission for researchers by arrangement with the Libraries Adviser, National Trust, 42 Queen Anne's Gate, London SW1H 9AS.

Wade Collection The books were collected by Mr Charles Wade, the original owner of the house, between 1900 and 1950, and given to the National Trust in 1951. They total c300 v and include works by old Greek and Latin authors of the 16th and 17th cent; Bibles and sermons; 17th cent popery etc. Three items from the collection are on loan to the Bodleian Library.

Cat in progress.

Evesham

Hereford and Worcester County Council Evesham Library, Market Place, Evesham, Worcs WR11 4RW. Tel (0386) 2291. Open Mon, Tues, Thurs, Fri 9 am-5.30 pm; Sat 9 am-4 pm. Admission unrestricted. Photocopying facilities and microfilm/fiche reader are available.

Barnard Collection Originally belonged to Etwall Augustine Bracker Barnard (*d*1953), a noted local historian who bequeathed it to Evesham Public Library. The collection consists of c180 items of newspaper cuttings, being articles on the history of Evesham and district which appeared in the *Evesham Journal*, and written by Mr Barnard from 1906–52, as well as a useful collection of photographs and other documents.

Local History Collection It consists of c600 books, pamphlets, directories, almanacs and photographs, mainly relating to the history of Evesham. Of particular interest are *Chronicon Abbatiae de Evesham ad annum 1418*, Ed William Dunn Macray, 1863; Samuel Ireland, *Picturesque views of the upper or Warwickshire Avon*, 1795; and T Nash, *Collections for the history of Worcestershire* (2 v and an index) 1799. The library also possesses a collection of some 200 glass negatives of Evesham and district collected by Arthur Ward, journalist, on the *Evesham Journal*, about the turn of the century.

Sheaf cat of 1974; post-1974 cat on County Microfiche Cat.

Hereford

All Saints Church, Hereford. The Vicarage, 9 South Bank Road, Hereford. Tel (0432) 2715. Open by written or telephone application to the Vicar.

All Saints Parish (Chained) Library was left to the Vicar and parishioners by William Brewster, MD (1655–1715), being the residue of his library after (according to his wishes) St John's College, Oxford, and the Bodleian Library had taken such volumes as they needed for their own stock. It contains 267 v, including bound volumes of pamphlets—a chained library in accordance with the terms of Dr Brewster's will—and are substantially works of religion and morality, but including works of history and travel. 44 items listed in STC, and 336 in Wing.

Detailed cat, with indices (in typescript) by F C Morgan, FLA, FSA (1963).

William Blades, *Books in chains*, 1890 (includes list of books at All Saints in appendix).

F C Morgan, 'Dr William Brewster of Hereford', *Medical History*, 8 (2), 1964, p137-48.

Hereford Cathedral Library, The Cathedral, Hereford HR1 2NG. Tel (0432) 58403. (Hon Librarian (0432) 3537.) Open Tues, Wed, Thurs 10 am-

12.30 pm; at other times by appointment only. Admission free for students and research.

The Cathedral Library The earliest volume has been in the possession of the Cathedral since before the Norman Conquest, and the collection has been added to through the ages largely by gifts and bequests. It comprises *c*11,000 works in *c*10,000 v, including 227 mss (chained) dating from the 8th cent, *c*1,230 chained printed books (in cases dating from 1611) which include 56 incunabula; *c*167 v printed 1500–50; *c*500 1551–1600; *c*1,530 1601–1700; and *c*800 v 1701–1800. Subject content is mainly theological, religious history and general history, some music, chiefly religious, including 56 mss dating 17th-20th cent. There is a collection of Jesuit books from the suppressed monastery at Cwm, and 3 albums of rubbings of all tooled bindings with identification.

Author cat of all printed books, with subject index (on cards); index of printers, publishers, donors etc, with a shelflist of all books in the upper transept and upper cloister libraries, and of early books shelved in the lower library (typescript). Descriptive cat and index of tooled bindings, with three albums of rubbings (typescript).

G Bill, 'Christ Church and Hereford cathedral libraries and the Bodleian'. In *Bodleian Library Record* IV, (3) 1952.

G Bowen, 'Jesuit library in Hereford cathedral'. In *Assoc of British Theological libraries bulletin*, (20), p13-24 and (21) p17-27, 1965.

B G Charles and H D Emanuel, 'Notes on old libraries and books'. In *National Library of Wales Journal*, VI (4), 1950.

Neil R Ker, *Medieval libraries of Great Britain: a list of surviving books*, 2nd ed, 1964.

F C Morgan, 'The Vicars choral library, Hereford'. In *Woolhope Club Transactions*, 1957 (includes a transcript of the donors' book). (op)

F C Morgan and C Penelope. *Hereford cathedral libraries (including the chained library and the vicars choral library) and muniments. Illus.* 2nd ed, 1975.

B H Streeter. *The Chained Library*. 1931 (op)

Lady Hawkins School Library, Kington Deposited by the Governors of the school on permanent loan with Hereford Cathedral Library. The school was founded in 1632 under the will of Dame Margaret Hawkins (née Vaughan), widow of Sir John Hawkins, and the books added by gift and purchase from that date until the 19th cent. The library comprises 397 books in 249 v (printed), and 1 ms and 5 v and 7 items of archives relating to the school. Printed books include 1 incunabulum; 7 v 1501–50; 25 v 1551–99; 78 v 1600–40; 156 v 1641–1700; 86 v 1701–49 and 44 v 1750–99. These include 33 (+ 2 fragments of end-papers and one end-paper not recorded) STC items, and 140 + 3 not recorded (6 in new ed of Wing) Wing items. Chiefly theological in scope, the collection includes some school books.

Typescript cat (alphabetical).

Hereford Library (Hereford and Worcester County Council), Broad Street, Hereford HR4 9AU. Tel (0432) 2456 & 68645. Open Tues, Wed 9.30 am-6 pm, Thurs 9.30 am-5 pm, Fri 9.30 am-8 pm, Sat 9.30 am-4 pm. Admission free to the public during hours of opening. Microfilm/fiche reader; coin operated photocopying machine.

Reference Library & Local Collection The library, founded 1871, includes many volumes from the Hereford Permanent Library (1815–1900). Most important bequest was by Walter Pilley, Mayor of Hereford (*d*1913). Smaller personal collections from Alfred Watkins (*d*1935), H E Durham, Michael and Madeleine Hopton, and W S Brassington. Of 28,000 separate works, in 25,000 v, *c*4,000 may be classed as rare. These are strong in local history; other main subjects being cider, apple and pear culture, beekeeping, agriculture and rural life, visual arts.

Author, subject (classified) card cat. Published cats: *Catalogue of books in the Reference Dept*, 1882 and 1901.

William Collins, 'The history of the Public Library and Museum', *An Echo from the City of Hereford*, no 1, March 1909.

T G Porter and J F W Sherwood, *Hereford Public Library: the first hundred years*, 1971 (unpublished typescript).

Kidderminster

Hereford and Worcester County Council, Kidderminster Public Library, Market Street, Kidderminster, Worcs. Tel (0562) 62832. Open Mon and Fri 9.30 am-5.30 pm, Tues and Thurs 9.30 am-7 pm; Sat 9.30 am-4 pm. Photocopying service.

The Library houses two special collections, with an unknown number of pre-1851 items, namely (a) *Kidderminster and surrounding area local collection*; (b) *Carpet and textile collection* which is extensive and comprehensive, including foreign works.

Author cat of carpet collection (Published: restricted circulation).

Local collection cat.

The Hurd Library, The Bishop's House, Hartlebury Castle, Kidderminster, Worcs. Enquiries *via* BUL: 021-472 1301 Ext 2439. Open by arrangement only *via* the Librarian, Birmingham University Library, to whom written application should be made well in advance of visit. Photocopying by Birmingham University in conjunction with the librarian of Hurd Library.

The Hurd Library An 18th cent library collected by Richard Hurd, Bishop of Worcester (1781–1808) incorporating items from the libraries of Alexander Pope, Ralph Allen and William Warburton. It comprises *c*3,000 titles in *c*5,000 v of predominantly 18th cent publications, with emphasis on Greek, Latin and orthodox English literature. Strong religious content, with history, biography and travel well represented. Contains 1 incunabulum (*Legenda Aurea*, Lyons, 1476), 78 STC items, and 227 Wing items. 42 books are positively identifiable as Pope's, and *c*100 titles were certainly given by George III. There are 22 folders of ms letters etc. The collection essentially survives as in Hurd's day, although some volumes have 'strayed'. Ms versions of catalogue from 1783, 1789, 1819, 1844 and 1909. Typescript modern version now in preparation.

E H Pearce, *Hartlebury Castle*, London, 1926.

Kington

Lady Hawkins School Library, Kington, Hereford, deposited with Hereford Cathedral, 1978. (qv)

Leominster

Leominster Public Library, South Street, Leominster, Hereford. Tel (0568) 2384. Open Tues-Sat 10 am-5 pm. Admission free. Reference library only. No reproduction facilities.

Friends Meeting Library 1689–1969 A collection of 191 books deposited by the Leominster Friends' Meeting House in 1971. This small collection is particularly strong in lives of Quakers, mainly over the previous 100 years. *c*24 works are pre-1850. The Leominster Friends Meeting dates back to before 1656.

Abbreviated typed list of books in the collection.

Tenbury Wells

St Michael's College (a preparatory school, not an institution of higher education), Tenbury Wells, Worcs WR15 8PH. Admission by appointment only, after preliminary letter addressed to the College.

The Library of St Michael's College Formed by the Founder of St Michael's College, Sir Frederick Onseley (*d*1889). (*NB* Not 'Sir Frederick Gore Onseley'). Number of printed items *c*2,000 v and *c*1,400 mss. These comprise a collection of musical source materials, printed and ms, but including no medieval items. Its scope is miscellaneous. The most famous item is Handel's conducting score of *Messiah*, now published in facsimile by Scolar Press Ltd. The collection includes 3 incunabula. The mss have been placed on deposit in the Bodleian Library, Oxford.

All printed materials prior to 1800 are listed in the *British Union Catalogue of Early Music*, and in *Repertoire Internationale des Sources Musicales* (in progress). Printed material catalogued in card form.

E H Fellowes, *The Catalogue of Manuscripts in the Library of St Michael's College, Tenbury*, Paris, 1934.

Worcester

Stanbrook Abbey, Callow End, Worcester WR2 4TD. Tel (0905) 830209. The Library is open by appointment, but as it is within monastic enclosure, there is no direct access for visitors. Books can be fetched for consultation in parlour to *bona fide* scholars.

The rare book collection numbers about 900 v, dating from 1538. It belonged to a community of English Benedictine nuns who founded Cambai, 1623; imprisoned during the French Revolution, but returned to England in 1796. Some of the books were recovered, others collected or received as gifts. STC catalogue being compiled in author, subject, chronological sequence and provenance.

There are four medieval mss and later mss of personal character; Breviaries; Recusancy Press volumes, including some privately printed, and probably very rare editions not found in UK, with evidence of owners and sources. The collection is augmented only by donations. *See* Neil Ker on 'Middle English Mss' in *Medium Aevum* XXXIV, 3 (1965).

Worcester Cathedral, c/o 8 College Precincts, Worcester. Enquiries *via* Birmingham University Library. Tel (021) 472 1301 Ext 2439. Professional assistance given to the librarian by Birmingham University Library staff. The library is open by arrangement with the Librarian to *bona fide* research workers who must send in advance a written application enclosing a letter of introduction. Photocopying by Birmingham University Library by arrangement with the Cathedral Librarian.

Worcester Cathedral Library Comprises the collection of the medieval Cathedral Priory continued by the collection of the Dean and Chapter since the Reformation, and includes *c*9,500 printed books, of which *c*8,500 are pre-1800 and relate mainly to theology, church history and classics. There are 41 incunabula and a large number of early printed books which are in fine early bindings (*see* an unpublished catalogue by D W Evans housed in the Library). The core of the printed books collection is the library of Bishop John Prideaux (consecrated Bishop in 1641). There is also a collection of manuscripts and printed music, mainly connected with the Worcester sequence of the Three Choirs Festival.

J K Floyer and S G Hamilton, *Catalogue of manuscripts preserved in the Chapter Library of Worcester Cathedral*. Worcester Historical Society, 1906.

C Gordon, *Worcester Cathedral Library incunabula*, Cambridge 1910.

M Day, *A catalogue of the printed books in the Worcester Cathedral Library*, Oxford, 1880.

Worcester City Library, Foregate Street, Worcester

WR1 1DT. Tel (0905) 22154, 24853. Open Mon, Tues, Thurs 9.30 am-1 pm, 2-5.30 pm, Fri 9.30 am-1 pm, 2-8 pm; Sat 9.30 am-4 pm. Open to the public—material available on request; some items by appointment. Microfilm reader, photocopier available.

Willis Bund Collection Personal collection of J W Willis Bund (*d*1928), housed in library for reference only. It contains 3,774 v, plus 515 Bibles. Chiefly on Worcestershire history, but also general items on English and Welsh history. Family ms. About half the collection is pre-1851.

Sheaf cat.

Archaeological Society Library A collection of 2,212 v, being the library of Worcestershire Archaeological Society housed in the Library for reference only. It comprises books and periodicals of historical, architectural and archaeological interest, with emphasis on Worcestershire. *c*1,000 v pre-1851.

Printed cat 1966.

Stuart Collection A collection of books covering the reigns of the Stuart monarchs, originally a donation, built up from existing stock and added to up to 1964. It comprises *c*1,593 v (of which *c*700 v are pre-1851) and collections of tracts.

Sheaf cat.

General Library Stock The present City Library was opened in 1881, acquiring assets of Worcester City and County Libraries, and some of the assets of the Worcester Natural History Society. It contains 16,314 v and is a large and varied collection of public library acquisitions; many pre-1851; some first editions, Dickens etc. Many v are in poor condition.

Printed cat for stock received between 1879–86, but is inaccurate. Remainder listed in sheaf cat.

Local Studies Library Built up from general library stock and specific additions since foundation of library in 1881. Reorganized since 1964. It contains 7,807 v of books and pamphlets, chiefly on the old county of Worcestershire, but especially strong on the City of Worcester. Microfilms of local newspapers, particularly the *Berrows Journal* from 1712. About one quarter of the collection satisfies the criteria laid down by the Rare Books Group.

Sheaf and card cat.

Hertfordshire

Berkhamsted

Berkhamsted School (Library), Castle Street, Berkhamsted, Herts. Tel (04427) 3961. Open by arrangement with the librarian after written application.

Berkhamsted School Library The School, founded as King Edward VI Grammar School, 1541, was greatly enlarged in the late 19th cent. The rare books in the library were given mostly by old boys in recent decades, and total *c*150 v (1 STC item). They are a mixed selection of classics and of English and European literature. Some historical works and school magazine belong to the period 1880 onwards. Signed presentation copies (*c*45 v) of works of Graham Greene (old Berkhamstedian and son of former headmaster) form part of the collection.

Author and title card index (incomplete).

Elstree

Aldenham School (Library), Elstree, Herts WD6 3AJ. Tel (092 76) 6131. Open by appointment with the librarian for serious research work only.

Aldenham School Library The School was founded in 1597 with endowment administered by Brewers Company, London. It was reorganised and enlarged in 1875, and the library was built up after that date from a diverse collection of books acquired by gift and bequest from old boys, mainly through the encouragement of Cecil A Stott, Librarian 1924–67. The library contains *c*350 v, of which *c*180 v form a special collection, and these include 1 incunabulum, 4 STC, 13 Wing, and 10 foreign 16th cent items, together with diverse works of 18th cent English literature. The main library stock includes *c*170 v, principally standard texts in history, classics and English, and foreign literature of 18th and 19th cent. The collection is occasionally augmented by donation.

Card cat (not comprehensive) of authors and subjects.

Haileybury

Haileybury and Imperial Service College, Haileybury College, Hertford SG13 7NU. Tel (099 24) 64430. Open by appointment with the librarian to academic researchers only. Research facilities and services.

Haileybury College Library The library has grown since the foundation of Haileybury College, 1862. School buildings erected 1809 for East India College (founded 1806 for training East India Co's administrators). The East India College closed in 1858 and its library removed to the India Office, London. However, a few books and records have been returned (see below). The Imperial Service College amalgamated with Haileybury in 1943 but did not contribute any books to the library. The books total c2,140 v (including periodicals: 275 v, and Delphin and Tauchnitz classics: c400 v) including 5 STC and 29 Wing. The subjects covered are classics, theology, English and European literature—the great majority being of early 19th cent. Small collection of letters and records of East India College, including minutes, etc of Wellesley Club, 1844–57 (2 v); *Haileybury Observer* (East India College magazine) 1842–57. In 1872 the India Board donated c197 v from the former College Library: about 65 v are now identifiable from library stamp, binding or inscription.

Author and subject cats. Printed cat 1891.

Some dispersal has taken place but no records kept. Occasional sales will continue.

Harpenden

Rothamsted Experimental Station (Library), Harpenden, Herts AL5 2JQ. Tel (058 27) 63133. Open Mon-Fri 9 am-5 pm. Admission by written appointment for serious research only. Photocopying facilities.

Rothamsted Experimental Station Library The Experimental Station is the oldest, and one of the largest, agricultural research stations in the world. Various experiments were carried out as early as 1843 on the estate of J B Lawes who was assisted by the chemist J H Gilbert. Several of the 'classical experiments' are still continuing under the aegis of the Lawes Agricultural Trust.

The library was formed largely by Sir John Russell, Director of the Station 1912–43. The books were acquired from a diversity of sources, mainly by purchase. Works in English total c2,500 v with 175 STC and 209 Wing items. Foreign books number c1,020 v and include 14 incunabula, 171 16th cent, 117 17th cent, 420 18th cent and 197 19th cent works. Together they form an important collection covering all aspects of agriculture.

The ms collection (less than 50 v) include a 14th cent text of Walter of Henley's *Treatise of Husbandry*, records of Rothamsted's 'classical experiments' since 1843, and papers of Sir J B Lawes and Sir J H Gilbert.

The collection of early agricultural books forms a small part of the stock of the Rothamsted Experimental Station Library which exists primarily to cater for current research work.

Author and subject card cats.

M S Aslin (ed), *Rothamsted Experimental Station, Harpenden. Library catalogue of printed books and pamphlets on agriculture published between 1471 and 1840.* 2nd ed 1940, p294 (op). *Supplement* 1949 p15 (op).

Prints Collection Contains prints purchased by Sir John Russell and an important collection bequeathed by Francis, 4th Baron Northbrook (1882–1947). Totalling c1,000, the prints are of British farm animals (principally cattle), dating mainly from the period 1790–1845. Occasional donations are added to the collection.

D H Boalch, *Prints and paintings of British farm livestock 1780–1910. A record of the Rothamsted Collection*, 1958. pxxvi, 127. (op)

Hatfield

Hatfield House Library, Hatfield House, Hatfield, Herts. Admission by written application to the librarian. Photocopying facilities.

The collection was formed by William Cecil, Lord Burghley (1520–98) and his second son, Robert Cecil, 1st Earl of Salisbury (1563–1612), and added to by successive generations of the family. Lord Burghley's principal library seems to have been at Burghley House in the Strand, Westminster, and was largely bequeathed to his elder son Thomas, later Earl of Exeter, although Robert received some legal and political works from there. Robert Cecil's books were kept at Salisbury House in the Strand and were probably not moved to Hatfield House until the beginning of the 18th cent.

It includes c8,000 v (incl pamphlets) in the Main Library and Book Room (40 incunabula, 423 STC, 284 Wing, 1,192 foreign books of 16th-17th cent). Main subjects are theology, classics, history and travel with several pre-1600 atlases. Tracts acquired by Lord Burghley and Robert Cecil comprise 378 pieces (incl 120 STC) in 68 v. Tracts are mainly concerned with British and continental politics and religious questions, particularly with France (1551–1612) and Netherlands (1568–91). Uncatalogued collection (c1,500 v) of French 18th cent literature and works on French Revolution, especially of Marat. Ownership inscriptions, armorial bindings, etc of Lord Burghley (175 v), Mildred Lady Burghley (14 v), Robert Cecil (52 v, though many others identifiable as his), and Roger Ascham (8 v). Great majority of books rebound by Joseph Pomfret in 1712, but c120 v (not including plain vellum) retain earlier bindings. The very important collection of mss, maps and state papers has been calendared by the Historical Manuscripts Commission.

(For further information about Lord Burghley's books, see under Burghley House.)

Marquess of Salisbury, 'The library at Hatfield House, Hertfordshire', *The Library*, 5th ser., v 18, 1963, p83-7.

H M C *Calendar of the manuscripts of the Marquess of Salisbury preserved at Hatfield House, Hertfordshire.* Pts 1-24 (1883–1976).

Hertford

Hertford Museum, 18 Bull Plain, Hertford SG14 1DT. Tel (0992) 52686. Open Mon-Sat 11 am-5 pm (March-Oct), 11 am-4 pm (Nov-Feb). Admission unrestricted. Photocopying facilities.

Hertford Museum Collection (incorporating some books and mss belonging to the East Herts Archaeological Society). The Museum was founded by the brothers Robert T Andrews (1838–1928) and William F Andrews (1838–1918). A private collection was opened to the public in 1902, and moved to the present premises in 1914. Herbert C Andrews (1874–1947), son of R T

Andrews, was Director 1928–47. Ownership transferred by the Andrews family to Museum Trust, which in 1948 was vested in Hertford Borough Council (Hertford Town Council since 1974). The nucleus of the book and ms collection formed by Andrews family, which has been much added to by other donors, including East Herts Archaeological Society.

The books total *c*590 v (including some periodicals) with 8 STC items. The principal subjects include Hertford and Herts, topography, genealogy, geology, natural history and literature by Herts authors. Outstanding collection of local election placards, 1825–68 (4 giant folios and 3 boxes), local newspapers (*Reformer* 1834–37, *County Press* 1832–34) and large vol containing pasted-in printed poems and Hertford bills and trade notices, *c*1780–1851. Fragment (2 leaves) of J de Voragine: *Golden legend*, W de Worde, 1498. Mss holdings include:

R T Andrews Collection Herts topographical and antiquarian notes (30 box files).

W F Andrews Collection Herts topographical prints, postcards, newscuttings, photographs, etc (16 box drawers, 13 boxes and 12 giant portfolios).

H C Andrews Collection Herts topographical and antiquarian notes, incl many draft articles (50 box files).

James Wilcox Collection English topographical sketches and watercolours by J Wilcox (1778–1861) of Much Hormead, Herts (11 v).

Newall Collection English topographical sketches by C A, H A and R A Newall, 1806–50 (10 v).

A Whitford Anderson Collection Architectural plans of Herts churches and houses prepared for *Victoria County History*, *c*1905 (1 giant portfolio).

Wigginton Collection Papers of Wigginton family of Hertford, kept together with 20th cent correspondence files of Herts Regiment of Militia (about 40 boxes).

Miscellaneous Unclassified mss, mostly of Herts local historical interest, and some sketch books, *c*1550–20th cent, *c*100 items).

Herts sale particulars, late 19th-early 20th cent.

Hertfordshire Library Service, County Hall, Hertford SG13 8EJ. Tel (0992) 54242 Ext 5486. Open Mon-Thurs 9 am-5 pm, Fri 9 am-4.30 pm. Admission free. Photocopying facilities.

Herts Local Studies Collection The County Library was formed in 1926. A Local Studies Librarian was appointed 1974, and the collection has been acquired mainly by purchase. It includes *c*240 v pre-1851, with 30 Wing items. They refer to Hertford local history, topography, Parliamentary Acts, works of local poets, etc. Earlier books are mainly Herts sermons. There is a pamphlets collection contained in 40 filing cabinet drawers.

Author and subject card index.

Junior Fiction Special Collection Mainly acquired by purchase since *c*1947, with occasional donations, the collection totals *c*5,000 v, of which *c*150 are pre-1851. The collection is added to regularly.

Card index of authors pre-1870.

Hertfordshire Record Office (Library), County Hall, Hertford SG13 8DE. Tel (0992) 54242 Ext 412. Open Mon-Thurs 9.15 am-5.15 pm, Fri 9.15 am-4.30 pm. Admission by prior appointment preferred. Photocopying and microfilming facilities.

Record Office Reference Library The Herts County Records Committee was formed in 1895, and the public search room opened in the County Hall 1939. The pre-1851 books number *c*300 v, including 2 STC and 33 Wing items. Pre-1851 periodicals etc total *c*465 v. The collection covers Hertfordshire local history, sermons and biographies, law books and dictionaries. It includes authors' own copies of principal Herts county histories, and 40 v (pre-1851) formerly belonging to Hitchin historian R L Hine (1883–1949). Also W B Gerish's collection of Herts topographical newscuttings, prints, etc (87 boxes). Many mss collections contain individual printed items.

Card index: author, subject and parish.

St Albans

Cathedral and Abbey Church of St Albans (Library), St Albans, Herts. Tel (0727) 61744 (Librarian). Open by written appointment with the librarian.

St Albans Cathedral Library (otherwise known as the Hudson Memorial Library). There was a Clerical Lending Library in St Albans Abbey in 1870. The St Albans diocese was founded 1877, since when numerous donations have been received. The library is endowed in memory of Canon C E Hudson, 1965, and now exists primarily as a modern working and lending library for the clergy and lay-workers of the diocese. It contains 470 v, comprising 11 STC; 31 Wing; 3 16th cent foreign; 33 17th cent foreign; 175 18th cent; 217 early 19th cent. The pre-1851 works form only a small proportion of the present Cathedral Library. Essentially a theological library, it is mainly composed of works of the church Fathers, sermons, visitation charges, books on church history and ritual. Section on St Albans Abbey includes: J Neale, *The Abbey Church of St Albans*, 1878, with annotations by 1st Lord Grimthorpe, restorer of the Abbey. Many of the books have the bookplate of T L Claughton, 1st Bishop of St Albans (1877–90). About 100 v (unlisted) were sold to Abingdon Press, 1977. The mss include a 15th cent book of devotions in English; illuminated monastic office book (2 v); notes on Pridmore collection of Herts views, *c*1900 (3 v) by H R Wilton Hall; transcripts of papers concerning the cathedral,

1884–1910, and *Cathedral Chronicle*, 1914–20 (5 v).
Card cat of authors and subjects.

City Museum, Hatfield Road, St Albans, Herts AL1 3RR. Tel (0727) 56679. Open 10 am-5 pm weekdays. Admission by appointment with the librarian.

Museum Library Herts County Museum was opened in 1899 and taken over by St Albans City Council in 1955. Library gradually acquired and contains *c*105 v pre-1851, including 1 incunabulum, 4 STC and 20 Wing items. The earlier books are mainly Bibles, Herts sermons, liturgical and historical, early 19th cent children's books, chapbooks and song sheets (*c*50 items), local posters and broadsides (*c*100). There are also local mss, Herts antiquarian notes, newscuttings, children's writing books, etc (*c*25 v).

Herts College of Agriculture and Horticulture, Oaklands, St Albans, Herts AL4 0JA. Tel (0727) 50651. Open Mon-Fri 9 am-1 pm (9 am-5.30 pm during term time). Admission by appointment with librarian. Photocopying facilities.

Barley Collection The collection was mainly purchased by the late C M Barley, College Librarian (1963–69), and includes *c*35 v pre-1851 (1 STC) on agriculture and natural history, mainly of the early 19th cent. Some volumes are illustrated.

Author and subject (UDC classification) card cats.

St Albans City Library, Victoria Street, St Albans, Herts. Tel (0727) 60000. Open Mon-Wed and Fri 9.30 am-7 pm, Thurs 9.30 am-1 pm; Sat 9 am-6 pm. Admission by arrangement with Local Studies Librarian. Photocopying facilities.

Local History Collection The first St Albans Corporation Library was opened in 1882, and the library was rebuilt on its present site in 1911. The collection, which was gradually acquired, contains *c*230 v pre-1851 which include 3 STC and 13 Wing, and refer mainly to the history of St Albans and the County of Hertford. There are many short pamphlets and Herts sections removed from larger works. The mss (about 10 v) include the works of local historians W B Gerish and R W W Hall. The collection also includes *c*125 printed maps of Herts 1607–1850.

Card cats of author and subject.

Lewis Evans Collection Purchased from Lewis Evans by Herts County Museum, St Albans, 1901, and added to subsequently, it was transferred to the City Library *c*1970. The collection contains *c*530 v pre-1851, including 7 STC and 102 Wing items. The books and pamphlets relate to Herts, and many of the earlier works consist of sermons and accounts of trials. Some prints and books originally part of the collection were not transferred from St Albans City Museum.

Card cats of authors.

Hertfordshire County Museum. *Catalogue of the 'Lewis Evans' Collection of books and pamphlets relating to Hertfordshire* Parts I, II. St Albans, 1906–08. (op)

Tring

Zoological Museum Library, 42 Akeman Street, Tring, Herts HP23 6AP. Tel (044282) 4181. Open Mon-Fri 10 am-noon, 1-4 pm to bona fide research workers by appointment with the librarian at Tring.

Lionel Walter Rothschild (1868–1937) the banker, afterwards 2nd Baron Rothschild of Tring, in 1889 established a zoological museum on the edge of his father's estate of Tring Park and staffed it as a centre of research with its own journal *Novitates Zoologicae* from 1894. He built up a library there which was especially rich in ornithological books. He bequeathed the museum and library to the British Museum (Natural History), of which it is now an out-station housing the Sub-Department of Ornithology.

See the obituaries of Rothschild in *Novitates Zoologicae* 41(1) (1938) p1-16.

Obituary notices of Fellows of the Royal Society 6 (1938), p385-6; *Nature* 2 Oct 1937; *The Times* 28 Aug 1937, p12; 30 Aug, p13; 9 Sept, p17.

A S Woodward and C D Sherborn, 'The Rothschild Museum, Tring', *Natural Science* 2 (1893), p57-63.

W J Loftie, *London afternoons*, London (1901), p154-9.

Rothschild Library Rothschild bequeathed *c*30,000 v, of which the collections of general works on natural history and scientific voyages, in addition to the ornithology collection, remain at Tring. (The entomology and certain other small specialised parts were transferred in 1938 to the appropriate departmental libraries at South Kensington, the mss to the General Library); *c*6,000 v of pre-1851 books, including *c*300 pre-1701 and *c*900 of 1701–1800.

Card cat (authors) not yet fully in general cat at South Kensington.

Sub-Department of Ornithology Library Established 1971, now containing *c*40,000 v, of which only a small proportion being pre-1851 or rare.

Card cat (authors); also in general cat at South Kensington.

Ware

St Edmund's College Library, Old Hall Green, Ware, Herts SG11 1DS. Tel (0920) 821504. Open by appointment with the librarian or the Curator of the Museum for the Recusant Collection for academic researchers only. A very limited photocopying service will probably be available.

The College Library incorporates *The Douay Museum Collection; The Gosselin Library*, and is itself divided into the *Griffin Library* and the *Main Library*.

The various libraries have been accumulated since the foundation of the College in 1793 to serve as a replacement for Douay, founded in 1568, and closed with the French Revolution. It served the dual purpose of a school and seminary—at first for the whole of the South of England, and subsequently for the Archdiocese of Westminster (until 1975). The school is still the property of the Diocese, and continues to be partially staffed by priests of the Diocese. The extensive college archives for the period from 1568 onwards (excepting the Douay Diaries) have been catalogued by Dr J Kitching 'Archives of St Edmund's College' HMC 1972.

The Douay Museum Collection Consists of *c*3,600 v, of which *c*1,100 are STC and *c*1,000 are Wing items. The collection was reorganized in the mid-1960s, and houses probably one of the finest collections of Recusant books in the country. It also has a large number of pamphlets. The subject material ranges from philosophy, theology, works of devotion, and works arguing the case for and against the Church of Rome. Many of the books are in their original bindings.

Card cat in process of revision, author and chronological sequences.

The Gosselin Library Contains c2,750 v, including *c*50 STC and *c*800 Wing items. The books consist mainly of works of theological and philosophical interest, although it has a sizeable church history section. Its most important feature is its large collection of *c*250 Jansenist books, many of which are first editions.

The library is as yet uncatalogued.

The College Library Contains *c*1,350 v which include a large collection of classical authors, literature and history, purchased partly by the school and partly built up by the frequent bequest of books to the college by priests and prominent Catholic laymen.

The College Library cat does not yet incorporate that of the Griffin Library.

There has been a partial dispersal of the stock in the mid-1960s when the museum collection was reorganized and specialized. The items sold were those that had no bearing on the subject core of the collection. No record was kept at the time of what was sold, but it is probably included in the College's incunabula (*c*10 v).

Allison and Rogers, *Catalogue*, and Clancy, *English Catholic books*, both include (some) St Edmund's locations.

Watford

Watford Central Library, Hempstead Road, Watford WD1 3EU. Tel (0932) 26230/26239. Open 9.30 am-8 pm, Wed 9.30 am-1 pm, Sat 9 am-5 pm. Photocopying facilities.

Local History Collection The Watford Public Library Committee was formed in 1871, and the library was opened on its present site in 1928. Many of the books have been acquired by gift and bequest. The collection has *c*90 v pre-1851, including 6 Wing, and relate to the local history of Watford and the County of Herts, sale particulars of local estates, 19th and 20th cent total *c*25 v, and newscuttings about local affairs, *c*1895 onwards (25 v). There are 76 printed maps of Herts, 1579–1868. The mss include accounts, minutes, diaries, etc of local residents and societies, *c*30 v.

Card cat of author and subject.

Chronological list of printed maps.

Typescript guide: *Source material for local studies in Watford Reference Library*, 1972.

Humberside

Beverley

Beverley Library, Champney Road, Beverley, North Humberside HU17 9BQ. Tel (0482) 867108/9. Open Mon, Tues, Thurs, Fri 9.30 am-7 pm, Wed 9.30 am-5 pm, Sat 9 am-1 pm. Admission free to members of the public during normal hours of opening. Open-access to shelves in Yorkshire collection. Access to Champney collection to students and others on request. Older material not normally lent. Photocopying facilities and microfiche readers available.

Champney Collection Acquired by bequest of J E Champney to Beverley Corporation in 1919, it contains *c*2,800 v with main emphasis on history and standard editions of English literature published 18th-19th cent. There are some Wing items and a few individually rare books. In 1955/6, 310 items (mostly post-1851) were removed from the Champney collection and then discarded. A list of these is available.

Yorkshire Collection Acquired by purchase of material on Yorkshire local history by Beverley Corporation 1906–74, and East Riding County Council 1925–74, as well as by various donations. It includes *c*5,500 v, 900 maps, 1,300 pamphlets, posters, broadsheets etc. There are *c*100 17th and 18th cent maps of Yorkshire and East Riding; 70 Civil War tracts; 6 scrapbooks, and much ms material on Beverley and district collected early 19th cent by Gillyatt Sumner. There are in the collection 11 STC and 100 Wing items.

The above collections together contain 111 pre-1700 and 800 1701–1851 items.

Ms author list and accessions register. Card cat, author and classified sequences.

Lockwood Huntley, *The Champney Bequest, July 1929: descriptive notes.* Beverley Public Library, 1929. (op)

Bridlington

Bridlington Library, 14 King Street, Bridlington YO15 2DF. Tel (0262) 72917. Open daily (except Thurs and Sat) 10.30 am-6 pm, Thurs and Sat 10.30 am-1 pm. Admission during opening hours on application to the librarian on duty in the Reference Library. Photocopying facilities available. Material cannot be borrowed.

Bridlington Collection Purchase of books on local history by Borough Librarians on behalf of former Bridlington Town Council started 1938. Stock now totals 3,202 v and pamphlets, of which *c*100 are pre-1851. The books deal mainly with Bridlington and surrounding villages, with a small number of volumes dealing with Yorkshire as a whole. The collection is currently added to as material becomes available. None of the items has ever been sold or otherwise disposed of.

Sheaf dictionary cat.

Driffield

Burton Agnes Hall, Burton Agnes, Driffield, North Humberside YO25 0ND. Tel (0262 89) 324. Admission by arrangement with the owner, Mr Marcus Wickham-Boynton, after written application.

Burton Agnes Hall Library This represents the Boynton family collection, built up over several generations, and consists of *c*1,300 v, of which 235 are 1700–1851, and 16 pre-1700. The pre-1851 books are mostly history, biography, 19th cent literature and sport. A number of books were sold by the family in the 1890s.

Sledmere House, Sledmere, Driffield, North Humberside YO25 0XQ. Tel (0377) 86221. Open strictly by arrangement with the owner, Sir Tatton Sykes, in writing.

Sykes Family Collection Built up by Sir Christopher Sykes (2nd Baronet) 1749–1801, and Sir Mark Masterman Sykes (3rd Baronet) 1771–1823. The best books in the collection were sold in 1824, but many more were added in the mid-19th cent. It now contains 6,415 v (5,322 titles), of which *c*1,500 are post-1850; 61 periodical titles in 1,004 v. There are *c*40 STC and *c*300 Wing items. Main subjects covered are architecture, classics, English and French literature, history, theology and topography. Of special note are a collection of 18th cent plays and political pamphlets covering the Popish plot 1735–45. Many books have very fine bindings. Mss include 3 compiled by Francis Drake, the antiquary, one being a ms copy of his *Eburacum*; 18 v of mss of novels by Lady M Sykes.

Cats include 2 for pre-1800; 1 for 1800; 1 for *c*1863; 1 in 1912 (printed); 1 in process of compilation 1979.

Grimsby

Grimsby Central Library, Town Hall Square, Grimsby, Humberside DN31 1HG. Tel (0472) 40405. Open Mon-Fri 10.30 am-8 pm; Sat 9 am-1 pm. Admission during opening hours without prior arrangement for reference only. Microfilm reader; photocopier available.

Local History Collection Grimsby Public Library was opened by the former County Borough Council in 1901, incorporating stock from the Mechanics' Institute founded in 1856. It became part of Humberside County Library in 1974. It contains *c*2,500 v (about half of which are pamphlets) mainly 18th and 19th cent. There are *c*800 pre-1851 items. It has not been possible to check for STC or Wing items, but number is not likely to be significant. The collection consists of works relating to the historic County of Lincolnshire, and to works by or about people born in the county. Newton and Wesley are well represented, much of the material in this category is in the form of statutes, tracts, printed sermons, poems and miscellaneous items by local people.

Card cat.

Hull

Burton Constable Hall, Burton Constable, Near Hull, North Humberside. Tel (0401) 62400. Admission by arrangement with the owner, Mr J R Chichester-Constable.

Burton Constable Hall Library The library was created *c*1700. Its fittings date from 1730. Books were collected by Cuthbert Tunstall, but the library was largely built up by his son William Constable (1721–91), who was a noted scientist and Fellow of the Royal Society. He also corresponded with Rousseau, and collected much French literature. The collection comprises *c*6,000 v, mostly 18th cent. There are *c*160 items which are pre-1700, and *c*600 which are post-1850. The main subjects represented are French literature; classics; history (notably French history); theology; English literature; a little Italian and Spanish literature; politics and law. The collection includes *Journal des sçavans*, Paris, 1684–1745 and Diderot's *Encyclopedie*, Paris 1751–65. Some 500 v sold between 1950 and 1960.

Ms cats of 1791, 1882 and 1942.

Hull Central Library: Local Studies Library, Albion Street, Hull HU1 3TF. Tel (0482) 224040 Ext 21. Open Mon-Fri 9.30 am-8 pm; Sat 9 am-4.30 pm.

Microfilm readers; photocopying; printing from microfilm; study space.

Humberside Libraries. Central Local Studies Collection Originally part of Hull's general Reference Library founded c1900 and enlarged as a separate department with its own staff in 1962. It has c20,000 accessioned items, plus large collections of pamphlet and ephemeral material. The subject field is mainly the old East Riding of Yorkshire and North Lincolnshire, new county of Humberside, with special emphasis on Hull. Its *Special Collections* include William Wilberforce and slaves (c1,100 v); Whaling (500 v and mss); Andrew Marvell (180 v including first editions); Winifred Holtby: printed and other material including mss letters, first editions etc.

Classified card cat.

Various information indexes.

Hull City Libraries. Select list of books on Hull and district: guide to the collections in the Hull Local History Library 1969 (op)

Humberside Libraries. Select bibliography of the County of Humberside 1980 (includes material in the Hull Collection).

Hull Central Library: Reference Library, Albion Street, Hull HU1 3TF. Tel (0482) 224040 Ext 42. Open Mon-Fri 9.30 am-8 pm; Sat 9 am-4.30 pm. No restrictions on admission. Microfilm readers and reader/printer; microfiche reader; photocopiers.

Background Materials Scheme Collection The collection forms part of a national subject specialisation scheme which began c1951, and contains 1,380 v, comprising books published between 1740 and 1759 in all subject fields.

Conventional card cat—dictionary type.

Napoleon Collection Purchased from a local collector of Napoleonic literature (J Wilson Smith) in 1958, and added to continuously since. The collection contains 1,100 v covering biographies of Napoleon and histories of the Napoleonic era.

Card cat—dictionary.

Hull Medical Society, Hull Medical Library, Hull Royal Infirmary, Anlaby Road, Hull HU3 2JZ. Tel (0482) 28541 Ext 337. Admission by arrangement with the Honorary Librarian. Photocopying facilities.

Hull Medical Society Library Built up by the Hull Medical Society over many years, the bulk of the collection consists of the Society's lending library which flourished from 1920 to 1940. Includes many presentations of small collections from individuals and institutions. It totals c8,000 v including 1,500 books of historical value, mainly on medicine, but also botany, pharmacy, anatomy and physiology. There are c40 16th cent; c200 17th cent; c500 18th cent, and c500 19th cent books. The earliest items are Galen: *De simplicium medicamentorum facultatibus libri XI, Theodorico Gerardo Gaudano interprete*, 1547, and Dioscorides: *De medica materia*, 1554. There are 17th cent editions of works by Galen, Hippocrates and William Harvey.

Card cat (still in progress).

Town Docks Museum (Hull Maritime Museum), Queen Victoria Square, Hull HU1 3DX. Tel (0482) 222737. Open Mon-Fri 10 am-5 pm; Museum only Sat 10 am-5 pm., Sun 2.30-4.30 pm. Admission to book collections by prior appointment, by telephone or in writing. Photocopying and photographic facilities available.

Town Docks Museum (Hull Maritime Museum) Whaling Collection It began with the opening of Hull's first Maritime Museum in 1912, and contains c600 v. The main subject areas include whaling, polar exploration and polar natural history—c150 v (dating from early 19th cent); merchant shipping—c200 v (mainly recent, from late 19th cent); fishing; maritime art and decorative arts. Of special note are: a collection of original mss and transcripts of log books of Hull whaling ships; minute books of Hull whaling ship owners, 1813–25; a small collection of rare pamphlets on whaling published 1826–35, including several not in the British Library *General catalogue*; and early editions of works by Sir John Ross (*A voyage of discovery*...1819; *Narrative of a second voyage*...1835; and *The last voyage*...1834).

Rough handlists only.

J R Jenkins, 'Bibliography of Whaling', *Journ Soc for the Bibliography of Nat Hist*, v 2, 1943–52, p71-166.

University of Hull: Brynmor Jones Library, Hull HU6 7RX. Tel (0482) 46311. Open (Term) Mon-Fri 9 am-10 pm; Sat 9 am-1 pm; (Vacation) Mon-Fri 9 am-5.30 pm; Sat 9 am-1 pm. Admission to members of the University. Others, for reference, at the discretion of the librarian, to whom written application should be made. Photocopying; paper copies from microfilm; microfilm and microfiche readers.

Brynmor Jones Library—special collections Built up by gift and purchase since the foundation of the library in 1929. The special collections amount to c10,000 items with a wide subject range, but special interests in the library as a whole include South-East Asian studies; British labour history; modern British and American poetry; private press books. The following special collections are noted:

The Brynmor Jones Collection, established in honour of the former Vice-Chancellor from whom the library takes its name, containing c300 intellectual landmarks or finely produced books published between 1890 and 1940, including the copy of *Mein Kampf* which belonged to Hitler's private secretary, and first editions of Hardy, Lawrence and Proust.

Holy Trinity Library and St Mary Lowgate Library The parish libraries of the two oldest churches in Hull, containing 471 and 145 v respectively.

The Hull Collection, containing *c*2,000 items relating to Hull and Humberside, including a large number of late 18th and 19th cent playbills of Hull theatres.

The Philip Larkin Collection (181 items) and the *Stevie Smith Collection* (172 items) devoted to the respective poets and including many first editions.

The Library of Busby Hall, a country house in North Yorkshire, containing *c*5,000 items.

Throughout the special collections there are 3 incunabula; 120 STC; 470 Wing; *c*220 16th and 17th cent foreign works, and *c*2,600 18th cent British and foreign works.

The library's mss collection includes substantial holdings of modern British poetry. The papers of Gavin Ewart and Anthony Thwaite and the archives of *Phoenix* and other poetry magazines are held.

Name cat and classified cat with subject index (cards).

Private Collections
Applications (stating reasons) from bona fide researchers for further information or access to the following collections should be made initially to the Librarian, Brynmor Jones Library, University of Hull.

I A collection of *c*1,750 v, of which *c*100 are pre-1851 and 10 pre-1700. It includes local material on Hull and East Riding of Yorkshire, including East Riding Antiquarian Society Publications (*c*200 v); architecture; heraldry and geneaology (*c*100).
II A collection of *c*2,700 v, of which *c*1,900 are pre-1851, and 30 v pre-1700 imprints. Main subjects are theology; sermons; Bibles; English literature; history; travel and topography; law; classics; and little natural history.

University of Hull: Institute of Education Library, Cottingham Road, Hull HU6 7RX. Tel (0482) 46311 Ext 7556. Open Mon and Fri 9 am-5.30 pm; Tues, Wed, Thurs 9 am-7.30 pm; Sat 9 am-12.30 pm (hours vary in vacations). Open to all members of the teaching profession in Humberside, and to others by arrangement. Microfilm and microfiche readers. Photocopying facilities. Paper copies from microfilm and microfiche may be made in the Brynmor Jones Library.

Historical Collection The Institute Library was founded in 1949, and began acquiring material for its Historical Collection from its earliest days. The bulk of the collection was acquired by secondhand purchase, but a collection of the oldest books from the Hull Grammar School Library was deposited in 1971. The collection is devoted to source material for the history of education, and falls into three broad categories: (1) writings about education up to *c*1910; (2) Government reports, etc on education *c*1820-*c*1920; (3) school books and children's books up to *c*1910.

The books total *c*2,200, which include 58 books from the Hull Grammar School Library, together with some 16th and 17th cent continental printed texts and first and other early editions of John Clarke (1686–1734), Headmaster of Hull Grammar School. There are *c*20 Wing and 2 STC items. *c*One-third of the collection is pre-1850.

There is a separate author/name cat on cards, and in some cases there are added subject entries in the main Institute Library classified cat.

All pre-1870 holdings and pre-1918 Government publications are recorded in C W J Higson, *Sources for the history of education*, Library Association, 1967 and *Supplement*, 1976.

Wilberforce House, 24/25 High Street, Hull HU1 1NQ. Tel (0482) 222737. Open Mon-Fri 10 am-5 pm; Museum only, Sat 10 am-5 pm, Sun 2.30-4.30 pm. Admission to library by prior appointment, on written application only. Photocopying and photography by request.

Wilberforce Library The library contains (a) the personal library of William Wilberforce (1759–1833) and books of members of his family; (b) a collection of local history etc donated at the time of the acquisition in 1906 by the City Council of Wilberforce's house for conversion to a museum and added to since. The collection contains *c*1,800 works, including the personal library of William Wilberforce of *c*400 works (mainly religion, politics, classics, philosophy, English literature), and the Local Collection of *c*1,400 works which include material on slavery (*c*300 works) and on Wilberforce (*c*70 works), but is otherwise devoted to the history of Hull and East Yorkshire. There are 12 STC and 57 Wing items; 4 foreign works to 1700 and *c*380 works published 1701–1851. There is also a collection of *c*100 prints (17th-early 19th cent) of members of the House of Stewart.

Author cat (cards) of Wilberforce Collection and Local Collection.

Pocklington

Garrowby Hall, Garrowby, York YO4 1QD. Admission by application in writing to the Librarian, The Brynmor Jones Library, University of Hull, Hull HU6 7RX.

Private Library of the 3rd Earl of Halifax Collected by the Halifax family over the last 150 years, the library comprises 4,000 v, of which *c*850 are pre-1851 (30 are STC and Wing items). Subject areas include biography (*c*700 v mainly political); history (*c*1,100 v); literature (*c*900 v); theology (*c*400 v); local history and customs (*c*200 v).

Card cat for main library only.

Pocklington School, West Green, Pocklington, York YO4 2NJ. Tel (07592) 3125. Admission by arrangement with the Headmaster. Photocopying machine available.

Pocklington School Library The library dates from the time of the present buildings (1830–50). Most of the older books in the collection have been given by staff and old boys (the latter including William Wilberforce). The bulk of the collection is a typical school library. The historical collection comprises *c*140 v, of which *c*100 are pre-1850. There are no STC items. There is only one Wing (William Bates: *The harmony of the Divine attributes or discourses*, 1697). Holdings are mainly in the fields of classics (especially Homer, Virgil), English literature (Crabbe and Swift), theology and topography. There are also early editions of Wilberforce: *A letter on the abolition of the slave trade*, 1807, and *A practical view of the prevailing religious system*, 1811 and 1826.

Typescript cat, compiled in 1978.

Scunthorpe

Scunthorpe Central Libraries, Carlton Street, Scunthorpe, South Humberside. Tel (0724) 60161. Open Mon, Tues, Wed, Fri 10.30 am-8 pm; Thurs 10.30 am-5 pm; Sat 9.30 am-1 pm. Admission unrestricted. Photocopy service, locking desks for private study, material mainly for use in the library.

Scunthorpe Local Studies Collection The collection has been developed in the last 20 years, and comprises 4,000 books, pamphlets etc covering the old geographical county of Lincolnshire, plus the new administrative county of Humberside, but with particular emphasis on Scunthorpe. In addition there are 600 items on Methodism and the Wesley family covering the life and writings of John Wesley and other members of the Wesley family. Only 150 v in the collection were printed before 1851, for the most part runs of the *American Magazine* (1785 onwards) and the *Methodist Magazine* (1787 onwards).

Note Epworth Old Rectory, originally the home of the Wesley family, is about 10 miles away from Scunthorpe. Now a museum owned by the World Methodist Council, it also contains a small library of books on the Wesleys and Methodism, similar to, but less extensive than, the Wesley Collection at Scunthorpe Central Libraries. Further information may be obtained from the Warden, Epworth Old Rectory, Epworth, Doncaster DN9 1HB. Tel (0427) 872268.

A new card cat is in progress.

Scunthorpe Museum and Art Gallery, Oswald Road, Scunthorpe, South Humberside. Tel (0724) 3533. Open Mon-Thurs 10 am-5 pm, Fri 10 am-4 pm. Admission by arrangement. Photocopying facilities.

Scunthorpe Museum Library A collection of books donated by various individuals and added to by purchase. There are *c*2,715 items, of which 435 are pre-1851, and include 3 Wing items. Subjects covered are mainly of local interest, including the standard early local histories and directories. Also a good collection of prints by Fowler, some associated mss, and one private press publication relating to Fowler.

Author cat.

Kent

Ashford

Wye College Library, Wye, Ashford, Kent TN25 5AH. Tel (0233) 812401 Ext 242. Open (Term) Mon-Fri 9 am-10 pm; Sat and Sun variable; (Vacation) Mon-Fri 9 am-5 pm; Sat 9 am-1 pm by appointment with the librarian. Photocopying facilities.

The College occupies the buildings of a medieval college for secular priests, which continued after the Reformation as a grammar school. The school was converted in 1894 into the South-Eastern Agricultural College, which in 1900 became a school of the University of London. In 1946 it was renamed Wye College. The library contains *c*29,000 v.

Agricultural and horticultural books 1540–1918 Acquired by gift and purchase from the foundation of the library *c*1900. 1,050 v, including *c*5 STC, *c*15 Wing, *c*2,000 ESTC, *c*200 English 1801–50 and *c*20 pre-1851 foreign. 70 sets of periodicals.

A cat of agricultural and horticultural books 1543–1918 in Wye College Library, 1977.

Crundale Rectory Library Richard Forster (*d*1728), Rector of Crundale, bequeathed his library to his successors the Rectors of Crundale 'for ever'. It was moved to Godmersham Vicarage when the parishes were amalgamated. Deposited in Wye College 1976. It comprises *c*900 v, mostly 17th cent theology, political and religious controversy, and the founder's reference books and general reading.

Cat in progress. Early ms cats in Canterbury Cathedral archives Y.4.30 and 31.

Local History Collection On Kent generally, including a small collection of early works; local villages, and Romney Marsh; local agriculture.

Canterbury

Canterbury College of Art, New Dover Road, Canterbury, Kent. Tel (0227) 69371. Open (Term) Mon-Thurs 9.30 am-6.30 pm, Fri 9.30 am-5 pm; (Vacation) Mon-Fri 9.30 am-12 noon, 2-4.30 pm. Admission by arrangement in writing.

Rare Book Collection The college was founded by the artist Sidney Cooper in the 19th cent. The collection is partly on permanent loan from the executor of Mr John Duthoit, and contains *c*200 v. Subject coverage is mainly 18th and 19th cent architectural and design history. There is a nearly complete file of the *Architectural Review* and Large-paper edition of Jones's *Grammar of Ornament.*

Typed list available.

Canterbury Public Library, The Beaney Institute, High Street, Canterbury, Kent CT1 2JF. Tel (0227) 63608, 69964. Reference library open Mon, Tues, Fri 9.30 am-6 pm, Wed 9.30 am-1 pm, 2.30-5 pm, Thurs, Sat 9.30 am-5 pm. Microfilm reader; photocopying facilities.

Local History Collection The Public Library was established in 1847 and the present premises date from 1899. The library is the successor to the Philosophic and Literary Institute (1825). This developed from a historical society founded in the 18th cent. The collection contains *c*5,000 books and pamphlets, which include a large number of works of the 16th-18th cent relating to the history and topography of Canterbury and East Kent. Many editions are grangerized.

Card cat (dictionary).

The Philip Found Shorthand Collection The nucleus of the collection is that of Philip Found, with additions. The collection owes much to the enthusiasm of Frank Higenbottam, who retired as City Librarian in 1974. It contains 1,000 books on shorthand, including some early English and French systems and a large Pitman section.

Sheaf cats.

Christ Church College of Higher Education, North Holmes Road, Canterbury, Kent. Tel (0227) 65548 Ext 32. Open (Term) Mon-Fri 9 am-9 pm; Sat 9.30 am-12.30 pm, 2-5 pm; Sun 2-5 pm; (Vacation) Mon-Fri 9 am-5 pm. Open for reference purposes to members of the public. Photocopier available.

Children's Historical Books Acquired by gift and some purchases, the collection totals 912 v of children's books, books on teaching methods, textbooks, mostly of the late 19th cent but some of an earlier date.

In general cat.

A J Edwards, 'Children's Books, an Historical Collection in Christ Church College Library' in M H R Berry and J H Higginson *Canterbury Chapters*, 1977.

Chatham

Royal School of Military Engineering, R E Corps Library, The Institution of Royal Engineers, Chatham, Kent. Tel (0634) 44555 Ext 309. Open weekdays 9 am-4.30 pm by appointment in writing. Room to work. Photocopier available.

General Modern Library This is a general collection with emphasis on military and civil engineering, military history and biography, some naval history, foreign campaigns etc. Included are the Connolly Papers, mss biographical sketches of Royal Engineer Officers (1700p) from inception to 1860 (available to students when microfilmed). Books total *c*20,000 v, including photographic albums and bound letter books.

Card cat classified-modified UDC.

Specialist Collection on RSME The RSME was opened in 1812 when the collection was started; the libraries of other garrisons have been added during the years through closures. The present collection includes many volumes on practical military matters by C W Pasley who was the precursor of the monitor system of teaching in his courses of instruction for illiterate soldiers, both in reading and writing geometry. The school was the first to instruct officers and men together.

Military Engineering This collection of *c*1,000 v is the only one in the UK which relates to the 18th and 19th cent as an entity, and includes many European publications.

Photographic Library A collection of albums of photographs of military groups and situations from *c*1850 onwards.

Gillingham

Gillingham Central Library, High Street, Gillingham, Kent. Tel (92) 51066/7. Open Mon, Tues, Thurs, Fri 9.30 am-7 pm; Wed, Sat 9.30 am-5 pm. No appointment necessary. The collection is housed in locked cupboards, but any item(s) may be seen on request. Microfilm reader, photocopier available.

Local History Collection for Gillingham The collection was started when the library was opened in 1936, and now totals *c*1,500 items, including books and pamphlets.

Card cat in Reference Library.

Published references available from Gillingham Library.

Maidstone

Kent County Library, Springfield, Maidstone, Kent. Tel (0622) 671411 Ext 3240. Open Mon-Fri 9 am-6 pm; Sat 9 am-12.30 pm. Normal public library conditions; restricted use for scarce and valuable books. Very limited seating. Photocopies and microfilm reader-printer available.

The Kent Collection The books have been acquired over the years since the Kent County Library service began in 1921. The total stock amounts to *c*8,500 v (including pamphlets) of which *c*2,000 are rare and/or valuable. It is a broad collection, covering the history and topography of the County of Kent and of individual towns and villages within the county, as presented in books and pamphlets. The first edition (1576) and the second edition (1596) of Lambarde's *A perambulation of Kent*, are held, and also a 1614 edition of his *Eirenarda* or *The Office of Justices of the Peace.* One of the two first editions (folio) copies of Edward Hasted's *History* has been grangerized and rebound in 22 v, and there is also a grangerized edition of William Berry's *Pedigrees of the families of Kent* (1830). 'The Dunkin Scrapbook' is a collection of Alfred Dunkin's clippings and illustration posthumously bound into 20 v, about 1860. Most of the early maps of Kent are in the map collection, and the microfilms include the Registers of the Archbishops of Canterbury, 13th-17th cent from the Lambeth Palace Library.

Card cat.

Kent County Library—local history cat 1939.

The library's holdings are recorded in *The Kent Bibliography*, compiled by G Bennett, edited by W Bergess and C Earl (Library Assoc, London and Home Counties Branch, 1977).

Maidstone Museum and Art Gallery, St Faith's Street, Maidstone, Kent. Tel (0622) 54497. Open 10 am-6 pm (Winter 5 pm). Admission by appointment. Room for study.

Maidstone Parochial Library The Library of All Saints Church deposited at the Museum in 1870. It contains 480 v comprising religious and classical authors of the 16th-18th cent, with few secular works.

Ms cat (bound) and easily available.

Maidstone Museum General Collection Built up since 1858, it is a working library of 2,000 v on pottery, armour heraldry, genealogy and books of local interest.

Maidstone Museum Antiquarian Collection Built up since 1858, it contains *c*200 v of the 16th-18th cent, including a ms volume of 16th-17th cent legal forms.

Rochester

Rochester Cathedral Library, Rochester Cathedral, Rochester, Kent ME1 1SR. Cathedral open daily until 5.30 pm, but admission to the library by appointment on written application to the librarian. A room for study.

The Library of the Dean and Chapter The library originated in the 16th cent and now holds *c*3,000 v covering a wide range of subjects, and comprising works on ecclesiastical history, law, theology; collections of sermons mainly by prelates of the Cathedral; collections of Bibles, Books of Common Prayer, lexicons—mainly of the 16th cent. There are numerous STC and Wing items.

No cat.

Printed Guide to Rochester Cathedral Library (available from the Cathedral bookstall).

Rochester Museum, Eastgate House, High Street, Rochester. Tel (0634) 44176. Open Mon-Thurs and Sat 10 am-5.30 pm. Admission by appointment. Room to study.

General Museum Collection Mainly reference books on pottery, coins, armour, archaeology, Kent history and topography, but the collection includes some rare items (ie pre-1850), including a copy made in the 18th cent of Sir Roger Manwood's 'Black Book' 1586, being the first narrative history of Rochester Bridge.

Card cat in museum.

The Percy Fitzgerald Dickens Library (1912) Percy Fitzgerald was a friend of the Dickens family, and his collection contains different editions, and editions in various languages of the works of Charles Dickens. Also the personal letters and papers of Dickens, scrapbooks etc; some rare plagiarisms including 'Oliver Twiss', 'Nickleberry married', etc.

Edward Hasted Collection The collection comprises the papers of Edward Hasted, and the family papers. It includes Hasted's copy of the first folio edition (1776) with bookplates of his son and subsequent owners, with a signed portrait miniature and ms notes giving Hasted's costing of the publication bound in; Hasted's *Commonplace Book* and portrait sketch 1801.

George Payne Collection Consisting mainly of the mss, journals and works of George Payne, an eminent Kent archaeologist who lived in Sittingbourne.

Walter Prentis (of Rainham) Natural History Library, 1901 The collection includes many 18th cent works on natural history, with John Gould's *Birds of Great Britain* 5 v (1862—73), London 1802; a Breeches Bible 1560; and a 'Great She Bible' 1614 which belonged to Sir John Hawkins Charity Hospital, Chatham, with ms inclusions.

Sittingbourne

Kent County Library, Swale Division, HQ Sittingbourne Central Library, Central Avenue, Sittingbourne, Kent. Tel (0795) 76545. Open Mon-Thurs 9.30 am-6 pm, Fri 9.30 am-7 pm, Sat 9 am-5 pm.

Material available for reference only. Photocopying possible.

Local History Collection for Swale Held in the three main libraries in Swale, and built up by them over the years. The stock contains *c*500 v. Also bound periodicals of local interest, often duplicated in three main libraries. The collection relates to Faversham, Sheppey, Sittingbourne and Swale, and includes much ephemera, most of which originated in the 19th cent, with a sprinkling of 17th and 18th cent works.

Card cats (author and subject).

Tenterden

The Ellen Terry Memorial Museum (National Trust), Smallhythe Place, Tenterden, Kent. Tel (058 06) 2334 and 3134. Open daily March-Oct (except Tues and Fri) including Sun and Bank Holidays, 2-6 pm (or dusk if earlier). Admission by appointment through the Libraries Adviser, National Trust, 42 Queen Anne's Gate, London SW1H 9AS. Books may be used on the premises only.

The Working Library of Ellen Terry The house and contents were presented to the National Trust by Ellen Terry's daughter, Edith Craig, in 1939. The materials comprising the library were assembled and shelved in 1968. 43 items have been added to the original collection, which now totals 1,406 v. Playbills are not included unless in bound volumes, including theatrical biographies —mainly published in the early and mid 19th cent; plays—an extensive collection, many the working and prompt copies of Ellen Terry herself, with her comments inscribed; early plays 1700–1830; a collection of separate Shakespeare plays, collected editions, criticisms and Shakespeariana; works on the theatre, stage design, production—45 books by Ellen Terry's son-in-law, Edward Gordon Craig; Ellen Terry—autobiographical, lectures, eg lectures on Shakespeare—large type lecture copy, *c*1910, press cuttings etc.

The comments of Ellen Terry in working copies of plays, biographies etc are of great value to the student of theatre. Inscriptions by donors and biographers are of historical interest.

Printed cat entitled 'Catalogue of the working library of Ellen Terry' compiled by F T Bowyer, National Trust, 1966 (copies available from Smallhythe Place).

Sissinghurst Castle (National Trust), Tenterden TN17 2AB. Tel (058 06) 250. Admission to bona fide scholars only upon application through the Libraries Adviser, National Trust, 42 Queen Anne's Gate, London SW1H 9AS.

The books at Sissinghurst Castle were collected by Vita Sackville-West and Sir Harold Nicolson over the period 1911 to 1962 (when Miss Sackville-West died) and from 1911–68 (when Sir Harold died). The books belong to their son, Nigel Nicolson, with the exception of Sir Harold Nicolson's books in the South Cottage, which were presented to the National Trust. The library contains *c*10,000 books, plus letters and diaries, and is arranged in three parts:

South Cottage Here are contained: (a) Harold Nicolson's books, which reflect his special interests in diplomatic and political history, biography and general literature. There are very full collections of Byron and Tennyson, of whom he wrote biographies; (b) works of reference used in literary and political biography. This is the working library of a prolific author in the mid-20th cent.

The Tower (First Floor)—Vita Sackville-West's Study All the books within the study reflect her own interests, and they include an excellent collection of 20th cent English poetry, a library of gardening books, and works on subjects upon which she wrote—Joan of Arc, Florence, Persia and the Elizabethans. A particularly interesting part of the collection is a complete set of works by Virginia Woolf, her closest friend. Almost all of them are signed.

The Main Library (a) *In the north wing of the front building* are housed books of common interest to Vita Sackville-West and Sir Harold Nicolson. There they placed a great many books which each reviewed from 1920 to 1960, including full sets of the novels of E M Forster, H G Wells, Graham Greene, Evelyn Waugh, David Garnett, Hugh Walpole, etc. Being review copies, they are all first editions. In addition this library contains some 4,000 v of biography, travel, letters, diaries and works of general historical interest; (b) *In the south wing of the front building* are the books collected continuously by Nigel Nicolson since his parents' death. Subjects include 20th cent military and political history, English domestic architecture and archaeology.

In addition, Sissinghurst Castle contains an extensive archive of mss including all the letters exchanged between the Nicolsons, and the diaries of Vita Sackville-West. The original diaries of Sir Harold Nicolson are kept at Balliol College, Oxford.

Cat being prepared by the National Trust.

Westerham

Chartwell House (National Trust), Chartwell, Westerham, Kent TN16 1PS. Tel (073 278) 368. Admission by arrangement with the Library Adviser, National Trust, 42 Queen Anne's Gate, London SW1H 9AS.

Winston Churchill's Family Library, Chartwell The Randolph and Jenny Churchill's family collection added to by Sir Winston Churchill and family. It contains *c*4,000 v covering the subject fields of naval and military history, biography; Churchill's own works in various editions (both in English and in foreign languages); 18th and 19th cent sets of literary works of foremost French and English authors.

Card cat.

Leicestershire

Coalville

Mount St Bernard Abbey, Coalville, Leicester LE6 3UL. Tel (0530) 32298. Open by appointment after prior application by letter to the librarian.

The Abbey was founded in 1835, but the library dates from the 1940s. It contains *c*19,000 v which include 49 STC and 80 Wing items. There are also about 35 18th cent books; the rest are modern. The pre-1640 books are recorded in 'Allison and Rogers'.

Leicester

East Midlands Gas, John Doran Museum, P O Box 145, De Montfort Street, Leicester LE1 9DB. Tel (0533) 551111. Open Tues-Fri 12.30-4.30 pm, except Bank Holidays. Admission free.

John Doran Museum This is basically an archive and museum of the gas industry in the East Midlands, but there are a few pre-1851 printed books relating to the subject.

Alphabetical and numerical inventories of the whole archive.

Card cat in progress.

Leicester Town Library, Leicestershire County Record Office, 96 New Walk, Leicester LE1 6TD. Tel (0533) 539111. Admission on application to the County Archivist. Books are consulted in the Record Office, and all its facilities are available to users.

Town Library of Leicester Sometimes called the Old Town Hall Library, it was originally (1587) the library of St Martin's Church; taken over by the Corporation of Leicester in 1632. It contains *c*1,000 books largely, but not entirely, theological. It is strongest in 17th cent works.

C Deedes, *The Old Town Hall Library of Leicester, a catalogue*. Oxford, 1919.

Frank S Herne, *History of the Town Library*. Leicester, 1891. (op)

Phillip G Lindley, *The Town Library of Leicester*. Leicester, 1975.

Leicester University Library, University Road, Leicester LE1 7RH. Tel (0533) 554455. Open (Term) Mon-Fri 9 am-10 pm; Sat 9 am-6 pm; Sun 3-9 pm; (Vacation) Mon-Fri 9 am-5.30 pm. Admission by application to the librarian.

English Local History Collection Founded in 1920 with a gift of the Hatton Topographical Collection (2,047 v) by Thomas H Hatton of Anstey Pastures, Leicester. It now totals 36,000 v, including 2,800 v of bound periodicals. Of these *c*1,600 v might properly be described as rare, and range from the 17th cent to date. The subject content of the collection is the history of all English localities, including those of the Scottish and Welsh border counties. Large collections of town, county and church guides are included.

No separate cat but entries included in the Main Library name and classified cats and printed Periodicals List.

Leicester, Leicestershire and Rutland College. *Great gift to the Library. The Hatton Topographical Collection*. Leicester. The College, 1921 (6pp). Reprinted from *The Leicester Daily Post* 11 and 14 Dec 1920. (op)

Transport History Collection Founded in 1953 with a gift of 250 books by Professor Jack Simmons of this University's Department of History, the collection now totals 25,000 v, including 2,600 v of bound periodicals and *c*7,000 timetables. Of these some 300 v are pre-1851. The subject content is the history of all forms of transport in all countries, but with special emphasis on railways in Great Britain. The collection consists in the main of printed materials.

No separate cat but entries included in the Main Library name and classified cats and printed Periodicals List.

George Ottley, *Guide to the Transport History Collection in Leicester University Library*. Leicester. The University Library, 1981. ISBN 0 906092 01 9 £1.20.

Mathematical Association Library Founded in 1908 by a gift of books to the Mathematical Association from William John Greenstreet, editor of *The Mathematical Gazette*. In 1954 the Library was housed in the Library of the University of Leicester. It contains 8,400 v, including

3,500 v of bound periodicals. Of these *c*350 items might properly be described as rare. The subject content is predominantly the teaching of mathematics, and includes early school textbooks and early mathematical and scientific works.

Books are entered in the University Library's card cat, and periodicals in the University Library's printed Periodicals List.

Printed cat, now considerably out of date: *The Mathematical Association, Books and periodicals in the Library of the Mathematical Association* (compiled by R L Goodstein), London, The Association, 1962.

R L Goodstein, 'Collections III: the Mathematical Association Library at the University of Leicester' in *British Journ for the Hist of Sci.* 7 Pt 1, no 25, March 1974, p100-3.

Loughborough

Co-operative College, Loughborough *see under* Nottinghamshire

Loughborough Parish Library, School of Librarianship, Loughborough Technical College, Radmoor Road, Loughborough, Leicestershire LE11 3BT. Tel (0509) 215831. Open, by arrangement with the Head of the School of Librarianship, to suitable persons, but is primarily used for teaching purposes in the School, and by the Department of Library and Information Studies, Loughborough University. Reference materials; photocopying available.

Ashby-de-la-Zouche Parish Library The library was largely formed by Thomas Bate (1675–1727), Rector of Swakestone, and bequeathed by him to the parish of Ashby. It was augmented a little in the 18th cent, but was badly neglected thereafter. Deposited in Loughborough Technical College in 1970, but is still owned by the parish. It contains *c*1,250 works, including 66 STC and 700 Wing items. Subject coverage is mainly theological, including a number of locally printed sermons of the 18th cent and other local books.

Ms cat available, and recataloguing is in progress by students.

W Scott, *The story of Ashby-de-la-Zouche*, Ashby, 1907, p335-8. (op)

Loughborough Parish Library The Parish Library was bequeathed to his successors by James Bickham, Rector of Loughborough 1761–85, and augmented by some of them. Some books were lost or destroyed in the 19th cent. It was deposited at the School in 1967. It contains *c*800 v, chiefly theological, but also a reading collection of classics, history and literature, mainly of Bate's period. Includes some presentation copies from Bickham's friends, Gray and Mason.

19th cent ms cats; recataloguing in progress by students.

Geoffrey Wakeman, 'Loughborough Parish Library', *Book Collector*, 25, 1976, p345-53.

Lincolnshire

Grantham

St Sulfram's Church, Grantham, Lincolnshire. Tel (0476) 61342. Open 9 am-12.30 pm, 2-6 pm. Admission by appointment on application in writing.

The Trigge Library In 1589 Francis Trigge, Rector of Welbourne, gave money to provide a library for the clergy and others 'for the better encreasinge of learninge and knowledge of divinitie and other liberall sciences'. There were a number of later benefactions in the 17th cent. The library contains 309 v, comprising about 300 works, mainly theological, but essentially a general 16th-17th cent collection. It contains 12 STC; 20 Wing. Most of the books are 16th cent continental. As one of the earliest parish libraries in the country, its outstanding characteristic lies in its being a chained library; 83 books are still chained, and 150 others show signs of having been chained.

A cat of 1609 in the borough archives.

Shelflist compiled in 1894 by Canon Nelson: photocopy at church, typescript in Bodley (Ms Eng misc *c*360).

Canon H Nelson, 'The chained library, Grantham', *Lincoln Diocesan Magazine*, v 9, 1893.

Angela Roberts, 'The chained library, Grantham', *Library History*, v 2, no 3, Spring 1971, pp75-90.

Lincoln

Lincolnshire Archives Office, The Castle, Lincoln LN1 3AB. Tel (0522) 25158. Open Mon-Fri 9.30 am-4.45 pm. (Opening hours of Search Room, library opening hours may sometimes be shorter.) Admission by appointment only. Xeroxing, microfilming, print-out from microfilm, microfilm reader.

Dixon Collection Collected by the late G S Dixon of Holton le Moor and other members of his family from the late 18th cent, it contains *c*1,200 books and pamphlets on local history and topography of the 18th and early 19th cent. It includes many children's books and items annotated by members of the family.

Exley Collection 200 books and 300 pamphlets on local history, particularly Lincoln city (19th/20th cent) collected by the late C L Exley of Lincoln.

Foster Library Collected by Canon C W Foster (*d*1935), it contains 2,500 books and periodicals, and 2,500 of pamphlets dealing mainly with 19th and 20th cent local and general history (especially ecclesiastical). The Collection is added to by Archives Office.

Law Books A collection of *c*1,000 16th-20th cent books—some from the now dispersed Lincolnshire Law Society Library and others previously housed in various Courts of Quarter Sessions and other administrative centres.

Lincolnshire Architectural and Archaeological Soc Library Built up by purchase, exchange and donations from *c*1850, the Library contains *c*1,000 books and serials, mainly architectural, of the 19th-20th cent.

Scorer Collection *c*200 books and 300 pamphlets on local history and architecture (19th/20th cent) collected by members of the Scorer family of Lincoln.

Wright Collection 600 pamphlets, 2,000 books collected by the late W M Wright of Wold Newton. Mainly 19th cent, the collection covers local history and topography, ecclesiastical history and sport.

Cat on cards, author/title and subject.

'The Foster Library', *L A C Archivists' Report*, 7 (1955–6), p7-11.

'The Scorer Library', *ibid.* p11-13.

'Wright of Wold Newton', *ibid.* 23 (1971–2), p10-11.

Tennyson Research Centre, The Central Library, Free School Lane, Lincoln LN2 1FZ. Tel (0522) 28621. Open Mon-Fri 9.30 am-7 pm; Sat 9.30 am-5 pm. Admission to bona fide students by written application. Photocopy and photographic services.

Tennyson Research Centre In 1963 Harold Lord Tennyson deposited the libraries of the poet, the poet's father, the poet's brother, Charles Tennyson Turner, many mss and a large collection of correspondence belonging to the Tennyson family. Other members of the Tennyson and Tennyson d'Eyncourt families have since contributed important items. The City Library's collection of Tennyson material was transferred to the Centre when it was opened in 1964. The Tennyson Society adds to the collection its purchases of both new and second-hand material of relevance.

The library contains *c*700 books from Dr George Clayton Tennyson, the poet's father, and *c*4,000 v from the poet's own library, and a comprehensive collection of books and articles about his life and works; a large number of proofs corrected by Tennyson; an almost complete set of first and other eds of his works. The mss include the most complete copy of *In Memoriam*; family papers, including the diaries of Emily Tennyson; household books and publishers' accounts; more than 12,000 family letters and the poet's correspondence with the leading figures of the period. The Centre also houses portraits and other illustrative material of Tennyson and his family, ancestors and friends.

Tennyson in Lincoln: a catalogue of the collections in the Tennyson Research Centre, Vols I and II, compiled by Nancie Campbell. The Tennyson Society, 1971 (v I), 1973 (v II). Vol III (comprising the ms material) is in preparation.

'Tennyson's books', by J C Hixson and P Scott in *Tennyson Research Bull.* 2.5, 1976.

'Tennyson and the Victorian age', (a leaflet available from the Centre).

Spalding

Spalding Gentleman's Society Library, The Museum, Broad Street, Spalding, Lincs PE11 1TB. Tel (0775) 4658. Open by appointment; to non-members by appointment and reference. Photocopier available on the premises.

The Society was founded in 1710 and the library was built up by the gift of a volume from every new member of the Society, as well as by other gifts, bequests and purchase. The Society Library contains *c*15,000 v including pamphlets and periodicals, and include the following collections:

General Library *c*10,000 v miscellaneous, mainly 19th cent, many from Newark Stock Library, Spalding Mechanics Institute, and Spalding Permanent Library. Notable items include 13th cent illum Bible; late 17th cent ms (Moroccan) of the Koran; Caxton's *Confessio amantis* (Gower), 1483; 2nd folio of Shakespeare; a collection of engravings relating to Lincolnshire, compiled by Sir Joseph Banks, 3 v (1806).

Card cat author and Dewey.

Catalogue of the books, manuscripts, pamphlets and tracts. . ., Compiled by E W Maples and George Goodwin, Spalding, 1893;

Various ms catalogues of parts of the collection.

Local History Collection *c*2,000 v including pamphlets and periodicals of the 19th and 20th cent; newspaper cuttings referring to S Lincs, *c*1870–90.

Everard Green (1844–1926) bequest *c*600 v, including periodicals of the 19th and early 20th cent, covering mainly heraldry and genealogy.

Ashley Maples (1868–1950) bequest *c*500 v, including periodicals of the 19th and early 20th cent, covering numismatology and natural history.

Presentation books *c*450 v, including pamphlets, mainly of the period 1650–1750 on miscellaneous subjects.

The School Library (given by the Society to the Grammar School) comprising 106 v of the period 1535–1747. Classics and mainly continental.

The Vestry Library (given by the Society to the parish church). *c*250 v, mainly theological works, of which *c*100 are STC items and *c*150 16th and 17th cent items.

London (Greater)

Alpine Club Library, 74 South Audley Street, London W1Y 5FF. Tel (01) 499 1542. Open Tues-Fri 10.30 am-12.30 pm, 1.30-5 pm by prior arrangement with the librarian.

The Alpine Club was founded in 1857 to promote mountain climbing and exploration throughout the world, and to disseminate knowledge of these subjects. In 1972 the library was formed into a charitable trust. In 1975 the Club absorbed the Ladies' Alpine Club, and the Library absorbed its library, and now contains *c*15,000 v on mountaineering and mountains and related subjects, including an outstanding collection on the Alps, especially in the 19th cent. Extensive archives and mss.

Card cat, published as *Alpine Club Library catalogue* (v 1), London, Heinemann, 1982 (author and classified).

Catalogue of books in the Library of the Alpine Club, 1880; 1888; 1899; subsequent accessions listed in *Alpine Journal*.

The Alpine Club, 1857–1957: catalogue of the centenary exhibition. . .1957, 1957.

T S Blakeney, 'The Alpine Club archives', *Alpine Journal* 71 (1966), p285-95.

E Pyatt and F Solari, 'The reorganization of the Alpine Club Library', *Alpine Journal* 74 (1969), p356-8.

N R Rice, 'A guide to the archives of the Alpine Club', *ibid.* 78 (1973), p71-7.

F H Keenlyside ed. 'Alpine centenary 1857–1957', *ibid.* 62 (295) (1957), 194p.

Books *c*10,000 titles, including *c*1,300 pre-1851, of which *c*250 are of the 18th cent, and *c*30 earlier (1518 onwards). They cover mountaineering (including the history of mountaineering clubs); travel and exploration (of which there is an exceptionally fine early 19th cent collection, including colour plate books) of the Alps, and the mountainous regions of Great Britain and other parts of the world; the natural history of these regions, chiefly geology and physical geography, especially volcanoes, glaciers; and alpine flora both in its natural habitat and its cultivation elsewhere.

Catalogue, 1982, p1-180.

Climbing guides *c*500 guides from all parts of the world, 19th and 20th cent.

Ibid. v 1, 1982, p185-98.

Pamphlets Probably *c*10,000, accumulated uncatalogued from the beginning of the library.

Cat in progress; to be included in *Catalogue*, v 2 (forthcoming).

Periodicals *c*900 titles in 4,500 v, including complete runs of almost all the leading mountaineering journals. Also early magazines of the Alpine districts, eg *Alpina*.

Ibid. v 1, 1982, p203-30.

Amalgamated Union of Engineering Workers (Engineering Section), 110 Peckham Road, London SE15 5EL. Tel (01) 703 4231. Open Mon-Fri 9 am-5 pm on written application to the General Secretary. Photocopier available.

The Amalgamated Society of Engineers, Machinists, Smiths, Millwrights, and Patternmakers was founded in 1851 as an amalgamation of many existing trade unions, and after further successive mergers with smaller unions in 1920 became the Amalgamated Engineering Union, in 1967 the Amalgamated Engineering Federation, and in 1971 the Amalgamated Union of Engineering Workers.

Sources in British Political History 1900–51. 1975, v 1, p6-9.

Research Department Library The present library dates from 1966, but incorporates earlier collections, some of which perhaps date from the appointment of G D H Cole as Research Officer in 1915. Mainly periodicals, but also 200 v of books, including John Burns' copies of Holyoake *History of co-operation* 1875 v 1, J L and B Hammond *Rise of modern industry* 1925, and B Webb *My apprenticeship* 1926; and possibly other works from the library of John (Elliot) Burns (1858–1943), most of which was transferred to the Library of the Trades Union Congress in 1959, having been given to the union of which he was a member in 1942–3; there remains a file of papers and correspondence relating to the collection, and there are books from it in the Museum (see below). There are 4 books from the collection of Tom Mann (1856–1941) who was General Secretary 1918–21, viz J M Davidson *Henry George* 1899, E J Dillon *Eclipse of Russia* 1918, J W Smith *China's roar* 1930 (author's presentation copy), and Cumming *Moscow trial* 1933. Many books from the library have been dispersed.

Card cat (author and subject) includes many discarded books.

Museum Collection The Engineering Section Museum was opened in 1977 to set out the history of the engineering industry and of the union in parallel with this. Most of the exhibits are artefacts, but one small case is filled with printed material relating to the history of the union. Further collections belonging to the Museum are housed in the Research Department Library adjacent; they include *c*30 books from the Burns Collection. There are collections of publications of the constituent unions before the mergers of 1851 and 1920: Mechanics' Friendly Institute rules of 1824; Friendly United Mechanics member's card, 1832; a collection given by Sir Robert Young (1872–1957) MP of W Thompson's copies of rules etc 1842–55 of the Philosophical Society of Journeymen Millwrights, and of the Journeymen Steam Engine Machine Makers and Millwright's Friendly Society; also reports and rules of the Steam Engine Makers' Society 1879–1918; publications of the Amalgamated Society of Engineers, including sets of annual and other reports (and *Monthly Journal* from 1905), rules, and occasional documents on lockouts, etc. Some 19th and 20th cent ephemera on the trade union movement, given by members. Trades Union Congress reports, etc 1867–1907.

Rough typescript lists, but no systematic cat.

AUEW Engineering Section Museum: a permanent exhibition of members' involvement in industry, 1981, p5-6, lists some of the printed material chronologically (gratis).

Anthroposophical Library, Rudolf Steiner House, 35 Park Road, Marylebone, London NW1 6XT. Tel (01) 723 4400. Open Mon-Fri 2-6 pm (Tues 7.15 pm) on application to the librarian.

The Anthroposophical Society in Great Britain was founded in 1923 to promote the work of Rudolf Steiner (1861–1925) and its application to medicine, education, remedial teaching and agriculture. The Society established the Anthroposophical Library in 1931 to collect literature on all aspects of anthroposophy. There is also a lending collection at the Rudolf Steiner Library, 38 Museum Street, London WC1A 1LP, established in 1935.

Rudolf Steiner Collection This comprises the complete works of Rudolf Steiner, both in German and in English, in most editions.

Published list of works in English.

Architectural Association Library, 34–6 Bedford Square, London WC1B 3ES. Tel (01) 636 0974. Open Mon-Fri 10 am-6 pm (5 pm in vac, closed part of summer vac) to members only; to others only after written application in order to consult material not available in any other accessible collection, strictly by appointment only. Photocopier available.

The Architectural Association was founded in 1847, following correspondence in *The Builder*, as a school to provide evening instruction for architectural students; it incorporated the Association of Architectural Draughtsmen, founded in 1842 by James Wylson (Robert Kerr, who became the Architectural Association's first President and Charles Gray were the co-founders). In 1901, the Architectural Association School of Architecture Day School opened, although the evening classes continued for some time. The Architectural Association Library, founded in 1862 following the failure of an earlier book club, is mainly a working collection for the school's staff and students and Members of the Association, with one departmental collection and a Technical Section (with over 5,000 articles, pamphlets and trade catalogues). The Association has a separate Slide Library (with over 60,000 slides).

Elizabeth Dixon, *The Architectural Association Library*, 1981 (a detailed history repr from the *Architectural Association Ann Rev* 1979).

Introduction to the Library (new edition every autumn).

General Collection The library contains *c*25,000 books (in addition to maps and theses) on architecture, building construction, and related subjects.

Card cat (author and classified) begun 1907.

Indexes of architects and localities.

Theses and essays in *The Architectural Association Library*, 4th ed 1978.

Rare Book Collection Several hundred books which include over 150 pre-1851; a book of 1493 (an incomplete *Nuremberg Chronicle*); several of the 16th cent; and *c*20 of the 17th cent. There are British and foreign books on architecture, building and landscape architecture, with works (mainly of the 18th cent) on drawing and perspective. There are many large 18th cent monumental editions with plates, especially of Inigo Jones (1573–1652), Batty Langley (1696–1751), and Andrea Palladio (1508–80). Some mss, including one of Humphry Repton's 'Red Books'.

Select list.

Published *Catalogue of the books in the library of the Architectural Association*, 1869; 1871; 1873; 1877; 1882; 1895; with supplements.

Collections incorporated in the Library The rare book collection, and some of the modern material, has been built up from bequests and donations. The most important collections included are those of Wyatt Papworth (1822–94) given *c*1870; W Gullier, 1888, including *Vitruvius Britannicus* and *New Vitruvius Britannicus*; Arthur Cates (1829–1901) bequest of part of his library, including early and rare continental works and 18th cent books on perspective; Thomas Garner (1839–1906), 223 books of 1611 onwards given by his widow; Thomas M Rickman (*d*1916), President, a bequest of *c*100 v from his library. Other bequests have come from Lt-Col Henry Louis Florence (1843–1916) (a library of art and architectural books); Edwin Otho Sachs (1870–1919); Henry M Fletcher (*d*1955); Alan Potter; Percy May, Hon Librarian (*d*1971); C W Clark (*d*1973) (80 v of books and 19th cent periodicals). Some of these collections, however, were reduced in dispersals of older material *c*1955.

(Note: For periodical holdings, see *Periodicals and serials in the Architectural Association Library*, 4th ed 1980.)

Armourers' and Brasiers' Company, Armourers' Hall, 81 Coleman Street, London EC2R 5BJ. Tel (01) 606 1199. Open by appointment with the Clerk to the Company.

Twenty-second in order of precedence of the City livery companies, chartered in 1453, but founded earlier. The archives are deposited in the Guildhall Library, but *c*200 books, mostly donated by liverymen, are kept at the Hall; 60 pre-1851, including 1 STC; 5 Wing and 17 ESTC, chiefly on the history of London and of the livery companies, or on arms and armour.

Ms cat.

S H Pitt, *Some notes on the history of the Armourers and Brasiers*, 1930.

W F Kahl, *The development of London livery companies*, Boston, 1960 (bibliography).

C J Ffoulkes, *Some account of the Company . . .*, 1927.

Armouries Library, London EC3N 4AB. Tel (01) 709 0765. Open Mon-Fri 10 am-12.30 pm, 2-5 pm by appointment.

The library is a historical collection maintained by the Department of the Environment for the staff of the Armouries, a museum collection first assembled for display in the 17th cent at the Tower where the Board of Ordnance had its HQ. The Armouries had only a few reference books until *c*1930 when more systematic acquisitions began, and the collection has been organized as a library only since 1945.

S Barter, 'The Library of the Armouries, H M Tower of London', *Bull Circle of State Librarians*, May 1972, p21-30.

General The library contains between 7,000 and 10,000 items on arms and armour and related subjects, of which at least 500 are pre-1851, mostly on European arms and armour, fortification, the Tower of London, fencing manuals from 1536, drill manuals from 1608, general military history, horsemanship, heraldry and orders of chivalry. The earliest items are the 1532 and 1536 editions of *Vegetius De re militari*, noted for their illustrations.

Card cat (author) and incomplete sheaf cat (alphabetical subject); these include articles in the library's collection of 20th cent periodicals.

Catalogues Collection Several thousand catalogues of collections, exhibitions, and sales, of arms and armour. This collection is comprehensive for recent decades, and includes many pre-1851 catalogues.

Sale cat indexed in separate card cat; cats of collections and exhibitions in general cat.

Collections incorporated in the library Collections acquired but not kept separate. The first major acquisition was the gift in 1942 by the collector-scholar Francis Henry Cripps-Day (*c*1863–1961) of a major portion of his private collection. In 1945 books were bought from the collection of the French arms scholar Charles Buttin. In 1963 *c*1,000 v, including some of the most noteworthy books and catalogues in the library were bought from the executors of Sir James Gow Mann (1897–1962) Master of Armouries.

Army and Navy Club, 36–9 Pall Mall, London SW1Y 5JN. Open only to members and their guests.

The club was founded in 1837 and has a small military and general library, but most of the rare books have been dispersed.

C W Firebrace, *The Army and Navy Club 1837–1933*, London, 1934.

Anthony Lejeune, *Gentlemen's clubs*, 1979, p27-31.

Art Workers' Guild Library, 6 Queen Square, London WC1N 3AR. Tel (01) 837 3474. Open by arrangement on written application to the librarian.

The Guild was founded at the height of the arts and crafts movement in 1884 by five young architects, with the aim of bringing together artists and craftsmen to mutual advantage. The library has been built up by gifts from Guildsmen, and now contains *c*2,000 v on fine art, architecture, applied and decorative arts, and the crafts, especially as they relate to the history of the Guild and the work of its members.

Card cat (author and classified, with separate classified section for rare books) (the cat cabinet is a handsome piece by a member, Theo Dalrymple).

H J L J Masse, *The Art Workers' Guild 1884–1934*, London, 1935.

The Art Workers' Guild, 1975 (leaflet).

Early printed books include 2 STC (Gerarde's *Herball* 1633; Guillim *Display of heraldrie* 1638,;1 Wing (Vignola *Regular architecture* 1669); a number of English and foreign 18th cent works including Chippendale *Ornaments* and several architectural books by Batty Langley and others.

Private press books A collection from the Kelmscott, Doves, Nonesuch, Vine and other presses.

Bindings A collection of books bound by members of the Guild and their students, and other eminent binders, including Anthony Gardner and Douglas Cockerell (1870–1945).

Arts and Crafts movement Many books on the movement and its mentors John Ruskin (1819–1900) and William Morris (1834–96), some by Guild members, especially William Richard Lethaby (1857–1931) first Principal of the Central School of Arts and Crafts (now the Central School of Art and Design with which the Guild has close links), and Charles Robert Ashbee (1863–1942). Works issued by the Guild's 1887 offshoot the Arts and Crafts Exhibition Society (now the Society of

Designer-Craftsmen) including *Catalogue of the first exhibition* (bound by J M Dent).

Arts Council Poetry Library, 9 Long Acre, London WC2E 9LH. Tel (01) 379 6597. Open Tues-Sat 10 am-5 pm (Fri 7 pm) to the public.

The library was founded in 1953 by the Arts Council of Great Britain to promote contemporary British poets; its scope has now been extended to include all poetry in English from *c*1910, by writers of all nationalities; translations into English of foreign poets are included, and these include 20th cent translations of older (including classical) writers. There are now *c*9,000 books, (excluding *c*11,000 duplicates intended for loan purposes), including a substantial collection of anthologies. The library buys all British poetry currently published, including many works issued by obscure publishers not to be found in the British Library, and all the current British poetry magazines (though some are held for five years only); the British collection is being enlarged retrospectively to include as much as possible of the poetry of earlier decades, with many rare editions supplied by the bequests of Sylvia Townsend Warner (1893–1978) consisting mostly of the Valentine Ackland collection, and Alec Craig. The overseas poets section contains a high proportion of works not in any other British library.

Card cat (authors; nationalities; anthology titles; bequests).

The Poetry Library of the Arts Council of Great Britain, Short-Title Catalogue 6th ed by Jonathan Barker, introd by Philip Larkin, London, Arts Council (distributed by Carcanet Press Manchester), 1981; 1st ed published in *Books* May 1953; 5th ed 1973 has introd by Alan Brownjohn.

H Spaldin, 'A poetry library', *Books*, no 321 (1959) p26-7.

The Athenaeum, 107 Pall Mall, London SW1Y 5ER. Tel (01) 839 5004. The library is private to members, but bona fide scholars may be admitted, on application to the librarian in writing well in advance of a desired visit, at the discretion of the Committee.

The Athenaeum was founded in 1824 by John Wilson Croker (1780–1857) as a club for men of literary and artistic distinction. Its library has always been a major feature, and it is by far the richest of the London club libraries.

Humphry Ward, *History of the Athenaeum...*, London, 1926, p98-111.

F R Cowell, *The Athenaeum...*, London, Heinemann, 1975, p24, 65-90 (abridged in *Library Association Record* 78(9) (1976), p423-37.

General Collections The library has been built up mainly from donations, and now contains over 60,000 v, including a high proportion of rare books (which for the most part have not been included in dispersals of recent decades). It was intended primarily as a working library in the humanities, particularly English history (on which it is exceptionally strong), the fine arts, natural history, and archaeology. The classic, chiefly Protestant, theologians are represented, with standard sets of the Fathers and the *Acta Sanctorum*. Members' donations include most of John Murray's own publications (1778–1843), and many of the bird books of John Gould FRS (1801–81). There are some 18th cent voyages, and a complete set of the Hakluyt Society.

Card cat (Library of Congress classification), superseding *A catalogue of the library of the Athenaeum*, 1845; *Supplement*, 1851; *Second supplement*, 1859.

Catalogue of the Servants' Library at the Athenaeum, 2nd ed 1909.

Donations listed in *Annual Report* 1831–1939, currently typed for each meeting of the Library Committee.

Turnor Bequests A collection chiefly of 18th and 19th cent foreign illustrated art books bought with money bequeathed by Charles Turnor FRS (1768–1853), Prebendary of Lincoln; also including Migne *Patrologia*.

List in *Second supplement*, 1859.

Slade Collection 31 books on art, mostly 18th and 19th cent foreign, bought with a bequest of £100 from Felix Slade (1790–1868) the patron of the fine arts.

List of books on art purchased under the directions of the will of the late Felix Slade, 1870.

Vernon Dante Collection A part of the collection on Dante formed by the Hon William (John Borlase-) Warren (-Venables) Vernon (1834–1919) the Dante scholar, given in 1908, *c*400 v (the remainder went to the Travellers' Club).

Periodicals After a dispersal in 1945 there remain complete sets from the beginning of a limited number of the major journals in science (including the *Philosophical Transactions*), history and art, with a few on other subjects.

Pamphlet Collections At least 10,000 pamphlets, bound in over 2,000 v, of the 18th cent to the present. In addition to extensive miscellaneous collections designated the Athenaeum Collection, the Miscellaneous Collection, and the Supplementary Collection, accounting for over half the total, there are: American Collection, 51 v; Bangorian Collection, 7 v 1709–29 (on the controversy surrounding Benjamin Hoadley (1676–1761) when as Bishop of Bangor he denied divine right); Bullion Collection, 4 v 1810–12; Corn Law Collection, 5 v 1796–1842; Slavery Collection, 6 v 1797–1830; Tractarian Collection, *Tracts for the Times* 6 v 1838–42 and Puseyite tracts 13 v 1839–44; Sermons (Church of England) 5 v 1793–1843, and Visitation Charges 14 v 1837–42; Union with Ireland, 8 v 1799–1800. Also a number of miscellaneous collections formed by Sir James Mackintosh (1765–1832) the philosopher, 21 v 1805–16; by Edward Gibbon (1737–94) the historian, 23 v, donated by a member of his family *c*1850; by Morton Pitt, 139 v 1695–1796; and by James Nasmith (1740–1808) the antiquary, 43 v 1759–1802.

Separate author cat in *Catalogue* 1845, p369–534; *Supplement* 1851, p189-270; *Second supplement* 1859, p161-253.

War Collections There were formerly special collections on the Napoleonic Wars, the Crimean War, the Russo-Turkish War, the Franco-Prussian War, the Boer War, and the 1914–18 War. Some parts of these collections have been given to other libraries, the remainder integrated into the general collection.

Austrian Institute Library, 28 Rutland Gate, London SW7 1PQ. Tel (01) 584 8654. Open to all Mon-Fri 9 am-12 noon, 3-6 pm.

The Library contains *c*6,000 v on Austrian history, art and music, including some valuable late 19th and early 20th cent colour plate books on Austrian art and theatre.

Bank of England, Threadneedle Street, London EC2R 8AH. Telex 885001.

The Bank was founded in 1694 as a joint-stock company mainly to lend money to the government in the emergency of war, and it remained a combined central and retail bank under private control until it was nationalized in 1946. The Bank's first formal library was founded in 1850, and known as the Clerk's Library, but now the Staff Library. It originally contained 18th cent and later general literature, but is now limited to current recreational reading, and its rare books have been dispersed, important books being transferred to the Reference Library. In addition to the collections described below, there are others in offices which are treated as private.

Catalogue of the Bank of England Library and Literary Association, 1851; 1863.

Sir John Clapham, *The Bank of England: a history*, Cambridge UP, 1944, 2 v (does not mention the collections directly, but alludes to some unique or rare items to be found in them).

'The Reference Library and Staff Library', *The Old Lady* 54 (230) 19 June 1978, p54-8.

Reference Library

Open Mon-Fri 9.30 am-5 pm by appointment with the librarian on written application, for material not available elsewhere.

The present Reference Library dates from 1931, when most of the collections previously kept in departmental libraries and on office reference shelves were centralized; the most important were the Directors' Library, established in the late 19th cent from material which had accumulated from the time of the foundation; the Bank Note Office Library dating formally from *c*1860, and the original Reference Library probably established in the early 20th cent. It now contains over 50,000 v which is mainly a working collection on economics and banking, and includes much 19th cent material, in addition to the segregated collections referred to below. Most of the rare books seem to have been received at the time of publication, but there have been some retrospective purchases (eg the Burdett-Coutts collection). The only identifiable major donation is that of John Gellibrand Hubbard (1805–89), MP, a Director 1838–41, afterwards 1st Baron Addington.

There are at least 4 STC; 148 Wing; 70 ESTC and 125 1801–50 items.

Card cat (author and classified) including rare book collections.

Bank of England Reference Library catalogue, 1936 (classified with author index).

Unpublished cat of Directors' Library, 1898.

Tracts Collection 120 v, including 4 STC; 91 Wing and 25 early ESTC items. Most of the early items are on usury. There are a number of items of 1694–7 on the Bank.

Pamphlet Collection *c*1,200 items in 112 v, mainly 19th cent on all aspects of banking, the role of the Bank of England, currency questions, Bank Charter Act, bullion, finance, the national debt, company law, economics, trade etc, almost all in English.

Burdett-Coutts Collection A collection without marks of ownership acquired from a bookseller, probably from the library of Angela Georgina Burdett-Coutts, Baroness Burdett-Coutts (1814–1906), the philanthropist and partner in the bank of Coutts & Co (Sotheby 15 May 1922). It contains 35 Wing and 9 ESTC pamphlets of 1694–1732 on the foundation of the Bank, banking, landbanks, currency, etc.

Ms list.

General Rare Books Collection Books on economics and trade from 1697 onwards, including many of the works of the great economists, not necessarily in the earliest editions; 12 items on the South Sea Company 1716–21; Reports of the Committee of Secrecy 1721, and related works; 1 v of broadsheets and pamphlets on the Royal Africa Co and African trade 1709–10, etc.

Bank History Collection Books on the history of the Bank of England include a grangerized Francis *History* 1847, and some interesting material on attempts to defraud the Bank, reports of trials etc. There is also a special collection of 19th cent government reports on the Bank. Some rare works on the architecture of the Bank's buildings, including a copy of *The old Bank of England* 1930 with the cancelled preface; and several of the works of Sir John Soane (1753–1837). There are some rare limited editions of histories of foreign central banks, which supplement the comprehensive collection of bank histories in the Reference Library.

T A Stephens, *A contribution to the bibliography of the Bank of England*, London 1897. (op)

An historical catalogue of engravings, drawings and paintings in the Bank of England, 1928.

Serials Collection Includes *Castaing's Course of the Exchange* then Shergold's, Lutyens', and Wetenhall's 1705–1888 (incomplete) with E A Buckman, 'Bibliographical notes on the Course of the Exchanges' (unpublished typescript 1977); an excellent set of London directories 1755–1839; *London Gazette* 1665– , and a few banking and general periodicals beginning in the 18th and early 19th cent; Acts of Parliament from 1693.

The Museum

Open Mon-Fri by appointment with the Secretary to the Bank, on written application, to see material not available elsewhere.

The Museum, which forms part of the Secretary's Department, contains mostly artefacts connected with the Bank's history, but also some miscellaneous printed material, including unpublished material printed for internal circulation, a collection of bank notes, with at least 13 items printed 1707–1850 (3 ESTC).

Typescript list of items originating in Secretary's Dept, some in Museum, others transferred to Reference Library or offices.

Baptist Missionary Society Library, 93 Gloucester Place, Marylebone, London W1H 4AA. Tel (01) 935 1482. Open Mon-Fri 9 am-5 pm to bona fide students by appointment.

The Society was founded in 1792 as a mission to foreign countries. It has been active principally in North India, South and South-East Asia, China, Africa and the West Indies. Its missionaries in Serampore in the early 19th cent printed grammars and translations of the Bible in Indian languages, many of which are not in the British Library or the India Office, but are in the Society's own collection. *c*5,000 v altogether. Also substantial archives.

No cat of printed books.

Mary M Evans, *Baptist Missionary Society papers*. 1964–5. 4 parts.

F A Cox, *History of the BMS, 1792–1842*. London, 1842.

J C Marshman, *The life and times of Carey, Marshman and Ward, embracing the history of the Serampore Mission*. London, 1859, 2 v.

F Townley Lord, *Achievement... 1792–1942*. London, Carey Press, 1942.

Official publications include *Missionary Herald* from 1819.

Baptist Union of Great Britain and Ireland, Baptist Church House, 4 Southampton Row, London WC1B 4AB. Tel (01) 405 9803. Open Mon-Fri 9.30 am-4.30 pm by appointment only, following written application well in advance of an intended visit, to the Department of Ministry.

The Baptist Union was founded in 1812–3 among the so-called Federation of Particular Baptist Churches, and gradually came to include the General Baptists of the New Connexion. The library is said to have effectively begun in 1863 with the gift of his own large collection by the retiring secretary Edward Steane (1798–1882) Minister of Camberwell. It has absorbed the library of the Baptist Historical Society, and has been built up mainly by donations. There are now *c*8,000 v on Baptist history and theology, with some miscellaneous works by Baptists. These include *c*120 v of pamphlets (over 1,000 items) *c*1780–1860, including sermons, controversial works, works on baptism, etc; many of these were printed for local churches, and some are probably not to be found elsewhere. Periodicals include the *Baptist Register* 1794–1802, the *Baptist Magazine* complete from 1809, and the *Calcutta Christian Observer* 1833–47 (except 1837–8). Books on theology, especially baptism, include classics of Baptist doctrine, mostly after 1800, but with some earlier works from Edward Legh *Critica sacra* 1641 onwards. There are a few 16th and 17th cent English Bibles; *c*400 hymnals, mostly after 1800, but with some earlier, from 1705 onwards; mainly, but not exclusively, collections intended specifically for Baptist congregations; histories of individual Baptist congregations, mostly 20th cent privately printed; *c*500 v of Baptist biography, including a few late 17th cent works.

Classified card cat with author index, superseding *A catalogue of the Baptist Union Library*, 1915.

Ernest A Payne, *The Baptist Union: a short history*, 1959, p97, 182, 189.

Barking Public Libraries, Valence Reference Library, Local History Collections, Becontree Avenue, Dagenham, Essex RM8 3HT. Tel (01) 592 6537 or 2211. Open Mon, Tues, Thurs, Fri 9.30 am-7 pm; Wed and Sat 1 pm, by appointment.

The Curator/Archivist administers from the adjoining borough museum Valence House the Borough Archives in addition to the printed local history collections in the Valence Reference Library, most of which came from the former Borough of Dagenham, with additions from the former Borough of Barking in 1965.

Card cat.

Essex, Barking and Dagenham Collection Books and pamphlets on the former county of Essex generally, and on Barking and Dagenham, exceed 3,000, of which *c*300 are pre-1851. There is also a collection of specific localities in Essex outside the Borough.

Dagenham Public Libraries, *Essex and Dagenham: a catalogue of books, pamphlets and maps*, 1957, 2nd ed, 1961; does not include the ephemera on Essex localities. (op)

Greater London Collection A collection on the present

administrative area of Greater London (including Middlesex) except those parts included in the Essex collection.

Card cat.

English Counties Collection A collection on the counties of England, except Essex and Greater London, mostly standard histories, including 5 Wing; *c*25 ESTC and *c*35 of 1801–50.

Card cat.

Selective typescript list, 1965.

Barclays Bank plc Head Office, Director's Library, 54 Lombard Street, London EC3P 3AH. Tel (01) 626 1567. Open Mon-Fri 9 am-5 pm on written application to the Archivist. Photocopying facilities.

The library was assembled in 1972 from various collections within the Bank, which has been on its present site since 1728, and into which many older banks have been merged. It contains *c*500 v, including over 50 pre-1851 on banking, commerce, industry, economics, law; histories of Barclays Bank and its constituents, and biographies of the Barclay family, including R Barclay *Apology for the true Christian divinity...with a memoir...1850*; topography and history of London and of England generally; and some miscellaneous material. There is also printed material in the bank's archives, especially of Martins Bank, successor to Gresham's Bank, together with cheques, banknotes, etc issued by the various banks.

Typescript subject list.

Barnet Museum Reference Library, 31 Wood Street, Barnet, Herts EN5 4BE. Tel (01) 449 0321. Open by prior arrangement with the Curator.

The Museum is administered on behalf of the London Borough of Barnet by the Barnet and District Local History Society, and houses the Society's library which has been built up since its foundation in 1927. There are *c*500 v, of which over 50 are pre-1851, mostly donated by members, including a large gift by Mr J Faulkner in 1935. They relate to Barnet and the surrounding area of Hertfordshire and North London.

Typescript subject list and shelflist.

Barnet Public Libraries, Central Library, The Burroughs, Hendon, London NW4 4BE. Tel (01) 202 5625 (Reference) Ext 55 (Archives). Telex 25665. Open Mon-Fri 9 am-8 pm; Sat 4 pm. Archives by appointment only.

The Borough libraries were formed in 1965 by amalgamating those of the Boroughs of Hendon and Finchley and the Urban Districts of Barnet, East Barnet and Friern Barnet.

Central Reference Library The general reference collection, built up from 1929, includes *c*200 pre-1851 books, chiefly history, topography and travel. *c*50 of these are pre-1801.

Typescript list of pre-1801 English books.

Sheaf cat to 1964 of Hendon libraries (author and classified); continued on microfiche to include all borough libraries.

A Welford, 'A brief history of Hendon Public Libraries', (typescript, 1969).

Archives and Local History Department (Entrance is in Church Walk, Egerton Gardens). It holds the official archives of the borough and its predecessors, and is a repository for manorial documents, in addition to printed material. The local history collection includes *c*100 pre-1851 items, chiefly histories of London, Middlesex and Hertfordshire, and sermons. The collection is mainly derived from the former Hendon collection (begun 1932) and the smaller Finchley collection (begun 1944), with some books from Chipping Barnet Library and from the Barnet Museum. There are separate collections given by C O Banks, author of *Finchley and Friern Barnet* (*c*1920), on Finchley, including his ms notebooks; by Major Norman George Brett-James on Mill Hill; and by P Davenport on Hendon. The library of the Mill Hill and Hendon Historical Society, *c*1,000 items, mostly 19th and 20th cent pamphlets, is deposited on loan.

Archives and records in the Local History Collection (1981?) Most pre-1801 items included in the Reference Library list.

Bedford College Library, Inner Circle, Regent's Park, London NW1 4NS. Tel (01) 486 4400. Open Mon-Fri 9 am-5 pm (to 9 pm also Sat 9 am-1 pm during term), on written application to the librarian. Photocopying; film and fiche readers.

In 1849 the Ladies' College, Bedford Square, was founded by Mrs Elizabeth Jesser Reid (1789–1866), daughter of William Sturch (1753?–1838), the Unitarian writer, for the liberal education of nonconformist women. She regarded the library as an important part of her foundation, and gave some of her collection of English, French and Italian literature to it; the remainder was donated after her death by her friend Elizabeth Ann Bostock to whom she had bequeathed it. In 1861 it was enlarged and renamed Bedford College for Women, moving to York Place, Baker Street, in 1874, and in 1878, when women were first admitted to degrees, its students began to take the University of London examinations, though it did not become a school of the University until 1900. In 1913 it was moved to its present site, and a building for the library was endowed by Lady Tate (widow of Sir Henry, 1819–99) which bears her name. Most of the books have been bought for the needs of the teaching faculties, mainly in the humanities, with a strong literary emphasis. The few bequests include books on botany and mathematics from Mark Pattison (1813–84),

1,000 v from Mrs Morton Sumner (*d*1901), 1,100 v from Mrs Louise d'Este Courtenay Oliver (1850–1919), and 1,500 v from Prof John George Robertson (1867–1933), Professor of German. The library of the Board of Dutch Studies has been incorporated into the collections. Christiana Jane Lady Herringham (*d*1929) the artist, wife of the University Vice Chancellor Sir Wilmot Parker Herringham, MD (1855–1936), donated an art and general collection (incl a few pre-1851 books), the only donation kept as a separate collection. The library contains 2,239 pre-1851 books, chiefly classical and modern literature and history, with some botany and agriculture, and a few on other topics; 1,649 English (45 STC, 110 Wing, 464 ESTC and 1,030 1801–50 incl, 358 of 1847–9 collected for the Background Material Scheme of the JSCLC) and 690 foreign (chiefly Dutch, French and Italian, with a few German and Spanish; 42 16th cent, 97 17th cent, 351 18th cent, 200 1801–50). The bulk of the Spanish Collection was transferred to Westfield College in 1964.

General author cat on cards. Chronological card index of pre-1901 books (before 1800 in separate sequences for English and foreign).

Marjorie J Tuke, *A history of Bedford College for Women*, London, OUP, 1939, p265–72. (op)

J Cowan, *A short history of Bedford College Library 1849–1972* (1973) (typescript).

Note The College is due, eventually, to be amalgamated with Royal Holloway College, Egham Hill, Surrey.

Bedford Estate Office, 29a Montague Street, Bloomsbury, London WC1B 5BL. Tel (01) 636 2713. Open by appointment only.

The Office administers the settled estates of the Dukes of Bedford on behalf of the trustees. The archives include printed surveyors' reports on them from 1745 onwards. The main library is at Woburn Abbey (see under Bedfordshire).

Beth Din and Beth Hamidrash Library, Adler House, Tavistock Square, London WC1H 9HN. Tel (01) 387 1066. Open Sun-Fri 10.30 am-12.30 pm to members of the Court of the Chief Rabbi only; enquiries to librarian by letter only.

A general reference collection of *c*6,000 v (with mss) in Hebrew and Aramaic on Jewish religion, law, literature, history and culture. Much pre-1851 printed material, including 12 incunabula. The library was founded by the purchase, after his death, of the collection of Chief Rabbi Solomon Hirschel (1761–1842). In 1889 the library bought that of Asher Asher (1837–89), first Secretary of the United Synagogue, rich in later Hebrew literature and Jewish customs.

H M Rabinowicz, 'The Beth Hamidrash Library—London', *AJA Quarterly* 7(4) (1962), p21–5.

'The Beth Hamidrash Library, London' in H M Rabinowicz, *The Jewish literary treasures of England and America*. New York, Yoseloff, 1971, p56-9.

Bermans and Nathans Ltd, Research Library, 40 Camden Street, London NW1 0EN. Tel (01) 387 0999. Open Mon-Fri 9 am-5.30 pm, by appointment after payment of a substantial fee.

This library, of the well-known firm of theatrical costumiers, contains over 3,000 v of reference works on costume and military uniform, and some of the theatre generally, with many rare colour plate books, and 19th cent magazines.

Bexley Public Libraries, Local Studies Library, Hall Place, Bourne Road, Bexley, Kent DA5 1PQ. Tel (03225) 26574. Telex 846119. Open Mon-Sat 10 am-5 pm (dusk if earlier).

The Local Studies Section was set up in 1972 to integrate the local history collections from the former boroughs of Bexley (founded 1896) and Erith (founded 1906), the Urban District of Crayford, and the Sidcup part of the UD of Chislehurst, with the Borough Archives and museum collections. *c*7,000 books and pamphlets on the Borough, and *c*4,400 on the former County of Kent, including STC and Wing items, and 60 ESTC.

Card cat.

Bible Society Library, 146 Queen Victoria Street, London EC4V 4BX. Tel (01) 248 4751. Open Mon-Fri 9.30 am-4 pm to bona fide scholars by prior arrangement; letter of introduction required. (Library exhibition open without formality to casual visitors 9.30 am-5 pm.) Photocopying at discretion; microfilming can be arranged.

In 1804 the British and Foreign Bible Society was founded as a non-denominational body to encourage the circulation of the Christian Scriptures, which it has translated wholly or partly into over 1,500 languages. It is now known as the Bible Society. (*See* John Owen, *The history of the British and Foreign Bible Society*, London, 1816–20, 3 v; George Browne, *The history of the... Society*, London 1859, 2 v; W Canton, *A history of the... Society*, London, 1904–10, 5 v; J M Roe, *A history of the... Society 1905–54*, London, The Society, 1965.)

Scripture Library The founders considered that a library was essential to the work of the Society and solicited donations. Granville Sharp (1735–1813) gave the nucleus of 39 v, and the collections have grown continuously ever since, until there are now *c*33,000 v of printed Bibles in nearly 2,000 languages and dialects (and some important mss). William Blair (1766–1822), the surgeon, gave 200 v of Bibles and foreign commentaries (the latter subsequently dispersed). 1,300 English Bibles collected by

Francis Fry (1830–86), the chocolate manufacturer, were bought in 1890. The collection of early Hebrew, Greek and German Bibles of Christian David Ginsburg (1831–1914), the OT scholar, was secured in 1909 by public subscription. In 1966 the Society bought the collection of fine editions formed by the Leipzig philologist Hans Conon von der Gabelentz (1807–74) and his sons Hans Georg von der Gabelentz (1840–93) and sold the duplicates. The English collection includes the first editions of all the major versions except Tyndale's 1526 NT, and amounts to *c*450 STC, *c*320 Wing, *c*600 ESTC and *c*450 of 1801–50. There are 81 incunabula (incl the Psalter printed in 1457 at Mainz by Fust and Schöffer) and perhaps *c*2,500 foreign pre-1851 editions altogether. The German collection contains all pre-Lutheran versions. All the great polyglots are held, and all the early illustrated Bibles.

Among the so-called 'missionary versions' are: John Eliot's Massachusetts Indian New Testament (1661); Ziegenbalg's Tamil New Testament (1714); Henry Martyn's Urdu New Testament (1814); Henry Nott's Tahitian St Luke (1818) and the first book of Scripture to be printed in a Polynesian language; Robert Morrison's Chinese Bible (1823); Bishop Samuel Crowther's Yoruba Epistle to the Romans (1850); and William Carey's many Indian versions.

Card indexes by languages; translators and editors; places of publication; printers; and miscellaneous (including popular titles). T H Darlow and H F Moule, *Historical catalogue of the printed editions of Holy Scripture in the Library of the British and Foreign Bible Society*, London, the Society 1903–11, 4 v (op). Vol I is superseded by A S Herbert, *Historical catalogue of printed editions of the English Bible...* London, the Society, 1968. Revised editions also published for African languages (1966–75), languages of the Indian sub-continent (1977), Oceanic (1963) and China (1966). Earlier printed cats 1822, 1857 and 1901 (English to 1640).

J Peatman, 'A history of the library of the British and Foreign Bible Society, 1804–1969' (thesis, Univ of Sheffield, MA, 1969).

D Jesson, 'The libraries of the British and Foreign Bible Society and the American Bible Society' (thesis, Loughborough Univ, MLS, 1977).

G Coldham, 'Treasures of Bible House Library', *The Bible in the world*, Spring 1971, p7-9.

A short guide to the Library. (*c*1972) (cat of the permanent exhibition).

The Library and its treasures, (booklet and eight postcards), *c*1970.

H M Rabinowicz, *Treasures of Judaica*, NY, Yoseloff, 1971, p63-5.

Central House Library The collections of books formerly kept in the offices of the Translations Department have recently been formed into a library, for the use of staff, of some 5,000 v altogether, of which probably fewer than 100 are pre-1851, chiefly biblical commentaries, and works on biblical studies and linguistics.

Classified card cat (with author index).

Archives The records include the annual *Report* from 1805 and copies of other Society publications.

Birkbeck College Library, Malet Street, London WC1E 7HX. Tel (01) 580 6622 Ext 239. Open Mon-Fri 10 am-10.30 pm (term), 9 pm (Easter vac), 8 pm (other vacs); Sat (term only) 10 am-5 pm, on written application to the librarian. Photocopying; microform reading and printing facilities.

The College originated in 1823 as the London Mechanics' Institution. Its founders intended it to be a working-class co-operative for the further education of its members, but almost immediately its management was taken over by George Birkbeck (1776–1841) and his friends, and it became an orthodox mechanics' institute. In 1866 it became the Birkbeck (Literary and Scientific) Institution, and in 1907 Birkbeck College. It became a school of the University of London in 1920, but is still primarily a college for mature and part-time students. Its library was almost totally destroyed when the College was bombed in 1941, but some rare books and the college archives were saved.

Thomas Kelly, *George Birkbeck, pioneer of adult education*. Liverpool, 1957, p76–145.

C D Burns, *A short history of Birkbeck College*. London, 1924.

General The library has been reconstituted, largely since the College moved to its present site in 1951, to meet teaching needs in the arts and sciences, and now contains *c*170,000 v. The library contains (apart from the special collections below) *c*400 pre-1800 books with 1 incunabulum. Most of these, and some of the rarer 19th cent books, are in a closed access collection; mainly works of English history or literature (especially 18th cent), with some Latin classics, and a few on other subjects. This collection contains some books surviving from the pre-war library.

Card cat to 1978 then microfiche (author and classified) includes all collections.

10 general printed cats 1833–1903, and *Catalogue of the books of the late Alexander Anderson...*, 1889, are of historical interest only.

R C Trevelyan Memorial Library Robert Calverley Trevelyan (1872–1951), classical scholar, poet and translator, collected a library, most of which was purchased after his death by his friends to form a special collection at Birkbeck College, opened in 1954. It contains 5,064 v, mostly classical and modern literature, with sections on the arts, history, philosophy, orientalia and travel, arranged for the most part in Trevelyan's bookcases and in the order in which he kept them. 266 books which had been kept by Mrs Trevelyan were added after her death by Julian Trevelyan, with some oriental prints. A few additions have come from other sources. The earlier editions, mostly literature, include *c*10 Wing; *c*35 ESTC; *c*90 English 1801–50; and *c*35 foreign 1650–1850.

Taylor Collection c150 rare books of the 16th-18th cent (and a few of the 19th cent) bequeathed by Eva Germaine Rimington Taylor (1879–1966), Prof of Geography 1930–44; mostly on geography, with surveying, astronomy, natural history and history of England.

Catalogue of the R C Trevelyan Memorial Library at Birkbeck College, 1959.

Hansard Society Library Housed at the Branch Library at 7–15 Graesse Street, London W1P 1PA. Tel (01) 580 6622 Ext 492.

The collection contains c500 v on politics and the constitution of Britain and Commonwealth countries from the library of the Hansard Society for Parliamentary Government, founded in 1944. Formerly on deposit, now donated.

Bishopsgate Institute Reference Library, 230 Bishopsgate, London EC2M 4QH. Tel (01) 247 6844. Open Mon-Fri 9.30 am-5.30 pm to all.

The Institute was opened in 1894 as a cultural centre by the Bishopsgate Foundation, an amalgamation of charities founded from the 15th cent onwards in the parish of St Botolph, Bishopsgate. Reference and lending libraries opened in 1895 (the latter transferred in 1966 to the City of London Library service). The Reference Library, which is still maintained by the Foundation though functioning as an ordinary public reference library, owes its importance to the collection-building activities of Charles William Frederick Goss (1864–1946) who was its Librarian from 1897 to 1941. It consists of a general reference collection of c30,000 v and the special collections below.

Card cat.

Leaflet. c1980, 'The Bishopsgate Institute and its collections'.

T C Harrowing, *The Bishopsgate Foundation and Institute: an address to the Bishopsgate Ward Club*. (1952).

Bishopsgate Foundation, *History of the Foundation*, 1894. (new ed) 1911.

Report of the Governing Body 1896–1913/14 (annual).

R Samuel, 'The Bishopsgate Institute', *History Workshop* 5 (1978), p163–72.

Christopher W J Harris, 'Charles William Frederick Goss' (North Western Polytechnic School of Librarianship thesis 1969, enlarged from *Library World* 72 (841), (1970), p7-10).

Many rare books unconnected with the special collections below have been sold (especially art books, Sotheby/Hodgson 25 January, 1979).

Serials Collection This comprises c500 titles, of which 317 began before 1901. Most of the latter are connected with 19th cent labour movements and secularism; many of these are in the Howell collection (qv). They also include some 18th and 19th cent general directories.

Typescript title list.

London Collection Contains c100,000 items, chiefly on the City, with special emphasis on the Bishopsgate area; these include c8,000 books and pamphlets, of which c3,000 are pre-1851. Especially strong on transport and crime.

Card cat (author and classified) with analytical entries for certain periodicals (eg *Gentleman's Magazine, Notes & Queries*).

London Directories c300 complete sets of all directories of the City published after 1830, and c100 of 1740–1830, several of which are unique copies.

C W Goss, *The London Directories 1677–1855*. London, 1932 (op). Later additions to the collection in Guildhall handlist of London directories.

London Guidebooks c600 from 1722 onwards, including 19 ESTC, 43 English 1801–50. and a number in foreign languages. Many unique.

Cat in David R Webb, 'Guide books to London before 1900'. (Thesis, Library Association, 1975.)

Howell Collection The library and papers of George Howell (1833–1910) Chartist and MP, purchased 1905; additions by purchase after 1950. The library is primarily on trade unions and the Co-operative Movement 1832–1910, with a few items published earlier and later. c3,500 books, some of which are on general political and economic subjects. c6,000 pamphlets, many of which are on radical politics; some rare or unique items are included, eg *Third address of the Bradford wool-combers*, 1825, preceding their strike. Nearly 200 periodicals, including general labour periodicals with which Howell was connected as editor or manager, sometimes marked to show authorship of articles, eg *Beehive* 1870–6, *Labour Tribune* 1886–7, and numerous sets of reports and journals of Trade Unions, eg the Steam Boiler Makers' Society 1837–1920. A ms biography by Howell of Ernest Jones (1816–69) the Chartist, with his diaries and related printed and ms material. Howell's extensive mss, diaries, correspondence, etc, including the archives of the Reform League, of which he was Secretary. Howell bequeathed to the Institute the minutes of the First International 1864–76 which he had acquired from an unknown source; these were suppressed by the Governors until 1943.

Dictionary card cat. It is planned to publish a cat in a series of subject volumes.

Periodicals in typescript handlist, also included in *Warwick Guide to British labour periodicals*, 1977.

George Howell collection—index to the correspondence. Rev ed, 1975.

F M Leventhal, *Respectable radical*, London, Weidenfeld, 1971, p213, 255-67.

——'Notes of sources', *Society for the Study of Labour History Bull.* no 10 (1965), p38-40.

Holyoake Collection The library of George Jacob Holyoake (1817–1906), socialist and freethinker, purchased 1906 with his ms diaries 1836–1900 and other mss (but not his correspondence, which is in Co-operative

Union Library, Manchester), with a few additions. *c*300 v on the co-operative movement, socialism, atheism, and related subjects. *c*300 editions of his own books and pamphlets written between 1841 and 1906, including the two pamphlets he wrote in the dark in Gloucester Gaol, and proof copies of some early books. *c*50 books to which he contributed. 30 periodicals and newspapers edited by him, with some markings of authorship of articles, including complete files of the *Oracle of reason* 1841–3 and *Reasoner* 1846–74. Articles contributed by him to other publications, mostly in the form of cuttings. *c*100 items about him. The 424 pamphlets in 65 v include in addition to his own writings, a variety of Chartist and secularist items, and the mss also contain some printed items, eg the *Objects, means and rules of the London Atheistical Society* 1842–3.

C W F Goss, *A descriptive bibliography of the writings of George Jacob Holyoake*, London 1906 (op) is not a bibliography but an annotated cat of the main part of the collection.

Dictionary card cat.

E Royle, *Victorian infidels*, Manchester, University Press, 1974, p170-98.

National Secular Society Library, deposited 1981. The Society, now the most militant of the anti-religious pressure groups, was founded in 1866 by Charles Bradlaugh (1833–91) through the agency of the *National Reformer* which he edited, and which became the Society's organ. The library contains *c*2,000 books and pamphlets, with a few periodicals, and archives on free thought, secularism, humanism, rationalism, with some material on philosophy, ecclesiastical history, and causes promoted by radicals such as socialism, divorce, feminism, and civil rights. Predominantly 1820–1920, with a few from *c*1750 onwards, and some after 1920. Bradlaugh's personal library is incorporated; his correspondence and miscellaneous papers, including some pamphlets and printed documents, assembled by his daughter and biographer Mrs Hypatia Bradlaugh Bonner (1858–1935) were donated to the Society *c*1970, with her own collection of books by Basil Bradlaugh Bonner. First editions of *c*40 early works by Mrs Annie Besant (1847–1933) who joined the Society in 1874 and became joint editor of the *National Reformer*, but was later converted to theosophy. Collections from several absorbed societies, including several hundred from the Leicester Secular Society received probably *c*1930, many being gifts from Frederick James Gould (1855–1938) the historian of rationalism. The lending collection of the Hall of Science Club and Institute, City Road, an abortive attempt by the Society to popularize secularism, printed and ms archives of the Rationalist Peace Association (1910–21) of which Mrs Bonner was Secretary. A collection acquired from Edward C Saphire, probably *c*1936 and a collection from Harry Sykes. Certain donations unconnected with secularism and some duplicates are not included in the deposit and are likely to be dispersed. The books and pamphlets (other than those among the archival collections) are at present arranged by authors regardless of provenance (for which usually the only evidence is in the books themselves).

Card cat (authors).

E Royle, *The Bradlaugh Papers. . . a descriptive index*, East Ardsley, E P Microform, 1975, a chronological list accompanying the microfilm reproduction of most of the collection, but not including all the printed material.

D Tribe, *President Charles Bradlaugh MP*, London, Elek, 1971, is both a biography and a history of the early years of the Society, and includes a bibliography of his works. Other sources on the Society's history include *The infidel tradition*, ed E Royle, London, Macmillan, 1976, p63-70, 86-9.

S Budd, *Varieties of unbelief*. London, Heinemann, 1977, p35-80.

H P Bonner, *Charles Bradlaugh*. London, 1894, v 2, p86-90.

London Co-operative Society Archives, deposited January 1982. The Society founded in 1919 by the merger of three local societies, had by 1928 absorbed most of the co-operate societies of London. Some archives of the constituent societies are included, the oldest being the Edmonton Co-operative Society beginning in 1808, mostly ms. There are three separate collections of printed material on co-operation, mostly after 1900: a general collection of *c*50 items; *c*100 pamphlets and leaflets collected by Harry Claydon; and 31 books and pamphlets collected by Mrs Caroline Seline Ganley (1879–1966) MP, President of the Society.

Typescript lists of printed and archival collections.

Brent Public Libraries, Grange Museum of Local History, Neasden Lane, Neasden, London NW10 1QB. Tel (01) 452 8311. Open Mon-Fri 12 noon-5 pm (Wed 8 pm); Sat 10 am-5 pm, by appointment only.

The Museum houses the local history collections and archives of the whole Borough, including those of the former Metropolitan Boroughs of Willesden and Wembley. The local author collections include William Harrison Ainsworth (1805–82) and William Henry Giles Kingston (1814–80), the novelists. *c*40 pre-1801 books, including 1 incunabulum. There are a few books from 1633 onwards on London and Middlesex, and a miscellaneous collection of early printed books, mostly collected from the Borough's reference libraries, consisting mainly of editions of Greek and Latin authors.

Card cat.

Typescript and ms lists of rare books.

Brewers' Company, Brewers' Hall, Aldermanbury Square, London EC2V 7HR. Tel (01) 606 1301. Open by appointment with the Assistant Clerk.

Livery company of the City, 14th in the list of precedence, founded in the 13th cent. The archives are deposited at the Guildhall Library. The Hall was destroyed in 1940,

but the new Hall contains a few printed items on brewing; 2 STC; 1 Wing; 2 ESTC; and 10 later; and a volume stuffed with 18th-19th cent ephemera.

No cat.

Mia Ball, *The Worshipful Company of Brewers*. London, Hutchinson Benham, 1977.

W F Kahl, *The development of London livery companies*. Boston, 1960 (bibliog).

Brewers' Society Library, 42 Portman Square, London W1H 0BB. Tel (01) 486 4831. Open Mon-Fri by appointment with the House Manager; general enquiries on the Library and Archives to Information Officer.

The Brewers' Society is a trade association of brewery companies, formed in 1904 by the amalgamation of the Country Brewers' Society founded in 1822 with the London Brewers' Association and the Burton Brewers' Association. The library, established in 1964, incorporates material transferred from earlier libraries of brewing, and now contains *c*5,000 v of printed material in addition to part of the Society's archives and those of the Country Brewers' Society from 1894.

Books The collection of books amounts to *c*2,000 v, chiefly on the history of brewing, including a few pre-1851 items. There is a large collection of histories of individual brewing firms, mostly privately printed or limited editions; the very scarce Alfred Barnard, *The noted breweries of Great Britain and Ireland*, 1889–91, 4 v, and other general histories of brewing; books on public houses, drinking and teetotalism; legal and general reference books; and a large number of government publications. There is a very small collection of early technical manuals of brewing, including *Every man his own brewer*, London 1768, and a nice copy of the very scarce second edition of *The art of brewing*, London 1826 (published by Knight and Lacey around the time of their bankruptcy).

Card index (authors and titles), somewhat incomplete.

Serials These comprise brewing trade directories, including the Brewers' *Almanack* complete from the 1895 edition (published 1894) to 1971. Trade and technical journals include scarce runs such as the *Brewers' Journal* from 1869 (v 5) to 1889, the *Brewers' Guardian* from 1871 to 1905, *Brewing Trade Review* 1877–1976, and complete runs of the Society's own organs and those of the Country Brewers' Society.

British Dental Association Library, 64 Wimpole Street, London W1M 8AL. Tel (01) 935 0875. Open Mon-Fri 9.30 am-5.30 pm on application to the librarian.

The Association was founded in 1879. The Library, now the most comprehensive dental library in the British Isles, was founded in 1920, and was largely built up by two practising dentists, Lilian Lindsay and her husband Robert: hence it was formerly known as the Robert and Lilian Lindsay Library. It contains *c*10,000 v of books and pamphlets on dentistry, and over 300 periodicals. The original nucleus was *c*100 books from the library of a former President, Thomas Gaddes (*d*1919?) donated by his widow. 150 books were bequeathed by John Howard Mummery (1847–1926).

British Dental Association, *Jubilee book*, 1930, p111-8.

E M Spencer, 'The Library', *British Dental Journal*, 122 (1967), p261-5.

Rare Book Room contains a collection of *c*750 items, of which *c*400 were printed before 1851, including 4 STC; 10 Wing; 16 16th cent foreign and 29 17th cent. Virtually all the classics of dentistry are represented in at least one edition, and there are a number of unique or very rare items, eg *Zene Artzney* Frankfurt 1536; J Digitus *Nutzliche und bewerte Artzneyen für allerhand Zahnwehe* Speyer 1587; J Horst *De aureo dente maxillari* Lipsiae 1595; C Allen *Curious observations in... chirurgery relating to the teeth*, London 1687; 14 periodicals of the 18th and 19th cent; a collection of dental manufacturers' catalogues 1839 onwards, and archives of the Association.

Catalogue of the Rare Books Room, (1964). *Additions 1964–1973* (1974).

R Cohen, 'Rare books in the BDA Library', *British Dental Journal* 118 (1965), p280-1.

British Esperanto Association Library, Butler Library, 140 Holland Park Avenue, London W11 4UF. Tel (01) 727 7821. Open Mon-Fri by prior arrangement with the librarian.

The library, which was founded in 1922, contains *c*12,000 v in and about Esperanto and other artificial languages, and 16,000 pamphlets. Includes much scarce 19th cent material.

Classified and title cat.

British Humanist Association Library, 13 Prince of Wales Terrace, Kensington, London W8 5PG. Tel (01) 937 2341. Open for research by appointment with the Secretary after written application.

The Ethical Union, founded in 1896 by the local societies which had grown up in the late 19th cent under the influence of the American ethical movement and which believed in the innate morality of man, was renamed the British Humanist Association in 1965 (when it absorbed a public relations body of the same name founded by the Union in partnership with the Rationalist Press Association in 1963). The library contains the Association's archives and publications, together with a general collection of *c*900 books on philosophy (especially ethics and political and social philosophy), psychology, education, humanism and freethought, religious apologetics, popular science, and related subjects. Apart

from an 1825 edition of Johnson's *Rambler*, all are post-1850 editions, but they include some scarce foreign 19th cent items on the ethical movement. There are also sets of journals of humanism, freethought, etc.

Typescript author list of books.

British Institute of Radiology, Mackenzie Davidson Library, 36 Portland Place, London W1N 3DG. Tel (01) 580 4085. Open by prior arrangement with the librarian, Mon, Wed, Fri 9 am-5 pm, Tues, Thurs 9 pm.

The Institute was founded in 1897 and absorbed the Röntgen Society in 1927. The library contains *c*7,000 v on radiology, radiation, physics and cancer.

Historical Collection Contains *c*160 pre-1914 items, mostly the books and journals of Sir James Mackenzie Davidson (1856–1919), after whom the library is named, given in 1923, with some from the Röntgen Society Library, 30 of which had been given in 1903 by Charles Phillips, author of *Bibliography of X-ray literature*. Earliest are so-called radiological incunabula of 1896–1900. Complete file of *Archives of Clinical Skiagraphy* from its beginning in May 1896, the world's first radiological journal, still current as the *British Journal of Radiology*.

P J Bishop, 'The Library's Historical Collection', *British Institute of Radiology Bulletin* 1(3) (July 1975), p3-5.

British Israel World Federation, Research Library, 6 Buckingham Gate, London SW1E 6JP. Tel (01) 834 7222. Open Mon-Fri 10 am-5 pm (except 2nd Thurs in the month) on notification of intent to visit by letter or phone, with identification and references.

A federation of societies united in the belief that the British are the lost tribe of Israel. A collection of books has been built up by donation and purchase, incl 1 Wing; *c*20 ESTC; *c*20 English 1801–50 on pyramidology and ecclesiastical history, with a few on genealogy.

Card index.

The British Library Reference Division

The British Library Reference Division was formed in 1973 (following the British Library Act, 1972 c54) from the British Museum Department of Printed Books (incl the National Reference Library of Science and Invention formed in 1966 from the Patent Office Library), the Department of Manuscripts, and the Department of Oriental Manuscripts and Printed Books. The India Office Library and Records was added in 1982.

A **British Library Reference Division. Department of Printed Books: General**

Great Russell Street, London WC1B 3DG. Tel (01) 636 1544 Ext 209. Telex 21462. Open 9 am-4.45 pm (Mon, Fri, Sat), 8.45 pm (Tues-Thurs) to holders of readers' passes, which are issued to those who can show that the material they need to use is not readily available elsewhere. Photocopying, microfilming, and various forms of reproduction, subject to restrictions for rare, pre-1801, and copyright works. Microform readers. Computerized bibliographical services through BLAISE-LINE (British Library Automated Information Service), which includes ESTC (see Ic). The special collections of rare books (known as Case Books, see Hh) are available only in the North Library. Nearly half the general collection is outhoused (mainly at Woolwich), esp law, science and art; at least 24 hours notice is required to deliver these books. Material indicated as being in departmental offices is accessible only by special arrangement with the curator in charge.

A*a* *Growth of the collections* The British Museum Library was founded, with the rest of the Museum, in 1753 (26 Geo II c22). The 'foundation collections' consisted of the library of Sir Hans Sloane, Sir Robert Cotton's mss (with the Edwards bequest of printed books), and the mss of Robert and Edward Harley, to which was added in 1757 the Old Royal Library. Over the next century the collections were developed mainly by gift or purchase of similar semi-private collections, principally the King's and Grenville libraries. Large-scale systematic purchasing of current and retrospective printed material, and effective legal deposit, both began with the administration of (Sir) Anthony Panizzi (Keeper 1837–56, Principal Librarian 1856–66). In 1757 the Library contained *c*51,000 printed volumes; in 1821, 116,000; in 1832 after the acquisition of the King's Library and the arrival of Panizzi, 219,000; on his retirement in 1866, 825,000. There are now over nine million in the Department of Printed Books (excluding the Newspaper Library with a further 2.4 million in the rest of the Reference Division). Of the books, about 20% are classified as literature, 13% history, 14% theology, 7% biography, 5% science and technology (after some transfers to the Science Reference Library), with smaller collections of other subjects. There are *c*140,000 periodical titles. The General Catalogue now records over 500,000 distinct editions printed before 1801, with a further 100,000 additional copies; and there are probably a further 150,000 items (mostly broadsides and ephemera) not individually catalogued. Much of the Library's strength in early and rare printed books has always come from its adherence to the canons of 19th cent philological and historical scholarship, according to which the earlier texts of a particular discipline, and the typographical antiquities of a particular country, are as indispensable to

the scholar as the encyclopaedic coverage of current texts, a policy anticipated in the collecting of George III. In many fields (eg incunabula and bindings) the collections are unrivalled.

Ab Surveys of the collections

Chief general guides: Notes for readers and *Reader guide* no 1- , 1977- available gratis from Reader Services section; see esp no 9, Alison Gould, *Named special collections in the Department of Printed Books*, 1981, and others cited in various sections below. A detailed guide to all rare and special collections is in preparation. The best general historical survey of the older collections is Arundell Esdaile, *The British Museum Library*, London, 1946. This is supplemented and continued by Edward Miller, *That noble cabinet: a history of the British Museum*, London, 1973, with bibliography, p372-85; and his *Prince of Librarians: the life and times of Antonio Panizzi*, London, Deutsch, 1967.

Supplementary secondary sources: Edward Edwards, *Lives of the founders of the British Museum, with notices of its chief augmentors and other benefactors, 1570–1870*, 1870 2 v; repr in 1 v, New York, Burt Franklin, 1969.

Sources for individual periods: (For early periods see also B-F below). *The diary of Humfrey Wanley* ed C E & R C Wright, London, Bibliographical Society, 1966, 2 v. [Panizzi, A], 'On the collection of printed books at the British Museum', in *Representation of the Trustees of the British Museum to the Treasury...*, PP 1846 (166), p233–59. *Report from the Select Committee on the British Museum*, 1835 (479), VII, and 1836 (440), X. *Report of the Commissioners...British Museum*, 1850 [1170], XXIV. Robert Cowtan, *Memories of the British Museum*, London, 1872. P Weimerskirch, *Antonio Panizzi and the British Museum Library*, Clifton, NJ. *AB Bookman's Yearbook*, 1981. Thomas Nichols, *A handbook for readers at the British Museum*, London, 1866. The *British Museum Quarterly* 1926–1973, and the *British Library Journal* 1975– contain articles on current acquisitions and special collections. *The British Museum Library, 1753–1953: special exhibition*, 1953.

Ephemera and cuttings collections relating to the British Museum: A collection of articles from magazines, 1834–1912 (11914.dd.2). Cuttings on the British Museum in the Fillinham Collection (1889.b.10, see Pf below). *An attempt to illustrate the British Museum* in the John Cullum Collection, incl a grangerized *Synopsis* 6th ed 1832 (C.119.e.3). Sir Frederic Madden's Collection (C.55.i.1).

Manuscript sources: Sir Frederic Madden's journals (microfilm in Dept of Mss; originals at Bodleian Library, Oxford). Ms diaries of Edward Edwards from 1844 onwards, in Dept of Printed Books (with some gaps, KC.4 e.1). Papers of Sir Henry Ellis (Add.MSS.41312-41319, 42137, 42506). Diaries of Cracherode, 1784–96 (Add.MS.47611). Thomas Birch papers (Add.MSS.4449-4451). British Library archives (by appointment only). British Museum archives (by appointment).

Ac General surveys of catalogues For an outline of the present state of the catalogues, see R S Pine-Coffin and R A Christophers, *How to use the catalogues*, 1980 (Reader guide no 7). All the official printed catalogues to 1947, with many unpublished and unofficial catalogues, are described in F C Francis, 'The catalogues of the British Museum. 1 Printed books', *Journal of Documentation* (1948), p14-40. A very detailed description of all the catalogues available to readers in 1865 is included in Thomas Nichols, *A handbook for readers at the British Museum*, London, 1866, p34-69.

Ad Pre-Panizzi author/name catalogues The first catalogue of the library, recording books (but not most tracts) in collections received to 1786, was printed as *Librorum impressorum qui in Museo Britannico adservantur catalogus*, 1787, 2 v; this was kept up to date in an interleaved copy with ms insertions. A revised edition was published with the same title 1813–19, 7 v; an interleaved copy of this is in 109 v (L.R.419 b.1), selectively incorporated additions to 1846 (except the King's and Grenville libraries, of which separate though incomplete catalogues were printed), and continued in use as the 'Old General Catalogue of Printed Books' until *c*1875.

Ae General catalogue The 'New General Catalogue of Printed Books' was tentatively begun in 1836, and the *XCI rules* drawn up in 1839 for its compilation were prefixed to the abortive *Catalogue of printed books in the British Museum*, 1841, v 1 (A only, no more published); from 1847 all new accessions were inserted on moveable slips in a new series of guardbooks. Between 1849 and 1880 all the entries from the Old General Catalogue and the King's Library Catalogue were revised from A to Z and incorporated in the New, while the tract collections were entered in the General Catalogue for the first time. By 1880 the catalogue had grown to 2,250 guardbooks using ms moveable slips, and the whole was published following considerable revision as *Catalogue of the printed books in the Library of the British Museum*, 1881–1905, 437 parts (incl *Supplement* containing all books catalogued to 1899). A revision of the letters A-DEZ only was published as *General catalogue of printed books*, 1931–1954, 51 v, then discontinued. The whole catalogue was reassembled into one sequence photographically and published as *General catalogue of printed books: photolithographic edition to 1955*, 1959–66, 263 v (op); reduced facsimile reprint New York, Readex Microprint, 1967, 27 v (in print). Three supplements of later catalogue entries (also available in Readex Microprint editions), which are incomplete for cataloguing of older collections, are published as *Ten year supplement 1956–65*, 1968, 50 v, *Five year supplement 1966–1970*, 1971–72, 26 v, and *Five year supplement 1971–75*, 1979, 13 v. A new photolithographic edition, incorporating all cataloguing to 1975, is currently being published commercially as *The British Library catalogue of printed books to 1975*, London, Saur, 1979– . Certain publications of 1901–75 are entered only in a temporary card index in the Reading Room begun in 1967 (many of those dated before 1971 are in a special collection pressmarked DEF); cataloguing of these for the General Catalogue is in progress. Accessions of pre-1971 books acquired to 1982 are added to the reading room copy of the catalogue; from 1983 onwards in a microfiche supplement following approximately similar rules. (Post-1970 books acquired after 1975 are entered in a different microfiche catalogue, see Aj.) Provenance is not indicated in the general catalogue unless the owner is eminent and has made ms notes in the copy; in such instances a cross reference is usually but not always made under his name.

Guide to the arrangement of headings and entries in the General Catalogue, 1940, the heading 'Rose' used to illustrate the filing rules (R.R.Enq; 11914.g.31). *Explanation of the system of the Catalogue* by F E Blackstone, 2nd ed 1888.

History of the General Catalogue by A H Chaplin in preparation. C B Oldman, 'Sir Anthony Panizzi and the British Museum', in *English libraries 1800–1850; three lectures delivered at University College London*, London, 1958, p5-32. Richard Garnett, *Essays in librarianship and bibliography*, 1899, p67-108. D Murray, 'Bibliography: catalogue of the British Museum', *Glasgow Bibliographical Society Records* 1 (1914), p1-105. 'A reconsideration of the British Museum rules for compiling the catalogues of printed books', in M Pigott ed. *Cataloguing principles and practice... lectures delivered at the University of London School of Librarianship and Archives in March 1953*, London, Library Association, 1958, p26-49. Barbara S McCrimmon, *Power, politics and print: the publication of the British Museum Catalogue 1880–1900*, London, Bingley, 1981. A H Chaplin, 'The General Catalogue of Printed Books, 1881–1981', *British Library Journal* 7 (1981), p109-19.

Af *Lists of accessions* Current accessions have been listed in *Annual list of donations and bequests to the Trustees of the British Museum, 1828–1830*, 1830–1; *List of additions made to the collections...1831–1835*, 1833–9; *List of additions to the printed books... 1836–1838*, 1843. Regular printed lists of entries for incorporation in the General Catalogue 1880–1982 were issued by language groups (antiquarian sometimes separate). Rare acquisitions are described in *Three hundred notable books added to the Library of the British Museum...1890–1899*, 1899; *Some notable books added to the Library of the British Museum ...1948–1959*, 1959; and *Notable acquisitions 1959–1960*, 1960; continued in *British Museum Quarterly* and *British Library Journal*. Records of acquisitions in the British Library Archives (accessible by appointment only) inc: till *c*1840 donations and major purchases in British Museum Trustees minutes; Ledgers of donations 1840–1952, thereafter annual card indexes under donors, and under language groups/authors.

Ag *Classified catalogues* A classified catalogue was begun (as a supplement to that of the King's Library) in 1824 but abandoned in 1834. With the introduction of moveable slips in the new general catalogue a 'Fourth copy' of every catalogue entry was filed in order of shelfmarks; from 1880 with entries from the printed accessions lists. The file of fourth copies continued to be maintained until 1975 (it may be seen only by special arrangement); used in conjunction with the classifications of the Old Library, the New Library, and certain other collections (see H), this forms a partial guide to the Library's holdings in particular subjects. It is supplemented by a computer-generated pressmark list derived from the current catalogue.

The Subject Index, begun unofficially in 1881, soon became an important activity of the Dept. Abridged catalogue entries were assigned to broad alphabetical subject headings, some of which were subdivided. The first cumulation *Subject index of the modern works added to the Library of the British Museum 1881–1900*, and a succession of quinquennial catalogues to 1945, published 1902–53, incl *Subject index of the books relating to the European War 1914–1918*, 1922 (all repr London, H Pordes, 1965–70). *Subject index of modern works acquired 1946–50*, 1961; *1951–55*, 1974; *1956–60*, 1966; *1961–70*, 1984, and *1971–75*, provisionally on microfilm and to be printed, all reproduce the full General Catalogue entry under alphabetical subject headings; they are no longer limited to recent publications, but include some current acquisitions of post-1880 material.

Ah *Subject index of modern works* See R Bancroft, 'The British Museum Subject Index', *Indexer* 3 (1962), p4-9.

Ai *Antiquarian subject index* The Antiquarian Subject Index, begun in 1971 to include all current accessions of books catalogued for the first time (except Slavonic and East European) from 1501 to 1800 (Scandinavian to 1850), consists of the full General Catalogue entries arranged under subject headings similar to those used in the Subject Index of Modern Works. Accessions of 1971–6 are in an edited sequence on microfilm in the North Library; 1977–9 on cards (not yet available).

Aj *Current catalogue* For acquisitions from 1975 of material published from 1971 onwards see the author/name/title catalogue to August 1982 published on microfiche as *British Library general catalogue, 1976–1982*, London, British Library Publications, 1982, and in book form, London, Saur, 1983, 50v.

Ak *Special catalogues* See *Guide to the union catalogues of books printed before 1801 and to other tools for locating antiquarian books in Western languages*, British Library Department of Printed Books, 1977, unpublished typescript, esp Appendix 10. The most important catalogues are cited in the appropriate sections below.

Al *Books dispersed and lost from the Library* It was the policy until 1832 to sell 'duplicates', which sometimes included variant issues or impressions, with the exception of those in a very few notable collections such as the

King's Library, and many were auctioned by Sotheby 4 Apr 1769; 6 Mar 1788; 21 Feb 1805; 18 May 1818; 19 Feb 1819; 24 Feb 1831; 12 Mar & 10 July 1832 (annotated catalogues of these sales collected at N.L.7.d). Since 1832 disposals of duplicates have generally excluded rare books, and have been normally by gift to or exchange with other libraries. *c*250,000 v were destroyed by bombing in 1941, but about half have been replaced by microfilms from the Bodleian, New York Public Library, Bibliothèque Nationale, and other libraries.

Most of the pressmarks of books now destroyed have been marked under personal author main entries in the reading room copy of the General Catalogue with the letter D-. Card indexes and lists of destroyed and missing books.

B **Foundation Collections**

The offer in 1749 by Sir Hans Sloane of his collections to the nation led, with the later addition of the Cottonian Library and the Harleian mss, to the foundation of the British Museum in 1753. Most of the books are now in the Old Library (see Ha-b) if not transferred to C. (see Hh); other material is in tract collections (Hg), or periodicals and academies collections (Hf).

Sir Gavin R De Beer, *Sir Hans Sloane and the British Museum*, London, OUP, 1953.

B*a* *Sloane collection* The collections of Sir Hans Sloane (1660–1753), MD FRS, President of the Royal Society, were bought from his executors under the British Museum Act of 1753; encyclopaedic in interest, but with emphasis on medical, scientific, and esp botanical literature: over 35,000 printed books (incl many sold as duplicates until 1832), with numerous periodical and other publications of continental scientific academies, forming the backbone of the Museum's scientific collections. Many of the books are identifiable from inscriptions or from Sloane's distinctive pressmarks. (See also Sloane MSS, *WBc*).

Ms cat in 8 v, with index 2 v (Sloane MSS.3972C-D), comp by Sloane and his librarians, covers his entire collection of printed books. Sloane's interleaved and annotated copy of J A van der Linden, *Lindenius renovatus, sive Joannis Antonidae van der Linden de scriptis medicis*, Norimbergae, 1686, 8 v (878.n.8), provides a catalogue of his medical books. Keys to his marks of ownership incl pressmarks are given in J S Finch, 'Sir Hans Sloane's printed books', *Library* 22 (1941–2), p67-72; J L Wood, 'Sir Hans Sloane's books', *Factotum* no 2 (1978), p15-18; and M A E Nickson, 'Sloane's codes: the solution to a mystery', *Factotum* no 7 (1979), p13-18. Sloane's marked copies of sale catalogues (eg of Sir Thomas Browne's books, 1711) among the Sloane Mss.

B*b* *Edwards Bequest* *c*2,000 works in 3,800 v bequeathed by the 'self-effacing' Arthur Edwards (*c*1680–1743), FSA, First Major of the Second Troop of Horse Guards, to the Cottonian Library, with an endowment to house the collections and acquire more printed books. The books, received in 1769, were predominantly on history and literature, esp post-1650 English, French of all periods, and pre-1610 Italian. The endowment continued and was amalgamated with the Royal endowment, providing many of the Museum's early purchases. It was finally extinguished in 1815 when the capital was used to buy *c*14,000 of the 80,000 v collected by Karl Marie Ehrenbert Freiherr von *Moll*, Secretary of the Mathematical-Physical Class of the Bavarian Academy of Sciences: *c*4,000 of these were on natural history, 3,000 on medicine, 1,000 on other scientific subjects; 3,000 on law and politics, and 4,000 on other subjects in the humanities.

'A catalogue of the books given to the Cottonian Library by Arthur Edwards Esq', ms by Richard Widmore, 1755–6 (C.120.h.2) arranged by language and size. The books bear a square red stamp, which continued to be used for purchases; his pressmarks were of four digits.

C **Old Royal Library**

The Library of the Kings of England had a continuous history since the restoration of Edward IV in 1471, but the printed book collection was not developed systematically except for two short periods under James I and Charles II, when the Lumley, Casaubon and Morris collections were acquired. Some books were dispersed in the Civil War. The right to legal deposit from 1662 was not effectively enforced (see Ja), and despite the ambitious librarianship of Richard Bentley, backed by Evelyn and Wren, and association with the Cottonian Library, it ceded the role of the national research collection to Sloane and the Harleys. It was only after the two latter and the Cottonian collections had been formed into the British Museum that it was given to the Museum in 1757. Among the *c*9,000 printed books, most notable are the presentation and royal association copies (eg Henry VIII's copy of *Summa de potestate ecclesiastica* 1475), many in fine bindings (incl some by Samuel Mearne for Charles II). They were arranged by provenance until 1790–1805 when they were merged in the general library, and most are still in the Old Library (see Ha-b); the bindings and a few of the notabilia are segregated at C.73 and C.78. The rich collection of historical periodicals is now in the P.P. and Ac. collections (see He). Most of the books bear an octagonal blue stamp.

Ms author cats *c*1698 (C.120.h.6) and 1761–70 (apply to Curator of Bindings), both with sometimes inaccurate indications of provenance. Lists 1661–6 mainly by language (Royal Mss.App.73 & 86). Ms cat of Henry VIII's library, transcribed *c*1760 (Mic.A.505). *Catalogue of Western manuscripts in the Old Royal and King's collections*, 1921, v 1, pxi-xxxii. *The Old Royal Library*, by T J Brown and M Scheele, 1957, exhibition cat. Edward Edwards, *Libraries and founders of libraries*, London, 1864, p143-78. Howard M Nixon, *English Restoration bookbindings*, 1974. *Royal English bookbindings in the British Museum*, 1957, exhibition cat.

Ca Lumley Library The Library of John, Lord Lumley (1534–1609), from Nonsuch Park, the largest private library of the period, *c*2,600 works when acquired in 1609, reduced to *c*1,500 in 1757 by sales of duplicates. Lumley inherited *c*1,000 v (incl 30 of his hundred incunabula) from Henry Fitzalan, 12th Earl of Arundel (1511?–1580), half of which had been bequeathed by Archbishop Thomas Cranmer. The collection was narrow linguistically (88% in Latin, Greek or Hebrew), but its vast subject range included theology, history, science, philosophy, politics, economics, and classical literature, in addition to music, jokes, and practical subjects such as cookery, cosmetics, military tactics, handwriting and dancing.

The Lumley Library: the catalogue of 1609, ed Sears Jayne and F R Johnson, London, British Museum, 1956. D G Selwyn, 'The Lumley Library: a supplementary checklist', *British Library Journal*, 7(1981), p136-48. J Dent, *The quest for Nonsuch*, London, Hutchinson, 1970, p163-6, 184-8

Cb Casaubon Collection Of the 2,000 printed books in the library of the classical scholar Isaac Casaubon (1559–1614), 366 (from the early 16th cent onwards) came to the Royal Library, mostly in 1614, but 47 possibly after the Restoration. 19 were sold as duplicates, but 8 further Casaubon items were acquired. The library was strong in the classics, orientalia, patristics, contemporary theological controversy, and law. There are many presentation copies.

T A Birrell, 'The reconstruction of the library of Isaac Casaubon', *Hellinga Festschrift: forty-three studies presented to Dr Wyntyre Hellinga...*, Amsterdam, Nico Israel, 1980, p59–68. A full catalogue by Birrell is in preparation.

Cc Morris Library The library of John Morris (*c*1580–1658), a wealthy dilettante and moderate Puritan, was acquired from his widow at Isleworth and integrated into the Royal Library in 1660–1. Some items were sold, and 1,462 titles have been identified as coming to the British Museum in 1757, reduced to *c*1,300 by sales of duplicates. Mainly classical, neo-Latin, and Italian vernacular literature, genealogy, heraldry, topography, travel, botany, history, and religion, incl the French wars of the Ligue and Jesuitica. Many books contain notes of provenance. There are a few incunabula, *c*120 STC, 60 Wing, 500 16th cent and 700 17th cent foreign items.

T A Birrell, *The Library of John Morris...*, London, British Library, 1976.

D Major Collections Acquired 1762–1827

Da Thomason Collection George Thomason (*d*1666), a London bookseller, collected most of the English pamphlets, small books, newspaper issues and fugitive documents published between 1640 and 1661. The collection came to the attention of George III and Bute in 1761 and was presented to the British Museum in the King's name in 1762, so that it was originally known as 'The King's Tracts'. It now consists of 14,942 pamphlets and 7,216 newspaper issues, with 97 mss, rebound in 1762 in the original chronological order (pressmarks E.1-E.1938; some of the broadsides at 669.f; newspapers distributed throughout the sequence in 1-814, and in 1252-3; microfilm edition, University Microfilms). This does not include 29 v which were stolen between 1762 and 1847, of which one (v 269) was restored in 1963 (C.124.h.1). The collection represents a high proportion of the total output of the period, particularly of London, but is weak in reprints and in Quaker tracts.

Catalogue of the pamphlets, books, newspapers, and manuscripts relating to the Civil War, the Commonwealth, and Restoration, collected by George Thomason, 1640–1661, 1908, 2 v, comp by G K Fortescue, chronological, with general index; repr Ann Arbor, University Microfilms, 1977. Thomason's autograph ms cat, 12 v (chronological) (C.38.h.21). The periodicals and newspapers are listed also chronologically with pressmarks in J B Williams, *A history of English journalism...*, London, 1908, p218-65. *The Thomason tracts: an index to the microfilm edition*, Ann Arbor, 1978– . F B Williams, 'Five lost Thomason tracts come home', *Library*, 19 (1964), p231-4. F Madan, 'Notes on the Thomason Collection', *Bibliographica* 3 (1897), p291-308. J J McAleer, 'The King's pamphlets', *University of Pennsylvania Library Chronicle* 27 (1961), p163-75. S G Gillam, 'The Thomason Tracts', *Bodleian Library Record*, 2 (1948), p221-5. Edward Edwards, *Memoirs of libraries*, London, 1859, v 1, p455-6. L Spencer, 'George Thomason', *Library* 5th ser 13 (1958), p102-18; 14 (1959), p11-27.

Db Garrick Collection The collection of David Garrick (1717–79), actor-manager and dramatist, of later 16th and 17th cent English plays, part of a larger library. It was built up in association with the contemporary editing of early English drama (in particular with the work of Edward Capell). Garrick had obtained, through Robert Dodsley, plays from the Harleian Library which included many from the sale (R Chiswell, 15 May 1682) of Richard Smith (1590–1675) that were originally from the collection of Humphrey Dyson (*d*1632). The collection as catalogued by Capell in the 1750s, when it was intended for the British Museum, came as a bequest in 1780. It consisted of some 1,300 individual plays and collections and, though reduced by *c*10% during the duplicate sales (there being some 50 plays in the Thomason collection for example) constituted *c*90% of all the English plays in the Museum until the arrival of the King's Library in 1828. Transfers to the collection were made from the Thomason Tracts and elsewhere. In the 1840s Panizzi rebound the plays and placed them in the Old Library (643-644, those bound in full morocco at C.34, with others at C.21). He also had some 22 Garrick items perfected. The Garrick copies in particular suffered from T J Wise's thefts of leaves to perfect Ashley copies.

George M Kahrl and Dorothy Anderson, *The Garrick collection of old English plays: a catalogue with an historical introduction*, London, British Library Publications, 1982. Ms cats by E Capell, [c1756] (643.1.30). Helen R Smith, *David Garrick, 1717–1779*, 1979 (British Library monograph no 1), with bibliography. George W Stone and George M Kahrl, *David Garrick: a critical biography*, Carbondale, Ill, 1979, esp p105-99, [Helen R Smith], 'The literary world of scholarship'. D F Foxon, *Thomas J Wise and the pre-Restoration drama: a study in theft and sophistication*, 1959. D Anderson, 'The Garrick Collection', *British Library Journal* 6 (1980), p1-6. F C Francis, 'The Garrick Library', in A Nicoll ed, *Shakespeare Survey* 3 (1950), p43-57.

Dc *Cracherode Collection* The Rev Clayton Mordaunt Cracherode (1730–99), FRS, FSA, Student and Canon of Christ Church, Oxford, lived at Queen Square, Westminster, and seldom went further afield than Piccadilly. He devoted his life to the collection of a series of objects that appealed to his refined and delicate taste: books, prints, medals, and shells. He became a Trustee of the British Museum in 1794, and bequeathed all his collections to it. He had *c*4,500 books, mainly early editions of the classics and the Bible and a 'specimen collection' of *c*100 incunabula, all in fine condition with particular emphasis on binding (eg Grolier and other early French bindings, together with many bindings made for Cracherode by Roger Payne). Cracherode's was the first 'select' collection to be segregated from the general library, and is still separate (671-688); though certain rare books were removed *c*1860–65 to Case Book collections (in C.17-24, eg Bibles at C.17-18 & 23, classics at C.19-20, early English books at C.21, books of hours at C.24), and the incunabula later (in IA.-IC.).

Cracherode's autograph cat (Add.Ms.11360). Adina Davis, 'Charles Mordaunt Cracherode (Portrait of a bibliophile 18)', *Book Collector*, 23 (1974), p339-54, 489-505. British Museum, *Bookbindings from the library of Jean Grolier*, 1965, exhibition cat. Mirjam M Foot, 'Roger Payne', in her *The Henry Davis Gift*, 1979, v 1, p95-114.

Dd *French Revolution Collections* A collection of *c*800 works on Napoleon and the Revolution known as the *Napoleon* Collection formed by Joshua *Bates* was dispersed in the Old and New Libraries. The Right Hon John Wilson *Croker* (1780–1857), Tory politician and essayist, friend of Wellington and Peel, and an early specialist in the history of the French Revolution, was the source of three distinct collections of French Revolution tracts which were bought by the Museum, and originally designated Bibliothèque de la Révolution: the first (pressmark F.) from a bookseller through the agency of Croker in 1817; the others (FR. and R.) from Croker himself in 1831 and 1856. The three contain over 50,000 books, pamphlets, and sets of periodicals, bound in 2,008 v. The 'F' collection (2,195 v) is particularly rich in publications of 1789–92, esp pamphlets; the 'FR.' (600 v) in official publications; and the 'R.' in theoretical and controversial pieces from about 1790 onwards, incl periodicals. Much additional material obtained from Croker (mainly with the first and second collections) is in the classified collections of the Old Library or in the Official Publications Library. These collections rendered the Museum second only to the Bibliothèque Nationale in Paris for its holdings in the field, and they were reinforced by later acquisitions, notably a collection of the writings of Jean Paul Marat (1793–1891) and books, pamphlets, and ephemera about him bound in 70 v, given in 1898 by Francois Chèvremont (645.a.1-55; another Marat collection is at Tab.618.a.1). There is a collection of newspaper cuttings of 1791–2 at 647.l.1.

A H Bleeck, *Catalogue of the Napoleon Library*, 1858. G K Fortescue, *French Revolutionary collections in the British Library: list of the contents of the three special collections of books, pamphlets, and journals*... rev ed by Audrey C Brodhurst, 1979. Audrey C Brodhurst, 'The French Revolution collections in the British Library', *British Library Journal* 2 (1976), p138-58. Tract collections now mostly entered in the General Catalogue; see esp under Marat, Napoleon I, etc. Galley proofs of most of the 'R.' collection entries are available in the North Library. These collections are supplemented by the microfilm of the Maclure Collection at the University of Pennsylvania (cat *The Maclure Collection*, Philadelphia, 1966, with reel index 1972).

De *Burney Collections* The library of the Rev Charles Burney, DD (1757–1817), classical scholar, friend of Porson and Parr, purchased on his death, comprised: (a) a collection of classical texts, esp the Greek dramatists, 13,500 v with annotations by Henri Estienne, Casaubon, Bentley, etc, incl many bought at the Pinelli sale, distributed mostly in the classification of the Old Library, with 164 v of uncatalogued working copies, fragments, and books of cuttings recently transferred to the Department of Mss (see Dd); (b) 349 v of cuttings, playbills, etc illustrating the history of the English stage (937-939), for which see Q below; (c) a collection of *c*700 v of newspapers and news-pamphlets, principally published in London, 1603–1818; less strong than Thomason for the Commonwealth, but the Library's main strength for the 18th cent (*c*400 titles, with many unique runs). The collection includes Irish papers from 1691, Scottish from 1708, English provincial from 1712, and many 18th cent American. London papers from other sources (eg Longleat House, and a bequest from Sidney R Turner *c*1970) have been incorporated into some volumes. The main file is pressmarked Burney but the 1801–18 papers and most of the earlier provincial papers have been removed and incorporated into the Newspaper Library (see Va-Ve).

Burney's own ms cat of his newspapers with later amendments; photocopy with current pressmarks in N.L. Gallery and at R.R. Enquiries (chronological). Card index by titles (incl also some pre-1801 newspapers in other collections). Typescript index. The pre-1801 newspapers are recorded only partially, and sometimes inexactly, in the General Catalogue. The papers of 1641–66 are listed chronologically (with the Thomason) in J B Williams, *A history of English journalism*..., 1908, p218-65, and some corantos, p215-7. The collection is available on microfilm (with gaps filled from other libraries) from Research Publications, New Haven, Conn; see their *Early English newspapers: immediate title availability* (R.R.Enq with shelfmarks) which includes 'The Burney collection of early English newspapers: a working bibliography'.

Df *Colt Hoare Italian Collection* Sir Richard Colt Hoare, Bt (1758–1838), FRS, FSA, of Stourhead, historian of Wiltshire, in 1825, 'anxious to follow the liberal example of our gracious monarch George the Fourth', gave *c*1800 works on Italian local history (657-666 in the Old Library), mostly acquired during his extensive travels in Italy, making additional gifts later.

Sir Richard Colt Hoare, Bt, *A catalogue of books relating to the history and topography of Italy collected during the years 1786, 1787, 1788, 1789, 1790*, priv pr 1812 (Hoare's copy with ms additions C.61.b.12). Also included in *Annual list of donations, 1828*, 1830, p14-35. W Woodbridge, *Landscape and antiquity*, Oxford, 1970, p77-104, 251-61.

Dg *Banksian Library* Sir Joseph Banks (1743–1820) FRS, elected President of the Royal Society and Official Trustee of the British Museum in 1778, collected *c*16,000 v, mainly of natural history journals, transactions of societies, and monographs (incl incunabula), the finest collection of his time, built up by his librarians Daniel Solander, Jonas Dryander, and Robert Brown, with an international network of correspondents. It was the first of its great pre-Panizzi systematic collections to be offered to the Museum, bequeathed to the Museum with a life interest to Brown in 1820 and transferred by Brown in 1827 (mostly 431-462, 953-965, and 977-990); his scientific tracts B.; a few of the catalogues owned by Banks which were in use in the Department of Botany, were transferred to the British Museum (Natural History, qv). Banks also gave 117 Icelandic books in 1773, and more (chiefly theology) in 1783; many of these came from the library of Halfdan Einarsson (867-870). His collection of book prospectuses of 1803–5 is at 899.h.1.

Jonas Dryander, *Catalogus bibliotecae historico-naturalis Josephi Banks*, 1798–1800, 5 v. Ms cat by S S Banks 1800–15. Ms inventory of the collection as received, 1827, 2v (460.g.1). Ms cat of Icelandic donations, *c*1778 (980.h.32); see also the 1885 cat. *The Banks letters: a calendar*, ed W R Dawson, 1958. Blanche Henrey, *British botanical and horticultural literature before 1800*, 1975, v 2, p254-8. Rüdiger Joppien, 'Die Gelehrtenbibliothek des Sir Joseph Banks', in *Buch und Sammler: private und öffentliche Bibliotheken in 18. Jahrhundert, Colloquium der Arbeitstelle 18. Jahrhundert Gesamthochschule Wuppertal Universität Münster.* Düsseldorf . . . 1977, Heidelberg, 1979 (Beiträge zur Geschichte der Literatur und Kunst des 18. Jahrhunderts, Bd 3, p115-27).

E George III, The King's Library

The largest (65,259 v books, and *c*30,000 pamphlets) and most encyclopaedic, both in range and historical depth, of the pre-Panizzi accessions, the collection was built up by a careful combing of the European as well as the English book trade. Commencing with the purchase in 1763 of the library of Joseph Smith, the collection was later broadened systematically by the King's Librarian Frederick Augusta Barnard, with the advice of Dr Johnson, 'upon a comprehensive and liberal design of embracing every field of knowledge', incl major fields in which the Museum was still weak, eg English literature, early English printing (over 800 incunabula, and *c*40 Caxtons), geography and topography, in addition to the classics, Italian, French, and Spanish literature, architecture, painting, sculpture, and philosophy. The library was offered to the nation by George IV in 1823, and the transfer was made to the specially built King's Library in the Museum in 1828 (pressmarks 1-304, arranged by subject and size; incunabula and some other rare books transferred *c*1860–70 to C.1-16), 30 choice items (27 of which had been a personal gift from Jacob Bryant in 1782) being removed for the new royal library at Windsor. The mss and maps were transferred to other parts of the library. It contains a volume of ephemera on costume at 146.i.10. The collection received its distinctive crown stamp *c*1843. In 1940 several hundred volumes from presses 139-145 and 275-276 were destroyed by a bomb; all but 60 have been replaced by other copies or are available elsewhere in the library.

Classified cat in ms by Barnard 1812–20, 12 v (102-103. gg). Of the former shelflist in 60 v, 2 v (for presses 1-2 and 217-221) survive. Author cat *Bibliothecae Regiae catalogus*, 1820–9, 5 v; copy with ms pressmarks (N.L. 21.b). J Brocke, 'The library of King George III', *Yale University Library Gazette*, 52 (1977), p33-45.

Ea *Joseph Smith* George III bought the 'Bibliotheca Smithiana' or second library of Joseph Smith (1682–1770), merchant and British consul at Venice, sold 28 January 1763, comprising incunabula, early editions of the classics, and Italian history and literature, to form the basis of his collection.

[G B Pasquali], *Bibliotheca Smithiana, seu catalogus librorum D Josephi Smithi. . .*, Venetiis, 1755 (823.h.26 annotated archive copy; 681.g.24; 123.e.10 different impression, annotated archive copy; 11907.cc.23 with ms additions).

Eb *Thorkelin Collection* George III bought part of a collection of books formed by Prof Grimr Jónsson Thorkelin (1752–1829) of Copenhagen, comprising 2,085 works on Danish, Norwegian and Icelandic literature, philology, and history.

Ms cat, 2 v (103.e.10 and 103.f.2). (Another part of the collection is in the National Library of Scotland.)

Ec *Pamphlets* The pamphlet collection, including smaller monographs bound separately but included in the Pamphlet Catalogue, numbers *c*30,000 items from *c*1550 to 1810, with a heavy preponderance of English and French political subjects. (Most are placed at 101-164, 193 and 225-226.)

Catalogue of the King's Pamphlets, ms author cat *c*1850, 18 v (L.R.419.b.2 wanting v 1-2).

E*d Letsome sermons* 110 v of 17th and 18th cent sermons collected by Sampson Letsome (*c*1730–*c*1760) (225.f.1-22 and 226.f.1-i.18), forming part of the pamphlets collection, and included in its catalogue.

[S Letsome], *Index to the sermons published since the Restoration*, London, 1734; 1751. S Letsome, *The preacher's assistant*, London, 1753.

F Major Collections of Early Printed Books Acquired after 1828

F*a Grenville Library* Thomas Grenville (1755–1846), statesman, Trustee of the British Museum, formed a collection of *c*16,000 works in 20,240 v, intended to be 'instrumental in exhibiting the progress of learning and marking the refinements of art', which he bequeathed, in very fine condition, complementing the King's Library in incunabula and post-incunabula (eg the Mainz Psalter; 14 Caxtons; the 1505 Aldine Virgil), in early voyages, Bibles and vernacular (esp Italian and Spanish) poetry and romances; and to some extent duplicating it (eg with fine copies of the Gutenberg 42-line Bible and the Shakespeare first folio). Grenville also acquired, but not systematically, some Grolier and de Thou bindings. The collection was placed in a special room (G.1-20240). The library includes a number of collections of ephemera whose contents are not individually catalogued: general collections at G.6192 and G.6463; ballads at G.559; 18th cent Italian chapbooks in verse at G.18101-18106; and a political collection relating to British and Irish affairs 1680–1760 at G.5851-5852, containing bills, petitions, broadsides, and tracts (many of which are not recorded by Wing, Higgs or Hanson), with ms indexes.

Catalogued selectively in *Bibliotheca Grenvilliana* parts 1-2, by J T Payne and H Foss, 1842–8, pt 1-2; completed except for the ephemera in part 3 by W B Rye, with general index of parts 1-3, 1872 (N.L.21.b with pressmarks and ms additions).

F*b Roxburghe ballads* A collection bought at the sale of the library of Benjamin Heywood Bright (*d*1843) (Sotheby 4 March 1845 lot 296), then in 4 v, but recently rebound in 8, of over 2,000 ballads in English 1567–*c*1790, but mostly of the 17th cent (C.20.f.7-10; microfilm Mic.A.7526-7527; xerox. The core of the collection was assembled for the Harleian Library (by John Bagford, but not to be confused with his private collection, see Gb), and bound in 3 v. At the dispersal it was bought by James West, President of the Royal Society, who made additions, as did the purchaser at the West sale (Langford 29 March 1773 lot 2112) Thomas Pearson (1740–81), in whose hands it was rebound in 2 v with printed indexes. At Pearson's sale (Egerton 14 Apr 1788 lot 2710) it was bought by John Ker, 3rd Duke of Roxburghe (1740–1804) who made additions incl a third volume containing 17th and 18th cent ballads. At the Roxburghe sale (Evans 18 May 1812) it was bought by Bright, who added a fourth volume, mostly of 17th cent material.

The fullest description is in *North British Review* 6 (1846), p25-58. The whole collection was published, with a brief introduction, by William Chappell for the Ballad Society, as *The Roxburghe ballads*, 1869–99, 9 v, and also by Charles Hindley in *The Roxburghe Ballads*, 1873–4, 2 v.

F*c Narcissus Luttrell's Collections* The library of Narcissus Luttrell (1657–1732) was bequeathed to his son Francis (*d*1740) and passed to Edward Luttrell Wynne (sold Sotheby 6 March 1786). Much was bought by James Bindley (1737–1818) and dispersed at the sale of his collections (Sotheby 2 Aug 1820). At this sale his collection of ballads, broadsides, and proclamations of the later 17th cent passed to the Duke of Buckingham (who removed engraved items for grangerizing) and was bought for the British Museum at the Stowe House sale (Sotheby 9 Aug 1849 lot 122) (C.20.f.3-5). Various other books and small collections have reached the library at different times from different sources, mostly scattered in the Old Library. Many have special value attached to them by Luttrell's ms annotations, which frequently include the exact day of publication. 45 folio broadsides and pamphlets 1688–9, from a volume which had belonged to Col C H *Wilkinson*, were purchased in 1961 (C.122.i.5; see *British Museum Quarterly* (1961–2) p103-4). His collection of early sale catalogues is at 821.i.1-4, 4 v, with probably some succeeding volumes. Xeroxes of the Newberry Library collection in 5 v of annotated tracts and broadsides from his library, 1659–1730, in 5 v, are also held (Cup.407.ee.15).

J M Osborn, 'Reflections on Narcissus Luttrell', *Book Collector* 6 (1957), p15-27. S De Ricci, *English collectors*, 1930, p29-30 (N.L.2.a). See also *British Museum Quarterly* 11 (1936–7), p20. W Y Fletcher, *English book collectors*, 1902 (1969), p139-43 (N.L.2.a). 'Narcissus Luttrell', *Harvard Library Notes* 18 (1927), p123-6 (Ac.2692.ba).

F*d Huth Bequest* 50 v were chosen from the library of the bibliophile Henry Huth (1815–78), under the will of his son Alfred Henry Huth in 1903, on condition that it should remain separate and that the British Museum should print a catalogue of it (Huth 1-50). These include 13 mss, 16 incunabula, several of the Shakespeare quartos, some of his source books, and 69 Elizabethan and 5 later ballads (Huth 50) bought at the Daniel sale (see Qd) in 1864 (and originally collected by William Fitch, the remainder of the Daniel portion of the collection being in the Huntington Library). The residue of the Huth Library was sold in 12 sales, Sotheby 1911–22, at which 113 further items were purchased and added to the collection (Huth 51-165).

Catalogue of the fifty manuscripts and printed books bequeathed to the British Museum by Alfred Henry Huth, London, British Museum, 1912; there is no published list of the later purchases. The complete Huth Library is described in *The Huth Library: a catalogue...with collations and bibliographical descriptions. . .*, London, 1880, 5 v. The sale catalogues are collected at 11902.t.5. Bernard Quaritch, *Contributions towards a dictionary of English book collectors*, London, Quaritch, 1969, p164-71. S De Ricci, *English collectors*, Cambridge, 1930, p148-54. The Huth ballads were printed in *Ancient ballads and broadsides. . .preserved in the library of Henry Huth*, London, Philobiblon Society, 1867.

Fe *Imitatio Christi Collection* A collection of 1,014 editions of the *De imitatione Christi* often ascribed to Thomas à Kempis or Jean Charlier de Gerson, from the collection of Edmund Waterton (1830–87) the antiquary, bought in 1895, to which editions from elsewhere in the Library have been added (IX.), arranged alphabetically by language (IX.Lat, &c). There is an additional collection (IX.App) which includes Waterton's, but not most of the Library's other books written about the *Imitatio*.

General Catalogue under Jesus Christ: [De imitatione Christi]. E Waterton, *Thomas à Kempis and the Imitation of Christ*, 1883.

Ff *Britwell Court Library* The Library acquired some valuable books from the series of sales 1900–27 of the library at Britwell Court, begun in 1834 by William Henry Miller (1789–1848) MP, and enlarged by Samuel Christy afterwards Christie-Miller (1810–89), and other members of the Christie-Miller family. The cost of the items which were acquired by the Library was reimbursed by S R Christie-Miller.

'Britwell books for the British Museum', *TLS* 26 May 1927, p380. *The Britwell handlist or short-title catalogue of the principal volumes. . .to the year 1800 formerly in the library of Britwell Court, Buckinghamshire*, London, 1933, 2 v; an author cat with provenances, and prices realized in the sales, but not buyers. *British Museum Quarterly* 1 (1926), p47-8, lists a few items. *Catalogue of the library of S Christie-Miller, Esq, Britwell, Bucks*, London, Chiswick Press, 1873–6, three parts.

Fg *Holkham Hall Library* 83 v containing 169 printed items purchased in Nov 1951 from the library at Holkham Hall of Thomas William Coke, 4th Earl of Leicester (C.132.h.1-50; incunabula in IA.-IC.). A further collection bought 1959 (1492.a.1-t.1 and in C.94), mostly 17th cent continental.

1951 purchase listed in *Book Collector* 1 (1952), p120-6, 185-8, 259-63; and in typescript list (by L A Sheppard) with ms pressmarks. See also *British Museum Quarterly* 17 (1952), p23-40; *Library* 2 (1921–2), p213-37, & 11 (1930–1), p435-60. C W James, 'Some notes on the library of printed books at Holkham', *Library* 4th ser 11 (1931), p435-60. W O Hassall, 'The books of Sir Christopher Hatton at Holkham', *Library* 5th ser 5 (1950), p1-13. W O Hassall, *A catalogue of the library of Sir Edward Coke*, New Haven, 1950. W O Hassall, 'Thomas Coke, Earl of Leicester (portrait of a bibliophile)', *Book Collector* 8 (1959), p249-61.

Fh *Chatsworth Library* Books purchased (Christie 30 June 1958) from the Duke of Devonshire's library at Chatsworth House (C.132.i.1-66; incunabula in IA.-IC.). They comprise 63 incunabula (mainly classics and French and Italian), 73 STC books, and 8 noteworthy bindings.

Listed in *Book Collector* 7 (1958), p401-6, & 8 (1959), p180-1,294, incunabula; 8 (1959), p52-8, later books; p59, bindings. *Catalogue of the library at Chatsworth House*, London, Chiswick Press, 1879, 4 v. W Crowther, 'Chatsworth and its library', *Library* 8 (1959), p439-45.

Fi *Broxbourne Library* The bibliophile Albert Ehrman (1890–1969) and his son John made frequent gifts to the Library. In 1977 John Ehrman gave 39 incunabula (in IA.-IC.) and 16th cent books (the English at C.145.f.1-14, the foreign at other C. pressmarks). More were bought at sales (Sotheby 14 Nov 1977 and 8 May 1978).

Mss and printed books presented by Mr and Mrs Albert Ehrman to the Friends of the National Libraries, the British Museum, and other libraries from 1925 to 1970, 1970, typescript. List of the 1977 gift and some of the purchases in *British Library Journal* 6 (1980), p86-107. *The Broxbourne books*, priv pr 1978, broadside, lists 17 donated and 6 purchased items. See also A Ehrman, 'The Broxbourne Library', *Book Collector's Quarterly*, 1931; A Ehrman, 'The Broxbourne Library', *Book Collector* 3 (1954), p190-6. H M Nixon, *Broxbourne Library*, 1956. H G Pollard and A Ehrman, *The distribution of books by catalogue*, 1965.

Fj *Evelyn Library* c318 items from the library of John Evelyn (1620–1706), formerly deposited at Christ Church Oxford, consisting mainly of books with Evelyn's annotations, bought with the help of benefactors (Christie 22–3 June, 30 Nov and 1 Dec 1977, 15–6 Mar, 12–3 July and 8 Nov 1978), with a few given or purchased later (Eve.). They include many books by Evelyn himself, Robert Boyle, the great contemporary divines from Lancelot Andrewes to Jeremy Taylor, and some English literary writers.

Most listed in accessions part H.78 (Evelyn); copy with additions to date (English Language Branch). *Times Higher Education Supplement* 1 Dec 1978, p3.

Fk *Patent Office Library* Almost all the pre-1801 books from the British Library Science Reference Library, formerly the Patent Office Library (see Y below), but not including some of its books dispersed after the printing of the catalogue, were transferred to the Department and catalogued in 1963–84 (mostly at 1651/1-1975, &c; quartos L.32/1-; folios L.35/1-133; large folios L.40/1-67; but some in C., some foreign books at other pressmarks, chiefly in 1502; some duplicates passed to other libraries). Includes much of the libraries of Richard Prosser (1804–54) and Bennet Woodcroft (1803–79).

Catalogue of the Library of the Patent Office arranged alphabetically: v 1, authors, 1898 (2181.e.3); 1881 (BS.29/5); v 2 subjects, 1883 (2181.e.3). Many are included in the Antiquarian Subject Index.

G Collections of Special Bibliographical Interest

Ga *Incunabula* The collection of xylographs and

incunabula amounts to over 11,000 v, incl those in the King's and Grenville Libraries, which are still shelved with those collections, and the Hebrew incunabula (which are in the Department of Oriental Manuscripts and Printed Books, see XEe). Building on the strengths of the Old Royal, Cracherode, King's, and Grenville collections (above), Panizzi and his successors were able to benefit *inter alia* from the availability of duplicates originating from continental monastic libraries in the late 18th cent (eg many bought from the Royal Library at Munich). The collection is strong for the early years of printing, and has a broad subject coverage. It was first segregated from the Library's other collections by Robert George Collier Proctor (1868–1903) who arranged them to follow the invention and spread of letterpress printing in Europe, by country, place, and printer; this arrangement is followed by the catalogue (known as BMC) which is a major authority in the field.

Catalogue of books printed in the XVth century now in the British Museum, 1908– , in progress pt 1-8: pt 1-3 Xylographica, and books printed with moveable types in Germany, 1908–13; pt 4-7 Italy, 1916–35; pt 8 France and French-speaking Switzerland, 1949; pt 9 Holland and Belgium, 1962; pt 10 Spain and Portugal, 1971; pt 11 England, and pt 12, Supplement, Italy, in preparation; Catalogue of Hebrew incunabula, in preparation; Indexes, not yet compiled. The introductions to each part include a survey by subject of the output of the country concerned. The Library's working copy of pts 1-8 with ms additions and corrections was reproduced lithographically in 1963, and of pt 9 in 1967. R G C Proctor, *An index to the early printed books in the British Museum*, 1898, Pt 1 (to 1500), 2 v; Pt 2 (1501–20), 2 v. Lilian G Clark, *Collectors and owners of incunabula in the British Museum: index of provenances for books printed in France, Holland and Belgium*, Bath, Harding and Curtis, 1962, a provisional index which will be superseded by the index in *BMC*; ms lists held by the Incunabula Section. An incunabula short-title catalogue (ISTC) in machine-readable form comprising holdings of BL and British, American, and other libraries is in preparation for publication on microfiche; see L Hellinga, 'Machine-readable catalogue of incunabula—ISTC', *Library* 6th ser 4 (1982), p367. Stanley Morison, *German incunabula in the British Museum*, London, Gollancz, 1928. A Stevenson, 'The quincentennial of Netherlandish blockbooks', *British Museum Quarterly* 31 (1967), p83-7. K Meyer-Baer, 'The liturgical music incunabula in the British Museum', *Library* 4th ser 20 (1939–40), p272-94, catalogue with pressmarks. C B Oldman, 'Panizzi's acquisition of incunabula', in D E Rhodes ed, *Essays in honour of Victor Scholderer*, Mainz, Pressler, 1970, p284-91. A W Pollard, 'The building up of the British Museum collection of incunabula', *Library* 4th ser 5 (1924–5), p193-214. Collection formed by William Blades (1824–90) relating to the Caxton Exhibition, 1877, in an interleaved copy of the catalogue, *Caxton celebration 1877*, 8 v. William Blades, *A catalogue of books printed by, or ascribed to... William Caxton, in which is included the pressmark...*, London, 1865. *William Caxton: an exhibition...*, 1976. H M Nixon, 'Caxton in the British Library', *British Library Journal*, (1976), p91-101. Lotte Hellinga, *Caxton in focus: the beginning of printing in England*, London, British Library Publications, 1982. Victor Scholderer, *Johann Gutenberg, the inventor of printing*, London, British Museum, 1963; 2nd ed 1970. V Scholderer, *Reminiscences*, Amsterdam, 1970.

Gb Bagford Collections A collection of title pages, fragments of printed books and other printed and ms material 1528–1715 assembled by John Bagford (1650–1716), the shoemaker-bibliophile, in *c*129 v, and mostly acquired for the Harleian collection in 1716 (Harl. 5892-5910, Harl.5914-5958, and some from other collections, eg Sloane 885, all retaining their numeration from the Department of Mss, where the associated ms material remains). They were intended for a projected history of printing, of which Bagford issued a prospectus in 1707. They include 3,355 pre-1701 English title pages, of which 549 are not recorded in STC or Wing. Also his collection of 17th cent ballads and miscellaneous fragments.

Melvin H Wolf, *Catalogue and indexes to the titlepages of English printed books preserved in the British Library's Bagford collection*, London, British Library, 1974; includes reprint of A W Pollard, 'A rough list of the contents of the Bagford collection', first published in *Transactions of the Bibliographical Society* 7 (1902–4), p143-59. The ballads are published in *The Bagford ballads*, ed J W Ebsworth, Hertford, Ballad Society, 1876–80, 2 v. W Y Fletcher, 'John Bagford and his collections', *Transactions of the Bibliographical Society* 4 (1898), p185-201. A F Johnson, 'John Bagford', *Gutenberg Jahrbuch* 1950, p227–9; repr in his *Selected essays on books and printing*, Amsterdam, 1970, p378-80. J Bagford, 'An essay on the invention of printing, with an account of his collections... by H Wanley', *Philosophical Transactions of the Royal Society* 25(1706–7), p2347-2410. R Steele, 'John Bagford's own account of his collection of titlepages', *Library* 8 (1907), p223-4. M Nickson, 'Bagford and Sloane', *British Library Journal* 9 (1983), p51-5.

Gc Ames titlepages 9 v (originally 5 v) of titlepages collected for the compilation of his *Typographical antiquities* by Joseph Ames (1689–1757): 7,425 of books printed before 1749 in England, Scotland and Ireland (Ames 1-6), and 3,013 printed in foreign towns beginning with the letters A-J (Ames 7-9). The collections were bought at the Ames sale (5 May 1760) by James West (1704?–1772) President of the Royal Society; 1 v was lost before the collection was bought at his sale (29 March 1773, 270.k.7), by a Mr Bull. They apparently came to the Museum as a gift. Also a scrapbook formed by him containing ms and printed alphabets (Ames 10).

A W Pollard, 'The Ames collection of titlepages', *Transactions of the Bibliographical Society* 7 (1902–4), p161-3. J Ames, *Typographical antiquities*, 1749 (C.124.f.1 with ms notes by Ames; C.60.o.5 with ms notes, cuttings and other insertions by Ames and William Herbert); augmented by William Herbert, 1785–90, 3 v, (C.138.ee.2 imperfect copy with Herbert's copious ms notes); enlarged by T F Dibdin, 1810–9 (821.ee.3 with ms letter by W Combe); Index by A W Pollard, 1899; the Herbert and Dibdin editions include notes on Ames and his collections. John Nichols, *Literary anecdotes*, 1812, v 5, p256-68.

Gd Modern fine printing and private presses There is a general collection of modern fine printing at Cup.500-503, incl 50 items collected by Sir Sydney Cockerell by or on William Morris 1879–1903 (Cup.502.f.11); and a collection arranged under names of private presses at Cup.510 (card index). The most valuable, however, are in C.98-106. The holdings of British private press books are at least as full as those of any other British library; those of American private press books are less full, but still compare favourably with those of other British libraries. Some modern first editions are collected at Cup.400.

P A H Brown, *Modern British and American private presses (1850–1965): holdings of the British Library*, 1976. John Barr, *The Officina Bodoni, Montegnola, Verona: books printed by Giovanni Mardersteig on the hand press, 1923–1977*, 1978, exhibition cat. *Catalogue of an exhibition of books illustrating British and foreign printing 1919–1929*, 1929. *Stanley Morison: a portrait*, 1971, exhibition cat. *An exhibition of books designed ... for Mr George Macy...*, 1952. Some archives of the Chiswick Press, incl a select bibliography on slips, are held in the Dept of Manuscripts (see WFb).

Ge Miniature books The collection of the judge Sir Julius *Caesar* (1558–1636) of 44 v of miniature editions of the classics, in a travelling case shaped like a large volume (C.20.f.15-58). A collection of miniature books formed by Edward *Arnold* of Dorking, mostly French almanacs, 1747–1823, in a case; presented by Andrew W Arnold (C.97.f.6/1-72).

The travelling library of Sir Julius Caesar, *Bookworm*, 6 (1893), p157-9, and *British Bookmaker* 7 (1893), p5-6. *A catalogue of the library formed by Edward Arnold*, Dorking, priv pr, 1921. 'The Arnold collection of French almanacs', *British Museum Quarterly*, 7 (1932–3), p24.

Gf Illustrated books Illustrated books are not normally segregated, but books with finely printed illustrations are kept at C.70, and books with ms illumination at C.22, partly from the Cracherode collection.

M Scheele, 'Illustrated printed books', in *English book illustration 966–1846*, London, British Museum, 1965.

Gg Bindings The superb collection of historical bindings comprises examples from the 12th to the 20th cent. The main emphasis is on English and continental bindings, but there are examples from the Far and Near East as well as from the USA. The Old Royal Library (many of whose bindings are collected at C.68-69), the King's Library, and the collections at C. pressmarks (chiefly C.24-27; C.60-83; C.108-109; and C.143) are richest in historical and fine bindings, incl items from the Felix Slade bequest of 1868, but the Cracherode and Grenville collections contain specimens as well. There are two special collections of bindings: *c*1,500 English and French bindings of 1780–1840, mainly signed, bequeathed by Charles F I *Ramsden* (*d*1958) (C.150-156); and the gift of Henry *Davis* (*d*1977) made in 1958, the most comprehensive collection of over 1,000 bindings on mss in addition to printed books (with 260 reference books) (Davis).

M M Foot, *The Henry Davis gift*, v1-2, British Library Publications, 1979-83, v3 forthcoming. M M Foot, 'The British bindings in the Henry Davis Gift', *British Library Journal* 3 (1977), p114-28. M M Foot, 'The Henry Davis collection, 1: The British Museum gift', *Book Collector* 18 (1969), p23-44. H M Nixon, 'Printed books', in F C Francis ed, *Treasures of the British Museum*, London, Thames and Hudson, 1971, p318-22. C J H Davenport, 'Bookbindings at the British Museum', *Bibliographical Society Transactions* 2 (1893–4), p93-6. Descriptions of individual bindings are included in H M Nixon, *Five centuries of English bookbinding*, 1978. For bindings acquired 1941–71 see his articles in *British Museum Quarterly* 17 (1952), p39-40 (Holkham); 26 (1962), p11-17; 27 (1964), p181-90; and *British Library Journal* 1 (1975). For Grolier bindings in the Library see his *Bookbindings from in the library of Jean Grolier*, 1965, exhibition cat; and for Restoration bindings, his *English Restoration bookbindings*, 1974. For an earlier selective survey, see W Y Fletcher, *English bookbindings in the British Museum*, 1896 (63 examples). H B Wheatley, *Remarkable bindings in the British Museum*, London, 1889. W H J Weale et al. *Early stamped bookbindings in the British Museum*, 1922. *Royal English bookbindings in the British Museum*, 1957, exhibition cat. C J H Davenport, 'Bookbindings at the British Museum', *Bibliographical Society Transactions* 2 (1893–4), p93-6. Sir H Thomas, 'English bookbindings', *British Museum Quarterly* 8 (1933–4), p127; 9 (1934–5), p33; 10 (1935–6), p171; mostly on gifts from Julian Moore. Collection of cuttings and illustrations relating to bindings (677.h.4). Leaflets on the trade (1865.c.3(186)).

Gh Franks Collection of Bookstamps A collection of *c*300 books of the 16th-18th cent whose covers are impressed with heraldic bookstamps, incl *c*150 French and over 100 English, formed by Sir Augustus Wollaston Franks (1826–97), in 2 v, with typescript index, *c*1890 (L.R.406.i.9).

A W Pollard, 'The Franks collection of armorial bookstamps', *Library* 2nd ser 3 (1902), p115-34.

Gi Hirsch Collection of Decorated papers The Olga Hirsch collection of decorated papers bequeathed in 1968 comprises over 3,500 sheets of paper and *c*130 books in paper wrappers or with decorated end-leaves. There are hand-made papers from the 16th cent onwards as well as machine-made papers. Various techniques of decorating paper are represented: there are brush-coated, sprinkled, sprayed, flock, marbled, block-printed, embossed, and metallic-varnish papers, as well as book jackets and 20th cent artist papers. (The collection may be seen by appointment with the Curator of Bindings.) Also a collection of reference books on the history of paper decoration.

Gj Sale catalogues There are many auction catalogues in the King's Library; most of the other catalogues acquired before *c*1860 are at 821, incl the Luttrell collection, and 11906.e. There is a major special collection of auction sale and booksellers' catalogues (S.-C.), which includes in its oldest portion (S.-C. followed by a number) a miscellaneous collection of mostly early catalogues. The main runs are arranged alphabetically under the names of the auctioneers, and catalogues among these are seldom catalogued under the names of the owners of the libraries sold. There are complete runs of the catalogues of all the major auctioneers in London from at least as early as 1800, with the exception of Christie's of which the main set (S.-C.C.) begins in 1832 (though incomplete thereafter), with a few earlier entered individually. The main run of Sotheby's and their predecessors (S.-C.S.) is the auctioneer's archive set annotated in ms with prices and buyers' names, from the first sale by Samuel Baker in 1744 to 1961. Other auctioneers' annotated sets include Hodgson and Co and their predecessors beginning with Robert Sanders in 1807, continuing until their activities were taken over by Sotheby in 1967; Evans 1812–45; Southgate Lewis 1825–52; Wheatley 1835–57; Phillips 1850–1974; and Puttick and Simpson 1846–1967. There are also catalogues of the Hodgson trade sales (incl books, books in quires, and copyrights) 1806–88 (C.124.i.1) and of remainders 1854–1902 (S.-C. Hodgson (3)); and of the Longman trade sales 1704 and 1718–68 (C.170.aa.1) deposited on loan by Longmans, Green & Co Ltd. Collections of provincial sale catalogues include 1889.d.14; 10351.i.8 chiefly Yarmouth and Norwich; and 07805.ee.17, Canterbury. Special collections of art sale catalogues include the collection 1753–1839 formed by William *Dyce* (1806–64) RA, of continental, mostly French, catalogues (562.e.18-77, the first 20 v from his sale, Christie 5 May 1865); and that given by Edward Machell *Cox* in 1955 (typescript list at 011919.g.1, with a few pressmarks in ms); his collection comprises *c*1,300 catalogues 1717–1944 but mainly 1840–1900 British and foreign; many of his copies are annotated, some by auctioneers; many are from the collections of Ernest Gambart, Dawson Turner, Sir Thomas Phillips, and other well known collectors (older catalogues mostly in S.-C. numbered sequence; others in the S.-C. named series, in 1482, or in the New Library classification). Various catalogues of sales of works of art are collected at C.119.h.3; and of coins and medals at 603.h.4-7. Runs of catalogues of the major booksellers and publishers have been added to the S.-C. collection in recent decades, but there are few complete runs, and since 1966 these have been retained only selectively.

List of catalogues of English book sales, 1676–1900, now in the British Museum, 1915, *c*8,000 items with pressmarks, arranged chronologically, with index of owners; (Bar T.19b with ms additions, but not completely up to date; N.L.2.a with ms additions mostly relating to holdings of other libraries by A N L Munby). A N L Munby and L Coral, *British book sale catalogues 1676–1800: a union list*, London, Mansell, 1977, is based on the *List*, but with very few British Library additions (annotated copy in English Language Branch). Card index of owners of collections sold at Sotheby and Christie 1974 onwards (English Language Branch with a private selective index 1901–73); a more selective index to 1975 is included in *Directory of British and Irish Libraries*, 1977, typescript (N.L.7.d). Ms list in 2 v (the first to 1901 with index and notes by E B Harris) of Hodgson sales 1807–1920 (S.-C. Hodgson (a)); other material is in Dept of Mss (see WFb). Typescript index, 1928, of Puttick and Simpson sales 1846–70 (C.131.k.15); these are not for the most part included in the 1915 *List* or in Munby and Coral. An alphabetical set of slips of all the entries in the catalogues of Bernard Quaritch for a large portion of the 19th cent (English Language Branch). F Lugt, *Répertoire des catalogues de ventes publiques intéressant l'art...*, 1938–64, 3 v, gives locations, but is very incomplete for BL holdings.

Gk Exhibitions The permanent but constantly modified exhibition of printed books was first established by Panizzi in the King's and Grenville libraries. Its changes are reflected in the numerous editions of the printed guide from 1851 to 1939. Temporary exhibitions on special topics seem to have originated *c*1870; many have been of major importance, incl those on Luther in 1885; Gibbon, 1894; Nelson, 1903; the Authorised Version, 1911; Shakespeare, 1923; Printing and the mind of man, 1963; and Caxton, 1976. There are hourly tours of the Reading Room for visitors. A private exhibition of the development of the Department of Printed Books was established in 1982.

Exhibition catalogues are catalogued individually under 'London. III. British Museum' or 'London III. British Museum.—Department of Printed Books'. There is no special collection of them, and a few do not survive. Some catalogues of temporary exhibitions that are of permanent utility have been noted in appropriate sections of this *Directory*. See also *Printing and the mind of man*, 1963.

Gl Literary prospectuses The *French Revolution* tracts include a collection of prospectuses of *journals* (F.1561(18)). A collection of book prospectuses 1803–5, came from the library of Sir Joseph *Banks* (899.h.1). A collection of literary prospectuses, with newspaper cuttings, etc 1757–1853, formed by James *Maidment* (1795?–1879), 2 v (816.l.47). Prospectuses of books and periodicals 1791–1805, with ms index (11902.c.26). Prospectuses and publishers' catalogues 1796–1842, 3 v, with ms index to v 1 (11902.bbb.23). A collection of prospectuses and advertisements for erotica in various languages given by Dr Eric John *Dingwall* (P.C.16.m.18). A similar collection 1899–1929 (P.C.16.i.l). A collection of prospectuses and catalogues of erotic and obscene books, pictures, and instruments, 1889–1929, formed by George *Mountbatten*, 2nd Marquis of Milford Haven (1892–1938), (Cup.364.g.48; see Charles Franklin, *They walked a crooked mile*, New York, 1972, p121-65). Two bibliographical collections *c*1890 onwards formed by Jeffrey Bruce *Rund* of New York, given in 1971 and later: one of catalogues and lists (some in ms) of erotic literature (Cup.803.f.20); the other miscellaneous (Cup.900.x.15).

G*m* *Miscellaneous bibliographical collections* A collection of tracings and printed *facsimiles* of early printing, watermarks (with paper specimens), etc, assembled with copious annotations by Samuel & Samuel Leigh *Sotheby* (C.135.k.1) (see the General Catalogue under Sotheby, S & S L). *c*30 books with *fore-edge paintings* (list R.R.Enq). *Book jackets collection* (BJ; 7 days' notice required for access) contains jackets selected from books received 1923–55 in yearly, thereafter monthly bundles (the General Catalogue under Collection, col 785, bottom entry), but few are now retained. *Bookplates collection* at C.66.f.3. *Watermarks collection* at C.135.k.2. *Proof sheets* of modern books mainly at certain presses in Cup.400-799.

H The Classified Libraries and General Collections

Little systematic segregation from the general library took place until the later 19th cent, except in the case of certain of the earlier named collections, principally Cracherode, the King's, and Grenville, which were always shelved separately. On the other hand the very dispersal of the other early collections and of later retrospective acquisitions throughout the general classified Old Library means that some subject access is provided to the general early and rare book stock.

F J Hill, *Shelving and classification of printed books in the British Museum, 1753–1953 (Library Association essay no 254)*, [1953].

H*a* *Montagu House Collections* In 1790–1804 the collections in Montagu House (the original British Museum building) were arranged by subjects in fixed locations; the collections listed above in B, C, D in part, and Dg, and other books added to the collections were incorporated in this classification until *c*1837, then *c*227,000 v; they are now mostly in the Old Library (see Hb). Smaller collections incorporated include that bequeathed by the Rev Dr Thomas *Birch* (1705–66) DD, a Trustee, of books and mss, mainly on biography (his own ms cat of his library is at Add.MSS.39826; see also WDc); that bequeathed by Speaker Arthur *Onslow* (1691–1768) rich in Bibles (these books bear a square green accession stamp); a collection of books on music given in 1778 and 1788 by Sir John *Hawkins* (1730–86); the bequest of Thomas *Tyrwhitt* (1730–86) FRS, the classical scholar, a Trustee, of over 900 v of Greek and Latin classics, and English literature, incl many annotated copies; the collection of Sir William *Musgrave*, Bt of Hayton Castle (*d*1799), Trustee of the British Museum from 1783, who gave in 1790 400, and bequeathed 1,500 books from his 'library of British biography', incl many bearing his annotations and numerous biographical ephemera (with his major collection of mss); the purchase by Parliament in 1813 of the collection of Francis *Hargrave* (1741–1821), Recorder of Liverpool, of law books (mainly annotated by him) and mss (his books bear a special stamp incorporating the initials FH); the collection bought in 1818 of 4,631 v of romance literature collected by Pierre Louis *Guingené*, of which 1,675 were Italian; and the collections given in 1818 by Lady Dorothea Banks of antiquities and books from her sister-in-law Sarah Sophia *Banks* (1744–1818), mainly on chivalry and tournaments, with some collections of ephemera (see P below).

H*b* *The Old Library* On the removal of the library from Montagu House to the 'New Wing' in 1838–40, a new classification based on numbered presses (and lettered shelves) from 300 to 1213 was devised. All the collections from Montagu House listed in Ha above were reclassified with these pressmarks, which were used for additions to 1850, and for early books to the present day (incl additional presses to 1699; the numbering no longer relates to individual presses. The gifts incorporated include the bequest received in 1835 from General *Hardwicke* of *c*300 v on natural history; and the library of the *Cymmrodorion Society* given *c*1845, which formed the core of the Celtic collection. Major purchases were 627 modern Greek books (esp liturgies) bought at the sales of the library of Frederick North, 5th Earl of *Guilford* (Evans 9 Nov and 17 Dec 1835, now mostly at 807-871); the collection bought in 1836 of Armenian works by the *Mechitarist monks* of S Lazzaro near Venice; and works bought at the sales of the libraries of Richard *Heber* and P A *Hanrott* 1834–7, mainly of English literature; of Edward *Skegg* (1773?–1842), bank clerk (Sotheby 4 Apr 1842); of Francis *Wrangham* (1769–1842), Archdeacon of Cleveland (12 July 1842); of George *Chalmers* FRS (1742–1825) (Evans, 27 Sept 1841, 7 Mar and 10 Nov 1842); the *Strawberry Hill* sale (25–9 Apr 1842), incl Sir Julius Caesar's travelling library (see Ge above); Thomas *Jolley*, orange merchant, sales 1843–55; Benjamin Heawood *Bright* (1787–1843) banker 1844–45 (Sotheby 3 Mar 1845, etc); Robert *Southey* (1774–1843) (Sotheby 8 May 1844); Augustus Frederick, Duke of *Sussex* (1773–1843) (Evans 1827–1839); 1 July 1844, Aug 30 and 30 Jan 1845. Presses 1700–1899 were added in the later 19th cent for large books, esp guardbook volumes of ephemera (see P below).

Allen T Hazen, *A catalogue of Horace Walpole's Library*, New Haven, 1969, 3 v. On Chalmers see T F Dibdin, *Bibliomania...*, London, 1876, p592-605. A Bell, 'Archdeacon Francis Wrangham', *Book Collector*, 25 (1976), p514-26; M Sadleir, 'Archdeacon Francis Wrangham', *Transactions of the Bibliographical Society* Supplement no 12, 1937.

H*c* *Reading Room and Reference Book Collections* 2000-2121 (now extended to 2183) were assigned to presses on open access in Panizzi's Reading Room (opened in 1857), with reference books mainly transferred from the Old Library. This collection was described in *List of the books of reference in the Reading Room* by W B Rye, 1859; 4th ed 1910, 2 v, with pressmarks added. Presses (BB.) added in 1881 for bibliographies were listed in the classified *Handlist of bibliographies, classified catalogues, and indexes, placed in the Reading Room of the British Museum for reference* by G W Porter, 1881; *List of bibliographical works in the Reading Room...* 2nd ed by G K Fortescue, 1889. 2200-2410 were added in 1881 for a closed access reference collection on the first floor gallery, listed in *A catalogue of books placed in the galleries of the Reading Room*, 1857. Though many of these books have now been moved elsewhere to make way for more modern reference books, these catalogues are still useful.

Dictionary card index of open access books is the only up to date catalogue. P R Harris, *The Reading Room*, London, British Library Publications, 1979. G F Barwick, *The Reading Room of the British Museum*, 1929. *British Museum Reading Room, 1857–1957: centenary exhibition...*, 1957. Select lists in *Reader guide* series.

H*d The New Library* Most monographs acquired 1850–1963 are in Watts's second subject classification (3,000-12,991). Standard-sized presses were numbered non-consecutively leaving gaps for expansion; in 1887 additional presses were interpolated, numbered with a preliminary zero. Shelves were lettered, and numbers denoting individual books were added in 1875-1911, with a further number in parentheses for pamphlets in volumes. Later the identification with presses and shelves was abandoned and the system became completely moveable.

The arrangement of subject headings (without the press numbers) is printed in John Macfarlane, *Library administration*, 1898, p153-61; ms scheme as used in 1877 in archives of Placers' Office.

H*e Serials* In 1850 periodicals published by commercial publishers and directories were removed to a new collection designated P.P. (Periodical Publications, arranged by subject. *Almanacs* are mostly at P.P. 2465, 1880-2 or 717.m (French see also Ge). A separate collection Ac. (Academies) was begun *c*1865 for periodicals and monographic series issued by institutions, in topographical and subject sequences. Other collections include A.R., administrative annual reports of private and local government bodies from the later 19th cent; and W.P. (Works in Progress). (For all new serials after 1970 see Hf.) The collection Dissertations, mainly uncatalogued, arranged by place, university, and year, apparently begun in the earlier 19th cent, is gradually being dispersed and placed at monograph pressmarks as cataloguing proceeds (list of runs, many of which are fragmentary or incomplete, at R.R.Enq).

Periodicals catalogued before 1970 are entered under 'Periodical Publications' followed by place of publication (usually with a cross reference from the title), almanacs under 'Ephemerides'; from 1970 under title (without cross reference from 'Periodical Publications' or 'Ephemerides'). Selective title indexes of periodicals and of almanacs at R.R.Enq. Directories under 'Directories' followed by place of coverage (from 1970 also under title). Serial and monographic publications of academic and most other non-governmental societies and institutions are catalogued under towns. Numerous indexes in Archives.

H*f The X. and P. collections* A new classification for general accessions superseded the New Library system in 1970. Pressmarks are made up with an X. for monographs or P. for periodicals; two digits for broad subject classification (preceded by an additional zero for monographs in progress); a third denoting size; a /; and a consecutive number.

H*g Tracts* Until *c*1835–1880 tracts were mostly kept in separate collections uncatalogued. English tracts of the 17th and 18th cent were designated E., and comprise 3 series: E.1-E.1938 form the Thomason collection (see Da); the remainder are from the foundation collections (see B) and later acquisitions to *c*1835: E.1940-E.2088 arranged in chronological order by date of publication, and E.2089-2272 mixed. Another general collection, both British and foreign, to *c*1830, was bound up into 2,497 volumes to which a bare numbering was given; these numbers were later prefixed with the letter T. and (with the exception of some duplicates) entered in the General Catalogue. Most scientific tracts seem to have been placed with the B. (Banksian) tract collection (see Dg). The French Revolution tracts (see Dd) were designated F.; FR. and R. Most tracts subsequently received have been placed in the classified collections of monographs, sometimes bound individually, sometimes in groups; but the Chadwick Tracts (CT.) are placed separately (see RJb).

H*h Case Books* A special category of rare books called 'Case Books' (C.) which now may be used only in the special rare books reading room (North Library), was instituted *c*1860–65 when Panizzi locked up certain books from the King's and Cracherode collections in C.1-24. The collection is arranged by bibliographical forms, by provenance, or by subjects, and now runs to C.182. C.170 contains books deposited on indefinite loan (other than those at P.C.16a). Many other collections (esp those in D-G above) with those at certain other pressmarks, are now also 'Case Books'.

H*i Private Case and restricted collections* The Private Case consists of books segregated on grounds of obscenity by a succession of Keepers of Printed Books, beginning in the 1850s (P.C.). It was originally a case in the Keeper's room and its contents were not entered in the General Catalogue or issued to readers except by his permission. The definition of obscenity was arbitrary and varied with the fashion of the time and the eccentricities of individual Keepers, so that its contents have always been susceptible to change, and many books have from time to time been moved from it to other pressmarks. At its largest extent it contained *c*4,000 v, now reduced to 2,000. A separate catalogue of the Private Case books was kept from its inception, consisting of two guardbook volumes of moveable slips, originally ms and later printed. The entries from the P.C. catalogue were transferred from it to the General Catalogue 1966–83. Special restrictions on access have been removed, apart from the requirement to give a written undertaking not to reproduce the material. When the library of Henry Spencer *Ashbee* (1834–1900) was bequeathed in 1900, many of the books were incorporated in the P.C. (list at R.R. Enq) and Tab.603-605; other parts of his library are at Cerv.1080-1, 1093-4 and 1102. The 27th Earl of *Crawford* (1871–1940), a Trustee, gave over 100 v. The *Eliot-Phelips* erotica collection formed by William Robert Phelips (1882–1919) and bequeathed by his son to the Guildhall Library was transferred to the P.C. in 1950. The erotica collection of Charles Reginald *Dawes* (1879–1964) was given to the library, and chiefly placed at P.C. pressmarks, in 1964 (his catalogue of his own collection is in the Placers' Archives). Another collection was given in 1964 by Beecher *Moore* (scattered in P.C.14), chiefly French limited editions, and a smaller collection was bequeathed by Alfred *Rose*. Books which for legal reasons, esp successful prosecutions for libel, or conditions of gift imposing a period of inaccessibility, cannot be made available under any circumstances, form a separate collection of several hundred volumes (SS.), not entered in the General Catalogue. Enquiries about whether such books are in the library must be addressed to the Keeper in writing, and will be answered only if the circumstances permit.

Patrick J Kearney, *The Private Case: an annotated bibliography of the Private Case erotica collection in the British (Museum) Library*, London, Landesman, 1981, with historical introd by G Legman. Rolf S Reade [pseudonym of A Rose], *Registrum librorum eroticorum*, 1936, 2 v; many of the works listed are accompanied by P.C. shelfmarks, often inaccurate; Peter Fryer, *Private Case—public scandal*, London, Secker, 1966, describes all the restricted categories; summarized in P Fryer, 'Censorship at the British Museum', *Encounter* 27 (1966), p68-77. E S P Haynes, 'The taboos in the British Museum Library', *English Review* 16 (1913–14), p123-34.

H*j Microforms* Microfilms are mostly placed at Mic.A. and Mic.B.; microfiche at Mic.F. or Cup.700; microcards at Cup.700. These collections are available on demand in the N.L. Gallery with many of the bibliographies and catalogues on which many of the series are based.

Items in most of the commercially published and some other series are not catalogued individually; in some cases there are separately published guides, catalogues, or bibliographies giving access to their contents, fuller particulars are given in *Microform collections in the humanities 1984* (Reader guide no 11, M E Goldrick, *Microform collections: official publications and the social sciences*, 1983 (Reader guide no 12).

I **English Language Collections** (by periods)

Just over half the Library's total collections are in English. Building on the partial strengths of the Thomason, Garrick, King's, Grenville and (for newspapers) Burney collections, it was the Panizzi administration that first developed the English language collections not only systematically but in depth. The library's English holdings in all periods to 1800 are the largest in the world, and every effort is made to increase and enhance them; on average 40 STC, 150 Wing and 900 ESTC items are added annually. Owing to poor enforcement of copyright deposit before 1850, and less vigorous retrospective purchasing, the collections for the earlier 19th cent are less comprehensive. Gaps in the collections are being filled, in the short term, by the various published microfilm collections, in association with the period union catalogues indicated below.

British and American authors, 1978 (Reader guide no 5). The collections are supplemented by the Readex Microprint series *Three centuries of English and American plays*, covering 1500–1800 (1830 for American), incl Lord Chamberlain Larpent's collection 1737–1824.

I*a Pre-1641* Over 15,000 items. The titles printed for the first General Catalogue were expanded by the Keeper, George Bullen, into *Catalogue of the books in the Library of the British Museum printed in England, Scotland and Ireland, and of books in English printed abroad to the year 1640*, 1884, 3 v, under authors, with indexes of subjects, incl headings such as ballads, and of printers and publishers. This was used as the basis for the publication of STC. For other references to STC books see T H Howard-Hill, *Bibliography of British literary bibliographies*, Oxford, 1969, p41-50. Microfilms of STC books published by Oxford University Microfilms. A W Pollard, 'Recent English purchases at the British Museum', *Library* 2nd ser 6 (1905), p1-28; 8 (1933), p37; 9 (1908), p323-32, 'Early English and Welsh school books', David Salmon collection.

I*b 1641–1700* 50,000 editions; at least 3% of the works in the General Catalogue were omitted from Wing; see John E Alden, *Wing addenda and corrigenda; some notes on materials in the British Museum*, Charlottesville, Univ of Virginia Bibliographical Society, 1958; a more comprehensive file of addenda on slips. See also Howard-Hill, p51-4.

I*c 1701–1800 The library holds c*143,000 18th century imprints in English or from the English-speaking world; of which *c*119,000 are from England, 8,800 from Scotland, 350 from Wales, 8,300 from Ireland, 3,800 from the US and 2,700 from other places.

Eighteenth-century short-title catalogue, British Library Publications, 1983 (on microfiche) includes entries for many ephemera not in GK; also accessible on-line through BLAISE-LINE; on this catalogue see R C Alston and M J Jannetta, *Bibliography, machine-readable cataloguing, and the ESTC*, London, British Library

Publications, 1978; *Factotum: newsletter of the XVIIIth Century STC*, 1978- (gratis from the project office); R C Alston, *Searching ESTC on BLAISE-LINE*, 1982 (Factotum occasional paper no 1). A selective micro-filming programme by Research Publications Inc, based on ESTC, began in 1982. See also catalogues of the Project for Historical Biobibliography, University of Newcastle: *Eighteenth-century British books: subject catalogue extracted from the British Museum General Catalogue of Printed Books*, Folkestone, Dawson, 1978, 4 v, containing ruthlessly abridged entries without pressmarks classified by Dewey; *Eighteenth-century British books: an author union catalogue, extracted from the British Museum General Catalogue... catalogues of the Bodleian... and... Cambridge*, 1981, 5 v, without pressmarks, from General Catalogue and published supplements to 1970; *Eighteenth-century British books: an index to the foreign and provincial imprints in the Author union catalogue*, Newcastle, Avero Publications, 1982, by town then date. See also Howard-Hill, p55-7.

Id 1801 onwards The working of the Copyright Act has ensured an all-round coverage of British and Irish imprints (see Ja) and some overseas imprints (see Ka), esp since 1870. Acquisitions by purchase and donation supplement these holdings by filling gaps found to exist in the collection. As well as the output of commercial publishers, the Library has a rich collection of the work of private presses (see Gd).

J **British Isles**

Ja Copyright receipts The copyright deposit privilege was acquired with the Old Royal Library (see C) in 1757, and has been claimed under the Copyright Acts of 1708 (8 Anne p261), 1801 (41 Geo III c107), 1842 (see 5+6 Vict c82), and 1911 (1&2 Geo V c46), this last requiring deposit of works published in England, Wales, Scotland and Ireland, including the Irish Republic where it is still in force. Until *c*1790 these books formed a separate collection; until 1814 they were stamped on the spine with a rose and crown; subsequently with an internal plain blue stamp. A copyright registration procedure was introduced in 1837, and later the stamp incorporated the day, month and year of receipt (previously inserted in pencil). In 1757–66 fewer than 50 per annum were so received; in 1814, 500; in 1815, over 1,000; in 1850 when Panizzi began a vigorous campaign to secure deposit, 5,000; in 1855, 10,000; in 1858, 20,000; in 1981, 39,400 books (and 315,000 other items). Since 1967, the scientific works have gone to the Science Reference Library (see Y below).

Records of the Copyright Record Office, now in Reference Division Archives, include Receipt Books (arranged chronologically) from 1850 onwards; Publishers' delivery books from 1861 (an index to the preceding arranged by publishers); Publishers' Delivery Ledgers from 1869 onwards (arranged by towns); Periodicals Ledgers from 1846 (arranged by publishers); Newspaper ledgers from 1873 with retrospective summary from 1867 (arranged by place of publication); and Author index to publishers' ledgers from 1880; correspondence is not preserved. Cowtan, p158-91. R C Barrington Partridge, *The history of the legal deposit of books...*, London, 1938; inaccurate in places. R Bell, 'Legal deposit in Britain', *Law Librarian* 8 (1977), p5-8, 22-6. Collections on the law of copyright 1817–9, cuttings (515.1.20(4*)); 1831–72 (1889.d.2(53)).

Jb Ashley Library The outstanding collection in over 5,700 editions of English literature formed by Thomas James Wise (1859–1937), named the Ashley Library after the road in which he lived, was bought after his death from his executors. Respectable in the 16th-17th cent (esp plays), strong in the 18th cent, it was unrivalled in its 19th cent material, esp the poets. Printed texts were accompanied by much ms material (now in the Department of Manuscripts, see WFb). It was specially distinguished for the condition of its books, many of which in the later period are in original bindings. Its quality is vitiated in two ways: firstly, many of Wise's early plays were made up with leaves stolen from other copies, incl some present British Library ones (those which did not return to the Library with Wise's copies are mainly in the Wren and Aitken collections at the University of Texas Library); secondly, Wise perpetrated a large number of forgeries and piracies of 19th cent texts; the Ashley Library contains an almost complete collection of these.

Some duplicates of editions in other BL collections are not yet entered in the General Catalogue. Thomas J Wise, *The Ashley Library*, 1922–36, 11 v, contains a complete catalogue of Wise's collection as it then stood (not all of which passed to the BL); copy annotated with pressmarks (N.L.5.c); facsimile reprint of this copy Folkestone, Dawsons, 1971. Wise's thefts of leaves are charted in D F Foxon, *Thomas J Wise and the pre-Restoration drama: a study in theft and sophistication*, London, Supplement in *Library* 5th ser 22 (1968). W B Todd, 'Some Wise ascriptions in the Wren catalogue', *Library*, 5th ser 22 (1968). The forgeries and piracies are the subject of J Carter and H G Pollard, *An enquiry into the nature of certain nineteenth century pamphlets*, London, 1934; 2nd ed, London, OUP, 1983, with N Barker and J Collins, *A sequel to An enquiry...*, 1983; and A Freeman, 'The workshop of T J Wise', *TLS*, October 1982. T H Howard-Hill, *British bibliography and textual criticism*, Oxford, Clarendon Press, 1979, p470-6 (Index to British literary bibliography, 5), contains 82 bibliographical references to Wise and his collections.

Jc Notable authors The collections include portions of many libraries formed by well known authors. A few, noted here, are kept as separate collections. 186 v owned by Samuel Taylor *Coleridge* (1772–1834), many of which are annotated copies, given by the Pilgrim Trust in 1951 (C.126.a.1-l.11; see *British Museum Quarterly* 16 (1952), p91-3; *Samuel Taylor Coleridge, 1772–1834: catalogue of an exhibition...*, 1972, X.909/24050). A collection bequeathed by William Carew *Hazlitt* (1834–1913), 17 v all with ms notes by him (1655/1-17; list at R.R.Enq). A collection of over 1,200 v owned by Rudyard *Kipling* (1865–1936), of editions (incl suppressed and pirated editions) and translations of his own works, known to him as 'the file', bequeathed in 1940 by his widow (File; listed in separate Accessions Part, 1940; see L Hanson in *British Museum Quarterly* 14 (1939–40), p93-5). A collection formed by Walter Savage *Landor* (1775–1864), given by Lt-Col J W N Landor, *c*45 v, many with ms notes (C.134.e.1-34). A collection formed by Herbert *Spencer* (1820–1903), mainly editions of his own works (1650/48-161). A small collection bequeathed by George Bernard *Shaw* (1856–1950) (not yet catalogued or placed), mainly of rehearsal copies of plays, and programmes; this was detached from the larger collection of papers in the Dept of Mss (Add.MSS.50508-50743, etc), which also contains some printed material ((Department of Mss.) Departmental pamphlets 1341–3; See A M Brown, 'The George Bernard Shaw papers', *British Museum Quarterly* 24 (1961), p14-21).

Jd Poetry and ballad collections See also Bagford (Gb), Roxburghe (Fb), Luttrell (Fc), and Huth (Fd). There is a cornucopia of ephemeral verse not catalogued individually. This includes 2 v of songs, *c*1807–*c*1860, assembled by the Rev J *Baker*, with a ms index (1876.d.41). A collection of ballads printed in London *c*1860–70, formed by Thomas Russell *Crampton* (1816–88) in 8 v (now lacking the sixth, 11621.h.11). A collection of ballads, printed chiefly by J & M *Robertson*, Glagow, 1779–1816, in 3 v, collected by Miss Elisabeth Davison (11606.aa.22-24). A collection of ballads, chiefly printed in London by J Catnach, J Pitts and others, mostly 1800–70 with a few earlier and with a few prose broadsheets; collected by the Rev Sabine *Baring-Gould* (1834–1924), in 10 v, with ms indexes (L.R.271.a.2); and another collection by him of ballads chiefly printed in Newcastle-upon-Tyne *c*1730–*c*1830 by J White, or in London, in 2 v with ms index, and donated by him (L.R.31.b.19). A collection of ballads *c*1780–1820, collected by Thomas *Bell* (11621.i.12); and another collection, formed by him of local poetry and songs relating to Newcastle, 1780–1830, in 2 v (11621.i.2). Single sheet poems and songs relating to Newcastle 1743–1820 (1880.b.29). Uncatalogued single sheet verse placed 1912–75 with ms index (646.b.1), 5 guardbooks. Elegies (11602.i.1 and 1871.e.2). Poems from newspapers 1770–95 (644.m.15). Songs 1730–50 (C.116.i.4(1-16)). Songs and poems, mostly political, 1733–1875 (1871.f.16). Songs 1807–60, 2 v with ms index (1876.d.41). Topical songs 1878–1907 (1874.e.4).

See also *Andrew Marvell...exhibition...*, 1978 (X.900/25621).

Je Dexter Library A collection of *c*200 editions of the works of Charles *Dickens* (1812–70), and of numerous printed works about him, formed by John Furber Dexter (1847–1917), bought in 1969 from his great-grandson David Stern (Dex; microfilm Mic B613/1-101). It includes first editions in the wrappers and publishers' boards with many variants and proofs, speeches, reading editions, piracies, imitations, advertisements, etc. Also mss, in the Dept of Manuscripts (Add.MSS.56081-56085). Original drawings by H K Browne ('Phiz'), George Cruikshank and others, and sets of plates extra-illustrating the novels, now in the British Museum Department of Prints and Drawings.

Charles Dickens, the J F Dexter collection: accessions to the general catalogue of printed books; manuscripts; prints and drawings, 1974. A H Cleaver and T Hatton (Dexter's son-in-law), *A bibliography of the periodical works of Charles Dickens*, 1933, is based on the collection.

Jf Lady Dickens Library 100 v of translations of the works of Dickens, collected by Lady Dickens, and given to the Library by Miss Charlotte *Roche* (012631.p.2-29 and 51; 12631.r.1-19; 12631.s.1-8; and various Oriental pressmarks) with a file of letters to Lady Dickens.

Ms cat (L.R.106.b.22). *British Museum Quarterly* 14 (1939–40), p59-60.

Jg Novels collections From 1817 to 1863 English novels were placed in a special collection (N.1-2572), and after a period when they were included in the general classification under English literature, in three further collections 1912–49 (NN.1-40051), 1950–61 (NNN.1-17199), and 1961- (Nov., for post 1900 works only). Uncatalogued paperback reprints from *c*1971 are in a collection designated H. (followed by the last 2 figures of the year of receipt), /, and a serial number. Smaller collections include a collection mainly of late 19th cent novels in editions of 1880–1914 in the publishers' bindings, given by Eric John *Dingwall* (C.109.m.1-41); a collection of 19th cent novels in publishers' boards or wrappers, mainly 2nd editions of works of Sir Walter *Scott* (1771–1832), from the collection of Cecil *Hopkinson*, bought in 1951 (1652/1-20); and 21 Victorian novelettes *c*1865–80 (12654.h.17 and 12655.ee.7). For American novels see Ka.

Ms cat of novels in the N. collection (N.1-1450 only), 1837–9, arranged by titles with author index (1505/313). See also *Jane Austen...exhibition...*, 1975.

Jh Drama collections For the Garrick collection, see Db above; there are also many plays in the foundation collections (B), the King's Library (E), the Grenville Library (Fa) and the Ashley Library (Jb). Alfred Vout *Peters* (*d c*1934) bequeathed 230 v of English works 1594–1930 in good condition, many in the original bindings, esp 18th cent editions of plays; see *British Museum Quarterly*, 9 (1934–5), p13.

F C Francis, 'The Shakespeare collection in the British Museum', in A Nicoll, *Shakespeare survey*, 3 (1950), p43-57; abbreviated in *Theatre Research* 6 (1964), p50-8. *Shakespeare exhibition, 1923: guide...*, 1923.

Ji General and miscellaneous collections Collections include several put together by Francis John Stainforth relating to English authoresses: a general collection of their pieces 1690–1861 (11621.k.2); newscuttings of poems by women *c*1865 (11649.bbb.49); and engraved and lithographed portraits of poetesses, *c*1610–*c*1860, with a few of their autograph letters, in 2 v (1876.f.22). A collection of books by Isaac Taylor, Independent Minister at Ongar, and members of his family, given by the Friends of the National Libraries in 1969 (Cup.404.a.1-29). A collection of 102 books by and about Sir Francis Bacon (1561–1626), formerly part of the Bacon collection at Lambeth Public Library (Lamb.1-102).

Charles Lamb... exhibition..., 1975. Richard Marks and Ann Payne, *British heraldry... to... c1800*, 1978.

Jj *Children's books and chapbooks* Until *c*1950 the acquisition of children's books was haphazard, and consisted mainly of works received by copyright deposit since 1850, but there is now an active acquisitions policy in this field. A separate collection of rare children's books (Ch.) was established in 1966, to which all pre-1801 and many other items from the New Library literature collections were transferred. There are also several special collections. A collection of chapbooks printed by William and Cluer *Dicey*, *c*1750–1800 (1079.i.13-15; catalogued individually; the printers are not identified in the chapbooks, but see V Neuburg, 'The Diceys and chapbook trade', *Library* 5th ser 24 (1969), p219-31). A collection of mostly anonymous chapbooks for children *c*1790–1860, formerly part of the collection of Henry Major *Lyon* (C.121.aa.5) with card index (C.121.aa.5a); also another part of his collection of children's books (sometimes called the Court Bookshop Collection) mostly 18th and 19th cent (now in the Ch. collection, formerly at 12835.a.1-95; title index without pressmarks in English Language Branch). A collection of 19th cent bloods and penny dreadfuls collected by Barry *Ono* (C.140.a-e; title card index without pressmarks at N.L. Issue Desk, catalogued individually in General Catalogue). Miscellaneous chapbooks 1815- (11601.aa.55(1) etc; 11601.aaa.47(1) etc). From 1910 to 1979 5,591 anonymous children's books (incl some of the 19th cent) were placed in a separate uncatalogued collection (card index of titles to *c*1940 in Placers' Office). A similarly uncatalogued collection of comics and strip cartoons from 1950 (CAR; index in Placers' Office) and of chapbooks (index).

An exhibition of early children's books, 1968. J Roberts 'The 1765 edition of Goody Two-shoes', *British Museum Quarterly* 29 (1965), p67-70. B Ono, 'Dick Turpin literature', *Coll Misc* 6 (1933), p105-7, 111.

Jk *Local collections* For older topographical books see John P Anderson, *The book of British topography*, London, 1881 (BB.KK.a annotated with pressmarks, not completely up to date); repr Wakefield, EP Publishing, 1976. Collections of pamphlets and ephemera on *Kent: The history and antiquities of Rochester*, 2nd ed, 1818 grangerized with annotations, letters, cuttings, illustrations, pamphlets, etc 1818–87, 3 v, by W B Rye for an intended history (C.55.g.2); 2 copies of John Russell Smith, *Bibliotheca Cantiana*, 1837, annotated by the compiler (C.45.i.18; C.45.k.5); and 6 v of 18th and 19th cent pamphlets on Rochester (10368.e.2-7); 6 v on Deptford and Greenwich (578.m.11-16); Margate handbills 1795–1801 on miscellaneous entertainments are included in Playbills 419-422 (see *Factotum* no 15 (1982), p16-18). A collection formed by John *Bell*, of pamphlets, broadsheets, and other material, 1733–1855, in 20 v, relating to Newcastle upon Tyne (L.R.264.b.1). A collection formed by Richard *Percival* on the parish of St Pancras, 1729–1830 (Crach.1.Tab.4.b.43); and his collection on Sadlers Wells Theatre (see Qg). The residue (sold Sotheby 4 Feb and 23 Apr 1891) from the collection of Edward *Hailstone* of Horton Hall, Yorkshire, bequeathed to York Minster Library, esp 18th-19th cent sermons (10347.de.1-g.4 except e.45-53 and f.45-48; see the entry under York Minster Library for full particulars. A collection of *bills of mortality* (see General Catalogue under London . - I). A collection of pamphlets, etc on *Southampton* 1774–1830 (C.131.ee.1). Tracts, sermons, etc mostly printed by J T *Jones* and Son of Carmarthen and Aberdare 1831–70 (4460.h.8). A collection on Highgate formed by George *Potter* (1837–1927) (the bulk of which is in the British Museum Dept of Prints and Drawings) included some extra-illustrated volumes which are in the Library (see catalogue under Potter, George).

Jl *Celtic languages and cultures* The Welsh collection was built up mainly around the library of the Cymrrodorion Society (see Hb). Special collections include books, mainly in Welsh, of the 18th-19th cent, formed by Bob Owen (1550/1-172). A collection of 109 Jacobite and anti-Jacobite printed ephemera 1701–*c*1766 and 3 mss formed by Gertrude *Schlich* and Dorothy Kathleen *Broster* (C.115.i.3 (1-109), see *British Museum Quarterly* 19 (1954), p31-2). An Irish collection *c*750 items 16th-19th cent collected by Matthew *Dorey* of Oxford, given by Lord Moyn *c*1933 (see *British Museum Quarterly* 8 (1934), p127.

Jm *Madan collections* A collection formed by Falconer Madan (1851–1935) and his son Francis Falconer Madan (*d*1961) of the works of Henry *Sacheverell* (1674?–1724), bequeathed to the Friends of the National Libraries who gave it to the Library (Sach.). Francis Falconer Madan's collection of editions of the *Eikon basilike*, and related works (not all of which are in the General Catalogue), 134 v (C.118.d) given *c*1961.

F F Madan, *A critical bibliography of Dr Henry Sacheverell* ed W A Speck. Lawrence, Kansas, Univ of Kansas Libraries, 1978 (Ac.2692.i.8), notes Madan copies and some pressmarks in other BL collections. F F Madan, *A new bibliography of the Eikon Basilike*, 1950 (Oxford Bib Soc pub new ser 3). *British Museum Quarterly* 24 (1961), p117; 26 (1962), p58-9 and 64.

K **Overseas English Collections**

Ka *British colonies, protectorates and dominions* Systematic collection from most of the British overseas territories before the mid 19th cent was not possible either because printing was only just becoming established, esp in Africa, or the book trade had not yet developed an overseas distribution system. The 1842 Copyright Act was the first to specify delivery to the British Museum of books published in any part of the British dominions, but proved unenforceable, as Panizzi approached the Colonial Office and the India Office for assistance. The Colonial Office ruled in 1867 that copies of official publications were to be so delivered, the India Office in 1877; but the history of deposit of commercial publications is complex, and based on legislation for deposit both locally and at the BM sponsored by the Colonial Office or the India Office in individual territories, beginning with the Ceylon *Ordinance no 1* of 1885. Registers of works deposited were drawn up and often printed, sometimes as a supplement to the Official Gazette. Most countries sent all the works recorded, but India sent the registers first and from these a selection was made. (For Canada see Kb. For the collections of colonial newspapers see Newspaper Library, Vg below.)

A list of the registers recording receipts from those countries which sent works to the Museum is in the BL Archives; the Registers themselves are in the Department of Printed Books and the Department of Oriental Manuscripts and Printed Books.

Graham Shaw, *Printing in Calcutta to 1800*, London, Bibliographical Society, 1981.

Kb North America and the Caribbean It was in the field of American imprints that Panizzi, building upon an almost total void, achieved his greatest success. Henry Stevens, his former American agent, estimated that the number of American works in the Library had increased from 1,000 in 1843 to 4,000 in 1846 and to *c*70,000 in 1873. The Library is now thought to hold about 6,000 or 16% of the pre-1801 editions recorded in Evans's *American bibliography*. 81 items forming part of the collection of early Americana donated by White Kennett (1660–1728), Bishop of Peterborough, to the Society for the Propagation of the Gospel, given in 1916 by the Society prior to the auction of the residue (see London. United Society for the Propagation of the Gospel). After 1880 the pace of acquisition slackened, and the resulting gaps are now being filled by the American Trust for the British Library. American novels received 1918–37 form a separate collection (AN.1-3766); at other periods they have been placed in the general collections with American literature. *c*40,000 Canadian items received by copyright 1895–1924 are not yet fully catalogued.

Henry Stevens, *Catalogue of American books in the Library of the British Museum...1856...*, 1859, 2 v; Henry Stevens, *Catalogue of Canadian books in the Library of the British Museum...including those printed in the other British North American provinces*, London, 1859; Henry Stevens, *Catalogue of Mexican and other Spanish American and West Indian books in the Library of the British Museum*, 1859; these three catalogues reissued together as *Catalogue of the American books in the Library of the British Museum...1856*, 1866. Henry Stevens, *American books with tails to 'em: a private pocket list of the incomplete or unfinished American periodicals, transactions...legislative documents, and other continuations and works in progress supplied to the British Museum and other libraries*, priv pr 1873. White Kennett, *Bibliothecae Americanae primordia: an attempt towards...an American library...given to the Society for the Propagation of the Gospel...*, London, 1713; list of the 81 items (at USPG). John A Wiseman, *Henry Stevens and the British Museum: an account of his agency and other activities in the service of the national library*, (Library Association, FLA thesis, 1973). I R Willison, 'The development of the United States collection, Department of Printed Books, British Museum', *Journal of American Studies* 1 (1967), p79-86. The collections are supplemented by several microform collections: *Early American imprints*, Readex Microprint (to 1800 Cup.901 a.1; based on Evans and *National index*, both at 2037.a; 1801 onwards, Cup.901.a.10; based on Shoemaker, 2037.aa); *American fiction 1774–1850* (Mic.A.4281-4453, 5133-5142, 5926, etc; based on index by L H Wright BB.G. a.1); *American periodicals 1741–1900* (Mic.A.130-416, 3621-4212, Mic.B.604/846-1966, 606/1-771; index Bar.T.16 b.29).

L Germanic Language Collections

Mixed special collections include the bequest of James Hilton, FSA, comprising 250 v mainly of German and Dutch works, all containing chronograms, dispersed at various pressmarks; incl a volume of broadsheets and pamphlets, chiefly congratulatory verses to those taking religious vows 1676–1767 (KTC.29.b.9), and a volume of single printed leaves and engravings with a ms index dated 1890 (LR.22.c.18); see 'The Hilton bequest of chronograms', *BMQ* 5 (1930–1), p119-20 (many are repr in J Hilton, *Chronograms...*, 1882–95, 3 v).

La German The German collections, ie all books from German-speaking countries, until the 18th cent greater numbers in Latin than in German, as well as books in German printed elsewhere, are notably rich in most areas for all periods, and amount to *c*400,000 items. There are over 20,000 works of the 16th, *c*30,000 of the 17th, and at least 50,000 of the 18th cent. The foundation and early collections have been systematically enlarged (with some unavoidable intermissions) from Panizzi's time to the present. All major authors are well represented, and there are particularly fine collections of Reformation material, political tracts, ephemera (incl Lieddrucke), early science, literature from the period of Weimar classicism, and of secondary sources and periodicals. Collections of ephemera, the separate items of which are mostly entered in General Catalogue, include 16 verse broadsides 1568–1663 (Tab.597.d.3); a collection on the Revolution of 1848 (1851.c.4-7; see General Catalogue under Berlin: appendix); 72 religious songs of the mid-16th cent (C.175.i.31; listed in *BLJ* 1 (1975), p71-83); 34 illustrated broadsides 1619–73 (Crach.1.Tab.4.c.1-2; see *BLJ* 2 (1976), p56-69); facsimiles *c*1820 of charters of German emperors and princes (1756.c.18).

Short-title catalogue of books printed in the German-speaking countries, and of German books printed in other countries, from 1455 to 1600 now in the British Museum, 1962.

A 17th cent STC is in preparation; see D Paisey, 'Deutsche bücher des 17. Jahrhunderts in der British Library', *Börsenblatt für den Deutschen Buchhandel* 33(24) (25 Mar 1977), pA106-A-109. *Thomas Mann, 1875–1955: a British Library exhibition...*, 1975.

L*b* *Dutch* Of well over 50,000 Dutch books in the library, probably *c*15,000 are pre-1801, by far the largest collection in the British Isles; *c*5,000 of these are pre-1701. There is a large collection of clandestine wartime printing (see special catalogue), and also a collection of propaganda published in Holland during the German occupation, given by Dirk de Jong (Cup.21.p.3-53).

Short-title catalogue of books printed in the Netherlands and Belgium and of Dutch and Flemish books printed in other countries from 1470 to 1600 now in the British Museum, 1965; a catalogue 1601-20 is in preparation.

Anna E Simoni, *Publish and be free: a catalogue of clandestine books printed in the Netherlands 1940–45 in the British Library*, The Hague, 1975.

——'Hendrik Nicolaas Werkman and the Werkmanniana in the British Library', *BLJ* 2 (1976), p70-88.

A Loewenberg, 'Early Dutch librettos and plays with music in the British Museum', *Journal of Documentation* 2 (1947).

The collections are supplemented by the microfiche series *Dutch pamphlets ca 1486–1648*, Interdocumentation Co, based on Knuttel, 1978.

L*c* *Scandinavian* The Scandinavian collections to 1850 are extensive, probably over 50,000 v, but in recent years fewer significant gaps have been found in the pre-1851 period than in late 19th and early 20th cent holdings. Numerous important early works from the Scandinavian countries, incl Finland, were acquired with the King's Library, the Sloane, Grenville, and Banksian collections. Banks' collections in particular contained a major collection of Icelandic books and many works on Scandinavian topography. Danish, Norwegian, and Swedish history, philology and literature were well represented in the King's Library. Recent accessions have included many 18th cent dissertations from Danish and Swedish universities.

The Icelandic entries were printed separately as *Catalogue of the books printed in Iceland from 1578 to 1880 in the Library of the British Museum* by T W Lidderdale, 1885, with supplements by W Fiske, 1886 and 1890.

T W Lidderdale, *Catalogue of editions of Edda arranged chronologically: with an alphabetical list of editions, commentators, and works commenting on Edda literature*, ms, 1884. The collections are now being supplemented by a microfilm collection in progress. *Scandinavian culture series*, General Microfilm Co; this comprises Scandinavian works printed up to 1700: Swedish titles from Collijn, *Sveriges bibliografi intill år 1600* and *...1600–talet*; Danish, Norwegian, and Icelandic titles from Nielsen, *Dansk bibliografi, 1482–1600*, Bruun, *Bibliotheca Danica (1482–1830)*, and Pettersen, *Bibliotheca norvegica (1643–1813)*; combined card cat with pressmarks (N.L. Gallery).

M **Romance Language Collections**

M*a* *French* Among the foreign language collections the French has always held pride of place, building on the magnificence of the King's Library (E), the French Revolution collections (Dd), and the Grenville Library (Fa). It has the largest collection of French rare books outside France, and in many fields surpasses any individual French library. *c*12,000 works are of the 16th cent, and *c*20,000 of the 17th. Special collections include: the Arnold collection of almanacs (Ge); a collection of French pamphlets received in 1823; a collection of papers, pamphlets, etc 1834–61 on a claim on the British government made by Clement Augustus Gregory Peter Louis Baron de *Bode*, and Clement Joseph Philip Pen Baron de *Bode* (C.120.h.9-21); a collection formed by John Geoffrey *Aspin* of the collected works of Pierre Corneille (1606–84) bought in 1976 (C.127.f.1-8); two collections of cuttings on Napoleon III assembled in 1873 by Frédéric *Justen*, entitled *Napoleon III et la caricature anglaise de 1848 à 1872* (1761.a.12), and *Napoleon III devant la presse contemporaine en 1873*, 3 v (1764.c.21). There is one of the most extensive known collections of mazarinades, comprising over half those in Moteau's (11 v at C.406.j; 18 v at C.115.b; 18v at C.115.c; and 13 v at 180.a-181.a).

Short-title catalogue of books printed in France and of French books printed in other countries from 1470 to 1600 in the British Museum, 1924; repr 1966; discussed in A Tilley, 'The early French books at the British Museum', *Library* 4th ser 5 (1924), p161-8; *Supplement* due for publication in 1984. V F Goldsmith, *A short title catalogue of French books 1601–1700, in the library of the British Museum*, Folkestone, Dawsons, 1969–73, unofficial. Mazarinades are entered in Goldsmith's cat but not General Catalogue; special cat by Madeleine Stern in preparation; Célestin Moreau, *Bibliographie des Mazarinades*, 1850, copy with ms pressmarks. The collections are supplemented by the microfilm series *French political pamphlets 1560–1653*, Bell and Howell (Mic.A.4845-4872; based on D V Welsh, *A checklist* and *Second checklist of French political pamphlets...in the Newberry Library, Chicago*, 1950–5. Peter Barber, *Diplomacy: the world of the honest spy*, 1979.

M*b* *Italian* The Italian collection is hardly less fine than the French, building on the King's Library (E), Grenville Library (Fa), Colt Hoare collection (Df), and the Guingené collection (Hb). There are probably *c*50,000 pre-1801 works in the Library. *c*12,000 works are pre-1701. A collection of mainly 16th cent Italian books given by W M *Voynich* in 1907 is kept separate (Voyn). A collection of *c*600 v on the *Risorgimento* was bought in

1969 from the bookseller Fritz Haller. 16 v of Italian pastoral letters of the 18th-19th cent from the library of J B Leon *Maret* were given in 1969 by Theodore Besterman (1602/152(2-19)). Collections of ephemera from the 16th cent onwards not entered in the General Catalogue are numerous (see the general descriptions under General Catalogue headings such as Rome, City of; Rome, Church of, appendix; Italy, appendix; States of the Church, — Camera Apostolica (274 edicts 1549–1718)); many of them are placed at Cup.652.n.1, and in presses 1896-1897. There is a complete set of the decisions of the Rota 1700–1863 (305-309).

Short-title catalogue of books printed in Italy and of Italian books printed in other countries from 1465 to 1600, now in the British Museum, 1958. A F Johnson, 'Italian sixteenth century books', *Library* 13 (1958), p161-74. 17th cent cat in preparation. *Risorgimento Collection: accessions to the General Catalogue*..., 1971 see also *Bibliografia storica del Risorgimento*, London, 1980. C H Clough, *Pietro Bembo's library as represented particularly in the British Museum*, rev ed, London, British Museum, 1971; enlarged from *British Museum Quarterly* 30 (1965), p3-17. *Petrarch*...*catalogue of an exhibition*..., 1974. *Giovanni Boccaccio: catalogue of an exhibition*..., 1975.

Mc *Spanish, Portuguese and Latin American* These collections are unrivalled outside the countries of origin, and include, for the period before 1601, *c*3,000 Spanish, *c*350 Portuguese, and 54 from Mexico and Peru (a quarter of the books known to have been issued in those two countries in the period). Spanish 17th cent imprints are well represented, and no important work is lacking. For the 18th cent Spain is particularly well represented (eg *c*200 Ibarra imprints). A collection of editions of Miguel *Cervantes* Saavedra (1547–1616) formed by Henry Spencer Ashbee (1834–1900), part of his library (with *c*15,000 v of other books identifiable from his bookplate but not kept together) given to the Museum after his death in 1900 (Cer.). The collection of John Rutter *Chorley* (1807?–1867) of Spanish drama and poetry and books on Spanish drama, many with annotations, given? (or from his sale, Puttick, 27 Nov 1867, 11903.bbb.25) 1867 (11726.h.9 and 11728.h.1-22, and see General Catalogue under Chorley); with his collection on Spanish drama and other subjects (C.182.a.1-b.1) and *Comedias* 1652–1704 (11725.b.1-21; c.1-20; d.1-8; see General Catalogue under Spain. Appendix—Miscellaneous) with ms annotations by Johann Ludwig *Tieck*. There are many collections of chapbooks: Spanish 1758–9 (11450.h.4-5); Spanish 1813–21 (12330.l.1-); Spanish 1800–75, mostly 'gozos' and devotional verses (1875.a.27); Spanish and Catalan verse chapbooks relating to religious festivals 1747–1886 (11451.k.2); 393 Catalan chapbooks 1790–1875 (11451.ee.7; 11450.h.21; and 1875.a.26); Portuguese romances, ballads etc 1835–62 (1074.g.23-28). *c*500 bought (Sotheby 13 Feb 1968) from the collection of mainly 19th cent pamphlets, formed by the political journalist Luis Lopez *Dominguez* (1810–1898?); with other items that belonged to Lorenzo *Lopez* (*d*1833) (Cup.405.a.1-405.i.2). A collection on the *Falkland Islands* assembled 1982–3, incl historical material and propaganda of the war of 1982.

Henry Thomas, *Short-title catalogues of Spanish, Spanish-American and Portuguese books printed before 1601 in the British Museum*, 1966; this is a reissue of his *Short-title catalogue of books printed in Spain and of Spanish books printed elsewhere in Europe before 1601 now in the British Museum*, 1921 (typescript index of printers) and his *Short-title catalogue of Portuguese books*, 1940, and *Short-title catalogue of Spanish-American books printed before 1601 now in the British Museum*, 1944; Portuguese and Spanish-American first published unofficially in *Revue Hispanique* 65 (1925), p265-315 (reprint 1926). F Goldsmith, *A short title catalogue of Spanish and Portuguese books in the British Museum*, Folkestone, Dawsons, 1974, unofficial. Henry Stevens, *Catalogue of Mexican and other Spanish American and West Indian books in the British Museum*...*1856*, 1859; reissued with his *Catalogue of American books*, 1856. Henry Thomas, *Early Spanish ballads in the British Museum*, Cambridge, Stanley Morison, 1927 and *Thirteen Spanish ballads printed in Burgos, 1516–1517*, Barcelona, 1931. Maria Cruz Garcia de Enterria, *Catálogo de los pliegos poéticos espanoles del siglo XVIII en el British Museum*, Pisa, Giardini, 1977. Francisco Aguilar Pinal, *Impresos castellanos del XVI siglo en el British Museum*, Madrid, CSEC, 1970. *José Toribio Medina, 1852–1930; centenary exhibition*, 1952. *Lope de Vega, 1562–1635: catalogue of an exhibition*..., 1962; see also *British Museum Quarterly* 25 (1962), p70-4. H G Whitehead, 'A collection of Latin American pamphlets', *British Museum Quarterly* 34 (1969–70), p1-9. H Thomas, 'The Cervantes collection in the British Museum', *Library* new ser 9 (1908), p429-43. H G Whitehead, 'Joaquin Ibarra, 1725–1785: a tentative list of holdings in the Reference Division', *British Library Journal* 6 (1980), p199-215.

N **Slavonic and East European Language Collections**

Among general collections is one of mid-19th cent facsimiles of Slavonic printing from books printed between 1564 and 1759, formed by S A Sobolevsky (1803.c.31).

Na *Russian, Ukrainian and Belorussian* The Russian language collection totals *c*250,000 items; over 8,000 monographs are added annually. There are *c*50 pre-1700 Cyrillic items, approximately half of which were printed in Russia, ie in the State of Muscovy, and half outside. Notable 16th cent imprints are Makarios' Gospels printed in Tîrgovişte (Wallachia), 3 works printed by Frantsisk Skaryna (1 in Prague, 2 in Wilno), and 4 Ivan Fedorov imprints (his Moscow *Apostol*, his Lvov *Bukvar* and his Ostrog Bible). 17th cent holdings include Smotritsky's *Grammatika* of 1648, the 1649 *Ulozhenie* of Tsar Aleksei Mikhailovich, and the *Kormchaya Kniga* (Nomocanon) printed in Moscow, 1649–53. 18th cent books with

Russian imprints total *c*2,500, of which *c*1,500 are in Russian or Church Slavonic, the remainder in other languages; incl important editions of Trediakovsky, Kherasov and Lomonosov, F A Emin's *Nepostoyannaya fortuna* of 1763, an almost complete run of *Rossiisky teatr* (SPb., 1786–94), the series *Drevnyaya rossiiskaya vivliofika* and the periodical *Magazin svobodno-kamenshchitsy*. 19th cent holdings are particularly rich in literary, linguistic and historical works. 20th cent rarities include a large collection of futurist books mainly of *c*1910–6, and a collection of 50 satirical journals 1905–7. Considerable bomb damage, esp to holdings of literary periodicals and monographs on law and art, has been partly made good by recent purchases or microfilming. Special collections include a collection (printed and ms) on the emancipation of women in Russia, 1891–1907, annotated by Peter Alekseevich Kropotkin (1884.a.11).

P J Fairs, 'Russian publications in the British Museum in the 19th cent', *Solanus* 1 (1970), p13-16. V Burtsev, 'Russian documents in the British Museum', *Slavonic Review* 4 (1926), p669-85. L Loewensohn, 'Russian documents in the British Museum', *Slavonic Review* 14 (1936), p380-8, 661-9. B P Pockney, 'Russian books in the British Museum', *Anglo-Soviet Journal* 31 (1971), p4-14. S P Compton, *The world backwards: Russian futurist books*, 1978. The collections are supplemented by the microfilm series *Cyrillic books before 1701*, General Microfilm Co (Mic.A.6010-6332, with card index of pressmarks based on entries in A S Zernova, *Knigi kirillovskoi pechati izdannye v Moskve*, 2705.an.1); and *Russian revolutionary literature collection, Harvard University*, Research Publications (Mic.B.79/1-47; *Descriptive guide and key*, BB.G.f.26). *Transliteration of cyrillic* (Reader guide no 3).

C Drage, *Russian and Church Slavonic books 1701–1800 in United Kingdom libraries*, in preparation.

N*b Polish* The Polish collection totals *c*100,000 v, of which perhaps 5,000 are pre-1801. The earliest books printed in Poland to reach the British Museum came from the King's Library. The bulk of the pre-1801 collection was acquired in the 19th cent and it suffered heavy losses in 1941. There are *c*2,000 titles in Latin, Polish, Church Slavonic and German, among which are 4 Cracow incunabula and *c*330 books printed in the 16th cent. The collection includes many rare items some of which are not mentioned in Estreicher's *Bibliografia polska*. Among the most notable titles are: *Commune incliti Poloniae Regni privilegium* (1506), *Zwierzyniec* (1562) and *Zwierciadło* (1568) by Mikołaj Rej, *Polonicae grammatices institutio* (1568) by Piotr Statoriusz, *Elegiarum libri IV* (1584) by Jan Kochanowski, *Victoria deorum* (*c*1595) by Sebastian Klonowic, *Historia polonica* (1611) by Jan Długosz and *Selenographia* (1647) by Joannes Hevelius.

Some categories of material are particularly well represented: (i) the earliest Bibles which include the Radziwiłł Bible (1563), once the property of Bishop J Załuski (1702–74), co-founder of the first national library in Warsaw, and the very rare Socinian New Testament (1577); (ii) 'constitutions' issued by the 16th-18th cent diets, including the Third of May 1791 Constitution; and (iii) Socinian literature published in Cracow and Raków (1577–1638), some of which is rare.

There is a special collection of 80 books presented to the Museum in 1832 by Prince Adam Czartoryski, mainly on Polish history and editions of Polish classical authors, a large proportion of which was printed before 1801.

H Świderska, 'The old Polish Diets: the Museum collection of official and semi-official publications, *British Museum Quarterly* 31 (1967), p78-83.

——'Prince Czartoryski and the British Museum', *British Museum Quarterly* 28 (1964), p811.

——'Socinian books with the Raków imprint in the British Library', *British Library Journal* 8 (1982), p206-17.

N*c Czech* There are Czech incunabula and a large number of 16th and early 17th cent books now very scarce. Among the incunabula of Czech provenance are: the only known copy of Clement von Graz's 'Von den heissen Bädern' (Brno 1495), first Bible printed in the Czech language (Prague 1488) and the first illustrated Bible in Czech (Kutna Hora 1489) with 117 woodcuts. Important printers of the 16th cent, the golden age of Czech printing, are represented by books of the highest quality typography from the presses of Melantrich z Aventýna, Daniel Adam z Veleslavína and the Czech Brethren. Special mention deserve Melantrich's *Mattioli's Herbář* (1562) and Czech Brethren's *New Testament* (1564), beautifully decorated hymnal *Písně Duchownj Ewangelistické* (1564) and the 6-volume *Bible of Kralice* (1579–93). The Library's copy of the English poetess Westonia's 'Parthenicon', printed in Prague 1606, contains, on a flyleaf, manuscript poetical address to the reader from the authoress, dated 1610.

N*d Yugoslav* Most of the older volumes in the Library's collections in the 'Yugoslav' languages were printed in Italy or Germany, although often by printers of Slav origin. There are, however, rare copies of the earliest works of the first printing houses in Montenegro (Obod/Cetinje), Senj, Rijeka and Ljubljana, including examples of early Glagolitic printing. The collections also contain a number of works, mainly Bibles and catechisms, printed by one of the most prolific of the Glagolitic printing houses, that of Primož Trubar, at Tübingen, later at Urach. These are often present in both the Glagolitic and Cyrillic versions, complete with the introductory texts written by Trubar himself. 16th and 17th cent works held are largely those written in the earliest forms of the Croatian language, liturgical works, and the doctrinal and lexical works of Divković, Levaković, Kašić, etc, and the works of the first Croatian philosophers and writers of imaginative literature, Marulić, Lucić, Ranjina, etc. Notable 18th and early 19th cent holdings, in addition to traditional doctrinal and liturgical works, include many 'Illyrian' dictionaries and linguistic works, with early Serbian works from writers such as Orfelin, Rajić and Dositej Obradović (incl 3 given during his visit to London), and first editions of the linguistic and folklore collections of Vuk Karadžić.

Ne *Bulgarian* The collections do not boast very many examples of the earliest Bulgarian printed books but there is a copy of the rare ABAGAR of Philip Stanislavov, printed in Rome in 1651. The earliest Bulgarian book in the collections, published in Eastern Europe, is the work on Bulgarian grammar by the monk Neofit of Rila Monastery, published in 1835 by Kragujevac, no 31 in Pogorelov's *Opis na starite pechatni balgarski knigi, 1802–1877.*

Nf *Baltic countries* The Baltic collection, covering the modern Lithuania, Latvia and Estonia, originated in connection with the German, Russian, Polish and Scandinavian collections. Written literature in the vernacular languages of the area, which appeared as a result of the Reformation, was of a religious nature. The earliest material includes such rarities as the Lithuanian *Postilla* by Jonas Bretkūnas (1591); the three surviving fragments of the Lithuanian Bible translated at Oxford by S B Chyliński, whose printing (in London, 1660?) was never completed; the first Latvian Bible (1685–9) and the first Estonian Bible (1739). The awakening interest in the vernacular languages is illustrated by G F Stender's *Lettische Grammatik* (1783) and *Lettisches Lexicon* (1789–91), *Manuductio ad linguam Oesthonicam* (1660) by H Goeseken and *Ehstnische Sprachlehre für beide Hauptdialekte* (1780) by A W Hupel. Material on secular subjects printed in the area before 1801 was mainly in German, Latin and Polish.

S Pruuden, *Catalogue of books and periodicals on Estonia in the British Library Reference Division*, London, BL, 1981.

Ng *Hungarian* The collection of the bibliophile István *Nagy* forms the backbone of the Hungarian collection. A collection of *c*4,000 v of Hungarian pamphlets and ephemera on Hungarian history, literature, theatre and culture 1770–1863, formed by László Imre *Waltherr*, bought in 1873 (mostly a separate collection pressmarked Hung).

L Czigány, 'The László Waltherr collection', *British Museum Quarterly* 33 (1969).

Nh *Romanian* Though early Romanian imprints are poorly represented, later editions of many of these have been acquired among the 19th cent publications of the Romanian Academy. Notable 17th and 18th cent first editions held include *Indreptarea legii*, 1652, the first Wallachian code of laws; the Wallachian Cyrillic alphabet, with syllabaries, prayers, etc, printed at Karlsburg, 1700; and Dimitrie Cantemir's *Divanul* of 1698.

O Special Subject Collections

Oa *Religion* The foundation collections with the Old Royal and King's libraries provided an unsurpassed collection on the Church of England and strong collections on the Reformation in continental, early printed liturgies, and Luther, and this tradition has been maintained. The collections are less strong in British nonconformity, particularly of the 18th and 19th cent, and Catholic recusancy, and many of the gaps in these fields are now having to be filled. There are many special collections placed in the general library. A collection of religious broadsides, mainly in verse, 1889–1902, formed by William Edward Armytage *Axon* (11436.l.7) incl offprint from *Library* ns 5 (1904), p239-55, 'Some twentieth-century Italian chapbooks'). A collection of over 300 v of articles, tracts, etc on the Catholic Apostolic (or Irvingite) Church, 1821–1905, formed by Clement *Boase* (1846–1913) (764.an; see *Catalogue of printed books: accessions: Boase Collection*, 1913, and his annotated copies of his *Catalogue of...writings by...Fellowship of the Apostles...in the library of Clement Boase* and *Appendix...contra Irvingism...*, 1885–7). The collection of Joseph Gibbins *Dufty*, of late 19th and early 20th cent works on Emanuel *Swedenborg* (1688–1772) and Swedenborgianism (mainly at 1552/1132, but dispersed in the general collections). A collection of tracts and sermons *c*1820–40 formed by the Rev Michael Augustus *Gathercole* (908.b.1-e.7). 18 v on the Jesuits, 1596–1904 mainly 17th-18th cent, collected by Moriz *Grolig* (*b*1873) (4789.ae). A collection of editions of John Bunyan from the library of Sir (Robert) Leicester *Harmsworth* (1870–1937) (C.111.d.1-e.25; see *British Museum Quarterly* 15 (1952), p17-18). Part of the collection of hymnals and works on hymnology formed by John *Julian* (1839–1913), and presented by him to Church House Library; the collection was divided in 1972, all works not already in the British Museum being donated to the Library (hymnals at 3440-03441; hymnal broadsheets and cuttings 1794–1917 with ms notes and index by Julian 3442.c.18; and other material elsewhere in the general collections; see also Lambeth Palace Library; ms cat 1982, 4 v, 11927.k.1). *Novello* collection of hymnals, acquired from the reference library of Messrs Novello, music publishers, in 1965, with scores now in the Music Library. A collection of hymnal broadsheets associated with Sunday schools in Sheffield and elsewhere, 1816–1869, assembled and indexed by John Daniel *Leader* (1835–99) (3442.c.17). The collection of liturgies and service books (all entered in General Catalogue under Liturgies) is very extensive. A collection of liturgical works formed by John Wickham *Legg*, was given in 1921 (Legg.1-303). Other substantial additions have been made more recently (see *British Museum Quarterly* 36 (1971), p14). A large quantity of works from the library of the Oblates of St Charles, Bayswater, was bought in 1967 (those which had been the personal property of their founder Cardinal Henry Edward *Manning* (1808–92) are placed at 1650/147). 16 v from a collection of pastoral letters 18th-19th cent in 19 v from the library of J B Léon Maret were given in 1969 by Theodore Besterman (1904–76) (1602/152; see General Catalogue under Collection). A collection of reports of deaconesses' institutions 1845–85 (4499.h.1). For the Imitatio Christi collection see above (Fe).

W E A Axon, 'Indulgences in the British Museum', *Library*, 2nd ser 7 (1906), p275-86. *Catalogue of an exhibition commemorating the four hundredth anniversary of the introduction of the Book of Common Prayer.* Henry Stevens, *The Bibles in the Caxton exhibition 1877.* Catholic Truth Society publications are not all catalogued individually (mostly placed at 3938.ff and 3943.fff; see General Catalogue under 'London III'; those published 1886-1944 entered in a separate guardbook cat, Cup.1264.cc.5). Cat of Luther exhibition, 1883. *Guide to the manuscripts and printed books exhibited in celebration of the Tercentenary of the Authorized Version. . .*, 1911.

Ob Politics A collection of political and some miscellaneous pamphlets *c*1915–45 formed by George *Orwell* (Eric A Blair, 1903–50) (1899.ss.1-21, 23-47; typescript index 1899.ss.48). A collection of ephemera 1906–36 on the women's suffrage movement formed and annotated by Maud *Arncliffe-Sennett*, in 37 v (C.121.g.1; see *British Museum Quarterly* 11 (1936–7, p173-4). A collection of documents of the Papal States 1536–1843 (Cup.652.n.1-2). One box of uncatalogued election posters (Election Posters). *Election addresses* (5 sets 1880–1924 in GK under England: Parliament: House of Commons: Addresses to electors; others catalogued individually); Norwich election 1837 (8025.e.46).

Catalogue of the Gibbon Exhibition 1894, 1895. Peter Hogg, *Slavery, the Afro-American experience*, 1979. H Stein, 'Six tracts about women: a volume in the British Museum', *Library*, 4th ser 15 (1934), p38-48.

Oc Crawford collection *c*5,000 books and pamphlets and 4,000 periodicals on philately and postal history bequeathed by James Ludovic Lindsay, 26th Earl of Crawford (1847–1913) (Crawford). It incorporates the collections of John Kerr Tiffany (1843–97) of St Louis, bought in 1901; and of Heinrich Fraenkel of Berlin, bought in 1907.

E D Bacon, *Catalogue of the Philatelic Library of the Earl of Crawford*, 1911; *Bibliotheca Lindesiana*, 1911, v 7, A bibliography of the writings, general, special and periodical forming the literature of philately (Cup.402.h.2 with ms pressmarks); Supplement, 1926; Addenda, 1938.

Od Hanover Military Library The library of the general staff college at Hanover, mainly 19th and early 20th cent books on military topics, confiscated by the British government at the end of World War II (M.L.).

Partly in General Catalogue.

Oe Sciences See also Sloane (Ba) and Banks (Dg). Collections include 69 German broadsides on comets etc. 1615–1748 (1875.d.4); and 17 broadsides on portents 1551–1645 in German, French, Italian and Spanish (Tab.597.d.2).

Catalogue of the works of Linnaeus and publications more immediately relating thereto preserved in the libraries of the British Museum, Bloomsbury, and the British Museum (Natural History), South Kensington, 1907. K K Doberer, *Bibliography of books on alchemy in the British Museum*, 1946 (2748.b.1 with ms pressmarks). T S Pattie, *Astrology as illustrated in the British Library and the British Museum*, London, British Library, 1980.

Of Law Early law books are placed at C.59 and C.108.

P Ephemera

For literary prospectuses see Gl; for ballads see the appropriate language sections (in I-N). Ephemera were included in the Grenville Library (see Fa) probably the first significant collection, apart from the Burney and other theatre collections (see P). Panizzi built up these collections systematically by purchasing at auctions, eg of the collections of Edward Skegg (Sotheby 4 Apr 1842). Large quantities of material were received in the later 19th cent by purchases, donation and copyright deposit. Almost all were bound into guardbooks on particular subjects (which sometimes contain ms indexes). After 1910 the inflow was much reduced. Current collections of antiquarian single sheets are at L.23c and C.117.g.1; others at Cup.21.g and Cup.648.

Aslib directory, London, 1928 (but not the later editions) under alphabetical subject headings lists the main ephemera collections with their pressmarks (but many are now changed). Many of the collections are represented in the General Catalogue by a single collective entry, either under 'Collections', or under the name of the donor or annotator, or in the appendix to the name of the person or place to which the collection relates. Most collections of early printed ephemera are listed in *Guide to the union catalogues of books printed before 1801 and to other tools for locating antiquarian books. . .*, 1977, Appendix 17, with indication of the extent to which the contents of each are individually catalogued, typescript (ESTC office; photocopy N.L.7.d). Alphabetical list of ephemera guardbooks used for miscellaneous acquisitions 1919–*c*1963 (Placers' Archives; photocopy at R.R.Enq); some pressmarks have now been changed. A comprehensive survey of ephemera collections in the British Library (and many other libraries) is in progress.

Pa Lysons' Collectanea *Collectanea; or a collection of advertisements and paragraphs from the newspapers, relating to various subjects. . .*; collected by the Rev Daniel Lysons (1762–1834) FRS, with titlepages specially printed at the Strawberry Hill Press. Of the original 22 v, 8 v were bought for the Library in 1860–3; 2 v, general, 1660–1825; (C.103.k.13); 5 v, general, 1661–1840 with ms notes and index (C.103.k.11); 1 v, 1726–56, mainly relating to 'Orator' J Henley (C.103.k.12).

A T Hazen, *A bibliography of the Strawberry Hill Press*, New Haven, 1942, p162-3, no 60. J G McManaway, 'The theatrical collectanea of Daniel Lysons', *Papers of the Bibliographical Society of America* 51 (1957), p333-4.

Pb Cox's Fragmenta 'Fragmenta': a collection of 98 v of parts of books, cuttings from newspapers, advertisements, playbills etc 1750–1833, made by Francis Cox, and bequeathed by him in 1834, 94 v, formerly assumed to be part of the Burney Collection (937.g.1-94).

C B Oldman, 'Francis Cox and his Fragmenta', *British Museum Quarterly* 30 (1966), p65-75.

P*c Dawson Turner collections* Various collections from the library of Dawson Turner (1775–1858) MA FRS (sold Puttick, 16 May 1859), bought from booksellers. A collection of prospectuses 1774–1846 formed by Dawson Turner, with ms title 'Prospectuses of books, engravings, lithographs, etc, collected with a view, not only of showing the state of the literature, arts and sciences of the passing day, but as too often illustrative of the vanity of human wishes, etc', in 4 v (1879.b.1 numbered in ms 1, 3, 4, 8); another collection (see General Catalogue under Yarmouth) of handbills, playbills, reports of the Yarmouth and Norwich Railway Company, of charitable societies, etc, chiefly 1830–62, 9 v (N.Tab.2012/6, formerly 1889.d.14); and a collection of handbills and cuttings on lotteries 1802–26 with ms preface (8225.bb.78)

'A bibliography of the printed works of Dawson Turner', *Transactions of the Cambridge Bibliographical Society* 3 (1959–63), p232-56.

P*d Yeowell collection* A collection made by James Yeowell (1803?–1875), sub-editor of *Notes and Queries*, in the mid-19th cent, of newspaper cuttings, excerpts from printed books, ms memoranda, and portraits, in preparation for a biographical dictionary which was never published, 48 v and 8 parcels (010604.p.1; other material is in Dept of Mss).

P*e Place collection* A collection of 180 v of newspaper cuttings, leaflets, etc on politics and economics, 1792–1852 formed by Francis Place (1771–1854) (Place; index R.R.Enq; his other collections, incl his autobiography which contains references to his library, are in Dept of Mss, see WDe).

F Place, *Autobiography* ed M Thale, Cambridge UP, 1972. F Place, *London radicalism, 1830–43: a selection from the papers...*, London Topographical Society, 1970.

P*f Fillinham collection* Part of the large library of ephemera formed by John Fillinham; comprising news-cuttings, advertisements, playbills, etc; this part, in 8 v, relates mainly to the British Museum, Carlisle House, White Conduit House, fairs, exhibitions, and menageries (1889.b.10; other parts are in other libraries).

P*g Prospectuses of public companies* A collection of prospectuses of public companies etc *c*1830–45 mainly formed by Thomas Glover (1880.e.1). Among the early 19th cent collections, prospectuses of railway companies are especially numerous; these include many which were donated in response to an appeal by Sir Henry Ellis in a letter to *The Times*, 1845; and many for lines which never came to fruition; the main collections are at 1881.b.23, 30+v; 1890.c.6 and e.2&9; and Maps.18.c.1-5; see also 578.m.11&16 (Kent); 717.m.19; 8228.i.31; 8223.e.10; 8235.k.56-57.

Ms index to names of railway companies with press-marks of volumes in which their prospectuses are to be found.

P*h Miscellaneous collections* A collection of news cuttings, parliamentary reports, pamphlets etc relating to the introduction of penny postage, 1839–40, 8 v (L.R.271.c.11). Two collections formed by St John *Crookes*: on the Durham election 1865 (1851.d.11); on the murder of J Millie 1838 (1891.f.6). A collection formed by W B *Cross* on the Bristol Riots of 1831, 3 v (L.R.271.e.3; plates L.R.271.c.12). A collection of miscellaneous newspaper cuttings 1712–85 with ms index formed by Sir John *Cullum* (1890.c.7). A collection of cuttings of the births, marriages and deaths columns from American newspapers 1832–50, collected by Samuel *Drake*, and lettered 'Death's Doings' (10811.dd.12). Obituaries, chiefly French, from 1818 (Cup.1253.d.30). A collection of newspaper cuttings and pamphlets on *Tristan de Cunha*, 1886–1946, formed by Douglas M *Gane*, in 5 v (10493.h.27). A collection of English and South African newspaper cuttings *c*1880–1930, formed by Herbert John Viscount *Gladstone*, 3 v (1899.b.11). A collection on balloons (8755.k.11), and another in the large collection of ephemera formed by Sarah S Banks (L.R.301.h.3-11; see Ha).

Q Performing Arts Collections

The first main collection of theatrical history (mainly ephemera) came in *c*200 v with the library of Charles Burney (see De above), placed at 937.g.95-96; 938.a.-f.; 939.b.1-2; 939.d.-e. and playbills below; see General Catalogue under his name for details of the main subcollections; they include *c*50 v of cuttings, notes, and playbills relating to Garrick. In the 19th cent theatrical ephemera of all kinds were kept in the Newspaper Room mostly uncatalogued, but with some partial rough indexes. There is an incomplete typescript index 1951 (revised from the old ms indexes now in the Placers' Office) by towns and theatres, of the main collections in the Playbills and Theatre Cuttings collections (but not all their miscellaneous volumes); a photocopy annotated with some of the holdings in other parts of the Library is kept at R.R.Enq. Substantial runs are now entered in General Catalogue under Place and Theatre, but not all the smaller collections and odd items.

H M Nixon, 'Theatrical holdings of the Department of Printed Books, British Museum', Ohio State University, *OSU Theatre Collection Bulletin* 8 (1961), p5-9. The collections are supplemented by the microfilm series *Covent Garden prompt books* (Mic.A.4873-4875); and the microfiche series *Libretti*, Kraus-Thompson (Cup.580.f.11, based on E Thiel's *Verzeichnis* of the collection at Wolfenbüttel to 1800, 11906.cc.4).

Q*a Playbills* The Burney collection remains separate (937.b.-e.; 937.f.1, 2; 937.g.96; chiefly Covent Garden, Drury Lane, and Haymarket Theatre, 1768–1817; details under his name in General Catalogue, but not indexed). Thereafter most collections are incorporated in the general collection of playbills (Playbills; in course of microfilming); the collection of the Theatre Royal, Drury Lane, 1780–1885, made by Sir Augustus H G Harris (1852–96) the Manager at Covent Garden (Playbills 1-45); extended from other sources 1754–1845 (Playbills 46-76 and 127-133), incl an annotated and indexed run 1814–21. A set of the Theatre Royal, Covent Garden, 1753–1845, in part annotated (Playbills 77-108). Haymarket Theatre 1777–1849 (Playbills 109-123, 134-143, 300, 305). Among the provincial collections runs for *c*40 provincial towns begin in the later 18th cent. The collection of foreign playbills 1845–56 (Playbills 303), provincial 1845–60 (Playbills 404), and London 1847–1908 (Playbills 305) formed by William James Russell (1830–1909), FRS, given by his family. A collection made by the critic William Archer (1856–1924) of London and provincial playbills, 1895–1924, in 7 v, arranged alphabetically (Playbills 335-341). The collection of the Hon Sidney Carr Glynn (Playbills 352-363) of playbills mainly of London theatres, 1791–1895. The collection of mostly London and foreign playbills and programmes 1847–1919 formed by William Barclay Squire (1855–1927) (Playbills 342-7, 349-51). The collection of Covent Garden opera programmes 1906–39 made by J Petherbridge (Playbills 439-451, 453-467). A collection of London and Birmingham theatre programmes 1883–8 (11795.tt.45). A miscellaneous collection 1750–1821, with portraits of actors (1763.a.5).

Qb Theatre cuttings A general collection of Theatre Cuttings (Th.Cuts.) was begun in the late 19th cent from the collections in the Newspaper Room, beginning with the collection on London theatres 1704–79, 6 v, formed by Sir Augustus Harris (Th.Cuts.16). The collection of W E Streatfield 1847–93, 28 v (Th.Cuts.7-34). Major collections include Covent Garden 1760–1834 annotated (Th.Cuts.38-39), Drury Lane 1777–1834 (Th.Cuts.40), King's and Haymarket theatres 1757–1829 (Th.Cuts.41-43), Lyceum Theatre 1781–1840 annotated (Th.Cuts.44-46), Olympic Theatre 1805–41 annotated (Th.Cuts.47-48), and Sadlers Wells 1740–1866 (Th.Cuts.49); see also below. A collection on actors, dramatists, composers, etc (Th.Cuts.75-76).

Qc Concert programmes Programmes of concerts given by Adila A A M *Fachiri* (1886–1962) and Jelly d'*Aranyi* (1893–1966) the sister violinists, with cuttings and documents, 1906–56 (Aranyi). There are two collections of Sir William Schwenk *Gilbert* (1836–1911): his own miscellaneous collection 1887–93 (7903.1.4); and a collection on the Savoy operas 1879–1940 with some of his own collection (Th.Cuts.78). A miscellaneous collection 1888–1913 formed by William Edmonds (Cup.1247.ccc.5). Two collections formed from 1878 onwards by Diana *Gordon* 1932–74 given in 1975 (X.431/2098; X.435/318). A collection formed by Ernst *Henschel* of German programmes 1892–1938 and English 1938–66 and related material (Henschel; see *British Museum Quarterly* 33 (1968–9), p91-2. A collection of programmes and other material relating to Sigfrid *Karg-Elert* (1877–1933) (Cup.900.p.1). Many collections of late 18th and early 19th cent programmes, annotated by Sir George Thomas *Smart* (1776–1867) (C.61.g.1-20; for details see General Catalogue under Smart). A collection formed by Arthur Henry *Stevens* (1819–86), 1878–1921 (7900.f.41). A collection of programmes of concerts conducted by Sir Henry *Wood* (1869–1944), 1898–1944, many with ms inscriptions by him and others (X.435/115). Programmes of music at *Alexandra Palace* 1854–80 (7901.a.44). Programmes of concerts in Berlin, Paris, etc 1843– (748.e.10). Over 3,700 English provincial programmes collected by D A *Dalgleish* (Cup.918), bought 1982, all of the 20th cent but chiefly 1950–80, incl complete sets over long periods for several major orchestras (see General Cat Microfilm under place/name of orchestra). Miscellaneous programmes (X.0435/4). Souvenir programmes of *cinemas* 1955– (W.P.5999). 47 concert programmes 1905–7 printed on crepe paper (1899.b.10).

A Hyatt King, 'A collection of musical programmes', *British Museum Quarterly* 33 (1969), p91-2.

Qd Daniel collections From the sale of the library of George Daniel (1789–1864) the book collector (Sotheby 20 July 1864). A collection of ephemera on the Shakespeare Jubilee of 1769, and David Garrick's part in it, and other subjects, with ms notes by George Daniel, 1746–*c*1860 (C.61.e.2); and a collection annotated by him relating to the sale of Shakespeare's house with miscellaneous Shakespeareana 1710–1864 (1889.b.17). See also Huth Bequest (Fd).

Qe Evanion collection A collection formed by Henry Evanion of pamphlets, handbills, and miscellaneous printed matter *c*1800–95 on theatres, fairs, etc (Tab.11748.a.).

Qf Biographia dramatica Four copies annotated mainly by Thomas Hailes *Lacy* (1809–73) of D E Baker, *Biographia dramatica*, London, 1812, with 6 ms v of his additions for a new edition (11795.d.f and k.).

Qg Percival collection A collection relating to Sadler's Wells Theatre 1683–1848, formed by Richard Percival, comprising pamphlets, broadsides, playbills, advertisements, songs with tunes, views, portraits, and autograph letters, in 14 v (Crach.1.Tab.4.b.4).

Qh Smith collection An annotated cuttings collection entitled 'Of plays, players and play-houses, with other incidental matter', by 'J H', probably Joseph Haslewood (1769–1833), continued 1820–37 by Richard John Smith (1786–1855, the actor 'O' Smith); 9 v (11791.dd.18). Also *A collection of material towards an history of the English stage* comprising memoirs, plates, playbills, cuttings from books, newspapers and magazines, collected *c*1825–40 and copiously annotated by Smith, in 25 v (11826.r. and s.).

Qi Stoker collection A collection made by Bram Stoker (1847–1912), of programmes of performances with which

Sir Henry *Irving* (1838–1905) was connected, 1879–1905 (C.120.a.1 and C.120.g.1).

Qj Winston collection A collection of memoranda, documents, playbills, newspaper cuttings, etc, relating to *Drury Lane Theatre* 1616–1830, arranged chronologically by James Winston (1779–1843), in 19 boxes (C.120.h.1). Probably from the sale (Puttick, 13 Dec 1849).

Qk Musicology A collection of original editions of Gilbert and Sullivan given by Charles Johnson. A collection formed by James Arthur *Watson* of periodical articles, newspaper cuttings, etc, on Wolfgang Amadeus *Mozart* (1791–1844), *c*1920–50, bound in 3 v (7901.t.30). A collection of opera libretti and related material *c*1820–1940 formed by Richard A *Northcott* (1871–1931) (Northcott). A collection on pianos 1876–1951 made by James L *Stephen* (07902.b.1/1-13).

Ms cat of books on music in the Library, (*c*1880) (C.175.b.38). The collections are supplemented by the microfilm series *Richardson collection of dance books*, University Microfilms (Mic.A.5363-5643, based on I K Fletcher, *Bibliographical descriptions of forty rare books relating to the art of dancing in the collection of P J S Richardson*, London, 1977, BB.E.dd.31.c).

R **British Library Reference Division. Official Publications Library**

Great Russell Street, London WC1B 3DG. Tel (01) 636 1544 Ext 234. Telex 21462. Open to holders of Reference Division readers' passes (see A above) 9.30 am-4.45 pm (Mon, Fri, Sat), 8.45 pm (Tues-Thurs). Photoreproduction as for Dept of Printed Books, incl microform readers; postal and telephone enquiries welcomed. Most official publications and many legal materials are stored at Woolwich (24 hours' notice required).

RA General

The Official Publications Library, a section of the Department of Printed Books, houses official government publications of all countries, together with open access and certain special collections on law and social sciences (though most works in these last fields are shelved in the main library).

The Official Publications Library (free leaflet).

M E Goldrick, *Microform collections: official publications and the social sciences*, 1983 (Reader guide no 12).

RAa History Before 1870 official publications were held in the Journal Room or Newspaper Room. Few were received other than by copyright receipt (see Ja and Ka). In that year exchange of official publications with American and other foreign libraries began, and this laid the foundation for a major expansion in the field. In 1931 the State Paper Room became a separate branch of the Department. In 1974 it was reorganized to provide access to the whole field of the social sciences, and renamed the Official Publications Library.

G Spinney, 'Frank Campbell, 1863–1905', *Government Publications Review* 4 (1977), p21-9; S P Green, 'The State Paper Room of the British Museum', *Government Publications Review* 1 (1973), p61-5; E Johansson, 'The reference work of the British Library Official Publications Library', *Government Publications Review* 3 (1976), p271-6.

RAb Catalogues No special catalogue for official publications in general. Some are entered under names of countries in the General Catalogue (see Ae), to a very limited extent appearing in the Subject Index (Ah), or by author and subject in the Current Catalogue on microfiche (Aj). Supplementary card cat of official publications in Western languages 1966–79 (and see other special catalogues below). Many pre-1980 official publications, however, are not catalogued at all, and readers are recommended to seek advice. Catalogues are supplemented by over 2,000 v (with dictionary card cat) of bibliographies, indexes, abstracts, and other reference works in the social sciences.

RB Official Gazettes (OG)

A worldwide collection of official government gazettes, incl a set of the *London Gazette* from its foundation as the *Oxford Gazette* in 1665 (indexes incomplete until 1830).

RC British Parliamentary Publications

RCa Acts of Parliament Statutes of the Realm, 1100–1713, 12 v; *Acts of the Parliament of Scotland, 1124–1707*, 12 v; *Public General Acts*, 1509– . *Local and Personal Acts*, 1753– , previously 'Public Acts not printed in the General Collection'. *Private Bills* (incl Acts and Bills entitled 'Acts'), 1715–1800. There are over 500 (many annotated) from the collection of Robert Harper, with collection of Private Bills of the reign of Queen Anne (incl some in ms copies) from the *Salt* collection.

Card index (chronological, incomplete) of Private and Local and Personal from 1702 onwards. Sheila Lambert, *The Harper collection*, 1973, typescript list; the Harper collection is also described and listed in her *Bills and Acts*, Cambridge, 1971, p4-8, 194-225.

RCb Abbot collection and other pre-1801 Parliamentary Papers 18th cent Parliamentary Reports, Accounts and Bills, collected by Speaker Charles Abbot, 1st Baron Colchester (1757–1829), best of the 5 sets (see under House of Commons Library for full details and bibliography). Also 'First series' of *Reports from committees of the House of Commons*, 15 v, 1773–1803.

RCc Post-1800 Parliamentary Papers House of Commons almost complete bound set in the official order of the House of Commons Library set. House of Lords complete, not bound in the official order before 1950.

House of Commons Sessional Papers 1800–1900, and *1900 to date*, Cambridge, Chadwyck-Healey, microfiche editions in progress (SPR.Mic.E.291 and 301). P Ford and G Ford, *Guide to Parliamentary Sessional Papers 1714–1805*, ed F W Torrington.

RCd Parliamentary Proceedings Commons *Votes and Proceedings* (the first official printed record of Parliament, and the oldest continuous one) 1680/1, 1689/90 to date, with *Appendix* of petitions 1803/4–1882 (incomplete). *Supplement to the Votes and Proceedings*, 1837 to date; *Division Lists*, 1836, 1837/8, 1861 to date; *Private business*, 1847–50, 1861 to date; *Report of Proceedings in Standing Committee*, 1889 to date. House of Lords *Minutes of Proceedings* 1825 to date.

Ms index to *Votes* for 1689–1735, 2 v; printed index for 1794/5–1803/4.

RCe Parliamentary Journals and Debates Complete sets of the official printed journals of both houses (B.S.Ref.6). Hansard complete (B.S.Ref.12-14). With the exception of Woodfall's Debates all the other major collections of debates are held in complete sets, and virtually all the minor items listed in the standard bibliography, together with several not there mentioned.

House of Commons Library, *A bibliography of Parliamentary debates of Great Britain*, London, HMSO, 1956, copy annotated with pressmarks (OPL.Enq.Desk), ESTC under Great Britain: Parliament. General Cat under England: Parliament.

RD House of Lords Appellate Jurisdiction

RDa House of Lords Appeal Cases Collections of appeal case documents 1660–1711 (*BP.33*, with card index of cases); 1714–1887, 95 v and 8 parcels (L.3.a.1); and 1729–1732, 1 v with partial index (BS.96/60).

RDb Peerage claims Collection of peerage claims, 1801–1920, 104 v (BS.96/24; ms index OPL Index).

RDc Divorce Cases Collections of divorce cases, 1817–1862, 4 v (L.19.p.2), and 1855–62 (BS.96/24(81*)).

RE British Non-Parliamentary Official Publications
Probably the best collection in existence, incl those not published by HMSO.

Card cat of all British non-Parliamentary official publications, 1900–46, known as the 'Rogers cards'. *Check list of British official serial publications*, Provisional, 2nd (etc) provisional issue, 1967– .

REa Defence departments A fine collection, from the 17th cent onwards, of Admiralty manuals, Army and Navy lists, drill books and manuals for firearms.

REb Foreign Office Confidential Prints An imperfect set, donated by the Foreign and Commonwealth Office, of the regular printed batches of confidential telegrams, despatches, etc, 1827–1913 (BS.14/3509).

REc Pollbooks and Electoral Registers Electoral registers for all constituencies of the UK, incl Northern Ireland. Imperfect before 1937, and not published 1939–1946. Some earlier pollbooks. Some recent electoral registers for Channel Islands.

Card index to current holdings and changed constituencies. Ms indexes to earlier registers and pollbooks; they are also mostly in the General Catalogue under names of constituencies, and in the Institute of Historical Research union list of pollbooks.

RF British Local Government Publications
These are among the collections of the general library, and entered in the General Catalogue under place names. Many of their reports are in the Annual Reports (AR) and Periodicals (P) collections.

RFa London County Council and Greater London Council (LCC) Exceptionally, the publications of these two county authorities for London forms a segregated collection in the Official Publications Library. A virtually complete set of the publications of the London County Council (1889–1964) and of its successor the Greater London Council.

In General Catalogue under London. Subject card cat (incomplete).

RG Ireland
Statutes at Large, Ireland, 1310–1761, 20 v; *Journals of the House of Lords*, 8 v, 1779–1800; *Journals of the House of Commons of the Kingdom of Ireland, 1613–1800*, 19 v, 1796–1800; *Votes of the House of Commons in Ireland, 1695–1768.*

Dermot Englefield, *The printed records of the Parliament of Ireland, 1613–1800*, London, Lemon Tree Press, 1978. Griffiths, *General valuation of rateable property in Ireland*, 1847–64, on microfilm (SPR.Mic.E.287).

RH Commonwealth Official Publications
All former colonies sent their official publications by copyright deposit (see Ka), mostly after 1860.

Partial subject index for each country on cards.

RHa India (I.S.) The collection effectively begins in 1867, the year of the Registration of Books and Indian Press Act, which required copyright deposit at the British Museum.

Francis B F Campbell, *Index-catalogue of Indian official publications in the Library*, (1899); continued on cards to 1939 (the 'Campbell cards').

RJ Foreign Official Publications
Official publications of all countries, and in all languages, obtained mostly by exchange, incl much unique material. All inter-governmental organizations are covered from their foundations (eg UN, UNESCO, EEC, CENTO). Rare early materials include some *Journals* and *Votes* of the American states before independence, the debates of the Russian Duma, and early European printed laws and royal gazettes.

Not all rare materials are entered in the General Catalogue. The collections are supplemented by microform sets of US Congressional Hearings, 1839–1975; Congressional Committee Prints, 1829–1970; State Session Laws, published by Hein, 1977/8– ; and the official documents of the Organisation of American States, mostly now received on microfiche.

RJ *Miscellaneous Collections*

RJa Papers of peers, politicians, and public figures Printed materials (largely uncatalogued pamphlets and ephemera, the more substantial items often being incorporated in the general library and entered in the General Catalogue) received with the papers that are now held in the Department of Manuscripts, from the 1st Earl of *Balfour* (1848–1930), 1876–1929; Rt Hon Sir Henry *Campbell-Bannerman* (1836–1908), 1871–1908; Edward Algernon Robert Gascoyne-Cecil, Viscount *Cecil of Chelwood* (1864–1958), 1917–46; Arthur Charles Hamilton-Gordon, Earl of *Aberdeen*, 1833–62; the family of the Rt Hon William Ewart *Gladstone*, to 1903; Lieut-Gen Sir Edward Thomas Henry *Hutton* (1848–1923), 1881–1917; 1st Viscount *Morley*, 1803–93; Charles Wentworth *Dilke* (1789–1864), and his namesakes, son (1810–69, 1st Bart) and grandson (1843–1911, 2nd Bart); and Sir Charles Wood, 1st Viscount *Halifax* (1800–85), 1854–8, William St John Frederick Brodwick *Midleton*, 1st Viscount Midleton, papers on the East; Hugh *Rose*, 1st Baron Strathnairn, papers on India 1860–76.

Card indexes of pamphlets and/or official documents in a few cases.

RJb Chadwick Tracts (CT) A collection of pamphlets, press cuttings, etc, mainly of 1790–1860, made by Sir Edwin Chadwick (1800–90). Mainly on subjects connected with public health.

Shelflist. All added to General Catalogue *c*1960.

RJc Stopes collection (Stopes) A collection of *c*3,000 pamphlets and printed ephemera, incl rare manufacturers' catalogues, from the personal library and papers of Marie Stopes, the remainder of which are dispersed in the main library of the Department of Printed Books (and entered in the General Catalogue), and in the Department of Manuscripts. They cover a wide range of medical and social subjects, mostly 1900–50. Another collection, esp annotated copies, 1877–1956, mostly of her own works (Cup.361.a.2(1-76)).

RJd Left pamphlets (SS.Pam.) A collection formed within the library *c*1950 of *c*1,000 pamphlets in English, published (mostly in Great Britain) by communist and socialist parties and organizations.

Card cat (classified). Another similar collection in 6 v formed by Palme Dutt, is in the general library (Cup.1262.k.1-6).

S **British Library Reference Division. Map Library**

Great Russell Street, London WC1B 3DG. Tel (01) 636 1544 Ext 265. Telex 21462. Open to holders of Reference Division readers' tickets Mon-Sat 9.30 am-4.30 pm. Photoreproduction services as for Department of Printed Books general collection, but some special restrictions apply.

The Map Library is a branch of the Department of Printed Books which holds the main printed cartographic collections of the British Library ie atlases, maps and charts. It has its own distinct system of pressmarks. It also holds 2 major predominantly ms collections, the maritime and topographical maps and charts from the King's Library, and the Crace Collection; but the main ms map collections are held in the Dept of Mss. Some atlases (both ms and printed) may also be found in the Department of Oriental Manuscripts and Printed Books, the India Office Library and Records, and the Department of Prints and Drawings of the British Museum. Atlases and related geographical material may also be found in the Department of Printed Books main library, eg in the Grenville Library (Fa above).

Reader's guide.

SA *General History of the Map Collections*

Notable atlases are to be found in the foundation collections (Cotton, Sloane, and Harley, see B above and W below), and in the royal collections (SB below).

Descriptions

H M Wallis, 'The map collections of the British Museum Library', In H M Wallis and S Tyacke eds *My head is a map*, London, 1973, p3-20.

Catalogues

The printed maps and atlases were first catalogued by William Hughes *c*1843 and re-catalogued under the direction of R K Douglas for the 1885 cat. Interleaved guardbook cat reproduced as *Catalogue of the printed maps, charts and plans in the British Museum: photolithographic edition to 1964*, 1967, 15 v and *Ten-year supplement 1965–1974*, 1978; dictionary arrangement under geographical headings, with additional entries for cartographers, engravers, etc. Many atlases are also entered under cartographers and publishers in the General Catalogue of Printed Books (see Ae).

SB *Royal Map Collections*

Notable atlases in the Old Royal Library given by George II (see C) are the 'Boke of Idography' of Jean Rotz, 1542 and the 'Saxton-Burghley atlas' once owned by Lord Burghley, containing annotated proof states of Christopher Saxton's atlas of county maps of England and Wales, 1579.

R A Skelton, 'The Royal map collections', *British Museum Quarterly* 26 (1962), no 1-2, p1-6.

——'The Royal map collections of England', *Imago Mundi* 13 (1956), p181-3.

H M Wallis, 'The Royal map collections of England', *Revista da Universidade de Coimbra* 28 (1980), p461-8; separate reprint Coimbra, Junta de Investigaçoẽs Cientificas do Ultramar, 1981.

SBa King George III's Topographical Collection The main part of the Royal map collections are in George III's topographical collection given as part of the King's Library in 1828. This contained the finest geographical collection of its day, including the world atlas comprising the finest and largest Dutch printed maps presented to Charles II by Johan Klencke of Amsterdam 1660, many atlases of the North American colonies and the theatres of war in America and the East, also such items as Moses Pitt, *The English atlas*, London, 1680, 4 v, William Berry, *A collection of maps and geographical tables by Sanson*, London, 1690, and the English edition of Gerard Mercator's *Atlas*, London, 1636.

Catalogue of maps, prints, drawings, etc forming the Geographical and Topographical Collection attached to the library of... King George the Third, 1829.

SBb King George III's Maritime Collection In 1828 the maritime part of George III's collection was presented for the time being by George IV to the Admiralty. In 1844 a major part of this material was given to the Museum and in 1952 a further 27 items were identified in the Admiralty Library as being part of George III's collection and presented to the Museum by the Lords of the Admiralty. The printed material includes Dutch sea-atlases of the 17th cent, and English and French of the 18th; of particular note is a beautifully coloured copy of Des Barres's *Atlantic Neptune*, 1781. Included with a number of the charts are examples of sailing directions, some of which are apparently unrecorded.

Ms cat of the 1828 transfer. *Catalogue of King George III's Maritime Collection*, [c1850], reproduced by the 'carbonic process' but not published. R A Skelton, 'King George III's Maritime Collection', *British Museum Quarterly* 18 (1953), p63-4.

SC *Other Map Collections*

Other important collections containing atlases and other geographical material are the Banksian Library (Dg), the Grenville Library (Fa) and the Crace Collection (SCa below).

SCa Crace collection A collection on London formed by Frederick Crace (1779–1859), the decorator of the interiors of the royal palaces.

A catalogue of maps, plans and views of London, Westminster and Southwark, collected and arranged by Frederick Crace, edited by... John Gregory Crace, London, 1878.

SCb Exhibition catalogues An exhibition to commemorate the bicentenary of Captain Cook's first voyage round the world..., 1968. *Prince Henry the Navigator...*, 1960. *William Roy...*, 1977. *Cartographical curiosities*, 1978. *The American War of Independence 1775–83*, 1975. *Sir Francis Drake 1577–1580*, 1977. *Christopher Saxton and Tudor map-making*, 1980.

T **British Library Reference Division. Music Library**

Great Russell Street, London WC1B 3DG. Tel (01) 636 1544 Ext 260. Telex 21462. Music Reading Area (adjacent to Official Publications Library) open Mon-Sat 9.30 am-4.45 pm (8.45 pm Tues-Thurs) to holders of Reference Division passes; but rare works must be consulted in the North Library. Photoreproduction as for Department of Printed Books.

The Music Library, a branch of the Department of Printed Books, was established in the mid-nineteenth century, and scores which had been classified with the book collections were gradually transferred to the new section, which became known as the Music Room and retained that name until 1973. Systematic purchasing began in the 1840s, with special emphasis on early material. The collection numbers over 1,250,000 items, and for breadth of representation of musical publications from all countries and periods is unsurpassed. The literature on music, however, remained almost entirely in the general library of the Department of Printed Books (see Qj), and with the exception of the Hirsch Library, there is still relatively little in the Music Library.

The literature relating to the whole Department of Printed Books (Ab) is supplemented by A Hyatt King, *Printed music in the British Museum: an account of the collections, the catalogues, and their formation, up to 1920*, London, 1979; A Hyatt King, *A wealth of music in the British Library (Reference Division) and the British Museum*, London (1983); C B Oldman, 'Panizzi and the music collections of the British Museum', in *Hirichsen's 11th Music Book*, London, 1961, p62-7. *A guide to the manuscripts and printed books illustrating the progress of musical notation...*, 1885.

Ta *Music catalogue*

The catalogue of scores begun in 1841 is still in use today. Like the General Catalogue of that period it consisted originally of guardbooks in which ms moveable slips were pasted. Though theoretically limited to scores, it includes many books which contain sections of music. Between 1884 and 1980 the slips for new entries were printed in 94 accession parts. William Barclay Squire extracted and revised all entries for pre-1801 publications from the guardbooks for the *Catalogue of printed music published between 1487 and 1800 now in the British Museum*, 1912. *Second supplement*, 1940; repr with both supplements Neadeln, Kraus, 1968. These formed the basis for a new series of guardbooks in which all accessions of music up to 1800 were entered (and also the basis of 60% of the entries in *British union-catalogue of early printed music before the year 1801...*, London, Butterworths, 1957, 2 v). All the entries from the present 408 guardbooks in both series are now being merged in a single sequence, together with those in v 3 of the Royal Music Library catalogue (see below), to be published as *The catalogue of printed music in the British Library to 1980*, London, Saur, 1980—. Pressmarks for works other than scores in the Music Library appear in the General Catalogue of the Department of Printed Books, prefixed with the letter M or the word Music; but those in the Hirsch Library as Hirsch without a prefix.

Tb Foundation and Old Royal Collections

The only substantial collection of printed music was in the Lumley Library (Ca). It has recently been discovered that the items listed in the 1607 catalogue, many of which are in the Music Library, represent only a small proportion of the whole because the cataloguer listed only the first item in tract volumes, and these were split up and rebound in the 19th cent so that they have hitherto escaped detection.

Tc Royal Music Library

Deposited on loan by George V in 1911, and donated by Her Majesty Queen Elizabeth II in 1957 in commemoration of the gift of the Old Royal Library by George II in 1757. In addition to printed music it contains important mss and *c*200 v of literature on music. The nucleus of the library was brought over from Hanover. George III's librarians had instructions to buy antiquarian items alongside new music for more practical purposes, so that the 16th and 17th cent are represented by many important items. The 19th cent additions consisted largely of presentation copies and music for domestic use. (Pressmarked R.M.).

W B Squire, *Catalogue of the King's Music Library*, London, 1927–9, 3 v; esp pt 3, p357-83, music literature. A Hyatt King, *Some British collectors of music...*, Cambridge, 1963, Appendix A, 'The Royal Music Library and its collectors'. A H King, 'The Royal Music Library in the British Museum', in *Beiträge zur Musikdocumentation: Franz Grasberger zum 60. Geburtstag*, Tutzing, 1975, p193-201. A H King, 'The Royal Music Library, some account of its provenance and associations', *Book Collector* 7 (1958), p241-52.

Td Hirsch Music Library

Bought in 1946, *c*20,000 items collected by Paul Hirsch, a native of Frankfurt who emigrated to Cambridge in 1936. It contains both books on music and printed music, with a few mss, and is extraordinarily comprehensive in its coverage. Among special strengths are early theory (incl many incunabula), opera full scores, first and early editions of great composers of all periods (esp of the Viennese classics), examples of early music printing processes, embellished books, fine printing and notable bindings (pressmarked Hirsch).

Kathi Meyer and P Hirsch, *Katalog der Musikbibliothek Paul Hirsch... Berlin...*, 1928–47, 4 v. A more comprehensive listing of the music is in *Music Accessions* pt 53 (1951), and of the books in General Library *Accessions*, 3rd series, pt 219b (1959). Kathi Meyer, *Die Musikbibliothek Paul Hirsch in Frankfurt a M*, 1927, offprint from *Taschenbuch für Büchersammler*.

U British Library Reference Division. Library Association Library

7 Ridgmount Street, London WC1E 7AE. Tel (01) 636 1544 Ext 200. Telex 21897. Open to members of the Library Association, and British Library staff; and by appointment to holders of Reference Division passes (and others at the librarian's discretion), Mon-Fri 9 am-6 pm (8 pm Tues-Thurs except mid-July–mid-Sept). Photocopying.

Ua General

The Library Association of the United Kingdom was founded in 1877 to promote libraries and the profession of librarianship, and received a royal charter in 1898. The library was founded in 1900, but did not become large until it was first housed in permanent quarters in 1934, absorbing the library of the Association of Assistant Librarians (founded 1895) in 1949, and becoming an integral branch of the Department of Printed Books when the British Library assumed financial and administrative responsibility for it in 1974. Its main holdings are in librarianship, on which it has the most comprehensive collection in Britain. It also has major collections on bibliography, documentation, and information science, and more selective coverage of authorship, publishing, computing, printing, bookselling, copyright, and censorship. The library of the Society of Indexers is deposited.

Guide leaflet (gratis). A Munford, *A history of the Library Association 1877–1977*, London, Library Association, 1976, esp p114-5, 217-9, 258, 286-7, 299-300, 320-1. Library Association, *Library and Information Bulletin*, 1967–74 then British Library Reference Division. *CABLIS: current awareness bulletin for librarians and information scientists*, 1975– , incl lists of accessions.

Ub Monographs

Over 50,000 books and pamphlets, incl the classics of librarianship from the mid-17th cent onwards: over 50 are pre-1851.

Library Association, *Catalogue of the Library*, 1958 (op), classified with author index; classified cat 1957–65 on cards; 1966–76 on cards; 1977– on fiche. Author cat on cards to 1976, fiche thereafter. Association of Assistant Librarians, *Catalogue of the Library*, 1949.

Uc Periodicals

Over 300 defunct and 1,000 current periodicals, from the mid-19th cent onwards.

Card index.

Ud Historical collection

A collection of press cuttings, plans, and photographs of libraries.

Ue Other materials

Special collections of theses and reports (mainly on microfiche).

L J Taylor, *FLA theses: abstracts...from 1964*, 1979.

V British Library Reference Division. Newspaper Library

Colindale Avenue, Colindale, London NW9 5HE.

Tel (01) 200 5515 Ext 29. Open to holders of readers' passes of the Dept of Printed Books or those issued for local use at the Newspaper Library, Mon-Sat 10 am-4.45 pm (accommodation esp on Sat is limited and readers may have to wait for a seat). Photocopying and microfilming.

The Newspaper Library is a branch of the Department of Printed Books, now holding *c*650,000 v. It was first established in the British Museum in 1885 as the Journal Room, afterwards the Newspaper Room; a separate repository for British provincial newspapers was built in 1902 at Colindale (then known as Hendon), enlarged to house all the newspapers and certain periodicals, with its own reading room, in 1932. It houses the Department's holdings of newspapers, and most other serial publications issued once a fortnight or more frequently (the chief exceptions being some 19th cent popular magazines such as the *Penny Magazine* and the *Pulpit*); also certain other British periodicals (mostly trade monthlies) which were transferred to the newspaper collection in the 19th cent (and a few later) because they were little used. Some of the English provincial, Scottish, and Irish papers were destroyed by bombing in 1940.

Newspapers in the British Library, [1980], leaflet (gratis). British Library *Catalogue of the Newspaper Library, Colindale*, 1975, 8 v; 1-4 reproduce the topographical guardbook cat subarranged by country and title, 1 London, 2 rest of British Isles, 3-4 overseas, 5-8 reproduce the card cat of titles (which superseded the title index to the topographical cat *c*1965; this was based on *Catalogue of printed books. . . Supplement: newspapers published in Great Britain and Ireland, 1801—1900*, 1905, which listed *c*75,000 titles). *Representation of the Trustees of the British Museum*, 1846, p5-31, P.P. 1846 (166), p233-59. British Library, *The newspaper collections and the future*, 1977. *Microfilms of newspapers and journals for sale*, 1983 (gratis). Esdaile, p140-4, 209-10. R Cowtan, *Memories of the British Museum*, London, 1872, p190-1, 412-5. British Library Reference Division, *Newspaper Library Newsletter*, 1980- ; esp no 5 (1982), p1-4, '1932—1982: 50 years service to readers and the public'. P J Weimerskirch *Antonio Panizzi and the British Museum Library*, Clifton, NJ, AB Bookman's Yearbook, 1981. Barbara S McCrimmon, *The publication of the British Museum's general catalogue. . .*, London, Bingley, 1981, p120-37 (inaccurate on deposit 1855—69).

Va *Origins of the British collections*

There was no copyright deposit of newspapers before 1869. However, by the Seditious Societies Act of 1799 (39 Geo III c79) and the Stamp Act of 1836 (60 Geo III c9) copies had to be deposited (in return for the published price) at the Stamp Office Advertisment of the Board of Inland Revenue at Somerset House. The lack of newspaper files at the British Museum was keenly felt, and when the Burney collection (mainly London papers) arrived in 1817 an arrangement was made with the Stamp Office to continue it by transferring their files of London papers every three years at the Museum's expense. This arrangement was extended to English provincial and Welsh papers in 1832, and later to the Scottish, and Irish Stamp Offices. There were many gaps in the Stamp Office files, esp of papers published outside London; many of these gaps were filled (though at what date is uncertain) with the second set of statutory deposit copies from the Advertisement Duty Office at Somerset House (terminating with the repeal of that duty in 1853). In 1855 (under the Stamp Act, 18 Vict c27) stamping ceased to be compulsory (being used only by publishers wishing to obtain free postage on newspapers and periodicals issued monthly or more often) and there was a reduction (in practice if not in theory) in the deposited files. In 1869 (under the Newspapers, Printers, and Reading Rooms Repeal Act, 32&33 Vict c34) stamping and paid deposit at Somerset House ceased altogether. From 1869 the Museum demanded deposit of newspapers under the Copyright Act of 1842 (5&6 Vict c82), until 1873 claiming provincial papers through the agency of W H Smith; but many were never received. From 1873 all English, Scottish and Welsh newspapers were claimed direct from the publishers, with the help of a series of test prosecutions of non-complying publishers. In the present century many of the earlier gaps have been filled by donations from publishers and others, or by microfilming publishers' or local library sets.

The Inland Revenue deposit copies have an archival importance, bearing statutory ms declarations of publisher's name and address on the Stamp Office copies, and identifications of paid advertisments in many of the Advertisement Duty Office copies; see John E C Palmer, *Manual for the bibliographical description of serials: preliminary draft*, 1980, typescript paper presented to the Annual Conference of the Research Society for Victorian Periodicals, Philadelphia, 1980, p28-30.

Vb *London newspapers after 1800*

Newspapers published in London to 1800 are not in the Newspaper Library, but will be found in the Burney Collection of the Dept of Printed Books, Great Russell Street (see De); the only exception being a complete set from 1788 of *The Times*. The collection contains *c*15,000 titles in 75,000 v, incl many foreign language titles, and is by far the most comprehensive in existence, with a large proportion of unique runs.

Vc *English provincial and Welsh newspapers*

The collection contains *c*10,000 titles in *c*400,000 v, of which *c*7,000 (and film) are pre-1801, and *c*300,000 of 1801—1900. Few original issues before 1720 are held; they include the *Stamford Mercury* 22 May 1718 (and a microfilm set from 1714), the *Worcester Post-Man* 26 Jan 1711, and the *Newcastle Courant*, 31 Dec/2 Jan 1715. From the mid-18th cent there are runs of most of the major papers.

Vd *Scottish newspapers*
The collection contains *c*1,300 titles in *c*30,000 v. It is considerably less comprehensive than for England and Wales until the end of the 19th cent, but even so compares well with collections in Scotland and includes a number of papers not held there. The earliest issues held are the *Edinburgh Gazette* 18/21 Sep 1699, and some numbers of the *Edinburgh Courant* of 1705 onwards.

Ve *Irish newspapers*
The collection contains *c*1,250 titles in *c*6,500 v, and for pre-1851 newspapers is more comprehensive than any collection in Ireland. The earliest paper held is *Pue's Occurrences* 26 Dec 1704. Coverage is erratic though in theory it ought from 1870 to be comprehensive by copyright deposit. Though many minor papers of the 19th cent are held, others of major importance (eg *Saunders's Newsletter*) are not.

Vf *Channel Islands and Isle of Man newspapers*
The collection contains *c*80 titles in *c*2,500 v. The Stamp Acts and Advertisement Duty were never extended to the Channel Islands or the Isle of Man, and therefore none of the papers of these islands were received from the Stamp Office or the Advertisement Duty Office. They were received by copyright deposit from *c*1895, and many continue after 1911.

It should be specially noted that the towns of these dependencies are entered in the 'England and Wales' section of the *Catalogue*, v 2, 1975.

Vg *Overseas newspapers*
The collection contains *c*9,000 titles in *c*35,000 v and *c*100,000 reels of microfilm. The first systematic acquisition of colonial and foreign newspapers, after an abortive attempt by Panizzi in 1840–1 which was frustrated by the Trustees, began in the later 19th cent, though some earlier runs have been acquired retrospectively. Many of those from Commonwealth countries are derived from deposit arrangements begun under Colonial Copyright (see Ka) through agents of the national or state governments, sometimes continuing after the legislation or agreements expired, and from substantial donations from both the Colonial Office and the Royal Colonial Institute (now the Royal Commonwealth Society) from 1859 until recently. English language 18th cent Commonwealth titles include early files of *Hickey's Bengal Gazette* 1780–2 and the *Quebec Gazette* from 1764. The library holds some issues 1842–5 of *Ko te karere o nui tireni*, a Maori newspaper. There are also a number of important continental papers; the earliest is *La Gazette*, afterwards *Gazette de France*, from 1631 onwards; and a few 17th cent papers (incomplete sets or odd issues) published in Austria, Spain and the Netherlands. The *Pennsylvania Gazette* 1 Aug 1754 and *Dunlap's Pennsylvania Packet* from 15 Nov 1775 are held. Commonwealth and foreign newspapers are the subject of the library's archival microfilming programme.

Vh *Ships' and forces newspapers*
There are *c*100 papers of the British armed forces published mostly 1943–6 in various parts of the world, but incl the *Cologne Post* 1919–29. Also some ships' newspapers, incl the 1852 facsimile of the *Illustrated Arctic News* 1850–1, and various Cunard and other passenger ships' bulletins.

Catalogue 1975, v 2, col 1319-1332, England: Armed Forces; col 1333-1334, Ship's Newspapers.

W British Library Reference Division. Department of Manuscripts

Great Russell Street, London WC1B 3DG. Tel (01) 636 1544 Ext 372. Telex 21462. Open Mon-Sat 10 am-4.45 pm; supplementary pass required in addition to Reference Division pass. Microfilming, subject to restrictions.

WA *General*

WAa Printed material in the Manuscript Collections Mss have been administered separately from printed books since the foundation of the British Museum, and mixed collections have usually been divided between the two departments; but there are many printed ephemera scattered among the ms collections, and also printed books, esp annotated and grangerized copies.

J P Gilson, *A student's guide to the manuscripts of the British Museum*, 1920, p41-4. Richard Sims, *Handbook of the library of the British Museum*, 1854, p19-80.

WAb Catalogues The manuscript numbers of many mss (except Add) containing pre-1801 printed material are listed in R C Alston, *A reference list of manuscripts containing printed items 1500–1800: a survey carried out as part of the Pilot Survey for an Eighteenth Century STC*, typescript, 1977, under revision; but no descriptions are included. Catalogues in current use are briefly listed in M A E Nickson, *The British Library: guide to the catalogues and indexes of the Department of Manuscripts*, 2nd ed 1982. Detailed descriptions of all the catalogues are given in T C Skeat, *The catalogues of the British Museum, 2: The catalogues of the manuscript collections*, rev ed 1962 (op).

WAc Published catalogues There are printed catalogues for most collections received down to 1955. These (with a few exceptions) include general descriptions of the collections in order of [illegible] numbers, and most volumes contain indexes of personal and place names, incl many not indicated in the general descriptions; other headings are sometimes also included in the indexes, but subjects are not indexed comprehensively. Until *c*1850, printed material in the collections is usually excluded from the descriptions and indexes (though until then often inserted in the General Catalogue of Printed Books); thereafter it is frequently indicated (both in general descriptions and index entries), but not systematically, and seldom described in detail. Indexing rules are given in J P Hudson, *Manuscripts indexing*, 3rd ed, London, BL Dept of Mss, 1980.

WAd Class catalogue Entries from the main descriptions in the printed catalogues to *c*1900 (and sometimes later) pasted into 150 v classified by subjects; certain subjects such as technology which in the 19th cent did not interest the department are excluded; the catalogue is no longer maintained. Its usefulness in locating printed material is restricted by the frequent exclusion of such material from the printed catalogues from which it was compiled, or lack of indication as to whether material is ms or printed. Sections of particular interest for printed material are v 82 Bibliography and Literary History (incl catalogues of libraries); v 91 Fiction and drama (incl Playbills); v 93*(A) Engravings; v 93*(B) Bindings, and owners, incl bookplates; v 102-104 Owners of manuscripts; and vol 2 p569-72, Newspapers. There is an alphabetical index of subjects, and a chronological index.

WAe Amalgamated index A cumulation on cards (to be published, Cambridge, Chadwyck-Healey, *c*1985) of the indexes of personal and place names (but omitting any of the other headings such as subjects) from the printed catalogues of Additional and Egerton Mss acquired 1756–1950, and of the Arundel, Burney, Cotton, Hargrave, King's, Royal, Sloane and Stowe collections. The Index Locorum of the Harleian catalogue is also included.

WAf Subject index A cumulation on cards under alphabetical headings (other than personal and place names) from the same printed catalogues from which the Amalgamated Index (WAe) was compiled. The index is not comprehensive or systematic, being derived from catalogues which for the most part exclude subject entries, but some of the printed material can be traced under headings such as Bookplates and bookstamps, Bookselling, Catalogues, Printing, Bibliography, Bindings, Proclamations, and Newspapers.

WAg Research index A small card index of the names by which mss or collections of mss are popularly known, with their locations in the British Library or other repositories.

WAh Photographic indexes Card indexes of microfilms of mss. Descriptive list of de-reserved photocopies (deposited under the Export Licensing Regulations). Holdings of microfilms received to 1975 and photocopies to 1968 are included in *Register of microfilms and other photocopies in the Department of Manuscripts*, London, List & Index Society (special series 9), 1976.

WB *Foundation Collections*

WBa Cottonian Mss The collection of Sir Robert Bruce *Cotton* (1571–1631), given to the nation in 1700 by his grandson; printed books added by Arthur Edwards are now in the Dept of Printed Books, see Bb above.

Catalogue, 1802.

WBb Harleian Mss The collections of Robert (1661–1724) and Edward (1689–1741) *Harley*, 1st and 2nd Earls of Oxford, bought by Parliament in 1753. The Harleian Library of printed books was not included, but dispersed in a sale. The mss, even after the transfer of the Bagford printed items to the Department of Printed Books (see Gb), contain considerable quantities of printed ephemera.

Catalogue, 1808–12, 4 v. C E Wright, *Fontes Harleiani: a study of the sources of the Harleian collection...*, London, British Museum, 1972.

WBc Sloane Mss The collection of mss bought from the executors of Sir Hans *Sloane* (1660–1753) with his printed books (see Ba) and museum specimens, also contains printed material, esp annotated catalogues. (For Bagford printed material, see Gb.)

Included in Samuel Ayscough, *Catalogue of the manuscripts preserved in the British Museum*, 1782. Ms cat in 18 v. E J L Scott, *Index to the Sloane manuscripts in the British Museum*, 1904.

WC *Other named collections containing substantial printed material*

There is very little printed material among the Royal, King's, and Arundel mss, but the main deposits are the following.

WCa Lansdowne Mss Collected by William Petty, 1st Marquis of Lansdowne (1737–1805), incl the papers of William Cecil, Lord Burghley; bought in 1807.

Catalogue, 1819.

WCb Hargrave Mss The legal collection of Francis Hargrave (but most of his books, incl many of the annotated copies are in the Department of Printed Books, see Ha).

Catalogue, 1818.

WCc Stowe Mss The mss collected by Richard Temple Nugent Brydges Chandos Grenville, 1st Duke of Buckingham and Chandos (1776–1839), at Stowe House, and sold after his death to the Earl of Ashburnham; bought in 1883. They include political pamphlets and newspapers of the early 18th cent.

Catalogue, 1895–6, 2 v.

WD *Continuing series of manuscripts*

All but the largest collections of mss, ie those in the closed named collections (most of which are enumerated above) are placed either among the Additional or the Egerton series of mss. Both series contain major quantities of printed material, the most important of which are noted separately below.

Both the Additional and Egerton accessions are included in the same set of catalogues, published usually at intervals of five years, *Catalogue of additions to the manuscripts (1756–1955)*, 1843–1982, 29 v. (For 1783–1837 only the Index is published; the catalogue is in ms.) Unpublished handlist for 1956–60. Quinquennial Rough Registers form a temporary catalogue for accessions after 1960, published from typescript as *Rough register of acquisitions...*, London, List & Index Society (Special series), 1975– : *1961–65*, 1974 (sp ser 8); *1966–70*, 1975 (8); *1971–75*, 1977 (10); *1976–80*, 1982

(15). Unpublished selective indexes; a more comprehensive index of personal names is provided by the NRA computerized name index.

WDa Additional Mss Miscellaneous individual mss and collections of mss have been placed in the *Additional mss* collection since 1756, beginning at Add.MS.4101 in continuation of the numbering of the Sloane Mss, and it is now by far the largest individual collection of mss in the Library.

WDb Egerton Mss In 1827 Francis Henry Egerton, 8th Earl of Bridgwater (1756–1829), bequeathed 67 mss and an endowment later supplemented by a cousin, out of which the Egerton collection has been continued to the present time.

WDc Birch papers (Add.Mss.4101-4478) The papers of Dr Thomas Birch (1705–66), a Trustee, bequeathed with his library (see Ha). The collection, among which a considerable quantity of printed material of the 17th and 18th cent is scattered, includes drafts of published and unpublished historical and biographical works by him and others, voluminous correspondence, his very extensive biographical collections, and the archives of the Royal Society while he was Secretary 1752–65.

Catalogue of additions. . .1756–1762, p1-181.

WDd Burney annotations (Add.Mss.59902-60165) 164 v from the classical library of Charles Burney (see De) have *c*1977 transferred from the Department of Printed Books: they are from his working collection, comprising copies of Greek and Latin texts with his copious annotations, annotated collections of cuttings from textbooks, and some of the books from which the cuttings were excised. (They are quite distinct from his main collection of mss called Burney Mss, which probably contains no printed material.)

WDe Place collection (Add.Mss.27789-27859; 35142-35154; 36623-36628) The papers of the radical reformer Francis Place (1771–1854), given at various times, contain voluminous quantities of printed material relating to the rise of the working class movement in the early 19th cent, and a small amount from the 18th; esp prospectuses, pamphlets, and magazines of political societies, trade unions, and educational and social institutions. (There is also a major collection in the Department of Printed Books, see Pe.) They include a political narrative 1830–5 (Add.Mss.27789-97); documents of the campaign against the Combination Laws 1734–1826 (27798-27806 and 36623-8); London Corresponding Society 1791–1847 (27811-7); Westminster Elections documents and cuttings 1766–1848 (27819-48); and an autobiography 1771–1847 with related documents (esp relating to the campaign against the taxes on knowledge) (35142-54).

WDf Prosser collection of lives of inventors (Add. Mss.54496-54507) Biographical collections on British inventors, arranged alphabetically under their names, comp by Richard Bissell Prosser (1838–1918), Chief Examiner at the Patent Office, incl many used by him in preparing articles for the *Dictionary of National Biography*; sold after his death (Hodgson 22 Aug 1918 lot 201) and again to be bought by the British Museum (Sotheby 29 Oct 1968 lot 382). They contain transcripts of ms and printed records, printed cuttings and pamphlets (mostly after 1820), and correspondence.

WE Loan collections

Collections deposited on permanent loan by their owners, mostly described in separate rough lists.

WEa Portland loan (Loan 29) A collection of mainly early 18th cent material (incl some printed) deposited 1947–50 by the Duke of Portland.

Historical Mss Commission calendars for parts of the collection.

WEb Bell collection (Loan 24) A collection of offprints collected by Sir Harold Idris Bell (1879–1967), former Keeper of the Department.

WF Major subject groups of printed material

WFa Plays performed in English theatres Plays submitted to the Lord Chamberlain for licensing 1824–51 (Add.Mss.42865-43038); 1852–99 (Add.Mss.52929-53708); 1900–68 (L.C. Plays). The scripts required by the Theatres Act, 1968, to be deposited in the Department of Manuscripts (Playscripts). Printed editions form *c*5% of these collections. (Plays submitted to the Lord Chamberlain 1737–1824 are in the Huntington Library; a microcard edition is in the Dept of Printed Books.)

Catalogue of additions to the manuscripts; plays submitted to the Lord Chamberlain 1824–1851, 1964, chronological list, with author and title index, which is also included in the Amalgamated Index. From 1852 ms chronological lists, and card indexes of titles (also of authors from 1968). *British Museum Quarterly* 7 (1932), p72-3.

WFb Book trade and bibliography The *Strahan* papers (Add.Mss.48800-48918) comprise the ledgers and other printing and publishing archives (incl printed inventories) of William Strahan (1715–85) and his sons and nephews (A and R Spottiswoode) 1734–1855 (see descriptions cited in T H Howard-Hill, *Index to British literary bibliography, v 4: British Bibliography and textual criticism*, 1979, p525-6). The *Chiswick Press* archives 1792–1885 part (Add.Mss.41867-41960) given in 1929 by its Manager C T Jacobi whose description of the collection is in 41960B, and part (Add.Mss.43975-43989) given in 1935. The *Bentley* papers, comprising the publishing and editorial archives of Henry Colburn and Richard Bentley, afterwards Richard Bentley and Son, 1829–98 (Add.Mss.46560-46682), with printed material in 46682 (see Alison Ingram, *Index to the archives of Richard Bentley and Son*, Cambridge, Chadwyck-Healey, 1977, to accompany microfilm edition of the collection). *Macmillan* archive (Add.Mss.54786-56035), records of Macmillan and Co and related firms 1852–1946, incl catalogues of publications (temporary card index of personal names). The archives of *Hodgson and Co* auctioneers (Add.Mss.54580-54723, 58128-58148), 1825–1967, incl surveys of libraries (see 'The Hodgson archive', *TLS* 18 Apr 1968, p405). The *Ashley* Mss (Ashley) comprise the mss from the Ashley Library and included in its catalogue (see Jb), together with annotations extracted from some of the printed books in the collection after its arrival at the British Museum (printed catalogue of the entire Ashley Mss collection in preparation). A collection of copyright assignments 1704–1822 with extracts from periodicals in three indexed volumes comp by William *Upcott* (1779–1845) (Add.Mss.38728-30; his topographical collections are in Add.Mss.15920-33). Archives of the *Society for the Encouragement of Learning* 1735–49 which provided a channel for authors to publish their writings (Add.Mss.6184-6192), preserved by Dr John Ward at Gresham College, and given in 1810 with their records, contain much information on the book trade (see C Atto, 'The Society for the Encouragement of Learning', *Library* 19 (1938–9), p263-88). See also correspondence and biographical collections of Thomas Birch (WDc).

WG Departmental Library, with the exception of Students' Room reference books and material indicated below, not accessible to readers.

WGa Sale catalogues The extensive collection of British and foreign sale catalogues includes many catalogues not in the Department of Printed Books collection (see Gj); many are annotated and provide information additional to that to be found in that department's annotated copies. There is also an extensive collection of dealers' catalogues from the 18th cent onwards. Post-1951 catalogues cannot be made available to readers.

Pre-1801 English are included in Coral. *List of catalogues of English book sales, 1676–1900, now in the British Museum,* 1915, annotated copy with pressmarks of all Dept of Mss copies (also containing ms numbers of some mss purchased). Dealers' catalogues to 1800 are also noted in this copy; those from 1801 to 1900 in a separate ms list. A J Watson, *List of catalogues of foreign book sales 1709–1922 in the Department of Manuscripts of the British Museum,* 1923, typescript. Card indexes of later catalogues.

WGb Facsimiles of Mss (Ms Facs) There is an extensive collection of facsimile editions of mss which has been on permanent loan from the Dept of Printed Books since 1905, supplemented by others subsequently purchased by the Department, and unpublished facsimiles.

Card index in Departmental Library. Those belonging to the Dept of Printed Books are in that department's catalogues also.

WGc Departmental pamphlets A collection housed in the Mss Students' Room of over 2,000 offprints and pamphlets in 196 v, relating to individual mss in the collections, begun *c*1898, but incl some earlier 19th cent items.

Card indexes under authors and ms numbers. Slips containing bibliographical references have been bound in with mss since the early 19th cent, but the works referred to are not necessarily held in the Department.

WGd General collection A collection for staff use relating to palaeography, mss, and related subjects.

Card index in Departmental Library.

X British Library Reference Division. Department of Oriental Manuscripts and Printed Books

14 Store Street, London WC1E 7DG. Tel (01) 636 1544 Ext 259. Telex 21462. Open 9.30 am-5 pm (Mon-Fri), 1 pm (Sat) to holders of Reference Division readers' passes; temporary passes may be issued in appropriate cases in the Oriental Reading Room on the second floor at Store Street. Photocopying, microfilming, and other forms of reproduction, subject to restrictions on grounds of conservation. Curatorial staff covering the languages of Asia and Northern Africa will give bibliographical advice and identifications. Oriental newspapers are outhoused and must be requested 48 hours in advance.

XA General

The Department was formed, as the Dept of Oriental Printed Books and Manuscripts of the British Museum, in 1891, when Oriental material was removed from the Dept of Printed Books, and added to the collection of Oriental mss which since 1867 had formed a sub-department of the Dept of Manuscripts; it was renamed Dept of Oriental Manuscripts and Printed Books on the inauguration of the British Library in 1973. In 1975 the Oriental Exchange Unit (responsible for acquiring Asian government publications) was transferred to it from the Dept of Printed Books. Certain oriental dictionaries, grammars and Bible translations acquired before the foundation of the Department remain in the Dept of Printed Books and will be found in its General Catalogue (see Ae above). Rare books, which constitute *c*35% of the total collection of *c*500,000 items, form part of each language collection and are not kept or catalogued separately.

Guide to the Department of Oriental Manuscripts and Printed Books, by H J Goodacre and A P Pritchard, 1977. K B Gardner et al, 'The Department of Oriental Printed Books and Manuscripts', *Journal of Asian Studies* 18 (1959), p310-8. A Gaur, 'Oriental printed books and manuscripts', in *Treasures of the British Museum,* ed F C Francis, London, Thames and Hudson, 1971, p238-60. A Gaur, 'Oriental material in the Reference Division', *British Library Journal,* 2 (1976), p120-32. R L W Collison, *Directory of libraries and special collections on Asia and North Africa. . . ,* London, Crosby Lockwood, 1970, p45-7. See also *British Museum Quarterly* 1926–73; and *British Library Journal* 1975- ; A P Pritchard, 'Index of articles in the *British Museum Quarterly* on material in the Dept of Oriental Mss and Printed Books', *British Library Journal* 2 (1976), p133-7.

XAa Catalogues Catalogues, on an author/title/subject basis are arranged by individual languages. Those on open access in the Reading Room comprise printed catalogues, card catalogues, and mss catalogues; there are also blue-slip catalogues, kept in curators' offices, but available on request. From 1980 there is a multilingual COM catalogue (excluding Hebrew, languages of the Far East, and a few others).

F C Francis, *The catalogues of the British Museum, 3: Oriental printed books and manuscripts*, rev ed 1959; partly out of date, but still useful. J D Pearson, *Oriental and Asian bibliography*, London, 1966, p164-70. Additional information can be found in exhibition catalogues, the most important of which are listed under language sections below. See also *Handbook of Asian scripts*, by R F Hosking and G M Meredith-Owens, London, British Museum, 1966.

XAb Periodicals and newspapers Periodicals and newspapers are entered in the catalogues of individual languages under the heading Periodical Publications followed by place of publication; in the microfiche cat they are entered by title and/or issuing body. *P.P. (Oriental newspapers) numerical and O.P. (oriental newspapers) alphabetical list*, ms and typescript. *c*1,100 titles, of which 18% are 19th cent; there are also rare and unique items relating to important political events among the 20th cent publications.

XAc Language collections (general) Most material has been acquired by purchase or donation, some by way of the Indian or colonial copyright (see Ka above). All language collections are still growing and rare items are added whenever the opportunity arises. The concept of rarity differs from language to language and is mainly related to the date when printing of it began. Only those language collections which contain substantial numbers of rare books are described individually below.

XB Far East
Guide, p63-9.

XBa Chinese (incl Tangut) Printing was invented in China, and items printed before 1644, together with select items 1644—1795 can be considered rare; there are *c*20 pre-1000, *c*10 of 1000—1200, *c*7 of 1200—1368, and *c*150 of 1360—1644. The nucleus of the collection, apart from a few volumes contained in the Sloane, Harleian, Old Royal, and Lansdowne bequests, was the library bequeathed by Fowler Hull of the East Indies in 1825. In 1843 Queen Victoria gave a number of works which had been acquired during the Opium Wars, and in 1847 the collection of Chinese books belonging to John Robert Morrison (1814—43), Secretary to the Hong Kong administration, 11,509 v, was purchased by the Government. The collection of mss and printed books brought back by Sir (Marc) Aurel Stein (1862—1943) from his expeditions to Central Asia 1900—1, 1906—8 and 1913—6 includes *c*20 items printed before 1,000 AD, incl *c*1,500 fragments in Tangut from the 11th and 13th cent. From 868 onwards, with the *Diamond Sutra*, the world's oldest complete and dated printed book, and the *Lei feng ta* scroll of 975, the library is able to illustrate the continuous evolution of Chinese printing: single volumes from early printings of the Chinese *Tripitaka*, such as the *Wan-shou Tripitaka* printed at Fuzhou between 1080 and 1112, predominate for the 11th and 12th cent, with a piece of secular printing of 1194, a 20 v collection of biographies of Song dynasty officials, *Xin kan ming chen bei zhuan yuan yan zhi ji*. There are classical, historical and literary works of the 13th and 14th cent, and many Ming and Qing works, notably a 14th cent Yuan edition of the prose writings of the poet Du Fu, *Du gong bu wen ji* and a 1610 Ming illustrated edition of the drama *Pi ja ji*. The development of the physical form of the Chinese book is well illustrated, from the woodslip to the paper roll, through the concertina volume and the 'butterfly binding', to the thread-bound style from the Yuan to the Qing periods. Both the earliest Buddhist rolls are illustrated, and there are outstanding examples of the work of the late Ming blockcutters, culminating in an early edition of the *Shi zhu chai shu hua pu* collection of colour-printed illustrations, thought to be the high peak of Chinese printing. Other outstanding items include over 20 *juan* of the 1567 *Yong le da dian*; a complete copy of the Qing encyclopaedia *Qin ding gu jin tu shu ji cheng* in 10,000 *juan*, printed from moveable copper type in 1726; over 100 early or rare editions of popular Chinese fiction; and a strong collection of missionary works and translations of Biblical texts.

R K Douglas, *Catalogue of Chinese printed books, manuscripts and drawings in the Library of the British Museum*, 1877; *Supplementary catalogue*, 1903. L Giles, *Descriptive catalogue of the Chinese manuscripts from Tunhuang in the British Museum*, 1957, with typescript title index, 1963, incl printed documents; *Hsi-hsia fragments from the Stein collection*, by E Grinstead, 1965, typescript. L Giles, *Chinese accessions*, 1931, typescript: Title index, 2 v: Author index, 1 v. Card cat of the whole Chinese collection (books and mss). *A bibliography of Chinese newspapers and periodicals in European libraries*, New York, Contemporary China Institute, 1975; this largely supersedes E D Grinstead, *Chinese periodicals in British libraries*, 1965. Lui Ts'un-Yan, *Chinese popular fiction in London libraries*, Hong Kong, 1967.

XBb Japanese and Korean There are *c*50,000 v of printed books, of which *c*10,000 are rare, ie those produced from the beginning of Japanese printing in the 8th cent to 1868, the year when Japan was committed to commercial and cultural relations with the West, with some rare 20th cent editions. (Books in European languages printed in Japan are in the Dept of Printed Books.) Outstanding items include: *Hyakumanto darani*, Empress Shotoku's 'million Buddhist charms', printed by imperial order 776–770, the world's earliest dateable printed work; *Joyuishiki-ron jukki*, printed at the Kofukuji temple in Nara, c1175, commentary on a Chinese Buddhist work in roll form; *Chokuhan shisho*, 1599, the four books of Confucian classics, preceded by the Classic of Filial Piety, printed from moveable type by order of Emperor Go-Yozei, one of the finest examples of Japanese printing; ...*Feiqe no monogatari*, printed by the Jesuits on Amakusa island, 1592–3, the historical narrative *Heike monogatari* and two other works, the only surviving copy; *Kanze-ryu utai-bon*, printed at the Saga Press near Kyoto, c1605–10, libretti of Nō plays; *Genji monogatari*, c1605, 54 v, Japan's first novel, by Lady Murasaki, printed from moveable type; and *Koshoku ichidai otoko*, c1693, the only recorded copy of the 3rd ed. 2nd impression of Ihara Saikaku's novel, illustrated by Hishikawa Moronobu.

R K Douglas, *Catalogue of Japanese printed books and manuscripts in the Library of the British Museum*, 1898 and supplement 1904; continued by card cat. Card cat of Korean books. *Check-list of Japanese periodicals held in British university and research libraries*, 2nd ed, comp P W Carnell, typescript 1976. D Chibbett, *The history of Japanese printing and book illustration*, Tokyo, 1977. *Japanese popular literature of the Edo period*, 1981.

Kaempfer collection c60 v of books and maps collected in Japan by the physician Engelbert Kaempfer (1651–1716) in 1690–1, from whose widow they came into Sloane's collection (Ba above). Blue-slip cat by K B Gardner. K B Gardner 'Engelbert Kaempfer's Japanese Library', *Asia Major* new ser 7 (19), pt 1-2, p74-8.

Von Siebold collection c1,100 blockprinted works of the Edo period (1600–1868), mostly after 1800, on Japanese literature, history, religion, philosophy, traditional science, geography, etc, collected in Japan by Philipp Franz von Siebold, whose son sold them to the British Museum in 1868. (See Y Y Brown, 'The von Siebold collection', *British Library Journal* 2 (1976), p38-55.

Satow collection c300 editions in 900 v of rare printed texts from Japan and Korea, bought from the diplomat Sir Ernest Satow (1834–1929) in 1884–99, with a few later additions; rich in early blockprinted editions and books printed with moveable type (c1590–1640).

Anderson collection, a large collection of Japanese illustrated woodcut books and works on Japanese art formed by William Anderson, acquired in 1882, 1894 and 1900 (certain items primarily of artistic interest have been transferred to the Department of Oriental Antiquities of the British Museum). Pre-1590 books are mainly Buddhist scriptural texts, canonical and non-canonical, and commentaries on them, or works on Buddhism by Japanese authors; after 1590 predominantly printed editions of Chinese classical texts and works of native Japanese literature. 18th and 19th cent publications include traditional medicine, science and technology, agriculture, Confucian and native Japanese philosophy, local topography and guide books, also illustrated novels, artists' manuals, and polychrome woodcut blocks of pure illustration. Rare 20th cent books are mostly first editions and de luxe productions of literary works issued in limited editions.

XBc Manchu The important collection of Manchu books includes over 200 blockprints.

Manchu books and manuscripts in the British Museum, typescript by Walter Simon, c1940. Walter Simon and H Nelson, *Manchu Books in London, a union catalogue*, 1977.

XBd Mongolian c500 items, incl 80 blockprints.

W Heissig, *Mongolian blockprints no 1-66 in the British Museum*, typescript. Card cat of Mongolian books.

XC South East Asia

Guide, p55-62.

B Moon, *Periodicals for South-East Asian studies: a union catalogue...*, London, 1977. Greater detail on holdings is given in P Herbert, *Checklist of Southeast Asia connected serials in the British Library*, typescript available on request in the Oriental Reading Room.

W R Roff, *Bibliography of Malay and Arabic periodicals published in the Straits Settlements and Peninsular Malay States 1876–1941*, London, OUP, 1972.

XCa Burmese and Thai There are over 6,000 items in Burmese and 1,200 in Thai. Many 19th and 20th cent books in Burmese libraries were destroyed during World War II, and are now available only in British collections. There are many runs of early newspapers and periodicals, and the only known copy of St *Matthew* translated by Adoniram Judson, Rangoon, 1817, the first book printed in Burma. The collection also include rare printings in minority languages of the area such as Shan, Karen and Chin. (Some early Burmese and Thai imprints, mainly grammars, language books, and Christian propaganda, are in the Dept of Printed Books.)

L D Barnett, *Catalogue of the Burmese books in the British Museum*, 1913; blue-slip cat of Burmese acquisitions 1914–58, then card cat. Card cat of Thai books.

XCb Malay and Indonesian A quarter of the Malay collection of over 2,000 items is pre-1925, incl a collection of Baba-Malay (Chinese Malay) literature. Of c4,000 Indonesian titles, c300 are considered rare; before Indonesian became a national language they formed part of the Malay collection. Among languages of the Indonesian family, rare material can also be found in the *Malagasy* and *Philippine* collections.

Card cat (separate sequence for Indonesian from 1950). *Periodical publications and newspapers: Malay and Indonesian*, by R Aboe Hasan, typescript, 1970.

XCc Vietnamese There are c800 printed books. Card cat. Printed cat in preparation.

XD South Asia

The collection of c230,000 books is one of the finest outside South Asia, incl many items not in the libraries of the region. c25,000 date from before 1867 (when the

Indian Press and Registration of Books Act was passed). c24,000 are of 1868–1914; post-1867 rare material includes works in minor languages (in some of which there was little or no printing till c1900), and books proscribed under the Indian Press Act of 1910 and deposited until 1947. The British Museum claimed deposit under Indian copyright 1867–1947 (and later in the case of Sri Lanka), selecting items from the quarterly lists of publications prepared by each presidency. The library has a fine representative collection of the output of the early missionary presses at Tranquebar, Vepery, and Serampore, and good collections of those of the early 19th cent, and of the vernacular presses established for Indians' own tastes, eg the pothi-format Sanskrit texts printed at Bombay and Poona. The collection is also important for those interested in the spread of lithography (esp for languages such as Urdu using the Persian script), and in the development of book illustration, the earliest being a Bengali music treatise *Saṅgītataraṅga*, Calcutta, 1818. There are many early works in Indian languages printed in Europe, incl the Malayalam catechism of Clemens Peanius, Rome, 1772; Schultze's Urdu translation of the New Testament, Halle, 1745; Psalms, Halle, 1745; the first work of Sanskrit literature printed in Europe, Hamilton's edition of the *Hitopadeśa*, London, 1810; and other Sanskrit works printed in Germany such as Schlegel's *Bhagavadgītā*, Bonn, 1823, and in Paris at the Imprimerie Nationale, such as Burnouf's edition of the *Bhagavatapurāṇa*, 1840–7. (The library's 3 16th and 17th cent books, and some 18th cent works esp dictionaries and grammars, with some Biblical translations, are in the Dept of Printed Books.)

Guide, p36-54. *Early printing in India*, 1978–9. *Proscribed Indian books*, 1968, xeroxed typescript; printed cat of proscribed books in preparation; see also N G Barrier, *Banned: controversial literature and political control in British India 1907–1947*, Columbia, 1974, with pressmarks; N G Barrier, 'South Asia in vernacular publications. . . in the British Museum and India Office Library', *Journal of Asian Studies*, 28 (1969), p803-10. G W Shaw and S Quraishi, *The bibliography of South Asian periodicals: a union list of periodicals in South Asian languages*, Brighton, 1982. G Shaw, 'An outline of early South Asian printing', *SALG Newsletter*, 10 (1977).

XDa Assamese and Oriya c1,800 Assamese and 2,500 Oriya items, incl the productions of the Cuttack Mission Press.

Catalogue of Assamese and Oriya books, [by J F Blumhardt], [1894–1900]. Blue-slip cat of Assamese acquisitions 1900–1945, Oriya 1900–57; card cat thereafter.

G Shaw, 'The Cuttack Mission Press and early Oriya printing', *British Library Journal* 3 (1977), p29-43.

XDb Bengali c16,000 Bengali books include many Biblical translations from the Serampore Mission Press in Bengal from 1801 onwards, with its linguistic and Indian literary productions, and the first Indian-language journal, the Bengali *Digdarśana*, Serampore, 1818.

Catalogue of Bengali printed books in the Library of the British Museum, by J F Blumhardt, 1886; *Supplementary catalogue. . .*, 1910; *Second supplementary catalogue. . .*, by J F Blumhardt and J V S Wilkinson, 1939; blue-slip cat of 1935–54 acquisitions, card cat thereafter.

G Shaw, *Printing in Calcutta to 1800*, London, Bibliographical Society, 1980.

XDc Gujarati and Marathi c9,000 Gujarati (incl books printed at the Surat Mission) and 8,000 Marathi items. They include Marathi works printed at the private press of Rajah Serfoji II at Tanjore, eg the Marathi version of Aesop, 1809.

Catalogue of Marathi and Gujarati printed books in the British Museum, by J F Blumhardt, 1892; *Supplementary catalogue. . .*, 1915; blue-slip cat of 1916–56 Gujarati and 1916–42 Marathi acquisitions, thereafter card cat.

G Shaw, 'The Tanjore Aesop in the context of early Marathi printing', *Library* 5th ser 33 (1978), p207-14.

XDd Hindi, Bihari, Urdu, Panjabi, Pahari, Sindhi, Nepali, and related languages c20,000 Hindi books, c22,000 Urdu, c4,000 Panjabi, c1,700 Sindhi, etc. They include books in Urdu and Panjabi printed at the Ludhiana Mission, and in Hindi at the Allahabad Mission Press.

Catalogues of the Hindi, Panjabi, Sindhi, and Pushtu printed books in the Library of the British Museum, by J F Blumhardt, 1893; *Supplementary catalogue of Hindi books. . .*, 1913; *Second supplementary catalogue of printed books in Hindi, Bihari. . . and Pahari. . . in the Library. . .*, by L D Barnett et al, 1957; *Panjabi printed books in the British Museum, a supplementary catalogue*, by L D Barnett, 1961; blue-slip cat of Sindhi books acquired 1894–1960; thereafter card cat. *Catalogue of Hindustani printed books in the Library of the British Museum*, by J F Blumhardt, 1889; *Supplementary catalogue. . .*, 1909.

G Shaw, 'The first printing press in the Punjab', *Library Chronicle* 43 (1979), p159-79.

XDe Kannada, Malayalam, Tulu and minor Dravidian languages c4,000 Kannada, c10,000 Malayalam items, and small numbers in Tulu and other minor Dravidian languages. They include Kannada books printed at the Bellary Mission, and Malayalam at the Cottayam Mission, and those printed in several languages at Mangalore and at Tellicherry by the Lutheran Mission from Basel.

Catalogue of the Kannada, Badaga and Kurg books in the Library of the British Museum, by L D Barnett, 1910; blue-slip cat of acquisitions 1911–64, thereafter card cat; *Supplementary catalogue* in preparation. *Catalogue of Malayalam books in the British Museum*, 1971, by A Gaur; thereafter card cat G Shaw, 'Printing at Mangalore and Tellicherry by the Basel Mission', *Libri* 27 (1977), p154–64.

XDf Sanskrit, Prakrit and Pali c25,000 Sanskrit/Prakrit and c2,000 Pali items. They include the first work printed in Sanskrit, Sir William Jones' edition of Kalidasa *Rtusamhara*, Calcutta, 1792.

Catalogue of Sanskrit and Pali books in the British Museum, by Ernst Haas, 1876; *Catalogue of Sanskrit, Pali and Prakrit books...acquired...1876–1892*, by C Bendall, 1893; *Supplementary catalogue...1892–1906* and *1906–1928* by L D Barnett, 1908–28; *Fourth supplementary catalogue...*, by J P Losty.

XDg Sinhalese c8,000 items.

Catalogue of the Sinhalese printed books in the Library of the British Museum, by M de Z Wickremasinghe, 1901.

XDh Tamil c20,000 Tamil items include most of the publications of the Tranquebar Mission Press, from 1714 onwards, eg the Tamil Old Testament 1723–8. Works in Sinhalese and Tamil printed by the Dutch at Colombo, incl the first *Singaleesch gebeede book*, 1737; works in Tamil from the Vepery Mission Press, such as the Malabar New Testament of 1772.

A catalogue of the Tamil books in the Library of the British Museum, by L D Barnett et al 1909; *Supplementary catalogue...*, 1931; *Second supplementary catalogue...*, by A Gaur, 1980; thereafter card cat. R Subbiah, *Tamil Malaysiana*, Kuala Lumpur, 1969, incl a list of all the Tamil books published in Singapore and Malaysia in the British Library.

XDi Telugu c15,000 items.

A catalogue of the Telugu books in the Library of the British Museum, by L D Barnett, 1912; blue-slip cat of 1912–65 acquisitions, card cat thereafter.

XDj Tibetan With over 3,000 items, the collection of xylographs and printed books is one of the most comprehensive in the world, and it is no exaggeration to call 80% of its material 'rare'. Woodblock printing started at Narthang in the first half of the 13th cent, lithography c1860 introduced by then Protestant scholar-missionary H A Jaeschke. In the early days the British Museum received many donations from merchants and travellers who had visited Tibet. The backbone of the collection is formed by the books and mss acquired by Col Austin *Waddell* in the course of the Younghusband Expeditions to Lhasa in 1904 (other parts of his collection are at the India Office Library, Oxford, and Cambridge). Substantial contributions were made in 1917 from the collections of Sir Aurel *Stein* (shared with the India Office Library), and in 1933 an important collection of blockprints was acquired from Sir Charles *Bell*. In 1904 further notable works were given by the Secretary of State for India, and the expulsion of the lamas in the late 1950s has added much by means of donation and purchase. The collection includes all aspects of Mahayana Buddhism (incl Tibetan translations of lost Sanskrit works), commentaries, Tantric treatises, and also history, biography, logic, philology, rhetoric, prosody, music, astronomy, medicine, and the indigenous Bön religion. Notable works held include a virtually complete set of the Narthang edition of the *Bstan-hgyur (Tanjur)* dating from the 13th-14th cent, 220 v of blockprints; the 13th cent commentary on the *Legs-bshad*; the rare 13th cent translation of *Kavyadarsá*; 14th cent histories of the kings of western Tibet; biographies (partly autobiographical) and collected works of the First (1570–1662), Second (1663–1737), Third (1737–80), Fourth (1781–1854), Fifth (1855–81) and Sixth (1883–1937) Panchen Lamas; of the Fifth (1617–82) and Sixth (1653–1705) Dalai Lamas; 18th cent Tibetan/Mongolian bilingual dictionaries; lithographed periodicals published by the Moravian Mission in Ladakh from 1906 onwards, and many translations of Biblical texts printed by them at Kye-lang 1861–1970. The collection also includes works in Bhutanese, Sikhimese, Ladakhi, Mongolian and Khotanese, and some minor languages such as Sherpa, the languages of Gyethang, Mongul, Yunnan, Kham, and Tamang.

Card cat. *Catalogue of Tibetan manuscripts, xylographs and printed books in the British Library*, by Lama Chime Radha, in preparation.

XDk Other minor languages 132 Kashmiri items (Blue-slip cat to 1966, then cards). 19 Saurashtra items (*Catalogue*, by L D Barnett, 1960).

XE Near and Middle East
Guide, p19-35.

XEa Arabic Of c40,000 titles nearly a quarter are 19th cent or earlier, and a high proportion of these are rare items: the collection provides a fairly comprehensive picture of Arabic typography and publishing. Important items include Arabic editions printed in Europe 16th-17th cent; Arabic items published in the Levant on missionary and other Christian presses from the 18th cent onwards; the first books printed on Arab soil, produced from the press which Napoleon brought to Egypt in 1798; most of the publications of the Bulaq press at Cairo from 1822 onwards; rare lithographed publications from North Africa, South Asia, etc from the 19th cent onwards; complete runs of periodicals and monographs published in Beirut after 1850; and unique runs of Arabic newspapers printed in London in the 19th cent.

Exhibition leaflet. *Early Arabic printing*, 1979. *Catalogue of Arabic books in the British Museum*, 1894–1901 v 1-2 by A G Ellis (c8,000 items); v 3, Indexes, by A S Fulton, 1935; v 1-3 repr 1967. *Supplementary catalogue...*, by A S Fulton and A G Ellis, 1926; *Second supplementary catalogue* by A S Fulton and M Lings, 1959; *Third supplementary catalogue*, by M Lings and Y H Safadi, 1976, v 1-2 authors, v 3 titles, v 4 subjects; blue-slip cat of later acquisitions; *Fourth supplementary catalogue* in preparation. *Union catalogue of Arabic serials and newspapers in the British libraries*, ed P M Achterlonie and Y H Safadi, London, 1977, incl some rare items.

XEb Armenian The collection, c10,000 titles, is one of the largest in Europe; c2,500 of these are of the rare period between 1512, when Armenian printing began, and 1850, the date when in written documents the old classical language was replaced by modern Armenian. Important items include Abgar, dpir *Psalter*, Constantinople, 1566; Yohannes Terznc'i, *Psalter*, Venice, printed by Juan Albertus, 1587, the only known complete copy; Yohannes of Julfa, *Psalter*, Livorno, 1644, the only known copy; the first edition of the Armenian Bible, Amsterdam, 1668, known as the Oskanean Bible, with woodcuts by Christoffel van Sichem; *Bařgirk' Hayoc'*, Livorno, 1698, dictionary compiled by Eremiya Maghrec'i; *Bařgirk' Haykazean Lezui*, Venice, 1749–69, the first scholarly lexicon; *Nor Bařgirk' Haykazean lezui*, Venice, 1836–37, compiled by three Mekhitarist Fathers; and the series of classics *Matenagrut'iwnk Naxneac* and patristics *Sop'erk Haykakank'* printed by the Armenian Catholic monks in Venice.

Vrej Nersessian, *Catalogue of early Armenian books 1512–1850*, London, British Library, 1980. *Early Armenian printing*, 1980, exhibition leaflet.

XEc *Coptic, Ethiopic, Amharic and Syriac* There are over 300 Coptic books, 1,500 Ethiopic, 1,000 Amharic (incl some early periodicals), and 1,100 Syriac. Most of the collections are 'rare' since items are difficult to obtain and much material was and is being destroyed in the course of local hostilities. Collections cover most subjects of interest to scholars.

Coptic: blue-slip cat to 1972 (incl items in Dept of Printed Books); card cat thereafter. Ethiopic: card cat. Amharic: card cat. Syriac: C Moss, *Catalogue of Syriac printed books and related literature in the British Museum*, 1962; card cat thereafter. *Exhibition of books, manuscripts and antiquities from Ethiopia...*, 1963.

XEd *Georgian and other Caucasian languages* c3,000 Georgian items, of which c150 are of the rare period from the beginning of printing in the language at Rome in 1629 for missionary purposes to 1850. Outstanding items include the first complete Georgian Bible, published in Moscow 1742–3, and devotional literature published in Rome after 1629. There are also many later 19th cent rare books from small provincial presses, and political and poetic material from Georgian emigré communities in Paris and elsewhere. During the Soviet period many books were deliberately destroyed and have become rare items. The main subjects covered are history, poetry, biblical and devotional literature, politics and economics. Some rare items were given by Sir (John) Oliver Wardrop (1864–1948); others came from the British and Foreign Bible Society, and exchange arrangements are now in force with Soviet Georgian institutions. The library also has a limited number of rare publications in obscure Eastern and North-West Caucasian languages, mostly of peoples that were illiterate before the Russian conquest of 1859–64, eg several rare texts collected and published in the late 18th cent by Baron P K Uslar, a pioneer Russian linguist.

D M Lang, *Catalogue of the Georgian and other Caucasian printed books in the British Museum*, 1962; blue-slip cat thereafter; *Supplementary catalogue* in preparation.

XEe *Hebrew* The Hebrew collection amounts to nearly 50,000 items. Rare Hebrew books consist of early material (c1469–1660), transitory material (predominantly liturgy and early newspapers often destroyed by frequent handling), and deliberately destroyed material (mostly before 1946). There are 99 Hebrew incunabula, and c250 books of 1501–1540, incl many that are unique. *The Foundation Collection*, given by Solomon Da Costa (1690–1769) to the British Museum in 1759, comprises 180 pre-1661 volumes which originally belonged to Charles II. In 1848 the collection of 4,420 books of H J *Michael* of Hamburg was bought, and in 1865 some important books from the collection of Joseph *Almanzi* of Padua. Pre-1801 items consist mainly of religious literature, Bibles, liturgies, law books, commentaries, novellae, etc. There are large holdings of *Haggadoth* and Hassidic works, with most of the Responsa of rabbis on Jewish law. The *Yiddish* collection, rivalled only by the Bodleian, is kept in the Dept of Printed Books, in whose General Catalogue it is recorded.

J Zedner, *Catalogue of the Hebrew printed books in the Library of the British Museum*, 1867; repr 1964. S Van Stralen, *Catalogue of Hebrew books in the British Museum acquired...1868–1892*, 1894, with index of titles incorporating titles in the 1867 cat. Blue-slip cat. *Second supplementary catalogue* in preparation. *Illustrations in early Hebrew printing*, 1979–80, exhibition leaflet; *Hebrew periodicals: a, alphabetical list; b, numerical list*, ms. H M Rabinowicz, *Treasures of Judaism*, New York, 1971, p15-62.

XEf *Persian* Of c12,000 titles c4,500 were published before 1925, the end of the Qajar era in Iran. Apart from some Indian copyright material (much of which is very rare) and some English translations from Persian, all items were purchased. This is the only major collection of Persian books that has ever been fully described in a published catalogue. Covers all traditional Islamic subjects, esp religion, literature and history. Includes some early examples of Indian printing in the Arabic/Persian script, and rare Iranian 19th cent lithographs.

E Edwards, *A catalogue of the Persian printed books in the British Museum*, 1922. *Union list of Persian periodicals*, ed U Sims-Williams, in preparation.

XEg *Turkish* Of c10,000 Turkish titles in the library, c2,500 were published before 1928 (when Arabic script publishing ended in Turkey and most areas of Russian-controlled Central Asia). The library holds one of the best Ottoman collections in the West, and one of the few still growing. Includes all traditional Islamic subjects, esp religion, literature, history, and politics; also Christian religious literature, mainly in Greek (Karamanlitic) or Armenian characters. Ottoman printed material from the second half of the 19th cent also covers most subjects of interest to the contemporary western world, and Central Asian Turkish material from 1917 and later of interest to Soviet Russia. A complete collection of the books published between 1729 and 1742 by Ibrahim Müteferrika. Also, a specially bound selection of books presented in 1893 by Ottoman Sultan Abdülhamid II. Card cat.

Y **British Library Reference Division. Science Reference Library**

25 Southampton Buildings, Chancery Lane, London WC2A 1AW. Tel (01) 405 8721 Ext 3344/5 (Holborn Reading Room); 3350 (British patents); 3411 (foreign patents); 3126 (Aldwych Reading Room). Telex 266959. Holborn Reading Room (in Patent Office Building, 25 Southampton Buildings) open to all without formality Mon-Fri 9.30 am-9 pm, Sat 10 am-1 pm; Foreign Patents Reading Room (in Chancery House, opposite Southampton Buildings), Mon-Fri 9.30 am-5.30 pm. Aldwych Reading Room (9 Kean Street, WC2B 4AT) Mon-Fri 9.30 am-5.30 pm. Computer search services at Holborn in addition to general and business information services, and linguistic help facilities. Photocopying; microform readers.

YA *General*

The Science Reference Library is primarily the national library for modern science and technology and for patents, trade marks, and designs; but it retains much old material, esp after 1799, inherited from the Patent Office Library, whose subject arrangement and open access policy have been continued, though much material is now outhoused. The Holborn Reading Room has the literature on the physical sciences and their related technologies, engineering and commerce. The younger Aldwych Reading Room now has the life and earth sciences, astronomy, pure mathematics and medicine, ie the non-inventive sciences.

Science Reference Library, 1981, free leaflet available from External Relations Section. *Aids to readers*, 1961–(gratis). *Notes to readers*, 1961– (gratis). *SRL News*, 1973– ; superseding *NRLSI News* 1969–73. *List of SRL publications*, 1971– .

YB *Catalogues*

SCICAT: author/name and classified catalogues on microfiche of accessions and recatalogued earlier material from 1975 onwards, cumulated fortnightly, available at Holborn, Aldwych, and Dept of Printed Books (Great Russell Street). Author/name and classified catalogues of 1930–75 accessions on cards at Holborn (for Holborn and Aldwych collections) and at Aldwych (for Aldwych collection). Author/name cat of pre-1930 accessions, bound volumes of slips photocopied from printed entries; material transferred to Great Russell Street is so marked. Classified pre-1930 slips in sheaf binders (available on request; not kept up to date). Special catalogues are indicated in the individual sections below (eg trade literature at YG).

There is an archival collection of superseded catalogues (which may be seen only by appointment), incl *Catalogue of the Library of the Great Seal Patent Office*, priv pr 1856, mainly Woodcroft's library; the published edition 1857–8, 2 v: v 1 list of 1,827 full titles (by provenance, no 1-388 Woodcroft, 389-1093 Prosser), v 2 dictionary index; *Catalogue of the Library of the Patent Office, arranged alphabetically in two volumes*, v 1, authors, 1881; (new ed) 1898; *Supplement and appendix*, 1910; supplements thereafter to c1930. *Catalogue of the Library of the Patent Office, arranged alphabetically in two volumes*, v 2 subjects, 1883.

YC *Historical summary*

The library continues the character and function of the Patent Office Library, opened in 1855 as a free public open access library (probably the first in Britain), and then associated with a museum (amalgamated with the South Kensington, now Science Museum, in 1884). The library was built around the collections bought from the first head of the Patent Office, Bennet Woodcroft (1803–79), and from his friend Richard Prosser (1804–54), both of which were rich in material of earlier centuries. Prosser's son, Richard Bissell Prosser (1838–1918), who was on the office staff, contributed greatly to the historical collection by donation and bequest. Woodcroft's successors, esp Ernest W Hulme and Alan A Gomme, widened the historical scope of the collections. Patent Office librarians were active both in promoting a dynamic programme of publication, notably of early patent specifications, and in the foundation and publication programmes of the first engineering historical societies such as the Newcomen Society. In 1960–2 the National Reference Library of Science and Invention (intended for a new building on the South Bank) was established as part of the Dept of Printed Books of the British Museum, enjoying the privilege of copyright deposit. In 1966 it took over the Patent Office Library and established its headquarters there, transferring some material (mostly after 1930) from the Great Russell Street building. The new library greatly expanded its foreign (incl oriental) language holdings, and developed for the first time a life sciences collection. In 1973 it became a part of the British Library, but no longer within the Dept of Printed Books. With the occasional exception of patents and related material, the library no longer acquires rare items.

Herbert Harding, *Patent Office Centenary*, HMSO, 1952. John Hewish, *The indefatigable Mr Woodcroft*, British Library, (1980). R M S Hall, 'Woodcroft's heritage: the collections at the SRL', *British Library Journal* 6 (1980), p65-76. F W Gravell, 'The Patent Office Library', in R Irwin and R Staveley, *The libraries of London*, 2nd ed 1961, p60-73. E W Hulme, 'English patent law: its history, literature and library', *Library*, 10 (1898), p42-55. M Webb, 'The National Reference Library of Science and Invention: a record of progress', *Journal of Documentation*, 22 (1966), p1-12. M W Hill, 'The Science Reference Library', in W L Saunders ed *British Librarianship Today*, London, Library Ass, 1976, p73-85.

YD *Patents, trade marks and designs*

Patents of invention are a form of legally sanctioned,

limited-duration monopoly. Their development is traceable from royal privileges granted in the Middle Ages to importers and improvers, through the monopoly legislation of the 17th cent, to the well-defined and complex system of today. Publication was a development of the mid-19th cent and later. SRL has the most comprehensive collection of patent specifications and related publications (parliamentary papers, law reports, periodicals, bibliographies, and historical studies) in the world.

Industrial property literature in the Science Reference Library: holdings from the UK, the European Patent Office and WIPO(PCT), (Aids to readers no 26).

YDa British A complete set of currently published specifications exists from 1852, but Great Britain is exceptional in having published between 1854 and 1858 the antecedent records from 1617 to 1852 (in the public records of Chancery) as a continuous series *Letters patent and specifications*, with general indexes, for which Woodcroft was personally responsible. The early progress of local systems (such as for Scotland, Ireland, the Isle of Man, and Berwick on Tweed, distinct until 1852) can also be traced through specialized documentation and rare indexes.

A A Gomme, *Patents of invention...*, London, Longmans, 1946. *Letters patent and specifications of Letters patent for invention enrolled...1617 to...1852...*, 1854–8. B Woodcroft, *Name index...*, 1854, repr 1969. *Titles...chronologically arranged*, 1854; *Subject matter index...*, 1857, 2 v; and Reference index of patents, 1855, 2 v, 2 ed, 1862. *Supplement to the series of Letters...patent...*, 1858, reprinting scarce tracts, v 1, no more published. These are continued by a complete series of indexes, published and unpublished, down to the latest week. UK name index of current year's applicants on cards, updated weekly, with separate cumulations for each of the seven previous years. Weekly computer name index to published applications, with quarterly cumulations. UK Patents Information Network, *PIN Bulletin, 1981– .*

YDb Foreign Patent laws following the British pattern were introduced into the United States in 1790, most other industrial countries by 1865, and virtually all by 1900. The resulting patent specifications, from the first published, are held, mostly in complete sets, together with their indexes. In many cases the holdings begin even before the establishment of the national patent office, with regional patents granted by the separate states, provinces and kingdoms of such countries as Australia, South Africa and the German Empire.

Separate foreign national indexes, and international indexes by INPADOC and DERWENT on fiche or online. Publications held and the historical background are explained in 4 separate guides by B M Rimmer, *Guide to the United States patent and trade mark literature*, 1980; *Guide to industrial property literature: France*, 1980; *Guide to official industrial property literature: the Netherlands, Belgium, Luxembourg, Benelux*, 1981; and *Guide to German patent and trade mark publications including East Germany*, 1979.

YE *Periodicals*

In total range the Library maintains the 19th cent pre-eminence of the Patent Office Library, but its principal responsibility for modern science, patents, and current technology within the Reference Division, with *c*32,000 current periodical titles, has affected the historical dimension of holdings. Issues of journals of individual industries and trades are now held mostly from 1910 onwards (most earlier runs have been transferred to British Library Lending Division or other libraries). Even so, the important earlier serial literature of the main scientific disciplines has been retained. The 18th and earlier cent are represented by the publications of the principal European academies of science, esp those of London, St Petersburg, Paris, Berlin, Vienna, Munich, and Turin. Important additions to the main stream in the 19th cent are transactions of British scientific societies (Dublin, Edinburgh); the principal foreign journals in chemistry and physics; proceedings of the main engineering institutions; the general science journals; notable independent journals of 'natural philosophy'; journals in the industrial property field; and the many inventors' magazines originating in the last quarter of the 18th cent. To these must be added the chief independent journals in engineering, aviation, and photography, and some short-lived titles from the 18th cent onwards, notably in botany and agriculture. The bibliography of technology was a 19th cent development reflected in the collection, particularly in patents, with the pioneering *Abridgments* begun after 1850, and such publications as the Prussian *Repertorium der Technischen Journal Literatur*, 1856–1909, covering the literature of 1823–1908 to which Woodcroft wrote an introduction and attempted an English counterpart, *Index to foreign scientific periodicals...in the...Library*, 1867–76. The needs of patentees generally are closely associated with such productions as Woodcroft's *Journal of the Commissioners of Patents* (1856–), an official gazette and news forum for inventors.

Periodicals are entered under their issuing bodies or titles in the general catalogues; there is also a separate card catalogue of periodicals at Holborn. All are also included in *KIST (Keyword index to serial titles)* on microfiche (published by BL Lending Division). Helena M Barton, *Industrial property literature: a directory of journals*, London, SRL, 1981. *Abstracting and bibliographical periodicals held*, 1972; 1975; 2nd ed 1982. *Trade directories in journals: a list of those appearing in numbered parts of serials*, 1980; 2nd ed 1981. *House journals held by the Science Reference Library*, by D King and M Thomson, 1978. Older catalogues include *List of scientific and other periodicals and transactions of learned societies in the free public library of the Patent Office*, 1861.

YF *Monographs*

Woodcroft's international interests are exemplified in the

wide holdings of books and pamphlets on patents in many languages. Among the overall collection of 30,000 monographs, particular strengths lie in physics and thermodynamics, electricity, railways and civil engineering, marine propulsion (a Woodcroft interest), textiles, and international exhibitions (which figure among the earliest donations). Other subjects well covered are architecture, weaponry, games, instruments, and horology, agriculture and forestry, photography and printing. Some post-1930 material has been transferred from the Dept of Printed Books (with a few earlier items), but SRL contains many earlier works and books not deposited by copyright at the British Museum. *c*15,000 pamphlets (many outhoused) reflect the rapid acceleration of the Industrial Revolution in 1800–25. Many of the older monographs on the non-inventive sciences recorded in the printed catalogue were dispersed between 1930 and 1960, and most remaining pre-1800 monographs in all subjects except patents were transferred to the Dept of Printed Books from 1963 to 1982 (see Fk above).

YG *Trade and company literature*
Since 1973 the Library has devoted considerable resources to rebuilding and enlarging the collection of company brochures. These cover *c*8,000 companies, and include a substantial collection of trade catalogues 1850–1940 recently returned from store, illustrating changing tastes in commercial art and printing as well as commercial and technical history.

Company name and subject indexes on slips 1850–1940, from 1940 company name index only on cards.

YH *Special collections*

YHa *Woodcroft collection of lives of inventors* A collection of biographical miscellanea on inventors, ms and printed, in *c*800 files, arranged alphabetically. Originally put together by Bennet Woodcroft as a private project, it has been much expanded since his death. (The collection is supplemented by the *Prosser* collection, now in the Dept of Manuscripts, see WDf.)

Index of names on slips; these are also included in pre-1930 general author/name cat.

John Hewish, *The indefatigable Mr Woodcroft*, (1980), p35-6.

YHb *Collectanea* A collection of articles, pamphlets, cuttings, etc, on inventions and innovations, arranged alphabetically by subject.

Index of subject headings on slips interfiled with names of Woodcroft collection: also included in pre-1930 general subject cat.

YHc *Aeronautica illustrata* Records of balloon ascents from the 17th cent onwards, 10 v, mostly broadsheets, pamphlets, and cuttings, with some ms material; comp 1850–60 by George James Norman, a bookseller, bought *c*1880.

Typescript list and index by B L Rimmer.

Z **British Library Reference Division. India Office Library and Records**

Orbit House, 197 Blackfriars Road, London SE1 8NG. Tel (01) 928 9531. Open Mon-Fri 9.30 am-6 pm; Sat 9.30 am-1 pm. Microfilming, photographic and electrostatic copying facilities. Microfilm/fiche readers. Readers' typing room.

In 1771 an archivist was first appointed to the East India Company which had received its charter in 1600. A library was established out of scattered collections only in 1801, largely through the efforts of its historiographer, Robert Orme (1728–1801), and was conceived primarily as a repository of oriental mss and printed books on oriental subjects, with a strong literary bias. Orme's own collection was incorporated after his death, together with the library captured from Tippoo Sultan, and those of Warren Hastings (1732–1818) and John Leyden (1775–1811). The collections were built up by a succession of eminent scholar-librarians, beginning with Sir Charles Wilkins (1749–1836). In 1858 the Company, which since 1784 had been subject to a government Board of Control, was succeeded by the India Office, and from 1867 to 1947 the Library enjoyed copyright deposit privilege for Indian published material; during this period the emphasis shifted to acquiring more printed material, including the major works in all European languages relevant to the sub-continent. In 1947, following the Indian Independence Act, the Library and Records passed to the Commonwealth Relations Office, then the Commonwealth Office, in 1968 the Foreign and Commonwealth Office, and in 1982 the British Library.

S C Sutton, *A guide to the India Office Library* 2nd ed corrected, London HMSO, 1971 (£1.50).

A J Arberry, *The library of the India Office: a historical sketch*, 1938 (chiefly describing mss collections); repr as *The India Office Library*, London, HMSO, 1967 (£5.50).

Report for the year...1951 (annually).

Newsletter (3 yearly).

Jack Burkett, *Government and related library...services*, 3rd ed, London, Lib Assoc, 1974, p62-4.

R A Rye, *Students' guide...*, 3rd ed, 1927 (op) p336-7, 392-6.

F H Brown, 'The India Office Library', *The Library*, ns 5 (1904), p256-65.

Sir Malcolm C C Seton, *The India Office*, London, 1926, p237-42 (op).

R Datta, 'The India Office Library: its history, resources and functions', *Library Quarterly* 36 (1966), p99-148.

Za *India Office Records*
The archives of *c*175,000 v of British India: East India Company (1599–1858) Commissioners for the Affairs of India, Board of Control (1784–1858), India Office (1858–1947), Burma Office (1937–48). These are complemented by a virtually complete set, 70,000 v of Indian and the relevant British official publications from

the beginning and 30,000 maps and atlases (printed and ms).

William Foster, *Guide to the India Office Records, 1600–1858*, 1919; repr 1966 (£1.50).

S C Hill, *Catalogue of the Home Miscellaneous series...*, London, 1927.

Joan C Lancaster, *A guide to the lists and catalogues of the India Office Records*, 1966 (gratis).

A classified list of reports and other publications in the Record Branch of the India Office 1883; new ed 1894.

India Office Records: report...1947–1967, London, 1970 (and annual report above).

Zb European manuscripts (Private papers)

The official records are complemented and supplemented by a large collection of private papers, 11,250 v, boxes, files, collections and individual manuscripts, to which *c*100 are added each year. Collections range from Viceroys, Governors General, etc to individuals in official and commercial life. Unpublished handlists for most large collections. Some printed material is included.

Catalogue of manuscripts in European languages belonging to the Library of the India Office, London, 1916– (in progress).

—v 1, pt 1, The Mackenzie Collections, by C O Blagden, 1916.

—v 2, pt 1, The Orme Collection, by S C Hill, 1916.

—v 2, pt 2, Minor collections and miscellaneous manuscripts, section 1, by G R Kaye, 1937.

—v 1, pt 2 and 2, pt 2, section 2 were printed but not published (awaiting indexes). These cats cover the collections up to 1937; after that only an unpublished card index is available; however see also *Index of post-1937 European manuscript accessions*, Boston, G K Hall, 1964 (repr from cards).

Accessions of private collections, 1937–1977, by Rosemary Seton, London 1979, (gratis).

Zc European printed books

This collection includes *c*114,000 books and pamphlets (*c*4,500 pre-1851, mostly post-1750) in western languages, wherever printed (except translations from oriental languages, which are placed with the originals). Subject scope is comprehensive (excluding pure science and technology) for the Indian sub-continent, selective for other areas of Asia. There are also *c*30,000 v of periodicals (1,000 v pre-1851), and 4,200 v of newspapers (250 pre-1851) almost entirely Indian imprints, including papers printed at Calcutta from 1780 onwards.

Author cat (on slips and cards) reproduced as *Catalogue of European printed books*, Boston, Mass, G K Hall, 1964. Earlier cats are still useful (eg that of 1888 and its supplement of 1895 (classified with author indexes) list the contents of tract volumes as well as indexing them under their authors). Title list of all serials, including official publications and directories.

Dorothy Walker, *Catalogue of the newspaper collection in the India Office Library*, 1977 (75p).

Zd Oriental printed books and manuscripts

The printed books, which include translations into western languages, total *c*254,000 v (at least 20,000 pre-1851), comprising 36,000 Tamil; 33,500 Hindi; 28,000 Bengali; 24,000 Urdu; 24,000 Sanskrit; 7,500 Arabic; 7,000 Persian; and small collections in *c*80 other oriental (mainly South Asian) languages. Chiefly literature, history, religion and philosophy; the classical languages also include some science and medicine. There are also 27,000 mss.

Catalogue of the Library of the India Office, v 2: oriental languages, pt 1: Sanskrit books rev ed 1938–57, 4 v (£22); pt 2-5 (op); pt 6, Persian books, 1937 (£10).

Catalogue of Burmese Printed Books, 1969 (£10).

Catalogue of Panjabi Printed Books added...1902–1964, 1975 (£17.50).

Catalogue of Urdu books in the India Office Library, 1800–1920, (supp to J F Blumhardt's catalogue of 1900), by S al-din Quraishi, London, 1982 (£5). These cats are supplemented by author/title and classified card cats.

Catalogue of Persian manuscripts in the Library of the India Office, v 1 and 2 by H Ethé, revised and completed by E Edwards, 1937. Reprinted 'compact' edition, London, 1980 (£22).

Catalogue of Urdu manuscripts in the India Office Library, by Salim al-din Quraishi and U Sims-Williams, London 1978 (£4).

Catalogue of Panjabi and Sindhi manuscripts in the India Office Library, by C Shackle, London 1977 (£2).

Catalogue of the Tibetan manuscripts from Tun-Huang in the India Office Library, by L de la Vallée Poussin, London, 1962 (£10).

Catalogue of the Sinhalese manuscripts in the India Office Library, compiled by D J Wijayaratne and A S Kulasuriya, ed by C H B Reynolds, London, 1981 (£8.50), and other published catalogues of printed books and manuscripts.

Ze Prints and drawings

Major collections of prints, drawings, watercolours, engravings, with some sculpture, furniture, oil paintings and other works of art; with more than 184,000 photographs.

Mildred Archer, *British drawings in the India Office Library*, London, 1969 (£35).

——*Company drawings in the India Office Library*, London, 1972 (£17.50).

——*Natural history drawings in the India Office Library*, London, 1962 (£9.95).

B W Robinson, *Persian paintings in the India Office Library*, London, 1976 (£35).

T Falk and Mildred Archer, *Indian miniatures in the India Office Library*, London, 1981 (£57.50).

British Medical Association, Nuffield Library, BMA House, Tavistock Square, London WC1H 9JP. Tel (01) 387 4499. Open Mon-Fri 9 am-5.30 pm (Wed 9 pm) by arrangement with the librarian. Microfilm reader; photocopier.

The Association was founded in 1832 at the Worcester Infirmary as the Provincial Medical and Surgical Association, changing to its present name in 1856, and moving its offices to London in 1871. The library was founded in 1887.

E M Little, *History of the British Medical Association 1832–1932* (1933).

Paul Vaughan, *Doctor's Commons: a short history of the. . . Association*, London, Heinemann, 1959, p120-1.

'The Nuffield Library of the BMA', *British Medical Journal* 1963 (1) p1218-9.

Sir D'Arcy Power, *British Medical Societies*, London, 1939, p99-108.

General Collection Begun by Ernest Hart (1836–98), editor of the *British Medical Journal*, who incorporated part of his own private collection. *c*85,000 monographs, of which *c*2,200 (including Hastings collection) are pre-1851, mostly donations from members, on medicine and related topics.

Card cat (authors).

Donations listed in *British Medical Journal* from 1888.

D Ryde, 'Ernest Hart', *Journal of the College of General Practitioners* 12 (1966), p345-7.

Hastings, Sir Charles (1794–1866), the Association's founder, who had earlier established the *Midland Medical and Surgical Reporter*: his medical library, *c*1,200 v, including 8 Wing items, 5 foreign 16th cent and 14 17th cent, made up of his own working library and the collection of his father Dr George Woodyatt, of Worcester. Presented after his death by his son George Woodyatt Hastings to the doctors of Worcestershire, who formed the Worcestershire Medical Society to receive it; they gave it to the BMA in 1932.

Catalogue of the Library of the Worcestershire Medical Society, Worcester, 1869.

W H McMenemey, 'Charles Hastings', *British Medical Journal*, 1966 (1), p937-42.

British Museum, Great Russell Street, London WC1B 3DG. Tel (01) 636 1555. Libraries open (subject to the conditions and restrictions indicated below for each collection) Mon-Fri 10 am-4.45 pm (unless otherwise stated).

The British Museum was founded in 1853, but its massive library departments (of printed books, manuscripts and oriental printed books and manuscripts) in 1973 were transferred to the British Library Reference Division (qv). The remaining printed material not included in the transfer, held in the Department of Prints and Drawings, the Department of Ethnology (Museum of Mankind), and the working libraries of the departments of antiquities form the basis of a new library system which is actively being built up around a new Central Library. The archives of the British Museum, which include material relating to departments of the present British Museum (Natural History) and British Library, are administered separately.

A Central Library

Formation of a central collection began in 1981, and as yet it contains few rare books; transfer of the more general material from the departments is anticipated.

Union list of periodicals in all the libraries (typescript).

Union cat of books under consideration.

B Department of Prints and Drawings

Open Mon-Fri 10 am-2 pm, 2.15-4 pm; Sat 10 am-12.30 pm to holders of tickets of admission to its Students' Room, for which written application should be made to the Keeper.

Print collections were transferred in 1808 from the Department of Printed Books to the Print Room, which was a sub-department of the Department of Antiquities. In 1836 it became the separate Department of Prints and Drawings. The collections of prints and drawings, which lie outside the scope of this directory, include major collections of proof copies, especially in the bequest of Felix Slade (1790–1868), of plates for book illustration. In addition, the Department has large and important collections of rare books.

The history of the department is sketched in A E Popham, *Handbook to the drawings and watercolours in the Department of Prints and Drawings*, 1939; and in *Treasures of the British Museum* (ed T C Francis), London, Thames and Hudson, 1971, p285-308.

Books of Prints The collection officially called 'Books of Prints', of over 10,000 v, including *c*6,000 pre-1851, contains several incunabula, and *c*1,500 v of the 16th cent. It includes collections of plates published in volume form, and also ordinary books combining text with illustrations. In the case of the early printed books, there are many volumes in the collection merely to illustrate features such as ornamental initials or woodcut title pages, so that the collection is very varied in its subject matter. In the case of more modern books, most are examples of illustration by famous artists issued in limited editions. There is a collection of artists' manuals and drawing books, including many on special topics such as botanical and landscape artistry. There are major collections of rare colour plate books on certain subjects, mostly the books portions of benefactions to the Department, eg on skating from the gift in 1931 of the collection of skating prints of Miss F Laura Cannan; on playing cards, partly from the playing cards bequest of Lady Charlotte (Elizabeth) Schreiber (1812–95); and on fans from her 1891 gift of fans and fan leaves. There is also a considerable British topographical collection, and a smaller foreign one. There is a collection of over 50 editions illustrated by Holbein, especially his *Dance of death* (including Edward VI's copy), most of which came with the Holbein bequest of William Mitchell (*d*1908). A collection of colour plate books of French costume bequeathed in 1899 to the Princess of Wales and her successors in that office is held on deposit.

Book index on cards, dictionary arrangement; but most

rare books have no subject entries; a few entries under donors.

Separate index slips for Topography.

Slips in shelf order also provide access by category, but this is mainly not a subject arrangement.

General indexes of artists (in guardbooks) include illustrators of books.

Freeman M O'Donoghue, *Catalogue of the collection of playing cards bequeathed to the... British Museum by the late Lady Charlotte Schreiber*, 1901, books, p214-9.

Lionel Cust, *Catalogue of the collection of fans and fan-leaves presented to... the British Museum by the Lady Charlotte Schreiber*, 1893, books, p129-31.

Typescript list of Cannan collection.

Book index under Holbein.

Collections of Bookplates Over 70,000 bookplates, the largest collection ever assembled by one man, bequeathed by Sir Augustus Wollaston Franks (1826–97), Keeper of British and Mediaeval Antiquities and Ethnography. They range from the 15th cent onwards, and about half are British. There are 20 attached to complete books. This collection includes the major collection (chiefly French, Swiss and Low Countries bookplates) which Franks had bought from Marie Ernest de Roziere (1829–1901); this is still separate. (The Franks collection of armorial bookstamps was placed in the Department of Printed Books, now in the British Library Reference Division, qv.) The collection of Max Rosenheim (*d*1911), over 11,000, was given by Mrs Theodore Rosenheim in 1932. *c*8,000 bookplates from the collection of George Heath Viner were given in 1950. To these have been added a considerable number of miscellaneous collections.

E R Gambier Howe, *Catalogue of British and American bookplates bequeathed to the British Museum by Sir Augustus W Franks*, 1903–4, 3 v; personally arranged alphabetically, followed by miscellaneous categories; annotated copy.

Franks's ms lists by country for foreign plates in his collection; the German is served by his interleaved and annotated copy of F Warneck, *Die Deutscher Bücherzeichen*, Berlin, 1890.

No cat of other bookplate collections, but see G H Viner, 'The origin and evolution of the book-plates', *Library* 5th ser 1 (1946), p39-44.

Collections of printed ephemera Large collections of printed visiting tickets, concert tickets, funeral cards, trade cards, shopbills, letterheads, banknotes, and the like; predominantly of the 18th and early 19th cent. These have been built up around the collection formed by Sarah Sophia Banks, given in 1818 (with other ephemera collections now in the British Library Department of Printed Books); this collection, of material mainly after 1775, into which some material from Franks and other acquisitions has been incorporated, includes over 5,000 English and 4,000 foreign visiting cards; 3,000 admission tickets, and 6,000 trade cards, shopbills, etc. A collection of trade cards and similar material bequeathed by Sir Ambrose Heal (1872–1959) is kept separate; this contains *c*9,000 items, mainly of 1740–1800, but with some late 17th and early 18th cent items, and some miscellaneous printed material.

Typescript alphabetical subject index to portfolios containing ephemera.

Ms inventories by place and trade for tradecards and shopbills in Banks and Heal collections, with index of names.

Slip indexes (separate for British and foreign) to names on visiting cards; shopbills, and admission tickets.

Books of Reference (Departmental Library) (Except for a small collection of catalogues in the Students' Room. Not directly accessible, but specific works can be made available to readers in Students' Room.)

*c*17,000 v of catalogues and histories of Western art and artists, including many early and rare works. A major collection of auction catalogues from the 17th cent onwards, including many not available elsewhere.

All monographs are entered under authors in the Book Index.

Unique copies of sale catalogues recorded in F Lugt, *Repértoire.*

C **Private departmental libraries**

The departmental working libraries are open only to staff, and to students of antiquities who are working on the collections with the sanction of the Keeper of the department; individual items not held elsewhere can, however, be made available to registered readers of the British Library Reference Division, Department of Printed Books (subject to at least 24 hours' notice). General enquiries about locating books in the collections should be addressed to the Librarian of the British Museum Central Library.

There are probably over 100,000 v in the working libraries of the department. Though runs of journals and modern monographs predominate, there are many rare books in most departments, sometimes including incunabula; the older books are not always related to the present interests of the department. There are particularly strong collections in nearly all departments of British and foreign catalogues of collections and of sale catalogues, including many early and rare items, and many not in the British Library. The rare books among the departmental collections mainly are derived from two sources, the library of the former Department of Antiquities, which was divided in 1860 between the Department of Coins and Medals, and the Department of Greek and Roman Antiquities, the two departments which now are richest in early printed books; and the bequest of Henry Christy (1810–65) the banker and ethnologist to his friend Sir Augustus Franks of several thousand volumes, including incunabula and much other rare material; Franks gave it to the British Museum as a staff library (originally intended as a lending library), and it was subsequently divided among the libraries of individual antiquities departments. A major beneficiary was the Department of British and Medieval Antiquities; in 1969 this was split into the Department of Prehistoric and Romano-British Antiquities (taking a third of its library) and the Department of Medieval and Later Antiquities (taking the remainder). The latter library includes many rare books from 1494 to the present century, on special subjects, especially jewellery, scientific instruments, horology, arms and armour, heraldry, seals, sculpture, glassware and ceramics; with some general books on the archaeology, topography and travels of particular countries of Europe. The other major department was that of Oriental Antiquities, from 1886 renamed the Department of Egyptian and Assyrian Antiquities, into which was incorporated the library of Percy Edward Newberry (1869–1949), head of the Archaeological Survey of Egypt; in 1955 this was divided into the Department of Oriental Antiquities, which has a small library, and the Department of Ethnography, which took the major share, now merged in the Museum of Mankind Library (see following paragraph).

Author index on cards or slips of each department's collection.

Sale cats recorded in F Lugt, *Répertoire des catalogues de ventes publique. . .*, 1938–64, 3 v.

D Department of Ethnography. Museum of Mankind Library

6 Burlington Gardens, London W1X 2EX. Tel (01) 437 2224 Ext 69. Open Mon-Fri 10 am-4.45 pm for bona fide research, on application to the librarian. Photocopier; microfilm reader.

In 1976 the staff library (*c*15,000 v) of the Department of Ethnography, known as the Museum of Mankind, was amalgamated with that of the Royal Anthropological Institute (*c*60,000 v) to form a public collection, now over 100,000 books and 1,000 periodicals.

General The library covers anthropology in a very broad sense, including subjects such as social anthropology and primitive art; it includes the archaeology of Central and Latin America, Oceania and Africa (but not of Europe or Asia); and linguistics of these last areas. The pre-1900 books form a segregated collection.

Card cat, author and classified.

Card cat of serials.

Royal Anthropological Institute Library The Royal Anthropological Institute (chartered 1907) was formed in 1871 as the Anthropological Institute of London (founded 1863) and the Ethnological Society of London (founded 1842 as an offshoot of the Aborigines Protection Society founded 1837). The library of the Ethnological Society, which formed the greater part of the merged library, included complete runs of virtually all British and foreign anthropological journals from 1843 or earlier, and these were later supplemented by numerous periodicals in related areas of knowledge, especially before 1914. The library received numerous donations, of which the most notable were the libraries of Prof Charles Gavriel Seligman (1873–1940) given in 1945 by his widow; and that of Sir (John) Eric (Sidney) Thompson (1898–1975), *c*1,000 items, on Maya archaeology.

Partial subject index to holdings provided by *London Bibliography of the Social Sciences, v 1-4 and First Supplement, 1931–4.*

L Mair, 'The Royal Anthropological Institute Library', *TLS* 6, July 1973, p788.

G W Sooching, 'What's in a name? The origins of the Royal Anthropological Institute (1837–71)', *Man* 6 (1971), p369-90.

Department of Ethnology Library The library was built up around the large ethnological portion of the Christy Library (see C above), which was mostly pre-1851, and contained probably *c*200 pre-1801 items.

Burton Library of the Royal Anthropological Institute Though housed in the Museum of Mankind, this collection is not the property of the British Museum, and it may be consulted only with the written permission of the Trustees of the Burton Library (c/o the Royal Anthropological Institute, 56 Queen Anne Street, London W1M 9LA); one month's notice is required.

In 1898 the personal library of Sir Richard Burton (1821–90), who was a founder of the Ethnological Society was divided; a portion (mostly books which he had given to Lady Burton) was given to Camberwell Public Library (now in the London Borough of Richmond Public Library, qv); but the bulk of his collection at Trieste when he died was given to Kensington Public Library, who transferred them in trust to the Institute in 1955. It comprises over 2,000 v, including 110 books and pamphlets by Burton, and 13 by Lady Burton. The remainder are mostly books and pamphlets of the mid-19th cent, with a few earlier, and 44 periodical runs, mainly on anthropology and travel, with others on related subjects such as religion and medicine. Many of the items are annotated by Burton, or contain his insertions.

B J Kirkpatrick, *A catalogue of the Library of Sir Richard Burton, KCMG held by the Royal Anthropological Institute*, London, the Institute, 1978, classified, with notes on the annotations.

N M Penzer, *An annotated bibliography of Sir Richard Francis Burton, KCMG*, London, 1923; notes copies in the collection, and describes it on p291-8.

British Museum (Natural History), Department of Library Services, Cromwell Road, South Kensington, London SW7 5BD. Tel (01) 589 6323. Open Mon-Sat 10 am-4.30 pm (restricted service on Sat) to bona fide research workers (apply to librarian for reader's ticket). Photocopying and photography; microform and slide viewers and projectors. Typing facilities. Bibliographic assistance.

The natural history departments of the British Museum, but not the main library collections on natural history, moved from Bloomsbury to South Kensington in 1881.

Small departmental libraries had been built up in the years preceding the move, and to these was added in 1881 a general library whose librarian had general oversight of the departmental libraries. The first librarian, Bernard Barham Woodward (1853–1930), later assisted by Charles Davies Sherborn (1861–1942), vigorously built up the collections by purchase, donation and exchange into a library of world renown. Stock now totals *c*750,000 v including 21 incunabula and those in the Zoological Museum (for which see under Hertfordshire, Tring). In addition to printed books, pamphlets and periodicals, all the libraries have important collections of mss and drawings.

Catalogue of the books, manuscripts, maps and drawings in the library of the British Museum (Natural History), 1903–15. 5 v (authors). *Supplement*, 1922–40, 3 v, (all repr 1964, Wheldon and Wesley). Continued on cards (of which microfilm to *c*1977 can be purchased).

The history of the collections contained in the Natural History departments of the British Museum, London, 1904, v 1, p3-76.

F C Sawyer, *A short history of the libraries and list of manuscripts and original drawings in the British Museum (Natural History)*, 1971.

Bulletin of the British Museum (Natural History), Historical series 4(2) (1971), p77-204.

R Irwin and R Staveley eds. *The libraries of London*, 2nd ed 1961, p31-47.

F Sawyer, 'The Library of the British Museum (Natural History)', *Bull of the Circle of State Librarians* 17 (3) (1969), p35-8.

A E Gunther, *The founders of science at the British Museum 1753–1900*, Halesworth, Halesworth Press, 1980.

Peter Whitehead, *The British Museum (Natural History)*, London, Summerfield, 1981.

J R Norman, *Squire: memories of Charles Davies Sherborn*, 1944, p93-116.

Natural history manuscript resources..., London, Mansell, 1980, p152-89.

A General Library

Special book collection contains *c*2,500 v of books and pamphlets (in addition to periodicals) on general natural history, travel, and exploration, of which there are 11 incunabula, including works by Bartholomaeus Anglicus, Pliny the Elder, and editions of *Hortus sanitatis* (others in Botany Library); 230 pre-1701 items (of which *c*60 are English) and *c*2,200 1701–1800.

Serials A large proportion of the *c*18,000 titles in the libraries are held in the General Library, including runs of most early scientific journals and institutional publications of academies from their foundations in the 17th and 18th cent.

List of serial publications in the British Museum, Natural History, 2nd ed, 1975.

Linnaeus, Carl (1707–78), the Swedish naturalist: a large special collection of works by and about him. (See also under D.)

A catalogue of the works of Linnaeus and...relating thereto...in the libraries of the British Museum (Bloomsbury) and the British Museum (Natural History), 2nd ed 1933. (*Index to authors...* 1936).

Sowerby There are major collections of mss of James Sowerby (1757–1822), James de Carle Sowerby (1787–1871), George Brettingham Sowerby (1788–1854), and William Sowerby (1827–1906). Though their own collections of books were not acquired, almost all their published works are held, and the mss shed important light on their bibliographical history.

'Papers on the Sowerby family', *Journ Soc for the Bibliography of Nat Hist* 6(6) (1964), p373-568, including description of the mss and bibliography.

R J Clevely, 'The Sowerbys and their publications in the light of manuscript material in the British Museum (Natural History)', *ibid* 7 (1976), p343-68.

A de C Sowerby, *The Sowerby saga*, Washington, 1952.

Ray Desmond, *Dictionary of...botanists*, 1977, p574-5.

Dictionary of scientific biography, 1975, v 12, p552-3.

Sloane, Sir Hans MD FRS (1660–1753), founder of the British Museum. His natural history collections (with their ms catalogues) were transferred from Bloomsbury in 1880–1 together with his annotated copy of his *Voyage* and Ray's *Historia Plantarum* which were in use in the Herbarium; also some of his books annotated by James Petiver (*d*1718), eg Rumph *D'Amboinische Rariteit-kamer.*

Owen, Sir Richard (1804–92), Superintendent of the Natural History Departments. His mss and annotated copies, mainly of zoological works were donated in 1915 by his daughter-in-law Mrs Emily Owen.

Natural history manuscript resources, no 229, 134.

B Mineralogy Library

Special Book Collection contains *c*600 v, in addition to periodicals, on crystallography, mineralogy, gemmology, meteorites, mining and early chemistry; 50 items are pre-1701 and 290 of 1701–1800. A collection of rare works on mineralogy was donated in 1965 by Sir Arthur Russell (1878–1964).

W Campbell Smith, *Early mineralogy in Great Britain and Ireland*, 1978 (*Bull of the British Museum (Natural History)*. Historical series 6 (1978), p49-64).

Murray Library A separate collection formed by Sir John Murray (1841–1914), naturalist of the Challenger expedition 1873–6, donated in 1921 by his son J L Murray. Contains works on zoology and oceanography, including 1,500 pamphlets, mss and printed books relating to the voyage of HMS Challenger.

C Palaeontology Library

The former Department of Geology and Palaeontology

has been renamed the Department of Palaeontology. The Library includes a collection of 897 books formed by Thomas Davidson (1817–85) the palaeontologist, on brachiopoda, given by W Davidson; and 226 geological pamphlets bequeathed by John Morris (1810–86).

Rare book collection is representative of early works on geology, palaeontology, and related subjects, and contains *c*1,600 pre-1830 books and tracts.

William Smith (1769–1839) is represented by his published books, maps and sections, and also by copies of the Smith mss at Oxford.

D Botany Library

A comprehensive collection on botany and related subjects.

Special book collection comprises *c*3,000 v pre-1801, in addition to periodicals, and includes 9 incunabula (including works by Aggregator, Barbarus Apuleius, Hermolaus Barbarus, Emilius Macer, and Yuhanna Ibn Sarapion).

Linnaeus, Carl (1708–78), Swedish naturalist. Special collection *c*400 v of botanical works by and about him. (See under A *supra*.)

Banksian collection Published works relating to Sir Joseph Banks (1743–1820), with mss, drawings and engravings relating to the Cook voyages and the Flinders voyage. The printed books from Banks's collection remained at Bloomsbury after 1881, with the exception of some annotated copies transferred with his herbarium; but microfilms of those in the British Library are held, together with microfilm collections elsewhere relating to Banks, collected as part of an international bio-bibliographical project based at the Museum.

Natural history manuscript resources no 229.13.

J Dryander, *Catalogus bibliothecae historico-naturalis Josephi Banks*, Londini, 1798–1800. 5 v.

Ray Desmond, *Dictionary of... botanists*, 1977, p35-6.

Miers, John FRS (1789–1879), engineer and botanist: 68 works from his library annotated in relation to his herbarium, given by J W Miers in 1879–80.

Journal of Botany ns 9 (1880), p33-6.

E Zoology Library

Special Book Collection 2,500 pre-1850 works in addition to periodicals covering the whole field of zoology (except entomology which is at Tring), including the early classics of zoology, travels, and anatomical and physiological treatises. One incunabulum (Pliny, 1469). The library includes many works donated by John Edward Gray (1800–75), Keeper of the Department.

Tweddale collection, formed by Arthur Hay, 9th Marquis of Tweddale (1824–78), and donated by his nephew Capt Robert George Wardlaw-Ramsay (1852–1921), in 1887. It contains 2,560 v, mostly ornithological, of books and *c*200 pamphlets, including many standard natural history works of the 18th and 19th cent and reports of some important voyages and expeditions.

F Entomology Library

The Library was formed when the department was split from the Department of Zoology in 1935. It covers entomology and related subjects, eg agriculture, including almost all works of importance to the subject. The Special Book Collection contains *c*2,000 pre-1851 books. Several large collections have been acquired, as follows:

Alexander Fary (1821–1905), bequeathed 611 v on coleoptera.

Thomas de Grey Walsingham, 6th Baron (1843–1919) donated over 1,000 v of books and periodicals with his collection of microlepidoptera in 1911.

Sir George Francis Hampson (1860–1936), 10th Bart, donated his collection in 1921.

Lionel Walter Rothschild (1868–1937) bequeathed his collection to the Zoological Museum (see under Hertfordshire, Tring); the entomological portion was then transferred to the Entomology Library.

British Optical Association Foundation Library, British College of Ophthalmic Opticians, 10 Knaresborough Place, Earls Court, London SW5 0TG. Tel (01) 373 7765. Open Mon-Fri to non-members by appointment with the librarian. Photocopying available.

The British Optical Association was founded in 1895, the Library in 1901 when it began to acquire rare books by purchase and by gift. In 1980 the Association was merged with several other bodies not possessing libraries into the British College of Ophthalmic Opticians, but the library has retained the name of the former association. The Library is a general historically biased collection covering the anatomy, physiology and diseases of the eye and their treatment, optics, optical instruments and spectacles. Altogether there are 11,000 v, including 375 pre-1851 items; 2 STC; 20 Wing; 20 foreign 16th cent and 61 17th cent. The library also houses the Keith Clifford Hall collection of the Contact Lens Society.

Card cat (authors).

Published cat in three author sequences: British Optical Association, *Library and Museum catalogue*, 1932; *Library catalogue*, v 2, 1935; v 3, 1957.

British Telecommunications, Telecom Technology Showcase, Study Centre Library, Baynard House, 135 Queen Victoria Street, London EC4V 4AT. Tel (01) 248 7444. Telex 8956163. Open Mon-Thurs 10 am-4.30 pm on prior application to the Curator. Photocopying facilities.

The Telecom Technology Showcase was opened in 1982

to exhibit part of the historical collections of British Telecom formerly at the Post office (London Region) Telecommunications Museum and at its Research Centre at Dollis Hill, though most of the historical printed material from the latter has been transferred to the library of the new British Telecom Research Centre at Martlesham; some of the printed material is on loan from the Post Office Archives Library. There are *c*200 v, together with printed ephemera, photographs, films etc which include the 19th cent textbooks of telegraphy, with some French material on pneumatic tube delivery in addition, and early works on wireless telegraphy.

Typescript shelflist of 6 broad subject sequences arranged chronologically. Catalogue being compiled for computerization via MDA object cards. Telecom Technology Showcase, *Souvenir brochure*, 1982 (75p).

B Fox, 'Telecom Technology Showcase', *New Scientist*, 13 May 1982, p448.

British Theatre Association Library, 9 Fitzroy Square, London W1P 6AE. Tel (01) 387 2666. Open to members only (not August) Mon-Fri 10 am-5 pm (Wed 7.30 pm); membership is open to all at a modest subscription on application to the Administrator.

The Association was founded in 1919 as the British Drama League, and became the British Theatre Association in 1972. The library was founded in 1920 when Miss Annie E F Horniman (1860–1937) gave her collection of mss and plays, including prompt copies from the Gaiety Theatre, Manchester. The library now contains over 250,000 v of plays (including multiple sets) and books on all aspects of the theatre. The vast majority are 20th cent editions, but there are a limited number of books of earlier centuries, especially 18th and 19th, received as donations. Also runs of theatre periodicals. The library of Gordon Craig (1872–1966) formerly deposited, was sold to the Bibliothèque Nationale in Paris.

Card cat.

The players' guide: being a catalogue of plays in the library of the British Drama League, 1925.

The players' library and bibliography of the theatre, 1930–4.

The players' library: the catalogue of the Library of the British Drama League, 1950, and supplements 1951, 1954, 1956.

Archer Collection William Archer (1856–1924), the drama critic, bequeathed his library, over 1,500 v of books and plays (including many French and Scandinavian) together with an extensive collection of programmes and cuttings, to the library of the national theatre, if any such library was to be set up within a reasonable time, or failing that, to the British Drama League, which accepted the collection on deposit, and now considers itself to be the owner.

Bromley Public Libraries, Local Studies Library, Central Library, High Street, Bromley, Kent BR1 1EX. Tel (01) 460 9955 Ext 261 or 262. Telex 896712. Open (on 2nd floor, above Reference Library), Tues and Thurs 9.30 am-8 pm; Wed and Fri 6 pm; Sat 5 pm. Microfilm and fiche readers; xerox copying facilities.

Branch local studies collections in branch reference libraries at The Priory, Church Hill, Orpington BR6 0HH. Tel (0689) 31551; Beckenham Road, Beckenham BR3 4PE. Tel (01) 650 7292; 206D Anerley Road, Anerley, London SE20 8TH. Tel (01) 778 7457. These are closed Thurs; evening opening varies.

General Borough archives and printed local history collections include those from the former Metropolitan Boroughs of Bromley and Beckenham, and the Urban Districts of Orpington, Penge and the Chislehurst portion of the UD of Chislehurst and Sidcup. Printed collections on the whole county of Kent. The Central Local Studies Collection contains *c*8,000 books and pamphlets, of which *c*150 are pre-1851, including a few Wing and *c*35 ESTC. Some books and volumes of cuttings from the bequest of William Baxter (*d*1934) were incorporated (his mss remain separate, with other ms collections). Also *c*50 pre-1851 books on English topography in the adjacent Reference Library. The branch collection at Orpington, *c*2,500 books and pamphlets, includes the Harlow Bequest on the former County of Kent, received in 1960 on condition that it should remain in Orpington; 259 books on Kent generally (including *c*30 pre-1851) and some local. Branch collections at Beckenham, *c*2,100 books and pamphlets on Beckenham and Kent, and Anerley, *c*1,000 also contain some pre-1851 books.

Card cat (dictionary) including branches, but not yet the Harlow bequest.

Typescript lists of collection at Beckenham; books on Kent in Harlow bequest; 18th cent books in Central Library (Local Studies and Reference Library).

Local locations given in Brian Burch, *A bibliography of. . . Bromley, Hayes and Keston*, Bromley Public Library, 1964 (but many early works have been acquired subsequently).

V Whibley, 'A bibliography of Orpington' (FLA thesis, 1972); and Library Assoc London and Home Counties Branch, *Kent bibliography*, 1977.

H Alderton, 'Baxter bequest', *Library Assoc Record* (4th ser) 2 (1935), p108-10.

H G Wells Collection Over 1,600 items (the world's most comprehensive collection) by, and on, Herbert George Wells (1866–1946) built up since 1952. The collection of Thomas Jeeves Horder, Lord Horder MD (1871–1955), was bought in 1958. Almost all the first editions are included; photocopies of scripts of Wells's broadcasts; some autograph letters; all known university theses on Wells.

Card cat (including *c*300 items not in printed cat).

A H Watkins, *The catalogue of the H G Wells collection in the Bromley Public Libraries*, 1974; interleaved copy kept up to date; includes articles, cuttings, ephemera and photos not in card cat.

Microfilm held of cat of Univ of Illinois collection of letters.

De la Mare Collection c300 v by and on Walter de la Mare (1873–1956) the poet, built up mainly since 1968. Many first editions and some mss are included; also photocopies of scripts of his broadcasts.

Card cat.

National Book League, *Walter de la Mare: a checklist...*, 1956 (annotated copy).

Crystal Palace Collection (the portion containing illustrations and some books, mostly duplicates, is at Anerley Branch Library), includes books, pamphlets, catalogues, advertisements, ephemera, maps, illustrations etc relating to the Crystal Palace, strongest for the period 1854–60, following the opening at Penge; also catalogues and other material on the Great Exhibition in Hyde Park 1851, and part of the collection of Alan Warwick, purchased recently (see also London Borough of Lambeth, Minet Library). There is a chronological archive mounted in 2 v of the correspondence of Samuel Leigh Sotheby (1805–61) of Woodlands, Norwood, a director of the Crystal Palace Company, and well known as an auctioneer; this includes also polemical pamphlets for and against the directors, and miscellaneous ephemera, with some numbers of the journals specializing in the company's affairs; the archive passed to his auctioneering partner John Wilkinson (1803–94) and later to the Hodgson auctioneering family of Bickley, who gave it to the library c1950.

In main card cat.

Brompton Oratory see under Oratory Library

Brooks's, 60 St James's Street, London SW1A 1LN. Library open only to members and their guests; enquiries to Hon Librarian.

The club was founded in 1764 as Almack's by William Almack (*d*1781), in Pall Mall, moving to its present premises designed by Henry Holland in 1778. In 1975 it absorbed the St James's Club founded c1870. It is now, as originally, non-political, but in the 19th and early 20th cent it was a fortress of Whigs and Liberals.

Before 1880 there was no formal 'library', only a collection of reference books that included Johnson's *Dictionary*, a set of the *Racing Calendar* (recently sold), and some other guides to the turf. A room was then set apart as a members' library, but the collection has been reduced by sales of books to members and others. It now contains c10,000 v, chiefly memoirs of politicians and other public figures, beginning with some early 19th cent editions of Edmund Burke (1727–97) who was a member. The Society of Dilettanti now has its headquarters at Brooks's where its collection of pictures by Reynolds and others hang; the portraits of individual society members 1741–7 be George Knapton grace the library, but the Society's own book collection is deposited at the Society of Antiquaries (qv).

Typescript author cat.

Henry S Eeles and Earl Spencer, *Brooks's 1764–1964*, London Country Life, 1964.

Memorials of Brook's..., 1907.

Anthony Lejeune, *The gentleman's clubs of London*, London, Macdonald, 1979, p64-71.

Ralph Nevill, *London clubs*, London, 1911, p99-128.

H Thorogood, 'London clubs and their libraries', *Library Review* 13 (1951–2), p232-8.

Brunel University Library, Kingston Lane, Uxbridge, Middlesex UB8 3PH. Tel (0895) 37188.

The library does not at present possess any rare book collections. A collection on the history of railways in Great Britian, now the private property of Mr Charles Ralph Clinker of Padstow, consisting of c4,000 books from 1734 onwards, with sets of periodicals, timetables, company publications, official documents, maps and photographs, particularly strong on the Great Western Railway (including part of the private collection of its Chairman, Sir Felix Pole) will in due course be made available to the public at this library under the terms of a deed already executed. Enquiries about the collection should be addressed to the librarian.

Buddhist Society Library, 58 Eccleston Square, London SW1V 1PH. Tel (01) 834 5858. Open Mon-Sat 2-6 pm to members, and to others who have made an appointment in advance.

The Buddhist Lodge was founded in 1924 at the instigation of Christmas Humphreys (still (1982) its President), and was until 1926 a branch of the Theosophical Society; it became the Buddhist Society in 1943. At the beginning, a lending library on the practice of Buddhism, it has by now been built up to c6,000 v. From c1930, periodicals and scarce material were acquired to form a reference collection, now c500 v, in addition to archives (including those of an earlier society, the Buddhist Society of Great Britain and Ireland from its foundation in 1907 to 1914). There are only 2 pre-1851 books (Ogilby *Asia* 1673, 3 v, and Sam Turner *Embassy to the court of Teshoo Lama in Tibet* 1800), but several rare modern books on Buddhism. There are complete runs of virtually all the Buddhist periodicals in English, including the very scarce *Buddhist Lodge Monthly Bulletin* 1925–6 with its successors, and *Eastern Buddhist* (Kyoto 1921–39).

Christmas Humphreys, *One hundred treasures of the Buddhist Society*, 1964, p21-6.

Building Societies Association, Information Officer's Library, 14 Park Street, London W1Y 4AL. Tel (01) 491 3388. Open Mon-Fri 9 am-5 pm

by appointment with the Information Officer. Photocopying facilities.

The Association was founded in 1869. The library comprises a portion of the Archives recently separated into a working collection for the Information Officer, books, journals and reports; over 50 v being of historical interest; 19th cent books on building society practice, and controversial works such as J E Bowkett, *The Bane and the Antidote or good and bad associations*, London, 1850; and over 20 histories, mostly privately printed after 1940, of individual societies. Periodicals from 1872.

Burke's Peerage Ltd, 56 Walton Street, Brompton, London SW3 1RB. Tel (01) 584 8134/1106. Open Mon-Fri 9.30 am-5.30 pm on written application to the Editorial Assistant. Photocopying available.

A collection of editorial copies of some (but by no means all) of the genealogical and heraldic works published by the firm, begun 1826 by John Burke (1787—1848), and continued by his son Sir John Bernard Burke (1814—92), Ulster King and Arms, and others. *c*150 v, including over 20 pre-1851 in the publisher's cloth (but not necessarily in good condition).

R Pinches, 'A bibliography of Burkes's, in *Burke's family index*, 1976, pxiii-xxx.

Burke's Peerage Incomplete set from 1st ed 1826, including 9 pre-1850. Some of the early editions include Burke's *Armorial bearings*, (engraved plates), 1839 and 1842 eds with second chromolithograph title pages. Other Burke publications include eg *Landed Gentry* 1863 and later; *Heraldic Illustrations*, 1844; *Orders of Knighthood*, 1858 (with chromolithograph plates).

Business Archives Council Library, Denmark House, 15 Tooley Street, Bermondsey, London SE1 2PN. Tel (01) 407 6110. Open Mon-Fri 10 am-5 pm on written letter of application to the librarian. Photocopying facilities.

The library contains *c*1,000 books and 1,000 pamphlets given since the Council's formation in 1934 by members, authors of business histories, and firms.

Card cat (classified, with index of names of firms, but not of authors).

Accession in *Business Archives* to June 1974, later in Business Archives Council *Newsletter*.

Annual Report includes section on the library.

Business histories Histories of companies, mostly British, a few US and of industries, with some biographies of businessmen, and related economic history. Many are privately printed, but none pre-1851. Strongest for banking, insurance, shipping, engineering, publishing, printing and textile manufacturing.

Pamphlets and brochures Many short histories of firms produced as publicity material, eg *A history of Henry Sotheran and Co*, 1936.

Early works on business practice A collection of mostly 19th cent works with a few 18th cent, eg Nemnich, *Comptoir lexicon*, 1733; Oldenburg, *Calculation of foreign exchange*, 1734; *Practical Merchant's Journal*, 1857—61.

Camberwell School of Arts and Crafts Library, 45-65 Peckham Road, London SE5 8UF. Tel (01) 703 0987 Ext 239. Open to members of the school Mon-Fri (not in vac) 9.30 am-7 pm (Fri 6.30 pm); to others only on prior written application to the librarian.

The College, now administered by the Inner London Education Authority, was opened by the London County Council in 1898. Its library which contains a general collection on art and design, mostly post-1900, totals *c*25,000 v, including a collection on printing. There are, however, some earlier works, especially botanical, notably Gerard *Herbal* (1633), Gesner *Historiae animalium* (1617—20), and Curtis's *Botanical Magazine* (1793—1801) and his *Flora Londinensis* (1798).

Card cat.

Crane Collection Begun in 1964 with *c*20 books by Walter Crane (1845—1915), the book illustrator, and by Lewis Foreman Day (1845—1910), given by Day's niece Mrs Mary Ormerod, then a governor of the School, who had known Crane and acquired a number of his 'toybooks'. The collection has been enlarged to *c*130 items, of which *c*90 are illustrated by Crane, *c*15 are about Crane and his work, and *c*25 of Crane's writings on politics and art, and books by Lewis F Day.

Camden Public Libraries.
The libraries were formed by the amalgamation, in 1965, of those of the former Metropolitan Boroughs of Hampstead, Holborn and St Pancras.

A Swiss Cottage Library

88 Avenue Road, London NW3 3HA. Tel (01) 278 4444. Telex 23909. Open Mon-Fri 9.30 am-8 pm; Sat 5 pm. Photocopying, carrels.

Reference Library General Collection The stock totals *c*51,000 v, including 29 of the 16th cent, 133 of the 17th, 430 of the 18th cent and 771 of the first half of the 19th cent, and 9 later noteworthy first editions. There are 50 STC and 112 Wing items. The library of Prof Henry Morley (1822—94), the populariser of literature, was bought by the Vestry to form the nucleus of Hampstead Public Library on its opening in 1896. It long remained a separate collection, containing early and later editions of standard literary authors, mainly English, but with some continental, and a few oriental; later it was merged in the general stock (though some books are now in the

Philosophy or other special collections). Early and rare works were also given by many other donors, especially on English typography and art. There are several unique items: 3 Elzevir, 1 Plantin, 1 Aldus.

Card cat (author and classified) to 1980; microfiche for later acquisitions.

Typescript lists of pre-1701, 1701–1800 and 1801–50 imprints.

Hampstead Public Libraries, *Author catalogue of the works in the Reference Department at the Central Library*, 1903 (Morley books marked M before classmark).

Beattie Collection (In Reference Library). The works of William Beattie MD (1793–1875) who practised medicine in Hampstead, moving among literary circles, and who wrote memoirs, travel books and poems. *c*200 items, printed and ms, acquired by Henry Morley. It is not clear whether all the books are from Beattie's own collection.

Separate card cat.

Special Collections Department Subject collections acquired under the Metropolitan Special Collections Scheme 1948–75, incorporating some books acquired earlier, and with a few later additions. The Philosophy Special Collection, *c*1,000 items, includes many early printed books from the Morley and other donations. The Agriculture/Horticulture/Domestic Science collection, with *c*1,500 items, includes numerous 19th cent cookery books.

Partly in Reference Library classified and author card cat; partly in Lending Library microfiche cat.

Eleanor Farjeon Collection (In Children's Library). A collection of her own works given by the Hampstead children's writer Eleanor Farjeon (1881–1965) in 1960, with later donations from her. *c*120 items, many containing her ms inscriptions.

A handlist of the collection of her works presented by Miss Eleanor Farjeon to the Hampstead Public Libraries, 1960.

The Book of Hampstead, 1960, p165.

Local Studies Library The local history collections formerly belonging to the Boroughs of Hampstead and St Pancras (that of Holborn is not yet (1982) transferred here). Includes some early printed items.

Incomplete card cat (classified; alphabetical subject and author).

Beginning in local history in Camden, 1972 (op), including bibliography and list of special collections.

Local history collections, 1981 (guidesheet).

Heal Collection A special collection within the Local Studies Library, given to St Pancras Public Library in 1913 by Sir Ambrose Heal FSA (1872–1959), furniture designer of Heal and Son of Tottenham Court Road. Printed ephemera on St Pancras, especially illustrations, posters, playbills and other theatrical material, pamphlets, etc; a few books of the 18th and 19th cent. Includes 21 works by George Whitefield (1714–70), Minister of the Methodist Chapel in Tottenham Court Road.

Separate dictionary cat.

The lost theatres of St Pancras: an exhibition of playbills and other material...from the Heal collection..., 1958.

B **Holborn Library**

32 Theobalds Road, London WC1X 8PA. Tel (01) 405 2706. Open Mon-Thurs 9.30 am-8 pm; Fri 6 pm; Sat 5 pm. Special collections by appointment only. Photocopiers, carrels.

General Reference Library This constitutes the residue of the reference stock of the former Metropolitan Borough of Holborn, after most of the older material has been transferred to St Pancras. *c*36,000 v with *c*50 pre-1851 items on various subjects, especially London.

Card cat (author and classified, for books catalogued before 1965, and 1965–79, microfiche thereafter).

Local History Collection Covers the former Metropolitan Borough of Holborn. Includes all parish histories, many histories of London, directories from 1804, playbills, and at least 50 local Acts.

Card cat (classified) from 1978 onwards.

Alphabetical subject cat pre-1978 with additional indexes for playbills, portraits, prints, streets, residents, maps and general information.

Children's Library Special Collection A collection misleadingly known as 'Early children's books', of *c*300 items, of which 1 is of 1777, *c*25 of 1801–80, the remainder are later classics of children's literature, mostly 1881–1937, especially boys' adventure writers, many in first editions in the publishers' binding, usually in fair or good condition. There are other similar books, but usually in less good condition in the general children's library of *c*5,000 v and a Children's Library staff collection containing a very comprehensive collection of works on the bibliography of children's books.

Author card cat, separately, of special, general and bibliographical collections.

Cat of illustrators which includes in one sequence all the children's books and books with noted illustrators in the other departments of Holborn Library.

C **St Pancras Reference Library**

100 Euston Road, London NW1 2AJ. Tel (01) 278 4444 Ext 2484. Open Mon-Fri 9.30 am-8 pm; Sat 5 pm. Photocopier, carrels.

The library contains the general reference collections of the former Metropolitan Borough of St Pancras, with much of the older stock formerly at Holborn, and a few books formerly at Hampstead. Total now *c*50,000 v, of which 1,740 v are pre-1851, including 3 STC; 6 Wing; 101 ESTC; and 330 items of 1801–50. The collection is strong in historical subjects and geography, travel and topography (almost equally divided between England and foreign countries, but all are English books); 25 post-1800 limited editions, and 4 private press books.

Handlists of pre-1801 and 1801–50 books may be consulted on request.

Card cat (author and classified) for all books catalogued 1965–80, continued on microfiche.

Earlier author cat may be seen on request.

D **Keats House**

Wentworth Place, Keats Grove, Hampstead, London NW3 2RR. Tel (01) 435 2062. House and permanent exhibition open to the public Mon-Sat 10 am-1 pm, 2-6 pm; Sun 2-5 pm. Library strictly by appointment only (not Sun). Photocopying.

Keats House, originally named Wentworth Place, is a public memorial to John Keats (1795–1821) the poet. It was built 1815–16 by his friends Dilke and Brown as a semi-detached pair of cottages, which became the centre of their literary circle; Keats lived here 1818–20, and Fanny Brawne 1819–29. It contains a permanent exhibition of Keats' memorabilia, and the Keats Memorial Library, with other rare books. It was bought in 1921 with money raised jointly by Amy Lowell (1874–1925) the Boston poetess, and the Keats House Committee sponsored by the Mayor of Hampstead; it was then given to the Borough of Hampstead, and opened in 1925. It now also serves as the headquarters of the Keats-Shelley Memorial Association, which bought, in 1906, and still maintains (with a library of *c*9,000 v) the house at 26 Piazza di Spagna in Rome where Keats died.

Keats House, Hampstead: a guide, 8th ed 1980; earlier eds, with varying titles, contain much additional information: 1st, 1926; 2nd, 1934; 3rd, 1939; 4th, 1953; 5th, 1963; 6th, 1966; 7th, 1974; 2nd-6th include cat of the changing exhibition of books and documents.

Keats House Committee, *The John Keats memorial volume*, London, 1921, pv-ix.

Catalogue of books and manuscripts at the Keats-Shelley Memorial House in Rome, Boston, G K Hall, 1969.

H Adshead, 'Keats House', *CLS Bulletin* (Charles Lamb Society) no 137 (July 1957), p165.

Keats Memorial Library (general) A Keats collection built up in Hampstead Public Library was greatly enlarged by the Dilke bequest in 1911. Large donations followed the purchase and opening of Wentworth Place, and in 1931 when a branch library was built in its grounds, the Keats collections were transferred there and became the Keats Memorial Library. The library has subsequently been built up by donation and purchasing, and most of the collection was moved into Wentworth Place in 1975. Now *c*8,000 books and pamphlets, including many association copies, relating to Keats and his circle, especially Leigh Hunt, Lamb, Shelley, Byron, Coleridge and Wordsworth; 200 v of periodicals; with ephemera, cuttings and illustrations. Donated collections have not (except as indicated below) been kept separate. Microfilms are held of the unique material acquired up to 1957 at Harvard (including the Houghton and Amy Lowell collections) and at Rome.

Card cat (authors) incomplete; new cat (authors and classified) being compiled, with index of provenances from currently available information (accessions register is incomplete).

Editions of Keats Nearly all published editions 1829 to date, including some not in the British Library.

J R MacGillivray, *Keats: a bibliography...*, Toronto, 1949.

Keats-Shelley Association of America, *Keats-Shelley Journ*, includes current bibliography 1952 to date.

Keats's Library 12 books of the 81 found in his chest, and divided by Brown himself and Keats's friends, are now in Keats House.

Frank N Owings, *The Keats Library*, Hampstead, Keats-Shelley Memorial Assoc (1978), items nos 3, 10, 12, 14, 17, 19, 21, 22 in the Dilke Collection; also 4, 7, 15, 16.

Dilke Collection Charles Westworth Dilke (1789–1864), the official of the Navy Pay Office and literary editor who befriended Keats in 1817 and introduced him to Fanny Brawne, was the financial adviser to the family after his death, and acquired a mass of books and documents relating to his affairs. These were inherited by his son Sir Charles (Wentworth) Dilke, 1st Bt MP (1810–69), founder of the *Gardener's Chronicle* and Commissioner of the 1851 and 1862 Exhibitions, and in turn by his son Sir Charles (Westworth) Dilke, 2nd Bt MP for Chelsea (1843–1911). The latter, after destroying Keatsiana 'by the bushel', deposited a select portion in Chelsea Public Library on its foundation in 1891. By his will this collection was bequeathed to Hampstead Public Library and became the core of the Keats Memorial Library. It includes 10 of Keats's own books, including school books with his notes, and inscribed gift copies of his poems; and the 1806 Shakespeare *Poetical Works* which he gave to Reynolds after copying out his sonnet 'Bright Star' into it on his last voyage to Rome.

Illustrated handbook to the Dilke Collection of Keats relics preserved at the Central Public Library, Hampstead (1911); includes annotated list (earlier list in *The Library* 3 (26) (1891), p59-60; another printed by Chelsea Public Library, 1906.

The Keats letters, papers and other relics forming the Dilke bequest in the Hampstead Public Library reproduced in 58 collotype facsimiles, ed with...notes ...by G C Williamson, London 1914 (op).

Charles (Armitage) Brown (1787–1842), school friend of Dilke, and friend of Keats from 1817, who was responsible for publishing some poems in the *New Monthly Magazine* and *Plymouth and Devonport Weekly Journal*, acquired a large collection of Keatsiana. On emigrating to New Zealand with his son Carlino (1820–1901) he gave most of the books and papers, with a ms memoir by himself, to Richard Monckton Milnes, later Baron Houghton (1809–85), for use in his *Life, letters and literary remains of John Keats* (1848); (these are now in the Houghton Library at Harvard). He retained his books not directly associated with Keats and a few mementos of him; Carlino's daughter Mrs Mona M Osborne (*d*1951) gave many of these in 1931, and bequeathed the remainder by her will. These include *c*90 books in which Brown, or members of his family, had inscribed their names, and Hunt's presentation set to Brown of the *Indicator* (1819–21) which he edited, with Hunt's ms comments and Brown's inscription.

Leigh (James Henry) Hunt (1784–1859), Brown's friend, Keats's propagandist and first biographer: part of his collection was given in 1931 by Mrs L E Hunt, widow of Leigh Hunt's grandson. Material on his son Thornton (Leigh) Hunt (1810–73) was given by W B Lawrence. These two gifts form a separate collection. Other material relating to Hunt, Brown and Keats was given in 1925 by Luther Albertus Brewer (1858–1933) the collector (whose main Hunt collection was bequeathed to the University of Iowa). Material that had belonged to the Hunt family physician, George Bird, who attended Keats, was given by Miss Alice Bird.

Fanny Brawne (1800–65), daughter of Mrs Samuel Brawne (widowed 1809), sister of Samuel (1804–28) and Margaret (1809–87) married to João Antonio Pereira, Chevalier da Cunha (1802–83). In 1833 she married Louis Lindo, afterwards Lindon (1812–72), and a mass of relics and family papers passed to their children Herbert Valentin (afterwards Brawne-Lindon) (1838–1909), Edmund Vernon (1834–77), and Margaret Emily Walworth (1844–1907) (who sold her portion including Keats's letters, to Fanny). Mrs Oswald Ellis (1883–1973) daughter of Herbert Brawne-Lindon, gave a substantial collection to Keats House in 1925.

Mrs O Ellis, *Sphere* 16 May 1925, p137, 190.

Ms history of the family at Keats House (by C E Baker).

Joanna Richardson, *Fanny Brawne* (1952), p140-52.

Keats family The library has letters kept by Keats's brothers George (1797–1841) and Tom (1799–1818), the latter with presentation copies of books from the Dilke collection. Their sister Fanny (Frances Mary, 1803–89) became a close friend of Fanny Brawne, and in 1826 married Keats's former acquaintance Valentin Maria Llanos y Gutierrez (1796?–1885), a Spanish diplomat and minor novelist. In 1833 she took a mass of Keats memorabilia with her possessions to Spain, but later gave Milnes access to them. The letters Keats wrote to her were in 1889 given to the British Museum, but the rest were divided among her children Juan (1831–1905), Rosa (1832–1905), and Isabel (1839–1926) who married Leopold Count Brockmann (*d*1888). Rosa's inheritance (which included many of the books) was surreptitiously acquired by the collector Fred Holland Day (1864–1933) of Boston publishers Copeland and Day; a portion, which in addition to some books included Fanny Brawne's letters to Fanny Keats, was given by Day on his deathbed, behind an elaborate veil of anonymity, and received at Keats House in 1934. Isabel's inheritance was divided among her children Ernesto Brockmann (1865?–1928), Elena Brockmann (1866?–1946), Enrique Brockmann (*d* after 1937) and Marguerite Brockmann. Elena and Enrique gave some items to Keats House in 1935 as did Marguerite's son Dr Ernesto Paradinas y Brockmann later, though much of their inheritance was sold (mostly to Harvard).

M Adami, *Fanny Keats*, London, 1937, esp p226-67; additions and corrections by H E Rollins in *PMLA* 59 (1,1) (1944), p200-11.

H E Rollins and S M Parrish, *Keats and the Bostonians*, Cambridge (Mass), Harvard UP, 1951, p37-54.

Charles Cowden Clarke (1787–1877), headmaster of Keats's school at Enfield, and literary influence on him, author of *Recollections of Keats*, successor to the publishing firm of John and Leigh Hunt, married Mary Victoria Novello (1809–98) daughter and biographer of the music publisher Vincent Novello (1781–1861) who was well known in the Keats circle. Their library and papers, used in Milnes's biography, were partly dispersed, some being acquired by Forman (see below), whence they have reached Keats House (others are at the Brotherton Library).

Benjamin Robert Haydon (1786–1846), the painter, was introduced to Keats by Cowden Clarke; his friend James Elmes (1782–1862) editor of the *Annals of the Fine Arts* (1816–20) printed Keats sonnets. Some items from his collection held.

Autobiographical *Life* ed Tom Taylor, 2nd ed 1853; *Correspondence*, 1876.

The Reynolds-Leigh-Taylor Circle James Rice (1792–1832), when convalescing at Salcombe in 1814, met William Leigh's daughters Mary (*b c*1793), Sarah, later Mrs Smith (1795–1845), and Thomasine, later Mrs Carslake (1796–1883), and their cousin Maria Pearse. Rice introduced his later solicitor partner John Hamilton Reynolds (1794–1864) the minor poet (Hood's brother-in-law), and the Rev Benjamin Bailey to the family circle. In 1816 Reynolds met Keats, and introduced him to Rice, Bailey and Brown, and also to the partners who were to publish Keats from 1817, John Taylor (1781–1864) and James Augustus Hessey (1785–1870). In 1931–2 Thomasine Leigh's granddaughters Miss Annie Leigh Browne (*c*1936) and Thomasine Mary, Lady (Norman) Lockyer, who had inherited from the three Leigh sisters, gave to Keats House a collection known as the Leigh Browne-Lockyer collection; it consists of 19 commonplace books containing literary compositions by members of the circle, various mss and letters, and 15 inscribed gift copies of printed books by Reynolds and others. Other material relating to Reynolds, Rice and Bailey came in the bequest of R H Bath. Some Taylor items came from Miss Olive Taylor, and from Edmund Blunden.

P Kaufman, 'The Leigh Browne collection', *Library* (5th ser) 17(3) (1962), p246-50.

Joseph Severn (1793–1879), the artist who accompanied Keats on his last voyage to Rome and became Consul there, had numerous Keatsiana which were divided among his several children. Some items from his son Arthur (1841–1931) were donated to Keats House, though almost his whole library and papers were dispersed 1930–1 (mainly by auction). His twin sister Eleanor, friend of Fanny Keats and wife of the Rev Henry Furneaux (1829–1900), gave some items, as did her daughter Margaret, wife of F E Smith, Lord Birkenhead. Other relatives who have given books and mss include Rayner Storr (*d*1917) of Hampstead, husband of Joseph Severn's niece, and his children Severn Storr (*d*1933) and Mary Lady (Stanley) Unwin.

Sheila Countess of Birkenhead, *Illustrious friends*, London 1965, p379-83.

Charles Lamb (1775–1834), essayist and poet, first met Keats in 1817, but his Keatsiana were dispersed with his library, mostly in America. In 1934 Edmund Blunden (1896–1974) the poet, critic, and biographer of Lamb gave a collection of 994 v, mostly on Lamb, which was long known as 'Lamb Corner', and is still kept separate.

Sir Sidney Colvin (1845–1927), Slade Professor at Cambridge, and Keeper of Prints and Drawings at the British Museum, who published Keats's letters in 1887, bequeathed the material used in preparing his biography *John Keats* (1917).

Harry Buxton Forman (1842–1917) CB, postal official and literary editor who was a major collector of Keatsiana, and who caused a storm in 1878 by publishing Keats's letters to Fanny Brawne, left a mass of Keats material to his son Maurice Buxton Forman (1900–57), who was also a Keats scholar. Much of his library was sold in New York in 1920, and at Sotheby's 4 May and 27 July 1936 (and later). In 1945 Maurice gave to Keats House *c*2,500 v on Keats, some of which were placed in Keats's own bookcases. (There were later sales of Forman collections, eg Sotheby 10 April 1972.)

Poetry Library A general collection of English poetry of all periods was donated *c*1930 by Robert Henry Hobart Cust (son of Robert Needham Cust); this included some rare Byroniana. This has been developed into a collection of the romantic poets. Additions include the R H Bath bequest, with many first editions, especially of Shelley (also some books owned by Shelley).

Literary criticism *c*6,000 v on Keats, Shelley, Byron, Leigh Hunt, Coleridge, Lamb, Wordsworth, Southey and Clare; and on the Romantic period generally.

Potter Collection A very comprehensive collection in 20 v 1815–1924 of reviews, articles, newscuttings and illustrations of the writers of the first half of the 19th cent especially Keats, Shelley, Hunt, Coleridge, Byron, Wordsworth and Hazlitt. Given in 1924 by Ambrose George Potter of 126 Adelaide Road, Hampstead, the bibliographer of Omar Khayyam. The collection had probably been formed by the Potter family from the beginning. A G Potter's father, George Potter (1837–1927), well known as a bibliographer, print-collector, and grangerizer, lived at Highgate and was the son of William Potter (1812–86) a shoemaker there who came from Hornsey, and who was said to have been an acquaintance of Coleridge.

Periodicals *c*200 v mainly 19th cent, containing first appearances of some poems, and articles on the Romantic poets.

Kate Greenaway Collection A collection of the work of Kate Greenaway (1846–1901) the illustrator of children's books who lived in Frognal, Hampstead, given to Hampstead Public Library in 1926 by her brother John Greenaway; now *c*1,100 items. The collection of books illustrated by her was complete from 1878 onwards, and many earlier books have subsequently been added. *c*90 original drawings, with all stages of printed proofs. A wide variety of ephemeral illustration, including alphabets, almanacs and calendars, birthday books, valentine and other cards.

Card cat being compiled.

Handbook to the Kate Greenaway collection, Hampstead Public Library (1930) is a narrative of her life and work with a few reproductions from the collection.

Bolton Museum and Art Gallery, Kate Greenaway exhibition cat lists many items from the collection.

R K Engen, *Kate Greenaway*, Macdonald (1981) (including chronological list).

Canning House Library, Hispanic and Luso-Brazilian Council, Canning House, 2 Belgrave Square, London SW1X 8PJ. Tel (01) 236 2303. Open Mon-Fri 9.30 am-5.30 pm to the public. Photocopier.

The Hispanic Council and the Luso-Brazilian Council (now amalgamated), were founded in 1943 as charitable trusts to foster cultural and commercial relations with, and to provide information on, the countries of the world where Spanish and Portuguese are spoken. A number of collections were donated in 1947 to launch the library. The collections of monographs, which are mainly after 1870, have been built up systematically to *c*45,000 v on subjects relating to the culture and commerce of Spain, Portugal, Latin America and the Caribbean. The periodicals collection has been reduced to *c*12 sets.

Card cat (author and classified), also published (see below).

I V Cohnen, 'Die Bibliothek des Hispanic and Luso-Brazilian Council', *Zeitschrift für Bibliothekswesen und Bibliographie*, 20(6) (1973), p470-4.

Luso-Brazilian Library *c*7,500 v on Brazilian and Portuguese subjects, including 600 deposited by the Anglo-Brazilian Society. Mostly in Portuguese, including perhaps 100 pre-1851.

Canning House Library. Luso-Brazilian Council... Author catalogue A-Z and subject catalogue A-Z,

Boston, Mass, G K Hall, 1967; *First supplement*, 1973. Continued on cards.

Hispanic Library c38,000 v (including the special collections below) on Spanish and Spanish-American subjects, mostly in Spanish, including perhaps 500 pre-1851.

Canning House Library. Hispanic Council. Author catalogue and *Subject catalogue*, Boston, Mass, G K Hall, 1967, 4 v (including Hudson Library); *First supplement*, 1973. Continued on cards.

Hudson Library c5,000 v on Argentina, Paraguay and Uruguay, collected by Sir Eugen (John Henry Vanderstegen) Millington-Drake (1889–1972) and donated to form the nucleus of a Hudson Institute which was incorporated in Canning House in 1947. Included is a collection of 66 editions of the writings of William Henry Hudson (1841–1922), the naturalist, in addition to works about him; and c50 editions of works relating to Robert Bontine Cunninghame Graham (1852–1936), the adventurer.

Canning Collection c50 editions of works by and about George Canning (1770–1827), Foreign Secretary and Prime Minister, after whom the library is named.

Dictionaries Collection c250 Spanish and Portuguese dictionaries, from 1763 onwards, but mainly of the 20th cent.

Portuguese and Spanish dictionaries in the Canning House Library, 1971.

Cardiothoracic Institute, Thoracic Library, Brompton Hospital, Fulham Road, Brompton, London SW3 6HP. Tel (01) 352 8121 Ext 4189. Open Mon-Fri 9.30 am-5.30 pm to staff of the Institute and associated hospitals, and to others by special arrangement with the librarian.

The Institute of Diseases of the Chest was founded in 1949 as a postgraduate school of the University of London attached to the Brompton Hospital, and its Library opened in 1950, taking over a few books already at the Hospital. In 1973 it became part of the Cardiothoracic Institute of the University, but the Cardiac Library remains distinct; the London Chest Hospital is now included with the Brompton, which was established in 1841 by Sir Philip Rose (1816–83) as the Hospital for Consumption and Diseases of the Chest. The Library contains a collection of letters to Dr Marcus (Sinclair) Paterson (1870–1932), first Superintendent of the Brompton Hospital Sanatorium at Frimley.

Card cat (authors and subjects chronologically sub-arranged), including all except Peacock collection.

P J Bishop and B G B Lucas, *The seven ages of the Brompton*, London (1982).

M Davidson and F G Rouvray, *The Brompton Hospital*, London, Lloyd-Luke, (1954) p134-7.

R M Nicholas, 'The development of medical libraries within the University of London' (MA Librarianship thesis, Univ of London 1976), p112-21.

P J Bishop, 'The Marcus Paterson collection', *Tubercle* 48(1) (1967), p63-74, *Bull of the Library of the Inst of Diseases of the Chest* 6(4), (1965), p6-10.

Historical Collection c500 v on chest medicine and surgery, including tuberculosis, 17th cent onwards, mainly donated by members of the medical staff of the Brompton.

Peacock, Thomas Bevill (1812–82), founder of the London Chest Hospital, and President of the Pathological Society. A collection of 318 v that remain of his library (deposited on loan by the London Chest Hospital in 1959, and probably to be returned there in 1983); 154 monographs in 203 v; 78 pamphlets and reprinted articles in 8 v; 107 v of journals. Subject content mainly on thoracic and general medicine, including scarce works on malformations of the heart; influenza, and climate. They are mostly early and mid-19th cent, with a few ESTC.

Card cat (authors).

P J Bishop, 'Thomas Bevill Peacock's Library', *Circulation* 38 (1968), p1011-3.

——'Thomas Bevill Peacock...collection', *Bull of the Library of the Inst of Diseases of the Chest*, 5(2) (1960), p6-14.

See also I H Porter in *Medical History* 6 (1962), p240-54.

Laënnec, Rene Theophile Hyacinthe (1781–1826). A collection of c50 editions and translations of his *De l'auscultation mediate.*

An exhibition...relating to R T H Laënnec..., 1972.

Tudor Edwards, Arthur (1890–1946), Surgeon at the Brompton: his collection of c50 v, mainly early works on thoracic surgery.

Young, Sir Robert (Arthur) (1871–1959), Physician at the Brompton; his collection of books and reprints, with early stethoscopes.

P J Bishop, 'Some of Sir Robert Young's books from the Library', *Bull of the Library of the Inst of Diseases of the Chest*, 5(1) (1960), p7. Obit in *BMJ* 1959 (2).

Brompton Collection Books by the staff of the Brompton, c100 v 19th and 20th cent.

Periodicals c15,000 v, mostly specialist journals in thoracic and related aspects of medicine, from the mid-19th cent onwards, including some scarce foreign titles.

List 2nd ed 1966 (now somewhat outdated).

Carlyle's House, 24 Cheyne Row, London SW3 5HL. Tel (01) 352 7087. House open to the public at times varying with the season. Library open only by prior arrangement with the National Trust Libraries Adviser, 42 Queen Anne's Gate, London SW1H 9AS. Tel (01) 222 9251.

The house of Thomas Carlyle (1795–1881), the historian

and essayist, bought in 1895 by public subscription through the Carlyle House Memorial Trust, and opened as a public museum, with a portion of his library; transferred in 1936 to the National Trust. Carlyle bequeathed much of his library to Harvard, the rest to his niece Mary Carlyle Aitken, whence it passed to his nephew Alexander Carlyle. A portion was sold (Sotheby 13–14 June 1932), another portion bequeathed by him to Carlyle's House (now in the care of the National Trust) where it had previously been deposited. Some books were removed to Ecclefechan (qv), the residue, *c*500 v (half foreign), mostly 18th-19th cent (with a few 17th cent) remain at Chelsea, chiefly historical and reference books.

Selective cat printed (several undated editions) as *Carlyle's House: catalogue* [1896], and later undated editions; also included in *Illustrated memorial volume of the Carlyle's House Purchase Fund,* [1897] and later eds; 5th ed entitled *Carlyle's House: illustrated descriptive catalogue*; 6th ed [1914] entitled *Carlyle's House: illustrated catalogue...*; another ed 1937, 2nd ed 1954 entitled *Carlyle's House, Chelsea: illustrated guide, The National Trust guide*, 2nd ed, 1977, p70-1.

R L Tarr, 'Thomas Carlyle's libraries at Chelsea and Ecclefechan', *Studies in Bibliography*, 27 (1974), p249-65 (inc cat).

Catholic Central Library, 47 Francis Street, London SW1P 1QR. Tel (01) 834 6128. Open Mon-Fri 10.30 am-6.30 pm; Sat 4.30 pm (not bank holiday weekends), to subscribers, and to the public for reference; those wishing to use rare books should write in advance to the Administrator for an appointment. Photocopying facilities.

In 1912 William Reed Lewis, a former US Consul in Morocco, who lived at Bexhill-on-Sea in Sussex, established the Bexhill Library, a free lending library in the porch of the Roman Catholic Church there, transferring it to his house in 1916, and offering a widely advertised postal loan service. In 1922 the Catholic Truth Society bought the collection for a nominal sum and re-established it in London as a subscription library, and in 1926 renamed it the Catholic Truth Society Lending Library. It received a number of bequests, and from these and other donations a substantial rare books collection was built up. At the end of 1936, when closure was threatened and the collections were already being moved, it was saved by the intervention of the Hon Mrs Henrietta Bower and the Associations of the Old Girls of the Sacred Heart Convents; in 1938 it was renamed the Catholic Central Library, and the CTS transferred ownership of the stock to the Catholic Central Library trustees in 1940. In 1959, when closure was again suggested, it was re-established by the Society of the Atonement, a community of Franciscan Friars of Graymoor (NY), formerly Episcopalian, who had become Roman Catholic in 1909. The Society now works for ecumenical understanding.

Herbert Keldany, 'London's Catholic Central Library', *Ecumenical Trends* (Graymoor Ecumenical Institute, Garrison, NY) 10(11) (Dec 1981), p174-6.

Henrietta Bower, 'Notes on the beginnings of the Catholic Central Library', (typescript), (1959?).

C Collingwood, *The Catholic Truth Society*, London, The Society, (1955), p8-9.

The General Library The library, of *c*60,000 v, comprises the Subscription Lending Library, which is a contemporary and historical collection on the theology of all major Christian denominations, ecumenism, the Bible, ecclesiastical history, biography and liturgy; a Reference Library of *c*2,500 v of denominational encyclopaedias, and standard reference works on biblical studies, church history and theology, with periodical runs; and the collections of older material described in the following paragraphs.

Card cat (dictionary) includes all parts of the library (pamphlets in a separate sequence) except some rare books not yet catalogued.

There is some analytical indexing, and for modern official documents in a separate Documentation Index.

Classified cat accessible on request.

Catalogues were printed previous to 1922, and again in 1922 by Catholic Truth Society, with supplement 1924, but no printed cats have been found in the library.

Quarterly list of new acquisitions now issued.

Reserve Collection This is a general collection of post-1800 editions of theology in all its aspects, including works mainly by Roman Catholic authors, but also of many by Anglicans and others; ecumenism; church history, especially the recusant and penal periods of English Catholic history; and biography, with a special collection of Cardinal John Henry Newman (1801–90). Miscellaneous works by well-known Catholic authors.

Closed Library Almost exclusively pre-1851, the library comprises over 500 v, English and foreign, mostly of the 17th and 18th cent. It is partly a remnant from the rare-book collections of the Catholic Truth Society, supplemented by a collection from the former St Joseph's Lending Library, South Street (later Farm Street), and donations from Westminster Cathedral. There are over 500 bound tracts in 50 v of the 18th and 19th cent, mostly relating to English Catholic history and related controversies.

There is a collection of over 50 reports of trials of Catholics and others in the late 17th and early 18th cent, especially those connected with Titus Oates and the 'Popish Plot'.

Serials Collection This includes the *Catholic Directory* and its predecessor the *Laity's Directory* from 1759 (with some unauthorized editions), and the *Ordo recitandi*; many of these are annotated copies; also *c*300 sets of theological journals from early 19th cent onwards.

A select list of journals, 1981.

19th cent Catholic and Laity's directories analytically indexed in pamphlet cat.

Pamphlets These include 111 boxes of general

pamphlets; also 149 v of Catholic Truth Society pamphlets, with its Catholic biographies and other publications, a virtually complete set from the Society's foundation in 1884.

Central School of Art and Design Library, Southampton Row, London WC1B 4AP. Tel (01) 405 1825 Ext 39. Open Mon-Fri 10 am-7 pm (Fri 5.30 pm) by appointment after written application to the librarian. Photocopier and audiovisual equipment available.

The school was founded in 1896 as the Central School of Arts and Crafts, and became the Central School of Art and Design in 1970. It is administered by the Inner London Education Authority for advanced instruction in ceramics, textiles, industrial design, jewellery, theatre design and graphics and fine art. The library has *c*25,000 v on these and related subjects, and incorporates a special collection of fine printing and illustrated books, 15th cent onwards.

Charing Cross Hospital Medical School Library, Reynolds Building, St Dunstan's Road, Hammersmith, London W6 8RP. Tel (01) 748 2040. Open Mon-Fri 9 am-9 pm (6 pm in Summer vac); Sat (except in Summer vac) 9 am-12 noon, to staff and students of the Hospital and Medical School, and to others by arrangement with the librarian. Photocopier; fiche reader available.

The Hospital was founded in 1815 as the West London Infirmary, becoming the Charing Cross Hospital in 1827. The Medical School, founded 1822, is now an undergraduate school of the University of London. The Library was established in 1835, and received a large collection from Dr Benjamin Golding (1793–1862). Other collections were received from William Shearman (1767?–1862) and Edwin Canton the surgeon, and many other 19th cent donors. The Library and the archives housed there suffered bomb damage in 1940. *c*8,000 monographs and *c*13,500 v of periodicals.

Card cat (author, subject and chronological).

R J Minney, *The two pillars of Charing Cross*, London, Cassell, 1967, p59.

R M Nicholas, 'The development of medical libraries within the University of London' (MA Librarianship thesis 1976, Univ of London), p61-7.

M I Jellett, 'The Library', *Charing Cross Hospital Gazette*, 52 (1954), p62- .

B Armitage, 'Charing Cross Hospital Medical School Library', *Technical Book Review*, 30 (1964), p16- .

Historical Collection Medical texts of 16th-20th cent, *c*2,000 v, of which *c*200 are pre-1851.

Charing Cross men Collection of their writings, *c*200 v.

Chartered Insurance Institute Library, 20 Aldermanbury, London EC2V 7HY. Tel (01) 606 3835. Open Mon-Fri (in Summer) 9.15 am-5.15 pm (Fri 5 pm); (in Winter) 10 am-6 pm by appointment, after written application to the librarian. Photocopying facilities.

In 1907 the Federation of Insurance Institutes of Great Britain and Ireland (founded 1897) was replaced by the Insurance Institute of Great Britain and Ireland, which in 1912 became the Chartered Insurance Institute. The hall and library were built in 1934, and the rare book collections have been built up by gifts since that date. It has absorbed the older library of the Insurance Institute of London.

H A Cockerell, *Sixty years of the Chartered Insurance Institute, 1897–1957*, 1957.

A Lee, 'The Chartered Insurance Institute Library', *Chartered Insurance Institute Journal*, (Dec 1979), p20-3.

General The library contains over 15,000 v on insurance and related subjects. The general collection includes many histories of insurance companies, including a large number that are privately printed and scarce. Items include rare German works especially of the Nazi period.

Card cat (author and classified) includes rare books collection (rare books have special history facet in the classification).

Rare Books Collection *c*200 v, mainly relating to insurance companies, insurance law and practice, fire fighting, actuarial science, economics, etc, mostly in English, a few in French and 2 Dutch. There are 3 STC and 1 Wing items. Included is a collection donated in 1934 by Sir (Albert) Ernest Bain (1875–1939), insurance broker, comprising 22 books (Babbage, Braidwood, Farren, etc), together with a large collection of firemarks and old insurance policies. Most of the pre-1701 books are on insurance law. There is a substantial collection of prospectuses, charters, bye-laws etc, mainly early 19th cent; some polemical literature, eg *Pernicious effects of sea insurance* Kirkcaldy 1834, and a small collection of the handbooks issued by insurance companies for their agents in the mid-19th cent. The set of the *Insurance Cyclopaedia* compiled by Cornelius Walford (1827–85) 5 v (1871–8) (A-Hon) is accompanied by his unpublished notes for the remainder, and *Index* to the notes by G O Nelli, 1976; also the notes for Walford's unpublished *Cyclopaedia of periodical literature*; but his library was bought by the Equitable Life Assurance Society of New York.

Museum The Institute's museum houses its collection of insurance policies (earliest printed policy is 1732) including at least 300 pre-1851; also the first book on insurance, De Santarem *Tractatus de assecurationibus*, Venice 1552.

Chartered Institution of Building Services, Delta House, 222 Balham High Road, London SW12 9BS. Tel (01) 675 5211. Open Mon-Fri 9 am-5 pm on

written application to the Secretary. Photocopying facilities.

The Institution of Heating and Ventilating Engineers (founded in 1897) and the Illuminating Engineering Society (1909) merged in 1976 to form the Chartered Institution of Building Services.

Archaeology Books c70 v, all but 4 from the library of the IHVE, forming a historical collection, though much of the older material has been dispersed. They include books on lighting, heating and ventilating from 1729 onwards, c10 of which are pre-1851.

Chartered Institute of Transport Library, 80 Portland Place, London W1N 4DP. Tel (01) 580 5216. Open Mon-Fri 10 am-4.30 pm to members; to other bona fide enquirers by prior arrangement with the librarian. Photocopying.

The Institute of Transport was founded in 1919 to promote the study of all branches of transport, especially by means of professional examinations. It was chartered in 196?. The library dates from 1921. The general library is concerned with all forms of transport, but originally was mainly devoted to railways, which still account for about half of the contents. There are long runs of the major periodicals from c1840 onwards. Some of the older material has been transferred to other libraries, especially the University of Leicester, to make space for current material. The stock totals c15,000 v, of which c100 are pre-1851.

Note The Reinohl collection of passenger tickets has been transferred to the London Transport Museum (qv).

Card cat (author and classified).

Accessions in *Chartered Institute of Transport Journ.*

George Ottley, *Railway history: a guide to... collections...,* London, Library Assoc Ref, Special and Information Section, 1973, p33-4.

Chelsea College Library, Manresa Road, Chelsea, London SW3 6LX. Tel (01) 351 2488. Open (Term) Mon-Fri 9 am-9 pm (5 pm Summer vacation, 6 pm other vacations); Sat 9 am-1 pm (term only), on application in writing to the librarian.

General Collection The college was founded in 1891 as the South West London Polytechnic; it became the Chelsea Polytechnic in 1922, Chelsea College of Science and Technology in 1957, and Chelsea College in 1971; in 1966 it became a school of the University of London. c110,000 v of books and c2,000 serials.

Author and classified card cat.

Chelsea College: a history, 1977.

A short guide to Chelsea College Library and specialized guides.

Charles Darwin (1809–82) Collection of books by and about him and his contemporaries bought from Sir Gavin de Beer (1899–1972) and subsequently enlarged, c110 v, including the first six editions of *Origin of species* and first editions of his other works.

Included in general cats.

A G Quinsee, 'The Darwin Collection', *Chelsea College newsletter*, June 1978, p1-3.

Chelsea Old Church, c/o Old Church House, 4 Old Church Street, London SW3 5DQ. Tel (01) 352 5627. Open by prior arrangement with the Vicar on written application.

Chelsea Old Church contains 5 v which were formerly established there and chained by episcopal injunction, but are now in secure storage. They comprise Fox's *Martyrs* 1684, v 1 and 3; the *Homilies*, 1683; *Book of Common Prayer*, 1723; and 'vinegar' *Bible*, 1717.

Typescript cat at Council for the Care of Churches Library.

Chelsea Physic Garden, 66 Royal Hospital Road, Chelsea, London SW3 4HS. Tel (01) 352 5646. Open to bona fide students by appointment only Mon-Fri 9 am-5 pm.

The Garden was founded by the Society of Apothecaries in 1673, and by 1681 they had transferred part of their library (re-established after being destroyed in the Fire) from Blackfriars to the Garden. The collection was greatly augmented by the bequest of the library and herbarium of Ray's friend Dr Samuel Dale (1659–1739); the presses made to receive this library are still in use. James Sherard (1659–1728) also bequeathed a herbarium and library. After further gifts and purchases the library of Isaac Rand (*d*1743), Praefectus Horti, was donated by his executrix. In 1770 all the books on *materia medica* and some others were transferred to Blackfriars, leaving 273 v of botany; in 1832 these too were removed. The Physic Garden then became a separate institution until 1893 controlled by the London Parochial Charities Board, and began to accumulate its own library at the Garden.

In 1953 the Society of Apothecaries transferred 331 books to the Garden; 249 of these were from the original library. The Society then sold the remainder of its library. In 1960 the Society was prevented from selling the books at the Garden after a legal opinion that the Dale bequest could not be considered the Society's property.

The collection is now divided into a rare books collection, containing 373 works, and a modern library. Many of the works are by past Praefecti and curators. 1 incunabulum (*Ortus sanitatis* 1491); 6 STC; 44 Wing; 38 ESTC; 158 pre-1701 foreign. Mainly botany and herbals.

Catalogue of the Library at the Chelsea Physic Garden, 1956.

William Bramley Taylor, *Catalogue of the Library of the Society of Apothecaries... with an introduction* by J E Harting, London 1913; books from Chelsea asterisked.

Chelsea Physic Garden, *Catalogue of books and publications*, 1936.

Early ms catalogues in Society of Apothecaries archives deposited in Guildhall Library, including general cat by S Alchorne, 1769.

Henry Field, *Memoirs of the Botanic Garden at Chelsea...rev...by R H Semple*, London, 1878, p48-9, 63-6, 76-7, 96-7, 118.

The Chelsea Physic Garden (by A P Paterson) (1976), p15-18.

Sholto C J H Douglas, 21st Earl of Morton, *The Chelsea Physic Garden*, 2nd ed, London, R Madley, 1973.

P E F Perredes, *London botanic gardens*, London 1906, p48-99.

W T Stearn, 'The Chelsea Physic Garden' in *Hunt Botanical Library; Catalogue*, Pittsburgh, 1961, 2, pt 1, plxxiii-lxxx.

Other histories of the Society are listed in W F Kahl, *The development of London livery companies*, Boston, 1960, bibliography p36-9.

Chelsea School of Art Library, Manresa Road, Chelsea, London SW3 6LS. Tel (01) 351 3844 Ext 23. Open Tues, Thurs, Fri 9.30 am-5 pm, Mon, Wed 7 pm for reference on application in person with proof of address. Photocopying, videotape viewing, microfilm/fiche readers.

The library, which originated as part of the library of the former Chelsea Polytechnic (founded 1891), now contains *c*38,000 items, mainly after 1850, but within the modern field containing much that is rare or not available in other British libraries.

Card cat (author/title and classified, with alphabetical subject index).

Periodicals listed in ARLIS, *A union list of periodicals on art and related subject fields*, 1978 (new ed due 1982).

Western European art 1850 to the present This collection, which was begun in 1920, but has been built up mainly since 1963 with intensive retrospective purchasing in addition to acquisition of currently published material, contains *c*5,000 books, 9,000 exhibition catalogues and pamphlets, and *c*400 periodical titles, of which 295 are defunct (many of these being very rare). About 40 per cent of the books are foreign works not available in English. Most of the catalogues raisonnés of the artists of this period are held, many of these being very scarce. The most extensive collections of books are on Cezanne (128 items plus periodical articles); Courbet (39); Daumier (48); Degas (61); Gauguin (55); Van Gogh (64); Manet (54); Monet (51); Munch (32); Rodin (50); Brancusi (18); Kandinksy (39); Klee (67); Matisse (90); Picasso (250); and Pollock (21). There is much relatively ephemeral material on younger artists.

United States art c1950 to the present This collection, mainly purchased since 1963 and the only such special collection in British libraries, now contains *c*500 books and *c*1,000 exhibition catalogues. It covers the period of Abstract Expressionism and subsequent movements, with some material on earlier artists who had some bearing on the development of Abstract Expressionism or subsequent movements.

Chemical Society Library, Burlington House, Piccadilly, London W1V 0BN. Tel (01) 734 8871. Telex 268001. Open Mon-Fri 9.30 am-6 pm to bona fide research workers on prior application to the librarian. Photocopying.

The Society was founded in 1841, but the Library became substantial only after moving to Burlington House in 1857. In the early years books were mostly donated by Fellows, of whom Michael Faraday (1791–1867) was especially generous. Systematic purchasing later enriched the collections. The general library contains *c*60,000 v.

F W Clifford, 'The Library of the Chemical Society', *Library World*, Feb 1916, p228-31.

T S Moore and J C Philip, *The Chemical Society 1841–1941*, 1947, esp p11-31.

Chemistry in Britain, Jan 1965.

Chemistry and Industry, 26 Oct 1940, p720.

Periodicals Collection *c*1,600 sets, incl *c*50 beginning before 1851.

Periodicals in the Chemical Society Library, 1960.

Pre-1850 books *c*2,000 in a segregated collection on chemistry of all periods, and alchemy; strong in 18th cent material.

Card cat (author and classified). About half are included in *A catalogue of the Library of the Chemical Society arranged according to subjects* (1886) and *...according to authors* (1903) but these catalogues include dispersed books (mostly non-chemical, transferred to Science Museum).

Roscoe Collection Donated by Sir Henry Enfield Roscoe (1833–1915) President of the Society, Prof of Chemistry at Owen's College. 126 v on alchemy and early chemistry (chiefly 1550–1750), incl a few mss. Several unique items; 65 works by Robert Boyle (1627–91).

Cat in *Proceedings of the Chemical Society* 22 (213) July 1906 (1907), p209-33.

Nathan Collection Formed by Sir Frederick Lewis Nathan (1861–1933), Chief Chemist at the Royal Military College of Science. A special collection on explosives, chiefly in connection with mining and gunnery. A few are pre-1851.

Christian Economic and Social Research Foundation, Research Centre Library, Alliance House, 12 Caxton Street, London SW1H 0QS. Tel (01) 222 5880. Open Mon-Fri 10.30 am-4.15 pm, preferably by appointment. Photocopying facilities.

The Foundation was established in 1953. The archives of the United Kingdom Temperance Alliance Limited (the educational branch of the United Kingdom Alliance) are serviced by the Foundation at the same address. The library is a collection of works on the alcohol problem, purchased or donated from various sources, including some of the historic Temperance Societies (eg the United Kingdom Alliance founded 1853), the remains of the library of the National British Women's Total Abstinence Union, and a collection assembled by Rosalind Frances Howard, Countess of Carlisle (1845–1921), daughter of the 2nd Baron Stanley of Alderley, and President of the World's Women's Christian Temperance Union. Its stock totals *c*2,200 v, including *c*50 pre-1851 items.

Card cat (author/title, and alphabetical subject).

Sources in British political history, v 1, 1975, p255-7.

Books and pamphlets A general collection of temperance literature which includes the publications of the early 19th cent reformers, especially Joseph Livesey (1794–1884), *Lecture on Malt Liquor* (1838). Also *Report of Public Discussion between F R Lees and J Bromley on the Question of Teetotalism* (1840) and *The Physiological Question* (discussion on alcohol between W Jeafferson and Dr F R Lees) 1843, *Essay on Drunkenness* by Thomas Trotter (1804). Some illustrated, eg P Burne *Teetotaller's Companion* (1847); some semi-ephemeral, eg *Pasco's Temperance Almanack* (1839).

Journals Include especially those printed, published or distributed by Livesey, and *The Temperance Doctor* (1836); *Moral Reformer* (1831–8, incomplete). Also *Truth Seeker* (1846–7), edit J R Lees.

Not included in BUCOP.

Ephemera and Memorabilia A collection made up of printed pledges from 1843 onwards, temperance medals, illuminated addresses, Good Templar regalia and memorabilia, lantern slides and George Cruikshank prints.

Christie, Manson and Woods Auction Rooms, 8 King Street, St James's, London SW1Y 6QT. Tel (01) 839 9060. Telex 916429. Admission to archives and library restricted; enquiries must be in writing. Photo-reproduction not normally permitted.

The archives include the only existing complete set of the firm's sale catalogues from its foundation in 1766. There is also an art and bibliographical reference library for the use of the cataloguers. (A collection of other auctioners' catalogues is deposited in the Tate Gallery Library.)

W Roberts, *Memorials of Christie's*, 1897, 2 v.

Church Commissioners, 1 Millbank, London SW1 3JZ. Tel (01) 930 5444. Open Mon-Fri by appointment only.

The Church Commissioners administer the stipendiary finances of the Church of England. They were formed in 1948 by the amalgamation of Queen Anne's Bounty for the Augmentation and Maintenance of the Poor Clergy (established in 1704 to dispose of the revenues previously enjoyed by the Crown through the First Fruits Office), and the Ecclesiastical Commissioners (established in 1836). Most of the early books in the library (part of which consists of collections of individual offices) are derived from Queen Anne's Bounty. *c*2,000 v, including *c*300 pre-1851 (mostly after 1700), mainly official reports, statutes, ecclesiastical law (treatises and reports of cases), finance (esp tithes), cathedrals and topography.

Typed shelflist. Author cat on cards.

A Savidge, *The foundation and early years of Queen Anne's Bounty*, London, SPCK, 1955.

G F A Best, *Temporal pillars*. Cambridge, 1964.

Church House Archives, Dean's Yard, Westminster, London SW1P 3NZ. Tel (01) 222 9011. Open by appointment Mon-Fri 10 am-5 pm.

Church House is the headquarters of the General Synod of the Church of England. The main reference library was dispersed in 1972 (mostly to Lambeth Palace Library, but part of the Julian hymnology collection to the British Library and elsewhere). The departmental working collections contain few rare books. The three minor collections listed here form part of the Archives.

The Central records of the Church of England: a report and survey presented to the Pilgrim and Radcliffe Trustees. London, Church Information Office, 1976.

Convocation of Canterbury *c*25 v remaining from the Library of the Lower House, *c*1701–*c*1890, with a ms cat dated 1898 recording *c*200. Books of ecclesiastical law, and pamphlets attacking Convocation.

Typescript list of the surviving books.

Church Defence Institution, set up in 1858 as the Church Institution, to oppose disestablishment, and amalgamated in 1896 with the Central Church Committee to form the Church Committee for Church Defence and Church Instruction. A remnant of its Library, *c*100 v of printed books, pamphlets and periodicals, *c*1840–*c*1910, mostly its own publications, mainly of ecclesiastical politics.

Typescript list.

Hopkins (Jane) Ellice (1836–1904) social reformer and founder of the White Cross League. 41 of her pamphlets among a collection of 144 pamphlets chiefly on sex education transferred from the Library of the Board for Social Responsibility.

Typescript list.

Church Missionary Society Library, 157 Waterloo Road, London SE1 8UU. Tel (01) 928 8681. Open Mon-Fri 9.30 am-5 pm to those with a suitable letter of introduction.

The Society was founded in 1799 by a group of prominent Anglicans from the Eclectic Society, which had been formed under the influence of the Evangelical Revival. It was originally called the Society for Missions to Africa and the East, but soon became known as the Church Missionary Society, and later extended its operations to Canada and the West Indies. The library dates from 1800, when 13 books were bought 'to assist the Committee in acquiring missionary information', and was built up steadily throughout the 19th cent as a reference library, into which the lending library was incorporated in 1908. The present collection of printed books, *c*20,000, includes *c*15 ESTC and *c*300 of 1801–50, almost exclusively English; these are mostly on the history of missions and the growth of the Church in Africa and Asia, and on other religions, with a few books on travel, languages and history. Part of the collection was dispersed in 1900 (also Hodgson 27 July 1966, lots 280-1, 816-8); the Bible collection has been given to the Bible Society Library. Major-General Edward John Lake (1823–77), editor of the *Church Missionary Record* bequeathed a collection partly consisting of editions of the Puritans, but this is now removed and mainly incorporated into the collections of Lambeth Palace, the Evangelical Library and Sion College. The archives of the Society have recently been deposited in Birmingham University Library.

Card cats.

Some of the pre-1851 books are in new dictionary cat, remainder in old author cat.

Also in subject handlists *Christian missions* (general works only), 1959, and *Languages*, 1961.

J M Woods and R Keen, 'Sources for African studies 14: Church Missionary Society', *Library materials on Africa* 6(3) (March 1969), p86-90.

See also Eugene Stock, *The history of the Church Missionary Society*, London, 1899–1916, 4 v.

City University Library, Northampton Square, London EC1V 0HB. Tel (01) 253 4399. Telex 263896. Open Mon-Fri 9 am-5 pm to members of the University; to others on written application. Photocopying facilities.

The City University was founded as Northampton Polytechnic in 1891, and was Northampton College from 1957 to 1966. The Library is sometimes called the Skinners' Library after the Skinners Company who paid for the building. (The Horology Collection has been transferred to Hackney College: see under London. Hackney.) The History of Advertising Trust collections are independent of the library (see London. Islington, History of Advertising Trust). The general library has over 100,000 books and 1,300 periodicals.

Microfiche cat.

Special Collections Room General rare books collection includes 20 items 1652–1850 on various, mostly scientific, subjects, transferred from the general stock. 4 Wing, 5 ESTC.

Walter Henry Angel Fincham collection on optics donated from his estate. He taught at Northampton Polytechnic 1904–50, and published the standard textbooks on optics in 1934. 61 items, including 28 pre-1851.

The Walter Fincham optics collection, 1977 (catalogue).

London Collection *c*300 items on the history of London, including a few pre-1851.

Rosemary King, *Catalogue of the London collection*, 1976.

London Society Library The library has been collected by the Society since its foundation in 1912, the older material being mainly from members' donations; it was deposited at the City University in 1976. It contains *c*1,000 v and *c*600 pamphlets (in 22 boxes), including 28 pre-1851 items in 68 v. There are 2 Wing items and 11 ESTC. Subjects covered are mainly the history and topography of London and its environs; the earliest book is De Laure *Present State of London*, 1681, but most of the older works are 18th and 19th cent, including many of the standard works on London. Nearly half the collection came from the residue of the library of Dr Philip Norman (1842–1931), of which the rarer part had been sold (Sotheby 28 July 1916 and 9-10 May 1932, much of which went to the Burns collection now in the Greater London History Library); this part was given to the Society by A D Power, and included 4 pre-1851 books and an extra-illustrated Maskell *Collection. . . of all Hallows, Barking* 1864 with bookplates of James Comerford and J Grimshire. Miss M S Crawley of Charlbury bequeathed 60 v, including Wheatley *London* 1891 grangerized by Daniels, and some late 18th cent newspapers; Thomas Harrison gave 170 v from his collection in 1938; Hanslip Fletcher (1874–1955) bequeathed three albums of press cuttings of his published sketches of London (and a few elsewhere).

Card cat 1981, included in City University microfiche cat.

Typescript list of pre-1850 books.

The Journal of the London Society contains notes on the more important library acquisitions (scanty after 1940); collections listed include Norman (part), no 174 (Aug 1932), p116-8; Crawley (part) no 233 (July 1937), p100-1.

Civic Trust Library, 17 Carlton House Terrace, London SW1Y 5AW. Tel (01) 930 0914. Open by appointment with the librarian.

A library of *c*4,000 v on architecture, planning, conservation and environmental studies in the current context.

Amenity Societies A comprehensive collection from 1957 onwards of the publications of *c*1,000 local amenity societies registered with the Trust, including their newsletters, reports, pamphlets and ephemera.

Civil Service Department, Central Management

Library, Room 1/1 CSD, Old Admiralty Building, Whitehall, London SW1 2AZ. Tel (01) 273 5577. Open 10 am-4 pm by appointment on application in advance.

The Department was created in 1969.

Northcote-Trevelyan Collection c1,000 items on the history of the Civil Service, especially the reforms of Sir Stafford Henry Northcote, afterwards 1st Earl of Iddesleigh (1818–1887), and Sir Charles Edward Trevelyan, 1st Bart (1807–1886) in 1853. Includes all major parliamentary reports on the Civil Service from the early 19th cent; *British Imperial Calendar* from 1810; East India College, and Civil Service examination papers; pamphlets and tracts (mostly post-1850, a few earlier).

Clothworkers' Company, Clothworkers' Hall, Dunster Court, Mincing Lane, London EC3R 7AH. Tel (01) 623 7041. Open by appointment with the Clerk.

Though the Clothworkers' Company is of early foundation and 12th in order of precedence of the City livery companies, its collection is small, since most of the library and archives were destroyed by bombing in 1941. The present collection has been built up largely since that date, and contains only a few pre-1851 printed items.

Thomas Girtin, *The golden ram: a narrative history of the Clothworkers' Company, 1528–1958*, 1958.

College of Arms, Queen Victoria Street, London EC4V 4BT. Tel (01) 248 2762.

The College is the corporate body of the Officers of Arms or heralds, who charge fees to applicants for arms and to the public for heraldic and genealogical research. The library is private, and strangers are admitted only under the auspices of a herald. Specific enquiries may be addressed to the Archivist.

The library contains over 30,000 v on heraldry, genealogy and related subjects, including several thousand pre-1851 items; probably few are not in the British Library (except some leaves recorded in STC). Extensive collections of mss.

Card index of books.

Printed cat of mss in preparation.

Catalogue of the Arundel manuscripts, 1829.

A R Wagner, *The records and collections of the College of Arms*, London, Burke, 1952.

Heralds of England: a history of the Office and College of Arms, the College, 1967.

Heralds' commemorative exhibition 1484–1934... catalogue, 1936.

Commonwealth Institute Library, Kensington High Street, London W8 6NQ. Tel (01) 602 3252. Telex 8955822. Open Mon-Sat 10 am-5.30 pm to any member of the public providing proof of identity. Photocopier; microform readers and audiovisual equipment.

The present library of the Commonwealth Institute (successor to the Imperial Institute founded in 1893) dates from 1962; on its establishment it was intended for the training of teachers, but was opened to the public in 1972. It contains over 150,000 v on all aspects of the Commonwealth, and is intended to demonstrate, mainly to the people of the UK, the culture, economies, political and social life and background information on all the 46 Commonwealth countries and their dependencies as they are today. Its coverage of historical material is skeletal, though there is a very small reserved collection of older rare books. Three-quarters of current acquisitions are published overseas, and a high proportion of these (especially in the Literature Collection) are not in any other British library.

Card cat.

Commonwealth Literature Collection c50,000 v, one of the most extensive collections anywhere. It includes all kinds of creative and critical literatures in English, with translations from other languages, and literary magazines from Commonwealth countries.

Checklists on Commonwealth literature (series in progress).

Children's imaginative literature Mainly in English, but some in other languages. There is an unusual collection of children's books from Britain which reflect the present multi-racial society.

Commonwealth Institute of Entomology Library, 56 Queen's Gate, London SW7 5JR.

The library is in the main a post-1914 working scientific library of entomology. Almost all pre-1851 and other rare books have been transferred to the library of the Royal Entomological Society (qv).

Communist Party of Great Britain. Library and Archive, 16 St John Street, Clerkenwell, London EC1M 4AL. Tel (01) 251 4406. Open Mon-Fri 9 am-5 pm by appointment on written application to the librarian. Photocopying facilities.

The Party was founded in 1920 by the merger of several left-wing groups, but no formal library was established until c1947. The archives, including the Party's own publications, show gaps on account of police seizures at certain periods, removal or destruction of material by Party members, and transfers to the Central Archive of the Communist International. The Party is said to own the most comprehensive English collection of Trotskyite publications in existence, but this is not accessible.

Sources in British political history 1900–1951, 1975, v 1, p49-50.

General The Library contains *c*2,000 v of books, *c*2,000 pamphlets, and a serials collection, relating mainly to the history of the Communist Party and of the working class movement. Pamphlets include most of those issued by the Party, and many published by progressive organizations which the Party has supported, and by other socialist parties; 28 boxes arranged roughly by subject, 40 by country, and *c*60 bound v of pamphlets.

James Klugmann (1912–1977), former editor of *Marxism Today* who worked in the Party's Education Dept was an omnivorous collector of older material, and bequeathed his library (contained in 800 large boxes) to the Party. The rarest books were given to the Marx Memorial Library (qv). Much of the vast remainder has been incorporated in the general collections of the Party library, where it is sometimes identifiable by his signature. There is a substantial collection of graphic material called the James Klugmann Picture Library: a portfolio containing loose cartoons, portraits, and a few broadsides on radical politics of the late 18th and early 19th cent. Other material includes a collection of Yugoslav partisan publications collected while he was in British Intelligence, now transferred to the Yugoslav Embassy (qv). Of his art book collection, a few have been retained, the rest sold, as have most of the duplicates of political books. A special collection is being retained of novels, poetry, broadsides, etc by working class authors, some of the 19th cent. Much more is yet unsorted.

19th cent European Revolutions Rare material includes 1 v of prints and ephemera on the 1848 revolution in Austria; a collection of works on the Paris Commune of 1870–1.

Biography A very extensive collection of biographies of radicals, socialists, communists, and labour movement leaders. Though mainly modern, it includes some scarce items; some early 19th cent works; and 2 albums of cuttings on Tom Mann (1856–1941).

Early Socialist and Marxist works A small collection, including pamphlets by William Morris, and some from the foundation of the Soviet State, eg Lenin *Lessons of the Revolution*, 1918.

Serials Mostly Communist Party publications. Also odd volumes and short runs of some 19th cent journals, eg *Leigh Hunt's London Journal* 1834–5, and *Pictorial Times* 1844, and various other political, satirical and humorous publications.

Company of Watermen and Lightermen, Watermen's Hall, 18 St Mary-at-Hill, London EC3R 8EE. Tel (01) 626 3911. Open by appointment after written application to the Clerk.

This company, 91st in order of precedence of the City companies, was founded in 1780 without a livery. The archives include a collection of printed documents issued by the company (deposited at the Guildhall Library Department of Manuscripts).

Watermen's Company Library Contains *c*100 v on London and the Thames, donated by liverymen, including 2 STC; 10 Wing; and 23 ESTC items; a collection of Wing items by John Taylor (1580–1653) the water poet; 300 prints of the Thames.

Card index (author/subject).

Congregational Library, 15 Gordon Square, London WC1H 0AG. Tel (01) 387 3727. Open (not August) Mon, Wed, Fri 10 am-5 pm; Tues, Thurs 6.30 pm, on written application in advance to the librarian. Photocopier; microfilm reader. (Reading room is shared with Dr Williams's Library.)

The Congregational Library was established in 1830–3 as a subscription library in Blomfield Street, EC2, on the initiative of Thomas Wilson (1764–1843) and his son Joshua, for the congregations of Independents who at this time were forming themselves into the Congregational Union in England and Wales. In 1872 it moved to the new Congregational Memorial Hall in Farringdon Street, and was placed under a trust. In 1972 many congregations of the Congregational Church joined with the Presbyterian Church of England to form the United Reformed Church, and the others were divided between the Congregational Federation and the Evangelical Federation of Congregational Churches. In 1978 the Library came under the Congregational Memorial Hall Trust (1978) Ltd, whose trustees are drawn from these three churches. In 1982 it moved into accommodation adjacent to Dr Williams's Library, which provides staffing, and whose readers have access to it. It is still owned by the Trust (2 Fleet Lane, Farringdon Street, London EC4A 4EB Tel (01) 236 2223).

I M Fletcher and J H Taylor, 'Blomfield Street Mission House and Congregational Library', *Trans Congregational Hist Soc*, 19 (1960–4), p256-62.

A Peel, 'The Congregational Library', *Ibid* 12 (1933–6), p340-5.

General The library contains *c*40,000 v of books and periodicals, and *c*30,000 pamphlets, about half being pre-1851, including 24 incunabula (2 unique); also mss. They are predominantly the works of the ministers ejected in 1662, with their associates and Puritan ancestors; works on the history of the free churches; and works written by Congregationalists. The nucleus of *c*4,000 v was given by Joshua Wilson (1795–1874), including many works of great rarity; he bequeathed further collections of 17th cent tracts and miscellaneous Puritan literature. Other donors include Robert Mackenzie Beverley (1798?–1868) who gave *c*200 v, and Sir John Bickerton Williams (1792–1855), *c*90 v. Some books were later dispersed.

Card cat in two sequences, incomplete (authors).

A catalogue of the Congregational Library, Memorial Hall, Farringdon Street, London EC 1895 (authors), supplemented by v 2, 1910, and a duplicated typescript

(A-E only); these exclude the Wilson bequest and the special collections below, except Cooke Library.

Special collections have ms or typescript lists.

Tracts and pamphlets There are probably *c*5,000 pamphlets in bound volumes, mostly of the 16th and 17th cent, and perhaps *c*25,000 unbound in boxes, mostly of the 18th and 19th cent.

Chronological ms lists of two bound series. Others perhaps in card cat.

Foreign books *c*1,600 v of works of the Continental reformers.

Ms list.

Sermons Over 4,000 sermons from *c*1600 onwards.

Ms list.

Hymnals and Sacred Music William Martin Cooke (*d*1892) MD bequeathed *c*200 hymnals and psalters (with and without music) and works on church music, of many Christian denominations from *c*1830 onwards, with a few earlier. In 1930 Harold Reeves gave *c*1,400 v known as the Payne collection of hymn books. There is also a general collection of *c*1,200 hymn books.

Cooke collection listed in *Catalogue* 1895, p347-57.

Separate ms lists of Payne and General collections.

Liturgical Collection 380 v of service books and forms of prayer.

J W Niblock, 'Official forms of prayer for public occasions 1660–1860, with a few earlier and later', *Trans Congregational Hist Soc* 7 (1916–8), p250-4, 326-7, 381-7; 8 (1922-3), p34-7, 144-6, 223-4; 9 (1924–6), p87-93.

Conservative Party. Conservative Research Department Library, 32 Smith Square, London SW1P 3HH. Tel (01) 222 9511. Open by appointment after written letter of application to the librarian, Mon-Fri 10 am-5 pm. Photocopier; microfilm reader available.

The Conservative Research Department was founded in 1929, but some of the books in the library are from the National Union Political Library going back at least to 1894; there are now *c*5,000 v. Most of the 18th and early 19th cent books were dispersed between 1939 and 1950. There is, however, much rare or unique printed material from the mid-19th cent onwards.

Sheaf cat (authors and subjects) separate sequences for books and pamphlets.

Archives (including much printed matrial) described in *Sources in British political history* 1900–51, 1975, p53-73 and G D M Block, 'Conservative Party archives', *Bull Assoc of Contemporary Historians* no 4 (Summer 1972).

——*A source book of conservatism*, London Conservative Party Centre, 1964 (op) is based on the collections in the Library.

Conservative Party The Party's own collection of National Union publications from 1868; election addresses from 1922, 350 v; election posters from 1929; campaign guides and election notes from 1887; *Rules* of the National Union of Conservative and Unionist Associations from its foundation in 1867; *National Union Gleanings*, 1893–1939 (including abstracts of speeches and bibliographies of articles); remarkable miscellaneous material on the Party, including a volume on the 1910 general election; typescript *Examination of Mr Lloyd George's speeches, 1896–1914* (*c*1920?).

Pamphlets 160 boxes containing *c*2,000 political pamphlets, mainly after 1945 but some going back to 1910. Boxed by subject, mostly in fine condition, including 3 issued by Mosley's New Party, many of the Conservative Party, Labour Party, Fabian Society, etc. Many older pamphlets are in bound volumes among the book collection. One of these contains 6 collected by E T Cook (1857–1919) on Tariff Reform, Home Rule, etc 1902–13.

Budget Protest League (1909–10). Pamphlets issued by the League, their Budget Week by Week (28 nos) and 31 of their posters (including two by Hassall).

Electoral history A collection of electoral histories, mostly privately printed or limited editions, including W R Williams, *Parliamentary history of Gloucester*, 1898; Lambeth, 1879; Bristol, 1882; Coventry, 1925. A volume published by T Slack, 1774, reprinting election addresses of candidates in Northumberland with the poll book, and some printed hearings of election petitions from 1895.

Biographies This section of the Library contains a few pre-1851 items, eg Twiss, *Life of Lord Eldon*, 1844 (with bookplate of James Brand). Small collections of the works of Churchill, and of Disraeli, including his *Vindication of the English constitution*, 1835.

Journals Holdings include *The Tory*, 1892–97, and *Ashridge Journal*, 1930–48.

Corporation of London Records Office, PO Box 270, Guildhall, London EC2P 2EJ. Tel (01) 606 3030 Ext 2251. Open (Room 221) Mon-Fri 9.30 am-5 pm.

The office was set up in 1876 to house the official archives of the Corporation of the City of London which had accumulated in the Town Clerk's Office since the Middle Ages. They incorporate thousands of pre-1851 printed documents, mostly, but not invariably of official origin, many unique. (Unofficial collections were transferred *c*1947 to the Guildhall Library.)

Alphabetical subject indexes cover most collections, listing many but not all printed items.

Philip E Jones and R Smith, *A guide to the records in the Corporation of London Records Office and the Guildhall Library Muniment Room*, London, 1951 (op).

Reference Library A small working collection on the administrative history of the City, including general histories from 1559, legal textbooks from 1565 with books on the Courts controlled by the Corporation, and works on the Quo Warranto controversy 1683–90; 2 STC; 13 Wing; 13 ESTC items included.

The Crown and Parliament A collection of 34 Royal proclamations from the 16th cent. Hundreds of Acts, mostly relating to London, from the 16th cent *Mirror of Parliament.*

Mayoral documents A collection of 42 Mayoral proclamations from the 16th cent; miscellaneous documents and ephemera.

Administrative and financial records The records of the Court of Aldermen and the Court of Common Council and its committees, the Chamber of London (responsible for finance), and certain other bodies contain much printed material, some of which is kept separate in a Printed Documents collection. Hundreds of Acts, Bills and Orders of the Court 1611–1850. Reports, mostly post-1700, numerous after 1800; miscellaneous ephemera, eg public notices.

Lists of Acts, Bills and Orders (incomplete).

Shelflist of Printed Documents collection.

Supplementary subject index for most post-1800 printed reports.

Many printed items in committee records not indexed.

Judicial records A collection of the Records of the Sessions (Gaol Delivery to 1834 and Peace) for City of London cases, including printed proceedings of Gaol Delivery for London and Middlesex 1683–1834 (many gaps); printed proceedings of the Central Criminal Court 1838–1913 (with gaps). Records of civic courts, eg Court of Husting and Mayor's Court, including various printed documents.

Notices by printers 1799–1839 delivered to the Clerk of the Peace under 39 Geo III c79 (Seditious Societies Act) are also filed with Sessions records; see W B Todd, *A directory of printers and others in allied trades London and vicinity 1800–1840*, London, Printing Hist Soc, 1972.

Irish Society records The Society, appointed by and from among the members of the Court of Common Council, was constituted by letters patent of 1613 and 1662 for the plantation of Ulster. Its archives, forming part of the Corporation records, include printed documents and a few books, eg *Hibernia Anglicana* 1690, and the Irish *Statutes at large* 1786–1801.

Council for the Care of Churches, Library, All Hallows Church, 83 London Wall, London EC2M 5NA. Tel (01) 638 0971. Open to all, Mon-Fri 9.30 am-5.30 pm, except during meetings (it is therefore advisable to phone in advance).

The Council is a permanent commission of the General Synod of the Church of England responsible for co-ordinating and advising Diocesan Advisory Committees for the Care of Churches and allocating grants. It has a working library on ecclesiology, especially ecclesiastical art and architecture, and church furniture and fittings; also liturgiology, ecclesiastical law, local history and topography and heraldry. It is strong in the ecclesiological movement of the mid-19th cent. It incorporates the collection of the Council's first Secretary, Dr Francis Carolus Eeles (1876–1954) the liturgiologist, and the bequests of G B Gosling (–1944), William Iveson Croome (1891–1967) FSA, Canon Basil Fulford Lowther Clarke (1908–1978), and Canon John Lawrence Cartwright (1889–1978). In the whole collection of *c*12,000 v there are *c*400 pre-1851 printed books, mostly English (incl *c*25 ESTC and a few earlier), and *c*150 pre-1851 v of periodicals; also a large collection of files on parish libraries in England and Wales, which include photocopies of many rare printed or ms catalogues.

Dictionary card cat.

Bulletin of the Association of British Theological and Philosophical Libraries, NS 19 (Nov 1980), p4-5.

Council for World Mission Library

The rare books portion of this library has been transferred on deposit to the Library of the School for Oriental and African Studies (qv).

Courtauld Institute of Art, Book Library, 20 Portman Square, London W1H 0BE. Tel (01) 935 9292 Ext 14. Open (term) Mon-Fri 9.30 am-7 pm; (vacations, not in August) 10 am-6 pm, but closed access material never fetched after 5.30 pm; to higher education staff and students on production of appropriate identification; to others for material not available elsewhere on written application in advance. Photocopying (self-service).

General collections In 1931 Samuel Courtauld (1876–1947), chairman of Courtaulds Ltd and patron of the arts, gave the lease of his house in Portman Square with paintings and an endowment to the University of London to found an institute to teach the history of art for honours degrees. The library has been built up from 1933 by purchase and donation which have included the major collections of rare books (mostly post-1850) of Courtauld himself, of the art critic Roger (Eliot) Fry (1866–1934), and of the statesman and patron Arthur Hamilton Lee, Viscount Lee of Fareham (1868–1947). Rare books, including most pre-1851 and many of more recent date, are now in a closed access collection, which also includes mss. (The Robert Witt collection of illustrations forms a separate library within the Institute.) *c*1,200 v pre-1851; 8 STC; strong in 18th cent, mostly in English, French or Italian. All aspects of the visual arts, especially aesthetics, architecture, catalogues of private collections, topography and guidebooks (recently enriched by the collection of the Institute's late Director, Prof Thomas Sherrer Ross Boase, 1898–1974).

Card cat (author and classified).

On Courtauld *see* D Cooper, *The Courtauld collection...with a memoir...by Anthony Blunt*, London, Athlone, 1954.

Sale catalogues Large collection, including *c*500 pre-1851; some not known to Lugt. Mainly English, with some important continental sales.

Annotated copy of Lugt.

Exhibitions A collection of *c*28,000 catalogues of exhibitions, and pamphlets on related controversies. *c*450 are pre-1851, mostly English and French.

Classified list.

Cricket Society Library, c/o Royal Overseas League, Park Place, St James's Street, London SW1A 1LR. Open to members only.

The Society was founded in 1945 as the Society of Cricket Statisticians, becoming the Cricket Society in 1948, the year of foundation of its library. The collection has been built up by donations and bequests to over 4,000 items, including some scarce books.

Library catalogue, 1978.

State Librarian 28(3) (1980), p36-7.

Journal (1961–).

Croydon Public Libraries. Central Reference Library, Katharine Street, Croydon CR9 1ET. Tel (01) 688 3627. Open Mon 9.30 am-7 pm; Tues-Fri 9.30 am-6 pm; Sat 9 am-5 pm.

The general reference collection includes one incunabulum (Petrus de Palude). The local history collection on Croydon and Surrey (the former county) includes playbills from *c*1830, and a collection of the 19th cent pamphlets on bells issued by Gillett and Johnston, local Bellfounders (usually known as the Tintinnabula Collection).

Card cat.

Cruising Association Library, Ivory House, St Katharine Dock, London E1 9AT. Tel (01) 481 0881. Open to members only.

A collection of over 10,000 v on all aspects of sail cruising, with some general and pre-1851 books on seamanship and voyages from the 16th cent onwards.

The Cruising Association Library catalogue, 1927; 2nd ed 1931; 3rd ed 1954.

Customs and Excise Library, H M Customs and Excise, Kings Beam House, Mark Lane, London EC3R 7HE. Tel (01) 626 1515 Ext 2509. Telex 886231. Open Mon-Fri 8.30 am-5.30 pm by appointment on written application to the librarian. Photocopier; microform reader. Historical research carried out for fees (minimum £10).

Dates from the foundation of the Board of Customs in 1671. In addition to the Printed Library there is an important historical collection of mss on London and the outports.

The Library *c*200,000 books, mostly modern, but there is a historical collection of *c*1,800 v on the history, theory and practice of HM Customs and Excise from the 17th cent onwards, mainly from the re-foundation of the department in 1671. This is very strong in 19th cent material. A complete set of the *Book of rates* include first ed 1550 and 1610 ed (unique in the UK). Some material was lost by war damage.

Card cat (including the rare books).

Graham Smith, *Something to declare: 1000 years of Customs and Excise*, London, Harrap, 1980.

Dorothy Johnstone, *A tax shall be charged*, London HMSO, 1975.

H Hall, *A history of the Customs revenues...*, London, 1885, 2 v.

Bibliographies on Smuggling, Robert Burns, Ports and Shipping, Beer and Whisky, (all available gratis).

Debrett's Peerage Office, 73 Britannia Road, Fulham, London SW6 2JR. Tel (01) 736 6524. Open Mon-Fri 9 am-5 pm by appointment only, after at least seven days' notice to the Editor. Photocopying facilities.

The editorial library comprises *c*300 v of genealogical and biographical reference works.

Debrett Publications The editorial archive of Debrett's own publications. It contains *c*50 v, including 15 pre-1851. It became very incomplete, but many of the gaps have been filled retrospectively. Mostly editions of *Debrett's peerage* from the first published in 1769 as *The new peerage* by R Davis, and continued by John Debrett (*c*1760–1822) whose name appears in the title from 1802. The *Baronetage* (begun 1808) is held from 1864. Other Debrett publications, mainly after 1850.

Other Publications These include similar works by other publishers retained for reference, especially from the collection of P Montagu Smith, a previous Editor; eg Kinber *Baronetage* 1771, and several early 19th cent works, but mainly post-1850, including some scarce items such as Burke's *Order of the British Empire* 1921.

Department of Education and Science Library, Elizabeth House, York Road, London SE1 7PH. Tel (01) 928 9222. Open Mon-Fri 9.30 am-5 pm on prior application to the librarian.

General A very large library on all aspects of education has been built up from a nucleus formed in 1854 for an exhibition by the Society of Arts. In 1857 the Department of Science and Art of the Committee of Council on Education took over most of the collection and put it on display as a permanent exhibition in the South Kensington Museum, but in 1867 they transformed it into a working library, which was soon much enlarged. In 1876 the Committee's Inspectors' Library was amalgamated with it (their books are designated 'CCEL' in the printed catalogue of 1893). In 1882 obsolete books from the Museum of Practical Geology were added. In 1883 those scientific books which were still of current interest and some of the older ones were segregated into a separate Science Library which has remained at South Kensington (see Science Museum Library). In 1896 the Education Library, then amounting to 6,000 v, was removed to Whitehall where a collection of books had recently been formed, and in 1899 it became the property of the newly created Board of Education, succeeded first by the Ministry of Education, and then by the Department of Education and Science.

Author cat on cards. Published classified cat: *Catalogue of the Educational Division of the South Kensington Museum*, 1st-9th ed, 1857–76; *Catalogue of the Education Library in the South Kensington Museum*, 10th ed, 1893; See also Society of Arts, *Official catalogue of the Educational Exhibition opened in St Martin's Hall July 4, 1854*, 1854.

Ministry of Education Library 1854–1954: Centenary Exhibition, (1954).

G E Butcher, 'The Library of the Department of Education and Science', *Bulletin of the Circle of State Librarians* 18(2) (May 1970), p27-36.

Jack Burkett, *Government...library...services*, London, 1974, p77-81.

Brooke, Rev Richard, of Selby, Yorks, presented his educational collection in 1865. It remained in the Science Museum Library until 1959 when it was transferred to the Ministry of Education. 700 v of textbooks from 1570 to *c*1855, strong in 17th cent, esp primers, grammars, reading and spelling books; also arithmetic and other school subjects, and moral and instructive children's books.

Author cat on cards. Relevant items in Alston. See also *Education in 1959*, London HMSO, 1960 (Cmnd 1088), p101.

Baines Collection Assembled from the nurseries and schoolrooms of the Baines family of Gloucestershire. Donated in 1955 by a Miss Eyre, said to have been a governess, *c*250 v of 18th and 19th cent (150 pre-1851) children's books, mainly schoolbooks and instructive works of fiction and general knowledge; some French.

Author cat on cards. See also *Education in 1956*, London, HMSO, 1957 (Cmnd 23), p65-6.

Textbooks formerly in the general collection, now shelved separately, incl *c*200 pre-1851.

In general author cat.

Pamphlets Three large collections of bound pamphlets on educational and related subjects (nearly all English, provincial publications being very well represented). The original collection begun at the South Kensington Museum called 'Education Miscellanies', 109 v (incl *c*15 ESTC items and *c*120 of 1801–50) includes part of the private collection of Sir Henry Cole (1808–82), the Museum's Director; also a set of volumes on the blind, the deaf and the mentally retarded. Another collection, called 'Tracts on Education', 12 v (incl *c*80 items 1821–50) includes many on peripheral subjects such as husbandry and religion. A third called 'Education Pamphlets' 32 v (incl *c*120 items of 1800–50).

All items are in general author cat. There are separate author and alphabetical subject sheaf cats of 'Education Miscellanies'.

Official Publications section of the library contains complete series of all government reports on education from 1839, and all publications of the Charity Commission from 1819.

Shelved by series. Many not in author cat.

Department of Health and Social Security, Main Library, Alexander Fleming House, Elephant and Castle, London SE1 6BY. Tel (01) 407 5522 Ext 6363. Open Mon-Fri 9 am-5 pm to postgraduate students, or accredited research workers, on written application to the librarian. Microform readers and photocopying facilities.

Founded in 1834 as the library of the Poor Law Commission, it covers history of public health, medical services, and the poor law; including reports of Poor Law Commission 1834–47, Poor Law Board 1848–58, etc. Poor Law pamphlets, 56 vols beginning with 6 Wing items; 44 vols on cholera, 15 on smallpox and 38 on vaccination.

Dictionary card cat.

Departments of Industry and Trade Libraries.

All pre-1851 printed material from these libraries have been dispersed, including the contents of the former Board of Trade Library, parts of which were donated to the Guildhall Library, the British Library Reference Division, and other public collections.

Dickens House Museum and Library, 48 Doughty Street, London WC1N 2LF. Tel (01) 405 2127. Open Mon-Sat 10 am-5 pm by appointment only, following negotiation of a fee with the Curator. Photocopying facilities.

General Dickens House was the home of Charles Dickens (1812–70) the novelist 1837–9 during the composition of *Pickwick, Oliver Twist, Nicholas Nickleby* and *Barnaby Rudge*. The Dickens Fellowship, founded in 1902, and now based here, bought it in 1922–4, and in 1925 handed it over to the Dickens House Trust as a museum. The library has been built up from the National Dickens Library begun in 1906, which was moved to Dickens House in 1925. There are c5,000 v of printed books, comprising virtually all the early and many later editions of Dickens, contemporary and later criticism, and large collections of cuttings and ephemera. There are also prints, photographs, lantern slides and important collections of mss which include, in addition to the Carlton, Staples and Suzannet collections mentioned below, the papers of Thomas Wright (1859–1936), (Mary) Gladys Storey (1892–1978), and Sir Felix Aylmer (1889–1979), and a collection of documents relating to the foundation of the *Daily News* in 1846.

Card cat (author, title and alphabetical subject).

Register of Accessions lists collections acquired since 1925.

The Dickens House Museum: guide and illustrated souvenir, (1980).

The Dickens House, 48 Doughty Street, (1926).

Dickens Fellowship, *The Dickensian* (1905–) with *Cumulative...index...1905–74*, Hassocks, Harvester, 1976 (see esp p65 Dickens House accessions, and under names of collectors).

'The Fellowship in retrospect', *Dickensian* 40 (1944), p25-35, 97-101, 127-32; 47 (1951), p22-7, 94-7.

A D St John Adcock, *Famous houses and literary shrines of London*, London, 1929, p233-44.

Kitton Collection The collection formed by Frederic George Kitton (1856–1903), the journalist, illustrator, and Dickens scholar, bought by Dickens Fellowship in 1906. Dickensiana, including scrapbooks containing newspaper cuttings, proofs for an abortive edition of Dickens, and other material.

Dickensian 1 (1905), p233; 2 (1906), p17, 71, 314.

F G Kitton, *Dickensiana: a bibliography of the literature relating to Dickens and his illustrators*, London, 1886;

The minor writings of Charles Dickens: a bibliography and sketch, London, 1900.

National Dickens Library Built around the nucleus of the Kitton Collection, which was paid for and augmented by a public appeal in 1907. In 1908 it was given to the Guildhall Library, and in 1925 given back to form the core of the library at Dickens House.

Dickensian 3 (1907), p74; 4 (1908), p46, 61-4.

J W T Ley, 'The National Dickens Library', *Ibid* 4 (1908), p117-20, 183-5, 244-6, 266-9, 298-300.

Matz Collection The Dickensian collection of Bertram Waldron Matz (1865–1925) of Chapman and Hall (founder of the Dickens Fellowship, and first editor of the *Dickensian*), lent to Dickens House in 1925, and bought in 1927 at the expense of Sir Charles C Wakefield. Over 1,300 books and pamphlets (with 387 portraits of him, and his reading desk), including over 70 editions of Dickens works (English, American and foreign); 70 v of selections from his works; 65 v of plays, readings, and recitations; 50 v of the novels issued independently; and 113 editions of *A Christmas carol* and the other Christmas books. Secondary material includes 50 v on *Pickwick;* 30 v on *Drood;* 86 v and 60 pamphlets on the topography of the novels; 80 v and 40 pamphlets on other special topics; 40 biographies of the novelist; 10 of his illustrators; and 53 of his contemporaries; 75 v of his critics; 1,200 magazine articles on Dickens 1836–1925 bound in 20 v with 15 v of newspaper cuttings; 20 v of privately printed Dickensiana; and 26 portfolios of special illustrations for the novels.

Dickensian 21 (4) (1925) 'B W Matz Memorial Number', including obit (p179-92 and notes on the collection (p193-5) extended in 23 (1927), p78-82.

Suzannet Collection Part of the Dickens collection formed by comte Alain de Suzannet (1882–1950) of La Petite Chardière, Lausanne, donated partly in his lifetime, but mostly by his widow in 1971 (the remainder being sold, Sotheby 22 Nov 1971). It contains 36 first and early editions of Dickens; 6 of Dickens's own reading copies; 12 editions of his speeches; 3 collected editions of his works; 62 works about Dickens; 21 playbills and programmes; 20 paintings, prints and drawings, 443 autograph letters and documents; 8 literary mss; and proofs of Dickens's works; 69 ms *Dickensiana;* 11 miscellaneous objects and ephemera; and 22 collections of letters and other documents relating to the Suzannet collection.

Michael Slater, ed. *The catalogue of the Suzannet Charles Dickens collection*, London, Sotheby, 1975 (classified, with reprint of sale cat and author index to the whole).

P Collins, 'The Dickens reading copies at Dickens House', *Dickensian* 68 (1972), p173-9.

Unique items (association copies and original documents) listed in *Dickensian* 30 (1934), p112-6.

Carlton bequest Over 100 books and pamphlets incorporated into the general collection, with letters, mss and papers bequeathed by William John Carlton (1886–1973), parliamentary reporter and latterly Librarian at the International Labour Office (his shorthand collection is at the University of London Library).

K J F (ie Fielding), *W J Carlton...with a list of his writings on Dickens*, 1973; *Dickensian* (1974), p46-7.

Leslie C Staples bequest The collection of Leslie C Staples (1896–1980), Treasurer of the Ellen Terry Fellowship, and a Trustee of Dickens House. Over 100 books; 11 autograph Dickens letters; 21 other ms letters; 80 pirated editions and plagiarisms of Dickens; and miscellaneous papers. Piracies etc include the work of Bos (Thomas Peckett Prest (?–?) and George William MacArthur Reynolds (1814–79) the Chartist journalist. Staples's voluminous collections of papers are being donated, but have not yet been received.

M Reynolds, 'The Leslie C Staples bequest', *Dickensian* 77(2) (1981), p125-7; obit 76(3) (1980), p131-7.

Peyrouton bequest The Dickens collection of Noel C Peyrouton (1924–68) of Boston (Mass), editor of *Dickens Studies.* It includes first editions; letters; and miscellaneous *Dickensiana* (c120 printed items in all, merged in the general collection).

Dickensian 64(2) (1968), p128; 65(3) (1969), p207.

Henry Collection The collection of first editions of the novels given in 1959 by Sydney Alexander Henry (1880–1960) MD, specialist in industrial diseases, comprising an outstanding collection of the part issues with numerous variants, and first editions in volume form in the original cloth (his collection on sweeps is at Kirkstall Abbey Folklore Museum).

Dickensian 55(3) (1959), p132; 56(2) (1960), p127.

Foyle Collection The collection of first editions (both volumes and parts issued) formed by Gilbert Samuel Foyle (1886–1971), one of the founders of W and G Foyle the booksellers. Given to Eastbourne Public Library, who deposited it on permanent loan at Dickens House in 1974.

Dickensian 70(2) (1974), p122-3.

Directorate of Ancient Monuments and Historic Buildings Library (Department of the Environment), Fortress House, 23 Savile Row, London W1X 2HE. Tel (01) 734 6010 Ext 323 and 325. Accessible for research by prior arrangement with the librarian.

Mayson Beeton collection on the history, topography and architecture of London and the home counties, transferred from the Property Services Agency. It was donated in 1947 to the Ministry of Works by Sir Mayson Beeton (1865–1947) MBE, son of Mrs Beeton the writer of books on cookery, to form the nucleus of an anticipated reference collection. *c*1,000 v, incl *c*300 pre-1851 (incl 1 of 16th cent, 9 of 17th, 11 of 18th cent); also *c*35,000 prints.

Mayson Beeton collection: subject index to books, 1978. (Occasional paper No 6).

Guide to the collection of topographical prints of London and the Home Counties 1420–1930. (Occasional paper No 1).

Drapers' Company, Drapers' Hall, Throgmorton Avenue, London EC2N 2DQ. Tel (01) 588 5001. Open by appointment only after written application to the Clerk. Photocopying facilities.

The company is third in order of precedence of the City livery companies. There are extensive ms archives at the Hall.

Thomas Girtin, *The triple crowns: a narrative history of the Drapers' Company, 1364–1964*, 1964.

W F Kahl, *The development of London livery companies*, Boston, 1960 (with extensive bibliography).

William Archer-Thomson, *Drapers' Company: history of the company's properties and trusts. . .*, London, the Company, 1942, 2 v.

Drapers' Company Library *c*1,000 v including 10 STC; 37 Wing; and 91 ESTC items, including in addition to official printed documents of the Company, books donated by liverymen, on the history of London and its livery companies, and other institutions of interest as Company foundations, eg Bancroft's School.

Card cat (author and subject).

Lambarde Collection The whole estate of William Lambarde (1536–1601), historian of Kent, was bequeathed to the Drapers' Company. The library includes the books he owned, including his own copy of his *Perambulation of Kent* 1576, and other works by him, together with family portraits and heirlooms.

Duchy of Cornwall Office Library, 10 Buckingham Gate, London SW1E 6LA. Tel (01) 834 7346. Open Mon-Fri 10 am-5 pm by appointment after written application to the Clerk of Records. Photocopying and microfilming.

The records of the Duchy of Cornwall, with associated mss, together with a library of 5,000 v on the history and topography of Devon and Cornwall, and other areas in which the Duchy owns property in Somerset, Wiltshire, Dorset and Kennington (London) or used to own in Oxfordshire, Lincolnshire, Berkshire and Sussex. Also material on tin mining (chiefly in the 19th cent).

Card cat.

Dulwich College Library, Dulwich Common, London SE21 7LD. Open Mon-Fri 9 am-4 pm to accredited scholars who have applied in writing well in advance.

Edward Alleyn (1566–1626), the Shakespearian actor who founded the Fortune Theatre, established in 1619 the College of God's Gift at Dulwich, with Master, Warden, Fellows and Scholars (for whose instruction Schoolmaster, Usher and Organist were later appointed). Alleyn bequeathed to it his books (probably more than the 26 of which appear in a surviving list) and his numerous personal papers including those of his wife's stepfather Philip Henslowe (*c*1555–1616) the theatrical manager. A very much larger collection of printed books was bequeathed by Alleyn's friend William Cartwright the younger (*c*1610?–87), but it reached the college incomplete. Job Brockett (*c*1644–1705), Vicar of Royston, bequeathed a theological collection. Donations and purchases continued regularly until 1740 when both school and library fell into neglect, and some visiting scholars began to take liberties with the collections; a few early English plays passed by exchange into the collections of Edmund Malone (now in the Bodleian) and David Garrick (in the British Library); and John Payne Collier (1789–1883) practised some of his forgeries and depredations here. The last major bequest was that of a Master John Allen (1771–1843), MD, Byron's 'helluo of books', consisting of the foreign portion (chiefly Italian and Spanish) of a collection which he had taken from Holland House while he was resident political and literary oracle to Henry Richard Fox, 3rd Baron Holland (1773–1840). In 1857 the Charity Commission reconstituted the foundation as a public school by statute 20-21 Vict *c*84 of which paragraph 33 regulates the Library.

About 5,000 of the 65,000 printed books are pre-1851, consisting of 13 incunabula, *c*1,080 STC, 1,153 Wing, c750 ESTC, c600 English of 1801–50, c600 foreign of 1501–1640, c180 of 1641–1700, c150 of 1701–1800 and 100 of 1801–50. They are kept with a few later books as a rare books collection associated with the college archives, arranged in broad subject groups regardless of provenance. The largest groups are of biblical literature, sermons, and controversial theology to 1740, particularly Anglican, but with a broad spectrum of Protestant and some RC authors; political and miscellaneous tracts, with substantial collections on the Civil War and on the Titus Oates Plot; English law including some rare collections of statutes; classical authors, chiefly in continental 16th and 17th cent editions; travel and maps, chiefly of 1750–1850. There is a small mathematical and scientific collection.

Catalogue of the Library of Alleyn's College of God's Gift at Dulwich, 1880. Arranged by authors, but very incomplete. Card index is more comprehensive but not detailed. A ms shelflist of 1729 and other documents on the Library are in the Archives. *Catalogues of the manuscripts and muniments of Alleyn's College of God's Gift at Dulwich* by George Warner, 1881, (includes historical introduction). Second series by F B Bickley, 1903.

William Young, *The history of Dulwich College*, 1889 v 2, p321-42.

G L Hosking, *The life and times of Edward Alleyn*, London, Cape, 1952.

W S Wright, 'Dulwich College Library', *Theatre Notebook*, 8(3) (1954) p58-60.

Dutch Church Library, Austin Friars, London EC2N 2EJ. Tel (01) 588 1684. Open by arrangement with the Church Secretary on written application.

The Dutch Church was founded by a group of Protestant refugee theologians sponsored by Cranmer, and led by John à Lasco, to whom in 1550 Edward VI gave the former church of the Augustinian Friars. In 1605 the Minister established a library around the collection of Marie Dubois, which was enlarged by donations from Dutch ambassadors, the Dutch East India Company, and other wealthy members of the congregation. In 1862 it was deposited at the Guildhall Library, but when the Church was rebuilt after bombing was taken back c1950. About half were then given to the Lambeth Palace Library (qv), most of the incunabula and a few other, mostly non-religious, works were sold (Sotheby 14 Dec 1959), while 500 remain, mostly pre-1701, including 4 incunabula; c20 STC; c20 Wing; especially Bibles and testaments in the original and classical languages and in Dutch; Anglican Prayer Books; theology, apologetics and devotional works; books by ministers of the Church or relating to its history; general church history; atlases and topographical works; and a unique collection of 8 pamphlets in Dutch on the Popish Plot 1604–5.

Catalogus van het Boekenbezit van de Dutch Church, Austin Friars, 1978 (£7.50); limited to books in Dutch.

A catalogue of Bibles, manuscripts, letters &c belonging to the Dutch Church...deposited in the Library of the Corporation of the City of London, 1879.

Catalogue of the Guildhall Library, 1889; items marked 'DC', the most complete list of the collection.

17th cent cats in ms (Listed in 1879 cat, p155), and list of benefactors 1606–1695.

J Lindeboom, *Austin Friars, history of the Dutch Reformed Church in London 1550–1950*, The Hague, Nijhoff, 1950, p169–73 (available from the Church).

Ealing Public Libraries, Ealing Central Reference Library, Walpole Park, Ealing, London W5 5EQ. Tel (01) 579 2424 Ext 3418. Open Wed and Sat 9 am-5 pm; Tues, Thurs, Fri 7.45 pm, to all, but prior notice is required for access to rare books. Photocopying facilities. Library is due to move to Civic Centre, Ealing, in 1984.

General Reference Library Pre-1851 books mainly in Local History Section (below), but some general and foreign, including 3 incunabula; 12 16th cent; 4 17th cent; and 14 of 1701–1850.

Author and classified cat from computer printout covers whole General Reference stock.

Card index to items from notable and private presses.

Bloe Bequest The library of John William Bloe (1872–1965) OBE, FSA, an architect who worked on the Victoria history of London, the Royal Commission on Historical Monuments, and the London Survey Committee. It contains c500 v on art, architecture, history and literature in English, French, German, Latin, Italian and Spanish. Of these, 151 v are pre-1851, including 1 incunabulum; 1 16th cent; 10 17th cent; and 140 1701–50.

Typescript list.

Local history collection An amalgamation of the collections of the former Boroughs of Ealing, Acton and Southall, the collection contains c1,400 books and pamphlets, with other material. Special collections of c200 v by (including translations into foreign languages) and about George Douglas Howard Cole (1889–1959), the political historian, including some scarce material. Also c200 v by and about (Henry) Austin Dobson (1840–1921) the poet and critic, many from his own collection or that of his son Alban, with some miscellaneous books from his library. Other local authors are generously represented.

Incomplete card cat.

Separate card cat of local authors.

Ealing Public Libraries, *Austin Dobson*, 1962.

Selborne Society Library Deposited by the Society, which began to collect a library in Ealing in 1895, the library consists of c100 editions of Gilbert White (1720–93) the naturalist of Selborne, including c35 pre-1851, and c50 works about him. (The mss are deposited at the Linnean Society.) There is also a collection of general works on natural history, including 8 pre-1851.

Ealing Public Libraries, *Selborne Society Library: a catalogue of mss, books and periodicals devoted to*

Gilbert White and natural history, 1958 (copy annotated with numerous subsequent additions).

London Natural History Society Library This library, formerly deposited, has been transferred to Imperial College (see under London. Imperial College).

Egypt Exploration Society Library, 3 Doughty Mews, London WC1N 2PG. Tel (01) 242 1880. Open Mon-Fri 10 am-noon, 2-4.30 pm to members; others at librarian's discretion by appointment after written application.

The Society was founded in 1882, and has built up a library of *c*4,500 v on Egyptology, including a substantial number pre-1851.

Author cat.

Electoral Reform Society, 6 Chancel Street, Southwark, London SE1 0UX. Tel (01) 928 9407. Open Mon-Fri 9.30 am-5 pm by letter of application to the Education Officer.

The Proportional Representation Society was founded in 1884 by Albert Henry George Grey, 4th Earl Grey (1851–1917) and others; in 1959 it was renamed the Electoral Reform Society of Great Britain and Ireland. The archives are in the care of the Secretary.

'The Electoral Reform Society', *Liberal News* 6 Jan 1972, p8-9. History in preparation.

Arthur MacDougall Library Books and other printed material collected by or donated to the Society. These number *c*300 books and 900 pamphlets, including over 20 pre-1851, and press cuttings from 1869, on proportional representation, electoral reform and suffrage.

Card cat (authors and subjects) including the collections below.

Pamphlets on proportional representation in England, the US and Australia A collection of 97 pamphlets in 4 v 1844–1907, including C L Dodgson, *Principles of parliamentary representation*, 1884 and supplements.

Droop Collection 176 pamphlets 1864–1918 in 8 v on proportional representation in Belgium, Denmark, France and Switzerland, collected and donated by A R Droop.

Enfield Public Libraries, Local History Section, Broomfield Lane, Palmer's Green, London N13 4EY. Tel (01) 886 6555 Ext 15. Open Mon-Sat 9 am-5 pm to bona fide students (entrance via Southgate Town Hall, Green Lanes). Photocopying.

Local history collection An amalgamation of the local collections of the former boroughs of Edmonton, Enfield and Southgate, including 176 pre-1851 items on local history and topography, local Acts of Parliament, directories. Works by local authors, including Charles Lamb (1775–1834), though the Lamb Society Library has been transferred to the Guildhall Library. A small collection of books published by the Cedars Press at Enfield 1907–10.

Classified cat with author and subject indexes.

English Folk Dance and Song Society, Vaughan Williams Memorial Library, Cecil Sharp House, 2 Regent's Park Road, London NW1 7AY. Tel (01) 485 2206. Open Mon-Fri 9.30 am-5.30 pm to members; to others at the librarian's discretion after prior written application. Photocopier; microform reader available.

In 1911 the English Folk Dance Society was founded by Cecil Sharp (1859–1924), who bequeathed his own library, containing many early and rare items, to form the nucleus of the Society's library which was, therefore, called the Cecil Sharp Library. The Folk Song Society, founded 1898, had a smaller library, also containing rare books, which included the bequest of Anne C Gilchrist. The societies were amalgamated in 1932 and their libraries were consolidated in the Cecil Sharp Library, renamed in memory of Ralph Vaughan Williams (1872–1958) after his death.

S Jackson, 'The Cecil Sharp Library', *Theatre Notebook* 7(1) (1952), p18-20.

The story of the English Folk Dance and Song Society, rev ed 1974. (Leaflet no 12).

M Dean-Smith, 'A classification...for the Cecil Sharp Library', *Journ of Documentation* 7(4) (1951), p215-8 (with history).

General The library, now with over 4,000 v includes, in addition to a few 17th cent (from 1651) items, *c*120 18th cent items, and *c*150 of 1801–50; these figures include editions containing music. It is divided broadly into three subject sections: Folklore and customs, including religion and magic and archaeology; the dance; and folk song (both texts and music) including balladry. There are *c*100 sets of periodicals, some very scarce; major collections of mss, also a separate audio library, broadsheets and other ephemera.

Card cat (author and classified) published as *The Vaughan Williams Memorial catalogue of the English Folk Dance and Song Society... books, pamphlets, periodicals, sheet music and manuscripts...to 1971*, London, Mansell, 1973.

'How to use the catalogue' (typescript, 1951).

Cecil Sharp House...1930–1951, 1951.

Diamond Jubilee Exhibition, 1958.

The English Folk Dance and Song Society: what it is and what it does, (*c*1947).

Evangelical Library, 78A Chiltern Street, London W1M 2HB. Tel (01) 935 6997. Open Mon-Sat 10 am-5 pm to subscribers and donors only; apply to librarian for conditions of membership. Photocopying.

General Geoffrey Williams (1886?–1975) laid the foundations of the library in 1903 when he was converted by a Baptist minister to a vigorous evangelical faith, and resolved to collect as much as he could, both old and new, on the Puritan tradition. By 1925 he had amassed a substantial library at his home in Beddington, Surrey, and began lending regularly to others. In 1928 he converted it to a subscription library called the Beddington Free Grace Library, giving a nationwide postal loan service. In 1931 he rehoused it in a room behind a local chapel and placed it in the hands of trustees, but remained Librarian until 1974. In 1931 Mr F Kirby of Staplehurst, Kent, who became the library's President, gave a substantial collection of his own. Growth by purchase and donation was rapid: 7,000 v by 1934; 40,000 v by 1943 when the collection was moved to London with the help of David Martyn Lloyd-Jones (1899–1981), MD, Minister of Westminster Chapel, who did much to publicize it and renamed the Evangelical Library; 80,000 v in 1980 (in addition to worldwide branches). It has always been primarily a lending library based on subscriptions, but has acquired from the founder and others substantial rare book and general reference collections.

Card cats (author and classified) include all collections except Wilberforce and M'Ghee, *Short history and explanation of the benefits of the Beddington Free Grace Library, 1935*; Geoffrey Williams, *The birth of a library for the Christian public*, 1951?; *The Evangelical Library Bulletin*, 1945– ; *The Annual Meeting of the Evangelical Library, 1956–67*, 1956–67; *The Annual lecture of the Evangelical Library*, 1951– ; Ms history by Stephanie Wright, *c*1975.

General Reference Library This collection includes sets of the works of the Protestant divines, standard commentaries on the Bible, works on the ejectment of 1662 and on revivals, the history of the older Protestant churches (with special emphasis on Baptists and Methodists), and dictionaries and concordances. At least 500 pre-1851 v included, from *c*1600 onwards.

Puritan Collection Comprises *c*1,500 v, and includes 17th and 18th cent editions of major Protestant authors such as Richard Baxter (1615–91), John Bunyan (1628–88), many of the editions from a donation from Ralph E Ford son of the organist of Bunyan Meeting, Bedford (the main part of whose collection was sold to the University of Alberta), Matthew Henry (1662–1714), John Gill (1697–1771), George Whitefield (1714–70), and many authors of smaller importance.

Robinson Collection *c*100 v of early works on Protestantism, mostly 17th and 18th cent, donated by a Mr Robinson *c*1960?

Wilberforce and M'Ghee collections from the National Club A collection combining the general church history collection of pamphlets assembled by Bishop Samuel Wilberforce (1805–73), traditional Anglican in outlook, with a collection of Robert James M'Ghee (1789–1872), Rector of Holywell, Hunts, strong in Irish church controversies and anti-Catholic polemics. The two collections were brought together to form the library of the National Club (*c*1845–*c*1918), an Evangelical Anglican gentlemen's club founded by the Earl of Winchelsea. *c*2,000 items (bound in 158 v) including *c*40 Wing; *c*150 ESTC; *c*200 of 1801–30; *c*800 of 1831–50.

Ms cat dated 1896 (dictionary arrangement).

T H S Escott, *Club makers*, London, 1914, p296-9.

Hymnology Collection *c*2,000 v including at least 1,000 pre-1851, with some scarce editions.

Included in general cat under author, editor or title.

Magazines Collection Including, besides complete runs of standard titles such as the *Gospel Magazine* and the *Evangelical Magazine*, some unusual popular evangelical periodicals, from the early 18th cent onwards. At least 500 v pre-1851.

Faculty of Homoeopathy Library, Royal London Homoeopathic Hospital, Great Ormond Street, London WC1N 3HR. Tel (01) 837 8833 Ext 72. Open Mon-Fri 10 am-5 pm by appointment.

The British Homoeopathic Society was founded in 1844 to promote in England the homoeopathic system of medicine pioneered in Germany by Samuel Christian Friedrich Hahnemann (1755–1843). In 1849–50 Dr Frederick Hervey Foster Quin (1799–1878) founded the London Homoeopathic Hospital in association with the Society, which established a School of Homoeopathy there, with a small library, in 1877. In 1929 the Faculty of Homoeopathy was founded to take over the teaching function; it absorbed the Society and its library in 1943. The hospital received a royal charter in 1928, and was renamed the Royal London Homoeopathic Hospital in 1948 on absorption into the National Health Service. The Society's archives (which include statistics of the cholera epidemic in 1854) are kept in the library.

The Royal London Homoeopathical Hospital, Great Ormond Street, London, 1849–1949...centenary brochure, containing a short history..., 1949.

Printed books The collection totals *c*1,600 v on all aspects of homoeopathic medicine, including *materia medica*, repertories, therapeutics, specific diseases, veterinary works, philosophies and histories. Most are English books of the 19th cent of which the library has the best homoeopathic collection in existence, including a number of scarce works *c*1830–50; also a few early German and American. (Non-homoeopathic books have been dispersed recently; some obsolete early, especially late 18th cent continental and American books, have been deposited in the Faculty Museum.)

Classified list.

Author/title card index.

Journals Sets of all the British homoeopathic journals beginning with the *Journal of Homoeopathy* in 1845; also numerous American, German, French and Indian periodicals on the subject. Most of the journals have been transferred recently from the Hospital to the Faculty Library.

Fawcett Library, City of London Polytechnic, Old Castle Street, London E1 7NT. Tel (01) 283 1030 Ext 570. Open Mon-Fri 10 am-5 pm (Mon in term 1-8.30 pm only) except when Polytechnic closed, to subcribing members only. Photocopier.

In 1867 the London Society for Women's Suffrage succeeded the Women's Suffrage Committee founded in 1866, and after several changes of name and function, it became in 1953 the Fawcett Society, named after its former leader Dame Millicent (Garrett) Fawcett (1847–1929). Its library, begun in 1926 as the Women's Service Library, was built up until 1967 by the tireless energies of its first librarian, Miss Vera Douie (*c*1895–1979) OBE, with a team of volunteers. From 1957 it has been controlled by the Fawcett Library Trust, and from 1977 deposited at the Polytechnic. It continues to be enlarged by gifts, bequests and trust funds. It is the only major British library specializing in works by and about women and the feminist movement.

Microfiche cat (author and classified) published as *BiblioFem* includes the older rare books (the remainder will eventually be incorporated); supplemented by author card cat.

A Pritchard and D Doughan, 'Access to the literature on women: the Fawcett Library and BiblioFem', *Assistant Librarian* 72(2) (1979), p22-8.

Women's Service Library: the first seven years, 1933.

'Fawcett Library's cash problem', *The Times* 15 Feb 1973, p25.

B Vernon, 'Almost all about women', *Manchester Guardian* 25 Nov 1959.

'How the Fawcett Library was saved', *Library Association Record* 79(1) (1977), p17.

R Strachey, *Women's suffrage and women's service: the history of the London and National Society for Women's Service*, 1927.

Margaret Barrow, *Women 1870–1928: a select guide to printed and archival sources. . .*, London, Mansell, 1981, esp p205-15.

Monographs The Library contains altogether *c*40,000 v of books and pamphlets on all aspects of the position of women in society, eg women's political rights (esp suffrage), employment, education, emigration, prostitution, feminist movements, the ordination of women (including a collection of the Anglican Group for the Ordination of Women), the family, and domestic economy.

Periodicals *c*800 runs, including women's general magazines from the mid-18th cent feminist organs from 1858 onwards (including a number of unique sets), and modern academic journals on feminism and related subjects.

Handlist on cards.

Archives Large collections of letters and records of societies, often including printed reports, etc. Letters and papers of individuals, with a few authors' mss and corrected proofs of published modern works.

Typescript lists.

Barrow, *Women 1870–1928* lists the main collections of this period.

Ephemera A major strength of the Library, the ephemera are mostly post-1850, but a few earlier items. Also collections of newscuttings and of portraits.

Cavendish-Bentinck and Treasures Collection *c*2,500 v early 17th to early 20th cent: feminist works, books on female education, miscellaneous early works by women, biographies of women, and some 19th cent children's books. *c*1,700 v of these are from the Society's rare book and historical collection known as The Treasures; *c*800 v belong to the Cavendish-Bentinck and Edward Wright Trust deposited 1931, and were from an independent library formed *c*1920 by combining the collection of Ruth Cavendish-Bentinck MD (1867–1953), the Fabian and suffragist, with the Edward Wright Library, founded by Sir Almroth (Edward) Wright FRS (1861–1947), an anti-suffragist, and Lady Wright, in memory of their son Edward who had supported the feminist cause; the books are chiefly first and early editions of female writers. This collection contains most of the pre-1851 books.

Josephine Butler Society Library and Archives The Society was founded in 1870 as the Ladies' National Association for the Repeal of the Contagious Diseases Acts, becoming *c*1915 the Association for Moral and Social Hygiene, and in 1953 the Josephine Butler Society. Its library and archives, deposited *c*1960, comprise *c*1,200 v, mainly pamphlets and books from 1860 onwards (with a few earlier) on prostitution, eugenics, and related aspects of sex. It includes a major collection of works by and about Josephine Butler (1828–1906) the social reformer and campaigner against prostitution.

Sadd Brown Library Contains *c*500 v devoted to women in the Commonwealth, mostly 20th cent, but including some scarce 19th cent items. Established and still maintained in memory of Mrs Myra Sadd Brown, the suffragette, by her family, and in conjunction with the Commonwealth Countries League.

Fellowship of St Alban and St Sergius, St Basil's House, 52 Ladbroke Grove, London W11 2PB. Tel (01) 727 7713. Open to non-members by appointment with the Secretary. Photocopying facilities.

The fellowship was founded in 1928 to bring about the reconciliation of the Church of England with the Russian Orthodox Church, but now performs a much wider role in the ecumenical movement in furthering mutual understanding between Christians of the East and West. The library has been built up from the foundation both for the use of members, and as a reference collection for the information service that the fellowship provides on the churches of the East.

Monographs A working collection of *c*3,000 books and 2,000 pamphlets, mostly in English, but with some in Eastern languages, on church history, liturgy, iconography and theology, most notably by the Orthodox (and Byzantine) but also of the Armenian, Coptic, Uniate (RC) and other Eastern churches, with some Bibles, hymnology, general and moral theology, mysticism, and philosophy of religion. *c*30 are of the 18th and early 19th cent, eg John G King *The rites and ceremonies of the Greek Church in Russia* 1772. Some of the more modern pamphlets and books are not likely to be found in other libraries.

Card cat (author and classified).

Periodicals *c*200 sets on the Eastern churches, and on the ecumenical movement, including a number of Eastern countries, and a complete set of *Put* (Kharkov 1925–40), the organ of Russian intellectual Christianity under Communist rule, and other journals not available elsewhere.

List due to be published during 1982.

Fishmongers' Company, Fishmongers' Hall, London Bridge North, London EC4R 9EL. Tel (01) 626 3531. Terms of access not stated.

The Company is fourth in order of precedence of the City livery companies, having been founded by the 12th cent.

The archives, ms and printed material of the Company down to *c*1850 are deposited in the Guildhall Library Dept of Manuscripts. There are also some records and books at the Hall, mainly concerned with the Company's current active interests in the fishing industry and fish trade, but also include some older material.

Marston Library A collection of books on the sport of fishing formed by Robert Bright Marston (1853–1927), editor of the *Fishing Gazette* and compiler of a supplement to the *Bibliotheca piscatoria*; continued by his daughter who presented it to the Company. At least 2,000 v, mainly 19th and early 20th cent, with some earlier items.

Natural history manuscript resources, 1980, p190-1, (239.1).

Flyfishers' Club, 24A Old Burlington Street, London W1X 1RL. Tel (01) 734 9229. Open to members only. Enquiries should be addressed to the Secretary.

Many fishing authors have donated their books to the library, and in some cases the original drawings for plates in published books on fishing. There are some unique copies, and a few pre-1851 books.

Eric Taverner and Douglas Service, *Fly-fishers' Club Library* catalogue, London, 1935 (op).

The book of the Flyfishers' Club 1884–1934, p55, 76-82.

Foreign and Commonwealth Office Library, Sanctuary Buildings, 20 Great Smith Street, London SW1P 3BZ. Tel (01) 212 6753. Open Mon-Fri 9.30 am-5.30 pm for official purposes only. Photocopying through British Library Lending Division.

Established in 1968 from the libraries founded at the Foreign Office in 1801, at the Colonial Office a few years later, at the Dominions Office (afterwards Commonwealth Relations Office) in 1925, and at the Ministry of Overseas Development in 1964. (The India Office Library and Records (qv) has remained independent.) It includes at least 3,000 pre-1851 books and pamphlets (two-thirds foreign) on early embassies, general history, travel, law and related subjects. The greater part is from the Foreign Office, recorded in, Colin L Robertson, *A short title catalogue of books printed before 1701 in the Foreign Office Library*, 1966 (577 works arranged by authors, with indexes of printers and places, including 28 STC and 141 Wing) and in, *Catalogue of printed books in the Library of the Foreign Office*, 1926, reprinted New York, Kraus, 1980, dictionary. Others are in *Catalogue of the Colonial Office Library*, Boston, G K Hall, 1964, 15 vols (author and classified). Supplementary card and sheaf cats. See, Jack Burkett, *Government and related library and information services*, 3rd ed, London, 1974 p58-61, *Library World*, 61 (620), June 1960, p251-3.

Francis Skaryna Byelorussian Library and Museum, Marian House of Studies, 37 Holden Road, Finchley, London N12 8HS. Tel (01) 445 5358 or 7774. Open by appointment only after written application to the librarian. Microform reader.

The collection originated in 1947 when Bishop Ceslaus Sipovič brought to London from Rome a collection of books to form the nucleus of a cultural centre for the British Byelorussian community; after considerable enlargement it was formally opened in 1950, and in 1958 officially named Bibliotheca Alboruthena. In 1960 Fr Leu Horosko, the librarian, added some rare books from his own collection. In 1969, at the time of a change of location, it was renamed after Francišak Skaryna, and has become a charitable trust. It is the only specialist Byelorussian library outside the USSR, and contains *c*12,000 books and 200 serials on all aspects of Byelorussia, especially literature, history and language, and less intensively folklore, religion, politics, economics, geography and travel, bibliography, art, architecture, music and theatre. There are also extensive collections of mss from the 16th cent onwards.

Card cat (also union cat of Byelorussian books in other British libraries).

A Nadson, 'The Francis Skaryna Byelorussian Library in London', *Solanus* 9 (1974), p10-15.

G de Picarda, *The Francis Skaryna Byelorussian Library and Museum*, London, (1971) (Anglo-Belorussian historical papers no.1).

Early printed books A collection of 24 books, the earliest being a fragment of the Bible translated and printed by Skaryna (1518), and several liturgical books of the Uniates, (Catholics using the Byzantine rite), 1690–1839, which are especially rare since they were suppressed and destroyed after 1839. In addition to other books in Byelorussian, there are a few in English on the Eastern churches, and a few in other languages.

A Nadson, 'Some rare and old books in the Francis Skaryna Library in London', *Journ of Byelorussian Studies* 3(4) (1976), p364-9.

Modern rare books A number of early 20th cent first editions of well known writers, especially poets; these were usually printed in very small editions, and in many cases these are the only copies outside the USSR.

Francišak Skaryna (*c*1485–1540), the first Byelorussian printer and translator of the Bible. In addition to microfilms of all books printed by him, the library holds all significant works about him and on the history of printing in Byelorussia.

C Sipovič, *Doktar Francišak Skaryna*, London, 1967.

Franciscan Friars Minor Provincial Archives, Franciscan Friary, 58 St Antony's Road, Forest Gate, London E7 9QB. Tel (01) 472 3900. Open by appointment only after written application to the Archivist at the Friary, 160 The Grove, Stratford, London E15 1NS.

The archives of the English Province of the Order of Friars Minor founded by St Francis of Assisi in 1209. They include records of friars working in England after the suppression of the Observant houses in 1583 (kept secretly in England), and of the house of the English Recollects at Douai (1618–1793), with printed material from both sources. There is also a modern book collection on the history of the Order in England.

It should be particularly noted that the collections are not recorded in A F Allison, 'Franciscan books in English, 1559–1640', *Biographical Studies* 3 (1955–6), p16-65, or in Allison and Rogers *A catalogue of Catholic books in English*.

Brief conspectus English Province (typescript list of ms records and of published writings of the English Franciscans indicating items held).

Card index to ms archives.

Card index to 13th-16th cent ordinations in England, compiled by Conrad Walmsley from the episcopal registers.

See also the bibliography in John B Dockery, *Christopher Davenport*, London, Burns and Oats, 1960, p160-72, which lists both contemporary and later sources for the Order in the 17th cent.

Writings of the English Franciscans Over 60 v by post-Reformation English Franciscans, in Latin or English, many printed abroad for distribution in England. They include J Gennings *Institutio missionariorum* 1651; G Perrot *Seaven trumpets* 1626; G Willoughby *Golden treatise* 1632; the *Opera omnia* 1665–7 and many individual editions of Christopher Davenport, known as Franciscus a Sancta Clara (1598–1680), including his controversial *Deus, natura, gratia*, 1646, which attempted the reconciliation of Anglican and Catholic doctrine; *A select collection of Catholic sermons*, 1741, compiled by Angelus Bix, comprising mainly sermons preached under James II; 7 by Arthur Pacificus Baker (1695–1774); and other 18th and early 19th cent works.

Books from English Franciscan Collections Over 100 v, mostly continental books of the 16th and 17th cent, with a few English, from Franciscan houses and personal collections of Franciscans, kept in the archives on account of their associations. They comprise some liturgical books from English houses and some individual friars, but most are textbooks and devotional books identifiable as having belonged to well known members of the Order. An unusual item from the house at Sclerder in Cornwall is Izaac Walton's copy of the Bede *History of the Church of Englande* Antwerp 1565.

French Protestant Church, 8 Soho Square, London W1V 5DD. The church and its library and archives are temporarily inaccessible (1981). Enquiries should be sent to the Librarian, c/o Hugenot Society Library, University College, London WC1E 6BT.

The church was founded by Royal Charter in 1550 in Threadneedle Street, and has had a library from the early 17th cent. The library includes the archives of the church and three congregations amalgamated with it, in addition to *c*1,480 printed books and many mss. The books include Bibles, theology, the classics, history and science. Three incunabula, *c*80 16th cent editions. Some interesting bindings. (Many books originally in the collection disappeared in the 19th cent.)

Interleaved typescript cat.

'Catalogue of such books...in the Library of the French Church, as are not in that of Dr Williams', in *Dr Williams's Library. Appendix ad catalogum*, 1814.

H Bordier, 'Les archives de St Martins le Grand', *Bulletin de l'Histoire du Protestantisme Français* 25 (1876), p416-26.

Schickler, Baron Ferdinand de, *Les églises du refuge en Angleterre* Vol 1 (1892), pxxii-xxiv.

Neil R Ker, 'Notes on some books in the Library of l'Eglise Protestante, Soho Square, London', *Proceedings of the Hugenot Society* 21 (1967), p143-7.

W Turner, 'The Archives and Library of the French

Protestant Church, Soho Square', *Proceedings of the Hugenot Society* 14 (1933), p555-61 and 'An early Hugenot library in Threadneedle Street', 18 (1949), p243-53.

Raymond Smith, *The Archives of the French Protestant Church of London*, 1952. (Hugenot Society quarto ser v 50), introd p1-14.

Friends House Library, Religious Society of Friends, Friends House, 173 Euston Road, London NW1 2BJ. Tel (01) 387 3601. Open (except week before Spring Bank Holiday, and 1 week in Aug) Mon-Fri 10 am-5 pm to members; others engaged in bona fide research should make written application in advance or arrive with a letter of recommendation. Photocopying, microfilming and photography, subject to restrictions.

The library is the central repository for archives and printed materials of the Society of Friends. It has grown out of the collections kept by the Recording Clerk who, from 1673 until the early 19th cent, was supposed to retain two copies of every work printed for the Society, and one of every anti-Quaker work. This collection became a separate library at the Society's headquarters at Devonshire House during the 19th cent, with a Librarian from 1901, moving with the Society's administration to Friends' House in 1926. It now contains over 50,000 v of printed books, pamphlets and periodicals, in addition to major collections of mss.

Card cat (authors) begun 1903, not including most pamphlets and a few books.

Selective subject index (not now added to) includes certain items (especially pamphlets) not in author cat.

Title index of books catalogued from 1976.

Devonshire House shelflist.

Anna L Littleboy, *A history of the Friends' Reference Library with notes on early printers and printing in the Society of Friends*, London, Friends Historical Soc, 1921.

M A Hicks, 'Friends' Reference Library, 1901–1959', *Journ Friends' Hist Soc* 49 (1959–61), p123-34.

'Devonshire House and its treasures', *Friend* 42 (50) (12 Dec 1902) p809-19).

Friends' Books c1,200 Wing, c2,000 ESTC, c2,500 of 1801–50. Includes the official archive of Quaker publishing through the Society's official printers the Sowle family (1680–1732), Thomas Sowle Raylton (1732–49), Luke and Mary Hinde (1739–75) and James Phillips (1775–99). There are gaps, and the collection was supplemented with major gifts from John Whiting (1656–1722), John Kendall (1726–1814), and Morris Birkbeck (1734–1816); Thomas Thompson (1776–1861) sold a collection to some Friends who gave it to the Society in 1831 (long kept separate, with a ms list, but not now identifiable). Many American Quaker publications are included.

Joseph Smith, *Descriptive catalogue of Friends' books...*, London, 2 v 1867; *Supplement* 1893 (interleaved copy marked with library holdings to c1957).

Adverse Books From 1673 a serious attempt was made by the Recording Clerk, aided by George Whitehead and William Penn, to obtain all works attacking the Society with a view to commissioning replies; it is a good representative collection of the 18th cent, but by no means comprehensive; from the early 19th cent it was no longer maintained. In 1814 Thomas Thompson (1776–1841) gave 70 adverse books. There are c800 Wing; c600 ESTC.

Joseph Smith, *Bibliotheca anti-Quakeriana; or, a catalogue of books adverse to the Society of Friends, alphabetically arranged; with biographical notices of the authors, together with the answers...*, London, 1873 (interleaved copy marked with library holdings to c1957).

Penn Collection A miscellaneous assortment in two albums of mss, transcripts, facsimiles, engravings, and newspaper cuttings, of and relating to William Penn (1644–1718), and the Friends at Philadelphia; with his tracts bound into volumes, including a unique copy of the first document issued by the Philadelphia Yearly Meeting *A general epistle given forth by the...Quakers* 1686. These supplement other works by Penn in the Library.

C M Andrews and F G Davenport, *Guide to the manuscript materials for the history of the United States...*, Washington, 1908, p350-4.

Tracts Several thousand tracts, bound by periods, from the 17th-20th cent; the first c300 are in contemporary bindings; the next 300 bound in the 19th and early 20th cent; continued in c400 boxes; c300 v of classified tracts; this collection includes odd numbers of periodicals, annual reports etc.

Mostly not in author cat, but some in subject index, especially under name headings.

Most volumes include ms list of contents.

Slavery tracts A separate collection of 37 v of 18th and early 19th cent tracts against slavery (with a few in favour). v 1-7 were assembled by Joseph Binyon Forster, and the remainder were from 3 other unidentified collections. There are also some tracts against slavery in the general tract collections, and anti-slavery journals among the periodicals. There is also the Thompson-Clarkson collection, assembled by Thomas Thompson (1776–1861) to illustrate *The history...of the abolition of the African slave-trade* 1808 by Thomas Clarkson (1760–1846); it is bound in 4 v, and includes tracts, newspaper cuttings, mss and portraits. All these collections are included in the microfilm edition *Anti-slavery collection from the Library of the Society of Friends* (London, World Microfilms, 1978–80).

Anti-slavery collection 18th-19th centuries from the Library of the Society of Friends, London, World Microfilms (1978), lists the complete contents of the collections filmed, and also the *Chronological bibliography of anti-slavery tracts* which also lists tracts in other collections, including that of the Anti-Slavery Society.

Richard Richardson (1623?–89), the Society's second Recording Clerk, gave 60 v from his library, mainly devotional and practical books 1600–60.

Kept as a special collection, uncatalogued.

Birkbeck Collection Part of the collection of Morris Birkbeck (1734–1816), mostly tracts bound in 28 v, deposited by the York meeting.

Periodicals A very extensive collection of Quaker journals from 1820 onwards, mostly after 1850, including some short-lived and scarce 19th cent journals.

Garrick Club Library, 15 Garrick Street, London WC2E 9AY. Tel (01) 836 1737. Open by appointment only (usually on Wed) after written application to the librarian.

The Club was founded in 1831 by Francis Mills, the art collector, who gave his collection of the correspondence of David Garrick (1717–79) to form the nucleus of the library, now *c*3,000 v, of theatrical history and *c*500 v of general works on theatre history. The Garrick Collection includes 6 v of cuttings, illustrations and anecdotes relating to Garrick collected by Sir Henry Irving (1838–1905); over 20 v of scrapbooks relating to Irving; archives of Drury Lane Theatre, known as the Northcote Collection. Over 45,000 playbills and programmes, mostly 1800–35, with some earlier; the Nixon Collection includes the earliest known playbill, that for *The Confederacy* at the Queen's Theatre, Haymarket, in 1705. Major collections of press cuttings. The large collection of plays includes *c*800 given by Lewis Crombie the newspaper proprietor in the early years of the Club, with 45 Spanish and 11 German. 97 v of French plays were given by Charles Kemble (1775–1854). Complete sets of early editions of Congreve and Wycherley given by John Payne Collier (1789–1883).

Guy Boas, *The Garrick Club 1831–1947*, The Club, 1948, p111-5.

H Thorogood, 'London clubs and their libraries', *Library Review* 13 (1951–2), p495-8.

R H Barham, *The Garrick Club*, priv pr 1896 (notes on early members, including their donations to the Library).

Geffrye Museum Reference Library, Kingsland Road, London E2 8EA. Tel (01) 739 8368. Open Tues-Sat 10 am-5 pm on written application to the Director. Photocopying facilities.

The Museum, on cabinet making and woodwork, was established in 1914 in the former almshouse of the Ironmongers' Company, where it is now maintained by the Greater London Council. The library is now a small collection of modern books and magazines on applied art, design, furniture, crafts etc. The rare books, *c*50 v are now segregated, mainly late 19th cent, with some earlier. They include pattern books for cabinetmakers, including Sheraton *Cabinet maker and upholsterer's drawing book* 1791–3, in its most complete state, and in exceptionally fine condition. General books on carpentry and joinery such as Swan *British architect* 1745. Cabinet makers' price books from 1803 onwards; 19th cent books on ornament; *The Workshop* v 1, nos 1-20 (1868).

Gemmological Association of Great Britain, Saint Dunstan's House, Carey Lane, London EC2V 8AB. Tel (01) 606 5025. Open (to non-members by prior arrangement only) Mon-Fri 10 am-4 pm.

Sir James Walton Memorial Library A library was begun in 1945 and was reorganized in collaboration with the National Association of Goldsmiths in 1958, when it was renamed after Sir James Walton (?–1955) who had been president of both associations. It has a collection of about 2,000 books (of which a small number are pre-1851) on all aspects of gemmology, including related facets of jewellery, lapidary, geology, mineralogy, precious metals and horology.

There is a dictionary catalogue on cards.

Geological Society of London, Burlington House, Piccadilly, London W1V 0JU. Tel (01) 734 5673. Open to members only Tues-Fri 10 am-5.30 pm. Photocopying facilities (to non-members through British Library Lending Division only).

The Society was formed in 1807 by a group of members of the British Mineralogical Society, and the Library, founded in 1809, soon became the focus of its activities, attracting substantial donations and bequests from fellows, including Sir Roderick Impey Murchison (1792–1871), George Bellas Greenough (1778–1855), William Smith (1769–1839), and most of the famous names in 19th cent geology. The emphasis in the Rare Book Collection is on mineralogy and palaeontology; zoology and botany were formerly included, but most of the non-geological books have been sold. The Collection illustrates the development of geology as a science, especially in 19th cent Europe.

Out of the library's 290,000 v of printed books and periodicals, about 5,000 pre-1851 remain, mostly published after 1800, of which two-thirds are foreign; there are some 18th cent and a few earlier works. Many copies are annotated by the 19th cent geologists, but some of these have been dispersed in sales, together with some of the periodicals and non-geological books (Sotheby 26-27 June and 23 October 1972; 19-20 March; 1-2, 8-9 and 29-30 October 1973; 4-5 February; 8-9 April; 29-31 July and 28-29 November 1974; 14-15 April 1975; 21-22 March and 21-22 November 1977).

The classified 'Catalogue of the books and maps in the Library of the Geological Society of London' by David T Ansted, 1846, was followed by a classified 'Supplemental catalogue', 1856, and two author supplements 'Alphabetical Supplement', 1860 and 'Third Supplement-catalogue' 1863. The Catalogue of the Library of the Geological Society of London compiled by James Dallas, 1881, is in order of authors (with topographically divided headings for Serials and for Surveys). Acquisitions were listed in the *Quarterly Journal* 1850–94, and then separately as *Geological literature added to the Geological Society's Library* 1895–1935, but the proportion of pre-1851 additions was small after 1900. A 'List of serial publications held in the Library of the Geological Society' appeared in 1978. There is a card catalogue of authors; a classified card catalogue, and a separate catalogue of the Rare Book Collection are in preparation.

Horace B Woodward, *The history of the Geological Society of London*, 1907, p47-8, 216-9 (the author's additional notes are in the Archives).

Extensive archives (in the care of the Secretary) include material on the Library, with a collection of mss and printed documents formed by Sir Richard Owen.

Sir Archibald Geikie, *The founders of geology*, London, 1905, and *Life of Sir Roderick Impey Murchison*, London 1875, 2 v.

Natural history manuscript resources, London, 1980, p191-7.

German Historical Institute Library, 42 Russell Square, London WC1B 5DA. Tel (01) 580 1757. Open Mon, Thurs 10 am-8 pm; Tues, Wed, Fri 5 pm to the public without formality. Photocopier; microfilm reader available.

The Institute was established in 1976 by the Verein zur Förderung des Britisch-Deutschen Historikerkreises e V (Anglo-German Group of Historians) which is a society of German and British historians with a special interest in each other's history. It is also known as the Deutsches Historisches Institut London, and is analogous to similar institutes in Rome and Paris, being financed, but not controlled, by the government of West Germany. It is a centre for research on modern, and particularly contemporary, history, to which research fellows are appointed.

The Library is a reference collection, now *c*20,000 v of books and periodicals, but growing rapidly; about two-thirds in German, otherwise mainly in English. Most of the collection is on post-medieval German and British history with the main emphasis on the 19th and 20th centuries, especially 1914 onwards, though it is intended to build up a comprehensive collection on earlier periods of German history also, and there are already some standard 18th and 19th cent editions of sources and monographs.

Card cat (author and classified).

German Lutheran Congregation, 22 Downside Crescent, Hampstead, London NW3 2AR. Tel (01) 794 4207. Admission by prior arrangement only, as the books are stored elsewhere.

The collections of the Hamburg Lutheran Congregation, founded in London in 1669 (now at Hackney, E8), and of St Mary's Lutheran Congregation, established at St Mary-le-Savoy in 1694 (afterwards in Cleveland Street, now at 10 Sandwich Street, London WC1). There are *c*50 v from 1549–1800; German Bibles, prayer books, theology (esp of Luther); German Protestant church constitutions; with mss.

Cat in preparation.

Goethe-Institut Library, 50-51 Princes Gate, Exhibition Road, South Kensington, London SW7 2PG. Tel (01) 581 3344/7. Library entrance is at the rear. Open Mon-Thurs 10 am-8 pm; Sat 10 am-1 pm to the public without formality. Photocopying; microfilm/fiche reader/printer.

The Goethe-Institut (sometimes referred to as the German Institute) was opened in 1958; it is a branch (one of several in the UK) of the Goethe-Institut at Munich founded in 1952 to provide a world-wide network financed by the government of West Germany for the promotion of German language, literature and culture. The library contains over 25,000 monographs, *c*150 serials, and collections of press cuttings and microfiches (including Marburger Index). Most of the books are in German, but there are also English translations and works written in English on Germany. The main emphasis is on German literature, language, art and history, but all fields of the humanities and social sciences relating to Germany are covered. Though few of the books held are rare, and almost all are after 1850, the Institute is directly linked to the West German inter-library loan system, and can procure for use in the library much of the material of the 17th, 18th and 19th cent held by West German libraries.

Card cat (authors and subjects).

'The Goethe-Institut in the United Kingdom' (leaflet).

Alison F Behr, 'A critical study of British Council, French Institute and Goethe Institute libraries in England, France and Germany...with special reference to literature...collections' (BA thesis, Polytechnic of North London School of Librarianship, 1981).

Goldsmiths' Company, Goldsmiths' Hall, Foster Lane, London EC2V 6BN. Tel (01) 606 8971. Open Mon-Fri 10 am-5.30 pm by appointment with the librarian. Photocopier available.

The Goldsmiths' Company is fifth in order of precedence of the City livery companies. (For the library given by the Company to the University of London, see University of London Library, Goldsmiths' Library.)

A **Goldsmiths' Company Archives**

The archives, mainly mss from the 14th cent, but including considerable printed material from the late 17th cent onwards.

Ms lists, but printed items not catalogued.

Some of the items are listed in W F Kahl, 'A checklist of books, pamphlets, and broadsides on the London livery companies', *Guildhall Miscellany* 2 (1962), p108.

See also Arthur Grimwade, *London Goldsmiths 1697–1837: their marks and lives...*, London, Faber, 1976.

B Goldsmiths' Hall Library

A collection begun *c*1950, perhaps incorporating a few books acquired earlier (most were destroyed by bomb damage) of *c*7,000 v, of which over 200 are pre-1851 (including 5 Wing and 20 ESTC items) on gold and silver smithing, for the most part of the artistic rather than the practical aspects, gemmology, metallurgy, assaying and hallmarking. There is a very comprehensive collection of trade journals from all parts of the world.

Card cat (author and subject) including the periodicals.

Twining Collection Books, pamphlets and photographs on the Crown Jewels and Regalia.

Gray's Inn Library, South Square, Gray's Inn, London WC1R 5EU. Tel (01) 242 8592. Open Mon-Thurs 9 am-4 pm (vac), 7 pm (term); Fri 6 pm (term) to judges and barristers of Inns of Court; to bona fide scholars at the librarian's discretion after written application. Photocopying facilities.

The Library of the Honourable Society of Gray's Inn dates from the mid-16th cent. It had been built up into a collection of *c*30,000 v by 1941, when all except the special collections below were destroyed by bombing. The new library now approaching 40,000 v has a general collection of British and Commonwealth law, including a few pre-1851 law reports, statutes, and treatises acquired mainly by donation.

Honourable Society of Gray's Inn, *A guide to the Library* (1980?).

Author card cat (recently superseding typescript looseleaf v) contains all collections except De Lancey.

P C Beddingham, 'A brief history of Gray's Inn Library: address to Gray's Inn Historical Society' (typescript, 1973).

——'A short account of Gray's Inn Library', *Law Librarian* 5(1) 1964, p3-5.

F Cowper and W Holden, 'Gray's Inn Library', *Graya* No 49 (1959), p9-24.

W R Douthwaite, 'Notes on the Gray's Inn Library', *Monthly Notes of the Library Association* 2 (1881), p2-7.

——*Gray's Inn*, London, 1886.

F Cowper, *A prospect of Gray's Inn*, London 1952.

J Drueller, 'Gray's Inn: a historical bibliography' (typescript, 1973).

Early printed book collection A collection of rare books of 15th-17th cent was evacuated with the mss and survived the bombing; mainly law with some English and foreign history, and English literature. *c*300 items including a few added post-1700. Four incunabula, including Statham's *Abridgement* 1475, and the only complete set of the works of Paulus de Castro, Milan 1488; 76 STC.

Shelflist. In general card cat and *Catalogue of the books in the Library of the Honourable Society of Gray's Inn*, 1872 (author cat with subject index; new editions 1886; 1906).

Bacon Collection Francis Bacon, Viscount St Albans (1561–1626), Lord Chancellor and Bencher of Gray's Inn. A collection of works by and about him. 75 first and other 17th cent editions of his writings, both philosophical and legal, some being donations from the younger Sir Francis Bacon (1587 and 1657) and Nathaniel Bacon (1593–1660); 89 later editions; 65 biographical and miscellaneous works, including some on the possibility of his authorship of the Shakespearean plays.

Card cat under Bacon.

De Lancey Collection Cornelius ver Heyden De Lancey (1889– ?) MA MD LIB LRCP RCS (Edin) BDSc LDS, advocate in Jersey, and art historian; in 1954 donated the French portion of his library; 1,445 v (about half pre-1851) of the period 1650–1925 of books in French, on French history, biography, politics, literature and art, with special emphasis on memoirs of the nobility of the 18th cent.

Typescript author cat.

Greater London Record Office and History Library, 40 Northampton Road, Clerkenwell, London EC1R 0AB. Tel (01) 633 6851 (liable to alteration).

The Record Office and Library, which are being transferred from County Hall to Clerkenwell during 1982, contain the historical portions of the archives and printed material belonging to the Greater London Council, with those inherited from the Middlesex County Council, and the London County Council (1889–1964) and its predecessors, the Metropolitan Board of Works (1855–88), the Metropolitan Buildings Office (1844–55), the School Board for London (1870–1904), the Board of Guardians of the Poor (1834–1930), and a number of smaller bodies. There are some unofficial collections, mostly deposited on loan. Large collections of maps and prints are also held.

Record Office and Library Report (for 1955–76, thereafter unpublished). Greater London Council, *Directory of GLC library resources*, 1971.

A Greater London History Library

Open Mon-Fri 9.15 am-5 pm by appointment, on written application to the librarian.

The library, founded as a general administrative reference and lending library *c*1860 by the Metropolitan Board of Works, became known under the London County Council as the Members' Library, though it was also open to the public for reference. It began to acquire a historical bias in 1911 with the Harben bequest, and this was followed by many donations and a vigorous purchasing policy in the historical field. In 1955 it became subordinate to the Record Office, and current material was gradually transferred to the new Research Library and other departmental libraries at County Hall. In 1978 it was renamed the Greater London History Library to reflect its changed scope. The library contains *c*100,000 v on London, including at least 50 STC and 100 Wing items. These include, in addition to the major collections listed below, collections given by a Mr Willis in 1956, H Bruce Penn in 1958, and George H Wincote of Acton in 1959–70; the collection on N W London of Godfrey Groves of Enfield was bought in 1980.

London County Council, *Members' Library catalogue* 1939 (classified). v 1: London history and topography (no more published). Some of the material for v 2 may be found in London County Council.

Catalogue of the contents of the Library, 1902, and *Supplement*, 1905.

Author and classified card cat contains works acquired from 1947 onwards; most older acquisitions are in dictionary card cat (accessible on request).

Quarterly *Accessions list* includes some rare books.

Special materials Over 1,000 local Acts (with separate index) including a collection of Acts on bridges 1708–1869; *c*200 directories; Bills of morality; a collection on New London Bridge 1767–1829. Ephemera (playbills, advertisements, programmes, etc).

Most of these collections not in the general cats.

Henry Andrade Harben (1849–1910), FSA, Lawyer and LCC Member, bequeathed his collection of *c*2,000 pamphlets, with ephemera, prints, maps and mss on Greater London, which became the core of the London history collection, not kept separate from later additions, including at least 10 STC and 15 Wing items.

Mostly in general printed card cat.

Books (but not pamphlets and ephemera) listed by author in *Catalogue of books, mss, prints, etc bequeathed by the late H A Harben Esq, to the London County Council*, (1918?), p1-21.

John (Elliot) Burns (1858–1943), trade union leader who represented Battersea at County Hall and at Westminster, amassed a library of over 12,000 items, parts of which are now in Wandsworth Public Library and the TUC Library, the remainder sold after his death. The Portion on London was withdrawn from the auction and sold privately to Julius Salter Elias, Viscount Southwood (1873–1946), who gave it to the LCC. *c*4,500 books and pamphlets, including much rare and early material, of both literary and social history interest.

Mostly in general card cat.

Catalogue of the famous library of the late Right Honourable William Burns...The first portion...on London, comprising...extra-illustrated...works on London and London life, including Lysons' Environs... and fine copies of Thomas Pennant...various editions 1793–1813; rare 16th and 17th cent books and tracts, including Arnold's London chronicle (?Antwerp, 1503)..., books with coloured plates, including Ackermann's Microcosm...Boydell, River Thames, 2 v 1794–6, Westell and Owen, Picturesque...Thames 1628, which will be sold, Sotheby & Co... 7 December 1943, 1943.

See also William Kent, *John Burns*, London, 1950, p316-49; Kenneth D Brown, *John Burns*, London, Royal Historical Society, 1977, p7-11, 189-90.

B Greater London Record Office

Open Tues-Fri 10 am-4.45 pm by appointment only. Descriptions below are limited to the more noteworthy printed material.

Typescript lists normally indicate printed material.
Card index (alph subject) includes printed material selectively.

Ida Darlington, *Guide to the records in the London County Council Record Office*, pt 1, 1965.

——'Local archives of Great Britain: 13: The County of London Record Office', *Archives* no 2 (1956), p477–86.

E D Mercer, 'Local archives...24: The Middlesex County Records', *Ibid* no 6 (1963), p30-9.

Middlesex Records The Middlesex Sessions records include printed Newgate calendars for 1820–53 (Class OB/CP), pollbooks 1749–1841 ms and printed (WR/PP), and an annotated set of Acts relating to Westminster 1773–1888 (MC/R). There are also the printers' notices issued under the provisions of the Seditious Societies Act 1799 for licensing presses, for the City of Westminster, and for Middlesex outside the limits of the cities 1799–1867 (incomplete, WR/LP and MR/LP).

Guide to the Middlesex Sessions records, the Office, 1965.

W B Todd, *A directory of printers...*, 1972.

London Records The records of the Metropolitan Commission of Sewers (1844–55, Class MSC) include 212 surveyors' reports printed for internal circulation, and other printed documents.

Parochial Records (Class P). The deposited records of many of the parish churches include printed material such as parish histories, service books, and appeals.

Foundling Hospital (Class A/FH). The deposited archives of the Foundling Hospital, founded in 1739, now called the Thomas Coram Foundation for Children, include much printed material of an administrative nature in addition to *c*50 miscellaneous v of books 1751–1937, mostly from the Hospital Library, 1 v of cuttings *c*1750–1890; 61 v of anniversary sermons 1813–79; various Bibles and Testaments 1825–1930; 33 service books *c*1749–1901; a substantial collection of Acts and Bills; and *c*150 v of official reports 1820–88 on charities.

St Thomas' Hospital archives and related collections (Class H.1/ST) (See also London, St Thomas' Hospital.) This very extensive deposited collection incorporates considerable quantities of 19th cent pamphlets, especially in the St John's House records (H.1/ST/SJ/A10-17) and Nightingale Training School records (H.1/ST/NTS). A factitious collection relating to the work of Florence Nightingale (1820–1910) known as the Nightingale Collection (H.1/ST/NC) consists of a mixture of letters, mss, pamphlets, cuttings and printed ephemera; it includes miscellaneous pamphlets on nursing to 1920.

Gas Companies There are extremely extensive deposits of records of the Gas Light and Coke Company (Class B(GLCC) and its predecessors from *c*1810. These include, in addition to prospectuses, bye-laws etc; a vast quantity of government publications; pamphlets; and newspapers relating to the industry.

Singleton's Eye Ointment Collection (Class B/SIN), deposited by Stephen Green Ltd, the present makers of the ointment once known as Doctor Johnson's Golden Ointment after its supposed 17th cent inventor Thomas Johnson, and renamed by Thomas Singleton (*d*1779). The records include printed material *c*1770–1910, including handbills and documents relating to litigation against counterfeiters. Among correspondence is a letter from George Norton, printer of Henley-on-Thames, with enclosure of catalogues of books, medicines and perfumery for sale.

Sons of the Clergy (Classes A/CSC and A/FSC). The Corporation of the Sons of the Clergy is an Anglican charity founded by charter in 1678 to support the dependents of clergy who had suffered for their loyalty. The main deposit of archives includes 7 reference books 1835–1911 (A/CSC/3182-3188). The deposit of the Festival of the Sons of the Clergy (A/FSC) includes handbills and specimens of printing 1871–1955, *A compleat list of the stewards...*, 1733, 14 sermons 1690–2, and 16 early 19th cent, and posters 1843–1950.

Archbishop Tenison's Grammar School, Kennington Oval (Class A/ATC). Deposited archives include Polano *Historie of the Council of Trent* 1620, and *Almanach de Gotha* 1765, 1774 and 1775, perhaps from Tenison's Subscription Library (see under London. Lambeth Palace Library, Section H). There are also mss and printed documents relating to the liquidation of the Subscription Library 1849–50.

Beaumont Institution and People's Palace (Mile End) (Class A/BPP) (See also under London. Queen Mary College.) Archives include printed documents 1812–89, and a collection of tracts by the Working Men's Lord's Rest Day Association 1883–9 against Sunday opening of museums, etc. *Palace Journal* no 1-16, which is perhaps the only surviving set.

Liberation Society and National Education Association Archives deposited by the Free Church Federal Council, of the Society for the Liberation of Religion from State Patronage and Control (founded 1844 as the British Anti-State-Church Association, renamed 1855, defunct 1957) and its offshoot the National Education Association (founded 1889, defunct 1959, and not to be confused with a like-named society with different objects founded 1964). The entire Liberation Society Library is included with its catalogue (Class A/LIB/271-916), comprising *c*600 v on the Church of England, especially in its relations with the State, patronage ritualism, RC tendencies, endowments etc. The National Education Association records (A/NEA) include *c*200 printed items, of which *c*80 are its own publications for the promotion of secular education.

A/NEA not yet fully listed, but see Bibliography in A P Derrington, 'The National Education Association of Great Britain 1889–1959', *History of Education Soc Bull* no 11 (Spring 1973), p18-33, where location 'no 1' indicates this collection.

Royal Society of Arts (Class A/RSA). The deposited records of the Society from 1840 include a large number of printed papers of the period 1841–55. (For the Library and earlier Archives see London, Royal Society of Arts Library.)

Ranyard Mission (Class A/RNY). The deposited records of the mission founded in 1857 by Mrs L N Ranyard for Anglican Biblewomen as the London Bible and Domestic Female Mission, renamed in 1868 London Biblewomen and Nurses Mission, and in 1952 the Ranyard Mission and Ranyard Nurses. They include much printed material, especially reports, magazines, pamphlets and ephemera.

Toynbee Hall (Class A/TOY). The archives of Toynbee Hall founded in 1884 by Samuel Augustus Barnett (1844–1913) afterwards Canon of Bristol, for the study of poverty, in memory of Arnold Toynbee (1852–83). There is much printed material including student magazines and pamphlets. Since the Library of the Hall, at 28 Commercial Street, London E1 was bombed, many of these are probably unique copies. Barnett's private papers are also held on deposit (F/BAR).

See J A R Pimlott, *Toynbee Hall...*, London, 1935.

Green Room Club, 8 Adam Street, London WC2N 6AA. Tel (01) 379 7946 or 836 2691. Open to members only.

The Club was founded in 1927. Its library of *c*500 v, mostly theatrical biography and history, includes a complete set in 67 v of the playbills of the Lyceum under Sir Henry Irving (1838–1905), a number of prompt copies, and some theatrical portraits.

Greenwich Public Libraries. Formed in 1965 from the amalgamation of the libraries of the Metropolitan Boroughs of Greenwich (founded 1905) and Woolwich (founded 1900).

A **Local History Library**

Woodlands, 90 Mycenae Road, Blackheath,

London SE3 7SE. Tel (01) 858 4631. Open Mon, Tues, Thurs 9 am-8 pm; Sat 5 pm. Photocopying and photography (except Martin collection, where it is limited by terms of the gift); microfilm reader/printer.

The Library is on the first floor (above an art gallery) of the house which George Gibson designed for John Julius Angerstein (1735–1823) the undewriter and art collector, friend of Johnson and Reynolds. It houses the archives and local history collections, both printed and ms of the Borough and its predecessors. The library of the Greenwich and Lewisham Antiquarian Society (containing mss and periodicals) is deposited here.

Woodlands Local History Centre, 1981 (detailed guide).

Woodlands Art Gallery, *John Julius Angerstein and Woodlands 1774–1974*, 1974.

Local Collection c5,000 books and pamphlets (*c*100 pre-1851) with maps and illustrations, on the Borough, including some material originally in the Kent collection. Local authors include Edith Nesbit (1858–1924) the novelist and versifier. Locally printed items include Erica Cotterill, *An Account* (1916) expressing her infatuation for G B Shaw in 5 v, perhaps the only complete set in a public collection; some astronomers, and a collection of local sermons.

Card cat (author and classified) continued by microfiche.

Bibliog in *Trans of the Greenwich and Lewisham Antiq Soc* 1 (1905–14).

Kent Collection c3,000 books and pamphlets, including a few STC and Wing, *c*200 ESTC and *c*500 1801–50, assembled by the Woolwich reference library, on the former county of Kent (material on the present Borough has been removed to the Local Collection). Strong in sermons preached in Kent.

Card cat (author and classified).

Martin Collection Comprises *c*10,000 items on Blackheath, Greenwich, Lewisham and Kidbrooke, or by authors who lived in the locality, given by Alan Roger Martin (1901–74) FSA; *c*3,500 books and pamphlets (including 1 STC, 4 Wing, 105 ESTC, *c*350 1801–50), together with ephemera, mss, and illustrations. Good coverage of sermons and church ephemera, sale catalogues, local periodicals, architecture, Greenwich Hospital, and Lewisham Grammar School. Some works on astronomy, an account of the association of Stephen Groombridge (1755–1832) with No 6 Eliot Place, Blackheath, which Martin bought and bequeathed to Morden College.

Typescript lists (in arbitrary shelf order).

'A R Martin', *Trans Greenwich and Lewisham Antiq Soc* 8(1) (1973), p86-9.

A R Martin, *No 6 Eliot Place Blackheath, the house and its occupants 1797–1972, ibid* 1974.

Periodicals and serials These include Directories from 1792 (6 pre-1851); pollbooks from 1734; local periodicals and newspapers from 1833; archaeological and historical periodicals, mostly, but not entirely, local to Kent and London (probably partly from Skipwith Bequest to Plumstead Library).

Poster Collection c500 local notices, playbills, and miscellaneous broadsides and ephemera, including 2 ESTC and *c*200 1801–50.

Subject cat on cards.

Nights and days out in Greenwich: posters, playbills, programmes and pictures, 1970 (exhibition cat).

Allan Glencross, *The Theatres of Greenwich and Woolwich*, 1970 (gratis from the library).

B **Woolwich Reference Library**

Calderwood Street, London SE18 6QZ. Tel (01) 854 8888 Ext 2333 (office hours) or 854 1939 (other times). Open Mon and Thurs 9 am-8 pm; Tues and Fri 5.30 pm; Sat 5 pm; rare books by appointment only.

The library was opened in 1900 and now houses *c*16,000 v including a segregated collection of pre-1801 books, containing 3 incunabula, 9 STC items, 17 Wing, 21 ESTC and 15 foreign; mostly on natural history, travel, literature, and English history. General stock includes a few 1801–50 books and 4 pre-1851 periodicals. A few pre-1801 works remain from a former special collection on engineering (the rest are at Plumstead).

Microfiche cat (author and classified) includes all the Borough reference libraries.

Card cat of pre-1801 books may be seen on request.

Serials on file, 1978.

C **Plumstead Library**

232 Plumstead High Street, London SE18 1JL. Tel (01) 854 1728/1759. Closed 1-2.15 pm, otherwise hours as Woolwich; by appointment only.

The library was opened (as a branch of Woolwich Borough Libraries) in 1904, and soon afterwards received the Skipwith Bequest, which seems to have remained a separate collection until *c*1930, when it was mostly integrated with the Reference Library collections at Woolwich (now probably mainly at Woodlands) and Plumstead; it was a general library strong on archaeological journals and historical books, but little, if any, of it remains at Plumstead.

Sports Collection (Metropolitan Special Collection. Dewey 790-799). This collection is still being enlarged under the LASER special collections scheme. It incorporates a special collection on mountaineering built up at Woolwich Reference Library from 1900, and includes *c*700 items, of which few are pre-1851; *c*500 on horse-racing, and some scarce 19th cent works. Cricketing reference books and annuals from mid-19th cent; a few rare works on chess.

Included in microfiche cat.

Guardian Royal Exchange Assurance plc, Head Office, Archivist's Library, Royal Exchange, London EC3V 3LS. Tel (01) 283 7101. Open Mon-Fri 9 am-5 pm on written application to the Archivist.

The Guardian and the Royal Exchange companies, both founded in the 18th cent and incorporating many other old insurance companies absorbed at various dates, were merged in 1968. Most of the books are from the Royal Exchange company, and seem to have been acquired on publication. They total *c*100 v, including *c*15 pre-1851 on insurance, mainly life assurance and actuarial works from 1805 onwards, with some 18th cent works on London and atlases, and many of the companies' publications, including magazines, agents' instruction books, and a volume of 18th and 19th cent policies collected by H Birck Sharpe.

Atlases and books on London are listed.

B Supple, *The Royal Exchange Assurance...1720–1970*, Cambridge Univ Press, 1970, p550-64 (a note on sources).

Guildhall Library, Aldermanbury, London EC2P 2EJ. Tel (01) 606 3030. Telex 887955. Open to all Mon-Sat 9.30 am-5 pm. Photocopying; microfilm and fiche readers.

General

A library established 1423–5 from the bequests of Richard Whittington and Richard Bury was removed *c*1549. The present library was founded 1824–8 as a collection on London and Middlesex for the use of the Corporation, opened to others by ticket in 1856, and converted into a public reference library in 1872. Damaged by bombing in 1940, it was rehoused in 1974.

Guides

Brief guide, 1976, and specialized guides (see below). Handlists of many collections in *Guildhall Miscellany*, 1952–73; *Guildhall Studies in London History*, 1973. Accessions noted in *Guildhall Library, Museum and Art Gallery Bulletin*, 1948–65. See also W E Miller, 'The materials for research in the Guildhall Library', *Opportunities for research in renaissance drama: report of Conference 23 (1959)...of the Modern Language Association of America*, (1960?), p24-7.

History (select references)

Library Committee minutes in Corporation of London Records Office. There is no systematic history. Outline in *The Corporation of London: its origin, constitution, powers and duties*, OUP, 1950, pp164-7. 15th cent library discussed by R Smith, *Guildhall Miscellany*, 1(1), Jan 1952, p2-9 and 1(6), Feb 1956, p2-6. W S Saunders, *Guildhall Library 1869*, is political. Growth expounded by C Welsh, *The Guildhall Library and its work*, 1893, and his articles in Corporation of London, *Literary dinner of the Library Committee...*, (1894), p31-41; The *Library* 1, 1889, p20-34, and ns 4(13) 1903, p68-73; and *Notices of Proceedings...of the Royal Institution*, 18 (1905–7), 1909, p467–82. The library at the turn of the cent described by E M Borrajo, *Library Association Record* 10, 1908, p381-95. Guildhall Library collection of cuttings (in chronological order) in Dept of Prints and Drawings.

A Department of Printed Books

Of the *c*147,000 books, pamphlets and ephemera (including special and deposited collections), at least 50,000 are pre-1851, including 84 incunabula, *c*1,100 STC, *c*5,000 Wing, *c*20,000 ESTC, *c*20,000 English of 1801–50, and up to 3,000 foreign of 1501–1850. The Department is built around the London collection, and was early extended into all aspects of English local and national history, topography, biography, genealogy, emigration, and the colonies. After 1872 the scope was widened to embrace literature and early foreign collections, aided by major bequests and the transfer of *c*5,000 duplicates from the British Museum in 1890 and part of the London Institution Library on its closure in 1913. More recently most of the foreign collections have been moved elsewhere.

Dispersals *c*28,000 v (including *c*10,000 pre-1851) were bombed, including the sale cats, Swedenborg collection, and Fanmakers' Company gift. The Corporation private lending library was partly dispersed and partly merged in the general collection. The library deposited by the Dutch Church in Austin Friars was mostly incorporated in Lambeth Palace Library, but partly sold (Sotheby 14 Dec 1959). The Bible collection has been given to the British and Foreign Bible Society. The Hebraica and Judaica are deposited in the Mocatta Library at University College. The Elzevier and Dutch collection was given to the University of London Library in 1950 and the Phelips Spanish collection deposited there, while the Phelips erotica went to the British Museum. The National Dickens Library was returned to the Dickens Fellowship in 1926 and is at Dickens House. The Glaziers' Company has reclaimed its collection.

General catalogues The first cat was in ms (now MS 15564). Classified cats published 1828 (with index of donors), 1840 and 1859 (with 15 supplements 1860–79). Last general printed cat (by authors) *Catalogue of the Guildhall Library*, 1889 shelf marked copy in cataloguing office. Card cats begun 1878, revised from 1945, include all gen, special and deposited collections except those specifically excluded below: author/name; general classified (broadly by Dewey); and London classified (see below under Ah).

Arrangement The Department's collections and special cats are grouped in this Directory as follows: Periods,

A(a); Official publications, A(b); Ephemera, A(c); Serials, A(d); Biography, genealogy, local history and directories, A(e); Law, A(f); Literature, A(g); London, A(h); Religion, philosophy and politics, A(i); Practical arts and commerce, A(j).

A(a) PERIODS. In classified cats entries usually arranged in reverse chronological order of publication.

Incunabula 84 in Proctor order, mostly German and Italian, 2 English, 2 unique. 46 bought from widow of Major Alfred Heales in 1900.

Cat, *Guildhall Miscellany* 1(7), Sept 1959, p63-74, with provenances.

STC and Wing c6,100. Strong emphasis on Parliament and the Civil War.

A list of books printed in the British Isles and of English books printed abroad before 1701 in Guildhall Library, 1966–7, by authors with concordances of STC and Wing numbers; addenda, *Guildhall Miscellany*, 3(1), Oct 1969, p85-9, and 4(4), April 1973, p156-60, and *Guildhall Studies*, 1980. Some broadsides in Noble collection and Dept of Mss not included.

ESTC All items in the library will appear in ESTC and in separate cat of Guildhall holdings.

A(b) OFFICIAL PUBLICATIONS. Majority not in gen cats.

Corporation publications, dispersed among Broadsides, Proclamations, and general collections.

Chronological slip index to c500 items 17th-19th cent incl mayoral proclamations, orders, etc, ms list of Court of Common Council acts, bills and orders (placed at L34"2) includes also holdings of the Records Office; 217 pre-1851 items.

Proclamations c1,300 filed chronologically.

Chronological slip cat. Included in pr.cat of pre-1701 books, but not in card cat. Most given as location in Steele's bibliography. Another collection in Records Office not included in any of these.

Parliamentary publications Many thousands of Statutes, Parliamentary papers (Commons complete from 1835; also facsimile series for pre-1801). Hansard complete, and many of the earlier compilations of debates and proceedings. Entries in author cat under Statutes and Parliament are selective (but complete for debates series). Complete finding lists of Statutes and pre-1835 Parliamentary papers in staff cat.

A(c) EPHEMERA. See also Proclamations under A(b); Dept of Prints and Drawings (B); Dept of Mss (C).

Almanacs c150 titles including over 1,000 pre-1851 v. Those published by the Stationers' Company are in Dept of Prints and Drawings.

Alphabetical list, *Guildhall Miscellany* 1(7), Aug 1956, p40-6. Chronological, in classified cat under 059.

Broadsides Main collection in Dept of Printed Books, c3,500 from 1580. Those in Noble and other collections of Dept of Prints and Drawings gradually being transferred to it.

Only those in Dept of Printed Books are catalogued: pre-1701 in pr.cat 1966–7; most in London classified cat, and in author/name cat under personal headings (but no title entries). Catchword index in staff area. Some not in card cats are in pr.cat 1889 and pre-war slip cat. 210 select ESTC items, *Guildhall Miscellany* 3(2), April 1970, p147-56.

A(d) SERIALS. Over 1,500 sets from 17th cent (See also under A(b), A(c), A(e)).

In author/name cat under title. No separate complete list. About three-quarters in *BUCOP*, a few only in *London Union List*. Alphabetical list for 17th cent, *Guildhall Studies* 1(2) Apr 1974, p94-105, 138 titles. Newspapers and newsbooks listed chronologically in classified cat under 072 and in *Catalogue*, 1889, under heading Newspapers. General periodicals in classified cat under 052 alphabetically; many periodicals in *Catalogue*, 1889, under title.

A(e) BIOGRAPHY, GENEALOGY AND HERALDRY, LOCAL HISTORY, DIRECTORIES. A strong general collection on English local history has been extended into personal and family history to complement the large deposits of genealogical source materials which are one of the major attractions of the library. The general collection of genealogy and heraldry was enlarged in 1902 by 31 rare pr books (with mss) from Joseph Jackson Howars (1827–1902). In 1941 c1,000 v (mostly pollbooks replacing a bombed collection) were bought from the executors of Eric N Geijer, Rouge Dragon Pursuivant. c400 v (mostly provincial directories) have come from the library of Sir Anthony Wagner, Garter Principal King of Arms.

A guide to genealogical sources in Guildhall Library, 2nd ed 1979, is of wide scope. See classified cat under 920-928 (collective biography) and 929 (genealogy and heraldry); author/name cat for individual biography.

London directories The largest collection in existence, including 3 Wing, 144 ESTC, and 201 of 1801–50.

Typescript handlist (including locations for directories not in library). Not in gen cats. Guildhall locations in C W Goss, *The London directories 1677–1855*, 1932 (op) are very incomplete. Typescript indexes (chronological, topographical, and trade sequences) of other lists (mostly ms) of London inhabitants.

National and provincial directories, including 8 ESTC and 23 1801–50 national (for England or Great Britain); 38 ESTC and c1,000 1801–50 provincial for places in British Isles (chiefly England).

Typescript handlist, with analytical entries for places in national and composite directories; more detailed analytical card index for pre-1820 directories. The older Guildhall locations are in Jane E Norton *Guide to the national and provincial directories of England and Wales*, London, 1950, (op). Not in gen cats.

Peerages c100 pre 1851.
See classified cat under 929.7201, and details of sets in shelflists.

Poll books c900 (pr and ms) relating to over 150 parliamentary and municipal constituencies 1700–1870.

Handlist of poll books and registers of electors in Guildhall Library, 1970 (op); copy with ms additions at Desk. Not in gen cats.

Professional directories Most of the lists of the older professions, eg *Army list* from 1740, *Navy list* from 1793, *Law list* from 1787.

Historical texts The library holds nearly all the publications relating to English and Welsh history in the series issued by the Record Commission and by antiquarian societies, inc c200 pre-1851 v listed by Mullins.
E L C Mullins, *Texts and calendars: an analytical guide to serial publications*, London, Roy Historical Soc, 1958.

A(f) LAW. General collection contains c100 pre-1851 monographs.

Remembrancer's Law Library c1,000 v of law reports 1653–c1880, given in 1885 by Samuel Prior Goldney, City Remembrancer, and subsequently enlarged; apparently originated as a private collection handed on by each Remembrancer to his successor.
Shelflist; also in card cats; and in *Catalogue*, 1889, designated 'RLL'. A card index of all law reports in the library and other departments of the Corporation, chiefly the Solicitor's Office and the Mayor's Court which hold some early sets, is available at the Desk; volumes elsewhere may be transferred for use of readers in the library.

A(g) LITERATURE. Towards the end of the 19th cent a general collection of English poetry and drama was built up, and was enriched by duplicates from the British Museum and several thousand literary works from the demise of the London Institution, including the first, third and fourth folio editions of Shakespeare. Purchases at sales included 746 v of general literature at that of James Anderson Rose, (Sotheby, 1 June 1891); 239 v early plays at that of Thomas Gaisford (Sotheby, 23 April 1890); 130 v at that of R M Holborn (Sotheby, 25 Jan 1893); 36 early Byron editions at that of Gennadius (Sotheby, 28 March 1895).

Chapman plays c1,400 editions including a few ESTC and c200 of 1801–50; given by Mary Anne Chapman, widow of George Chapman (1814–92) the swordsman, in 1895 (with books on Fencing, see A(j)).
Shelflist.

Hamilton plays Over 400 bequeathed by Walter Hamilton (1844–99), drama and book critic, including c150 ESTC, c100 items of 1801–50.
Shelflist.

Lamb, Charles (1775–1834), essayist. The Charles Lamb Society Library, founded 1935, deposited 1979. c2,900 books and pamphlets by or about Lamb.
Separate card cat; being incorporated in general cat.

Settle, Elkanah (1648–1724), the last 'City poet'. A collection of 75 items including the poems on civic occasions and mayoral shows, many in his presentation bindings.
List, *Guildhall Miscellany* 2(9), Aug 1967, p418-23.

Wise, Thomas James (1859–1937) 95 items, mostly donated by him between 1893 and 1932, of his forgeries and piracies, works edited by or privately printed for him, and other donations.
K I Garrett, *Thomas J Wise and Guildhall Library*, 1970 (op) lists the collection, also 54 formerly included which were bombed, but not the Shelley reprints donated by Wise's accomplice Harry Buxton Forman (1842–1917) which were also destroyed.

Gresham College General library of 321 pre-1851 works of general literature and travel, including 3 incunabula and Music Library of which only scores now remain. Deposited in 1958, when a part of the library duplicating books already at the Guildhall was given to the University of Malta. The College was established in 1581, but most of the library came from the Hollier bequest in 1871.
Shelflist. See also typescript list dated 1930 (placed at Gresham 381), and *Catalogue of books, pictures, prints, etc presented by Mrs Laetitia Hollier to, and also of books and music in the Library of Gresham College*, 1872.

A(h) LONDON. The City of London forms the core of the library, but the rest of the former London County Council area is also covered intensively. Altogether c25,000 items, including c9,000 pre-1851. Major donations include 42 v rare tracts from Henry Butterworth in 1829, many of 632 v from W T Wingrove brassfounder in 1889, and many of 273 v of architecture from Willoughby Mullins, c1895. See also Corporation publications in A(b) above; Department of Prints and Drawings (B); Department of Mss (C).

Guide to the London collections, 1978, covers all three departments; p7-8 list special indexes. Special classified card cat arranged by the *Classification for London literature based upon the collection in the Guildhall Library*, 3rd ed 1966 (op). Also pre-war classified cat including bombed items and also some surviving ephemera not in current cat.

Handlists The following handlists on London topics are in the *Guildhall Miscellany*:
Calamities, wonders, and topics of the Town 1603–1902 (excluding almanacs and chapbooks), 385 selected items, chronological. 2(10). Oct 1968, p463-82.
Education before 1970; 227 selected items, classified.

3(3), Oct 1970, p218-32.

Fire of 1666 and rebuilding: 168 items, authors. 2(8), Sept 1966, p369-76.

Livery companies, chronological: 723 entries with 130 Guildhall locations. 2(3), April 1962, p99-126. Complement to W F Kahl, *The development of London livery companies*, Boston, Mass, 1960, p36-104 (bibliography with Guildhall locations).

Pageants: collection of 80 pamphlets describing Lord Mayors' shows, royal occasions, etc; classified. 2(6), Oct 1964, p257-69.

Plague and Bills of mortality 1532—1858; classified; 148 titles on plague and numerous sets of bills (including deposited collection of Parish Clerks' Co and that in Records Office). 2(7), Sept 1965, p306-17; 2(8), Sept 1966, p367-8.

Thames to 1900: classified; including 31 pre-1851 items, 9 on frost fairs. 4(3), Oct 1972, p184-93.

Theatres to 1900: 215 items, many from Hamilton bequest (See A(g) above); chronological, mainly limited to first editions. 4(2), April 1972, p121-35.

A(i) RELIGION, PHILOSOPHY AND POLITICS

Cock collection, 210 v mostly relating to Sir Thomas More (1478—1535), Lord Chancellor, and mostly pre-1851; formed by Alfred Cock, QC (1849—98), and bought for the library by public subscription after his death. Includes first and later editions of *Utopia* and other works (including translations) by More, works about him, and some editions of Erasmus.

The Alfred Cock memorial. Catalogue of books, portraits, &c, of or relating to Sir Thomas More, collected by the late Alfred Cock, QC, 1903 (op). All printed books in the library by or about More (including those from Cock) listed, *Guildhall Miscellany* 4(1), Oct 1971, p44-60. A note on Cock is included in 'The Thomas More Exhibition...1977', *Moreana* 15, 1978, p121-2.

Hackney College (or Tyssen) collection of liberal dissenting theology c1,800 items, including some Wing, c500 ESTC, c1,000 of 1801—50. Sermons and tracts written by, about, or against Unitarians, and by others expressing Arian or Socinian beliefs (including Presbyterians, Congregationalists, Baptists, and Anglicans); with a few miscellaneous books by Unitarians, donated by John Robert Daniel-Tyssen, FSA (1805—82) solicitor in Hackney, 1860 (the rest of his collection became the public library of Hackney). The college was founded in 1786 by the Unitarian Society, but closed in 1796, and part of the library was sold to repay creditors (Sotheby, 21 July 1802). Tyssen acquired many of its books and added others from notable dissenting collections, eg that of Walter Wilson (1768—1863) (Sotheby, 5 July 1847). College lecturers are well represented: Joseph Priestley (1733—1804) 314 items; Thomas Belshal (1750—1829) 78; Richard Price (1723—91) 66; Gilbert Wakefield (1756—1801) 61; Andrew Kippis (1725—95) 25; Abraham Rees (1743—1825) 12; and Hugh Worthington (1752—1813) 11. Also includes Robert Aspland (1782—1845) 54 items; Samuel Palmer (1741—1813) 46; John Pye Smith (1774—1851) 34; and c200 others, mostly ministers of chapels in the neighbourhood of Hackney.

Shelflist of main collection (Store 1073-1074), but some items are in general collection, especially Biography. Classified cats chiefly under L18 and 288. 30% listed in *Supplement* (first) 1860 to pr cat, p49-88. 80% in *Catalogue*, 1889. Handlist of 178 of the Priestley items, *Guildhall Miscellany* 3(4) April 1971, p287-300 (most not recorded as locations in Crook's bibliography). See also H McLaghlan, *English education under the Test Acts*, Manchester, 1931, p246-55.

Wilkes, John (1727—97), Lord Mayor, MP, and Libertarian. In London and general collections. Handlist of 154 selected items by or about him, *Guildhall Miscellany* 3(1), Oct 1969, p75-84.

A(j) PRACTICAL ARTS AND COMMERCE

Clockmakers' Company This livery company founded a library in 1813 and deposited it in 1873 (with a museum and archives). c1,000 books, including c300 pre-1801. Supplemented by Antiquarian Horological Society collection deposited 1973 including a few pre-1851.

John Bromley, *The Clockmakers' Library: the catalogue of books and manuscripts in the library of the Worshipful Company of Clockmakers*, 1977, superseding a series of printed cats from 1830 (some of the books they record have been sold). Temporary card cat of Antiquarian Horological Society, not yet in gen cat. 'Horological Index' on cards of sources on clocks and clockmakers. Card index compiled privately by Clive Osborne of sources for over 300,000 makers may be consulted by special arrangement.

Cookery 239 books including 75 pre-1851, mostly from the widow of Alderman John Staples (chairman of Library Committee, and Master of Cooks' Company); augmented by Cooks' Company, and by 76 of 195 v bequeathed by Robert Miller in 1899.

Author handlist, *Guildhall Miscellany* 1(9), July 1958, p52-9.

Fencing 54 works 1553—1900 (not kept together), mainly from the widow of George Chapman (1814—92) founder of the London Fencing Club, chiefly technical, including military manuals.

Author handlist, *Guildhall Miscellany* 2(5), Oct 1963, p227-9.

Gardeners' Company Library founded 1891 in Guildhall Library on deposit; since 1967 has acquired only rare books. c300 items, 100 pre-1851, from 1608.

A catalogue of the horticultural library of the Worshipful Company of Gardeners in Guildhall Library, 1967, authors; classified cat under 631-635.

Lloyd's marine collection, deposited by Lloyd's. c3,000 v on shipping movements and casualties. *Lloyd's list* from 1740 (with index of vessels from 1838), and *Lloyd's register* from 1764. (Monographs all post-1850.)

Typescript handlists. Not in card cats.

Shorthand Historical collection, 106 items, mostly pre-1851.

Author handlist, *Guildhall Miscellany* 2(1), Sept 1960, p39-52; chronological in classified cat under 653.4 (to 1800 also in Alston v 8).

Stock Exchange, deposited 1979, including 6 runs of pre-1851 share price lists (some unique), prospectuses of companies from *c*1800 (but not reports till 1869), and a few pre-1851 books on trading in securities.

Classified cat under 332.63 and L64.6. Prospectuses uncatalogued.

Wine trade collection Founded 1908 as library of the Wine Trade Club under aegis of Andre Louis Simon (1877–1970); taken over on club's demise in 1966 by the Institute of Masters of Wine, which has enlarged and deposited it. 1,421 books and pamphlets (307 pre-1851), 97 v of periodicals; and mss. All aspects of wine trade, including alcoholism.

A catalogue of books belonging to the Institute of Masters of Wine deposited in Guildhall Library. 1972 (op); typescript supplements. Classified cat under 663.2 also includes six 17th cent books deposited by Vintners' Company.

B Department of Prints and Drawings

Prints, cuttings, maps, photographs, with the printed ephemera listed below:

Guide to the London collections, 1978, p1-6. Many special indexes, but printed ephemera not individually catalogued.

Prints *c*30,000, chiefly 18th-19th cent topographical, including extra-illustrated books. The illustrated books from the bequest of old master prints of William Hughes Willshire (1816–99) have been transferred to the Department of Printed Books incunabula and general collections.

M W Barley, *A guide to British topographical collections*, 1974, p74-6, includes each extra-illustrated book in the alphabetical list of collections.

Cuttings 43,000; including collection on London bought from Theophilus Charles Noble, historian of City institutions, and still added to. Noble's books are in Department of Printed Books, and the broadsides and other significant ephemera are gradually being transferred to that dept.

Playbills *c*15,000, and theatre programmes of 120 London and 250 provincial theatres, 18th-19th cent, mainly from the Hamilton collection (see under A(g) above), with indexes.

Fires Fire Protection Association collection; ephemera and prints to 1947 of all places and periods. Fire of Parliament in 1834.

Playing Card Makers' Company, formerly Phillips collection. 800 historic packs of cards; small library, including a few pre-1851 books. On deposit.

Catalogue of the collection...formed by Henry D Phillips, 1903, including books.

Miscellaneous collections 2,333 bookplates (most post-1850) with indexes. *c*1,600 trade cards etc (mainly 1750–1850) with indexes, with some small unindexed collections. Invitations, programmes, menus, etc of 1,300 civic occasions from 1727. John Fillinham's collection on London public gardens. Fairs, especially Bartholomew Fair. The mayoralty of John Key in 1830–1.

C Department of Manuscripts

(Does not include the Corporation archives, which are administered independently in the Corporation of London Records Office.)

*c*85,000 ms units, which include some printed ephemera. Records of parishes, wards, manors, estates, and institutions of the City of London. Diocese of London archives. Mss relating to the City. Pre-1851 printed material, chiefly in deposits of 76 livery companies, and 144 businesses and 29 societies beginning before 1851.

Philip E Jones and R Smith, *A guide to the records of the Corporation of London Records Office and the Guildhall Library Muniment Room*, 1951 (op). *Guide to the London collections*, 1978, p10-42, including lists of names of firms, societies, and livery companies whose records are deposited. *Guide to genealogical sources*, 1979. Cat in ms, with classified and name indexes on cards; sometimes noting presence of printed material.

Note All the surviving archives, printed and manuscript, of the following livery companies are deposited in the appropriate departments of the Guildhall Library: Bakers' Company; Barbers' Company; Basketmakers' Company; Blacksmiths' Company; Bowyers' Company; Broderers' Company; Butchers' Company; Carmens' Company; Carpenters' Company; Clockmakers' Company; Coachmakers and Coach Harness Makers' Company; Cooks' Company; Coopers' Company; Cordwainers' Company; Curriers' Company; Cutlers' Company; Distillers' Company; Dyers' Company; Fan Makers' Company; Farriers' Company; Feltmakers' Company; Fletchers' Company; Founders' Company; Framework Knitters' Company; Fruiterers' Company; Gardeners' Company; Girdlers' Company; Glass Sellers' Company; Glaziers' Company; Glovers' Company; Gold and Silver Wire Drawers' Company; Grocers' Company; Gunmakers' Company; Haberdashers' Company; Horners' Company; Innholders' Company; Ironmongers' Company; Loriners' Company; Musicians' Company; Needlemakers' Company; Painter-Stainers' Company; Pinners' Company; Parish Clerks' Company; Pattenmakers' Company; Paviors' Company; Poulters' Company; Playing card Makers' Company; Plaisterers' Company; Plumbers' Company; Saddlers' Company; Salters' Company; Scriveners' Company; Shipwrights'

Company; Silk Throwsters' Company; Spectacle Makers' Company; Turners' Company; Tin Plate Workers' Company; Tobacco Pipe Makers' and Tobacco Blenders' Company; Upholders' Company; Vintners' Company; Wax Chandlers' Company; Weavers' Company; Wheelwrights' Company.

Guildhall School of Music and Drama Library, Silk Street, Barbican, London EC2Y 8DT. Tel (01) 628 2571. Open Mon-Thurs 9 am-7.15 pm, Fri 5.30 pm (term); Mon-Fri 9.30 am-4.45 pm (vacation), (usually closed 12.30-1.30); to members of the School; to others by appointment only.

Though the School was founded by the City Corporation in 1880, the Library has been actively organized only since 1973. It contains over 42,000 v of music scores, drama texts, musicology, and to a more limited extent works on the drama. There are special collections of guitar and double-bass music and vocal scores. Alkan Society collection (mainly scores, but some books) is deposited.

Microfiche cat (author and classified) separate for music and for drama (special collections in course of being incorporated).

Hugh Barty-King, *GSMD: a hundred years' performance*, London, Stainer and Bell for the School, 1980, p146.

Westrup Library The working library of Sir Jack Westrup (1904–75), Heather Prof of Music at Oxford, bought by the Worshipful Company of Musicians, who deposited it on permanent loan at the Guildhall School in 1977 to form the core of the Reference Library. *c*4,000 v of books on music, mostly 20th cent, but including a few of the 18th and 19th cent with 870 scores.

Card cat, to be superseded by microfiche.

Rosencweig Collection *c*100 v of 19th and 20th cent on Jewish music, with some scores, deposited on permanent loan by Harry Rosencweig. Currently being enlarged.

Mostly uncatalogued, some on microfiche.

Bingham Collection A collection of 20th cent English literature, *c*2,000 v, mostly plays from *c*1920 to *c*1955, including much very recondite material. It was given to the School in 1969 by W Rapier Bingham.

Included in microfiche cat.

Gunnersbury Park Museum, Gunnersbury Park, London W3 8LQ. Tel (01) 992 1612. Books can be seen by appointment 9 am-5 pm.

The Museum was opened in 1929 with local interest collections purchased in 1927 from Major Sadler (see below). It is housed in the mansion where the family of Lionel Nathan Rothschild (1809–79) lived until 1925. It now belongs to the boroughs of Hounslow (whose Librarian administers it) and Ealing. The general reference library, built up for staff use, covers archaeology, local and social history. With the special collections below, there are *c*800 v, of which *c*250 are pre-1851; also prints, drawings and maps.

Card cat by authors of all the printed collections.

R G L Rivis, *The Gunnersbury Park Museum 1927–1955* [1960].

Chiswick Press *c*40 v printed at the press during its earliest period, acquired to exemplify the products of the 1804 Stanhope Press (the earliest surviving example) which was used at the Chiswick Press until *c*1860, and is now on display in the Museum.

Sadler, Major Frederick His collection of books of local interest, *c*400 v (including *c*100 pre-1851), chiefly works of local authors, eg Richard Baxter (1615–91) the Presbyterian (9 first editions); Edward G E L Bulwer-Lytton, Lord Lytton (1803–73) (24 early editions of his novels); Lady Mary Wortley Montagu (1689–1762); and Sir Matthew Hale (1609–76). Also topographical works on Middlesex and Greater London.

Typescript list.

Children's books *c*150 v (including *c*80 pre-1851) of the period 1801–1920, but mostly 1820–80 bought and donated to complement the collection of toys. Includes gift books, annuals, and magazines. *c*25 v by Mrs Sarah Trimmer (1741–1810) of Brentford, together with other moralists.

Guy's Hospital Medical School, Wills Library, St Thomas Street, London Bridge, London SE1 9RT. Tel (01) 407 7600 Ext 3374. Open Mon-Fri 9.30 am-5 pm to applicants engaged on bona fide research who send letter of introduction in advance and produce identification on arrival.

General Thomas Guy (1645?–1724), a bookseller, financier and philanthropist, who was a governor of St Thomas's, founded his new hospital across the street from the old in 1722–6. The two hospitals shared common facilities, including the reference library at St Thomas's. Teaching at Guy's was institutionalized by the erection of a lecture theatre in 1760, and in 1771 a lending library was set up by the Physical Society (see below). A rift between the hospitals, begun 1825 and completed 1837, compelled Guy's to set up its own Medical School and a reference library was possibly in existence in the latter year. In 1852 the Medical School acquired the large Physical Society collection, and it was successively enriched by the collections of Dr Henry Marshall Hughes (1805–53); Dr Benjamin Harrison jr (1771–1856) FRS, Guy's Treasurer; John Hilton (1804–78) FRS, Surgeon; Dr Philip Henry Pye-Smith (1839–1914); and Arthur Edward Durham (1834–95), Surgeon. In 1903 a governor, Sir Frederick Wills bart. (1838–1909) financed the construction of a library in the new Medical School building and gave his name to it. The school is now an undergraduate school of the University of London.

Card cat excludes most rare books and special collections.

S Wilks and G T Bettany, *A biographical history of Guy's Hospital*, London, 1892.

Sir Hector C Cameron, *Mr Guy's Hospital*, London, Longman, 1954.

Guy's Hospital Gazette 1872– , and four supplementary historical volumes.

Special number in commemoration of the bicentenary ed L G Housden (1925).

Guy's Hospital 1725–1948 ed H A Ripman (1948).

Centenary edition ed T B Barnes (1972).

Guy's Hospital: 250 years ed C E Handler (1976).

The hospital archives, containing a few references to the Library, are deposited in the Greater London Record office.

R M Nicholas, 'The development of medical libraries within the University of London', (MA Librarianship thesis, Univ London, 1976), p20-30.

Physical Society held at Guy's Hospital The library of this Society does not now form a separate collection, being integrated into the historical and periodicals collections, but it is by far the largest single source of rare books in the Wills Library, and most of its volumes can be identified by the lettering of the Society's name on their bindings. In 1771 the demand for professional meetings and for library facilities within Guy's led to the formation of the Physical Society held at Guy's Hospital, which was open to all medical men in London, and built up a large lending collection (over 1,000 v by 1823). The resident Apothecary was customarily the librarian. Competition from an offshoot, the Pupils' Physical Society, and from other medical societies in London, led to the Society's dissolution in 1852, when its library, then exceeding 1,500 v, was given to the Medical School.

The Society's minutes (incomplete) are in the Wills Library.

Laws (ms) 1775 and later printed editions.

A list of the officers... with... catalogue of the books, 1786.

A catalogue of books 1823 (interleaved copy with ms additions).

J R Wall, 'The Guy's Hospital Physical Society', *Guy's Hospital Reports* 123 (1974), p159-70.

J M H Campbell and I H Dodd, 'The history of the Physical Society', *Guy's Hospital Gazette* Special no... of the bicentenary (1925), p107-19.

W Hill, 'Wills Library antiquities', *Ibid*, 81 (1967), p1-11.

Guy's men A collection of works by men connected with the hospital, including a few non-medical, with *c*20 ESTC; *c*120 of 1801–50.

William Wale, *List of books by Guy's men in the Wills Library, Guy's Hospital*, 1913. (Repr from *Guy's Hospital Reports* 67 (1913), p265-333. A few copies have portraits added.)

Historical Collection Containing all pre-1851 books formerly in the general collections (including those from the Physical Society) shelved by author. *c*2,300 English and foreign, including 2 incunabula; 11 16th cent; *c*100 17th; and at least 500 18th cent, covering the traditional medical topics, and psychology, botany, zoology and chemistry. First editions of many of the medical classics.

Incomplete author cat on cards.

G E R Winston, 'Old books in the Wills Library', *Guy's Hospital Gazette* 43 (29 Nov 1929), p176-82.

Periodicals Collection includes *c*800 v pre-1851 (nearly all English), some of which are publications of short-lived medical societies, mostly from the library of the Physical Society.

Cat of the collection (computer printout) includes very few of the older titles.

Hackney College, Hackney Centre, Keltan House Annexe Library, 89-115 Mare Street, London E8 4RG. Tel (01) 985 8484. Open during term only Mon-Thurs 8.45 am-7 pm; Fri 8.45 am-5 pm.

Horology Collection Begun by Northampton Polytechnic about 1930, and transferred in 1959 when this subject was removed from the curriculum. About 300 v (increasing), of which a small proportion are rare or pre-1851; some former volumes are lost, and many early books are represented by facsimile reprints.

Card cat.

Hackney Public Libraries, Central Library, Mare Street, London E8 1HG.

In 1965 the libraries of the Metropolitan Boroughs of Hackney, Stoke Newington, and Shoreditch were amalgamated into those of the London Borough of Hackney. The local history collections are being centralized with the Borough Archives, but the Central Reference Library (formerly the Metropolitan Borough of Hackney collection) at Mare Street, which has only a handful of pre-1851 books, and the Stoke Newington Reference Library, are retaining their other collections.

Catalogue of the books in the Central Public Library, Mare Street, Hackney, 1908 (now dictionary card cat).

Golden jubilee of the Hackney Public Libraries, (1958).

A **Stoke Newington Reference Library**

Church Street, London N16 7TH. Tel (01) 800 1282. Open Mon-Fri 9 am-9 pm, Sat 5 pm, but for rare books and special collections strictly by appointment only.

Reference Library (general) The collections of the Metropolitan Borough of Stoke Newington, whose Reference Library was established in 1890. *c*1,200 pre-1851 books are held, including 29 STC; 134 Wing; 635 ESTC; 4 foreign books of the 16th cent; 7 17th; and 6 18th cent. The pre-1701 are almost entirely from the Sage bequest (qv), but many later books on historical and literary subjects are from other donations.

Card cat (author and classified).

Separate author cats for 16th, 17th and 18th cent may be consulted on application.

K A Manby, 'The libraries of Stoke Newington and Hornsey 1890–1900', *Journ of Librarianship* 6(2) (1974).

Sage bequest The library of Edward John Sage (1827?–1905), local historian bequeathed with prints, portraits and other material; no longer a separate collection, but Johnson and Walpole collections (below) are mainly from this source. It consists predominantly of English literature from the 16th-19th cent, books on Stoke Newington and the vicinity (now in Local Collection), and some miscellaneous early printed books. At one time probably over 2,000 v. (The portion on Essex assembled by his father Edward Sage, who was Deputy Steward of the Manor of Barking, is deposited in the Essex Record Office.)

Provenance identified in card cat, but there is no separate list (except for the Essex deposit, issued by Essex Record Office 1952–3).

Obits in *Notes & Queries* (10th ser) 4, p540; *North London Guardian* 8 Dec 1905.

Johnson, Samuel (1709–84) LLD, lexicographer. A collection of 178 books by and about him, including 26 pre-1801 editions of Johnson and Boswell from the Sage bequest (some of which are Johnson and Boswell association copies).

Author cat under Johnson and Boswell.

Walpole, Horace, 4th Earl of Orford (1717–97). A collection of Walpole's works and books printed on his press at Strawberry Hill, from the Sage bequest, together with later biographical material. Includes 25 pre-1801 Walpole editions, in addition to other Strawberry Hill Press items.

Local history collection The collection is notable for its sub-collections of the writings of local authors, who include Daniel Defoe (1661?–1731) (413, including *c*40 pre-1801 items); Isaac Watts (1674–1748) the hymnodist (176, including 63 pre-1801); Edgar Allan Poe (1809–49) poet and novelist (116 items) and the Aikin family, including John Aikin (1747–1822) and Anna Laetitia Aikin; Mrs Barbauld (1743–1825) (209 items); Richard Price (1723–91) (19 items). These author collections are expected to remain at Stoke Newington after the general local history collection has been transferred to the Archives Dept.

Card cat (author and classified).

Stoke Newington Public Libraries

Daniel Defoe, 1660–1731: commemoration in Stoke Newington of the tercentenary of his birth, an exhibition..., 1960.

Metropolitan special collection: Africa and Asia A collection on the history and topography of Africa and Asia, collected from 1950 under the Metropolitan/LASER Special Collections Scheme, and still added to. Contains a few pre-1851 books, though predominantly modern. (Administered by staff of the Lending Library.)

Card cat (classified) but pre-1801 items included also in Reference Library 16th, 17th and 18th cent lists.

B **Archives and Local History Department**

Rose Lipman Library, De Beauvoir Road, London N1 5SQ. Tel (01) 249 3669. Open by appointment only Mon-Fri 10 am-7 pm, Sat 5 pm.

The archives of the former boroughs of Hackney, Shoreditch and Stoke Newington, including some literary mss from their libraries and some printed material, have been centralized here. The printed local history collections from Shoreditch and Hackney (Tyssen Library) have already been brought here, and those from Stoke Newington are likely to follow. The printed collections include pre-1851 directories, topographical books and a collection of *c*1,000 playbills for theatres in Shoreditch *c*1831–90.

Card cat (author and classified).

Tyssen Library Originally a library (with extensive ms transcripts from archives) on Hackney assembled by John Robert Daniel-Tyssen (1805–82) FSA, solicitor, and brother of the Lord of the Manor of Hackney. He had given the portion on New College and the Hackney unitarians to the Guildhall, but when he died his sons gave the remainder to the parish vestry, who opened it to the public at Hackney Town Hall. It was enlarged by numerous donors over the next few years, and became the nucleus of the local history collection in the Borough reference library in Mare Street, Hackney, when it opened in 1908, whence it is being transferred during 1982. The original Tyssen portion is not now distinct from later accretions, and the whole library, still called the Tyssen Library, is to be merged with the local history collections from Shoreditch. The original gift included, among *c*2,000 printed items, a few STC, and *c*100 Wing items, many of the early items not being closely connected with Hackney; also *c*1,000 ESTC items (predominantly sermons, and genealogical works, with a wide variety of other subjects, including literary works). The Tyssen mss include a collection of ephemera on elections in Hackney 1840–70 (D/F/TYS/10).

J T Whitehead, *Catalogue of the Tyssen Library...*, 1888.

Ms working cat.

Ms cat of books donated to the Tyssen Library by W Amhurst Tyssen Amherst, MP 1887 (D/F/TYS/61).

Ms cat of donations to the Tyssen Library after the original gift, mostly from George Chambers (included in supplement to Hackney Metropolitan Borough printed cat).

Dawson Library, (Shoreditch Parish Library) deposited on permanent loan. The only surviving parochial library in London. Collected 1710–62, for his personal use, by sailor and excise officer John Dawson (1692–1763) and bequeathed by him (with reference in his will to the Parochial Libraries Act 1709, and special conditions) to the Vicar of St Leonard, Shoreditch, then John Denne (1693–1767) Archdeacon of Rochester, a well known antiquary, and his successors for ever. The conditions were ignored and the books were kept in the church, whence many disappeared. The collection was transferred to Shoreditch Public Library on its opening in 1892 by the Vicar, Septimus Buss (1836?–1914), without authority, and from 1894 to 1979 it was kept as a separate collection in Hoxton Branch (later Shoreditch District) Library in Pitfield Street. It was slightly damaged in the 1939–45 war, and uniformly rebound 1956–8. Of the 879 v received in 1765, 635 remain (in addition to 6 v stray from elsewhere). All in English, 1620–1762, they include 4 STC and 49 Wing items; 231 have ms contents lists by Dawson, 42 ms text indexes and 24 ms illustration indexes by him, 8 have ms chronological tables, and 14 his marginal notes. There is a small number of books on his professional interests (including several early works): mathematics, excise gauging, and navigation. Large collection of travel and voyages; history, mainly in standard sets, including the *Universal history*, and many of the histories of Parliament; English literature, especially mid-18th cent plays and novels. Other subjects include: devotional and other religious books (chiefly Anglican and ecclesiastical history; classical and continental literature in translation; dictionaries, encyclopaedias, and biographical reference books; moral and political philosophy, including first edition of Hobbes *Leviathan* 1651; law and other practical subjects; 12 runs of newspapers and periodicals, including the only known (though incomplete) set of the revived *The Country Journal, or the Craftsman* Nov 1749–Dec 1752.

Card cat 1894 (dictionary), 1956 (author).

Tony Brown, 'John Dawson, his life and library' (Thesis, Library Ass 1973) 3 v (including author cat in v 2).

Ms cat by William Burgess, Parish Clerk, 1765 (D/F/DAW/1 copied from Dawson's ms cat now missing; printed in John Ware, *An account of... charities... of... Shoreditch*, London, 1836, p161-7).

Dawson's ms diaries (D/F/DAW/2 and 3/1-2) and autobiography (stolen from the collection, later Phillipps ms 6839, now in Kirklees Borough Library).

M Benson, 'John Dawson's Library (typescript with the collection).

W C Plant, 'John Dawson and his books', *Library Assistant* 1(15) (March 1899), p165-73.

Sir Henry Ellis, *The history and antiquities of St Leonard Shoreditch...*, London 1798, p12, with author's ms note in British Library copy 577.b.17(2).

Sir Walter Besant, *Shoreditch and the East End*, London, 1908, p18-9.

Herbert J Bradley, *The history of Shoreditch Church*, London, 1914.

Survey of London, 1922, v 8, p102.

Hammersmith and Fulham Public Libraries. The libraries of the former Metropolitan Boroughs of Hammersmith and Fulham (both established in 1887) amalgamated in 1965, and until 1979 called the London Borough of Hammersmith Public Libraries.

A **Archives Department**

Shepherds Bush Library, 7 Uxbridge Road, London W12 8LJ. Tel (01) 743 0910. Open by appointment only, Mon, Thurs, Fri 9.15 am-5 pm, Tues 8 pm. Photocopying facilities.

The Department holds the official ms and printed archives of the Borough and its predecessors, with some unofficial ms collections, and miscellaneous deposited collections, including the ephemera collected by Sir William Bull (1863–1931) FSA, MP for Hammersmith (mostly after 1890). (It also oversees the printed local history collections at Hammersmith and Fulham, see below.)

Typescript hand lists.

P Taylor, 'The London Borough of Hammersmith Record Office', *Archives* 9 (1970), p192-6.

Buxton Forman Collection Containing 395 printed and ms documents on William Morris (1834–96) collected by Harry Buxton Forman (1842–1917) CB, sold at Sotheby 10 April 1972 (by his granddaughter Mrs Madeleine Buxton Holmes) and bought by Hammersmith Public Library. Included are letters and mss on socialism; 28 pamphlets of the Socialist League and its offshoot the Hammersmith Socialist Society by Morris, Ernest Belfort Bax (1854–1926) and others; anti-socialist pamphlets; numbers of *Commonweal* and *Liberty*; proof sheets of works by Morris (including a probable Forman forgery); ephemera printed at the Kelmscott Press, and catalogues and advertisements (including booksellers') for its products.

Descriptive lists of deposited records: DD/341/1–395: material relating to William Morris from the collection of H Buxton Forman, 1972.

B **Hammersmith Reference Library**

Shepherds Bush Road, London W6 7AT. Tel (01) 748 6032. Open (by appointment only except general reference section), Mon, Tues, Thurs 9.15 am-8 pm, Fri 5 pm, Sat 9 am-1 pm, 2-5 pm. Photocopying facilities. Library is in the part of Shepherds Bush Road formerly called Brook Green Road, between Hammersmith Broadway and Brook Green; a new library is planned in Hammersmith Broadway.

General reference collection This amounts to *c*50,000 v, of which *c*500 are pre-1851 items, mainly in the humanities, especially travel, English history, London history and English literature, especially 18th cent plays;

c30 monographs and reports on law (all that remains from the former special *MSC* law collection). (Many other older books have been dispersed to the British Library Lending Division and other libraries.)

Card cat (author/name and classified).

Early children's books c1,120 v built up from a collection of c300 bought in 1943 from William C Cater, of Fulham, who had exhibited his collection in the library in 1931. Editions of the period 1775–1910, including 7 ESTC; some foreign. Most are in publishers' cloth. Many instructional books, especially scientific, of early 19th cent; c20 magazine sets.

Card cat (authors; indexes of titles and illustrators).

Early children's books: a catalogue of the collection in the London Borough of Hammersmith, 1965.

Local history collection c11,000 books and pamphlets (c300 pre-1851) on the Hammersmith area (pre-1965 borough), with ephemera, and over 10,000 illustrations. The collection includes c30 Wing, c30 ESTC. Local author collections include Sir Alan Patrick Herbert (1890–1971): all the first editions of his works, some later editions, and works about him. Extensive theatrical ephemera, including a collection on Brandenburgh House—chiefly cuttings, 1792–1821.

Card cat (author and classified).

Guide to the local history collection, 1977 (op).

Private press collections These include all the 72 v printed at the Kelmscott Press 1891–8 by William Morris (1834–96) and his heirs, some donated by Morris and his family soon after publication, the remainder bought in 1948, and a volume of its advertisements and type specimens; 14 of the 51 v printed at the Doves Press 1900–16 by Thomas James Cobden-Sanderson (1844–1922) and (Sir) Emery Walker (1851–1933); 9 of the 32 v printed at the Eragny Press 1894–1914 by Lucien and Esther Pissarro (1863–1944, c1872?–1951).

G S Tomkinson, *A select bibliography of the principal modern presses...*, London, First Edition Club, 1928 (annotated copy).

William Morris (1834–96) A collection of his works and biographical and miscellaneous material relating to him, containing 100 works by him, 172 books and pamphlets about him, 14 items on Morris & Co, 4 re the Hammersmith Socialist Society, 8 books on the pre-Raphaelites; a small collection of works from Morris's library, and 521 cuttings on him. (See also *supra* under A Buxton Forman Collection).

A list of the material relating to William Morris kept in the Local History Collection of the Hammersmith Reference Library, 1979.

A list of the cuttings on William Morris held in the Hammersmith Local History Collection, 1978.

Early and fine printing A collection containing c100 rare books segregated from the General Reference Collection, but included in its catalogue, including the products of the Aldine Press, Estienne, Plantin, Elzevier, Bodoni, Baskerville, and the Chiswick Press. Some are from a private collection bequeathed by Samuel Martin (1852–1933), first Borough Librarian, others from the Shuter bequest of money. There are 4 STC, 5 Wing, 5 ESTC items.

C **Fulham Reference Library**

598 Fulham Road, London SW6 5NX. Tel (01) 736 1127/8. Open (special collections by appointment only) Mon, Tues, Thurs 9.15 am-8 pm, Fri 5 pm, Sat 1 pm and 2-5 pm.

General reference collection c30,000 v, of which 3,000 are on art (including modern limited editions), and c1,000 v on history. c150 are pre-1851, including many on the architecture and topography of London.

Card cat (author and classified).

Fulham Public Libraries, *Catalogue of the Central Libraries (Lending and Reference)* 1899.

Susan Holland, 'Fulham Public Libraries 1886–1939' (typescript, 1974).

Local history collection c6,000 books and pamphlets, of which c100 are pre-1801 (1 STC), and 10,000 illustrations. Includes small collections of, and on, Samuel Richardson (1689–1761), Samuel Foote (1720–77), Queen Caroline (1768–1821), Granville Sharp (1735–1813), and Sir Edward (Coley) Burne-Jones (1833–98), together with the Cecil French bequest of his paintings. The 19th cent pamphlet and illustrations collection of Charles James Feret, author of *Fulham old and new* (1900, the ms of which he donated) was donated to the library by William Hayes Fisher, MP.

Card cat (author/name) and classified.

Religion (Metropolitan Special Collections etc) c30,000 v. All aspects of religion are included, but mainly general and comparative religion (Dewey 200-219), c20,000 v, Bible (220-9, a small collection to be built up as LASER special collection in succession to that at Lewisham), and non-Christian religions (260-289), c800 which are the current special responsibilities of the Borough under the LASER scheme. There are at least 600 pre-1851 works, including many on the Quakers (some from the 'Swash' collection). Also on the Church of England, Church law and Councils of the Church, many in these categories being in an uncatalogued group.

Card cat (author/name and classified).

A guide to the religious serials and periodicals held in the Metropolitan Special Collections by the London Borough of Hammersmith Public Libraries, 1974.

Haringey Public Libraries

A **Archives and Local History Departments**

Bruce Castle, Lordship Lane, Tottenham, London N17 8NU. Tel (01) 808 8772. Telex 263257.

The Archives and Local History departments comprising material from the former Boroughs of Tottenham,

Hornsey (in part) and Wood Green, are housed with the borough Museum and the Middlesex Regimental Museum in the former manor house of Tottenham Manor. There are *c*20 pre-1851 books and printed ephemera in these collections, relating to Tottenham and a large neighbouring area. Local authors collected include Charles Bradlaugh (1833–91) the atheist, 'Neil Bell' the novelist (ie Stephen Southwold 1887–1967), and William Hone (1740–1842) the bookseller.

Bruce Castle Museum: a guide to the building and collections (*c*1980).

Morten postal history library, deposited on permanent loan by the Union of Communications Workers. Originally a private collection formed *c*1850–80 by W V Morten, a telegraph linesman of Nottingham, containing books, pamphlets, and a very large quantity of ephemera and documents on the history of postal and telecommunications and associated services from the 15th cent to the present. All British, and particularly strong in the period 1700–1840. Printed material includes 18th cent road-books and other topographical works, odd numbers of 17th and 18th cent newspapers (and enormous files of cuttings from such and later papers of items relating to the mails), 17th cent pamphlets (some of which have no clear connection with the subject of the collection), 18th cent official notices, and a variety of miscellaneous ephemera.

Card cat (author and classified) of part of the collection.

Guide to the collection in preparation.

B **Hornsey Reference Library**

Haringey Park, London N8 9JA. Tel (01) 348 3351. Open Mon-Fri 9.30 am-8 pm; Sat 5 pm.

General reference collection The collection of the former Borough of Hornsey, begun 1899, including several hundred pre-1851 books, from the 17th cent onwards, now being segregated into a separate rare book collection. They cover a wide range of subjects, especially British history and literature and technology, eg Moxon *Mechanick exercises*.

Microfiche cat (author and classified).

Local history collection A small collection supplementing that at Bruce Castle, containing a handful of pre-1851 items. It also includes a collection of *c*120 editions of works illustrated by William Heath Robinson (1872–1944), together with a number of his original designs.

Card cat (author and classified).

Harrow Public Libraries, Civic Centre Reference Library, PO Box 4, Civic Centre, Station Road, Harrow, Middlesex HA1 2UU. Tel (01) 863 5611 Ext 2055. Telex 923826.

The Borough Libraries were formed in 1965 from a portion of the former Middlesex County Libraries, founded in 1922.

Local history collection The collection, which covers the Borough and the County of Middlesex generally, is almost entirely modern, but there are a few pre-1851 items from 1795 onwards, including some on Harrow School.

Local History Collection (1979?) (Guide).

Card cat.

Harrow School, Vaughan Library, Headmaster's House, High Street, Harrow-on-the-Hill, Middlesex HA1 3HW. Open Mon-Sat 9 am-1 pm, 2-5 pm; Sun 11.45 am-12 noon, 2.15-4 pm, by appointment after written application.

The School was founded in 1615 (replacing an earlier school at Harrow), and the Library in 1768 by Dr Robert Carey Sumner (1729–71) when Master. It had its own room at least from 1820, and was exclusively for the use of the Monitors, who were required to donate books on leaving; in 1862 it moved to the new Vaughan Library building with 3,500 v, now enlarged to *c*10,000 v, and was gradually opened to the whole school. The rare books are mainly segregated, many being late 18th and early 19th cent works of literature, history, and travel, including some colour plate books. Several hundred items are pre-1851; these include 4 incunabula and at least 8 STC. Many have been given by Old Harrovians, and there are four collections relating to distinguished alumni:

Richard Brinsley Sheridan, (1751–1816). The collection includes T Moore, *Memoirs of Sheridan* 1825 (presentation copy from W Linley to Miss Tickell, extra-illustrated with some ephemera such as Sheridan's tickets for the trial of Warren Hastings, and important mss and ms letters to Sheridan). W Fraser Rae *Sheridan* 1896 (extra-illustrated with many ephemera and prints relating to Sheridan, including contemporary playbills and ms autograph letters from Sheridan to the Regent, and from others, given by Wilfred Sheridan in 1901).

George Gordon Byron, 6th Baron (1788–1824). Five of his schoolbooks (one annotated by him) received in the bequest of Harry Panmure Gordon (1837–1902) which also brought Byron mss and relics. His *Ode to Napoleon* 1814, a volume containing various proofs and revises with his ms corrections, given by John Murray in 1898. Some other printed works of Byron, including *Don Juan*. His copies of *The World* 1753–56, de Stael *Dix annees* 1821 (given by A R Bayley 1914), and Forster *Arabian nights* (given by Byron to Sir John Claridge).

Henry John Temple Palmerston, 3rd Viscount (1784–1865). His copy of Morell *Latin dictionary* 1738, signed and dated 1795.

Anthony Trollope, (1815–82). His *Chronicles of Barsetshire* 1879, 8 v, with his presentation signature. Also the ms of part of his *Framley Parsonage* (given by G Smith, the publisher).

Theology collection Includes various Bibles (Barker 1607, 'vinegar' 1717 on vellum, etc). *Decretals* 1473 (in contemporary binding, bookplate of Georgius Klok).

Fine printing and binding The collection includes the *Book of Common Prayer* 1637, with needlework binding relaid into a binding by Hering. Other bindings by Hering, Walther, etc; *Seneca* 1502 bound in 1779 for King Louis; Bodoni *Catullus* 1794 given by H Yates Thompson.

Bigg collection of Aldines A collection of 160 v printed by the family of Aldus Manutius in Venice in the 15th and 16th cent, many in contemporary bindings, given by E A Bigg in memory of his brother L O Bigg who had collected them in Italy.

A A Renouard, *Annales de l'imprimerie des Aldes* 1834 (annotated copy).

Miscellaneous rare books These include works of English literature such as Chaucer 1532; classics such as Cicero *Epistolarum*. . . , Milan 1481; John Locke's copy of Speed *Theatrum* 1616, and various travel books; Salvin and Brodrick *Falconry* 1855 (Brodrick's copy with the original watercolours instead of printed plates); some French literature, including Racine and Molière.

Catalogue of the Monitors' Library, 1830.

Catalogue of the Harrow School Vaughan Library, 1877; 2nd ed 1887.

Card cat (author and alphabetical subject) includes rare books; typescript list of 50 rarest books and mss.

E D Laborde, *Harrow School yesterday and today*, London, Winchester Publications, 1948, p89-90, 123-35 (op).

Havering Public Libraries, Central Reference Library, St Edward's Way, Romford, Essex RM1 3AR. Tel (0708) 44297 Ext 355. Open Mon-Fri 9.30 am-8 pm; Sat 5 pm.

The Borough includes the libraries of Romford, Upminster and Hornchurch. The local history and archive collections are now centralized in the Central Reference Library.

General Reference Collection It includes *c*200 pre-1851 v on most subjects in the humanities, especially English topography and ecclesiastical history, from the 17th cent onwards.

Local History Collection *c*3,000 books on the Borough and the former county of Essex, including 210 v pre-1851, mostly post-1700; numerous editions of poetical works of Francis Quarles (1592–1644) such as *Feast of Wormes* and *Emblems*. H Repton, *Observations on*. . . *landscape gardening* 1803. A few early scientific books such as Bacon *Essayes* 1632, B Franklin *New Experiments* 1754, W Derham *Physico-theology*, 12th ed 1754.

Henry George Foundation Library, 177 Vauxhall Bridge Road, London SW1V 1ER.

The rare book collection belonging to the United Committee for the Taxation of Land Values, formerly in this library, is now deposited at the Museum of Rural Life of the University of Reading.

Heythrop College Library, 11 Cavendish Square, London W1M 0AN. Tel (01) 580 6941. Open 9 am-5 pm (Mon-Fri in vacation and Sat in term only), 7 pm (Mon-Fri in term), to staff of the University of London with identification; to others with letter of introduction. Photocopier; microfilm and fiche readers.

The Library began in 1614 as the library of the seminary of the English Jesuits at Louvain. It moved to the English Academy at Liége in 1626, and to St Mary's Hall at Stonyhurst in Lancashire in 1794. In 1848 the theological section of the college and the theological part of the library moved to St Beuno's College near St Asaph, while the philosophical part remained at Stonyhurst. In 1926 the two parts were reunited at Heythrop College at Heythrop in Oxfordshire. The College moved to London in 1970 when it became a school of the University of London. The library incorporates collections from many other religious communities, as well as the private libraries of bishops and nobility. Edward Louth Badely (1803–68), a lawyer prominent in the Oxford movement and RC convert, bequeathed *c*5,000 books, including editions of the Fathers, medieval theologians and canon lawyers, and Anglican divines; together with classical and English literature, and many rare legal books. The whole library contains *c*200,000 items, divided into a historical (pre-1801) and a modern section.

Card cat (author/title).

'Heythrop College Library', *Libraries Bulletin (University of London)* no 10 (1977), p14-17. *Bulletin of the Association of British Theological and Philosophical Libraries* no 2 (1957), p6-8; no 23 (1966), p13-16; New Series no 13 (1978), p4-5.

Pre-1801 collection *c*15,000 items, including c43 incunabula, *c*850 STC, *c*1,500 Wing, and *c*3,000 ESTC. The core is of books by and about the Jesuits. This is surrounded by a large theological collection, preponderantly RC, but including much polemical material of 17th and 18th cent (especially in a collection of *c*6,000 bound pamphlets) which contains Anglican and Protestant contributions, philosophy, early science (mostly Liége) including rare editions of Sir Isaac Newton (1642–1727), literature and history.

Dictionary card cat being compiled, but part of the collection only in general cat. 18th cent English items in ESTC.

Highgate Literary and Scientific Institution, 11 South Grove, Highgate Village, London N6 6BS. Tel (01) 340 3343. Open Mon-Sat 10 am-1 pm and Mon, Tues, Thurs, Fri 3-6 pm, to members; others admitted at the discretion of the librarian.

The Institution was founded in 1839 by Harry Chester (1806–68) FRS, the educationist, with the help of Charles Knight (1791–1873) the publisher, and William Cutbush (*c*1800–*c*1860) the nurseryman, and others, as a library, social centre, and forum for lectures, for subscribers, but also for educational and reference purposes open to the general public.

Harry Chester, *The Highgate Literary and Scientific Institution: introductory address*, 1839.

Highgate Literary and Scientific Institution, 1839 (rules, with list of donations).

Extensive ms and printed archives from 1839 in the Library, including *Annual Report*.

John H Lloyd, *The history, topography and antiquities of Highgate*, the Institution, 1888, p472-5.

Highgate Literary and Scientific Institution 1839–1956, [1956] (brief outline).

A E Barker, 'Improving the minds of Highgate: the story of the Literary and Scientific Institution', *Camden History Review* no 8 (1980), p13-16.

J Pateman, 'Source of mental enjoyment: Highgate Literary and Scientific Institution'.

Exhibition: The Highgate Literary and Scientific Institution, its history and personalities: souvenir catalogue, 1980.

Lecturers, souvenir catalogue, (1981).

General The library began with donations of 300 v, and has been built up from donations and purchases to *c*45,000 v, of which one-fifth is fiction, the remainder mainly general literature and history, with a wide spread of other subjects in the humanities. Though political and religious controversy have been barred from the outset under the constitution, there are, nevertheless, general books on politics and religion in the library. Scientific books were collected until *c*1930, but the scientific collection was completely dispersed *c*1948. The lending library is still strong in 19th cent editions, including probably *c*400 pre-1851. There is a small reference library, which includes all the special collections below.

Author cat on cards in lending library also includes most of the reference library but not all the books in special collections.

A catalogue of the Library of the Highgate Literary and Scientific Institution, March 1839; new editions 1846; 1863; 1872; 1881; 1890; and 1896.

Local History Collection Over 250 v, including many early and extra-illustrated books. The focus of the collection is Highgate (now divided between the boroughs of Camden, Haringey and Islington), and there are *c*100 early pamphlets on the village, including many scarce 19th cent items and a collection of 33 on the controversy in 1709–10 concerning the sermons and impeachment of Henry Sacheverell (1674?–1724); the archives of the Highgate Dispensary (1787–1840) and the Highgate Book Society (founded 1822). There are sets of local parish magazines from 1863 onwards. There are also many books on Islington and other neighbouring parts of London, and a small collection on the City (including livery companies) and more distant boroughs. Many of the rare and extra-illustrated books in the collection are from the bequest of John Henry Lloyd (1830–1910), historian of Highgate, the Institution's Vice President.

Coleridge and his circle A collection of *c*150 v by and on Samuel Taylor Coleridge (1772–1834), the poet, including 2 autograph letters, originally forming part of the Local History Collection; these include early editions of his works. There is also a similar number relating to others in the romantic circle, and these include some early editions of Robert Southey (1774–1843).

Talbot Baines Reed, (1852–93), writer for boys, and historian of typography. After his death a collection was given in his memory, consisting of his own works, and other 19th cent adventure stories, but the latter were afterwards dispersed, and there remain *c*15 of his own books.

Reed Memorial: catalogue of boys' books presented to the Institution..., 1894.

Private Press books A collection given *c*1972 by Ronald T Gibbon of about 30 privately printed items, chiefly of the Gregynog and Nonesuch presses.

Hillingdon Public Libraries, Uxbridge Library, 22 High Street, Uxbridge, Middlesex UB8 1JN. Tel (0895) 50708. Telex 934224. Open to all Mon-Fri 9.30 am-8 pm; Sat 9.30 am-5 pm. Photocopying.

Local Collection Until 1965 part of Middlesex County Library Local Collection, and contains *c*120 pre-1851 printed works. Local material includes a dozen Civil War tracts connected with the Treaty of Uxbridge; rare Chartist periodicals conducted by John Bedford Leno (1826–94) for the Uxbridge Young Men's Improvement Society from 1846 onwards; some early children's books, and a collection of 96 books (*c*50 pre-1851, from 1658 onwards) deposited by the Uxbridge Society of Friends, consisting of Quaker biography, theology, and devotion.

Dictionary card cat, excluding Quaker collection of which there is a separate typescript list.

History of Advertising Trust, c/o City University, 23/31 Whiskin Street, London EC1R 0BP.

The History of Advertising Trust has in recent years been building up a collection on the history of advertising at 53 Goodge Street, London W1P 1FB (Tel (01) 636 7196), with a view to making it publicly accessible when suitable premises can be found. It is intended during 1982 to move the collection to 23/31 Whiskin Street and to provide permanent staffing for a study centre. The collection includes the Robert Opie collection of examples of consumer packaging from *c*1830 onwards. The Beaverbrook Foundation has promised money to build up the Sir Max Aitken Press Archive, which will acquire material exemplifying and relating to the press and press advertising, from the 17th cent onwards.

History of Advertising Trust, *Found! a home for the history of advertising. Wanted, the funds to run it: a memorandum from the Rt Hon Lord Barneston, President. . .*, (1982).

Journal of Advertising History.

B Smith, 'Can the ad industry cash in on its long forgotten past?' *Campaign* 3 Nov 1978.

Home Office Library, 50 Queen Anne's Gate, St James's Park, London SW1H 9AT. Tel (01) 213 3646. Telex 24986. Open Mon-Fri 9.15 am-5.15 pm to genuine researchers by appointment. Photocopying.

The Home Office was formed in 1782 by the amalgamation of the 'home' functions of two former Secretaries of State (ie of the Northern and Southern Departments) both of whom had home and colonial responsibilities, and their collections of books were put together to form a library. This now contains *c*50,000 works including pamphlets, runs of periodicals, state papers, parliamentary papers, statutes etc. *c*3,000 of these are pre-1851, including perhaps *c*1,000 pre-1801 from 16th cent onwards. Subject field is wide; mainly history, topography, biography, government. Periodicals include *Annual Register* from 1758; *Monthly Mercury* 1688–1735.

Dictionary card cat. *Catalogue of the Home Office Library*, 1852, 1876, 1915 (omitting part of the collection included in previous eds).

The Home Office: handbook rev ed 1972.

D B Gibson, 'The Home Office Library: its history, functions, scope and resources', *Law Librarian* 3(3) (1972), p36-9. *Powers and duties of the Principal Secretary of State for the Home Department*, Pt 1, 1881 (op).

Royal Commission on Civil Establishment, *2nd Report*, 1888 [C5545], p451 (op).

17th cent pamphlets *c*500 in 17 v on a wide variety of subjects, including some parliamentary papers.

Printed cat in preparation.

18th cent pamphlets *c*1,000 in 34 v. (Similar to preceding.)

Irish Office Library A representative selection was made from this library when the office was disbanded and incorporated into the general collection (the remainder being dispersed). All aspects of Ireland are included.

Ms cat of the original library from 1834.

Honourable Artillery Company's Museum, Armoury House, City Road, London EC1Y 2BQ.

The Honourable Artillery Company is the world's oldest volunteer regiment, founded in 1537; its headquarters was built in 1735. The library on the regiment's history, which contains some pre-1851 books, is not open to the public. Access strictly by written application to the Curator.

Hounslow Public Libraries, Chiswick District Reference Library, Dukes Avenue, Chiswick, London W4 2AB. Tel (01) 994 5295 or 1008. Open to all Mon-Sat 9 am-8 pm (5 pm Thurs and Sat). Photocopying.

(The local and special collections here are due to be moved to the planned new Central Library in Hounslow Town Centre *c*1988, where they will be united with the small Heston and Isleworth local collection now in the Reference Library at Treaty Road, Hounslow TW3 1DR, Middlesex.)

Brentford and Chiswick local collection *c*5,000 v, including *c*400 pre-1851 (excluding Hogarth and Chiswick Press which are separate segments within the local collection), built up from 1884, with archives, maps, prints etc.

Card cat (author and alphabetical subject).

Fred Turner. *After twenty one years: a short history of Brentford Public Library from 1889–1910.* 1911.

——*History and antiquities of Brentford.* Brentford, 1922, p151-78.

Hogarth, William (1697–1764) Over 500 prints with books and pamphlets about him or illustrated by him. (Also a small museum collection administered by the Borough Librarian on public view at Hogarth's House, Hogarth Roundabout, Great West Road, London W4 2QN. Tel (01) 994 6757.)

Card cat.

Chiswick Press A collection of books printed at the Press 1809–52, mostly acquired before 1900, *c*1,000 v.

Author card cat.

Layton collection (In store, but accessible by prior appointment.) Thomas Layton (1819–1911) FSA, Chairman of Brentford Urban District Council, a most omnivorous collector, lived by Kew Bridge, whose tolls he owned, and stuffed his house with a gargantuan and utterly chaotic plethora of books and prints, mixed up with objects and antiquities of every conceivable kind, most of which had been dredged up from the Thames. By the time he died, the collection had overflowed into numerous extensions and garden sheds, and some of it was rotting away with damp. He bequeathed it all to the people of Brentford to form a museum in his memory, but this proved impracticable, and the trustees deposited the collections at Brentford Public Library. The museum objects are now mainly in the Museum of London and ownership of the library collection is to be transferred to the public library so that it can be conserved, catalogued, and housed in the planned new Central Library. Of the books found in 1911, at least 10,000 v which were duplicates, so-called 'useless' material, or irreparably damaged, were dispersed, and *c*11,000 v now remain. About half are pre-1851, almost all in English, with a few French and Italian. 6,800 are on English topography and local history, including many of the London and county histories. Histories of England start with Holinshed 1577, and there are many collections of sources such as Rushworth, *Historical collections*. There are also collections of voyages, of travels; books on archaeology; literary miscellanies of the 18th and 19th cent, and a vast range of miscellaneous subjects. Also *c*2,000 v of periodicals from the 17th cent onwards, chiefly general, literary, and archaeological, and 3,000 prints.

Ms author list (also typed subject and author lists at Hounslow Library HQ).

Obituary in *Proceedings of the Society of Antiquaries NS24* (1911–12) p232.

Fred Turner, *History and antiquities of Brentford*. Brentford, 1922, p179-204.

D Whipp and L Blackmore, 'Thomas Layton', *London Archaeologist* 3(4) (1977), p40-6.

Horniman Museum and Library, London Road, Forest Hill, London SE23 3PQ. Tel (01) 699 2339. Open to all Tuesday-Saturday 10.30 am-5.45 pm, Sunday 2-5.45 pm.

This very heterogeneous collection of natural history, anthropological and folklore specimens with their related literatures was formed by Frederick John Horniman (1835–1906, MP) chairman of the Horniman Tea Company (founded by his father) during 40 years of travel to and from the Far East. He opened the collection to the public at his home in Forest Hill in 1890, appointed a librarian in 1895, moved it to the purpose-built museum in 1897, and presented it in 1901 to the London County Council, from whom the administration passed to the Inner London Education Authority.

Virtually all the rare books are from Horniman's own collection. Some 2,000 items are pre-1851, including many entomological books, with some fragmented runs of early periodicals, general works on natural history, and a small collection of 18th cent botany (not included as a location in Henrey). There is also a large collection on foreign travel and topography, and some early musicology. The collection of Bibles has been dispersed (the more important items to Lambeth Palace Library). There are also some mss.

The subject catalogue, with author index, published as *A handbook to the library* in 1905, and reissued with a supplement in 1912, includes virtually all the rare books. There are also author and subject catalogues on cards. Individual items are described in *Journal of the Society for the Bibliography of Natural History*, 1(9), 15 November 1939, and 3(3), January 1956, p158-64.

R E R Banks, 'Horniman Museum Library', *State Librarian*, 24(2), July 1976, p19. *The Times*, 6 March 1906, p10.

Horniman's dream: a proposal to expand the Museum (London, GLC, 1974).

House of Commons Library, Palace of Westminster, London SW1A 0AA. Tel (01) 219 3666. Telex 916318.

The Library is private to MPs. Parliamentary and official documents (A and B below) may be used by the public in the House of Lords Record Office. Other material (C and D) that is not accessible elsewhere may occasionally be made available during recesses if prior application is made in writing to the librarian. Entry is via St Stephen's Entrance in St Margaret Street, and Central Lobby.

In the 18th cent most printed parliamentary documents were stored in the Journal Office, which by 1780 was overflowing. In 1800 a repository was provided in Abingdon Street where parliamentary papers were reorganized into permanent reference collections; there was also a collection of printed papers and tracts in the Speaker's House. In 1818 the first librarian was appointed, a committee room was fitted up as a library for the use of Members, and some of the collections from Abingdon Street and elsewhere were transferred to it. In 1827 a new library was built to contain books 'of historical and constitutional information' (originally to the exclusion of science, theology and literature). A number of old collections of books and pamphlets from various offices and committee rooms were still being moved to the library in 1834 when the fire destroyed two-thirds of the 6,000 v in the library itself and all other collections in the House of Commons except that in the Speaker's Gallery (D1). Barry's new library opened in 1852 encouraged expansion to 30,000 v by 1856, including books on general subjects and the classics of English, French, Greek and Latin literature, which continued to be added to to the end of the century. More recently some important, mainly 19th cent pamphlet collections, have been added. Many rare books have been dispersed, but the library (*c*130,000 v) still has some notable items in addition to its parliamentary holdings. The Library Department is divided into a Parliamentary Division, containing the reference library which includes all the older and rare material, and the now more prominent Research Division which provides specialized information and research services for Members. (There is also a Branch Library (tel 219 4272) which has some parliamentary collections and provides a parliamentary information service to the public.)

The Library of the House of Commons: handbook, 1959 and 1963, including guide to holdings (omitted from rev ed 1966 and 1970). (op)

D Menhennet, 'The House of Commons Library' in: Study of Parliament Group.

D Menhennet, 'The Library of the House of Commons', *Law Librarian* 1(3) (1970), p329-31.

The House of Commons in the twentieth century, ed S A Walkland, Oxford, Clarendon Press, 1979, p611-40.

D Englefield, *Parliament and information*, London, Library Association, 1981, p20-52 (including lists of official reports and printed catalogues).

M Rush and M Shaw, eds *The House of Commons*

services and facilities, London, Allen & Unwin, 1974. (New ed in preparation.)

R Buchanan, 'The Library of the House of Commons', in: *Of one accord: essays in honour of W B Paton*, ed F McAdams, Scottish Library Association, 1977, p9-21.

A Parliamentary Papers

In 1800 at the time of the Union with Ireland and of the removal of the Journal Office to Abingdon Street there was a major revolution in the system of parliamentary printing and publishing. In a movement set in train by Charles Abbot, afterwards Baron Colchester (1757–1829), who was Speaker 1802–17, Luke Hansard (1752–1828) the printer to the House was employed to establish permanent reference collections from the surviving papers of the past, and to provide a system for numbering and binding up all documents ordered to be printed by the House, and all Command Papers presented to it in printed form, from 1801 onwards in a set for the use of Members. Hansard and his sons became engaged in compiling and printing indexes to past and current collections on a prodigious scale. These indexes refer to the volume numbering and ms pagination of the sets bound up for the Commons Library, and after 1800 also to the new sessional publication numbers. The sets in the library therefore set the standard on which all other collections of its documents are based.

C G Parsloe and W G Bassett, 'British parliamentary papers: catalogues and indexes', *Bulletin of the Institute of Historical Research* 11 (1933–4), p24-30.

S Lambert, 'Guides to parliamentary printing 1696–1834', ibid 38 (1965), p111-17.

H H Bellot, 'Parliamentary printing 1660–1837', ibid 11 (1933–4), p85-98.

S Lambert, 'Printing for the House of Commons in the eighteenth century', *The Library* (ser 5) 23(1) (1968), p25-46.

Maurice F Bond, *Guide to the records of Parliament*, 1971, p232-6 and p134-5 (bibliography).

P and G Ford, *A guide to Parliamentary Papers*, 3rd ed, Shannon, Irish UP, 1972.

Hansard papers (House of Lords Record Office, Hist Coll 105).

A1 *First Series of Reports, 1715–1802.* A retrospective collection, *Reports from Committees of the House of Commons which have been printed by order of the House, and are not inserted in the Journals*. 4 v, 1773, reprinted from papers originally printed 1715–73, v 5-15, 1803, covering 1774–1802. Hansard's *General index* dated 1803 but published 1820.

General index to the Reports from Committees of the House of Commons 1705–1801 printed but not inserted in the Journals (facsimile reprint) with a new introduction by John Brooke. Bishops Stortford, Chadwyck-Healey, 1973.

Catalogue and breviate of parliamentary papers 1696–1834, Repr Oxford, Blackwell, 1953.

A2 *Abbot collection 1731–1800* (sometimes misleadingly called Second Series). *c*2,000 separate papers bound in 110 v chronologically within three series. Bills, Reports, and Accounts and Papers. Collected in 1800–5 from all the printed documents of which Abbot and Hansard could find surviving copies. (For the 1659–1740 collection reorganized by Abbot see D1 below.)

Catalogue of papers printed by order of the House of Commons... in the custody of the Clerk of the Journals, 1807. Reprinted with collations of this and 3 other slightly different sets by Sheila Lambert (1978).

E L Erickson, 'The sessional papers, last phase', *College and Research Libraries* 21 (1960), p343-58.

A3 *Parliamentary Papers from 1801, bound by session.* Public Bills and House of Commons Papers numbered sessionally, and Command Papers published in continuous numbered series, bound together by session, until 1968–9 in four groups of volumes: Public Bills; Reports from Standing and Select (including Joint Select) Committees; Reports of Commissioners (and certain other non-parliamentary bodies); and Accounts and Papers (including White Papers, Estimates, Treaties, etc). Sessional volume numbering and ms pagination corresponds with references in the printed sessional and general indexes to Commons papers, which also (except General Index 1852–99) give the sessional number of each paper.

Introduction to the series in *General index for 1900–1948/9.* K A C Parsons, *A checklist of British Parliamentary Papers (bound set) 1801–1950.* CUP, 1958 (Collation of numbers of volumes by session in each category). General indexes listed in Parsloe and Bassett p25.

A4 *Second Series, 1801–1826.* In 1825–7 Hansard, hoping to be allowed to publish a 'Second Series of Reports of Committees and Commissioners' in continuation of the first, bound up copies in 154 v in a classified subject arrangement in five identical sets, of which one was deposited in the library (later broken up to form the Third Series). In 1828 he added classified sets of the Accounts and Papers in 152 v and the Bills in 56 v, both still in the library, and called the Second Series.

Sel.Ctte. *3rd report*; 1825 (516), V p21-102 (including preliminary select list). Listed volume by volume in *Classification of parliamentary papers and a breviate of their contents, 1801–1826.* 1830 (81). IV, p143-314. Indexed in *General index to the sessional papers from 1801–1826.* 1829 (including both Second Series and sessional v numberings).

A5 *Third Series of Reports, 1801–61.* A classified set of Reports of 1827–32 (but not Accounts and Papers or Bills) was formed, and later rearranged in combination with the Second Series to form a Third Series of Reports 1801–61 comprising Reports of Committees 1801–59 in 218 v, and of Commissioners 1801–61 in 140 v. They are probably incomplete for the last few years. 191 digestive indexes to originally unindexed reports were printed and bound in.

No complete list, but see *Catalogue and breviate 1696–1834* and supplement 1837 (498.-I), LII, p1. No complete index, but volume-page numbers noted in ms in a copy of Index to the *Reports from Select Committees of the House of Commons 1801–1845*, 1845 (396-II, XLII, p311). Analytical indexes to committee reports are indexed in *Indexes to reports of the House of Commons 1801–34*; 1837 (498), LII, p1, and most bear the sessional number 1837 (498) though printed later; those for commission reports, various numbers 1845–54 (see Parsloe and Bassett, p26-9).

B **Parliamentary and Official Documents (other than Parliamentary Papers)**

Some of the collections (eg the business papers of the House to 1900, including from 1680, *Votes and Proceedings*) have been transferred to the House of Lords Record Office. East India Papers have been transferred to India Office Library. The collections below are still retained in the library.

Maurice F Bond, *Guide to the Records of Parliament*, HMSO, 1971, p197-248. (Indicates the printed documents available without differentiating the holdings of Record Office and Library.)

B1 *Statutes*. Public General Acts complete from 1715 (with some earlier volumes from 1543); Local and Personal from 1798; Private from 1815. The complete series of Road Acts (1760–97, 37 v). Some miscellaneous collections.

B2 *Journals*, or official record of the proceedings of both Houses. Those of the Commons printed since 1762 in a current series, *c*200 v. Retrospective series 1547–1761, published 1742–1762, 28 v, General Indexes, 16 v.

D Menhennet, *The Journal of the House of Commons: a bibliographical and historical guide*, 1971. (Library document no 7.)

B3 *Debates* and other unofficial records of the proceedings of both Houses. Hansard complete. Most of the other collections listed in *A bibliography of parliamentary debates* (Library document no 2, 1956) are held (those missing are mostly in the Lords' Library, qv, section A3).

B4 *Miscellaneous*. Complete sets of Foreign Office State Papers. Rolls Series, and Record Commission publications.

C **Reserve Collections (Books)**

The older books withdrawn from open access (some of which are in the Victoria Tower) include *c*250 pre-1701 (mostly English), *c*650 1701–1800, *c*1,500 1801–50. Strong in Parliament (including a good collection of reports of election cases), politics, law, English history and topography, county histories, antiquities, and biography. Some major 17th cent atlases, and early travels and voyages, many finely illustrated, including one of the few copies with coloured plates of Viscount Kingsborough, *Antiquities of Mexico*. Collections of 81 early editions of William Prynne (1600–69), and many of William Cobbett (1762–1835) bound in 12 v. Latin and some Greek classics, English literature, and ecclesiastical history. The French collection (mainly donated by the Parlement after the fire) has been much reduced by transfers to the Université de Caen and elsewhere.

Card cat (author and subject). *Catalogue of the books in the Library of the House of Commons*, 1910 includes entries for *c*800 books now dispersed; interleaved copy with printed additions slips and deletions (to 1943 only) available to readers. Some books accidentally omitted will be found in earlier printed catalogues (listed in Englefield p51-2).

D **Reserve Collections (Pamphlets)**

Substantial collections of historical pamphlets, some of which had already been transferred to the library, perished in 1834. To the one surviving collection many were added by donation and purchase until the end of the century, and a few subsequently.

Not in main author or subject cat. Rough lists in volume order printed as appendices in the cat of 1856 and 1857, and more extensively in *Catalogue of the pamphlets in the Library of the House of Commons*, 1889. Card cat begun *c*1965 contains entries (sometimes incomplete) for each collection separately.

D1 *Parliamentary collection, 1559–1740*. In the mid-18th cent a clerk (Zachary Hamlyn?), personally employed by the Clerk of the House, assembled from collections going back to 1490 a working library and compiled a ms cat of it in 3 v. In 1805 Speaker Abbot removed a portion to the Speaker's Gallery, rearranged it and bound it in 88 v (to which an unnumbered volume was later added) with a ms list (v 90) and chronological index (v 91). In 1834 the main collection and its cat were destroyed, but all but one volume of those in the Speaker's Gallery were rescued, and transferred to the library in 1836. 1,110 items dated 1559–1740, mostly in English (some Latin and French), *c*50 STC, *c*670 Wing (including 325 of 1641–43). The earliest are ecclesiastical, from 1600 90% parliamentary, including monarchs' speeches, Charles I's messages and answers, speeches of MPs and Peers, proceedings of conferences, lists of members, declarations and ordinances proceedings on impeachments, papers laid before Parliament, contemporary accounts of debates, etc. A few documents of the Scottish Parliament, and political pamphlets: items on Ireland, and the City of London. One or two mss, eg an official inventory of the property of Queen Henrietta Maria made after her death in 1669; this appears, as do some of the printed items, to have been in a private collection.

Cards by authors (incomplete). Abbot's list and index (which omit about 5 v) are more reliable than the chronological list printed in the *Catalogue of pamphlets* (derived from the rough lists of contents prefixed to each volume, as were ms author and classified indexes compiled in 1836–40 but now missing).

Bond, *Guide* p234-5. Select Ctte on Public Records, *First Report*, 1800. Appendix B2. Library Ctte, *Report*, 1831–2 (600). V. p245, 23-5); 1837 (468). XIII. p65.

Orlo Williams, *The clerical organization of the House of Commons 1661–1850*, OUP, 1954, p192.

S Lambert, 'The beginning of printing for the House of Commons 1640–42', *The Library*, ser 6 3(1) (1981), p43-61.

D2 *Chiswell collection*, named after Trench Chiswell (1735?–1979, born Richard Muilman) FSA, of Debden Hall, MP for Aldborough. *c*120 tracts 1782–95 on political and parliamentary subjects (of which India and America are well represented), originally bound into Chiswell's (afterwards the Library's spare) set of Debrett's *Parliamentary Register*, adjacent to the speeches to which they were related. They were extracted *c*1890, some items were discarded, and two-thirds were then bound in 12 v (one of which is missing). The residue were bound into a New Series of 8 v *c*1950.

Cards in shelf order. *Not in Catalogue of the pamphlets.*

D3 Colman, Jeremiah James (1801–98) MP for Norwich, mustard manufacturer and book collector. Part of his collection donated in his memory by his son Russell James Colman (1861–1946) in 1940. *c*1,500 pamphlets, *c*1810–80 (*c*450 pre-1851) bound in 139 v alphabetically by subject groups, on a very wide range of subjects, predominantly in the social sciences, of which the strongest are slavery and India.

Cards under authors.

Helen C Colman, *Jeremiah James Colman*. Priv pr 1905.

D4 *Miscellaneous pamphlet collections. The Catalogue of the pamphlets* (1889) includes some smaller collections: 19 on the scarcity of 1800–1; 68 of 1807–16 on bullion and currency; 392 on the disruption of the Church of Scotland 1836–46 bound in 25 v by subject; 73 on the West Indies (and slavery) 1679–1826. It lists part (with listing completed in ms in library copy) of the 'Miscellaneous Series of Pamphlets', 162 v including 96 ESTC and 460 English of 1801–50, mostly bound by subjects in volumes corresponding roughly to years of accession (*c*1820–*c*1900), predominantly economic and social, especially Corn Laws, currency, Union with Ireland, slavery, and opium. Collections received after 1910 have remained individual collections (cards in shelf order but no other list): gift by Marcus Samuel (1873–1942) MP for Wandsworth of 63 Civil War tracts (mostly 1640–5); 14 of 1805–6 on the election of Sir John Leslie (1766–1832) as Professor of Mathematics at Edinburgh; 37 of 1809–54 on reform; 23 of 1810–13 on Madras; 4 of 1811–24 by David Ricardo (1772–1823); United States 1850–2; 31 on India 1769–92; the *Parliamentary Register* or proceedings of the Irish Parliament to 1798.

House of Lords Library, House of Lords, London SW1A 0PW. Tel (01) 219 5242. Telex 916318. The Library is private to Peers, but open also to MPs. Material, not available elsewhere, is made available to the public by temporary transfer to the House of Lords Record Office (see below). Applications for direct access by appointment (granted only in exceptional cases) should be made in writing to the librarian; entry is by Chancellor's Gate (near the Victoria Tower in Old Palace Yard).

In 1826 the Clerk Assistant in the Parliament Office was made responsible for maintaining a reference collection of statutes, journals, reports, papers, law books and certain other works. These were assembled from existing office collections into a small library designed by Sir John Soane (1753–1837). In 1834 the library was damaged by fire, but almost the whole collection was rescued. In 1848 a new library designed by Sir Charles Barry (1795–1860) was opened, and purchases and donations became both numerous and wide-ranging. Successive librarians have maintained an excellent general collection of English history and related subjects, in addition to the specialized legal and parliamentary material. Rare books are still occasionally added. There are now *c*100,000 v, of which at least 25,000 are pre-1851 (including 1 incunabulum).

Catalogues Recataloguing is in progress; a new 'Unified Card Catalogue' (author, and for almost all collections alphabetical subject) will eventually include all printed material before 1950, with a MARC-based microfiche cat thereafter. Pre-1801 holdings are also being recorded in a separate cat (arranged by author and imprint) as well as being included in ESTC and the revisions of STC and Wing. Hitherto some collections have had separate cats, some none. The printed *Catalogue* 1908 includes only the general collections, excluding parliamentary and law.

History. Preface to *Catalogue* 1908. Christopher Dobson, *The Library of the House of Lords: a short history, with an appendix listing its principal contents*, rev ed, 1972. *The Library of the House of Lords: a short guide*, 1972. *The House of Lords Library Bulletin*, 1977–, with notes on collections. *The Library of the House of Lords: report of the Working Group*, 1977, (1976–7 HL 84).

D Englefield, *Parliament and information*. London. Library Assoc. 1981, p52-8.

The Short guide 1972 (op) is now partly out of date.

A **Parliamentary Documents** (Enquiries should be made through the House of Lords Record Office).

A1 *Statutes.* 37 sessional v before 1708; Public General Acts complete from 1708; Local and Personal Acts from 1798; A rare set of Private Bills from 1719 (not complete in early years). A number of prints of individual acts from 1649.

A2 *Parliamentary proceedings and papers.* Lords' Journals, a very rare but incomplete set of Lords' sessional papers 1788–1800; Lords' Standing Orders from 1825; Commons' Journals; Commons sessional papers 1731–1800 (less complete than the Abbot collection set in the House of Commons Library); and Sessional Papers of both Houses complete from 1801.

K A Mallaber, 'The House of Lords' Sessional Papers', *Journal of Librarianship*, 4(2) (1972), p106-14.

A3 *Parliamentary debates.* Hansard and almost all the retrospective and near-contemporaneous compilations in complete sets, a comprehensive collection. A number of proceedings of individual parliaments of the 17th cent, eg the Exclusion Parliament of 1680. Also editions of numerous individual speeches.

A bibliography of parliamentary debates of Great Britain, 1956. (House of Commons Library documents no 2.) Based on the holdings of both Houses, but does not give locations.

A4 *Scotland.* Acts, 2 collected editions from the 16th cent, 3 from the 17th cent and 1 from the 18th cent; 23 sessional collections from the period 1633–1707. Acts of the General Assembly of the Church of Scotland 1639–49, 1690, 1694– .

A5 *Ireland.* Journal of the Irish House of Commons, rev ed 1796–1802. Journal of the Irish House of Lords, published 1783–1800; Statutes at Large, 2nd ed, 1786–99; Sessional vol of statutes for 1800; Lords Standing Orders, 1778 and 1784 eds; Caldwell's Debates, 2nd ed, 1779; Parliamentary Register...Debates...Commons, 2nd ed, two but differing sets.

B Law, but excluding legislation

The law collection, established in the Parliament Office in the 18th cent, formed the greater part of the material transferred to the library when it was formed in 1826. It is the working collection of the Law Lords for the hearing of appeal cases and also serves the staff of the Lord Chancellor's Office who work in the Palace of Westminster. The main law collection forms the preponderant part of the library.

B1 *Truro collection*, formed by Thomas Wilde, Lord Chancellor Truro (1782–1855), mainly as his working law library (with ms notes of cases), but including a number of rare and unusual works, donated by his widow Augusta Emma D'Este (1801–66). Over 2,000 v, a comprehensive collection of English Law 1650–1850, with many earlier books from 1490. 128 v contain *c*1,120 pamphlets, 1688–1855, but the great majority are 1790–1850; mainly legal but also include various other subjects. Except for some folio and quarto v and the pamphlets, it is shelved as a collection in the Truro Corridor. A ms cat came with the collection.

B2 *Peerage law and cases.* A comprehensive collection from 1673 onwards.

Separate card cat to peerage cases.

C General Collections

The general collection of books was built up by purchase and donation mostly during the periods 1848–60 and 1897–1920, especially 1904–14 during the librarianship of Edmund Gosse (1849–1928), when the literary and historical purchasing was substantial. A wide range of subjects is covered, especially British history (including English local history), genealogy, English, Latin and Greek literature, European history, and travel. There are *c*4,000 pre-1851 books in addition to the collections below.

C1 *Peel tracts. c*2,000 bought 1897 and then bound by subjects in 305 v; 70% relate to Ireland, especially during the period 1782–1800; others are on political, economic, and social subjects. The collection was purchased from Sir Robert Peel, 3rd Bart (1822–95), who was Chief Secretary for Ireland 1861–5. It was probably collected by his grandfather the first Sir Robert Peel (1750–1830) when Chief Secretary for Ireland 1812–16, but it does not include his 'Bibliotheca Hibernicana' of 125 major works on Ireland, of which a cat was published in 1823.

Author-subject list in *Catalogue* 1908, p492-722.

C2 *Charles I and Commonwealth.* A collection of *c*400 contemporary printed items was built around the Death Warrant of Charles I (in the library's custody, 1851–1977, now on display in the Royal Gallery); these include a series of 126 Fast Sermons, 1641–47, and 56 works by William Prynne (1600–69) published 1628–61.

C3 *Miscellaneous tracts.* A collection of 41 v containing 297 pamphlets 1712–1885. Miscellaneous subjects; including 32 items, 1712–85, relating to North America. Scattered through the general collections are *c*50 contemporary tracts relating to the Popish Plot.

C4 *French gift.* In 1834–6 the Chambre des Pairs gave 1,872 v of French material both official and unofficial, with some substantial works of history and genealogy, eg Anselme, and the *Almanach Royal* from 1692. The ms catalogue sent with the gift records 103 v of French law before 1789; 1295 v of French law after 1788; 474 v of 'documents divers'. The collection has been enlarged by subsequent donations and purchases, including a set of the *Encyclopédie* from the library of the guillotined Béatrice de Choiseul-Stainville, Duchesse de Gramont (1730–94).

C5 *Farnham gift*, donated *c*1845 by Henry Maxwell, 7th Baron Farnham, then sitting as an Irish representative peer. *c*1,500 tracts bound in 363 v predominantly on religious matters, from the Protestant establishment viewpoint, but including a number on Irish affairs. At least 2 STC, 15 Wing and 265 ESTC but mainly 1800–40. There is also a separate collection of 60 rare Catholic and anti-Catholic works 1523–1794 bound in 56 v (including 1 STC, 10 Wing and 16 pre-1701 foreign).

The 60 rare books are listed in *Bulletin* 1980, no 1, p5-11. The tracts are uncatalogued at present.

C6 *Newspapers* 1757–1823. Sets mostly incomplete of 15 titles, bound in 60 v.

List.

C7 *Roxburghe Club.* 25 of its publications from 1838 donated by former librarians Sir Charles Clay and Christopher Dobson, the latter being Secretary to the Club, and others.

List in *Bulletin* 1980, no 2, p16-20.

House of Lords Record Office, Palace of Westminster, London SW1A 0PW. Tel (01) 219 3073 or 3074. Search Room (in Victoria Tower, entry via Chancellor's Gate in Old Palace Yard) open 9.30 am-5.30 pm to the public. Material from the Lords' Library may be consulted here; also from the Commons' Library by prior arrangement with its librarian. Photocopying and microfilming.

In 1509 the Parliament Office (headed by the Clerk of the Parliaments), previously a department of Chancery, became a part of the House of Lords where the original Acts of Parliament and other records were preserved. From 1621 the records were mainly housed in the Jewel Tower, where they escaped the fire of 1834. The Record Office was transferred to the purpose-built Victoria Tower in 1864, with a search room which since 1946 has been public. It now houses the archives of both Houses, and has increasingly become the repository for older printed documents transferred from the two parliamentary libraries. It also houses some historical collections of mss and printed books, and an office reference collection which includes a few early law books. It is staffed to answer enquiries from the public about the documents of either House whether printed or manuscript, unlike the two libraries which provide this service only for Members (each House has an Information Office which answers enquiries by post or telephone from the general public, but only about current business).

Maurice F Bond, *Guide to the records of Parliament*, London, HMSO, 1971, and *A short guide to the records of Parliament* 3rd ed 1979. *Record Office memoranda* 1953– includes both the annual *Report* (with notes of accessions) and sectional guides and calendars (see especially no 25 (1961) *The use of finding aids* and no 50 (1973) *Sources for economic history*). M F Bond, *The records of Parliament, a guide for genealogists and local historians*. Chichester, Phillimore, 1964. M F Bond, 'Materials for transport history among the records of Parliament', *Journal of Transport History* 4(1) (May 1959), p41-5. M F Bond, 'The Victoria Tower and its records', *Parliamentary Affairs* 8 (1955), p482-91. D Englefield, *Parliament and information*, London Library Association, 1981, p95-8.

A *Acts of Parliament*, forming part of the House of Lords records, described in *Guide*, p93-103. Original Acts are held in ms from 1497 until 1849 (1850 in the case of Private Acts) when they began to be specially printed on vellum. The Record Office also holds the sessional printed volumes of Public Acts from 1715 (with a few earlier volumes), of Local and Personal Acts 1798–1875, and of Private Acts from 1815 (before which there are no official sets, only copies of individual Bills or Acts printed at the expense of the parties); and some retrospective compilations.

Sheila Lambert, *Bills and Acts*, Cambridge, 1971.

B *House of Lord records* (other than Acts), described in *Guide*, p106-96 (including printed documents held in the Lords' Library). The pre-1851 printed documents held in the Record Office itself include the Journals from 1510 (with indexes and calendars) printed 1767– (p31-2), Minutes of Proceedings printed from 1825 (p33-4), collected Debates (p37-9), Petitions on Bills (p67), some printed Private Bills from 1705 (p84), State Trials (p111), Lords' Appeal Cases and writ of Error Cases from 1702 (p117-8), and Peerage Claims cases from 1734 and evidence from 1794 (p162-3).

C *House of Commons records*, described in *Guide*, p199-248 (including printed documents held in the Lords' and Commons' libraries). Pre-1851 printed documents held in the Record Office itself include Journals (1547–) with indexes, printed from 1762 (p211-2), Votes and Proceedings 1680–1900 with Appendices from 1826 and Supplement from 1836 (p213-4), Private Business from 1847 (p218), Notices of Motions from 1849 (p214-5), Division Lists from 1836 (p215), some Committee Proceedings, chiefly after 1800 (p218-25), Public Bills from 1731 (p227), a few 18th cent Parliamentary Papers (p233-4), and an incomplete duplicate file transferred from the Controller's Office of HMSO of individual Parliamentary Papers from 1822 (1,458 boxes, accessible by prior arrangement only).

D *Historical Collections*, primarily of mss, but some include printed books, described briefly in *Guide*, p269-99 (supplemented by accessions lists in *Report*) and some in more detail in *A guide to historical collections of the nineteenth and twentieth centuries*, 1978 (Memorandum no 60). Typescript lists of most. Calendars of some in *Memoranda*. Those containing significant printed pre-1851 material are mentioned individually below.

D1 *Ashbourne papers*, deposited 1972, formed by Edward Gibson, 1st Baron Ashbourne (1837–1913), Conservative MP, Lord Chancellor of Ireland, including printed documents 1800–1913 (not included in the list published 1974).

D2 *Marriage law papers*, a collection formed and deposited by a firm of parliamentary agents, *c*450 items ms and printed in 3 v relating to the efforts of Unitarians to obtain reforms of the marriage laws 1819–36. (List).

D3 *Catesby collection* of prints and 28 printed books of 1621–1912 belonging to the Catesby family and mostly collected in the early 20th cent, deposited in 1965 by Peter A Catesby of Catesby Ltd. Most relate to the Gunpowder

Plot and its conspirators, especially Robert Catesby (1573–1605). (List no 45.)

Imperial College of Science and Technology, South Kensington, London SW7.

Imperial College is a federation established in 1907 of the Royal College of Science (founded 1845 as the Royal College of Chemistry), the Royal School of Mines (founded 1851) and the City and Guilds College (founded 1884); in 1908 it became a school of the University of London. It has a central library (the Lyon Playfair) and 13 major departmental libraries, which are mainly working scientific collections without old or rare books.

The Royal Charter of the Imperial College of Science and Technology, 1957.

A Lyon Playfair Library

Imperial College Road, London SW7 2AZ. Tel (01) 589 5111 Ext 2100. Telex 261503. Open Mon-Sat 9.30 am-5.30 pm (Mon-Fri 9 pm term and Easter vac) to bona fide research workers by appointment only; no book delivery after 5 pm. Photocopying facilities.

The Lyon Playfair Library contains over 200,000 v on the sciences. It also houses the archives of the College and of its constituent parts, and the deposited libraries of the London Natural History Society, the Operational Research Society, and the Tensor Society of Great Britain. The papers of many eminent scientists are held with the archives.

Card cat (authors) is union cat of all libraries in the College.

Classified cat of Lyon Playfair Library only.

Natural history manuscript resources, 1980, p200-2.

Annan Collection c600 works collected by Robert Annan (*b*1885) and given by him in 1972 to the Royal School of Mines, but housed in the Lyon Playfair Library, on the history of the laws and practice of mining, together with mineralogy, metallurgy and assaying (except ferrous metals and coal); also the modern industrial archaeology of mining and metallurgy, and archaeometallurgy. 1 incunabulum; 3 STC; 33 Wing items; 284 other pre-1851 works. Over 10 mss. All important printed books on mining are present, usually in at least the first edition.

Cat in preparation (1982).

Robert Annan, *Historic books on mining*, London, Science Museum, 1960 (exhibition cat); repr 1968.

——'Early literature of metal mining', *Trans Inst Mining and Metallurgy* 70 (1960/1), p161-75.

'The Robert Annan bequest [ie gift]', *Royal School of Mines Journ*, no 22, p73-5.

B Civil Engineering Library

Dept of Civil Engineering, Imperial College Road, London SW7 2BU. Tel (01) 589 5111 Ext 1313. Telex 261503. Open Mon-Fri 10 am-5.30 pm (6 pm in term) to bona fide research workers by appointment only on application to the librarian. Photocopying can be arranged in the Department.

Civil Engineering History Collection A special collection built up within the library from *c*1962 when the Institution of Civil Engineers gave some early works it wished to discard; it is being actively enlarged by donation and selective purchasing. Now *c*750 works illustrating the development of civil engineering from the mid-17th cent onwards, one third of which are rare. It is strong in hydraulic engineering; docks and harbours; irrigation, especially in the Indian sub-continent; structures, especially iron and concrete; tunnelling; canals; foundations and retaining walls. Related topics (applied mechanics; fluid mechanics; material properties and testing) are also well represented. The collection includes *c*250 pre-1851 items (1643 onwards); 2 v of newspaper cuttings and ms notes on canals *c*1760–1836; drawings and photographs.

Printed cat in progress (1982): *A bibliographical catalogue of the collection of works on soil mechanics 1764–1950*, 1981.

Included in main author cats of Civil Engineering Library and Lyon Playfair Library.

C Watts Library

Department of Geology, Royal School of Mines, Prince Consort Road, London SW7 2BP. Tel (01) 589 5111 Ext 1613. Open Mon-Fri 10 am-12 noon, 2-4 pm to bona fide research workers on written application to the librarian. *No* photocopying.

The Watts Library is named after William Whitehead Watts (1860–1947), Professor Geology at the Royal College of Science, who gave much of his own library to the Department.

Rare Books Collection c300 early editions of geology and palaeontology books.

Geology: early editions of geology books in the Watts Library, Imperial College, [1971]. (op)

Imperial War Museum, Department of Printed Books, Lambeth Road, London SE1 6HZ. Tel (01) 735 8922 Ext 260 (Library enquiries), 237 (appointments). Open Mon-Fri 10 am-5 pm by appointment, on at least 24 hours' notice; closed last two full weeks in October. Photocopier; microfilm/fiche reader.

The Museum illustrates the history of conflict in the 20th cent, especially the two world wars and other operations in which British and Commonwealth forces took part. It was formed in 1917, reconstituted by statute under trustees in 1920, and opened to the public at the Crystal Palace in the same year. In 1924 it moved to Kensington, and in 1936 to its present building, formerly that of

Bethlem Royal Hospital, whose chapel has been converted into the Reading Room. The library escaped the bomb which fell on the Museum in 1941, but was damaged by arson in 1968. There are also separate Departments of Art (including a poster collection); Film; Photographs; Documents; and Sound Records.

Imperial War Museum handbook, 1976.

Department of Printed Books, Imperial War Museum, 1980 (leaflet).

General The library holds well over 100,000 v of books, 30,000 pamphlets, and 20,000 v of periodicals and newspapers, with large collections of maps and technical drawings; a major proportion has been donated. The primary focus of the library is on the wars in which Britain and other Commonwealth countries have taken part, whether officially (as Vietnam), or unofficially (as in the Spanish Civil War), from 1914. There is also a less intensive coverage of other 20th cent international and civil wars of all nations. The principal strengths of the collections are reflected in the sub-sections below.

Card cat (author and classified).

Subject guide to booklists, 1976, lists *c*500 lists which are available gratis.

Unit histories An outstanding collection in several thousand volumes of histories of fighting units; of armies, from regiments down to battalions, of navies down to individual ships, and of air forces down to squadrons; many are privately printed or scarce. The British portion includes some 19th cent histories; and a number of works printed in Germany 1945–6. The German portion, *c*700 v including some older works, was obtained almost entirely after World War I in lieu of reparation payments. There are also extensive French and American sections.

Technical manuals The most comprehensive public collection on arms, munitions, equipment and vehicles.

Personal experience Several thousand volumes of autobiography and memoirs, some privately printed, arranged by theatres of conflict geographically.

War poetry Over 2,000 items, chiefly of the world wars, though the collection on the Second was depleted in 1968. There is a high proportion of privately printed and very recondite items.

Catherine W Reilly, *English poetry of the First World War: a bibliography*, London, George Prior, 1978 (annotated copy).

Newspapers and periodicals Well over 2,000 sets. A substantial collection of trench newspapers of 1914–8 (though damaged in 1968) in a variety of formats in letterpress, lithographed, and spirit duplicated forms; the French collection is especially extensive. British unit magazines of all periods. General military periodicals include some American, Commonwealth, and foreign. Special donated collection of publications on the forces of Kenya in World War II.

List of current journals, 1980. A comprehensive list is in preparation.

Uncatalogued collections of ephemera 180 boxes of ephemera with many volumes of newscuttings collected by the Women's Work Department of the Museum from 1917 to *c*1925, relating to the role of women in World War I (the periodicals have been transferred to the Periodicals Collection). A collection of *c*8,000 aerial propaganda leaflets, the largest in Europe. Stationery of the world's armed forces. Ration books and documents. Theatre programmes, comprising programmes both of performances in military surroundings or under military auspices, and of plays relating to war. Military menus.

Uncatalogued collections not yet available to readers These include half of the collection of the Military Intelligence Library established in Paris in 1944, received through the Cabinet Office. Also a current collection of ephemera of the conflict in Northern Ireland.

Industrial Participation Association, Suite 25, Buckingham Court, 78 Buckingham Gate, London SW1E 6PQ. Tel (01) 222 0351. Open Mon-Fri 9 am-5 pm by appointment only, at Director's convenience, after written letter of application to the Director.

The Association was founded in 1884 as the Association for Promoting Co-operative Production, becoming in 1904 the Labour Co-partnership Association, in 1926 the Industrial Co-partnership Association, and in 1972 the Industrial Participation Association. The Director's office contains the following collections (in addition to the Association's own publications): *c*500 v donated from 1884 onwards, mostly on the co-operative movement, industrial democracy, profit sharing and co-ownership. They include *c*100 v from the 19th cent.

Books from the collections of Association and other co-operators Books and pamphlets from the collections of Edward Owen Greening (1836–1923), Thomas Blandford (1862?–1899), and especially John Malcolm Forbes Ludlow (1821–1911) the Christian Socialist (including a volume of Christian Socialist tracts *c*1850–8); and from members of the Association.

Books from other libraries of co-operation Several from Co-operative Institute (London); 2 rare Owen items from the Circulating Library of the Guild of Co-operators (*New moral world* 1842–7, 7 pts with the wrappers in 1 v, and *Millenial Gazette* no 1-16, 1856–8); and others from similar collections.

Miscellaneous Books on economics, eg Babbage *Economy of machinery* 1832 (author's presentation copy to Lord Althorp). 80 pamphlets published by the Co-operative Union (mainly late 19th-early 20th cent). *Co-operative Magazine* 1828–9.

Sources in British political history 1900–1951, 1975, v 1, p114.

Journal 1894– .

Annual Report 1885–1938.

Inland Revenue Library, Somerset House, London WC2R 1LB. Tel (01) 438 6477. Open Mon-Fri 9 am-4.30 pm for government business, or by special written permission on application in writing to the librarian. Photocopying facilities.

The Library of the Board of Inland Revenue, containing *c*75,000 v on taxation, has been built up mainly since 1921, though containing early material; most of the earlier archives have been transferred to the Public Record Office within the last decade, including important documents relating to the newspaper stamp duty (the copies of newspapers deposited until 1855 at the Board's Stamp Duty Office are now in the British Library Newspaper Library).

Board of Inland Revenue, *A short history of Somerset House* (*c*1978).

The historical material consists of *c*300 v on taxation, inland revenue, the Exchequer and related subjects. The collection is mainly post-1850, but includes some interesting earlier items, eg a collection of printed licences, certificates, etc; Income Tax bills, acts and tables, 1799 onwards, and earlier legislation on other taxes (including Sorbell's Acts and ordinances 1640–56).

Inner Temple Library, Honourable Society of the Inner Temple, Inner Temple Lane, London EC4Y 7DA. Tel (01) 353 2959. Open Mon-Fri (not last two weeks August) 10 am-6 pm (5 pm in Aug and Sept) to judges and barristers only. Bona fide research scholars who apply in writing for an appointment may be admitted at the librarian's discretion. Special arrangements for photography of rare books.

A library is known to have been established at this Inn of Court by 1505, but it remained small until the later 17th cent when a succession of major benefactions began. In 1661–2 Mrs Anne Sadleir, eldest daughter of Sir Edward Coke (1552–1634) donated her collection of printed books and mss; the books were mostly devotional and sermons, and have been wrongly labelled as coming from her father's library. The Fire of 1666 caused some loss to the collections. The Treasurer William Petyt (1637–1707), son of the William Petyt whose library is preserved at Skipton, bequeathed 182 printed and 209 ms v, with endowments. Other donations, all of which were of both books and mss came from Francis Maseres (1731–1834) FRS FSA, Treasurer (including his own works on mathematics and physics); the Hon Daines Barrington (1727–1800), Recorder of Bristol; Alexander Luders (*c*1750–1819), Treasurer; John Austin (1790–1859), Lecturer at the Inn; and John Leycester Adolphus (1795–1862) editor of *King's Bench Reports*, who donated the 1785–1800 series annotated by Sir George Sowley Holroyd (1758–1831). Herbert Jacob's library of printed books was acquired in 1726. Some of the rare books (and many of the library records) were destroyed in 1941–43, but most of the older material, and all the mss were saved. Some non-legal books have been sold (Christie 1 Dec 1976; 11 and 25 Oct 1978). It now has a general law collection of *c*100,000 v (including excellent collections of reports from the 17th cent, statutes, treatises, Roman and Roman-Dutch law and jurisprudence; 6 incunabula. Also a 16th-19th cent non-legal collection (mostly English, French and German literature, English and foreign history, heraldry, genealogy and antiquities, and some science and mathematics).

Card cat (authors). Cats of printed books in ms 1713, 1726, 1733, 1773. *A catalogue of printed books... manuscripts*, 1806 (no copy in library, but in British Library and Lincoln's Inn). *A catalogue of the printed books and manuscripts... arranged in classes*, 1883. *An alphabetical catalogue of the printed books*, 1843. In 1892 a loose-leaf typewritten cat was introduced, for later acquisitions, and was in use until recently.

J Conway Davies, *Catalogue of manuscripts in the Library of the Honourable Society of the Inner Temple*. London, OUP, 1972, 3 v. v 1 contains a history of the Library and description of the major donations and biographies of donors, with some information on printed books. v 3 lists records of the library. See also Historical Mss Commission *2nd* and *11th report* (1871, 88).

W W S Breen, 'A sketch of the Inner Temple Library', *Law Library Journal* 64(1) (1971), p5-12.

H H L Bellot, *The Inner and Middle Temple*, London 1902, esp p47-50.

J B Williamson, *The history of the Temple*, London 1924, esp p648-51.

IPC Business Press Ltd, Quadrant House, The Quadrant, Sutton, Surrey SM2 5AS. Tel (01) 661 3500 Ext 3927. Open Mon-Fri 9 am-5 pm on application to the Divisional Archivist, subject to payment of fee (£3 per ½ day, £5 per day). Photocopying.

Kelly's Directories Collection

An editorial archive of directories published by the firm, by Kelly's Directories Ltd, and by other absorbed publishers, it contains *c*2,000 v. 130 v are pre-1850; these alone are referred to below:

London directories The *Post Office London directory* (founded 1800 by Post Office letter carriers, who were the compilers until 1847, bought in 1836 by Frederick Kelly, Chief Inspector of Inland Letter-Carriers, and published by his brother W Kelly trading as Kelly & Co at Boswell Court), 1801–50 editions (published Autumn preceding), 40 v. Others by Kent, 1768–1807, 5 v; Pigott, 1823–38, 3 v; Lowndes, Boyle, Holden, Lochie and Robson, 1768–1836, 16 v.

Town directories Bristol (Matthews), 1793–1842, 5 v; Liverpool (Gore), 1805–39, 6 v; Manchester (Dean), 1808–21, 4 v; (Pigott), 1813–41, 6 v; (Slater), 1844–8, 3 v. Single issues for other towns.

County directories Pigott 1826–50, 15 v; Kelly 1840–50, 8 v; both covering large groups of counties. Others, 1822–50, 9 v.

Special trades directories Laxton's builder's price books, 1850.

Typescript list by publisher.

Index by county and title.

C W Goss, *The London directories 1677–1855*, London, 1933.

J E Norton, *Guide to the national and provincial directories. . .*, London, 1950.

——'The Post Office London directory', *Library* (5th ser) 21 (1966), p293-9.

Institut Francais Du Royaume-uni, 15 Queensberry Place, South Kensington, London SW7 2DT. Tel (01) 589 6211. Open Mon-Fri 10 am-6 pm (Mon-Tues 8 pm) to subscribers, and for reference only to the public; closed two weeks at Christmas and Easter, six in Summer.

The Institute was established by the government of France in 1910 to foster cultural relations with the United Kingdom. A small library, founded in 1913, was opened to the public and systematically built up from *c*1935, now holds *c*65,000 v (including at least 100 pre-1851, but almost all are post-1800), mainly literature, history and art, almost all in French.

Card cat (author and classified).

Acquisitions lists 1957– .

M Ventre, 'La bibliotheque de l'Institut francais de Londres', *Bulletin de l'Association des Bibliothecaires Francais* no 21 (Nov 1956), p151-4.

Institute of Actuaries Library, Staple Inn Hall, 1 Staple Inn, London WC1V 7QJ. (Entrance to Staple Inn is between 2 and 3 Holborn, 20 yards East of the South exit from Chancery Lane tube station.) Tel (01) 242 0106. Open Mon-Fri 9.15 am-5 pm by appointment, on written application to the librarian. Photocopying facilities.

The library dates from the foundation of the Institute in 1848, and from 1886 it was housed in the hall of Staple Inn, formerly an Inn of Chancery but now devoted to other uses; it had been evacuated when the hall (now rebuilt) was demolished by a bomb in 1944.

Reginald C Simmonds, *The Institute of Actuaries 1848–1948*, Cambridge UP for the Institute, 1948, p277-87. (op)

Library Guide (1981) does not mention the segregated rare book collections.

General The library contains *c*10,000 v on actuarial science and its applications; mathematics; statistics; insurance; economics; demography; and law. Much of the material is of historical interest, including several hundred pre-1851 books. 160 v of these are in segregated rare books collections described below. Most of the rare books are derived from donations, including the gift in 1849 by Edwin James Farren, Actuary of the Asylum Life Office, of part of his collection, and many donations from Augustus de Morgan (1806–71), including most of his own works. Purchases were made at the outset, and from 1865 to 1874 with a fund in memory of Peter Hardy (1813–63) FRS, whose own extensive library passed to his son R P Hardy, also an actuary, who gave a few rare books from it. Major dispersals from the library took place at various times between 1880 and 1940; these included many of the mss and proof copies for which it was once famous.

Card cat (author and classified); separate author cat for 160 rarer books.

Catalogue of the Library of the Institute of Actuaries, 1880 (author; classified index); 1894 (dictionary); 1907 (dictionary); 1935 (author); all op.

Additions to the library, 1908– (annual, previously in *Journal*). The first printed cat was included in the Institute's *Constitution and list of members* 2 v, 1849–51.

Mathematics Collection, including probability, logarithm tables, etc; mainly 18th-19th cent, but including some of the rarest books in the library and 3 STC items, and a number of association copies; Babbage *Specimen of logarithm tables* 1831 in 21 parts on coloured paper has ms note 'only 1 copy having been printed' and letter of presentation to W Streatfield, and many books by Abraham de Moivre (1667–1754).

Mortality Statistics Collection The collection includes *General Bill of the mortality of the clergy of London* 1662, bound with *London's dreadful visitation. . .*, 1665. Standard classics such as Graunt *Natural and political observations* 1665, and Short *New observations* 1750.

Theory of Life Assurance and Annuities Collection Many works of the 18th and 19th cent, eg 1771 and later editions of Price *Observations on reversionary payments*; Brand *Treatise on annuities* 1775; Babbage *Comparative view* 1826.

Insurance Prospectuses Collection The collection is said to have been started in 1906 by the gift from the Clerical, Medical and General Assurance Society of a bound volume of pre-1839 prospectuses. This probably refers to a 3 v set in which the first contains prospectuses (with reports to policy-holders and specimen policy conditions) 1832–38, the second prospectuses collected in 1838, and the third prospectuses 1836–42. There is another 3 v set bound up by the Colonial Life Assurance Co in 1846 covering English, Irish, Scottish and foreign offices. Also a volume of statutes of French and German companies of the 1850s.

Tracts Collection *c*70 v of pamphlets mainly of the 19th cent covering life assurance, statistics, friendly societies, mortality rates, etc, with some French, German, and Dutch insurance literature. They include a collection bought in 1880 from Cornelius Walford (1827–85).

Author entries for v 1-20 included in *Catalogue*, 1880; v 1-69 in 1907 edition.

Newmarch Collection This contains 6 v of pamphlets, mainly on life assurance, collected by William Newmarch (1820–82) FRS, Manager of Glyn Mills and Co's bank, bequeathed to the Royal Society, who have deposited the collection on permanent loan.

Serials The collection includes, in addition to the Institute's own publications from 1849, the *Journal de l'assureur* 1848–51 and some other scarce mid-19th cent sets.

Law A small legal section includes Weskett *Digest... of insurance* 1781, and Trusler *Useful... information re... estates*, 1811 (with ms notes).

Institute of Advanced Legal Studies Library, 17 Russell Square, London WC1B 5DR. Tel (01) 637 1731. Open Mon-Thurs 10 am-8 pm, Fri 5.30 pm, Sat 12.30 pm to graduates of British universities on written application; others may be admitted for advanced research, normally subject to payment of a fee. Photocopying.

The Institute and its library were founded in 1947 within the University of London to provide a focal point for legal research in the United Kingdom.

E M Moys, 'The Library of the Institute of Advanced Legal Studies, London', *Law Library Journal* 49 (1956), p23-30.

General The library contains *c*150,000 v on all branches and jurisdictions of law. In practice, as a result of a co-operative acquisitions policy agreed with other law libraries, it tends to specialize, at the exclusion of most oriental and East European, in the jurisdictions of the British Isles, Commonwealth, US, Latin America and Western Europe, together with public international law, comparative law, and jurisprudence. There are *c*1,000 pre-1851 monographs, some on subjects not included in the current specializations. The whole library is arranged by a single subject classification, without separate special collections.

Card cat (author/name and alphabetical subject) reproduced as *Catalogue of the Library of the Institute of Advanced Legal Studies, London*, Boston, (Mass), G K Hall, 1978, 6 v ($480).

Post-1981 acquisitions on microfiche cat.

Classified shelflist.

Collections Incorporated In its early years the library was built up from many substantial donations from institutions and individuals; rare books are virtually all from such sources. The most important were: a large collection from the House of Commons Library; Hispanic and Luso-Brazilian Councils (the whole law collection from Canning House Library); *c*170 v including rare English material bequeathed by Prof Sir Percy Henry Winfield (1878–1955), in addition to *c*300 similar items from the 16th cent onwards which he gave earlier; a German collection to 1929 bequeathed by Charles Huberich; the Canadian Law Library (of the Canadian government), formerly kept in the library of the Judicial Committee of the Privy Council; a 17th-18th cent collection mainly of Roman Law from the library of Percival Frere Smith, received in 1955; a collection of *c*60 v, many of which are pre-1851, on the law of the Channel Islands, received mainly as duplicates from the Guille-Allès Library and the Priaulx Library, both in Guernsey; and the library of Prof Herbert Felix Jolowicz (1890–1954) containing much early and rare material, especially on Roman Law, given by his widow in 1956.

Accessions Register 1953 onwards.

Serials Collection Law reports, reviews, and other serials make up 60 per cent of the holdings of the library, and include sets of English law reports and statutes, the largest collection in existence of Commonwealth law reports, and a very extensive collection of US law reviews. A large collection of the reports of US state jurisdictions was received from the Inner Temple Library.

Institute of Advanced Legal Studies, *Union list of legal periodicals...*, 4th ed 1978 (£12.50), does not include law reports.

All serials included in general cat.

Institute of Archaeology Library, 31 Gordon Square, London WC1H 0PY. Tel (01) 387 6052. Open Mon-Thurs in term 10 am-8.30 pm, Fri in term and Mon-Fri in vac 10 am-5.30 pm to staff, students, and members of the University of London with identification; to persons of academic standing after prior written application.

The library has been built up as a working and teaching collection to serve the Institute since it was established by the University of London in 1937. *c*35,000 v of serials and books, of which *c*3,000 are pre-1851. It incorporates substantial donations from the libraries of Sir (Robert Eric) Mortimer Wheeler (1890–1976), W H G Drummond, Sir (Charles) Leonard Woolley (1880–1960), Vere Gordon Childe (1892–1957), and Prof Alfred Frederick Eberhard Zeuner. There is a special collection of mss on nautical archaeology and of excavation reports.

Card cat (author, with alphabetical subject index). Institute of Archaeology, *Annual Report* 1937– ; *Bulletin*, 1959– .

Institute of Army Education, Services Central Library, 54 Kimber Road, Wandsworth, London SW18 4PQ. Open Mon and Tues 8.30 am-5 pm, Wed-Fri 4.30 pm on written application to the librarian. Photocopying facilities.

A central lending library for the Army is said to have begun in 1923, but it dates in its present form from the establishment of the Army Central Library in 1948, with which a similar but small library from RAF Northwood was amalgamated in 1974 to form the Services Central Library, serving the Army and the RAF. It incorporates many collections formed in the 19th cent by various regiments, corps and garrisons, including several branches of the Royal Engineers, and the Army Education Corps HQ Library at Shornclife 1920–39 known as the Sir John Moore Library. There are also many books from the Victoria Library of the Military Society of Ireland. There are over 100,000 v, including *c*90 pre-1851.

Card cat (author and classified).

A C T White, *The story of Army Education*, London, 1963. (op)

D McEwan and R A Wafer, 'The Army library service', *Library Assoc Record* 60 (1958), p37-40.

Unit Histories *c*600 v of histories of individual divisions, brigades, regiments, and corps, including *c*60 pre-1851 from the series by Richard Cannon, many with hand-coloured plates, and some other pre-1851 and rare later items.

Army Central Library, *Military History Collection* (1962?) (limited to the unit history collection despite its title).

Military History A very large collection, mainly modern, but with some earlier, such as Bentivoglio *War of Flanders* 1678, a collection on the Napoleonic Wars which includes contemporary works, and *c*170 v mainly contemporary on the Russo-Japanese War. The section on the campaigns in India includes some confidential War Office histories. Complete sets of official histories of the two world wars.

Biography A collection, mainly modern, of military figures. Some pre-1851 books such as Gumble *Vie du General Monck*, Rouen 1672, and a number on Napeoleon, with a few non-military people.

Institute of Bankers Library, 10 Lombard Street, London EC3V 9AS. Tel (01) 623 3531. Open Mon-Fri 9 am-5 pm by appointment after written application to the librarian. Photocopier available.

The Institute of Bankers was founded in 1879 to regulate professional standards in banking following a campaign in the *Bankers' Magazine*. The library began with an appeal for donations in the same year, but has been built up mainly since 1930. It now contains *c*30,000 v.

Edwin Green, *Debtors to their profession: a history of the Institute of Bankers 1879–1979*, London, the Institute, 1979, p53, 67, 130-1, 158-9.

P Jilkes, 'The Library of the Institute of Bankers', *Journ Inst Bankers*, Feb 1980, p19.

Books total *c*25,000 of which *c*150 v are pre-1851. These include books on banking practice, eg 10 works by James William Gilbart (1794–1863), mainly in English; a collection in 1 v on the Chesterfield and North Derbyshire Bank (including histories of banks and banking, after 1860, but including many privately printed and presentation copies, miscellaneous works on social and economic conditions).

Card cat (author and classified).

Catalogue of the Library [6th ed], 1935 (classified, without index), includes most of the rare books.

Pamphlet Collection 141 v acquired by the library and uniformly bound, 1707–1950, comprising *c*1,200 items, of which *c*150 are pre-1851.

Library Catalogue. Section 2. Pamphlets, 1949 2 v (authors; and serial list contents of each volume).

Catalogue of the Library, 1935, includes contents of v 1-91.

Not in general card cat.

Periodicals Collection Over 500 sets. These include an interesting set (perhaps the only complete or near-complete one in existence) of the *Circular to Bankers* and *Bankers' Circular* (1827–50), the private organ of Henry Burgess (the editor and virtually the sole author) and his Committee of Country Bankers; it is the set addressed to Heywood Bros and Co, Manchester, in the early numbers of which several additional ms pages are added to each issue by Burgess.

Paper Money Collection In 1905 the Institute bought the collection of banknotes and other forms of paper money built up by Maberly Phillips the historian of private banking, *c*1,000 specimens of British and Irish banks from 1709 onwards and 2 foreign. Modest additions have been made to the collection. Several of the specimens are unique.

Institute of Bankers, *Catalogue of the 'Maberly Phillips' collection of old bank notes, drafts, etc collected and mounted by Maberly Phillips*, 1906.

Institute of Brewing, 33 Clarges Street, London W1Y 8EE. Tel (01) 449 8144. Open Mon-Fri 9 am-5 pm. Admission by written application to the Assistant Secretary. Photocopying facilities.

Institute of Brewing Library The origins of the Institute of Brewing Library lie in the formation of Moritz's Laboratory Club (founded 1886) and several provincial Institutes of Brewing which merged to form the Institute in 1903. The original library was formed by the London Section of the Institute, but was totally destroyed during an air raid in 1940. The present small library seems to consist mostly of books presented to the Institute, especially by the Chemical Society Library and by the library of the Institute's associated research body, the Brewing Industry Research Foundation (now the Brewers Research Society), who presented all of their older books to the Institute in 1975. The Institute occasionally purchases old books on brewing but the main source of its acquisitions are gifts from members. Its stock totals 400 v, including *c*40 printed pre-1850. Most of the library consists of late 19th and early 20th cent works, shelved by subject, and including the older material, especially on chemistry, organic chemistry, sugar and carbohydrate chemistry, fermentation, mainly later 19th cent, including Pasteur *Studies in fermentation* 1879; a few books in German, including Mayer *Lehrbuch des Gährungschemie* 1879; barley, malt and other brewing materials (all 19th cent and later); theory and practice of brewing: mainly works of the 18th and 19th cent, including *London and County Brewer* 4th ed 1742, 5th ed 1744; Combrune *Essay* 1758 and his *Theory and practice of brewing* 1804; Richardson *Statistical estimate*... 1784 and 1788; Hughes *Treatise on the brewing of beer*... 4th ed Uxbridge printed for the author 1798 (unbound, uncut, original stab sewing, contemporary sig of Jas King (?) presented to the Institute of Brewing by H J Gray, Director Cascade Brewery, Hobart, Tasmania, 13 March 1979); Morrice *Theory of Brewing* 1802 (sig on title page of Viscount Curzon Oct 1802); few histories of brewing (but very few histories of breweries): all late 19th or 20th cent, including J P Arnold, *Origin and History of Beer*, Chicago, 1911; Gauging excise duty, etc, including 1 v of 8 pamphlets on import duties on beer, all published in Belgium 1830s–40s.

Author/UDC subject *Library Catalogue* was published in 1965 (op) which included some older books. In 1981 the collection was recatalogued by the librarian of the Brewers Research Society in the form of a typed list in rough alphabetical order by author.

The books are shelved by subject.

Institute of Cancer Research Library, Royal Cancer Hospital, Chester Beatty Institute, Fulham Road, London SW3 6JB. Tel (01) 352 5946. Open Mon-Fri 9 am-5.45 pm to staff of Institute and Hospital; to other bona fide research workers by prior arrangement at the librarian's discretion.

The Hospital was founded in 1851 by William Marsden (1796–1867) as the Free Cancer Hospital, becoming the Cancer Hospital, in 1936 the Royal Cancer Hospital, and in 1954 the Royal Marsden Hospital. The Chester Beatty Research Institute was founded at the Hospital in 1909–11, in 1951 being incorporated into a more comprehensive Institute of Cancer Research attached to the Hospital, and becoming a postgraduate school of the University of London. The Institute of Cancer Research Library incorporates the former Chester Beatty Research Institute Library; it is financed by the Medical Research Council, and is the largest British library for cancer research. It contains 26,000 v of periodicals (including 672 current titles) and 12,000 v of monographs on cancer and general medicine.

Card cat.

R M Nicholas, 'The development of medical libraries within the University of London' (MA Librarianship thesis, Univ of London 1976), p110-2.

D A Brunning and C E Dukes, 'The origin and early history of the Institute of Cancer Research of the Royal Cancer Hospital', *Proc Roy Soc of Medicine* 58 (1965), p33-6.

Frieda Sandwith, *Surgeon compassionate*... *William Marsden*, London, Peter Davies, 1960, p193-213.

The Royal Cancer Hospital, Fulham Road, London 1851–1951, 1951.

Historical Collection A small collection of classic and early works on cancer.

Thurstan Holland, Charles (1863–1941), Liverpudlian GP, pioneer in radiology, bequeathed his library on radiology and allied subjects to Woodburn Morrison, Prof of Surgery at the Hospital, from whom it passed to the library.

Chester Beatty Research Institute Library, *An annotated catalogue of early radiological literature*, 1958.

Institute of Chartered Accountants Library, Chartered Accountants Hall, Moorgate Place, London EC2P 2BJ. Tel (01) 628 7060 Ext 210. Telex 884443. Open Mon-Fri 9 am-5.30 pm by appointment, after letter of application to the librarian. Photocopying; microfilm reader.

The Institute of Chartered Accountants in England and Wales was formed in 1880 by the merger of five smaller bodies, one of which, the Institute of Accountants in London, founded in 1870, had a small library which became the basis of the Institute Library. It has been built up by systematic purchasing from 1882, and with the Kheil collection in 1913 became the leading British accountancy library, reinforced in 1957 by the absorption of that of the Society of Incorporated Accountants and Auditors (see below), with c35,000 v.

[Sir Harold Howitt and others], *The history of the Institute of Chartered Accountants in England and Wales 1880–1965 and of its founder accountancy bodies*..., London, Heinemann, 1966, p211-4.

Reference Library General Collection Includes some rare books not in the Historical Collection. 50 v of histories of accounting firms, mainly privately published in the 20th cent, given by the firms, covering the UK, US, and Australia. Law reports include 99 pre-1851 sets in 335 v, many given by Cooper Bros, including 5 Wing (Latch 1661, Palmer 1675, Popham 1682, Ventris 1696, Chancery 1697). Miscellaneous collection of donated books strong in histories of livery companies. All known Institute publications.

Card cat (author and classified).

Library catalogue, 1887; 1903; 1913 (dictionary), repr New York, Arno Press, 1980; 1937, 2 v, repr *ibid*, (v 1 author and alphabetical subject; v 2 chronological).

List of histories of accounting bodies and firms, the Library, 1980 (gratis).

List of periodicals and law reports in the Library, the Library (due 1982).

Checklist of publications of the Institute of Chartered Accountants in England and Wales (due 1983); most also listed in *Catalogue* 1913 and 1937.

Accessions (including Historical Collection) in

Accountant 1894–1914, 1936–57; *Accountancy* 1958–70.

Account of Library appears annually in the Institute's *List of members and firms.*

Historical Accounting Literature Collection A segregated collection, into which the four individual special collections referred to below have been merged: books on bookkeeping and accounting 1494–1914, 3,000 v include 16 STC (3 not in 1st ed); 33 Wing; *c*150 foreign pre-1701. The foreign books are in 17 languages, chiefly French, German, Dutch and Italian, including most of the books on bookkeeping to 1700 and a representative selection afterwards. Also included are two issues of Pacioli *Summa de arithmetica* 1494 containing the first published exposition of double-entry bookkeeping; and works on other subjects by him, and about him. Many of the English works on bookkeeping are represented by numerous editions, eg Dafforne *Merchants Mirrour* 1635 (not in STC, Sir James Hope of Hopetoun's copy), 1651, 1660, 1684; J Mair *Bookkeeping* 1st-8th eds 1736–65. Collection of the works of Edward Thomas Jones (*d*1843?) including translation of his *English system* 1799 into French, Dutch, German, Italian and Russian, and many of the works influenced by or critical of him. A strong collection of Dutch works includes Ympyn *Nieuwe instructie* 1543 the first Dutch book on bookkeeping (1 of 3 known copies, bought at the Dietrichstein sale 1933); 7 mainly 18th cent works, several of considerable rarity and importance were bought at the sale of the collection of Gerrit Jan Honig in 1969. Books of tables and ready reckoners, including scarce STC and Wing items. Merchants' handbooks, especially those with sections on bookkeeping, including many editions of Peri *Negotiante* 1636–1707, Savary *Parfait negociant* 1676–1763 (including Dutch and German translations). Encyclopaedias of commerce, eg Postlethwait 1751–74, Rolt 1756 etc. Some works on commercial law before 1800 include Straccha 1556, Malynes 1622–36, and Beawes 1771–83. Material on company law and bankruptcy, which is entirely English, begins at 1850.

Card cat (author and language sub-arranged chronologically) for books on bookkeeping, other subjects in broad subject sequences sub-arranged by author: reproduced as *Historical accounting literature: a catalogue of the collection of early works on bookkeeping and accounting in the Library of the Institute. . . ,* London, Mansell, 1975 (£35); *Supplement*, the Institute, 1975 (£1). (See also the older printed catalogues above.)

H W Thomson and B S Yamey, *Foreign books on bookkeeping 1494–1750*, 1966 (50p).

R H Parker ed *Bibliographies for accounting historians*, New York, Arno Press, 1980. ($30).

See also M F Bywater and B S Yamey, *Historic accounting literature, a companion guide*, London, Scolar, 1982, p9-29 (detailed history of the collection).

Coffy Collection Part of the collection of R P A Coffy (*d c*1867?), liquidator and lecturer in accountancy in Paris, received as part of the Kheil collection: 56 French works on bookkeeping 1716–1865, including 4 pre-1801, and 41 of 1801–50; several translations of Jones *English system* and books influenced by it, and some sophisticated French writers, including 2nd ed of Coffy's own *Tableau synoptique* 1833.

Chronological typescript list.

A ms list by Coffy 1859 of 32 books includes 20 that are in the collection; the remainder have been identified by binding and other evidence.

Kheil Collection The collection was begun by Karel Petr Kheil (1817–81), owner of a private school of commerce in Prague, and its 1,800 books were divided between his two sons, those on commerce going to N M Kheil (1840–1923), and those on bookkeeping to Karel Petr Kheil jnr (1843–1908). Both sons ran commercial schools and formed substantial libraries, that of N M Kheil bequeathed partly to the National Library in Prague, and partly to the Academy of Commerce there. K P Kheil jnr, a major historian of bookkeeping, began to compile a bibliography of bookkeeping from 1494 onwards on the basis of his own collection; his library contained *c*10,000 books at his death, the portion on bookkeeping was bought by the Institute in 1913 through Nijhoff (the fate of the remainder is unknown). 1,634 v (but some of these were later dispersed as duplicates) including 1 STC; 9 Wing; 29 pre-1601 foreign; 88 per cent were not in the British Museum. Strong in 17th cent Dutch and German books, but the bulk of the collection consists of books published in the lifetime of the Kheils, especially in Slavonic languages, including many presentation copies. Includes the very rare Peele *Maner and fourme* 1553 (STC 19547).

Identified in card cat and by bookplate, but not specially indicated in printed cats.

The collection includes Kheil's ms accessions list, chronological list, and list by language and subject; and some correspondence relating to the acquisition of the collection.

K P Kheil, 'The bibliography of bookkeeping', *Accountant* 18 (1892), p595-6, includes a list of the rarest items by author and date only.

J Blebs, 'Über das Leben und Werk von Karl Peter Kheil', *Der Österreichische Betriebswirt* 3/4 (1965), p129-65.

Society of Incorporated Accountants and Auditors The Society was founded in 1885, and its library in 1887. A small collection of pre-1885 books on bookkeeping was built up from donations, and a collection of 126 18th-19th cent books (of unknown provenance) was bought in 1905. The collections came to the Institute Library when, in 1957, the Society was amalgamated with the Institute. There were in all *c*300 v but probably over half were dispersed as duplicates. The books are mostly 18th and 19th cent standard English works on bookkeeping, but there are a few very rare items, including an otherwise unknown variant of STC 18794, and the unique E Jones *Defence of the English system of bookkeeping*, Bristol, 1797, from the 1905 purchase. 2 STC; 2 Wing.

Society of Incorporated Accountants and Auditors,

Catalogue of the Library..., 1939 (dictionary, op); p63-72 author list of pre-1885 books.

Accessions were occasionally listed in *Incorporated Accountants Journal*, especially 1890–6 and July 1905, p240-1.

A A Garnett, *History of the Society of Incorporated Accountants*, London, OUP for the Society, 1961 (available from the Institute, £1).

R R Coomber, 'Early accounting books and early books of account', *Accountancy* 68 (1957), p433–4.

Judson Collection A collection of books on actuarial science collected by Charles Judson (*d*1947) ACA, and presented to the Institute in 1941. 104 v, of which 9 are pre-1851 and 25 pre-1914; they include books and interest tables etc in English, French and German, mainly late 19th and early 20th cent.

Included in Historical Collection card cat and *Historical accounting literature*, 1975, p231-3 and elsewhere.

Complete list with notes by Judson in *Accountant* 105 (1941), p152-3.

Institute of Child Health Library, 30 Guildford Street, London WC1N 1EH. Tel (01) 242 9789. Open Mon-Fri 9 am-6 pm to staff and students of the Institute and Hospital; to others by prior arrangement with the librarian.

The Hospital for Sick Children, Great Ormond Street, was founded in 1852 by Charles West. The Institute, attached to the Hospital, was founded in 1946 as a postgraduate school of the University of London. The library, which grew out of the hospital library, contains *c*4,000 v of monographs and *c*4,000 v of periodicals on paediatrics and general medicine.

T T Higgins, *Great Ormond Street 1852–1952*, London, Odhams, (1957).

R M Nicholas, 'The development of medical libraries within the University of London' (MA Librarianship thesis, Univ of London, 1976), p122-4.

Charles West (1816–98), MD, founder of the Hospital. His personal library, the typical working library of a mid-Victorian physician, housed in the Institute Library, but the property of the Hospital. Part was donated in 1875 on his resignation from the Hospital, the remainder by his family in 1923. (A few books were accidentally destroyed some time later.) *c*700 works of 1717–1888, including 12 18th cent on paediatrics and most other fields of medicine; 54 editions of his own writings.

Ms classified cat by West.

Hospital for Sick Children, *The West Library: catalogue* (*c*1957).

F S Besser, 'Notes on Dr Charles West', *History of Medicine* 6 (1975), p47-50.

Royal College of Physicians, *Libellus de aegritudine puerorum: a paediatric anthology*, 1967.

Institute of Classical Studies Library *See* Joint Library of the Hellenic and Roman Societies.

Institute of Commonwealth Studies Library, 27 Russell Square, London WC1B 5DS. Tel (01) 636 4808. Open (term) Mon-Wed 7pm, Thurs-Fri 6 pm; (Vac) Mon-Fri 9.30 am-5.30 pm to staff and postgraduate students of British and overseas universities on production of letter of introduction or appropriate identification; some archival collections restricted. Photocopying by arrangement (not on the premises).

The Institute was established by the University of London in 1949 to promote advanced study of the Commonwealth, and maintains a general library of *c*90,000 books on the social sciences and recent history of the Commonwealth, and *c*1,000 periodicals.

West India Committee Library deposited 1977 on permanent loan by the Crown Agents. From an association of merchants and planters founded *c*1750 the Committee developed into an association in Great Britain of individuals, firms and organizations interested in the Caribbean. The library was founded by Sir Algernon (Edward) Aspinall (1871–1952), Secretary to the Committee 1898–1938, and reached 10,000 v in 1974 when it was sold to the Crown Agents. Some books have been transferred to other libraries. The pre-1851 and rare books section comprises *c*200 v (11 not in the British Library Reference Division); 230 pamphlets; 17 ms items; 22 maps; 13 collections of prints and drawings. Historical and descriptive works on the West Indies; pamphlets relating to slavery and the sugar trade.

Card cat (author, subject, topographical).

Catalogue of the Library of the West India Committee, 1941.

Douglas Hall, *A brief history of the West India Committee*. St Lawrence, Barbados, Caribbean University Press, 1971.

'The Library and its future', *West Indies Chronicle* 84 (1460) (Sept 1969), p435.

'The WIC Library', *Chronicle of the West India Committee* 82 (1437), (Oct 1967), p493.

West India Committee. *Report of the Executive Committee for the year 1972/73*, 1973.

Political parties collection Collected by the library since 1961, *c*5,000 items: pamphlets, election manifestos, campaign literature, policy statements, conference reports, posters, car stickers, published by political parties, liberation and other pressure groups and trade unions in countries of the Commonwealth, mostly after 1960.

Indexes by country and issuing body. V Bloomfield, 'African ephemera'.

International Conference on African bibliography, Nairobi 1967 Proceedings, ed J D Pearson, London, Cass, 1969.

V Bloomfield, *Commonwealth elections, 1945–1970: a bibliography*, London, Mansell, 1976.

Institute of Cost and Management Accountants Library, 63 Portland Place, London W1N 4AB. Tel (01) 637 4716. Open Mon-Fri 10 am-5 pm by appointment after written application to the librarian. Photocopying facilities.

The Institute was founded in 1919 as the Institute of Cost and Works Accountants, changing to its present name in 1970. It has a general working library of *c*12,000 books and *c*8,000 pamphlets, with 132 periodical runs.

Historical Collection *c*400 v, including 1 pre-1851, segregated from the general library in 1976, with some donations from members following an appeal at that date. Mainly on cost accounting, factory organization and administration, and bookkeeping, 1731 onwards, but mostly after 1900.

Card cat (authors) separate from main cat.

'Any old books', *Management Accounting*, Dec 1976, p436.

Institute of Dental Surgery, Eastman Dental Hospital, Gray's Inn Road, London EC1X 8LD. Tel (01) 837 7251 Ext 17. Open Mon-Fri 9 am-5.30 pm to University of London registered readers; to others only after written application to librarian or Dean. Photocopying by arrangement.

The Eastman Dental Clinic was founded in 1930, becoming a teaching hospital in 1948. The Institute was set up as a postgraduate school of the University of London in association with it in 1947, and its library opened in 1950. *c*1,900 monographs, including 8 pre-1851 dental textbooks and *c*100 periodicals in *c*3,000 v.

R M Nicholas, 'The development of medical libraries within the University of London' (MA Librarianship thesis, Univ of London, 1976), p125-6.

Institute of Education Library, 11 Ridgmount Street, London WC1E 7AH. Tel (01) 637 0846. Open Mon-Fri 9.30 am-6 pm (Summer vac), 7 pm (rest of year, extended to 8 pm Mon-Thurs in term); Sat (not Summer vac) 9.30 am-12.30 pm to registered students of the Institute; others wishing to use rare books should apply to the librarian. Photocopying; microform readers.

In 1902 the London Day Training College was founded by the London County Council, with the assistance of the University of London. In 1932 it became an institute of the University and was renamed the Institute of Education. In 1982 it became a school of the University.

Library Guide (revised annually).

N W Beswick, 'The Institute of Education Library' (brief typescript history 1981).

General The library, formed in 1909, has been built up mainly since 1925, and especially after 1956, and now contains *c*250,000 v of books and periodicals, consisting mainly of 20th cent working collections, and it is the largest British education library after the Department of Education and Science, covering all aspects of education.

Card cat (author; topographical; and alphabetical subject).

Comparative Education Library A special collection on comparative education was formed *c*1932, and was greatly enhanced by the gift by the then Director Sir Fred Clarke (1880–1952) of his own collection (his ms papers are also held, with the exception of a portion still retained by his family). The Africa Department of the College in 1927 had formed another library of its own; it became the Colonial Dept and later the Department of Education in Tropical Africa; this collection has recently been incorporated into the Comparative Education Library. The whole library contains several thousand v, mostly after 1850 but includes a few early 19th cent items.

Catalogue of the collection of education in tropical areas, 1964 (3v), *Catalogue of the Comparative Education Library*, 1971 (6 v), and *First Supplement*, 1974 (3 v), all published Boston, G K Hall, reproducing card entries in three sequences; authors; topographical; and alphabetical subject.

T Bristow, 'The University of London research library for comparative education', *Comparative Education Review* 9 (1965), p213-8.

Hans Collection Dr Nicholas Hans (1888–1969) Russian-born Reader in Education at the Institute, bequeathed his books and papers, which are kept as a special collection associated with the Comparative Education Library, having earlier endowed a fund for the purchase of expensive books for the library. The papers include published and printed proofs of his own works, as well as mss and correspondence. His library contained 1,145 printed items, mainly 20th cent, but with a few earlier from *c*1770 onwards; strongest on education in continental Europe, India and Australia, with much background material on these areas.

In memoriam Nicholas Hans: the man, his books, his papers, the Library, 1975 (*Education Libraries Bulletin* supplement 19), includes author cat of library and list of papers.

Hayward Collection *c*200 v from the library of Dr Fran Herbert Hayward (*b*1872), LCC inspector of schools and prominent writer on education, who was also a historian of ethics and humanism. All books are after 1890, and relate chiefly to religion, freethought, education, psychology, and philosophy (including unconventional philosophies). A noteworthy feature of the collection is the extensive nature of pencilled annotations and insertions of reviews (some by himself), letters, and other material.

Historical Collection A collection of all pre-1919 monographs and pre-1860 periodicals segregated from the general library (but not from the special collections above), *c*1,500 v, predominantly after 1800, but include *c*20 English and foreign books of the 16th-17th cent, and *c*200 of the 18th cent. They include both school books (including grammars, Comenius etc) and books of educational theory; strong in the education of women. Several early 19th cent periodicals, eg *Children's Magazine* 1824–44, *Guida dell'Educatore* 1836–45 (incomplete).

Chronological card cat; also in general card cat.

Pre-1901 items except periodicals mostly in C W J Higson, *Sources for the history of education*, London, Library Association, 1967, and Supplement 1976.

The periodicals are *not* included in *Union list of periodicals* of the Librarians of Institutes and Schools of Education, 4th ed 1977.

Institute of Geological Sciences Library, Geological Museum, Exhibition Road, South Kensington, London SW7 2DE. Tel (01) 589 3444 Ext 257. Telex 8812180. Open (except three weeks in Jan) Mon-Fri 10 am-4 pm to the public (prior notice required for rare books). Photocopying and photography. Microfilm/fiche readers.

The Institute was established in 1965 as a research establishment of the Natural Environment Research Council, and its library is the national reference library of geology, incorporating the library (founded 1843) of the Geological Survey and Museum, and that (founded 1947) of the Overseas Geological Surveys. Almost all the rare books are derived from the former collection. *c*250,000 v overall.

Jack Burkett, *Government... library... services*. 3rd ed 1974, p160-1.

Sir John Smith Flett, *The first hundred years of the Geological Survey*, London, HMSO, 1937.

T W Newton, 'The Jermyn Street library of geology', *The Library* 7(79) (1895), p229-30.

Small Library, and Pamphlet Collections The Geological Survey of Great Britain was founded in 1839 to carry out geological surveys of the British Isles. Its founder and first Director, Sir Henry Thomas de la Beche (1796–1855) FRS, donated his private collection of scientific books (bearing his bookplate) to form the nucleus of its official Library at Craig's Court, Whitehall. In 1851 the Museum of Practical Geology and the Royal School of Mines were established at a new headquarters in Jermyn Street, and the library grew rapidly, receiving major collections from the libraries of George Bellas Greenough (1778–1855), Thomas Weaver (1773–1855), William Henry Fitton (1780–1861) and William Thomas Brande (1788–1866). The library of Sir Roderick (Impey) Murchison (1792–1871) donated after his death by his nephew Kenneth R Murchison. After 1871 the Royal School of Mines became divorced from the Geological Survey and was incorporated in the Royal College of Science at South Kensington (now Imperial College), and after the last of its departments had moved, about a third of the books were transferred to the Library of the Science Museum in several stages (1883–1905), mainly to meet the needs of the College; these were chiefly on mining and metallurgy, with some on non-geological subjects. In 1935 the Museum and Library moved to South Kensington, and in the late 1950s, 150 v were returned to the library from the Science Museum. Pre-1900 books are segregated in the 'Small Library' of *c*4,660 v. There are also 440 v of bound pamphlets, including 161 v from the Murchison Library (in classified order); 12 v from that of Andrew Crombie Ramsay (1814–91); and 3 internally assembled series, known as 'Museum Pamphlets' collected in the mid-19th cent; 'Survey Pamphlets' bearing directly on the work of the Geological Survey, and the 'A-Z pamphlets'; 50 v, bound by subject. There are probably *c*1,800 pre-1851 items altogether: these include 4 STC, 46 Wing, 213 ESTC, 4 foreign 1524–1600 and 32 items of 17th cent. They include a wide scatter of subjects related to geology, especially volcanoes, mineral water springs, natural theology, surveying, magnetism and electricity, agriculture, general natural history and travel.

The library has general card cats, author and classified, for books catalogued before 1961, and those catalogued (or recatalogued) 1961–80. MARC cat 1981– . These include almost all pre-1851 items. Chronological card file to 1830 available on request. Ms cat 1850 (by title) and *c*1875 (author). *A catalogue of the Library of the Museum of Practical Geology and Geological Survey*, compiled by H White and T W Newton, 1878. (Interleaved copy with ms additions to 1903, and deletions showing dates of transfer to Science Museum. Includes the Museum and Murchison pamphlets.)

Archive Collection 19th cent ms correspondence, field notes, drawings, etc of the Geological Survey with a collection of printed and ms material on the coal fields of Northern England.

Institute of Germanic Studies Library, 29 Russell Square, London WC1B 5DP. Tel (01) 580 2711 or 3480. Open Mon-Fri 9.30 am-6 pm, on application to the Deputy Director. Xerox copier; microfiche reader.

The Institute was founded within the University of London to promote German language and literature as the Institute of Germanic Languages and Literature, renamed in 1962. The main Reference Library contains bibliographical and lexicographical material, and critical editions of authors. *c*29,000 books; 1,500 periodical titles, and 6,000 pamphlets and ephemeral items. Important mss collection.

Card cat (author/title classified).

Sixteenth and seventeenth century books in the library of the Institute, 1967. (op)

An outline Guide to resources for the study of German language and literature, The Institute, 1978, p30-1.

Priebsch-Closs Collection Over 2,000 v from the libraries of Professor Robert Priebsch (1866–1935) and Professor August Closs (1898– ?). First and early editions of 18th and early 19th cent German authors. Over 100 literary annuals.

Included in general cat of the library.

Translations German and German-English dictionaries, 16th cent onwards.

Alternative periodicals and little magazines A comprehensive collection of German literary periodicals from 1945 includes most of these.

German language literary and political periodicals, 1960–1974, supplementing *Periodical holdings*, 1970.

Stefan George (1868–1933) A special comprehensive collection of works by and on George and his circle.

Institute of Historical Research Library, Senate House, London WC1E 7HU. Tel (01) 636 0272. Open Mon-Fri 9 am-9 pm; Sat 9 am-5 pm, by arrangement with the Secretary-Librarian, to graduates researching historical subjects. Photocopier; microform readers; typing room; calculators; slide projectors.

The Institute of Historical Research, a postgraduate institute of the University of London, was founded in 1921. Its library contains *c*130,000 v of bibliographies and reference books, historical journals, primary texts, and other source material for the history of the nations of Western Europe and their expansion into North America, the Commonwealth, and elsewhere. It does not collect ordinary monographs. The collections have been built up systematically by donation, purchase, and transfer from other libraries, and are organized on an area basis, supplemented by general subject collections. There are over 4,000 pre-1851 items.

General author cat on cards; periodical titles are included in this, and also in BUCOP and the University of London microfiche union list.

The Institute is a major publisher of bibliographies on British history, but these are not limited to the holdings of the Institute Library. They include *Writings on British history, 1934– , 1937–* , current; and E L C Mullins, *A guide to the historical and archaeological publications of Societies in England and Wales, 1901–1933*, 1968.

General Subject Collections The Ecclesiastical History Collection is strong in the papacy and Church Councils. Military and Naval History includes material from the library of Col Lionel James (1871–1955), Military Correspondent of *The Times*.

British and Irish History The English national collection is strong in pre-1800 law reports, state trials, and yearbooks. The local collections include some 18th and 19th cent directories, and a large collection of Poll Books.

J M Sims, *A handbook of printed English parliamentary poll books*, London, the Institute, 1983; also recording locations elsewhere for items not held.

European History The collections incorporate many important sets transferred from the House of Lords Library; and are particularly strong for the Low Countries, France and Germany.

United States and Canada The collection includes parts of the libraries of Manton Marble (1834–1917) on the US in the 18th and 19th cent; and of Henry Percival Biggar (*b*1872) on Canada.

Imperial and Colonial History The collections, on colonization in general and by particular European nations, especially the British, include books from the colonial library of George Louis Beer (1872–1920).

Latin America The Latin American library includes a special collection of 1,209 printed documents of the government of Mexico, comprising decrees, proclamations, circulars, and miscellaneous broadsides, covering virtually every major event from 1744 to 1843, bound in 6 v, with a ms index, from the library (now divided between many institutions) of the civil engineer George Robert Graham Conway (1873–1951).

Michael P Costeloe, *Mexico state papers 1744–1843: a descriptive catalogue of the G R G Conway collection in the Institute of Historical Research, University of London*, London, Athlone, 1976.

Institute of Laryngology and Otology Library, 330 Gray's Inn Road, London WC1X 8EE. Tel (01) 837 8855 Ext 122. Open Mon-Fri 9.30 am-5.30 pm; Sat (except before a Bank Holiday) 9.30 am-12.30 pm to staff and students; to other bona fide enquirers at discretion of library assistant.

The Institute was founded with a library in 1946 as a postgraduate school of the University of London, in association with the Royal National Throat, Nose and Ear Hospital (founded 1939 by the amalgamation of two hospitals in Gray's Inn Road and Golden Square). The library contains *c*2,000 v of monographs and *c*3,000 v of periodicals, mostly on otology, rhinology and laryngology, from the foundation of the speciality *c*1880, and related sciences.

Card cat (author/name/classified).

R M Nicholas, 'The development of medical libraries within the University of London', p130-1.

Historical Collection *c*250 v (including some general medicine), 7 are pre-1851, and *c*100 of 1851–1900.

Institute of Latin American Studies Library, 31 Tavistock Square, London WC1H 9HA. Tel (01) 387 4055/6. Open Mon-Fri 9.30 am-5.30 pm to members of the University of London; others should write to the librarian for an appointment.

The library of the Institute, established by the University of London in 1965, contains *c*5,000 v only, and is mainly limited to bibliographies and general reference books on Latin America and the Caribbean, not including rare books.

British Union Catalogue of Latin Americana This catalogue, maintained in the library, contains *c*300,000 cards which record *c*273,000 British locations (in addition to the holdings of the Library of Congress); *c*2,500 of these are for pre-1851 books, almost all after 1800.

British Union Catalogue of Latin Americana: new Latin American titles (issued at frequent intervals 1968–77, then discontinued; includes the pre-1851 notifications). Publication of the complete cat is under consideration.

Institute of Marine Engineers Library, Memorial Building, 76 Mark Lane, London EC3R 7JN. Tel (01) 481 8493. Open Mon-Fri 9 am-5 pm after prior application to the librarian. Photocopying.

The Institute was founded in 1889, and its library of *c*6,000 v which dates from the same year, has been built up by purchase and donation. Most of the older technical works have been dispersed, but there is a Historical Collection shelved separately, of *c*250 v, mainly late 19th and early 20th cent which includes a few rare items from *c*1850, and some privately printed histories of shipbuilding and shipping firms. Periodicals begin in 1847. There are also some mid-19th cent mss.

Card cat (author and classified); some older material not yet catalogued. Accessions lists in *Transactions* 1890–*c*1960.

B C Curling, *History of the Institute of Marine Engineers* 1961. (op)

Institute of Neurology, Rockefeller Medical Library, National Hospital, Queen Square, London WC1N 3BG. Tel (01) 278 9052. Open Mon-Fri 9 am-6 pm on application to the librarian.

The National Hospital, Queen Square, was opened in 1860 for the treatment of nervous diseases, with a library from 1927. A medical school was established at the hospital in 1938, and the library transferred to it; it is now a postgraduate medical school of the University of London. The library now contains over 15,000 v.

Card cat (including the Historical Collection).

R M Nicholas, 'The development of medical libraries within the University of London', p132-6.

Sir Gordon M Holmes, *The National Hospital, Queen Square, 1860–1948*, Edinburgh, Livingstone, 1954, p90.

B B Rawlings, *A hospital in the making*, London, Pitman, 1913.

Historical Collection *c*900 v on neurology, mostly from the National Hospital, many being authors' presentation copies. 60 v are pre-1851 (some autographed), mostly early 19th cent neurology, including neuroanatomy.

Shelflist.

Institute of Ophthalmology Library, Judd Street and Tavistock Place, London WC1H 9QS. Tel (01) 387 9621. Open Mon-Thurs 9.00 am-5.30 pm; Fri 9.00 am-3.00 pm after written permission from librarian in response to a proved need. Restricted photocopying.

The Institute was founded in 1947 as a postgraduate school of the University of London. It is associated with the Moorfields Eye Hospital, which is an amalgamation of the former Royal London Ophthalmic Hospital at Moorfields, the Central London Ophthalmic Hospital, and the Royal Westminster Ophthalmic Hospital. The Institute Library incorporates the collections from their three medical schools, of which that at Moorfields was by far the largest. The library contains a very comprehensive collection of books and periodicals on ophthalmology and related sciences, *c*15,000 v.

Author/title card cat.

R M Nicholas, 'The development of medical libraries within the University of London' (MA Librarianship thesis, Univ of London, 1976), p137-43.

Royal London Ophthalmic Hospital, Moorfields The hospital was opened in 1805 by John Cunningham Saunders (1773–1810) as the London Dispensary for Curing Diseases of the Eye and Ear, becoming the London Ophthalmic Infirmary in 1822, and the Royal London Ophthalmic Hospital in 1836. Its medical school was established in 1811, to which a library was attached *c*1830, when a collection was built up by John Richard Farre (1775–1862) the hospital's surgeon. Much of the library is now in the Historical Collection (see below).

Edward Treacher Collins, *The history and traditions of the Moorfield Eye Hospital, London*, 1929, p72; v 2 by F W Law, London, H K Lewis, 1975.

R C Davenport, '150th anniversary of the Moorfields School of Ophthalmology', *British Medical Journal*, 1961 (1), p1033.

Collections added to the Institute Library The library was opened in 1947 with a donation of 510 v from Sir John Herbert Parsons (1868–1957) FRS, followed in 1948 by 180 v from Sir (William) Stewart Duke-Elder (1898–1978), and a portion of the Bowman Library of the Ophthalmological Society was added at the same time (the greater part being at the Royal Society of Medicine, qv).

Historical Collection of pre-1921 books on ophthalmology and visual science. 739 v from 1583 onwards. Also drawings and papers of Edward Nettleship (1848–1913).

In general card cat. Separate author/title cat to letter 'O'.

Pre-1801 English books listed in M H T Yuille *et al*, *Literature on ophthalmology*, London, the Institute, 1972, (op), but photocopy available from the librarian.

Institute of Orthopaedics Library, Royal National Orthopaedic Hospital, 234 Great Portland Street, London W1N 6AD. Tel (01) 387 5070. Open Mon-Fri 9.30 am-5.30 pm to staff and postgraduate students of the Institute and Hospital; to others by prior arrangement with the librarian. Photocopying facilities.

The Infirmary for the Cure of Club Foot and Other Contractures was founded in 1838 by William John Little (1810–94), and in 1864 chartered as the Royal Orthopaedic Hospital. The National Orthopaedic Hospital was founded in 1860 by Thomas Carr Jackson (1823–78). The two were amalgamated in 1905 into the Royal National Orthopaedic Hospital, which in 1908 absorbed the City Orthopaedic Hospital (founded 1851). The attached Institute is a postgraduate school of the University of London, founded with its library in 1946. There are now *c*8,000 v, including *c*4,000 monographs on orthopaedics and related sciences.

Card cat (authors). Library guide.

R J Whitley, 'The hospital founded in 1838 by W J Little', *Medical and Biological Illustration* 25 (1975), p240-4.

R M Nicholas, 'The development of medical libraries within the University of London' (MA Librarianship thesis, Univ of London 1976), p144-9.

Historical Collection Orthopaedic books, especially on orthopaedic surgery, acquired by purchase and donation, especially by H Jackson Burrows (former Dean). *c*200 v of 1665–1850; *c*240 of 1851–1900. Also photographic and radiographic records of Dr C J Hackett (*b*1905) for use in osteo-archaeology.

Institute of Psychiatry Library, De Crespigny Park, Denmark Hill, London SE5 8AF. Tel (01) 703 5411. Open to members Mon-Thurs 9 am-9 pm; Fri 7 pm; Sat 12.45 pm; to other bona fide research workers by prior arrangement only at the librarian's discretion.

The Institute was founded in 1948 as a postgraduate school of the University of London, attached to the Maudsley Hospital (opened in 1923 by the London County Council) and the Bethlem Royal Hospital (Bedlam, founded by monks 1247), transferred in 1547 to the City, moved to Beckenham in 1930). The library incorporates that of the Maudsley Hospital Medical School which was attached to the University from 1924, and now contains *c*30,000 v on psychiatry, psychoanalysis, psychology, neuroscience, sociology, and related sciences.

R M Nicholas, 'The development of medical libraries within the University of London', (MA Librarianship thesis, Univ of London 1976), p147-9.

E G O'Donoghue, *The story of Bethlehem Hospital*, (1914).

Anthony Masters, *Bedlam*, London, Joseph, 1977.

P H Allderidge, 'Historical notes on the Bethlem Royal Hospital and the Maudsley Hospital', *Bull of the New York Academy of Medicine* 47 (1971), p1537-46.

The archives of Bethlem Royal Hospital are at Monks Orchard Road, Beckenham BR3 3BX. Tel (01) 777 6611, open by appointment only.

Historical Collection *c*100 works on psychiatry, mainly in English, of the 19th and early 20th cent.

Mayer-Gross Collection Works on psychiatry bought from the personal library of Dr Willi Mayer-Gross (1889–1961), mainly in German, *c*1900–50.

Guttmann-Maclay Collection Books, mainly in English, with some French and German, on art, especially of the mentally ill, from the libraries of Dr Eric Guttmann (1896–1948) and Dr Walter Symington Maclay (1901–64). (The Guttmann-Maclay collection of psychopathological works often secured from patients, donated to the Institute, is mostly housed in the Maudsley Hospital.)

Institute of Psycho-Analysis Library, 63 New Cavendish Street, London W1M 7RD. Tel (01) 580 4952. Open Mon-Fri 10 am-5.30 pm to members of the British Psychoanalytic Society only; to others only by prior arrangement with the Honorary Librarian.

The library was founded in 1926. In addition to a general collection of *c*15,000 v on psychoanalysis, there is a collection of virtually all the editions of the works of Sigmund Freud (1856–1939).

Institute of United States Studies Library, 31 Tavistock Square, London WC1H 9EZ. Tel (01) 387 5534. Open Mon-Fri 9.30 am-5.30 pm to members of the University of London; others should write for an appointment. Photocopier, microform reader available.

The Institute was established by the University of London in 1965 for postgraduate study. The library is limited to bibliographies and basic reference works in all aspects of American studies, fewer than 2,000 v, and does not contain rare books. The library maintains the Union Catalogue of American Studies Material, which records the American holdings of 21 libraries in the UK, over 123,000 titles, of which a substantial proportion are pre-1851.

Institute of Urology Library, 172 Shaftesbury Avenue, London WC2H 8JE. Tel (01) 836 5361. Open Mon-Fri 9.30 am-5.30 pm to staff and postgraduate students; to other research workers by prior arrangement with letter of introduction.

The Institute was founded in 1947 as a postgraduate school of the University of London. It is attached to St Peter's Hospital (founded in 1860 as the Hospital for Stone) and St Paul's Hospital (founded 1947). The library, which contains *c*2,500 v on urology and nephrology, has been built up mainly by donation.

Card cat.

R M Nicholas, 'The development of medical libraries within the University of London', (MA Librarianship thesis, Univ of London 1976), p150-1.

C Morson, 'The history of a postgraduate medical institute', *Inst of Urology Report 1967–8*, p9-16.

——ed, *St Peter's Hospital for Stone 1860–1960*, London, Livingstone, 1960, p1-10.

Historical Collection A small collection of classic books on urology, from 1811 onwards.

Winsbury-White Collection A collection of reprints of articles formed by Horace Powell Winsbury-White (1889–1962), founder of the *British Journal of Urology*.

Institution of Civil Engineers Library, Great George Street, London SW1P 3AA. Tel (01) 222 7722. Open Mon-Fri 9.15 am-5.30 pm to members only; rare material to research workers by arrangement, following written application.

The Institution, founded in 1818, is the world's oldest professional engineering institution. Its library dates from 1820 with the first of the gifts of Thomas Telford (1757–1854), first President, which formed the nucleus. At first the collections were built up mainly by donations, notably those of Colonel Frederick Page (1769–1834), William Chapman (1749–1832) the canal engineer, and Thomas Young (1773–1829) MD FRS.

General The library contains *c*85,000 items in most branches of engineering. Over 5,000 are pre-1851, mostly post-1700, with a few earlier, including incunabula; many are English and foreign classic texts on science and engineering; also extensive collections of pamphlets, including several not held elsewhere. Many books and periodicals formerly held have been dispersed, but the tracts and parliamentary papers are virtually intact. There are two special collections worthy of note: (all other collections are merged in the general collections).

Vulliamy, Benjamin Lewis (1780–1854), Master of Clockmakers' Co, his collection on horology, 270 v, donated 1853, including 3 items dated 1476, 1558 and 1593 and 19 17th cent (see *Appendix to the Catalogue: Catalogue of the Horological Library bequeathed by B L Vulliamy* (1854?), *Minutes of Proceedings of the Institution of Civil Engineers* 14 (1859), p155-9.

Vitruvius 40 editions of his *De architectura*, including 1 of 1496, 16 of 16th cent and 23 1701–*c*1860.

Catalogue of the Library of the Institution of Civil Engineers, 1895 (superseding 1851 and 1866 eds) with 3 supplements for acquisitions of 1895–1904, 1905–10, 1911–15; continued on cards; author cat only.

George Ottley, *Railway history: a guide to... collections...*, London, Library Assoc Reference, Special and Information Section, 1973, p42-4.

A W Skempton, *Early printed reports and maps (1665–1850) in the Library of the Institution of Civil Engineers*, London, the Institution, 1977 (limited to professional surveys of British engineers).

Institution of Electrical Engineers, Savoy Place, London WC2R 0BL. Tel (01) 240 1871. Telex 261176. Open Mon-Fri 10 am-5 pm by prior appointment with the Archivist (or the librarian in the case of the Periodicals Collection). Xeroxing and microfilming and readers.

The Institution was founded in 1871 as the Society of Telegraph Engineers, and changed to its present name in 1888. In 1921 it acquired a royal charter making it a qualifying and regulating body for the profession. The library was established in 1880, and was soon enormously enlarged by the acquisition of the Ronalds and Thompson libraries. The librarian is now responsible only for the care of current books, and the periodicals collection. All rare books and special collections of printed books are in the care of the Archivist. The Archives also contain the major collections of personal papers (almost exclusively ms) of Michael Faraday, Jacob Brett, Cooke and Wheatstone, and a variety of collections belonging to the National Archive for Electrical Science and Technology. There is a general rare book collection (*c*200 items) with its own card cat in addition to the special collections. There are 7 incunabula.

R Appleyard, *The history of the Institution of Electrical Engineers 1871–1931*. London, the Institution, 1939, p253-6. Leaflet guide 'The Archives of the Institution of Electrical Engineers' (*c*1980).

L Symons, 'Rare books and manuscripts', *IEE News* no 59 (Nov 1980), Library centenary supplement, p17-24.

Ronalds Library Sir Francis Ronald (1788–1873) FRS, whose experimental telegraph was demonstrated in 1816 and who developed a system based on synchronously rotating discs, was Hon Superintendent of the Meteorological Observatory at Kew, where he made important developments in instrumentation. He travelled extensively abroad, especially in Italy, and built up a collection on the history of electricity and magnetism which is rich in foreign works. The library of *c*2,000 books and 4,000 pamphlets was bequeathed to his brother-in-law Samuel Carter with a request that it should be kept intact for the use of scientists. It was deposited at the Institution in 1876, and donated in 1976. The collection is strongest for the 18th and 19th cent and includes numerous association copies. There are 6 STC items.

Catalogue of books and papers relating to electricity,

magnetism, the electric telegraph, etc. Including the Ronalds Library. Compiled by Sir Francis Ronalds, with a biographical memoir. Ed. A J Frost. London, Society of Telegraph Engineers, 1880.

Silvanus Thompson Memorial Library Silvanus Phillips Thompson (1851–1916) FRS, DSc, LLD, Physicist and Principal of Finsbury Technical College, and a noted scientific biographer, amassed an electrical library of 12,900 items, including many of the choicest and rarest of the early works. After his death the collection was bought for the library by subscription. It included 13 (chiefly medieval) mss; 34 Faraday mss; 900 pre-1825 rare books (of which Thompson himself had issued a cat in 1914); 2,500 other 19th cent scientific books (now known as the Study Collection); 1,200 v of periodicals; and 8,000 pamphlets. The rare book collection includes 7 incunabula, 18 STC, 60 Wing items. Mainly on the development of the theory of electricity and magnetism, and early navigation, gemmology. It includes Peter Peregrinus *De Magnete* 1558 and 2 14th cent mss of it, one of which was the printer's copy. Numerous association copies and fine bindings. Thompson designed his own bookplate for the collection.

Handlist of the magnetic and electrical books in the library of Silvanus Phillips Thompson. London, priv pr at the Chiswick Press, 1914. Card cat of Study Collection.

J S and H G Thompson, *Silvanus Phillips Thompson: his life and letters*. London, 1920, p227-52. *Proceedings of the Royal Society* 94A, (1917–8), pxvi-xviii.

Oliver Heaviside (1850–1925), the developer of duplex telegraphy who predicted the existence of the ionosphere, left a collection of ms working papers and notes, together with *c*150 19th and 20th cent pamphlets.

Card cat of pamphlets.

Periodicals Collection There are *c*1,000 sets in the library, of which 111 are wholly or partly pre-1801, including those from the Thompson collection. They include virtually all the British 19th cent journals on physics, electricity, magnetism, and telegraphy, including rare items such as *Annals of electricity* 1836–43, and *Transactions and Proceedings of the London Electrical Society* 1837–43, with many of the American, German, French, and Italian. Also a number of more general scientific periodicals of 18th and 19th cent.

Typescript list of pre-1901 titles.

Institution of Gas Engineers Library, 17 Grosvenor Crescent, London SW1X 7ES. Tel (01) 245 9811. Open Mon-Fri 9.30 am-5 pm to members; to other bona fide enquirers by arrangement following written application.

The Institution and its library were founded in 1863 to serve the gas industry. The library contains over 10,000 v of books and journals, in addition to mss and archives.

Historical Collection Contains early works on the gas industry, especially gas manufacture and lighting.

Institution of Mechanical Engineers Library, 1 Birdcage Walk, St James's Park, London SW1H 9JJ. Tel (01) 222 7899 Ext 265. Telex 917944. Open to members of any institution affiliated to Council of Engineering Institutions, Mon-Fri 9.30 am-5.30 pm. Others should apply in writing in advance.

The Institution was founded in 1847 by a group of railway engineers, one of whom, the eminent George Stephenson (1781–1848) had been denied admission to the Institution of Civil Engineers. The library has been built up gradually from that date by donation and purchase. All engineering topics are included, but the older books are predominantly on railway engineering, *c*120,000 v altogether, of which perhaps 2,000 are pre-1900. Most of the early books are from the Napier Memorial Collection (now dispersed among the general stock) named after Robert Napier (1791–1876), President of the Institution who left a legacy for book purchase. (There have been some disposals of older books.) Also important ms collections. Incorporates the collection of the Institution of Railway Signal Engineers.

Card cat superseding *Library catalogue* (1876), (1881), (1887), and (1896).

A list of periodicals. . . in the Library. . ., 1969 and later editions.

Chartered Mechanical Engineer, 1954– includes accessions lists.

Library and information services handbook.

Institution of Mining and Metallurgy Library, 44 Portland Place, London W1N 4BR. Tel (01) 580 3802. Telex 261410. Open Mon, Tues, Thurs, Fri 9.45 am-5 pm, Wed 9.45 am-7 pm to members, and to visitors at the librarian's discretion on payment of £5 per day (not charged to students or retired persons). Photocopying service.

The Institution was founded in 1892, and its library has been built up since 1894 by bequests of members and by donations; a few gaps have also been filled by purchases. The Historical Collection contains mss and about 230 printed books, mostly pre-1900. It includes 92 pre-1851 books, 39 English and 37 foreign. The English books include 4 STC, 13 Wing, 22 ESTC items, and 37 of 1801–50; the foreign books include 3 of the period 1501–1600, 1 of 1601–1700, 5 of 1701–1800, and 7 of 1801–50. They are mostly standard works on metallurgy (as distinct from alchemy), and mining, and a few on peripheral subjects such as the geology and topography of Cornwall and Derbyshire, with some dictionaries. There is a chronological list with author index. There are also a few pre-1851 books in the general collection, of which there is a card catalogue.

Islington Public Libraries

The Borough Libraries were formerly those of the Metropolitan Boroughs of Islington (established 1907) and Finsbury (1887), the nucleus being *c*1,000 books from the collection given by Robert Major Holborn of Highbury; the local history collections remain divided by the former boundary (with some overlap).

A Central Reference Library

2 Fieldway Crescent, Holloway Road, London N5 1PF. Tel (01) 609 3051. Open Mon-Fri 9 am-8 pm; Sat 5 pm.

The Collection, including local history, contains *c*52,000 items, of which *c*200 are pre-1851 printed books and pamphlets. The general collection has been built up by purchase and (particularly for older books) by donation. The earlier books cover a wide range of subjects in the humanities, especially art, travel, history, and religion from 1582 onwards and include *c*20 17th and early 18th cent tracts defending the Church of England; 5 STC items; 2 Kelmscott Press books given by the widow of William Morris.

Card cat (author and classified).

Eric A Willats, *History of the Islington Public Libraries*, London, priv press (*c*1961).

Islington Collection (including the districts of Islington, Barnsbury, Highbury and Holloway). Books, pamphlets, and documents, including many items given by members of the former Islington Antiquarian and Historical Society S T C Weeks, A G Licrece and Frank V Hallam (*d*1953); local directories from 1852, and the major histories of London generally from 1633. Extra-illustrated copies of the 4 main 19th cent histories of Islington. Archives of the Borough.

Subject cat on slips available on application. *The story of Islington* (*c*1969) (annotated bibliog).

Sickert, Walter Richard (1860–1942), RA. In 1947 the Sickert Trust and Mrs Oswald Sickert gave 43 etchings, 4 oils and 18 drawings by Sickert and his wife Therese Lessore (*d*1945) from those which remained in their studio, together with their collection of circus programmes and works by other members of the Sickert family. The Sickertiana collection has been greatly enlarged and includes all biographical and critical works on the painter.

Walter Richard Sickert 1860–1942: a handbook to the. . . material in the possession of Islington Public Libraries, 1964.

Walter Richard Sickert 1860–1942: catalogue of the Islington Libraries Sickert Collection (*c*1970?) (limited to pictorial material).

B Finsbury Library

245 St John Street, London EC1V 4NB. Tel (01) 609 3051 Ext 66. Open by appointment Mon, Tues, Thurs 9 am-8 pm; Wed, Fri 1 pm; Sat 5 pm.

Local history and theatre material relating to the southern part of the Borough, comprising the former Metropolitan Borough of Finsbury, including the parishes of Clerkenwell, St Luke's, St Sepulchre, Charterhouse, and the Liberty of Glasshouse Yard. Housed in the same building as branch reference and lending libraries.

Ms histories of Finsbury public libraries by E V Lewis (1965) and Valerie Dawson (1969).

Finsbury Collection (general). *c*4,623 books and pamphlets (in addition to 4,623 prints, documents and cuttings, and pictures by Geoffrey Stearns Fletcher, together with his published books). Some ESTC and early 19th cent and later locally printed books. Books on the theatre, from *c*1800, complementing the documentary collections below. Directories from 1814.

Sheaf cat (dictionary).

Sadler's Wells Collection Enlarged from a collection bought from Mr W L Borrell of Pentonville Road in 1922, relating to the theatre at Sadler's Wells, founded in the 17th cent by a tavern keeper, Richard Sadler, as a music room, and the home of circus, drama, music, opera, ballet, and every kind of entertainment; from 1804–16 it was called the Aquatic Theatre, and 1838–72 the Theatre Royal, Sadler's Wells. There are *c*100 playbills of 1793–1820; *c*1,000 of 1821–50; *c*700 1851–70; and a few later. Ephemera and portraits relating to Joseph Grimaldi (1779–1837) and other performers and managers. Books and pamphlets about the theatre from 1712. Plays produced there (mostly ms prompt copies), songbooks etc. Cuttings of press notices and advertisements from 1737. Views, miscellanea.

Dennis Arundell, *The story of Sadler's Wells 1683–1977*, Newton Abbot, David and Charles, 1978.

Other local theatres Playbills, ephemera and cuttings relating to Bagnigge Wells from 1780, White Conduit House 1825–40, and the (new or Royal) Grecian Theatre at the Eagle Tavern, City Road 1832–80 (including *c*250 playbills), and a few on other music halls and places of entertainment.

Italian Institute of Culture Library, 39 Belgrave Square, London SW1X 8NX. Tel (01) 235 1461. Open Mon-Fri 9.30 am-5 pm, by arrangement with the librarian. Photocopier available.

The Institute, officially called Instituto Italiano di Cultura del Regno Unito, is maintained by the government of Italy to provide facilities for the study of Italian literature, history, art, religion and culture. Its library contains *c*20,000 v, built up since 1950; these include *c*500 pre-1851 from the 16th cent onwards, mostly Italian classics, prose and poetry, history and art.

Card cat (author and classified).

Dante Collection 502 v relating to Dante Alighieri (1265–1321). They include 26 pre-1851 editions of Dante, and 15 pre-1851 biographical and critical works on him.

The Iveagh Bequest Kenwood, Hampstead Lane, London NW3 7JR. Tel (01) 348 1286. Though the house and Adam Library are open to public view daily 10 am-5 pm (7 pm in Summer), books can only be examined by appointment after written application well in advance to the Curator.

The Iveagh Bequest, generally known as Kenwood, is a museum of art administered in trust for the nation by the Greater London Council under the Iveagh Bequest (Kenwood) Act (19 and 20 Geo 5 Ch lxix). It was originally Kenwood House, built in the 17th cent, and rebuilt by Robert Adam (1728–92) for William Murray, 1st Earl of Mansfield (1705–92), Lord Chief Justice; the 6th Earl dispersed the entire contents in 1922. In 1925, after a public campaign to prevent its demolition, it was acquired by the Kenwood Trust financed by Edward Cecil Guinness 1st Earl of Iveagh (1847–1927) the brewer, who installed his own collections of pictures, furniture and books, all of which were bequeathed on condition that the house should be renamed The Iveagh Bequest and opened to the public by the London County Council (and other administrative trustees, who continued only until 1951).

Sir John Summerson, *The Iveagh Bequest Kenwood: a short account of its history and architecture*, London, GLC, 1967; rev ed 1977.

Survey of London, 1936, v 17, p114-32.

Arthur T Bolton, *The architecture of Robert and James Adam*, London, 1922, v 1, p303-20.

Frederick Mullaly, *The silver salver: the story of the Guinness family*, London, Granada, 1981 (1982).

Adam Library
This collection is so called because it was housed by the first Earl of Iveagh in the room designed by Robert Adam to accommodate Lord Mansfield's books (which had all been dispersed before 1923). Iveagh filled the whole room (including bookcases added in the 19th cent) with his own library and fresh purchases. When the room was recently restored to Adam's original design, the additional bookcases were removed and many of the books transferred to other parts of the house, but Iveagh's whole collection is still known as the 'Adam Library'. It contains *c*4,200 v, including *c*5 STC; *c*8 Wing; *c*140 ESTC. About a quarter were Iveagh's personal collection, three-quarters the Irish collection; the two are now intermingled, but are described separately below.

Card cat (authors).

Original shelflist.

Iveagh Collection Lord Iveagh's personal collection is almost entirely of the 19th and early 20th cent. It is a very general collection consisting mainly of politics, literature, English history (especially standard sets such as the Victoria County History), and guides to the turf. There are a few rarer books, notably Speed's 1632 atlas, Sir Thomas More *Works* 1557, *The accomplished cook* 1685, E Worsley *Reason and religion* Antwerp 1671, the first edition of Dickens *Master Humphrey's clock* 1840–1, and some illustrated books, including *The third tour of Doctor Syntax*.

Irish Collection A collection which Lord Iveagh acquired, perhaps specifically to fill the shelves at Kenwood, mostly from a substantial portion of the library formed by Matthew D'Orey (*d* *c*1915?) of Dublin, with his bookplate. The part remaining in the Adam Room Library consists chiefly of 18th and 19th cent standard works on Irish history. The whole collection, however, covers all aspects of Irish culture, including topography, literature, religion (especially Protestantism), balladry and art. Interesting items include a volume of mid-19th cent cheap Dublin magazines, and a volume of newspapers of the Irish rebels of 1848.

Catalogue of the late Mr Matthew D'Orey's rare and valuable books (*c*1916?) (author cat of *c*4,000 books); Kenwood has photocopy of copy in National Library of Ireland.

British Empire Club Library
A collection formed at the British Empire Club, 12 St James's Square, between 1927 and 1941, *c*380 items entirely of the 20th cent, including many presentation copies from authors and from others, especially from the British Empire League; most relate to overseas countries, chiefly those of the British Empire. The library was acquired by Rupert Edward Cecil Lee Guinness, 2nd Earl of Iveagh (1874–1967), a member of the LCC, who gave it to Kenwood. A few of the books have been given to other libraries.

Art Reference Library
A collection, mostly of the 20th cent, built up since 1970 to meet the needs of the curatorial staff of The Iveagh Bequest, who also have responsibility for the other GLC houses (Rangers' House at Blackheath and Marble Hill House at Twickenham). There are over 500 v of monographs, strongest on the Flemish, Dutch and English schools of painting which are those represented in the collection at Kenwood.

Japan Society Library, Japan Information Centre, 9 Grosvenor Square, London W1X 9LB. Open by arrangement with R A Scoals, Central Reference Library, London Borough of Ealing, Tel (01) 579 2424 Ext 3418, to any serious student. Photography by users is permitted, but no facilities provided.

The Society and its library were founded in 1892 by a group of individuals with interests in Japanese studies, especially history and art. The library contains *c*5,000 works, of which *c*20 are pre-1851, on Japanese history and culture, including *Atlas japanensis* 1670 and rare newspaper *Japan Weekly Mail* *c*1875–1914. Some mss.

Partial cat on cards.

Jesuit Residence, 114 Mount Street, Mayfair, London W1Y 6AH. Tel (01) 493 7811.

A **Community Library**

Open by previous appointment only 9.30 am-1 pm, 2-7.30 pm at the librarian's discretion. Photocopying; microfilm reader accessible.

In addition to the former library of the Jesuit Residence established in 1849 in Mount Street, the Community Library now includes some works from the defunct parish library of St Joseph's and the main bulk of the Jesuit Writers' Library formerly in Farm Street, which included a collection bequeathed by Alexander Fullerton and the collection of Joseph Stevenson (1806—95) SJ, historian and archivist, but which was seriously damaged by bombing in 1940. *c*20,000 items altogether, including *c*6,100 rare items; 5 incunabula; *c*105 16th cent items; 2,435 17th cent; 1,595 18th cent; and 1,670 of 1801—50. There are 220 STC and 384 Wing items. Strong in Jesuit history and Jesuit writers. Also general Catholic theology, hagiography, patrology, bibliology and Church history.

Incomplete author cat on cards.

B **Gillow Library of the Catholic Record Society**

Open to members of the Society, and in exceptional circumstances to others, by prior arrangement with the Society's Hon Secretary, 114 Mount Street (temporarily inaccessible, probably to end of 1982).

The Catholic Record Society was founded in 1904 for publishing sources in English Catholic history, especially of biographical information on recusants. The Gillow Library was the working library of Joseph Gillow (1850—1921) one of its founders, and biblio-biographer of English Catholics. His widow donated it to the Society, and it has been modestly enlarged by other donors. Over 2,000 v, of which *c*500 are pre-1801 (mostly post-1700); many with bibliographical annotations; also mss.

Author cat on cards.

C **Archives of the English Province of the Society of Jesus**

Open by previous appointment only, at the Archivist's discretion. Photocopying; microfilm reader.

The Archives are mostly post-1700, but photocopies of the earlier mss at Stonyhurst are held. A substantial collection of printed material, including over 100 recusant books, is included.

F O Edwards, 'The Archives of the English Province of the Society of Jesus at Farm Street', *Journ Soc Archivists* 3(3) 1966, p107-15.

Books not in Allison and Rogers or Clancy.

The Jewish Museum, Woburn House, Upper Woburn Place, London WC1H 0EP. Tel (01) 388 4525. Access to books and mss by appointment only, normally on a Monday. No separate reading room; photocopying facilities.

The Museum was founded in 1932 by Wilfred Sampson Samuel (1866—1958), the Anglo-Jewish historian, with a view to combining it with a Jewish Central Library which did not materialize. The Museum was originally deposited in the Library of Jews' College, then at Woburn House, and subsequently was housed in its own accommodation there. It is a museum of Jewish ritual art. In addition to 17 Torah and 62 Megillah scrolls, 25 illuminated marriage contracts (1524—1896), and 25 15th-18th cent religious mss, there are 15 printed books and ephemera dating from 1515 to 1835 (2 in silver bindings—with another 2 such bindings on mss), 147 bookplates, 70 trade cards, 104 prints (mainly portraits), and 73 paintings and drawings. These are fully described (with provenances) in Richard D Barnett (ed) *Catalogue of the permanent and loan collections of the Jewish Museum*, London, Harvey Miller, 1974 (with introduction by Cecil Roth). There is also a collection of archives on miscellaneous matters of Jewish interest, but these are not included in the catalogue.

Cecil Roth, 'The Jewish Museum', *Connoisseur* v 92, p151-9, 229-32, Sept/Oct 1933.

Jews' College Library. Admission on application to the librarian at Finchley Synagogue, Kinloss Gardens, London N3. Tel (01) 346 8551.

Jews' College is a mainly postgraduate institution, recognized by the University of London, for the education and training of Jewish ministers, educators, and laymen, founded in 1855, its library established from earlier collections brought from elsewhere in 1860, and increased by benefaction, deposits and purchases to a present size of *c*65,000 v of books and 20,000 pamphlets. There are extensive collections on the Bible and biblical criticism, Talmudic and Rabbinic literature, Hebrew and other philology, Jewish literature, music, folklore, and general culture, and Anglo-Jewish history. The Rare Book Collections comprise *c*15,000 v of books (including 8 incunabula) down to the 19th cent and 5,000 pamphlets, and are associated with important collections of mss. Except for a few, mainly large, collections, most donated libraries have not been kept separate.

Card cat (authors; subjects; Hebrew titles); available on microfilm.

Ruth P Lehmann, *Jews' College Library, a history* 2nd ed 1967.

Bulletin of the Association of British Theological and Philosophical Libraries no 8 (1959), p7-10.

A M Hyamson, Jews' College, London 1855—1955, 1955. *Annual Report.*

H M Rabinowicz, *The Jewish literary treasures of England and America*, New York, Yoseloff, 1962, p52-5.

Jewish encyclopaedia under the names of the colleges and the major donors.

A M Hyamson, *Plan of a dictionary of Anglo-Jewish*

biography, 1949. (Gives bibliographical references for most of the donors named here.)

Jews' College Jubilee volume, 1906.

Sussex Hall Library, acquired 1860 In 1845 Hananel de Castro (1796–1849) and others founded a mechanics' institute at Sussex Hall, former site of the New Synagogue, called the Jews' and General Literary and Scientific Institution, with a library soon to be enriched by the collection of Grace Aguilar (1816–47), poet and novelist. When the institution closed in 1859, Jews' College was still without a library, and Lewis Meyer Rothschild (1810–84, also known as Benjamin Mayer Lewis) the philanthropist bought the library from Sussex Hall, then *c*1,000 v, and gave it to the college to form the nucleus of its library at Finsbury Square. It was a general collection and contained few Hebraica.

Catalogue (held at Mocatta Library, University College).

A Barnett, *Transactions of the Jewish Historical Society* 19 (1959), p65-79.

Collections added to the Library at Finsbury Square, 1860–1881 In 1861 the foundation of a library of Hebrew Philology was laid by the gift of *c*250 v from the library of Michael Josephs (1763–1849) the lexicographer by his son Walter Josephs (1804–93) the educationalist. Further collections were given in 1864 by Barnett Meyers (1814–89), the philanthropist; in 1870 by Eleazar Moses Merton; and in 1871 by Louis Werner. The Hebrew and semitic library of Oscar Menahem Deutsch (1829–73) of the British Museum was bought by Rothschild after his death and donated. The first college treasurer, Jacob Henry Moses (1805–75) bequeathed his library; the second, Charles Samuel (1821–1903), in 1877 donated the biblical and rabbinical library of Alexander Henry Keyser of Amsterdam. In 1877 the Rev (later Sir) Philip Magnus (Bart) (1842–1933) gave a collection of historical works. Abraham Benisch (1811–78), editor of the *Jewish Chronicle* and founder of the Society for Biblical Archaeology and of the Anglo-Jewish Association, bequeathed his library.

Green Library, deposited 1883 The library of Aaron Levy Green (1821–83), a leading minister, and first Hon Secretary of the college deposited by his widow, Mrs Phoebe Green, and later donated, with an endowment for its maintenance, as a separate library. *c*6,000 v including rare works of 15th and 16th cent, mainly theology and Hebraica, strong in talmudic and rabbinical literature, responsae and novellae, English and German sermons, and Anglo-Jewish historical and polemical pamphlets.

Collections added to the Library at Tavistock Square, 1881–99 Collections came from the libraries of J Jacobs of Hull in 1884; Henry A Franklin, a teacher of English in Germany; and Frederic David Mocatta (1828–1905) FSA, both in 1890; and Lionel Louis Cohen (1832–87), financier and MP, in 1895. In 1899 Mr S Hoffnung gave a collection from his father's library.

Montefiore Library, deposited by the Montefiore Trustees, 1897 and 1958 Sir Moses (Haim) Montefiore, Bart (1784–1885), FRS, the philanthropist, opened a theological seminary in 1869 near his home at Ramsgate and named it Judith Montefiore College. He gave part of his personal collection to found the college library, and bequeathed all his Hebrew books and mss to it. The collection was built up by the first two Principals, both renowned scholars, Louis Loewe (1809–88) who had been first Principal of Jews' College, and Moses Gaster (1856–1939) later Chief Rabbi of the Spanish and Portuguese Congregation. Sir Moses bequeathed his fortune to a Trust, governed by that Congregation, which continued the college until a reorganization in 1896–7. The library was then divided: 4,000 of the printed books (including the Zunz and Schiller-Szinessy collections below) and most of the mss (including the Halberstamm collection) were transferred to Jews' College; the remainder, 800 books and some mss stayed at Ramsgate to serve a modified college there until its final closure in 1958, when they rejoined the main collection at Jews' College.

Card cat of books; printed cat of mss 1904 (repr 1969).

D A Jessurun Cardozo, *Think and thank: the Montefiore Synagogue and College*, OUP, 1933.

Jewish encyclopedia (under Judith Montefiore College; Montefiore; Ramsgate; Loewe; Gaster).

Zunz, Leopold (1794–1886), originator of the Wissenschaft des Judentums, had amassed a collection which was purchased for the Montefiore Library in 1891, of 20,000 books, together with 1,070 German pamphlets *c*1700–1880 bound in 38 v, mainly on Jewish emancipation in Germany.

M Gaster, *Catalogue of pamphlets belonging to the library of Zunz*, now in *Judith Montefiore College*, (1892).

Schiller-Szinessy, Solomon Mayer (1820–90), Rabbi, and Reader in Rabbinics at Cambridge; part of his library bought *c*1891.

Löwy Library, donated 1900 Albert Löwy (1816–1908), LLD, a noted preacher and scholarly minister at the West London Reform Synagogue, collected *c*9,000 v. These were bought by Claude Goldsmid Montefiore (1858–1938), given to the college and integrated into the general collections. Mainly Judaica, oriental and western philology, translations of the Bible, Syriac and other liturgies, philosophy, folklore, German, Italian, and Arabic literature, sets of periodicals, and pamphlets on Jewish communities in England.

Collections added to the Library at Queen Square, 1900–32 *c*100 rare books were bought from the library of Gerald Friedländer (1871–1923), minister and writer. Collections were given from the libraries of Alfred Louis Cohen (1836–1903), John Stranders, Albert Henry Jessel (1864–1917), Sir Israel Brodie (1864–1979), later Chief Rabbi, and in 1926 Dr Israel Abrahams (1858–1925), President of the Jewish Historical Society.

Collections added to the Library at Woburn House, 1932–45 Benefactions included part of the library of Solomon Levy, Minister of the New Synagogue from 1895 to 1938; and *c*150 rare books from the library of Joseph Polack, Lecturer in Hebrew at Bristol, bought and donated by Herbert Marcus Adler (1876–1940), educationalist, who also gave from his own biblical and rabbinical library on several occasions. Arthur Ellis Franklin (1857–1938) gave hundreds of books from 1933 to 1937. *c*250 books from the library of Bernard Spiers (1829–1901), doyen and writer, were donated by his son Herman in 1933. In 1938 German-Jewish books and periodicals were bought from the library of Rabbi Dr Adolf Salvendi (1837–1914). *c*250 books, mainly talmudic commentaries, from the collection of Dr George S Wigoder (1864–1934) were donated by his widow in 1938.

Büchler Library, received 1948 Purchased anonymously for the library, the complete library of Principal Adolf Büchler (1867–1939), historian and theologian, consisting of reference books, periodicals, and a collection of pamphlets known as the 'Büchler Miscellanies' relating to the growth of the Wissenschaft des Judentums in 19th cent Germany.

Committee on Restoration of Continental Jewish Museums, Libraries and Archives *c*9,000 v deposited in trust by the committee 1947–52. These are Hebraica and Judaica plundered by the Nazis from Jewish homes on the continent 1932–45; those without identifiable owners were deposited at various institutions, including Jews' College. They include many rarities, and are rich in talmudical and rabbinical works, responsa, and Hebrew commentaries on the Bible.

Collections added to the Library at Woburn House, 1946–57 The collection on hazanut (liturgical music) of Hermann Mayerowitsch (1882–1945) precentor of the Great Synagogue, was given by his widow in 1947. In 1947 Prof Selig Brodetsky (1884–1954) gave his collection of Hebraica. In 1953 Louis Rabinowitz of New York gave 100 American Judaica, and the family of Chief Rabbi Joseph Herman Hertz (1872–1946), who had been a benefactor in his lifetime, gave a memorial collection of Israeli literature and modern Judaica.

Aria College Library, deposited 1957 Aria College was founded at Portsea by the will of merchant Lewis Aria (*d*1874). It closed in 1957, and its library of Judaica and general literature was transferred to Jews' College.

Collections added to the Library at Montagu Place, 1957–80 In 1958 the library of rabbinical literature formed by Aron Blumenthal was deposited by his son Samuel; a ms cat of it was given in 1970. In 1959 German Judaica were obtained from the libraries of the deceased M Bauer, Dr J Ehrlich, and the Rev J D Irger. In 1960 Sir Simon Marks gave a substantial collection of 17th and 18th cent pamphlets.

Dr Johnson's House, 17 Gough Square, (Fleet Street), London EC4A 3DE. Tel (01) 353 3745. House open to the public 11 am-5 pm (5.30 pm in Summer); library open by prior arrangement with the Curator (access is impracticable during public opening of house, and is therefore granted only in exceptional cases).

The house is the only one surviving of many residences of Samuel Johnson (1709–84), the one where he compiled the greater part of the *Dictionary*; bought by Cecil Harmsworth in 1911 and given in trust to the nation. Primarily a collection of literary and other relics on permanent exhibition. There is a small library, including material donated to the Trustees *c*1930 by the Johnson Club, mostly received as a gift from the Honorary Member Robert Borthwich Adam, the younger (1863–1940) of Buffalo, NY. Exhibits include books from the library of Johnson's friend Elizabeth Carter (1717–1806), the translator and verse writer, including her translation of Epictetus and Euripides with her bookplate; Johnson's copy of Homer bequeathed by him to his physician William Cumberland Cruikshank (1745–1800), given by Augustine Birrell; and other copies of books associated with Johnson and his friends.

Card cat.

Johnson's House, Gough Square (1967) (with list of exhibits).

Dr Johnson's House, 17 Gough Square, 1914.

A St John Adcock, *Famous houses and literary shrines of London*, London 1929, p68-88.

Joint Library of the Hellenic and Roman Societies, Institute of Classical Studies, Institute of Archaeology Building, 31 Gordon Square, London WC1H 0PY. Open Mon-Fri 9.30 am-6 pm, Sat (not August) 10 am-5 pm to members of either society of the Institute of Classical Studies, or of the Institute of Archaeology. Others wishing to see the Wood donation or other material not available elsewhere must write in advance to the Librarian.

General Library The Society for the Promotion of Hellenic Studies was founded in 1879, and the Society for the Promotion of Roman Studies in 1910, known respectively as the Hellenic Society and the Roman Society. From the latter date they have maintained the Joint Library which incorporates a small collection which the Hellenic Society had built up by donation and exchange from 1880. In 1925 Walter Leaf (1852–1927), Chairman of the Westminster Bank and Homeric scholar gave 211 v of books and *c*200 pamphlets (v 251-66 in the library collection), about half of which were editions of, or works on Homer. Other major donations include the Overbeck collection of pamphlets. In 1953 the University of London established the Institute of Classical Studies with a library of current textbooks and reference books owned separately from, but administered as a single unit with the societies' Joint Library. In 1957 the combined libraries moved into the present building of the University of London. Their collections together amount to over 50,000 v, of which *c*3,000 v (all belonging to the societies) are pre-1851 (almost all being after 1800), on Greek and Roman literature, history, philosophy, religion and culture in the widest sense, including to a limited degree Greece of the Byzantine and modern periods (but almost exclusively its literary aspects).

Guardbook cat (author and classified). Author cat in *Journal of Hellenic Studies* 8 (1888); accessions lists in subsequent volumes to 59 (1939), thereafter published separately (selective from 1954).

A catalogue of books in the Library of the Society for the Promotion of Hellenic Studies, 1903. *A classified catalogue of the books, pamphlets and maps in the Library of the Societies for the Promotion of Hellenic and Roman Studies*, 1924.

J E Southan, *A survey of classical periodicals*, 1962 (Bull Supplement No 13).

George A Macmillan, *A history of the Hellenic Society 1879–1929*, 1929, pxiv-xvi.

Wood donation A collection formed by Robert Wood (1717?–71) explorer, Homeric scholar and politician, relating to his expedition from Rome to Syria and other countries of the Middle East 1749–51 to identify and record ancient sites, donated in 1926 to the Hellenic Society by A H Wood and other descendants. 27 (originally 28) items, including fine copies of first editions of all Wood's published works, viz *The ruins of Palmyra* (1753) and ...*of Baalbec* (1757) and *An essay on the original genius and writings of Homer* (1775). Also the official ms record of the tour, and the ms diaries on which it was based kept by Wood himself and his companions the archaeologist John Bouverie (*d*1750 on the tour) and James Dawkins (1722–57), together with sketches made by the Italian draughtsman Torquilino Borra. Interleaved copy of Clarke's Amsterdam 1743 Homer used in the preparation of the *Essay*, together with other related ms material.

Journal of Hellenic Studies 46 (1926), pxxii, xliv, xlix-l, liv, lix, lxvii-lxix, lxxi, lxxix; 47 (1927), p102-28, plates xv-xix.

Keats House (Keats Memorial Library), Wentworth Place, Keats Grove, Hampstead, London NW3 2RR. Tel (01) 435 2062. Open Mon-Sat 10 am-6 pm by appointment after completion of appropriate form naming two referees. Photocopying facilities.

Keats Memorial Library was founded in 1897 by Hampstead Public Library, and removed to Keats House on gift of the house to Hampstead Borough Council (1925). It contains *c*6,000 books and *c*600 ms items all devoted to Keats and his circle (including John Keats, P Bysshe Shelley, Lord Byron, Charles Lamb, Leigh Hunt, William Wordsworth, Samuel T Coleridge, J H Reynolds), contemporary periodicals containing reviews of Romantic poetry. The Potter Collection contains 20 v newscuttings *c*1800–1924.

Card index to books. Collection on view to public listed in *Guide* 6th ed 1966.

Kensington and Chelsea Public Libraries. Open to all Mon-Sat 10 am-5 pm (Wed and Sat), 8 pm (other days). Photocopying; microfilm readers and reader/printer available.

Formed from the libraries of the two former separate boroughs of Kensington and Chelsea, both of which had been founded in 1888. The Kensington library incorporated a private 'Free Public Library' founded by James Heywood MP at Notting Hill Gate in 1874. Some books formerly at Chelsea have been moved to Kensington or dispersed elsewhere.

Incomplete chronological card index of pre-1801 books.

B R Curle, 'Libraries for all...in Kensington and Chelsea 1874–1974', 1974. (Typescript in Kensington Local Studies Collection).

A **Central Library**

Phillimore Walk, Kensington, London W8 7RX. Tel (01) 937 2642.

1 *Reference Library General Collection* *c*70,000 v, of which perhaps *c*10,000 are pre-1851 (including collections A2-4 below); at least 5,000 1801–50 but many earlier English and some foreign from early 16th cent. (Sir Richard Burton's library is now at Museum of Mankind).

Card cat (author and classified). Closed dictionary cat in office includes some older books not yet in current card cats (chiefly collection A3).

2 *London and English topography* Collections built up by first Kensington Librarian Herbert Jones. *c*3,300 v on London (*c*300 pre-1851), *c*5,000 provinces (*c*200 pre-1851).

In card cat. Also classified handlists (closed in 1950) for London and for England, each with author index.

3 *Genealogy, heraldry, biography* Older collection has been greatly enlarged under MSC scheme; at least 100 pre-1801.

Partly in author and classified card cat; remainder in old dictionary cat.

Genealogy: the special collection, [1978].

4 *Whiteford Collection* Sidney T Whiteford (*d c*1900), teacher of painting, *c*2,000 books on the humanities, of which *c*200 are pre-1851, chiefly general literature; most 18th and 19th cent English. Donated by Richard Whiteford, *c*1920.

In card cat. Also handlist.

5 *English book illustration* *c*700 illustrated books, including a notable collection of *c*170 with wood engravings of the 1860s and many earlier, mostly purchased.

In classified cat mostly at 741.64 and under illustrators. Chronological handlist 1851–70 compiled in 1922, with indexes of artists, engravers, publishers and authors.

6 *Kensington Local Studies Library*, comprising material on the area of the former Metropolitan Borough, including over 100 pre-1851.

Card cat (author and classified).

7 *Early English children's books* A collection of *c*5,000 v formerly built up at Chelsea Children's Library *c*1930–70, now transferred temporarily to the Central Junior Library pending re-evaluation (accessible only by appointment with the Children's Librarian). Mostly post-1870, but some earlier. 37 v of works by Maria Edgeworth (1767–1849), early collections of riddles, and a few other pre-1851. (The foreign part of the collection has been transferred to Tower Hamlets, Bethnal Green Branch Library.)

Author-title cat on cards.

B **Chelsea Library**

Reference Library, Old Town Hall, King's Road, Chelsea, London SW3 5EZ. Tel (01) 352 6056 or 2004.

1 *Reference library general collection* The first Librarian of Chelsea, John Henry Quinn (1860–1941), built up a good general collection beginning from the early 16th cent, leaning particularly towards art and travel. There are now, after transfers to Central Library (especially biography) and to other libraries, *c*40,000 v, including *c*1,000 pre-1851 (including collections B2-4).

Rough card index by authors of all pre-1801 books. Most pre-1851 material is in dictionary sheaf cat (closed), remainder in current card cat (author and classified). Donations listed in annual *Report* to 1939. Printed cat 1891 and partial 1895, and *Quarterly list of additions* 1912–28 include books no longer held.

2 *Costume collection* begun 1950 under MSC scheme includes early books.

3 *Botany collection* begun 1950 under MSC scheme includes early books.

4 *Chelsea Local Studies collection* includes *c*100 pre-1851.

Separate dictionary card cat.

5 *Bookplates* *c*3,500 from 16th to 20th cent, arranged by periods and styles. Includes collections bequeathed by local residents Mrs Jacqeline Cockburn and Mr S H J Johnson.

Lists of Cockburn and Johnson collections. Card index of artists and owners.

B N Lee, *Early printed book labels*, 1976.

King's College Hospital Medical School Library, Denmark Hill, London SE5 8RX. Tel (01) 274 6222 Ext 2028. Open Mon-Thurs 9 am-7 pm, Fri 6 pm to members of the University of London; to other qualified persons with letter of introduction.

In 1839 King's College became affiliated to the University of London, and in the same year it built a hospital for its Faculty of Medicine, with a departmental library there. In 1910 the Medical School separated from the College, taking the postgraduate section of the medical library. In 1913 the Hospital and School moved to their present site.

Jean B Wood, 'The development of the medical library of King's College London' (MA Librarianship thesis, Univ of London, 1969).

R M Nicholas, 'The development of medical libraries within the University of London' (MA Librarianship thesis, Univ of London, 1976), p55-60.

David Jenkins and A T Stanway, *The story of King's College Hospital*, Huntingdon, Hambledon Press, 1968, especially p30.

D S Ramsay, 'The Medical School Library', *King's College Hospital Gazette*, 45 (1966), p99-103.

F J C Hearnshaw, *Centenary history of King's College, London, 1828–1927*, London, 1929.

General Collection The library has over 24,000 v devoted to medicine, surgery, the medical sciences, dentistry, medical history and biography, nursing, midwifery, and physiotherapy. Until 1947 it was built up mainly by donation. The nucleus was the Todd bequest (see Historical Collection below). Later 19th cent donors are not systematically recorded; those of the 20th cent include (Sir) John Phillips (1855–1928), Herbert Willoughby Lyle (1870–1956), Edward Worrell Carrington (*c*1889–1915) MC, surgeon, Sir Hugh (Reeve) Beevor (1858–1939) 5th bt, Urban Pritchard (1845–1925) Professor of Aural Surgery, Sir Ernest Playfair (1871– ?), Frederic James Burghard (1864–1947) CB, and Vice-Dean Harold Waterlow Wiltshire (1879–1937) DSO OBE.

Card cat of whole library.

Ms author cat 1865.

Accessions register 1914–45.

Ms reports by Librarian 1939–52.

Reports by College Librarian 1904–10 and Minutes of Library Committee from 1904 are held at King's College Library.

Historical Collection contains *c*1,100 pre-1851 books including 1 incunabulum (d'Argellata *Cirurgia* 1497), and incorporates part of the collection of Robert Bentley Todd (1809–60) FRS, first Dean of the Medical School. (The remainder forms the Todd Collection at King's College Library, qv.)

Incomplete list. Included in main cat.

'King's men' Collection First segregated in 1946, it is now being actively enlarged. It includes a general section of the history of the Medical School and the Hospital, with the archives of Societies; and an alphabetically arranged collection of the published writings of individuals, with books about them. The collection of Joseph Lister, Lord Lister (1827–1912), *c*40 v, includes

some books from his own collection (most were bequeathed to the Medical Society of London), and some of his apparatus.

Included in main cat.

H Willoughby Lyle, *King's and some King's men* with *An Addendum. . .*, Oxford UP, 1935, 1950.

King's College Library, Strand, London WC2R 2LS. Tel (01) 836 5454. Open Mon-Fri (term) 9.30 am-8.45 pm; Christmas and Easter vac 5.45 pm; Summer vac 4.30 pm; Sat (not Summer vac) 12.45 pm, to members of the University, and others on written application to the librarian. Rare books cannot be fetched in the evening: several days' notice required for rare books at Egham Depository.

King's College was founded 1828–31 by George D'Oyly (1774–1846) DD, Rector of Lambeth, as an Anglican counterpart to University College, for the study of religion and morals, classics, mathematics, science, philosophy, English literature, history, modern languages, medicine and law. In 1836 the University of London was set up to conduct examinations for students of University College and King's College, and in 1908 King's College became a school of the reconstituted University.

F J C Hearnshaw, *Centenary history of King's College, 1828–1927*, London 1929.

G Huelin, *King's College London 1828–1978*, 1978.

A **General**

The Library, opened in 1831, is organized in a series of scattered subject collections, under a common administration. Rare books are mostly centralized. Subject coverage of the pre-1851 books is a fairly exact reflection of the list of original faculties above. Of *c*435,000 works in the whole library, *c*12,000 are pre-1851. Specialized collections are listed below under the subject libraries with which they are associated unless they are too general.

Card cat (author/name and classified) continued from 1981 on microfiche, includes all subject libraries and most special collections, containing entries for books, pamphlets, and periodicals.

There is also a separate cat for each subject collection.

Superseded cat in ms *c*1841, and 1880 (continued to 1910), and published *Catalogue of the Library of King's College, London* (*c*1870); 2nd ed 1874 (classified). Printed accessions lists for 1876–95 and 1914–52; ms accessions registers for most periods.

General collection of rare books *c*4,500 v on various subjects, comprising all pre-1801 items not forming part of any special collection; pre-1801 items abstracted from most of the special collections; and certain post-1800 items of rarity. These include 15 incunabula; 155 STC items; 275 Adams; 460 Wing; 850 foreign 17th cent; 2,000 ESTC.

Shelf cards in above categories; included in general author and classified cats.

Bone Collection Miss Margaret Bone gave 25 v in 1932 from her family's library: early printed books 1498–*c*1820, now incorporated in the general Rare Books Collection.

Hutton Collection 14 early printed books, 1489–1632, given in 1959 by a Fellow in appreciation of the services of Robert Hutton as Librarian of the College. Kept together as a special collection.

Included in general cat.

Philip Hammersley Leathes, of Peckham, who endowed divinity prizes for medical students, gave a collection of 18th cent books and mss (also coins, which were sold in 1850).

In general collections; no list, and they have not yet been identified.

London Institution Library A collection of *c*3,000 v. Part of the library was received in 1916 in exchange for 2,500 v from Marsden Collection and 500 v from Oriental Section of General Library loaned to School of Oriental and African Studies. Subject fields include English pre-1485 history; European medieval and modern history; colonial history (except American); naval history; Shakespeare studies; and natural science, which include STC; Wing; and pre-1701 foreign items. Pre-1801 items incorporated in general Rare Books Collection; others in various sections.

Catalogue of the Library of the London Institution, 1835–52, 4 v.

Documents relating to King's College London, 2nd ed, 1933, p226.

William Marsden, (1754–1836) FRS, philologist, Secretary of the Navy, donated *c*1,300 books in 1835, mainly philology, with a wide range of languages. Also early Bibles, including the unique Genesis in Algonquin (Cambridge, Mass, 1655), and travel. (The Oriental books are deposited at the School of Oriental and African Studies; the Slavonic and East European at the School of Slavonic and East European Studies.) The collection includes 6 mss; 20 STC items; *c*100 Wing; *c*350 ESTC; *c*100 foreign 16th cent; *c*300 17th and *c*350 18th cent items.

Sheaf cat.

William Marsden, *Bibliotheca Marsdeniana philologica et orientalis: a Catalogue of books and manuscripts collected with a view to the general comparison of languages. . .*, London, 1827 (annotated copy).

Souter Collection The books and papers of Prof Alexander Souter (1873–1949) Vice-Chancellor of Aberdeen University, bought 1949, and mostly incorporated in the Classics and Theology libraries, except for pre-1801 items, which are in general Rare Books Collection. *c*1,750 v on classics and patristics, 16th-20th cent.

Included in general card cat (author and classified).
Accessions register.

College Collection c650 v about the College, or by its members, many donated by them and bearing presentation inscriptions.
Card cat (authors).

B Theology, Ecclesiastical History, and Philosophy Libraries

These libraries and their associated special collections contains c30,000 v, of which c3,000 are pre-1851, especially strong in biblical studies (the collection on the Orthodox Church has been transferred to the Burrows Library).

Theology collection author cat (main and special collections in one sequence) and classified cat (separate for each collection).

Exhibition of Bibles from the collection in the College Library to mark the 350th anniversary of the... Authorised Version... Catalogue, 1961.

Box Library of Hebrew and Old Testament Studies The library of Canon George Herbert Box (1869–1933), Prof of Hebrew of King's, bought in 1932, and supplemented by occasional accessions in the field of Judaica. It contains c4,900 v on the language, literature, and history of the Near and Middle East, in editions from the 16th cent onwards, including many in Hebrew, Syriac, and other oriental languages. (Pre-1801 items are incorporated in the general Rare Books Collection.)
In general card cat (author and classified).

Rainbow Collection The library of Dr Bernarr Rainbow, Director of Music at the College of St Michael and St John, Chelsea, given in 1973. It contains c400 hymnals of all the major and numerous minor denominations of Christians and Jews, including c100 pre-1851.
Author/title and classified cat. Also in general cat.
M Elliott, 'The Rainbow collection of hymnbooks at King's College, London', *Bull Assoc British Theological and Philosophical Libraries*, new ser no 9 (June 1977), p 5-7.

Ratcliff Collection The library of Canon Edward Craddock Ratcliff (1896–1967), Prof of Liturgical Theology 1945–7, bought in 1972. There are c1,000 v of liturgical theology, including c30 STC and many Wing and ESTC items. (Pre-1801 items incorporated in general Rare Books Collection.)
Separate classified card cat.
Author entries incorporated in general card cat.

Relton Library The library of Prof Herbert Maurice Relton (1882–1971), Prof of Dogmatic Theology, given in c1947. It contains c2,000 v of theology, including c20 pre-1701 English and foreign items. (Pre-1801 items incorporated in general Rare Books Collection.)
Separate classified card cat.
Author entries incorporated in general card cat.

Wordsworth Collection The library of John Wordsworth (1843–1911), Bishop of Salisbury 1885–1911, deposited in 1916 by his widow, and in 1960 given by his children. It contains 542 v theology and history, mostly 18th-19th cent, with a few earlier.
Handlist in author order.

Miscellaneous absorbed collections Mrs E K Saunders bequeathed a collection, received in 1930, on religious life in 17th cent France. Major-General Sir Frederick (Barton) Maurice, Prof of Military Studies, in 1926 gave 353 v, mainly of theology from the library of his grandfather (John) Frederick Denison Maurice (1805–72) Prof at King's and founder of the Working Men's College. In 1949 William Oscar Emil Oesterley (1866–1950), Prof of Hebrew, gave his father's and his own collections mainly of Judaica. The Philosophy Library, containing a few thousand (mainly modern works) incorporates the bequest of Dr David Laurence Smarya Pole (d1977), Lecturer in Philosophy.
Accessions registers.

C Laws Library

Contains c20,000 v in current use, no old editions are kept. The pre-1851 items are English law reports. All aspects of English and international law are covered as well as European community law, French, German, USA and East European law.
Author and classified cat on cards to 1981, then fiche.

Cohn Collection The library of Prof Ernst Joseph Cohn (1904–76), visiting Prof of European Law. c3,500 v of European law, nearly all German or Swiss, including rare items published during World War II, reports and periodicals.
Card cat (author and classified).

Italian Law A collection, in Italian, of about 500 v presented by the Italian Government in 1977 to form a basis for a proposed course in Italian law. The collection is not kept up to date.
In general cat.

D History and War Studies Libraries

These contain c30,000 printed items, including 1,500 pre-1851 (mainly on British history).
Author and classified cat on cards to 1981, then fiche.

Laughton Collection Selected items from the library of Sir John Knox Laughton (1830–1915), Prof of History 1885–1912, given by his friends in 1916, and incorporated in the History section of the library, except pre-1801 items which are in general Rare Books Collection. The collection is mainly on naval history, including some 18th cent sailing manuals.

Fossey John Cobb Hernshaw, (1869–1946), Prof of History, 1902–34. A collection comprising his library, now incorporated in the History Library, c1,250 v.

Gerald Sanford Graham Rhodes Professor of Imperial History, 1949–70. A collection of volumes from his library, bought in 1970, now incorporated in the History Library. *c*500 v are on Imperial, Commonwealth and naval history, especially the history of Canada.

Liddell Hart Centre for Military Archives The library and papers of Sir Basil (Henry) Liddell Hart (1895–1970), military historian and strategist, bought 1973; and other papers bearing on 20th cent military affairs given or deposited after 1964. The collection contains *c*6,000 books and 290 metres of archives, mainly on British military affairs. An appreciable amount of the printed material consists of authors' presentation copies to Liddell Hart and his copies of his own works.

Card cat (author and classified) in preparation.

Index to archives.

'The War Studies Library at King's College', *Aslib Proceedings* 29(8) (1977), p295-301.

E Classics Library

*c*14,000 items, including perhaps *c*3,000 pre-1851, especially 18th-19th cent continental editions (many of these now stored at the Depository at Egham).

Enk Library The library of Prof Petrus Johannes Enk (1885–1960) of Groningen, bought in 1961 partly with grant from the Nuffield Foundation. *c*14,000 v on classics, including many foreign 16th-19th cent items.

Inventory of Professor P J Enk's classical library, 1960, with Supplement 1969 and *Subject index to . . . pamphlets*, 1972.

Card cat (author and classified) being compiled.

King's College calendar for 1963–64, pxx.

Walters Collection Bequeathed by William Charles Flamstead Walters (*d*1927), Prof of Classics 1901–23. Classics, with a noteworthy collection of books, pamphlets, and mss on Livy. Integrated into Classics Library, except pre-1801 which are in general Rare Books Collection.

No separate cat.

Warr Collection Books on classics from the library of George Charles Winter Warr (1845–1901), Prof of Classics, bequeathed in 1908 by Mrs Constance Warr.

Bookplate.

F Burrows Library of Byzantine and Modern Greek

c9,000 items on all aspects of the Greek language, history, religion, and civilization formed mainly from the collections listed below; the whole library is now called the Burrows Library, though the Burrows bequest as well as all other bequests, total no more than half the entire collection, in which all the following are merged together.

Card cat (author and classified).

Burrows bequest *c*2,500 v from the library of Ronald Montagu Burrows (1867–1920), DLitt, Principal of King's. A general library of Greek and Byzantine studies, including works on Levantine travel, with some Wing and ESTC items. Includes a substantial section on the Orthodox Church. Many items are in the Depository at Egham.

Miller donation 800 v given in 1932 by William Miller (1864–1945), Athens correspondent of the *Morning Post*; on Frankish, Turkish and modern periods of Greek history.

Stroud-Read Collection 679 v given in 1942 (separated from the main collection at the University of London Library) by Mrs F Stroud-Read, from the library of her late husband Mr F Stroud-Read, on medieval and modern Greece, including substantial numbers of 16th-17th cent British and foreign items.

Stroud-Read's own cat still exists, available in the office.

Miscellaneous donations Substantial additions were made in 1935 by the Anglo-Hellenic League, Demetrios Caclamanas, and Marco Pallis; and in 1947 by A Vlasto from his late father's library.

G Modern Language Libraries

Separate libraries for French (*c*17,000 items on open access), German (*c*12,000 on open access), Italian (*c*1,000 on open access), Spanish (*c*10,000 on open access), Spanish-American (*c*5,000 on open access), and Portuguese (*c*7,000 on open access). *c*2,000 in these collections are pre-1851.

Saurat donation *c*600 v on French, German, and English literature, incorporated in the respective language libraries; from the library of Denis Saurat (1890–1958), Prof of French.

List on file.

Kantorowicz Collection Library of Dr Ludwig Kantorowicz, given in 1946 by Mrs Regina Kantorowicz and her two sons. *c*6,000 items in German on literature, history, science, and Judaica; including a few pre-1851 items. Some 2,000 items absorbed into subject collections (identifiable by bookplate) and *c*4,000 in the Depository at Egham.

Sheaf cat (authors and subjects) by Kantorowicz.

Frida Mond (*d*1923), bequeathed her library, *c*300 v of books, also mss of German literature, mainly Goethe and Schiller. Now incorporated in the German library.

H G Atkins, *The Frida Mond Collection at King's College: a descriptive catalogue* (*c*1925). All but 65 items also in German and Main cats.

Frederick Norman (1897–1968) OBE, Prof of German; 350 books from his library donated by his widow; *c*250 books are at the Depository at Egham.

List on file.

Richardson Collection The library of Linetta Palamidessi de Castelvecchio, afterwards Mrs Richardson (*c*1886–1975), Serena Prof of Italian at Birmingham, acquired from her late husband Canon Robert Douglas Richardson (1893–) in 1975. *c*1,400 v on Dante and Italian Renaissance literature, including *c*20 pre-1851 items.

In general author cat.

Villasante Library A collection from the library of Julian Martinez Villasante, given by Miss Villasante in 1946, and incorporated in the Spanish Library.

In general cat.

Accessions register.

Anglo-Spanish Society When the Society was dissolved in 1947, its library was donated and incorporated in the Spanish Library.

Prestage Collection The library of Edgar Prestage (1869–1951), Prof of Portuguese 1923–36, bought in 1948. *c*2,000 v of 16th-19th cent especially history and literature. Mainly incorporated in Portuguese library; pre-1801 books in general Rare Books Collection.

In general author and classified card cats.

H English Library

*c*23,000 items on English language and literature, of which *c*1,500 are of 1801–50. *c*1,000 pre-1801 items have been transferred to the general Rare Books Collection.

Skeat and Furnivall Library The libraries and papers of the lexicographers Prof Walter William Skeat (1835–1912) given in 1913, and of Dr Frederick James Furnivall (1825–1910) given in 1911. In 1971 the papers were removed to the Archives, and the pre-1801 books to the general Rare Books Collection; later books were incorporated in the English library, except annotated copies, which remain a separate collection. Predominantly Old and Middle English, Elizabethan and Shakespearian. Also includes linguists, comparative philology and the publications of early 19th cent literary and linguistic societies.

Card cat (author and classified) of annotated books.

Shelf cards for unannotated items.

Some bookplates; many signatures.

Aitken bequest 400 v from the library of William Francis Aitken received in 1937 from his sister-in-law Mrs E M Parsons, in accordance with his known wish.

No list. In main cat.

Charles Williams Society Library, deposited on loan 1977. *c*40 editions of the works of Charles Williams (1886–1945), publisher, poet and miscellaneous writer; including many first editions and proof copies. (Works about him, held by the Society, are not included in the deposit.)

Separate card cat (authors).

Lois Glenn, *Charles W S Williams: a checklist*, Kent State UP 1975 (copy annotated by Charles Williams Society).

Annual report of the Delegacy 1977–8.

Reed Collection 350 v given in 1941 by Prof Arthur William Reed (1873–1957), Prof of English 1927–39, incorporated in the English library.

Bookplate. No list.

I Science Libraries

There is a general science library with additional subject libraries in Biophysics, Earth Sciences, Engineering and Plant Sciences. Rare material is mostly being collected into the Wheatstone Library, but in certain subject areas, eg mathematics, there are still many pre-1851 books elsewhere in store. Perhaps *c*2,000 pre-1851 items (including some in general Rare Books Collection).

Wheatstone Library *c*3,000 v collected from 1976 to illustrate the history of science, in editions of 18th-20th cent, mostly transferred from other sections of the library. (It should not be confused with the Wheatstone Collection, which was formerly known as the Wheatstone Library.)

Card cat (authors), and in general cat.

Wheatstone Collection The library of Sir Charles Wheatstone (1802–75) FRS, Prof of Physics 1834–75, bequeathed to the College. It contains *c*3,000 v and 40 boxes of pamphlets, mainly on electricity, especially telegraphy and kindred subjects, but a wide range of other scientific topics is represented. Mostly 19th cent, but some ESTC.

Card cat (authors).

Original ms cat by V G Plarr.

Calendar for 1876–77, p62-3.

Adams Bequest A scientific collection mainly on physics, bequeathed by William Grylls Adams (1836–1915), Prof of Physics. Many are now in the Wheatstone Library, the remainder in subject collections.

Bookplate.

James Bequest 200 v from the mathematical library of Charles Gordon F James (*d*1926), a lecturer in mathematics, incorporated in the mathematics collection.

Ruggles Gates Collection The books and papers of Reginald Ruggles Gates (1882–1962), Prof of Botany 1921–44, given in 1968 by Mrs Laura Ruggles Gates. *c*60 books and *c*1,000 pamphlets on human genetics, including a few pre-1851.

Uncatalogued.

Stebbing Collection The library of the Rev Thomas Roscoe Rede Stebbing (1835–1926), Fellow, an authority on crustacea, bequeathed by his widow. *c*500 v on zoology, including a few pre-1851 items.

Typed list of pamphlets. Otherwise uncatalogued.

Titley Collection The bequest of Dr Ian Francis Titley (*d*1946), education lecturer, of *c*200 v on the history of science, including some pre-1851. Incorporated in Wheatstone Library, except pre-1751 which are in general Rare Books Collection.

No separate cat, but identifiable by bookplate or accession number.

Todd Collection The library of Robert Bentley Todd (1809–60) FRS, Prof of Physiology and first Dean of the Medical School, the 'Doctor of London' of Thackeray's *Roundabout papers*, was given by his widow in 1860. The majority of the medical books were transferred, with the postgraduate section of the Medical Library in 1910, to King's College Hospital Medical School Library. The remainder, incorporated in various subject libraries, are being collected together as a special collection, now *c*160 v on medicine and science.

In main or Wheatstone Library cats; identifiable by widow's presentation label or by signature.

Card cat of those in special collection.

N McIntyre, 'Robert Bentley Todd, 1809–1860', *King's College Hospital Gazette* 35 (1956), p79-91, 184-98.

F F Cartwright, 'Robert Bentley Todd's contributions to medicine', *Proc Roy Soc of Medicine*, 67 (1974), p893-7.

Kingston-upon-Thames Public Libraries, Central Library, Fairfield Road, Kingston-upon-Thames, Surrey KT1 2PS. Tel (01) 549 0226. Open to all Mon-Thurs 9 am-7 pm, Fri 8 pm, Sat 5 pm.

Central Reference Library, including Local History Collection (Kingston and Surrey). A collection has been accumulated by purchase and donation from 1882, the majority of the pre-1851 items being in the Local History Collection; *c*80 books, *c*200 pamphlets, 25 broadsides. (Also engravings, maps, lithographs etc.)

Card cat of general reference collection; separate card cat for local history. Punched card index to broadsides and illustrations.

Kingston-upon-Thames. Kingston Libraries, Information Service, Fairfield Road, Kingston-upon-Thames, Surrey KT1 2PS. Tel (01) 546 8905. Open Mon, Wed, Thurs, Sat 9 am-5 pm; Tues, Fri 7 pm.

The Information Service, formerly called the Reference Library, includes a collection on English history, especially county histories, with some pre-1851 items. (The collection on Surrey and Kingston has been transferred to the Recreation Dept Heritage Unit.) The collection of works by and about John Galsworthy (1867–1933) formerly at New Malden Reference Library has been dispersed into various lending libraries.

Card cat.

Kingston-upon-Thames, Recreation Department, Heritage Unit, Fairfield West, Kingston-upon-Thames, Surrey KT1 2PS. Tel (01) 546 5386. Open Mon-Sat 10 am-5 pm.

The Heritage Unit combines a museum, an art gallery, and the Borough Archives, with the local history collection recently transferred from Kingston Libraries.

Local History Collection, on Kingston and the former County of Surrey. Built up by purchase and donation from 1882. *c*60 books; *c*200 pamphlets and *c*25 broadsides are pre-1851; in addition to engravings; maps; lithographs etc.

Card cat.

Robert Cedric Sherriff (1896–1975). A collection of his plays and novels.

Kingston Polytechnic, Knights Park Library, Knights Park Centre, Kingston-upon-Thames, Surrey KT1 2QJ. Tel (01) 549 6151 Ext 259. Open (to non-members only if they can prove genuine need) Mon-Thurs (in term) 9 am-7.30 pm, Fri (in term) and Mon-Fri (in vacation) 9 am-5.30 pm. Photocopying and information services.

Art Library Special Collection About 500-600 mostly rare items, of which about 50 are 19th cent and 25 earlier, though the bulk of the collection is on 20th cent French decorative arts and architecture, including children's books and other material not available elsewhere.

Author and classified cats of the whole library on cards and fiche; cat of the Special Collection is being prepared for publication.

Laboratory of the Government Chemist, Cornwall House, Stamford Street, London SE1 9NQ. Tel (01) 928 7900 Ext 604. Open by prior arrangement with the librarian Mon-Fri 9 am-5 pm. Photocopying facilities.

The Laboratory was founded around 1840 and has always been closely associated with the Customs and Excise, though it now has additional functions, and is administered by the Department of Industry. It has always had a substantial working collection of reference books, now amounting to 7,000 v, and 14 items of 1800–50 on excise duties and chemical analysis remain in the library.

Labour Party Library and Archives, 144–152 Walworth Road, London SE17 1JT. Tel (01) 703 0833. Open Mon-Fri 10 am-5 pm to members of the Labour Party; to others on written application to the Librarian and payment of fee (£1 daily or £5 annually). Photocopier; microfilm/fiche reader/printer facilities.

The library was begun in 1918 as a press cuttings collection, and until 1956 was part of the library at Transport House maintained jointly with the TUC and the Transport and General Workers Union. It is now an adjunct to the Labour Party Research Department.

P Francis, 'The Labour Party Library', *Librarians for Social Change* no 21 (1979) p4-5.

The library usually has a paragraph in the Labour Party *Annual Report.*

Sources in British political history 1900–1951, 1975, v 1, p127-41.

P Bird, *The archives of the Labour Party* (due for publication 1982).

General Library Primarily concerned with providing books, magazines, and press cuttings of current political interest, with the emphasis on the Labour Movement, the library includes *c*3,000 older pamphlets etc, kept separate from the main bookstock, of the Independent Labour Party 1892–1932, the Labour Representation Committee 1900–6, the Labour Party from 1900, including many publications of constituency parties, and election addresses from 1906.

Card cat (author and classified).

Labour Party bibliography, (1967) covers the ILP, LRC and LP, based on Library holdings; chronological, including some journals, with author and subject indexes (op).

Middleton Library The personal library of J S Middleton, General Secretary of the Labour Party 1934–44, with some later books added by his widow; kept separate, in author order. *c*600 v, mainly on socialism, government, politics, etc for the period 1918–39, including presentation copies from authors (eg Maiskey *Before the storm,* 1944) and other colleagues (eg Stewart *Keir Hardie* 1921, from Ramsey MacDonald). Many of MacDonald's works, including his *Margaret Ethel MacDonald 1870–1911,* priv pr 1911, presented to Middleton's wife by Malcolm MacDonald. Some novels of Wells and Bennett, and Walt Whitman's *Poems and prose* 1890 (author's presentation copy to Edward Carpenter).

Separate card cat (authors); not in general cat.

O'Brien Collection A collection of Bronterre O'Brien (1805–64) the Chartist, given by Miss W Mathews in 1972. 170 letters, *c*1857, with copies of his *Human slavery* 1885 and *Robespierre.*

Pickles Collection The collection of Fred Pickles (*d*1933), member of the IP, given by his family. Letters from Eleanor Marx, Besant, Blatchford, Crane, Holyoake, Hardie, Kropotkin etc. Pamphlets, mainly published by the Socialist League; issues of *Labour Leader;* a curious *List of works on economics, labour and social subject in... Bradford Central Library,* Bradford Independent Labour Party, 1893.

Vincent Papers Bought at auction *c*1960, a small archive collection of Henry Vincent (1813–78) the Chartist, comprising 125 ms letters; 50 issues of Chartist newspapers, including a good but incomplete run of the *Western Vindicator* nos 2-39 (1839) by Vincent; and a few of the *Chartist Circular* (1840).

Lambeth Palace Library, Lambeth Palace Road, London SE1 7JU. Tel (01) 928 6222. Open Mon-Fri 10 am-5 pm on production of letter of introduction, at the librarian's discretion.

Lambeth Palace has been the chief residence of Archbishops of Canterbury from the 12th cent, but had no permanent library (as distinct from their individual private collections) until 1610, when Bancroft bequeathed his books to his successors to form a public library. It has been built up mainly by gifts and bequests of archbishops, and was maintained at their private expense until 1866, when it passed to the Ecclesiastical (now Church) Commissioners. From 1964 it has been assisted to buy rare books and mss by the Friends of the Lambeth Palace Library. It is now the chief library for historical and administrative purposes of the Church of England, and the principal repository of its archives. The present collections of printed books are described below generally in Section A, and by subjects in B-F; the printed material in the mss and archives in G; and the collections from which the library was formed (not now maintained as separate collections) in H.

John Le Neve, *The lives and characters... of... bishops...,* London, 1720, v 1 (pt 1): Canterbury.

A C Ducarel, *The history and antiquities of the Archiepiscopal Palace of Lambeth,* London, 1785, p47-76; reissued in John Nichols, *Bibliotheca topographica Britannica,* 1790, v 2 (no 27), repr New York, Kraus, 1968.

John Nichols, *Literary anecdotes,* London, 1812–15, 9 v repr New York, Kraus 1966; many refs in indexes, v 7, p220, 611.

William Clarke, *Repertorium bibliographicum,* London, 1819, v 1, p93-106.

Thomas Allen, *The history and antiquities of the parish of Lambeth and the Archiepiscopal Palace,* London, 1826, p186-96.

'Library of Lambeth Palace', *Gentlemen's Magazine* new ser 2 (1834), p151-4.

B Botfield, *Notes on the cathedral libraries,* London, 1849, p189-258.

Edward Edwards, *Memoirs of libraries,* London, 1859, v 1, p714-25.

John Richard Green, *Stray studies from England and Italy,* London 1876, p107-66, 'Lambeth and the archbishops'.

'Lambeth Palace Library and its associations' [by S E Kershaw], *Church Quarterly* 6(12) (1878), p439-51.

J Cave-Brown, *Lambeth Palace and its associations,* Edinburgh, 1883, p58-111.

Dorothy Gardner, *The story of Lambeth Palace,* London, Constable, 1930, p209-19.

Lambeth Palace Library: a short history, 1957, description rather than history.

A Cox-Johnson, 'Lambeth Palace Library 1610–1664', *Trans Camb Bibliographical Soc* 2 (1958), p105-26.

M R James, 'The history of Lambeth Palace Library', *ibid* 3 (1959), p1-31.

Lambeth Palace Library 1958–1963 [by E G W Bill], [1963].

E G W Bill, 'Lambeth Palace Library', *The Library* 21(3) (1966), p192-206.

Lambeth Palace Library, *Annual Report* 1953– .

Friends of Lambeth Palace Library, *Annual Report 1964–5.*

Extensive archive 'Library Records' and some stray items among the general mss.

J B Oldham, Notes on bindings (Ms 1468 fol 26-46).

A **Printed Book Collections** (General)

*c*65,000 books (in 75,000 v), *c*40,000 pamphlets, and over 1,000 periodicals (of which 130 are current). The collections are arranged by subjects, regardless of date, provenance, or physical form, except incunabula and pre-1641 English which are separate. The library is mainly concentrated on the history of the Church of England and related subjects, but almost the whole field of Christianity other than current theology is covered.

Author cat on cards; this superseded an earlier card cat and *Catalogue Bibliothecae Bodleianae*, 1843, interleaved and noted up with Lambeth holdings and now obsolete shelfmarks; this in turn superseded a ms dictionary cat used 1718–1850 (L.R.F.17419) begun by copying E Gibson's cat *c*1711 (L.R.F.12-14); for other early catalogues see *C* below.

S R Maitland, *A list of some of the early printed books in the Archiepiscopal Library at Lambeth*, 1843, lists selectively in 3 chronological sequences *c*150 pre-1500, *c*300 foreign 1500–19, and *c*200 English 1500–49, with dictionary index.

Chronological lists in ms by Maitland 1466–1549 (L.R.F.28) and 1600–33 (L.R.F.29).

Classified cat on cards is very incomplete and omits many pamphlet collections (but note the separate catalogues of these, *H* below).

Incunabula There are 193 incunabula, of which 190 are in a special collection arranged chronologically, and 3 among the mss.

Cat by C A Webb (ms); entries also incorporated in general author cat.

English 1501–1640 *c*3,500 STC books arranged roughly in chronological order in a special collection. For specific subjects, see sections *C* and *D* below, especially the Marprelate tracts at *C*.

Annotated STC. *c*2,900 recorded in Ramage, *Finding list.*

S R Maitland, *An index of such English books printed before. . . MDC as are now in the Archiepiscopal Library at Lambeth*, 1845.

Author list of *c*1,400 items.

Chronological lists by S R Maitland, 1466–1549 (L.R.F.28) and 1600–33 (L.R.F.29).

English 1641–1700 (Distributed among subject classes). Over 6,000 Wing items, including many pamphlets (see also sections *C* and *D* below).

Annotated Wing records almost all holdings.

Foreign 1501–1700 (Distributed among subject classes). *c*3,000 of the 16th and *c*6,000 of the 17th cent. (Many more were bombed, see *H*.) For specific subjects, see section *E* below.)

B **Christian Literature**

Bibles (Class E) *c*1,700 editions of the Bible and its parts, including *c*800 in English. In 1782 Thomas Percy (1729–1811), bishop of Dromore, gave 42 English psalters. The collection of early Bibles was greatly enriched by gifts from Charles Manners-Sutton (1755–1828), archbishop 1805–28. The Horniman Museum donated its collection in 1965.

Author cat (under Bible) lists most English editions of the Bible and its parts to *c*1770, Botfield, p193-216 (with a transcript of a ms cat of the Percy Collection) and the more important foreign editions.

Friends Annual Report 1974, p3-4 on English 16th cent versions.

H M Rabinowicz, *Treasures of Judaica*, New York, Yoseloff, 1971, p66-8.

Liturgies (Sub-sections under churches class H; Anglican at H5141-5147). Liturgies, particularly the Book of Common Prayer, are well represented. The collection has been greatly enlarged by donations of recent years, especially from Francis Carolus Eeles (1876–1954) DD, the liturgiologist, in 1954 (with mss 1501–31, which include printed fragments); Alan Campbell Don (1885–1966) DD, author of *The Scottish Book of Common Prayer*; and Canon Bernard John Wigan (*b*1918). A collection of Old Catholic liturgical works assembled by Claude Beaufort Moss (1888–1964) DD, author of *The Old Catholic Movement*, was given by his executor (with some mss).

Author cat (under names of churches).

Many references in *Friends Annual Report*, eg 1974, p5-6, 1977, p6-7, 1978, p3-4.

S W Kershaw, 'List of forms of prayer (for special occasions) 1558–1866', ms, 1883 (L.R.F.30), now very incomplete.

Theology and sermons The collection is particularly strong in 18th cent theology, for which it owes much to the Secker bequest (see under *H*). It contains over 1,000 bound v of separate sermons, mostly Anglican, and over 100 v of visitation charges; a fine collection of early editions of Fathers and continental theology (reduced by bomb damage). Bequests include 142 works from the library of William Selwyn (1806–75) FRS, Lady Margaret Professor at Cambridge. Lincoln's Inn gave 386 works, mostly 17th-18th cent in 1910, and more in 1953.

Contents of 18 v of sermons listed at end of 1773–90 pamphlet cat (L.R.F.24), and others in 1802 pamphlet cat (L.R.F.27).

Printed list of Selwyn bequest in 'Catalogue of modern books' (L.R.F.31) fol 73-4.

List of Lincoln's Inn 1910 donation (L.R.J.12).

C English Church History

Possibly a third of the library relates specifically to English church history, including controversies between Anglicans and other denominations and political aspects.

Church of England A large collection of ecclesiastical history and biography.

English political history (class KA; pamphlet class N). At least 5,000 items, including *c*3,000 from the pamphlet collections (see under *H* below). 16th-19th cent.

Pamphlet cat 1773–90 (L.R.F.23-24) under Politics, and specific subjects.

Marprelate controversy, 1588–95 (in 1501–1640 English collection). The most comprehensive known collection of the anti-episcopal 'Marprelate tracts', probably mostly from the Bancroft bequest. It includes first and later editions of the seven satirical tracts written under the name 'Martin Marprelate' by John Penry (1559–93) and probably Job Throckmorton (1549–1601), printed on intinerating presses, 1588–9. Also the replies commissioned by Whitgift and by Bancroft, then his Chaplain, including Bancroft's *Sermon preached at Paules Crosse.* The ms report of the examination of two of the printers, Valentine Symms and Arthur Thomlyn, 10 Dec 1589, acquired in 1972 (Ms 2686 fol 25-7). Also the pseudo-Martinist tracts and replies to them, 1590–95.

STC under Marprelate.

D J McGinn, *John Penry and the Marprelate controversy*, New Brunswick, Rutgers, 1966, p239-55 (Bibliog).

NewCBEL v 1, col 1957–64.

Friends Annual Report 1972, p3-6.

See also W Pierce, *An historical introduction to the Marprelate tracts*, London, 1908.

Leland H Carlson, *Martin Marprelate, gentleman*, San Marino, Huntingdon Library, 1981.

Bangorian controversy, 1717–19 There are *c*100 tracts in the dispute provoked by Benjamin Hoadly (1676–1761), when Bishop of Bangor, by his sermon preached before the King on 31 March 1717, denying scriptural warrant for church organization. The collection includes the replies of William Law (1686–1761), Thomas Sherlock (1678–1761), and many others.

List in Pamphlet cat (L.R.F.23) under Bangorian Controversy.

Bibliography in Hoadly *Works*, 1773, v 2, p379–401 (see also v 1, p689–701).

D English Local History and Topography (class KA670-690)

Strongly represented in the early benefactions. Works on cathedral and parochial churches and parish histories are still added. In 1979 a collection of topographical pamphlets was donated by Dr R H Little.

S W Kershaw, 'Early topography in Lambeth Palace Library', *Bibliographer* 1 (1881–2), p45-8.

Kent In 1875 a collection on the topography of Kent and those parts of the dioceses of Canterbury and Rochester, then in Surrey, was actively begun and exceeded 500 items by 1900.

S W Kershaw, 'Catalogue of the Kentish and Diocesan collection', 1890, (L.R.F.35), revised 1903 (L.R.F.36).

——*in Archaeologia Cantiana* 9 (1874), p176-88 and 29 (1911), p206-16.

E Ecclesiastical History Outside England

There are collections on virtually all Christian churches, including in addition to those noted below as being of special interest, Roman Catholics, Old Catholics, Lutherans, Quakers, etc.

Anglican churches outside England Collections on the Episcopal Church in Scotland from the 18th cent; Anglican churches in the British Empire in the 19th cent; North America in the 17th and 18th cent, including 27 v of pamphlets, together with printed material in the Fulham Papers (papers of the bishops of London formerly at Fulham Palace); the Archbishops' Papers, and other ms collections.

Pamphlet Catalogue 1773–90 (L.R.F.23) under America.

C M Andrews and F G Davenport, *Guide to the manuscript materials for the history of the United States to 1783*, 1908, p286-301, citing titles; supplemented by B R Crick and M Alman, *A guide to manuscripts relating to America*, rev ed 1979, p114-5.

Moravians *c*200 items on the Unitas Fratrum or Moravian Brethren, especially the controversy when Heinrich Rimius (*d*1759) came to England from Prussia, *c*1750 and began to publish anti-Moravian tracts. His collection of books and mss was acquired from his executor for Secker by the anti-Moravian Bishop of Exeter, George Lavington (1684–1762).

List of Rimius collection of books, *c*1760 (L.R.F.20).

Six tracts among Secker Papers (S.R.18-20) cited in list of these.

Pamphlet cat (L.R.23) under Moravians.

Swedish Church John Wordsworth (1843–1911), Bishop of Salisbury, author of *The National Church of Sweden*, gave a collection on the established episcopal church of Sweden, with books on Swedish political history.

Eastern Churches Collections on the Orthodox Church and on other Eastern churches, mostly acquired in the present century, reflecting Lambeth's role in the ecumenical movement; mostly modern, but including some earlier works. The Anglican and Eastern Churches Association has donated hundreds of books, and its founder, Canon John Albert Douglas (1868–1956), Secretary of the Church of England Council on Foreign Relations, bequeathed his personal papers and a large collection of books.

Cat of Douglas papers by V Wallace, 1972, typescript; correspondence on the bequest (L.R.K.3.4).

F Miscellaneous Subjects

Chronology and the calendar Collections on reform of the calendar and related subjects acquired from William Bowyer the younger (1699–1777) Archbishop Secker and others; mostly of the 18th cent, both English and foreign. Also 16th-17th cent almanacs.

Pamphlet cat 1775–90 (L.R.F.23) under Kalendar.

Five tracts among Secker Papers (S.R.10) cited in list of these.

Literature The early benefactions were strong in classical and modern literature, but much, except the pre-1800 English, was damaged by bombing. (The later Farquharson classics donation is deposited in the University of Kent at Canterbury.)

Social sciences There are collections on sociology (class M), including a small but valuable collection donated in 1966 by the Church of England Temperance Society, mainly 19th-20th cent (with its archives); education (class P); law (class O).

G Printed Material in Collections of Manuscripts and Archives

The collections of mss, Archbishops' Papers, and other archives are very extensive; many include considerable quantities of printed material. Certain collections have been mentioned in *A* above in connection with related book collections. The printed items, other than incunabula, are not yet included in the catalogues of books, but are often listed in the catalogues of mss.

Leaflet *Published catalogues of manuscripts and archives* lists the 30 most important catalogues, but for many collections there are typescript lists.

The basic list of mss is H J Todd, *A catalogue of the Archiepiscopal manuscripts in the Library at Lambeth*, 1812, repr New York, Gregg, 1965) superseded in several sections by more modern catalogues), continued for later acquisitions by a series of catalogues by E G W Bill, 1972– .

H Chief collections from which the library has been built up

Donated collections receive bookplates, but are not kept distinct. Archbishops' arms or bookplates are useful guides to provenance, but from the 18th cent may sometimes rather indicate date of binding (eg of the Cornwallis pamphlets). A Register of Donations begun 1959 omits the larger collections. The larger general benefactions are listed below; those of specific subjects have been listed above. The library in its early years somehow acquired parts of the libraries of John Foxe (1516–87) the martyrologist, Robert Dudley, Earl of Leicester (1532–88), and Sir Christopher Hatton (1540–91).

Richard Bancroft (1544–1610) bequeathed 6,065 v to his successor Abbot on condition that the collection should be made public. About half is theological, mostly Bibles and commentaries, Fathers, Protestant and Catholic theology about equally divided, with controversial tracts, sermons, etc. The non-theological part included much history and topography, law, and classical literature. 29 items at Lambeth, most of which seem to have been acquired by Bancroft from John Lumley, Lord Lumley (1534–1609), have been identified as having come from Archbishop Cranmer's library. Bancroft had also acquired the whole of Archbishop Whitgift's library from his executors.

Classified shelflist, 1612 with preface by Abbot, two copies (L.R.F.1-2).

Cox-Johnson, *ibid* p105-8.

Ducarel, p48-52.

C A Mackwell, 'A list of Archbishop Cranmer's books in Lambeth', *Friends Annual report* 1973, p29-31.

George Abbot (1562–1633), Archbishop 1611–27, arranged Bancroft's collection, and bequeathed his own, with instructions for cataloguing it. The contents were similar, but there was more modern literature than classical. *c*2,667 v.

Cat by W Baker, 2 v, by size and author (two copies, L.R.F.3-4).

Two cat of the complete library (L.R.F.5-6).

Cox-Johnson, *ibid* p108-10.

R A Christophers, *George Abbot...a bibliography*, Charlottesville, Univ Pr of Virginia, 1966.

Commonwealth Laud's private library was dispersed after his arrest, and books from the official Lambeth Library were also beginning to disappear when, in 1646 Parliament ordered their removal to Cambridge University Library (reversing a decision to send them to Sion College). They were mostly returned *c*1665, with a few strays from Cambridge.

Classified shelflist of complete library immediately prior to despatch from Lambeth (Bodleian Ms 3335) and copy with Cambridge shelfmarks (Cambridge UL.Ms.Oo.7.51).

Author cat *c*1650 (Cambridge UL.Ms.Ff.2.34 and copy Mm.4.1).

Cat of Cambridge UL with items returned to Lambeth noted (Cambridge UL.Ms.Oo.7.73).

Part of list of books received back at Lambeth in order of receipt of barrels, prefixed to cat of Sheldon bequest (L.R.F.7).

Cox-Johnson, *ibid* p110-26.

Gilbert Sheldon (1598–1677), Archbishop 1663–77, bequeathed his own collection, *c*2,500 books; mostly theology, sermons, biblical commentaries, Fathers, classics, history.

Author list (L.R.F.7).

Le Neve, p87.

Cat of the entire Library, *c*1680 (L.R.F.9); 1684, by P Colomesius (L.R.F.10).

Thomas Tenison (1636–1715), Archbishop 1694–1715. In 1684 he deposited most of his collection to found a parish library at St Martin-in-the-Fields, but on appointment as primate retrieved some of those books and added them to the private collection that he kept in his study at Lambeth. The 1,500 v which were in the study at his death were bequeathed to Lambeth, with some mss (others bequeathed to Edmund Gibson came by the latter's bequest).

Author cat of his collections (L.R.F.11) distinguishes his study and St Martin's books.

P A Hoare, 'Archbishop Tenison's library at St Martin-in-the-Fields', 1684–1861 (DipLib thesis, Univ of London, 1963).

Thomas Secker (1693–1768), Archbishop 1758–68, bequeathed his whole library except duplicates: *c*2,000 v of books, and 163 v of pamphlets. Includes Fathers; sermons of leading Anglican and Nonconformist divines. Also his Papers, including pamphlets on Methodists (S.R.16) and Moravians (see *E* above); and on America, including Society for the Propagation of the Gospel, with pamphlets (see under *E* above).

Dictionary cat by A C Ducarel of books offered (L.R.F.21) and books accepted and received (L.R.F.22).

Botfield, p255-8.

B Porteus, 'A review of the life. . . of. . . Secker' prefixed to 1770 and later editions of Secker's *Works*.

Cornwallis and other pamphlet collections Frederick Cornwallis (1713–83), Archbishop 1768–83 bequeathed no library, but gave his name to a collection of *c*10,000 pamphlets, including *c*1,500 of 1715–68 from the Secker bequest, which had accumulated unbound and uncatalogued throughout the Palace since the 16th cent. In 1773 they were arranged by subjects by A C Ducarel and bound with the Cornwallis bookplate, but it is likely that few, if any, had belonged to him personally. These and some pamphlet collections acquired later are now scattered through the subject classification. In 1902 the London Library gave 358 v, mostly on education, church history, theology, and sermons, to Church House Library; these were transferred to Lambeth in 1946.

Cat by A C Ducarel, 1773, with additions to *c*1790 (L.R.F.23-24), lists the vols under broad subject headings alphabetically, listing the pamphlets in each; dictionary index (L.R.F.25) of subjects and names in individual pamphlets.

List of 34 v added later, *c*1802? (L.R.F.27).

Cat by S W Kershaw, 1886–7, 2 v.

Cat of London Library collection by H T Cox, 1888 (L.R.J.13).

Archibald Campbell Tait (1811–82), Archbishop 1868–82. *c*650 books from his library donated 1883 on theology, history, education etc for the period *c*1840–80.

Author list in 'Catalogue of modern books' (L.R.F.31) fol 1-71.

Dutch Church Library In 1954 a portion of the Dutch Church Library (probably about half, comprising perhaps *c*700 v of theology and Protestant history), were given to Lambeth Palace Library and incorporated in the collections (see under London. Dutch Library, for the history and catalogues of the collection; there seems to be no list of what was given to Lambeth).

Edwin James Palmer (1869–1954), Bishop of Bombay, in 1843 gave a collection of books 1721–1872 inherited from his ancestors, mostly on English church history.

Samuel Burney (1885–1969), founder of the Society of St Peter and St Paul, bequeathed his library of early printed books and pamphlets, and 19th-20th cent Anglo-Catholic theology.

Congregation of Oblates of St Charles, Bayswater This house was founded in 1857 by Cardinal Henry Edward Manning (1808–92), and acquired many of his own books. In 1969 most of its library was sold, much of it to Lambeth, including many rare Anglican books and pamphlets of 17th-19th cents.

Church House Library Church House Library dispersed various parts of its collections from 1930 onwards. It was closed (except for some modern departmental working collections) in 1972, when there were *c*10,000 v, of which two-thirds came to Lambeth, mainly post-1800. The collection was strong in church history, Fathers, Councils of the Church, and ecclesiastical law; the last (including 16th and 17th cent works) came mainly from the executors of Walter George F P Phillimore (1845–1929), 1st Baron Phillimore, the ecclesiastical and international lawyer.

Card cat from Church House.

(C T R) Christopher Perowne (Canon) donated many works from 1960 onwards, including early printed books, topographical works, books on the Huguenots, etc.

Register of Donors 1960, 1968, etc.

Bomb damage, 1941 Pre-1800 English books had been evacuated with the mss but several thousand foreign and 19th-20th cent English books were destroyed or damaged (eg several incunabula, some Fathers, most classical and modern literature, science, and some philosophy).

Rough lists of books damaged and destroyed (L.R.J.10.4).

Lambeth Public Libraries

The libraries, now administered as part of the Directorate of Amenity Services, are formed from those of the former Metropolitan Borough of Lambeth, with the addition of certain libraries from that of Wandsworth.

A Minet Library

Archives and Surrey Collection, 52 Knatchbull Road, Myatt's Fields, London SE5 9QY. Tel (01) 733 3279. Open Mon-Tues and Thurs-Sat 9.30 am-5 pm, by appointment with the Archivist.

William Minet (1851–1933) FSA, President of the Huguenot Society, gave the original building for a public library, opened in 1890 as the Minet Library, together with his Surrey collection (his Huguenot collection is in the Huguenot Library at University College London). Until 1956 the Minet Library was administered as an independent public library jointly by the Metropolitan Boroughs of Camberwell (in whose area it lay before boundary changes in 1900) and Lambeth; from then until 1964 by the latter alone. The Surrey collection is now administered with the Borough Archives, independently of other collections in the Minet Library.

Surrey Collection (general) Comprises *c*6,500 books and pamphlets, with numerous ephemera, on the County of Surrey as it was before the creation of the London County Council in 1888, including, in addition to the present county, the area of Greater London to the South of the Thames eastwards to the then boundary with Kent beyond Bermondsey. The collection is still currently being built up for the whole of this area—its history, topography and archaeology, architecture, elections, genealogy and heraldry, militia, sport, natural history, religion, theatres, social life, biography, transport, etc. It is the most comprehensive collection on Surrey in existence, with all the general histories of Surrey and its parishes, many extra-illustrated copies—and nearly all the histories of London; over 800 local Acts; *c*250 pre-1851 sermons; cuttings collection from *c*1680, including in addition to items from early newspapers, some complete ephemera; directories of London from 1787 and Surrey from 1791; *c*200 sale catalogues from 1728, mainly of South London estates; extensive collections of prints, maps etc. The collection includes *c*5 STC; *c*50 Wing; and *c*225 ESTC items.

W Minet and J Courtney, *A catalogue of the collection of works relating to... Surrey contained in the Minet Public Library*, 1901; *Supplement*, 1923.

M Y Williams, *A short guide to the Surrey collection*, 1965.

'Guide to London history resources: London Borough of Lambeth' (typescript, 1981).

M W Barley, *A guide to British topographical collections*, 1974, p84-5.

Parliamentary elections The collection includes poll books for county constituencies 1719–1826; registers of electors 1836 and 1865 for the county; 1843 onwards for the Borough of Lambeth (with 1833– in ms); an archival collection on Lambeth elections 1834–52, especially the campaigns of Charles Tennyson D'Eyncourt FRS (1784–1861), Whig MP for Lambeth 1832–52; including election addresses, posters, poll-cards etc.

George Hill, *Electoral history of the Borough of Lambeth*, 1879.

Theatres and places of entertainment Playbills, programmes and ephemera of many South London theatres and music halls, especially Surrey Theatre 1816–78 (with plays performed there 1830–45, and cuttings 1782–1889); Vauxhall Gardens bills, programmes and cuttings 1822–59 (with songs sung there 1750–1800). Astley's (later Sanger's) bills 1823, the Royal Cobourg (later Old Vic), Bower Saloon, etc.

Crystal Palace Collection Built up mainly from two major purchases, the more recent being of part of the collection of Alan Warwick of Norbury (see also under Bromley Public Libraries). Mostly after the removal to Penge by the Crystal Palace Co in 1854 (programmes, cuttings, pamphlets etc) but including some scarce catalogues of the Great Exhibition in Hyde Park, 1851. Books on the history of the Great Exhibition and the Crystal Palace.

Magdalen Hospital Trust archives The archives of Magdalen Hospital, founded by Jonas Hanway in 1757 in Blackfriars Road, 1757–1975. The early material consists mainly of printed reports, rules and histories.

B Brixton Reference Library

Brixton Oval, London SW2 1JQ. Tel (01) 274 7451. Open Mon-Tues and Thurs-Fri 9 am-9 pm, Wed and Sat 5 pm; special collections by appointment only (Bacon and Dumas are temporarily housed at Minet Library, where they may be seen only by prior arrangement with the Brixton Reference Librarian, during the same hours as the Surrey Collection).

The Brixton Reference Library was opened in 1893 as the reference department of the Tate Library of the Borough of Lambeth, financed by Sir Henry Tate (1819–99) the sugar magnate and patron of the arts. In its early years it owed much to donations.

General Reference Collection Formerly one of the finest London public library collections, it still retains most of its older stock. A very extensive collection of complete sets of Victorian literary and scientific periodicals was severely pruned *c*1930–47, but is still the best in London outside the City and Westminster. It contains *c*1,000 pre-1851 books and pamphlets, of which perhaps 100 are pre-1701. They cover most subjects, including some fine editions in architecture, engineering, natural history, travel, literature and bibliography.

Two complementary card cats (dictionary) one of which is accessible only to staff.

Local Studies Collection Contains some basic works on Lambeth, Surrey and London from 1631.

In general cat.

Blake Collection Contains *c*200 v of editions of the

artistic and literary works of William Blake (1757–1827) and works about him, chiefly mid-19th cent. Originally formed as a local author collection, it is not intended to be much enlarged in the future.

In general cat.

Bacon Collection c700 editions of the works of Francis Bacon, Viscount St Albans (1561–1626) from 1597 onwards (the predominant part) and of works about him and on the Shakespearian authorship controversy. There are c90 pre-1641; c130 1641–1700; c90 18th cent, all including some foreign editions. Some scarce periodicals (eg *Fly-leaves of the Ladies' Guild of Francis St Alban* 1914–28) and some German and French controversial works. The collection seems to have been begun c1912, and at least part is said to haved come from the library of Sir Edwin Durning-Lawrence (1837–1914) who was a member of the Library Committee (whose main Bacon collection is in the University of London Library).

Ms cat (chronological) and separate card cat. It is not known whether either cat accurately represents the collection in its present state.

Dumas Collection The works of Alexandre Dumas the elder (1802–70), c120 v, chiefly in first and early editions (at least one inscribed by the author), and contemporary English translations; periodicals edited by Dumas: *La Psyché* (1826–9); *La Mousquetaire* (1866–7); and *D'Artagnan* (1868); biographical works on Dumas, and criticisms of his writings, 19th cent. Mss on Dumas by Harry A Spurr (c1865–1906), author of *The life and writings of Alexandre Dumas*, 1902, brother of Mel B Spurr the comedian and entertainer; also a collection of ephemera comprising early cheap editions of his plays, articles and cuttings about him, and prints and other pictorial material.

Law Society Library, 113 Chancery Lane, London WC2A 1PL. Tel (01) 242 1222. Telex 261203. Open Mon-Fri 9 am-5 pm, to Members and their articled Clerks only. The library is private, and non-members cannot be admitted except by special dispensation from the Council. Photocopying for Members.

The Law Society is the professional body of solicitors practising law in England and Wales, and has statutory duties. It was founded in 1825 as the Law Institution, afterwards the Incorporated Law Society, superseding earlier societies. Its library originated in 1828 when three benefactors presented sets of standard legal and other reference works. On the demise of the College of Advocates at Doctors' Commons, many of its books were purchased by the Society. It has been built up steadily by donation and purchase, and until c1900 acquired books of English history and other non-legal subjects. More recently some of the non-legal rare books have been dispersed. It is now a comprehensive library of all branches of English law, and selected branches of Scottish, Irish, EEC and other jurisdictions. c70,000 v, including at least 5,000 pre-1851; 77 incunabula (some unique, and mostly from the Mendham collection).

First printed cat 1841. *Catalogue of the Library*, 1851 (classified); 1869 (dictionary). *Catalogue of the printed books*, 1891 (dictionary) with *Supplement* 1906. Loose-leaf typescript cat for later acquisitions.

F P Richardson, 'The Law Society Library: a short historical description' *Law Librarian* 1(2) (1970), p15-9.

Law Society's Gazette, 1903– , including lists of acquisitions and other information on the Library.

Acts of Parliament Complete sets of the retrospective collections of *Statutes at Large*, *Statutes of the Realm*, etc. Very extensive collection of Private Acts, mainly assembled by William Salt the antiquary and banker (1808–63), including many of Anne and George I received from the British Museum as duplicates in 1861. Ms copies of many for which no printed editions available.

Mendham Collection Collected by the anti-RC polemicist Joseph Mendham (1759–1856) Curate of Sutton Coldfield. Bequeathed to his nephew John Mendham (1800?–69) Rector of Clophill, Beds, whose widow donated c5,000 items selected by Charles Hastings Collette (1816–1901) the Protestant Controversialist solicitor of Lincoln's Inn Fields. Some have been sold, but there remain c1,000, chiefly history and theology, especially books and pamphlets relating to the post-1688 controversy between the Anglican and RC churches; Bibles, Liturgies (RC and Anglican); editions of the *Index*; Fathers, Mss.

Catalogue of the Mendham Collection, being a selection of books and pamphlets from the library of...Joseph Mendham... and *Supplement* 1871–4.

W K Riland Bedford, *Three hundred years of a family living*, Birmingham, 1889, p129-30.

Leathersellers' Company, Leathersellers' Hall, 15 St Helen's Place, London EC3A 6DQ. Tel (01) 588 4615. Archives and books may be seen by appointment only, on written application to the Clerk; owing to lack of staff this is restricted at present, but the Clergy and Gentlemen of the Hundred of Lewisham are legally entitled to use Colfe's School Library.

The Company is 15th in order of precedence of the City livery companies. It has kept its ms and printed archives at the Hall.

William H Black, *History and antiquities of the worshipful Company of Leathersellers*, priv pr 1881.

Colfe's Grammar School Library The School was founded in 1652, to revive a dormant Elizabethan foundation, by Abraham Colfe (1580–1657), Vicar of Lewisham, who appointed the Leathersellers' Company as trustees. At the same time he opened a Library with a donations book for the use of the School and of the Clergy and Gentlemen in the Hundred of Blackheath. It began with 12 books which were soon increased to several hundred by the bequest of Colfe's own books. The School, originally called the Free Grammar School at Lewisham, became known as Colfe's Grammar School, and is now Colfe's School, at Horn Park Lane, SE12 8AW. The books from the original library were removed to Leathersellers' Hall several years ago, and have not recently been made accessible, nor have facilities to describe them for the *Directory* been given on account of shortage of staff at the Hall. It is not known how closely the collection corresponds with the printed catalogue, where the main strength is in 16th-17th cent Bibles and commentaries, Fathers, general theology, and classical literature.

Bibliothecae Colfanae catalogus: catalogue of the Library in the Free Grammar School at Lewisham founded by. . . Abraham Colfe, by William Henry Black, London, Company of Leathersellers, 1831 (classified; historical introduction; list of donors on pxliv-xlvii); annotated copy in British Library.

Ms cat of Colfe's collection 1657.

Leland L Duncan, *A short history of Colfe's Grammar School, Lewisham*, Lewisham, 1902 (repr from *The Colfeian*).

Leo Baeck College for the study of Judaism and the Training of Rabbis and Teachers Library, 33 Seymour Place, Marylebone, London W1H 5AP. Tel (01) 262 7586. Open Mon-Thurs 10 am-5 pm, Fri 10 am-2 pm, to bona fide students and researchers. Photocopying.

The College and its Library were founded in 1956. The latter contains about 10,000 v, of which *c*40 are pre-1851; 6 of 16th cent, including 1553 ed of Maimonides *Morehnevukhim*; 8 of 17th cent; 24 of 18th cent; 1 of 1801–50. Most in Hebrew, a few German.

Card cat.

Lewisham Public Libraries

A **Archives and Local History Department**

The Manor House, Old Road, Lee, London SE13 5SY. Tel (01) 852 5050. Open Mon, Tues, Thurs 9.30 am-8 pm; Fri, Sat 5 pm by appointment.

The collections for the whole Borough, including the former Metropolitan Boroughs of Lewisham and Deptford, were centralized here in 1965. The archives include deposits of manorial and diocesan records.

L L Duncan, *History of the Borough of Lewisham*, Lewisham Public Libraries, 1963.

E and J Birchenough, *The Manor House, Lee.*

C W J Harris, 'C W F Goss' (North Western Polytechnic thesis 1969) enlarged from *Library World* 72 (841) (1970), p7-10.

Local History Collection Collections of local authors include John Evelyn (1620–1706) and Thomas Campbell (1777–1844) the poet, in each case a few editions only. Pre-1851 books on the history and topography of Kent, London and Lewisham. Kent poll books 1734–1865, and a few early Kent directories.

Card cat.

Society of the Treasury of God The library and archives of the Society, founded in 1886 by Anglicans to encourage personal tithe-giving by disseminating literature on the subject, dissolved in 1953. The Society's last Treasurer gave the collection to Deptford Public Library to form part of its special collection on Christianity; the archives were transferred to the Manor House in 1969, and the library in 1982. The library contains *c*90 books on tithes, including Selden (1618), Montagu (1621), Comber (1682), Leslie (1700) and a number of ESTC items; 5 v of rare tracts 1837–1900, with some numbers of magazines of the tithe movement, and numerous individual tracts, mostly issued by the Society (some in multiple copies).

List in preparation.

H J Rengert, 'The Society of the Treasury of God', *Bull Assoc of British Theological and Philosophical Libraries* no 17 (Dec 1962), p4-7.

B **Lewisham Reference Library**

366 Lewisham High Street, London SE13 6LG. Tel (01) 690 1247. Open Tues-Fri 9.30 am-8 pm; Sat 5 pm.

*c*30,000 v on the humanities and social sciences. Most pre-1851 books were dispersed between 1940 and 1968, but a few early 19th cent topographical books remain.

Card cat (author and classified).

C **Bookstore**

305 Hither Green Lane, London SE13 6RS. Open by appointment only Mon-Fri 9.30 am-1 pm, 2-5 pm.

Collections built up under the Metropolitan Special Collections Scheme, formerly at Deptford. The library of the Society of the Treasury of God is now in the Archive Dept. Two sections are worthy of mention:

The Bible (Dewey 220-229) *c*3,500 v, including *c*150 pre-1851 Bibles, concordances and commentaries from the 16th cent onwards. (This collection is closed, now being continued by London Borough of Hammersmith and Fulham.)

Christian theology (Dewey 230-239) *c*400 v, still being enlarged, including a few pre-1851.

Card cat (author and classified).

Lincoln's Inn Library, Honourable Society of Lincoln's Inn, London WC2A 3TN. Tel (01) 242 4371. Open Mon-Fri 9.30 am-7 pm by prior

arrangement with letter of introduction; last resort only.

Scope: The library comprises 20,000 pre-1851 items, including 34 incunabula; 1,300 STC and 3,170 Wing (mainly pamphlets). The library covers all aspects of law, English and foreign; yearbooks and law reports (outstanding collection for 16th-19th cent); statutes, all major Kings' Printers' editions; Private Acts 1727–1838, 149 v; Road Acts 1754–96 40 v; Parliamentary papers; topography, local history. General subjects (Theology sold Hodgson 11 Dec 1969; French and English literature 5,000 v sold earlier).

Growth: John Nethersale (*d*1497) bequeathed money to house existing collection, but was not large till the 17th cent. Special collections included in general collection are: Ranulph Cholmeley (*d*1563) City Recorder, don; John Donne (1573–1631) the poet, don; John Brisco, don; Miles Corbet, don; George Anton, don; Charles Fairfax, don; Sir Roger Owen, don; William Prynne (1600–69), don, including many of his own pamphlets; John Brydall (*c*1635–*c*1710), 69 v of pamphlets, chiefly theological and political don 1706; John Coxe (1695–1783) law, history and general literature, 5,000 v bequeathed; Charles Purton Cooper (1793–1873) foreign and civil law 2,000 v, purchased 1843; some books of Isaac Reed (1742–1807) Shakespearian editor bought at sale (King 2 Nov 1807); law tracts 125 v bought from executors of Serjeant George Hill (1716–1808); 58 v printed and ms material on the trial of Warren Hastings (1732–1818) collected by John Adolphus (1768–1845). Some non-legal books have been sold (eg Sotheby 9 Nov 1978, 21 Feb 1980, 6 Nov 1980).

Catalogue of the printed books by W H Spilsbury, 1859, supersedes 1835 author cat.

A catalogue of pamphlets, tracts, proclamations, speeches, sermons, trials, petitions from 1506 to 1700, 1908 chronological.

Cooper collection partly cat in ms.

see E Halfpenny, 'Letters from Lincoln's Inn', *The Library* (s5) 12, 1957, p256-9.

Collections described by W H Spilsbury in *Trans London & Middlesex Arch Soc*, 4, 1873, p45-66; Hist in his *Lincoln's Inn* 2nd ed 1961, p292-3.

See also R A Rye *The student's guide* 3rd ed 1927, p355-7; E Edwards, *Memoirs* 1859, 1, p726-33; R Walker in *Law Librarian* 8 (1) 1977, p3-4; *The libraries of London*, ed R Irwin and R Stavely 2nd ed 1961, p292-3.

Linnean Society Library, Burlington House, Piccadilly, London W1V 0LQ. Tel (01) 734 1040. Open Mon-Tues, Thurs-Fri 10 am-5 pm; Wed 2-5 pm, to Fellows; to others by introduction of a Fellow, or by written application to the librarian in advance.

The Linnean Society of London was founded in 1788 for the study of flora and fauna (the idiosyncratic spelling 'Linnean' being embodied in its Royal Charter). Its library, dating from the same year, has been built up by bequest, donation, exchange and purchase, and now holds *c*70,000 v on the biological sciences. Of the collections acquired from individuals, only those of Linnaeus and Insch are kept as separate entities. The Society also houses the libraries of the British Ornithologists' Union (containing very few rare books), the Avicultural Society (periodicals only), and the Herpetological Society (modern works only).

A T Gage, *A history of the Linnean Society of London*, 1938.

Notes on the Library, 1978.

'Catalogue of the exhibits. . . on the occasion of the 150th anniversary celebrations', *Proceedings* 150(4) (1937–8), p294-308.

Ray Desmond, *Dictionary of British and Irish botanists and horticulturists*, London, Taylor and Francis, 1977, under names of collectors etc, with extensive bibliographical references.

Monographs Collection Of the *c*30,000 books and pamphlets (including special collections), *c*10,000 are pre-1851, *c*3,500 pre-Linnaean (ie 1707), 8 incunabula, *c*500 of the 16th cent and *c*1,500 of the 17th cent. Predominantly taxonomy, with a slight preponderance of botany over zoology, strong in herbals (some with contemporary colouring), and a good collection of bestiaries. Substantial collection on Darwinism and other evolutionary theories. Some pre-1800 mineralogy and a little early geology and palaeontology. Post-1840 non-European entomology is no longer collected, and the former holdings in this field, other than special association copies, have been sold.

Card cat (author and classified) of post-1750 books.

Pre-1751 author cat in ms (to be incorporated in the main cat).

Printed author cats: first in *Transactions* 5 (1800), p277-93.

Catalogue of the Library of the Linnean Society of London, London, Richard Taylor, 1827.

Catalogue of the Natural History Library of the Linnean Society of London Pt 1: separate works, 1866, and supplements in Pt 2, 1867 and Pt 3, 1877.

Proof copy, A-G, of abortive cat [1894].

Catalogue of the Library of the Linnean Society of London, new ed 1896.

Catalogue of the printed books and pamphlets in the Library of the Linnean Society of London, 1925.

Index of provenances being compiled during recataloguing.

Accessions with names of donors listed (not always completely) in *Transactions* 6(1802)-21(1855), then in *Journ of the Proceedings* 1855–65, then in most volumes of *Proceedings* 1866–1963/4.

Register of donations (incomplete) 1788–99 and 1822-(still current).

(Sales of entomology and duplicates Sotheby 10 June 1963, 20 Dec 1965, 7 June 1976, 15 May 1978, 2 July 1979; Christie 28 Nov 1974.)

Periodicals Collection Of *c*40,000 v in *c*3,000 sets, *c*400 are wholly or partly pre-1851, including a very wide range of the publications of natural history societies and scientific institutions throughout Europe, Asia and America. Some sets not in the mainstream of the Society's interests have been sold, including all post-1840 non-European entomological journals.

Title cat on cards.

Entries for periodicals are incorporated in the printed cats of 1896 and 1925. They are listed separately under place of publication in *Catalogue... Part 2*, 1867, and in proof of abortive cat [1893]. The *List of current periodicals*, 1964, does not show holdings. A long Presidential address on foreign periodicals by G Bentham is printed in *Proceedings* 9 (1865), pix-lxxxiii.

Manuscripts Mss of Linnaeus (see Linnaean Library below) and a large number of important collections of working papers and correspondence, in some cases with printed material included.

Card cat.

Published lists of two collections only in *Catalogue of the manuscripts in the Library of the Linnean Society of London*: Part 1: the Smith papers, 1934 (p113-4; printed matter); Part 4: Calendar of the Ellis manuscripts, 1948.

Natural history manuscript resources, 1980, p213-35.

Linnaean Library The collection of Carl Linnaeus (1707–78) Prof of Botany and Medicine at Uppsala, and founder of the modern system of taxonomy and nomenclature. His library, herbarium and zoological specimens from the museum that he had established at Hammarby, passed to his son Carl (1741–83) and then to the elder Carl's widow. In 1784 they were bought by Sir J E Smith (see below) who made them available to Society members when meetings took place at his house from 1788–95. They were then removed, but were bought by the Society in 1829 from his widow with his own collections. The books and pamphlets were incorporated into the general lending library, but segregated again in 1857. They totalled *c*2,700 items in *c*1,600 v, including bound volumes of tracts, on a wide variety of biological and other subjects, but principally flora, fauna, and mineralogy; there are some medical tracts, but the books on medical subjects were sent back to Hammarby in 1894, and are now at Uppsala University. There are numerous copies of his own works, many of them annotated for the preparation of future editions. Works of others are also often annotated by him, his son, or others. The collection of his mss is also very extensive.

The printed cat of 1866, 1896 and 1925 identify the copies belonging to Linnaeus, but omit many of the medical and most of the non-biological items.

S Savage, *Synopsis of the annotations by Linnaeus and contemporaries in his library of printed books*, 1940 (Catalogue of the manuscripts in the Library of the Linnean Society of London, Part 3).

Cat by Linnaeus *c*1751–3 among his mss, shelflist by Smith also, and later ms list. (Also a typed list of books sent to Hammarby, 1892.)

J M Hulth, *Bibliographia Linnaeana*, Uppsala, 1907, partie 1, livraison 1 (works by Linnaeus); no more published.

Unpublished handlist of Linnaean mss.

See also under British Museum (Natural History) the cat by B H Soulsby.

William T Stearn and G Bridson, *Carl Linnaeus (1707–78): a bicentenary guide to the career and achievements of Linnaeus and the collections of the Linnean Society*, 1978.

B D Jackson, 'History of the Linnean collections', *Proceedings* 1887–8, p18-34.

Exhibition of a selection from the Linnean collections, 5th International Botanical Congress, 1930, London, Linnean Society [1930], with history.

Memoir and correspondence of the late Sir James Edward Smith, ed by Lady Smith, London, 1832, v 1, p91-134.

T M Fries, *Linné: lefnadsteckning*, Stockholm, 1903, v 2, p413-30; English adaptation by B D Jackson, *Linnaeus*, London, 1923, p342-57.

Wilfrid Blunt, *The complete naturalist: a life of Linnaeus*, London, Collins, 1971, p236-8.

Dictionary of scientific biography, v 8, p374-81.

Ball, John (1818–89) FRS, First President of the Alpine Club. Some of his books received from his executors in 1890 (others at Kew etc).

Obit, *Proceedings* 1889–90, p90-2.

Banks, Sir Joseph (1743–1820). He donated part of his library in 1789.

Register of donations.

Brown, Robert (1773–1858), Society's Librarian. Bequeathed 297 items (mostly botany) and 48 more were bought at sale of the residue (Stevens 27 June 1859).

Ms lists of the bequest and those bought.

See also *Proceedings* 1859, pxxv-xxx; 1887–8, p54-67; 1888–9, p34; 1931–2, p17-54.

Dictionary of scientific biography, v 2, p516-22.

Cuming, Hugh (1791–1865), plant and shell collector, donated many books and bequeathed a small conchology library containing some choice rarities.

Obit, *Proceedings* 1865–6, plvii-lix.

Currey, Frederick (1819–81) FRS, Treasurer. 189 v from his mycology library donated, with his mss by his family.

Obit, *Proceedings* 1881–2, p59-60.

Druce, Francis (1873–1941), Treasurer. Gave some early herbals and other books (but most of his library bombed).

Obit, *Proceedings* 1940–1, p293-4.

Insch, James (1877–1951), tea planter, bequeathed his library, *c*100 v (some early), kept as a special collection.

List, *Proceedings* 1951–2, p286-92, Obit, 1950–1, p253.

Jackson, Benjamin Daydon (1846–1927). General Secretary, editor of *Index Kewensis*. Bequeathed his library.

Obit, *Proceedings* 1927–8, p119-23.

Pearson, Arthur Anselm (1874–1954), President of the British Mycological Society. Bequeathed his mycology library.

List, *Proceedings* 165 (1955), p31-42. Obit, 168 (1955–6), p31-42.

Smith, Sir James Edward (1759–1828) FRS, President. His library, mss and herbarium came with those of Linnaeus.

Biog in *Proceedings* 1887–8, p22-8.

Wallace, Alfred Russel (1823–1913) FRS, evolutionist, spiritualist and eccentric. His library (except the entomology, now at Hope Library, Oxford) donated with his mss by Thomas Henry Riche.

List, *Proceedings* 1914–5, p62-70.

Weiss, Frederick Ernest (1865–1953) FRS, President, Prof of Botany at Manchester. Bequeathed a collection.

Obit, *Nature* 171 (1953), p285-6. *Times* 9 Jan 1953, p8.

Woodward, Bernard Barham (1853–1930), Librarian of the British Museum (Natural History). Bequeathed his collection on conchology.

Obit, *Proceedings* 1930–1, p201-2, 207.

Lloyds Bank plc, Head Office, 71 Lombard Street, London EC3P 3BS. Tel (01) 626 1500 Ext 3235. Open Mon-Fri 9 am-5 pm, by appointment, on written application to the Archivist. Photocopying facilities.

Archivist's Office Library A collection of books transferred from various offices and branches of the Bank. *c*150 v, including *c*10 pre-1851, mainly on the history of banking and of Lloyds Bank.

Directors' Library A collection formerly called the Board Room Library which now furnishes the Directors' sitting rooms, *c*300 v, including *c*10 pre-1851 (2 Wing; 1 ESTC), mainly miscellaneous reference books and general literature, the provenance of which is unknown.

Shelflist on cards.

Lloyd's. Corporation of Lloyd's Library, Lime Street, London EC3M 7HA. Tel (01) 623 7100. Open Mon-Fri 10 am-4.30 pm by appointment on written application to the librarian.

Lloyd's was incorporated in 1871, but had been conducting insurance (originally at Edward Lloyd's coffee house) from the 1680s. (Lloyd's Register of Shipping (qv) is now a distinct organization with its own collections.) The library dates from 1928, but probably includes books from earlier office collections.

Dictionary cat on cards in course of compilation.

Historical Collection *c*150 v mainly relating to maritime law and insurance law, with some on insurance practice. Mostly after 1800, but a few earlier, including 1 STC and a set of *Lloyd's List* from 1741 (lacking 1742–6, 1754, 6 and 9, and 1778).

Nelson Collection (A museum administered by Lloyd's Information and Publicity Dept). A collection in memory of Horatio Nelson, Lord Nelson (1758–1805). The nucleus was acquired in 1910 with the re-purchase of some of the plate presented by Lloyd's to Nelson in honour of his victory at the Battle of the Nile, 1798. In 1928 E Lamplough gave a large collection of ms letters, and the publication of a catalogue of the collection encouraged further donations (including books which are a relatively small part of the whole) shortly afterwards. There are *c*38 works, including 16 pre-1851; many bear a bookplate of the 'Symington Collection'. They are books on Nelson's life, naval career and family, some in display cases.

Typescript list, but excludes the items in the display cases.

Lloyd's Register of Shipping Records Centre, Archivist's Office Library, 22-23 Shand Street, Bermondsey, London SE1 2ES. Tel (01) 709 9166. Open Mon-Fri 9 am-5 pm by appointment on written application to the Archivist.

A collection of material removed *c*1970 for the personal use of the Archivist from Lloyd's Register of Shipping Technical Library (qv), now *c*450 v forming the greater part of the historical collection of Lloyd's. It incorporates much of the collection formed by Augustin Francis Bullock Creuze (1800–52) FRS, Principal Surveyor to Lloyd's, and author of books on naval architecture; this includes 5 18th cent and many later French works of shipbuilding and naval architecture, and 6 v of early 19th cent pamphlets containing many inscribed presentation copies to Creuze. Most of the standard 18th cent English treatises on shipbuilding are also held, together with works on shipping and voyages, with pilots, marine dictionaries and some miscellaneous works; also mainly modern collections of naval memoirs and works on wrecks.

In course of arrangement. See the printed cats of the Technical Library which include most of the collection.

Lloyd's Register of Shipping Technical Library, 71 Fenchurch Street, London EC3M 4BS. Tel (01) 709 9166. Open Mon-Fri 9 am-5 pm on written application to the librarian. Photocopying facilities.

Lloyd's was founded in 1760, but not established in its present form until 1834. A library was in existence by 1884, but much was dispersed *c*1970, the more important material being mostly deposited at the Guildhall Library. The remaining historical material is divided between the Technical Library and the Records Centre (qv). There are *c*150 v of English and foreign works of historical interest, chiefly pre-1851, including the *Register* (complete only after 1828, earlier issues being transferred to the British Library, facsimiles only being retained) housed in the office of the Shipping Information Service; *Rules* from

1859; some copies of the rival Liverpool Register 1862 onwards; early monographs on naval architecture, shipbuilding, marine dictionaries, naval history, voyages, the Corporation of Lloyds, and some miscellaneous technical works of the later 19th cent—the earliest is C van Yk, *De Nederlaandsche sheeps bouw-konst*, Amsterdam, 1697; and bound volumes of pamphlets, including a collection by Sir Samuel Bentham (1757–1831) of the 1820s.

All catalogues include material no longer in the library; printed catalogues include some at Records Centre.

Card cat (author and classified, the latter incomplete).

Lloyd's Register of Shipping, *Library catalogue* 1926 (subjects) (op).

Catalogue of books in the Library, 1961 (dictionary) (op).

London College of Fashion Library, 20 John Princes Street, London W1M 9HE. Tel (01) 629 9401 Ext 279. Open Mon-Fri 9 am-4.30 pm (vac); Mon-Thurs 7 pm (in term); Fri 4.30 pm (in term) on application to the Chief Librarian. Photocopier available.

The College (originally the College for the Garment Trades) is administered by the Inner London Education Authority, and its library (on two sites) has over 35,000 v, including a number of pre-1851 books in the collections noted below.

Card cat (author and classified) at each library, with union cat at Oxford Circus.

Oxford Circus Library (at the address above) Special collection of beauty therapy and hairdressing books, including *Hairdressers' Journal* from 1882. Extensive coverage of fashion design in book, journal, slide, illustration, and photographic formats. Clothing manufacture and management.

Curtain Road Library, 100 Curtain Road, Shoreditch, London EC2A 4BA. Tel (01) 739 4002. Specialist books and periodicals on tailoring, furriery, clothing, manufacture and management.

London College of Furniture Library, 41-71 Commercial Road, Stepney, London E1 1LA. Tel (01) 247 1953. Open Mon-Thurs 8.45 am-7.15 pm, Fri 5 pm, but in vacation only by special arrangement, and usually until 4 pm on application to the librarian. Photocopying; microform reader; typing room.

The College was founded in 1889 as the Shoreditch Technical Institute, later becoming the Technical College for the Furnishing Trades. There is a segregated special collection of older and rare books withdrawn from the current library (now *c*20,000 v), or given or purchased in the last few years, including the gift in memory of Percy Wells in 1957 from his daughters, which included a number of 19th cent works. This collection contains *c*300 v on joinery, carpentry and building construction; the history of furniture design and manufacture; architecture and interior design; design and ornament; and musical instrument manufacture. There are standard works of the 18th cent by Chippendale, Sheraton and Hepplewhite. Later rare works include a number of publications of the Great Exhibition of 1851. One of only two known complete sets of the *Cabinet Maker* from 1882 to date.

Card cat (author/name and alphabetical subject).

Library guide (gratis).

Periodicals in the Library, 1981.

London College of Printing Library, Elephant and Castle, London SE1 6SB. Tel (01) 735 8484. Rare book collections may not be seen except by appointment with the librarian in person, after written application giving plenty of notice, and with a letter of introduction. Open Mon-Thurs 9 am-7.15 pm, Fri 5.45 pm (in term); 9.30 am-4.30 pm in vacation (not August). Photocopier; micro-film/fiche reader/printer; audiovisual equipment available.

The London College of Printing was built on its present site and acquired its present name in 1963, incorporating the London School of Printing and kindred trades (afterwards Graphic Arts) from Stamford Street, SE1, which in its turn has absorbed the St Bride Printing School (founded 1894) in 1922, but not its Library (for which see St Bride Printing Library). It is administered by the Inner London Education Authority.

General The library contains *c*80,000 v, of which about one third are on fine art (one of the subjects taught) and a quarter on the current technical aspects of printing. Virtually all the 19th and 20th cent English textbooks of printing are held.

Card cat (author and classified to 1980, continued by microfiche).

Rare Book Collection A segregated collection of *c*1,000 items, of which about two-thirds are private press books, mostly after 1920, including 25 of the Golden Cockerel Press, 37 of the Nonesuch Press, and a very extensive post-1960 collection (with a few American). There are a few of 1850–1920, including 2 of the Kelmscott Press and 10 other Morris items. *c*100 late 19th and early 20th cent illustrated (including children's) books (especially Rackham). *c*100 pre-1851 books; a few are on printing, eg Senefelder *Complete course of lithography* 1819, but most are on miscellaneous subjects and have been acquired simply as specimens of printing from 1549 onwards. There is an uncatalogued collection of tracts 1660–91 on ecclesiastical controversies. Some 19th cent lithographed books and a substantial uncatalogued collection of 19th and 20th cent ephemera.

In general cat.

Special card index under authors and presses.

Periodicals c800 sets, mostly on printing and art. Many of the scarcer, older and rare titles have been given to the St Bride Printing Library, but some 19th and early 20th cent runs, including some humorous, satirical and other illustrated magazines, have been transferred to the Rare Books Collection.

Periodicals in the Library, 1980.

London Hospital Medical College Library, Turner Street, Whitechapel, London E1 2AD. Tel (01) 377 8800. Open Mon-Fri 9 am-5.30 pm to members of the University of London, and to others on written application in advance. Photocopier available.

The Hospital was founded as the London Infirmary in 1740 by a surgeon, John Harrison, and six backers. The Medical School as a separate institution dates from 1785, when the Library was established; in 1909 it became a school of the University of London. There are now c10,000 v of books and c14,000 v of periodicals.

Author cat on cards (incomplete) in two sequences.

R M Nicholas, 'The development of medical libraries within the University of London' (MA Librarianship thesis, Univ of London, 1976), p37-40.

E W Morris, *A history of the London Hospital*, 2nd ed, London, 1910, p186-203 (see also 3rd ed, 1926, p169-83).

A E Clark-Kennedy, *The London*, London, Pitman, 1962–3, 2 v, does not mention the library, nor does the popular adaptation *London Pride*, London, Hutchinson Benham, 1979, or Polly Toynbee, *Hospital*, 1977.

Historical Collection A collection of c400 (formerly over 1,000) books mostly dating from the early days of the College Library, separated from the main collection (which also contains a few pre-1851 books). It spans a period from 1535 to the late 19th cent of mostly classic medical authors. Many bear the bookplates of Thomas Jeremiah Armiger (1742–1844) Demonstrator of Anatomy; William Wood; Augustus Bradshawe; Henry Corbet; and the Rev C Buckeridge.

Catalogue [c1880]. Not in current card cat.

J P Entract, 'Historical books in the Library', *London Hospital Gazette*, 1953, p83-4.

Alumni Collection Works including non-medical writings by staff and students, with the two following individual collections.

J P Entract, *The London Hospital bibliography* (typescript).

Treaves, Sir Frederick (1853–1923), surgeon to Edward VII, who trained at the London and was Surgical Registrar, gave his library of travel and memoirs, including his own writings, eg *The elephant man and other reminiscences*.

W R Bett, 'Sir Frederick Treves', *Annals of the Royal College of Surgeons of England* 12 (1953), p189-93.

Sir Newman Flower, *Just as it happened*, New York, 1953, p109-23.

Bashford, Sir Henry Howarth (1880–1961) author (using pseudonym 'Peter Harding') and government medical officer. A collection of his works, including novels set against the background of the Hospital, poems and children's books.

Peter Harding, *The corner of Harley Street*, London, 1913.

British Medical Journal 1961 (2), p588-9.

London Library, 14 St James's Square, London SW1Y 4LG. Tel (01) 930 7705. Open Mon-Sat 9.30 am-5.30 pm (Thurs 7.30 pm) to subscribers; temporary membership available to visiting scholars, and a special scheme (the London Library Trust) for remission of fees to students; all enquiries must be made to the librarian in writing, well in advance of an intended visit.

The London Library, now the world's largest subscription library, was opened in 1841 for 'the supply of all good books in all departments of knowledge' for loan to scholars and other serious readers prepared to pay a substantial subscription. The impetus came from Thomas Carlyle (1795–1881) who complained of poor facilities at the British Museum, and launched a campaign in the *Examiner* in 1840, supported the next year by a pamphlet from his politician friend William Dougal Christie (1816–74). Its policies have always been guided by eminent literary men from the time the first desiderata lists were drawn up by Gladstone, Grote, Hammond, Mill, Mazzini, and other scholars. From 3,000 v the collection has grown by systematic purchasing and an exceptionally large number of donations and bequests to over 1 million.

W D Christie, *An explanation of the scheme of the London Library, in a letter to the Earl of Clarendon*, London, 1841.

Frederic Harrison, *Carlyle and the London Library...*, London, 1907.

C T Hagberg Wright, *The London Library...*, 1926, and *The London Library...1913–1940*, 1941.

S Gillam, 'The history of the London Library', *Journ London Soc* no 390 (Sept 1970), p36-43.

Miron Grindea ed, *The London Library*, Ipswich, Boydell Press (1977?) repr from *Adam*, nos 387-400 (1977).

Diana Dewar, 'The London Library: its first hundred years' (BA Librarianship essay, Birmingham Polytechnic, 1975).

A General Library

The main emphasis of the collections is literary and historical, both British and foreign (including some modest collections in oriental languages), and all subjects in the humanities are well covered. Books on science, medicine, and law are never purchased, but have not been excluded from donations, and there is a substantial collection on botany. The collection of 19th cent literature is particularly fine, and there are substantial earlier collections from the 16th cent onwards, though books are bought for the utility of their texts and not for their rarity.

Author cats printed 1842–4, 1847, 1865, 1875–81, 1888, 1903–11, superseded by Catalogue of the *London Library* new ed by C T Hagberg Wright and C J Purnell, 1913–4, 2 v, with supplements 1920, 1929 and (to 1950), 1953; continued on cards.

Subject index, 1909, with supplements 1923, 1938 and (to 1953), 1955; continued on cards.

List of Parliamentary Papers, by C T Hagberg Wright, 1903; supplemented by card cat.

B Book Collections

Individual bequests and donations are not (unless otherwise indicated) preserved as separate entities, but merged in the appropriate subject collections, and unless a separate list or catalogue is indicated below, none is known to exist, though collections on narrowly defined subjects can easily be found in the *Subject index*.

Ingram Bywater (1840–1914), Regius Prof of Greek at Oxford, had a fine library which was sold (Hodgson 7 June, 14 July and 2 Dec 1915). The London Library bought a substantial part of this collection.

Franco-Prussian War 1870–1 The library in 1914 acquired a large collection, which included 7 v of satirical ephemera, including issues of satirical journals.

(Jean) Sylvain van der Weyer (1802–74) A collection of Belgian books bought at the sale of his library.

Sir Leslie Stephen (1832–1904) His working collection of 18th cent philosophy, used when writing his *History of English thought in the eighteenth century* (1876).

Allan Library A collection of *c*12,000 v on theology and related subjects in the humanities, 16th-19th cent, collected by Thomas Robinson Allan (*c*1800–84) to form the nucleus of a large central library on Methodism, mostly purchased 1860–80 in England and abroad, and incorporating rare book collections that had been formed by the Rev Paul Orchard and the Rev Richard Brown. In 1884 it was opened as a combined reference and subscription lending library at the City Road Methodist HQ, but it was unsuccessful, and in 1920 the entire collection was bought by the London Library. (On 14 June 1966 all the incunabula in the London Library were sold at Sotheby's (lots 1-88), most being from the Allan Library). The library includes English (mainly Puritan) divines, RC theology and liturgy, and missionary works (including early Americana); also travel, history, printing, and emblem books.

A catalogue of books chiefly theological collected by Thomas Robinson Allan in usum amicorum, Leipzig, Teubner (*c*1875) (two copies with complementary ms additions, one with printed continuation).

Catalogue of a collection of Bibles...formed by... Allan..., 1881 (with ms additions).

Book Collector 16(2) (1967), p211-5.

(Henry) Austin Dobson (1840–1921), poet and literary editor, in 1921 gave his collection of 18th cent prints, and after his death his 18th cent books were added by his family.

Col Ramsay Weston Phipps (1838–1923), author of *The armies of the first French republic* (1926–39), in 1921 gave a collection on Napoleon I and his era.

Frederick Cornwallis Conybeare (1856–1924), Fellow of Univ College Oxford, bequeathed his Armenian collection of *c*500 items.

Subject index, 1938, p58-61 etc.

Obit in *Proceedings of the British Academy* (1926).

L Maries, *Frederick Cornwallis Conybeare*, Paris, 1926 (with bibliography).

Henry Brodribb Irving (1870–1919), son of Sir Henry, accumulated *c*400 v of literature on criminals and criminal trials, which were given *c*1925 by his widow. His drama collection was given *c*1938 by Laurence Irving.

Lt-Col John Henry Leslie (1858–1943), military historian, in 1921 gave a collection on the Royal Artillery, and at later times much of his general collection of military history. (This was complemented by a smaller collection of regimental histories, given in 1925 by W H Bernau.)

Alfred Collingwood Lee (?–*c*1925?), a public health official, and author of *The Decameron, its sources and analogues*, bequeathed his collection of Romance literatures.

Sir Sidney Lee (1859–1926) 50 v from his collection of early Italian poets acquired *c*1925.

Henry Yates Thompson (1838–1928), the collector of illuminated mss, left a collection of reference books, facsimile editions, and rare books, which were given to the library by his widow.

Francis George Baring Northbrook, 2nd Earl of (1850–1929), ADC to his father when Governor of India, bequeathed his library on a miscellany of subjects.

P A Cohen, gave a collection of finely printed and illustrated works between 1928 and 1950.

Mrs Seymer, *c*1931 gave several thousand v of travel books, especially 18th cent voyages.

Subject index, 1938, p1013-5.

George (Allardice) Riddell, 1st Baron (1865–1934), Chairman of *News of the World* and George Newnes Ltd bequeathed his library, *c*3,000 v of miscellaneous books.

Miss A A Petavel, bequeathed *c*1934/5, *c*50 items on Mary, Queen of Scots.

Donald Bradley, Baron Somervell of Harrow (1889–1960), Lord of Appeal. His collection of private press books, *c*100 v.

Aylmer Maude (1858–1938) His collection, given *c*1939 consists of *c*150 editions of Tolstoy in Russian and translations into various languages, *c*100 books about him, and several hundred on Russian literature in general.

Alfred Edward Hippisley (1848–1939), Secretary to the Chinese Commissioners of Customs, and author of *The Chinese Revolution* (1912), gave *c*1930, a collection on the history of China in several hundred volumes 17th-20th cent (some in Chinese).

Subject index, 1938, p186-92, etc.

Sir Ernest (Alfred Thompson) Wallis Budge (1837–1934), of the British Museum bequeathed a large selection from his library, chiefly Ethiopic and other oriental books and mss, amounting to over 1,000 items.

Subject index, 1938, p340-1.

Robert Bontine Cunninghame-Graham (1852–1936) MP, bequeathed *c*500 Spanish-American books, including many rare items.

John Frederick Baddeley (1854–1940), St Petersburg correspondent of the *Standard* and author of *Russia, Mongolia and China* (1919) gave, at various times, large numbers of books, and included, in 1921, his noted collection of books and pamphlets on the Caucasus, and his mother's collection on London, chiefly prints, in 1922, including an extra-illustrated copy of Pennant's *London*; also a bequest.

'Index Caucasica' (typescript subject index to his Caucasus collection). Memoir by C H Wright in *The rugged flanks of Caucasus* (1940).

Edward Heron-Allen (1861–1943) FRS, marine biologist and litterateur, bequeathed his library, including a special collection of *c*400 editions of Omar Khayyam in numerous Eastern and Western languages, and critical works on the poet; with 10 portfolios of pamphlets, ephemera, and cuttings relating to him.

Subject index, 1953, supplemented by ms cat of portfolios.

Alexander Henry Higginson (1876–19?) of Boston, Mass and Dorchester, Master of the Cattistock Hunt, sporting author and author of *British and American sporting authors* (1951), collection on hunting and field sports.

*c*2,000 v kept as a separate collection.

Miss Frances Perry *c*1953 gave a collection on the history of 16th cent France.

Miss Thérèze Mary Hope (?–1958?), historian of Hatfield Peverel, bequeathed her collections of rare books, including early printed books, fine printing and private presses, and books on Essex.

Miss Susan Minet (1884–1976), in 1967 gave a collection of several thousand books on the 16th, 17th and 18th cent, English and foreign, that had belonged to the Minet family, of Huguenot descent, including some bearing the inscription of Lieutenant-General William Minet (1762–1827) and of his father Hughes Minet (1731–1813). (The Huguenot books from the Minet family library are in the Huguenot Library at University College London, and the books on Surrey at the Minet Library of the London Borough of Lambeth Public Libraries.)

C Pamphlet Collections

The following collections have been kept as individual entities. Other collections of pamphlets received are merged in the general collections, eg 18th cent pamphlets given in *c*1925 by the Royal Agricultural Society, and the collection of 17th cent pamphlets given *c*1927 by Miss S Buxton.

Per nozze pamphlets This collection consists of *c*1,000 Italian poems, letters and other writings, published in the 18th and 19th cent mainly in Vicenza.

Claude Joseph Goldsmid Montefiore (1858–1938), the Jewish philanthropist, bequeathed 664 v of pamphlets almost entirely on Jewish subjects; they include *c*150 written by him and his family.

D Periodicals

The Library's collection comprises many hundreds of runs, many of them complete, of the standard periodicals within its range of subject interests. 18th and 19th cent periodicals are well represented. There is a strong British emphasis, but European and American serials will also be found.

No separate cat but included in author cat under title, and subject index where appropriate.

London School of Economics and Political Science, British Library of Political and Economic Science, 10 Portugal Street, London WC2A 2HD. Tel (01) 405 7686. Telex 24655. Special Reading Room open Mon-Fri (except Aug) 10 am-6.30 pm, 7.15-9 pm; Sat (except July-Aug) and Mon-Fri (Aug) 10 am-5 pm, on application to the Librarian in advance. Photocopying and microfilming; microform readers available.

The London School of Economics, now a school of the University of London, was founded in 1895 by a group led by Sidney Webb, afterwards Lord Passfield (1859–1947). The British Library of Political Science (as it was named until 1925) was established by public subscription in 1896, to serve both the School and a wider public. Webb's own collection on trade unions was donated to form the core of the collection, which has been built up by substantial donations and systematic purchasing into one of the world's great social sciences libraries.

R Irwin and R Stavely, 'The libraries of London', London, *Library Assoc*, 1964, p197-208.

A H John, *The British Library of Political and Economic Science: a brief history*, 1971.

'The British library of Political and Economic Science

reference services', *Aslib Proc* 24 (1972), p459-63.

D A Clarke, 'The BLPES and the collection of primary materials' *Ibid* 23 (1971), p201-2.

C G Allen, 'The library as a research collection', *LSE Magazine* Dec 1967, p4-6.

LSE: the new library, 1978.

E C Blake, 'Sources for African Studies', *Lib Materials on Africa* 5 (1967), p10-13.

Guide to the Library, 3rd ed 1980.

Outline of the resources of the Library, 3rd ed 1976.

A reader's guide to the British Library of Political and Economic Science, 3rd ed 1945, not wholly superseded by the *Guide* or the *Outline*.

Notes for readers, revised annually.

B Hunter, 'Russian and East European material in the British Library of Political and Economic Science', *Solanus* no 4 (1969), p8-15.

A **General**

The Library contains over 2½ million items, including *c*650,000 v of books, and over 11,000 serial titles, covering the whole range of the social sciences, with particular strengths in economics, commerce, business administration, trade unions, transport, statistics, political science, international law, and the social and economic aspects of history. It includes very large collections of the publications of British and foreign governments. Older and rare material, hitherto mainly mixed in with the current classified collections, is now being segregated (see B), but some pre-1851 material remains in the general collections. The 19th cent collections of British social, economic, and trade union history are outstanding; coverage of earlier periods is less systematic.

Author cat on cards to 1979.

A London bibliography of the social sciences: being the subject catalogue of the British Library of Political and Economic Science..., 3 v (and author index), 1931–2; supplements to 1979.

From 1980 microfiche cat (author, classified and alphabetical subject).

Card cat of non-governmental periodicals to 1979.

Edward Fry Library of International Law This library was founded in 1920 by the family of Sir Edward Fry (1827–1918), endowing a collection which is held on deposit. The nucleus was the collection on international law of Prof Lassa Francis Lawrence Oppenheim (1858–1919) and a selection from Fry's own library. There are large collections of pamphlets, treaties and periodicals; also law reports and digests of decisions.

Author and classified card cat.

In main author cat and *London bibliography*.

Schuster Library of Comparative Legislation The collection was originally formed by Ernest Joseph Schuster (1850–1924), and given by him to the Society of Comparative Legislation, who after leaving it on deposit for 10 years, donated it in 1936.

Transport Collections The library has received an exceptional number of gifts of collections covering the historical aspects of transport, and the coverage of 19th cent railways is especially comprehensive. The nucleus came from the collection of Sir William Acworth (1850–1925), the School's first Lecturer in Railway Economics, which included much parliamentary material, early timetables, and reports of railway and canal companies. Another collection was formed by Septimus Bell in 1848–50, and consists of 8 v with indexes of ephemera, cuttings and maps, relating to the development of certain British railways 1795–1850, and the defeat of canal competition. A similar collection *c*1860–1910 in 8 v made by E V Ivatts on the British railways in their heyday.

G Ottley, *Railway history: a guide to... collections...*, London, *Lib Assoc Ref Section*, 1973, p24-5.

Book Trade Collection The nucleus of a collection on publishing, bookselling, and all economic aspects of the book trade, was given by Mr A D Power (*d*1959) in 1934, supplemented by his bequest. In 1935 the Publishers' Association gave the collection on the French and German book trade which Geoffrey Sydney Williams (1871–1952) had donated to them, with the donor's approval. It has been greatly enlarged by subsequent gifts and purchases, and now contains *c*4,000 items, including *c*100 pre-1851 (mostly post-1800).

Classified cat of a collection of works on publishing and bookselling in the British Library of Political and Economic Science, 1961 (without author index).

Catalogue of a collection of works on publishing and bookselling..., 1936 (arranged by authors).

B **Rare Book Collections**

The collections in this section are accessible only in the Special Reading Room.

General rare books collection Books transferred from the general collections on account of their rarity, chiefly under the classifications OU OW OX OY OF and SR. *c*12,000 v and being enlarged. Mainly on economic and political subjects. 1485–1968, mostly 1600–1850; with some topographical works. Includes many books bought from the estate of Harold Laski (1893–1950).

In general author/name card cat only.

Bonar Collection 1,064 works from the library of James Bonar (1852–1941), economist, on economics, religion and philosophy, 1569–1927.

In general author/name cat only.

Cannan Collection 1,034 books on economics 1572–1931 from the library of Edward Cannan (1861–1935), Professor of Political Economy, and his private papers 1876–1938.

Books in general author/name cat only.

Separate cat of papers.

Civil War tracts Over 1,000 tracts of *c*1640–1660 are held; most are from a collection purchased in 1932.

Hutchinson Collection 1,880 books bought with a bequest of money from Miss Constance Hutchinson (*d*1895) on socialism, anarchism, syndicalism, communism, and other radical and revolutionary movements, including original theoretical works, attacks on left wing movements, Utopian novels in English, French, German and Italian, 19th and 20th cent. The serials from the collection are now in the classified collection of serials.

In general author/name cat only.

See also W L Guttsman, 'Sources on the history of the British Labour Movement in the British Library of Political and Economic Science', *Soc for the Study of Labour History*, Bull no 8 (1964), p23-30, which describes similar material elsewhere in the Library.

Jevons Collection 144 v of tracts on political and economic subjects 1616–1871 collected by William Stanley Jevons (1835–82), FRS, Professor of Political Economy at University College.

Cats in Special Reading Room.

London School of Hygiene and Tropical Medicine Library, Keppel Street, Bloomsbury, London WC1E 7HT. Tel (01) 636 8636. Open Mon-Fri (term) 9.30 am-7.30 pm; (vac) 9.30 am-5 pm; Sat (not August) 9.30 am-5 pm to any bona fide enquirer. Photocopying; microfilm/fiche reader.

The London School of Tropical Medicine was founded by the Seaman's Hospital Society in 1899 at the Albert Dock Hospital, and became a school of the University of London in 1905. The Library of the Tropical Diseases Bureau of the Colonial Office, founded in 1908, was added in 1921 to the school library. In 1924 the London School of Hygiene and Tropical Medicine was established by the University as a postgraduate school into which the earlier school was incorporated. In 1931-9 the library of the Society of Medical Officers of Health and that of the Ross Institute were incorporated. There are *c*65,000 v of books and periodicals, and some archival collections, including the papers of Sir Ronald Ross (1857–1932) and Ross Institute archives.

Card cat, reproduced as London School of Hygiene and Tropical Medicine *Dictionary catalogue* and *Supplement*, Boston, G K Hall, 1965, 1971, 8 v. (Superseded published cats 1904 and *c*1911.)

Cat of Ross archives to be published 1982.

Cyril Barnard, *London School of Hygiene and Tropical Medicine: history of the Library*, 1947.

Sir P Manson-Bahr, *History of the School of Tropical Medicine in London 1899–1949*, 1956, p88-92, 261-2.

Historical Collection *c*400 pre-1840 and some later volumes on epidemiology, tropical medicine and public health. Purchased from 1924 onwards, or donated, many by Dr Andrew Duncan, Sir Patrick Manson, Sir George Buchanan, Sir Arthur Newsholme, and Sir Shirley Murphy.

Brownlee, Dr John (1868–1927) bequeathed *c*139 classic historical monographs on epidemiology and infectious diseases to the Medical Research Council, from whom the collection was obtained, including 2 STC and 3 Wing items.

Reece, Dr Richard James (1862–1924) of the Local Government Board, in 1925 donated his collection on smallpox and vaccination, including material by and about Edward Jenner (1749–1823), and polemical works. 282 monographs, 7 v periodicals, 624 pamphlets and 54 scrapbooks of newspaper cuttings.

W R LeFanu, *A bio-bibliography of Edward Jenner*, London, Harvey and Blythe, 1951.

London Transport Museum Library, 39 Wellington Street, Covent Garden, London WC2E 7BB. Tel (01) 379 6344. Open by prior arrangement with the librarian, Mon-Sat 10 am-6 pm.

The Museum was opened in 1978 to house the former London Transport Collection at Syon Park (previously part of the British Transport Museum at Clapham). A library has been built up recently to complement the display collections. It contains books, pamphlets, and periodicals, together with ephemera, on all forms of transport in London. (Part of the closed London Transport headquarters library, formerly at 55 Broadway, SW1, is deposited on loan.)

Reinohl Collection Over 1 million passenger tickets, with some newspaper cuttings, and a few miscellaneous ephemera, from the beginning of the 19th cent onwards, mounted in 180 massive volumes, probably the largest ticket collection in existence. Over three-quarters are British, principally of bus transport (and especially the horse-bus era), also including water, rail and air transport; some American, colonial, and foreign. Donated by the Chartered Institute of Transport.

Loose leaf handlist.

Lord's Day Observance Society, 47 Parish Lane, East Penge, London SE20 7LU. Tel (01) 650 1117. Students admitted on written application in advance to the Secretary. Open Mon-Fri 9 am-5 pm.

The Society has built up since its foundation in 1831, a collection of over 100 v on the observance of Sunday as the Lord's Day.

Magic Circle Library, 84 Chenies Mews, London WC1E 6AH. Library (which will move to a new address within the next two years) is normally open to Members only; others should apply in writing to the Secretary.

The Magic Circle was founded in 1905 as an association of conjurors. It has built up a library of over 4,000 v on conjuring and related subjects. In 1949 the older and 'rare' books were formed into a separate reference library, now over 500 v, and include 3 STC items; 9 Wing; 31 ESTC; 36 English 1801–50; and *c*200 English 1851–1900, with a number of foreign books from 1618 onwards, and over 30 sets of British and American periodicals, 1791 onwards, including some not held elsewhere. The books are mainly on legerdemain and visual illusions, but there are some on other forms of deception, charlatanism, astrology, spiritualism, cyphers, and similar subjects. The earliest items are Thomas Hill *Natural and artificial conclusions* 1581, and the first edition of Reginald Scot *Discoverie of Witchcraft* 1584. There are a number of books from the libraries of famous magicians, and the collection of the bibliographer Trevor Henry Hall (*b*1910) was acquired *c*1975, which included many early works.

Magic Circle, *A catalogue of the Reference Library and Lending Library*, 1952, now seriously incomplete.

Earlier lists were published in the Circle's private organ, the *Magic Circular* in 1906, 1907, 1908, 1912, 1913, 1919, and 1922, with continuing accessions lists, and separately in 1927 and 1940, with supplement 1948.

Trevor H Hall, *A bibliography of books on conjuring in English from 1580–1850*, Lepton, Palmyra Press, 1957; author list, without locations, are not limited to his own collection; supplement in his *Old conjuring books*. . ., 1972.

Magic Circle (including the Hall collection) is included among the locations in the more detailed R Toole Stott, *A bibliography of English conjuring 1581–1876*, Derby, Harpur, 1976–8, 2 v.

Marine Society, Hanway Collection, 202 Lambeth Road, London SE1 7JW. Tel (01) 261 9535. Open Mon-Fri 9 am-5.30 pm on written application to the Secretary, with suitable references. Photocopying facilities.

The Marine Society was founded in 1756 by the philanthropist Jonas Hanway (1712–86). In 1774 he presented the 'Thomas Hanway Mausoleum', which now serves as a bookcase for the collection which included some books and mss given by Hanway specifically to be placed there (mostly now lost), and others donated later, especially a collection of Hanway books made by H Macfall. Over 50 v, including 23 by Hanway, several lives of him; 8 pre-1851 editions of the Society's printed rules; books on its history; its *Annual Report* from 1834 (incomplete); and some mss and cuttings. (The Society also has a 20th cent collection on the merchant navy, and runs the Seafarers' Education Service and College of the Sea Library.)

Typescript chronological list.

H T A Bosanquet, *Marine Society: a catalogue of the pictures and other works of art at the Society's offices*, 1905 (op); some of the books listed on p18-19.

Marx Memorial Library, 37A Clerkenwell Green, London EC1R 0DU. Tel (01) 253 1485. Open Mon and Fri 2-6.30 pm, Tues-Thurs 2-9 pm, Sat 11 am-1 pm, on payment of subscription and additional research fee.

The Library was founded in 1933 as a riposte to Nazi book-burning, in celebration of the jubilee of Karl Marx (1818–83) by the Marx Commemoration Committee, mainly on the initiative of the Labour Research Dept, and the publisher Martin Wishart. Until *c*1945 its official name was the Marx Memorial Library and Workers' School. It is housed in Marx House, originally a charity school, later the home of the radical London Patriotic Club, and from 1893 to 1922 the socialist Twentieth Century Press, from which Lenin edited *Iskra* from April 1902 to May 1903.

Andrew Rothstein, *A house on Clerkenwell Green*, London, Lawrence and Wishart, 1966 (op), is a history of the building and its occupants; p73-80 describe the library.

Quarterly Bulletin of the Marx Memorial Library, 1941– .

General The library contains *c*25,000 books, 50,000 pamphlets and numerous runs of periodicals (in addition to substantial collections of visual material), on Marxism, the history of socialism, and of the working class movement, including early radical movements and republicanism. Numerous bequests and donations have been incorporated into the general collection.

Card cat (author and alphabetical subject) reproduced as *Catalogue of the Marx Memorial Library*, Boston, G K Hall, 1979, 3 v ($275).

Marx Memorial Library, *Catalogue* 1971– (classified cat of selected, mainly the more current, loanable, material, 15 parts so far issued); also cats of special collections (see below).

Lenin Collection A collection housed in the Quelch Room, where Harry Quelch (1858–1913) edited *Justice* for the Twentieth Century Press and Lenin edited *Iskra* from April 1902–May 1903; it comprises *Iskra* no 25 and a collection of Russian language works on Marxism, mainly modern, and a few other rare items and association copies, eg Robert Owen *New Moral World* 1836 (signed copy), and Marx *Das Kapital* 3rd ed 1883–5, the copy used by the translator of the English edition, S Moore, with signature and some ms notes in v 1 of Engels the German editor.

Serials and Pamphlets Collection The library claims to have the largest collection of the pamphlets of British workers' organizations; these include extensive sets of pamphlets, with many of the serials, issued by the British Socialist Party, the Communist Party of Great Britain, Independent Labour Party, Labour Party, Minority Movement, National Unemployed Workers' Movement, Social Democratic Federation, Socialist Labour Party, and others; a complete set of the *Clarion* ed by Robert Blatchford (probably unique).

Bernal peace library The works of Prof John Desmond Bernal (1901–71) FRS, and contemporary works on disarmament.

J D Bernal peace collection, 1981 (cat £2).

International Brigade Collection A collection on the Spanish Civil War (1936–9), consisting mainly of contemporary pamphlets, press cuttings, ephemera, mss, and some books, collected by the International Brigade Association, and donated in 1975.

Books, pamphlets, periodicals and photographs concerning the War in Spain, 1982 (cat £2).

'Priceless records of the War in Spain', *Quarterly Bulletin* no 77 (Jan/Mar 1976), p3-6.

N Green, 'The Spain archive', *Ibid* no 84 (Oct/Dec 1977), p18-9.

Torr Collection A collection assembled by Miss Dona M Torr (1883–1957), editor of the correspondence of Marx and Engels, given after her death to the Communist Party, later transferred; *c*500 v, mainly on socialism, Marxism, and history, including some 19th cent items.

Williamson American Collection A collection of US books and pamphlets on socialism, Marxism, etc, formed by John Williamson (1913–74) former Librarian, who was deported from the US in 1955.

M Williamson, 'The John Williamson collection', *Ibid*, also no 76 Oct/Dec 1975.

Dobb Bequest Maurice Herbert Dobb (1900–76), Fellow of Trinity College Cambridge, bequeathed *c*1,000 books, of which *c*330 are kept as a separate collection, and of these *c*200 are on economics, including all the classical works of 18th-20th cent, and *c*90 on the role of the trade unions in economic development, especially in the Eastern bloc, the raw material for Dobb's *Soviet Economic Development since 1917.*

M Robinson, 'Dobb Reference Library', *Quarterly Bulletin* no 89 (Jan/Mar 1979), p3-5.

A Rothstein, 'Maurice Dobb'. *Ibid* no 80 (Oct/Dec 1976), p3-4.

Klugmann Collection Contains most of the rare books from the vast library formed by James Klugmann (1912–77), editor of *Marxism today*, the whole of which was bequeathed to the Communist Party of Great Britain (qv) and transferred to the Marx Memorial Library (*c*1,500 v on the history of radicalism are kept as a separate collection, including at least 1 STC, *c*60 Wing (mostly relating to the Revolution and Protestantism); books and pamphlets by radicals and socialists of the late 18th and early 19th cent including Wilkes, Paine, Cobbett, Owen, Saint-Simon, Fourier, Proudhon, etc, with 1 v of Comtist pamphlets of the 1850s in English and French; works on constitutional struggles, including *Tracts* of the Society for Constitutional Information 1783; 12 pamphlets on the Reform Bill 1831; Chartism, Luddist riots etc; trials of radicals and treason trials, including 1 v 1774–1820 of tracts and reports, chiefly on Cato Street, and other items on Carlisle, Horne Tooke (with many of his works, mostly from the collection of James Whatman), and others; works on the trial of Queen Caroline, including her *Memoirs* 1820 and 1821 (Hone's ed with 60 songs, pamphlets and broadsheets, many by Hone, in 3 v); tract collections, including Society for the Promotion of Permanent and Universal Peace 1819, 1 v of anti-slavery tracts by the Rev Benjamin Parsons (1797–1855), Congregational Minister at Ebley, Gloucester, locally printed, and 1 v of his *Tracts for fustian jackets* 1848 (formerly in the Cowper and Newton Museum, Olney, from William Wright's collection), and 1 v on the Irish question. Some books on atheism, especially by Charles Bradlaugh (1833–91), and 2 v from his library on this subject received from E B Watson. Bound runs of newspapers and periodicals include many scarce early 19th cent titles.

Cat being compiled for publication.

Marylebone Cricket Club Library, Lord's Ground, St John's Wood, London NW8 8QN. Tel (01) 289 1611 Ext 8. Open (via Grace Gate in St John's Wood Road) by prior arrangement with the Archivist, Mon-Fri 9.30 am-5.30 pm and during the hours of cricket (including Sat), but non-members should not ask to see material which is available in the British Library.

The library is administered with the MCC archives, dating back to the foundation in 1787 (though most early records perished in the fire of 1825), the museum and extensive collections of paintings and other works of art.

Diana Rait Kerr and I Peebles *Lord's 1946–70*, London, Harrap (1971), p318-20.

Collections from which the library has been built up
Until 1930 there was only a small collection in the Pavilion. Several major and innumerable minor donations have now been incorporated into a unified collection arranged by a subject classification, to which some purchases have been added.

Ashley-Cooper, Frederick Samuel (1877–1932), prolific cricketing author and editor of *Cricket* collected *c*4,000 books and pamphlets on the game, which he sold in 1931 to Cahn.

Typescript list by Cahn.

G N Weston, *Bibliography of the cricket works of... F S Ashley-Cooper*, priv pr, 1933.

Irving Rosenwater, *F S Ashley-Cooper...*, priv pr 1964.

Cahn, Sir Julien, 1st Bt (1882–1944) of Stanford Hall, Notts, the noted cricket captain, collected *c*4,000 v of cricket books, to which he added the Ashley-Cooper collection; all except duplicates were given to the MCC by Lady Cahn after his death.

Typescript list, 1942.

Ford, Alfred Lawson, collected probably *c*2,000 v on cricket, given by H R Ford after his death in 1930.

Wilson, Evelyn Rockley (1879–1957), Master of Winchester College, collected *c*1,000 books, together with pictures, ceramics and other objects which he bequeathed.

The present collections
There are *c*12,000 v on all aspects of cricket (including a few on other sports), British and foreign, forming the most comprehensive cricket library in existence.

Sheaf cat (author/title and classified), gives provenances, but does not index them.

The whole collection is included in E W Padwick, *Bibliography of cricket*, London, Library Assoc 1977, though this does not normally print locations of printed items; the entries include much material, unique to the library, some of its ms and factitious collections, and some unpublished lists of them.

Cricket: a catalogue of an exhibition...presented by the National Book League with the co-operation of the Marylebone Cricket Club, arranged by Diana Rait Kerr, Cambridge UP, 1950 (includes descriptions of over 100 rare items from the MCC Library).

Laws of cricket *c*80 editions, including 43 before 1851, many in broadside format.

R S Rait Kerr, *The laws of cricket*, London, 1950, p114-27; bibliog (copy with typescript additions by the author and others inserted).

Books and pamphlets on cricket A collection of *c*8,000 v. At least 50 pre-1851 items, including some anti-cricket propaganda, the earliest being G Swinnock, *Life and death of Tho Wilson* (1672). Many scarce privately printed editions.

Cricket annuals and reference books of scores Virtually all the late-18th and 19th cent publications, including Lillywhite's guides and *Cricket scores*, and Wisden from 1864, in complete sets.

Cricket magazines *Cricket* complete from 1882, and almost all other British publications. Many foreign, including *The American Cricketer* (1877–1929).

Cuttings Collections Mostly in scrapbooks: 1763–83 (mainly Kent); 1807–33 (including fire at Lord's 1825); 1825–49 (with ms index by Ashley-Cooper); 1838–40 (given in 1941 by Hampstead Public Library); 1841–6 (5 v collected by Sir Charles William Atholl Oakeley, 1828–1915, 4th Bt); 1848–51; 1851–2 (All England XI, with watercolours and ms descriptions by one of the team, Nicholas Wanostrockt, 1804–76, headmaster of a school at Blackheath, who played under his pen-name N Felix).

Other sports *c*40 v, mostly after 1880, on real (royal) tennis, which is still played at Lord's; and a few on other sports.

Masons' Company, 9 New Square, Lincoln's Inn, London WC2A 3QN. Tel (01) 405 6333.

The Company is 30th in order of precedence of the City livery companies, but no longer has a Hall within the City. Its older archives are deposited in the Guildhall Library Department of Manuscripts (it is not known whether these contain printed books or documents); authorization from the Clerk to the Company must be obtained before they may be consulted at the Guildhall. There are no books or records at the Hall before the late 19th cent.

Mercers' Company, Mercers' Hall, Ironmonger Lane, London EC2V 8HE. Tel (01) 726 4991. Open Mon-Fri 9.30 am-5.30 pm by appointment with the Archivist.

The Mercers' Company is first in order of precedence of the City livery companies, having been founded in the Middle Ages. It has been concerned in the foundation of a number of educational institutions. The music and general libraries from Gresham College are deposited (with the exception of some general books given to the University of Malta) at the Guildhall Library. St Paul's School (qv) has a major library, which has been enlarged with most of the rare books from the Mercers' School (closed in 1959).

W F Kahl, *The development of London livery companies*, Boston, 1960 (with extensive bibliography).

The Mercers' Company..., (1972).

Sir John Watney, *History of the Mercers' Company*, London 1914.

Mercers' Company archives These are mostly the mss archives of the company. Printed material amounting to *c*200 items has also been incorporated; these include 4 STC items; 15 Wing; and 45 ESTC. These are mainly histories of London and of livery companies, Mercers' Company documents and works relating to connected institutions such as Gresham's College. There are some service books from Mercers' Chapel.

Ms lists, supplemented by card cat, with classified index.

Trinity Hospital Greenwich collection Holy Trinity Hospital (an almshouse) was founded by the company in 1614. This collection comprises some papers and books belonging to Charles Heathcote Tatham (1772–1842), the architect, who was Master of the Hospital from 1837 to 1842. (Most of Tatham's collection had been sold before he became Master.)

Merchant Taylors' Company, Merchant Taylors' Hall, 30 Threadneedle Street, London EC2R 8AY. Tel (01) 588 7606. Open by prior appointment with the Clerk.

The Merchant Taylors' Company is one of the oldest of the City livery companies, being sixth or seventh in order of precedence. Educational foundations supported by the company (with libraries) include St John's College, Oxford, and Merchant Taylors' School (qv). The archives of the company are separate from the library.

Company library Contains *c*1,000 v, including 1 incunabulum; 20 STC; 36 Wing; and 75 ESTC items. They include histories of London, and of the livery companies of Merchant Taylors' School, St John's and other institutions of interest to the company; also works by members of the company, the School, or St John's, and includes sermons, plays, literature etc. (Material not connected with the company was sold in 1980.)

Card cat (author and subject).

Merchant Taylors' School, Sandy Lodge, Northwood, Middlesex HA6 2HT. Tel (092 74) 23857. Open to academic researchers only by arrangement with the librarian.

Goad Library Merchant Taylors' School, founded in 1561, moved to its present site in 1933. The school library was founded in 1662 by John Goad (Headmaster 1661–81), although it incorporated several books at the school from the late 16th cent. John Goad saved many books when the school buildings were destroyed in the Fire of London, 1666. The Goad Library was formed as a separate collection *c*1960, comprising books listed in the 1826 school library catalogue, together with other rare books added subsequently—many presented by members of Merchant Taylors' Company or former pupils of the school. The collection includes *c*550 pre-1851 v; 1 incunabulum; 26 STC; 66 Wing; 83 16th cent; and 134 17th cent foreign works. Classical authors and works on theology are well represented, with some history, geography, literature, etc, and books by or about persons connected with the school. The collection is added to by donations. Of the 297 titles originally listed in the 1826 catalogue, 212 remain.

Ms cats 1662 and 1773 at Merchant Taylors' Hall; 1826 (printed) and 1876 (ms) cats at the school.

Typescript cat by Cormac Rigby, 'John Goad's Library. A history of the foundation and growth of the library at Merchant Taylors' School with a definitive catalogue', 1961.

R T D Sayle, 'Annals of Merchant Taylors' School Library', *Trans Biblio Soc* (4th ser) 15 (1934–5), p457-80 (with transcript of cat of 1662 and excerpts from the archives).

H B Wilson, *The history of Merchant Taylors' School...*, London, 1812, p341, 351-2, 459, 528, 993, 1030-1.

Merchant Taylors' School: its origin, history and present surroundings (ed W C Farr), Oxford, 1929, p72.

Merton Public Libraries. Open Mon, Tues, Thurs, Fri 9 am-7 pm; Wed, Sat 5 pm.

There are a few rare or early books among the collections below.

Mitcham Library, London Road, Mitcham, Surrey CR4 2YR. Tel (01) 648 4070.

Local History *c*1,500 items on cricket.

Morden Library, Morden Road, London SW19 3DA. Tel (01) 542 2842.

Local History *c*60 items on Horatio Nelson, Viscount Nelson (1758–1805).

Wimbledon Reference Library, Wimbledon Hill Road, London SW19 7NB. Tel (01) 946 7979.

Local History and English Topography, including extra-illustrated books on Surrey.

*c*400 items on tennis.

Methodist Church Overseas Division Library

All rare books from the library have been placed on deposit at the library of the School of Oriental and African Studies (qv).

Metropolitan Police, New Scotland Yard, Broadway, London SW1H 0BG. Tel (01) 230 1212 Ext 4398.

The Metropolitan Police Museum includes printed material from pre-1850. Much of the Museum's collection is stored and inaccessible until the completion of a recently instituted programme to make an inventory and form a catalogue. It is expected that this will be completed *c*1987.

Middle Temple Library, Honourable Society of Middle Temple, Middle Temple Lane, London EC4Y 9BT. Tel (01) 353 4303. Open (to non-members as a library of last resort, by prior arrangement only) Mon-Fri 9.30 am-7 pm. Photocopying.

(a) *General collection* Robert Ashley (see c below) bequeathed his library with an endowment for its upkeep after the earlier library had disappeared. The library has been enlarged by regular donations and purchases up to the present, when (after some disposals, eg to St Edmund's College, Ware) the pre-1851 printed books number at least 8,000, including 83 incunabula. In addition to British and foreign law, a wide variety of subjects is represented. There are medieval and later mss. General author catalogue on cards and printed catalogues overlap but are incomplete, many older works not being catalogued at all.

C E A Bedwell, *A catalogue of the printed books in the Library of... the Middle Temple alphabetically arranged, with an index of subjects*, 1914, 3 vols is still in print. Author cats of 1845, 1863 (with supplements 1868, 1877), and 1880 are less full and accurate, but *Catalogus librorum*, 1734 (with supplement 1766) is detailed and useful. Classified cat: *Bibliotheca illustris Medii Templi Societatis in ordinem iuxta rerum redacta*, 1700. Ms handlist of books printed 1500–25.

See J B Williamson, *The history of the Temple*, London, 1924, p381-4.

S G Turner, *The Middle Temple Library*, 1958, reprinted from *Law Times.*

R A Rye, *The students' guide to the libraries of London*, 3rd ed 1927, p357-60.

(b) *Pre-1701 tracts* are in 177 v, chiefly historical, political and legal; 73 unidentified v came from the Petyt donation (see e below). Contents of many v listed seriatim in *Catalogus*, 1734. Ms title list compiled in 1888 (with location marks). Most not in author cats.

(c) *Ashley, Robert* (1565–1641), literary translator, bequeathed his library of *c*5,000 v, probably including the Donne collection (d below), which became the nucleus of the general collection; ms handlist of 73 items identified as his, all non-legal.

(d) *Donne, John* (1573–1631), the poet. A collection of 71 v from his library, chiefly theology in Latin, among those sold at his death, came probably through the Ashley bequest (c).

J Sparrow, 'Donne's books in the Middle Temple', *Times Literary Supplement*, 29 July 1955, p436, and 5 Aug 1955, p451. G Keynes, *A bibliography of Dr John Donne*, 4th ed, Oxford, 1973, p258-79 and 379.

(e) *Petyt, William* (1636–1707). Treasurer of the Inner Temple, son of William Petyt of Skipton, gave 45 v in 1698, of which 43 have been identified (ms handlist) in the general collection, on a wide variety of subjects, in addition to 73 v in the tract collection (b above).

(f) *Eldon, John Scott, Earl of* (1751–1838), successively Solicitor General, Attorney General and Lord Chancellor, the prosecutor of Horne Tooke. A collection of 346 v from his library were deposited in 1934, and deal chiefly with law, but including religion, philosophy, and other subjects, and belong mostly to 18th-19th cent but with some 17th and late 16th cent material.

H A C Sturgess, *A catalogue of Lord Chancellor Eldon's law books from the Library at Encombe*, 1934, under authors. (op)

(g) *Phillimore, Walter G F, Baron Phillimore* (1845–1929), appeal judge and ecclesiastical and international jurist; his library was donated by his executors, and included *c*100 pre-1851 books, though most are later; merged in general collection, but recorded under authors in H A C Sturgess, *A catalogue of books chiefly on foreign and international law collected by the late Baron Phillimore of Shiplake, and presented to the Library... 1929*, 1930. (op)

(h) *Sowler, R S*, gave 7 oddments which are in *A descriptive list of a few rare...books presented...by Robert Scarr Sowler*, (1868).

Middlesex Hospital Medical School Library, 8 Riding House Street, London W1P 7PN. Tel (01) 636 8333 Ext 7479. Open Mon-Fri 9.30 am-10 pm (Aug 6 pm); Sat 9.30 am-12.30 pm to staff and students: to others by prior arrangement at the librarian's discretion. Photocopying.

The Hospital was opened (as the Middlesex Infirmary) in 1745: teaching facilities and a library were included at the outset. In 1835 a separate Medical School was inaugurated, with a library of its own from 1845, later becoming a school of the University of London. From 1955 the Library was officially called the Boldero Library, after Sir Harold Boldero (1889–1960), who had been Dean, now contains *c*18,000 v. Some of the books now in the library were donated by the Middlesex Hospital Medical and Philosophical Society, founded 1776 and still active.

Card cat (author and classified) including Middlesex Collection.

R M Nicholas, 'The development of medical libraries within the University of London' (MA Librarianship thesis, Univ of London 1976), p70-1.

J Hickling, 'The Medical School Library', *Middlesex Hospital Journ* 72 (1972), p63-5.

J Magonet, 'The Librarians', *Ibid* 63 (1963), p21-3.

Hilary St George Saunders, *The Middlesex Hospital 1745–1948*, London, Parrish, (1949).

Joan Bright, *The story of the Middlesex*, London, The Hospital, 1950.

Herbert C Thomson, *The story of the Middlesex Hospital Medical School*, London, Murray (1935).

Erasmus Wilson, *The history of the Middlesex Hospital during the first century...*, London, 1845.

Middlesex Collection Books by Middlesex Hospital and Medical School authors, predominantly those of the 19th cent, and works about them. There is a substantial collection of Sir John Bland-Sutton (1855–1936) the surgeon and friend of Kipling. *c*200 v.

Middlesex Polytechnic, Bounds Green Site Library, Bounds Green Road, Bounds Green, London N11 2NQ. Tel (01) 368 1299. Open Mon-Fri 9 am-5 pm to registered students, and others with genuine research need. Photocopying.

Silver Studio Collection *c*800 v associated with the major collection 1880–1963 from the London design studio for wallpaper and fabric designs. *c*50 books pre-1851. Deposited 1963.

Card cat.

Middlesex Polytechnic, Cat Hill Site Library, Cat Hill, East Barnet, Hertfordshire EN4 8HU. Tel (01) 440 7431. Open Mon-Fri 9 am-5 pm to registered students, and others with genuine research need. Photocopying. Information.

The library, formerly the library of Hornsey College of Art, has a general collection on art, of which *c*50 v are pre-1851.

Card and microfiche cat of whole collection.

Middlesex Polytechnic, Trent Park Site Library, Cockfosters Road, Enfield Chase, Hertfordshire EN4 0PS. Tel (01) 449 9691. Open Mon-Fri (term) 9 am-9 pm, (vacation) 9 am-5 pm to registered students, and others with genuine research needs.

The library was formerly that of Trent Park College of Education, with which the library of New College of Speech and Drama has been incorporated. The general collection includes 35 pre-1851 v, dealing mainly with the theatre or dramatic works.

Card and microfiche cat of whole collection.

Middlesex Yeomanry and Signals Historical Trust, Elmgrove Road, Harrow, Middlesex HA1 2QA. Tel (01) 427 6890. Open by appointment with the Curator, after written application in advance.

The Trust houses a collection of printed books, mss, letters and maps directly relating to the history from 1797 to 1982 of the Uxbridge Yeomanry, including Brighton Troop; the Middlesex Yeomanry Cavalry; the Middlesex Yeomanry Signals Regiment; and the Middlesex Yeomanry Airborne Formations. All pre-1851 printed items are in photocopy, but there are later privately printed histories, and instruction manuals of the two world wars, many of which are unique copies.

Midland Bank plc Head Office, Archivist's Library, Poultry (PO Box 125), London EC2P 2BX. Tel (01) 606 9911. Open Mon-Fri 9 am-5 pm on written application to the Archivist. Photocopying facilities.

The library has been assembled in the last few years from various offices in the bank. There are *c*150 v, including *c*25 pre-1851 (from 1762 onwards), mostly on banking and economics; histories of banks and other businesses; and miscellaneous pamphlets, mainly relating to the United States in the late 18th cent. Serials include *Banking Almanac* 1847–50, 1855–6, 1884.

Ministry of Agriculture, Fisheries and Food, Main Library, 3 Whitehall Place, London SW1A 2HH. Tel (01) 217 6266. Telex 889351. Open 9.30 am-5 pm Mon-Fri to the public; advanced notice preferred. Photocopying.

General Collection When the Board of Agriculture, founded in 1889, became the Ministry of Agriculture and Fisheries in 1919, the library was already of major importance. Now *c*160,000 v including *c*350 v pre-1851, mostly the works of famous British agriculturalists, and sets of county reports of the Board of Agriculture and Internal Improvement of 1793–1820, with some foreign books and works on sciences allied to agriculture.

Chronological list of early agricultural works in the Library of the Ministry of Agriculture and Fisheries, by G E Fussell, HMSO, 1930 (op).

Card cat.

Cotton, William Charles (1813–79), Vicar of Frodsham, Cheshire, bequeathed his library to his successors in the vicarage. A section on beekeeping was separated from the rest and deposited on loan at the Ministry in 1932; 220 books, mostly pre-1851 on bees and apiculture in all its aspects, in England, French, German, Italian, Dutch and Latin.

Ms list.

Cowan Memorial Collection of British Beekeepers' Association, named after their founder Thomas William Cowan (1840–1926), donated by them to the Ministry in 1929. 1800 v on bees and related subjects, of which 150 are pre-1851 (16th cent onwards).

Card cat. Included in *Chronological list.*

Punnet, Reginald Crundall (1875–1967), FRS, Prof of Genetics at Cambridge, who worked for the Board of Agriculture 1914–18. Collection bought 1960. 195 v (58 pre-1851, mostly after 1800) on poultry science and poultry genetics.

Card cat.

Ministry of Defence Library, Old War Office Building, Whitehall, London SW1A 2EU. Tel (01) 218 0016. Open Mon-Fri 10 am-4 pm by prior postal application to the librarian.

The Ministry of Defence libraries have been extensively reorganized since the former libraries of the Army, Navy and Air Force came under a common administration, though the Naval Historical Library remains separate. The present HQ library incorporates the older collections of the War Office Library (established 1683 but diminished by bomb damage) and part of the collection formerly at the Royal United Service Institution (diminished by a major theft, and partly dispersed to other libraries; there remains a collection of 19th-20th cent books on military history administered by MOD, for the use of members).

Army history The historical collection of *c*2,000 pre-1851 (16th cent onwards) is not segregated from the general library; it covers all military subjects, and is particularly strong in geographical and biographical aspects, including all Army lists from 1750 onwards. Drill books and manuals from mid-16th cent. Many illustrated books on British and foreign military uniforms.

Card cat and special index of references to all aspects of Army history.

Catalogue of the War Office Library, 1906–12: pt 1: authors; 2: official publications (including many foreign);

3: subjects. Supplemented by printed accessions lists to date, and *Supplement* 1916.

Classified catalogue of books in the Library of the War Department, 1864.

Catalogue of the Library of the Royal United Service Institution, 1908, 2 v; authors, subject, index (previous editions 1837; 1865; 1890).

D W King, 'War Office Library', *Library World* 61(720) (1960), p254-5.

Arthur S White, *A bibliography of regimental histories of the British army*, 1965 (based on MOD holdings).

Jack Burkett, *Government... library... services...*, 3rd ed, London, Lib Assoc 1974.

Moravian Archive Library, Moravian Church House, 3 Muswell Hill, London N10 3TJ. Tel (01) 883 3409. Open Mon-Fri 10 am-5 pm to bona fide research students and other researchers with written recommendation from authorized person or institution.

The library is the reference collection of the British Province of the Moravian Church and its overseas missions in Labrador and elsewhere. It contains over 10,000 v on Moravian history and theology built up, mainly at the former HQ of the Province at the Fetter Lane Church, since the introduction of this Protestant church to England in the early 18th cent and its recognition by an Act of 1749. It incorporates *c*2,000 v from the library of the Moravian Theological College at Fairfield, Manchester, received after its closure in 1958, and some material deposited by other Moravian provinces. There are many early works both in German and English, including Moravian pamphlets from 1552 onwards, and the Kralitz Bible of 1596. The collection of Moravian hymnology is very extensive, both in German and in English. There is a complete set of *Periodical Accounts* of missions from 1790 to the present (from 1972 entitled *Viewpoint from Distant Lands*), and despatches from the mission field. Extensive collections of diaries, and mss include correspondence of John and Charles Wesley with James Hutton and other Moravians.

Card cat (authors and titles).

W G Malin, *Catalogue of books relating to the history of the Unitas Fratrum or United Brethren... now generally known as the Moravian Church*, Philadelphia, 1881.

J E Hutton, *A short history of the Moravian Church*, London, 1895.

Independent libraries in England, London, 1977, p115-7.

Morden College Library and Archives, St German's Place, Kidbrooke, London SE3 0PW. Tel (01) 858 3365. Open by appointment with the librarian or the Archivist on Tues or Thurs only, after written application in advance.

Morden College was opened in 1700 in one of Wren's most delightful buildings, as a home for retired merchants in reduced circumstances, by Sir John Morden (1623–1708), a Levant merchant and property dealer. He bequeathed it to the Company of Merchants trading into the Levant (or Turkey Company). When, in 1825, the company was dissolved, the College was transferred to the East India Company, and soon afterwards to a board of trustees drawn from aldermen of the City of London. The object of its charity has been extended to the managerial classes as a whole and their unmarried daughters. The library for residents is now known as the Kelsall Library.

Morden College, a brief guide and handbook, 1955; 2nd ed 1960; 3rd ed 1966; 4th ed 1972 (list of muniments exhibited in 1st and 2nd eds is replaced in the 3rd and 4th eds by a list of 16 rare books in the library).

T Frank Green, *Morden College, Blackheath*, London Survey Committee, 1916, p20-1, 26-42.

A E Martin Harvey, *Sir John Morden and his College*, London, Morden Society, 1925.

Proceedings of the Levant Company respecting the surrender of their charters, 1825.

Reginald Saw, 'Charles Kelsall and his Library' (typescript, 1960; copy also at Greenwich Local History Library).

General The present library of *c*3,000 v has been built up almost entirely from donations and bequests, all of which are now merged in a general subject arrangement, most being from the Kelsall collection. The three following paragraphs indicate the course of acquisitions and dispersals in chronological order, with the catalogues of their respective periods.

There is at present no accurate catalogue, but in 1960 it was said that there were 9 English and 15 foreign pre-1701 books, and 289 English and 48 foreign of the 18th cent.

College Library, 1825–60 A library for residents was first established from a gift in 1825 of £50 (made by Henry Smith and Thomas Jackson of Camberwell) to buy books. This attracted numerous subsequent donations, the library of this period being mainly general literature and history. By 1854 there were 1,529 v.

Catalogue of books in the Library of Morden College, Blackheath 1835 (dictionary).

Ms cat 1841.

Catalogue, 1854 (dictionary).

Kelsall Bequest Charles Kelsall (1782–1857), dilettante and amateur architect bequeathed *c*2,500 books (including 300 inherited from his father Thomas Kelsall (1736–96) of Maze Hill, India merchant), with money to erect the building which still houses the library, known as the Kelsall Library. Kelsall, who was a cousin of Lady Clive of India, travelled the length and breadth of Europe and the Near East in search of classical purity in literature, art, architecture, and religion, building his library as he went, and from time to time publishing books and pamphlets where he happened to be (760 copies of these appeared with 230 items from his library in a sale, Sotheby 1 July 1831); at home he published some more major works, *Phantasm of an university* (1814), a *Letter from Athens* (1812) anticipating Byron's support for Greek independence, *Horae viaticae* (1836), and made several contributions to the *Pamphleteer*; his pseudonyms include Mela Britannicus, Laurea Arpinata, and Junius Minimus. About half his collection is in English, the remainder in French, Italian, Spanish, Latin and Greek, from 1565 onwards. Many are works of literature (especially 16th cent editions of the classics, and Italian); others are on travel, history, politics, art and architecture (including a first edition of Palladio). Most can be identified by a distinctive binding, some by his bookplate, the majority by Kelsall's ms inscription at the front of each volume recording date, place and price of acquisition, sometimes with earlier provenance, eg in a copy of a general history of the *Turks, Mongols and Tartars* (1730) bearing Gibbon's bookplate he notes that it was bought from the purchaser of Gibbon's library in Lausanne. A few of the annotations, eg on his own pamphlets, identify the printers and publishing history of anonymously printed editions; others contain notes on the author or critical comments.

Catalogue of the Library at Morden College, Blackheath, 1864.

Mela Britannicus (pseud of Kelsall), *Esquisse de mes travaux, de mes voyages, et de mes opinions*, Londres (ie Frankfurt), 1830 (autobiography which mentions some of his purchases).

H S Ashbee, *Mela Britannicus*, Paris, 1893 (repr from *Annuaire de la Societe des Amis de Livres)*.

David Watkin, *Thomas Hope 1769—1831 and the neoclassical idea*, London, John Murray, 1968, p70—82, 243-4.

C E Collyer, 'Notes relating to the Kelsall Library and Kelsall' (ms in college archives).

The post-Kelsall Library The building endowed by Kelsall was used to house both his own bequest and the earlier college library, but they were kept distinct. In 1864 there were altogether 1,878 works in 3,898 v; a large subsequent collection was built up, probably entirely from donations, and by 1907 there were 4,712 v. In *c*1955 there was a dispersal, when what the then librarian described as 'half a ton of duplicates and rubbish' was sold to dealers for a 'generous' £100, in addition to the sale of almost the whole of Kelsall's print collection. Probably only a small proportion of Kelsall's books were included in the dispersal, but much of the earlier college library seems to have gone, and the vast majority of the post-Kelsall acquisitions.

There is no list of the works sold, and no catalogue of the library subsequent to the dispersal. The Kelsall and other collections have been merged in a new subject arrangement which renders it difficult to find books from the 1907 catalogue.

C E Collyer, *Catalogue of books in the Kelsall Library*, London, 1907 (inaccurate, and without places or dates of publication).

Archives The records, ms and printed, of the college from its foundation include a collection of maps of estates owned by the college; the remnant of Kelsall's print collection, consisting of a few early 19th cent published volumes of plates; Kelsall's sketchbooks and architectural drawings, and the ms of his unpublished guide to Spain *c*1800, with a number of his published pamphlets (others will be found in the Library)—several are not in the British Library.

Museum of London, London Wall, London EC2Y 5HN. Tel (01) 600 3699. Library departments open by appointment only 10.30 am-5.30 pm. Limited photocopying.

The Museum was established jointly by the City Corporation, the Greater London Council, and the Department of Education and Science, and opened in 1976. It incorporates the collections of the former London Museum (whence most of the older printed material is derived) and of the Guildhall Museum. Early printed books and printed ephemera are included in the collections on display in the galleries, which follow a chronological sequence.

The Museum of London 1975 to 1979: the first report, 1980.

General Library

A general collection of working tools for museum staff, including the standard works on British archaeology, mostly modern; augmented by the gift of 700 books, with maps and other material, collected by Marjorie Blanche Honeybourne (1899—1977).

Card cats (author and subject).

London Collection *c*5,500 books of all periods, including the standard histories from 16th cent onwards, with maps and mss. (The printed ephemera have been transferred to the Ephemera Collection.) Some of the books are grangerized.

Included in author card cat of the general collection; subject cat separate.

London and Middlesex Archaeological Society Library Deposited 1979 after removal from Bishopsgate Institute, it contains *c*750 books on the history and topography of London, of which *c*30 are of the period 1701—1850. *c*100 sets of periodicals, mostly of provincial archaeological societies 1840 onwards.

London and Middlesex Archaeological Society, *Catalogue of Library at Bishopsgate Institute...*, 1972.

Bell, Walter George (1867—1942), journalist and historian, bequeathed a collection on the Plague and the Great Fire to the London Museum. *c*120 Wing; *c*20 ESTC; *c*10 1801—50.

Card cat (author and subject).

Tangye, Sir Richard (1833—1906) Collection Head of the Tangye engineering firm, Sir Richard amassed a collection of Cromwelliana of all kinds in the course of writing his study of the Cromwells, *The two Protectors*, 1899. In 1889 he had bought, prior to an advertised auction, the 'Cromwellian Museum' of a congregational minister of Hackney, John De Kewer Williams (1817–95), which included, *inter multa alia*, 142 rare books and pamphlets. By 1905 the museum, then removed to Tangye's retirement home in Newquay and a place of resort for scholars, had at least 800 printed works. In 1912 almost the whole collection was presented to the London Museum by his son Sir (Harold) Lincoln Tangye, Bart (1866–1935). It contains 8 STC items; *c*270 Wing; *c*55 ESTC; *c*70 English 1801–50; *c*150 foreign pre-1851 items, and mss and other material.

Card cat (author and subject).

Printed items also included in published cat.

The Cromwellian collection of mss, miniatures, medals etc in the possession of Sir Richard Tangye, Glendorgal, Newquay, Cornwall. Priv pr 1905. (Annotated copy in Library.)

Stuart J Reid, *Sir Richard Tangye*. London, 1911, p201-15.

E Walford, 'A Cromwellian museum', *Antiquarian Magazine* 4 (1883), p16-23, 80-4.

Catalogue of the Cromwellian Museum of the Rev J De Kewer Williams...which will be sold...Sotheby...6 May 1889 (1889).

Modern Department. Special Printed Collections Room

London theatre collection, built up from a continuing series of donations, including those of the actors John Martin-Harvey (1863–1944), and Robert North Green-Armytage (*d*1966). *c*1,400 plays (many being prompt copies). Playbills, *c*2,000 arranged by theatres; programmes, prospectuses for rebuilding theatres, and miscellaneous ephemera. Strong in 19th cent especially Sir Henry Irving (1838–1905); some ESTC items.

Card cat.

Juvenile drama 700 v bequeathed by Jonathan King (1836–1912), including plays, character sheets, scenery for toy theatres, etc. A remnant of an originally vast collection of printed ephemera formed by this stationer of Islington, most of which was destroyed by fire or dispersed. (Part of his collection of valentines and greetings cards is also here.)

An appreciation of the unique collections of the late Mr Jonathan King [*1912*].

A short description of a collection of tinsel pictures, theatrical plays (etc)...*presented to the London Museum by Jonathan King* [1912].

Frank Staff, *The valentine and its origins*, London, Lutterworth, 1969, p130-2.

Children's books *c*400, mostly modern, but including some 1701–1850, formed as an adjunct to the museum's toy collection, and being enlarged into a representative collection of juvenile book publishing of all periods.

Title card cat.

Suffragette Collection, formed at the museum of the Suffragette Fellowship in Cromwell Road, and incorporating the archives of the Women's Social and Political Union, afterwards the Women's Party. Donated to London Museum in 1950, and now being actively enlarged. *c*1,000 books and pamphlets, including a collection of early 19th cent works on the social position of women. Also ephemera, mss, photographs.

Miniature books *c*80 early 19th cent and 9 ESTC; chiefly almanacs. Mostly from the collection of Sir Hubert (Edward Henry) Jerningham (1842–1914) FSA, MP, former Governor of Mauritius. Supplemented by a collection of almanacs donated 1919 by Baron Emile Beaumont d'Erlanger (1866–1945?).

Pleasure gardens A collection of ephemera collected by Warwick William Wroth (1858–1911) FSA, numismatist of the British Museum and author of *The London Pleasure Gardens of the eighteenth century*, 1896.

Miscellaneous printed ephemera, including those formerly in the London collection. *c*3,000, including *c*1,000 pre-1851 items (*c*100 pre-1701). Includes broadsides and proclamations of 17th-18th cent, lottery tickets, trade cards, and a collection of Newgate.

Indexed by type.

National Army Museum Library, Royal Hospital Road, Chelsea, London SW3 4HT. Tel (01) 730 0717. Open Tues-Sat 10 am-4.30 pm (closed Sat of bank holiday weekends), to holders of readers' tickets, for which an application form must bear the written recommendation of an educational institution or employing organization or other appropriate authority. Photocopying, microfilming and photography; microform readers.

The Museum and its library were founded in 1960 and opened to the public in London in 1971. They illustrate the history of the British Army from 1485 to the present day, the Indian Army to 1947, and the armies of the Commonwealth countries to the dates of independence. The library contains *c*35,000 v of books, in addition to mss, prints, drawings and photographs.

Army lists (mainly on open access). Almost complete sets of all the officially published lists from 1754 onwards, and of Hart's lists from 1840 onwards.

Books The collection has been built up from gifts and bequests, supplemented by careful purchasing (eg at the Royal United Services Institute sale, Christie 25 Oct 1978). It contains *c*1,500 pre-1851 items (not segregated from the general collection, all on closed access), including *c*20 STC and *c*100 Wing. There are good collections of drill manuals from *c*1770 of regimental standing orders from *c*1770, and of regimental and campaign histories; military biography (especially from *c*1840), and books (mainly in English though including foreign authors) on the art of war as practised since 1485.

There are also many older books by British soldiers on subjects such as foreign topography and administration. Collections acquired include, among others, some holdings of the Oriental Club (qv) received in 1961; the library and papers of General Sir James Outram, Bt (1805–63), received in 1963; the bequest of books, papers and pictures of Cecil C P Lawson (*d*1967), military artist and author of *A history of the uniforms of the British Army* (including Rowlandson's *Loyal Volunteer Corps*, Ackermann 1799). In 1970 the collection of 90 illustrated books and 425 prints formed by Col Chichester de Windt Crookshank (1868–1958), author of *Prints of British military operations* (1921) was deposited on permanent loan by the British Museum.

Card cat (authors, biography, regiments and corps, topography, campaigns chronologically, and subjects alphabetically), including books and all other documentary materials.

Notable acquisitions listed in National Army Museum *Annual Report*.

Periodicals Collection *c*300 sets, including a very good regimental collection from *c*1870, general military science journals, with some general magazines (chiefly those useful for military biography and genealogy) from the late 18th cent.

Ministry of Defence, *Union catalogue of periodicals*, 1976; new ed in preparation.

National Book League, Book House, 45 East Hill, Wandsworth Town, London SW18 2QZ. Tel (01) 870 9055. Open Mon-Fri 9 am-5 pm by appointment with the Mark Longman Librarian or Children's Librarian.

The National Book Council was founded in 1925 to promote books and reading. In 1944 it was renamed National Book League. It is a charitable foundation financed partly by membership subscriptions (especially those of publishers) and fees, and partly by the Arts Council.

National Book League handbook, 1981 (gratis).

A **Mark Longman Library**

The library of the National Book Council was founded in 1929 when its Secretary Maurice Marston gave *c*200 books, and was often known as the Morrison Library. A separate collection, the Winterbottom Production Library (on book manufacture) was eventually incorporated into the main collection, which after 1944 was called the National Book League Library. In 1975 it was renamed after Mark Frederick Kerr Longman (1916–72), formerly Chairman of the League, and President of the Publishers' Association, who had given financial assistance to it. It now contains *c*9,000 v (in addition to mss and archives), on all aspects of bibliography, book production, and the printing and book trades. There are *c*25 pre-1851 books from the 16th cent onwards (with 2 incunable leaves) including several works on various subjects acquired as specimens of printing in addition to standard 18th and 19th cent bibliographical works, and Hansard *Typographia* 1825.

Card cat (authors).

Library guide.

Books about books: catalogue of the Library of the National Book League, 5th ed Cambridge, 1955 (op), and earlier eds 1933; 1935; 1938; 1944 and supplement 1948.

Many exhibition catalogues and readers' guides, but these often include books not in the Library.

Robin Myers, *The British book trade from Caxton to the present day*, London, Deutsch, 1973, 2 v, partly based on the library's collection.

Books: journal of the National Book League 40th anniversary number (Nov-Dec 1965), p194-226.

A Clarke in *Bookseller* 21 Aug 1976.

Linder Collection The works of Beatrix Potter (1866–1943) given in 1970 by Leslie Linder her biographer to trustees, who have deposited them in the Library: 280 original drawings and paintings; and 38 first and other early editions of her works.

The Linder collection of the works and drawings of Beatrix Potter, The League, 1971 (catalogue).

Peter Rabbit's 7th birthday exhibition: a souvenir catalogue, *Ibid*, 1976.

Becker Collection Books, letters and photographs relating to May Lamberton Becker (1873–1958) the American editor, reviewer and pioneer of children's books in the US, given by her daughter, the typographer Beatrice Warde (1900–69). Also a set of her Rainbow Classic editions of well-known children's books published by World Publishing Co of Cleveland and New York.

Periodicals A fine collection of runs of bibliographical, printing and book trade journals from 1852 onwards. In addition to *c*60 still current there are a very large number of older, including some very valuable, sets, eg *The Fleuron; Typographica; Curwen Press Newsletter*; many of these are kept with the archive collection.

Pérez Collection of bookplates Luis Marino Pérez (*b*1882), a Cuban sugar merchant, in 1965 through the British Council gave his collection of over 12,000 British bookplates *c*1610–*c*1910, arranged by broad periods and styles; it includes bookplates of famous men such as Dickens and Gladstone, and a number from institutions.

Card index of names.

Luis Marino Pérez, *British bookplates: description of a collection. . .*, Havana, 1962 (op).

Other Bookplate Collections In 1974 the American collector G T Banner gave a collection of bookplates from the libraries of American colleges, firms, and other institutions. In 1975 Richard Smart gave a collection of bookplates designed by the Australian artist Adrian Feint during the 1920s. A collection has also been formed in the Library of the entire work of the late Leo Wyatt (the designer of the League's own bookplates) which also includes book illustrations and titlepages.

Book Illustrations Collections A collection called Twentieth Century Engravers is being formed of the work of modern artists specializing in woodcuts and etchings, eg Joan Hassall and Reynolds Stone. A collection of the work of Diana Stanley, including the original artwork for *Worzel Gummidge* (the first Puffin imprint, 1941), and correspondence with Mary Norton concerning their collaboration in *The Borrowers*. A collection bequeathed by Arnrid Johnston, illustrator of later Puffin books, of the books she illustrated and her correspondence, with some original illustrations.

Weaver Collection of James Joyce The important collection of *c*200 editions of James Joyce (1882–1941), collected by Harriet Shaw Weaver (1876–1961), publisher of the *Egoist*, including a large number of the author's presentation copies to her, placed in the library in 1957, was sold in 1977 to the University of Tulsa, Oklahoma.

Harriet Weaver and James Joyce: the catalogue of the Harriet Shaw Weaver collection of James Joyce housed in the library of the National Book League (1976).

B **Centre for Children's Books**

In 1981 the Arts Council gave a special grant to create the Centre, which incorporates some collections previously begun by the League. Children's Reference Library, established in 1966, holds all British children's books published within the last two years, with some pre-publication copies.

Card cat (authors, titles, illustrators and translators).

Periodicals *c*40 periodicals containing reviews of children's books.

Signal Poetry Collection All British poetry books for children currently in print (being established 1982).

Reference Collection *c*600 v about children's literature.

Hans Christian Andersen Collection Given by the British section of the International Board on Books for Young People. British editions of Andersen's works, and a Danish album of Andersen documents.

Encyclopaedias A small but growing collection of encyclopaedias suitable for children.

St Nicholas Collection Eleanor Farjeon's set of *St Nicholas Magazine* 1883–85, 1887, 1890–1900, given by Grace Hogarth.

National Coal Board Headquarters Library, Hobart House, Grosvenor Place, London SW1X 7AE. Tel (01) 235 2020 Ext 34071. Telex 882161. Open Mon-Fri 9 am-5.15 pm to those with a genuine need to use the collection; outsiders should make an appointment in advance. Photocopying.

The main library has a collection of 40,000 books and pamphlets for the use of headquarters staff, which includes a historical collection of *c*500 v, including reports of Inspectors of Mines and of Royal Commissions on Mining; early mining journals; and some 18th and 19th cent mining and coal trade Acts; and 72 miscellaneous pre-1851 items. Some of the items were donated by the Institution of Mining Engineers when their library was removed from London; others by gift and purchase.

Included in microfilm cat of main library.

National Council for Civil Liberties, Civil Liberties Library, 21 Tabard Street, London SE1 4LA. Tel (01) 403 3888. Open Mon-Fri 9 am-5 pm by appointment after written application to the Research Officer. Photocopier available.

The Council and its library (now financed by the Cobden Trust) were founded in 1934. The archives and press cuttings collections are deposited in Hull University Library. The library now contains *c*1,500 books and 2,500 pamphlets. In addition to a complete set of NCCL publications since 1934, there is a collection of fascist and anti-fascist, and anti-British publications; *c*100 items of the 1930s, of which some are not available elsewhere, and some anti-semitic material.

National Council for Voluntary Organisations, Information Department Library, 26 Bedford Square, London WC1B 3HU. Tel (01) 636 4066. Open Mon-Fri 9 am-5 pm by appointment after written application to the librarian. Photocopying available.

The Council was founded in 1919 as the National Council of Social Service, whose main function has been to co-ordinate and promote the raising of money by charities, changing to its present name in 1981; in 1938 it absorbed the British Institute of Social Service and its library, which was added to the Council's existing collection. Since 1979 the library has been organized as part of a separate Information Department.

The Library now has *c*10,000 v, of which probably between 10 and 50 are pre-1851 books, with later material, on the development of the voluntary movement in the 19th cent; mostly general and specific accounts of charities.

Card cat (author and subject) of whole library.

Guide to library services and resources, 1981.

M Barnett, *Voluntary social action*, London, NCSS, 1976 (£2.50; a history of the Council, with a few references to the Library).

National Gallery Library, Trafalgar Square, London WC2N 5DN. Tel (01) 839 3321. Open Mon-Fri 10 am-5 pm by appointment with the librarian. Photocopying facilities.

The Library includes:

Eastlake, Sir Charles Lock (1793–1865, Director

1855–65), his collection bought 1869 and slightly enlarged; chiefly Greek and Roman antiquities; guidebooks; history of painting, architecture and other arts; monographs on artists; cats of public and private collections. *c*2,000 items almost entirely pre-1851; *c*10 STC; *c*30 Wing; *c*100 ESTC; *c*300 English 1801–50; *c*15 16th cent; *c*100 17th cent; *c*500 18th cent; *c*1,000 1801–50 foreign (mainly Italian, with some French and a few Spanish).

Catalogue of the Eastlake Library in the National Gallery, 1872. Library has copy with additions to 1904. Author and classified card cats.

Sale catalogues *c*3,500 items.
Index by owners' names.

National Liberal Club, 1 Whitehall Place, London SW1A 2HE. The Club was founded with Gladstone as President in 1882, and has always been associated with the Liberal Party. The Gladstone Library was sold to the University of Bristol in 1977 (qv), but the general library, *c*20,000 v, of which no particulars are available, remains at the club for the exclusive use of members. Strong in English politics; English and German literature.

H Thorogood, 'London clubs and their libraries', *Library Review* 13 (1951–2), p495-8.

National Maritime Museum Library, Romney Road, Greenwich, London SE10 9NF. Tel (01) 858 4422 Ext 264. Open Mon-Sat 10 am-5 pm (closed 1-2 pm Mon and Sat) to holders of readers' tickets; apply to Head of Readers' Services. Photocopying and microfilming facilities.

The Museum was opened in 1937 as the National Museum for Maritime History, including Royal Navy, merchant shipping, fisheries, pleasure craft, cartography, nautical astronomy and marine archaeology. The library is administered together with a major collection of mss in the Department of Printed Books and Manuscripts.

Sir J Caird, 'A museum in the making', *Syren and Shipping* 2, Jan 1935, and offprint (2 pages).

G Callender, 'The National Maritime Museum, Greenwich', *Museums Journal* 37 (1937), p45-56.

Guide to the manuscripts in the National Maritime Museum, London, Mansell, 1977–80, 2 v.

General The library contains *c*45,000 books, 45,000 pamphlets, and 20,000 v of periodicals and other serials. The primary focus of the collection is the maritime history of Great Britain in war and peace, including naval architecture, trade and exploration, navigation and nautical astronomy, fisheries, piracy and cartography. There is also a considerable amount of foreign material in these subjects, and some on the topography of maritime countries. There are over 20,000 pre-1851 items, including *c*20 incunabula. The donated collections listed below are not kept separate, but merged in the general library.

Author card cat (incomplete) of pre-1977 material being superseded by a computerized cat (author/title/series and classified) from which it is hoped eventually to produce separate lists of the major donations as identified from the provenances recorded in the books.

Catalogue of the Library, London HMSO, 1968–76 (discontinued, includes items not held): v 1, *Voyages and travel*; v 2, *Biography*; v 3, *Atalases*; v 4, *Piracy and privateering*; v 5 pt 1, *Naval history to 1815*.

Information Index (for ships, persons, places, events and general maritime subjects) being transferred from cards to computer.

Anderson Collection Given by Roger Charles Anderson (1883–1976) LittD, editor of the *Mariners Mirror* and President of the Society for Nautical Research, from 1937 onwards, the main collection was donated in 1970. It contains *c*1,300 books, including many rare works on naval history and naval architecture.

Included in computer cat, but not yet separately listed.

Caird Collection Sir James Caird, Bt, of Glenfarquhar (1864–1954), shipowner, was the main benefactor of the Museum, and gave material regularly from its inception, including books, atlases, charts, mss, paintings and museum objects of all kinds.

Typescript list of the books.

The Caird Collection of maritime antiquities; including the collection made by Sir James Caird...the Wyllie Collection, the Mercury Collection and the Macpherson Collection..., priv pr 1934?–1937, v 1-4 and Supplement to v 1; a printed accessions list with prices paid by Caird and many provenances; the general books section was never printed.

Gosse Collection A collection of *c*250 books on piracy and privateering, many pre-1851, formed by Philip Gosse (1879–1959) MD MRCS LRCP, and bought by Caird, and given by him to the Museum in 1939.

Included in computer cat and in *Catalogue* v 4.

Macpherson Collection Collected by Arthur George Holdsworth Macpherson (1873–1942), SNR RNVR, bought by Caird in 1929 and given to the Museum. *c*12,000 items, including 312 atlases, 96 books 1555–1902, also prints and drawings on the maritime history of the English-speaking peoples (also charts, instruments and paintings).

The Caird Collection, v 3, p81-136.

Maskelyne Collection Collected by Nevil Maskelyne (1732–1811), Astronomer Royal from 1765, given by his descendant, J E Arnold-Forster, in 1952; 133 pamphlets, papers and books on astronomy, mathematics, navigation and kindred subjects.

Included in computer cat, but not yet separately listed.

Miscellaneous donations Other collections acquired include those formed by Charles Napier Robinson

(1849–1936), Commander RN, editor of *Brassey*; Capt Henry Daniel; the Reynolds polar collection; the Styping collection on flags and funnels; and the Bowen collection of nautical press cuttings. These are almost entirely material printed after 1850.

National Museum of Labour History, Library, Limehouse Town Hall, Commercial Road, London E14 7HA. Tel (01) 515 3229. Open Mon-Sat 9.30 am-5 pm, after written letter of application agreeing to become an associate member of the museum (subscription £1 pa). Photocopying; microfilm readers.

In 1966 the Trade Union, Labour, Co-operative Democratic History Society (until that year called the Socialist History Society) acquired the Southgate collection and established the Walter Southgate Trust, with the object of establishing a museum, library and study centre of trade unionism and the labour movement. The museum eventually opened, in makeshift premises, in 1975, after the acquisition of the Syd Marks collection, the Socialist Sunday Schools collection, and the National Council of Labour Colleges collection, which have been incorporated together with innumerable smaller collections. The museum is now financed mainly by the Labour Party, several trade unions, and the TUC.

Caroline Gibbs, 'The National Museum of Labour History', *History Workshop* no 10 (1980), p191-3.

P Johnson, 'What's left...memorabilia of the labour movement', *Art and Antiques* 24(5) (24 July 1976), p24-7.

Visual History (published twice yearly by the Society).

Museum Display Collection This includes some of the rarest printed material, eg Southgate's copy of *Rights of man* and Clio Rickman's *Life of Paine* 1819, ephemera such as a unique enrolment form of the Grand National Consolidated Trade Union, copies of *Black Dwarf* and early newspapers, the magazine of the London Corresponding Society, notices announcing meetings, etc.

National Museum of Labour History, (1976) (select guide to exhibits).

Archive Collections A great variety of collections, which include much printed material such as annual reports, notices and reports of meetings, etc, relating to several branches of the Labour Party, and a number of trade unions (including AEU, ASRS, NUAW, NUPE, Stevedores, etc), and the Socialist Sunday Schools. Combined archive from several unions relating to the Grunwick dispute 1976–8.

Sources in British political history 1900–1951, 1975, v 1, p181-2.

National Council of British Socialist Sunday Schools, *A catalogue of...material of the Socialist Sunday School and later the Socialist Fellowship (1894–1971), presented to the Trade Union, Labour and Co-operative History Society for safe keeping at their museum at Limehouse* [c1974?].

The Times, 6 Oct 1978, p6 (Grunwick archive).

Library (general) The library now contains c2,000 v which are catalogued and accessible. There are also at least ten times that number in store, unsorted and completely inaccessible to readers. They relate to the labour movement, radicalism, socialism, co-operation, trade unions, etc, during the last 200 years. Collections already catalogued include material on slavery, the game laws, Napoleon, the Luddites, Queen Caroline (1768–1821), the Cato Street conspiracy, the Duke of Yorke/Mrs Clarke scandal, the agricultural riots of 1830, David Ricardo (1772–1823), mechanics' institutes, the Poor Laws, the Factory Acts, etc.

Card cat (classified) including general, Southgate and Fry Collections. There is no author cat.

Southgate Collection The personal library of Walter Southgate (*b* c1889), a founder-member of the Labour Party and trade unionist active 1918–39. c550 v of books, and over 600 pamphlets. Most of the books are late-19th and 20th cent works on socialism, trade unionism, etc. A few pre-1851 books include Glasse *Art of cookery* and Shelley *Essays* 1845 (with contemporary circulation list of the Dover Book Society).

Typescript list.

Fry Collection c200 items from the personal collection of Henry B Fry of Reigate, founder of the Socialist History Society, and the museum's first Secretary. Mainly socialist pamphlets 1918–39, but with some early radical literature, including Paine *Common sense* 1752 (on display).

Special Printed Collections A collection of material connected with *The Clarion*, edited by Robert Blatchford (1851–1943), the Clarion League, and the Clarion Cycling Club; Plebs League publications; National Council of Labour Colleges collection; newspapers published during the General Strike 1926; 3 books belonging to James Maxton; journals from women's and immigrant groups.

National Physical Laboratory, Queens Road, Teddington, Middlesex TW11 0LW. Tel (01) 977 3222. Open (on prior application in writing to the librarian) Mon-Wed 9 am-5.30 pm, Thurs 9 am-5 pm, Fri 9 am-4.30 pm. Photocopying by arrangement.

The library of the Laboratory, which was founded in 1900 as a government research station, contains a small collection of books by English, French and German scientists on physics, chemistry and mathematics. 37 of these are pre-1851, and appear mostly to have been donated by members of the Laboratory's staff before 1930. There are also a few volumes of periodicals. There is a typescript list of the pre-1851 books.

National Portrait Gallery Library, 15 Carlton House Terrace, London SW1Y 5AH. Tel (01) 930 1552. Open Mon-Fri 10 am-5 pm by appointment with the librarian. Photocopying.

The nucleus of the library was the bequest of part of his private collection kept at the Gallery by its first Director, Sir George Scharf, KCB (1820–95). It has been built up subsequently into a large working library on portraiture, iconography, costume, heraldry, techniques of engraving and painting, and aesthetics. There are also collections of sale and exhibition cats from the 18th cent onwards. *c*30,000 v including *c*2,600 pre-1851 books, including 20 STC, *c*50 Wing; *c*2,100 English 1701–1850, and *c*400 foreign. (Also *c*20,000 engraved portraits in Macdonald collection.)

Dictionary card cat. Exhibition and auction cats indexed by year and name of collection (auction cats also in Fritz Lugt *Repertorium*).

National Register of Archives, Royal Commission on Historical Manuscripts, Quality House, Quality Court, Chancery Lane, London WC1. Tel (01) 242 1198. Open to the public Mon-Fri 9.30 am-5 pm.

The Royal Commission on Historical Manuscripts, better known as the Historical Mss Commission, was established at the instigation of George Harris (1809–90) in 1869 as a branch of the Public Record Office; it became independent in 1958. Its function is to locate and catalogue mss and papers (which may include printed material) in the possession of private individuals and unofficial institutions, and do what it can to ensure their preservation and public accessibility. In 1945 the lists and indexes were placed in the hands of a separate department, the National Register of Archives for England and Wales. There is a public search room containing a complete file of reports and lists of the Commission and of the NRA, with a short title index to these; an index of persons of major importance (DNB status) appearing in the lists; a selective subject index (useful for tracing certain categories of printed material, in that it includes, for instance, a heading Newspapers); and a topographical index. Most of these indexes are kept up to date in computer files. Most, but not all, of the reports of the National Register of Archives for Scotland (based at the Scottish Record Office) are also held.

'The Centenary of the Royal Commission on Historical Manuscripts', *Journ Soc Archivists* 3(9) (Apr 1969), p441-66, especially 'National Register of Archives', p452-62, and 'The use of the resources', p462-9.

R A Story, 'Indexing archives', *Indexer* 5(4) (Autumn 1967).

National Secular Society, 698 Holloway Road, Upper Holloway, London N19 3NL. Tel (01) 272 1266.

The Society's Library is deposited at the Bishopsgate Institute (see under Bishopsgate Institute Library).

National Society for the Prevention of Cruelty to Children Library, 1 Riding House Street, London W1P 8AA. Tel (01) 580 8812. Open Mon-Fri 9 am-5 pm by appointment on application to the librarian. Photocopier available.

The London Society for the Prevention of Cruelty to Children, founded in 1884, was enlarged into the National Society in 1889. In 1910 the formation of an international library (as part of the Bureau of Child Welfare) was begun with the intention of making it the core of an international society, but this project was cut short by the war in 1914. The library, then made up of 670 v and a press cuttings collection, became a dormant collection at the Society's offices, to which little was added, and from which about half the books were dispersed. A new library was established in 1974 as part of the National Advisory Centre on the Battered Child. When the Centre closed in 1981, the library moved to the Society's headquarters to form part of the National Advisory and Consultancy Service. The residue of the earlier library has been incorporated, mostly into the Historical Collection.

Guide to the NSPCC Library and its services, 1982 (gratis).

Library Bulletin 1979– (monthly).

Annual Report includes paragraphs on the library.

General The general collection contains books, pamphlets and periodicals on child abuse, family violence, child psychology, psychotherapeutics, and social work. Since 1974 nearly all British and American material has been acquired, with a selection from other countries.

Card cat (author and classified).

Subject index to periodicals.

Historical Collection and Archives In addition to what remains of the Society's Archives, there are *c*100 v of pre-1914 printed works on poverty, the Poor Law, and social welfare; child abuse and children's employment, mainly after 1880, but with a handful earlier, eg *The Courier* 14 Oct 1816 containing Astley Cooper's evidence to the Commons on children employed in factories. Publications of the NSPCC and related and similar foreign Societies. A collection of material by and about Benjamin Waugh (1839–1908) founder and first Director of the Society, his books and pamphlets, the *Sunday Magazine* 1882–93 edited by him, with a file of press cuttings, articles, obituaries, etc 1902–68.

Card cat (author and classified) separate from current library cat is in course of compilation.

National Turf Protection Society, 23 Pembridge Square, London W2 4DR. Tel (01) 229 1461. Open on application to the Secretary.

The Society maintains a collection of three million documents, ms and printed, on horse racing built up since its foundation in 1902.

National Westminster Bank plc, Head Office, Archivist's Library, 41 Lothbury, London EC2P 2BP. Tel (01) 726 1000. Open Mon-Fri 9 am-5 pm by appointment on written application to the Archivist. Photocopying facilities.

The National Westminster Bank is the product of a long series of mergers. The books in the Archivist's Library are older works from the collections of the County Bank, the London and Westminster Bank, the National Provincial Bank and the District Bank. They total *c*200 v, including directories of banks from 1838, and of Manchester from 1838; a few books on economics, trade and commercial law from 1651; 6 v of pamphlets (*c*80) published 1832–57, including presentation copies to, and items by, James William Gilbart (1794–1863), apparently collected by him while General Manager of the London and Westminster Bank. Also *c*10 books by Gilbart, some privately printed. Reports and other documents printed for internal distribution in the banks in the 19th cent. Histories of constituent and other banks.

Card cat (author and subject) being compiled.

Naval and Military Club, 94 Piccadilly, London W1V 0BR.

This club was founded in 1862 and has a library which is for the exclusive use of members. Many of the rare books from its collection have been transferred to the National Army Museum Library (qv).

New Church Library. General Conference of the New Church, Swedenborg House, 20 Bloomsbury Way, London WC1A 2TH. Tel (01) 242 8574. Open by appointment to bona fide scholars on written application to the librarian.

The General Conference maintains a Library and Archives under the supervision of its Library and Documents Committee. The Church was established in 1789 and its Archives have accumulated continuously from that date. A Reference Library was established in 1913. *c*2,000 books, 600 bound v of periodicals and mss. A considerable proportion is pre-1851. Works by and about Emanuel Swedenborg and his teachings and the history of the New Church (mainly in Great Britain) from mid-18th cent onwards.

Card cat of books and periodicals. Loose-leaf index of pamphlets.

Newham Public Libraries. Stratford Reference Library, Local Studies Library, Water Lane, Romford Road, Stratford, London E15 4NJ. Tel (01) 534 4545 Ext 334 (except after 5 pm and on Sat 534 1305). Open Mon, Tues, Thurs, Fri 9.30 am-7 pm; Wed, Sat 5pm by appointment only.

The local history collection of the former County Borough of West Ham, to which the much smaller collection from East Ham was added in 1965, covers the Borough of Newham intensively, and Essex and Greater London to a limited extent. It consists of *c*6,000 books and 3,500 pamphlets, of which *c*150 are pre-1851 works (including a few STC and Wing items) relating to Essex; *c*25 pre-1851 directories; a volume of cuttings and broadsheets 1650–1900 relating to Wanstead House, Wanstead, Essex, and its occupants, collected by Hiram Stead, together with an annotated copy of the sale catalogue, 1822; a collection on James Keir Hardie (1856–1915) MP formed by Herbert Bryan; a collection on Gerard Manley Hopkins (1844–89) (a more important Hopkins collection is accessible nearby by appointment with the Provincial Archivist at the Friary, 160 The Grove, Stratford E15 1NS); general literature by Essex authors; sermons preached in Essex churches; and a few rare books not relating to Essex, from the general collections of the Reference Library. The Borough Archives are also held here.

Card cat (author and alphabetical subject).

Guide to the Local Studies Library, [1978].

North London Collegiate School, Canons Drive, Edgware, Middlesex HA8 7RJ. Open by appointment only after prior written application to the Archivist.

The School was founded in 1850 in Camden Town by Frances Mary Buss (1827–94), the pioneer of girls' education. In 1939 it moved to its fourth home in Canons Park in the expanded mid-Georgian mansion after the estate was sold in 1929 (without the Canons books, which were sold in 1932, mostly to the Huntington Library and a private collector). The School Library has few rare books, apart from an unopened copy in boards of *Sense and sensibility* 1813 3 v (2nd ed), being now a working library. The Archives, on the other hand, contain much interesting printed and ms material on the history of the School, the education of girls, and the role of women.

The library includes works illustrated by Robert William Buss (1804–75), the father of the School's founder who was a historical and theatrical painter, illustrator and engraver, pupil of George Clint (1770–1854). Specimens of his book illustrations include the first two parts of the first issue of *Pickwick papers*, with two illustrations by him commissioned after the sudden death of Seymour; 2 Harrison Ainsworth novels; Frances Trollope *The widow married* London 1840 3 v; his own *English graphic satire* 1874; and several other books.

Norwegian Seamen's Church, 1 Albion Street, Rotherhithe, London SE16 1JB. Tel (01) 237 5587. Accessible by appointment with the Pastor who acts as librarian.

2,000 Norwegian books, mainly on Norwegian history, and some fiction; 19th and 20th cent.

Office of Population Censuses and Surveys Library, St Catherine's House, 10 Kingsway, London WC2B 6JB. Tel (01) 242 0262 Ext 2236. Open Mon-Fri 9 am-4 pm to the public (prior notice preferred). Photocopying.

In 1837 the General Register Office was established to act as a central registry of births, marriages and deaths. The Office was formed in 1970 with the merger of the General Register Office (incorporating the Census Office) and the Social Survey Department.

The Library contains *c*45,000 items, of which *c*500 are pre-1851, on demography, statistics (vital, population and medical), epidemiology, public health, dissenting churches. Holds the only accessible complete set of all published reports for each population census since 1801. Annual reports of the General Register Office from 1837. *Tables of the revenue, population, commerce etc of the United Kingdom* from 1820. Census of Ireland from 1821. Annual reports of the Poor Law Commissioners from 1831. Historic works on vital statistics and on the movement to improve public health, 17th-19th cent by John Graunt (1620–74), John Snow (1813–58), William Farr (1807–83) FRS, Florence Nightingale (1820–1910), and others. Henry Eyre on the Holt waters (1731); William Langham's *Garden of Health* (1579).

OPCS Library (brief guide, *c*1979). Office of Population Censuses and Surveys.

Population and health statistics in England and Wales, The Office, 1980. (Includes a history of the General Register Office.)

Card cat. Classified shelflist.

Oratory Library, Brompton Oratory, Brompton Road, London SW7 2RW. Tel (01) 589 4811. Application must be made in writing to the Father Librarian for an appointment; admission is granted only to see material which is not available in other London libraries. Photocopying by special arrangement.

The Congregation of the Oratory of St Philip Neri (the first of the order of secular priests known as the Oratorians) was established in Rome in 1575. The London Oratory (second in England to Birmingham) was established in the City in 1850, and moved to Brompton in 1854 (hence it is now popularly known as the Brompton Oratory). The Library is the private collection of the Fathers of the Congregation and was mainly assembled between 1854 and 1900 by Fathers and benefactors. It contains *c*18,000 books, mostly 1550–1900, and periodicals in 50,000 v and *c*2,000 pamphlets (mostly 19th cent). There are 78 incunabula. Mainly theology, Church history, hagiology, liturgy and canon law. Major benefactions, except the Lewis library, are dispersed by subject throughout the library.

Separate cats of incunabula and pamphlets.

Dictionary card cat of the other books (author entries for most; subject entries for some).

Ms lists of certain special collections.

[R Kerr], 'The Oratory in London' a long serial history in *The Oratory Parish Magazine* 1 (1921)–12 (1932); library described in 5 (1925), p45-6, 83-5, and see also 1 (1921), p111; 4 (1924), p481-2, 519, 557; 5 (1925), p45-6; 7 (1927), p181.

The London Oratory 1849–1949, London, Catholic Truth Society, (1949), p13, 24.

R A Rye, *Students' Guide*, 1927, p417-20.

Oratorian Literature Collection A major collection of books about the Oratorians, both in England and abroad, including much ms material. Also a comprehensive collection on the life of their founder St Philip Neri (1515–95) of Florence.

Oratory Parish Magazine 8 (1928), p91-3.

Antrobus, Ignatius (1837–1903) Superior and Father Librarian for 25 years, historian and translator of Pastor's *Lives of the Popes*, bequeathed over 5,000 v, mainly on European church history, and strong in 16th and 17th cent works.

Oratory Parish Magazine 10 (1930), p73-5.

Benedictines Collection The collection includes the folio editions issued by the Congregation of St Maur and others, and a very fine general collection of Maurist literature.

Dalgairns, John Dobree (1818–76) of Guernsey, Faber's successor as Superior, and a distinguished member of the Metaphysical Society, bequeathed his collection which reflects mainly his interest in the history of philosophical speculation.

English recusant literature A substantial collection, including *c*80 STC.

A F Allison, 'Early English books and the London Oratory: a supplement to STC', *The Library* 5th ser 2(2/3) (1947), p95-107. Also in Allison and Rogers.

Faber, Frederick William (1814–63), first Superior, friend of Wordsworth and Newman, former Anglican priest converted 1845, bequeathed his library, collected mainly after 1845, including a large collection of mystical theology and devotional works, including many rare continental treatises on the spiritual life, and the mss of his own works. *c*3,000 v.

Ronald Champman, *Father Faber*, London, Burns Oats, (1961), p291-321.

John Edward Bowden, *The life and letters of Frederick William Faber*, London, 1869, p412-3, 469-93.

'The Oratory in London' in *Oratorian Parish Magazine* 5(9) (Sept 1925) – 6(1) (Jan 1926).

Jansenism The best collection in London, including the rare periodical *Nouvelles ecclesiastiques* 1729–89.

Knox, Thomas Francis (1822–82), canonist and ecclesiastical historian, was in 1874 appointed by the Sacred Congregation of Rites to research the English martyrs under Henry VIII and Elizabeth. During this work he accumulated a large collection of early printed and ms material covering a rather wider field of 16th cent church history in England and abroad, which was acquired by the Oratory.

Lewis, David (1814–95), former Anglican curate to Newman at Oxford, lawyer and translator of classic devotional works, bequeathed his very fine library, housed now in a separate room, but included in the general catalogue, of *c*10,000 v. Strong on canon law, French history of 16th and 17th cent and Scotist theology; with many works on St Teresa of Avila, St John of the Cross, and the Spanish mystics; controversial works, incunabula.

Shipley, Orby (1832–1916), ecclesiastical historian, liturgiologist, and hymnologist, an Anglican clergyman converted in 1878, bequeathed a substantial collection strong in early and rare books covering a wide field in liturgy, hymnology and the history of religious devotion and practice.

Order of St John Library, St John's Gate, Clerkenwell, London EC1M 4DA. Tel (01) 253 6644. Open Mon-Fri 10 am-5.30 pm by appointment only. Photocopying.

The Order of St John Library belongs to the Grand Priory in the British Realm of the most venerable order of the Hospital of St John of Jerusalem, now a British Order of chivalry under the Sovereign and separated from the Sovereign Military Order of Malta, (which is now known as the Knights of Malta, founded *c*1200 at Jerusalem as an Augustinian order of hospitallers, moved to Rhodes in 1310, Malta 1530, and dispersed in 1798). The Priory of the English Branch of the original Order was established at Clerkenwell *c*1150, dissolved in 1540, revived in 1556, but from 1558 was inactive; revived in 1831 by Anglicans helped by the French Knights but repudiated in 1858 by the head of the Order in Rome. Since it received its Royal Charter in 1888 it has been mainly associated with the St John Ambulance Brigade which has been extended throughout the Commonwealth, and it is open to Christians of all denominations, including Roman Catholics.

Order of St John Library Consists of a small collection assembled from 1838, was formally organized into a library in 1858, and has been enlarged by purchase and donation to *c*3,500 books and *c*1,200 pamphlets. It is now the most important collection outside Malta on the history of the Knights of Malta, and includes besides works about the Order and the Crusades in general, a large collection of its own publications, including *c*65 of its Acta and *c*80 v of *Relazioni*; *c*40 items on the topography of Malta and the Eastern Mediterranean; and 50 on heraldry. Collection on the English Order; 7 incunabula; 45 16th cent items; *c*10 STC and Wing; 50 v of mss bound, and *c*2,000 other ms items; they include the Rhodes Missal of 1503 which is richly illuminated and was used at admission ceremonies.

Card cat (authors, titles, subjects). Previous cats in ms *c*1858 and *c*1865, printed 1893 and 1895.

Catalogue of the Grand Priory of the Order of the Hospital of St John of Jerusalem by B H Soulsby; recording only 438 items).

H W Fincham, *Notes on the history of the Library and the Museum of the venerable Order of the Hospital of St John of Jerusalem*, 1945 (op).

Oriental Club, 11 Stratford Place, Oxford Street, London W1N 0ES. Library open to members only.

The Club was founded in 1824 as a meeting place for those who had resided abroad, serving as a London base for those employed abroad, and a meeting place for them in retirement. A library was built up from the beginning from donations by members, who were expected to give copies of the books they had published. Major benefactions of the 19th cent included the large classical library of the Hon Mountstuart Elphinstone (1779–1859), Governor of Bombay. Much of the library was sold (Knight, Frank and Rutley, 18 Dec 1961), and some books remain, and the collection has subsequently been enlarged by purchase. The collection, now *c*5,000 v was formerly strongest on India, but equal weight is now given to other Oriental countries.

Catalogue by John Rutherford, 1874.

Alexander F Baillie, *The Oriental Club and Hanover Square*, London, 1901, p55, 76, 274-9.

Annals of the Oriental Club 1824–1858 ed S Wheeler, 1925, pvii-xv.

R A Rye, *Students' guide to the libraries of London* 3rd ed 1927, p48.

Denys Forrest, *The Oriental: life story of a West End Club*, 2nd ed, London, Batsford, 1979, p103-8, 213, 244-5.

Fergus Innes, *The Oriental Club Library* (nd).

G Evans, 'The Oriental Club', *Antique Collector* 42 (1971–2), p231-41.

Anthony Lejeune, *Gentlemen's Clubs*, 1979, p174-9.

Oxford University Press London Library, Ely House, 37 Dover Street, London W1X 4AH. Tel (01) 629 8494. Open by appointment only Mon-Fri 9 am-5.30 pm.

The Reference Library of books published by the Press includes a few pre-1851 works such as Clarendon's *History of the Rebellion*, but the future of the library is in doubt (the main collection is at Oxford).

Palestine Exploration Fund Library, 2 Hinde Mews, Marylebone Lane, London W1M 5RH. Library is

for the use of subscribers only; enquiries from non-members about its contents should be addressed to the Fund's Honorary Librarian, Department of Western Asiatic Antiquities, British Museum, London WC1B 3DG. Tel (01) 636 1555 Ext 382.

The Palestine Exploration Fund was founded in 1865 to give support to the archaeological investigation of the Holy Land. It has built up a library of *c*2,000 v on the archaeology, palaeography and history of the area within the modern states of Syria, the Lebanon, Jordan and Israel. Though the library is predominantly of modern works, there is a substantial rare books collection.

Passmore Edwards Museum Library, Romford Road, Stratford, London E15 4LZ. Tel (01) 534 4545 Ext 376. Open by appointment only, Mon-Fri 10 am-6 pm, Sat 5 pm, following written application to the Curator, allowing at least one week for reply.

The library began from donations at the foundation, in 1880, of the Essex Field Club at Buckhurst Hill, transferred with the club's other collections to the Chelmsford Museum in 1893. The collections moved to the present building, erected by the Borough of West Ham and J Passmore Edwards in 1900, where they were officially named the Essex Museum of Natural History in the Passmore Edwards Museum, and while remaining the club's property, were maintained partly at the Borough's expense. In 1956, ownership, control and financing were transferred to an independent board of governors, though staffing is now provided by the London Borough of Newham.

Percy Thompson, *A short history of the Essex Field Club, 1880–1930*, 1930 (Essex Field Club special memoirs v 7).

M Christy, 'The Essex Field Club and its work', in Essex Field Club *Yearbook and calendar for 1911–12*, p5-15.

Essex Collection A collection on the former county of Essex, *c*1,500 printed items, of which *c*100 are pre-1851, including *c*40 pre-1701, together with mss and archives. It contains standard histories of the county and of the towns within it, and works on subjects treated in the local context, especially archaeology and geology. Directories, poll books, road books, specimens of local printing, pamphlets and ephemera. The collection is being actively expanded by the acquisition of early printed and ms material in addition to modern.

Card cat (author and alphabetical subject superseding dictionary).

General Collection A collection of *c*6,000 items which include *c*100 pre-1851, which are chiefly on geology, palaeontology, botany, zoology (chiefly birds), and archaeology (chiefly of England). This collection includes Essex authors, eg John Ray (1627–1705) who is represented by 7 early editions.

Card cat (author and classified).

Percival David Foundation of Chinese Art, 53 Gordon Square, London WC1H 0PD. Tel (01) 387 3909. Open Mon-Fri 10.30 am-4.30 pm, if and when staffing permits, to registered students of the University of London attending related courses, and to others on written application, stating purpose, at the discretion of the staff.

The personal library of Sir Percival (Victor) David, 2nd Bart (1892–1964) who, in 1951, presented it, together with his collection of Chinese ceramics, to the University of London, who assigned it to the School of Oriental and African Studies. It contains *c*3,000 works, both European and Chinese, on the history of Chinese art, mainly ceramics, including a collection of 37 rare books. Additions are mainly by donation, and are limited to ceramics.

Card cat.

M Medley, The Library of the Percival David Foundation, *Libraries Bull (University of London)*, no 21 (1981), p5-6.

Pewterers' Company, Pewterers' Hall, Oat Lane, London EC2V 7DE. Tel (01) 606 9363. Open by appointment with the Clerk.

Most of the Company's archives to 1900 (probably including printed material) are deposited in the Guildhall Library Department of Manuscripts, but there are some boxes of unsorted records at the Hall. There is a small library at the Hall, which includes 6 pre-1851 books on London, beginning with the Stow *Survey* 1720.

A short history of the worshipful Company of Pewterers' of London and a catalogue of pewterware in its possession (1968).

Pharmaceutical Society of Great Britain Library, 1 Lambeth High Street, London SE1 7JN. Tel (01) 735 9141. Open Mon-Fri 9 am-5 pm to fellows, members and students of the Society; also to bona fide researchers. Photocopying.

The Society and the Library were founded in 1841. *c*68,000 v.

Historical Collection The collection has been built up from the gifts by members, and now contains *c*1,525 pre-1851 v (2 incunabula, 59 16th cent books and 277 17th cent), herbals; London, Edinburgh and Dublin Pharmacopoeias from 1618; books on alchemy, chemistry, *materia medica*, pharmacy and pharmacology; with prints, caricatures, and ms letters. 550 v (chiefly illustrated botanical works which came from the library of Daniel Hanbury FRS (1825–75), one of the Society's founders, which was given by his brother Thomas in 1892.

Card cat (author and classified).

Separate author cat of pre-1860 books.

Catalogue of the Library of the Pharmaceutical Society, 10th ed, 1911 (dictionary, incomplete).

R G Todd, 'Treasures of the Society's historical collection', *Chemist and Druggist* 208 (5095) (3 Dec 1977), p844.

Pharmaceutical Society *Calendar* lists additions 1934-5—1963-4.

Poetry Society Library, 21 Earls Court Square, London SW5 9BY. Closed to all except members.

This once fine library has been much reduced by sales, which have included most of the rare books; there is no longer a librarian. There are still several thousand volumes of, and on, English poetry of all periods.

Polish Institute and Sikorski Museum Library, 26 Pont Street, London SW1X 0AB. Tel (01) 584 7399. Open Tues 2-8 pm; Wed-Fri 10 am-4 pm on application to the librarian. Photocopying by arrangement.

The Institute is an amalgamation of the Polish Research Centre, founded by the emigré Polish government in 1939, and the Sikorski Historical Institute, established by private interests in 1945, combined in 1965. Both institutions had accumulated large archives from World War II in addition to libraries, chiefly those of the exiled government (now housed at 20 Princes Gate).

Instytut Polski i Muzeum im Gen Sikorskiego, 1970.

The Polish Research Centre: a record of Anglo-Polish achievement, 1939—57 (1957).

Books There are over 30,000 books, chiefly on Poland, and to a more limited extent, other East European countries, in the 20th cent, but donations cover a much wider field of Polish history, including many 19th cent and a few 18th cent works.

Card cat (author and subject).

Periodicals c2,000 titles, almost all Polish, including the Polish wartime underground press, and publications of the Polish armed forces.

Polish Library, The Polish Centre, 238-46 King Street, Hammersmith, London W6 0RF. Tel (01) 741 0474. Open by arrangement with the librarian, Mon, Wed 10 am-8 pm; Tues, Fri 5 pm; Thurs, Sat 1 pm.

The Polish Library in London was established in 1943 by merging two collections which had been built up since 1941 by the Polish government in exile. It was originally a centre for books in Polish published outside Poland from 1939, but soon added current and historical collections in all languages relating to Poland. In 1945 the government transferred it to the Polish Research Centre, and from 1948 it was the Polish University College Library until the college ceased in 1953. It then became the Polish Library, controlled since 1967 by the Polish Social and Cultural Association for the Polish community in the United Kingdom.

M L Danilewicz, 'The Polish Library in London', *Solanus* no 1 (Nov 1966), p4-9.

——*Biblioteka Polska w Londinie*, 1959.

Annual Reports in Polish in *Komunikat Informacyjny POSK* (1967—9), then in *Wiadomosci POSK*.

The Polish Library 1942—1979, 1979.

Polish Research Centre, *Apel na Polski Fundusz Bibliotekzny*, 1959.

General The library has over 100,000 works, of which 70 per cent are in Polish, relating to Polish literature, culture, history, arts and social science subjects.

Author cat on cards.

Historical Collection c5,000 pre-1939 items, of which a substantial number are pre-1851.

M L Danilewicz and Z Jagodzinski, *Katalog Wystawy Zbioriow Historycznych*, 1970.

Conrad Collection A collection built up in the library from c1944 of works by and about Joseph Conrad (1857—1924). Over 400 editions, about half being editions of his writings: these include 25 English first editions; many other early editions in English or Polish, and translations into a variety of languages.

Jadwiga Nowak, *The Joseph Conrad collection in the Polish Library in London: catalogue*, nos 1-399, the Library, 1970.

Joseph Conrad, 1857—1924, 1956 (exhibition cat, compiled by Janina Zabielska which includes some items not held in the Polish Library).

Lanckoroński Foundation Collection This is the residue of the Lanckoroński Library from Rozdol in Poland, and Vienna, much of which was dispersed in two world wars, deposited in 1968—9 by the Lanckoroński Foundation of Fribourg in Switzerland. It contains c2,000 v and 550 etchings and engravings, of the 16th-20th cent. Strong in Polish law, 18th cent political journalism and almanacs; 18th and 19th cent military administration and Polish literature, with many examples of books printed by Michel Gröll (1722—98), and a complete set of the Polish classics edited by Count Tadeusz Antoni Mostowski (1766—1842). The library was founded by Count Maciej Lanckoroński, Palatin of Braclaw (d1771) and his educationist son Count Antoni Lanckoroński (1760—1830). The latter's son Kazimierz, the economist, added a collection on Poland under Austrian rule. Around 1900, major additions were made by Count Karol Lanckoroński (1848—1933), the archaeologist, author and explorer.

M L Danilewicz, 'The Lanckoroński Foundation collection', *Solanus* no 5 (March 1960), p11-2.

Mieczyslaw Paszkiewick, *Jacek Malczewski w Azji Mniejszej*, 1972 (exhibition cat with reproductions, also published in English as *Jacek Malczewski in Asia Minor and in Rozdól*).

Ami Lanckoroński, *Alle meine Bücher*, 1970.

Polish emigré publications c15,000 works published by Poles outside Poland since 1 September 1939, world-wide, the most comprehensive collection in existence.

Catalogue of periodicals in Polish or relating to Poland and other Slavonic countries published outside Poland since September 1st 1939, 2nd ed 1971.

Bibliography of books in Polish or relating to Poland, published outside Poland since September 1st 1939, 1953– (also a quarterly list).

Bibliography of works by Polish scholars and scientists, published outside Poland in languages other than Polish, 1964– .

Josef Garlinsky, *Polska prasa podziemna w zbiorach londynskich 1939–45*, London, 1962.

Bookplates c39,000 bookplates of Polish and other collectors.

Pollock's Toy Museum, 1 Scala Street, London W1P 1LT. Tel (01) 636 3452.

The collection originated with J K Green, the publisher of juvenile theatrical prints and plays; his plates were acquired by John Redington (1819–76) of Shoreditch, and passed to his son-in-law Benjamin Pollock (*d*1937), who reprinted the plays, and then to Miss Louisa Pollock. The collection was bombed, but has been re-established by trustees, and the exhibits include toys, especially toy theatres and children's books.

Pollock's Toy Museum and toy theatres (c1960).

Frederic Boase, *Modern English biography*, v 6, 1921, col 457 (detailed history under Redington).

Polytechnic of the South Bank Library, Faculty of the Built Environment Library, 202-230 Wandsworth Road, London SW8 2JZ. Tel (01) 928 8989 Ext 7214. Open Mon-Fri (term) 9 am-9 pm (vac) 9.30 am-5 pm, on written application in advance. Photocopier, microform reader available.

The Brixton School of Building (till 1943 officially named the London County Council School of Building) was established in 1904 and built up a substantial library, including rare books, mainly by donation. In 1970 its professional courses became affiliated to the new Polytechnic of the South Bank, whose Faculty of Construction Technology and Design was created in 1973, and occupied the present building in Wandsworth Road, now renamed and incorporating the bulk of the School's library. It contains over 54,000 v of books, together with periodicals on building, engineering, architecture, interior design, and the decorative and fine arts; also town planning, estate management, and the related social sciences, with audio-visual and material samples libraries.

On-line VDU author and subject cats include book, periodical and slide holdings.

Reserved Stack Collection Contains c1,250 v, mainly British books of successive architectural movements, culminating in a strong collection of the period 1880–1910, with many fine illustrated books. The earliest book is Stow's *Survey of London* 1633, and there is a 17th cent account of Lemercier's château at Richelieu. The 18th cent books include the Palladian works of Isaac Ware (*d*1766), Giacomo Leoni (1686–1746), and a complete *Vitruvius Britannicus*. The 19th cent is represented by two sets of the works of John Britton (1771–1857), *True principles* 1841, and works by John Ruskin (1819–1900), Owen Jones (1809–74), among others. The *fin de siecle* works include those by Richard Norman Shaw (1831–1912), John Belcher (1841–1914), etc. An important aspect of the collection is the set of building manuals, technical instructors and architectural pattern-books from the 18th cent to the present day. All the building crafts and architectural skills are represented.

A detailed cat is being prepared for publication; also in main cat.

Port of London Authority Library and Archives, 1 Thomas More Street, London E1 9AZ. Tel (01) 488 4883. Open to persons engaged in bona fide research, by appointment only with the librarian, Mon-Fri; plenty of notice is recommended, and it should be noted that the library is likely to move to a new location at about the end of 1984. Photocopier available.

The Port of London was established as a statutory corporation in 1909 to take over the companies which then owned and operated docks on the River Thames, and also to become the navigation authority for the river below Teddington Lock (previously in the hands of the Conservators of the Thames). The authority took over the ms and printed archives of the Navigation Committee from 1770, and of the absorbed dock companies from the beginning of the 19th cent, together with various accumulated collections of books. These were all incorporated into a reference library which was formally established in 1928. Until 1939 the book collection was very actively enlarged by purchase and donations to include not only the history of the docks, but a wide variety of related subjects. In addition to printed books, the library has large collections of maps (including Rocque's Survey and some others in atlas form), photographs (deposited at the Museum of London), paintings and prints. It is intended, when the proposed Dock Museum is completed, to place the entire library on deposit there.

Bertram Stewart, *The Library and Picture Collection of the Port of London Authority*, London, Richards Press, 1955, p3-17.

General The collection of printed books and pamphlets comprises over 10,000 v, of which at least 100 are pre-1851, from the 17th cent onwards. In addition to London and the London docks, the subjects include the Thames to its source; the history of ships, shipping, and individual shipping lines; other British ports; pilots for the Thames, the English Channel, and foreign waters, including some scarce 19th and 20th cent editions.

London There is a very extensive general collection on London, which includes many of the standard histories of the 18th cent and a few earlier, eg William Gough *Londinum triumphans* (1682), and also some rare 19th cent works. The main emphasis is the topography of the riparian boroughs.

London Docks The printed material includes rule books etc of the dock companies, several issues of the series of tracts printed 1793–1800 by William Vaughan (1752–1840) FRS, and others advocating dock construction in London; the series of government reports on this subject issued 1793–1802, and innumerable later official publications, collections of relevant Acts and over 100 v of newspaper cuttings from *c*1870 onwards.

Post Office

A **Headquarters Library**

St Martins-le-Grand. This reference library, established in 1937, had 70,000 v by 1968, but all rare and most other books from it have been dispersed, partly to the Archives, the Museum, and British Telecom (qv).

B **Post Office Archives Reference Library**

Post Office Headquarters, St Martins-le-Grand, London EC1. Tel (01) 432 1234. Open Mon-Fri 10 am-4.30 pm on application to the Archivist. Photocopying facilities.

The archives of the General Post Office were first organized as the Muniments Room (later known as the Records Room) in the late 19th cent, and have always included books and other printed material. Some books formerly held, have been transferred to the Museum and to British Telecom. There are *c*2,000 v, including 1 STC; 4 Wing; and 10 ESTC items.

Typescript subject lists each chronological; foreign material by country.

A guide to the Post Office Records (1969) (gratis).

History of Postal Services Collection Works on the establishment of postal services include *A discourse briefly showing the true state and title of the Comptroller or Post Master General* (1637?); *A full and cleare answer to a false and scandalous paper,* (1642?); and *An ordinance touching the office of postage of letters,* 1654; all other pre-1701 material is in photocopy. There are many works on postal reform in the late 18th and early 19th cent, and a pamphlet collection which includes 3 v on the Chalmers/Hill controversy 1887–91 over the invention of the penny post. The collection on post-1850 history is comprehensive, embracing Post Office publications; directories and almanacs; road books; foreign posts; Post Office Savings Banks; telecommunication.

C **National Postal Museum**

London Chief Post Office, King Edward Building, King Edward Street, London EC1A 1LP. Tel (01) 432 3851. Open Mon-Thurs 10 am-4 pm, on application to the Curator by letter or phone. Photocopying facilities.

The Museum was established in 1965 with finance and a superb stamp collection given by R M Phillips, a property developer, and houses three collections:

Museum Display Collection The whole of the R M Phillips collection of British stamps is on display, with a collection of printed documents and ephemera, mostly from his collection (with many unique copies), on the early development of the penny post and of stamps 1837–40; also later material.

Museum Reference Library A collection of mainly modern works on philately and postal history, with that part of the Phillips collection not on display, most other books before 1900 being from the HQ Library; works on the history of postage and the Post Office from 1844 onwards, and Post Office publications from 1854.

Postal History Society Collection A collection given (*c*1970) by the Society relating to the operations of the Mercantile Committee which agitated for Post Office reform in 1838, with material on this subject added from other sources. One volume contains all 70 printed items issued by the Committee in 1838, including circulars, pamphlets, the *Post Circular* with a specimen of no 1 containing an article by Rowland Hill not in the published version. Copies of *Scenes at Windsor Castle* [by Henry Cole] 1838 as issued 'with *Nicholas Nickleby* and separately, and other Cole items. Another set of the papers of the Committee formed by Sir George Gerard De Hochepied Larpent, Bart (1786–1855) lacks 9 items, but includes 14 others to 1844 which were not publications of the Committee, mostly by Hill.

Press Club Library, International Press Centre, 76 Shoe Lane, London EC4A 3JB. Tel (01) 353 2644. Open to members; others should write to the librarian for an appointment.

The Club was founded for working journalists in 1882 by George Augustus Sala (1828–96), but its membership is now slightly wider. A reference library consisting mainly of donations from members of their own works on a wide variety of subjects was first systematically organized in 1921; rare books are limited to the collections below.

Early Newspaper Collection A collection of *c*550 specimens of typical newspapers in the English language from the 17th cent to *c*1930, mostly published in London.

It incorporates the collection of Henry Sell the advertising agent, and contains 76 corantos and newsbooks to 1660 published in London; *c*100 London papers 1660–1760; *c*100 of 1760 until the abolition of Stamp Duty in 1855; and *c*75 on 1855–1930. *c*35 Scottish and Irish papers; 12 early magazines; 20 sport and stage papers; and 13 specimens of the dominion press before 1900; 16 curiosities, such as parodies, and Berthold's *Handkerchief* printed on cotton in 1831 to avoid Stamp Duty. There are also 12 Proclamations 1642–1705 regulating the press, 2 Acts, and 9 miscellaneous ephemera 1768–1841.

The evolution of the English newspaper... as illustrated by the catalogue of the Press Club collection, 1935 (an enlarged version of *Catalogue of an exhibition illustrating the history of the English newspaper*, 1932).

War newspapers A collection of specimens of papers produced throughout the world by the allied forces in World War II, amounting to 209 titles.

Catalogue of London Press Club Library on journalism, vol 3: collection of the newspapers, magazines, news bulletins, wall newspapers etc printed, typed or handwritten by or for the Forces... during the 1939–45 War... by... Andrew Stewart [1948].

Toye Vise, *A staircase in Fleet Street* (1939).

Anthony Lejeune, *Gentlemen's clubs, 1979*, p194-9.

The Press Club 1882–1942... souvenir, 1942.

'The Printer's Devil' Public House, 98 Fetter Lane, London EC4A 1EP. Tel (01) 242 2771. Open to customers during licensing hours.

In 1953–5 Whitbread and Co rebuilt one of their older pubs and renamed it 'The Printer's Devil' in honour of the principal trade of the surrounding area. They furnished it for the reopening by acquiring a collection of *c*500 specimens of pre-20th cent printing and some related objects to be framed and line the walls. The collection was arranged and catalogued by historians of printing, but has subsequently been reorganized for a new layout of bars which has caused the disappearance of some of the former exhibits. The Saloon Bar contains pages of letterpress printing, including leaves from incunabula and other fine books, titlepages, 18th cent type specimen sheets, broadside ballads, and advertisements for and illustrations of early composing machines. The stairs from the Saloon Bar to the Wine Bar contain a collection of engraved and woodcut portraits of famous printers from the 15th to the 19th cent. The Sports Page Bar contains illustrations and related material in colour and monochrome, including the work of Bewick, Blake, Gould, and Beardsley. The Wine Bar on the first floor contains a largely new collection of mostly 20th cent theatrical and cinema posters.

Whitbread and Co Ltd, *Catalogue of the collection of items at The Printer's Devil, Fetter Lane, London EC4, illustrating the history of printing...*, [1955] with essays 'The printed page' by A Lloyd-Taylor and 'The printed illustration' by John Lewis.

Property Services Agency (Department of the Environment), Whitgift Centre, Croydon, Surrey CR9 3LY. Tel (01) 686 8710 Ext 4520. Open Mon-Fri 9.30 am-5 pm (after prior application) to research students requiring material not available elsewhere.

PSA Library Historical Collection The agency (known as PSA) reorganized from the Ministry of Public Building and Works in 1972 is an integrated part of the Department of the Environment and is responsible for the provision and maintenance of the buildings and constructions required by the State. Central control of the Royal building dates from 1878, and a library was established at the Office of Works *c*1860; volumes from this library form the present historical collection. (The documents and drawings passed to the Public Record Office *c*1952; the Mayson-Beeton collection on London to the Directorate of Ancient Monuments.) It contains *c*5,000 v, of which *c*100 are pre-1851, covering architectural and building history, especially in London.

In card cat of PSA main library. J Burkett, *Government... library... services*, 3rd ed London, Library Assoc, 1974, p84-5.

The History of the King's Works ed H M Colvin, HMSO, 1963– .

Public Record Office. Each branch is open Mon-Fri 9.30 am-5 pm to holders of readers' tickets, for which a letter of recommendation from a person of standing is essential. Photocopies and microfilms may be ordered.

General Documents of departments of the Crown (but not those of Parliament) were formerly kept at the Tower of London. In 1801 the Record Commission was set up to look after them and publish the more important series. In 1838 the Commission was superseded by the Public Record Office, with much wider responsibilities, but still under the administration of the Master of the Rolls. The records (ms and printed), libraries, reading rooms, and staff are divided between the original repository at Chancery Lane, and a new repository at Kew. The extent to which printed documents are preserved in the public records varies greatly in different classes (from some of which it has been removed at various times), but overall the quantity is colossal; it is not limited in scope (including incunabula for instance) and is by no means confined to material officially issued. Much general printed material seems to have crept into the files by accident, and much else by design, particularly in the case of material thought to be possibly subversive or to infringe laws relating to revenue duties whether a prosecution resulted or not.

V H Galbraith, *An introduction to the use of the public records*, Oxford, Clarendon Press, 1934, repr 1971.

Guide to the contents of the Public Record Office, London HMSO, 1963–8, 3 v (v 1-2 op): see below. Earlier guides by F S Thomas 1853, S R Scargill-Bird 1891, 1896 and 1908, and M S Giuseppi 1923–4 are more detailed in parts and occasionally still useful.

A comprehensive series of lists and indexes, with general card indexes to these, is available in the reading rooms at Chancery Lane and Kew; some have been published by HMSO (see *List of record publications*, gratis), others by the List and Index Society whose HQ is in the Chancery Lane Branch.

Card index to documents that have appeared in print.

Typescript lists of classes at Chancery Lane and at Kew.

New accessions from 1966 onwards are recorded in the *Annual Report of the Keeper of Public Records.*

A-B Chancery Lane Branch, Chancery Lane, London WC2A 1LR. Tel (01) 405 0741.

A **Public Records**

The branch houses all the records described in v 1 of the *Guide* (except those of Stationers' Hall), mostly legal (both judicial and curial), and those of the older administrative departments such as the Palatinates. Other records now here are those of the State Paper Office (see *Guide* v 2, p1-14); of legal administration; the Probate and Census records, and certain special collections and gifts and deposits.

1 Gazettes A collection of foreign gazettes extracted from State Papers Foreign now forms a separate group (SP 116-) including many rare Dutch and German, with a number of unique items from *c*1660 onwards. Some gazettes remain in their original bundles among the State Papers Foreign from 1700, and Colonial Office papers (CO; at Kew). Seized gazettes, mostly 1750–1800, are among the Miscellaneous Papers of the High Court of Admiralty (HCA); these are strong in French, French colonial, and French colonial revolutionary gazettes.

D Paisey, 'German newspapers of the 17th cent in the Public Record Office, London', *Gutenberg Jahrbuch*, 1978, p168-72.

List of German gazettes available in Reading Room.

Calendars of all gazettes, and other printed items from State Paper Office and certain other collections (whether segregated or not) on cards in Office Library may be seen by appointment.

2 Pamphlets Material formerly extracted from State Papers Domestic and State Papers Foreign, *c*1540–1800 has now been returned to these classes. They include a very large collection of French *arrets* of the 18th cent. There are a few among HCA 30, mostly French and Dutch.

Included in index (see A1 above).

Printed material in State Papers of George I and II noted in typescript calendars.

3 Proclamations Some proclamations are scattered among the State Paper Office papers and treated with the pamphlets (see A1 above), but most are separate collections: 1625–1804 in SP 45; others in collections at Kew, especially the Privy Council Office (PC) and Colonial Office (CO) (see index to *Guide* v 2).

B **Office Library**

A library established originally by the Record Commission, now serving the staff both of the PRO and the Historical Mss Commission, not open to holders of PRO Reading Room tickets, except by appointment after written application to the librarian. It contains (including the branch library at Kew) over 100,000 v on subjects mainly related to English history and the public records.

1 General Collection The collection covers mostly British history, topography, and law, with some material on continental history, particularly the subjects and periods associated with the Public Records at Chancery Lane. There are *c*1,300 pre-1800 items.

Card cat (dictionary).

2 Watson Collection The library of George Watson, genealogist, on French genealogy, several thousand volumes, donated *c*1935. The collection is not normally accessible, but specific items may sometimes be made available.

List.

C-D Kew Branch, Ruskin Avenue, Kew, Richmond, Surrey TW9 4DU. Tel (01) 876 3444.

C **Public Records**

The branch houses the records of modern administrative departments of the Crown, and to a limited extent of nationalized industries and similar bodies, including all the records described in v 2 and 3 of the *Guide* (except State Paper Office records). Nearly all the classes include some printed documents, most a substantial number. The records of the Foreign Office (FO) and the Colonial Office (CO) are probably the most outstanding in this respect; the latter includes for many territories the most complete sets in existence of official publications from the 17th-19th cent. Home Office papers (HO) also include much 18th cent material (little of which is noted in the printed calendars), especially ephemera of the period of agrarian unrest 1796–1800, while the Inland Revenue records (IR) also include some important 19th cent specimens of newspapers and other publications infringing the Stamp Acts.

D **Office Library**

The library is a branch of that at Chancery Lane, and (with the specific exceptions below) the same restrictions on access apply.

1 General Collection A collection of books relating to

subjects connected with the Public Records at Kew, mainly after 1800.

Card index (dictionary).

2 Parliamentary Papers The collection of Parliamentary Papers from 1801 onwards is comprehensive; the pre-1801 collection is fragmentary. All papers are available on request to readers using Public Records in the main Reading Rooms.

3 British Transport Historical Records Library (available to readers in the main Reading Room). This collection was originally the working library associated with the archives of the British Transport Commission set up in 1947 to incorporate the records of its antecedent railway companies and other transport undertakings such as canals from the 17th cent onwards which had been merged in them. These archives were transferred to the care of the PRO as the British Transport Historical Records (RAIL), and the library with them, but the latter is now less active than the archives. It includes much of the printed material originally in the archives, and includes extensive collections of early prospectuses, timetables, surveyors' reports, etc in addition to pamphlets and standard monographs on railway history. Many of the specialist railway journals are held from 1835 onwards, in a separate collection (ZPER).

Card cat.

George Ottley, *Railway history*, 1973 (Library Assoc Reference, Special and Information Section).

Subject guides to library resources no 1, p30-1.

L C Johnson, 'Historical records of the British Transport Commission', *Journ Transport History* 1 (1953–4), p82-96.

'British Transport Commission archives; work since 1953', 5 (1961–2), p159-65.

'British Transport Historical Records Department', *Archives* 6 (1964), p163-71.

On material in other collections, especially the Railway Dept of the Board of Trade, see D B Wardle, 'Sources for the history of railways at the Public Record Office', *Journ Transport History*, 2 (1956), p214-34.

'Punch', 23-27 Tudor Street, London EC4Y 0HR. Tel (01) 583 9199. Open Mon-Fri 9 am-5 pm by appointment only, on application to the library.

Punch has been published since 1841, but the present library seems to date from the 1940s, now 1,000 v, of which at least 50 are pre-1851, but it incorporates material preserved in the editorial offices from early years, and many books from the collection of Alexander Meyrick Broadley (1847–1916) the journalist, and from the paper's publishers Bradbury Agnew.

No cat, but partly alphabetically arranged by author on the shelves.

R G G Price, *A history of Punch*, London, 1957 (op), p346-52 'Source'; many of the books described as being in the Managing Director's Office are now in the library.

History of Punch The collection begins with the author's extra-illustrated copy of A Bunn, *A word with Punch* 1847, with many ephemera to support his hostility. Among the more notable items are M H Spielmann *History of Punch*, 1895, the extra-illustrated copy of P E Spielmann; and *Mr Punch, his origin and career* (1870?) bound by Riviere with two later items, and extra-illustrated with illustrations, proof-pulls and letters for presentation to Joseph Swain the paper's engraver.

Books by contributions to 'Punch' A large mainly 20th cent collection, but with many earlier items such as J Leech, *Follies of the year* 1844–64, and books by R Doyle and G A A Beckett, mostly from the library of Bradbury Agnew, some having originally been their publications.

'Punch' publications A substantial but probably incomplete collection, including *Punch's Pocket Book* 1843–81.

Serials Complete set of *Punch*, in Chairman's Office, from 1841, complete with all wrappers, advertisement pages and supplements; *The Times* reprint of 1900, and the earlier reprint. A variety of British and foreign imitations of *Punch*.

Queen Elizabeth College Library, Campden Hill Road, Kensington, London W8 7AH. Tel (01) 937 5411. Open Mon-Fri 9.30 am-9.15 pm (term, 7.30 Fri), 5.30 (vac) on written application to the librarian.

The College was founded in 1908 as the Home Sciences Dept of King's College for Women. In 1915 it became an independent school of the University of London called King's College of Household and Social Science. It changed to its present name in 1953.

General The library contains *c*40,000 v, mainly on chemistry and the biological sciences. There is a large special collection on food science, which includes a Historical Collection on food, including cookery, with some pre-1851 books.

Queen Mary College Library, 327 Mile End Road, London E1 4NS. Tel (01) 980 4811 Ext 472. Open Mon-Fri 9.15 am-9 pm (5 pm in Christmas and Summer vac); (closed one week at Christmas and Easter) to members of the University; to others by appointment following written application.

The New Philosophical Institute, also known as the Philosophical Institution, was established at Mile End in 1840 by John Thomas Barber Beaumont (1774–1841), founder of the County Fire Office, and continued after his death under a trust administered by the Drapers' Company as Beaumont's Philosophical Institute, which was replaced in 1884 by the People's Palace for East London. Its lectures were replaced by the People's Palace

Technical Schools in 1887, renamed in 1896 the East London Technical College; in 1905 East London College; and in 1934 Queen Mary College; it has been a school of the University of London from 1907. The library of the People's Palace was transferred in 1901 to the adjacent public library (see Tower Hamlets Public Libraries), except for technical and scientific books which were kept in a small students' library in the lecture rooms. In 1921 this collection became the nucleus of a new college library. After the acquisition of a few major collections until 1930, it has been built up as a working library for teaching and research.

George Godwin, *Queen Mary College*, 1939, p105-11.

W S Beaumont, *A brief account of the Beaumont Trust and its founder...*, London, 1887.

The archives of the People's Palace for 1885–*c*1925 are in the library.

General Collection Rare books are derived from the early years of the library's growth, mostly from the few special collections below which are now merged in the general classified arrangement. Of the 220,000 v in the library, there are *c*2,500 pre-1851, mainly in English literature from the 16th cent onwards, and British history, with some German, French and classical literature. There are several English items of 1615–9 acquired under the Background Material Scheme of the Joint Standing Committee on Library Co-operation, and *c*50 other STC items; *c*72 Wing; and *c*500 ESTC. The collections below (except the original part of the Johnson Collection) are now merged in the general library.

Card cat (author and classified) to 1980, then microfiche.

Lee, Sir Sidney (1859–1926), Shakespearian scholar and editor of *DNB*. The College bought his Elizabethan and Shakespearian collection after his death, *c*3,000 v, to form the backbone of a library of English literature. The Shakespeare collection now amounts to *c*1,500 items.

De Quincey, Edmund, Chairman of the Governors (*d* *c*1930) bequeathed *c*300 v, chiefly travel, history and art.

Stronge, Edmond, 640 v from his library given by Mrs Arthur P Richardson.

Johnson, Samuel (1709–94), lexicographer. The library acquired a special collection of editions of Johnson, around which has grown a Johnsonian collection of *c*500 items (including works by and concerning Johnson and Boswell). These include *c*60 pre-1851 editions.

Railway Club, Keen House, 4 Calshot Street, Islington, London N1. Open to members only; enquiries should be made in writing to the Hon Secretary.

The Club was founded in 1899 for those interested, professionally or otherwise, in railways, and now shares premises with the Model R Railway Club. Members, who are now usually railway enthusiasts with historical inclinations, are elected by a Committee. The Club has built up a library of *c*1,500 v containing books from 1820, journals from 1835, timetables from 1843, and directories from 1848, relating to British railway operation and history (with a very few on foreign railways). Also a collection of passenger tickets, mostly pre-1923.

Card cat (authors and subjects).

George Ottley, *Railway history: a guide to... collections...*, London, Library Assoc Reference, Special and Information Section, 1973, p59.

Rationalist Press Association Library, 88 Islington High Street, London N1 8EL. Tel (01) 226 7251. Open by appointment with the Association's Secretary.

The Propagandist Press Fund was established in 1888 to reform the laws of blasphemy. Its publishing arm, the Propaganda (or Propagandist) Press Committee, was set up in 1890 by Charles Albert Watts (1858–1946), printer of the *Freethinker*, and George Jacob Holyoake (1817–1906), and in 1893 the renamed Rationalist Press Committee. In 1899 these bodies were replaced by the Rationalist Press Association to stimulate freethought, promote secular education, and to publish propaganda for these causes. It is now the principal publishing arm of the humanist movement.

The library contains the archives and all publications of C A Watts and Co to 1960, and a general collection, probably *c*4,000 v of works on rationalism, humanism, secularism, freethought, and related subjects such as anthropology, psychology, philosophy, and theology. Though the books are mainly modern, they include some scarce early works. In 1924 the widow of Sir Hiram Stevens Maxim (1840–1916) the ballistic and aeronautical engineer gave his collection of *c*130 v dating from 1711–1915 on science, religion, freethought, and China. The library's greatest strength is its complete files of humanist, rationalist and freethought journals, including the *Republican* (1819–26) and the *Reasoner* from 1846; also many foreign publications. The papers of Henry Stephens Salt (1851–1939) Secretary of the Humanitarian League are also held.

Catalogue of the Library of the Rationalist Press Association, 1937 (classified; previous edition 1923).

Frederick J Gould, *The pioneers of Johnson's Court*, London 1935.

Susan Budd, *Varieties of unbelief*, London, Heinemann, 1977, p126-32; 165-79.

A G Whyte, *The story of the RPA*, London, 1949.

Raymond Mander and Joe Mitchenson Theatre Collection Ltd, Beckenham Place, Beckenham Place Park, Beckenham, Kent BR3 2UP. Open by appointment on written application. Photocopying.

The collection of two actors who have been collecting theatre publications all their lives. It was located at their home from 1946 to 1982, and was formed into a charitable trust in 1977, and is now housed by the London Borough of Lewisham at the above address. The collection has been greatly augmented by donations, including the complete collection of C B Cochrane (1872–1951). Probably *c*8,000 v, in addition to a roomful of ephemera.

No cat yet, but register of acquisitions (excluding plays and programmes).

'Treasure house of stage history', *Beckenham Journal* 30 Aug 1947.

Playbills and theatre programmes A very large collection from *c*1760 arranged by theatres. Also some bound collections, including Manchester Theatre Royal 1820–40, and E Compton's collection in 3 v of bills of theatres he played in 1808–77. Also large collections of press cuttings.

Biographical dictionaries and directories A comprehensive collection from Baker *Biographia dramatica* 1772 onwards.

Plays A large collection, mainly 19th and 20th cent, including many prompt copies. There are also some 17th and 18th cent editions, and the standard 18th and 19th cent sets and series. Prompt copies of Shakespeare from *c*1780, and large collections of Barry, Coward, Maugham, Shaw, and Wilde; many of the Shaw items being pre-publication rehearsal copies, some with his ms notes. Many plays from the library of Sir Herbert Beerbohm Tree (1853–1917) usually presented by the authors in the hope of productions.

Libretti Operatic libretti, especially of Gilbert and Sullivan.

Biographies and memoirs of actors, playwrights &c An extensive collection of standard works on 18th and 19th cent actors and dramatists such as Garrick, Cibber, Mrs Siddons etc, with some less well known works such as Macfall *Irving* 1906 (most copies of which were destroyed by the author).

History of theatres and the theatre The collection includes most of the standard works from 1800 onwards, and some ms material. Also critical works on the theatre.

Theatrical design, including costume, ballet, pantomime &c The collection includes some scarce works, and a collection on theatre posters, including *Le Maître d'affiche* 1896 on vellum.

Serials A small collection of 19th cent theatrical organs, including *The Thespian* 1838, *Grumbler* 1839, *The Town* 1838, and *Oxberry's Weekly Budget* 1843–44.

Redbridge Public Libraries, Central Reference Library, 112B High Road, Ilford, Essex IG1 1BY. Tel (01) 478 4319. Open Mon-Fri 9 am-8 pm; Sat 5 pm; an appointment is necessary to see the Brand Collection, which is not housed in the library.

Local History Collection The collections of the former Borough of Ilford, to which were added, in 1965, the smaller collections of Woodford and Wanstead, together with the Borough Archives. A few pre-1851 items are included, chiefly directories and standard histories of Essex.

Card cat (classified; author entries in general cat).

Brand Collection on Essex The private library of Frederick Joseph Brand (1857–1939) of Ilford (organist of St John's Church, Loughton, local historian and compiler of the *Essex index*) was purchased after his death, and after the sale of some rare books, *c*2,000 v remain, all English, including *c*500 pre-1851 (*c*5 STC, *c*40 Wing). Apart from some general literature and a few miscellaneous early editions, all relate to the former county of Essex, or are by Essex authors, or printed in Essex, and cover history, topography, roadbooks (and maps), genealogy, ecclesiastical history, church architecture, monumental inscriptions, directories, poll books etc. Also included are large collections of prints, photographs, and mss (chiefly Brand's own transcriptions of documents). 40 Essex sermons 1643–1826 bound in 2 v, *c*300 Essex pamphlets 1726–1938 bound in 15 v. 2 v of cuttings from newspapers and books 1700–1870 (with ms index); topographical periodicals and proceedings of archaeological societies of 19th cent; literary and antiquarian pamphlets published privately by Brand, including some printed at home on his own hand press, and 72 broadsheets printed at the private press of Charles Clark of Great Totham 1843–5.

Card cat, author and classified, may be seen by arrangement. Brand's own ms dictionary cat in 1 v. Not included in Reference Library general cat or local history cat.

G M Benton, 'In memoriam Frederick Joseph Brand', *Trans Essex Archaeological Soc* 23(1) 1942–5, p192-5.

Reform Club, 104 Pall Mall, London SW1Y 5EW. Tel (01) 930 9374. The Library is private to members; others may use it only through the personal introduction of a member, or by special arrangement with the librarian.

The Reform Club was founded in 1836 by Edward Ellice MP (1781–1863), the Hudson's Bay merchant, and promoter of the Reform Bill of 1832, as a resort for Liberal politicians; its Library was established in 1842 with a major collection of Parliamentary Papers, and other donations and purchases. Collections, chiefly of history, politics, topography, and general literature were built up. In the present century much, but by no means all, of the older material has been dispersed. The pamphlets collected by Sir Anthony Panizzi (1797–1879) were sold (Sotheby 28 July 1964 lot 392); most of the other pamphlet collections were given to the University of London Library, and the Parliamentary Papers were deposited there. The sets of Commons and Lords Journals were sold (Hodgson 18 Nov 1965 lots 264-5) and major runs of 17th-19th cent periodicals (Sotheby 28-29 July 1965 lots 326-330). The Club has extensive archives.

Catalogue of the Library of the Reform Club, 1883; 2nd ed 1894.

Annual Report of the Library Committee.

George Woodbridge, *The Reform Club 1836–1978*, priv printed, 1978, p99-114, 175-8.

Louis Fagan, *The Reform Club...*, London 1887, p124-9.

J M Crook, *The Reform Club*, 1973.

H Thorogood, 'London clubs and their libraries', *Library Review* 13 (1951–2), p232-8.

Richard III Society, Barton Library, 3 Campden Terrace, Linden Gardens, Chiswick, London W4 2EP. Tel (01) 995 3068. Open by appointment only after written application to the librarian. Other enquiries relating to the Society must be addressed to the Correspondence Secretary, 4 Oakley Street, London SW3 5NN.

In 1924 the gynaecologist Samuel Saxon Barton (1892–1957) formed the Fellowship of the White Boar, an informal group which aimed to secure the reassessment of the role of Richard III in English history. This was transformed into a public society in 1956, and later renamed the Richard III Society. Barton bequeathed 21 rare books in trust to form the nucleus of a library, to which Mrs Vivien Beatrix Lamb, Hon Assistant Secretary, and others added further donations. There are now 474 books (including 167 novels) of which 30 v are pre-1851; and 770 pamphlets and papers. All are devoted to the life and times of Richard III (1452–85), King of England, including biographies, chronicles, and other source materials, social and political history, topography, costume, battles, and heraldry; fictionalized treatments, including plays (17 in typescript) and novels. 2 STC: Habington *Historie* 1640 (STC 12586) with signature of Daines Barrington (1727–1800); Sir T More *Historie of the pitifull life...of Edward the fifth 1640* with Barton's bookplate; 3 Wing; B299 with signature of Buddle Atkinson; B5306; B5307 with ms notes by N C Scatcherd (1781–1853); 18th cent books include *The parallel* 1744 and 2nd ed 1744; Walpole *Historic doubts*, 1768; and Hutton *Battle of Bosworth* 1788.

The Barton Library: catalogue, part 1: books, 1978 (in 5 subject sequences of authors), continued on cards. *Part 2: pamphlets and papers* is in preparation.

George Awdry, *The Richard III Society, the first fifty years: a personal account*, Upminster, the Society, 1977.

The Ricardian (1961– , quarterly).

Richmond upon Thames Public Libraries

A Central Reference Library

Little Green, Richmond, Surrey TW9 1QL. Tel (01) 940 5529 or 9125. Open Mon-Fri 10 am-6 pm, Sat 5 pm by appointment (much material is stored elsewhere). Photocopying.

Reference Collection General reference collection totals c25,000 including 1,000 pre-1851 items, mostly donated between the opening in 1881 and 1930; c20 STC; c50 Wing; c400 ESTC items, mainly history, topography, coins, and English literature. Some private press books 19th-20th cent; some 18th-19th cent literary periodicals.

Card cat (author and classified) which includes also Twickenham Reference Library, but works catalogued from 1980 (including earlier works recatalogued) are in microfiche cat.

Typescript union cat of periodicals in the borough.

Local History Collection Covers the part of the Borough to the South of the Thames (the pre-1965 Borough of Richmond with the Urban District of Barnes), and general works on Surrey. Contain c2,000 books and pamphlets, of which c200 are pre-1851 and c80 pre-1701, in addition to ephemera. Also part of the Borough archives.

Card cat (author and classified) accessible on request (including Twickenham local history collection).

Local history notes, including descriptions and catalogues of some collections.

Long Collection The library of Alfred Long, a local resident, was donated c1920 and integrated for the most part into the collections; the greater part is in the Local History Collection and the Theatre Collection. There is a residue of uncatalogued ephemera on Richmond, including some rare early 19th cent pamphlets, known as the Long Collection.

Local Authors The collection includes 64 editions, mostly 18th cent of James Thomson (1700–48) the poet; 80 mostly first editions of Mary Elizabeth Braddon (1837–1915) the novelist; 8, mostly presentation copies, of John Henry Newman (1801–90), cardinal; and 9 of (Alphonsus Joseph Mary Augustus) Montague Summers (1880–1948) the historian of witchcraft.

Separate author card cat, also in Local History cat.

Authors of note who lived in Richmond upon Thames: an index, 1971.

James Thomson (Local History note no 17).

Sladen Collection Douglas (Brooke Wheelton) Sladen (1856–1947), editor of *Who's Who*, novelist and travel writer, gave his library and papers (c1925), then over 10,000 v, to Richmond Public Library. Most of the books consisting of general literature and history, including numerous publishers' review copies, were integrated c1930 into the Lending Library (partly destroyed by bombing). His collection of reference books, strong in biographical and genealogical dictionaries, until recently remained separate, but after the dispersal of part to other libraries, it is now in the Richmond general reference collection. A special collection remains of 49 of Sladen's own works, mostly first editions of proof copies, with a chronological archive of his correspondence with literary figures 1888–1921, interspersed with pamphlets, ephemera, and cuttings.

Sladen's works in cat of local authors.

National Register of Archives is listing the archive.

Theatre Collection Hundreds of playbills (with other ephemera) relating to the Theatre Royal, Richmond, 1765–1884, mainly from the Long Collection.

Ms list of performances in chronological order with indexes of plays and dramatists.

Playbills announcing Kean's performances (Local History note no 45).

The Theatre Royal, Richmond (ibid no 27).

Vancouver Collection 45 books by, or relating to, Capt George Vancouver (*c*1758–95) of Petersham, the explorer who sailed with Cook to Australasia and North America.

Captain George Vancouver Collection: catalogue, 1971 (Notes on local history no 25).

B **East Sheen District Library**

Sheen Lane Centre, Richmond Road, London SW14 8LP. Tel (01) 876 8801. Open Mon-Wed and Fri 10 am-6 pm; Sat 9 am-5 pm by appointment with the District Librarian.

Burton Collection Deposited in 1969 by Camberwell Public Library (London Borough of Southwark). Part of the library of Isabel Lady Burton (1831–96), wife of Sir Richard Francis Burton (1821–90) the explorer: given to Camberwell Public Libraries (part of the collection seems to have been subsequently dispersed; Sir Richard's own library is at the Museum of Mankind). There are 38 editions of works by Sir Richard, including some presentation copies to Isabel, and some with her ms notes and some with his; 11 editions of works edited by Sir Richard; 3 editions of works by Isabel; *c*30 biographical items on both, to which additions are being made. Also 33 objects collected by, or associated with, Sir Richard; and the volume of reproductions of Albert Letchford's paintings to illustrate Burton's edition of *Arabian nights*; 16 oil paintings by him and two other paintings of the Burtons and their homes.

The Burton Collection [catalogue], 1972 (Notes on local history no 33), with supplement for miscellaneous items.

N M Penzer, *An annotated bibliography of... Burton*, 1923, though recording the Kensington copies, fails to note the Camberwell ones.

C **Twickenham Reference Library**

Local History Department, Carfield Road, Twickenham, Middlesex TW1 3JT. Tel (01) 892 8091. Open Mon, Tues and Fri 10 am-1 pm, 2-6 pm; Sat 9 am-1 pm, 2-6 pm by appointment only; books may be transferred to main Reference Library for use there on Wed and Thurs if adequate notice is given.

The Local History Collection of that part of the Borough which lies on the Middlesex (North) side of the Thames, ie the former Borough of Twickenham (with its archives). A few pre-1851 books are included in this collection, mostly by local authors or works on Middlesex generally, in addition to the collections below. (A branch at Orleans House Gallery houses the print collection bequeathed in 1962 by the Hon Mrs Nellie Ionides.)

Card cat (author and classified), local authors separately.

Pope Collection Editions of the works of Alexander Pope (1688–1744) the poet, of Twickenham, of which 20 are pre-1801; 5 1801–50, and 16 later; *c*70 items on Pope and his writings, and 13 prints of his villa.

Catalogue of the Pope collection (Notes on local history no 31) omits most of the 19th cent editions in the collection. Included in local history card cat.

Walpole Collection Contains 8 books printed at the Strawberry Hill press, and 27 other books by Horace Walpole, Earl of Orford (1717–97), of which 10 are 18th cent editions. All significant books about Walpole and Strawberry Hill.

Classified cat (L.027.4 Tl:083) and local author cat under Walpole.

A T Hazen, *Bibliography of the Strawberry Hill Press*, New Haven, 1942 (nos 1, 3, 5, 7, 20, 27, 30 and 31 French).

Roehampton Institute

The Roehampton Institute is a federation established in 1975 of four previously independent teachers' training colleges, until 1982 affiliated to the University of London Institute of Education, but from 1983 to the University of Surrey. Library services are provided by the Institute for the colleges, which retain ownership of rare and other books acquired before 1975.

Each college library has author and classified card cat for acquisitions to 1981 (each available on microfilm together with a union cat from 1976 in each of the others). From 1982 there is a combined cat of all the libraries on microfiche. These include all the general collections of the college libraries, but few of the rare books.

A **Whitelands College**

West Hill, Putney, London SW15 3SN. Tel (01) 788 8268 Ext 244. Open (term) Mon-Fri 8.45 am-8 pm, Sat 9.30 am-12.30 pm; (vac) Mon-Fri 9 am-12 noon, 1-5 pm by appointment with the Librarian or Archivist.

The College was founded at Chelsea in 1841 by the National Society for the Promotion of Education of the Poor in the principles of the Established Church, as Whitelands Training Institution for Schoolmistresses. It moved to its present site in 1931, and became co-educational in 1966.

Whitelands College monographs, 1981– , annual: no 1, May Queen Festival 1881–1981 by M Cole; no 2, Whitelands College, the history, by M Cole, (both include information on the library).

Whitelands College Library The College Library, now c90,000 v, is a working collection in the subjects taught, chiefly the sciences, education, divinity, history and English literature. There are very few pre-1851 books in the humanities, but most have been tranferred to the archives.

Whitelands College Archives (general) Over 1,000 v, nearly all the pre-1880, and many other books formerly in the College Library, have recently been transferred to the Archives, where they are in the course of arrangement. They consist of a miscellaneous collection, which includes 2 imperfect incunabula, and the special collections below.

A catalogue of books belonging to Whitelands Training Institution Library, 1870, is a shelflist mainly of historical interest.

Whitelands College Archive catalogue, by H Henstridge, the College, 1979, lists on p87-9 19 association copies which were donated to the Archives, but none of the books recently transferred from the Library; it also includes miscellaneous printed cuttings and ephemera collections.

Ruskin donations John Ruskin (1819–1900) became a patron of the College through his friendship with the Principal, the Rev John Pincher Faunthorpe (1839–1924), and his gift to the College in 1877 of a complete set of his own works (supplemented by each new work on publication) gave the small College Library a great impetus. Within a few years he had given several hundred other books which are identified by a special bookplate (and sometimes by his own inscription), and which have been now segregated into a special collection. They include a substantial number of 18th and 19th cent finely illustrated works on botany, ornithology, architecture, and other subjects, but many show signs of their former everyday use in science and art classes. He gave the first edition of Johnson's *Dictionary* 1755.

Gifts of the May Queens In 1881 Ruskin inaugurated the famous ceremony still performed annually of the May Queen, elected from first year students by her peers to have charge of charitable works for the ensuing year. Ruskin personally gave a set of his works to each May Queen, who was to retain one and distribute the others among her chosen handmaidens with bookplates (personally inscribed by Ruskin) bearing her chosen mottoes. They were originally produced from editions printed on handmade paper and specially bound. Many May Queens have bequeathed their gifts to the College, sometimes with letters from Ruskin (connected with his customary invitation to them to visit him at home) inserted.

Early children's books c250 v of 18th and 19th cent children's books, the vast majority of which came from the bequest of Miss Matilda Sharpe. Most are from the first half of the 19th cent, and these include scarce books and some magazines such as the *Children's Friend* and the *Children's Weekly Visitor*.

Printed handlist.

B **Southlands College**

65 Wimbledon Parkside, London SW19 5NN. Tel (01) 946 2234. Open Mon-Fri 9 am-8 pm, Sat 9 am-12 noon, on written application to the librarian. Photocopier, microform reader available.

Southlands College Library The College was founded in 1872 to replace Westminster College in the training of Methodist women teachers, when the latter became restricted to men. Its library was first organized in 1880, and now contains c70,000 v mostly modern books on history, geography, local history (especially London), the theatre, music, education and religious studies, with 450 current periodicals. There are a few earlier editions of English literature.

Wesley Historical Society Library (deposited on loan); open only to members and holders of subscribers' tickets, for which application should be made to the Secretary of the Society.

The Library contains c11,000 items (excluding ephemera) on the history of the Methodist Churches in England. There is a very extensive collection of the works (especially sermons) of, and about, John and Charles Wesley, and the other members of the Wesley family; missionary notices from 1818; missionary reports from 1804; circuit plans from 1805 (and some literature on cirplanology); c500 pre-1851 pamphlets; c200 hymnals, including 20 of the 18th cent and c40 of 1801–50; class tickets from 1818; an extensive collection of Methodist periodicals; local church histories and locally printed ephemera; a very extensive cuttings collection from 1791 onwards; ms correspondence; microfilms of material in other Methodist libraries.

Card cat (author, topographical and classified).

C **Froebel Institute Library**

Grove House, Roehampton Lane, London SW15 5PJ. Tel (01) 876 2242 Ext 39. Open Mon-Fri 9 am-9 pm (term), 5 pm (vac), by appointment on written application in advance to the librarian. Photocopier; microform readers available.

The Institute was founded in 1892 to train teachers in infant and junior schools according to the education theories of Friedrich W A G Froebel (1782–1852), and is now a general college of education with a school on the site. The library contains c70,000 v mainly on education, the social sciences and the humanities, and is now strong in history (having absorbed much of the library of the Historical Association, the remainder of which is in the other Roehampton Institute libraries), art and French literature. The library, founded in 1879 of the now adjacent National Froebel Foundation (originally the Froebel Society) has been largely dispersed, but a portion now mostly in the Early Childhood Archive has been acquired by the Institute, including parts of the collections of Fanny Franks, E R Murray and Frances Roe.

Historical Association, *Library catalogue*, London 1962 (classified with author index).

National Froebel Foundation, *Education Library 1947 catalogue*, London, reissued with supplement 1955.

Froebel Society and Junior Schools Association, *Catalogue of the Froebel Society and Fanny Franks Memorial Lending Library. . .*, London, 1924.

Early childhood archive There are over 1,000 v on educational theory by Froebel, Montessori, Pestalozzi, and other educationists, mainly 19th and early 20th cent editions; over 50 editions of Froebel, mostly in English, and numerous items of the Froebelian movement; many runs of Froebelian and a few other 19th and 20th cent educational periodicals.

Separate author cat on cards, not yet complete, and partly in general cat.

Early children's books A collection of *c*300 v, mostly late 19th and early 20th cent from the collection of Miss Margaret Stanley-Wrench, given to St Gabriel College, supplemented by other donations, especially from Eglantyne Mary Jebb (1889–1978), Principal of the Froebel Institute. There are also some items from the former Rachel Macmillan College collection.

Cat in course of arrangement. Separate card cat of Stanley-Wrench collection.

D **Digby Stuart College Library**

Roehampton Lane, London SW15 5PH. Tel (01) 876 8273. Open Mon-Fri (term) 9 am-8 pm, (vac) 9 am-5 pm; Sat (term only) 9.30 am-12.30 pm, after written application to the librarian. Photocopier available.

The College was founded as a women's teachers' training college at the adjacent Sacred Heart Convent (see under Society of the Sacred Heart Archives for the rare books still in the Convent). It later became St Charles's College, and was re-named Digby Stuart College after the surnames of two earlier Superiors of the Convent. Its rare book collection has mainly been sold, but *c*20 pre-1850 works on London and a few others have been retained. There is a special collection of *c*120 children's books of the late 19th and early 20th cent.

N M Rothschild and Sons Ltd, Archives Reference Library, P O Box 185, New Court, St Swithin's Lane, London EC4P 4DU. Tel (01) 280 5329. Open by appointment only, Mon-Fri 9.30 am-4.45 pm, to approved scholars who agree to adhere to certain special conditions after written application, giving two appropriate references, to the Archivist.

After establishing a business in Manchester (1798) N M Rothschild founded a permanent banking concern in the City from 1809 onwards. The associated library is now being actively enlarged with the aim of building up a comprehensive collection on the history of the bank and of the Rothschild family. It contains over 430 v, including *c*10 pre-1851, of books on the business activities of the Rothschilds; books on their social and collecting activities, and books dedicated to them, including catalogues of sales of their collections; history of banking and finance; and some miscellaneous Hebraica of the 18th and early 19th cent.

Card cat (author and classified).

Computerized IBM-d Base II catalogue.

G A Knight, 'The archive service of the House of Rothschild in London', *Zeitschrift für Bankgeschichte* Heft 12 (1978), p60-3.

Royal Academy of Arts Library, Burlington House, Piccadilly, London W1V 0DS. Tel (01) 734 9052. Open Mon-Fri 2-5 pm to Members and Friends of the Royal Academy; also to all serious students by appointment after written application to the librarian.

The Royal Academy and its library, both founded in 1768, are the oldest British fine art institution and the oldest special library in the field.

Sidney C Hutchison, *The history of the Royal Academy 1768–1968*, London, Chapman and Hall, 1968.

——'Historic records of artists', *Apollo* 89(83) (1969), p64-5.

William Sandby, *The history of the Royal Academy of Arts. . .*, London, 1862.

General The Library now contains *c*15,000 books and pamphlets, of which about half are pre-1851, and many later are rare. (There are also major collections of drawings and engravings.) The older books have been acquired almost exclusively by donation from academicians, the founding collection coming from Richard Dalton (1715?–91), Librarian to George III. Although there are many modern books on the applied arts, the older are almost exclusively devoted to painting, sculpture, architecture, topography and archaeology, and the theory of art, including mathematics and perspective, together with general works on the history of art and biographies of artists, especially of academicians. There are also some catalogues of art collections. There are some early atlases of human anatomy, a few books on zoology and botany, and some general reference works such as the *Encyclopedie*. The earliest book is Dürer *Apocalypsis* Nuremberg 1511.

Card cat (author and alphabetical subject).

A catalogue of the books in the Library of the Royal Academy of Arts, 1877; supplement 1901; the two together are very incomplete, even for the older books.

Obsolete printed cats 1802 and 1841.

Ms shelflist, including drawings of the books on each shelf, *c*1815.

Register of donations 1769–1840.

Royal Academy Exhibitions The file of exhibition catalogues is complete from the beginning. There are three important extra-illustrated sets: one to 1850, put together by James Hughes Anderdon (1790–1879) with much ms material inserted; another by Basil Jupp; and a third containing illustrations taken from magazines.

Royal Academy of Dramatic Art, 62 Gower Street, London WC1E 6ED. Tel (01) 636 7076. Open during term by appointment with the librarian.

The Academy was opened in 1906, the library in 1968, and now contains *c*9,000 v.

Restoration and 18th cent plays A collection of *c*90 v of 18th and early 19th cent editions of English plays written *c*1660–1800, mostly acquired in the 1920s by the Johnson family from London club libraries, and recently donated to the Library by Celia Johnson.

Card cat (authors and titles), including the special collection.

Royal Academy of Music Library, Marylebone Road, London NW1 5HT. Tel (01) 935 5461. Open on written or telephoned application in advance 9.30 am-5 pm (6.30 in term); Sat (term only) 10 am-1 pm. Most printed material is inaccessible till *c*1982. Microfilming can be arranged.

A large collection of music scores and early literature on music has been built up from bequests since the foundation in 1822 by John Fane, 11th Earl of Westmorland (1784–1859), who bequeathed his music library to the Academy. Notable collections incorporated include those of Richard John Samuel Stevens (1757–1837) the glee-writer, and of Charles Ainslie Barry. There are 5,000 v of musicology, including *c*60 pre-1801 and perhaps *c*500 of 1801–50. There is also a collection of early music periodicals.

Card cat (the musicological works are included in *RISM* Vol 3, VI).

R A Rye, *The students' guide*, 3rd ed London, 1927, p281-2.

F Corder, *A history of the Royal Academy of Music*, London, 1922. (op)

Royal Aeronautical Society Library, 4 Hamilton Place, Hyde Park Corner, London W1V 0BQ. Tel (01) 499 3515. Open Mon-Fri 10 am-4 pm by appointment with the librarian. Photocopying available.

The Society was founded, as the Aeronautical Society of the United Kingdom, in 1866, and chartered in 1918, absorbing the Institution (previously Institute) of Aeronautical Engineers in 1927. A library was built up from 1867, mainly by donation, but was dispersed *c*1892. In 1897, active enlargement resumed, and it is now a collection of major importance, exceeding 25,000 v.

General Historical Collection Comprising *c*500 books, 17th-19th cent, including presentation copies from famous 19th cent British and foreign aviators. In 1922 the collection was enlarged with a grant from the Carnegie United Kingdom Trust. Covers all aspects of aviation, including bird flight, from the 17th cent onwards.

Card cat (authors, including Cuthbert-Hodgson).

A list of the books, periodicals and pamphlets in the Library of the Royal Aeronautical Society, 1941 (op).

Cuthbert-Hodgson Collection Books, ephemera, and mss on flight. Begun before 1820 by John Cuthbert, scientific instrument maker of St Martin's Lane, from whom it was acquired by the omnivorous collector John Fillinham, a friend of Cuthbert's, and later by the electrical engineer George Edward Dering (*c*1830–19 ?). At the sale of Dering's books (Hodgson) it was bought for his private collection by a partner in the auctioneering firm, John Edmund Hodgson (1875–1952) the historian of aeronautics (he was also the Society's Hon Librarian). Hodgson rearranged, annotated, and enlarged the collection, and sold it to Sir Frederick Handley Page (1885–1962) the President, who donated it to the Society in 1947.

Frederic John Poynton (1869–1944) MD, collected a large number of prints and ephemera relating to early flight, which he bound in 12 large folio volumes and donated to the Society *c*1935.

Royal Air Force Museum, Department of Printed Books, Aerodrome Road, Hendon, London NW9 5LL. Tel (01) 205 2266. Open Mon-Fri 10 am-12.30 pm, 1.30-4.30 pm on written application to the librarian.

The Museum was opened in 1972 by the Ministry of Defence. A library has been built up by purchase, donation (including the library of the Royal Aero Club in 1974), and transfers from the former Air Ministry Library and several RAF stations. It also houses the British Airways Museum Library, chiefly timetables and advertising ephemera of British Airways and its predecessors, which awaits the establishment of a permanent British Airways Museum. There are over 100,000 v, of which 10 are pre-1851.

Card cat (author, title and subject) in progress.

Recent accessions 1974–8 (ceased publication).

The Royal Air Force Museum, Hendon: 100 years of aviation history, London, Pitkin Pictorials, [for the Museum], 1975.

Guide to Library and Archives in preparation.

Royal Air Force Museum and Battle of Britain Museum publications 1972–1979 (gratis).

The Library includes the following collections:

Ballooning literature A small section which includes all the 10 pre-1851 books in the library, including 4 items of 1784–6.

History of flight and aviation A collection of standard histories and a number of rare works on the subject, some foreign.

Air display programmes A large collection, especially of those connected with Hendon Aerodrome from 1912 onwards.

Official publications of the RAF and Air Ministry The archival set of RAF technical and instructional literature from 1918 onwards, *c*65,000 items, and *c*16,000 air diagrams, wallcharts, pamphlets etc, many of which are unique copies.

History of the RAF A large collection of memoirs after 1917.

Serials In addition to standard aviation journals, there is a very extensive collection of publications from both world wars, including many produced by individual squadrons and units of the RAF and RNAS.

Periodicals catalogue, 1975. (op)

Royal Army Medical College, Millbank, London SW1P 4RJ. Tel (01) 834 9060 Ext 220. Open Mon-Fri 9 am-5 pm by prior appointment on application to the Commandant. Photocopying; microfilm reader.

The library was founded as an adjunct to an Army Medical Museum by Sir James McGrigor (1771–1858) Bt, KCB, FRS, when Principal Army Medical Officer at Hilsea; in 1816 it was transferred to York Hospital, Chelsea. In 1860, when the Army Medical School was established at Fort Pitt, Chatham, the library was transferred there, moving to Netley with the school in 1863 and to Millbank in 1907. The collections of earlier books have suffered at times from neglect, war damage, and deliberate dispersal, but now form a historical collection within the library belonging to the Chattels Fund Trust. Most of these books were donated; some of the most important collections (not now separate) are listed below. Now *c*400 v of 16th-19th cent on military and general medicine, including 10 of the 16th cent and 50 of the 17th. Also mss.

Catalogue of books of historical value belonging to the officers of the Royal Army Medical Corps (1970), 2 v.

Superseded cats include *A catalogue of the Library of the Army Medical Department* (1833); *A catalogue of books in the Library of the Medical Department of the Army* (1852).

M Davies, 'The library of the Royal Army Medical College', *Journ of the Royal Army Medical Corps* 116(1) (1970), p51-2.

See also J B Neal, 'The history of the Royal Army Medical College', *Journ of the Royal Medical Corps* 103 (1957), p163-72; R L Blanco, *Wellington's Surgeon General...McGrigor*, Durham NC, Duke, 1974, p67-8; A Peterkin and W Johnston, *Commissioned officers in the medical services of the British Army*, 1968, 2 v.

Waring gift, mainly 19th cent clinical works.

Fayrer, Sir Joseph (1824–1907) Bt, naval and military surgeon: collection of his works, his own library, and his ms papers, donated by his sons 1916, including the ms of his *Recollections* (Edinburgh 1900).

Johnston, William (1843–1914), compiler of the *Roll of Commissioned Officers*, bequeathed a collection of printed military orders, regulations and ephemera.

Spiller Collection on India, especially topography and the mutiny of 1857–9.

Macpherson, Sir William (Grant) (1858–1927), author of the *History of the Great War*, Deputy Director General, gave a substantial collection on military medical administration, tactics, and history.

Home, Sir Everard (1756–1832) FRS, surgeon; deposited his collection of theses and 18th and early 19th cent pamphlets on permanent loan by the Royal Hospital, Chelsea.

Muniment Room (Separately administered by the Curator of the RAMC Historical Museum.) Over 1,000 documentary items, including mss published or privately printed books and pamphlets, cuttings etc. Mostly after 1800, but a few 18th cent.

Catalogue of the contents of the Muniment Room at the Royal Army Medical College, 1975.

Royal Artillery Library and Archives, Royal Artillery Institution, Old Royal Military Academy, Academy Road, Woolwich, London SE18 4JJ. Tel (01) 856 5533 Ext 2523. Open by appointment only Mon-Fri 10 am-12.30 pm, 2-4.30 pm, after written application at least seven days in advance stating precise subject of enquiry. Photocopier available.

The Royal Artillery Library was founded in 1809 as a subscription library for officers of the Royal Regiment of Artillery, and was incorporated in the Royal Artillery Institution on its foundation in 1838. It now holds also the regimental archives.

F Duncan, *The history of the Royal Artillery (1716–1815)*, 1874, 2 v.

H W L Hime, *The history of the Royal Regiment of Artillery 1815–1853*, 1908.

Sir John Headlam and Sir Charles Callwell, *History of the Royal Artillery (1860–1914)*, 1931–40, 3 v.

General Library The library contains *c*25,000 v on everything connected with artillery, both British and foreign, including *c*1,500 pre-1851 printed items.

Card cat (author and alphabetical subject).

A catalogue of the Royal Artillery Library at Woolwich, 1814; 1858 (new ed).

Catalogue of the Royal Artillery Library, Woolwich: Military Section (1895?).

Catalogue of the Royal Artillery Institution Library (Military Section), 1913.

Published cat of modern books, various editions.

Pre-1820 Collection 923 printed books and pamphlets (with a few mss) segregated from the main library, comprising its holdings to the year 1819. There are 45 STC; 57 Wing; *c*200 ESTC; and 19 16th cent; 70 17th cent and *c*225 18th cent foreign items.

Some interesting association copies include Wolfe's annotated copy of John Barker, *Treasury of fortification* (1707), taken from his body after he was shot; Wellington's copy of *Aide memoire...des Officiers d'Artillerie* (Paris, 1809).

Typed shelflist.

Cleaveland mss A miscellaneous collection somewhat similar to the Dickson mss, covering the period 1267–1757, collected by Lt Gen Samuel Cleaveland (*d*1794).

Dickson mss A collection formed by Major-General Sir Alexander Dickson (1777–1840) GCB, of mss, diaries, letters, prints, and maps from 1294 onwards, with a few pamphlets, given to the Royal Artillery Institution by his son, General Sir Collingwood Dickson.

The Dickson manuscripts, Woolwich, 1908–9, and *Minutes of Proceedings of the Royal Artillery Institution*, 28 (1902), p45-52, 133-46, 235-49, 335-50, 431-46, 477-94, 583-98; 29 (1903), p81-96, 184-92, 279-90, 407-22, 489-92.

Royal Asiatic Society Library, 56 Queen Anne Street, Marylebone, London W1M 9LA. Tel (01) 935 8944. Open (except August) Mon-Fri 11 am-5 pm to Fellows, and by appointment only following written application to research workers. Microfilming available.

The Society was founded in 1823 on the initiative of Henry Thomas Colebrooke (1765–1837), the Sanskrit scholar, as the Asiatic Society of Great Britain and Ireland, becoming the Royal Asiatic Society in the same year. The library dates from the foundation, and has been built up mainly by gifts and exchanges. In 1918 the Society of Biblical Archaeology, founded 1870, was absorbed with most of its library. (The Chinese collection is deposited at the University of Leeds.)

S Simmonds and S Digby, *The Royal Asiatic Society, its history and treasures*, Leiden, 1979.

C A F Beckingham, 'The Royal Asiatic Society 1823–1973', *SALG Newsletter* no 7 (Jan 1976), p1-10.

F Legge, 'The Society of Biblical Archaeology', *Journ Royal Asiatic Soc*, 1919, p25-36.

General The library now contains perhaps *c*30,000 v of printed monographs, of which *c*6,000 are pre-1851 (including a few STC and Wing), and *c*400 sets of periodicals. There are also important collections of oriental (with a few western) mss, and of prints and drawings. There is a fairly comprehensive collection on the languages, literatures, history and art of South Asia; slightly less strong on other parts of Asia, N E Africa, Ethiopia, and Oceania; the former collections on Eastern Europe have been dispersed. There are also collections on the archaeology, anthropology, religion and customs of these areas. Most are in Western languages, but there are some books in oriental languages.

Catalogue of the printed books published before 1932 in the Library of the Royal Asiatic Society, 1940 (authors, omitting Turkish, Armenian and Chinese books, and all pamphlets); continued on cards.

Author cat of pamphlets in *Catalogue of the Library of the Royal Asiatic Society*, 1893, p367-423.

Some pamphlet collections listed in *Catalogue of the printed books in the Royal Asiatic Society's Library*, 1830 (classified).

W Wenzel, 'List of Tibetan mss and printed books in the Library', *Journ Roy Asiatic Soc*, 1893, p699-716.

Accessions sometimes listed in *Journal of the Royal Asiatic Society* and in *Proceedings of the Society of Biblical Archaeology*.

Collections incorporated in the Library Sir George Thomas Staunton (1781–1859) gave *c*3,000 v (mostly on China) to begin the library, and Sir Alexander Johnston (1775–1849), Chief Justice of Ceylon in the following years gave numerous works on the island; Lt-Col James Tod (1782–1835), first Librarian, bequeathed his oriental books, mss and coins; Dr Nicholas Wiseman (1802–65, later Cardinal) in 1834 gave early oriental books; Thomas Gordon (1788–1841), Major-General in the Greek army, bequeathed his Persian, Turkish and Arabic books; Basil Hall Chamberlain (1850–1935), Prof of Japanese at Tokyo, gave 205 v of Japanese poetry in 1881; Sir William Edward Maxwell (1846–97), the colonial administrator, bequeathed Malay books and mss. Throughout the 19th cent the British and Foreign Bible Society was a donor of Bibles in oriental languages. In 1938 Lewis C Loyd gave the collection of works of Sir Richard (Francis) Burton (1821–90) formed by Oscar Eckenstein. In 1943 the widow of the missionary William Pettigrew gave his books and papers relating chiefly to old Manipuri. In 1967 the library acquired much of the collection of Prof Charles Ambrose Storey (1888–1967).

Schrumpf Collection The library has *c*700 Armenian books built around the collection formed by Gustav A Schrumpf (1844–92) an Alsatian who taught at University College School given in 1893, with additions donated by Minas Tchéraz; books from 1796 to 1892.

M Tchéraz, 'The Schrumpf collection of Armenian books', (author cat), *Journ Roy Asiatic Soc* 1893, p699-716.

Archives The Society's records include printed material, chiefly early transactions.

Royal Astronomical Society Library, Burlington House, Piccadilly, London W1V 0NL. Tel (01) 734 4582 or 3307. Open Mon-Fri 10 am-5 pm to members; to others with a letter of recommendation from a Fellow or person of equivalent scientific standing. Photocopying.

The Library was founded in 1820 at the inception of the Society, and has been increased continuously by donation and purchase. It is now claimed to be the most comprehensive collection of astronomical and geophysical works in the Commonwealth, and to contain 95 per cent of the literature of astronomy before 1800. There is a notable collection of star catalogues and star atlases. The library holds *c*25,000 items altogether, including *c*2,000 pre-1801; *c*500 1801–50; 55 incunabula. (Certain books formerly in the library, chiefly on subjects other than astronomy, were sold in 1889 and 1912.) Important mss (eg Herschel) and archives.

Card cat supersedes *Catalogue of the Library* 1838; 1850; 1886 (with supplements 1900, 1926).

'The Library of the Royal Astronomical Society. Prepared by the Library Committee', Quarterly *Journ of the Royal Astronomical Society*, 8 (1967), p299-303.

Archives include material on the Library; see J A Bennett, 'Catalogue of the archives and manuscripts', *Memoirs of the Royal Astronomical Soc* 85 (1978), p1-90.

History of the Royal Astronomical Society 1820–1920, ed J L E Dreyer and H H Turner, London, 1923, p64, 243-4.

Society of Mathematicians of Spitalfields, founded 1717 by Joseph Middleton and others as the Mathematical Society meeting in Brown's Lane Spitalfields, had a general scientific library (with some other books acquired from a historical society absorbed in 1783) and loan collection of instruments, but its core was mathematics and astronomy. The Society with its Library and Archives, but not the instruments, was absorbed into the Royal Astronomical Society in 1844, when it had over 2,500 v, including important works by Flamsteed, Euler and Clairaut, in addition to many works of great interest in the history of mathematics. The collection was not kept separate, but the books have a distinctive binding and bookplate.

A catalogue of books belonging to the Mathematical Society, Crispin Street, Spitalfields, 1804. With Historical Preface. (An archival interleaved and amended copy is in the British Library 11900.d.18.)

The articles of the Mathematical Society meeting...in Brown's Lane...(with) *Catalogue*, 1784. (British Library B.733.(3)).

History..., 1923, p99-104.

Grove-Hills Library The library was bequeathed by Col Edmund Herbert Grove-HIlls (1864–1922), President of the Society, and housed in a special room. It contains over 500 pre-1700 books of mathematics and astronomy (with 3 later), including 40 incunabula. Also incorporated are editions of works by astronomers such as Joannes de Sacro Bosco, Copernicus, Tycho Brahe, Kepler, Galileo, Newton, Hevelius, etc. Important editions of Euclid. Fine editions from presses of Aldus and Ratdolt.

Catalogue of the Grove-Hills Library of the Royal Astronomical Society, 1924.

British Astronomical Association Library Housed on the same premises, but administered separately, is primarily a modern lending library for its members, but possesses a handful of early 19th cent books on astronomy which will be made available on request through the Royal Astronomical Society Library.

Catalogue of the Library of the British Astronomical Association, 1954.

Royal Automobile Club, 89 Pall Mall, London SW1Y 5HS. Tel (01) 930 2345. Telex 23340. Club library available to members only.

The club was founded in 1897, and has built up a reference library of over 12,000 v of books and 200 periodicals on motoring, including scarce material on the early motoring era and vintage cars.

Royal Botanic Gardens Kew. Library and Archives Division, Kew, Richmond, Surrey TW9 3AB. Tel (01) 940 1171. Open Mon-Thurs 9 am-5.30 pm, Fri 5 pm to staff and government officers; to bona fide research workers at the Director's discretion, on written application only. The public has right of access to the official records in the Archives, but only by appointment.

George III amalgamated the gardens of Richmond Lodge and Kew House, and after enlargement they became a government responsibility in 1841. The first Director, Sir William (Jackson) Hooker (1785–1865), then found that the library had disappeared, and brought his private collections to serve official purposes. The Library has been built up jointly with the Herbarium as a working collection for the staff and for the preparation of research publications such as the *Index Kewensis*. It now comprises comprehensive collections of books, pamphlets, serials, drawings, and mss on all aspects of botany, plant utilization, and horticulture, amounting to over 300,000 items. The nucleus of the book collection was the gift in 1852 of *c*600 v from the library of William Arnold Bromfield (1801–51) by his sister Eliza, including fine copies of the works of the older botanists. In 1854 George Bentham (1800–84) gave his herbarium and a collection of *c*1,000 textbooks which he had collected while preparing the *Genera Plantarum* with Hooker. In 1867 Hooker's mss and herbarium, and 4,000 v from his library, were bought; they included many finely illustrated works, the nucleus of the Travels collection, and 228 v of pamphlets. The Rev Miles Joseph Berkeley (1803–89) FRS donated his library and herbarium of cryptogamia in 1879. John Ball (1818–89) FRS, MP, first

President of the Alpine Club, bequeathed a collection rich in continental works. In 1892 Thomas Hanbury (1832–1907) FLS donated *c*30 15th-17th cent books which had been used by his brother Daniel Hanbury (1825–75) FRS, partner in the family pharmaceutical firm and co-owner of the garden they had founded at La Mortola near Vengimiglia, in the writing of *Pharmacographia: a history of...drugs.... In 1974 the scientific trustees of Norman Douglas Simpson (1890–1974) FLS, compiler of the Bibliographical index of the British flora* gave 992 books from the unsurpassed British botanical collection of 6,000 v which he had amassed, the greater part of which is at the Cambridge Botany School. Since 1884 many rare books have been bought with funds provided by the Bentham-Moxon Trust, founded by Bentham's bequest and supplemented by the Moxon family.

Report issued annually 1844–82.

'Review of the work of the...Gardens', Appendix to *Bulletin of Miscellaneous Information* 1887–1942 and to Kew *Bulletin* 1946–58, 1972–6, thereafter as 'Annual Report'; not published 1883–6, 1943–5, 1959–71.

Ms lists of Bromfield, Bentham and Hooker collections in the Archives.

Hanbury described in *Bulletin* 1893, p22-4 (see also 1907 No 4, p132-6).

Functions and work of the Royal Botanic Gardens, Kew and Wakehurst Place rev ed Kew, 1981, p12-13.

Herbarium and Library: the opening...of the New Wing...1969. Kew, 1969. A history and description.

Mea Allan, *The Hookers of Kew 1785–1911*, London, Joseph, 1967.

R G C Desmond, 'The Library of the Royal Botanic Gardens, Kew', *Bulletin of the Circle of State Librarians* 17(3) 1969, p29-32.

——'Kew Herbarium and Library', *Journal of the Kew Guild*, 8(74) (1969) p1081-6, and *Supplement* (1970) 'The Queen's Garden and the Herbarium', p5-21.

R Davidge, 'The Library of the Royal Botanic Gardens, Kew', *London Librarian* 9, 1960, p3-9.

See also the extensive bibliographies to the articles in Ray Desmond, *Dictionary of...botanists*, 1977.

Serials Collection It contains *c*3,000 sets of periodicals and other serials including *c*200 wholly or partly pre-1851, botanical and natural history journals and publications of academies, British and foreign.

List of periodical publications in the Library, London, HMSO, 1978, superseding list in 1899 cat.

Monographs The whole library contains *c*120,000 books and *c*140,000 pamphlets. *c*7,000 of these are pre-1851, mostly in the special collections below, but many 1801–50 works are in the general collections. Early 19th cent pamphlets in Opuscula collection by authors.

Author card cat of all the collections published as *Author catalogue of the Royal Botanic Gardens Library, Kew, England*, Boston, G K Hall, 1974, 5 v (superseding 'Catalogue of the Library' in *Bulletin of miscellaneous information*. Additional series 3 and *Supplement* 1919 continued by accessions lists in 'Review of the work' section of *Bulletin*). *Classified catalogue...* Boston, G K Hall, 1974, 4 v excludes Kewensia Archives and certain other collections.

Pre-Linnaean Botany Collection *c*2,000 items, including *c*25 incunabula, *c*150 1501–1700 English, *c*1,400 1501–1700 foreign.

British items in Henrey.

Linnaean Botany Collection *c*250 editions of Linnaeus, and *c*2,000 other items to *c*1830.

Floras Collection *c*8,000 systematic floras of all parts of the world.

Classified cat v 4, p285-368.

Travels *c*2,400 items including nearly 1,000 from Hooker's collection, collected for their botanical descriptions and accounts of the discovery of plants in foreign countries. Almost all in English, mostly late 18th and 19th cent.

Classified cat v 4, p285-368.

Kewensia Books, pamphlets, and a few mss on the Royal Botanic Gardens and on the history of the surrounding locality. Official Kew publications are all included.

In author cat but not classified cat.

Archives The official records of the Gardens are kept here under the terms of the Public Records Act 1958; these include some printed items. A large number of miscellaneous mss are also included.

Natural history manuscript resources, London, Mansell, 1980, p242-61, lists the collections selectively. Some items are in the author cat. Handlist superseding list of mss in 1899 cat.

Botanic Gardens Collection *c*1,000 pamphlets and other monographs on other public gardens, mostly in a special collection.

Classified cat 712.56.

Biographies of botanists A collection of *c*9,000 items in classified cat (920), of which many are in special collections 'Biographers' or 'Obituary and biography tracts'.

Botanists' libraries This collection consists of *c*40 sale catalogues collected alphabetically under names of collectors.

Author cat under 'Botanists' libraries'.

Royal College of Art Library, Kensington Gore, London SW7 2EU. Tel (01) 584 5020 Ext 318. College library open Mon-Fri 10 am-5 pm; Colour Library Mon-Thurs 2-5 pm, by appointment only, on written application to the librarian. Photocopying and photography; microform reader.

The College was incorporated by Royal Charter in 1897 (as the successor of the National Art Training School, founded in 1837 as the School of Design, whose library was transferred to what is now the Victoria and Albert

Museum in 1852). It received University status in 1968, but until 1953 depended entirely on the Museum Library.

The College Library Established 1953, it now contains *c*38,000 titles on the visual arts, especially design, visual perception, aesthetics; the history and criticism of other arts; with some books on history, religion and philosophy. 42 titles are pre-1850.

Card cat.

H Brill, 'The Royal College of Art Library', *ARLIS Newsletter* No 3 (1970), p3-6.

Colour Reference Library Established in 1977 with the purchase of the collection of Don Pavey, ARCA, it is the most comprehensive special collection on colour and allied subjects in existence, with over 3,000 v, including *c*1,100 monograph titles (24 pre-1850) excluding a large collection of pamphlets and offprints, and 30 periodical runs. It includes both scientific and artistic treatments of the subject, historically as well as currently. There are collections of outstanding examples of colour printing and the application of colour in various fields; and colour atlases, and samples charting changing preferences in applied colour.

Card cat.

Royal College of Music Library, Prince Consort Road, South Kensington, London SW7 2BS. Tel (01) 589 3643. Open in term only, Mon-Fri 10 am-5 pm after previous written application, but only for work which cannot be carried on elsewhere.

Parry Room Reference Library When the college was founded in 1883, the library of the Sacred Harmonic Society (which included *c*600 pre-1851 musicological works) was bought by public subscription to form the nucleus of the college library. The library was enlarged from the collections of the Concerts of Ancient Music (donated by Queen Victoria), of the Musical Union (transferred from the Victoria and Albert Museum in 1900), of Sir George Grove (1820–1900) donated 1897–8, and of Sir C Hubert Parry (1848–1918). There are now *c*200 musicological works of the 18th cent, with a few earlier. There is also a collection of music periodicals beginning in the 18th cent.

Catalogue of the library of the Sacred Harmonic Society. New ed 1872 and *Supplement* 1882. Pre-1801 musicological works in *RISM* pt B VI.

H L Colles, *The Royal College of Music 1883–1933*, London, 1933. (op)

Department of Portraits and Ephemera Collection of concert programmes (in addition to engravings, photographs and scores).

Royal College of Nursing of the United Kingdom. Library of Nursing, 1a Henrietta Place, London W1M 0IB. Tel (01) 409 3333. Open Mon-Fri 9 am-5 pm (Tues-Thurs in term 6 pm) for bona fide research; those wishing to consult rare material must write in advance to the librarian.

The College of Nursing was founded in 1916 and chartered in 1928. The Library of Nursing was founded in 1921 by the College to provide a library service for the nursing profession generally, but full services are now restricted to members of the College and students of the Associated Institute of Advanced Nursing Education. It contains *c*32,000 v on nursing and related medical and social sciences.

Card cat.

A M C Thompson, 'The Library of the Royal College of Nursing', *Library Assoc Record*, 54 (1952), p332-4.

Gerald Bowman, *The lamp and the book: the story of the RCN*, London, Queen Anne Press, 1967, p39, 101.

Pre-Nightingale Collection A miscellaneous collection, over 100 v of books from the 17th cent onwards, on subjects related to the care of the sick and medicine, including general medical works, especially domestic medicine, midwifery, pharmacy, etc, and some 19th cent works on hygiene and public health.

Florence Nightingale Collection Contains 20 books from the library of Florence Nightingale (1820–1910), mainly religious and literary works (some inherited from her mother), given in 1973 by Miss Stella Bonham-Carter; a few of her own works, and *c*30 books about her.

Nursing History Collection (after 1859) Several thousand volumes, including virtually every edition of every British nursing textbook, and most of the other published literature on the history of nursing; and complete runs of the *Nursing Record*, and virtually all other pre-1920 nursing periodicals; a major collection of 19th cent British government publications on nursing and public health.

Alice M C Thompson, *A bibliography of nursing literature, 1859–1960 and 1961–70*, London, Library Association and the College, 1968–74; most of the works listed are in the collection.

Royal College of Obstetricians and Gynaecologists Library, 27 Sussex Place, Regents Park West, London NW1 4RG. Tel (01) 262 5425 Ext 12. Open Mon-Fri 10 am-5 pm to Fellows and Members; to others with suitable introduction. Photocopier.

The College was founded in 1929 as the British College of Obstetricians and Gynaecologists, receiving a Royal Charter in 1938. It regulates professional qualifications. The library dates from the first Blair-Bell gift in 1932, and was originally a historical collection only, later extended to include current literature. It contains *c*3,500 monographs and *c*8,000 v of periodicals.

Sir William Fletcher Shaw, *Twenty-five years: the story of the Royal College of Obstetricians and Gynaecologists*, London, Churchill, 1954, especially p110-1, 124-5.

Annual Report of the Council, 1930–

W F Shaw, 'The birth of a College' and 'The College: its past, present and future', *Journ of Obstetrics and Gynaecology of the British Empire* 57 (1950), p875-99; 61 (1954), p557-66.

J L Thornton and P Want, 'The Royal College of Obstetricians and Gynaecologists', *St Bartholomew's Hospital Journal* 77 (1973), p36-9.

Sir John Peel, *Lives of the Fellows of the... College... 1929–1969*, London, Heinemann, 1974.

Historical Collection (general) This Collection has been built up mainly by donation, particularly from the major benefactions listed below: (these are not maintained as separate collections), and contains *c*1,700 pre-1851 items on obstetrics, gynaecology, and related subjects, including 2 incunabula; 18 STC and *c*100 Wing items, and 38 16th cent and *c*100 17th cent foreign. Also mss. Arranged within centuries alphabetically by authors.

General author and subject cats on cards.

Abridged author entries in *Catalogue of the Library up to 1850*, 1956, greatly enlarged in *Short-title catalogue of books printed before 1851*, 1968.

J L Thornton and P C Want, 'Antique books in the Library of the... College...', *British Journ of Obstetrics and Gynaecology* 88(4) (1981), p337-45.

E Holland, 'The Library of the... College... to... 1850', *Journ of Obstetrics and Gynaecology of the British Empire* 64 (1957), p282-7.

J L Thornton and P C Want, 'Obstetrics and Gynaecology' in *Use of medical literature*, ed L T Morton, 2nd ed, London, Butterworth, 1977, p348-78.

Blair-Bell, William (1871–1936) Founder of the College and of the Library. His series of gifts began with the writings of William Smellie (1697–1763) and he finally bequeathed *c*450 v from 1478 onwards.

Dobbin, Roy (Samuel) (1873–1939), Prof of Midwifery at Cairo, donated books at various times. He collected a library with the intention of using it to write the history of British obstetrics, and then enlarged it to cover the whole field of medical literature. He deposited the rare books at the Royal College of Surgeons, who declined to purchase them. 150 of the books were then bought for the Obstetricians in 1935 with money raised by the widow of Sir Henry Simson (1872–1932) from his patients. Strong in 16th and 17th cent anatomy, especially Andreas Vesalius (1514–64) and in the literature surrounding Michael Servetus (1511–53) and the history of the pulmonary circulation.

Ms handlist by Dobb, 1931, with notes of previous owners.

J L Thornton and P C Want, 'Roy Samuel Dobbin, book collector and benefactor of the... College...', *Proc of the XXIII Congress of the History of Medicine, London 1972*, v 2, p1087-98 (with summary of the correspondence at the Library of the Royal College of Surgeons).

Peel, op cit p134-6.

Holland, Sir Eardley (Lancelot) (1879–1967), President, author of the standard *Manual of Obstetrics*, gave numerous books. He sold part of his collection (Sotheby 25 July 1960); a number of the lots were bought by the College. Mainly 18th and early 19th cent.

Peel, op cit, p202-5.

Phillips, Miles (Harris) (1875–1965), Prof of Obstetrics at Sheffield, assembled an 18th and 19th cent collection. Part donated during his lifetime, part bought at the sale of the residue (Knight 17 Nov 1965).

Gunn, Alistair (Livingston) (1903–70), Hon Librarian Gynaecologist to Lewisham hospitals, bought in 1955 the obstetric portion of the library of Alfred Myer Hellman (1880–1955) American gynaecologist and bibliophile, consisting of 47 editions of rare foreign works 1513–1635. He collected a further 257 later editions, and gave the whole collection to his wife, who sold it anonymously (Bonham 10 Oct 1979). *c*30 items, *c*12 from the Hellman portion, were bought by the College.

Alfred M Hellman, *A collection of early obstetrical books: an historical essay with bibliographical descriptions of 37 items, including 25 editions of Roesslin's Rosengarten*, New Haven, priv pr 1952; additions in *Academy Bookman* 11(2) (1958), p2-11; see also 8(1) (1955), p2-13 (memoir).

F Gibb, 'Milestones in the midwifery story', *Daily Telegraph* 10 Oct 1979, p7 (sale).

Alfred M Hellman, *The physiology and pathology of book collecting*, New York, priv pr 1949.

Obituaries of Gunn in *British Medical Journal* 1970(4), p562; *Journal of Obstetrics and Gynaecology of the British Empire* 78 (1971), p1901.

Royal College of Organists' Library, Kensington Gore, London SW7 2QS. Tel (01) 589 1765. Open (except Aug) 10 am-5 pm by appointment on written application to the librarian.

The College Library contains *c*200 books and pamphlets on the organ in addition to records and scores. It also houses the library of the Organ Club, open to members, which contains a much larger collection of literature on the organ.

Royal College of Physicians of London, 11 St Andrew's Place, Regents Park East, London NW1 4LE. Tel (01) 935 1174. Open Mon-Fri 10 am-5 pm to Fellows, Members and Licentiates; also to bona fide research workers by prior arrangement with the librarian. Photocopying and photography; microfilm and fiche readers.

A College Library

The College of Physicians was founded in 1518 to regulate the practice of medicine in and around London. Its Library dates from the same year, and until the 19th cent was not limited to medical subjects.

A brief introduction to the Library, (1981).

A history of the Royal College of Physicians, Oxford,

Clarendon Press, 1964–72, v 1-2 by Sir George Clark; v 3 by A M Cooke.

C E Newman and L M Payne, 'A history of the College Library', *Journ Roy Coll Physicians* 3(3) (1969); 4(3) (1970); 5(4) (1971); 7(2) (1973); 8(3), 9(1) 1974; 11(2) (1976); 11(3) (1977); 12(2) (1978).

C Dodd, 'Christopher Merrett, FRCP (1614–1695), first Harveian Librarian', *Proceedings of the Roy Soc of Medicine* 47 (1954), p1053-6.

Extensive archives, including ms Annals of the College, and ms 'Short History' by F J Farre, 1883.

Charles Knight, *London*, 1842, v 2, p17-32.

General Collection The Library is now devoted to the history and biography of medicine, with a modern collection of works in this field supported by primary texts in all medical subjects, predominantly from donations of former centuries. The General and Dorchester collections together contain *c*18,000 books, including 106 incunabula; 3,000 books of the 16th cent and 5,000 of the 17th; 300 STC; and 750 Wing items. Also collections of mss and portraits.

Name cat on cards.

Catalogue of the Library of the Royal College of Physicians of London, 1912, authors (for earlier catalogues see below).

Bibliothecae Collegii Regalis Medicorum Londinensis Catalogus, 1757.

Catalogue, 1827, in ms.

(Some of the non-medical books and duplicates have been dispersed, Sotheby 23 and 31 July 1962; 14 Dec 1964.)

Over 100 exhibition cats (duplicated typescript) cumulating into volumes (sometimes indexed): subjects include John Dee, 1953; Sir Hans Sloane, 1953 and 1960; John Caius, 1955; Thomas Linacre, 1960; William Harvey, 1957 and 1958; Sir Joseph Banks, 1978; and 'A brief introduction to the Library', 1959.

Books surviving from before the Fire of 1666 140 books were saved from the destruction of the original College Library. These include perhaps 3 of the collections which Thomas Linacre (1460?–1524) gave to found the library and some from the collections of William Gilbert (1549–1604), author of *De Magnete*, and Matthew Holsbosch (*d*1629), a physician from Germany, who gave 680 books in 1628–9.

List of the books saved from the Fire, by C Merrett, 1680 (printed in E Boswell, 'The Library of the Royal College of Physicians in the Great Fire', *The Library* 4th ser 10 (1930), p313-26.

Francis Maddison et al *Essays on the life and work of Thomas Linacre*, Oxford, Clarendon Press, 1977.

Catalogus librorum (by C Merrett) 1660, listing 1,278 titles (British Library copy 821.h.2 appears to be unique).

Collegii Medicorum Londinensium fundatores et benefactores (1662).

G Keynes, *The life of William Harvey*, Oxford, Clarendon Press, 1966, p397-403.

K D Keele, 'William Harvey: the man and the College of Physicians', *Medical History* 1 (1957), p265-78.

Dorchester Library, bequeathed by Henry Pierrepont, 1st Marquis of Dorchester (1606–80) FRS, scholar, chemist, and respected amateur physician; maintained as a separate collection. A typical gentleman's library, described by a contemporary as 'the best for physic, mathematics, civil law and philology in any private hand'. 2,101 works (in 3,270 v) comprising 825 on mathematics and physical sciences, 508 on law, 192 on medical and biological sciences, and 578 on non-scientific subjects. 27 incunabula (including Caxton's *Recuyell* (*c*1473) and the unique copy of the first book on dancing (Paris *c*1488); 50 STC; 39 Wing. Many association copies, some from the library of John Dee (1527–1608) mathematician, astrologer and alchemist. Most are finely bound and in excellent condition.

Cat by T Salusbury on vellum 1664 with later additions. Distinctive cards in general author cat.

L M Payne and C E Newman, 'The Dorchester Library', *Journal* 4 (1970), p234-45.

J F Fulton, 'The Library of Henry Pierrepont, first Marquis of Dorchester', *Journ of the History of Medicine* 14(1) (1959), p89-90.

The Library of the Marquis of Dorchester, 1958 (exhibition cat).

Benefactions from Fellows and Members, not now separate. Richard Hale (*c*1673–1728) gave large sums of money to buy books; these once formed a separate collection. Thomas Crowe or Crow (*c*1674–1751), compiler of the London *Pharmacopoeia*, bequeathed his books not in English, mostly medical works in Latin and the Greek and Latin classics. Thomas Gisborne (*c*1727–1806) Physician to St George's Hospital, gave in 1794 and bequeathed 750 v and a collection of pamphlets; three-quarters were medical. Matthew Baillie (1761–1823), Physician to George III, bequeathed his medical library of *c*900 books (including *c*180 pre-1701). Andrew Bain (*c*1758–1827), Physician Extraordinary to the Prince Regent from 1811, bequeathed all his medical and chemical books. Richard Powell (1767–1834) Physician at Bart's and reviser of the *Pharmacopoeia*, bequeathed his library. Arthur Farre (1811–87) FRS, Physician-Accoucheur to the Royal Family, bequeathed over 1,000 rare obstetrical and other works. The Edward Meryon (1809–80) collection on prostitution, and his pamphlets from the library of Charles Witt (*c*1796–1883), Surgeon at Northampton, have been partly dispersed. (David) Lloyd Roberts (1835–1920), gynaecologist, bequeathed a fine library of 3,000 v, including 46 incunabula and over 300 16th cent books.

Register of Donors does not list the large collections.

William Munk, *The Roll of the Royal College of Physicians*, v 1-5, 1878–1968, notes benefactions of Fellows and Members.

Evan Bedford Library of Cardiology Presented in 1971 by David Evan Bedford (1899–1978) CBE, MD, FRCP, the eminent cardiologist. 1,112 items (289 pre-1851; 3,of 16th cent; 37 17th cent and 7 Wing).

The Evan Bedford Library of Cardiology: catalogue of books, pamphlets and journals, 1977, in broad subject groups, with index of authors, subjects and associations.

Serials c250 sets, of which c100 are wholly or partly pre-1851, including publications of British and foreign medical academies and societies, early general medical periodicals, and a collection of medical directories.

A list of serial publications in the Library of the Royal College of Physicians of London, 1950, prepared for incorporation in the *British union-catalogue of periodicals*.

Barlow bookplates A collection of 2,700 bookplates of medical men and institutions, donated by Horace Mallinson Barlow.

B **Deposited Libraries**

Permission in writing from the Librarian of the depositing institution should be obtained before applying to College Librarian for access.

British Association of Dermatologists, Willan Library The Association was founded in 1920, and built up a collection of the works of Robert Willan (1757–1812), the father of scientific dermatology. In 1967 Sir Archibald (Montague Henry) Gray (1880–1967) bequeathed his dermatological collection to form the nucleus of a general library of dermatology, strong in historical texts. c558 v including 50 pre-1851; 1 Wing.

Author cat on cards.

Sir A Gray, 'The British Association of Dermatology', *British Journ of Dermatology* 72 (1960), p243-8.

G B Dowling, 'The British Association of Dermatology 1920–1970', *Ibid*, 3 (1970) Special jubilee issue, p119-25.

Heberden Society Library The Society was founded in 1936 as the Committee for the Study and Investigation of Rheumatism, and became the Heberden Society in 1937, after William Heberden the elder (1710–1801) who first described the nodules of arthritis on the fingers. The Library was founded in 1938 when the Hon Secretary, William Sydney Charles Copeman (1900–70) CBE donated his historical collection to the Society, and it has been built up subsequently by gifts and purchases, primarily as a historical collection on rheumatism, gout and related diseases. c650 v from 1534 onwards, including c250 pre-1851; 5 16th cent items; 16 17th cent (including 7 Wing); 115 18th cent. c60 serials and conference series, all post-1850.

Heberden Society, *Catalogue of the Library* 3rd ed 1976, containing pre-1915 author cat.

Modern author cat.

Serials and conference proceedings and miscellaneous (objects, mss, prints etc).

1st ed entitled *The Library of the Heberden Society*, 1960, and 2nd ed, 1966, include only a small proportion of the present library.

W S C Copeman, 'The Heberden Society', *Medical News* 21 June 1968, p6.

Osler Club Library The Club, founded in 1928 to perpetuate the memory of Sir William Osler (1849–1919) and to foster the study of medical history, was re-established in 1947, when 12 books, all that survived from its bombed library, became the nucleus of a new collection. c320 v by and about Osler; other material, including early medical texts, has been dispersed. It incorporates the comprehensive collection of Osler's works formed by Dr (Louis) Carlyle Lyon (1899–1970).

M E S Abbott, *Classified and annotated bibliography of Sir William Osler's publications*, 1939.

E F Nation et al. An annotated checklist of Osleriana, Kent State Univ Pr 1976, by authors.

Royal College of Physicians, *Osleriana*, 1975 (exhibition cat).

A W Franklin, 'The Osler Club of London', *Medical Press* 222 (5749) (13 July 1949), p32-4; abridgment *The Osler Club of London: a brief history*, Oxford Univ Pr 1965.

The Osler Club of London (1962) includes a history of the Club omitted from later editions. *St Bartholomews Hospital Journ* 65 (1961), p53-4.

Royal College of Psychiatrists Library, 17 Belgrave Square, London SW1X 8PG. Tel (01) 235 2351. Open Mon-Fri 10 am-4.30 pm to college members; to bona fide students by prior arrangement with the librarian.

The College was founded in 1841 by Samuel Hitch (c1800–c82), physician to the Gloucestershire General Lunatic Asylum, as the Association of Medical Officers of Asylums and Hospitals for the Insane. In 1865 it became the Medico-psychological Association (1888–1925 'of Great Britain and Ireland'), in 1925 the Royal Medico-Psychological Association. In 1971 it was reconstituted under a new charter as the Royal College of Psychiatrists, a body regulating statutory qualifications in psychiatry. Its library was founded in 1854, and now contains c6,000 v.

Catalogue of the Library of the Royal Medico-Psychological Association, 1928 (authors; subject index).

Card cat being compiled.

A Walk, 'The Royal College of Psychiatrists', *St Bartholomew's Hospital Journ* 77 (1973), p135-9.

History in *General Index to the First twenty-four volumes of the Journal of Mental Science*, 1879.

Historical Collection Classic and early books on psychiatry. c500 v, mainly 19th cent, some 17th and 18th cent works, but one book of 1483.

Cat in preparation.

Royal College of Surgeons of England Library, 35 Lincoln's Inn Fields, London WC2A 3PN. Tel (01) 405 3474 Ext 8. Open (except Aug) Mon-Fri 10 am-6

pm to staff and diplomates of the College; to others introduced by a Fellow, or by the Dean of a medical school, or at the librarian's discretion. Photocopying and photography; microfiche reader.

The mediaeval Company of Surgeons, joined with the Barbers into the Barber-Surgeons from 1540 to 1745, when their library was sold, was reconstituted by charter in 1800 as the 'Royal College of Surgeons of London' ('of England' from 1845). A library, which was stipulated in the charter, was begun immediately, and became an important adjunct to the Museum formed by John Hunter, which had been bought for the nation by Parliament in 1799 and passed on to the College with endowments; it still serves the Hunterian Museum, and other research departments which have been added to the College in the present cent. In 1828 it was first made available for professional use, and thereafter was rapidly built up by purchase, donation and exchange, until by 1900 it was the largest medical library in the British Empire. More recently it has become restricted to surgery and its specialities (including anaesthesia and dental surgery) the sciences basic to surgery (especially anatomy, pathology and physiology); together with the history of medical science. Books of earlier periods include comparative anatomy, materia medica, zoology, and other subjects. There are now *c*45,000 v of monographs, *c*50,000 pamphlets and *c*110,000 v of periodicals.

Z Cope, *The Royal College of Surgeons: a history*, London, Blond, 1959, p257-73.

Royal College of Surgeons of England, *Souvenir of the centenary*, London, 1900, especially p24.

A record of the years from 1901–1950, 1951, p15-17.

Annals of the Royal College of Surgeons of England (1947–), including accessions lists and other information on the Library; similar information in *Calendar* 1865–1940.

W R LeFanu, 'The history of the College Library', *Annals* 9 (1951), p366-82.

——'Medical libraries of the world, 1', *Medicine Illustrated* 3 (1949) p36-7.

E H Cornelius, 'The Library of the College: a short account of its history, present state, and future development', *Ibid* 46 (1970), p41-6.

J B Bailey, 'The Library of the Royal College of Surgeons', *The Library* 1 (1889) p249-61; abridgment in *Medical Press* ns 48 (1889), p163.

——'The Royal College of Surgeons of England', *Bull Med Lib Assoc* 25 (1937), p233-5.

Rare Book Collection (General) *c*7,500 v, separated from the main library in the 1950s. 57 incunabula, including the first printed medical book (Nicolaus, *Antidotarium*, Venice 1471), classical texts, plague and syphilis tracts of the 1480s and 1490s and the earliest herbals. *c*145 STC books and *c*490 Wing, including several works not recorded elsewhere. Over 600 foreign 16th cent books, including an outstanding series of anatomical atlases and surgical texts, editions of classical and Arab medicine, herbals, zoology, and books by British writers (eg Turner on birds, Cologne 1544; Wotton on animals, Paris 1551–2; and Kinloch's Lucretian poem on generation, Paris 1596); *c*1,000 foreign 17th cent items, mainly anatomy and surgery, with the principal physiological texts (eg Aselli, Descartes, Harvey 1628, Malpighi, Pecquet); *c*2,500 English and foreign 18th cent books, including important first editions in most branches of medicine; extensive pamphlet collections; comprehensive series of editions of the leading British surgeons. Later 19th cent books include the chief French and German anatomy and physiology texts. Select modern books of scientific importance, rarity, or special association; especially prominent British surgeons, with extensive collections of the Spanish neurologist Santiago Ramon y Cajal (1852–1934), and the pioneer American neurosurgeon Harvey (Williams) Cushing (1869–1939).

Included in general card cat (dictionary, being separated into author and alphabetical subject).

Cat of incunabula in *Annals of Medical History* ns 3 (1931), p674-6.

English books printed before 1701 in the Library of the Royal College of Surgeons of England, Edinburgh, Livingstone, 1963 (available from the Library).

Catalogue of the Library of the Royal College of Physicians of England, 1831 (authors); Supplements 1840 (pt 2), 1849 (v 3 pt 1), 1853 (v 3 pt 2); classified *Index* in v 3, 1853; *Additions to the index*, 1855.

A classed catalogue of the books contained in the Library, 1843.

Periodicals A general collection of *c*4,000 sets, strong in the publications of British and foreign scientific academies. It has been slightly reduced in recent years to those more strictly related to surgery, but the major collection of the 18th and early 19th cent journals remains almost intact.

List of the transactions, periodicals and memoirs in the Library of the Royal College of Physicians, 1890, 2nd ed 1931.

Also in *World List* and *BUCOP*.

Hunter Collection A separate collection of works by and about John Hunter (1728–93), his contemporaries and pupils. 30 editions of Hunter are included. Others include Matthew Baillie (1761–1823) FRS, the morbid anatomist, his nephew, and Sir Everard Hume Bt. (1756–1832) his son-in-law, both of whom were major donors to the library. Related mss are held in the Hunter-Baillie collection.

W R LeFanu, *John Hunter: a list of his books*, London, the College, 1946.

——'The Hunter-Baillie manuscripts', *Trans Hunterian Soc* 12 (1953/4), p88-101.

List of books, manuscripts, portraits, &c, relating to John Hunter in the... College..., 1891.

'The Hunter-Baillie collection', *British Med Journ*, 1926 (2), p120-1.

Campbell, John Menzies (1887–1974), historian of dentistry. His collection of historic works on dentistry, c500 items (in addition to c1,000 advertisements 1709 onwards), including 30 pre-1801, mostly 1750–1860 British and American, with a few French; sets of journals. Given in 1969 on condition that it should be incorporated into the general collections, his collection of instruments and dental equipment having been given in 1964 to the Royal College of Surgeons of Edinburgh.

J Menzies Campbell, *Dental books, etc gifted to the Royal College of Surgeons of England* (1974).

——*A dental bibliography, British and American, 1683–1880*, London, 1949.

M E Ring, 'In memoriam J Menzies Campbell', *Bull Hist Dentistry* 22 (1974), p71-82.

Keynes Collection on blood transfusion c60 books and pamphlets given by Sir Geoffrey (Langdon) Keynes (b1887) c1975 on condition that they should form a separate collection. 16th-20th cent.

Included in Keynes, *Bibliotheca bibliographici*, 1964.

Collections dispersed among the general rare book collections These include c600 17th cent and other editions given by the widow of William Sharpe, c1820; the library bequeathed by William Long, Master in 1800 of surgery and medicine, strong in anatomy, natural history, travels by medical men, and vaccination, including first editions of pamphlets by Edward Jenner (1749–1823); over 650 editions (including 4 incunabula) sold for a nominal sum by Sir Anthony Carlisle (1768–1840) FRS, President; a small collection of books from Sir Richard Owen (1804–92) Conservator of the Hunterian Museum (his papers, which include proofs of published works, are in the ms collection); donations and bequest of early printed books from Sir John Tweedy (1849–1924) President; numerous donations of rare books from Sir Charles (Scott) Sherrington OM FRS (1857–1952); and the bequest of c3,000 books and mss by Sir Arthur Keith FRS (1866–1955), anthropologist, Conservator of the Hunterian Museum.

Ms lists of most, but some items no longer in the Library.

Handlist of Owen Collection (see also *Natural history manuscript resources* 271.42; *Annals* 30 (1962), p117-24; 15 (1954) p272-3).

Ms autobibliography by Keith (see also *Ibid* 271.32; *Autobiography*, London, 1950; *Ibid* 38 (1966), p233-5; 39 (1966), p17-29).

Archives and special materials The College archives, and the Lock Hospital archives include some official printed documents. There are important collections of mss, portraits, photographs, and medals. Also a collection of c2,000 bookplates of medical men, mainly British.

V G Plarr, *Catalogue of manuscripts*, 1928.

Natural history manuscript resources, London, Mansell, 1980, p262-7.

Royal College of Veterinary Surgeons, Wellcome Library, 32 Belgrave Square, London SW1X 8QP. Tel (01) 235 6568. Open Mon-Fri 10 am-5 pm to those on the registers of the College; to bona fide research workers on introduction by a MRCVS or a librarian. Photocopying.

The College is the governing body of the veterinary profession in the United Kingdom, founded with a Charter in 1844. Its library, founded c1853, was until 1954 known as the Central Library for Animal Diseases, and from 1954 to 1964 as the Memorial Library. It has been built up mostly by donation and bequest, but suffered war damage. It now contains c27,000 v on veterinary science, animal nutrition, and comparative medicine.

Card cat. *Catalogue of modern works 1900–1954*, 2nd ed, 1955.

B Horder, 'The Royal College of Veterinary Surgeons Wellcome Library', *Veterinary Annual* 9 (1968), p42-7.

G F Boddie, 'The Memorial Library of the Royal College of Veterinary Surgeons', *Veterinary Record* 67 (1955), p99-101.

Historical Collection Made up of c2,500 v, 1528–1850, the collection includes 13 STC, 20 Wing, 3 foreign 16th cent and 13 17th cent items; also mss, mostly on veterinary subjects, especially farriery, but some on general medicine. It includes books from the collections of George Fleming (1833–1901), William Percivall (1792–1854), and John Field (fl 1856); 56 works on farriery by Bracy Clark (1771–1860), and many books from a large collection donated in 1969 to the library in memory of John Anderson, Secretary of the British Veterinary Association.

Catalogue of the Historical Collection: books published before 1850, 1953; supplement 1959 (both op, together recording c800 items).

Royal Commonwealth Society Library, 18 Northumberland Avenue, Charing Cross, London WC2N 5BJ. Tel (01) 930 6733 Ext 58. Open Mon-Fri 10 am-5.30 pm to members and accredited students. Photocopier; microform readers.

The Colonial Society was founded in 1868 to spread knowledge of the peoples and countries of the British Empire. In 1869 it was renamed Royal Colonial Society, in 1870 Royal Colonial Institute, in 1928 Royal Empire Society, and in 1958 Royal Commonwealth Society. The library from the outset has played a major role in the Society's affairs.

Trevor R Reese, *The history of the Royal Commonwealth Society 1868–1968*, London, OUP, 1968.

'A century of the Library', *Library Notes* ns no 133, 135, 137-9, 141, 143, (1968).

D H Simpson, 'Treasures of the Royal Commonwealth Society Library', *Commonwealth Journal* 11(1-5) (1968).

——'An internationally famous library' in *Royal Commonwealth Soc 1868–1968: centenary souvenir*, 1968, p55-9.

——'Educational material in the Library of the Royal Empire Society' *Education Libraries Bulletin* no 1 (1958), p12-15.

'The Library of the Royal Commonwealth Society as a centre for research', *Library Notes*, ns no 229 (1979), p1-4.

Many collections are described in *Library Notes* (1950–).

General The library contains *c*400,000 books, pamphlets and periodicals for the most part, but including maps, mss, drawings and watercolours. Though in its early years it depended to a considerable extent on donations (which have to some degree continued) it has been built up by current and retrospective systematic purchasing from early in the present century into the most important collection for the study of the Commonwealth. Major strengths include early exploration, biography and early imaginative literature from the Commonwealth. *c*35,000 v and 5,000 pamphlets, mainly from the general section, were bombed in 1940. The library is arranged topographically by a special classification, and individual donations and bequests are not kept as separate collections.

Personal authors and societies cats on cards.

The biography catalogue of the Royal Commonwealth Society, London, the Society, 1961; also cards.

The subject catalogue of the Royal Empire Society, 1930–7, 4 v, topographical with subject divisions each chronologically arranged; repr with important new introductions Folkestone, Dawson, 1967; supplement reproduced from cards published with the misleading title *Subject catalogue of the Royal Commonwealth Society*, Boston (Mass), G K Hall, 1971, 7 v and *Supplement* 1977, 2 v; also on cards.

The manuscript catalogue of the Library of the Royal Commonwealth Society, London, Mansell, 1975; supplements in *Library Notes* no 217 (1976) and 225 (1978).

Superseded catalogues include 'Library catalogue', *Proc Roy Colonial Inst* 8 (1876–7), p457-79 (alph.subject); *Catalogue of the Library of the Royal Colonial Institute*, (1881) (authors); 1886 (topographical, author index); 1895 (chronological, author and subject indexes).

First supplementary catalogue, 1901.

Periodicals Collection *c*2,500 sets, including many published in the Commonwealth which are not available elsewhere.

Card cat.

List of newspapers, magazines, and other periodicals taken at the Royal Empire Society, 1935.

Many are indexed in author and subject cats.

Government Publications Over 100,000 v, one of the best collections in existence of the publications of the British, Colonial and Commonwealth governments, and the East India Company, strong overall in 19th cent material.

Card cat.

Voyages and travels A very fine collection of the general collected editions of early voyages was badly depleted in 1940, but much remains or has been replaced. There is also a substantial collection of early atlases.

R A Skelton, 'Maps in the Society's Library', *Library Notes* ns no 176-7 (1971–2); includes atlases.

Europe and the Mediterranean (excluding Cyprus). The Gibraltar and Malta collections were bombed, but small collections remain on the Channel Islands and the formerly British territories of Heligoland, Capri, the Ionian Islands, and Minorca.

Cobham Collection on Cyprus On Cyprus there is more early material than for any other country. A large proportion came from the bequest of Claude Delaval Cobham (1842–1915), Commissioner of Larnaca; well over 1,000 v, including *c*130 pre-1851 from the early 16th cent onwards. Substantial pamphlet collections are included.

'The Cobham Cyprus collection', *Library Notes*, ns no 12 (1957), p1-2.

Subject catalogue v 4, p23-63; Cobham items are asterisked.

C D Cobham, *An attempt at a bibliography of Cyprus*, Nicosia 1886 (chronological); 2nd ed 1889; 3rd ed 1894; new ed arranged alphabetically with additions (by others), 1929.

Asia Collection The collection, which is almost exclusively in English and other Western languages, is strong on the Indian Empire. The British Association of Malaysia has deposited its historical collection: this is mainly biography and memoirs, especially of the 20th cent, but with some earlier material; mainly ms, but includes cuttings and ephemera.

Australasia A very fine collection, particularly for early voyages and the exploration of New Zealand. There is a notable edition, published by the Society in 1962, of the drawings of William Westall (1781–1850) on Flinders's voyage to Australia; the original drawings which were owned by the Society have been transferred to the National Library of Australia.

Africa The collection includes many early and rare works on African exploration. That part of the library of the Royal African Society (founded 1901 and until 1935 called the African Society) which survived bombing and did not duplicate works already held was absorbed in 1949, and a remnant of its archives deposited.

America The collection is noteworthy for the many sets of publications of North American historical and geographical societies, and the Hakluyt Society. There is a substantial collection of the works of Hakluyt, Purchase and other explorers.

The West Indies collection is of interest for its very extensive pamphlet literature, which includes many on slavery and the slave trade, some of which are thought to be unique; many of these came from the collection of Nicholas Darnell Davis (1846–1915), a West Indies administrator who gave them to the Library.

D H Simpson, 'Treasures in the Society's Library', *Commonwealth Journal* 11(1) (1968), p15-17.

Kipling Society Library A collection of over 1,000 v of works by, or about, Rudyard Kipling (1865–1936), deposited by the Society, whose headquarters are in the building. The Society was founded in 1927, and the library was started soon afterwards; it has been built up almost entirely from donations. The most valuable portion is the bequest, kept separately, of Col M A Wolff (*d*1954), of over 150 early editions of Kipling works, including some very scarce early items. Other benefactors include Capt Ernest Walter Martindell, the bibliographer of Kipling. There are some association copies, and curiosities of bibliography such as *Putnam* printed by Kipling on two sheets of crepe paper at Rottingdean in 1900.

Card cat.

'The Kipling Society Library', *Library Notes* n s no 134 (1968), p1-3.

'The Kipling Society Library', *Kipling Journal* 35 (166) (1968), p12-14.

Royal Entomological Society Library, 41 Queen's Gate, South Kensington, London SW7 5HU. Tel (01) 584 8361. Open Mon-Fri 9.30 am-5 pm to Fellows; to others with introduction from a Fellow. Photocopying.

The Society was founded in 1833 as the Entomological Society of London; the word Royal was prefixed in 1933. The Library was founded at its first meeting, and has been built up by purchase and donation. In addition to the collections below, there are extensive holdings of mss, drawings and photographs.

S A Neave, *History of the Entomological Society of London, 1833–1933*, especially p75-85.

Natural history manuscript resources, London, Mansell, 1980, p268-71.

Archives contain information on the library.

General Collection The first major donation came in 1852 when 67 v of entomology from the library of the botanist William Arnold Bromfield (1801–51) MD, were given by his sister Eliza, and in 1884 the library of the Society's founder William Spence (1783–1860) FRS was donated by his son W B Spence (*d*1900). After the acquisition of the Stainton Library (see below) Robert McLachlan (1837–1904) FRS bequeathed part of his collection which included 12 v of pamphlets on Hemiptera collected by John William Douglas (1814–1905). The collection on Lepidoptera of J J Joicey was bought in 1932. The monographs collections, including rare books, comprise *c*7,000 books and *c*50,000 pamphlets. Most are specialized works on entomology; there is very little general zoology and natural history.

Author card cat reproduced as *Catalogue of the Library of the Royal Entomological Society, London*, Boston, G K Hall, 1980, 5 v (earlier author cats in *Transactions* 1 (1835–7), pxcvii-civ; new ser 5 (1858–61), pl-lii.

Catalogue of the Library of the Entomological Society of London, ed G C Champion, 1893; *Supplementary catalogue of the Library. . .*, 1900.

Accessions lists in *Proceedings*; previously in 'Proceedings' section of *Transactions*.

Rare Books Collection *c*1,250 v of books and pamphlets, including the Stainton books (below). It is a very complete collection of systematic works from 1609–*c*1800, and many later, and includes many of the large and expensive illustrated monographs produced in the 18th and early 19th cent. (Many 19th cent books are in the general collections.)

Stainton, Henry Tibbats (1822–92) FRS, President, took over the library (already open to other entomologists) of James Francis Stephens (1792–1852), then 768 items, and published a catalogue of it. Stainton added to the collection, and when he died his widow gave to the Society all entomological items it did not already possess, *c*600 books and 31 periodicals; about half pre-1851. They are not separated from other collections, but bear a distinctive bookplate.

Supplementary catalogue, 1900, identifies Stainton items.

H T S(tainton), *Bibliotheca Stephensiana: being a catalogue of the entomological library of James Francis Stephens. . . now removed to Mountsfield, Lewisham, where it may be consulted by any entomologist every Wednesday evening as heretofore*, 1853.

Transactions new ser 2 (1852), p46-50.

Proceedings of the Royal Society 52 (1893), pix-xii.

Apiculture A collection on apicultural methods, supplementing the general collection on bees. *c*20 books given in 1839 by the Rev Frederick William Hope (1797–1862) and *c*120 given by the Apiarian Society in 1863 from 16th cent onwards.

Transactions 2 (1837–40), plxxxvii-xci; 3rd ser 1 (1862–4), pxiii-xxiv.

Periodicals Collection *c*11,000 v; *c*600 sets, of which 270 are current, and *c*60 wholly or partly pre-1851. Mostly specifically on entomology; strong in the publications of foreign societies, including some concerned with general natural history (but some of the latter dispersed in 1976).

List of periodicals, 1981 (superseding that of 1951), by title.

Catalogue 1893 contains a geographical list.

Royal Free Hospital Medical Library, Pond Street, Hampstead, London NW3 2QG. Tel (01) 794 0500 Ext 3201. Open Mon-Fri 9 am-7 pm, on written application to the librarian. Photocopying facilities.

The Medical Library combines the libraries of the Hospital and of the School of Medicine, which were separate until 1981. The School was founded in 1874 by Miss Sophia Jex-Blake (1840–1912) as the London School of Education for Women; in 1877 it became associated with the Royal Free Hospital (founded 1828). In 1947 it received its present name, and became a co-educational school of the University of London. The Library contains c30,000 v, mainly current medical works, and some earlier, including c70 pre-1851, mostly from the former School Library.

Isabel Thorne, *Sketch of the foundation and development of the London School of Medicine for Women*, 1913.

Margaret Todd, *The life of Sophia Jex-Blake*, London, 1918, p415-51.

S Jex-Blake, *Medical women* 2nd ed, Edinburgh, 1886.

R M Nicholas, 'The development of medical libraries within the University of London' (MA Librarianship thesis, Univ of London, 1976), p88-91.

Royal Free Hospital School of Medicine, *An exhibition to commemorate the centenary*, 1974 (with history and bibliography).

N I Swift, 'The foundation of the London School of Medicine for Women', *Magazine of the Royal Free Hosp Med School* 8 (1946), p16-20.

'Report of the Library', *Magazine* 1 (1895), p32.

Historical Collection Made up of c700 items and nine books of press cuttings on the history of the School and of the campaign for the medical education of women in the 19th cent, including pamphlets, letters and portraits.

Card cat (names/subjects).

Royal Geographical Society Library, 1 Kensington Gore, London SW7 2AR. Tel (01) 589 5466. Open Mon-Fri 10 am-5 pm to members only; others may be admitted only by special resolution of the Library Committee. Photocopying (restricted).

The Society and its library were founded in 1830, absorbing the African Association (founded 1788) and its archives in 1831. The library contains c100,000 v. There is an independent Map Room, which includes thousands of atlases and gazetteers from the 15th cent onwards, not available to non-members. Archives include minutes, correspondence, etc from 1830, and papers relating to Scott's first expedition, Mary Henrietta Kingsley (1862–1900), David Livingstone (1813–73), and Sir Henry Morton Stanley (1841–1904).

Catalogue of the Map Room, 1845.

Topographical card cat.

G R Crone, 'The Library of the Royal Geographical Society', *Geographical Journ* 121 (1955), p27-32.

——*The Royal Geographical Society: a record, 1931–1955*, 1955, p3-4, 26-7.

——*Modern geographers*, London, 1970.

——*Publications of the Royal Geographical Society: a chronological list of periodicals, special publications and maps 1832–1964*, 1964 (Library ser no 7).

Hugh R Mill, *The record of the Royal Geographical Society*, 1930 (esp p238-40).

Ian Cameron, *To the farthest ends of the earth: the history of the...Society*, London, Macdonald & Jane's, 1980, p205-9.

Clements R Markham, *The fifty years' work of the Royal Geographical Society*, London, 1881, p100-6.

Year-book and record 1898 (1898), p40-50.

C Kelly, 'The Royal Geographical Society archives', *Geographical Journ* 141 (1975), p99-107; 142 (1976), p117-30; 143 (1977), p73-85, 266-78.

Monographs There are c65,000 v of books on exploration and travel, geography (all branches), cartography and survey, and biographies of explorers and geographers. They include 7 15th cent works (also 2 in Map Room); 167 16th cent; 451 17th cent; 1,642 18th cent and 3,387 of 1801–50. In addition there are 30 pamphlets of the 18th cent and 550 of 1801–50. Pre-1851 books are mainly on world voyages, travels in all parts of the world, some biography and some early academic books, eg 18th cent general world geographies.

Catalogue of the Library of the Royal Geographical Society, 1895 (author cat superseding editions of 1852 and 1865 with supplements 1871 and 1882).

Classified catalogue, 1871.

Card cat (author and subject) in two sequences divided at 1910.

Periodicals The collection totals c35,000 v (1,800 titles), including publications of foreign academies and learned societies. In addition to geographical periodicals there are a few literary journals and reviews of the early 19th cent.

See separate sections of the printed author cats.

Card cat of authors of articles.

Brown Collection Bought in 1896, it was formed by Dr Robert Brown (1842–95), exponent of popular geography, with special interest in botany. 348 v of books and 57 pamphlets on travel, mainly in Morocco, with some works on neighbouring territories: Algeria, Sahara, West Africa, Spain, Portugal, and Gibraltar. Mostly of the 19th cent but with c10 v of the 16th, c25 of the 17th, and c30 of the 18th cent.

In general cat.

Feilden Collection on the Polar Regions Given in 1912 by Col Henry Wemyss Feilden CB, (1838–1921), who had a distinguished military career, especially in the South African War (1900–1), and undertook scientific research in the Arctic, including Greenland, Spitzbergen and Arctic Russia. 16 v of 'Arctic Tracts' and 299 other works on exploration in the Polar Regions, mostly on the Arctic, but with a few on the Antarctic. Two of the books are of the 17th cent, c10 of the 18th, c80 of 1801–50, the remainder mostly of 1851–1900.

In general card cat.

Hotz Collection on Persia and neighbouring territories Given in 1925 by Mr A P H Hotz CBE, FRGS, (d1930), Dutch Consul in various Asian countries, the collection contains 672 v of books of both geographical and historical interest, including travel books, mainly on Persia, but also covering neighbouring Asian territories, chiefly Turkey, the Middle East, and India. It contains 23 v of 16th cent, 104 v of 17th, 112 v of 18th, 118 v of

1801–50, 231 v of 1851–1900, and 84 v of 1901–*c*1923.

Separate card cat.

'Generous gift to the Society's Library', *Geographical Journ* 66 (1925), p376-7.

Fordham Collection of Road Books Bequeathed by Sir (Herbert) George Fordham (1854–1929), Chairman of Cambridgeshire County Council 1904–19. His collection of 747 works on road travel, formed between 1900 and 1929, mostly on the British Isles, but France and, to a more limited extent, other European countries are also represented, and a few are on North America and India; mostly itineraries and guides, but atlases and maps are included.

Separate card cat.

M J Freeman and J Longbotham, *The Fordham Collection: a catalogue*, Norwich, Geo Abstracts, 1981 (Historical geography research ser no 5).

——'The Fordham Collection...an introduction', *Geographical Journ* 146 (1980), p218-31.

H G Fordham, *Paterson's Roads*, OUP, 1925: *Road-books and itineraries, bibliographically considered*, 1916; *The road-books and itineraries of Great Britain 1570 to 1850*, CUP, 1924; *The road-books and itineraries of Ireland, 1647 to 1850*, Dublin, 1923; *The road-books of Wales...1775–1850*, 1927; *John Ogilby*, OUP, 1925.

Gunther Collection on Southern Italy Bequeathed by Dr Robert Theodore Gunther FRGS (1869–1940), Director of the Museum of the History of Science, Oxford, and Fellow of Magdalen College, the collection contains 265 v on Southern Italy and Sicily, with special reference to volcanoes (eg Vesuvius), and to antiquities. Included are 1 v of the 15th cent, *c*5 v of the 16th, *c*10 v 17th cent, *c*35 v 18th cent, 65 of 1801–50, and 149 later volumes.

In general card cat.

Rough shelflist on cards.

Rennel Collection A collection bequeathed by Francis James Rennell Rodd, 2nd Baron Rennell of Rodd (1895–1978) KBE CB diplomat and banker, President of the RGS 1945–8, made up of 454 v of geographical and historical interest—the earlier ones reflect mainly his interests in Asia and the Middle East, the later ones his interest in Africa. There are 10 v of the 17th cent, 59 of the 18th cent, 91 v of 1801–50, 59 v of 1851–1900, and 245 of a later date.

Separate card cat (copy also held at British Library Dept of Printed Books). Brief description in *Geographical Journ* 145 (1979), p368, will be superseded by a more detailed description in the issue for March 1982.

Other collections, not kept separate Collections of major significance incorporated in the general library include the bequest (with an endowment) of the geographical portion (following earlier gifts) of the library of George Bellas Greenough (1778–1855), the geologist, President of the RGS; the gifts and bequest of the geographical library of Sir Walter Calverley Trevelyan, 6th Bart (1797–1879), the naturalist; the bequest of Michael C Andrews, *c*1935 of a collection on historical cartography; and the collection of atlases and rare geographical books of the bibliographer Henry Yates Thompson (1838–1928), given by his widow *c*1935.

Royal Horticultural Society, Lindley Library, 80 Vincent Square, London SW1P 2PE. Tel (01) 834 4333. Open Mon-Fri 9.30 am-5.30 pm to members and to bona fide gardeners on application to the Secretary.

The Society was founded in 1804 and soon assembled a library, but this was sold (Sotheby 2 May 1859) with most of the archives. A new library was established in 1862 from gifts and purchases. In 1865 it was augmented by the Strachan donation, and by the bequest of part of the library of Sir Joseph Paxton (1801–65) of Chatsworth. In 1866 the International Horticultural Conference, organized by Maxwell Tylden Masters (1833–1907) MD FRS, found itself with surplus funds, which he handed to the Society to purchase the outstanding library (including 138 v of pamphlets still remaining as a separate collection) of Professor Sir John Lindley (1799–1865) FRS, who had been the Society's Secretary. This collection was vested in the Lindley Library Trust, with Masters as chairman, and remained separate from the Society's Library, though housed on its premises, until 1910; 135 v of botanical pamphlets from Masters's own library were added to it, and it also received books from Queen Victoria. In 1910 the two libraries were combined as the Lindley Library, with a new trust under the aegis of the Society's Council. In 1934 it was enriched by *c*250 books, mostly of 17th-19th cent bequeathed by Reginald (Radcliffe) Cory (1871–1934) FLS, industrialist and plant collector; these included a number of copies from the Society's pre-1859 library, and contained many early 19th cent French books with coloured illustrations, with some unique items and association copies, eg of Poiret, *Leçons de Flore* 1819–20 specially printed on vellum and hand-coloured for Louis XVIII. The collection of Dr Fred Stoker author of *A gardener's progress* (1938), came in 1964. Benefactions are not normally kept together, but dispersed throughout the library. The collections now amount to 37,700 v of periodicals, books, pamphlets, and drawings. There are *c*1,000 sets of periodicals which include most of the early British publications in botany and horticulture, and many foreign. *c*3,500 pre-1851 books and pamphlets, including *c*40 STC; *c*100 Wing; *c*500 ESTC and *c*300 pre-1701 foreign, mostly botany, horticulture and silviculture, with a good collection of early herbals.

Author cat on cards, and published *Catalogue of the Lindley Library* 1898, and *The Lindley Library: catalogue of books, pamphlets, manuscripts and drawings*, 1927, supplemented by annual lists of *Books and pamphlets... deposited in the Library* (1927–38) issued separately and in Proceedings section of *Journal* 1928–39.

Subject cat limited to accessions from 1952. British items included in Henrey.

Harold R Fletcher, *The story of the Royal Horticultural Society*, London, OUP, 1969, makes frequent reference to the Library, and describes it with emphasis on the rare books, p410-19.

R A Chittenden, 'The Lindley Library', *Journal* 64(8) (1939), p350-2.

A Simmonds, 'The history' and P M Synge, 'The publications of the Society', *Journal* 79 (10) (1954), p457-88, 528-36.

'Centenary of the Society', *Journal* 29(3) (1904), p221-68.

Exhibition of manuscripts, books, drawings, portraits, medals and congratulatory addresses on the occasion of the Society's 150th anniversary celebrations, 1954.

Extensive bibliography on Lindley in Ray Desmond, *Dictionary of...botanists*, 1977, p386; see also *Dictionary of scientific biography*, 1973, v 8, p371-3.

Earl of Morton in *Journal* 90 (1965), p457-62.

On Cory see *Proceedings of the Linnean Society* 1933–4, p151-4.

Royal Humane Society, Brettenham House, Lancaster Place, London WC2E 7EP. Tel (01) 836 8155. Open, after written application to the Secretary, Mon-Fri 9.30 am-5 pm.

The Society was founded in 1774 to save the lives of those rescued from drowning. Archives include *c*300 printed works in 100 v, about half pre-1851.

Printed archives of the Society They comprise (a) Annual reports 1774–1976, 82 v; also 4 v 1808–17 in paper covered boards as issued. *Transactions* v 1 (1795) lettered for presentation to Prince Regent. 30 sermons presented to the Society 1777–1827, bound in 3 v. Festival proceedings 1845 and 1850; (b) *Literature.* 20 v of pamphlets and 4 books, 1723–1835, on life preservation, resuscitation etc.

Royal Institute of British Architects, British Architectural Library, 66 Portland Place, Marylebone, London W1N 4AD. Tel (01) 580 5533. Open Mon 10 am-5 pm, Tues-Fri 8 pm, Sat 1.30 pm to the public; those wishing to consult rare books should make written application in advance to the Librarian. Photocopier; microfilm/fiche readers.

The Institute of British Architects was founded in 1834, and formed a library at the outset. It became Royal in 1866. In 1925–7 it absorbed the Society of Architects and most of its library. It has recently been named the British Architectural Library, and is in two parts: the Sir Banister Fletcher Library, which houses the printed collections and the major collections of mss and archives; and the Drawings Collection of over ¼ million items, now housed with the Heinz Gallery (and open by appointment only at 21 Portman Square, W1H 9HF).

D Dean, 'A great library in need', *Architectural Review* 157 (940) (1975), p324 6.

P Goldring, 'Yours for the asking: the Royal Institute of British Architects Library', *RIBA Journal* 72 (1965), p122-5.

D Dean, 'The richest mine of information and ideas in our world', *Lib Assoc Record* 79(6) (1977), p315.

There are separate printed cats of drawings and some mss collections.

See also *Index of architects*, 1956; *Architectural Periodicals Index* 1972– .

Goodhart-Rendel card index to English 19th cent church builders.

Philippa Bassett, *List of the historical records retained by the...Institute...*, Birmingham, Centre for Urban and Regional Studies, 1980.

The Drawings Collection is published on microfilm by World Microfilms.

Sir Banister Fletcher Library (general) The library is named after Sir Banister (Flight) Fletcher (1866–1953) who stipulated in his will (bequeathing much of his money and property to the RIBA) that it should be thus renamed. It contains *c*100,000 books, 15,000 pamphlets, and 2,000 serials. During the 19th cent it was built up almost entirely by donation and bequest; it includes the bequests of the complete libraries of James Fergusson (1808–56) the historian of architecture; Thomas Leverton Donaldson (1795–1885) Prof of Architecture at University College; and Arthur Cates (1829–1901). *c*4,000 items are pre-1851.

R Dircks, 'The Library and collections of the Royal Institute of British Architects', *RIBA Journal* (3rd ser) 28 (3-4) (1920), p49-64, 81-92 (detailed description especially of rare books).

Card cat (author and classified) superseding *Catalogue* 1838 (copy; with ms additions); (1846) (copy with ms additions to 1856); 1865 with supplements 1868 and 1877; 1889 (copy with ms additions to 1910); 1937, 2 v repr Folkestone, Dawson, 1972.

Pre-1841 Collection Over 3,000 items, forming a representative collection on European architecture and design, recently segregated from the general collection. There are 4 incunabula, including Alberti *De re aedificatoria*; *c*25 STC items, including Shute, *The first...groundes of architecture*; *c*55 Wing. Also strong in 17th cent French books, including the *Cabinet du Roi*.

Chronological card index; also in general cat.

Descriptive catalogue of books and pamphlets in the British Architectural Library printed before 1841, by N Savage (due 1984).

Subject areas of special strength are:

Theory of architecture Early general treatises, including perspective, geometry, etc.

Vitruvius, De architectura, 57 different editions, from the *editio princeps* (*c*1482) to 1837.

Pattern Books (English), for town and country houses, published in the 18th and 19th cent; and for architectural details, ornament, carpentry, metalwork, furniture, etc, and for technical detail of construction.

Topography 17th-19th cent English, French and Italian topographical books, maps, guidebooks and general travel literature.

Antiquities Books on Greek and Roman antiquities, such as those published by the Society of Dilettanti (who gave some unpublished plates to the Library early in the 20th cent), and similar standard works; an almost complete set of Piranesi's works; also works on British antiquities.

Landscape architecture Books on landscape gardening and design and the Picturesque Movement.

Pamphlets c15,000 pamphlets from c1800 onwards, mostly bound in collections by period and subject. They included an early 19th cent collection on architectural competitions, containing much unusual material.

In general and pre-1841 cat.

Handley-Read Collection A special collection bequeathed by Charles Handley-Read on the decorative arts and architecture, in Victorian Britain, c1,500 v.

Shelved separately, but in general cat.

Modern Movement Collection A special collection begun recently, now c100 v of works on the Modern Movement in architecture, including a number of extremely scarce items published 1900–30.

Royal Institution Library, 21 Albemarle Street, Piccadilly, London W1X 4BS. Tel (01) 409 2992. Open Mon-Fri 10 am-5 pm to members by arrangement after prior written application; longer hours for members. Photocopying; information service.

The Royal Institution of Great Britain was founded in 1799 by the inventor Benjamin Thompson Count von Rumford (1753–1814) as a general society for the advancement of useful and scientific knowledge. He gave c200 scientific books in 1801, including all his own works, to found a library. To these was added the collection of Thomas Astle (1735–1803) FRS, the antiquary and palaeographer, which was purchased after his death; it included the library of his father-in-law Philip Morant (1700–70) the historian of Essex. Other donors included Michael Faraday (1791–1867) whose books, presented on numerous occasions, bear his inscription. During the 19th cent the collection was built up rapidly as a general library, leaning towards science. After the institution became more exclusively scientific, the library narrowed its intake, and has dispersed the major proportion of its older non-scientific books. There are now over 55,000 v, of which c10,000 are pre-1851, chiefly 16th-18th cent British and foreign; sets of major scientific periodicals, and an important and large collection of mss of eminent scientists, and large photographic archives.

Card cat of pre-1901 books (author and classified) supersedes obsolete printed *Catalogue of the Library* by W Harris (1809, 2nd ed 1821) and *New classified catalogue* by B Vincent (1857–82, 2 v).

Natural history manuscript resources, London, Mansell, 1980, p277-9.

K D C Vernon, 'The Royal Institution and its library', *Lib Assoc Record* 61 (1959), p283-9.

——'The reorganisation of the Library of the Royal Institution', *Proceedings* 36 (1957), p1-8.

——'The foundation and early years of the Royal Institution', *Ibid* 39 (1963), p364-402.

K Vernon, 'The Library of the Royal Institution 1799–1954', *Proceedings Roy Inst* 35 (1951–4), p879-89.

Notes on the Library of the Royal Institution and a list of periodicals. . ., 1958.

Thomas Martin, *The Royal Institution*, London, Longman, 1948.

Henry Bence Jones, *The Royal Institution: its founder and its first professors*, London, 1871, p204, 212-3, 258-9.

A S Forgan, 'The Royal Institution of Great Britain 1840–1873' (PhD thesis, Univ of London, 1977).

Royal Institution of Chartered Surveyors Library, 12 Great George Street, Westminster, London SW1P 3AD. Tel (01) 222 7000. Open Mon-Fri 9.30 am-5.30 pm on application to the Librarian. Photocopying; microform reader available.

The Institution was founded in 1868 as the Institution of Surveyors. In 1881 it became the Surveyors' Institution, in 1930 the Chartered Surveyors' Institution, and in 1946 the Royal Institution of Chartered Surveyors. In 1970 it absorbed the Chartered Auctioneers' and Estate Agents' Institute (see below).

F M L Thompson, *Chartered Surveyors: the growth of a profession*, London, Routledge, 1968, p207.

J C Rogers, 'The Surveyors' Institution', *Surveyors' Institution Transactions* 42 (1909–10), *Library* p335-7.

The General Library The Library contains c33,000 v on agriculture and estate management, building construction, law of property, estate agency, techniques of surveying, and related subjects. There is a reserved collection of post-1875 books not in current use in addition to the Historical Collection.

Card cat (dictionary) of general library and part of historical collection.

Surveyors' Institution, *Library catalogue* 3rd ed 1893 (dictionary).

Accessions listed in *Transactions* 1869–1955.

Chartered Auctioneers' and Estate Agents' Institute Library The Institute of Auctioneers and Surveyors, founded in 1888, in 1889 was renamed the Auctioneers' Institute of the United Kingdom; its library was established in 1891. The Institute of Estate and House Agents was founded in 1872, and in 1904 renamed the Estate Agents' Institute. In 1912 these two institutes were amalgamated to form the Auctioneers' and Estate Agents' Institute of the United Kingdom, in 1947 becoming the Chartered Auctioneers' and Estate Agents' Institute. In 1970 its library, then c4,800 v was merged, mostly into the RICS Library's post-1875 collection, and some earlier books, probably *c*50 of the 18th and 19th cent, mainly on agriculture and law, into the Historical Collection.

Auctioneers' Institute of the United Kingdom, *Classified catalogue of the reference and lending library*, 1911 (with author cat).

Auctioneers' and Estate Agents' Institute of the United Kingdom, *Ibid*, 2nd ed 1921 (classified and author).

D H Chapman, *The Chartered Auctioneers' and Estate Agents' Institute: a short history*, London, 1970, p69.

Notes on Library in *Annual Record* 1912–19 and *Journal* 1921–39.

Historical Collection A special collection of pre-1875 materials established in 1959 from the existing collections, almost entirely donated when Cyril Ernest Kenney was appointed its Honorary Curator. (The Institution failed to acquire Kenney's very famous private collection, though it is said that a few non-book items may have been bought from him privately, and it was sold, Sotheby 28 June 1954; May and October 1965; March, June and Oct 1966; May 1967; March and Oct 1968). The collection contains *c*1,500 v, including 1 incunabulum, 35 STC; 78 Wing items and *c*20 foreign pre-1701, mainly on land measurement and surveying, agriculture, estate agency, valuation, building and law. The special strengths of its pre-1851 portion are described in separate sections below. It also includes maps, mss, and surveying instruments.

Typescript shelflist; some of the books are included in the general card cat.

Mathematics and Land Surveying This section incorporates the collection formed by Thomas Miller Rickman (1827–1912), President, part given in 1908, part bequeathed, *c*150 v which included Paccioli, *Summa* 1494, some scarce 16th cent continental works, and a good 17th-18th cent English collection. The collection as a whole is strongest in English books of the 18th and 19th cent but there is a collection of *c*20 arithmetic books of the 17th cent.

Rickman gift listed in *Surveyors' Institution Transactions* 41 (1908–9), p608-14; 43 (1910–11), p724; 44 (1911–2), p656-8.

Estate Law and Management Standard books on land law, including 6 STC; 7 Wing; and many later. A strong collection in 18th and 19th cent agriculture and estate management, including *c*50 v of reports of the Board of Agriculture, and many works relating to stewardship; also 3 STC and 13 Wing. Books on estate agency practice begin with Inwood *Tables* 1820 given by the author.

Topography There is an extensive collection of English and foreign atlases from 1606 onwards (also printed and ms sheet maps, as well as histories and descriptions of English counties and towns, including 1 STC and 12 Wing; 12 such works (in 34 v) were given by Francis Charles Hastings Russell, 9th Duke of Bedford (1819–91) in 1874 in response to a published desiderata list. There were also some books on more distant places, but these have been sold (Sotheby 27 July 1966, lots 1-83).

Bedford gift listed in *Institution of Surveyors Transactions* 5 (1872–3), p355.

Building and Architecture A few foreign works from the 16th cent onwards, many English 1687 and later, including some of the works of Batty Langley (1696–1751).

Sale Catalogues 1 v of catalogues 1774–90, mainly of coins, seals and medals, apparently collected by Thomas Astle (1735–1803), and given by S Moger to the Chartered Auctioneers. Book sale catalogues include Fonthill 1823, and there are several of art sales.

Royal Institution of Naval Architects, 10 Upper Belgrave Street, London SW1X 8BQ. Tel (01) 235 4622. Open 9.30 am-12.30 pm, 1.30-5 pm to members; to others only at the discretion of the Secretary. Photocopying.

The Institution has built up a collection on naval architecture, housed in a room called the Denny Library (a name sometimes mistakenly applied to the collection) now totalling *c*10,000 items. In 1930 it received by donation from R L Scott, the famous naval architecture collection which had been assembled by John Scott (1830–1903) of the Scott family shipbuilding firm at Greenock. When Scott died, his library of *c*12,000 v was sold (Sotheby 27 March 1905), but the portion on naval architecture, which formed a single lot, *c*1,200 v, remained unsold. The Institution acquired both the books and the mss but later sold most of the printed books (Christie 4 Dec 1974), including almost all the pre-1801 and some later books from this collection, and many books from its general collection at the same time. The library has a residue of *c*700 pre-1851 printed books, from the 16th cent onwards.

Library catalogue, 1920.

Betty M Cooper, *Catalogue of the Scott collection of books, manuscripts, prints and drawings*. London, the Institution, 1954. No catalogue currently maintained.

K C Barnaby, *The Institution of Naval Architects 1860–1960*, 1960, p303.

Royal Literary Fund Archives, 11 Ludgate Hill, London EC4M 7AJ. Tel (01) 248 4138. Open Mon-Fri by appointment only, after written application to the Archivist.

The Literary Fund was established in 1790 to provide assistance to authors in financial difficulties; it was incorporated in 1812, and became the Royal Literary Fund in 1842.

Nigel Cross, *Printed guide to the Royal Literary Fund Archives*, London, World Microfilms (due 1982) will include a historical introduction, and an alphabetical index of application; it is designed to accompany the microfilm edition *Archives of the Royal Literary Fund* (due to be published by World Microfilms, 1982), but will also be available separately; it includes descriptions of those parts of the archives not included in the microfilm.

David Williams (1738–1816), dissenting minister and founder of the Fund: all his published works, *c*12 items.

Not included in the microfilm edition.

See British Library cat; also E V Lucas, *David Williams, founder of the Royal Literary Fund*, London, 1920.

Annual reports The only known complete set of the Fund's *Annual Report*, 1792 to the present.

Included in the microfilm edition.

Reference Library The small general reference collection includes a few 18th and early 19th cent bibliographies and general reference books.

Not included in the microfilm edition.

Files on applicants, 1790–1918 *c*3,000 files relating to every applicant, including many authors now famous, eg Coleridge, Chateaubriand, Peacock, Clare, Hogg, Hood, Mayhew and Jefferies. Each file contains the letters of application and acknowledgment, letters in support, any correspondence concerning the case, and frequently printed advertisments, public appeals etc; also press cuttings of bankruptcy proceedings, obituaries, etc. Each application is normally accompanied by a list of the applicant's published works (both monographs and articles) which can be important for bibliographical purposes, especially in the case of works published anonymously; very occasionally the actual printed pamphlets by the applicant are included in the file. Many files contain biographical information not found elsewhere.

Microfilm edition includes all the files in their entirety, including any printed matter, together with a cat of documents, and indexes of applicants, sponsors, and names.

Card cat of pamphlets.

Administrative records, and files of applicants after 1918 All the archives of general administration of the Fund, and the files of later applicants, including some printed documents.

Not included in the microfilm edition.

Royal National Institute for the Deaf Library, 105 Gower Street, London WC1E 6AH. Tel (01) 387 8033. Open Mon-Fri 9 am-5 pm to the public. Photocopying.

The library dates from the foundation of the Institute in 1911, and owes much to Selwyn Oxley (1890–1951) bibliophile and missionary to the deaf. It comprises 435 pre-1851 items, including 2 STC, 37 Wing, 7 16th cent, and 18 17th cent works. Mainly education of the deaf, with some medical works.

Cat on cards: author, subject and chronological.

Royal Naval College Library, Greenwich, London SE10 9NN. Tel (01) 858 2154 Ext 86. Open to College students and staff only (others are not admitted since most of the books held are thought to be available also at the National Maritime Museum and other libraries). Photocopier; microform reader; typing room.

The College, which is administered by the Ministry of Defence, occupies the buildings used by the Royal Hospital from 1694–1873. The present library was established in 1970 by the merger of seven separate collections. There are now *c*36,000 v of books and 190 periodicals, relating to the Navy, naval history, the history of England, and related arts and sciences. There is a collection of perhaps 100 rare books from 1630 onwards, and also a number of separate bequests, but these do not for the most part include rare books.

Card cat.

J Blacklaw, 'Library services at the Royal Naval College', *State Librarian* 29(1) (1981), p6-7.

Royal Opera House Archives, Floral Street, Covent Garden, London WC2E 7QA. Open only after prior written application to the Administrator with suitable letter of introduction.

Collections of playbills, books, prints, cuttings, etc relating to the Theatre Royal, Covent Garden (1732–1808), the second Covent Garden Theatre (1809–56 with a virtually complete run of bills 1813–40), and the later theatres. The collection has been built up mainly since 1952, partly via the Arts Council from the Harold Holt Theatre Collection.

Harold Hobson, 'Royal Opera House', in A M C Kahn, *Theatre collections*, 1955, Library Association Reference and Special Libraries Section (South Eastern Group) Library resources in the Greater London area no 4, p25-6.

Royal Photographic Society Library (see under Avon).

Royal Society for Asian Affairs Library, 42 Devonshire Street, London W1N 1LN. Tel (01) 580 5728. Open Mon-Fri 10 am-4.30 pm to members; to non-members at discretion of Secretary.

Founded 1901 by Alfred Cotterell Tupp (1840–1914) as Central Asian Society (from 1931 Royal), its scope soon spread to cover the whole of Asia, but its present name was adopted only in 1975. The Library, almost entirely donated or bequeathed, includes 90 pre-1851 from 17th cent, mostly in English. Mss. Anglo-Mongolian Society collection on Mongolia deposited.

Author and topographical cats on cards.

P M Sykes, 'The founding and progress of the Royal Central Asian Society', *Journal of the Royal Central Asian Society* 21(1), Jan 1934, p5-9.

Royal Society Library, 6 Carlton House Terrace, St James's, London SW1Y 5AG. Tel (01) 839 5561. Telex 917876. Open Mon-Fri 10 am-5 pm to Fellows and to any one introduced by a Fellow; to others engaged on bona fide research, at the Librarian's discretion after written application in advance. Photocopying and microfilming; microform reader/printer.

The Royal Society of London for Improving Natural Knowledge was founded in 1660 by 12 individuals including (Sir) Christopher Wren (1632–1723) and Robert Boyle (1627–91), and received a Royal Charter in 1662. It was at Gresham College in Bishopsgate until 1710; it then moved to Crane Court, Fleet Street; in 1780 to Somerset House; in 1856 to Burlington House; and to its present home in 1967. It is the oldest continuous academy of scientists in the world. The library has always played a major part in its life, and has been built up by purchase, donation and exchange to *c*150,000 v.

The record of the Royal Society of London 4th ed 1940, p150-4 (see also 1897, 1901 and 1912 editions).

C Sherrington, 'The Society's Library', *Notes and Records of the Roy Soc* 1 (1938), p21-7.

Sir Harold Hartley, *The Royal Society: its origins and founders*, 1960.

Thomas Birch, *The history of the Royal Society* (to 1687), London 1756–7, repr with a new introduction by A R Hall, New York, Johnson Reprint, 1968.

Thomas Sprat, *The history of the Royal Society*, London, 1667.

Sir Henry Lyons, *The Royal Society 1660–1940*, Cambridge, 1944.

C R Weld, *A history of the Royal Society, London*, 1848, 2 v.

M Purver, *The Royal Society: concept and creation*, London, Routledge, 1967.

L Rostenberg, 'John Martyn, "Printer to the Royal Society"', *Papers of the Bibliographical Soc of America* 46 (1952), p1-32.

Periodicals Collection *c*100,000 v 17th-20th cent. A few months after the start of the *Journal des Scavans* in Paris, the Society's first Secretary, Henry Oldenburg (1615?–77), issued the first number of the *Philosophical Transactions* in 1665, and this soon became an official publication of the Society; it was Britain's first scientific periodical, now the world's oldest to be published continuously. The collection includes a complete set (with the mss of the papers to 1867 in the Archives). There is a comprehensive collection of the publications of scientific academies to 1800, mostly in complete sets. Thereafter the collection is selective, being mostly limited to the scientific serials of each national academy of science (the more specialized were sold, Sotheby 16 Feb 1970, and most of the commercial scientific periodicals dispersed earlier). There is a comprehensive collection of publications of bodies federated to the International Council of Scientific Unions, many of which are not available elsewhere in the British Isles.

Catalogue of the periodical publications in the Library of the Royal Society, 1912. (Alphabetical by title. Interleaved working copy shows disposals.)

Catalogue of the scientific books in the Library of the Royal Society: transactions, journals, observations and reports, surveys, museums, 1881 (Lists transactions of academies under place, followed by miscellaneous periodicals by title, and other categories, including non-serial publications now in books collection).

W P D Wightman, 'Philosophical Transactions of the Royal Society', *Nature* 192 (4797) (1961), p23-4.

E N da C Andrade, 'The birth and early days of the Philosophical Transactions', *Notes and Records of the Royal Society of London* 20 (1965), p9-27 (see also 15 (1960) p183-97).

Books The collections now cover the history of science and scientific institutions, with special emphasis on the Royal Society itself, the writings (not exclusively scientific) of its Fellows, and works relating to them. As a result of past benefactions, the scope of the rare books holdings is very much wider, though reduced by dispersals. There are 46 incunabula. *c*40,000 v in a general collection, 1501–1950 (about half pre-1851) of books arranged, within very broad subject classes, by authors; the subjects include all the pure sciences, medicine and engineering; with smaller collections on biography, British history, travel and topography, and antiquities. Pamphlets are bound in a miscellaneous collection of 1,400 v. There is a segregated collection, *c*400 v of the works of Sir Isaac Newton (1642–1727), including first editions of all his major works (the ms of the *Principia* being in the Archives) and works about him; 600 v of works by other early Fellows (elected to *c*1690, eg 47 v by Boyle) are also segregated; this collection includes many authors' presentation copies; also shelved with it are early works by some important non-members, eg Descartes. Incorporated into the collections are the remnants of some major benefactions of general libraries, but their non-scientific portions were mainly dispersed in 1713, 1745, 1872 and 1925. First and foremost was the Norfolk or Arundel House Library, of whose 4,000 v donated in 1667 by Henry Howard, 6th Duke of Norfolk (1628–84) perhaps 500 remain; it was mainly collected by his grandfather Thomas Howard, Earl of Arundel (1586–1646) while Ambassador to the Holy Roman Empire, and included the complete library of Bilibald Pirckheimer (1470–1530) the humanist of Nuremberg who collected books from the noble houses of Europe (identifiable from his bookplate, designed by Dürer). This collection was rich in incunabula (*c*40 of which remain) and other rarities, most of which were sold (Sotheby 4 May 1925, including everything in *Catalogue of a collection of early printed books in the Library of the Royal Society* by R F Sharp, 1910); the books that remain are mostly on astrology, alchemy, medicine and navigation. Another general library was bequeathed by George Ent, Esq FRS (164?–1679), probably son of Sir George Ent (1604–89) to whom the collection has wrongly been attributed; of its *c*500 books and tracts, *c*100 remain, mostly mathematics and medicine. Another donor, John Aubrey (1626–97) FRS, gave mainly literary works, some of which are still identifiable. Henry Dircks (1806–73), civil engineer, gave and bequeathed *c*200 books and pamphlets on machines and the history of invention, including five editions of Hero of Alexandria, and six of the Marquis of Worcester's *Century*. Henry Bowman Brady FRS (1835–91), naturalist and pharmacist, bequeathed his library on protozoa, 110 v of books and 70 v of pamphlets, offprints etc, with an endowment for its continuation.

Card cat (author/name) to be published, Frederick, Maryland, Univ Publications of America, 1982.

Catalogue of the scientific books in the library of the Royal Society: general catalogue, 1883 (authors).

Earlier printed cats (which include books no longer in the library) are *Bibliotheca Norfolciana* (1681, with appendices listing Ent library and miscellaneous author donations).

Catalogue of the Library (1825, authors).

[A Panizzi], *Catalogue* 1839 (Scientific books, classified) and 1841 (Miscellaneous literature, authors). A collection of annotated copies of these cats in the library.

J Buchanan-Brown, 'The books presented to the Royal Society by John Aubrey', *Notes and Records of the Royal Society of London* 28 (1974), p167-93.

Lists of donations 1660–87 in Birch's *History*; 1769–1869 in *Philosophical Transactions* 59-159; 1869–96 in *Proceedings* 18-59; 1897–1975 in *Year Book*; 1975–8 in *Additions to the Royal Society's Library*.

Archives The Archives collection includes both the extensive official records from the Society's beginning, including documents relating to the Library, and miscellaneous mss, chiefly the scientific papers of Fellows, of which there are large and important collections. Both categories, particularly the first, include printed (though mostly unpublished) material.

The essential key is R K Bluhm, *A guide to the Archives of the Royal Society and to other manuscripts in its possession*, 1956 repr from *Notes and Records* 12(1) (1956), p21-39.

General author cat on cards.

J O Halliwell, *A catalogue of the miscellaneous manuscripts*, 1840.

A H Church, *Some account of the Classified Papers* (1606–1741) and ...*Letters and papers*...*1741–1806*. Oxford, 1907–8 (including broadsides etc).

See also the guides to British sources on the US (by C M Andrews and F G Davenport (1908), p355-68 (including printed sources; supplement in B R Crick and M Alman, rev ed 1979, p147-8); Sweden (by Krigsarkivet, tr A Tapsell 1958); Africa (by N Matthew and M D Wainwright 1971); Asia (Wainwright and Matthews 1965); S and SE Asia (*ibid*); Far East (*ibid* 1977); Australia etc (by P Mander-Jones 1972).

Natural history manuscript resources, 1980, p280-5.

Royal Society of Arts Library, 6-8 John Adam Street, Adelphi, London WC2N 6EZ. Tel (01) 839 2366. Open Mon-Fri 9.30 am-12.30 pm, 1.30-5.30 pm to bona fide research students and historians, after written application to the Curator-Librarian. Photocopying facilities.

The Society, founded in 1754 as the Society for the Encouragement of Arts, Manufactures and Commerce, was renamed the Royal Society for the Encouragement of Arts, Manufactures and Commerce in 1908, but is generally known as the Royal Society of Arts. Its original object was to provide cash rewards to inventors and artists of promise, but after 1840 it changed its interest to popular education and industrial art.

Sir H T Wood, *The history of the Royal Society of Arts*, London, 1913 (op).

D Hudson and K W Luckhurst, *The Royal Society of Arts, 1754–1954*, London, 1954 (op).

K W Luckhurst, 'Some aspects of the history of the Society of Arts, London, 1754–1952' (PhD thesis, Univ of London, 1957).

General Built up mainly by donation until recent times, the library now contains *c*15,000 v. In its first century it received numerous gifts from authors and members, the greater part of which seems to have been sold in 1840–4 to pay the Society's debts. It was then relatively inactive until 1948 when it was reorganized into a Lending Library containing most of the post-1830 material of *c*6,000 v, and a Reference Library containing the special collections indicated below.

Card cat (author and classified) of post-1830 books; some of these are also in *Catalogue of the Library of the Royal Society of Arts* (Lending Section) (1953).

D G C Allan, 'The history and scope of the Society's Library', *Journ Roy Soc Arts* 109 (5054) (1961), p105-14.

The Royal Society of Arts Library (1981) (leaflet, gratis).

Pre-1830 Collection This is the remnant of the Society's early library, with a few more recent additions. Nothing remains of the books bought with the legacy of William Benson Earle, except 6 v of the *Description des arts and metiers*. The collection is extremely varied, and includes 3 STC, the earliest being Lucar, *Art of shooting* 1588; agriculture is the most extensive single subject.

Separate card cat (author and classified).

A catalogue of the books, pamphlets and maps, belonging to the Society..., 1790 (by size).

A catalogue of the books, maps, prints, drawings and tracts belonging to the Society... by John Robinson, 1804 (classified).

Catalogue of the Library of the Society..., 1828 (dictionary).

Tracts Collection 13 boxes of disbound pamphlets are all that survive of 112 v; very varied subjects, mainly late 18th and early 19th cent.

Separate card cat (authors only).

Publications of the Royal Society of Arts Collection This includes the *Transactions* 1783–1851; the *Journal* 1852 to date; and *c*150 separately published items. There is also some printed material in the Archives (chiefly in the portion deposited at the Greater London Record Office). For a list, see Hudson and Luckhurst, *Royal Society of Arts*, p377-84. See also cat of Archives; and articles on them in *Journal of the Royal Society of Arts* 106 (1957–8), 107 (1958–9), 108 (1959–60).

Serials There are *c*150 sets, mainly on science, art and architecture, including *c*30 beginning before 1851; some of these are shelved as serials, others with the pre-1830 books (eg *Journal des Scavans* 1677–1771; *Ladies Monthly Museum* 1804–20). There are some very long runs, eg the *Bath and West and Southern Counties Society Journal* 1780–1940.

List in Journal of the Royal Society of Arts 99 (1951), p137-42.

Exhibition Catalogues Collection A collection of catalogues, jury reports, etc, of international and certain other exhibitions. The earliest are those of the Society of British Artists annual exhibitions 1824–46. There is an archival collection on the Great Exhibition of 1851, in 5 v, containing ms and printed material, especially ephemera, collected by its Commissioner who until 1850 was the Society's Secretary, John Scott Russell (1808–82; also the *Proposal of HRH Prince Albert for making a Great Exhibition* 1851 with the signatures of various promoters and subscribers to the exhibition; and the Minutes of the Proceedings of HM Commissioners for the Exhibition 1850–67. Many catalogues of later exhibitions, including Paris 1925 (12 v).

Batsford Collection In 1977 Sir Brian (Caldwell Cook) Batsford (*b*1910) gave his own private collection of 650 books published by Batsford and Co since 1874, some autographed by authors, many in fine bindings. A further 90 published before 1945 were given by the firm of Batsford from the office file in 1981. Many of the books relate to the history of English architecture, decorative arts and crafts, and topography.

The books will be entered in the card cat.

The Batsford Collection, 1981 (broadsheet).

'Opening of the Batsford Collection', *Journ Roy Soc Arts* 129 (1981), p752-3.

Royal Society of Health Library, 13 Grosvenor Place, London SW1X 7EN. Tel (01) 235 9961. Open 9 am-5 pm to Members and accredited enquirers.

The Society was founded in 1876 as the Sanitary Institute of Great Britain, becoming the Sanitary Institute in 1888, the Royal Sanitary Institute in 1904, and the Royal Society for the Promotion of Health in 1955, which remains its full legal name, but is now usually shortened to Royal Society of Health. Its library contains *c*35,000 v on environmental health and preventive medicine.

Historical Collection This collection totals *c*300 v of Victorian public health literature, including the works of eminent sanitary reformers such as Sir Edwin Chadwick (1800–90), Sir John Simon (1816–1904) KCB FRS, and Lemuel Shattuck (1793–1859) of Boston. Books on food adulteration, infectious diseases, and sanitary engineering. Incorporates the collection of the Parkes Museum of Hygiene, founded at University College in 1879 in memory of Dr Edmund Alexander Parkes (1819–76) FRS, Professor of Hygiene at the Army Medical School.

Royal Society of Medicine Library, 1 Wimpole Street, London W1M 8AE. Tel (01) 580 2070. Telex 298902. Open Mon-Fri 9.30 am-9.30 pm; Sat 9.30 am-5.30 pm to members; to visitors introduced by a Fellow, or by special permission of the librarian. Photocopying, microfilm and fiche readers.

The Society and its library were formed in 1907 from a merger of medical societies and their libraries, which are enumerated in *B* below.

Maurice Davidson, *The Royal Society of Medicine... 1805–1955*, London, the Society, 1955, p118-37.

Sir D'Arcy Power, *British medical societies*, London, 1939, p267-76.

P Wade, 'The history and development of the Library' and 'The Library in retrospect and prospect', *Proc Roy Soc of Medicine* 55(8), p627-36; 69( ), p751-4.

A The present collections

The Library is now the most extensive general medical library in the British Isles, with over 450,000 v, *c*30,000 of these (including over 10,000 temporarily housed in the Wellcome Institute Library) are pre-1851. Mainly medical, with a representative selection of general science, philosophy, botany etc. There are 13 incunabula.

Dictionary card cat of all collections. Accessions register with names of donors from 1907.

Chalmers Collection The collection of Albert John Chalmers (1870–1920) of Khartoum, the parasitologist, donated in 1921 by his widow. In addition to *c*1,400 books and periodicals on tropical medicine, there are *c*350 early medical works, including 5 incunabula (eg Celsus, *De medicina* 1478), 64 16th cent items, and 109 17th cent. This collection is strong in herbals.

(Some non-medical items dispersed.)

Periodicals Over 9,000 titles, of which *c*500 are wholly or partly pre-1851, and 2,300 are current. Strong in the publications of early foreign medical and scientific academies.

List of the periodicals in the Library, 1938. Included in *BUCOP*.

Card cat (also in general dictionary cat).

B **Merged societies and absorbed collections**

In 1905 the Royal Medical and Chirurgical Society invited the other leading medical societies with headquarters in London to amalgamate with itself to form a new large body with specialist sections. The Medical Society of London declined, but most others accepted, and were merged in 1907 into the Royal Society of Medicine. The libraries of most were merged at the same time.

Royal Society of Medicine, *Record of the events and work which led to the formation of that society by the amalgamation of the leading medical societies of London with the Royal Medical and Chirurgical Society*, London, 1914.

'Historical account of the Library of the Royal Chirurgical Society of Medicine', *Library World* 15 (1912–3), p33-9.

The Archives (mss, with a few printed items) of the RSM and of most of the absorbed societies are held in the Library (individual references being noted below); they are listed in Royal Commission on Historical Manuscripts, *Rept on the records of the Roy Soc of Medicine 1805–1968*, 1978.

Royal Medical and Chirurgical Society The Medical and Chirurgical Society of London was founded in 1805 by a seceding group of members of the Medical Society of London, receiving a Royal Charter in 1834. From the outset it aimed to build up a good library which depended less on donations than on systematic purchasing of British and foreign medical works, both current and historic. The collection, with *c*80,000 monographs and a major periodicals collection, was by far the largest constituent of the amalgamated library.

A catalogue of the Library of the Medical and Chirurgical Society of London, 1816–9, 2 v (3 sequences of authors; more detailed than later cats).

Catalogue of the Library of the Royal Medical and Chirurgical Society of London, 1844; 1856 (with subject index); 1879, 2 v plus subject index, and six supplements 1879–92.

Lists of donations in *Medico-Chirurgical Transactions* 1809–1907.

Norman Moore and S Paget, *The Royal Medical and Chirurgical Society of London centenary 1805–1905*, Aberdeen, 1905.

Laryngological Society Founded 1893.

Archives, I 57-60.

Library records 1899–1902, 159.

Obstetrical Society of London The Society was founded in 1858 by Edward Rigby (1804–60) MD FLS, and he bequeathed his 220 gynaecological and obstetrical books to form the nucleus of a library. It was built up, at first mostly by donation, later by purchasing, into a fine collection of *c*15,000 v.

Rigby bequest, *Transactions of the Obstetrical Society of London* 3e(1861) (1862), p29, 453-80.

Author cat with names of donors, 4 (1862) (1863), p285-338; supplement at end of each annual v.

Author cat, 17 (1875) (1876) supplement.

Subject index 7 (1865) (1866), p309-35; 22 (1880) supplement.

H G Arth, 'The London Obstetrical Society', *Proc Roy Soc of Medicine* 62 (1969), p363-6.

Medical Times and Gazette 1 (1861), p24.

Medical Circular 18 (1861), p33.

Odontological Society of Great Britain Founded in 1856 as the Odontological Society of London, its library by 1907 had *c*5,000 books, which remained a distinct collection for many years after the merger. It absorbed the College of Dentists of England (1862–3).

Catalogue of the Library of the Odontological Society of Great Britain, 1879, dictionary, lists *c*300 items only.

'Notes on the Odontological Society', *British Dental Journal* 102 (1957), p69, 81-2, 141-2.

Transactions of the Odontological Society 1856–1907.

Archives, I 94-122.

Other societies absorbed in 1907 The remaining societies absorbed, mostly with small collections of books were (with dates of foundation and archive references): Pathological Society of Great Britain (1846, I.125-42); Epidemiological Society of London (1850, I.37-40); Clinical Society of London (1867, I.19-27); Dermatological Society of London (1882, I.28-31); British Gynaecological Society (1884, I.47-55); Neurological Society (1886, I.61-9); British Laryngological, Rhinological and Otological Association (1888, I.56); Dermatological Society of Great Britain and Ireland (1894, I.32-5); Otological Society of the United Kingdom (1899, I.123-4); British Electro-Therapeutic Society (1901, I.136); Therapeutical Society (1902, I.143-5).

Societies absorbed after 1907 The following societies and their books were absorbed (with dates of independent existence and archive references): Society of Anaesthetists (1893–1908, I.1-4); British Balneological and Climatological Society (1895–1909, I.5-10); Society for the Study of Diseases in Children (1900–08, I.11-18).

Ophthalmological Society of the United Kingdom Founded in 1880 by Sir William Bowman, Bt (1816–92) FRS, its library began in 1884 and was provided mainly at his expense and that of his family after his death, when it came to be known as the Bowman Ophthalmological Library. The Society is still independent, but the library was mostly merged in the RSM Library in 1947; there were *c*3,000 books, of which *c*400 were pre-1851 (but part was transferred to the Institute of Ophthalmology.

Provisional cat printed 1885.

Catalogue of the Library of the... Society..., 1887; 2nd ed 1893; 3rd ed 1899; 4th ed 1901.

Sir D'Arcy Power, *British medical societies*, London, 1939, p172-85.

'Ophthalmological Society...brief history', *Annals of the Royal College of Surgeons of England* 56 (1975), p52-3.

Transactions of the Ophthalmological Society... (1880–) contains lists of accessions.

R R James, 'Sir William Bowman', *British Journ of Ophthalmology* 9 (1925), p481-94.

B Chance, 'Sir William Bowman', *Annals of Medical History* 6(2) (1924), p143-58.

Royal Society of Musicians, 10 Stratford Place, Marylebone, London W1N 9AE. Tel (01) 629 6137. Open Mon, Wed, Fri 10 am-4 pm by appointment only, after written application to the Secretary.

The Society was founded in 1738 as the Fund for the Support of Decay'd Musicians or their Families, acquiring its present name in 1785 and a Royal Charter in 1790; in 1866 it absorbed the Royal Society of Female Musicians. Its archives contain music scores (mainly ms) and letters of Haydn, Weber, Beethoven, Mozart, etc, most of the music being that performed at the Society's own concerts. Printed material includes an annual list of subscribers to the Fund from 1742.

George Frederic Handel (1685–1759), was prominent in the work of the Fund and in promoting its concerts. The collection includes *Lives* by Mainwaring 1760 and Coxe 1799; Burney's *Account* of the Fund's Handel Commemoration performances 1785 (which includes a history of the Fund); Libretto of *Acis and Galatea* 1762 (bound with *c*20 programmes of London concerts of the 1750s).

Music Festivals Programmes and accounts, including Cross *Grand Music Festival... York Cathedral* 1825 (with 4 large 2-page colour lithographs by Wolstenholme printed by Hullmandel); John Parry *Royal Musical Festival* at Westminster Abbey 1834 (with 3 leaves of facsimile embossed concert tickets); programmes of concerts of ancient music 1841–7, and Handel Festival 1857 and 1859. *Annals of the Norwich Music Festival*, 1896 (limited ed).

P Drummond, 'The Royal Society of Musicians in the eighteenth century', *Music and Letters* 59 (1978), p268-89 (with bibliography).

Royal Statistical Society Library, 25 Enford Street, London W1H 2BH. Tel (01) 723 5882. Open Mon-Fri 10 am-5 pm to Members; to others with letter of introduction from a Fellow.

The Society was originally the Statistical Branch of the Royal Society, gaining independence as the Statistical Society of London in 1834, and becoming the Royal Statistical Society in 1887.

Annals of the Royal Statistical Society 1834–1934, 1934; *1934–71* in *Journ Roy Statistical Soc* (ser A) 135(4) (1972), p545-68.

The Library contains over 40,000 v, after a reorganization in which about half the collection was transferred, on deposit, to the Department of Industry's Business Statistics Branch at Newport, Gwent (qv) to form the nucleus of the Porter Library; this included 19th and 20th cent textbooks. *c*500 sets of periodicals.

The Library [1980?] (brief guide).

Card cat (authors) superseding earlier cats.

Ms author cat 1855, printed as *Catalogue of the Library*, 1859; *Supplement* 1875; new editions 1884 (with subject index 1886), 1908, 1921 (dictionary).

List of periodicals in *Journal* A120 (1957), p510-26.

Collections from which the library was formed In the 19th cent the scope of acquisition was very wide, and included much social history and sociology in addition to most of the pioneer works in theoretical statistics (for early works a greater latitude of acquisition still prevails). It depended to a large extent on major donors, including (Lambert) Adolphe (Jacques) Quetelet (1796–1874), Charles Babbage (1792–1871) and George Richardson Porter (1792–1852). The most notable benefactor of all was George Udny Yule (1871–1951), who made large donations in 1906 and 1931, and bequeathed his remaining collections; a substantial proportion were early books, and now form part of the Yule Library (see below). There are extensive collections of pamphlets including virtually the complete papers of the major statisticians Karl Pearson (1857–1936), Yule, Francis Ysidro Edgeworth (1845–1926), and Major Greenwood (1880–1949) FRS.

Yule Library A special collection of early printed statistical works has been formed since 1950 to include both Yule's books that fall into this category, and those from the general collection. This collection now ends *c*1820, though there was an intention to extend it to perhaps 1900. *c*400 items in chronological order by date of publication.

Cat (loose leaf).

Royal Thames Yacht Club, 60 Knightsbridge, London SW1X 7LF. Tel (01) 235 2121. Open by appointment only, on written application to the Club Secretary.

The Club, founded in 1775 as the Cumberland Fleet, is one of the world's oldest yacht clubs, but the library was established probably after 1860 when it first acquired permanent premises. It contains *c*500 v, mostly received by donation from members; *c*25 v are pre-1851, mainly from the library donated by Sir George Metcalf (1848–1931). They include works on naval architecture such as *Elements and practice of rigging* 1794, and 19th cent standard works by Charnock (1800–3), Serres (1805), and Sir John Scott Russell (1875); yacht design and yachting technique; yachting memoirs; biographies; and accounts of cruises, mainly after 1900.

Author and subject card cat in progress.

D Phillips Birt, *The Cumberland Fleet: 200 years of yachting 1775–1975*, the Club, 1975. (op)

B Heckstall Smith, *A catalogue of the prints, portraits*

and oil paintings in the Club House of Royal Thames Yacht Club, 1938. (op)

Royal United Services Institute for Defence Studies, Whitehall, London SW1A 2ET. Tel (01) 218 5062.

The Institute was founded in 1831 for officers of the armed services, as the Naval and Military Library and Museum, renamed the United Service Museum and Library in 1835, the Royal United Service Institution in 1860, and in 1970 it received its present name. The library was built up by gifts and bequests during the 19th cent into a collection of major importance for military history, with many rare and several unique printed items, and important collections of mss. Following a series of thefts in the 1960s the library was transferred to the control of the Ministry of Defence's Librarian, but the rare books were kept by the Institute as an investment asset to secure its finances; the cream of these were auctioned (Sotheby 30 Oct 1967 and Christie 25 Oct 1978) when some of the books were bought by the National Army Museum, and other libraries (these were also sold at Hodgson 10-12 May 1933 and 23-24 Nov 1955). The greater part of the mss were given to the National Army Museum. Public access to the library has ceased.

Catalogue of the Library, 1837; 1865; 1890; 1908.

Royal Veterinary College Library, Royal College Street, Camden Town, London NW1 0TU. Tel (01) 387 2898 Ext 231. Open Mon-Fri 9.30 am-5 pm by appointment with the librarian (longer hours to staff and students). Xerox copier; microfilm and fiche readers.

The Veterinary College of London was established on its present site in 1791, and was chartered in 1875 and 1956. In 1949 it became an undergraduate medical school of the University of London. The Library was formed at the foundation when Granville Penn (1761–1844) contributed 50 books to the College. It has been built up by donation and purchase to *c*30,000 v.

Historical Collection of pre-1851 books containing *c*2,000 v on farriery, agriculture, medicine, surgery, animal husbandry, the veterinary art, etc. In addition to Penn's books, it incorporates the deposited library of the Veterinary Medical Association (founded 1836) which includes part of that of the London Veterinary Medical Society (which had 345 books when it was dissolved in 1836), and the bequest of Professor James Beart Simonds (1810–1904). Numerous books were donated by William Youatt (1776–1847).

A catalogue of the books, pamphlets and periodicals in the historical collection to 1850, 1965 (Supplement to *Veterinary Record* 1 May 1965).

R Catton, 'The historical collection in the Library of the Royal Veterinary College', *Veterinary Record* 77(18) (1965), p503-6.

——'Some association copies in the historical collection in the Royal Veterinary College Library', *British Veterinary Journal* 120 (1964), p583-6.

Saddlers' Company, Saddlers' Hall, Gutter Lane, Cheapside, London EC2V 6BR.

The entire collection of books and most of the archives of this livery company were destroyed in the fires of 1821 and 1940.

St Bartholomew's Hospital Medical College Library, West Smithfield, London EC1A 7BE. Tel (01) 600 9000 Ext 3602. Open Mon-Fri 9 am-6 pm (Charterhouse Square 5 pm in Aug, 10 pm other months) to members of College and Hospital; bona fide scholars who apply in advance may be admitted at librarian's discretion. Photocopier; microfiche reader/printer; microfilm reader (Charterhouse Sq).

The Hospital, founded as a monastic institution in 1123, was reconstituted in 1546 under the City Corporation. Medical training was provided from *c*1660, and the College formally established 1825–34. A non-medical library was established by the Governors in 1667, but this seems to have lapsed. The present library dates from 1800, and is maintained by the Medical College (since 1921 a school of the University of London) to serve both College and Hospital. The Main Library is within the Hospital; this houses collections *d*, *e* and *h*. The pre-clinical Branch Library is in the Medical College in Charterhouse Square; collections *f* and *g* are, for the time being, stored there.

The library contains *c*40,000 v, including *c*19,000 v of monographs, of which *c*3,000 are pre-1851, *c*21,000 v of periodicals (nearly all post-1900). The archives of both the Hospital and the College are administered independently by the Archivist to the Trustees of the Hospital, but archives of the library are in the Charterhouse Branch Library.

V C Medvei and J L Thornton eds, *The Royal Hospital of Saint Bartholomew 1123–1973*, London, The Hospital, 1974, especially p308–31, 382–3.

G Whitteridge and V Stokes, *A brief history of the Hospital of Saint Bartholomew*, London, The Hospital, 1961, p59-64.

Sir D'Arcy Power, *A short history of St Bartholomew's Hospital*, London, The Hospital, 1923, p56-62.

R M Nicholas, 'The development of medical libraries within the University of London', (MA Librarianship thesis, Univ of London 1976, p31-6).

(a) *The former constituent collections* The Medical and Philosophical Society of St Bartholomew's Hospital was founded in 1795 by John Abernethy (1764–1831) FRS, and in 1800 established a lending library financed from subscriptions. In 1805 the control of the library was vested in Trustees of the Hospital, who made an annual subvention towards its cost. The Society became inactive in 1830 (being in 1832 replaced by the Abernethian Society). The Hospital then provided accommodation for the collection, and opened it to all doctors and medical students on a subscription basis. It grew to over 2,000 books, remaining a subscription library until 1879, when it became the nucleus of a new official reference library serving both the Hospital and the College. During the 19th cent the library received numerous donations, including parts of the libraries of Abernethy, through his son-in-law Sir George Burrows, Bt (1801–87), Sir William Lawrence, Bt (1783–1867) FRS, Edward Stanley (1793–1862) FRS, and Sir James Paget (1814–99).

A catalogue of the Library of St Bartholomew's Hospital, 1865.

Catalogue of the Library of St Bartholomew's Hospital and College, 1893.

J C Crawhall, 'An historical note on the Abernethian Society', *St Bartholomew's Hospital Journal* 65, 1961, p33-5.

Norman Moore, *The history of the Abernethian Society*, London, 1895.

J L Thornton, 'John Abernethy 1764–1831', *St Bartholomew's Hospital Journal* 68, 1964, p287-93.

(b) *General arrangement of Historical Collections* The Historical Collections, *c*6,000 v, contain first and sometimes later editions of works of classic importance in the history of medicine, from the earliest times to the recent past. Works by Bart's men, now in the Athenae Collection (infra) are soon to be incorporated into the Historical Collections. Each writer's works are placed together, with works about him, alphabetically within the century in which he was most prominent.

Included in general author cat on cards; not yet in subject cat.

(c) *Athenae Collection* Over 3,000 v of works by and about Bart's men, including any person associated with Hospital or College as student or medical, nursing or lay staff. The collections include non-medical as well as medical writings, both books and articles. They are arranged alphabetically, and are soon to be arranged by centuries and merged with the Historical Collections; details are therefore included with those below. A separate section on the history of the Hospital and the College is to become part of a new Medical History Collection.

Included in general author cat on cards; not yet in subject cat.

Sir D'Arcy Power, 'Some books by Bartholomew's men', *St Bartholomew's Hospital Journal* 35, 1927–8, p146-9, 164-7.

(d) *16th century and earlier* Among Bart's men included are Thomas Vicary (*d*1561), and Timothie Bright (1551–1615). Others include Galen, Hippocrates and Ambroise Paré (1510–90), Andreas Vesalius (1514–64), etc.

Sir Geoffrey Keynes, *Dr Timothie Bright... with a bibliography...*, London, Wellcome Historical Medical Library, 1962.

J L Thornton, 'In our library', *St Bartholomew's Hospital Journal* 2 (1940–1), p125 (Paré); 151-2 (Paracelsus); 50 (1946–7); p143-4 (Bright); 54 (1950); p134-6 (Bullein).

(e) *17th Century* Chief among Bart's men was William Harvey (1578–1657). Others include Thomas Bartholin (1616–86); John Browne (1642–1702); Samuel Collins (1618–1710); William Cowper (1666–1709); Nicholas Culpeper (1616–54); Robert Hooke (1635–1703); Marcello Malpighi (1628–94); and Jacques Guillemeau (1550–1613).

Sir Geoffrey Keynes, *A bibliography of... Harvey...*, 1953, and *...Hooke...*, 1960.

J L Thornton, 'In our library', *St Bartholomew's Hospital Journal* 2 (1940–1), p98 (Hooke); 3 (1941–2), p60 (Wiseman); 78 (Tyson); 50 (1946–7), p46 (Needham), p127 (Yonge); 51 (1947), p61-2 (Harvey); 53 (1949), p16-17 (Guillemeau), p219-20 (Culpeper).

——'Writings on William Harvey by Bart's men', 61 (1957), p176-8.

(f) *18th Century* (In Charterhouse Square Branch Library). The most significant Bart's man of the period is Percivall Pott (1714–88). The collection includes the classics of scientific anatomy by authors such as Bernhard Siegfried Albinus (1697–1770), Matthew Baillie (1761–1823), Hermann Boerhaave (1668–1738), William Cheselden (1688–1752), John Hunter (1728–93), William Hunter (1718–83), Giovanni Battista Morgagni (1682–1771) founder of pathological anatomy, and his pupil Antonio Scarpa (1752–1832), who came to London in 1780.

J L Thornton, 'In our library', *St Bartholomew's Hospital Journal* 2 (1940–1), p230 (Haller bibliographies); 50 (1946–7), p73 (John Hunter); 55 (1961), p168-9 (Moyle); 68 (1964), p8-11 (Pott).

(g) *19th Century* (In Charterhouse Square Branch Library). Bart's men include John Abernethy (1764–1831) FRS, and Sir James Paget. Also Charles Darwin (1809–82); and the anatomical atlases etc of Jones Quain (1796–1865) and Erasmus Wilson. Sir Astley (Paston) Cooper (1768–1841), Sir Charles Bell (1774–1842), Thomas Young (1773–1829) FRS.

J L Thornton, 'In our library, *St Bartholomew's Hospital Journal* 3 (1941–2), p16 (Bodington), 41 (Cooper), 96 (Bell); 50 (1946–7), p59 (T Addison), 164-5 (anaesthesia); 51 (1947), p6 (Young), 174-5 (Oliver Wendell Holmes).

(h) *20th Century* Bart's men include Sir D'Arcy Power (1855–1941) surgeon, historian and bibliographer, and Richard Gordon (otherwise Dr Gordon Ostlere, *b*1921) anaesthetist and novelist; innumerable editions and translations of his novels in addition to medical works.

J L Thornton, 'In our library', *St Bartholomew's Hospital Journal* 51 (1947), p174-5 (Harvey Cushing); 2 (1940–1), p210-11 (Power).

St Bride Printing Library, St Bride Institute, Bride Lane, Fleet Street, London EC4Y 8EE. Tel (01) 353 4660. Open to the public without formality Mon-Fri 9.30 am-5.30 pm, although some materials (in special collections) may not always be available without previous appointment. Photocopying and photography; microform reader available. Entry to the Printing Library is easiest from St Bride's Passage.

The library contains *c*40,000 v and *c*1,400 serial titles in the general collections, together with specimens and artefacts that illustrate the progress of printing and the related trades. Microform readers; photography and photocopying facilities.

A General development

The St Bride Foundation was formed in 1891 from a merger of charities in the parish of St Bride, then a major centre of printing and its allied trades. In 1894 the St Bride Foundation Printing School opened, and in 1895, the Blades Library and a modern technical library—initially financed by J Passmore Edwards—opened to serve the school. Holdings of historical and technical works were further strengthened by the addition of the Reed and Southward collections in 1900–2. Thereafter, benefactions continued at a slower pace and, under the librarianship of Robert Alexander Peddie (1903–18), the various complementary collections were amalgamated.

In 1922 the Printing School removed to Southwark to form the nucleus of the London School of Printing, but the 'Technical Reference Library' remained at the Institute. It was subsequently called the St Bride Typographical Library, but in 1952 was formally renamed the St Bride Printing Library. Since 1966 it has been administered by the City Corporation and the collections have been substantially expanded.

The initiative that secured the Blades Library and most of the other major benefactions came from Charles James Drummond (1848–1929), chairman of the Governors of St Bride Foundation, sometime secretary of the London Society of Compositors, and chairman of the Institute of Printers and Allied Trades. During many years he was instrumental in acquiring thousands of books for the library, often acting as a channel for gifts from others.

A brief outline of the contents of the William Blades and Passmore Edwards libraries, compiled by J Southward (1895).

R A Peddie, 'The St Bride Typographical Library: its methods and classification', *Library Assoc Record* 18 (1916), p235-58.

W T Berry, *The St Bride Typographical Library*, London: British Typographers' Guild, 1932.

J Mosley, 'Typographic treasures at St Bride's, *Penrose* 71 (1978/9), p85-98.

B Benefactions

Blades Library The collection formed by William Blades (1824–90), partner in the printing firm Blades, East and Blades, bibliographer, and biographer of Caxton. Begun when he was a printer's apprentice and pursued with steady purpose from the beginning, the collection was described in 1895 as 'the largest of its kind that exists in a separate and independent condition'. After Blades death, Drummond arranged for its purchase with funds set aside by the Governors, augmented by public subscription. It contains *c*2,000 v and *c*1,500 pamphlets (*c*300 pre-1701 and *c*400 18th cent), including all Blades' own works, both books and articles, together with his scrapbooks, notebooks and memoranda; works in any language on printing (often annotated) especially its antecedents, origins, history, and early technology; sets of periodicals, and portraits of printers and typefounders; many early printed books as specimens of a printer's work, and several early facsimiles. Blades was the first to recognize the value of type specimens in bibliographical investigation, and these are well represented. Many of the 'pamphlets' are pages extracted from Victorian journals of improvement, separately wrappered and catalogued.

All the incunabula, except two, were sold in 1952, and some duplicates have been sold, mainly in 1911–12. A number of Blades' books not related to printing were transferred to the Institute's General Library. Blades' substantial collection of medals, which formed the basis of his work *Numismata typographica*, was acquired by the Guildhall Museum, which is now part of the Museum of London.

Catalogue of the William Blades Library, compiled by J Southward, 1899, Dictionary.

W Blades, *The Pentateuch of printing, with a memoir of the author and list of his works by T B Reed*, London 1891.

W B Thorne, 'William Blades: the man and his library', *Library Assistant* 2 (1899–1900), p155-62.

Catalogue of an exhibition in commemoration of the centenary of William Blades, compiled by W T Berry, 1924.

Butler Shorthand Collection *c*3,000 items donated by Edward Harry Butler, journalist and author of *The story of British shorthand* (1951). A comprehensive collection of shorthand manuals from the 17th cent to 1956, mainly English but including some for other European languages, together with runs of shorthand periodicals, and general literature printed in various shorthand systems. In course of arrangement.

W A Dwiggins Collection Books, pamphlets, and ephemera designed by William Addison Dwiggins (1880–1956). Annotations by Dorothy Abbe, who presented the collection in 1958.

The books of WAD: a bibliography of the books designed by W A Dwiggins, compiled by Dwight Agner. San Francisco, 1977.

George W Jones Collection *c*150 v (6 pre-1701 and 1

18th cent) donated in 1909 by George William Jones (1860–1942), 'artistic printer', including type specimens, specimens of printing, periodicals and prints. His remaining early books were sold by Sotheby 1-2 July 1936.

Accessions 10817-963 included in the *Catalogue*, 1919.

'Geo W Jones: master craftsman', *British Printer* 55 (1942/3), p28.

L Jay, *Si monumentum requiris, circumspice: notes on the libraries of George W Jones*. Birmingham School of Printing, 1942; reprinted in *The Torch* 3, *ibid*, 1950.

London Society of Compositors The collection of technical works, printing handbooks, and early printing-trade union journals, retained by the LSC after its library was closed and sold in 1896, was donated in 1902. For many years thereafter, donations of LSC archival material, and other unions' publications were received from this source.

Accessions 2855-79, 7568-95, 18947-58, 18960-19028, and passim (included in the *Catalogue*, 1919).

Peet Collection c100 v bequeathed by William Henry Peet (1849–1916), head of the advertising department of Longmans and authority on the history of thc publishing trade. Mostly biographies of publishers, booksellers and printers, and histories of firms.

Accessions 19760-801 (partial list in the *Catalogue*, 1919, pxiv-xvi. *Printers' Register* 56 (1916/17), p115.

Reed Collection The books of Talbot Baines Reed (1852–93), partner in the typefounding firm Sir Charles Reed and Sons, first Secretary of the Bibliographical Society, author of *A history of the old English letter foundries*, and of stories for boys, bought by J Passmore Edwards in 1900 at Drummond's request and donated to the Institute. The collection consists of c2,000 v (c350 pre-1701 and c375 18th cent), including all Reed's books on subjects relevant to the library: manuals of printing technique, histories, type specimens, and bibliographies; books as specimens of early, notable, exotic or unusual types, particularly Irish, mostly annotated; 18 v of children's books published by John Newbery (1713–67); chapbooks and almanacs. All the incunabula were sold in 1952, and some duplicates have been sold, mainly in 1911–12. All of Reed's books not related to printing, which had been received with the collection, were returned to his widow.

Accessions 5001-6500 (included in the *Catalogue*, 1919).

Ms author and classified cat by Reed (accessions 8792-3); revised classified cat [1901] (accession 10555, typescript).

T B Reed, 'On the use and classification of a typographical library', *Library* 4 (1892), p33-44.

Memoir by John Sime in Reed's *Kilgorman*, London, 1895, pvii-xxiv.

S Morison, *Talbot Baines Reed*, Cambridge, 1960.

P M Handover, 'Some uncollected authors XXXV: Talbot Baines Reed, 1852–1893 [with a checklist]', *Book Collector* 12 (1963), p62-7.

Southward Collection The books of John Southward (1840–1902), author of printing textbooks and journalist of the trade, bought by the Institute of Printers and Kindred Trades in 1902, and donated to the St Bride Foundation Institute. They total c550 v, mainly 19th cent works on printing and related trades, especially trade literature, including Southward's own extensive writings, his notebooks, scrapbooks and sets of periodicals.

Accessions 2880-3202, 3937-51, 3981-90, 3996-4014, 4162-210, 4575-94, 10046-82, 11950-65, 11977-84, 13664-77, 13681-5, 13694-703, and passim (included in the *Catalogue*, 1919).

The Times 11 July 1902, p8; 17 July 1902, p8.

Printers' Register 42 (1902/3), p35.

Taylor Papers These amount to c100 v and 70 boxes, the personal and family papers of Richard Taylor (1781–1858), printer and publisher of scientific journals, together with account books and records of his business, including documents relating to the development of Koenig's powered printing machine of 1810. Many printed documents issued by societies with which Taylor was connected were deposited by Taylor and Francis Ltd in 1969.

Handlist of account books.

Index to personal and business papers.

N Barker, 'Richard Taylor: a preliminary note', *Journ of the Printing Hist Soc* 2 (1966), p45-8, 2 p of plates.

Beatrice Warde Collection Drafts, typescripts and texts of published work by Beatrice Warde (1900–69), publicity manager of the Monotype Corporation and editor of *Monotype Recorder*. Including typescript checklist of publications and lectures. Presented by the Monotype Corporation in 1970.

Wilson Collection of Street Literature c500 broadsides, c1820–40, donated in 1953 by George F Wilson.

J Farlow Wilson Collection c100 v donated in 1916 by the executors of John Farlow Wilson, printing manager of Cassell and Company, a governor of the Institute, and author of *A few personal recollections by an old printer* (1896). Mainly 19th cent ephemera on printing; some early books; newspapers.

Accessions 19308-401 (partial list in the *Catalogue*, 1919, pxiii-xiv).

J Bassett, 'Eminent living printers: John Farlow Wilson', *Inland Printer* 8 (Chicago, 1890/1), p344-5.

Printers' Register 55 (1915/16), p157.

C General subject collections

The principal subject collections covering lettering, type and composing, printing processes and history; but publishing, newspapers, shorthand, advertising, paper-making, illustration, graphic design, inkmaking, book-binding, copyright and bibliography are also strongly represented. All subjects are treated historically. The collections relevant to the *Directory* are:

Monographs A collection of *c*20,000 items comprising books, pamphlets and ephemeral materials. Manuals of printing in all languages from the 17th cent to *c*1940, thereafter less comprehensive; especially complete collection of the literature of typefounding. Official publications: relevant Acts of Parliament and decrees (eg of Star Chamber) from 17th cent; British parliamentary papers; and French *arrêts* regulating the book trades.

Printed author cat: *Catalogue of the Technical Reference Library of works on printing and the allied arts*, 1919.

Supplementary cat on cards.

Classified card cat (own scheme).

Bookbinding and warehouse work: a guide to the literature available up to 1957, compiled by the staffs of the London School of Printing and Graphic Arts Library, National Book League Library, [and] St Bride Printing Library, 1959. Classified.

'An annotated list of printers' manuals to 1850'.

Journ of the Printing Hist Soc 4 (1968), p11-32 (additions and corrections *JPHS* 7 (1971), p65-6).

G Barber, *French letterpress printing: a list of French printing manuals...1567–1900*. Oxford Bibliog Soc, 1969.

Periodicals Collection *c*1,200 titles, covering all aspects of the library's work, including many foreign titles, particularly of the period before 1920. Printing trade journals from early dates in Germany (1834), England (1840), France (1851), USA (1866). House journals of printing firms and their suppliers from mid-19th cent. Short runs of periodicals published in South America, Africa, and Asia. Several of the library's trade periodicals are the publishers' editorial files, eg *Publishers' circular* (1837–1970), *British and Colonial printer* (1878–1953), *Newspaper World* (1898–1953).

Catalogue of the periodicals relating to printing and allied subjects in the Technical Library of the St Bride Institute, 1951. Annotated. Library copy has typescript subject and topographical indexes.

More complete cat on cards.

Index under name headings (author and subject) to articles from 1930 (in some cases earlier) to date.

Directories A collection of *c*800 v of trade directories, mainly of printers, newspapers, papermakers, and the book trade. Some foreign; French from the late 18th cent.

Included in the serials cat.

Archives In addition to the papers of firms and individuals listed above, several printing organizations have deposited archives with the library, eg Association typographique internationale (correspondence concerning type design copyright); Double Crown Club (minutes and records, albums of ephemeral printing); Electrotypers and Stereotypers Managers' and Overseers' Association (minutes and records); Printing Historical Society (minutes and records); Wynkyn de Worde Society (minutes and records, ephemeral printing).

D Trade literature

The library has extensive collections of trade literature, much of which is not entered in the general catalogues, but arranged in appropriate classified sequences. Many of the library's benefactors have contributed to these collections, and their items often carry annotations.

Type specimens A special collection of over 10,000 items: books, pamphlets and single-sheet specimens. The foundations of the collection were laid by Blades and Reed, and strengthened by Bremner and Southward, by regular purchase and donation, and by deposit by typefounders and printers. The typefounders' specimens are arranged by country, then foundry; the printers' and other users' specimens are similarly arranged. The collection of British specimens is the largest in existence, and includes 95 pre-1831, 23 of which no other copy is known. There are *c*100 pre-1831 foreign specimens.

Book trade prospectuses and catalogues *c*2,000 items, including booksellers announcements and catalogues (general, 18th-19th cent; 20th cent limited to booksellers specializing in the library's subjects); auction sale catalogues; private press prospectuses; and modern publishers' literature of printing interest.

E Trade documents

The general subject collections contain *c*1,000 items on trade unions, guilds, employers' organizations, and working conditions; these include several hundred documents published by the printing trade unions. Most of the items in the special collections below are not entered in the general catalogues.

St Bride Collection of Trade Documents *c*340 items, mostly printed, but some ms or typescript, on labour relations in the printing trade (1785–1913), mostly of the London Society of Compositors and its predecessors.

[Catalogue of] Broadsides, leaflets, etc relating to the printing trade in London up to the year 1900 [1785–1889], 1931.

Typescript, alphabetical and subject (accession 26318).

Many of the documents are printed in Ellic Howe, *The London compositor...1785–1900*, London: Bibliographical Society, 1947.

Some are printed in E Howe and H H Waite, *The London Society of Compositors: a centenary history*, 1948.

Cambridge University Press Collection of Trade Documents *c*80 printed items, issued 1795–1919, assembled by Stanley Morison (1889–1967), mainly from the collection of Charles Thomas Jacobi (1855–1933), managing partner of the Chiswick Press. Deposited by Morison at Cambridge, and presented by the University Press in 1975.

Handlist of printing trade documents issued by the London associations of master printers, booksellers, compositors, press-men and machine-men, 1795–1919, now preserved at the University Press. Cambridge, 1936.

Also chronological. Morison's copy of the 1931 cat of the St Bride Collection, in which are inserted entries for this collection (accession 34021).

London Society of Compositors Trade Reports c1,700 printed items, issued by the London Society of Compositors or its predecessors, 1821–1937; including annual and quarterly reports, scales of prices, fair lists, documents issued in furtherance of trade disputes, advance of wages movements, election of officers, and management of the union.

Mostly arranged chronologically in annual volumes.

F Specimens of printing

The library has *c*10,000 items: books, pamphlets and single sheets, not relevant to the subject collections, but which are preserved as specimens of printing. There is also a small group of Western and oriental mss.

Printed Books Collection c3,000 v (*c*750 pre-1701 and *c*1,000 18th cent) of all periods, including the work of the early printers, private presses, and notable modern printing offices. The items printed by Giambattista Bodoni (1740–1813) include 83 broadsheets (fogli volanti). Many of the early books came from the Blades Library or Reed Collection, together with *c*100 incunabula. Today the incunabula number 2 and *c*100 leaves; the remainder were sold by Hodgson 6 March, 1952.

Included in general cat by author.

Selected cat on slips arranged by country then printer (*c*1,400 items, mainly the earlier works).

Chronological cat in progress.

Typescript list of Bodoni fogli volanti.

Newspapers c50 17th cent news pamphlets and *c*500 specimen issues of newspapers, 17th-20th cent; chiefly British, with some American and French. Originally from the J Farlow Wilson Collection, but augmented since.

Title index on slips.

Typescript chronological list, 1921 (Accession 24833).

Broadsides c1,150 broadsides and ballad sheets, *c*1820–40, many printed by James Catnach (1792–1841), but including the work of several other printers. *c*500 were donated in 1953 by George F Wilson, having been obtained at the sale of the collection of William Samuel Fortey (*d*1901), successor to the business of Catnach.

Cat of the Wilson Collection of Street Literature now in the Printing Library of St Bride Foundation Institute. Typescript 1954. Classified cat by subject, with index to printers (accession 29635). Complete cat in preparation.

An exhibition of street literature presented by the Printing Library: catalogue of exhibits (1954).

W T Berry and G Buday, 'Nineteenth century broadsheets', *Penrose Annual* 49 (1955), p28-30 with 8 p of plates.

Chapbooks c260 chapbooks, songbooks and reciters, arranged by place of publication, chiefly British, *c*1750–1900. Many of these derive from the Reed Collection. All are folded, but many are unopened.

Ms title cat by Reed (accession 9618).

Typescript list by place of publication (1950). (Accession 29052).

Almanacs A collection of 163 items (25 pre-1701 and 100 18th cent), principally from the Reed Collection. All are London published, some loose but most bound in year sets.

Book Jackets A collection of *c*1,000, chiefly British and German of *c*1950–60, but some earlier. Arranged by country then publisher.

Ephemera c6,000 pieces, many mounted in albums, mainly 18th-19th cent, but some later, including valentines, greetings cards, trade cards, labels, menus, handbills, posters etc.

St Dominic's Priory, Library of the Dominican Friars, Southampton Road, Gospel Oak, London NW5 4LB. Tel (01) 485 5491. Open by prior arrangement with the Librarian or Prior.

The Dominicans intended to establish a large library at the Priory, and put up a substantial building for that purpose, only part of which is now used. The collection is a miscellaneous one, *c*15,000 items, including *c*500 pre-1800, on theology and related disciplines.

Author/title cat but very incomplete. Many books formerly held have been dispersed.

Dominican Collection A special collection on the Dominican Order, including *c*200 v of acts of general chapters, and other publications on the history and spirituality of the Order, especially in England.

St George's Hospital Medical School Library, Hunter Wing, Cranmer Terrace, Tooting, London SW17 0RE. Tel (01) 672 1255. Telex 945291. Open Mon-Fri 9.30 am-6 pm; Sat 9.30 am-12.30 pm to staff and students; other bona fide research workers by prior arrangement at librarian's discretion. Photocopying.

St George's Hospital was established at Hyde Park Corner in 1733 by a minority of the subscribers to the Westminster Public Infirmary who objected to a new site planned for it. The Medical School replaced William Lane's private anatomy school in 1836; it became a school of the University of London in 1900. The Library was also founded in 1836; it suffered bomb damage in World War II. The Hospital and Medical School have now moved entirely to Tooting, where there was already a branch hospital and library. The Library contains *c*9,000 monographs (including *c*500 pre-1851) on medical sciences, and *c*21,000 v of periodicals.

Card cat, author/name and subject.

Library donations book 1836–71, minutes 1852–1921.

R M Nicholas, 'The development of medical libraries

within the University of London' (MA Librarianship thesis, Univ of London, 1976), p72-6.

'The Library', *St George's Hospital Gazette* 6 (1898), p168; 32 (1941), p32.

Sonia P Anderson, *Report on the manuscripts and library records of St George's Hospital Medical School Library...18th-20th century*, London, Historical Mss Commission, 1973.

J Blomfield, *St George's 1733–1933*, London, 1933, p54, 70, 91.

A Perret, 'The historical development of St George's Library' (Ms, 1980, St George's Library archives).

St George's History Collection Contains c1,700 v, being the works and biography of St George's men, including the mss of Sir Benjamin (Collins) Brodie the elder (1783–1862) FRS, surgeon to the Hospital and to Queen Victoria, and works of the pupils of John Hunter (1728–93).

Separate cat (also in main cat).

St John's Hospital for Diseases of the Skin, 5 Lisle Street, Leicester Square, London WC2H 7BJ. Tel (01) 437 8383. Open Mon-Fri 9.30 am-5.30 pm to staff and postgraduate students; to others by prior arrangement with letter of introduction. Photocopying.

St John's Hospital was founded in 1863 by John Laws Milton (1820–98); the library in 1883. A School of Dermatology was set up within the Hospital in 1885, superseded in 1923 by the London School of Dermatology, which in turn was superseded by the Institute in 1946, from 1959 a postgraduate school of the University of London. The library of c2,000 v of monographs on the skin and its diseases, was transferred from the hospital to the Institute in 1948.

R M Nicholas, 'The development of medical libraries within the University of London' (MA Librarianship thesis, Univ of London, 1976), p127-9.

M J Fenton, 'London Hospital for Diseases of the Skin', *British Med Journ* 1968(3), p251-2.

Historical Collection Contains c250 v of classic and rare works on dermatology 1660–1900.

L C Parish, 'Books...in English before 1975', *International Journ of Dermatology* 15 (1976), p206-14.

J M Shaw, 'Early printing in dermatology', *Archives of Dermatology* 106 (1972), p112-16.

St Joseph's College, Lawrence Street, Mill Hill, London NW7 4JX. Tel (01) 959 8254. Open by appointment with the librarian or the archivist on written application in advance. Photocopier available.

The Society of St Joseph was founded in 1866 as a Roman Catholic order of missionary priests (known as the Mill Hill Missionaries), with a college which was the first British missionary seminary. The college is now affiliated to the Missionary Institute, London, with HQ at Mill Hill, a general teaching institution for Catholic missionaries, which maintains its own research library.

Library of St Joseph's College The library contains c35,000 v. All aspects of theology are represented, but it is strongest in Biblical and patristic studies, liturgy and catechetics, and Church history, with the social and political background of the Society's present and past mission fields, especially East Africa, Borneo (a very strong collection), India, New Zealand, South America (including the Falkland Islands), and the Pacific. The open access collection of modern works is supplemented by a reserved collection of mainly 19th cent books; this includes some unusual works in anthropology and a small 19th cent collection on linguistics. The periodicals collection includes runs, mostly from their foundation, of many theological journals founded in the 19th cent.

Card cat (author, title, subject), with subject index to periodicals from 1960 onwards.

Archives of the Society of St Joseph The archives include the papers of the Society's founder, Cardinal Herbert Vaughan (1832–1903), and printed works by and about him. The collection on the history of the mission and its colleges and houses is being strengthened by the transfer of some older printed material from the library. There is a major biographical section, which includes ms diaries. There is a modest collection, being enlarged, of works printed in vernaculars in the mission field; so far, mainly catechisms. A few vernacular magazines and a large collection of 20th cent European mission journals.

A very detailed card index is in the course of compilation.

W Mol, 'The Archives of the Mill Hill Missionaries', *Catholic Archives* no 2, (1982), p19-27.

——'Our Archives', *Millhilliana*, 1 (1981), p31-6.

D Henige, 'The Archives of the Mill Hill Fathers', *African Research and Documentation* no 22 (1980), p18-20.

St Katherine Cree Church, 86 Leadenhall Street, London EC3A 3DH. Tel (01) 283 5733. Open by arrangement with the librarian on written application.

A Sunday School library

A collection of c600 v remaining from the 766 v formerly in use in the Sunday School at the Church, brought by Dr W M Whittemore (Rector 1873–95) from St James Duke Place where he was Perpetual Curate 1850–73 when the two parishes were amalgamated in 1873. They are almost all of the period 1825–90, mainly publications of the Society for Promoting Christian Knowledge, the Religious Tract Society, and the Sunday School Union. It is in two sections: theology, devotional works, history, biography etc, and mainly novels and tales for children, with some improving non-fiction works. Magazines are included in both sections.

Hand written shelflists corresponding to a shelf arrangement in order of accession number.

K E Campbell, *St Katherine Cree Sunday School Library 1977* (1 page of typescript notes on the collection, available from the Librarian).

B **Industrial Christian Fellowship Library** (Deposited)

The Navvy Mission Society was founded in 1877; in 1918 it merged with the Christian Social Union to form the Industrial Christian Fellowship. There is a library of *c*4,000 modern books in addition to the two special collections below.

Founders' Library Books by former prominent members of the 1914–39 period such as Charles Gore (1853–1932), William Ralph Inge (1860–1954), William Temple (1881–1944), etc.

Navvy Mission Society Collection The Society's archives, with books and periodicals. There are three very scarce late 19th cent books on navvies; the Society's *Quarterly Letter to Navvies* 1878–1920, and its *Annual Report* from 1877–8 onwards. Almost all the printed material is from the collection of Mrs E Garnett (1839–1921).

Author cat on cards.

St Mary's Hospital Medical School Library, Norfolk Place, Paddington, London W2 1PG. Tel (01) 723 1252 Ext 17. Open Mon-Fri 9 am-7 pm (Wed 5 pm) to students and staff of Hospital and School; to others by prior arrangement at librarian's discretion.

The Hospital was opened in 1852, the Medical School in 1854, becoming a school of the University of London in 1948, when the Wright-Fleming Institute of Microbiology (founded 1907 as the Inoculuation Dept) was incorporated. The library contains *c*30,000 v on clinical medicine.

Card cat (author and alphabetical subject).

R M Nicholas, 'The development of medical libraries within the University of London', (MA Librarianship thesis, Univ of London 1976), p78-82.

Sir Zachary Cope, *The history of St Mary's Hospital Medical School*, London, Heinemann, 1954.

St Mary's Hospital... six hospitals, a medical school, and an institute of research, London, The Hospital, 1955.

St Mary's Men Collection A collection of their published writings. *c*300 19th cent items.

Card cat (separate).

St Pancras Reference Library, 100 Euston Road, London NW1 2AJ. Tel (01) 278 4444 Ext 2484/5/6. Open Mon-Fri 9.30 am-8 pm (Sat 5 pm). Rare material may be consulted on request. Public photocopiers available.

The rare books collection is made up of early acquisitions and miscellaneous donations, especially history and topography. It comprises 468 items published pre-1800; 771 1801–50; 25 limited editions post 1850.

St Paul's Cathedral Chapter Library, St Paul's Cathedral, London EC4M 8AE. Open by appointment with the Librarian, after written application, but during current reorganization only to consult material not available elsewhere.

Though the foundation of the cathedral goes back 1,300 years, the present library dates from the 15th cent; it was damaged by fire in 1561 and 1666 (when books evacuated to Sion College were destroyed in the burning of that library). It contains well over 15,000 v of printed books and pamphlets, mainly of the 17th, 18th and 19th cent, but there is an appreciable number of 16th cent books, and 21 incunabula. There is also a major collection of printed and ms music. The cathedral archives were transferred to the Guildhall Library Department of Manuscripts on deposit in 1981.

W M Atkins, 'St Paul's Cathedral: a short history of the library', *Record of the Friends of St Paul's Cathedral*, 1954, p14-20.

A R B Fuller, 'A note on the Cathedral Library', *Dome: the magazine of the Friends of St Paul's Cathedral* no 5 (1967–8), p16-18.

B Botfield, *Notes on the cathedral libraries*, 1849, p297-327.

W S Simpson, *Gleanings from old St Paul's*, London, 1889, p35-48.

W J S Simpson, *Memoir of... W Sparrow Simpson...*, London, 1899, p37-44.

R A Rye, *Students' guide*, 3rd ed 1927, p420-6.

H M Rabinowicz, *Treasures of Judaica*, New York, Yoseloff, 1971, p96-100.

Edward Edwards, *Memoirs of libraries*, v 1, p688-90.

W R Matthews and W M Atkins, *A history of St Paul's Cathedral*, London, 1964, p265, 291, 308.

'The Library at St Paul's', in W J Loftie, *London afternoons*, London [1901], p250-61.

A **Individual collections**

The present printed book collections (of *c*13,500 v) received their impetus from Compton who, in effect, refounded the library after the Fire of 1666, and this was added to throughout the 18th and 19th cent. Individual bequests, donations, and purchased collections have not been kept distinct (except in the tract collections).

Author cat on cards is incomplete (also author cat in ms, 18th and 19th cent).

W Sparrow Simpson, *St Paul's Cathedral Library: a catalogue...*, 1893, is a highly selective list of about

3,000 items, mostly of the special collections, in classified order.

Shelflist, 1862.

Full list of cats and published descriptions in E Anne Read, *Checklist of books...relating to cathedral libraries*, Oxford Bibliographical Society, 1970, p33-6.

Benefactions Book lists the Compton Collection in full, but little else.

Henry Compton (1632–1713), Bishop of London, gave 1,892 v in 1692, of the 16th and 17th cent; about a quarter are foreign; chiefly Fathers, ecclesiastical history, especially church councils, and controversial theology, including nonconformist and RC works, and numerous sermons.

List in Benefactions Book; identified by bookplate. See also Simpson, op cit, p15.

Robert Gery (*c*1652–1707), Vicar of Islington. His library was bought in 1708.

John Mangey (1727 or 8–82), Prebendary of St Paul's. His library of 1,511 v was bought in 1783 for a nominal sum; most of it had been inherited from his father Thomas Mangey (1688–1765), Prebendary of Durham.

Henry Hart Milman (1791–1868), Dean. His library was donated.

B Tract collections

The series of bound volumes of tracts described below were organized and listed separately by W Sparrow Simpson in the late 19th cent. (Others among the general and special collections are not included here; the total number of tracts and pamphlets in all collections is said to be *c*80,000.)

Ms shelf cat in 5 v, with two dictionary indexes (one for Sumner, one for the others).

Charles Richard Sumner (1790–1874), Dean of St Paul's, afterwards Bishop of Winchester. 6,348 political and religious tracts, mostly of the period 1800–60, from the sale of his library (Sotheby 11-13 March, 1875), bought 1875.

Tract cat v 1 fol 129-208, v 2 fol 158-209, v 3 fol 1-200, v 4 fol 1-161; separate index vol.

William Hale (1795–1870), Archdeacon of London. 1,405 tracts on theology, archaeology, history, and politics, *c*1790–1871, from the sale of his library, bought in 1871.

Tract cat v 2 fol 1-121.

William Josiah Irons (1812–83), Prebendary of St Paul's. *c*33 v of tracts which he collected, given by his widow. Mostly early and mid-19th cent, especially the religious controversies of the times: Tracts for the times, ritualism, Colenso dispute, sermons; with some on history and philosophy.

Tract cat v 5 fol 51-85.

Robert Gregory (1819–1911), Dean of St Paul's. *c*300 tracts collected by him.

Alphabetical index in Tract cat v 5 p158-84.

Sacheverell controversy A collection of 159 tracts bound in 6 v bought in 1893, on the controversy fired by the sermon preached in St Paul's on *The perils of false brethren* by Henry Sacheverell (1674?–1724), in 1709 and his subsequent impeachment; this collection adds to 72 others on the subject elsewhere in the library.

Typescript list (49.B8) of the 159 and the 72.

Tract cat v 5; see also 1893 *Catalogue* p122-5.

Miscellaneous tracts Hundreds of volumes, from the 18th and 19th cent, mostly relating to religious controversies; the Tractarian controversy features strongly.

C Christian literature

Bibles The collection is especially strong in early English versions. Humphrey Wanley (1672–1726), librarian to the 1st and 2nd Earls of Oxford, gave a collection of early Bibles, eg Tyndale's New Testament (Worms 1525). William Stanley (1647–1731), Dean of St Asaph, gave Walton's polyglot (1657) and Castell's *Lexicon* (1669).

Ms cat 1862 (37.B2) in shelf order with full collations and notes on condition. Botfield, p299-312.

Liturgies RC and Orthodox liturgical books, British rituals, Books of Common Prayer with translations, Sarum missals etc, ritual and devotional books.

Theology The library is rich in the Fathers and Councils of the church; also Anglican sermons. A complete set of the Bampton Lectures was given by Dr James Augustus Hessey (1814–92), Archdeacon of Middlesex. A collection of editions of the *Index Expurgatorius* was given in 1871 by Charles Marshall (*c*1810–83), Prebendary.

D Special collections

St Paul's A collection of works on the cathedral itself and its clergy, and related activities taking place around it, including probably well over 1,000 sermons preached by the cathedral clergy and others in the cathedral, and over 100 Paul's Cross sermons. Plays acted by the children of St Paul's. Works on Sir Christopher Wren. Works on the funerals of Nelson and Wellington.

Simpson, *Catalogue*, 1893, p71-122.

London Works on London generally, the City parishes, St Paul's School, livery companies and the Fire, the Plague etc. There is a large number of ephemera on the City.

Simpson, *op cit*, p125-210.

St Paul's School Library, Lonsdale Road, Barnes, London SW13 9JT. Tel (01) 748 9162. Open during term Mon-Fri 8.30 am-5.45 pm to bona fide scholars who apply in advance in writing.

Growth. John Colet (1467?–1519), Dean of St Paul's, founded the school in St Paul's churchyard under the tutelage of the Mercers' Company and perhaps bequeathed his collection, but the first evidence of a library is a ms cat dated 1582–3 (printed in *Admission registers*, 1884, p451-4). Most books were destroyed in the 1666 Fire, but some earlier books, including two Pepys donations survive. The library was re-established in 1670, and moved with the school to Hammersmith in 1884 (where from 1914 it was known by the name of F W Walker, a previous High Master), and to Barnes in 1968. It incorporates the classics library of 1,300 v of Dr F H Marvell Blaydes (1818–1908) strong in Greek dramatists, and Madame Léon Paul Blouet's French collection *c*600 v.

Rare Books Room 900 pre-1851 and modern first editions with 11 incunabula; 169 16th cent; 245 17th cent items. Srong in classics, especially Aldines. Collections of books by and about Colet; Erasmus; notable High Masters, eg Wm Lily (1468?–1522); and Old Paulines, eg Milton, G K Chesterton, Compton Mackenzie, Ernest Raymond, and Montgomery of Alamein. Extensive oriental collection of Edw Thomas (1813–86) the Indian antiquary deposited by N L Naimaster. Some books are on loan to Osterley House.

Catalogues 1697 in Thos Gale mss at Trinity College, Cambridge, records 454 v (see *The Pauline* 8 (42), 1890, 129-31). *A catalogue of all the books. . . with the names of the benefactors* by George Charles, 1743, records 830. *A catalogue of the Library*, 1836, compiled by Benj Jowett (1817–93) while Captain of the School; *Supplementary catalogue*, 1859. From 1893 most accessions noted in *The Pauline*.

Sir M McDonnell, *A history of St Paul's School*, 1909, p437-40 [op], supplemented by his *Annals of St Paul's School*, 1959.

Early history in *The Pauline* 32 (211), 1914, p140-4.

C W Picciotto, St Paul's School, London, 1939 [op], p103.

St Thomas's Hospital, Lambeth Palace Road, London SE1 7EH. Tel (01) 928 9292.

The Hospital, founded in 1551 in Southwark, reviving the monastic Spital St Thomas, moved to Surrey Gardens in 1864, and to its present site in 1871. The bulk of the Hospital archives are deposited in the Greater London Record Office.

B Golding, *An historical account of St Thomas's Hospital, Southwark*, London 1819.

F G Parsons, *The history of St Thomas's Hospital*, London, Methuen, 1932–6, 3 v.

E M McInnes, *St Thomas's Hospital*, London, Allen & Unwin, 1963.

——'St Thomas's Hospital and its archives', *Journ of the Soc Archivists*, 1 (1959), p277-82.

A **St Thomas's Hospital Medical School Library**

Tel Ext 2367. Open Mon-Fri 9 am-9 pm (6 pm in vac), on written application in advance, at the discretion of the Librarian. Photocopier; microfilm reader available.

The Medical School was instituted in 1842 to replace the unofficial training which had grown up from *c*1660, becoming a separate institution in 1858, transferred to the University of London in 1949. The Library, founded *c*1667, came to be housed in the Medical School, but until 1949 was provided by the Hospital, whose Special Trustees now maintain the Historical Collection.

A L Crockford, 'History of St Thomas's Hospital Medical School', *St Thomas's Hospital Gazette*, 54(4) (1956), p129-34.

Historical Collection The original Hospital Library, built up mainly by donation, absorbed the libraries of the Webb Street School of Anatomy and Medicine (1819–42) of Richard Dugard Grainger (1801–65), and of the Theatre of Anatomy of Sir Joshua Brookes (1761–1833) FRS in Blenheim Street. It incorporates collections donated from the libraries of Sir John Simon (1819–1904), Joseph Lister, Lord Lister (1827–1912), Charles Murchison (1830–79) FRS, Richard Gullet Whitfield (*d*1871) with those of his father Richard and of John Whitfield the 18th cent surgeon, Sir William McCormac (1836–1901), and Henry Cline (1750–1827). It is made up of *c*6,000 v of printed books, pamphlets and periodicals, including *c*3,500 pre-1851; with *c*150 v of mss, letters etc, also prints and photographs; two incunabula; *c*10 STC; *c*20 Wing. Most medical subjects represented. Strong in anatomy (with a noteworthy collection of English and continental anatomical atlases), including the works of William Cheselden (1688–1752), surgeon at St Thomas's; surgery; clinical medicine. Periodicals from 17th cent onwards, with some German.

Author cat on cards, being revised for publication.

F A Tubbs, 'The uses of libraries', *St Thomas's Hospital Gazette* 49 (1951), p208-10.

——'Cheselden and St Thomas's', *St Thomas's Hospital Gazette* 67 (4) (1969), p3-5.

R M Nicholas, 'The development of medical libraries within the University of London', (MA Librarianship thesis, Univ of London, 1976), p15-19.

B **Nightingale Training School for Nurses**

Nightingale Library. Admission by appointment only to bona fide scholars; apply to District Nursing Officer. Tel Ext 2126. General enquiries on the collection to the Art Historian to the Special Trustees for St Thomas's Hospital, York House, 199 Westminster Bridge Road, London SE1 7EH. Tel (01) 928 4506.

The School was founded in 1860 with money raised for Florence Nightingale (1820–1910) by public subscription, the first public training school for nurses in Great Britain, forming part of the Hospital. When she died, her books were divided between relatives and her friend Miss Elisabeth Bosanquet; some of these were passed on to the Hospital to form a collection in memory of Florence Nightingale (others, and the bulk of her ms papers, are in the British Library). The collection was formerly part of a Nightingale Museum, now removed, which it is hoped to re-assemble (some Nightingale mss are now deposited with the Hospital Archives in the Greater London Record Office). The collection includes 25 printed items on the Crimean War, in addition to the 'Crimea broadsheets'; 67 from her personal library, including books received as presents in childhood, and books on nursing, theology, natural history, memoirs and travel; 25 of her own writings, including books and pamphlets on the army, nursing, statistics, and India; 56 of her inscribed presentation copies to other people; and 53 biographical items about her.

Typescript lists.

W J Bishop and S Goldie, *A bio-bibliography of Florence Nightingale*, London, Dawson, 1962.

Sir Edward Cook, *Life of Florence Nightingale*, London, 1925, v 2, p437-58 (list of published writings) and 457-66 (biographica).

Lucy Seymer, *The writings of Florence Nightingale*, London, Cornwall Press, 1947 (Florence Nightingale oration no 2).

——*Florence Nightingale's nurses: the Nightingale Training School, 1860–1960*, London, Pitman, 1960.

M J Smyth, 'The Nightingale Museum', *St Thomas's Hospital Gazette* 52 (1954), p170-2.

The Nightingale Training School, St Thomas's Hospital 1860–1960, priv pr 1960.

Salvation Army Archives, 101 Queen Victoria Street, London EC4P 4EP. Tel (01) 236 5222. Open Tues-Fri 10 am-noon, 2-4 pm, by arrangement with the Archivist/Librarian.

Archives, and *c*2,600 v of printed material on the Salvation Army and by its officers from its foundation in 1878, and the earlier evangelism of its founder William Booth (1828–1912).

Savage Club, 9 Fitzmaurice Place, London W1X 5DE. Tel (01) 493 1094. Library open to members only.

The Club was founded in 1857 by George Augustus Sala (1828–96), and draws its members mainly from journalism and the lighter end of the theatre. Its library was diminished by a bomb which fell on the Club in 1940, but still has *c*3,000 v, including a few pre-1851 books from 1666 onwards, and a large collection of theatre programmes.

H Thorogood, 'London clubs and their libraries', *Library Review* 13 (1951–2), p495-8.

Aaron Watson, *The Savage Club*, London, 1907.

P V Savage, *Brother Savages and guests*, London, 1957.

Savile Club, Brook Street, London W1Y 1YE. Tel (01) 629 5462. Open only to members.

The Club was opened in 1868 as the New Club, by a group of members of the Eclectic Club, for literary and commercial men. Its library has received donations from many distinguished members of first editions of their works, most notably Robert Louis Stevenson (1850–94), Rudyard Kipling (1865–1936), H G Wells (1866–1946), Sir Compton Mackenzie (1883–1972), Baron C P Snow (1905–80), Nigel Balchin (1908–70), Eric Linklater (1899–1974), Stephen Spender (*b*1909), and J B Priestley (1894–1981).

Charles Graves, *Leather armchairs*, 1963, p100-2.

A Lejeune, *Gentleman's clubs*, 1979, p256-63.

The Savile Club, 1868 to 1923, priv pr 1923.

The Savile Club 1868–1958, priv pr 1958.

School of Dental Surgery, Stobie Memorial Library, Royal Dental Hospital of London, 32 Leicester Square, London WC2H 7LJ. Tel (01) 930 8831. Open Mon-Fri 9.30 am-5.30 pm to staff and students; to other bona fide research workers by appointment after written application in advance.

The Dental Hospital of London was founded in 1858 by the Odontological Society, but their library was incorporated in that of the Royal Society of Medicine when the societies merged in 1907. The present library dates from 1949 when the school became part of the University of London, but it was partly destroyed by fire in 1958. It holds *c*5,000 books on dentistry and related medical subjects, and *c*200 periodicals.

Card cat (author/title and classified).

Antiquarian collection A collection of 99 early books on dentistry from the library of Warwick James (*b c*1875), consultant surgeon to the Hospital.

Separate author cat.

R M Nicholas, 'The development of medical libraries within the University of London' (MA Librarianship thesis, Univ of London 1976), p86-7.

'Stobie Memorial Library', 1976 (ms history).

J M Campbell, 'The origin and development of the Royal Dental Hospital', *Royal Dental Hospital Magazine* 18 (1951), p39-42.

'Royal Dental Hospital and School', *British Medical Journal* 1858 (1), p1351.

School of Oriental and African Studies Library, Malet Street, Bloomsbury, London WC1E 7HP. Tel (01) 637 2388 Ext 281. Open Mon-Fri 9 am-8.30 pm (but 5 pm in Christmas and Easter vac), Sat (not Bank Holiday weekends) 12.30 pm to members of

the School; others must apply in writing to the Librarian for permission to use the library. Photocopiers, photographic service. Specialist regional advisers for bibliographical advice.

The School of Oriental Studies was formed in 1916 under a government scheme by acquiring the premises and library of the London Institution at Finsbury Circus; it became part of the University of London in 1918, incorporating the oriental departments previously at King's College and University College. Its name was expanded in 1938 when it began the teaching of African Studies.

Library guide, 4th ed 1980, very detailed.

A Lodge, 'The history of the School of Oriental and African Studies Library', in University of Sheffield Postgraduate School of Librarianship and Information Science, *University and research library studies* (ed W L Saunders), Oxford, Pergamon, 1968, p84-110.

J D Pearson, 'The Library of the School of Oriental and African Studies', *Journ of Asian Studies* 17 (1957), p183-8.

R J Hoy, 'The Library of the School of Oriental and African Studies', *Bull of the Assoc of British Theological and Philosophical Libraries*, no 12 (June 1960), p6-8.

The School of Oriental and African Studies, University of London, 1917–1967, an introduction, 1967.

B Bloomfield, 'The Library of the School of Oriental and African Studies', in *Acquisitions from the Third World: papers of the Ligue des Bibliotheques Europeennes de Recherche, Seminar. . .1973* ed D A Clarke, London 1975, p245-63.

General The library contains over 500,000 v of books and 10,000 sets of periodicals, and other serials, on the languages and cultures of Asia (including the Pacific) and Africa. It was established in 1917 around the oriental section of the London Institution Library (founded 1805) by exchanging collections mostly by deposit on indefinite loan; the non-oriental collections were traded for the oriental collections from other University of London libraries. King's College provided *c*2,500 v with mss from the oriental portion of the library of William Marsden (1754–1836), and its general oriental library of 500 v. University College provided the Morrison Collection on China and a general collection of *c*2,000 v, which included the collection of Sandford Anthony Strong (1863–1904) given by his widow. Individual donations and bequests are with rare exceptions not kept separate, but are incorporated in the appropriate regional or subject libraries, where the more important are described below, apart from the libraries of Sidney Herbert Ray (1858–1939) and General Sir William (Henry) Mackinnon (1852–1929) which relate to the whole of Asia. The Rev Louis Henry Jordan (1855–1923) bequeathed *c*1,200 v on religions other than Judaism and Christianity, with an endowment to enlarge the collection, which is divided among the appropriate divisions.

Card cat (author, topographical/subject, and title, Chinese and Japanese titles in separate sequences), reproduced as *Library catalogue*, Boston (Mass), G K Hall, 1963, 28 v, and supplements, 1968, 16 v; 1973 and 1978.

Serials under heading Periodical Publications.

Separate cat for official publications on India; materials on music; and mss, also some deposited libraries, most of which are not included in main cat.

The Library compiles the *Union catalogue of Asian publications*, London, Mansell, 1971, 4 v, and Supplement, 1973; thereafter unpublished on cards (locations given on request; access to unpublished portion only by special arrangement); in addition to books (but not periodicals) published in Asia in all languages it includes books in Arabic and Ethiopian languages from Africa.

A Rare Books Collection

All pre-1800 books, and many later books, are segregated; these include 6,541 pre-1851 and 218 later items. They are included below in the descriptions of the regional and other divisions to which they belong. Special collections are also now being formed of boys' adventure stories set in Asia and Africa (eg G A Henty, G M Fenn, etc).

Handlists available on request. The three incunabula (from Auboyneau collection) are in the University handlist.

Catalogue of books printed between 1500 and 1599 in the Library of the School. . ., preliminary ed by Lesley Forbes, 1968, with detailed descriptions but not provenances, of 360 items; chronological; indexes of places, printers and authors.

William Marsden, *Bibliothea Marsdeniana philologica et orientalis: a catalogue of books and manuscripts collected with a view to the general comparison of languages. . .*, London, 1827.

S Goddard, 'Boys' adventure stories set in the Third World', *SALG Newsletter* (South Asia Library Group), no 15 (Jan 1980), p6-7.

B South Asia Division

The original nucleus of the Library, built around the collection of Indian books from the London Institution to which were added the Marsden and other collections from the colleges. In 1917 the school bought the library of John Faithfull Fleet (1847–1917), and in 1919 that of Dr Ernst Haas (18?–*c*1918), Professor of Sanskrit at University College, was given by his family. In 1963 the Northbrook Society deposited *c*1,000 v on oriental religion, literature, and art from the Sir Dinshaw Petit Library. The collections are strongest in language and literature. *c*59,000 books, pamphlets and journals, predominantly in the languages of the region.

Ancient Indo-Aryan languages A collection of *c*8,000 books and pamphlets (and mss) in Sanskrit, Pali and Prakrit. Notable books include William Carey's

Hitopadesa 1804 (in Magari script, an early specimen from his Serampore Press, from the library of the College of Fort William), and *Isvarasya sarvavākyāni* 1811 (Sanskrit translation of the Pentateuch by the Serampore missionaries).

Modern Indo-Aryan languages A collection of *c*22,000 books and pamphlets (with 200 journals and mss) in all the languages, ie Bengali, *c*3,300, including N B Hallhead *Grammar* 1778, W Carey *Grammar* Serampore 1801; Gujarati, *c*1,600; Hindi, *c*5,200, including the New Testament from Carey's Serampore Press 1812; Marathi, *c*2,600, including two books printed at Goa in Konkani 1640–59; Sinhalese, *c*1,700; Urdu, *c*4,500, including *Grammar* 1796 and several others by J B Gilchrist, with the 1822 Pentateuch from Carey's Serampore Mission Press; Panjabi, *c*1,400, including the New Testament translated into Lahnda, Serampore, 1819; Canarese, Malayalam, and other Dravidian languages, *c*4,300; Tamil, *c*2,200, including Ziegenbalg's grammar printed at Halle in 1716, and the dictionaries of Fabricius 1779 and 1786; Telugu, 430, including the first book in the Telugu fount, Carey's grammar printed at Serampore 1814, and A D Campbell's grammar.

C **Far East Division**

The division holds *c*160,000 v on the Far East and Eastern Siberia.

China and Tibet Collection The Chinese collection contains *c*8,000 v and 15,000 pamphlets in Western languages, *c*94,000 in Chinese and *c*2,000 in Japanese. It was built up round the library of 9,371 works in *c*15,000 v with many rarities, collected by the missionary Robert Morrison (1782–1834) in Macao in the 1820s, brought to London by him to encourage Chinese studies there, and given to University College in 1837; with other collections received from the college in 1917. Sir Reginald Fleming Johnston (1874–1938), tutor to the last Chinese Emperor, and Prof at the School, bequeathed his library of more than 15,000 v, which included many palace editions and works on Buddhism. The Tibet collection contains *c*500 v in Western languages, and over 200 blockprint editions, including 118 given by Mr M Pallis in 1940. There are a few unusual items published by the Chinese government for the Tibetans, including a magazine and almanacs *c*1915.

D S G Goodman and T Sach, 'Chinese local newspapers at the School...', London, 1979.

SALG Newsletter no 16 (June 1980), p4.

Mongolia and Manchu A collection of *c*1,400 v on Mongolia in Western languages and in Mongol; Western books on Manchu and *c*100 Manchu 18th-19th cent items.

W Simon and H Nelson, *Manchu books in London: a union catalogue*, 1977.

Japan and Korea The Japanese and Korean collections began with a few hundred books from the London Institution, but now contains *c*6,000 in Western languages, 60,000 in Japanese, and 4,000 in Korean, with over 800 periodicals. They include the collections of the Rt Hon Sir (Spencer Cecil) Brabazon Ponsonby-Fane (1824–1915) and Sir Harold George Parlett (1869–1945). In 1927 *c*400 v, mainly blockprints, were given by Mrs S de Watterville in memory of her brother Lt-Col E F Calthrop, Military Attaché in Tokyo. The collection is strongest in language, literature, history and religion, especially after 1868.

D G Chibbett *et al*, *A descriptive catalogue of the pre-1868 Japanese books, manuscripts and prints in the Library...*, 1975.

B F Hickman, *A catalogue of books dealing with the Ainu in the Library...*, 1975.

Y Yasumura, *List of Japanese periodicals in the Library...*, 1979; also in P W Carnell, *Checklist of Japanese periodicals...*, Sheffield, 1976– .

B C Bloomfield and B F Hickman, *A preliminary directory of library resources for Korean studies...*, London, 1978.

D **Other regional divisions**

South East Asian and Pacific Division There is much material on this area from the Marsden Collection, but most of the growth in the collection has been recent. The collections of older books are strongest in history, literature and religion. Material on Australasia relates mainly to the aboriginal populations.

Islamic Near and Middle East Division, including Egypt A collection of *c*42,000 items in Persian, Arabic, Turkish and other languages of the region, and *c*20,000 in European languages. It was built up around the collections of the London Institution, Marsden, and the colleges. The most notable addition of rare books has been the Auboyneau Collection, bought in 1947, and originally formed by Gaston Auboyneau (1865–1911), Manager of the Imperial Ottoman Bank, comprising several thousand books on the history, geography and travel of Turkey and the Near East, mostly in European languages, from the 15th to late 19th cent, including three incunabula. Other collections acquired include that of William Hartmann (1844–1926), *c*300 books and over 4,000 pamphlets bought in 1920; of Sir Thomas (Walker) Arnold (1864–1930), *c*2,500 v bought *c*1930, and kept together as the Arnold Memorial Library; and rare books on Islamic law and other subjects from the library of Sir (James) Norman (Dalrymple) Anderson (*b*1908) Prof of Oriental Laws. A Kurdish collection was given in 1957 by Cecil John Edmonds (1889–1979); a collection on Sudan in the Mahdi period by Prof Peter Malcolm Holt (*b*1918) in 1978; and *c*400 Persian books collected by N M Rashid the Urdu poet by his widow. Rare books were bought from the library of Lt-Col David Lockhart Robertson Lorimer (1876–1962) and his unpublished linguistic material was donated in 1962.

Bibliotheque de Monsieur Gaston Auboyneau: manuscripts, imprimés, gravures, documents..., (*c*1948).

Auboyneau collection also partially listed in G Auboyneau and A Fevret, *Essai de bibliographie pour servir a l'histoire de l'Empire ottoman*, Paris, 1911, fasc 1: Religion. Moeurs et coutumes (no more published).

Non-Islamic Near and Middle East Division A collection of *c*21,000 items. The Ancient Near East Collection, *c*7,000 v, benefited from the bequest of Cyril John Gadd (1893–1969) Prof of Ancient Semitic languages and civilizations, and includes T Fuller *A Pisgah—sight of Palestine* 1650 with Coleridge's marginalia, and H Ludolf's Amharic grammar and lexicon, both published at Frankfurt 1698; also some early printed Ethiopian works, several with the bookplate of Ras Tafari (afterwards Emperor Haile Selassie I). The Modern Collection contains *c*8,000 items in Hebrew and 6,000 in European languages, mainly modern Israel and on the Hebrew language, and mostly 20th cent works, though an 18th and 19th cent collection is being built up (Biblical and Rabbinical studies, and Judaica in general, are not collected).

Africa Division (excluding Egypt) A collection of *c*30,000 items, acquired almost exclusively after 1930, with 1,750 serials. The Society of Libyan Studies Library, which contains much archaeological material, is maintained as a separate collection within the division.

E Subject divisions

General and Social Sciences Division This section contains *c*120,000 items on general subjects, economics, law, social sciences, geography, anthropology, phonetics and linguistics, political science, and sociology. Mainly modern, but with 19th cent material on linguistics, and an interesting collection, *c*1,000 v, on American Indian languages, and a collection on gypsies and gypsy languages given by Dr J Sampson in 1931 which includes Borrow's translation of the Bible into Spanish Romany (Madrid 1847).

Art and Archaeology Division In 1957 the Asian collection of the Courtauld Institute of Art was deposited on loan, 3,750 v, and used to form the core of a new division (formerly housed at the Percival David Foundation). Originally mainly on the Far East, it now covers the whole of Asia, with more limited material on Africa and general art history. Now *c*25,000 books and 280 periodicals mainly in Western and Far Eastern languages.

F Libraries deposited in the Archives and Manuscripts Division

Council for World Mission The archives and library of the Council for World Mission, until 1966 called the Congregational Council for World Mission, formed in 1966 by the amalgamation of the London Missionary Society (founded 1795, and until *c*1829 called the Missionary Society) and the Commonwealth Missionary Society (founded 1836 and until 1955 called the Colonial Missionary Society).

The Library, *c*13,000 books and pamphlets is mainly derived from the London Missionary Society, which in its early years was undenominational and included Anglicans. The serials issued by the societies are held in complete runs in the archives. Originally the LMS library was built round the collection of 3,800 items of the 16th-19th cent mainly on China and the Far East, bequeathed by the medical missionary William Lockhart (1811–96); but most of the Chinese material was sold to the National Library of Australia before the collection was deposited at the School. It includes a wide variety of material in about 100 languages. It mainly relates to Protestant missions and travel in nearly all parts of the world, but is strongest on India, the South Seas, and Africa (including a collection of pamphlets on South Africa 1800–60). There are a few general periodicals, notably the *Asiatic Journal* from 1817, and *Indian Mail* 1837–57.

Separate card cat.

G Mabbs, *Catalogue of the books contained in the Lockhart Library and in the General Library of the London Missionary Society*, London, 1899.

C Stuart Craig, *The archives of the Council for World Mission, an outline guide*, the School, 1973.

Methodist Church Overseas Division The archives to 1945 and library have been deposited since 1975. It was formerly the Methodist Missionary Society, an amalgamation in 1932, of the Wesleyan Methodist Missionary Society founded in 1786 and the Primitive Methodist Missionary Society founded in 1870. *c*6,500 books and pamphlets, especially on India, China, Africa, and the West Indies, with reference books, Bible translations, grammars and dictionaries, and sets of reports and journals of the Methodist churches and their missions.

S Goddard, 'The library and archives of the Methodist Missionary Society', *Africa Research and Documentation* no 19 (1973), p18-19.

Typescript guide to the archives.

G G Findlay and W W Holdsworth, *The history of the Wesleyan Missionary Society*, London, 1921–4, 5 v.

Conference of Missionary Societies in Great Britain and Ireland The archives of the Conference (founded 1912) and of the British office at Edinburgh House of the International Missionary Council (now amalgamated with the World Council of Churches). Also *c*500 v remaining from their libraries, on missions in various parts of the world, mainly Asia and Africa, after the bulk was transferred to the World Council of Churches in Geneva.

Independent libraries in England..., London, 1977, p102-3.

W R Hogg, *Ecumenical foundations: a history of the International Missionary Council...*, New York, Harper, 1952.

School of Slavonic and East European Studies Library, Senate House, Malet Street, Bloomsbury, London WC1E 7HU. Tel (01) 637 4934. Open Mon-Fri 10 am-7 pm (6 pm in long vacation); Sat 1 pm to holders of readers' tickets, for which written application must be made in advance to the librarian.

The School of Slavonic Studies was founded in 1915 as a department of King's College, extending its name to include all East European Studies in 1929, and becoming an independent school of the University of London in 1932. The library was first established from the King's College Slavonic collections, later supplemented by the Slavonic section of the library of the London Institution (see London, School of Oriental and African Studies), collections given by the governments of Czechoslovakia, Yugoslavia and Poland, and by the Academy of Sciences in Prague. Many private collections have also been donated.

D Bartkiw, 'The Library of the School of Slavonic and East European Studies', *Solanus* 2 (1967), p3-6.

Director's report on the work of the School, 1954– .

A guide to the Library, 1971.

General The library contains over 200,000 v of books, pamphlets and serials relating to all parts of the USSR (both in Europe and Asia) and Poland, Czechoslovakia, Jugoslavia, Bulgaria, Rumania, Albania, Hungary and Finland. *c*2,000 items are pre-1851, of which the greater part are on the history, language, literature and topography of Russia, Hungary, Rumania and Jugoslavia, and also the Balkans in general, with smaller collections on the other countries. There are also ms and archives collections.

Gen author cat on cards; also separate author cat of each class (usually a country).

Subject cat of books acquired after 1974.

Retrospective classified cat in preparation.

Acquisitions to the Library, 1950– .

J E O Screen and C L Drage, 'Church Slavonic and Russian books, 1552–1800, in the Library of the School of Slavonic and East European Studies', *Slavonic and East European Review* 57(3) (1979), p321-47 (chronological cat of 113 items from 1552 onwards, with provenances; indexes of printers and names; 19 from Marsden collection, 14 from Gaster, 46 from Russian Orthodox Church).

C L Drage, 'Eighteenth-century Church Slavonic and Russian books in United Kingdom libraries', *Solanus* no 13 (June 1978), p1-13.

T H P Penton, *A checklist of Russian imprints, 1801–1860, in the Library of the School of Slavonic and East European Studies*, the School, 1978 (Bibliographical guides, no 2).

T Penton, 'Nineteenth and early twentieth century Russian author inscriptions in the Library of the School. . .', *Solanus* no 15 (July 1980), p12-21 (11 items).

Gaster Library The library, consisting of *c*3,500 items, is the residue (bought in 1952) of the library of Dr Moses Gaster (1856–1939), Chief Rabbi of Sephardic Jews in Britain, and a pioneer in the study of early Rumanian literature, after the purchase, in 1936, of the most valuable Rumanian books by the Rumanian Academy Library, and other dispersals (eg some mss to John Rylands Library). The collection is made up mostly of secular and religious Rumanian books and pamphlets from 1643 to the 19th cent, with items in other languages from 1531 onwards, eg Gospels in Church Slavonic (Belgrade 1552) and many liturgical works.

Typed slip cat received with the collection, but not all in general author cat.

D Deletant, 'A survey of the Gaster books in the School of Slavonic and East European Studies Library', *Solanus* no 10 (June 1975), p14-23.

Marsden Collection A portion from the collection at King's College Library (qv) of *c*60 books, including 19 Russian pre-1801, and the first Finnish grammar, Eskil Petraeus, *Linguae finnicae brevis institutio* (Åbo, 1649).

Not all catalogued (see William Marsden, *Bibliotheca Marsdeniana*, 1827).

Iványi-Grünwald Collection A collection formed by Béla Iványi-Grünwald (1902–65), Hungarian historian (who lived in Britain after 1939), and bought by the School in 1968. It contains 972 titles of books, pamphlets, and periodicals (with 158 maps, prints, music and mss), on Hungary written in English, or by Hungarian authors in English translations, and includes 27 STC and Wing items; 31 ESTC items and 94 books and pamphlets of 1801–50.

Separate author card cat and also in main author cat.

L Czigány, *Hungarica: English books, prints, maps, periodicals, etc relating to Hungary collected by Béla Iványi-Grünwald*, Alphamstone (Suffolk), Mrs Jocelyn Ivanyi, 1967. (op)

Science Museum Library, Imperial College Road, London SW7 5NH. Tel (general) (01) 589 3456; (enquiries, direct line) (01) 581 4734. Telex 21200. Open (except public holidays and Saturdays preceding these), Mon-Sat 10 am-5.30 pm to the public, but reader's ticket required to consult rare books, archives and pictorial collections. Photocopying, photography, and microfilming; microform readers; beta-radiography (for studying watermarks). Enquiries accepted by phone, telex, post, or in person, and short bibliographies compiled, especially on historical aspects of scientific subjects.

The Library is administered by the Science Museum, under the Department of Education and Science, as a national reference library in pure and applied science, specializing in the history of science, technology and medicine. It has *c*500,000 v of printed works, in addition to pictorial and archive collections.

Growth of the collections The Library was founded in 1883 as the Science Library of the South Kensington Museum (now, in part, the Victoria and Albert) by amalgamating most of the scientific works from the Education Library of the South Kensington Museum (now the Department of Education and Science Library) with part of the Library of the Museum of Practical Geology (now the Institute of Geological Sciences Library). The Science Museum, formed within the South Kensington Museum in 1885, became independent in 1893, taking with it the Science Library, which was then enlarged by adding most remaining non-geological books from the Geological Museum. It became a public scientific reference library, and from 1926–62 a national lending library. Subsequently it has become the national library for the history of science and technology, and has come to include the medical sciences, not previously covered, within its field, though here the collections are as yet small.

H J Parker, 'Science Museum Library', *Libri* 3 (1954), p326-30.

David Follett, *The rise of the Science Museum under Henry Lyons* (1920–33), 1978.

H T Pledge, 'The Science Library' in R Irwin and R Staveley eds, *The libraries of London*, 2nd ed, 1961, p48-53.

J A Chaldecott, 'The Science Library: a survey of the development of the Science Museum Library', *Technical Book Review* 11 (1964), p8-9.

M J Bailey, 'A visit to the new Science Museum Library', *Bull of the Circle of State Librarians* 19(2) (1971), p26-7.

'S C Bradford', *Journ of Documentation* 33 (3) (1977), p173-9.

Monographs Collections Numbering *c*120,000 v, mostly on the physical sciences, and modern works on the history of science, technology and medicine, the collections include 2,650 v which are pre-1801, including 5 incunabula; 45 STC; and 224 Wing items; *c*330 foreign 1501–1640 and *c*240 1641–1700. They include major classics in the history of science by Boyle, Copernicus, Galileo, Harvey, Kepler, and Newton. An outstanding 19th cent collection.

Card cat (author and classified).

Judit Brody, *A catalogue of books printed before 1641 in the Science Museum Library*, 1979.

Catalogue of the Science Library in the South Kensington Museum, 1891 (10th ed of the science portion of *Catalogue of the Educational Division of the South Kensington Museum)*; supplement 1895.

Exhibition cats, notably *A hundred alchemical books* (1952); *Historic astronomical books* (1954); *Historic books on mining* (1968); *Historic books on machines* (1953).

Weekly accessions lists from 1931.

Subject lists in *Bibliography series*.

S A Jayawardene, *A handlist of reference works for the historian of science*, 1982.

Serials Collection The collection, which contains *c*400,000 v including *c*6,000 current titles, was enlarged greatly between 1920 and 1960, but a substantial proportion was later transferred to Boston Spa, and is now in the British Library Lending Division. The library retains the principal scientific and technological serials, and a comprehensive collection of those on the history of science.

Current periodicals, 1965.

Periodicals on open-access: a short-title list of periodicals received since 1945 (on microfiche, regularly updated).

Holdings included in *World list* and *BUCOP*.

Sion College Library, Victoria Embankment, London EC4Y 0DN. Tel (01) 353 7983. Open Mon-Fri (with certain exceptions) 10 am-5 pm to Fellows and subscribers; others wishing to consult rare books must write in advance with letter of recommendation; entrance at S E corner in John Carpenter Street. No copier, but microfilming can be specially arranged.

Sion College was founded in London Wall by the will of Thomas White (1550?–1624), Rector of St Dunstan-in-the-West and founder of the Oxford chair of moral philosophy, as a meeting place for the London clergy, with (until 1875) an associated almshouse, Sion Hospital. It is governed by a Court of President, two Deans and four Assistants, all elected by the Fellows, who are ex-officio the incumbents of City and adjacent parishes; since the Sion College Act 1956, there are also two lay Fellows. The library was an afterthought, built over the almshouse (with lodgings for students nearby), endowed and opened in 1630 by White's relative and executor John Simpson (or Simson, *c*1560–1633), Rector of St Olave, and by the wills of Abraham Colfe (1580–1657), Vicar of Lewisham and John Wynne (*d*1673) a dyer. In 1666 1,682 folio and 187 quarto v were saved from the Fire by temporary removal to the Charterhouse, but over 1,000 v including a locked rare books collection (with all the books from Old St Paul's) were destroyed. Donations have always been numerous, but the period 1698–1712 saw six large benefactions which brought the Library's total to almost 10,000 v, of which half were theological, the remainder covering every serious subject. In practice it was a public library, chained until 1720, and open to anyone on the recommendation of a Fellow. Its importance was recognized by the grant of the copyright deposit privilege in 1710. From 1836 a Treasury grant has been substituted, more foreign books have been bought, and acquisitions have been narrowed gradually to theology, philosophy, and ecclesiastical history. The College moved to the present building in 1886 with *c*70,000 v; 6,000 v were lost by war damage in 1940. After partial rebuilding the premises are now shared with the City Livery Club, and the library has been aided by the Pilgrim Trust. The College archives, and some biblical and liturgical mss are held in the library.

E H Pearce, *Sion College and Library*, Cambridge, 1913.

W Reading, 'History of... Sion College' appended to 1724 printed cat.

W H Milman, 'Some account of Sion College', *Transactions of the London & Middlesex Archaeological Society* 6 (1890), p53-122.

E Edmonston, 'Unfamiliar libraries 9: Sion College', *Book Collector* 14(2) (1965), p165-77 (many of the books and mss here singled out for mention have been sold).

E Edmonston, 'The Library of Sion College', *Bulletin of the Association of British Theological and Philosophical Libraries* no 5 (1958), p1-4.

B Botfield, 'Sion College Library', *Miscellanies of the Philobiblon Society* 6 (1860–1). *Notices of libraries*, p21-8.

William Clarke, *Repertorium bibliographicum*, London, 1819, v 1, p152-3.

Sion College founded by Thomas White, DD [by John Russell, 1845] and rev ed [by William Scott], 1859.

R A Rye, *Students' guide*, 3rd ed London, 1927, p181-5.

A Classified Collections

ie the printed books and pamphlets classified by subjects and entered in the general catalogues (excluding only the segregated Pamphlet Collections). Special collections, except the Port Royal Library, are broken up and distributed in the general classification. In 1895 63,801 v were classified into: theology 24,880; history 14,013; philosophy 1,257; philology 1,255; literature 8,019; bibliography and literary history 7,170; social sciences 2,244; science 2,445; useful arts 1,364; and fine arts 1,154. Pre-1851 items now probably number *c*30,000, including 56 incunabula, 1,658 STC and *c*4,000 Wing (with perhaps as many more in Pamphlet Collections). Bibles (see Botfield, p22-7) include the four great polyglots, all significant English and many foreign editions. Fine collection of liturgies and catechisms. (Science and medicine sold Hodgson 21 April 1938; some mss and (mostly 16th cent literary) rare books Sotheby 13 June 1977 reported in *The Times* 14 June 1977, p18).

The 'Book of Benefactors 1629–1888' also known as the 'Vellum Book' records chronologically with titles, (but with major omissions) the donations, purchases from endowments, and copyright receipts, but pamphlets are usually ignored, and titles of these never given.

Author-title cat on cards begun 1891, complete except for some segregated rare books; also interleaved printed cats.

Catalogus universalis librorum omnium in Bibliotheca Collegii Sionii (1650) author cat by John Spencer (three annotated copies, others at British Library and Dr Williams's); he also made ms lists of books saved 1666, and of the Old St Paul's and locked collections burned.

William Reading, *Bibliothecae Cleri Londinensis in Collegio Sionensi catalogus* (1724) classified, gives many provenances, with author index, history, and list of donors (including individual items in smaller collections); two interleaved copies.

Interleaved Bodleian 1843 cat shows holdings after first reclassification and two further copies (complementing each other, part of U-Z burned 1940) after the last reclassification, these overlapping the card cat and continuing to *c*1905.

Shelflist on ms slips following *Order of classification of Sion College Library* by W H Milman, 2nd ed (1889).

Classified list of books purchased 1882–7 and... *added 1887–1910* 10 v (1883–1914).

Typescript list of incunabula, 1958 with amendments. Annotated STC.

Travers, Walter (1548–1635), Minister of the Temple, the famous puritan opponent of Richard Hooker, bequeathed *c*150 books which are listed in the Book of Benefactors, consisting of rabbinics, patristics, Bibles and dictionaries in many modern languages, alchemy, and medicine; together with many others which are not listed.

Spencer, John (*c*1610–80), Librarian 1631–80, donated several hundred books 1631–58.

Jesuit Library seized at Holbeck near Leeds in 1679 during the Popish Plot. Transferred to Sion by the King at the College's request expressed through Archbishop Sancroft, but many books were lost on the way, and probably fewer than 500 (many of them liturgical books) were received

Ms list (1679) lists *c*750 books found in the library and to have been 'delivered'.

Berkeley, George (1628–98), 1st Earl of Berkeley, Master of Trinity House, and Governor of the Levant Company, inherited from his aunt's husband Sir Robert Coke (1587–1653) of Holkham, Royalist son of Sir Edward, a fine theological general and literary collection (including incunabula) formed for the use of the London clergy who had been deprived by the parliamentarians. He incorporated this collection into his library at Durdans near Epsom, but in 1681 transferred 555 v, described in the following year as 'the best and most useful part' of the combined collections, to Sion; the remainder of the Durdans Library was received by bequest in 1698. *c*300 v folio and *c*1,000 smaller books, for which a bookplate 'E Bibliotheca Durdanensi' was specially printed.

Three incomplete mss lists of the Durdans Library: classified by subjects. 1667: undated shelflist, marking transfers of 1681; author cat with additions to at least 1687. Booke of Benefactors, p97-103 (entered retrospectively in 1709, under the year 1682) seems to include the highlights of both portions. *'Berkley'* in 1724 cat.

Lawson, John (*c*1632–1705), MD of Gratwin Street, President of the Royal College of Physicians, friend of Archbishop Tenison, frequent user of and occasional donor to the Library, bequeathed *c*1,100 v predominantly medicine and science (now sold), with some literature, modern history, political tracts, and other works.

Book of Benefactors, p106-20. *'J L'* in 1724 cat.

Compton, Henry (1632–1713), the anti-Jacobite son of the Earl of Northampton and Bishop of London, inherited from Edmund Castell (1606–85) DD, Prof of Arabic at Cambridge, all his oriental and other Bibles, which had formed a working library used in the preparation of Walton's polyglot (though some were destroyed in the Fire). He donated most of them to Sion in 1707, and the residue with his own theological collection came by bequest in 1715 (originally segregated).

Book of Benefactors, p120-2, 224-6. *'Hen Ep Lond'* in 1724 cat, Castell books usually distinguished.

Jamesian Library Thomas James (*c*1650?–1711), bookseller and mathematical printer to the King, in Mincing Lane, and a descendant of Bodley's first Librarian, collected a general library of English books to form a public library after his death. His widow Eleanor presented it to Sion College on condition that it should remain separate, as the 'Jamesian Library'. This condition was met by placing the books in an outbuilding, whence many were stolen, but in 1720 the library was incorporated into the general collections. *c*2,400 books and 1,329 pamphlets; literature predominates; but history, theology, and innumerable other subjects are represented.

Book of Benefactors, p128-58. *'T J'* in 1724 cat.

Chiswell, Richard, the elder (1639–1711), bookseller at the Rose & Crown in St Paul's Churchyard, specialized in publishing the works of contemporary Anglican divines. In 1697 he sent for the Library catalogue in order that he might fill the gaps by donation from his stock, but the number and titles are not recorded. He also kept an archival collection of his publications, writing 'DRC' on the back of each one, which he intended for Sion after his death. These books (*c*200) (with 11 v of tracts) were brought in by his assistant Benjamin Cowse, and dispersed among the general collections.

Book of Benefactors, p124-7. *'R Chiswell'* or *'R C'* in 1724 cat.

Waple, Edward (*c*1660–1712). President in 1704, Vicar of St Sepulchre, and Archdeacon of Taunton, made many donations in his lifetime, and bequeathed 1,860 books of theology, history, and a wide range of other subjects, with many political tracts. Many foreign books are included. Contemporaries described the collection as 'very well chosen'.

Book of Benefactors, p162-223. *'E W'* in 1724 cat.

Quaker collections, pro- and anti-, *c*250 items, mostly donated by Francis Bugg (1640–*c*1727) the apostate from Quakerism, whose polemics are well represented. Also 17 v of Quaker tracts donated 1804 by the Society of Friends.

Rawlinson, Richard (1690–1755) LLD, topographer and nonjuring bishop, was a donor according to the Book of Benefactors of some hundreds of historical and other books, both English and foreign, on numerous occasions.

Clements, William (1712?–99), Librarian from 1762, seems to have been son of Henry Clements (*d*1719) the bookseller of St Paul's Churchyard. He bequeathed his personal library, mainly theology, *c*500 books, with some pamphlets which are incorporated in the Russell collection.

Book of Benefactors, p342-9.

Copyright 1710–1836. The Library claimed by 8 Anne *c.*19 from the warehouse-keeper at Stationers' Hall a copy of every work whose copyright was entered in the Register there (chiefly popular works), and additionally from 1814 under 54 George III direct from the publisher any newly published work whose publisher had failed to deliver to Stationers' Hall, regardless of whether it was entered in the Register. Books added from this source averaged *c*50 pa before and *c*400 pa after 1814, excluding pamphlets, and ignoring material (including latterly all the music and probably most of the novels) which was claimed in order to be sold. Many of the pamphlets seem to be incorporated in the Russell collection.

'St' in 1724 cat and so marked in some of the books.

Port Royal Library, of works by the nuns and Jansenist scholars of the Abbaye de Port-Royal-des-Champs and on its history, collected by Mrs Mary Anne Schimmelpenninck (1778–1856) the Moravian of Bristol. It began in 1811 with the gift to her as a consolation at a time of penury by Hannah More (1745–1833) which stimulated her to write a series of books on the abbey (finally collected into *Select memoirs of Port Royal,* 1829). She built it up with the help of Henri Grégoire (1750–1831) the revolutionary Bishop of Blois, and other clergy of Jansenist sympathies. She bequeathed it to Robert Aitken (1800–73) the Methodist preacher who became Vicar of Pendeen in Cornwall, and his widow donated it in 1874 on condition that it should remain segregated. 389 v 1666–1861 (nearly all in French and before 1790), with 26 v of miscellaneous French theology. In 1876 her cousin and biographer Miss Christiana C Hankin donated her own collection of the suppressed portraits and other engravings executed before the dissolution of 1708, mainly by Marie Anne Hyacinthe Horthemels (1682–1727).

A complete catalogue of the Sion College 'Port Royal' Library. . . and of Port Royal portraits and other engravings. . . , Aberdeen, 1898 (issued with *Classified list of the books added 1895–7*).

C C Hankin, *Life of Mary Anne Schimmelpenninck* 3rd ed London, 1859, p358-63.

Budd, Theodore (*c*1820?–1900), Vicar of Briningham in Norfolk, bibliophile, and writer on biblical history, bequeathed his collection 'to the public'. His executors after a court hearing donated it to Sion College. A ms list gives titles of *c*1,500 rare books and tracts (*c*1550–1710) on theology, history and politics, but indicates that there were over 2,000 more unbound books, pamphlets, sermons, and tracts (whose nature is unknown).

*c*300 identified in *Classified list of books added. . . 1900–1910* (1914).

B **Pamphlet Collections**

30,240 pamphlets mostly received *c*1798–1890 (including *c*22,000 of *c*1580–1851) were set apart and not entered in the general catalogue. They are formed into five collections, each with its own catalogue: the 'Russell' and 'General' of miscellaneous origin, and three individual benefactions. (Pamphlets acquired from 1891 have been classified with the books and entered in the general card cat.)

Holdings of sermons indicated in John Cooke, *The preacher's assistant*, Oxford, 1783, v 2.

Russell collection, named after John Russell (1787–1863) Headmaster of Charterhouse, Canon of Canterbury, and Rector of St Botolph without Bishopsgate, because it was in 1845, during his presidency, that it was assembled and bound, but there is no evidence as to whether he contributed anything to it. Said to contain 5,855 pamphlets, including some sermons and archdeacons' charges, bound in 411 v. Only 4,776 are in the Russell cat, nearly all non-theological (perhaps the remainder were entered in the general cat). On a very wide variety of subjects, including medicine. Of those in the Russell cat, *c*200 are of *c*1750–97, *c*1,000 of 1798–1814, *c*4,000 of 1815–35, and *c*50 later; this distribution and the nature of the pamphlets suggest that they are mainly copyright receipts, though there are also some donations (eg from the Clements bequest).

Ms author cat in 2 v in 1878.

General collections of 11,779 pamphlets mostly acquired 1845–91 dating from mid-16th cent onwards, bound soon after acquisition. (Some earlier collections which had been analysed in 1724 are probably also included.) Predominantly theology and politics, but with a wide scatter of other subjects.

Author cat on slips closed 1891 and pasted into 4 v after incorporating slips for Gibson collection (but not Goode or Scott as the titlepage implies).

Gibson, Edmund (1669–1748), canon lawyer, Librarian at Lambeth, and Bishop of London, collected 3,765 pamphlets in 358 v which passed to his son Edmund (1713?–71) Rector of St Bene't, Paul's Wharf, and were donated by the latter's executor in 1798–9. Mainly controversial theology, especially anti-popery tracts, and politics.

Ms shelflist with name index by Robert Watts, *c*1800. Also in author cat of General Pamphlet Collections.

Goode, William (1801–68), Dean of Ripon, leading evangelical and editor of the *Christian Observer*, amassed a library of colossal size and range, much of which was sold (Sotheby 10 May 1869). 1,670 pamphlets from the sale, *c*1701–*c*1860, chiefly sermons and controversial theology.

Ms author cat 1876.

Scott, William (1813–72), Vicar of St Olave, tractarian, and editor of the *Christian Remembrancer*, President in 1858. 7,171 pamphlets 1840–70 donated at various times, chiefly theology (especially liturgy), education and musicology, with some on miscellaneous subjects.

Ms author cat 3 v, 1876.

Skinners' Company, Skinners' Hall, 8 Dowgate Hill, London EC4R 2SP. Tel (01) 236 5629. Open by prior arrangement with the Clerk.

The Hall was extensively damaged in 1941 and 1944. Though some ms archives survive, there is no printed material except livery lists from 1792.

Duplicated list of archives 1965.

Sir John Soane's Museum, 12-14 Lincoln's Inn Fields, London WC2A 3BP. Tel (01) 405 2107. Museum open Tues-Sat 10 am-5 pm; Library by appointment on written application to the Director.

The artistic and literary collections of Sir John Soane (1753–1837), architect to the Bank of England, in the house and museum which he built 1792–1824, were bequeathed by him by an Act of Parliament (3 Will.IV. c.4) with an endowment, to Trustees (drawn from City aldermen, the Royal Society, the Royal Academy, the Society of Antiquaries, and the Society of Arts) to provide the first public architectural museum and library in Britain. From 1947 it has been assisted by government funds, now received through the Department of Education and Science.

John Britton, *The union of architecture, sculpture and painting. . . the house and galleries of. . . Soane*, London, 1827.

Sir John Soane, *Description of the house and museum. . . of Sir John Soane*, London, 1832; 1835; abridged as *A general description of Sir John Soane's Museum*, 1840, to 10th ed, 1920; A T Bolton, *Description of the house and Museum*, 11th ed, 1930; superseded by Sir John Summerson, *A new description of Sir John Soane's Museum*, 1955; rev ed 1966.

Susan G Feinberg, *Sir John Soane's Museum: an analysis of the architect's house-museum* (PhD thesis, Univ of Michigan, 1979).

Pierre Du Prey, *Soane's architectural education*, New York Garland, 1977.

Sir John Summerson, *Sir John Soane 1753–1837*, London, 1952.

M Binney, 'An extension to the Soane Museum', *Country Life* 25 May 1972, p1306-9.

'Observations on the house of John Soane', *European Magazine* 62 (1812), p381-7.

'The Soanean Museum', *Mirror* 21 (598) (1833), p209-14.

Museum Library The library's stock totals *c*7,783 v of printed books and 680 pamphlets, with architectural drawings and mss. There are 4 incunabula; 54 STC items; *c*162 Wing; *c*1,400 ESTC; 43 16th cent and *c*192 17th cent foreign books. The library is now divided as below.

Author cat in ms; recataloguing in progress for new published cat.

Catalogue of the Library of Sir John Soane's Museum, 1878.

General Library Contains *c*3,000 v of books and pamphlets, including general reference books, especially dictionaries of all kinds; English literature (chiefly 17th cent), especially romances, plays (including 1st, 2nd and 3rd folios of Shakespeare), and some poetry; 75 mostly 1st editions of Daniel Defoe (1661–1731); 17th cent philosophy, theology and politics, including English tracts printed abroad; alchemy, spiritualism, and the occult are represented; mathematics and various scientific subjects.

Art and Architecture Library *c*4,000 v of books and pamphlets. First or other editions of most of the continental classics of architecture, 16th-18th cent, with numerous works of smaller importance. Also 17th-19th cent English architectural books.

Sale catalogues There are several hundred catalogues of art and book sales 1784–1836 (with a few earlier), mostly annotated by Soane or his agent with a view to possible acquisitions.

Card index may be consulted on request.

Architectural Drawings *c*32,000 drawings of the 16th-19th cent, including the collections of Soane himself; Henry Holland (1744–1806) and his successor Charles Heathcote Tatham (1772–1842) bought at his sale in 1834; Robert Adam (1728–92) and James Adam (1730–94); Sir William Chambers (1726–96); George Dance the younger (1741–1825), Soane's first master. An extra-illustrated copy of Pennant's *London* (1805) from the collection of the banker Henry Fauntleroy (1785–1824), who was executed for forgery, containing 1,531 prints and drawings.

Socialist Party of Great Britain Library, 52 Clapham High Street, London SW4 7UN. Tel (01) 622 3811. Open Tues 7-9 pm, or by arrangement, after written application to the Librarian. Photocopying.

The Party was founded in 1904 to promote genuine socialism by a disaffected group of the Social Democratic Federation. The library of *c*500 v and 2,000 pamphlets has been built up since 1904, mainly by donations from members, on Marxism, economics, social science, Russia, Bolshevik theory, and anti-Bolshevism.

Sources in British political history 1900–1951, 1975, v 1, p241-2.

Socialist Standard 1904– , especially Jubilee ed Sept 1954 (containing history and list of publications of the party).

Annual Report includes section on the Library.

Books Mostly 20th cent, the books include some scarce editions of Marx, D de Leon, Dietzen, Kautsky, Labriola, Vail, etc published by Charles Kerr of Chicago, mainly in the 1920s. There are some privately printed items and interesting association copies.

Socialist Party pamphlets All of the pamphlets published by the Socialist Party of Great Britain since 1905, and many of those published by its foreign parties in Australia, Canada, Ireland, New Zealand, and the United States (the World Socialist Party).

Other Pamphlets An extensive and interesting collection of pamphlets published from 1890 onwards by a wide variety of Marxist, pacifist, socialist, Trotskyist, communist and radical organizations, and the publications of a variety of anti-socialist organizations such as the British Empire Union and the Anti-Socialist Union.

Society for Promoting Christian Knowledge, Library and Archives, Holy Trinity Church, Marylebone Road, London NW1 4DU. Tel (01) 387 5282. Open by appointment only, on written application to the Librarian/Archivist.

The SPCK was founded in 1699, the first of the Church of England missionary societies, to promote religion at home and abroad, developed out of a scheme of Dr Thomas Bray (1656–1730) to establish parochial libraries, but when in 1701 he founded the Society for the Propagation of the Gospel to take over its work in America, it became mainly a publishing organization. In its early years, it was closely associated with the work of Charity Schools.

W K Lowther Clarke, *A history of the SPCK*, London, SPCK, 1959.

W O B Allen and E McClure, *Two hundred years... of the Society for Promoting Christian Knowledge*, London, SPCK, 1898.

Leonard Cowie, *Henry Newman: an American in London* 1708–43, London, SPCK, 1956.

The Library houses a collection of well over 10,000 items, and consists almost exclusively of the Society's own publications, of which until 1973 it held an almost complete set from its foundation. They include the *Book of Common Prayer* in innumerable European and oriental languages, the Apocrypha (because it was not printed by the Bible Society), and enormous collections of tracts in English, Welsh, and some foreign languages, from the mid-17th cent onwards, many of the early issues being printed at the Society's expense, but not necessarily bearing its name in the imprint. There was a major dispersal from the tract collections 1973–77 when a very large number of 18th and 19th cent exact duplicates and also many (mostly 19th cent) new editions were sold (some to the British Library, others to booksellers).

The Archives The Society has very important collections of mss which contain considerable detail relating to the publication of the tracts. The binding of these has been partly paid for out of the proceeds of the sales of tracts from the Library.

Society for Psychical Research Library, 1 Adam and Eve Mews, Kensington High Street, London W8 6UG. Tel (01) 937 8984. Open by appointment only on written application to the Librarian who may at his discretion grant access for bona fide scientific research (usually subject to payment of a fee).

The Society was founded in 1882 for the scientific investigation of reported phenomena not capable of explanation by the established theories of science; the society as such has no collective opinions or theories, being merely a forum for research and discussion. It was realized at the outset that a collection of the published evidence was the first prerequisite for such studies, and a Literary Committee was established to encourage donations and make purchases. Since the publication of the *Catalogue* and its supplements, much 19th cent and some other rare material has been dispersed.

Mrs H Sidgwick, 'The Society for Psychical Research', *Proceedings* 41(126) (1932), p1-26.

W H Salter, *The Society for Psychical Research: an outline of its history*, the Society, 1948.

General The library now contains well over 5,000 v on all aspects of psychical research and related studies, including spiritualism, hypnotism, telepathy, psychology, psychiatry, theosophy, the occult, and witchcraft. There are at least 25 Wing and 50 ESTC items.

Library catalogue of the Society for Psychical Research, compiled by Theodore Besterman, Glasgow Univ Press, 1927 (interleaved copy annotated with additions); Supplements 1928, 1929, 1931, 1934.

Cat and supplements also printed in *Proceedings* 37(104) (1927), whole issue; 38(108) (1928), p103-207; 39(113) (1929), p193-246; 40(120) (1931), p1-58; and 42(133) (1934), p1-47.

Cats and accessions lists also printed in *Proceedings* 1883–9 and in *Journal* from 1949.

Tracts There are over 100 v bound mostly by subjects: these include collections on apparitions; death and survival; dowsing; dreams; hallucinations; hypnotism; philosophy; psychical research; psychoanalysis; psychology; spiritualism; supernormal healing; telepathy and clairvoyance; theosophy; and collections of tracts by or about Sydney G L R Alrutz (1868–1925) of Sweden; Sir William Crookes (1832–1919); Karl Baron von Reichenbach (1788–1869); and Emanuel Swedenborg (1688–1772).

Included with books in *Library catalogue.*

See also Preface to first supplement, which explains the arrangement of the Tract collection.

Serials Over 200 runs of journals, society publications, conferences, etc, on psychical research, spiritualism, psychology, psychiatry and the occult, including some rare early 19th cent publications.

Library catalogue, p1-25, and supplements, but many there listed have been dispersed.

Edmund Gurney Memorial Library on hypnotism In 1889 a special collection on hypnotism was begun in memory of Edmund Gurney (1847–88) one of the Society's founders, and was built up by donations to several hundred volumes. In 1923 it was merged in the general collection.

List of original nucleus in *Proceedings* 5 (1889), p575-89.

Society of Antiquaries Library, Burlington House, Piccadilly, London W1V 0HS. Tel (01) 734 0193. Open (not August) Mon-Fri 10 am-5 pm to members; to other scholars and research workers by prior written application to the Librarian.

The Society of Antiquaries of London was formally instituted in 1717; it had grown out of a more informal group led by Humfrey Wanley (1672–1726), John Bagford (1650–1716), and John Talman (*d*1726), which began in 1707, and was not connected with the Elizabethan society similarly named. The library did not expand until the society first acquired a permanent home in 1753; it has been at its present address since 1875. In addition to books, it contains extensive and important collections of the society's archives, mss (some medieval), maps, seals, prints, drawings, watercolours, photographs and rubbings of monumental brasses and bell inscriptions. The William Morris collection is housed at Kelmscott Manor (see under Oxfordshire).

Joan Evans, *A history of the Society of Antiquaries*, London, OUP, 1956 (op), contains numerous references to the Library, not all of which are indexed.

The Society of Antiquaries of London: notes on its history and possessions, London, The Society, 1951, p13-16. (op)

J Hopkins, 'The Society of Antiquaries and its Library', *Libraries Bulletin (University of London)* no 9 (Jan/Mar 1977), p5-8.

C Kortholt, *De Societate Antiquaria Londinensi*, Leipzig, 1735.

Archaeologia, 1770– .

Antiquaries' Journal, 1921– .

General collection of printed books The library is primarily a special collection on archaeology and antiquities; including also liturgy, genealogy and heraldry, bibliography, topography, prehistory, and classical archaeology. The collections on British archaeology are unrivalled, and include all the Elizabethan antiquaries and every edition of Camden *Britannia*, all the standard county and city histories. Also held are many of the great atlases, both British and foreign, from the 16th cent onwards. It was formerly the practice for fellows to donate all their published works; this led to the acquisition of large collections not related to the society's objects, and many of these have been dispersed, especially in 1895 when large transfers to the Guildhall Library and British Museum (Natural History) were made, and collections sold; but many books on miscellaneous subjects remain. There are now probably c130,000 v, perhaps about half are pre-1851, including c2,000 pre-1701; c15,000 pamphlets. Donations and bequests have not been kept as separate collections, but some of the more important, chiefly those of which there are lists, are described in separate paragraphs below.

Card cat (author, alphabetical, subject, and topographical) begun 1924, including subject entries for journal articles, superseding printed author cat, none of which was ever complete, and which concentrated on material of current interest at time of publication.

A catalogue of the printed books in the Library of the Society of Antiquaries of London, comp Nicholas Carlisle, 1816.

List of printed books in the Library of the Society. . ., 1861; *Supplement*, 1868.

Printed books in the Library of the Society. . ., 1887 (with subject index); *Supplement*, 1899.

Shelflist of pre-1700 books, compiled 1967.

Incunabula There are 51 incunabula, almost all of which were bequeathed in the 19th and early 20th cent. 28 are from the Ashpitel collection, and three from the William Morris collection at Kelmscott Manor. The earliest is Rodericus Sancius de Arevalo *Speculum* 1471; there are four printed by Koberger, including the Bible of 1478.

J C Clayton, 'Incunables in the Library of the Society of Antiquaries of London: a handlist', *Antiquaries Journal*, 60 (1980), p308-19 (offprint £1).

A more detailed cat in ms available on request.

Fine printing There is a large number of finely printed books scattered throughout the collections; these include four printed by Wynkyn de Worde, *Chronicle of England* 1502; *The arte or crafte* 1503; *Ortus vocabulorum* 1514; *Cicero* 1534; five of Tottell; eight of the Aldine press; and 66 of Elsevier. Later works include Baskerville and Roxburghe Club editions (see also below the collections deposited by the Roxburghe Club and the Society of Dilettanti, and the Society's own collection of William Morris at Kelmscott Manor, Oxfordshire).

Society of Antiquaries publications and other early journals A complete set of the Society's publications from 1722, including *Archaeologia* from 1770 and *Proceedings* 1843–1920, with *Vetusta monumenta* 1747–1897. Most other serial publications of antiquarian interest before 1850, including a very extensive collection of foreign periodicals.

Local society publications 19th and 20th cent collections include the most extensive holdings in existence of the publications of county, borough and other local archaeological and record societies.

Applied arts Extensive collections on monumental sculpture, brasses, arms and armour, and the decorative arts. Many books on ceramics have been bought with money given by Hugh Owen in 1894. Many on heraldry have been bought from a fund bequeathed by Colonel Croft Lyons c1927.

Proclamations collection In 1725 members were urged to procure for the library as many proclamations as they could find, and a guardbook was provided to receive them. The King's Printer later agreed to donate all royal proclamations on publication. After the President, Martin Folkes (1690–1754) died, 2 v of proclamations 1239–1625, both ms and printed, were bought at the sale of his private collection at Sotheby's, 2 Feb 1756 (lot 5125); these had originally been part of the famous collection of proclamations formed by Humphrey Dyson (*d*1631), and passed through the Richard Smith sale (15 May 1682, first lot on p370). 12 v of proclamations, broadsides, etc were bought by Thomas Hollis (1720–74) of Lincoln's Inn at the sale of Charles Davis, bookseller in Holborn, 3 Dec 1723 (lot 94), and given by him to the Society; the proclamations were added to the general collection when the volumes were broken up in 1852, and are thought to have originally come mostly from the Dyson collection. There are now c2,000 items.

Ms cat 1865.

H Dyson, *A booke containing all such proclamations as were published during the raigne of. . . Elizabeth*, London, 1618, with table.

R L Steele, 'Humphrey Dyson', *Library* 3rd ser 1 (1910), p144-5.

W A Jackson, 'Humphrey Dyson's Library', *Papers of the Bibliographical Society of America* 43 (1949), p279-87.

'Humphrey Dyson and his collections', *Harvard Library Bull* 1 (1947), p76-89.

Broadsides Collection A collection of c1,000 items, first formed into a separate collection in 1852, mainly from the Davis purchase (see Proclamations collection), by the Society's archivist Robert Lemon; it includes over 300 STC, 300 Wing, and 100 ESTC items. Among these are a printed indulgence of 1513, numerous ballads with 8 on Cromwell, a number of petitions, and a unique copy of *A short answere to the boke called Beware the cat* 1540; 33 items mainly relating to the City of London 1828–52 given by Arthur Taylor, printer to the Corporation, in 1853; 87 of the 19th cent given by Edward Peacock of the National Association for the Revision of the Present System of Taxation in 1862, and 4 v of broadsides from the library of Major John Roland Abbey (1896–1969) were given in the 1960s. (See also the Prattinton collection below.)

Catalogue of a collection of printed broadsides in the possession of the Society of Antiquaries of London, Comp P Lemon, 1866 (in print at £5).

Prattinton collection Peter Prattinton (1776–1840) of Bewdley bequeathed a collection on the history of Worcestershire, comprising mss, 100 v of books, c1,500 pamphlets, together with handbills and printed ephemera now bound in 5 v. The printed material is mostly post-1770. Material on the county as a whole includes histories, Acts, pollbooks, election bills and pedigrees. The section on Bewdley contains material of societies, tradesmen (71 items, mainly 19th cent), town notices, (45 18th cent); broadsides and catalogues of sales (203, mainly 18th cent); Bellman's notices requesting contribution (8, all 1776); poor relief; turnpikes; Charity and other schools; Bewdley Circulating Library catalogues 1822 and 1824, and booksellers' notices and catalogues. The Kidderminster, Stourport and Wribbenhall section includes 98 playbills and notices (19th cent). The Severn section includes Severn Humane Society reports 1791–1829, and material on Worcester Music Meeting 1809–27.

E A B Barnard, *The Prattinton collections of Worcestershire history*, Evesham, 1931, especially p119-20 (op), classified with author and subject indexes; supplemented by his 'List of the printed papers and miscellanea with index and of the pedigrees and portraits in the Prattinton collections. . . of the Society of Antiquaries', typescript 1932, carbon copy in British Library.

Fairholt collection on pageantry Francis William Fairholt (1814–66), the book illustrator, bequeathed this collection which he had assembled while contributing to the Percy Society's publications, to form the nucleus of a special collection on pageantry. There are 179 v (together with prints) on pageantry in general, coronations, royal marriages and entries, funerals, tournaments, etc in English, Dutch, French, German and Italian, 1530–1865. Many finely illustrated and exceptionally rare items are included. In 1918 it was supplemented by a collection on French and English coronations from the library of the Rev E G Dewick, FSA, given by his son.

[C S Perceval], *Catalogue of a collection of works on pageantry bequeathed. . . by F W Fairholt*, 1869 (classified, without index).

Charles Lyttleton (1714–68) President A collection of 90 books and an important collection of mss given in 1755.

John Robert Daniel Tyssen (1805–82) of Hackney, gave one of his many collections (others to Hackney Public Library, etc) to the Society in 1857. It contains 413 v on London, especially the Hackney area, includes also guides to other towns; mainly late 18th and early 19th cent.

Reported without list in *Proceedings* 4 (1857), p101.

Arthur Ashpitel (1807–69), architect and political writer, bequeathed (with a collection of Greek vases) *c*2,400 v of books, including many of the rarest in the library, in which a special bookplate was inserted. They include 28 incunabula, most of the Elsevier collection, many fine architectural works by Palladio, Piranesi, etc, books on the occult and witchcraft of 17th-19th cent, and 23 chapbooks (13 from Stirling *c*1820).

Ms cat in 2 v.

C Ferguson, 'Chapbooks in the Library', *Proceedings* 2nd ser 15 (1895), p338-45.

Report in *Proceedings* 2nd ser 4 (1869), p375-6; obit p299-301.

George Edward Cokayne (1825–1911), Clarenceux King of Arms, in 1895 gave over 1,100 books to fill important gaps in the collections.

Report without list in *Proceedings* 2nd ser 15 (1895), p236.

Sir Augustus Wollaston Franks (1826–97) A collection of *c*800 books given in 1895, and later he bequeathed the books remaining in his library on architecture, art, history and genealogy not already held, *c*1,350 books, *c*400 tracts, and heraldic drawings, engravings and mss.

Report without list in *Proceedings* 2nd ser 16 (1897), p416-17.

Albert Way (1805–74), in 1869, gave books and prints to form the nucleus of a collection on seals. After his death selections from his library were given by his widow; these included *c*150 dictionaries, hundreds of Yorkshire almanacs, 25 tracts in Yorkshire dialects, and various other items, including the unique *Catholicon abbreviatum* 1497 (and collections of archaeological drawings and seals).

Proceedings 2nd ser 6 (1874), p198-200 (obit), 207-12 (list of dictionaries), 435 (list of Yorkshire material).

Royal Archaeological Institute Library In 1843 was founded the British Archaeological Association for the Encouragement and Prosecution of researches into the Arts and Monuments of the Early Middle Ages. In 1845, following a dispute, it broke into two parts, the larger of which was in 1846 renamed the Archaeological Institute of Great Britain and Ireland, and in 1867 the Royal Archaeological Institute of Great Britain and Ireland. Its library, mainly 19th cent periodicals and books, was from 1892 housed in the University College, but in 1900–2 was broken up, all material not already held being absorbed by the Society of Antiquaries; *c*2,000 items on archaeology and English and European history.

Royal Archaeological Institute, *Catalogue of the Library*, 1890 (authors; topographical index).

J Evans, 'The Royal Archaeological Institute: a retrospect', *Archaeological Journ* 106 (1949), p1-11.

Arthur William George Lowther (1901–72) of Ashtead, architect and British archaeologist, bequeathed his library of rare books. *c*400 v printed books 1600–80, and *c*1,600 Civil War tracts were retained, the remainder sold.

Obit in *Archaeological Journ* 53 (1973), p405-6; 56 (1976), p35-6.

Society of Dilettanti Library, deposited. The archival collection (not complete) of the publications of the Society of Dilettanti, founded in 1732 as a dining club for those who had been to Italy on the Grand Tour, from 1764 to 1914, active in sponsoring archaeological expeditions to Greece and the Eastern Mediterranean, and publishing the results in magnificent folio volumes, now reverted to its original purpose and based at Brooks's (qv). A major gap in the collection has recently been filled by the purchase of Richard Payne Knight *Account of the remains of the workshop of Priapus.*

Lionel Cust, *History of the Society of Dilettanti* ed by Sir Sidney Colvin, re-issued with supplementary chapter, London, 1914.

Sir Cecil Harcourt-Smith, *The Society of Dilettanti: its regalia and pictures*; together with an *Outline of its history 1914–1932* comp by G A Macmillan, London, 1932; including bibliography of the publications of the Society, p121-5.

The Society of Dilettanti, 1977 (illustrated brochure).

G A Macmillan, 'A romance of publishing', *Times Literary Supplement* 30 Dec 1915, p499.

Roxburghe Club Library, deposited. The Club was founded at the time of the sensational sale in 1812 of the Duke of Roxburghe's library by Thomas Frognall Dibdin (1776–1847) and others, for the printing in limited editions of rare English texts. The library comprises a collection (not quite complete) of its own publications. The Club's private archives also contain Dibdin's copies of the Roxburghe sale catalogue and *Roxburghe revels*, and a few other printed items.

Hon Clive Bigham, afterwards Viscount Mersey, *The Roxburghe Club: its history and its members 1812–1927*, Oxford, 1928, p131-50.

Nicholas J Barker, *The publications of the Roxburghe Club 1814–1962, an essay... with a bibliographical table*, Cambridge, the Club, 1964.

Society of Apothecaries, Apothecaries' Hall, Blackfriars Lane, London EC4V 6EJ.

The archives, ms and printed material of the Society, which is 58th in order of precedence of the City Livery companies, are deposited in the Guildhall Library Dept of Manuscripts. All rare books in its Library were sold *c*1958, but not the collection which had been transferred to the Chelsea Physic Garden (qv). Some books remaining at the Hall were recently discovered, and a successful appeal was made for donations to establish a new library. Now including 2 STC items; 11 Wing and 50 ESTC.

Society of Chiropodists Library, 8 Wimpole Street, London W1M 8BX. Tel (01) 570 3227. Open Mon-Fri 9.30 am-4.30 pm to Members; to others only by prior arrangement with the Secretary of the Society.

The Society was founded in 1945 by the merger of the British Association of Chiropodists (founded 1931), the Chelsea Chiropodists' Association (1926), the Chiropody Practitioners (1942), the Incorporated Society of Chiropodists (1912), and the Northern Chiropodists' Association (1925). It has one of the largest chiropodial libraries in Europe.

J C Dagnall, 'The origins of the Society of Chiropodists', *Chiropodist* 25 (1970), p315-20.

Seelig Collection An historical collection on chiropody, formed by Walter Seelig (1898–1955), historian of chiropody.

J C Dagnall, 'The history of chiropodial literature', *Journ of the Society of Chiropodists* 20 (1965), p173-84.

Society of Genealogists Library, 37 Harrington Gardens, London SW7 4JX. Tel (01) 373 7054. Open Tues, Fri, Sat 10 am-6 pm; Wed, Thurs 8 pm after written application to the Librarian, subject to the payment of a substantial fee by non-members according to time. Photocopier; microform reader. Research Dept carries out research for hourly fees.

The Society and its library were founded in 1911, and the collections have been built up by purchase and donations from members and others.

General The library is a general working collection for genealogical research containing over 42,000 v, with but 1 STC and 1 Wing item, and some ESTC. The major collection of printed material dates from the early 19th cent on genealogy, family history, topography, heraldry, directories and biographical reference books.

Card cat (author and subject, with separate topography and biography sections).

Using the library of the Society of Genealogists, 1980.

Accessions printed in *Genealogists' Magazine*.

Documentary collections and indexes Collections of documents have always been a major feature of the library, but those that are mainly ms rather than printed are not described in detail in this Directory. The most important are the Family Documents collection (which includes many printed pedigrees); the Great Card Index, recording biographical details of several million individuals especially of the 18th and early 19th cent; Boyd's Marriage Index 1538–1837 in typescript covering fully or partially over 4,300 parishes in England (about 12 per cent coverage) compiled by Percival Boyd (1866–1955) and collaborators from those transcripts of registers that were readily accessible; Boyd's Inhabitants of London, indexing *c*60,000 individuals from printed and ms sources; the collection of Frederick Simon Snell (1872–1914) on Berkshire; the collection of Arthur Campling (1871–1947) on East Anglia; the collection of Walter and John Macleod assembled 1880–1940 on Scotland; and the collection of Mrs Vernona Thomas Christian Smith (neé Torry, *d*1902) on the West Indies.

A J Camp, 'Collections and indexes of the Society of Genealogists', *Genealogists' Magazine* 13(10) (June 1961), p311-17.

Genealogists' Handbook 5th ed by P Spufford and J Camp, London, the Society, 1969.

A list of parishes in Boyd's Marriage Index, 4th ed 1980.

Local histories A large collection of histories of counties, towns and parishes, mainly late 19th cent, but some earlier from *c*1700 onwards.

Parish register copies The largest known collection of copies of British parish registers, including virtually every printed edition (mostly 19th cent); and the rare *Register of Portman Square dissenting baptisms, 1782–1820*. Also included are some of the registers from Garratt's Hall Library.

Catalogue of the parish register copies in the possession of the Society of Genealogists enl.ed 1980.

National index of parish registers 1966– (in progress 1982).

Trade directories These cover London from 1734; English provinces from 1783, including rare *Salop directory* by Tibram and Co 1828; some Scottish and Irish including an unusual set of Dublin directories 1746–1847; smaller runs of Indian from 1799, Australian from 1857, Canadian and US from late 19th cent. Imperial directory from 1812.

Catalogue of directories and poll books in the possession of the Society of Genealogists enl.ed 1979.

Pollbooks A collection for English and Welsh constituencies from 1754; many are from collections given by Sir Isaac Pitman (1813–97) and A E Oldaker.

Catalogues of directories and poll books, 1979.

Professions Army lists from 1740; Navy from 1756; Clergy 1829, 1841 and 1850 onwards; medical from 1845 (with 1 register 1769); law from 1813.

Apprenticeship indentures 18 v of indentures, including printed indenture forms 1641–1732, collected by Frederick Arthur Crisp (1851–1922).

Privately printed genealogical books Rare items among many include Ruvigny *Plantagenet blood royal* (1903) and *Brooke Quaker pedigrees* (1940) (1 of only 2 existing copies).

Peerages and genealogical dictionaries Virtually every edition of the standard works published since 1800, eg Walford, *County families* 1860–1920, Burke etc.

Heraldic visitations All printed editions of the visitations of the officers of the College of Arms (1530–1687).

Periodicals Virtually all British genealogical journals, and many sets of transactions of local archaeological societies.

Society of the Sacred Heart Provincial Archives, Sacred Heart Convent, Roehampton Lane, London SW15 5PH. Tel (01) 876 4414. Open by prior arrangement only, on written application to the Sister Archivist.

The Society of the Sacred Heart was founded in 1800 as a Roman Catholic order of nuns who have traditionally been concerned with education. The Society's college, adjacent to the Convent, became Stuart College with its own library, and now forms part of the Roehampton Institute (qv). The Convent library was severely damaged by bombing, but some of the books that were rescued have been transferred to the Archives, which are intact. There are *c*500 v on the history of the Order and biographies and writings of its members, mainly after 1850. There are *c*20 v of 17th and 18th cent French books of devotion and instruction used in the Society's French houses until the expulsions of 1904, when they were brought to England. One of these, *La vie du père J Rigoleuc*, Paris, 1686, from the convent of Beauvais, bears the inscription of the Society's founder (St Madeleine) Sophie Barat (1779–1865).

Sotheby, Parke Bernet and Co's Auction Rooms, 34 New Bond Street (and Bloomfield Place), London W1A 2AA. Tel (01) 493 8080. Telex 24454.

Sotheby's traces its history back to 1734 when Samuel Baker, the bookseller, first began to hold sales of books, and the firm has had 14 different names (see BL cat). The complete archival set of its sale catalogues to 1971, with the auctioneer's ms record of buyers' names and prices has been transferred to the British Library Reference Division, as has the similar set from Hodgson's rooms (established in 1807, continued as part of Sotheby's from 1967). There are substantial reference collections on art and bibliography for the exclusive use of the firm's cataloguers; there is no public access.

Frank Hermann, *Sotheby's*, London, Chatto, 1980.

Hodgson and Co, *One hundred years of book auctions*, London, 1908.

South London Botanical Institute, 323 Norwood Road, Tulse Hill, London SE24 9AQ. Tel (01) 674 5787. Open to all Tues and Thurs 6 pm-9 pm, or by appointment.

In 1911 Allan Octavian Hume (1829–1912) CB, botanist and ornithologist, and retired Indian Civil Servant, author of *The game birds of India, Burmah and Ceylon* (Calcutta 1879–81), bought the house at 323 Norwood Road to house his herbarium and library which he opened to the public. The collection has subsequently been built up as a library of taxonomic botany, particularly strong in British floras. There are now *c*5,000 v, of which *c*500 are pre-1851.

Card cat.

Sir William Wedderburn, *Allan Octavian Hume*, London, 1913, p113-21.

J E Lousley, 'W R Sherrin, Curator of the South London Botanical Institute from 1919–1955 (obituary)', *Proceedings of the Botanical Society of the British Isles*, 1 (1955), p553-6.

South Place Ethical Society, Conway Hall, 25 Red Lion Square, London WC1R 4RL. Tel (01) 242 8032/3. Open by appointment only after written application to the Secretary.

The Society originated in 1793 as a non-conformist Christian group, later known as Philadelphians or Universalists, meeting at Parliament Court Chapel in Artillery Lane, Bishopsgate, under the ministry of Elhanan Winchester—a pioneer of the universalist faith—(1751–97) from Virginia. Their next minister, William Vidler (1758–1816) who founded the chapel library, led them into Unitarianism as the Society of Religious Dissenters. In 1824 they moved to a new chapel at South Place in Finsbury, and became known as the South Place Unitarian Society. Later they became the South Place Religious Society. In 1887 Stanton Coit (1857–1907), an Emersonian from America, became minister on condition that the name be changed to the South Place Ethical Society, and the next 40 years witnessed the library's greatest expansion, absorbing part of the McIntyre Memorial Library, given in 1896 to the Union of Ethical Societies by Lavinia Vidlake in memory of Jane Anne McIntyre, mainly for the use of the School of Ethics and the Emerson Club (the Union, now renamed the British Humanist Association, has a library of modern works at 13 Prince of Wales Terrace, London W8 5PG). In 1929 the Society with its library of *c*10,000 v, moved to Red Lion Square. Since 1891 the Society has been recognized as a charity for the advancement of education and for purposes beneficial to the community. The library is reduced to *c*6,000 v, of which *c*150 are pre-1851, ie from mid-18th cent onwards. There is a core collection of philosophy, radicalism, and freethought, and of works relating to the Society's history, associated with the archives, which seem to begin *c*1850 with a few important mss, such as the autobiographies of William Lovett (1800–77), the Chartist (whose chair is in the office), and G J Holyoake (1807–96); the Society's periodical from *c*1883 and its lectures etc from *c*1840; a collection of works by Fox (with the *Monthly Repository*); and 12 v of English and American pamphlets collected by Conway, given by his family. There is also an extensive library of general subjects, built up as a lending library for members, which is particularly strong in early 19th cent English literature; it also includes the social sciences, and popular science with a collection on Darwinism.

Card cat (authors and titles). Separate cat of freethought collection.

S K Ratcliffe, *The story of South Place*, London, Watts, 1955.

Susan Budd, *Varieties of unbelief*, London, Heinemann, 1977, p15-20, 217-26.

A short history of the South Place Ethical Society (1927).

Moncure D Conway, *Centenary history of the South Place Society*, London, 1894.

F E Mineka, *The dissidence of dissent...*, Chapel Hill, NC, 1944, p169-203.

Southwark Cathedral Library, Chapter House, St Thomas Street, London SE1 9RY. Tel (01) 407 3708. Open Mon-Fri 10 am-4 pm by appointment, after written application to the Provost. Enter via Provost's Office between nos 7 and 9 St Thomas Street.

The Priory Church of St Mary Overie became, after the ejection of the Augustinian Canons in 1539 (and the dispersal of their library), the Parish Church of St Saviour, Southwark, in the Diocese of Winchester, until 1877 when it was transferred to Rochester; in 1893 it became a Collegiate Church and was rebuilt. In 1905 it became the Cathedral and Collegiate Church of St Saviour and St Mary Overie, for the new Diocese of Southwark.

Brian Tunstall, *The pictorial history of Southwark Cathedral*, London, Pitkin (1961).

Arthur Tiler, *The history and antiquities of St Saviour's Southwark*, London 1765.

M Concanen and A Morgan, *The history...of...St Saviour's Southwark*, Deptford, 1795.

Bailey Library Though the Cathedral Library now contains books associated with the church from the 16th cent onwards, some of which have probably been in the care of the church continuously, after 1539 there was no organized library until 1902, when Mrs Harriot Bailey, widow of the Rev Hammond Roberson Bailey, gave his collection of *c*2,000 books which long formed an unofficial library in the Chapter House gallery, with added donations from Samuel Mumford Taylor (1859–1929) successively Rector, Precentor and Sub-Dean, the Rev Cecil Thomas Wood (1903–80) and others, but the collection was greatly diminished by theft and neglect.

Chapter Library In 1959–61 an official Chapter Library was created by William Cuthbert Brian Tunstall (1900–70) FSA and the Friends of the Cathedral from the Bailey Library (part of which had been lent to Lambeth Palace) and a collection of recent acquisitions which had been kept at the Foster Hall. Further donations were received from Tunstall (chiefly early printed books) from the library of the South London Church Fund (Bibles and other texts, commentaries, and modern theology), and from Mrs C E Forrester. Most of the modern collection has, within the last few years, been transferred to the Southwark Ordination Centre at Bletchingley, and the remainder, now *c*1,000 v, with the archives, is somewhat neglected and its future is in doubt.

General cat missing (perhaps at Bletchingley).

Southwark Cathedral Library 17th October 1963 (history and exhibition cat).

Some pre-1701 books are recorded in the Cathedral Libraries Catalogue of the Bibliographical Society.

Andrewes Collection *c*50(?) editions of works by Lancelot Andrewes (1555–1626), Bishop of Winchester (who is buried in the Cathedral), mostly of the 16th cent; a few modern, with some biographica. Andrewes was one of the translators of the Authorised Version of the Bible, and his own copy of it is in use in the Cathedral. It is not clear whether any of the collection of his writings is from his own library; it has been added to at numerous times, and some books have recently been donated by his descendants.

Typescript list.

Henry Sacheverell (1674?–1724), High Church Tory controversialist, Preacher and Chaplain of St Saviour's. His own copy of the Samuel Newman's *Concordance*, 1698, and 2 1710 editions of his *Tryal*.

Theology and ecclesiastical history The major part of the library is a general collection, mostly English late 19th and early 20th cent, but including 11 STC; 14 Wing; *c*30 ESTC; *c*60 English 1801–50; 6 foreign 16th cent, 19 17th, and 19 18th cent, with a very few later foreign books. Bibles, prayer books, and lexicographic works form a substantial part of the collection; also sermons, miscellaneous theology, and a small amount of ecclesiastical history, with a handful of classical texts.

Southwark *c*100 v on the Cathedral and the topography of Southwark, almost all after 1800, but with earlier histories of London from the 17th cent onwards.

Southwark Catholic Diocesan Archives, Archbishop's House, 150 St George's Road, London SE1 6HX. Tel (01) 928 5592. Open by appointment with the Archivist after written application in advance.

The Diocese was established in 1851 from part of the Diocese of Westminster which had been created in the previous year. There is a general reference library of *c*2,000 v of 20th cent books in addition to the collections below. There are no catalogues except of the earlier part of the Tierney Collection.

Tierney Collection Part of the library formed by Canon Mark Aloysius Tierney (1795–1862), Professor at St Edmund's College, Ware; the greater part of which was auctioned (Sotheby 1–4 Dec 1862); supplemented by early printed books collected by Dr Daniel Rock (1799–1871), Canon of the Cathedral. Probably acquired *c*1900. It includes 8 incunabula and 34 items of 1501–1640, with a large collection of later printed books; also mss. Mainly ecclesiastical history and theology, of wide-ranging character.

'Catalogue of mss, incunabula, other early printed books, and rare books in the possession of the Bishop of Southwark' 1921 (in ms, lists printed books to 1640 only).

Religious Orders A collection of 133 v of rules of religious Orders operating at some time in the Diocese, including some pre-1851.

Styche Collection A collection of *c*30 miscellaneous foreign books of the 16th and 17th cent, formed privately by a former Diocesan Archivist, the Rev Percival Styche. Some are on ecclesiastical history, but others are on natural history, geography and extraneous subjects.

Canon Fletcher Collection A small collection of documents, mostly ms, but with some printed items relating to the Church in England from 1787 onwards.

Southwark Public Libraries.

Leaflets issued by Southwark Library Service include *An introduction to the Library, Museum and Art Gallery Services*, (1976), and *Special Collections* (1977).

A **Newington Library**

155 Walworth Road, Newington, London SE17 1RS. Tel (01) 703 3324 or 5529 or 6514. Open Mon, Tues, Thurs, Fri 9.30 am-8 pm, Wed 1 pm; Sat 5 pm, but rare books may be consulted only by prior arrangement with the Reference Librarian. Photocopying facilities.

Principal Reference Library General Collection Includes 4 incunabula, 6 books of 16th cent; *c*100 17th, hundreds 18th and 19th cent. Shakespeare 2nd and 4th folios; 7 William Morris editions. Henry Syer Cuming (1815–92) of Kennington Park Road, son of Richard Cuming (1777–1870), the antiquary, bequeathed his museum and library of rare books, from which much of the general collection is derived.

Card cat (incomplete).

18th cent items in ESTC.

Borough of Southwark, *Souvenir of the opening of the Cuming Museum and the inauguration of the open access system in the Borough Libraries*, 1902.

Dante Collection In 1900 a number of books were donated to the then Newington Public Library by R C Jackson as part of a Dante Memorial in memory of Henry Clark Barlow (1806–76), a local scholar who founded the Dante lectures at University College, London. A much larger number was deposited on loan, and eventually purchased in 1949 by the Borough for a nominal sum. *c*800 v, including 10 of 1515–1600; 1 of 1601–1700; and 18 of 1701–1800.

Card cat.

Dante Sextenary celebration (exhibition cat).

Greek and Latin Literature Started in 1950 as the Borough of Southwark's allocation under the Metropolitan Special Collections Scheme (which was discontinued in 1975), the collection was extended backwards to include earlier works, of which 8 are of the 16th, 66 of the 17th and 191 of the 18th cent, nominally closed 1976, but still occasionally added to by donation.

Card cat.

B **John Harvard Library**

211 Borough High Street, Southwark, London SE1 1JA. Tel (01) 403 3507. Open Mon and Thurs 9.30 am-12.30 pm, 1.30-8 pm; Tues and Fri 9.30 am-12.30 pm, 1.30-5 pm; Sat by appointment only.

Southwark Local Studies Library Library and archive collection formed in 1965 from the collections of the former boroughs of Bermondsey, Camberwell, and Southwark. *c*5,000 v of books, together with numerous pamphlets, newspapers, and archives. Includes collections of books by, and about, John Ruskin

(1819–1900), *c*140 including most first and later editions to 1965, some from his own library; Charles Haddon Spurgeon (1834–92), Baptist preacher at the Metropolitan Tabernacle; Michael Faraday (1791–1867), *c*70 19th cent items, with a few later; and Eliza Cook (1818–89), her complete published work, including *Eliza Cook's Journal*. There is also a collection on the Globe Theatre, but the general Shakespeare Collection has been dispersed. Also a large collection of 19th cent playbills of the Surrey Theatre, South London Palace, and Royal Surrey Zoological Gardens. A collection on John Harvard (1607–38) founder of Harvard College, after whom the library is named.

Card cat.

Handlist of archives.

Spurgeon's College Library and Heritage Room, 189 South Norwood Hill, London SE25 6DJ. Tel (01) 653 0850. Open by appointment with the Librarian, following written application in advance. Xeroxing.

General Collection Baptist theological college founded in 1856 by Charles Haddon Spurgeon (1834–92) the popular preacher, whose own collection formed the core of the library, and whose correspondence, with proof copies of sermons and pamphlets, and other archival material is held. A substantial number of pre-1851 works is held, mainly Puritan writings.

Card cat (excluding Philpot).

The special collections include (a) *c*80 items donated by A H Philpot (*d*1966) OBE, a trustee of the College; (b) a collection of early Bibles. Lists of both collections available.

Stationers' and Newspaper Makers' Company, Stationers' Hall, Stationers' Hall Court, Ludgate Hill, London EC4M 7DD. Tel (01) 248 2934. Archives open by appointment on written application to the Archivist, usually on Wed; libraries on application to the Assistant Clerk, usually on Mon 10 am-4 pm.

The Stationers' Company, a medieval guild, received its first charter in 1557. Its members claimed the monopoly of printing and publishing; its Register of copyright entries, begun in 1544, and at first the compulsory instrument of a government licensing system, has continued to the present day on a voluntary basis. The royal patents granted to the Company in 1603 for printing psalters, almanacs, and primers, originated a publishing enterprise known as the 'English Stock', which survived until 1960, though the patents lapsed in the 17th and 18th cent. In 1933 it absorbed the Newspaper Makers' Company (founded 1931) and the combined company is 47th in order or precedence of the City livery companies.

Cyprian Blagden, *The Stationers' Company: a history, 1403–1959*, London, Allen and Unwin, 1960 (p300-3, 'A note on the records' with select bibliography of secondary sources).

[Philip Unwin], *The Stationers' Company, 1918–1977...*, London, E Benn, 1978.

T F Howard-Hill, *Index to British literary bibliography, v 4: British bibliography and textual criticism*, Oxford, Clarendon Press, 1979, p520-4.

A Archives

The principal records of the Company, the Registers and Court records (see below), are for their most important periods available in published transcripts. The Company did not retain legal deposit copies of books for which it was the collecting agent under certain Copyright Acts or create archival collections of works published by or for the Company, with the very limited exceptions indicated below; but there are extensive ms records of the 'English Stock'.

'Catalogue of records at Stationers' Hall', *Library* 4th ser 6 (1926), p348-57.

Court records and Apprentices Books These constitute the ms records, and printed transcripts to 1640; also the registers of apprentices and the printed compilations based on these and the main records of the Court. Printed livery lists from 1733 onwards.

W W Greg and E Boswell eds, *Records of the Court of the Stationers' Company 1576 to 1602, from Register B*, London, Bibliographical Society, 1930.

William A Jackson ed, *Records of the Court of the Stationers' Company 1602 to 1640*, London, Bibliographical Society, 1957.

D F Mackenzie, ed, *Stationers' Company apprentices: 1605–1640*, Charlottesville Bibliographical Soc of the Univ of Virginia, 1961: *1641–1700*, *1701–1800*, Oxford, Oxford Bibliographical Soc, 1974–8.

Registers of copyright In 1544 the 'Register of copies licensed by the Company to be printed' was begun; the right that entry in the Register conferred came to be known as copyright. Since the company had the right to refuse entry, the 'licence' soon came to be used by governments as a form of censorship, enforced by Star Chamber decrees of 1566, 1586 and 1637, and Licensing Acts of 1649 and 1662. When the last Act expired in 1695, entry became in effect voluntary, but was recognized by all Copyright Acts before that of 1911, when it became non-statutory. The original ms Registers are held in the Archives, except those for 1842–1924 (which with many related printed and ms documents are at the Public Record Office, Kew Branch); also the published transcripts to 1708, and the privately printed indexes for 1710–73 and 1842–1907.

E Arber ed, *A transcript of the Registers of the Company of Stationers of London 1554–1640*, London 1875–94, 5 v indexed (with other ms and printed records of press licensing) repr New York, Peter Smith, 1950.

[G E B Eyre *et al* ed], *A transcript of the Registers of the worshipful Company of Stationers 1640–1708*, London,

Roxburghe Club, 1913–4, 3 v; repr New York, Peter Smith, 1950; indexed in William P Williams ed, *Index to the Stationers' Register, 1640–1708...*, La Jolla (Calif), Laurence McGilvray, 1980; a new edition and index is being compiled by Carol Evans.

The scheme for publishing the transcript after 1708 is in abeyance; but see *Index of titles and proprietors of books entered in the Book of Registry of the Stationers' Company (pursuant to 8 Anne c.19) from 28th April 1710 to 30th Dec 1773*, London, pr by Taylor and Francis, (*c*1909?) (authors); *Index of entries (literary) in the Book of Registry of the Stationers' Company (pursuant to 5 and 6 Vict, cap.45) from 1st July 1842 to 15th March 1907*, London, Harrison and Co, 4 v, 1896–1907 (by author's surname or title in first v to 1884, thereafter by title with index of authors and publishers); *Index of entries (commercial)...from...1842 to...1884*, 1896 is a similar index to entries for labels, advertisements, etc; other indexes are in ms only.

Hyder E Rollins ed, *An analytical index to the ballad-entries (1557–1709) in the Registers...*, Chapel Hill, 1924, repr Hatboro (Pa), Tradition Press, 1967.

R Barrington Partridge, *The history of the legal deposit of books...*, London, 1938.

Loose Records These are made up of 23 boxes of papers, including some collections rediscovered in the Hall since 1940. Though most are ms, there are also many printed items, the chief of which include:

Box A, on licensing and copyright: Lord Chancellor Ellesmere's *Speech* 1609.

Acts against unlicensed printing 1649, 1661, 1718, 1761, 1774.

Copyright Act 1842. Proclamations of 1679, 1685, 1688.

Box E, printing in Oxford and Cambridge: material on the almanac dispute and a proclamation of 1791.

Box F, Company affairs: Stamp Act 1757; 3 pamphlets on the charter, 1741–62.

Box G, Hall business: 16 ephemera 1692–*c*1890.

Box P, papermaking: Act 1794 repealing duty, etc.

Box R, miscellaneous: 25 pamphlets and cuttings (modern); and a collection of specimen newspapers, mostly single sheets, 1694–1923, English and American.

Ms handlist in progress.

S Hodgson, 'Papers and documents recently found at Stationers' Hall', *Library* 4th ser 25 (1944–5), p23-36 (printed collections p33-6).

Almanac Collection The Company claimed the monopoly of printing almanacs from 1603–1779, but now has none before 1620, and has substantial sets only after 1720, and strongest for the 19th cent in several hundred volumes. There is a substantial collection of the 'Raven' or 'London' vest pocket almanacs of the 18th and 19th cent (and some blocks for their printing); and a major collection of broadsheet almanacs 1835–90, bound in four very large volumes. Most have come as donations in the present cent, including a very large collection from Sidney Hodgson (see below).

Temporary rough handlist, later to be incorporated in Library card cat.

C Blagden, 'The distribution of almanacs in the second half of the seventeenth century', *Studies in Bibliography* 11 (1958), p107-16. The collection was not used by B Capp for his location list of pre-1701 almanacs in *Astrology and the popular press*, 1979.

Pamphlet Collection A collection of *c*100 items, mostly from 20th cent donations, chiefly pamphlets, with a few substantial books, associated with the history of the Company; including 1 incunabulum leaf, 14 STC and 21 Wing items, 40 ESTC, and 9 of 1801–50. They include livery lists 1787–1831; documents printed for the private use of the Company; works on licensing, printing, and the book trades; works published by the Company or by its Masters on their own account; pamphlets connected with St Cecilia's Feast held in the Hall 1670–1720.

Uncatalogued.

B **Library**

A substantial number of books relating to printing and the book trades were formerly donated by members of the Company for preservation with the Archives. These have recently been segregated into a library, which is available for research to members of the public. It contains *c*3,000 v on the printing and publishing trades, chiefly in Great Britain, the Stationers' Company, other livery companies, and related subjects. The collection is mostly modern, but there are some older standard works such as the anecdotes of Bowyer (1790) and Nichols *Literary anecdotes* (1812–17). There is a major collection of biographies of London printers, publishers, papermakers, and newspapermakers, and histories of their firms. The Hodgson and Day collections, which are not kept as separate collections, have provided the greater part of the library.

Card cat (author/title and classified).

Heal Collection A collection on London printers and publishers to 1800 formed by Sir Ambrose Heal (1872–1959), in 13 v, containing advertisements cut from contemporary newspapers, facsimiles of title pages, articles from 20th cent newspapers and journals etc.

Sidney Hodgson (1876–1973), FSA, the auctioneer, Master of the Company, gave many books to the Company in his lifetime (including part of the almanac collection above), and many more from his collection were donated by his son Wilfrid B Hodgson after his death. They included a collection of works printed by past Masters of the Company, 1613–1739, with Richardson's *Grandison* (to which *Pamela* and *Clarissa* have been added by other donors); and some works printed for the Company.

Kenneth Day (1912–81), member of the Court of Assistants of the Company, and Production Manager of Ernest Benn Ltd, bequeathed his library of *c*800 v and several thousand smaller items (pamphlets, ephemera and correspondence); mainly on 20th cent typography, including many type specimen sheets, and some scarce items associated with Stanley Morison (1889–1967), with some earlier rare material.

In the course of arrangement.

Obit in *Printing World* 2 Dec 1981, p8.

C **Bibliographical Society Library**

(Deposited on permanent loan.) The Bibliographical Society was founded in 1892. Its library, dating from the same year, has been built up almost exclusively from donations, many being from distinguished bibliographers, both British and foreign, eg part of the library of Sir John Young Walker MacAlister (1856–1925), editor of *The Library*. Acquisitions policy has changed from time to time and books have been dispersed.

Ms author cat of MacAlister's library.

Archives An almost complete set of the publications of the Bibliographical Society, both periodicals and monographs, is included.

Monographs (general) These include *c*2,000 v on the techniques of analytical or historical bibliography, the history of printing and the book production arts and the book trades, book collecting, private (and to a very limited extent institutional) libraries, with some material on English literature, and bibliographies. *c*50 pre-1851 items, mostly after 1700.

Card cat (author/name) superseding earlier dictionary cat.

Rough hand-list of books in the Library, 1897; supplements 1898 and 1899.

Handlist of books in the Library of the Bibliographical Society, 1907, 1935 (op and very incomplete).

Book Collecting A strong section which includes over 150 catalogues of collections and book sales (in addition to runs of booksellers' catalogues), including 3 of the 18th cent and 22 of 1801–50, several of which are not in the British Library.

Bibliographies c600 items, of which *c*300 are author bibliographies, especially of the more significant writers of English literature; many bibliographies of more minor figures have been dispersed. There is an almost complete set of the author bibliographies compiled by Thomas James Wise (1859–1937) donated by himself, and his *Ashley Library* catalogue. Other bibliographies include 18th and 19th cent standard works by Ames, Dibdin, Palmer, etc.

Facsimiles A selection of photographic facsimiles of title pages of *c*1,000 STC books. A collection of photographic facsimiles of a selection of early 16th cent types.

Periodicals *c*100 titles (many not in complete runs) including a few scarce late 19th and early 20th cent publications.

Offprints A collection, mainly donated by authors of the articles, including substantial numbers from Konrad Haebler (1857–1946), Anatole Claudin (1833–1906), Leopold Victor Delisle (1826–1910), and Marie Pellechet (1840–1900).

Uncatalogued.

Supreme Court Library, Royal Courts of Justice, Strand, London WC2A 2LL. Tel (01) 405 7641 Ext 3587. Open at the Librarian's discretion for reference to material not available elsewhere, Mon-Fri 9 am-5 pm (closed bank holidays and following day).

The library was established in 1968, and the collection of over 200,000 v, which consists entirely of printed law books, has been actively built up since 1972 by large-scale transfers from the various courts and departments of the Royal Courts of Justice, from other government libraries, and by purchase. Many of the books formerly belonged to the libraries of the older courts (eg the Court of Exchequer), the private collections of judges, and the library of Doctors' Commons (ie the College of Advocates and Doctors at Law), part of which was bought by the government (from the sale, Hodgson 22 Apr 1861) for the Court of Admiralty and the Court of Probate.

There are 8 works of the period 1501–99, 79 of 1600–99, 315 of 1700–99, and 956 of 1800–50.

College of Advocates in Doctors' Commons, *Catalogue of the books in the library of the College*, 1818.

Thomas Hart, *History of the origin and progress of the Chancery Library now called the Probate Library*, London, 1895.

Swiss Cottage Reference Library, 88 Avenue Road, London NW3 3HA. Tel (01) 278 4444 Ext 3039. Open Mon-Fri 9.30 am-8 pm; Sat 5 pm. Rare materials may be consulted on request. Coin-operated photocopiers available.

The collection of early books in literature, topography and history in the Reference Library dates from the opening of Hampstead Central Library in 1897. The nucleus came from the Henry Morley Collection of *c*8,000 v purchased by the Hampstead Vestry, 1896 which has been added to by later donation and purchase. Many items listed in STC and Wing (up to 1700). These comprise 29 v 1501–1600; 133 v 1601–1700. Items published later comprise 430 v 1701–1800; 771 v 1801–50. Some noteworthy items include Lyly's *Euphues and his England* 1580 (unique copy?); 3 Elsevier Press books (1638, 1641 and 1647 respectively); an Aldus Smyrnaeus Quintus (1505?); an example of Zaehnsdorf binding (1822) and a Riviere binding (1916).

Special Collections Dept (Ext 3010) The collection formed (from 1948–75) part of the Metropolitan Special Collections Scheme. Previously Hampstead libraries had an interest in philosophy and psychology partly as a result of the Henry Morley collection purchased by

Hampstead Vestry in 1896. The collection covers philosophy, psychology, agriculture, horticulture, domestic science, and includes many Victorian and Edwardian cookery books.

Catalogued in general reference and lending cats.

Tallow Chandlers' Company, Tallow Chandlers' Hall, 4 Dowgate Hill, London EC4R 2SH. Tel (01) 248 4726.

All books in the library at the Hall are after 1885. The earlier printed material relating to the Company is included with the archives deposited in the Guildhall Library Department of Manuscripts.

Tate Gallery Library, Millbank, London SW1P 4RG. Tel (01) 828 1212 Ext 255. Open by appointment with the Librarian to researchers for material not available elsewhere; application must be made in writing stating subject of research in detail, and must be accompanied by *two* written references from persons of standing. Open Mon-Fri 10 am-5 pm. Photocopier; microform reader available.

The gallery was endowed by Sir Henry Tate (1819–99), the sugar magnate, and opened in 1897, as a branch of the National Gallery specializing in British art. From 1932 it was officially called the Tate Gallery (originally the National Gallery of British Art, and from 1917 when modern foreign art was added to its scope, the National Gallery, Millbank). In 1954 it became fully independent. The library has been built up mainly since 1970 when it was first organized as a separate department, in conjunction with the gallery archives.

John Rothenstein, *The Tate Gallery* rev ed, London, Thames and Hudson, 1966.

The Tate Gallery: an illustrated companion, 1979.

General The library is an adjunct to the gallery collections, and therefore covers British painting from the 16th cent and foreign painting and sculpture (and British sculpture) from the late 19th cent.

A C Symons and B Houghton, 'Tate development responds to increased demands', *Library Association Record* 79(6) (1977), p311-3.

Books and pamphlets A collection of *c*20,000 items, including several hundred pre-1851, from *c*1700 onwards. Strong in monographs on individual artists, and catalogues of their work. Includes a fine collection on the modern art movements of the early 20th cent with many scarce works.

Card cat (author and alphabetical subject).

Exhibition catalogues A collection of *c*80,000 catalogues on the artists and topics relevant to the gallery; both British and foreign (many not available elsewhere in Britain); including Royal Academy from 1769; British Institution, early 19th cent. The collection is being actively enlarged. Its coverage is extended by a complete microfiche of the Knoedler Library in New York (fiche of 26,000 items).

Separate card cat: one-man exhibitions (by artists); group/thematic (by location of exhibition and selectively by subject).

Periodicals and sale catalogues A collection containing *c*3,000 v including sets of standard auction catalogues (also microfilm of Sotheby's 1734–1945). Also a miscellaneous collection bound chronologically in 50 v (deposited on permanent loan by Christie's) of various London and provincial auctioneers' catalogues, 1903–38 (unindexed). Art periodicals from later 19th cent; *Gentlemen's Magazine*.

List on cards of periodicals.

Index of private collectors.

Theosophical Society Library, 50 Gloucester Place, London W1H 3HJ. Tel (01) 935 9261. Open Mon and Fri 11 am-5 pm; Tues-Thurs 6.45 pm (except Aug and two weeks round Christmas) on written application. Photocopying facilities.

The Society was founded in 1875 by Madame Blavatsky; the Library began in 1883 on the opening of the London branch, and now contains *c*20,000 v, including *c*150 items of pre-1851 date in the general library (in addition to those in the Blavatsky collection). It is mainly devoted to theosophy, comparative religion, mysticism, and occultism, but many other subjects are represented. It includes most of the publications of the Theosophical Society, including transactions of individual lodges and branches, and 63 v of theosophical pamphlets.

Author/title cat on slips.

Besant Collection *c*100 v of works written by Annie Besant (1847–1933) the theosophist, many of them published by the Theosophical Society; they include most of the books she wrote, and 9 v of her pamphlets.

Typescript author list; and in main slip cat.

See also T Besterman, *A bibliography of Annie Besant*, the Society, 1924 (op) which is mainly based on the collection.

Madame Blavatsky Collection The library of Helena Petrovna Blavatsky (1831–91), the founder of theosophy and of the Society, is divided between this collection and another at the Society's international HQ at Adyar, Madras, India. It contains *c*300 v (including 1 STC; 49 Wing; 29 foreign pre-1701), mainly on alchemy, arcana, astrology, magic, mysticism, occultism, physiognomy, platonism, rosicrucianism, and religion, though many other subjects are included, in English, French, German, Latin and Russian. Some posthumous editions of Blavatsky's own writings have been added to the collection which also includes many works by Jacob Boehme (1575–1624), Edward Blount (*fl*1588–1632), and Thomas Taylor (1758–1835) the Platonist.

Typescript author list (several sequences by size); and in main slip cat.

Tower Hamlets Public Libraries

In 1965 the libraries of the Metropolitan Boroughs of Bethnal Green (founded 1922), Poplar (founded 1892) and Stepney (founded 1892) were amalgamated to form the libraries of the new London Borough. In 1901 the library of the People's Palace for East London was incorporated into the Stepney reference and local history collections, including many books which were transferred after 1965 to the Central Reference Library at Bethnal Green, but almost all rare books from Bethnal Green have recently been sold.

A **Local History Library**

Central Library, 277 Bancroft Road, Mile End, London E1 4DQ. Tel (01) 980 4366 Ext 47. Open Mon, Tues, Thurs, Fri 9 am-8 pm; Sat 6 pm; closed Wed. Photocopier, microfilm reader.

Includes the local history collections and archives of all three former metropolitan boroughs. A few pre-1851 books from the People's Palace are here or in the adjacent branch reference collection.

C C Black and O Dymond, *Catalogue of the books in the library of the People's Palace...*, 1889.

The People's Palace archives are at Queen Mary College (qv).

General Library Altogether the library contains *c*12,000 books and pamphlets on all local subjects. *c*900 are pre-1851 (23 pre-1701) or are literary first editions. 20,000 illustrations (500 pre-1851), including 250 from the London collection bequeathed by Ernest James Bartlett (1870–1942) of Bethnal Green to his public library (items not relating to the borough were transferred to other libraries). Directories from 1811.

Card cat (author and classified).

Local History (*c*1975) (illustrated guide).

Bethnal Green Public Libraries, *The Bartlett bequest...*, 1947.

Local authors collection Includes Thomas Burke (1887–1945); Jerome K Jerome (1859–1927); George Lansbury (1859–1940); Israel Zangwill (1864–1926); W W Jacobs (1863–1943); Arthur Morrison (1863–1945); and the poet and Borough Librarian Stanley Snaith (1903–76). *c*20 v of locally preached sermons, *c*1650–1800.

Cuttings Collection A large collection which includes ephemera, pamphlets, and playbills (1800–80).

Shipping Collection A special collection on merchant shipping was formed in the Poplar local collection from *c*1900. To this was added (*c*1947), a collection formed by Daniel R Bolt, a Poplar councillor, which was strong in 19th cent material, including rare books, and contained Bolt's very extensive ms records and indexes of company fleets and data on individual ships (mostly 1840–1900). Now *c*1,500 books, 350 pamphlets, and 5,000 illustrations, mostly 1850–1914, but including some earlier works from 1800 on naval architecture and the Port of London and rare later items.

B **Art Library**

Whitechapel Area Library, 77 Whitechapel High Street, London E1 7QX. Tel (01) 247 5272. Open Mon-Fri 9 am-8 pm; Sat 5 pm.

A general library of *c*8,000 v on painting, sculpture, drawing and the graphic arts, which also incorporates the collection on furniture formed by Bethnal Green Public Library. Mainly 20th cent including some rare works on furniture design, with a very few of the 19th cent.

C **French and German Literature Library**

Limehouse Library, 638 Commercial Road, London E14 7HS. Tel (01) 987 3183. Open by appointment only.

The collection has been built up from 1947 under the Metropolitan and LASER Special Collections Scheme, now *c*20,000 v. Some pre-1851 books are included.

Trades Union Congress Library, Congress House, 23 Great Russell Street, London WC1B 3LS. Tel (01) 636 4030 Ext 222. Open Mon-Fri 9.15 am-5.15 pm on written application to the Librarian. Photocopying facilities.

The TUC was founded in 1868. From 1922 it had a joint library at Transport House with the Labour Party and the Transport and General Workers' Union. In 1955–6 it moved to Congress House, taking a portion of the joint library which then became autonomous. The library now contains over 60,000 v, mostly late 19th and 20th cent material on the history of trade unionism, including rule books, annual reports, union publications, etc. Most of the rare material is in the Burns and Tuckwell collections (qv).

Card cat (dictionary).

A **Burns Collection**

Part of the library of John (Elliot) Burns (1858–1943) MP, remaining after the gift or sale of other parts comprising *c*3,000 v on the labour movement, given in 1942–3 to the Amalgamated Engineering Union, of which he had been a member (though some of the labour material was sold or given to the British Museum); the Union gave it to the TUC in 1959. Some books bear his annotations.

Sheaf cat (author and alphabetical subject).

Separate typescript list of Owen and Cobbett items.

Y Kapp, 'A choice of books: an account of the finding and losing of John Burns AEU Library', *Our History* (Communist Party of Great Britain. History Group) pamphlet no 16 (Winter 1959) including list of selected items.

Pre-1851 works These include six Wing items on revolutionary movements in England and Naples; a number of ESTC books, chiefly on poverty, poor law, John Wilkes (1727–97), including *The North Britain* no 1-46; also a comprehensive post-1800 collection on radicalism, chartism, socialism, the rise of the labour movement, and on social conditions and reform.

Robert Owen (1771–1858) *and Owenism* The collection comprises *c*100 works by Owen, including several copies presented to persons as diverse as William Lovett (1800–77) the Chartist, and the Queen of Spain. Also works by Robert Dale Owen (1800–77); 15 Owenite pamphlets and periodicals collected by Lovett; works about Owen and by followers of Owen, and later co-operators; numerous Owenite and co-operative periodicals, including two possibly unique issues of the *Gazette of the Exchange Bazaars* 1832. Contemporary press cuttings are inserted in some of the books and pamphlets.

William Cobbett (1762–1835) A large collection including many of his serials in both US and British printings, some with signatures of John P Cobbett and Mary Cobbett. Many of his books and pamphlets, including the Court Martial proceedings of 1809 and other scarce items. An album of Cobbett's corn-stalk paper guarding his business letters 1831–2.

Chartism and radical movements Many Chartist and radical serials, including the *Chartist Circular* of 1841. Many reports of trials, including that of Peterloo 1819 and those of the Chartists in 1843.

Trade Unions A large collection, mainly late 19th cent, of material on the old and new unionism, 4 v of pamphlets on the eight hours movement; 6 v of pamphlets from 1868 on unemployment; 2 v on Trades Disputes Bill; 1 v on the International Trades Union Congress 1891–6.

Political Pamphlets Major collections of mostly scarce late 19th and early 20th cent pamphlets collected by Burns while current. Some are bound into volumes by subjects, including 11 v on South Africa and the Boer War (with some items in Afrikaans), and smaller collections on the Eastern Question, African and Chinese labour, local government, pacifism, poor law, poverty, pensions, temperance, etc. Collections of pamphlets issued by the Independent Labour Party, Labour Party, Fabian Society, British Socialist Party 1917–8, etc.

B **Tuckwell Collection**

A collection made by Gertrude Mary Tuckwell (1861–1951) between 1890 and 1920, mostly while Secretary of the Women's Trade Union League. Part was deposited when the League entered the TUC in 1922, the remainder in *c*1958. It contains 720 envelopes of material, mainly cuttings, but including printed reports, pamphlets and ephemera on the political and economic struggles of women 1890–1920.

Uncatalogued; the collection is being microfilmed.

J Morris, 'The Gertrude Tuckwell Collection', *History Workshop* Journal no 5 (Spring 1978), p155-62.

Legislation on female workers Items on the work of women factory inspectors, the work of the Trade Boards, etc.

Women's Employment Items on women's wage rates, female munition workers, and wartime substitution for men.

Women in Trade Unions Much on the Women's Trade Union League and the National Federation of Women Workers, including annual reports, leaflets, pamphlets etc; also of organizations connected with these, especially items relating to Mary Reid Macarthur (1880–1921) the Federation's Secretary, and material on women's trade unions collected in the US 1907–9.

Women's Political Organizations Material on Women's Labour League, Women's Industrial Council, Women's Co-operative Guild, National Union of Women's Suffrage Societies, East London Suffrage Federation, etc; and on women in the Labour Party, co-operative movement, British Socialist Party, Independent Labour Party, etc.

Travellers' Club, 106 Pall Mall, London SW1Y 5EP. The Library is exclusively for the use of members and their guests.

The Travellers' Club was founded in 1819 on the initiative of Lord Castlereagh for gentlemen who had travelled at least 500 miles from London. Its library contains many thousand volumes, including several thousand of voyages and travels. A large proportion are early 19th cent, though some books have been sold. Part of the Dante collection of William Warren Vernon (1834–1919) was given to the Club (the remainder to the Athenaeum).

Sir Almeric Fitzroy, *History of the Travellers' Club*, London, 1927, p133-6.

G Evans, 'The Travellers' Club', *Antique Collector*, 45(4) (1974), p69-74.

P Fleetwood-Hesketh, 'The Travellers' Club', *Country Life* 140(3637) (17 Nov 1966), p1270-4.

H Thorogood, 'London clubs and their libraries', *Library Review*, 13 (1951-2), p495-8.

Treasury and Cabinet Office Library, Treasury Chambers, Great George Street and Parliament Street, London SW1P 3AG. Tel (01) 233 7921. Telex 262405. Open 9.30 am-5 pm to bona fide research workers on application to the Librarian.

The Treasury Library was founded in the mid-18th cent and the collection has been built up to meet the working needs of the Treasury, with the later addition of the Cabinet Office. Now *c*60,000 items, including *c*100 pre-1851 (after some disposals to other libraries) relating to economics, public finance, government and public administration. Includes annual volumes of statutes from

1692, a collection of court guides and official directories of the late 17th cent, the Lister collection of prints of the Whitehall area, and a collection of early reports of proceedings in Parliament.

Catalogue of the Treasury Library, 1910, Pt 1: authors; 2, Subjects.

Card cat.

Treasury Solicitor's Department Library, 3 Central Buildings, Matthew Parker Street, Westminster, London SW1H 9NH. Tel (01) 233 7168. Open to department's staff; to others by appointment.

A general law library of *c*25,000 v serves the department. It includes a major collection on the common law and some historical material. *c*50 1501–1850 items. Includes some works on the customary law of the Duchy of Normandy.

R Toole Stott, *Catalogue of the legal library of the Treasury Solicitor*. 6th ed, 1977. (Previous eds 1963, 1967, 1971, 1974, 1975.)

Trinitarian Bible Society, 217 Kingston Road, South Wimbledon, London SW19 3NN. Tel (01) 540 3021. Open Mon-Fri (except Aug-Sept) 9 am-5 pm by prior arrangement with the Secretary, at whose discretion non-members may sometimes be admitted.

In 1831 a group of members of the British and Foreign Bible Society, including its Hon Librarian, Thomas Pell Platt (1798–1852), Fellow of Trinity College, Cambridge, proposed to exclude Unitarians by incorporating an explicit definition of Christian belief in the rule on qualification for membership. After being out-voted, they mounted an unsuccessful campaign to rescind the decision, and then called a public meeting to found an independent 'Trinitarian Bible Society' to which title was later added 'for the circulation of Protestant or Uncorrupted versions of the Word of God'. The Society prints and distributes the divinely inspired canon of the Scriptures, defined to exclude the Apocrypha, in translations, sometimes specially commissioned, of a conservative evangelical character, emphasizing the Trinity and the fully co-equal divinity of Christ. It opposes texts and translations influenced either by the Vulgate and Roman Catholic theology, or by the 'higher criticism' and liberal theology, preferring the Massoretic and Byzantine textual traditions and the 'received' texts of the 16th cent based on them to codices more recently found in Egypt. In the English language the Society circulates the Authorized version only.

Andrew J Brown, *The Word of God among all nations: a brief history of the Trinitarian Bible Society 1831–1981*, London, Trinitarian Bible Soc, 1981.

The library and the foundation of its collections The origins of the library are obscure, but it seems to have been first assembled in the early 20th cent from the collection of the Rev Dr J Sale-Harrison, part of the collection of William Goode (1801–68), Dean of Ripon and editor of the *Christian Observer* (perhaps from the sale, Sotheby 10-17 May 1869), and that of William Elliott, first Pastor of the Protestant Evangelical Church at Epsom 1855–63 and afterwards of the Compton Street Chapel Plymouth, where the biblical scholar Samuel Prideaux Tregelles (1813–75), was an Elder. These collections, amounting to *c*2,000 v have grown, mainly by donation, to a present total of *c*5,000 v, of which *c*1,500 are pre-1851.

Card cat.

Bibles This collection has been greatly strengthened by recent gifts and purchases. It is strong in early English editions, eg the Great Bible of 1561, the Bishops' of 1585, and the Genevan of 1578–1640. Some major polyglots. Many editions in Hebrew, Greek and Latin, chiefly from France and the Netherlands 1503–1650. There is a variety of translations into modern languages.

Biblical scholarship A wide variety of commentaries, concordances and dictionaries, including some early works.

Theology and church history Editions of the Fathers and Protestant divines; and church history and biography. These come almost entirely from the foundation collections.

Trinity College of Music, Bridge Memorial Library, 11 Mandeville Place, London W1M 6AQ. Tel (01) 935 5773 Ext 16. Open Mon-Fri 9.30 am-5.30 pm to bona fide students, on written application. No copier available.

The College was founded in 1872 as the Church Choral Society and College of Church Music, and from 1875 to 1904 was called Trinity College London. It is now a college with teachers recognized by the University of London. The library is named after Sir (John) Frederick Bridge (1844–1924) the organist, composer and musical antiquary, but it is not known whether he contributed to its collections. It contains *c*700 v of uncatalogued books and mss on music of the 18th and early 19th cent, built up mainly from donations in the early years of the college, in addition to scores.

The Academic Gazette... of Trinity College... 1884–1916, includes occasional notes of donations.

Trinity House Lighthouse Service, Trinity House, Trinity Square, Tower Hill, London EC3N 4DH. Tel (01) 480 6601. Telex 884300.

The Corporation of Trinity House owns a rare book collection, which is described in part in *Country Life* for 5 July 1919. There is at present no librarian, and therefore there is no access for the time being. Enquiries should be directed to the Public Relations Officer.

Tylers' and Bricklayers' Company, 6 Bedford Row, London WC1R 4DQ. Tel (01) 242 8223. Open by prior arrangement with the Clerk.

The Company is 37th in order of precedence of the City Livery companies, but it no longer has a Hall within the City. There are no books held at the office, except the annual printed list of members complete from 1760 to 1960. Some printed books owned by the Company (some unrelated to the Company itself) are included with the archives deposited at the Guildhall Library Department of Manuscripts.

Walter George Bell, *A short history of the worshipful Company of Tylers and Bricklayers*, London, 1938.

United Africa Company International Ltd, Public Relations Department Library, PO Box 1, UAC House, Blackfriars, London SE1 9UG. Tel (01) 928 2070. Open Mon-Fri by appointment on written application to the Librarian. Photocopying facilities.

UAC International Ltd, formerly the United Africa Company, is a wholly owned subsidiary of Unilever plc. The older books were originally the property of individuals working for the Company, or of the Company. In 1943 they were centralized in the Unilever Central Library, but later returned to the United Africa Co where they were first catalogued and organized in 1960. There are *c*1,100 works, including *c*100 pre-1900, on Africa, especially West Africa, chiefly travel, discovery, exploration and history, with a scattering of other subjects. They include 1 STC; 1 Wing; *c*30 ESTC; and *c*30 1801–50 English.

United Africa Co Ltd, *Catalogue of books in the Public Relations Department Library* (1966?) (duplicated typescript). The Company's archives begin in 1777 (see N Matthews and M D Wainwright, *A guide to... documents... relating to Africa*, 1971).

United Grand Lodge of England, Library and Museum, Freemasons' Hall, 55-60 Great Queen Street, London WC2B 5AZ. Tel (01) 405 3633. Open Mon-Fri 10 am-5 pm to members and their guests; written requests for information or research facilities from non-members who are serious researchers are considered on their individual merits.

The library was formed in 1837 from a collection of 250 books and 2 mss. It was first systematically organized 1887–1914 by Henry Sadler who was successively Sub-Librarian and then the first Librarian and Curator. It now contains (in addition to the archives of the United Grand Lodge and Supreme Grand Chapter of England) *c*35,000 v of printed and ms works. *c*500,000 letters, documents and printed ephemera, and *c*20,000 prints, drawings and photographs. It is devoted to freemasonry, with the main emphasis on its history in England with its philosophy, ritual and symbolism, but covering all aspects of the craft, wherever practised, with more limited coverage of allied subjects such as Rosicrucians, orders of chivalry, trade guilds and livery companies, religions, and friendly societies.

It contains many unique copies, and is particularly rich in 18th and 19th cent works, many in fine contemporary Masonic bindings, and has the most comprehensive collection in existence of British Masonic newspapers and periodicals. The famous private collection of Wallace E Heaton, who was chairman of the Library and Museum Committee 1942–52, containing many unique and rare items, was given in 1939. The libraries of the Grand Lodge of Mark Master Masons and of the Quatuor Coronati Lodge (of Research) No 2076 are deposited on permanent loan. Gaps in the collections are actively being filled, and new publications comprehensively acquired.

Note The Library acts as an information centre for Masonic bibliography and art, and can refer enquiries in appropriate circumstances to the libraries of other lodges in London and elsewhere in England which have not permitted their collections to be described in this directory.

The library is arranged by a classification devised by A R Hewitt, Librarian and Curator 1960–72.

Card cat (author and alphabetical subject) supersedes the inadequate printed cat, which are chiefly of historical interest.

Catalogue of the Library at Freemasons' Hall by H W Hemsworth, (1869) (dictionary).

Catalogue of books in the Library at Freemasons' Hall, 1888 (dictionary), *Supplementary catalogue*, Hull, 1895.

Catalogue of manuscripts and Library at Freemasons' Hall... by Sir A Tudor-Craig, 1938 (United Grand Lodge catalogues v 3) (dictionary).

Catalogue of rare and early works on freemasonry from the 'Wallace Heaton' collection presented to the United Grand Lodge of England by Robert E Card and Wallace E Heaton, 1939 (Haphazard).

Lodge of the Quatuor Coronati No 2076 [cat in loose sheets], 1888–92, and *Index to the catalogue slips*, Margate, 1893.

Annual supplement, privately printed.

United Oxford and Cambridge University Club, 71 Pall Mall, London SW1Y 5ES. Tel (01) 930 4152. Open to members of this club, and of certain other clubs.

The United University Club was founded in 1822 for graduates of the universities of Oxford and Cambridge; its library had rare books (some sold Sotheby, Hodgson's Rooms, 11 Dec 1969).

The Oxford and Cambridge Club was founded in 1830 as an overflow from the United, and also had a library with valuable books (some sold Sotheby, Hodgson's Rooms, 4-5 April 1968 and 5 March 1970). The two clubs were amalgamated in 1972 into the United Oxford and Cambridge University Club, in the former premises of the Oxford and Cambridge, with a combined library of c20,000 v, strong in history and the classics.

Catalogue of the Library of the Oxford and Cambridge Club, 1887; supplement 1909.

Anthony Lejeune, *Gentlemen's clubs*, 1979, p180-7.

United Reformed Church History Society, W B Shaw Library, United Reformed Church House, 86 Tavistock Place, London WC1H 9RT. Tel (01) 837 7661. Open by prior arrangement only, on written application to the Society's Research Secretary at the above address; normally Tues, Thurs and Fri 12 noon-3.30 pm.

The library originated when the Presbyterian Historical Society was founded in 1913. It came to be known as the W B Shaw Library after William Buttars Shaw, who was a major donor of rare books in the early years. In 1972 the Society amalgamated with the Congregational Historical Society to form the United Reform Church History Society (which had no library of its own).

General The library contains c8,500 v of books, pamphlets and periodicals on history of Presbyterianism (mainly in England) from the 17th cent to the present, including the Independents of the 17th to 19th cent, the Presbyterian Church of England from its foundation in 1876 until its merger in the United Reformed Church in 1972, the United Reformed Church from its creation then, and to a very limited extent the Congregational Churches absorbed in 1972.

Card cat (author, title and alphabetical subject).

Bulletin of the Association of British Theological and Philosophical Libraries new ser no 14 (1979), p2-3.

Confessions of faith A collection of over 200 v, including the original ms of the Westminster Confession, which strayed from the House of Lords records and was bought for presentation to the library in 1943, both the printed editions of 1646, and many later editions of this and the Shorter Catechism, and works about them, with later confessions and commentaries.

Presbyterian writings The works of 17th cent Independents and Puritans, especially after the Restoration, and of Presbyterians down to the 19th cent (and to a limited extent later). There are c150 v by Richard Baxter (1615–91), mostly in early editions, and some 19th cent fiction by Presbyterians.

Miscellaneous collection c2,500 pamphlets, mainly on 18th and 19th cent controversies in which Presbyterians were involved. Presbyterian periodicals of the 19th cent. Presbyterian (including American) and other nonconformist historical society journals; biographies of Presbyterians; histories of individual churches; and some of their ephemera, mostly locally printed in the 20th cent; some magazines of defunct churches, mostly 19th cent.

United Society for the Propagation of the Gospel, Library and Archives, 15 Tufton Street, London SW1P 3QQ. Tel (01) 222 4222. Open Mon-Fri 9.30 am-5.30 pm by appointment to scholars and bona fide research workers who make prior written application to the Librarian or the Archivist, with a letter of introduction. Photocopier.

The Society is an Anglican mission formed by the amalgamation in 1965 of the Society for the Propagation of the Gospel in Foreign Parts (founded 1701 by Dr Thomas Bray (1656–1730) and others, mainly to minister to English settlers in North America and elsewhere), and the Universities Mission to Central Africa, founded in 1857 by Dr David Livingstone (1813–73) as the Oxford and Cambridge Mission to Central Africa, to promote religion and the extinction of the slave trade. A number of other missions have been absorbed, and these include some working in Asia, but Africa and the West Indies are the areas principally reflected in the collections. The very extensive archives are a major source on the early history of North America, and of Africa.

C F Pascoe, *Two hundred years of the SPG*, 1901.

I Pridmore and M Holland, 'The Archives and Library of the United Society...', *Library Materials on Africa* 8(2) (1970), p105-8.

A G Blood, *History of UMCA 1857–1957*, 1957, 3 v.

Rosemary Keen, *Survey of the archives of missionary societies.*

White Kennett Fund White Kennett or Kennet (1660–1728), Bishop of Peterborough, one of the founders of the SPG, collected books on America for an intended history of American missionary activity which he never wrote. In 1713 he gave the collection, then c400 books and tracts 1508–1714 to the Society; other volumes were added by Sir Hans Sloane (1660–1753) and others, including some of general literature and travels. When the SPG's interests moved away from America, this collection fell into disuse, and about half (including most of the rare items) disappeared, mainly between 1865 and 1890. In 1916 the British Museum received by gift, the 81 remaining items, of which it possessed no copy, and the residue was sold (Sotheby 30 July 1917, 226 lots), leaving only two copies of the printed catalogue. The proceeds of the sale were invested to produce an income which now provides the entire library book fund.

W Kennet, *Bibliothecae Americanae primordia: an attempt towards...an American library...given to the Society for the Propagation of the Gospel...*, London, 1713 (chronological).

Ms author cat (including additions) 1865.

List of books given to the British Museum, 1916 (printed General Catalogue titles in order of headings).

Annotated sale cat with buyers' names.

'The sale of the White Kennett Library', *Mission Field*, July 1917.

Charles Deane, *An account of the White Kennett Library...*, Cambridge, Mass, 1883.

General Library In 1856 a new library was begun by the SPG relating to parts of the world in which the Society was interested, other than America. This was always known as the Lending Library, despite the fact that it included numerous rare books, many of them early, which were never available for loan. In 1965 the UMCA Library, which consisted almost entirely of modern works, was absorbed into it. There are now *c*30,000 v, of which *c*350 are pre-1851, of which the principal strengths are indicated below.

Card cat (dictionary).

Classified shelflist.

SPG Lending Library catalogue, (1920); (1927) (reference books asterisked); *Supplement* 1936; continued by annual *White Kennett list* from 1943 and accessions register.

List of rare books evacuated, 1941.

Colonial Church Chronicle 9 (1955–6), p277.

Books in Western Languages Most of the early material is on missions (including particularly those of the Jesuits) in Asia, Africa, India and Canada, with some interesting items on Tristan de Cunha; and the history, geography and travel (especially journeys of missionaries) of these areas, their religions, customs, and political conditions. There are a number of items relating to Thomas Bray, and H Torselin *La vie due...pere...François Xavier*, Douay 1608.

African and Asian Languages *c*2,000 items, mainly of the 19th cent, but with a few earlier and later, on or in the languages of Africa and Asia, especially grammars and dictionaries; and Bibles and prayer books (chiefly the *Book of Common Prayer* or its parts) in these languages.

Separate card cat.

Pamphlets *c*1,500 pamphlets from 1835 onwards, mostly unbound in boxes arranged by country, relating directly or indirectly to missions in North America, Africa, India and Australasia.

Mostly uncat.

Biographical Directories In addition to standard general works, there are sets of the *Ecclesiastical and Universal Annual Register* 1808–10 and *Clergy List* 1841–1911 (incomplete).

Missionary periodicals published at home *c*200 sets, including some 18th cent Jesuit organs, and a number of publications beginning *c*1840 in London to stimulate interest (including juvenile interest) in overseas missions, and gift books, eg *Gospel Missionary*, *Christian Keepsake* and *Children's Missionary Magazine*, standard journals such as the *Missionary Register*.

Card cat both under titles and under heading Periodicals.

Overseas Periodicals *c*300 sets of official and unofficial magazines of Anglican overseas dioceses, including many not held elsewhere, from the mid-19th cent onwards. Those beginning in the 19th cent include titles from South Africa, Zanzibar, India, Australia, Nassau and Hawaii.

Card cat both under titles and under heading Periodicals (Diocesan) sub-arranged by place.

University College Library, Gower Street, London WC1E 6BT. Tel (01) 387 7050. Telex 28722. Mss and Rare Books Reading Room open Mon-Fri 9.30 am-5 pm (6 pm by prior arrangement only) on written application to the Librarian; most other reading rooms remain open to 7 or 9 pm, and on Sat mornings (except Summer vac); but certain deposited libraries have restricted access as indicated in each case. Photocopying; microfilming; and all types of photography; various types of microform readers and reader/printers available.

The College, which was the first non-sectarian college of higher education in England, was founded in 1826–8 as the University of London. In 1836 it was renamed University College, and a new University of London was set up as a joint examining body. In 1900 the College was incorporated in the federally reconstituted University of London. The library dates from 1829, but in the 19th cent grew slowly and depended mainly on benefactions; in the 20th cent it grew rapidly through an elaborate system of subject libraries with a central administration and catalogue, assisted by some important libraries deposited by learned societies. A few science departments have fully independent libraries, but only that of the Galton Laboratory, mentioned below, has rare books.

General author/name cat on cards includes (to 1982 after which it is continued on microfiche) all subject library and general collections, most special collections, and some deposited collections.

Classified cat for most subject libraries.

Catalogue of books in the General Library, 1879, 3 v; supplement 1897; annual lists of additions to 1900; all include books no longer in the library.

Ms cat to 1849 by F A Cox.

A E Tooth, 'Cataloguing rules and practice...at University College', *Journ of Documentation* 12 (1956), p88-93; 16 (1960), p71-9.

K Garside, 'The basic principles of the new library classification at University College London', *Ibid* 10 (1954), p169-92.

Library Guide (Annual).

J W Scott, 'The Library of University College London' in R Irwin and R Staveley eds, *The libraries of London*, Lib Assoc, 1964, p157-96; reissued separately by the College.

R W Chambers, 'The Library of University College London', *Lib Assoc Record* 11 (1909), p350-8; repr in H Hale Bellot, *University College London 1826–1926*, London, 1929, p417-26, with further information in other chapters.

L Newcombe, 'The Library of University College, London' (unpublished typescript, 1926).

R Martin, 'University College Library', *Library World* 65 (1964), p296-8.

R A Rye, *Students' guide...*, 1927, p194-200.

Notes and materials for the history of University College London (by W P Ker), London, the College, 1898.

A General

The Library contains *c*870,000 v, excluding deposited libraries. The more valuable rare books are available for consultation in the Mss and Rare Books Room in the D M S Watson Library. Information on the special collections containing rare books is set out below.

Strong Room Collection, chronological sequence The most valuable rare books drawn from all collections in the library, comprising 182 incunabula; *c*600 STC v and 63 broadsheets; and *c*100 selected foreign 16th cent items.

Card cat (authors) in Mss and Rare Books Room, and in main author cat.

Incunabula included in *Incunabula in the libraries of the University of London...*, 1963.

Strong Room Collection, subject sequence *c*1,230 v of rare books, including many of those published 1501–1700 from the library's various collections.

Card cat (author and classified) in Mss and Rare Books Room. Also in main cat.

Store Collections The less valuable older books, including probably *c*16,000 pre-1851, distributed among stores related to subject libraries, especially classical studies, French, Italian, German and English literature, history and philosophy. Many of the older books in certain subjects (indicated below) were among 100,000 v destroyed by bombing in 1940 (but the more valuable had been evacuated).

Periodicals *c*20,000 runs, distributed by subjects mostly in or near the related subject libraries; many of the older titles are stored at Egham (see also Little Magazines Collection below).

Periodicals card cat, and partly in *Union List of Serials in Libraries of the University of London* (microfiche).

Catalogue of the periodical publications, 1912, listing 1,441 titles, is of historical interest only.

College Collection *c*3,000 books by and about members of the College. Printed and ms material on the history of the College, including the Library from its foundation to the present. College archives (in part; some are held by the Records Officer of the College). Papers of College societies.

Classified card cat in Mss and Rare Books Room; and in main author cat.

English Works published 1820–29 The general collections and especially the History Library are strong in the literature of the decade of the College's foundation, and there are several thousand publications of 1820–9. Further works have been added under the Background Material Scheme of the British Library (formerly of the Joint Standing Committee on Library Co-operation), but they are not kept as a separate collection.

In main cat; also a special author cat for 1820–9, not complete, containing *c*1,500 entries.

Rotton Library Sir John Francis Rotton (1837–1926), a member of the College Committee, bequeathed his library of over 30,000 v on the literatures of Italy, England, France, Germany, Greece and Rome, with some economics, law and fine art. The English literature is strongest in the 18th cent, with some rare editions of Pope. The books are mostly in fine bindings. Originally scattered, it is now a separate collection. It includes *c*200 editions of the 16th cent.

Shelf cat on cards, and in main cat.

B Manuscript Collections which include printed material

The ms collections are numerous and often include occasional printed items. Those containing substantial collections of rare printed material are described below. Larger printed collections ancillary to ms collections are treated separately in later sections under subject libraries.

Manuscript collections in the Library of University College London: a handlist 2nd ed, the Library, 1978 (Occasional publication no 1).

For many of the more important collections there are published handlists.

Society for the Diffusion of Useful Knowledge The Society was founded in 1826, largely at the instigation of Henry Brougham, Lord Brougham (1778–1868), to promote the publication, in several major series, of works for the self-education of all classes of the community at low prices. In 1846 the Society gave a complete set of its publications to the College, and when it was wound up in 1848, its complete archives. Both have suffered war damage, but the set of publications is now again almost complete.

The Society for the Diffusion of Useful Knowledge, 1826–1848: a handlist... compiled by Janet Percival, the Library, 1978, p2-7 (with bibliography).

The Brougham Papers which have many connections with this collection are also held.

Routledge and Kegan Paul archives The archives of Routledge and Kegan Paul Ltd and its predecessor publishing firms were deposited in 1975–6. They include an incomplete set of their printed catalogues: 41 v from George Routledge and Co 1852–1909; 7 v from Kegan Paul, Trench, Trübner and Co 1877–1910; 27 v from Routledge and Kegan Paul 1912–47; and 30 v from Routledge and Kegan Paul Ltd, 1948–73. There are also some prospectuses and other printed material from the last.

The archives of Routledge and Kegan Paul Ltd (1853–1973) publishers: a handlist compiled by Gillian Furlong, the Library, 1978 (Occasional publication no 6), p17-8, 25-8 (complete list, with notes on illustrations included).

C English and Related Collections

The library of the Philological Society was integrated into the collections in 1887, and the private collection of William Paton Ker (1855–1923), Professor of English, given by his daughters in 1924, was also incorporated. The English and Phonetics libraries suffered severely from war damage.

Ogden Library An important part of the library of Charles Kay Ogden (1889–1957), consisting of some 5,000 v, including a number of mss and early printed books, and over 62,000 letters from the correspondence of Lord Brougham, purchased by the Nuffield Foundation in 1953 and deposited in the College Library to serve as a basis of studies in the field of human communication; in 1956 presented to the College in perpetuity by the Trustees of the Foundation. It comprised *c*50,000 v on orthology and all aspects of the English language. There are 21 incunabula and 394 STC items.

University College London Communication Research Centre, *The Ogden Collection pt 1: a short title list of the special books (incunables and printed books)*, (1953).

Ben Jonson, *Works* ed C H Herford and P Simpson, Oxford, Clarendon Press, 1925–52, v 1 appendix 4, p250-71 and v 11, p593-603 (books in Jonson's library).

Minsheu collection described in F B Williams, 'Scholarly publication...a leading case', in Joseph Quincy Adams memorial studies, Washington, Folger, 1948, p755-73.

Chambers Collection In 1943 *c*700 v, including the rare books from the library of Raymond Wilson Chambers (1874–1942), successively College Librarian and Professor of English, were given by his sister. They are mostly English language and literature, with some Scandinavian and other languages. Many are annotated by Chambers. There are *c*20 editions of works by Sir Thomas More (1478–1535).

In main cat.

His papers are among the ms collections (see published handlist).

Orwell Collection A collection on Eric Arthur Blair (1905–50), 'George Orwell', begun *c*1960 to accompany the Orwell Archive. *c*3,500 v, including almost all editions and translations of his works, a very extensive collection of books and articles on Orwell and his times, his own library, and a set of the publications of the Left Book Club.

Card cat and typescript lists in Mss and Rare Books Room.

Not in main cat.

James Joyce Centre The Centre was established in 1973 jointly with the trustees of the estate of James Joyce (1882–1941), to provide the basic materials for Joyce scholarship. It contains *c*1,200 printed editions, including the first editions of all his major works, most other early and later editions of all his writings, the Garland archive published in 63 v of facsimile of his innumerable ms drafts; translations into foreign languages, mostly received by a continuing arrangement with the Society of Authors; the residue of the papers of Harriet Shaw Weaver (1876–1961) publisher of the *Egoist*, along with some papers deposited by her biographer Jane Lidderdale.

Card cat in Mss and Rare Books Room. Also in main cat.

James Joyce Centre: a list of holdings..., 1973 (the first nucleus only).

Joyce and the Joyceans: an exhibition compiled by Geoffrey Soar and Richard Brown..., 1982.

James Joyce Broadsheet, issued by the Centre every four months.

Little Magazines Collection A collection of literary and creative uncommercial little magazines and alternative press magazines, built up since 1964–5 by comprehensive subscriptions and retrospective acquisitions. There are *c*3,000 catalogued titles, mainly British, but with many from North America and Commonwealth countries. Uncatalogued collections include the Smoothie Publications Archive 1965–75 deposited by John L Noyce of Brighton from all the publishers listed in his list *Alternative publishers* (2nd ed 1975) (30 boxes); and the Quest Library (6 boxes).

Card cat in Mss and Rare Books Room, and in main Periodicals cat.

Little Magazines: an exhibition held in the Library... 1966, 1967.

Ezra Pound in the magazines: an exhibition..., 1977.

G Soar, 'Little Magazines at University College London', *Times Lit Supplement* 23 March 1967, p256.

——'Little Magazines at UCL: 11 years on', *Assistant Librarian* 71(10) (Oct 1978), p106-10.

Poetry Store Collection *c*6,000 items from small presses, not in serial form, complementing the Little Magazines Collection, and including both poetry and experimental prose. Also works about the little magazines, small presses, and alternative literature groups, and the movements associated with them.

Classified card cat 1976–81, and in main cat under authors; from 1982 in microfiche cat, including entries under names of presses in author/name section.

Scott Collection (Housed at Egham) A collection of works by and about Sir Walter Scott (1771–1832) the novelist and poet, built up around a nucleus given by Sir Arthur (Salusbury) MacNalty (1880–1969) MD, now 287 v (in addition to over 100 in other collections). Most of the early editions are included.

Separate cat on cards, and in main cat.

Laurence Housman Collection *c*500 editions of the published writings of Laurence Housman (1865–1959). They were bought in 1978, and include almost all the verse and prose (both fiction and non-fiction) editions from the library of Ian Kenyur-Hodgkins. The Little Plays of Francis from the previous collection at the College (where they were regularly produced until *c*1935) have been added.

In main cat.

Marked copy of sale cat issued by Warrack and Perkins 1978.

Ouida Collection The complete writings of the novelist Ouida (pseudonym of Marie Louise de La Ramée, 1839–1908).

In main cat.

Leacock Collection A complete set of the first editions of all the works of Stephen (Butler) Leacock (1869–1944) the humourist.

D Language Collections

Italian Collections The library has been fortunate in a series of notable benefactions which have enriched the Italian Library general collection, now *c*15,000 v, including a major collection of Petrarch, and the two special collections below (Castiglione and Dante). The bequest of Dr Henry Clark Barlow (1806–76) included the nucleus of the Dante Collection. In 1921 Sir Herbert Thompson (1859–1944) gave a collection of rare books that included the nucleus of the Castiglione Collection, and additions to the Dante Collection. Professor Edmund Garratt Gardner (1869–1935) bequeathed his library. Also *c*1,500 v from the library of Huxley St John Brooks (*d*1949) were bought after his death, of which 1,002 were added to the Dante Collection. (The Rotton and Stokes libraries also include many Italian rare books.)

Barlow bequest marked 'B' in *Supplement to the Catalogue*, 1897.

Italian at University College: an exhibition of books and letters..., 1975.

Castiglione Collection First established from a collection in the Thompson gift of 1921, and later enlarged, a collection of editions of Baldassare Castiglione (1487–1529), perhaps the most complete in existence, from the Aldine editions of 1528 (the first), 1533, 1541, 1545 and 1547, to the 20th cent; 102 editions, including 70 pre-1800; 10 STC.

B Castiglione, *The Book of the Courtier...*, translated and annotated by Leonard Eckstein Opdycke, London, 1902, p417-22, list of editions to 1900.

Dante Collection Originated with the Barlow bequest (including the foundation of a Dante lecture) in 1876, with additions from the Morris Library received 1875, the Mocatta Library 1906, the Whitley Stokes Collection 1910, Rotton Library bequeathed 1926, the Thompson gift 1921 (including two incunabula), the Gardner bequest 1935 and the Brooks purchase 1949. The collection now contains over 5,000 items (more than double the printed list), including 36 pre-1600 editions of the *Divina commedia*, beginning with those printed by Vendelin da Spira, Venice, 1477, and Nicolas de Lorenzo, Florence, 1481.

R W Chambers, *Catalogue of the Dante Collection in the Library of University College London...*, 1910 (authors); includes the Rotton Collection, not then transferred to the Library, designated by the initial 'R' (copy annotated with additions).

Dante at University College London: an exhibition..., 1977.

German Collections The German Library was partly destroyed in 1940, but in 1945 acquired the library of the Anglo-German Academic Bureau (Deutsch-Englische Vermittlungstelle). It now holds *c*20,000 v, including many of the 19th cent series of literary texts, and some 17th and 18th cent editions.

In general author cat.

Classified cat.

Anglo-German Collection Over 400 items in *c*350 v collected by the library, English translations of German literature and vice versa, especially 18th cent texts and 18th cent editions.

Shelf cards.

In general author cat.

French Collections The French Library contains *c*20,000 v, including *c*1,000 pre-1851; it is strong in Renaissance literature. (There are also many French books in the Rotton Library.)

Scandinavian Library The Scandinavian Library was destroyed in 1940, but many of the rare books had been evacuated; these included books from the collection of John Daulby, including inscribed presentation copies from Norse scholars, given by the widow of William Caldwell Roscoe (1823–59) who had inherited them. In 1953, 2,200 v were bought from the Icelandic collection of Herra Snaebjörn Jonsson of Reykjavik, including many early works; *c*800 v on Iceland were bequeathed *c*1964 by Miss Ingibjörg Olafsson. The libraries of the Viking Society for Northern Research (most of which was bombed), the Norwegian Club, and the Norwegian Embassy have been absorbed (the last, hitherto on deposit, still forms a separate collection). The library now holds *c*30,000 v, including *c*400 pre-1851.

Viking Society, *Northern research: a guide to the library holdings of University College London*, 1968– , 5 v.

Catalogue of Swedish books, and books relating to Sweden, in the Library of University College, London, 1952– .

J Wilks, 'Danish libraries in Britain', 1: University College', *Denmark* Sept 1947, p6-7.

Catalogue of the Royal Norwegian Embassy Library, London, 1968.

J A B Townsend, 'The Viking Society, 1892–1967', *Saga-book of the Viking Society* 17 (1967–68), p102-15.

E Celtic and Folklore Collections

Whitley Stokes Library The library of Whitley Stokes (1830–1909) the Indian legal administrator and folklorist, given in 1910 by his two daughters; mainly on Celtic subjects, folklore, folk literature, philology, and oriental religions. Originally *c*3,500 v (including some books now transferred to the Dante collection), it is maintained as a separate library with regular additions of books on Celtic subjects, and now totals *c*4,000 v, including some rare editions. Many autograph letters from Celtic scholars to Stokes are inserted in books in the collection.

Classified cat with author index; also in main author cat.

Typescript handlist of books containing autograph letters.

Folklore Society Library (Accessible only by appointment with the Society's Secretary at the College. Tel (01) 387 5894 direct line, on Tues, Wed and Thurs.)

The Society was founded, as the Folk Lore Society, in 1878, and has kept its library on deposit at the College since 1911; it has recently moved its headquarters there. The library is one of the world's largest collections on folklore and related fields. It contains *c*15,000 v and 5,000 pamphlets on all branches of folklore throughout the world, including calendar customs, religion and the supernatural, ballads, and ritual drama, with some background material in archaeology and anthropology. There are many rare and early books.

The Folklore Society, founded 1878 (descriptive brochure).

Gaelic Society of London Library The Society was founded in 1830 as An Comunn na Gaëlic or Gaelic Society, though claims have been made that this was a continuation of earlier societies with similar objects. The library, deposited since 1973, contains *c*700 v, mainly on the history of Scotland and Scottish Gaelic literature, with very small collections on other Gaelic languages and peoples. *c*20 books are pre-1851, and there is a collection of *c*200 tracts of 1649–1776 in 19 v purchased by the Club *c*1835 from an unnamed literary gentleman; mainly relating to the Jacobite rebellions of 1715 and 1745; with Sir George Mackenzie *Jus regium* 1684.

Catalogue of books, tracts, and papers, belonging to the Gaëlic Society of London... Ainm-chlar leabhraichean, thrachd, agus phaipeirean, a bhuineas bo Chomunn na Gaëlig Londuin..., 1840 (author cat including the tracts).

Library list, 1971.

Mrs Norman Stewart, *A brief history of the Gaelic Society of London 1777 to 1964*, (1964).

F History and Social Sciences Collections

The complex of History Libraries (at Gordon Square), including the main History Library (which incorporates Economic History), Latin-American History Library, and the London History Library, contain *c*70,000 v. The original library on economics called the Ricardo Library, founded in 1839 as a result of raising a fund by subscription is now scattered, part being in the history reserve collections. The History Library is strongest in English history, including English local history in which there is much pre-1851 material. The Latin-American History Library, one of the best collections in its field, contains *c*10,000 v including, perhaps, *c*500 pre-1851, mostly post-1800. (There are further important Latin-American collections in the Geography Library and the Spanish Library.)

The Bentham Collection, Hume Tracts, Halifax Tracts, and Lansdowne Tracts, are housed at the Mss and Rare Books Room.

Bentham Collection *c*400 books and 200 pamphlets. A comprehensive collection of the published writings of the College benefactor Jeremy Bentham (1748–1832) the utilitarian, and of books and articles about him; they complement the Bentham mss which were given by his executor Sir John Bowring (1792–1872) in 1849, and which include drafts and notes for published and unpublished works, and letters. These collections are at the centre of the project for publishing a new edition of Bentham's works. *c*4,000 v from Bentham's own library were bequeathed by him to the College, and integrated into the general collections. The portion of his library on jurisprudence was bequeathed to (Sir) Edwin Chadwick (1800–90) who presented it in 1853.

Notes on the bequest of books in Bentham papers clv 80.

Books in main author cat, but no subject cat.

Card cat in Mss and Rare Books Room.

A Taylor-Milne, *Catalogue of the manuscripts of Jeremy Bentham*, 2nd ed, 1962.

Abbot Collection of Parliamentary Papers One of four sets of *c*2,000 papers of 1731–1800 collected by Charles Abbot, Baron Colchester (1757–1829) when Speaker, but not quite identical with the others. This was originally the Speaker's set, and was deposited on loan by the Stationery Office in 1906, with an incomplete set in 110 v of Parliamentary Papers 1801–50.

See bibliography under London. House of Commons Library. A.

Hume Parliamentary Library Joseph Hume (1777–1855) radical MP left a major collection on Parliament, 2,232 v, which was given to the College in 1855. The books were incorporated into the general library. *c*5,000 tracts in 352 v, 1810–50, on economics, politics, education, religion, and social reform remain a separate collection known as the Hume Tracts; many are presentation copies inscribed by their authors.

In main author cat.

No complete list.

London Institution Library The London Institution, founded in 1805, built up major collections of earlier printed material in British and foreign history and literature. In 1918, after its Library had been acquired by the School of Oriental Studies, a proportion of the historical books (incorporated into the Library) and all the tract collections were received on loan in exchange for oriental collections. In addition to the tract collections described in the next six paragraphs, there are over 300 v of political and miscellaneous tracts.

In main author cat.

A catalogue of the Library of the London Institution,

1835–52, 4 v, especially v 2; the tracts and pamphlets, 1840 (alphabetical subject cat with name index).

Halifax Tracts 3,582 tracts of 1559–1749 in 145 v collected by George Montague-Dunk (1716–71) bought at the sale of his library (Sotheby 21 Nov 1806, lot 1748), relating to all aspects of English history. They include many originally collected by Walter Yonge (1581?–1649) MP, and the royalist Fabian Phillips (1601–90), mostly relating to the Civil War.

Lansdowne Tracts 2,024 tracts of 1679–1776 on Belgium, and of 1761–99 on France in 247 v from the Bibliotheca Lansdowniana built up by Abbe Etienne Dumont for William Petty, 1st Marquis of Lansdowne (1737–1805), from the sale of his library (Sotheby 6 Feb 1806, lot 5916), and on economics, politics, law, history, and theology 1589–1780 (Sotheby 5 May 1806, lot 1051). The Belgian collection had originally been begun by Gilbert Affleck, MP for Cambridge, in the early 18th cent.

Not in main cat.

Shelf cat incomplete.

London History Library A collection of over 5,000 v and many pamphlets on Greater London (the present GLC area). It originated with a bequest of *c*700 v received in 1873 from the executor of Capt Henry Ward (*d*1867), and became a separate library in 1922. There are 9 STC; 36 Wing; over 300 ESTC; and over 500 1801–50 items. Tract collections of the 18th and 19th cent include 10 v called Ward Tracts from the Ward bequest, and 12 v called SOS Tracts from the London Institution. There are *c*200 v of histories of the City livery companies.

Author card cat.

Very incomplete classified cat.

Typescript author list of pre-1701 books.

Ward collection also has separate author cat in ms, and is included in *Catalogue* 1879 identified as 'W'.

1914–18 War Collection (Stored at Egham) Over 3,000 pamphlets and several hundred books on the First World War. Predominantly propaganda of the allied cause. It includes a set of the *Daily Review of the Foreign Press*.

Uncatalogued, but books are arranged in alphabetical order of authors.

Olden Collection (Stored at Egham) *c*900 items primarily on the rise of Nazi Germany, with some works on earlier German history, mostly after 1900; a few works of literature are included. They are from the collection of Rudolf Olden (1885–1940), author of works on Hitler and Nazism, and were acquired in 1947.

Special author cat in History Library, and in main cat.

Royal Historical Society Library (Housed in the D M S Watson Library; the Society's headquarters are at the College, and permission to use the library must be obtained from the Secretary. Tel (01) 387 7532).

The Society was founded in 1868, and its library was first systematically organized in 1875, but was dormant for long afterwards. It began to grow rapidly after 1900, particularly with the bequest of the more valuable part of the library of Sir George (Walter) Prothero (1848–1922). At first a general historical library, it was reorganized in 1934 to specialize exclusively in British history, with a strong emphasis on source materials. At the same time some special collections were transferred to the British Museum, Public Record Office, Northamptonshire Record Society, and King's College London War Studies Library, while overseas material (chiefly on the colonies) was given to the Institute of Historical Research. The backbone of the library is now formed by a collection, *c*5,000 v of editions of British history texts and calendars in the series published by the national record offices, Historical Mss Commission, and similar bodies, and of most national and many local historical societies; over 200 of these are pre-1851. There is a complete set of the Society's own publications.

Card cat.

Not in main cat.

Library catalogue of the Royal Historical Society, (*c*1878).

Catalogue of the Library of the Royal Historical Society, 1915.

E L C Mullins, *Texts and calendars: an analytical guide to serial publications*, the Society, 1958, corrected reprint 1978; a bibliography of publications in series; all are held in the library except those listed on p671-4.

Alexander Taylor Milne, *A centenary guide to the publications of the Royal Historical Society 1868–1968 and of the former Camden Society 1838–1897*, Ibid 1968.

R A Humphreys, *The Royal Historical Society 1868–1968*, Ibid 1969.

Law Library There has been a separate Law Library from 1829. It attracted, in addition to part of Bentham's Library (see above), the collections of William Blackburne of Lincoln's Inn, given by his sister in 1847, originally 2,486 v of law reports and treatises, and of John Richard Quain (1816–76), Judge of Queen's Bench and Fellow of the College, of *c*1,000 monographs. These have been incorporated in the general collection, but only a proportion of each seems to have survived. The collections now include *c*100 pre-1851 treatises and controversial works on English law, mostly post-1650, and over 100 sets of English law reports, mostly published between 1770 and 1840. The Library now specializes in Roman Law, with 1,800 books on this subject, of which *c*50 are pre-1851, mostly foreign, and Russian and Soviet law, *c*1,900 v, including *c*150 v of the 19th cent, mostly diplomatic and treaty material.

Supplement to the Catalogue, 1897, marks Quain items 'Q'.

Ms cat of 1849–50 was destroyed.

B Tearle, 'The Law Library at University College London', *Law Librarian* no 10 (1979).

W E Butler, 'The Russian and Soviet law collection at University College London', *Solanus* 13 (1978), p40-1.

G Religious History Collections

The teaching of theology was barred by the original rules of the College, and there is no subject library in theology, but over 2,000 v in this subject were given in 1870 by Sir Ralph Daniel Makinson Littler (1835–1908) QC from the library of his father the Rev Robert Littler, incorporated into the general collections. Three societies for sectarian religious history have deposited the following collections:

Huguenot Library (deposited as an independent library within the College). Open to members of the Huguenot Society and approved scholars by appointment only, Tues-Fri 10 am-12.30 pm, 2-4 pm; membership is freely available on payment of subscription.

La Providence, or the Hospital for Poor French Protestants, now at Rochester and known as the French Hospital, was incorporated by royal charter in 1718, and began a library in 1876. The library of the Huguenot Society of London, founded with the Society in 1885, was deposited at the Hospital 1885–8, and from 1900. In 1957 both collections were amalgamated into a joint library called the Huguenot Library, and deposited at the College. It contains *c*4,500 v and *c*500 tracts, *c*1550 onwards, including *c*1,200 pre-1851 items. Mainly on the history of the Huguenots, particularly strong on the dispersals 1650–1720 (with some pre-1700 general Protestant history) in England (including Commonwealth tracts), France, the Low Countries, Germany and America. Liturgies of the French Reformed Church and of the Church of England in French translation, with some Bibles and general theology, especially Moyse Amyrault (1596–1664) and Jean Daillé (1594–1670). Huguenot biography, genealogy and family history, including many privately printed books, and the collection of pedigrees assembly by Henry Wagner (*d*1925?) FSA; archives of the French Hospital; archives (with some gaps) of the Royal Bounty (1687–1876), including printed reports from *c*1707; various ms collections.

Card cat (dictionary, with some analytical entries).

A few books included in main cat of College Library.

Purchases and donations listed in *Proceedings of the Huguenot Society Bibliotheque de la Providence: catalogue of the Library of the French Protestant Hospital, Victoria Park Road, London*, by Reginald S Fâber, London, 1887 (authors); rev and enlarged ed 1890 (omitting Huguenot Society books); 3rd ed, Canterbury, priv pr 1901.

A rough handlist of the Library of the Huguenot Society, Lymington, priv pr, 1892; also in *Proceedings* 4 (1891–3), p3-21.

C Marmoy, 'The French Hospital', *Proceedings of the Huguenot Society* 21 (1965–70), p335-54; 22 (1970–6), p235-47.

R D Gwynn, 'The distribution of Huguenot refugees in England', *Proceedings* 21 (1965–70), p404-36; 22 (1970–6), p509-68; includes a list of churches with references to the material on them in this and other collections.

Raymond Smith, *Records of the Royal Bounty...*, (Huguenot Society Quarto ser v 51).

R A Austen-Leigh, 'Fifty years of the Huguenot Society of London'.

Franciscan Society Collection (Stored at Egham) The International Society of Franciscan Studies was founded in 1902 by Paul Sabatier (1858–1928), and a British Branch with Sabatier as its President was established in the same year, with a library from the outset. In 1907 the branch was reorganized as the British Society of Franciscan Studies, which was primarily a society for publishing texts and studies on Franciscan history and the religious life in the Middle Ages; it also became associated with productions of the 'Little Plays of St Francis' by Laurence Howman at University College, the proceeds from which supported the Society. The library was built up mainly by gifts and exchanges, until by 1938 there were over 150 v. The Society then deposited the library at the College, and dissolved itself. The collection includes, in addition to the Society's publications, a general collection on St Francis of Assisi and the history of the Franciscan order; mainly early 20th cent, but with 3 of the 17th; 8 of the 18th; 4 of the earlier, and 31 of the later 19th cent.

International Society of Franciscan Studies in British Branch, *Catalogue of the Library*, (1904); typescript list of additions to 1938; both in author order.

Shelf cat on cards, in author order; also in main cat.

Accessions in annual *Report*.

British Society of Franciscan Studies Extra series v 2: Franciscan essays 2, by F C Burkitt (et al), with a prefatory note on the history and work of the Society, Manchester, 1932.

Mocatta Library (An independent library deposited at the College, open by appointment only to members of the Jewish Historical Society and of the College; temporary admission to other scholars applying in writing at the Librarian's discretion.)

Frederick David Mocatta (1828–1905) bequeathed his collection to the Jewish Historical Society to form the nucleus of a library of Anglo-Jewish history, and of Biblical, Hassidic and Cabbalistic literature, which was formed by depositing it at University College. The libraries of Israel Abrahams (1858–1925), Sir Hermann Gollancz (1852–1930), Lucien Wolf (1857–1930), and Hartwig Hirschfeld (1854–1934) were among the gifts which made it the foremost library in its field. In 1940 the whole library was destroyed, except the mss, early editions of Josephus, and some other rare books from the Wolf and Gollancz collections which had been evacuated. The library has been rebuilt to almost its former size, now *c*12,000 books and 6,000 pamphlets, including *c*3,000 pre-1851 items, mostly from donations.

The Guildhall Library in 1941 gave its Hebraica and Judaica collection, which had been built up around the gift in 1846 of *c*400 early Hebrew books by Philip Salomons, mostly from the collection of his father Levi Salomons (1797–1873), and with gifts of books from Mocatta, so that it was especially appropriate that it should be used to replace the original Mocatta collection;

over 2,000 items, from 1550 onwards, chiefly liturgies, Bibles, commentaries, editions of the Mishnah, works on Cabbalah, philosophy, history, geography, literature, and bibliography. Other collections incorporated in the library are described in the published bibliographies cited below.

Card cat (authors; subject, incomplete).

The first collection was listed in R A Rye, *Catalogue of. . . the library of Frederick David Mocatta*, 1904; and C Roth, *Magna bibliotheca Anglo-Judaica*, 1937.

Most of the Guildhall Collection is listed in *Catalogue of Hebraica and Judaica in the Library of the Corporation of London, with a subject index* by A Löwy, London, 1891.

The collections are described in H M Rabinowicz, *Treasures of Judaica*, New York, Yoseloff, 1971, p69-79 (and the old library, p80-7); and J W Scott, 'The Mocatta Library', in *Remember the days: essays on Anglo-Jewish history presented to Cecil Roth* ed J M Shaftesley, London, Jewish Historical Soc, 1966, p323-31. See also E Levine, *The origin and growth of the Mocatta Library*, London, 1933.

Sir H Gollancz, *A contribution to the history of University College*, priv pr 1930.

C Roth, 'The reconstruction of the Mocatta Library', *Journ Jewish Biblio*, 3, 1942, p2-4.

The Gaster Papers, 1976 (Library of University College London. Occasional Publication no 2).

'The new Mocatta Library', *Jewish Chronicle*, 16 Dec 1932, p22-4.

H Art and Archaeology Collections

Yates Library of Classical Antiquity and Archaeology James Yates (1789–1871) FRS, Unitarian minister, left an endowment and *c*350 v to found the library which bears his name. In 1903 Dr Frederick Septimus Leighton's library of 2,580 v was given by his children to the College, and mainly went to the Yates Library. *c*500 v on Roman archaeology were bequeathed by Bunnell Lewis (1824–1908) Professor of Latin at Cork. In 1961 Norman Hepburn Baynes (1877–1961) bequeathed *c*2,500 v on ancient history (but his Byzantine collection went to Dr Williams's library).

Edwards Library of Egyptology Miss Amelia Ann Blanford Edwards (1831–92), the novelist, who had endowed the chair of Egyptology, bequeathed her Egyptological library to form the core of a departmental collection, with an endowment. Sir Alan Gardiner, President of the Egypt Exploration Society, bequeathed over 1,800 v in 1963.

Fine Art Library Established at the Slade School in 1872, it was later moved to the main library. It was originally formed from the Edwin Field Memorial Fund, and gifts of books from Mrs Harriet Grote (1792–1878) and others.

Environmental Studies Library A separate Architecture Library, which included gifts received earlier, was established in 1905; 140 v of rare illustrated works were given in 1859 by Samuel Angell (1800–66), Architect to the Clothworkers' Company.

Ms cat *c*1885–92 in College Collection.

I Scientific Collections

Many of the science libraries were destroyed or damaged in 1940, and apart from the segregated special collections mentioned below, most earlier bequests do not survive in their entirety, if at all.

Handlist of scientific periodicals, 1964.

J Percival and W A Smeaton, 'Library and archive resources in the history of science at University College, London', *British Journ for the Hist of Sci* 11 (1978), p191-5.

Natural history manuscript resources, 1980, p288-9.

History of science: principal archive and manuscript sources in University College London, (1981?), includes collections not held by the Library.

Graves Library John Thomas Graves (1806–70), Professor of Jurisprudence, then Poor Law Inspector, bequeathed his mathematical and scientific library, over 14,000 items. It now serves as the Library's special collection of rare mathematics books, and early mathematics books have been added from elsewhere, including a few books from the bequest of William Kingdon Clifford (1845–79) FRS, Professor of Applied Mathematics, whose library was incorporated in the general mathematics library; it is enlarged by regular purchases from the Rouse Ball Fund. 75 of the library's incunabula are from Graves. Mainly early mathematics; also history of physics, applied mathematics, and to a smaller extent chemistry and the biological sciences, (with 51 mss). It includes 260 editions of Euclid in 19 languages, including all the first 19 of 83 pre-1641 editions, and the first translations into Italian 1543, German 1562, French 1564, English 1570, Arabic 1594; also a collection of John Holywood, or Joannes de Sacro Bosco)(*d*1256), including a 14th cent ms and 8 incunabula; first editions of Newton's *Principia* and *Opticks*, Priestley, Boyle, Kepler, Galileo and Napier; Thomas Salusbury's *Mathematical Collections* of 1661–65, and important runs of early periodicals English, French and German, including complete sets of transactions of the Royal Society, the Berlin Academy, the Royal Irish Academy, and the Académie des Sciences, with the rare journal *Observations sur la Physique* from 1771; complete runs of the standard mathematical journals from the early 19th cent onwards. There are some important association copies, and fine modern bindings. Of 1,143 17th cent items in the collection, 298 are not in the British Library.

In general author cat.

Shelf cat on cards.

Included in Physical Sciences Library classified cat.

Graves's own ms author cat (incomplete); these entries were incorporated in *Catalogue* 1879.

A R Dorling, 'The Graves mathematical collection',

Annals of Science 33 (1976), p307-10.

C Thomas-Stanford, *Early editions of Euclid's Elements*, London, Biblio Soc, 1926.

Douglas McKie, *Science and history*, London, 1958, p15.

Obit in *Proc Roy Soc*, 19 (1871), pxxvii-xxviii.

Physical Sciences Collections The Physical Sciences Library has since *c*1950 built up a collection of rare books, mostly 1601–1850, now 2,750 v, called the History of Science Sources Collection; partly by transfer from the general collections, partly from new purchases. The collection covers physics, astronomy and chemistry, in which it is particularly strong, owing much to the libraries of two Professors of Chemistry, George Fownes (1815–49) bequeathed, and Thomas Graham (1805–69) given by his nephew J C Graham in 1879. It also contains a few books on zoology and botany.

In Physical Sciences Library, author and classified cats. Also in main author cat.

Fleming Collection *c*500 v from the library of Sir (John) Ambrose Fleming (1849–1945), first Professor of Electrical Engineering 1885–1926, given by his widow in 1945.

In main cat.

London Mathematical Society Library (Deposited since 1929) The Society was founded in 1865 under the presidency of Augustus De Morgan when Professor of Mathematics at the College. The library holds *c*7,000 v, including monographs (mostly post-1850), tracts, and over 250 sets of periodicals; also a collection known as LMS Sources, mainly of 1701–1850, *c*150 v.

Natural Sciences Collections The Natural Sciences Library has since *c*1950 built up a Natural Sciences Rare Books Collection, mostly 1601–1850, now 1,925 v on botany, zoology, geology (see below), and geography; mostly transferred from the general collections.

In general author cat.

Geologists' Association Library In 1907 the library was deposited in the College, bringing with it not only a valuable collection of books and pamphlets, but a flourishing exchange scheme which brings into the College Library over 300 periodicals. It is incorporated into the College Library's Natural Sciences Library.

Geologists' Association, *Catalogue of the Library*, London, Univ College, 1879 (authors).

——*Catalogue of the geological books in the library of University College, London, including the Library of the Geologists' Assoc...*, by W Bonser, 1927 (classified).

J Nash, 'Periodicals in the Geologists' Association and University College libraries', 73: 1963 (1964), p467-81; reprint available (title list).

Johnston-Lavis Collection Collected by Henry James Johnston-Lavis (1856–1914), and bequeathed to the College, it contains 444 v on vulcanology, especially strong on Italian volcanoes, and incorporating the collection of Leopold J Fitzinger.

In general author cat.

Natural history manuscript resources, 1980, 291.15.

Smith Woodward Collection The library on palaeontology of Sir Arthur Smith Woodward (1864–1944) FRS, bought in 1945: 400 books, over 100 v of periodicals, and an outstanding collection of *c*10,000 reprints.

Tansley Collection (Stored at Egham) A collection of offprints and pamphlets on plant ecology throughout the world collected by Sir Arthur George Tansley (1871–1955); *c*7,380 items from *c*1890–1940, in 257 boxes.

Special author cat.

Dawes Hicks Collection The library of 3,929 books and 408 pamphlets bequeathed by George Dawes Hicks (1862–1941) Grote Professor of Mind and Logic to rebuild the psychology and philosophy libraries that had been bombed, supplemented by 1,300 v on psychology given in 1942 by the widow of Dr Gustav Adolf Wohlgemuth.

Hertfordshire Natural History Society Library Deposited in 1935 and contains some 2,200 v of books and periodicals, including some early herbals and a copy of the 10th ed of Linnaeus *Systema naturae*, 1758.

J Hopkinson, *Catalogue of the Library of the Hertfordshire Natural History Society and Field Club*, London, 1885; *Supplementary catalogue*, 1890.

Malacological Society Library The Malacological Society of London was founded in 1893, and deposited its library from 1930. *c*500 v (including over 200 pre-1801) from 16th cent onwards, on molluscs and conchology, with some older books on general natural history and travel; mainly from the bequest of Percy E Radley. Rare works include Martini and Chemnitz *Systematisches Conchylien-Cabinet* 1769–88, and Cuvier *Anatomie des mollusques* 1817, with Cuvier's own woodblock library stamp and inscription.

Malacological Society of London, *Library catalogue (Radley bequest)*, 1927.

Galton Bequest The personal library of Sir Francis Galton (1822–1911) the discoverer of fingerprints, and founder of the Galton Laboratory of National Eugenics, now part of the Department of Genetic Engineering. Several hundred volumes on a wide variety of scientific topics, including many inscribed presentation copies; housed in the laboratory's independent departmental library, which also includes a large collection of 19th cent pamphlets. Galton's papers, including proofs of his published works, are available in the Mss and Rare Books Room.

Galton's own card index.

Galton Laboratory, *A list of the papers and correspondence of Sir Francis Galton (1822–1911) held in the Manuscripts Room, the Library, University College London*, compiled by M Merrington and J Golden, 1976, p35, 37.

Karl Pearson, *The life, letters and labours of Francis Galton*, Cambridge, 1924, v 2, p12.

J Medical Collections

The Medical Library was established at University College *c*1828. At the same time a Medical Society was formed within the college which had its own lending library, mostly incorporated in the College Medical Library in 1900. In 1826 the North London Infirmary was founded to provide clinical practice for the students of the College, becoming the North London Hospital in 1834, and University College Hospital in 1837; in 1886 part of the Medical Library was transferred there, and when the hospital Medical School separated from the College in 1907, a much larger part. In 1981 the Medical School Library again became part of University College Library, and was renamed the Clinical Sciences Library.

Catalogue of books in the Library belonging to the Medical Society of University College, 1843.

A catalogue of the books in the Medical and Biological Libraries, 1887; three annotated copies, one by Thane and one showing transfers to the Medical School.

Catalogue of the periodical publications in University College, 1912, annotated to show medical holdings to *c*1960.

R M Nicholas, 'The development of medical libraries within the University of London' (MA Librarianship thesis, Univ of London, 1976), p50-4.

Jean B Wood, 'The development of the medical library of King's College, London with consideration of other medical libraries. . .(Especially at Univ Coll) in the 19th century', (MA Librarianship thesis, Univ of London, 1969).

Medical Donations The Medical Library received many gifts and bequests in the later 19th cent. The largest was the formerly separate Sharpey-Grant Library, founded by the bequest of Robert Edmond Grant (1793–1874), Professor of Comparative Anatomy of his collection of *c*4,000 v, with an endowment, at the instigation of William Sharpey (1802–80) FRS, Professor of Physiology, who, in 1874, added his own collection and catalogued the whole library; part of Sharpey's collection was general literature, incorporated into the main library. Other bequests of professors' private collections include those of Professor Sir Richard Quain (1800–87); Professor Edmund Alexander Parkes (1819–76) FRS (partly transferred with the Parkes Museum to the Royal Society of Health); Nathaniel Rogers (*d*1884), 466 v.

Clinical Sciences Library The former University College Hospital Medical School Library, now *c*25,000 v, including 4,000 pre-1851. It includes a Historical Collection of *c*600 v of classic, early and rare medical books, including *c*230 v from the library of Sir John Tweedy (1849–1924) given shortly after his death, all rare, with one incunabulum. The libraries bequeathed by Sir John (Eric) Erichsen (1818–96), surgeon to Queen Victoria, and Marcus Beck (1843–93), another surgeon at the Hospital, form a combined separate collection. There is a major collection of pathological drawings by Sir Robert Carswell (1793–1857), and a bequest of general and popular 20th cent literature by Professor Max Leonard Rosenheim, Baron Rosenheim of Camden (1908–72).

Card cat (dictionary).

Current periodicals list, 1979.

Donations Book 1907–53.

D R Merrington, *University College Hospital and its Medical School: a history*, London, Heinemann, 1976, p99.

A T Picton, 'How to use the Library', *Univ Coll Hosp Mag* 35 (1950), p45; 36 (1951), p56-9.

Thane Library of Medical Sciences The pre-clinical library, *c*60,000 v, with a medical history collection of *c*1,600 v, mainly pre-1851, from the early 17th cent onwards, and a collection of medical tracts.

University of London Library, Senate House, Malet Street, Bloomsbury, London WC1E 7HU. Tel (01) 636 4514. Telex 269400. Open (except Summer vac) Mon-Thurs 9.30 am-9 pm; Fri 9.30 am-6.30 pm; Sat and Summer vac Mon-Fri 9.30 am-5.30 pm, to members of the University of London, and (normally only in vacation) to members of other universities (and exceptionally others needing to see material not available elsewhere) on written application in advance to the Librarian. Several days notice required to see material stored in Depository Library at Egham, Surrey. Photocopying and microfilming; microfilm and fiche readers and printers available. Computerized information services.

The University of London was founded in 1836 as an examining body; in 1900 it was reorganized as a federation of colleges and institutes. The University Library originated in 1838, but its development dates from its formal opening in 1876–7 (following the gift of De Morgan's library) in the new University HQ in Burlington Gardens; an era of rapid expansion followed, culminating in the receipt of the Goldsmiths' Library in 1903. In 1900 the Library moved to South Kensington, and in 1937–8 to the familiar ivory tower surmounting the new Senate House in Bloomsbury. It has been built up mainly as a central research library in the humanities and social sciences, but also provides for undergraduate readers. In 1973 the University set up a Library Resources Co-ordinating Committee to administer and develop its central library services and co-ordinate libraries throughout the University.

J H P Pafford, 'The University of London Library', in *The Libraries of London*, ed R Irwin, London, Library Association, 1949, p125-38; 2nd ed R Irwin and R Staveley, 1961, p140-56.

——*The University Library* (address to Convocation, 1959).

Histories of the University cited in H Silver and S J Teague, *The history of British Universities. . .a bibliography*, London, 1970, p124-35.

Guide to the University of London Library, 1981;

earlier eds contain more information on special collections, especially *General Information*, 1919 and 1923, and *A Reader's Guide*, 1938.

Report of the Library Committee for 1926 includes a history of the Library.

University of London. Library Resources Coordinating Committee, *Guide to the libraries of the University of London*, London, Univ of London Library, 1983.

A General

The library contains well over 1 million v, including *c*120,000 pre-1851 items, of which 130 are incunabula; *c*700 STC; and *c*4,500 Wing items. In addition to the special collections described below, the general collection includes much early and rare material, especially in history and in English and romance languages and literatures. There are open access subject libraries of mainly modern books for Geography and Geology, History, Philosophy, Psychology, and romance languages and literatures. An unusually comprehensive collection of published and privately issued catalogues of collections of mss and other aids to the study of mss is held in the Palaeography Room, which serves readers of the library's extensive collections of mss. A very extensive collection of bibliographies and works on all aspects of bibliography and librarianship (with its own card cat in the Middlesex North Library) includes some notable fine and rare books on the history of printing. The library also contains many books in fine bindings.

Card cat to 1980 (authors); microfiche cat (authors and classified) thereafter.

Catalogue of the Library of the University of London, including the libraries of George Grote and Augustus De Morgan, 1876 (authors). Abbreviated and extended as *Hand-catalogue of the Library brought down to the end of 1897*, 1900.

Lists of accessions from 1876 onwards, usually selective, have been published with a few intermissions.

Certain parts of the library have classified and author cats of their own, but most of these contain modern works only.

Incunabula in the libraries of the University of London: a hand-list (by M F Wild), London, Univ of London Library, 1963 (authors; index of printers and places).

R A Rye and M S Quinn, *Historical and armorial bookbindings exhibited in the University Library descriptive catalogue*, 1937 (describes 83 items by country); annotated copy in Goldsmiths' Library.

The palaeography collection: author and subject catalogue, Boston (Mass), G K Hall, 1968, 2 v.

J M Gibbs and P Kelly, 'Manuscripts and archives in the University of London Library', *Archives* 11 (1974), p161-71.

R A Rye, *Catalogue of the manuscripts...*, 1921.

P Kelly, *Modern historical manuscripts...*, 1972.

M Canney, 'Sources for African studies', *Library Materials on Africa* 5(3) (1968), p79-83.

Periodicals Section *c*15,000 runs of serials, including a strong, mainly English language, collection of the 19th cent, and earlier British and foreign titles. The collection effectively began with the receipt, in 1879, of the periodicals section of the library then being dispersed of the British Association for the Advancement of Science. The literary and general section was strengthened in 1925 by 5,000 v from the dispersed library of the London Institution. There is an almost complete set of the journals published by state historical societies in the United States (many deposited by the Institute of Historical Research), and other runs of American periodicals from the United States Library and the Latin American Library.

Card cat (including all serials in special collections except Carlton, for which typescript list is held in Periodicals Office).

List of periodicals, 1956.

List of current periodicals, 1969; *Additions and amendments* 3rd ed 1973.

Union list of serials in the libraries of the University of London (microfiche) in course of compilation; see L Rogers, 'The University of London's Union List of Serials', *Aslib Proc* 34 (1982), p192-7.

British Government Publications Library Mainly 19th and 20th cent. Pre-1801 material is limited to Lords' and Commons' Journals, Lords' papers 1714–1805 (Oceana reprint) and Commons' sessional papers 1731–1800 (microprint edition), all the remainder being held in the Goldsmiths' Library (see below), which also has certain early 19th cent series. Commons papers (mostly from a set bought from the Reform Club) are complete from 1860 onwards, with some in chronological sequence from 1811; and a fairly full set in subject sequence 1816–35. Commons *Votes*, Lords *Minutes*, Division Lists and Standing Orders of both houses; all slightly incomplete. Public General Acts from 1832, and standard collections of statutes.

British Government Publications and related material: alphabetical finding list, 1981.

United States Library The nucleus of *c*15,000 works (mostly post-1945) was given from the former American Library in London by the United States Information Service in 1966, and amalgamated with the University Library's own American holdings which included earlier material. It has been enlarged to over 30,000 v on the whole range of American studies, especially literature and history, with much black studies material, and some coverage of art, architecture, philosophy, religion, sociology, travel, Indians, and other subjects. Works on music are held in the Music Library, periodicals in the Periodicals Section, and bibliographies in the Bibliography Collection.

Peter Snow, *The United States: a guide to library holdings in the UK*, Boston Spa, British Library Lending Division, 1982, p296-9.

Latin American Library Over 24,000 v on most aspects of Latin American and Caribbean studies, especially history, politics, economics and the humanities and social sciences generally, well supported by reference works and bibliographies, with some early works, chiefly on travel. Periodicals on these subjects are held in the Periodicals Section.

B Goldsmiths' Company's Library of Economic Literature

The Goldsmiths' Library contains *c*60,000 books and pamphlets, of which *c*35,000 are pre-1851, with 3 incunabula; 236 STC; 2,395 Wing; and *c*14,000 ESTC items, and *c*600 pre-1701 foreign; *c*600 18th and 19th cent periodicals; and *c*500 royal and parliamentary proclamations (mostly of the 17th cent) and *c*1,400 broadsides of 1641–1868. It covers economic literature very broadly, and is rich in early and rare works illustrating the development of economic thought, principally in the British Isles, but also in France (especially in the 18th cent), the Netherlands, Germany, Italy, Spain and the USA. It is strong on financial and monetary policy; agriculture; early English and French socialism, especially works by, and about, Robert Owen (1771–1858), Claude Henri de Saint-Simon (1760–1825), and Charles Fourier (1772–1837); guilds, railway history; slavery; the temperance movement; the growth of industry and trade; and the condition of the people generally. It is arranged chronologically. A large collection of official publications (to which almost all the pre-1801 material from elsewhere in the University Library has been transferred) includes *Statutes of the Realm* and other 18th and 19th cent collected editions of English, Scottish and Irish statutes; Acts published individually from 1649 (King's Printers' editions bound in annual volumes); Lords' Journals in ms 1510–1628 and 1719–43; Commons' *Votes* 1689–1800 complete; a good collection of 18th and 19th cent editions of parliamentary debates, and the rare *Irish Parliamentary Register 1781–1801*. Reports from *Committees of the House of Commons 1715–1800* 1803–6; and the *Census of Ireland*. The Goldsmiths' Library mss are administered as part of the University Library's mss collection. The main collections from which the library was built up are described below. Current additions are mainly pre-1850.

Catalogue of the Goldsmiths' Library of Economic Literature, by M Canney et al, Cambridge UP, 1970– v 1-2 printed books (with historical introduction by J H P Pafford) in chronological order; v 3 in preparation); additions to v 1-2 periodicals, mss; v 4 (in preparation) general index.

University of London Library, *The Goldsmiths' Company's Library of Economic Literature 1903–1953*, 1954.

The printed books and pamphlets to 1850, together with those at the Kress Library at Harvard University, are published on a chronological series of microfilm reels by Research Publications, Woodbridge (Conn), 1978–82, with *Goldsmiths'-Kress library of economic literature: a consolidated guide* listing the contents of each reel.

Card cat (author); also included in general cats.

Included in *A London bibliography of the social sciences*, London, 1931–7, under alphabetical subject headings, with a continuation on sheaf slips from 1952 onwards.

Catalogue of the collection of English, Scottish and Irish proclamations in the University Library (Goldsmiths' Library of Economic Literature)..., 1928; chronological, annotated, with other locations and references, with indexes of printers and publishers, subjects and names.

Catalogue of the collection of broadsides in the University Library (Goldsmiths' Library of Economic Literature)..., 1930, similar, with a supplement to the catalogue of proclamations.

George Ottley, *Railway history: a guide to... collections...*, London, Lib Assoc RSI Section, 1973, p71-2.

G J Broadis, 'Books on inland navigation in the Goldsmiths' Library' (Univ of London, Diploma in Librarianship bibliography, 1962).

Robert Owen, 1771–1858: catalogue of an exhibition of printed books...1958, 1959.

The Foundation Collection of Foxwell and the Goldsmiths' Company The nucleus of the Library was the first library of Herbert George Somerton Foxwell (1849–1936), Professor of Political Economy at University College, London, which he collected between 1875 and 1901, and then sold to the Goldsmiths' Company, who donated it to the University in 1903, *c*30,000 v (his later library became the Kress Library of Harvard University, and is available in the Goldsmiths' Library in the Goldsmiths'-Kress combined microfilm). It was strongest in the period 1750–1850, and set the pattern for the continuing growth of the collection, to a size now twice as large. Most of his books are in fine condition, many having been obtained at major sales (particularly that of Sir James Gibson-Craig (1765–1850) and his son, Sotheby 27 June 1887, 23 March and 15 Nov 1888), with an exceptional number of copies from the collections of well-known personalities such as Adam Smith, Arthur Young, David Ricardo, Jeremy Bentham, Karl Marx, etc, and a number of integral collections, eg the tracts and broadsides on the factory movement and related subjects collected by its leader Richard Oastler (1789–1861); the collection of broadsides and proclamations assembled by Frederick Henry Maitland, 13th Earl of Lauderdale (1840–1924); *c*30 v of pamphlets, mostly political, collected by George Agar-Ellis, 1st Baron Dover (1797–1833); and other collections of pamphlets formed by David Ricardo (1772–1823), William Cobbett (1762–1835) and others.

H S Foxwell, 'The Goldsmiths' Company's Library of Economic Literature', in (Sir Robert) *Palgrave's dictionary of political economy* ed Henry Higgs, London, 1925, v 1, p870-2. His correspondence and papers relating to the collection are in the Mss Dept with handlist in Palaeography Room.

J M Keynes and C E Collet, 'Herbert Somerton Foxwell', *Economic Journal* 46 (1936), p589-619, including bibliog.

Sabatier Collection The first of a series of major additions funded by the Goldsmiths, bought in 1906; *c*1,000 items on French monetary history, especially during the revolutionary period, but extending from 1651 to 1852.

Sheffield Collection In 1907 the library bought (Sotheby 4 Nov) part of the collection of John Baker Holroyd, 1st Earl of Sheffield (1735–1821), of Sheffield Place, Sussex, a leading economic authority of his time, comprising 260 books and pamphlets; 54 Acts and Proclamations of 1650–1; and 6 v of his scrapbooks.

List of economic books and tracts, Acts of Parliament, broadsides and proclamations from the Library of the Earl of Sheffield, presented by the Goldsmiths' Library. . . 1907, (1908) by subjects; *Supplementary list of economic tracts. . .*, (1908).

Identified in *Catalogue.*

Rastrick Collection John Urpeth Rastrick (1780–1856), civil and mechanical engineer, especially of railways, bequeathed his books and papers to his son Henry, after whose death in 1893 they were sold; in 1908 *c*250 items from the collection were bought with an *ad hoc* grant from the Goldsmiths, and incorporated in the transport history section of the library (except ms, notebooks, specifications, and estimates, in the University Library mss collection). There are 211 printed books of 1768–1887, mostly 1821–50, and almost all railway (with a few canal) engineering reports and prospectuses, including some very rare items.

List of manuscripts, maps and plans, and printed books and pamphlets. . .from the collection of John Urpeth Rastrick, and his son. . .presented. . .to the Goldsmiths' Library, 1908, chronological.

Identified in *Catalogue.*

J Simmons, 'The Rastrick Collection, University of London', *Locomotion*, June 1939, p33-6.

Introduction in T D Rogers, *The Rastrick Papers. . .in the University of London Library, a handlist*, 1968.

J Gibbs in *Bulletin of the National Register of Archives*, 1967, p32-4.

James Turner Temperance Collection *c*500 v acquired *c*1930 from the collection of James Turner, temperance advocate of Manchester, on the temperance movement in the 19th cent, including some rare periodicals, now forming part of the Library's Temperance Collection.

Identified in *Catalogue.*

Reform Club Pamphlets Bought from the Reform Club in 1964, comprising most of the pamphlets then in the Club's Library, except the Panizzi Collection. They consisted of *c*360 v containing *c*4,000 pamphlets on political, economic and social subjects of *c*1770–1910 (but mostly pre-1880); *c*50 per cent were duplicates and were sold to the University of Toronto, the remainder being incorporated in the library.

Ms lists by author, subject and volume.

Relevant items listed in *London bibliography of the social sciences*, with the Reform Club location, and in *Catalogue of the Goldsmiths' Library* v 1-2.

Family Welfare Association Library (deposited) Founded in 1869 as the Society for Organising Charitable Relief and Repressing Mendicity, and from 1871 to 1946 called the Charity Organisation Society, the Family Welfare Association deposited its library of *c*5,000 v of books and pamphlets on permanent loan in the Goldsmiths' Library in 1963 (its periodicals are at the National Institute of Social Work Training; its archives at the Greater London Record Office). Mostly late 19th and early 20th cent, with *c*100 pre-1851 items; *c*300 v of pamphlets and over 100 v of government publications. It covers all social questions, with the emphasis on those directly affecting the Society's work, especially poverty and the Poor Law, education, mental and physical health, and the blind. Donations include those of Thomas Mackay, Sir Charles Stewart Loch (1849–1923), and William Harris, who gave a collection of books on the care and teaching of the blind. The library also contains the bequest of William Pare (1805–73), the co-operator, many of whose books are in distinctive bindings, marked by his initials, including a scrapbook and much other material relating to Robert Owen (1771–1858), assembled for an intended biography which he never accomplished; the bequest was to any institute or trust founded on Owen's model, and it is not clear whether it was received by the Charity Organisation Society in the first instance.

Typescript author cat 1962, excluding pamphlets and some government publications.

Pamphlets, mostly arranged by subject, are uncatalogued.

C L Mowat, *The Charity Organisation Society 1869–1913*, London, Methuen, 1961, p48-9.

M Rooff, *A hundred years of family welfare. . .*, London, 1972, p49, 92-3, 230.

Annual Report from 1870.

Reporter 1872–84, continued as *Charity Organisation Review* 1885–1921.

Sources in British political history 1900–1951, 1975, v 1, p97-8.

C **Special Collections**

Most of the larger gifts and bequests of rare books are maintained as separate collections, listed below in order of acquisition.

Some are included in main cat, some have separate cats.

Durning-Lawrence Library The private collection of Sir Edwin Durning-Lawrence, Bt (1837–1914), protagonist in the Bacon-Shakespeare authorship controversy, bequeathed by his widow in 1929, subject to a life interest, which soon lapsed. *c*5,750 v. Partly an extensive collection of early editions of Francis Bacon, Viscount St Albans (1561–1626), and works on the Shakespearian authorship controversies. The remainder contains books on a variety of other subjects, with many early editions of Elizabethan and Jacobean authors and dramatists, of the works of Daniel Defoe (1661?–1731), and of emblem books. Noteworthy items include the first four Shakespeare folio editions; the Latin Bible printed by Koberger at Nuremberg in 1477; Coverdale's Bible of 1535; and the first translation into English by Thomas Shelton of *Don Quixote* 1612–20. There are *c*20 incunabula, and *c*40 mss. Some items have been added from a small endowment fund, from the Bacon collection at Lambeth Public Libraries, and from other donations.

Ms cat by Sir Edwin Durning-Lawrence's librarian.

The more noteworthy items are listed in *Report of the Library Committee* for 1931.

See also A Gordon, *The Lawrences of Cornwall*, (London, priv pr, 1915), with bibliog of his writings.

Quick Memorial Library A collection given in 1929 by the Education Guild, formerly the Teachers' Guild of Great Britain and Ireland. The greater part had originally been the library of the Rev Robert Herbert Quick (1831–91), schoolmaster and writer of books on education; this had been enlarged by other collections donated to the Guild, including that of William Henry Widgery (1857–91), a teacher at University College School. The library contains *c*1,000 v, including 90 v of pamphlets, to the late 19th cent, on education. It is rich in early school textbooks, eg C Holliband, *The Italian schoole-maister* 1597 and the first English translation of Lily's Grammar 1641. Most of the leading educational thinkers from the Renaissance to the mid-19th cent are represented, eg Roger Ascham *The scholemaster*, 1571, Mulcaster *Positions* 1581, and Locke *Some thoughts concerning education* 1693. There are also biographies, histories of schools, and encyclopaedias of education. Subsequent acquisitions on the history of education are placed in a section adjacent to this library.

In general cat but no separate cat.

Quick locations are specifically noted in C W J Higson, *Supplement to Sources for the history of British education*, London, Library Assoc, 1976.

D E Bormer, 'The Quick Memorial Library and other books on education in the University of London Library', *Univ of London Inst of Educ Bull* no 25 (Autumn 1957), p1-3.

Crofton Collection Formed by Cecil Frederick Crofton, the actor, who donated it in 1932. *c*550 v in miniature format, chiefly reprints of English and French literary works published in the 18th and 19th cent. A few additions have been made.

Typescript author list; also in main author cat.

Austin Dobson Collection A collection of the works of (Henry) Austin Dobson (1840–1921), the poet and critic, begun by his youngest son Alban Tabor Austin Dobson (1885–1962), round a nucleus of material inherited from his father's own collection; he also bought virtually all the Dobson editions at the sale of a portion of the poet's library (Sotheby 13 March 1922). After much enlargement, he gave most of the collection to the University Library (and a small portion to Ealing Public Library) in 1946. It has been subsequently enlarged by gifts from Alban's son Christopher Selby Austin Dobson (*b*1916), formerly Librarian of the House of Lords, and from other members of the family; and by purchases with assistance from trust funds. *c*3,500 items, including almost every edition of every work written or edited by Dobson, together with mss, proofs, and printed editions with his ms corrections and annotations.

There is a major collection of his contributions to magazines and newspapers built round the collection assembled in 50 v by Francis Edwin Murray, author of *A bibliography of Austin Dobson* (Derby, 1900), from the Murray sale, Sotheby 17–18 July 1924, lot 540.

The mss include almost all his published and many unpublished poems, some in more than one version, and his correspondence to and from artists and writers. There is also a selection of books about him.

University of London Library, *Catalogue of the collection of the works of Austin Dobson...*, 1960; a classified short title cat, compiled by Alban T A Dobson; see also his *A bibliography of the first editions...of Austin Dobson*, London, 1925.

H M Young, *Handlist of letters and manuscripts of H Austin Dobson...in the University...Library*, Historical Mss Commission, 1976.

Alban T A Dobson, 'Austin Dobson: some of his books of association', *London Mercury* 10 (1924), p511-9.

'Gift to University of London Library: Austin Dobson Collection', *The Times* 2 July 1946, p7.

Chichester Collection *c*120 v bought from Chichester Cathedral Library in 1947, mainly 17th and 18th cent editions of the classics.

Typescript list with the collection; in main author cat.

See also *Bibliothecae Ecclesiae Cicestrensis librorum catalogus*, Chichester, 1871.

Harry Price Library of Magic (Access restricted to those who can show that they need to use it for approved academic research) The collection of Harry Price (1881–1948) the publicist of psychical research, developed from a childhood collection of books on conjuring into a library of all aspects of abnormal and occult phenomena. He deposited it, 1922–7, with the Society for Psychical Research; in 1927–36 at the National Laboratory for Psychical Research which he had founded in 1926, then (after unsuccessful proposals for founding a University chair of psychical research) at the University of London Library, bequeathing it in his will. In 1937 it contained 4,376 books; 5,343 pamphlets; 725 v of periodicals; with ephemera, press cuttings, mss, photographs and slides; it has been modestly enlarged from an endowment. *c*800 items are pre-1801.

The collection on witchcraft includes several incunabula and the first edition 1584, and all later editions of Reginald Scot *Discoverie of Witchcraft.* 58 editions of Nostradamus (1503–66) 1533 onwards, with works about him, acquired from Carl Ludwig Friedrich Otto, Graf von Klinckowström (1884–1969), the historian of dowsing, who had published a bibliography based on the collection; and later prophets and religious eccentrics, especially Joanna Southcott (1750–1814); with some works on astrology and almanacs 17th-20th cent.

Major collections on psychical phenomena, including psychical research, spiritualism and hypnotism, with first editions of all the occult works of Daniel Defoe (1661–1731), Oliver Goldsmith's *The mystery revealed...* (1762), containing the first account of a seance; some very scarce British and foreign 19th cent items; and a complete set of Sir Arthur Conan Doyle's works on the subject. The conjuring collection is outstanding, and contains *c*100 pre-1840 English textbooks, including the first by Samuel Rid, 1614, one of four known copies of *Hocus Pocus junior* 1634, and 15 of the 17 editions of that by Henry Dean, 1727; with pamphlets on oddities such as the purported birth of rabbits to Mary Toft (1701–63); and British and American conjuring periodicals, including the *Conjuror's Magazine* 1791–93 complete with all plates, and many very scarce later runs. Collections on hand shadows, spectral illusions, and similar tricks; and on playing cards. Chapbooks, and children's books, including several with illustrations incorporating ingenious mechanisms for animal noises, moving figures, etc. Music hall and theatre bills and programmes 1766–1900, including Vauxhall and Ranelagh gardens. An enormous collection of press cuttings, mainly on Harry Price himself.

National Laboratory of Psychical Research, *Short-title catalogue of works on psychical research, spiritualism, magic, psychology, legerdemain, and other methods of deception...*, compiled by Harry Price, Hon Director, 1929, issued as *Proceedings of the National Laboratory of Psychical Research* 1(2) (1929), p67-422. Supplement published as *Short-title catalogue of the Research Library...Supplement*, compiled by Harry Price, London, 1935 (Univ of London Council for Psychical Investigation Bull 1).

Graf C von Klinckowström, 'Die ältesten Ausgaben der propheties des Nostradamus: ein Beitrag zur Nostradamus-Bibliographie', *Zeitschrift für Bücherfreunde* Neue Folge 4/2 (1913), p361-72.

The most outstanding items are noted in *Report of the Library Committee for 1936*.

A Wesencraft, 'The Harry Price Library', *Libraries Bull* (Univ of London Library Resources Co-ordinating Committee), no 12 (Jan-Mar 1978), p10-13; no 13 (Apr-June 1978), p5-9, 15.

Trevor H Hall, *Search for Harry Price*, London, Duckworth, 1978, p109-35, 212-28.

Journal of the Society for Psychical Research 20 (1922), p270-1; 21 (1923), p33-4.

H Price, 'My library', *Magic Wand* 12 (1923), p133-8.

——'The National Laboratory Library', *British Journ of Psychical Res* 1(10) (Nov/Dec 1927), p307-16.

Many other articles on the Library by H Price listed in *Catalogue* 1927, p69.

Elzevier Collection *c*700 v from the press of the Elzevier family, and *c*440 v from other 17th cent Dutch presses, formerly in the Guildhall Library, who gave it to the University of London in 1950.

A Willems, *Les Elzevier: histoire et annales typographiques*, 1880 (marked up copy available on request).

Sterling Library The private library of Sir Louis Sterling (1879–1958), book collector and pioneer of the gramophone industry, *c*4,200 v received in 1956, supplemented by purchases from an endowment fund and other gifts. Now *c*6,000 v almost all rare, including seven incunabula; also 700 mss. Mainly first and early editions of the great writers of English literature from Chaucer to the present day; strongest after 1750. There are 110 STC and 133 Wing items include all four Shakespeare folios, with firsts of *Paradise Lost* and *Regained* and *Anatomy of melancholy*. The 18th cent books are in unusually fine condition; 16 items by Samuel Johnson (1709–84) include both the *Dictionary* 1755 and its *Plan* 1747. There is an important collection of books by, and about, George Crabbe (1754–1832), given by Dr John Henry Pyle Pafford (*b*1900), a former Goldsmiths' Librarian; and other early 19th cent books include some copies with interesting associations, eg Lamb *Specimens of English dramatic poets* 1808 first ed inscribed to Southey; 20th cent books include notably good collections of John Masefield (1878–1967), enriched *c*1971 by the bequest of presentation copies and first editions from his sister Mrs Ethel Stockdale-Ross; of W B Yeats (1865–1939); and of Sean O'Casey (1880–1964) inscribed to his son Neill, given by Mrs Eileen O'Casey; *c*600 private press books and limited editions include a complete set of Kelmscott Press editions and a set, presented by Sir David Hughes Parry (1893–1973), Chairman of the Court, of specially bound Gregynog Press editions; over 250 illustrated books include nine published by Rudolph Ackermann (1764–1834), 13 aquatinted by Henry Alken (1784–1851), and 26 designed or engraved by George Cruikshank (1792–1878). Sterling also gave 17 portraits of English authors, part of a set collected by Philip Dormer Stanhope, 4th Earl of Chesterfield (1694–1773) for Chesterfield House, Mayfair.

In main author cat.

The original collection listed in *The Sterling Library: a catalogue of the printed books and literary manuscripts collected by Sir Louis Sterling and presented by him to the University of London*, 1954.

'Private libraries, 15: Sir Louis Sterling', *Times Lit Supp* 4 Feb 1939, p80.

'A great patron of literature', *John O'London's Weekly* 10 Sept 1954.

Record of proceedings at the opening of the Sterling Library by the Chancellor...the Queen Mother..., 1957, with detailed inscription.

C Dobb, 'John Masefield collections in the University of London Library', in Geoffrey Handley-Taylor ed, *John Masefield, OM the Queen's Poet Laureate: a bibliography...*, London, Cranbrook Tower Press, 1960, p19-21.

Bromhead Library The library of Col Alfred Claude Bromhead (1876–1963) CBE, co-founder of the Gaumont cinemas in 1898, and Commander of the Order of St Maurice and St Lazarus, given by his family in 1964. *c*4,000 items, mostly rare, and mainly on London. *c*120 STC items (including broadsheets), and *c*700 Wing, including a collection of Civil War pamphlets. Important items include Arnold's *Chronicle* of 1503; works of Dekker and Greene; and a collection of 17th cent Lord Mayor's pageants. *c*200 prints and maps, and 15 mss.

Col Bromhead's own card cat available on request.

Not in main cat.

Malcolm Morley Library Collected by Malcolm Morley (1890–1966) actor-manager and stage director, and given by his widow in 1966. *c*4,000 v of books and 200 v of periodicals, comprising plays, mainly in 19th and 20th cent editions, and works on theatrical history and stagecraft. The collection includes sets of plays such as Dick's Standard Plays, and French's and Lacy's Acting Editions.

In main author cat; no separate cat.

G W Nath, 'Malcolm Morley', *Theatre Notebook* 20 (1966), p70-80, 98-9.

M Morley, 'Fragmented autobiography', *Theatre Survey* 11 (1970), p86-98; 12 (1971), p67-78.

Ethel M Wood Biblical Collection The collection was formed and bequeathed by Ethel Mary Hogg, afterwards Mrs Wood (1876–1970) CBE, daughter and biographer of Quinton Hogg (1845–1903), and historian of the Polytechnic. It contains *c*350 items, mainly English and American Bibles and books connected with biblical studies. 1 incunabulum; 45 STC items (including the Great Bible 1539, Genevan 1560, Bishops' 1568), and 25 Wing; 1 13th cent ms.

No separate cat; partly in main cat.

Carlton Shorthand Collection Collected and bequeathed by William John Carlton (1886–1973), bibliographer of shorthand. *c*12,000 printed items, with *c*200 mss on all aspects of stenography, comprising books, pamphlets, and periodicals of all countries and systems, in 60 languages and dialects; one of the most comprehensive collections in existence, with examples of applied shorthand, such as early sermons, trials and speeches printed from shorthand; works by well-known authors printed in shorthand; books on the history and bibliography of shorthand, etc. The 15 STC and 85 Wing items include John Willis's anonymous *Art of stenographie* 1602 and editions of Thomas Shelton's *Tachygraphy* and *Tutor*, and of William Mason's *Pen Pluck'd from an eagle's wing.* The collection included *c*40 v bought at the sale of the Earl of Crawford's library (Sotheby 8 July 1948) which had come from the collection of Cornelius Walford (1827–85), and previously from that of James Henry Lewis (1786–1853) sold Sotheby July, 1871.

Incomplete typescript list; not in main cat, except STC items.

Most of the pre-1801 English books located in R C Alston, *A bibliography of the English language*, corrected reprint of v 1910, Ilkley, 1974, v 8.

W J Carlton, 'Lord Crawford's stenographiana', *TLS* 17 July 1948.

'The Carlton Shorthand Library', *Ibid* 22 Apr 1960.

H G Wells Collection Formed in 1962 under an agreement between the H G Wells Society and the University Library whereby both should contribute to the collection. It contains *c*100 v, comprising an almost complete set of first editions of the works of H G Wells (1866–1946), and other early editions of his books and pamphlets.

In main author cat; no separate cat; but see the Society's *H G Wells: a comprehensive bibliography*, 2nd ed 1968, annotated copy.

D Donations and Bequests Incorporated in the Main Library

Many bequests and donations have been incorporated into the general collections, sometimes after being kept separate for a time. The more important are listed below in order of acquisition.

It was formerly the practice to record provenance from major collections, usually by initials within square brackets, in the card and printed cats; the initials used for each collection have been identified below.

De Morgan Library The library of Augustus De Morgan (1806–71), Professor of Mathematics at University College London, bought by Samuel Jones Loyd, 1st Baron Overstone (1796–1883), and given by him to the University in 1871. There are *c*4,000 books and pamphlets (also over 500 mss), mainly on mathematics and astronomy, with a scattering of other subjects. Many important editions, including the first five printed Euclids 1482–1516; the first two of Gilbert *De magnete* 1600, 1628; the first (1543) and second (1566) of Copernicus *De revolutionibus*; and first and other early editions of Sir Isaac Newton, including *Principia* 1687; *c*18 incunabula; early almanacs; a major collection of De Morgan's published works and many books annotated by De Morgan.

No separate list.

Identified as [D.M.] in *Catalogue* (1876).

Annotated copy of his *Arithmetical books* 1847 in Palaeography Room.

S E De Morgan, *Memoir of Augustus De Morgan*, 1882.

Grote Collection The library of George Grote (1794–1871), historian and Vice-Chancellor, bequeathed to the University, *c*5,000 v and 2,500 pamphlets, mainly Greek and Latin classics, and books on Greek and Roman history and archaeology; supplemented by regular additions bought by his widow.

No separate cat.

Identified as [G.G.] in *Catalogue* 1876, *Accessions* 1876–1886, and later accessions lists.

Harriet Grote, *The personal life of George Grote*, London, 1873.

Another part of Grote's Library is said to have been sold in the anonymous sale at Puttick and Simpson, 31 March 1851.

Shaw-Lefevre Russian Library The library of Sir John (George) Shaw-Lefevre (1797–1879), Vice Chancellor, given by his widow in 1880. *c*160 works in Russian, nearly all printed in the period 1801–78. Among other rarities it contained the first Russian translation of *The Vicar of Wakefield*, Moscow 1786.

List appended to *Hand Catalogue* 1897.

Lady Welby Library A collection of books formed and extensively annotated by the Hon Victoria A M L Stuart-Wortley, afterwards Lady Welby-Gregory (1837–1912) given by her husband Sir Charles Welby-Gregory. *c*1,500 v and *c*1,000 pamphlets, mostly 19th cent on theology, philosophy, economics, education, science and philology.

List of books in the Lady Welby Library, (1913) excluding the pamphlets. [L.W.L.] in card cat.

Preedy Memorial Library The library of Lieut John Benjamin Knowlton Preedy (*d*1917), formerly of the University Extension Dept, was given by his mother in 1922 in his memory, with an endowment for its enlargement to form a special collection of archaeology and art.

Catalogue of books on archaeology and art and cognate works belonging to the Preedy Memorial Library and other collections in the University Library, 1935–7, 3 pts classified with author index and *Supplement* [P.M.L.] in card cat.

Waller Memorial Library The collection of Augustus Desiré Waller (1856–1922), Director of the University Physiological Laboratory, comprising 93 pamphlets collected by him, some books, and the papers of his father Augustus Volney Waller (1816–70) FRS, Professor of Physiology at Birmingham, given in 1923 and 1946.

Special bookplate.

See under Waller in card cat.

Hitchcock Collection The library of George Stewart Hitchcock (*d c*1925), Unitarian minister, then RC priest, given by his widow in 1926; mostly books on theology, and philosophy.

[H.C.] in card cat.

A pilgrim of eternity: the history of a Unitarian minister, G S Hitchcock, London, 1911.

Mrs Humphry Ward Collection Books and pamphlets on the 1914–18 War used by (Mary Augusta) Mrs Humphry Ward (1851–1920) the novelist while writing her *Letters to an American friend* (1916), and other war books. Her husband gave the collection after her death to General Sir Neville Gerald Lyttleton (1845–1931) whose widow gave it to the University Library in 1931.

Manton Marble Collection Books and pamphlets on the history of the United States 1860–1910, with emphasis on currency, collected by Manton Marble (1834–1917), and given in 1937.

Playne Collection of books on the social history of 1914–18, given by Miss Caroline Playne in 1938.

Stroud Read Collection The collection of F Stroud Read (*d*1941), Warden of the University Union, of books on history and travel, especially of the Near and Middle East, given by his widow in 1941. (See also under King's College.)

Rye Memorial Library The collection of Reginald Arthur Rye (1876–1945), Goldsmiths' Librarian, of books on Egyptology. *c*400 v given by his widow in 1948.

Snell Memorial Library A collection of books on natural religion and philosophy, bought from an endowment fund established in 1948 in memory of Henry Snell, 1st Baron Snell (1865–1944).

Troup Horne Collection Bequeathed by George Francis Troup Horne (1881–1953), Secretary of Birkbeck College, as a memorial to Margaret Cuming Troup Horne (1841–1953). *c*600 works in 700 v illustrating the development of the short story in the English language; mainly 20th cent, with a few earlier and rare items (eg of Kipling). Also *c*400 v of private press books, and *c*1,000 v of other works.

Bell Collection The theological library with numerous ecumenical works of George Kennedy Allen Bell (1883–1958), Bishop of Chichester, given in 1962.

Jane Collection The botanical library bequeathed by Professor Frank William Jane (1901–63).

Harmsworth Collection The library of Alfred Charles William Harmsworth, 1st Viscount Northcliffe (1865–1922), on journalism, given in 1966.

Hallett Collection Books on Spinoza bequeathed by Professor Harold Foster Hallett (1886–1966).

E **Deposited Collections**

Collections deposited in the University Library on loan, arranged below in order of date of first deposit.

Some are included in general author cat.

Eliot-Phelips Collection Formed by William Robert Phelips (1846–1919) and his son Edward Frederick Phelips (1882–1928) of Montacute House in Somerset, and bequeathed by the latter to the Guildhall Library who deposited it in 1950.

It is known as the Eliot-Phelips collection in memory of Clara Louisa Eliot, sister of E F Phelips and wife of the Hon Edward Granville Eliot. *c*3,000 v of books on Spain, and in Spanish. The main emphasis is on history, especially of Madrid, but there are also many works of literature and books on travel, and a variety of other subjects, including philosophy, religion, geography and mathematics. Many books are of the 17th cent and some of the 16th; also 30 mss.

Incomplete cat on slips.

Most items included in main author cat.

Francis Bacon Society Library The Society, from its foundation in 1885 to 1948 called the Bacon Society, deposited its library in 1956, but in 1979 withdrew all 11 incunabula, and 14 STC and Wing items. There are now *c*1,500 items, including *c*120 STC and 130 Wing, mainly works by and about Francis Bacon, Viscount St Albans (1561–1626), and other authors of the late 16th and early 17th cent.

No separate cat.

In main author cat.

Porteus Library The library of Beilby Porteus (1731–1809), Bishop of London, housed at Fulham Palace until its deposit in 1958. *c*4,000 v including 300 v of pamphlets, covering ecclesiastical affairs, and a wide range of other subjects such as slavery, the French Revolution, travel and topography. The bulk was published 1750–1809, but there are a few earlier books, including one incunabulum, and a later collection, mainly volumes of sermons and charges, added by William Howley (1766–1848).

Subject cat on cards available on request.

Cataloguing in progress for main author cat.

D T Richnell, 'The Library of Bishop Porteus', *Lib Assoc Record* 61 (1959), p156-8.

Robert Hodgson, *The life of the Right Reverend Beilby Porteus. . .*, London, 1811, p100-42.

Graveley Parish Library The parish library of Graveley in Cambridgeshire, originally the private library of Henry Trotter (*d*1766) Rector of the parish, bequeathed by him to his successors for the use of the clergy of the neighbourhood. When the rectory was sold the books were transferred to Jesus College, Cambridge, the corporate patron of the living. In 1960 the college deposited the collection in the University of London Library. *c*1,400 v of the 17th and 18th cent, mainly theology and history.

Card cat at Jesus College; photocopy with the collection.

Also in main cat.

Central Council for the Care of Churches, *The parochial libraries. . . of the Church of England*, London, 1959, p80.

Theatre Museum Library In 1963 the Society for Theatre Research deposited its library, *c*2,500 v on the history of the theatre, including biographies, plays, periodicals, and some Russian and East European items. The British Theatre Museum Library, founded in 1963 at Leighton House in Holland Road, was deposited in 1966, then *c*3,200 v, but later much enlarged; covering the history of the British theatre including plays, theatrical journals, theatre programmes and ephemera, the nucleus being the Henry Irving Archive; also containing prompt copies etc deposited by the English Stage Company, and collections presented in memory of Cyril Swinson, author and publisher, and of George Bishop and Ernest Short, both theatre critics. The two libraries are now amalgamated, and will form the nucleus of the library of the National Theatre Museum due to be opened in Covent Garden *c*1984 under the auspices of the Victoria and Albert Museum.

There are temporary records of the books in both libraries in the main cat.

Belgian Library The former library of the Belgian Institute placed on permanent loan in the University Library in 1967 by the Belgian Government. *c*4,000 books, mainly in French or Flemish, on Belgian art, history, literature, etc, and includes a good collection on the Belgian Congo. Regular additions are made by the Belgian Embassy, and in 1972 the retiring ambassador, Baron J van den Bosch, gave *c*500 v from his personal library, with further gifts in 1979 and 1982.

In main author cat, also separate set of these author entries available on application.

The collection is in process of being incorporated in the general library.

F **Music Library**

This library, established in 1925, contains major collections of books and scores, including a number of special collections, of which two contain rare books.

Card cat of books and scores.

Books also included in main cat.

Some pre-1801 items included in *RISM*.

Littleton Collection A collection bought at the sale (Sotheby 13-16 May 1918), of the library of Alfred Henry Littleton (1845–1914), chairman of Novello and Co, Master of the Musicians' Company 1910–11, by the Carnegie United Kingdom Trust, who gave it in 1932. 31 rare and valuable works on music, including examples of early compositions, and some important theoretical works of the 15th-17th cent, eg the first printed treatise on music by Gafurius 1480. 5 incunabula; 11 STC and 4 Wing items.

Typescript list available on application.

See also auction cat and *A catalogue of a hundred works illustrating the history of music printing from the fifteenth to the end of the seventeenth century in the library of Alfred Henry Littleton*, 1911.

Plainsong and Mediaeval Music Society Library The library was formed by the Society from its foundation in 1888, deposited in 1956 and sold to the University in 1967. *c*450 v on plainsong and mediaeval music, including liturgical and musical books from the library of the Rev Thomas Helmore (1811–90); notably a Plantin Roman missal of 1598; a Roman antiphonal of 1622; and a Roman gradual of 1674.

Card cat.

Plainsong and Mediaeval Music Society, *Catalogue of the Society's Library*, Burnham (Bucks), Nashdom Abbey, 1928.

Two rare items were sold by the Society to others *c*1965.

Victoria and Albert Museum, National Art Library, Cromwell Road, South Kensington, London SW7 2RL. Tel (01) 589 6371. Open Mon-Thurs 10 am-6 pm, Sat 10 am-1, 2-5.30 pm, to the general public; regular readers should obtain readers' tickets, by applying in writing. An endorsed ticket (apply on form obtainable from the Library) is required to consult special collections or mss. Reading Room accommodation is very limited. Photocopying, but not of pre-1800 or valuable or fragile material; microform readers.

The library originated at the Government School of Design founded at Somerset House in 1837. In 1852 it moved to the Museum of Ornamental Art established by Sir Henry Cole at Marlborough House to perpetuate the Great Exhibition, becoming a branch of the Department of Practical Art. In 1856 the department was merged in the Department of Science and Art, and the museum was absorbed into the South Kensington Museum with its library becoming the Art Library (later the National Art Library) among several libraries there. In 1899 the museum, after shedding its non-art functions, was renamed the Victoria and Albert, and in 1900 placed under the Department (later Ministry) of Education, now the Department of Education and Science.

R N Wornum, *An account of the library of the Division of Art at Marlborough House*, London, 1855.

W H J Weale, *The history and cataloguing of the National Art Library*, London, 1898.

I Whalley, 'The National Art Library, Victoria & Albert Museum', *Bulletin of the Circle of State Librarians*, Sept 1972, p41-4.

E M B King, *The South Kensington Museum Art Library... until 1900* (MA thesis, Univ of London, 1975).

Anna S Cocks, *The Victoria and Albert Museum: the making of a collection*, Leicester, Windward, 1980, p164-8.

A General

There are probably *c*750,000 monographic items, of which at least 500,000 are foreign, on the fine and applied arts; with early and rare printed books on these and related subjects such as topography, archaeology, heraldry, anatomy for artists, costume, stage design, pageantry, social history, aesthetics, photography as an art-form, and illustrated books; also *c*3,500 periodical titles, and over 50,000 exhibition catalogues.

Publications Her Majesty's Stationery Office, *Sectional List no 55*, lists all HMSO publications on the museum and library; it also lists some of those published by the Museum itself, but these are obtainable only direct from the Museum.

Donors *List of the bequests and donations to the... Museum...*, 1889; (new ed), 1901; chronological list of donors, with numbers of books, pamphlets, etc, and general descriptions; with index of names.

Periodicals *c*3,500 sets, of which *c*1,500 are current.

List of papers and periodicals received..., 1881.

Sale catalogues One of the largest collections in the world, and includes many of great rarity. There are complete sets of those of Christie; and of the art sales of Sotheby.

Card cat by town, auctioneer, and date of sale; separate index of owners. Holdings to 1900 listed in F Lugt, *Répertoire des catalogues de ventes publiques intéressant l'art ou la curiosité*, 1938–64, 3 v.

Exhibition catalogues Over 50,000, by far the most comprehensive collection in the British Isles. There is an outstanding collection on the Great Exhibition, 1851, including that given by its organizer Sir Henry Cole (1808–82) with catalogues of later exhibitions (see also Cole bequest below). There are also important holdings of catalogues and reports of 19th and early 20th cent international exhibitions. Sir Charles Wentworth Dilke, 1st Bart, MP (1810–69) in 1867 gave his collection of 297 v, 862 pamphlets, 155 programmes, and prints, on the Great Exhibition 1851, the Paris Exhibition 1855, and the International Exhibition 1862.

Handlist by place and date. Typescript list of cats from 1890 onwards reproduced in ... *Catalogue* 1972, v 11.

Trade catalogues Extensive collections of trade catalogues and pattern books relating to the arts covered by the Library, especially furniture, textiles, jewellery, silversmithing, and ironwork.

Old English pattern books of the metal trades: a descriptive catalogue of the collection in the Museum, 1913.

Old trade catalogues: some notes on the collection of 18th and early 19th century trade-lists of ironmongery..., 1913.

Trade directories A collection of *c*1,000 London and provincial directories from the 17th cent onwards, including 72 pre-1851 London directories; it includes the bequest of a collection made by Edward and Eva Pinto, incorporating part of that formed by Sir Ambrose Heal (1872–1959).

M E Keen, *Edward Henry and Eva Pinto bequest*, the Museum, 1979.

——*A bibliography of the trade directories of the British Isles in the National Art Library*, 1979; by place, with name/title index.

Cole bequest The bequest of Sir Henry Cole (1808–82), Director of the South Kensington Museum. In addition to an important collection of mss, it included guide books, a collection of the travelling charts which he compiled for the *Railway Chronicle* 1844–6, some miscellaneous works printed after 1860, and a series of printed and ms 'Miscellany Volumes' *c*1830–75. (See also Exhibition catalogues above.)

Typescript list of Cole papers, mainly the ms material.

Oriental books The library has always had many oriental books but active purchasing began with the creation of its Far Eastern Department in 1970; it now has the major UK collection of Oriental books on the arts. The Japanese books, *c*12,000 v, are strong in museum and exhibition catalogues, books on the fine and applied arts (especially the more unusual aspects of applied arts) and archaeology (including *c*250 pre-1851). The Chinese and Korean books are concentrated on the archaeological aspects of art history, *c*3,000 v including 25 pre-1851. The collection is strong in early art periodicals, including *Chrysanthemum* 1881– , and *Kokka* 1889– (the most complete set in W Europe).

E F Strange, *Japanese books and albums of prints in colour*, London, 1893.

E F Strange, *Books relating to Japanese art*, London, 1898.

L C Dawes, *Japanese illustrated books*, HMSO, 1972.

B D Galbraith, *A catalogue of oriental periodicals in the National Art Library*, the Museum, 1973, £1.10.

B Art of the Book

The Library is also a Museum Department responsible for collecting and exhibiting books and mss illustrating the art of book making; these collections comprise illuminated mss (mediaeval and later) and specimens of calligraphy; fine printed books as specimens of the history of the typographer's art; fine illustrated books as specimens of the history of book illustration; and fine bindings, both European and Islamic. There are extensive supporting reference collections on the history of the bibliographic arts, mainly orientated towards artistic aspects.

Calligraphy The collection includes both specimens of handwriting, and the largest known collection of printed copy-books. The latter include the collection formed by Sir Ambrose Heal (1872–1959) (except the duplicates of items already held, which were bequeathed to the Fitzwilliam Museum, Cambridge).

Sir Ambrose Heal, *The English writing masters and their copy books 1570–1800*, 1931; bibliography with locations including the Museum and Heal collections.

J I Whalley, *A provisional check list of writing books and books on calligraphy received... before 1890*, 1954.

Four hundred years of English handwriting: an exhibition of manuscripts and copy books 1543–1943..., 1964.

J I Whalley, *English handwriting 1540–1853: an illustrated survey...*, London, the Museum, 1969.

J I Whalley & V C Kaden, *The universal penman*, London, HMSO, 1980.

Typography A major collection of books as specimens illustrating the history of printing, including 185 incunabula.

Card index of printers and publishers of pre-1801 books.

T M MacRobert, *Printed books: a short introduction to fine typography*, London, HMSO, 1957.

Early printers' works, London, HMSO, 1962; illustrating 30 15th-16th cent books from the collection.

G D A McPherson, *Incunabula: a provisional checklist of pre-1500 books in the Library*, 1970; typescript; by place and date; annotated copy.

A J Sloggett, *Catalogue of miniature books in the Library*, 1971 (Supplement to *List of accessions*).

Illustrated books A superb collection. It includes a major collection of 20th cent *livres d'artiste*, with works illustrated by Picasso, Matisse, etc, mostly bought during the keepership of A J Wheen 1939–62, and since 1976. Special collections include 400 v bequeathed by H H Harrod; and a collection of the work of Thomas Bewick (1753–1828), with letters and documents, also 4 albums of proofs of his engravings (in the Dept of Prints & Drawings).

Typescript list of Harrod bequest; residue listed in Supplement to *Monthly list of accessions*, 1969.

T M MacRobert, *Appendix to Hofer: 17th century book illustrations in the Library*, (1960); repr in *Motif* 5 (1960?).

Frances Hicklin, *Bewick wood engravings*, London, HMSO, 1978, £1.00.

A S Hobbs, 'Illustrated fables: a catalogue of the library's holdings', *Library Monthly List* Jan 1972, p68-89.

Private press books This major collection includes a complete set of the productions of the Stanbrook Abbey Press from 1876 onwards.

G D A McPherson and J I Whalley, *Stanbrook Abbey Press and Sir Sidney Cockerell: a centenary exhibition*, London, HMSO, 1976.

Catalogue of an exhibition in celebration of the centenary of William Morris, 1934.

P Hogarth, *Arthur Boyd Houghton: introduction and checklist of the artist's work*, London, HMSO, 1975.

Bookbindings c2,000 v, of which many are on permanent display. Henry John Beresford Clements (*d*1940) bequeathed a collection of over 1,150 British armorial bindings. In recent years the library has commissioned or purchased bindings from Ivor Robinson, Sally Lou Smith, James Brockman, Elizabeth Greenwood, and others.

Photographic Catalogue of Bookbindings: with descriptions and finding list in typescript.

W H J Weale, *Bookbindings and rubbings of bindings in the National Art Library*, 1894–8.

John P Harthan, *Bookbindings*, 2nd ed 1961.

Denis Woodfield, *An ordinary of British armorial bookbindings in the Clements collection, Victoria and Albert Museum*, 1958, based on ms cat by Clements.

H J B Clements, 'Check list of English armorial book stamps', *Book Collector's Quarterly* no 14-17.

Two modern binders: William Matthews & Edgar Mansfield..., London, Designer Bookbinders, 1978, exhibition cat.

C Literature Collections

Though literature is not now a primary concern of the Library, major collections were bequeathed during the 19th century.

Dyce collection Alexander Dyce (1798–1868), Curate of Nayland and editor of English poets, bequeathed over 15,535 printed books and 61 mss, in addition to pictures, prints, and drawings. They include several incunabula, *c*250 STC, *c*800 Wing, *c*4,000 ESTC, and *c*2,200 1801–50 English items; *c*850 16th and 1,200 17th cent foreign. Literature predominates, especially the Greek and Latin poets and some other classical authors; the major Italian authors, especially Ariosto, Boccaccio, Dante, Petrarch, and Tasso, and some later plays, poems and romances; works of 16th-17th cent scholars and critics; Fathers of the Church, and Anglican divines; French literature, chiefly Rabelais, Montaigne, Moliere, and Racine; and a large collection of English literature (chiefly poetry and drama) from the late 16th cent onwards, with many of the Shakespeare quartos, 398 playbills 1726–1837, and a collection of pamphlets and annotated cuttings on Edmund Curll (1675–1747) the bookseller.

Dyce collection: a catalogue of the printed books and manuscripts bequeathed by. . . Alexander Dyce. . ., 1875, 2 v.

Handbook of the Dyce and Forster collections in the South Kensington Museum, (1880), p1-52.

Forster collection John Forster (1812–76), editor of the *Examiner*, friend and biographer of Dickens, bequeathed most of his library, *c*18,500 books (in addition to mss including 39 v of Garrick letters, drawings, and engravings). It comprises mostly the classics, Italian and French poetry, English poetry (especially 1750–1825), English drama (mainly Restoration, but including first and second folios and other Shakespeare items), *c*500 v chapbooks and children's books, Swiftiana, English dictionaries, history and travel. There is an almost complete set of first editions of Dickens, many being autographed presentation copies, with many mss and proof copies (mostly bequeathed to Forster by Dickens). 150 proclamations and broadsides collected by the first Lord Holland (1629–60). *c*10,000 pamphlets in 1,000 v; with a substantial collection on Charles I and the Commonwealth, including 10 v of sermons preached before the Long Parliament; 14 v bought at the sale of Macaulay's library originating from the collection of Monck Mason of Dublin. Granger, *Biographical history of England*, extra-illustrated with over 5,000 portraits.

Forster collection: a catalogue of the printed books bequeathed by John Forster, 1888.

Forster collection: a catalogue of the paintings, manuscripts, autograph letters, pamphlets, etc, bequeathed by John Forster. . ., 1893.

Handbook of the Dyce and Forster collections, 1880, p53-91.

A Burton, 'The Forster Library as a Dickens collection', *Dickens Studies Newsletter* 9 (1978), p33-7.

A Burton, 'Some recent work on the Forster Collection', *John Forster Newsletter* 1 (1978), p11-20.

Dickens Exhibition 1912, 1912.

Charles Dickens: an exhibition, 1970, London, HMSO, 1970, £0.20.

Jones collection *c*780 v bequeathed by John Jones (*c*1800–82), military tailor of Regent Street and Piccadilly, with pictures, furniture, and objects of vertu, on condition that it should remain a separate collection, in his own bookcases. Chiefly English poetry and history, with some works on art. Includes first-third folios of Shakespeare, the 1561 Chaucer, some rare Wing editions, and Covent Garden playbills 1818–9.

Catalogue of the Jones bequest in the South Kensington Museum, 1882.

Catalogue of the Jones collection, part 2, 1924, p113-5, description but not a catalogue of the books.

Handbooks of the Jones collection, 1883.

D **Children's Books**

(NB The Renier and Linder collections, and later possibly the others, are to be transferred to the branch museum at the Bethnal Green Museum of Childhood, Cambridge Heath Road, London E2 9PA. Tel (01) 980 2415.

The Library has always collected children's books as part of the history of the art of the book. By 1960 it had *c*2,500 v, a figure which was doubled by the Little acquisition, but eclipsed by the arrival of the Renier collection.

Title index on cards, with cross references from authors.

Victorian children's books selected from the Library of the Victoria and Albert Museum: an exhibition at the Bibliothèque Royale, Brussels. . ., 1973, 210 items.

J I Whalley, 'Children's books at the Victoria and Albert Museum', *Children's Book News*, 5 (1970), p112.

Exhibition of illustrated books for children, historical section, catalogue, 1932, 676 items, including copies from the Little collection.

Victorian books exhibition: children's books: a list comprising exhibited books and additional works, 1967.

Little collection *c*2,500 v collected by Guy Little, who bequeathed them *c*1960.

Renier collection Over 45,000 children's books, with toys and games, formed by Anne (Cliff) Renier, author of *Friendship's offering, an essay on the annuals and gift books of the 19th century*, 1965, and her husband, Fernand Gabriel Gustave Renier (*b*1905); given in 1970.

Author card cat.

'What the children like': a selection. . . from the Renier collection. . ., 1970, exhibition cat.

A Renier, *The basket of flowers by Christoph von Schmid: a checklist of copies in the Renier collection*, Stroud, 1972.

Linder bequest Books by and on Beatrix Potter (1866–1943) bequeathed by Leslie (Charles) Linder (whose other collection of Potter material is at the National Book League), especially first edititions; with mss, watercolours (forming the bulk of the collection), letters, etc, received in 1973.

Union cat of Beatrix Potter holdings in V&A and other collections in preparation for publication.

National Book League, *Peter Rabbit's 75th birthday exhibition: a souvenir catalogue*, 1976.

L Linder, *Beatrix Potter 1866–1943*, London, National Book League, 1966, exhibition cat.

A history of the writings of Beatrix Potter, London, (1971).

E Miscellaneous Collections

Hutton collection A collection of 400 v on fencing from the library of Capt Alfred Hutton (1840–1910), writer on swordsmanship.

Handlist by authors.

Townshend collection The Rev Chauncy Hare Townshend (1798–1868), mesmerist, friend of Dickens, bequeathed a selection of his collections of art treasures, including 831 v of books (the residue to the Wisbech Museum).

Piot collection Pageantry and ceremonial, 16th-19th cent books.

Ms author list.

Larionov collection 350 v on ballet, mainly early 20th cent Russian and French.

Author/subject handlist.

F Branches

Ham House, Richmond, Surrey TW10 7RS. Tel (01) 940 1950. The Library is furnished with books from Henham Hall, Suffolk (built in 1797 for Earl Stradbroke, demolished 1953). 2,163 v, mainly typical country house reference books and sets of novels of the 18th and 19th cents.

Typescript author list in cat office in main V&A Library.

Osterley Park House The original collection housed by the Child family in the library designed by Robert Adam at Osterley Park House was sold by Victor A G Child-Villiers, 7th Earl of Jersey, in 1885 (see sale cat). There seems also to have been a later collection, of which a typewritten cat was issued in 1926. The present collection, mainly sets of 18th and 19th cent reference books, novels, and odd volumes, is deposited on loan by St Paul's School and the Athenaeum Club to furnish the shelves available.

J F Bennett, 'The library of Osterley Park House, Middlesex', in Ealing School of Librarianship, *Ealing occasional papers in the history of libraries*, no 1, 1972, p9-11.

G Theatre Museum Library

The Theatre Museum was founded in 1974, but will not have premises of its own until 1985 when it will be relocated in Covent Garden, London WC2. The library, based partly on the existing collections of the V&A, but with numerous donations recently added, is stored mainly at the V&A, but partly at the University of London Library (qv, section E).

Card cat, author and classified, now being compiled for completion in advance of relocation.

Enthoven collection c20,000 v, given by Mrs Gabrielle Enthoven (1868–1950) in 1925, it contains over 6,000 prints and cuttings, and a large number of printed plays, including 150 Drury Lane prompt copies, and over 100,000 London playbills and programmes (especially strong for Garrick, Mrs Siddons, and Kean and Macready).

C Hail, *Victorian illustrated music sheets*, London, HMSO, 1981, based on Enthoven and Beard collections.

Vic-Wells Association Library c2,000 v, mainly on theatre.

Card cat.

H R Beard collection c2,000 v of books and libretti, mainly 19th cent.

Typescript list.

Anthony Hippisley Coxe collection c1,000 v on circus.

Printed cat in preparation.

London Archives of the Dance c1,000 v mainly on ballet, especially early 20th cent, including the collections formed by Cyril Beaumont (1891–1976), and Pigeon Crowle.

Card cat in preparation.

British Theatre Museum Association collection c1,000 v on theatre, mainly 19th and 20th cents.

Prompt scripts The collection of prompt copies in the Enthoven collection is supplemented by the collection of prompt scripts formed by William Poel (1852–1934); 19th cent prompt copies from the Drury Lane Theatre; Old Vic prompt scripts of c1940–60; and the deposited collection of the English Stage Company.

Victoria Institute or Philosophical Society

This Society sent its library for pulping during the 1939/45 war. The file of its own publications is on deposit at Dr Williams's Library (qv). Its mss are deposited at the Tyndale Library, Cambridge.

Victorian Society Library, 1 Priory Gardens, Bedford Park, London W4 1TT. Tel (01) 994 1019. Open Mon-Fri 9.30 am-5.30 pm to members; others should write to the Hon Secretary. Photocopier available.

The Victorian Society was founded in 1958 and has built up a library on the Victorian and Edwardian periods, with special emphasis on their architecture, art and crafts.

Pevsner Collection A complete set of the series *Buildings of England* edited by Sir Nikolaus Pevsner (*b*1910); together with a collection, donated by him, of the material used in its compilation.

Wallace Collection Library, Hertford House, Manchester Square, Marylebone, London W1M 6BM. Tel (01) 935 0687. The library is solely for staff use, but scholars wishing to see unique

material may apply in writing to the Director of the Wallace Collection.

The museum, in the rebuilt Hertford House, contains the collections bequeathed to the nation by the widow of Sir Richard Wallace, Bt (1818–90), inherited from the 3rd and 4th Marquises of Hertford; mainly European paintings, especially French 18th cent, and arms and armour both European and Oriental. The library reflects these interests, but does not include the book collection of Lord Hertford (which was sold to Bumpus).

D Mallett, *The greatest collector: Lord Hertford and the founding of the Wallace Collection*, London, Macmillan, 1979.

French art A collection of works on French painting, sculpture, ceramics, and furniture.

Arms and armour A collection of works on arms and armour, chiefly of the Middle Ages and Renaissance in Europe.

Sale catalogues A very large collection of 18th and 19th cent art sales catalogues, of which a number of unique copies are recorded by Lugt.

Waltham Forest Public Libraries

(The pre-1851 books in the Walthamstow and Leyton reference libraries, other than those in the local history collections, are being dispersed.)

A **Vestry House Museum of Local History**

Vestry Road, Walthamstow, London E17 9NH. Tel (01) 527 5544 Ext 391. Search Room open by prior arrangement with the Archivist, Mon-Fri 10 am-5.30 pm, Sat 5 pm. Museum open without notice.

The Museum was opened in 1931 by Walthamstow Borough Libraries, at the instigation of Walthamstow Antiquarian Society (founded 1915) which is still actively involved in its affairs. In 1965 when Walthamstow was amalgamated with Leyton and Chingford to form the London Borough of Waltham Forest, it became the repository for the archives of the Borough and its predecessors, with overall responsibility for printed local history material throughout the Borough. The printed collections of over 10,000 v are now being centralized at the Museum, with a small branch collection remaining in the reference library at Walthamstow.

Card cat (author and classified) includes the branch collections (it entirely supersedes the embryonic list by Z Moon, *Essex literature*, Leyton Public Library, 1900).

Guide to the archive and local history collections, 1982 (Survey of local resources in London: Waltham Forest).

Local historical material (London Borough of Waltham Forest, Resources Available, v 1), 1974.

S D Hanson, *Walthamstow bibliography*, 1971.

Walthamstow collection Built around the collections formed by the Walthamstow Antiquarian Society (given to the Borough in 1931) and that at Walthamstow Reference Library, where a small branch collection remains (High Street, London E17 7JN, open Mon, Tues, Thurs, Fri 9 am-8 pm, Sat 5 pm, closed Wed).

Some pre-1851 books are included, eg sermons preached in Walthamstow.

Leyton collection A collection relating to the area of the former Borough of Leyton, built up from the foundation of Leyton Public Library in 1893.

Wire collection Books, pamphlets, cuttings and a major photographic archive, relating mainly to Leyton and the immediate vicinity, formed by Alfred Philip Wire (1843–1914), Headmaster of Harrow Green School, donated to Leyton Public Library. It has been partly integrated into the general Leyton collection, but is being resegregated.

Typescript list (also included in Leyton collection cat).

Essex collection A collection on the former County of Essex, built up mainly by Leyton Public Library. *c*50 pre-1851 items on the general history and archaeology of the County; many pre-1851 items (four pre-1701) on individual localities outside Waltham Forest (predominantly those in the Western half of the county); some sermons, including a collection in 10 v of Congregationalist sermons preached for the Essex Home Missionary Society, 1827–44; 13 Poll books 1734–1865. A few pre-1851 directories, and some rare later ones; (*Berret's Walthamstow directory*, 1877; *Shillinglaw's Walthamstow directory*, 1882; Jones and Sons, *Directory of Woodford... Chingford...*, 1893).

Z Moon, *Essex literature...*, Leyton Public Library, 1900, lists the collection in embryo, but is entirely superseded by the card cat.

Sale catalogues Several hundred catalogues, early 18th cent onwards, of sales of estates, houses, or contents.

Separate section in classified cat; also under place names.

John Drinkwater (1882–1937), poet and dramatist, from the Leyton collection of local authors. *c*150 editions of works by him, together with mss, and books about his work, given at various times by his widow.

John Strype (1643–1737), antiquary, and Vicar of Leyton; from the Leyton local authors collection. 44 v of works by him, with extensive biographical collections.

Powell scrapbooks A collection assembled by the Powell family of Buckhurst Hill, bordering Epping Forest in Essex, in 6 v *c*1800–1911, relating both to the family and to the locality; consisting of news cuttings, letters, printed ephemera, and photographs.

Ambrose George Barker (see also under B, Socialist publications) A small portion of his collection of political and social pamphlets is held among his papers in the archive collection.

Museum collection c100 19th cent (with a few earlier) children's books acquired to complement a collection of toys.

B **William Morris Gallery and Brangwyn Gift**

Water House, Lloyd Park, Forest Road, Walthamstow, London E17 4PP. Tel (01) 527 5544 Ext 390. Library open Tues-Sat 10 am-1 pm, 2-5 pm by appointment with the Keeper after at least three days' notice; exhibition gallery open without notice same hours and first Sunday in each month.

General The gallery was opened in 1950 by Walthamstow Borough Council in Water House, the boyhood home of William Morris (1834–96), to collect and display the work of Morris and of the movements associated with him. The nucleus came from small collections assembled by Walthamstow Antiquarian Society and Walthamstow Reference Library. In 1936 Sir Frank Brangwyn (1867–1956), who in his youth had worked briefly for Morris, presented his collection of paintings and works of art by trust deed to the Borough, and these are now housed at the Gallery. Brangwyn's friend, Arthur Heygate Mackmurdo (1851–1942) bequeathed his collection of furniture, textiles, Century Guild designs, books and mss. The library collection includes part of the Morris collection of his biographer Prof John William Mackail (1859–1945) and his wife Margaret, daughter of Sir Edward Burne-Jones (1833–98), bought (Christie 3 Dec 1954, including Morris notebooks) or given earlier. Much was bought at the sale of Sir Sydney Cockerell (1867–1962) Morris's personal assistant and his literary executor. The Kelmscott collection was completed at the sale (Sotheby 20 July 1964) of the private press collections of Sir Ambrose Heal (1872–1959) and of Sir Rex Benson (1889–1968) (Sotheby 8 Oct 1964). Donors include Miss E M Lefroy of Sunningdale whose parents had obtained material from Morris and Co as customers in the 1890s, and Miss L Demain-Saunders, who gave a Kelmscott collection to Walthamstow Public Library which was transferred in 1951.

The library now contains c2,000 v of books and periodicals, in addition to pamphlets, cuttings, illustrations and mss (of which important collections are held). There is a general collection of Morris's literary works, c150 v including most modern editions, and c100 v on the biography and work of Morris himself. There are a few books from Morris's own library (dispersed by Richard Bennet of Riversdale, Manchester, partly through Sotheby 5 Dec 1898), including Gerard's herbal (1636).

The William Morris Gallery and Brangwyn Gift, Walthamstow: a memorial to William Morris, the nineteenth century artist, poet and craftsman, (1951) (summary cat).

Catalogue of the Morris collection, 1958; 2nd ed 1969 (brief cat of mss and books p44-61).

In fine print: William Morris as book designer, 1977 (extensive exhibition cat with detailed descriptions).

Card index (author and subject) of most of the library; recent acquisitions included in London Borough of Waltham Forest microfiche cat.

See also P Needham, ed *William Morris and the art of the book*, OUP, 1976.

Typographical experiments Specimens of Morris's early trials, including material for *The earthly paradise; Love is enough* and *Cupid and Psyche*, with proofs of illustrations by Sir Edward Burne-Jones (1833–98).

Joseph R Dunlap, *The book that never was*, New York, Oriole Press, 1971.

Kelmscott Press All 53 books printed at the press by Morris, with many trial pages, and designs by Morris and Burne-Jones; some of the leaflets and ephemera printed at the press. *The works of Geoffrey Chaucer* (1896) and a selection of other products of the press, with blocks and proofs, are displayed in the exhibition gallery.

Pre-raphaelites and the Arts and Crafts movement The collection includes periodicals of the movement: *The Germ* no 1-4 (1850); *Oxford and Cambridge Magazine* no 2, 4-6, 8 and 11 (Chiswick Press, 1856); *The Savoy* (1896); *The Yellow Book* (1894–7); Mackmurdo's organ *The Hobby Horse* (1884–93), lacking 1893, no 3. Many pamphlets (especially from Mackmurdo's collection); Mackmurdo's typescript history of the Arts and Crafts movement; material of and on Selwyn Image (1849–1930) Master of the Art Workers' Guild and Slade Prof at Oxford; books illustrated by Brangwyn. Later books on the movement, interpreted broadly to include, for instance, John Burley Waring (1823–75), the Swedenborgian architect and writer on industrial art, Sir Edwin Landseer Lutyens (1869–1944), and Gertrude Jekyll (1843–1932) the interior and garden designer.

Exhibition cats include three of the Arts and Crafts Exhibition Society; very comprehensive collection of later cats of Morris exhibitions. Hundreds of auction cats. These are complemented by a general reference collection of art books and periodicals.

Socialist publications Morris's mouthpiece *The Commonweal*, v 1-2 (1885–7), and several editions of *The people's charter*. Many pamphlets by Morris and others, including virtually all those issued by the Socialist League (not necessarily first editions); many are from the collection of Ambrose George Barker, historian of Walthamstow Working Men's Club, and include several of the forgeries by Harry Buxton Forman (1842–1917) (other works from Barker's collection are at the Vestry House Museum (A above), but the greater part of his library was dispersed after his death).

Wandsworth Public Libraries

A **Battersea Reference Library**

265 Lavender Hill, London SW11 1JB. Tel (01) 223 3082 Ext 3. Open (entrance in Altenburg Gardens) Mon-Sat 9 am-9 pm; Sun 2-6 pm. Special collections by appointment only. Photocopier.

General reference collection The collection from the former Metropolitan Borough of Battersea, opened 1890. A good all-round collection was built up 1890–1920, including many older books, most of which have been retained. It contains *c*30,000 books, of which *c*1,000 are pre-1851, *c*100 pre-1701. Strong in travel and topography, including one edition of almost every English county history from Lambarde's *Kent* (1576) onwards; histories of London; literature. Some fine natural history works, from Evelyn onwards. Works by local authors include Simon Patrick (1626–1707) Vicar of Battersea, afterwards Bishop of Chichester, and Henry Elsynge (1598–1654), Clerk of the Commons.

Card cat (author and classified) in two sequences (books catalogued before 1960, 1961–80); the latter includes many older books recatalogued; including Blake and Thomas.

Microfiche cat for later accessions will eventually incorporate the older acquisitions.

Blake collection *c*150 v by and on William Blake (1757–1827), formerly collected as a local author, but now only modestly being enlarged. Almost entirely modern editions, but includes a few scarce items.

Thomas collection 76 books and 10 periodicals by, and on, Edward (Philip) Thomas (1878–1917), the poet and critic, of Battersea. With ms letters (stored elsewhere; advance notice required for access).

Archives and local history collection Includes the Borough archives, and *c*2,000 books and pamphlets relating to the Borough. A few of these are pre-1851. Local authors' works in the two following collections.

Card cat (author and classified).

Swinburne collection Works of Algernon Charles Swinburne (1837–1909) the poet, first and other early editions, and biography (including an unpublished ms).

Henty collection (Formerly part of Early Children's Books collection, now attached to Archives and Local History collection). 233 copies of works by George Alfred Henty (1832–1902), the writer of adventure stories, in 278 v. The best Henty collection anywhere, lacking only one first edition, and for the most part in publishers' cloth in fine condition. Includes 79 bequeathed by his widow Elizabeth in 1927, and presentation copies.

Typescript cat.

P Newbolt, 'G A Henty', *Antiquarian Book Monthly Review* 4(3) (March 1975), p83-92; 4(11) (Nov 1977), p438-47.

R S Kennedy and B J Farmer, *Bibliography of G A Henty and Hentyana*, priv pr (1956) (annotated).

Architecture and building collection Formed under the Metropolitan Special Collections Scheme, and not now added to. *c*15,000 items, including *c*20 of the 18th cent and *c*100 of 1801–50.

Sheaf cat (author and classified) available on request; not in cat of General Reference Collection.

Mountaineering collection has been dispersed.

B **West Hill Reference Library**

36 West Hill, Wandsworth, London SW18 1RZ. Tel (01) 874 1144. Open Mon-Wed 9 am-8 pm; Fri-Sat 9 am-5 pm. (Special collections by appointment only.) Photocopier available.

General reference collection *c*30,000 items, including *c*250 pre-1851 (mostly post-1700), including a variety of subjects in the humanities, and horticulture and botany.

Card cat (author and classified) discontinued 1980; later accessions in microfiche union cat.

Early children's books (administered by the Borough Children's Librarian). The Henty collection (now at Battersea) prompted Wandsworth Public Library in 1959 to acquire from a bookseller and from a local resident, a nucleus of a historical collection of children's books, later enlarged by purchase and donation. Now *c*4,000 items dating from 1673–1940, including *c*40 pre-1801 and *c*700 of 1801–50, with *c*140 v of serials. Most books after *c*1850 are in publishers' bindings (but not necessarily in fine condition). Children's books are given a wide interpretation, to include chapbooks, instructional and school books (*c*500 v, especially early 19th cent science and history), in addition to all varieties of literature intended for juvenile recreation and amusement. Many late 19th cent annuals, with some magazines.

Card cat (author/title; indexes of illustrators and titles) to be published in a new greatly enlarged edition to supersede D Aubrey, *The Wandsworth collection of early children's books*, 1972 (author cat op).

Blackmore collection A collection formed by Trovey Blackmore, a 19th cent resident of Wandsworth Common, on the north African countries bordering the Mediterranean, and Gibralta, *c*60 editions from *c*1650 to *c*1840 (uncatalogued). Probably a residue of a larger collection, the remainder being dispersed to the appropriate subject libraries.

Europe special collection A collection originally begun under the Metropolitan Special Collections Scheme, and still actively being built up. It totals *c*40,000 books on history, geography, travel and archaeology of the countries of Europe (except the British Isles); and these subjects in general. There are *c*1,000 pre-1851 (*c*250 pre-1701, early 17th cent onwards); a number of 18th and 19th cent atlases; collections of voyages.

Warburg Institute, Woburn Square, London WC1H 0AB. Tel (01) 580 9663. Open Mon-Fri 10 am-6 pm; Sat (not Aug-Sept) 1 pm to staff of the University with identification; to others at the discretion of the Director following letter of introduction from tutor or other appropriate scholar. Photocopier; microfilm and fiche readers.

The private library of Aby Warburg (1866–1929), on the humanistic tradition in art history, was opened in 1905 in Hamburg to research students as the Kulturwissenschaftliche Bibliothek Warburg (with teaching facilities from 1920). It was moved to London 1933–4, housed by the University of London in 1936, and enlarged into a university school of art history, the Warburg Institute in 1944.

The Warburg Institute, 1978.

F Saxl, 'The history of Warburg's library 1886–1944', in E H Gombrich, *Aby Warburg: an intellectual biography*, London, Warburg Institute, 1970, p325-38; see also p348-52 (bibliography).

David Farrer, *The Warburgs*, London, Michael Joseph, 1975, p126-47.

G Bing, 'The Warburg Institute', *Library Association Record* 36 (1934), p262-6.

W F Ryan, 'The Slavonic and East European holdings of the Warburg Institute', *Solanus* 12 (1977), p17-19.

Warburg Institute Library c250,000 v of books and 1,000 periodicals on the history of European art, science, religion, literature, and culture, especially the Classical tradition. Very strong on Byzantine art, the humanists, the Reformation, Renaissance art, and Italian history. About a quarter of the stock is not in the British Library. It includes 11 incunabula, over 1,000 books of 16th-17th cent (chiefly foreign), and over 10,000 of 1701–1850.

Author cat on cards (unpublished).

Classified cat on cards, reproduced as *Catalog of the Warburg Institute Library*, 2nd ed Boston, G K Hall, 1967, 12 v; *First supplement*, 1971.

British Numismatic Society Library Housed at the Institute, and consists of c5,000 v, with the Society's archives. A collection on the coins and currency, medals and tokens of Great Britain, Ireland, and the English-speaking world, from the earliest times. It includes a very extensive collection, bound in over 500 v, of numismatic auction catalogues.

Wellcome Institute Library, Wellcome Institute for the History of Medicine, 183 Euston Road, London NW1 2BP. Tel (01) 387 4477. Open Mon-Fri 9.45 am-5.15 pm to approved readers following written application. Photocopying and microfilming; microfilm/fiche reader. Carrels.

The library grew out of the private collection of (Sir) Henry (Solomon) Wellcome FRS (1853–1936) which he assembled from c1890. In 1898 he placed it under a Librarian as an adjunct to a medical museum which he formed within his drug firm Burroughs Wellcome, now internationally known as The Wellcome Foundation Ltd. The Museum was opened to scholars in 1913, the library in 1949, as the Wellcome Historical Medical Library, after its 300,000 v had been reduced to 200,000 by judicious weeding. The Wellcome Trust, a charity set up by Sir Henry's will, took over the management in 1960. In 1964 they were amalgamated into the Wellcome Medical Museum and Library, which in 1968 became the Wellcome Institute of (from 1973 'for') the History of Medicine. In 1976 the Trustees deposited the Museum on loan at the Science Museum. The library, now c400,000 v has been built up, mainly by purchasing, into the world's most notable specialist library of the history of medicine. It combines one of the largest collections of the 15th-19th cent primary printed texts and major ms collections, with an extensive collection of reference books and modern secondary material on the history of medicine and related sciences.

The Wellcome Trust: its origin and functions, 1963, p20-1.

The Wellcome Historical Medical Library: a brief account of its history, scope and purpose, 1950, and (rev ed) 1954; later editions without the subtitle are severely abridged.

Helen Turner, *Henry Wellcome: the man, his collection and his legacy*, London, Heinemann, 1980, p52-72.

F N L Poynter, 'The Wellcome Historical Medical Library', *Book Collector* 4(4) (1955), p285-91.

——'The Wellcome Historical Medical Museum and Library and its services to research', *Verhandlungen des XX internationalen Kongresses für Geschichte des Medizin*, Berlin Aug 1966, Hildesheim, 1968, p411-18.

——'The Wellcome Historical Medical Library', *Indian Journal of the History of Medicine* 1(2) (1956), p1-5.

E Freeman, 'The Library of the Wellcome Institute', *Libraries Bulletin, Univ of London Library Resources Co-ordinating Committee*, no 8 (1976), p7-8.

M L Ettinghausen, *Rare books and royal collectors: memoirs of an antiquarian bookseller*, New York, Simon and Schuster, (1966), p64-7.

Wellcome Foundation Ltd, *Sir Henry Wellcome: a biographical memoir* (1953).

C M Wenyon, 'Henry Solomon Wellcome', *Obituary Notices of the Royal Society* 2(6) (1938), p229-38.

J E McAuley, 'Libraries—V [The Wellcome]', *Dental Magazine and oral topics*, Sept 1958, p154-5.

A **Primary texts in medicine and science**

The collection contains c60,000 pre-1851 editions of books and pamphlets in medicine and the biological sciences, to a much more limited extent the physical and social sciences, and a few other subjects. Wellcome aimed to have the first edition of every significant advance in medicine or science, and all subsequent early editions of every major medical book; the few significant medical gaps have been mostly filled since his death. Also an immense range of medical material of lesser importance, but including a remarkable proportion not known to be held elsewhere.

General author cat on cards (the printed period author cats below are more thoroughly revised).

Chronological cat to 1850 on cards.

Indexes of provenances for incunabula and mss only.

Accessions registers from 1897, not very informative before 1910, and thereafter do not usually itemize substantial collections.

Supplementary information in early reports of Museum and Library, and file of sale cats. (For subject access see section C below.)

Incunabula A collection of 614 complete incunabula and 22 fragments; 117 are not in the British Library, and many of these not be found elsewhere in the British Isles; 126 are pre-1481; *c*200 are medical or scientific, including in addition to the classics of Aristotle, Galen, Hippocrates etc, contemporary works such as the *Dicta* of Hugo Senensis (1485) and Bernard de Gordon *Lilium medicinae* (1480). The non-scientific cover a wide range of subjects, and were no doubt acquired by Wellcome as specimens of the science of printing. His several major purchases of incunabula included 65 from the sale of part of the library of William Morris (1834–96) from Kelmscott House (Sotheby 5 Dec 1898); the integral collection of 51 of Dr Joseph Frank Payne (1840–1910) the medical historian and Emeritus Librarian of the R C P Lond (Sotheby 12 July 1912); 115 out of 824 items in the sale of Kurt (August Paul) Wolff (1887–1963) the literary publisher from Munich (Frankfurt, J Baer, 1926); and 11 finely bound specimens from the Fürstliche Dietrichstein'sche Fideicomiss-Bibliothek from Schlos Nicolsburg (now Mikulov) (Lucerne, Gilhofer & Ranschburg, 21 Nov 1933) included annotated copies which had belonged to Hieronymus Münzer (1437–1508) town physician of Nuremberg and his friend Hartmann Schedel (1440–1514) author of the *Nuremberg Chronicle.*

F N L Poynter, *A catalogue of incunabula in the Wellcome Historical Medical Library*, 1954 (op) lists all but four by author, with indexes of names, subjects, associations, printers, places, chronological.

Paul Needham et al, *William Morris and the art of the book*, Oxford Univ Pr 1976.

Janus 15 (1910), p720 (obit of Payne).

1501–1640 A collection of 6,582 works, of which 572 are English (STC) and 6,010 foreign. It includes the classical Greek, Roman and Arabic medical writers in fine copies of the great Renaissance editions issued by the scholar-printers Aldus, Froben, the Estiennes, Junta, Oporinus etc. All the editions of the anatomies of Vesalius and his forerunners, the works of the pioneers of surgery, and, of course, Harvey.

Catalogue of printed books in the Wellcome Historical Medical Library, 1962, v 1: Books printed before 1641.

1641–1850 A collection of *c*41,000 works consisting of *c*1,700 Wing; *c*10,000 ESTC; *c*5,000 English 1801–50; *c*2,500 foreign 1641–1700; *c*14,000 1701–1800; *c*8,000 1801–50. Includes first and later editions of the major English scientists such as Bacon, Newton, Boyle and continentals such as Galileo, Kepler, and Descartes.

Catalogue of printed books. . ., 1966– , in progress: v 2: 1641–1850, A-E; v 3: F-L.

After 1850 (Stored elsewhere: 1 week's notice required) The collection of modern texts of *c*33,000 v, mostly of medicine and science.

Catalogued only in author card cat.

B Special forms of primary material

Mostly not included in general author cat.

Periodicals and other serials A collection of 2,670 titles, of which *c*900 are wholly or partly pre-1851, and *c*200 are current, including those of the history of medicine and science (under C below). Mostly medical.

Title cat on cards (incomplete).

'Periodicals in the Wellcome Foundation: a union list', 1961 (incomplete), copy with amendments at Enquiry Desk, together cover entire holdings.

Tracts and pamphlets Nearly all such collections are now in the general catalogue, and form part of the general collection, but a few special collections remain, eg *c*300 v of tracts on cancer, including some early material (part catalogued); *c*900 items on neurology, mostly 1850–1920 (typescript author list); *c*60 v of the works of French scientists *c*1840–1920 (assembled in France *c*1930 for Wellcome, with a typescript author cat; the larger works transferred to the general collection).

Printed ephemera A collection of thousands of uncatalogued items, mostly after 1700 (earlier items being transferred to general collection). Mostly medical, especially from England, France, Italy and Austria; advertisements, posters, proclamations, diplomas etc.

Documentary collections Extensive and important collections of mss, letters, and miscellaneous papers are held in the Department of Manuscripts, and in the Contemporary Medical Archives Centre: these occasionally include printed documents. Separate prints and portraits collections in the Department of Prints.

Catalogue of Western manuscripts, 1962–3, 2 v in 3, continued on cards.

Author cat of autograph letters on cards.

Engraved portraits. . . catalogue, 1973.

C Medical topics

All the former special subject collections of primary texts, except the Cyriax collection and a few tract collections have been dispersed among the general stock where there is no subject arrangement.

Old alphabetical subject index in Reading Room is very incomplete; it includes only those books (about half the pre-1851 medical books and a few others) which had been catalogued by the time of its closure in 1938, *c*75,000 entries.

For bibliographical aids, see section E below.

Pharmacology Major collections of herbals, materia medica, pharmacology, and pharmaceutical practice of all periods, Wellcome's dominant interest: in 1918–9 he bought the collection of Louis Debacq, a Parisian pharmacist, rich in early and rare material.

Partly in old subject index under Herbals, Pharmacopoeias, Pharmacy, etc.

J K Crellin, 'Pharmaceutical history and its sources in the Wellcome Collections', *Medical History* 11 (1967), p215-27; 13 (1969), p51-67; 14 (1970), p132-53; 16 (1972), p81-5; 17 (1973), p266-87.

Orthopaedics (Cyriax collection) kept separately. The residue of the collection of Edgar Ferdinand Cyriax (1874–1955), chiefly pamphlets, offprints, and mss, after some items had been selected by the Royal Society of Medicine (qv). Predominantly on orthopaedic manipulation, including works by several members of the Cyriax family.

Separate subject cat and also in general author card cat.

British Medical Journal, 1955, v 1, p435.

Other medical specialities Major special collections now incorporated in the general collection (with numbers of items in subject index, not complete) include: Plague and the Great Plague of 1665 (*c*1,000); Smallpox (*c*900); and Venereal Diseases (*c*500).

D Peripheral subjects

No longer kept as special collections.

Alchemy and occultism A superb collection, *c*2,000 items, mostly 17th and 18th cent, including over 100 editions of Paracelsus, derived mainly from the purchase, in 1931, of the library of Dr Ernst Darmstaedter (1877–1938) of Munich, author of *Arznei und Alchemie.*

Typescript lists of Darmstaedter collection, ms 2038-2042.

Printed author cat.

Old subject index under Alchemy; Medicine; Magic, etc.

Voyages and travels This formerly very large collection was partly dispersed in 1939, but still remains significant. Books retained contain descriptions of tropical diseases, indigenous materia medica, and ethnomedicine.

In author cat but only *c*20 in old subject index under Voyages and travels.

Tobacco A collection of 182 items 1621–1939, including 30 pre-1701, mostly English and French.

Exceptionally, included in *Subject catalogue*, 1980; also in author card cat.

Cookery Several hundred cookery books 16th-19th cent.

In author cat but no subject approach (except for *c*100 in old subject index).

Ethnography Concentrates on American Indians (Wellcome's special interest), but extends into all sorts of highways and byways of anthropology and archaeology.

E Secondary collections

Major collections on the history and bibliography of medicine and science, partly compensate for the lack of a comprehensive subject catalogue of the primary texts.

Wellcome Institute for the History of Medicine, *Subject catalogue of the history of medicine and related sciences*, Munich, Kraus, 1980, reproducing card cat, in three sections: topographical (classified by countries with alphabetical subdivisions) 4 v; biographical, 5 v; and subject (topics alphabetically) 9 v. This includes Wellcome holdings of material published 1954–77 (and historical articles in many medical periodicals not held); also most earlier historical monographs and earlier articles in certain medical history periodicals held by Wellcome.

Quarterly continuation *Current work in the history of medicine*, cumulated on cards.

Reference collection A very extensive classified collection, mostly on open access, of bibliographies, biographies, encyclopaedias, and histories of medicine and the biological sciences, of all periods.

In subject and author cat.

Periodicals room All the specialist periodicals of the history of medicine, other science history journals, and a few major medical journals of the 19th cent, on open access.

In card cat of periodicals (see B).

Indexed in *Subject catalogue.*

Reprints and pamphlets A collection of *c*100,000 offprints and reprints of articles, pamphlets and similar material, mostly on topics in the history of medicine.

Filed by author, biographer, or institution.

In *Subject catalogue*, but most not in author cat.

F Non-European Collections

Held in separate departments, each containing mss with primary and secondary printed sources.

All except Guerra included in printed author cat.

North America Purported to be the best collection of early medical Americana outside the US, it includes 550 US imprints 1720–1820, 21 per cent of R B Austin's total of 2,106 in *Early American medical imprints*, and some others of medical interest. Arranged chronologically.

Cat of printed books in preparation. (Mss see Latin America).

Robin Price, 'Wellcome Institute for the History of Medicine: American collections', *American Studies Library Group Newsletter* no 4 (1979), p13.

Latin America A collection of *c*6,000 printed books; primary texts arranged by place of printing, then chronologically. Wellcome's collection was particularly strong in books on American Indians. In 1927 he bought the library of Dr Nicolás León (1859–1929) which strengthened the collection of Mexican imprints, including the first American medical periodical *Mercurio volante* 1772–3, and mss. In 1962 was added the much larger collection of Dr Francisco Guerra (*b*1916), the Spanish bibliophile and historian of medicine, including 360 items printed in New Spain and Mexico 1557–1833, and 71 from other Latin American colonies; a good collection of works on materia medica and pharmacopoeias; theses of the University of

Mexico 1598–1820 (xerox copies) and 1860–1950; and 65 Mexican and other periodicals, including some rare early official and literary journals.

An annotated catalogue of Americana in the Library of the Wellcome Institute for the History of Medicine: books and printed documents 1557–1821 from Latin America and the Caribbean Islands; and manuscripts from the Americas 1575–1927, in the press; arranged by place and date, with author and subject indexes.

Robin Price, 'Latin American materials in the Wellcome Institute', *Bull of the Soc for Latin American Studies*, no 23 (1975), p17-22.

Oriental collections These amount to *c*3,000 printed books and over 10,000 mss arranged in nearly 40 language collections. Most were collected by Dr Paira Mall on a series of expeditions 1910–26 to remote places in the East. In 1972 the collection of Gustave Alexandre Liétard (1833–1904) French physician and orientalist, on the history of oriental (chiefly Indian) medicine, was acquired (mostly mss). Block-printed books in Chinese (525 including *c*300 medical, especially on acupuncture and moxibustion), Japanese (140) and Tibetan (46). Books printed in Arabic (*c*200), Hebrew (*c*60 including incunabula), Sanskrit (hundreds), Hindi (*c*150), and Urdu (*c*120), and Persian (*c*120); smaller printed books collections include Armenian, Turkish, Tamil, Panjabi, Malayalam, and Telugu.

Cats of mss being published by languages.

N Allan, 'The oriental collections in the Wellcome Institute', *Journ of the Roy Asiatic Soc* (1981), no 1, p10-25.

——'The Wellcome Institute and its Library, with special reference to South East Asia', *South East Asia Library Group Newsletter* (Oct 1980), no 22, p1-4.

——'Gustave Alexandre Liétard', *Medical History* 25 (1981), p85-9.

G Deposited libraries

Libraries deposited in the Wellcome Institute Library by other institutions may normally be used by its readers without additional formality. The Library of the Osler Club has been removed to the Royal College of Physicians (qv). The Library of the Society for the Study of Addiction is now deposited, but contains mainly 20th cent works.

Medical Society of London The Society was founded in 1773 by John Coakley Lettsom (1744–1815) FRS who presented a number of books to its Library in the early years; his own collection was mostly sold (Sotheby 26 March 1811 and 3 April 1816), some books being acquired by the Society and others by the British Museum. In 1800–2 the library of the President, James Sims (1741–1820), *c*5,800 v, much of which he had acquired from the sale of Antony Askew MD (1722–74) and classicist (Sotheby Feb-March 1775), was bought. Joseph Lister, Baron Lister FRS (1827–1912) bequeathed the choicest portion, *c*2,500 v of his medical library, including at least 150 pre-1800 (Sotheran sold the remainder by catalogue). The library had eventually reached 30,000 v when in 1966–71 it was dispersed. *c*2,400 v, consisting of most of the rare medical books not already held by the Wellcome Institute, and all the remaining mss were deposited there. Duplicates, some foreign medical books, and non-medical material were dispersed to members, or through the book trade; *c*3,500 items intended for a Sotheby sale, were pre-empted by Dr Jason A Hannah, and have since been given to the University of Toronto. A collection of *c*1,000 books, consisting mainly of association copies, remains at the Society's headquarters (11 Chandos Street, Cavendish Square, London W1M 0EB); enquiries about these books should preferably be made through the Wellcome Institute.

Complete card cat (authors) in preparation.

Old card cat of tracts.

Printed author cats: 1970 (no copy extant?)

A catalogue of books contained in the Library of the Medical Society of London, 1803 (in British Library); (new ed) 1829 (interleaved copy deposited, enlarged and corrected to 1929); supplemented by Appendix 1846 and (new ed) 1856.

Annual reports on library 1880–1940 in *Proceedings.*

Thomas Hunt, *The Medical Society of London 1773–1973*, London, Heinemann, 1972, p89-104.

F Hickey, 'The Library of the Medical Society of London 1773–1969' (thesis, Aberystwyth College of Librarianship Wales, 1969).

G Bethell, 'An account of the Library', *Trans Med Soc of London* 37 (for 1913–4) (1915), p362-72.

Sir D'Arcy Power, *British medical societies*, London, 1939, p28-36.

Warren Dawson, *Manuscripta medica... catalogue of the manuscripts in the Library...*, 1932.

James J Abraham, *Lettsom*, London, 1933, p128-30, 303-4, 319-20, 392-4.

O H and S D Wagensteen, 'Lister, his books...', *Bull His Med* 48 (1974), p100-28.

Royal Society of Medicine A portion of this Library's general collection (qv) deposited here for reasons of space, mostly 18th and 19th cent.

Separate author cat on cards.

Hunterian Society of London Hunter-Baillie mss deposited in Wellcome Institute Library. Printed Books and Museum deposited in Wellcome Museum of the History of Medicine, Science Museum, Exhibition Road, South Kensington, London SW7 2DD. Tel (01) 589 6371, with whom an appointment must be made for access.

The Society was founded in 1819 as a general medical society meeting in the City of London, where it still meets though it no longer has premises. It is named after John Hunter (1728–93) the celebrated surgeon. It had a library formed soon after the foundation, which reached *c*3,000 v in the early 20th cent. In 1866 it was deposited at the London Institution, which closed in 1912. In 1914 the collection was given to the University of Cambridge, except for a handful of books of John and William Hunter and their nephew. This collection has been built up since 1929, with the help of gifts of books and mss from members of the family, into a museum of Hunteriana—books, mss and objects. It now has *c*300 v of printed books (*c*100 of the 18th cent, *c*100, 1801–5, *c*100 more recent), by and about John Hunter, his wife, Anne, born Home (1742–1841) the poetess, his brother William (1718–83) the anatomist, his nephew Matthew Baillie (1761–1823) the morbid anatomist, his niece Joanna Baillie (1762–1851) the dramatist, and other members of the family. The mss consist of an extensive collection of Hunter family correspondence (including the collection known as the Hunter-Baillie mss) and the Society's archives. (John Hunter's medical mss were destroyed by his executor Everard Home.)

'Catalogue of the manuscripts, books, furniture, pictures and engravings, and other items belonging to the Hunterian Society of London', typescript [by Jessie Dobson, 1975], p127-74.

Author cat of printed books; Hunter family preceding the main alphabetical sequence.

R Fowler, *A catalogue of the Library of the Hunterian Society of London*, 1869.

Sir D'Arcy Power, *British medical societies*, London, 1939, p78-90.

E F G Stewart, 'The Hunterian Society', *Practitioner* 202 (1969), p572-80.

H I Fotherby, *Scientific associations. . .with a history of the Hunterian Society*, London, 1869.

W R LeFanu, *John Hunter: a list of his books*, London, 1946, with locations.

Trans Hunterian Soc includes annual report of Curators; see also 31 (1972–3), p111-5 and 32 (1973–4), p229-31.

John Wesley's House and Museum, 47 City Road, London EC1Y 1AU. Tel (01) 253 2262. Open by prior arrangement only to serious students.

The main collection of the Methodist Church archives and printed books has been deposited at the John Rylands University Library, Manchester. John Wesley's personal library of *c*500 18th cent v and 50 pamphlets remains in its original bookcase with his letters.

West London Institute of Higher Education, Borough Road, Isleworth, Middlesex TW7 5DU. Tel (01) 568 8741. Archives open Mon-Fri 9 am-5 pm by appointment after written application to the Chief Librarian or the Archivist (Library collections longer hours).

This site of the Institute was formerly the Borough Road Training College, an undenominational men's college of the British and Foreign School Society. The library includes a special collection of *c*3,000 v on linguistics.

Archive Centre. British and Foreign School Society archives The records, mainly ms, include a complete set of annual reports and other printed material of the British and Foreign School Society, from its foundation in 1808, by Joseph Lancaster (1778–1838) and others, to promote Nonconformist systems of education. Until 1814 it was named the Royal Lancastrian Institution for the Education of the Poor.

H Bryan Binns, *A century of education*, 1908.

Sources in British political history 1900–1951, 1975, v 1, p22.

West London Institute of Higher Education, Maria Grey Site Library, 300 St Margaret's Road, Twickenham, Middlesex TW1 1PT. Tel (01) 891 0121 Ext 215. Open to all Mon-Fri 9 am-5 pm (vacation), 9 pm (term); Sat (term only 9 am-noon). Photocopying facilities; microform reader and camera; typewriter room.

The Maria Grey Training College for Women Teachers, founded in 1878, now forms part of the West London Institute in affiliation with the University of London Institute of Education.

Murray Library of early children's books and periodicals, *c*800 v donated by Miss Elsie Riach Murray (1861–1932), Vice-Principal of the College 1899–1932. *c*150 v are pre-1851.

Card cat.

Westfield College, Caroline Skeel Library, Kidderpore Avenue, Hampstead, London NW3 7ST. Tel (01) 435 7141. Open Mon-Fri 9 am-5 pm (9 pm in term), Sat (term only) 9 am-5 pm to members of the University of London with identification, and to others on written application in advance.

The College was founded in 1882 by a wealthy religious philanthropist Miss Dudin-Brown and her friend Miss Constance Louisa Maynard (1849–1935) its first Mistress, as a college for women, with a vigorous evangelical Anglican background, preparing for the examinations of the University of London. Since 1902 it has been a teaching college of the University, principally in the humanities, and since 1964 it has been open to men. In 1971 the library was moved to a new building named after Caroline Skeel, Professor of History at the College. Purchasing has been mainly limited to the requirements of the teaching faculties, but the library has benefited greatly from donations (not kept as separate collections), notably 5,000 v of English literature, history and politics from the psychologist George Lichtheim (1912–73), mostly modern; classical literature and history from George Dyson, donated by his son Peter Dyson *c*1976; *c*200 v from Eleanor Mary Carus-Wilson (1897–1977), Professor of Economic History at the London School of Economics, chiefly on medieval English. In 1964 the Spanish collection at Bedford College was transferred here.

Author and classified card cats.

Typescript lists of major donations.

Westfield College, University of London, 1882–1932, London, 1932, op.

Catherine B Firth, *Constance Louisa Maynard*, London, Allen & Unwin, 1949.

Centenary history in preparation.

Rare books collection Contains 2,312 v, of which *c*1,800 are pre-1851 (nearly all pre-1851 having been removed from the general collection), including 15 STC and 44 Wing. Chiefly English, French, Spanish and German literary texts from 17th cent; primary texts in English history, 18th and 19th cent; *c*50 20th cent English literary first editions; and some natural history (chiefly botany).

Separate author and classified card cats (also in general cats).

John Lane archive (Not accessible without having first obtained written permission from the Archivist, Dept of English, Westfield College.) Deposited by the publishing firm John Lane, the Bodley Head. Mostly mss, but includes some proof copies.

Westminster Abbey Chapter Library, East Cloister, London SW1P 3PA. Tel (01) 222 5152 Ext 28. Open Mon-Fri 10 am-1 pm, 2-4.45 pm to scholars and members of the public with specific enquiries, on written application to the Librarian; enter via Dean's Yard and South Cloister. Photocopying. Postal information service. Annual exhibition (1 month).

Though the Benedictine monastic community dates from 1065, the pre-Reformation library was destroyed. At the Reformation the Abbey became an Anglican collegiate church, and its library was re-established in 1574 by Dean Gabriel Goodman (1529–1601). The library was built up from donations and from a customary sum of £10 exacted from each prebendary when he assumed office. It was reconstituted as a general public library by Dean Williams in 1625 (see below) but had ceased to consider itself as such when Richard Widmore, the Librarian in 1757, became one of the first assistant keepers at the British Museum. It was enriched in 1775 by the Pearce bequest, but no later additions of substance have been made, except to the collection on the Abbey. The library contains both printed books and mss, with an important collection of ms and printed music on the 15th and 16th cent. The Muniment room houses further miscellaneous mss in addition to the archives. The printed books form a general collection of the period to 1775. Individual collections, except the Camden tracts, and the Abbey collection, are not kept separate. *c*14,000 v, *c*1,000 STC items, perhaps *c*1,800 Wing, 60 incunabula, including a Latterburius (Oxford 1482) on vellum and a Pynson *Dives and pauper* (1493). Numerous Bibles, including the polyglots of 1514-17 (in Academia Complutensi), 1572 (Antwerp, Plantin), and 1657 (ed B Walton); many in the ancient languages; and most of the significant English editions. The first complete Welsh Bible (with the rare errata leaf) presented according to an inscription on 28 July 1588 by its translator William Morgan (*c*1545–1604) later Bishop of St Asaph, who enjoyed the hospitality of the deanery during its preparation. A wide variety of liturgies. Fathers of the Church. Theological treatises and sermons, mainly by Anglican divines and the more eminent continental Protestant and Catholic theologians. Ecclesiastical history. English history and topography; law; antiquities; heraldry. English and foreign philology, including Johnson's Plan of his *Dictionary* uncut and unopened, 1751. Classical and modern literature. A scattering of other subjects such as medicine and science.

Card cat of general library. Ms author cats 1726, 1798. Register of Benefactors 1623–1744.

J Armitage Robinson & M R James, *The manuscripts of Westminster Abbey* [with a history of the Library]. Cambridge, 1909.

B Botfield, *Notes on the cathedral libraries*, 1849, p430-64.

L E Tanner, *The Library and Muniment Room* 2nd ed, 1935. (Westminster papers no 1).

H M Rabinowicz, *Treasures of Judaica*, New York, Yoseloff, 1971, p101-5.

L E Tanner, *Recollections of a Westminster antiquary*, London, Baker, 1969, p106-19.

R A Rye, *Students' guide*, 1927, p426-31.

William Latymer (*c*1515–83), Dean of Peterborough and Prebendary of Westminster, Chaplain to Queen Elizabeth, bequeathed the greater part of his library.

William Wheatley, *The history of Edward Latymer and his foundations*, rev ed, London, Latymer Upper School, 1953, p25-7.

John Williams (1582–1650), Dean 1620–42, Bishop of Lincoln and subsequently Archbishop of York, who completely reorganized the Chapter Library to turn it into a general collection with public access, purchased the gentleman's library formed by a Mr Baker of Highgate, and donated it, together with other books, including part of the collection that William Camden (1551–1623) the antiquary, had bequeathed to Sir Robert Cotton. The Camden pamphlets, over 400 items in 60 v, now form a separate collection.

John Hacket, *Scrinia reserata* In the Savoy, 1693, Pt 1, p7-8, 46-7.

Printed cat of Camden pamphlets in preparation.

Nicholas Onley (*c*1640–1724) DD, Prebendary of Westminster, bequeathed his library of *c*630 books and pamphlets, mainly English and foreign theology, classical literature, and a few of English literature. Also his own ms sermons in 3 v.

Michael Evans (1651?–1732), Prebendary of Westminster, bequeathed his library of *c*400 books and pamphlets (the latter including *c*30 v of sermons and controversial theology, also some choice items of English literature).

Zachary Pearce (1690–1774), Bishop of Rochester, editor of Cicero and Milton, bequeathed his printed books, *c*6,000, about half of which are foreign. They include Greek, Latin, Italian, French, and English literature, with a taste for plays: there is a presentation copy from Pope, and first editions of Milton. Moral philosophy, especially classical and continental. Works of Anglican divines, some by RCs, and by dissenters such as Toland, and some continental reformers. Dictionaries and philology. Practical books, such as Y-worth *Practical distilling*, Manwayring *Seaman's dictionary*, and some medical handbooks.

Pearce's ms author cat 1758 with later additions and deletions.

Westminster Abbey collection Books about the Abbey and the associated Westminster School, and biographies of clergy connected with the Abbey. Over 1,000 v, beginning with Camden *Reges* (1600) and continuing to the present. It includes a collection of 4,000 prints donated by Percy Edward Langley, with its own card index.

Bindings The more notable bindings are segregated in a special collection. The collections contain over 300 early blind-tooled bindings. A collection of *c*80 English decorated bindings 1660–1920 formed by Mr K H Oldaker is on deposit.

Ms list of blind-tooled bindings by J B Oldham: see also his *Blind panels*, 1958 and *English blind-stamped bindings*, 1952.

Burlington Fine Arts Club, *Exhibition of bookbindings*, 1891.

W J H Weale, *Bookbindings and rubbings... in the National Art Library*, 1894, pt 2.

British bookbindings presented by Kenneth H Oldaker to the Chapter Library, Westminster Abbey, London, 1982.

Westminster City Libraries

A **Central Reference Library**

St Martin's Street, London WC2H 7HP. Tel (01) 930 3274. Telex 263305. Open Mon-Fri 10 am-7 pm; Sat 5 pm. Photocopying; microfilm reader.

General Reference Collection This totals *c*20,000 v (following recent dispersal of some older material) including 1,234 pre-1851 and other rare works, mostly in English literature and history, built up by purchase and donation since 1856. Arthur Penrhyn Stanley (1815–81), Dean of Westminster, bequeathed his library of *c*3,200 books. The collection includes four items of 16th cent; 57 of 17th, and 226 of 18th cent.

Card cat (dictionary) with entries under dates, names of private presses, and associations.

Union list of periodicals (in Westminster Libraries), 1970 (including some now dispersed).

Fine Arts Library Until 1970 this library formed part of the general reference collection, which was always strong in art, and purchases were made in this field, and became responsible for this subject in 1950 under the Metropolitan Special Collections Scheme. *c*25,000 v, of which *c*2,000 are pre-1851, or otherwise rare.

Dictionary card cat.

Preston Blake Library Contains most of the collection of Kerrison Preston (1884–1974) and Merstham donated in 1967. It totals 1,100 items, including 126 rare works by or on William Blake (1757–1827) the poet and painter, consisting of books, pamphlets, articles, and newspaper cuttings; ms letters of Blake; his *Poetical sketches* 1783 with his own ms alterations; *Book of Job* 1826; proof copy of *Dante* 1827; all Trianon Press facsimiles. Some of the rare items had belonged to the artist Walford Graham Robertson (1866–1948).

Card cat.

William Blake: catalogue of the Preston Blake Library..., 1969; *Cumulative supplement*, 1976.

Kerrison Preston, *William Blake, 1757–1827: notes for a catalogue of the Blake Library at the Georgian House Merstham*, Cambridge, 1960; typescript supplement 1965.

Sir G L Keynes and E Wolf, *William Blake's illuminated books: a census*, New York, 1953.

B **Central Music Library**

160 Buckingham Palace Road, London SW1W 9UD. Tel (01) 730 8921. Open Mon-Fri 9.30 am-7 pm; Sat 5 pm. Photocopying.

The collection was originally formed by Mrs Christie Moor in 1946, and built up by the purchase, donation and bequest of a number of fine private collections. Deposited in 1947, it is now integrated with the Public Library's own large music collection. *c*90,000 items altogether, in addition to a large collection of printed music scores, there are 26 18th cent English, French, German and Italian books about music, and *c*200 mss letters of musicians.

Card cat (author and classified) of books on music; also available in microform regularly updated.

C **Archives and Local History Department (Westminster)**

Victoria Library, 160 Buckingham Palace Road, London SW1W 9UD. Tel (01) 730 0446 Ext 23. Open Mon-Fri 9.30 am-7 pm; Sat 5 pm.

Contains archives and printed material relating to the former Metropolitan Borough of Westminster (City of Westminster) and its constituent parishes, Westminster as a whole, and a general printed collection on London. Directories from 1740 (26 to 1800, 72 of 1801–50).

Cuttings from newspapers 1668–1836 relating to the parish of St Martin-in-the-Fields.

Card cat and numerous special indexes.

Theatres Collection Over 20,000 programmes; playbills of West End theatres from *c*1800, especially Covent Garden and Drury Lane. 5 v of playbills of the Theatre Royal, Glasgow.

Card index to programmes.

D **Archives and Local History Department (Marylebone and Paddington)**

Marylebone Road, London NW1 5PS. Tel (01) 828 8070 Ext 4030. Telex 263305.

The collections cover the areas of the former Metropolitan boroughs of St Marylebone and Paddington, but include some material of wider interest. *c*6,000 books and pamphlets, including *c*350 pre-1851; *c*1,000 theatrical and musical ephemera, including *c*400 pre-1851. Also illustrations, maps, etc.

The local history and archive collection, Marylebone Library (Current leaflet).

Guide to London's local history resources: 1, City of Westminster.

Ashbridge collection A bequest by Arthur Ashbridge (1858–1943) of Pinner, who was District Surveyor of St Marylebone 1884–1918, to St Marylebone Public Library, on condition that it should be kept separate and intact, and without addition. It contains *c*3,000 items, including *c*600 pre-1851 books, pamphlets and ephemera 17th-20th cent, in addition to maps and prints. Most relate to Marylebone, but some are of much wider interest. The pre-1851 material includes atlases of the environs of London, all the standard histories of the parish (and some of London), some extra-illustrated, descriptions of places of entertainment, including Regent's Park, Madame Tussaud's waxworks, Lord's (with items on cricket generally); and executions at Tyburn, from 1660 onwards, including 25 v of criminal biography in general; and the Cato Street conspiracy, 1820; ephemera, including playbills; and cuttings from newspapers, periodicals and books.

Ann Cox-Johnson, *Handlist to the Ashbridge collection on the history and topography of St Marylebone*, 1959 (classified, with dictionary index). Many items omitted are included in annotated copy in the Library.

Marylebone collection This represents the local history collection from the library of the former borough, now closed, built up from the opening of the library in 1923. It includes a collection on Marylebone Gardens 1718–80 with cuttings, programmes, songs etc performed there, and a collection from the foundation in 1832 (as the Royal Pavilion West) of the Theatre Royal, Marylebone.

Card cat (author and classified) with supplementary indexes.

Paddington collection This represents the local history collection from the library of the former borough, now closed, built up from the opening of the library in 1920. It includes *c*80 v of gardening books (some with coloured plates) by John Claudius Loudon (1783–1843) and his wife Jane Loudon (1807–58).

Card cat (dictionary) with supplementary indexes.

London and Westminster collections A collection containing works on London or Westminster generally, including pre-1851 topographical books and directories; and works on Marylebone and Paddington acquired after the closure of the Marylebone and Paddington collections. *c*80 v of local Acts and Bills.

Card cat (author and classified) with supplementary indexes.

Sherlock Holmes collection This was begun when a Sherlock Holmes exhibition was held by the library in 1951; it has been built up into the largest British collection on Sir Arthur Conan Doyle (1859–1930) and the character he created. It contains 485 books, 500 pamphlets, 132 periodicals and 50 miscellaneous items; the Holmes stories by Conan Doyle in many languages, both Western and oriental; Holmes stories by imitators, and others works by Conan Doyle. Works in Sherlockian scholarship, British and foreign, including recondite magazines such as *The Baker Street Cab Lantern*, published by the Solitary Cyclists of Sweden.

Card cat, to be published *c*1983.

Westminster Medical School Library, 17 Horseferry Road, London SW1P 2AR. Tel (01) 828 9811 Ext 2318. Open Mon-Fri 9 am-5 pm to any properly accredited enquirer on application to the Librarian. Photocopying.

Westminster Hospital was opened in 1719, and had a library by 1832. Westminster Medical School was founded as a private school by George James Guthrie (1785–1856) with a library; it was annexed to the Hospital in 1849, and is now an undergraduate school of the University of London. The present library, which dates from the rebuilding of 1938, incorporates both collections and totals *c*14,000 v.

Card cat. The library archives were destroyed 1920–39.

R M Nicholas, 'The development of medical libraries within the University of London' (MA Librarianship thesis, Univ of London, 1976), p83-5.

John Langdon-Davies, *Westminster Hospital*, London, John Murray, 1952.

J G Humble and P Hansell, *Westminster Hospital*, London, Pitman Medical, 1966.

Walter G Spencer, *Westminster Hospital*, London, 1924.

General Historical collection This collection includes the classics of medicine, 549 v including 53 pre-1851 titles from 1656 onwards; also 17 v engravings.

M Hutt, 'History of medicine in the Library', *Broad Way: Westminster Hospital Gazette*, March 1963, p42-4.

Westminster collection This collection contains 89 works by Westminster men, including 15 pre-1851 titles. It includes works of William Cheselden (1688–1752), including *Osteographia* 1733 and *Anatomy* 1750. Guthrie's works are virtually complete. Also mss.

Westminster School Library, 17 Dean's Yard, Westminster Abbey, London SW1P 3PB. Tel (01) 222 6904. Open at the Headmaster's discretion to those who apply in writing in advance.

A school was attached to the Benedictine Abbey in the 14th cent, and it was refounded by Henry VIII, and again by Queen Elizabeth in 1560 when the Abbey became a Collegiate Church. It was governed by the Dean, with the Dean of Christ Church Oxford and the Master of Trinity Cambridge, who are *ex officio* governors of the present public school. The Library (which was in existence in 1584) was greatly enriched by the famous Headmaster, Richard Busby (1606–95) whose collection of 451 books (of which *c*350 remain) was added to it, and whose name was attached to the whole library. In the early 19th cent it fell into neglect. In 1883 the Scott Library, named after Charles Brodrick Scott (1824–94) DD, Headmaster, was opened, and the Busby Library was rehoused in a part of it, together with the 16th and 17th cent library furniture. Many of the less important older books were sold in 1888. Donations have included 50 books in oriental languages from the College of Fort William, Calcutta, in the 19th cent; *c*200 v of the Delphin Classics series given by a Mr McLeay in 1892; and the bequest by G A Henty (1832–92) of editions of all his works. The Busby Library includes books on the traditional school subjects, in which editions of the classics are pre-eminent, and contains over 2,000 v, including 7 incunabula and 23 post-incunabula. There is a collection of the Latin plays acted at Christmas in accordance with a custom dating back to the foundation, and a collection of foreign translations of the Bible.

Westminster School Library, no 1-2 (1933).

John Sargeaunt, *Annals of Westminster School*, 1898.

L E Tanner, *Westminster School*, 2nd ed, 1951.

John D Carleton, *Westminster School*, 2nd ed, London, Hart-Davis, 1965.

Benefactions are sometimes recorded in *The Elizabethan*, the school magazine.

Wiener Library, 4 Devonshire Street, Marylebone, London W1N 2BH. Tel (01) 636 7247. Open Mon-Fri 9 am-5.30 pm to accredited researchers with a letter of introduction, who may become members on payment of a moderate fee. Photocopiers and microform reader/printers.

The library was established in 1933 in Amsterdam by Dr Alfred Wiener (1885–1964) a German-Jewish refugee in association with the Jewish Central Information Office which he set up there. In 1939 it moved to London and became an integral part of the Ministry of Information. After the war it was re-established as an educational charity called officially the Institute of Contemporary History and Wiener Library, but commonly known as the Wiener Library. By 1980 it held over 80,000 books and pamphlets, in addition to large quantities of other material, and was the world's foremost library on Nazi persecution. The greater part (comprising almost all material not prevented by terms of gift from leaving London) was then transferred to the University of Tel Aviv. At the same time almost all the transferred material which was not subject to copyright restrictions, was microfilmed for use in the library in London; this included nearly all the rare pamphlets and ephemera, but not the books and more recent material. The library is still actively being enlarged by the acquisition of both rare and current material.

P Kluke, 'Die Wiener Library und die Zeitgeschichte', in *On the track of tyranny: essays presented by the Wiener Library to Leonard G Montefiore...*, London, 1960, p157-79.

S Schwartz Abraham, *Views of Jewish history: a comparative study of libraries focusing on the European Jewish community* (Diss, Univ of Chicago, 1975).

A Wiener, 'L'histoire et les buts du Jewish Central Information Office (Wiener Library)', in *Les juifs en Europe (1939–1945)*, Paris, Editions du Centre, 1949, p125-8.

Jewish Central Information Office, *The Wiener Library: its history and activities 1934–1945*, London, 1945.

P Flather, 'Catalogue of hate', *Times Higher Education Supplement*, 5 March 1982, p8.

Wiener Library Bulletin 1946–

Journal of Contemporary History 1966– .

General The library now contains *c*30,000 books and pamphlets (partly on microfilm), and *c*1,600 runs of periodicals on persecution, especially of the Jews in 20th cent Europe; with extensive ms archives of Jewish refugee organizations and eye witness reports of atrocities. The printed material includes the whole history of 20th cent Germany, and of Palestine and Israel; of persecution and totalitarianism (both of the left and the right) and its political background, and of religious minorities, with the main emphasis on Europe. There is a large collection of Nazi and other anti-semitic propaganda as well as anti-fascist material.

Card cat (author and classified) of books and pamphlets; separate card cat of periodicals.

Wiener Library catalogue series, 2. From Weimar to Hitler: Germany 1918–33, 2nd ed 1964; 3. German Jewry: its history, life and culture, 1958; 4. After Hitler: Germany, 1945–63, 1963; 5. Prejudice: racist, religious, nationalist, 1971; 6. German Jewry, Pt 2, 1978; 7. Persecution and resistance under the Nazis, 1978 (reissue of no 1, same title, 2nd ed with supplement, 1960 including the illegal publications collection).

Illegal publications A special collection of several hundred pamphlets and periodicals in German containing anti-Nazi and other Jewish propaganda printed in Switzerland and France 1939–45, with false German imprints and smuggled into Germany for distribution there.

Nazi school books A collection of Nazi primary school books of the 1930s with anti-semitic texts and illustrations.

Press cuttings collection Over two million cuttings from 1933 onwards, on persecution worldwide, with the emphasis on Europe, classified by subject. To 1950 they are on microfilm.

Williams and Glyn's Bank Head Office, Archives and Museum, 67 Lombard Street, London EC3P 3DL. Tel (01) 628 5400. Open Mon-Fri 9 am-5 pm on written application to the Librarian. Photocopying facilities.

The bank was formed in 1970 by the merger of Glyn Mills & Co, the National Bank, and Williams Deacon's Bank, incorporating absorbed banks founded in the 17th cent; it is now a subsidiary of the Royal Bank of Scotland. Most of the older books have long formed part of the archives, which is organized separately from the library. There are *c*300 v, including *c*25 pre-1851, consisting of histories of banks and banking and biographies of its directors (with some miscellaneous books which had belonged to them). The museum contains a large collection of the banks' cheques, banknotes, etc from the early 18th cent; also share certificates, prospectuses, etc, with some miscellaneous ephemera, especially of the Society for Promoting the Interest of the Trading Community in the mid-19th cent.

Title card cat of bank histories; otherwise uncat.

Child's Branch, 1 Fleet Street, London EC4Y 1BD. Tel (01) 626 5400.

Child's Branch was founded in 1690, and was acquired by Glyn Mills and Co in 1924. *c*50 v (25% pre-1850) are shelved with the ms archives of the bank, consisting of miscellaneous works presented to the bank; a few books used in the bank; two contemporary pamphlets relating to Sir Francis Child (1684–1740), and R G Hilton Price's own copy of *Marygold of Temple Bar* 1882, with ms revisions for the 1902 edition, many inserted prints, photographs and original ms documents.

No cat or list of the collection, which is shelved in random order.

Dr Williams's Library, 14 Gordon Square, London WC1H 0AG. Tel (01) 387 3727. Open (not August) Mon, Wed, Fri 10 am-5 pm; Tues, Thurs, 6.30 pm to subscribers and the public; those wishing to consult rare books or mss are recommended to write in advance. Photocopier; microfilm reader; microfilming can be arranged through the University of London Library.

Dr Daniel Williams (1643–1716), a Presbyterian minister, bequeathed his fortune to education (especially the training of ministers) and his library to the public. Dr Williams's Trust, set up under his will (as interpreted by the Court of Chancery) to administer these bequests, opened the library in 1729 in Red Cross Street, Cripplegate; it has been in Bloomsbury since 1865, and at its present address from 1890. It is primarily a library of theology and English nonconformist history, but with other subjects represented in the older collections and in a few modern special collections described below. It is principally financed by the endowments of Dr Williams's Trust. The Library is described below: A in general; B-E in terms of constituent collections (whether now separate from the general collections or not) in chronological order by centuries when received; F New College Library, recently acquired. The adjacent Congregational Library, which is accessible to readers at Dr Williams's, is described in a separate entry.

R T Herford and S K Jones, *A short account of the charity and library established under the will of the late Rev Daniel Williams, DD*, London, 1917. (op)

John Creasey, *Dr Williams's Library 1729–1979: a brief introduction* (1977) (gratis).

Friends of Dr Williams's Library, *Lecture*, 1947– annually, especially Stephen K Jones, *Dr Williams and his library*, 1948 (1947 lecture); Ernest A Payne, *A venerable dissenting institution: Dr Williams's Library 1729–1979*, 1979.

K Twinn, 'Sources for church history 2: Dr Williams's Library', *Local Historian*, Aug 1970, p115-20.

——'An ivory tower in Gordon Square', *Camden History Review* 1 (1973), p17-18.

Dr Williams's Trust, *Papers relating to the late Daniel Williams, DD and the Trust*, 1816.

'Dr Williams's Library by Z Z', *Congregational Magazine* new ser 1 (1825), p18-22.

Walter D Jeremy, *The Presbyterian Fund and Dr Daniel Williams's Trust: with biographical notes of the trustees*, London, 1885.

A **General Description**

The Library contains *c*135,000 v; about half are pre-1851, including 31 incunabula, over 2,000 STC items, 2,500 Wing, and *c*30,000 ESTC (about half of which are pamphlets), covering Christian theology, ecclesiastical history, other religions, and philosophy, but especially strong in English material from 1580 onwards; most subjects in the humanities and some scientific books are also included in the older collections, especially before *c*1820, though very haphazardly. Archives of the Trust are held, together with many collections of mss, including some items of major importance, most notably the minutes of the Westminster Assembly, and a ms of George Herbert's poems.

The older catalogues, in ms and printed, are described historically in the *Short account*, 1917, p82-115; printed catalogues listed on p130-1.

Author/name cat on cards includes all collections (New College and Baynes still being added) with some minor exceptions noted below.

There is an old subject cat (in ms) by Thomas Hunter.

Early English dissent Dissenting history is the primary focus of the collections, including (apart from the Congregational Library) *c*40,000 pre-1801 items, with *c*1,000 STC; 12,000 Wing and 19,000 ESTC. All denominations are included, but there is a strong emphasis on the older groups, especially the English Presbyterians and their successors the Unitarians, with the Separatists and their successors, the Independents and the Congregationalists, now reinforced by the New College and Congregational libraries.

Bibliography of Early Nonconformity to 1800, compiled 1947–55 as the first phase of an abortive union catalogue project; in three sequences of sheaf slips (author/name; alphabetical subject; date of printing), limited to England, but including both sides in controversies, so that there is some material from Anglicans, Catholics, Scotland, Wales and Ireland; incomplete for Quakers; on its methods and limitations see Notes on the *Bibliography of Early Nonconformity*, 1957 (Occasional paper no 5); reduced facsimile, often barely legible, published as *Early nonconformity 1566–1800: a catalogue of books in Dr Williams's Library*, Boston (Mass), G K Hall, 1968, 12 v.

G F Nuttall, *The beginnings of English nonconformity 1660–1665: a checklist*, London, priv pr, 1960; a union list including several other libraries.

Histories of congregations and their ministers An unrivalled collection of histories of individual dissenting congregations and their ministers is brought together in the Nonconformist History Room, and is now complemented by another collection in the Congregational Library; many of these are privately printed and are not available in other libraries. The same room houses sets of nonconformist historical society publications, denominational directories, and standard histories. Also in the room is the index known as the 'Directory of Congregational biography' *c*1640–1956, compiled by Charles Edward Surman (*b*1901) to record references to all known ministers of Congregational churches including those originally Presbyterian which became Unitarian or Independent. Important complementary ms collections include those of John Evans (1680–1730), Josiah Thompson (1724–1806), Walter Wilson (1781?–1847), with three extra-illustrated copies of his *History... of dissenting churches* 1808–14, John Edwin Odgers (1843–1925), and George Lyon Turner (1844–1920).

Nonconformist congregations in Great Britain: a list of histories and other material in Dr Williams's Library, 1973; includes analytical entries for periodical articles and parts of books; also mss.

Index to the John Evans list of dissenting congregations... 1715–1729, 1964 (Occasional paper no 11).

Handlist of mss, indicating printed pamphlets in certain collections; see also K Twin, *Guide to the manuscripts*, 1969.

'The Evans list and... dissenters in the early 18th century', Appendix in Michael R Watts, *The dissenters*, Oxford, Clarendon Press, 1978, v 1, p491-509.

'The Morrice mss', *Trans Congregational Hist Soc* 4 (1909–10), p294-8.

Continental collection This forms a separate collection of *c*5,000 v of 17th cent writers, chiefly French Protestants, especially Moÿse Amyrault (1596–1664), Jean Daillé (1594–1670), Pierre Jurieu (1637–1713), and Blaise Pascal (1623–62). Many of these were from the foundation collections.

In general author card cat.

Lists also in *Occasional papers* no 4: Amuraldus, 1958; no 7, Dallaeus, 1958.

Bible *c*5,000 commentaries, texts, and other works on the Bible. They include a collection of foreign versions given by the British and Foreign Bible Society in 1820.

Fathers of the Church A collection brought together in the Church History Room includes complete sets of Migne *Patrologia Graeca* and *Latina*, and many other editions of the Fathers, especially 17th cent, *c*900 v altogether.

Liturgies 168 Unitarian forms of prayer, *c*150 other nonconformist, and a large number of Anglican and RC liturgies; not a separate collection.

General card cat under heading Liturgies.

Hymnody 707 hymnals, including 3 Wing; 70 ESTC; 193 English 1801–50; 332 English 1851–1900; 84 English post-1900; and 28 foreign; kept as a collection (606), mostly built up in the 19th cent. In 1955 a collection of 91 hymnals and psalters from Hove Public Library was added; in 1964 *c*300 shelved separately from the main collection came in the bequest of Miss Ingibjorg Olaffson.

General card cat under heading Hymnals (arranged chronologically).

Judaica and Hebraica *c*900 v 16th-20th cent, first segregated by the Unitarian minister Robert Travers Herford (1860–1950) who compiled a ms cat while Librarian.

Periodicals Over 1,000 titles, including *c*400 beginning before 1851; *c*30,000 v, including long, mostly complete, runs of the major and older nonconformist organs such as the *Evangelical Magazine*, the *Monthly Repository*, the *Arminian Magazine*, and also the anti-slavery journals; also many small and obscure papers such as the *Bulletin of the Isle of Man Communist Christian Church*; a collection of American evangelical magazines of 1820–40; many of the major Victorian review journals such as the *Fortnightly Athenaeum*, and the *Edinburgh*; a collection of French literary reviews and general periodicals 1660–1740; and many other journals, especially those on religious, historical and philosophical subjects.

General card cat under heading Periodicals.

Pamphlets and tracts Of perhaps 3,000 v altogether, over 2,000 bound v are kept together as a collection, mostly bound by subject regardless of provenance. They include particularly extensive collections of funeral sermons, mostly for nonconformist ministers, of Unitarian tracts, and of pamphlets on slavery; and collections of parliamentary sermons; and on the Bangorian and Trinitarian controversies, and on popery.

Historical series A collection of important series on English history, mostly published in the 19th cent is brought together in the Series Room, including the reports on the Historical Mss Commission; the Commons 1st series Reports, 1773; *Statutes at large*, the *Mirror of Parliament*, *State Trials*, etc.

Special bindings and bibliographical curiosities A collection of over 40 items brought together from other collections.

B Foundation collections

The library bequeathed by Williams in 1716 contained *c*7,641 books in 6,241 v, in addition to 127 v of tracts. It was a general and wide-ranging collection comprising two private libraries, his own and that collected by his late friend William Bates. The 1727 catalogue does not distinguish them, but many are identifiable from inscriptions. This library was kept distinct from later additions until the 19th cent when it was merged in the general library.

Bibliothecae quam vir doctus, & admodum Reverendus, Daniel Williams, STP bono publico legavit, Londini 1727; by size and language compiled at Williams's home at Hoxton by Isaac Bates.

William Bates (1625–99), Rector of St Dunstan-in-the-West, who had been an Assistant at Sion College but was ejected from his living in 1662, and was described at his funeral as 'an earnest gatherer and devourer of books, a living library' who 'knew how to choose and was curious in his choice'; in 1700 Williams bought his library for a large sum. In addition to an extensive theological collection, it included choice editions of classical, French and English literature, including plays, among them a Shakespeare first folio, two with Ben Jonson autographs, and first editions of Beaumont and Fletcher, and Dryden.

John Howe, *A funeral sermon for...William Bates, DD*, London, 1699, p77-9.

Daniel Williams (1643–1716), the self-taught Welsh Pastor at Wood Street, Dublin, later at Hand Alley, London, and acknowledged leader of the Presbyterians, was a prolific pamphleteer against Antinomianism. His book collection, however, was wide-ranging though mainly theological; it included some books from his first wife, sister of the Countess of Meath.

Daniel Defoe, *Memoirs of the life...of...Daniel Williams, DD*, London, 1718.

Roger Thomas, *Daniel Williams, 'Presbyterian bishop'*, 1964 (Annual lecture, 1962).

C Collections added in the 18th century

The library was opened to the public in 1729 with no fund to buy additional books; it was built up by gifts of money and books from trustees and others. The library soon became the Headquarters of the Three Denominations (Presbyterians, Independents, and Baptists around London) and was known as the Dissenters' Library. Many books on subjects other than theology were added when they were offered, but the main intention was to have a library of current theology for the use of nonconformist ministers. In order to buy desiderata other books were sold, especially older editions when newer ones were given to the library. Individual donations and bequests were not kept distinct, but merged in a general library of post-foundation collections.

Book of Benefactors 1729–88 (MS 12.65) and transcript with continuation to 1881 (MS 12.66), lists most gifts.

Bibliothecae quam...Daniel Williams...legavit catalogus ed 2, 1801; a very inaccurate abridgement of a ms cat of 1768 with additions to 1800.

B Manning, *The Protestant Dissenting Deputies*, Cambridge, 1952.

John Evans (1680–1730) DD, Minister at New Broad Street, previous colleague of Dr Williams at Hand Alley Chapel. Out of his library, *c*10,000 v, which was sold after his death, the trustees bought, in addition to the Morrice and other important collections of mss, a large number of rare 16th-17th cent tracts, including the Marprelate Tracts, and collections on the struggles of the Puritans, and some books.

Bibliotheca rarissima: or a catalogue of the library of the late...Dr John Evans...sold by auction...17 Dec 1730 by Thomas Ballard, London, 1730.

Samuel Horsman (1698?–1751) MD, Treasurer of the Royal College of Physicians, gave scientific books from 1732 onwards.

Edmund Calamy, the fourth (1697?–1755), a Trustee, gave *c*100 biblical and theological works 1732–49.

John Archer (*d*1733), Presbyterian Minister at Hackney, bequeathed 473 books chiefly on theology, including a unique volume of pamphlets by members of the Pilgrim Fathers' Church in Holland in the early 17th cent.

Thomas Rowe, Minister at Yarmouth, in 1737 gave *c*560 v of literature, philosophy and theology.

Philip Gibbs (*dc*1760), Independent Minister at Lime Street, bequeathed 733 books on theology, science, and general literature.

William Harris (*c*1675–1740) DD, a Trustee, editor of Dr Williams's works, bequeathed 1,959 v.

Jeremy, op cit, p113-14.

Thomas Hollis (1720–74) FRS, of Lincoln's Inn, republican and dilettante, acquired a library of finely bound books; many donations from him 1760–70 are recorded in the Book of Benefactors as given 'by an unknown hand'. His friend and heir Thomas Brand Hollis (*d*1804) of The Hyde, near Ingatestone, inherited the main part of the collection, and in 1798 gave from it 16 first editions of Milton, five related works, and some others. The bulk of the library was next inherited by his friend John Disney (1746–1816) DD, a former Anglican who joined the Unitarian ministry at Essex Street with Lindsey; he gave many gifts of books and mss (Mss 87), including a fine collection of nonconformist liturgies, clerical subscription, the Francis Blackburne Confessional controversy, and many others from his own and from the inherited collection between 1793 and 1805 (the residue was sold, Sotheby 22 Apr 1817).

Robert Wastfield (*d*1776), a cultured layman, bequeathed *c*350 books on theology, science, literature, and other subjects.

D Collections added in the 19th century

In 1805 the trust was for the first time permitted to spend money on books for the library, and the discarding of unwanted material ceased. At around the same time the trustees became preponderantly Unitarian; in 1829 the Unitarians separated from the Three Denominations whose headquarters moved elsewhere, the Baptists and the Congregationalists set up their own libraries, and Dr Williams's acquisitions became narrower in scope, including fewer works on general subjects. The collections below have not been kept separate, except where indicated.

Book of Benefactors to 1881 (MS 12.66) and 1881– (Librarian's Office) lists most donations below.

Appendix ad catalogum Bibliothecae Danielis Williams, STP, 1808 (accessions from 1801 by size and language); rev ed 1814.

Catalogue of the Library in Red Cross Street, Cripplegate, founded pursuant to the will of the Reverend Daniel Williams..., v 1, 1841 (author cat of the books, based on the bad cat of 1801, with additions to *c*1835); v 2, 1841 (author cat of tracts and sermons to 1840); Appendix, 1854; v 3, 1870 (author cat of books and tracts acquired *c*1835–70); Supplements, 1878, 1885; there is a guardbook author cat combining v 1 and its three supplements.

John Charlesworth (1742–1821), Rector of Ossington, Notts, gave 1807–8, *c*300 books on theology, history, philosophy, education and literature.

Abraham Rees (1743–1825) DD, FRS, Presbyterian minister, a Trustee, encyclopaedist, and leader of the Three Denominations, is said to have given a collection of books.

Robert Aspland (1782–1845), a Trustee, Unitarian minister of the Gravel Pit, founding editor of the *Monthly Repository*, made numerous donations 1820 onwards.

R Brook Aspland, *Memoir of...Robert Aspland*, London, 1850.

Philip Mallet (*d*1812), editor of Hobbes, bequeathed 70 v of philology, 1571 onwards.

David Davison (*d*1858), MD (Glasgow), Presbyterian minister of Jewin Street Chapel 1825–40, in 1840 gave *c*100 v of theology.

Henry Crabb Robinson (1775–1867), Foreign editor of *The Times* and well known in literary circles gave many books in his lifetime, and *c*100 books of history and literature were given from his estate by his executors. His ms diaries and letters were received on the death of his surviving executor in 1877. 39 v of books (five with marginalia by Coleridge) retained by his executor, Edwin Wilkins Field (1804–71) were given by his family in 1916.

J C Addyes Scott of Stourbridge, in 1874 gave *c*200 v, chiefly theology and history.

Christopher Walton (1809–77), Methodist jeweller in Ludgate Hill, in 1875 deposited, and later bequeathed his collection on condition that it should be kept apart as the Walton Theosophical Library; *c*1,000 v on mysticism, theosophy, philosophy, etc, including *c*600 pre-1801.

In general card cat. Also separate author cats to 1800 and 1801 onwards, possibly incomplete.

George Henry Lewes and George Eliot Library George Henry Lewes (1817–78) the journalist, bequeathed his library to his cohabitant Marian Evans (1819–80, George Eliot the novelist); it passed with the addition of her own books to his son Charles Lee Lewes (1842–91) who, in 1882, gave two-thirds of the combined collection on condition that it should remain a separate collection bearing his father's name. *c*2,400 items, mostly 1801–81, but including 22 of the 16th cent, 41 17th and 117 18th cent; 40 per cent English, remainder German, French, Italian and Dutch; 50 per cent on science and medicine, the rest on history, literature, philosophy and theology, with a few on other subjects. There are many annotated copies.

William Baker, *The George Eliot-George Henry Lewes Library*, New York, Garland 1977; history, analysis and cat.

Items identified as 'GHL' in *Catalogue Supplement 2*, 1885, and card cat.

E Collections added in the 20th century

Acquisitions have been mostly limited to theology, church history, philosophy (but with progressive reduction in comprehensiveness), and those aspects of history most closely related to these subjects. The collections below have not been kept separate, except the largest, eg Baynes. New College Library is described separately in Section F.

Only the smaller collections are usually listed in the Book of Benefactors 1881 to present.

Catalogue of accessions 1900–1950, 1955; *1951–1960*, 1961; *1961–1970*, 1972; *1971–1980*, 1982; limited to publications after 1900.

Annual lists in *Bulletin* 1921– including some of the pre-1801 accessions.

Classified sheaf cat of modern works acquired from 1950 onwards.

British and Foreign Unitarian Association, Essex Hall Library Numerous gifts, 1870 to the present, but most frequent after 1900, eg a collection of bound Unitarian pamphlets *c*1910.

Miss Matilda Sharpe in 1915 gave a collection of rare books, incorporated in the general collections, *c*50 items in 63 v, 1622–*c*1910.

Book of Benefactors.

Miss Helen Alexandrina Dallas in 1917 gave *c*500 items, mostly modern, on behalf of the Association of St John the Evangelist, of miscellaneous theology, mysticism and poetry.

Separate author cards.

Book of Benefactors.

W K Marriott in 1915 gave the Library of the Fanshawe family, *c*500 v including 100 v of pamphlets, housed in the Lindsey Room. It includes the collection formed by John Conybeare (1693–1755) Bishop of Bristol, the defender of revealed religion against Tindal; chiefly controversial theology.

*Arnold F Jones, c*1915 gave a collection of works on the Bible, literature and dissenting theology.

Typescript author list in Book of Benefactors.

Liberation Society and related collections The Liberation Society was founded in 1844 as the Anti-State-Church Association, in 1855 becoming the Society for the Liberation of Religion from State Patronage and Control, better known colloquially as the Liberation Society. In *c*1945 and at certain earlier times it gave hundreds of pamphlets (mostly its own publications) from office collections which are kept as a special collection. (After its demise in 1957 its main library went to the Greater London Record Office.) One of its most prominent members, Thomas Bennett (*d*1934) LLD, solicitor of Grimsby, and author of *The people's guide to disestablishment and disendowment* in 1923 gave 125 scarce works on this subject 1711–1924, including some Liberation Society tracts, together with a collection now known as the Bennett Donation of 54 v of law reports on church endowments and establishment 1679–1798, chiefly extracted from larger collections; he also bequeathed 53 law textbooks 1658–1916. In 1971 the Rev R E Cooper gave the collection of Liberation Society and other tracts written by the Baptist Minister Dr John Clifford (1826–1923) that had belonged to the author, bound in 5 v (but his mss were destroyed later). There is further Liberation Society material in the mss and general collections.

Bennett Donation in *Bulletin* 5 (1923), p119, 138; his Tracts listed in *Bulletin* 10 (1925) but probably not all in general cat; Book of Benefactors 1919.

Clifford in general card cat.

Miss C Scott in 1928 gave *c*50 Unitarian and other sermons, pamphlets and miscellaneous literature 1691–1860.

Book of Benefactors.

W B Bellars His personal library given in 1929 by G F Bellars; *c*120 books of Italian literature and history 1775–1901.

Rayner Storr (1835–1917), compiler of the concordance to the *Imitatio Christi*, assembled a collection of editions of Thomas à Kempis 1493–1952 in 98 v which was given by his children in 1933; shelved with the Library's other editions of Thomas.

Card cat and shelflist.

Lindsey Room Mostly the library of Theophilus Lindsey (1723–1808) Vicar of Catterick, then Unitarian Minister at Essex Street, friend and son-in-law of Archdeacon Francis Blackburne (1705–87); given in 1810 by his widow Hannah Elsworth (*d*1812, Blackburne's stepdaughter) to the chapel for the use of the resident minister, where it attracted some additional donations (the Lindsey items have his bookplate). Deposited in 1928, given to Dr Williams's *c*1977. There are 397 v of books and 102 v of pamphlets, mainly Unitarian or on a variety of subjects in nonconformist theology, with some foreign books, 16th-19th cent. Also a collection of the works of Joseph Priestley (1753–1804) Unitarian minister and scientist; 53 editions, some donated by him, from the New College collections, supplementing 72 other Priestley items in the library, including a collection of pamphlets formed by the Rev Samuel Parks (or Parkes) FLS.

Alexander Gordon, *Addresses*, London, 1922, p240-82.

Richmond College 78 v on theology probably given *c*1941, and five deposited tracts *c*1970.

Sir George Francis Hill (1867–1948), Director of the British Museum; 109 v from his library, given in 1965 by Dr Anthony Bedford Steel (1900–73), Principal of Univerity College, Cardiff; on Cyprus 1573–1946, but mostly after 1900.

M Aird Jolly (*d*1957), bequeathed 105 v on Cornwall 1720–1950, mostly modern.

John William Lister (*d*1951), Borough Librarian of Hove, bequeathed *c*300 books on the Catholic Apostolic Church 1820–1917, including some very rare items.

Typescript author list (at S.701.E.18).

There is also a collection not easily accessible to non-members at the adjacent Catholic Apostolic Church headquarters.

Norman Baynes Byzantine Library Norman Hepburn Baynes (1877–1961), author of *The Byzantine Empire* (1925), and Prof of Byzantine history in London, bequeathed his Byzantine library, with an endowment for its maintenance and enlargement. It contains *c*6,500 v in 12 languages, nearly all modern, but with *c*50 of 1701–1850. In addition to all facets of the history and archaeology of Byzantium and of the Roman Empire, there are books on comparative religion and a number of related subjects, and *c*1,800 pamphlets. Many works came from the library of John Bagnall Bury (1861–1927) whose literary executor was Baynes.

Author cat on cards, intended for publication.

I Elliott, 'The Norman Baynes Byzantine Library', *Bull Assoc British Theological and Philosophical Libraries* no 23 (Sept 1966), p11-12.

J M Hussey, 'An appreciation of Norman Hepburn Baynes', 1967 (Supplement to *Bulletin* no 72).

An address presented to Norman Hepburn Baynes with a bibliography of his writings, Oxford, priv pr, 1942.

Samuel Noble (1779–1853), engraver and Swedenborgian Minister of the New Church, Cross Street, Hatton Garden, founder of the Swedenborg Society, bequeathed a library to the church; *c*400 v of this were given by the New Church, Finchley, to Dr Williams's in 1971, consisting of English and continental Protestant theology.

List of pre-1800 items in *Bulletin* no 79 (1974), p23-9.

F New College Library

New College was founded in the Congregational tradition in 1850 by the merger of three colleges, Coward, Highbury and Homerton, which had originated in the 18th cent as academies for the higher education of dissenters excluded from the two universities. In 1900 it became part of the Theological Faculty of the University of London. Hackney College was merged with it in 1924, and from then until 1936 it was called Hackney and New College. In 1976 the College was closed, and its library, already pruned in 1926–7 and at Hodgson's 28 July 1937, was divided. The incunabula went to the University of London Library; the 351 remaining STC books and all other pre-1851 books identified as having come to New College from its three constituent colleges in 1850, with three special collections and certain other books, to Dr Williams's. Other books were given to the Bible Society Library, or sold to Spurgeon's College, London, and a number of other academic libraries, and at Sotheby 31 Jan 1977, and to R Booth at Hay-on-Wye.

G F Nuttall, *New College London and its Library*, 1977 (Dr Williams's Library lecture).

H McLachlan, *English education under the Test Acts*, Manchester, 1931.

General The library contains *c*13,000 v, kept together as a collection, but apart from the Doddridge collection and some sub-collections, not grouped by provenance; and the very extensive archives of the College and its predecessors. The collections of the individual colleges are, however, described below from the historical viewpoint. Now predominantly theological, many of the books on other subjects having been included in the dispersals.

Author card cat from New College gives provenances. Being recatalogued for Dr Williams's card cat and Bibliography of Early Nonconformity.

Archives contain cats in ms from the colleges, identified with shelfmark below (some of the attributions in the *List of the Archives* made by the National Register of Archives, 1968, are wrong).

Doddridge collection A collection of books identified as having come from the personal library of Philip Doddridge (1702–51), with his mss, and study furniture, now in the Doddridge Room. His books formed the core of the library of his academy (later Coward College); they have recently been segregated into a special collection. *c*500 books, mostly Bibles, classics, editions of Richard Baxter (1615–91), school books, Roman Catholic and anti-papal books. They include books acquired from his uncle Philip Doddridge (*d*1715), and others bought from the widow of John Jennings (*c*1686/7–1723), founder of Kibworth Academy; gifts mainly of classical literature and philosophy from his brother-in-law John Nettleton, a minister in Essex, and from Samuel Clark (1684–1750), minister at St Albans.

G F Nuttall, 'Philip Doddridge's Library', *Trans Congregational Hist Soc* 17 (1952), p29-31; see also p19-28, 32-5.

——*Calendar of the correspondence of Philip Doddridge DD (1702–1751)*, London, HMSO, 1979 (Historical Manuscripts Commission Joint Publication no 26; also issued as Northamptonshire Record Society Publication no 29, 1977).

Coward College Library In 1729 founded as an academy (which was in effect partly a continuation of that at Kibworth, at Market Harborough), moved to Northampton in the same year. Its library of *c*200 books, into which its own larger collection was incorporated, became that of the Daventry Academy (1752–89), which acquired books from the collections of Isaac Watts (1674–1748), Caleb Ashworth (1722–75), Thomas Belsham (1750–1829), Job Orton (1717–83), including some books given by Doddridge, and Henry Miles (1698–1763) FRS. It then became again the Northampton Academy (1789–99), when it acquired books from John Horsey (1754–1827), and then the Wymondley House Academy (1799–1833) when it absorbed the library of William Parr (1754–1819). From 1833 it was Coward College at Byng Place near Gordon Square in London. By 1850 the library had *c*3,500 books, and was strong in Hebraica, Bibles, the classics, ecclesiastical history, travel, and natural history.

Cats: (*c*1789), author (L89); (*c*1810?), duplicates (L85); 1821–9, author and shelf (L73); *c*1840, classified (L82).

'Donors of books to the Northampton Academy', and 'The Northamptonshire Book Society' (five books in the collection) in Nuttall, *Calendar of... Doddridge* (see above), p372-4.

Correspondence on the cats (414/31; 416/22; 419/23; L53/1/120).

Highbury College Library One of the origins of Highbury College Library was the library established in 1741 at the Academy at Moorfields, moved in 1744 to

Wellclose Square, which in 1762 became the first Hoxton College. In 1785 the college was dissolved for unorthodoxy, but the library remained, and was transferred in 1791 as a special collection (which until 1977 was kept separate) of more than 3,000 v called 'The Coward Trustees' Books', to the new Hoxton Academy. This academy, which had its own small library established in 1779, had originated as the Societas Evangelica or Evangelical Academy, an undenominational training centre for preachers. In 1826, on removal to Highbury, it was renamed Highbury College. Its library contained more unorthodox books than those of the other colleges.

1819 author cat and undated near duplicate of the Coward Trustees collection (L75 and L76/1).

Undated 18th cent author cat of Hoxton Academy library (L79).

Classified cat 1847 (L81) with undated numerical list (L80) and partial subject index (L90).

Arthur D Morris, *Hoxton Square and the Hoxton academies*, priv pr 1957; 'Hoxton' (Early nonconformist academies), *Trans Congregational Hist Soc*, 6 (1913-15), p139-42.

Homerton College Library The College originated as the King's Head Society at Deptford in 1730, and among tutors who gave their own works were John Conder (1714–81), Thomas Gibbons (1720–85), and Daniel Fisher (1731–1807). After several migrations it became the Homerton Academy in 1769. Its library acquired a collection of books by John Owen (1616–83), Vice Chancellor of the University of Oxford, 12 of which were included in the bequest of Mrs Elizabeth Cooke (*d*1763) of Stoke Newington and had been given by Owen to her grandfather Sir John Hartopp (1637?–1722); others came in a gift of *c*200 books received in 1793 from the library of Richard Rawlin (1687–1757) Minister of Fetter Lane Chapel. It became Homerton College in 1820, and was ruled by John Pye Smith (1774–1851) who bequeathed his library of 2,000 v, including many foreign and rare works. In 1840 it became affiliated to the University of London. The library contained over 3,000 v by the time of the merger in 1850, and was strong in Biblical criticism and controversial works.

Cat: (*c*1800) by size (L87); 1814, authors (L88); 1817, authors (L86/1); 1824 classified (L83).

'Homerton Academy', *Congregational Magazine* new ser 1 (1825), p133-6, 187-93.

List of Owen collection, *Trans Congregational Hist Soc* 20 (1965), p45-6.

William Walford, *Autobiography*, London, 1851, p100-19, 153-64.

Hackney College Library Hackney College originated in 1796 as the Village Itinerancy Association, formed by dissenters, Anglicans and Methodists; in 1803 it became the Evangelical Association for the Propagation of the Gospel, in 1839 Hackney Theological Seminary, and in 1871 Hackney College (with no connection with the 18th cent Unitarian college of that name). In 1889–95 Dr Philip H Lockhart, a Governor, gave *c*1,000 v, mainly Puritan books and tracts from his father's library. The surviving proportion of this library is probably comparatively small.

Alfred Cave, *The story of the founding of Hackney College*, London, 1898.

Report from 1817, usually annual.

Western College, Bristol collection This college, which originated from various academies from 1752 onwards in the West of England, closed in 1969. Most of its library was then sold (some at Sotheby 13 Feb 1922), but some books with the bookplates of Taunton Academy (1780–94) and Axminster Academy (1796–1828) were transferred to New College Library.

'Taunton Academy', *Trans Congregational Hist Soc* 4 (1909–10), p236-41.

J C Johnstone, 'The story of Western College', *Ibid* 7 (1916–18), p98-109, 130-1.

Funeral sermons A collection of *c*1,900 sermons 1577–1866 preached at the funerals of nonconformist ministers and others, bound in *c*120 v. It was begun as a private collection by Roger Flexman (1708–95), Dr Williams's librarian, and later came into the possession of Walter Wilson (1781–1847) who used it in his *History... of dissenting churches*. From him it is thought to have passed to Charles Godwin, a bookseller in Bath where Wilson died, who added to it considerably. It is not known when or how it reached New College.

Cat in ms of preachers and subjects.

White collection *c*500 items on life after death, the majority collected by and probably bequeathed to New College by Edward White (1819–98) Congregational minister at Camden Town, and author of books on conditional immortality, which are included in the collection.

Wimbledon Lawn Tennis Museum, Kenneth Ritchie Memorial Library, All England Lawn Tennis and Croquet Club, Church Road, Wimbledon Park, London SW19 5AE. Tel (01) 946 2244. Open by prior appointment with the Curator, Tues-Sat 11 am-5 pm (except during the Championships).

The museum was established with the library in 1977 to house and develop the historical collections accumulated by the Club. The library contains *c*500 books and 65 sets of periodicals on lawn tennis from the 1870s onwards, including some scarce early material, with programmes and ephemera, and is the most comprehensive British collection on the game. There are also books on earlier games, especially real (royal) tennis.

The Kenneth Ritchie Wimbledon Library: catalogue, the Museum, 1979.

H Godfrey, 'The Wimbledon Lawn Tennis Museum', *Museums Journal* 78(1) (1978), p13-15.

Woolmen's Company, 3rd Floor, 192 Vauxhall Bridge Road, London SW1V 1HF. Tel (01) 834 3631.

The Company is 43rd in order of precedence of the City livery companies, but the Hall was bombed (with the destruction of most of the archives and books) in 1940. What little remains is deposited in the Guildhall Library Department of Manuscripts.

H B A DeBruyne, *A history of the Woolmen's Company*, 1968.

Working Men's College Library, 44 Crowndale Road, London NW1 1TR. Tel (01) 387 2037. Open 4.45 pm-9 pm Mon and Thurs during vacation; Mon-Fri during term to members of the College and of the Frances Martin College; outsiders will not be admitted unless they can prove a genuine need to see materials not available elsewhere.

The College was founded by the Christian Socialists in 1854, and the library reflects the growth of the College. It incorporates donations from College teachers including (John) Frederick Denison Maurice (1805–72), John Malcolm Forbes Ludlow (1821–1911), Sir Charles (Prestwood) Lucas (1853–1931) Principal of the College, Frederick James Furnivall (1825–1910), Albert Venn Dicey (1835–1922), Sir John Lubbock, Baron Avebury (1834–1913), and Goldsworthy Lowes Dickinson (1862–1932). *c*800 v are rare or pre-1851 (including volumes of periodicals), with some mss; they deal mostly with the Christian Socialist movement and the social history of the 19th cent, with some miscellaneous literary items such as early editions of Kingsley, Ruskin, etc.

Card cat of whole library.

The Working Men's College magazine 1859–62. *The Working Men's College Journal* 1890–1932, continued as *The Journal* 1933– .

Yugoslav Embassy Library, 5 Lexham Gardens, Earl's Court, London W8 5JJ. Application for access should be made in writing to the Cultural Attaché.

The Klugmann collection of partisan literature A portion transferred from the Communist Party of Great Britain (qv) of the library bequeathed by James Klugmann (1912–77). This portion contains a collection of the publications of the partisan forces and political agencies, mostly in mimeographed form, assembled while he was employed by British Intelligence during World War II.

Zoological Society Library, Regent's Park, London NW1 4RY. Tel (01) 722 3333. Open Mon-Fri 9.30 am-5.30 pm to Society members, and also to holders of library reference tickets on application and payment.

The Zoological Society of London was founded in 1826, and almost immediately began to receive donations of books which were formed into a library. In 1835 the Secretary, Edward Turner Bennett (1797–1836) gave 218 v. It has been built up to *c*150,000 v, covering all branches of zoology. Also mss, drawings and photographs.

H Scherren, *The Zoological Society of London*, London, Cassell, 1905.

Lord Solly Zuckerman ed *The Zoological Society of London 1826–1976 and beyond*, 1976 (Symposia of the Zoological Society no 40), p233-52.

P Chalmers Mitchell, *Centenary history of the Zoological Society of London*, 1929, p107-30.

G B Stratton, 'The Zoological Society of London', *British Book News* 95 (1948), p358-60.

Natural history manuscript resources, London, Mansell, 1980, p299-300.

Rare books collection Received mainly by donation, it totals *c*30,000, and includes *c*1,000 pre-1701 items. A noteworthy bequest came in 1888 from the widow of Corresponding Member M J M Cornely of Tours, 840 rare books. Most of the 16th and 17th cent natural histories of Gesner, Aldrovandi, Topsell, etc. A copy of the limited edition which Linnaeus edited for Queen Louisa Ulrica of Sweden, of C A Clerck *Icones insectorum rariorum* 1759.

Card cat (names and titles) superseding *Catalogue of the Library of the Zoological Society of London* (1854; 1872; 1880; 1887; 5th ed 1902).

Accessions lists to 1909 included in annual *Report*.

Periodicals collection Containing *c*3,000 sets, of which *c*170 are wholly or partly pre-1851, including both zoological and general natural history and scientific journals.

List of the periodicals and serials in the Library of the Zoological Society of London, 1949.

Manchester (Greater)

Bolton

Bolton Public Libraries, Civic Centre, Le Mans Crescent, Bolton BL1 1SD. Tel (0204) 22311 Ext 351. Open Mon, Tues, Thurs, Fri 9 am-7.30 pm, Wed 9 am-1 pm, Sat 9 am-5 pm. Admission by written application. Microfilm readers, photocopying facilities.

Holdings of books published up to 1850 (This material has no generic designation.) Most of the earlier, pre-1700 material was acquired either in the late 19th cent, largely by donations from various sources, but mainly by a systematic purchasing policy. The collection totals *c*7,000 v, including 2 continental incunabula; *c*70 STC and 350 Wing items; and over 650 ESTC. Main subject areas of the pre-1851 stock are fine arts, ornithology, bibliography and book illustration, belle-lettres, local history and topography. Most of the stock is located in the central general reference library, with some also in the technical and reference library and small portions in the reference departments of Farnworth and Westhoughton libraries.

Most of the material is listed in the library's general card cats, but following several serious thefts, entries for the rarer items were withdrawn, and a separate author index was compiled for staff use.

The Bowyer Bible On Robert Bowyer's death in 1834, the Bible was bequeathed to his business partner, Mrs Mary Parkes, who sold it by lottery in 1843–4. After passing through various hands (details in Sparke's monograph) it was acquired in 1856 for £550 by Robert Heywood, a former Mayor of Bolton. On his death in 1868, it was inherited by his son, whose widow, Mrs John Heywood presented it to Bolton Public Library in 1917. The Bible, which is housed in a specially-created bookcase, is an extra illustrated copy, grangerized into 45 v by the publisher/printseller Robert Bowyer, of Thomas Macklin's Bible, originally published in 7 v (v 1-6, 1800; v 7, 1816), and at the time 'the most costly edition of the Bible ever issued from any press' (Sparke). Bowyer's copy was completed in 1826, with the addition of his own title-page, and over 6,000 illustrations, which he had apparently been collecting for his specific project since soon after the publication of Macklin's first volume in 1800. There are also 200 drawings of head- and tail-pieces by P J De Loutherbourg (1740–1812). Bowyer estimated that the illustrations and binding cost over £3,000, with the cost of the special oak cabinet bringing the total to £4,000.

Ms indexes: (a) a sequential list of the illustrations, indicating for each the subject, location in the Bible, and artist; (b) an alphabetical list of the artists, indicating the number of illustrations by each.

Archibald Sparke, *The Bowyer Bible: a monograph.* Bolton Libraries Committee, 1920. 4to. 10pp. (op, but copies available for use in the library).

Private press books and other limited editions (this material has no generic designation). The collection was mainly built up as a systematic policy during the librarianship of Archibald Sparke, (1904–31), and consists of *c*2,000 editions, mostly post-1851. The private press books include Kelmscott (19); Doves (29); Ashendene (3); Vale (18); Eragny (10).

Rare items are only listed in an author index compiled for staff use only (for reasons of security); other material is listed in general card cat.

Walt Whitman Collection The collection was based initially on the Whitman collection of Dr J Johnston, which was built up from some time before 1890, in which year Johnston visited Whitman in America. Johnston was a leading member of a group of admirers who met regularly from about 1885, and corresponded with Whitman over several years, and at some stage constituted themselves into the Bolton Whitman Fellowship. They maintained close contact with the intimate circle of Whitman's friends in America, and also with, among others, leading figures among Whitman's many admirers in Britain. Johnston donated his collection to the library in 1924, and it was subsequently augmented principally by donations from Americans. There are *c*2,000 items, a small proportion being post-1918, but the great majority comprises printed, and, particularly, ms material of the late 19th and early 20th cent. The editions of the various works of Whitman include more than 30 pre-1900, mostly American, including the first two editions (1855 and 1856) of 'Leaves of Grass'. Some bear Whitman's autograph, occasionally accompanied by a greeting. The large number of biographical and critical works also include many pre-1900 editions, also mostly published in the USA. The 1919 books by, or about, Whitman total 130. Issues of periodicals containing contributions by, or about, Whitman, of which perhaps 100 are pre-1919. The collection also includes 1,000 or so letters (the majority from Americans), including one or two from Whitman himself, to members of the Bolton societies; a few diaries compiled by members of the Bolton societies recording their visits to Whitman in America; portrait in oils of Whitman by Sidney Morse; some photographs of Whitman, his house, his tomb, etc. There are also many early reports, public addresses etc, by members of the Bolton Whitman societies, both in print and in ms.

Harold Hamer, *A catalogue of works by and relating to Walt Whitman in the Reference Library, Bolton.* Bolton Libraries Committee, 1955, 52pp.

Separate card cat.

Bolton School (Boys' Division), Chorley New Road, Bolton BL1 4PB. Tel (0204) 40201. Open school hours in term time only; admission by written application. Photocopying facilities.

A grammar school, adjacent to, and associated with, Bolton parish church, and probably originally a chantry school, is known, from a will, to have been in existence by 1516 and may have been instituted in the late 15th cent. By the 1630s the school was on the verge of ceasing to exist. There is no record of there having been a collection of books at the school up to this time, nor any indication that any of the books in the present library are survivals from any such collection. Various members of the local Lever family had been associated with the school from early in its history. During this period the family's fortunes had long been in decline, but revived in the 17th cent with the growth of the local textile trade. In the 1640s Robert Lever, who had become prosperous in London as a merchant of Lancashire textiles, refounded the school with a bequest wherefrom a new building, still adjacent to the parish church, was completed in 1665.

Chained Library The earliest surviving reference to the acquisition of books for a school library dates from 1661, and by 1682 the collection comprised 10 v. In 1735 a list, still extant, was compiled of the 47 books then in the library. Of the 15 that survive, most are Latin classics or religious works in English, the remainder being mainly lexions or grammars.

From 1694 the library was housed in a bookcase, presented by James Lever, a descendant of the founder, which is of the kind which J W Clark in his 'The care of books...', 2nd ed, 1909, categorizes as the stall-system consisting of a combination of an almery and a lectern. It still houses 56 of the library's present stock of 113 v, of which 53 are chained.

The library's stock of 113 v, comprising 137 works, dates from 1608 to the mid-19th cent; 96 v are of the 17th cent (including the only foreign edition printed in Hanover in 1619); 53 of STC period and 42 of Wing period. There are 24 books of the 18th cent and 8 of the 19th, the latest dating from 1859. There are also 9 items which, having lost their title-pages and being Latin classics, and similar works which have been published at many periods, are difficult to date without detailed examination. The majority of the books are theological, and in the case of the 17th cent books, and one or two of the early 18th cent, most of which derive from the original library of the parish church, are commonly Puritan and frequently anti-Catholic. Most of the non-theological works are Latin classics, grammars or lexicon. STC items for which there are very few locations given in Ramage, or in the 2nd edition of STC, are STC 7145, 7397, 12120 and 13740. There are also a number of STC period titles, editions or issues which do not appear to be listed in STC, though one or two are noted in Ramage, invariably with very few locations. There are: a 'corrected and enlarged' edition, 1633, noted by Ramage, of STC 19311 (dated 1632); a 2nd edition, 1633, printed by Augustine Matthews noted by Ramage, of part 2 of STC 7394, printed by J Beale; a 4th edition, 1613, of STC 25701-3; a 1614 reprint of STC 25704 (dated 1604); a 1632 reprint, noted by Ramage, of STC 1440 (dated 1619); issues or editions of STC 20931, 20932 and 21385 which exclude the name of the printer; an issue or edition of STC 25690 which excludes the name of the publisher, but includes the name of the printer, Cantrell Legge, which is not given in STC for 25690. Owing to the absence of the title-page from the library's copy of Birckbek's *The Protestants' evidence*, it has not been established whether it is the very rare 1st edition of 1634 (STC 3082) or the much less rare 2nd edition of 1635 (STC 3083). Another work which lacks its title-page, and consequently the details of authorship, has been identified as being probably STC 7148, which appears to be very rare. Another work of unknown authorship from this period, containing *The first book of divinitie of God the creator* and *The second book of divinitie of Immanuel, God and Man, our redeemer*, has a prefatory note by John Downame, but no such work is attributed to him in STC. Two works of the early 18th cent by Thomas Bray (1685–1730), Commissary of Maryland, both of them printed in London, appear to be rare, viz *Papal usurpation...1711–12*, and *Propositium de martyrologio generali...*, 1714, which latter does not appear to be listed in '18th century British books'. Nor does the anonymous *A short, easy and delightful method of family religion...*, printed by S Holt for W Hawes, 1707.

Wendy J Sherrington, 'A catalogue of the chained library at Bolton School. 1979. Introduction' (13 pp). (University of Sheffield thesis).

R C Christie, *Old church and school libraries of Lancashire*. 1885. (Chetham Society publications, ns no 7). p56, 111-20.

B H Streeter, *The chained library: a survey of four centuries in the evolution of the English library*. 1931. p299-302.

Manchester

Manchester Central Library, St Peter's Square, Manchester M2 5PD. Tel (061) 236 9422. Open Mon-Fri 9 am-9 pm, Sat 9 am-5 pm. While the book rarities are available for consultation by all bona fide researchers, it is necessary to produce proof of identity and residence. Additionally, prior notice is necessary in connection with the rarer material, including mss, some older printed books and some later ones, eg pre-1914 private press books. Consultation of items labelled as book rarities, identified by 'BR' prefixed to the call number, requires the completion of a special application form. Restricted photocopying facilities.

Book Rarities From the inception of the Manchester Free Library in 1852, a policy was adopted of acquiring, in addition to current publications, books, both British and foreign, from all earlier periods and covering the whole range of subject matter. This policy was aided by the donation of special collections which were compiled by businessmen and others during the city's commercial and cultural heyday in the 19th cent. Successive bibliophilic librarians maintained the policy of purchasing older material, although on a diminishing scale as economic conditions became less favourable, and in recent years such acquisitions have increasingly become restricted to material of local interest. The library designates *c*4,000 items as book rarities on the basis in most cases of their being incunabula (30+), privately printed, having fine plates or other rare illustrations, or particularly fine bindings. In addition there are several thousand other items which are rare insofar as they were published pre-1850, including large numbers from the 16th and 17th cent. The latter include *c*60 items published up to 1640, including 2 incunabula printed by Wynkyn de Worde in 1497 and 1498 (STC 9996 and 13440b). The library's holdings are not included in Ramage.

The rare books are distributed among the various subject-departments, notably Social Sciences, Technical (science and technology), Language and Literature, Arts, Music (Henry Watson) and Local History; and the library's rare bookstock is described hereunder on a departmental basis. In some departments part of the rare material is contained in special collections, which were mostly received as donations and which are the subjects of separate reports. Some of these collections are housed as separate entities, while others have been integrated into the departments' general stocks.

Card and microfiche cats: Card cats housed in the Catalogue Hall cover the holdings of all the departments, other than the Henry Watson Music Library, as follows: name cat in a single sequence; subjects, by Dewey, in two sequences according to period of accession, viz 1950–March 1977 (which contains entries for a small proportion of the library's rare stock, including a few incunabula) and April 1977–date (which contains, few, if any, entries for rare items). Subject entries for the vast majority of the rare books (ie those not entered in the 1950–77 cat) are contained in the microfiche cat of pre-1950 accessions. The general cats in the Catalogue Hall serve as the departmental cats of the Social Sciences and Technical libraries, which are adjacent to the hall. All the other departments house, in addition, individual name and subject cats. (Nora K Firby, 'The Manchester Reference Library and its catalogues...', in *Manchester Review*, v 10, Spring 1963, p1-18.

Printed cats: The first general printed catalogue, compiled by Dr Andrea Crestadoro and published in 1864, lists 26,534 items in author order, with a subject index. It includes separate listings of incunabula (only four at that time), 16th cent books (*c*40), and of books of various periods which were 'considered to be scarce, rare, unique or curious'. A supplement published in 1879, listing 24,647 accessions, is inconvenient to use because the books are listed in nine sequences representing different periods of acquisition. More helpful is the *Index of names and subjects*, published in 1881, which lists the whole of the library's stock as at 1880, to which it remained the main key until the addition of entries for this earlier stock in the card cats was completed in the 1950s. (George Eric Haslam, 'The catalogues of the Manchester Reference Library' in *Manchester Review*, v 5, Winter 1949–50, p358-61). In addition to the general cats there are printed cats for some of the special collections, sometimes labelled as 'occasional lists'.

Arts Library

The older stock has been built up largely by retrospective purchase from the foundation of the Manchester Free Library in 1852 and transferred to the department on its inception in 1960. The policy adopted was of acquiring important older material of foreign as well as British books and periodicals. The library also houses the collection of sales cats, the earliest of which dates from 1678. There are 10 from the 17th cent, *c*70 from the 18th cent, and *c*200 from 1801–50. They are indexed in a shelf-list by date of sale and by name of collection or owner.

The theatre collection includes *c*18,600 playbills and programmes of Manchester theatres up to 1900. *c*220 playbills are 18th cent, the earliest dating from *c*1743. The collection is listed in the department's card cat at 792.094273, sub-arranged by theatre. Also, special indexes are being compiled under titles of plays and under names of leading performers. A list of the holdings relating to each theatre, which gives separate dates for the playbills and the programmes, is given in *Manchester Review*, v 10, Summer-Autumn 1963, p43.

Departmental card cats, with additional or alternative indexing for some material as indicated above.

Elizabeth Leach, *Guide to the Arts Library*, 3rd ed, 1974.

——'The Manchester theatre: resources of the Arts Library', in *Manchester Review*, v 10, Autumn 1965, p217-25.

Sidney Horrocks, 'The Manchester theatre: sources for research in the Manchester Reference Library', *ibid*. v 6, Winter 1951, p161-4, 200. (This article, written before the creation of a separate Arts Library, is up-dated by Miss Leach's article of 1965, but contains some information which is not repeated in the later article.)

Language and Literature Library

The latest of the main subject-departments to be established, in 1963, with stock which had been acquired by the General Reference Library since 1852. Much of the material is contained in various special collections, for which separate reports follow. Most of the very early material, including incunabula is, however, contained in the department's general collection and consists mainly of continental editions of the Latin classics and commentaries on them. Works in English include a few pre-1641 items. Possibly the rarest of these is John Lydgate's *The life and death of Hector*, published in 1614 by Thomas Purfoot, which was not listed in the first edition of STC but is numbered 5581.5 in the second edition. Also quite rare is the 1635 edition of George Wither's *A collection of emblems...*, for which the library's copy contains the separate title-pages of each of the five joint publishers, as represented by STC 25900–25900d. The department is particularly rich in pamphlet material issued from the mid-18th to the early 19th cent, due to the acquisition of over 5,000 such items in the early 1850s. (Manchester Free Library. *Third Annual Report*, 1855, p12). Consisting mainly of plays, poems and lectures on a wide range of subjects, the majority of which are not essentially literary in that they cover theology, philosophy, history, biography, topography, science, medicine, technology and the arts as well as literature, they were bound in 552 v as the Literary Tracts Collection. Although their arrangement is only rudimentarily systematic, individual items can be traced in the library's general printed *Index of names and subjects*, published in 1881. The majority are also entered in the department's card cats and in the general cats in the Catalogue Hall. (*Manchester Review* v 10, Winter 1963–4, p68-9.) The department also has a substantial collection of older material in the field of English dialect, especially Lancashire, mainly due to the donation to the library of the collection of the English Dialect Society in 1878. The contents of the Society's collection, together with the material already possessed by the library, were published in 1880 in the 28-page *Catalogue of the English Dialect Library (in the) Free Reference Library, King Street, Manchester.* Arranged systematically, mainly under English counties, followed by single sequences for Scotland, the Isle of Man and Ireland, it lists over 500 items, of which *c*120 relate to Lancashire and *c*60 to Yorkshire. Many of them are pre-1850, including some pre-1800. In the field of literature in general, the department possesses first editions of many British writers, particularly of the 19th and 20th cent; also mss of some local authors, notably Robert Neill and J L Hodson. There are also complete files of many long-established periodicals, including, for example, *Blackwood's Magazine* from 1817.

Departmental name and subject cats.

Also various printed, typescript and card cats for the special collections which are described hereunder.

Michael Harkin, 'The Language and Literature Library', *Manchester Review*, v 10, Winter 1963–4, p65-73.

Alexander Ireland Collection Formed by Alexander Ireland (1809–94) who came to Manchester from Edinburgh in 1843, and became managing partner of the *Manchester Examiner*. While still at Edinburgh he had already become acquainted with many of the leading British writers of the day, and had formed friendships with some of them, including Scott and Wordsworth. He later compiled published bibliographies of Lamb, Hazlitt and Leigh Hunt (*Papers of the Manchester Literary Club*, v XXI, 1895, p1-9). In 1895 the collection was purchased by Thomas Read Wilkins and presented to the library.

The collection contains *c*450 books, of which *c*150 are pre-1851; also runs of literary periodicals, separate literary articles, newspaper cuttings and letters. Included are books, articles, etc by, or about, Charles and Mary Lamb, William Hazlitt, James Leigh Hunt, Thomas and Mary Carlyle, and Ralph Waldo Emerson. Coverage of authors varies, but many are represented by numerous first editions of their works and by other rare material.

John Hibbert Swann, *Catalogue of the Alexander Ireland Collection*, 1898. 25pp (occasional list no 5) (arranged systematically under individual writers). The book material is also entered in the general cats.

A typescript list of the ephemera is in preparation.

Bellot Chinese Collection Collected in China in the 1840s by Thomas Bellot, naval surgeon and orientalist, on whose death in 1857 the collection was bequeathed to the library. The collection consists of 58 printed books and 4 boxes of ms material. Printed books include rare dictionaries, works on religion, archaeology and the fine arts, illustrated drawing books and acupuncture charts. Of the 58 printed books, one dates from 1661, 11 from the 18th cent, 32 1800–50, and 14 are undated.

Typescript author list of printed books.

W E A Axon in *Trubner's Library Record*, July 28, 1870, and repeated in Axon's *Handbook of the public libraries of Manchester and Salford* (1877), p174-6.

Broadside Ballad Collection Acquired before 1879 (presumably purchased, but not known from whom), the collection includes *c*2,000 broadsides, mounted in 13 v. Two v consist of black-letter ballads, mostly of the 17th cent, but including a few from the late 16th cent. They comprise 112 printed broadsides which contain one or two ballads; also 2 ms ballads. The remaining 11 v contain mainly 19th cent items, with some from the late 18th cent. They include many printed in the provinces, particularly Manchester.

A typescript list of the black-letter ballads, in the order of their mounting in the 2 v.

The later ballads are indexed on cards by title or first line and by subject.

Robert Langton, 'The black-letter ballads in the Free Reference Library, Manchester', 1885 (offprint of an article in *Trans Lancs and Cheshire Antiq Soc*, v II, 1884).

The 11 v of later ballads have been microfilmed; copies can be supplied.

Brontë Collection Covering the Brontë family as a whole, the material was collected by Joseph James Gleave of Whalley Range, Manchester, and presented to the Moss Side Free Library early in the present century. The collection was later transferred to Manchester Central Library, and has since been dispersed among the library's general reference stock. It contains 150 v and pamphlets in the original collection, plus magazine articles and newspaper cuttings.

John Albert Green, *Catalogue of the Gleave Brontë Collection at the Moss Side Free Library*. 1907. 32pp (includes also a number of items in other Manchester free libraries).

——*Brontë Collection... list of additions, 1907–16.* 1916. 24pp (lists mainly late 19th cent and later material).

Both of these lists include the cuttings etc.

The books and pamphlets are also listed in the library's general cats.

Chapbook Collection Probably acquired in the 19th cent, the collection contains *c*1,000 items in *c*80 v, and covers a wide range of material in chapbook form, including some in Italian and a little in French. The largest part of the collection, however, consists of *c*500 chapbooks (in *c*40 v), emanating from all over Britain from *c*1770 to the mid-19th cent. They vary in page size from *c*4″ × 2″ to *c*7½″ × 4″, and in price from ½d to 6d, the dearer ones sometimes containing one or more titles such as *Mother Bunch, Mother Shipton, Tom Hickathrift* and *Guy of Warwick*; also some which were specifically intended for younger children, varying from *Cinderella*, issued in 8pp at ½d by Catnatch to E Hodgson's series of toy books, issued *c*1820–30 as the *Royal Nursery Library* at 4d each, with a coloured illustration on each of their 12 pages. Many others were apparently intended for older readers in that they are at the upper end of the price- and size-range, and largely deal with sensational and violent subjects—murders, brigandage etc, sometimes condensed from Gothic novels. Other adult categories include biography and a few adaptations of 19th cent authors, for instance one or two works of Byron and Scott at 6d, with coloured copper-engraved frontispieces. Each item is listed in two card indexes, one of which lists the contents of each volume, while the other lists each item by author or title and refers to the volume containing it. A typescript list of chapbooks published in Manchester was compiled in 1935. Most of the *c*60 items are undated; dated ones range from 1792 to 1853.

Other chapbook-form material in English consists of *c*20 v of moral stories, mostly issued by religious societies, etc; also 50 songs of the Victorian period in 5 v. Foreign language material consists mainly of 270 chapbooks in Italian, published at Florence *c*1894–1902, all but one or two of them in verse. There is also a volume of 55 religious stories in French, published 1839–41.

For a fuller listing than that given in the card indexes, the library's pre-1950 subject cat (on microfilm) should be consulted; the material is mostly listed at 398.5, with some also at 398.4, 398.51, 398.77 and 398.8.

Hilda McGill (part of an article on early children's books), *Manchester Review*, v 9, Spring 1960, p17-19.

(Samuel Taylor) Coleridge Collection Collected in a private capacity from the 1800s or earlier by John Albert Green, Librarian of Moss Side Library and later of Special Collections at Manchester Central Library; purchased by the library for £250 after Green's death in 1931. The collection includes 740 v of books and pamphlets, of which 175 are pre-1851; also many magazine articles, newspaper cuttings, portraits and lantern slides. It contains many first editions, including *Poems*, 1796, *Wallenstein*, 1800, *The Friend* (periodical) 1809–10, *Omniana, Remorse*, 1813, *The statesman's annual*, 1816, *Sibylline leaves, Zapolya, Biographia Literaria*, 1817, and *Aids to reflection*, 1825. There are more than 50 editions of *Lyrical ballads*, howbeit not the first of 1798. The numerous collected editions of Coleridge include Pickering's 1828, Galignani's continental edition, Paris 1829, the Philadelphia edition 1831, and Moxon's 1852; there are also *c*40 v of selections; *c*60 anthologies containing work by Coleridge; 30 v of criticism, and more than 60 biographies; also more than 100 other works which include impressions or recollections of Coleridge.

In addition to the entries in the library's general cats, there is a separate card cat of the collection.

A E Dillon, 'The Coleridge Collection at the Manchester Reference Library', *Library Assoc Record*, July 1931, p254-6.

S Horrocks, 'The Coleridge Collection', *Manchester Review*, v 6, Summer 1952, p255.

De Quincey Collection Based on the collection which was donated in *c*1898 by Dr W E A Axon to Moss Side Public Library, which was subsequently absorbed into Manchester Public Libraries. While Axon's contribution remains the most important part of the collection, there are substantial later additions, including much 19th cent material, of which a few items are pre-1851. Of the total collection of *c*1,000 items (mainly *c*400 books and *c*600 periodical articles), mostly of the 19th cent, *c*200 items are pre-1851. Included are the first five editions of *Confessions of an English opium eater*, and most other 19th cent editions in English published in Britain and the USA; also a few rare 19th cent translations into French and German, and the first edition of the novel *Klosterheim* (1832). The exhaustive collection of items published in magazines, principally *Blackwood's*, represents the first publication of most of De Quincey's essays; and in the case of many anonymous items identified by Axon were, at least as late as 1912, the only form of publication, as they had not been included in the author's canon (and there does not appear to have been a bibliography of De Quincey's writings published since Axon's time). De Quincey accessions are added to the general stock but not to the collection.

John Albert Green, *Thomas De Quincey: a bibliography based upon the De Quincey Collection in the Moss Side Library.* 1908. v vii, 10pp (lists many items not then in the collection, many of which were, however, subsequently acquired). A 14-page typescript supplement was produced in 1977; it lists very little older material. The collection is not indexed in the library's general cat.

William E A Axon, 'The De Quincey Collection at Moss Side'. 1900, 15pp (a bibliographical essay, wider in scope than the Moss Side collection; offprint of an article in the *Library Assoc Record*, Aug 1900).

(Thomas) Fuller Collection Collected by John Eglington Bailey, FSA (1840–88), a Manchester merchant, book-collector, antiquary, and a prolific writer of articles on the history of churches and clergy in South Lancashire and North Cheshire, and an authority on Thomas Fuller (1608–61). The collection was purchased on Bailey's

death in 1888 and presented to the library by Messrs Taylor-Garnett and Co. It comprises *c*170 editions in *c*230 v, and contains three categories of books: (a) *c*50 17th cent editions of Fuller's works, comprising the first and other earliest editions of them, including, for instance, the first four of each of the *History of the Holy War* (1639, 1640, 1647, 1651) and *The holy state* (1642, 1648, 1652, 1663); (b) *c*60 17th and early 18th cent titles, mainly by other people named Fuller; (c) *c*60 19th cent editions, comprising books about Fuller, and reprints of his writings.

Listed in the general cats.

'The Fuller collection...', 1891 (occasional list no 2) (an author list, unannotated) (the sole surviving copy is kept at the centre counter in the Great Hall).

Gaskell Collection The nucleus of the collection was donated in 1895 by Dr W E A Axon to Moss Side Public Library, which was subsequently absorbed into Manchester Public Libraries. The collection was subsequently developed by Mr J A Green, the Librarian at Moss Side, the acquisitions including donations from Mrs Gaskell's daughters, and in 1913 by purchases from their estate. Donations of American editions were received from a Mr D Hutchinson of Newport and Washington, USA, in 1911, 1915 and 1922. The printed books by, and about, Mrs Gaskell (1810–65), including recent editions, probably total *c*500. Of these, about a quarter comprise editions of her works published before her death in 1865. There are also 77 v and 3 issues of periodicals containing serialisations of her novels and other contributions by her. There is also a small amount of contemporary ms material, and *c*300 miscellaneous items dating from the 19th cent, apart from later items, consisting mainly of newspaper cuttings and periodical articles and various kinds of pictorial material, such as postcards, associated with Mrs Gaskell and/or her writings.

It is an extensive collection which includes the first published form, both serialized and in volumes, of all Mrs Gaskell's works, except for *Cranford*, of which the earliest edition is the second, reprinted in the same year, 1853, as the first. Included are the first two editions of the *Life of Charlotte Brontë*, 1857, which contain the passages which were suppressed in later editions. There are also some early continental editions, including the Tauchnitz edition of *Mary Barton* in 1849, the year after its first publication in Britain. There are also many early UK reprints and also ultra-cheap paper-covered reprints from the turn of the century, some of which are now quite rare: the penny editions of Newnes and Stead and the sixpenny ones of Methuen. The ms material includes two stories, 'Crowley Castle' and 'The crooked branch', six letters written by Mrs Gaskell, and one from Charles Dickens in 1852. A small part of the collection comprises the published works of the author's husband, the Rev William Gaskell (1805–94), mainly pamphlet sermons and addresses.

John Albert Green, *A bibliographical guide to the Gaskell Collection in the Moss Side Library*. 1911, 68pp. (Preceded by a short preface, it lists, without annotation, but in systematic order, *c*600 items which comprise most of the rarer material in the collection.)

Ms list, which is kept up to date as material is added and thus, as compared with Green's cat, includes a large proportion of more recent, less rare material. Systematically arranged, it is also very detailed, listing, for instance, all the individual excerpts from newspapers and periodicals, and also noting Mrs Gaskell's contributions in each issue of the periodicals which contain her work. There are cross-references to corresponding entries in Green's cat.

Book material in the collection is also listed in the library's general cats.

Marion V Malcolm-Hayes, *Notes on the Gaskell Collection in the Central Library Manchester*, 1945, 26pp. (Still in print; reprinted in *Memoirs and Proceedings of the Manchester Literary and Philosophical Society*, v 97, 1946–7; contains much information regarding Mrs Gaskell's background in regard to its effect on her writing career.)

S Horrocks, 'The Gaskell Collection', *Manchester Review*, v 6, Autumn 1953, p483 (a brief survey).

Local History Library

Created as a separate subject-department in 1957 to accommodate relevant material collected since 1852; also to undertake more effectively the various existing projects and to initiate new ones in connection with creating as exhaustive as possible a collection of material of all kinds relating to all aspects of the history of a region within, broadly, a 25-mile radius of the Centre of Manchester.

Apart from a wide variety of other materials, the collection contains, including post-1850 items, some 12,000 titles or editions of books and *c*130,000 illustrative items such as prints and photographs. The large number of directories dates back to 1772 for Manchester, and to 1818 for Lancashire. The many long runs of pre-1851 newspapers include many which commenced in the 18th cent, of which the earliest dates from 1733–78. Many have been microfilmed. The collection of broadsides and posters contains many items which are undated but includes *c*12 from the 17th cent, over 400 from the 18th cent and over 800 from the first half of the 19th cent. This collection, which is arranged in chronological order, has its own card indexes, arranged respectively by date and by subject. Other materials include histories of various kinds, census returns and files of newspaper clippings.

Card cats.

Manchester Public Libraries. *The Local History Library: a guide to its resources*. 1965.

D Read, '"Manchester News-Letter": A discovery at Oxford', *Manchester Review*, v 8, Spring 1957, p1-5 (describes the extant issues of the first Manchester newspaper, of which the library only possessed a single issue, of 1725, until a microfilm copy of 22 unique issues of 1724 was obtained from All Souls College, Oxford.

The article was reprinted from the *Manchester Guardian*, Aug 31, 1956).

(Henry Watson) Music Library

By far the greatest number of the rare books were part of the collection of 16,700 v of music and books about music, including over 2,000 pre-1800 items, which were collected by Dr Henry Watson in the later 19th cent, and which he donated to the City of Manchester in 1899. Subsequent donations included rare early-17th cent editions of English music, given by Mr S W Bebbington of Knutsford in 1906. In addition to thousands of items dating from the first half of the 19th cent there are *c*2,700 dating before 1800, some as early as the 16th cent. Consisting mainly of printed scores, the pre-1800 material includes several hundred books on music, and nearly 500 mss, of which all but *c*50 comprise the important Aylesford Collection, consisting mainly of Handelian scores and instrumental and vocal parts, and also *c*50 rare early 18th cent mss of Italian music. There are *c*100 editions for which the Henry Watson copy is the only one recorded in BUCEM. In addition there are some items which are not listed in BUCEM, some of which, being continental editions, are therefore not listed in the STCs, but listed in the BL general catalogue and possibly the catalogues of some other libraries. They include the first editions of Glareanus' *Dodecachordi*, Basle, 1547; the first two volumes of Praetorius' *Syntagma musicum*, Wolfenbüttel, 1614–20; Kircher's *Musurgia universalis*, Rome, 1650; also the second edition of Zarlino's *Le institutione harmoniche*, Venice, 1562. British editions which are not listed in BUCEM, and for which Wing does not indicate the Henry Watson location include Mace's *Musicke's monument*, London, 1676 (M120); and Ptolemy's *Harmonicorum libri tres*, Oxford, 1682 (P4149). At least one edition in the library is not recorded in either BUCEM or STC, namely the third edition, 1603, of Dowland's *First book of songes or aires* printed by E Short, which falls between 7092 and 7093 in STC. The library has copies of the rare second and third books of Dowland's 'songs or airs' of 1600 (STC 7095) and 1603 (STC 7096); also the very rare undated *Lachrimae* printed by J Windet, dated by BUCEM and STC at 1604—the Henry Watson catalogue gives (1605) but there is no reason to assume that the copy is other than STC 7097. There are also copies of the very rare compilations of Tobias Hume, namely *The first part of ayres, French, Pollish...*, 1605 (STC 13958) and *Captain Humes poetical musicke*, 1607, in 2 v (STC 13957). The library also has vocal parts, some of them very rare, of Byrd's collections, namely the superius and medius of *Psalms, sonets and songs of sadnes and pietie*, printed by T Este (sic) in (1590?) (STC 4254)—not the 1588 edition which BUCEM credits to the library; the superius and contratenor parts of the four-part 1610 edition of *Songs of sundrie natures* (STC 4258); also a copy of *Parthenia* (STC 4252), undated, but containing a ms note to the effect that it was published in 1611, which agrees with STC but not with BUCEM, which places it at 1615. The note also refers to a second edition of 1613, which is not recorded.

The library also contains an outstanding collection of 18th cent Handelian material, including the very important Aylesford mss, the bequest of Sir Newman Flower's collection in 1965, for which the library has published a catalogue (see reference below). The major part of the collection comprises 368 v of Handelian mss (some of these volumes also contain some printed scores), which were produced either by John Christopher Smith senior, Handel's copyist and amanuensis or, after *c*1730, mainly by a group of copyists working under Smith's supervision. The copies were commissioned as the personal property of Charles Jennens, Handel's friend and librettist—of *Messiah*, among other works. On Jennens' death in 1773, the mss were inherited by Heneage Finch, 3rd Earl of Aylesford (1715–77), in whose family they remained until 1918, when they were auctioned by Sotheby's. With the exception of a few items which went to the King's Music Library, the collection was purchased by Flower, who subsequently added to the collection (James S Hall, 'The importance of the Aylesford manuscripts', *Brio*, v 4, no 1, Spring 1967, p7-11). Of the 368 v of Handelian mss, 68 contain full scores of operas and oratorios. The other 300 v, apart from a few which contain airs and arias, contain instrumental and vocal parts, including, according to Hall, orchestral parts for 75% of the full scores. The parts constitute the most significant material in the collection for researchers into Handel's music (see L W Duck, 'The Aylesford Handel manuscripts: a preliminary check-list', *Manchester Review*, v 10, Autumn 1965, p228-32). The Aylesford parts are extremely rare, and in some cases unique, owing to the fact that the sets which were produced for performance were lost in conflagrations at the theatres where they were housed. The Flower bequest also included *c*280 printed Handel scores of the 18th cent in 150 v; also *c*60 printed libretti, mostly of the 18th cent, with a few from the early 19th cent in 26 v. A number of the printed editions in the Flower collection duplicate copies which the library had acquired from Henry Watson's original bequest of 1899. The latter, however, also contained 86 18th cent editions of Handel's works, which thus supplement those in the Flower collection. These have been listed in L W Duck, 'Handel: early printed editions in the Henry Watson Music Library', *Manchester Review*, v 12, no 3, Winter 1972–3, p73-81. The list was compiled so that, used in conjunction with the printed catalogue of the Flower collection, 'the Handel resources of the Henry Watson Music Library may be referred to without the necessity of consulting the departmental card catalogues'. In addition to the Handel material in the Flower collection there are 52 v of early 18th cent ms copies of the works of Italian composers of the first decade of the century. An annotated listing has been published in: M Talbot, 'Some overlooked manuscripts in Manchester', *Musical Times*, v 115, 1974, p942-4 in which the writer suggests that they were

Handel's personal copies. Among the mss in the original Henry Watson collection is one described by the library's former librarian, John Russell, as being 'of great value to musical scholarship'. It is a volume of 200 pages, dating from *c*1660, containing *c*216 pieces of music for the viol-da-gamba, mostly in lute-tablature, by British composers, including both well-known and forgotten ones. A transcription made for the Libraries Committee by Dr Lee Southgate in 1913 has not yet been published. Of particular interest among the contents of the collection is a song which is referred to in a Shakespeare play, and which was previously thought to have been lost (*Manchester Review*, v 1, July 1936, p13). Leonard Duck also refers to this in *Manchester Review*, Autumn 1960, p73-4; and also to a ms copy of organ parts for Purcell anthems, believed to be in the writing of John Blow, which had recently been used 'by a well-known authority in preparing performing versions'. Three earlier ms items of interest are a 14th cent psalter from the Rhine Provinces, a 14th cent antiphoner and a slightly later Italian antiphoner (see Russell, *loc cit*). Among various material of more local interest are many sets of concert programmes, mostly of series initiated in the 19th cent and many of them complete, eg the Halle Concerts; they include an almost complete set for the Gentleman's Concerts (1799–1895) (*Manchester Review*, v 9, Autumn 1960, p77).

Card cats covering a wide range of approaches to music (*Manchester Review*, v 10, Spring 1963, p16-17) include for instance, exhaustive indexes to songs in collections, by title, date and subject.

Separate name and subject cats for pre-1800 material.

Index of important periodical articles which were published before the advent of 'The Music Index' in 1950.

Arthur D Walker, *George Frederic Handel: the Newman Flower Collection in the Henry Watson Music Library*, 1972.

There are brief and virtually identical surveys by Leonard Duck in *Manchester Review*, v 9, Autumn 1960, p73-4, and in *Manchester Public Libraries: A guide to the Henry Watson Music Library*, 3rd ed, 1970, p11-12. Also various articles on the library's Handeliana, some of which are referred to above.

Social Sciences Library

Located in the Great Hall, which formerly housed the General Reference Library, following the transference of the language and literature stock to form a separate subject-department. Covering the Dewey classes 001–399 and 900–999, the department houses the largest collection of rare material in the library as a whole, acquired by the General Reference Library since 1852. Much of the rare stock is contained in various special collections, for which separate reports are appended. The majority of the oldest material, however, is contained in the department's general collection of book rarities, which includes the majority of the 30+ incunabula and other early books in the possession of Manchester Public Libraries. All but 2 of the incunabula are continental; the only 2 English items, both of which were printed by Wynkyn de Worde, are STC 9996 and 1344b. Of the other *c*40 items in Pollard and Redgrave the rarest appear to be STC 568, 570, 4925, 7170, 9194, 11917, 13893, 23326 and 24487.5. An item which does not appear to be listed is a 1545 reprint of STC 21790. A copy of a sermon by Bishop Thomas Cooper, which lacks the title-page and has no colophon and therefore no imprint, but which has the caption-title *A sermon no lesse godlie then sic necessarie, preached in the Minster at Lincolne... on the xxvii day of August, 1575* may be STC 5691 (the trimmed page is $c14\frac{1}{2} \times 9\frac{1}{2}$ cm and the chain-lines are vertical). In addition to large numbers of older, or otherwise rare, books and pamphlets, the department holds complete files of many long-established periodicals and newspapers, including the *Oxford London Gazette* from its inception in 1665.

The stock of the department is recorded in the general reference cats in the adjoining Catalogue Hall.

Card cat, except for the pre-1950 subject cats which are on microfilm.

Printed cat for the holdings on genealogy, published in three parts, 1956–8 (ref: Walford, v 2).

Printed cats or typescript shelflists for most of the special collections, as indicated in the separate reports hereunder.

Bataillard Gypsy Collection Collected by M Paul Bataillard of Paris, an eminent authority on the subject, and purchased by the Libraries Committee in 1895. It contains *c*350 books and pamphlets; also several thousand sheets of ms notes (in French), and covers the history, language and customs of gypsies throughout Europe. The printed material is in French, German and other European languages, as well as English. It dates mostly from the 19th cent, with some from the 18th cent. There is also a volume containing 108 19th cent photographic portraits of gypsies which were collected by M Bataillard. Entitled *Ethnographie tsigane*, it is shelved at Q397 B26.

There is no separate cat. The printed books are listed in the general cats and are classified at 397-397.9.

Early Children's Books (pre-1900) Accumulated over the years, the collection contains *c*650 pre-1850 items out of a total collection of *c*1,000, the remainder dating from 1850–99. On the authority of Hilda McGill, the collection is claimed to 'exemplify the many changes which have taken place in the education and amusement of children by way of books'. The earliest item is the 1602 edition of William Clerk's *A short dictionarie for children, Latin and English* (not in STC?), and there are a number of other 17th cent items. The many 18th cent items include the 41-vol *Le cabinet des fees...*, published at Geneva and Paris, 1785–9.

No separate cat; listed in the general reference cats.

Hilda M McGill, 'Early children's books in the Manchester Reference Library', *Manchester Review*, v 9, Spring 1960, p12–20.

Local and Personal Acts A complete set of local, private and personal Acts relating to the region from 1802 was acquired from the North Western Gas Board in the 1960s, since when the collection has been kept up to date. The period 1802–50 is covered by 154 v. (A further *c*620 v cover the period 1851–1981.)

The individual Acts are not listed in any of the library's cats, there being only a single entry for the collection as a whole. The individual Acts are, of course, listed in the HMSO *Index of Local and Personal Acts 1801–1947*, published in 1949, and in its supplements.

Political Pamphlets Collection Presented in 1932 by the National Reform Union, the Liberal Party pressure group which was concerned with parliamentary reform. The collection of *c*2,000 items in 108 v consists of material published in the second half of the 19th cent, and although it is likely that comparatively few of the individual items are rare, the collection is so exhaustive that it provides a valuable insight into 19th cent Liberalism and the Free Trade Movement. Subjects covered include land reform, the Irish question, education, free trade, parliamentary reform, foreign and colonial affairs, Liberalism and Conservatism. The material is arranged systematically under broad subject headings.

Individual pamphlets are entered in the general cats.

A separate index to the volumes reached v 69; it cannot, however, be located at present (1982).

Private Press Collection Built up from the 19th cent by purchase and donation. An appraisal of the collection in connection with the compilation of a printed catalogue resulted in substantial purchases in the 1950s and 1960s of the work of many of the historic presses. Of the total of *c*1,700 editions produced by private or other fine presses, (while *c*1,000 are from minor modern presses), possibly as many as 500 may be considered to be rare by virtue of their age, typographic quality and/or limitation of size of edition and, in many cases their historical significance. The collection covers the whole range of British private and semi-private presses, also a few American and continental ones. The historic presses are well represented; so too are a number of little-known presses of various periods which produced very small editions of as few as 10 or 20 copies. The pre-Kelmscott presses are represented both by the better known ones, Strawberry Hill (10 items, published 1757–84) and that of C H O Daniel (6 items, 1899–1908); and also by a number of lesser-known ones, the earliest being that of Peter Whitfield at Liverpool (2 items, 1748 and 1749). Of the major pre-1914 presses, the Kelmscott is represented by 18 main works, mostly from the early years of the press, 1891–3; also the great *Chaucer* of 1896. There are 14 Doves items (1903–14), including the 5-v Bible of 1903–5. There are 10 Eragny items (1899–1906) and 13 Vale (1896–1904), the latter including many of the earliest, and 4 from 1896. The 13 Ashendene works (1903–35) include 4 pre-1914, namely 3 from 1903–4, and the 1909 *Dante*; also the Spenser folios of 1923 and 1925 and the *Don Quixote*, 1927–8. Of the 'next rank' and post-1918 presses, there are 23 Essex House (1898–1912), mostly of the early period to *c*1903; 35 Cuala (1908–44), including 4 (1904–7) from the initial Dun Emer period and 7 from 1908–15; 26 Gregynog (1923–46), mostly early, including many from the 1920s; 136 Golden Cockerel, of which 9 (1921–3) belong to the H M Taylor period; 32 (1924–33) to the Gibbings period; 45 (1934–44) to the pre-war and wartime Sandford period; and 50 (1945–76) to the post-war period. Of the 90 Nonesuch titles (1923–57) nearly all are pre-1940.

Manchester PL Reference Library subject cat: section 094, private press books. 1959–60, 2 v. (Arranged alphabetically by presses (127), with an introductory note on each, it lists 743 editions, giving details of typefaces used, illustrations, colour-printing, paper, binding, size of edition and occasionally, provenance, eg gifts of Kelmscott books by Mrs Morris; call-numbers are also given.) The catalogue, which is still in print, lists the great majority of the older, rarer material. However, a significant amount of such material was acquired after the publication of the catalogue, including a few important Doves and Ashendene editions; 13 Golden Cockerel; 11 Cuala (including the only 4 in the collection from the initial Dun Emer period, dated 1904–7); 8 Gregynog (including 6 published between 1926 and 1934) and 10 pre-1940 Nonesuch titles. These and other relevant items are listed at 094.10942 etc in the classified card cat which covers accessions from 1950 to March 1977. The private press material which is similarly listed in the card cat which covers accessions from April 1977 comprises, in 1982, only the work, mainly recent, of minor modern presses.

Shorthand Collection The collection was almost wholly built up, particularly as regards the oldest and rarest items, by John Eglington Bailey, FSA (1840–88), a Manchester merchant, writer, book collector, antiquarian, authority on, among other things, shorthand and founder of the Manchester Phonographic Union. On Bailey's death the collection was purchased and presented to the library in 1889 by Councillor Henry Boddington, with a few additions. It contains 1,230 printed books and *c*105 mss relating to shorthand, on the authority of John O'Donnell in 1906, by which time the collection, at least as regards its rarer content, was complete. There are also over 200 books on cryptography, spelling reform, international language, etc. As well as books in English and Latin, it includes many in modern European languages. The collection includes many very rare items, particularly of the 17th and early 18th cent. Among the rarest are: Thomas Andrews's *Rudiments. . . of shorthand* published in Dublin in 1744, whose existence is not recorded in Westby-Gibson's bibliography of 1887; an edition of Samuel Botley's *Maximo in minimo*, printed for Edmund Parker and claiming to have 'never been done till now', undated, but allocated by Westby-Gibson to 1674, which is not recorded in Wing. The collection also includes the edition 'printed and sold by Samuel Botley. . .', also allocated by Wing, to 1674 (B3806); the 2nd edition, 1674 of William Hopkins's *The flying pen-man* (H2752); and the 1669 edition of Jeremiah Rich's *The pen's dexterity completed* (R1347). An undated edition of Henry Barmby's *Shorthand unmaske'd* is possibly very rare, but the date allocated to it, 1700, possibly derived from Westby-Gibson, is probably more than 70 years too early, as the publisher, Stanley Crowder was not, on the authority of Henry Plomer, active until *c*1755, and the earliest recorded edition otherwise is that of 1772. (Wing is rather misleading regarding Crowder in that it places at 1700 another work (H1893) which Crowder published jointly with four others, none of whom, like Crowder, were active until *c*1750 or later.) The collection is shelved as a separate entity, with its own individual system of call-numbers. The general stock of the library also includes some older material, including some of the 18th cent which is listed in the library's general catalogue.

Manchester Public Free Libraries. The Shorthand Collection. 1891. 42pp. (Occasional list no 3). (An author list, unannotated. The titles, often very lengthy, are quoted with adequate fullness. Names of publishers are, however, not given, thus sometimes making it difficult to determine, in the case at least of 17th cent works, the precise edition or issue represented, particularly if they are, as in so many cases, undated. Identification can sometimes be achieved by reference to Westby-Gibson.) The contents of the collection are not listed in the library's general cats. Nor is the printed cat listed; it is thus necessary to memorize its call-number, 016.653 M1; an unnumbered copy is also kept at the stack desk.

John O'Donnell, *British shorthand libraries*. 1906. p123, 124-5.

Thomas Greenwood Library for Librarians The initial collection was built up in the early years of the present cent by Thomas Greenwood (1851–1908), a native of Woodley, near Stockport, who moved to London in 1876, where he became a successful publisher. An industrious advocate and public speaker in support of free public libraries, he was also the author of *Free public libraries*, published in 1886, among other writings on the subject. When the municipal library system had become well established, Greenwood began to concern himself particularly with library education, one outcome being his publication in 1903 of the first edition of James Duff Brown's *Manual of library economy*. At about the same time, he began to collect every available publication which was concerned with libraries. Then, conceiving the idea of a library for librarians, he extended the scope of his collecting in an endeavour to build up as complete a library as possible of every kind of material that was relevant to librarianship, bibliography and, such as there was at the time, library education. A further extension of scope was the inclusion of material to illustrate the physical history of books, including the various materials used at different times and places. In 1904, when the collection had grown to *c*10,000 v, Greenwood donated it to Manchester Public Library, together with a legacy of £5,000. The collection expanded until it comprised *c*26,000 v by 1958, before being dispersed among the general stock of the library. *c*1,000 v in the collection are pre-1850.

As a result of Greenwood's donation, the Social Sciences Library possesses an exhaustive collection of material concerned with bibliography and associated subjects published over the centuries both in Britain and abroad, including for instance, Conrad Gesner's *Bibliotheca universalis*, 1545. The collection included many mss, both European and Oriental; also early printed books, including incunabula, notably the *Nuremberg Chronicle*, 1493, as well as examples of fine binding.

Included in the general cats in the Catalogue Hall. Most of the items are not, however, rare. More useful is *Manchester Public Libraries. Classified catalogue of the Thomas Greenwood Library for Librarians*. 1915, 64pp.

S Horrocks, 'Thomas Greenwood and his library', *Manchester Review*, v 8, Spring 1959, p269-77.

Sutton Witchcraft Collection Acquired in 1920 from Oliver Jepson Sutton, a son of Charles William Sutton, Chief Librarian 1879–1920, it consists of 30 books, some pamphlets and miscellaneous material. Although the collection is quite small, 15 of the books are pre-1851 and a few date from the 17th cent. Moreover, it is supplemented by a number of older items on the subjects which were already in the stock of the library. The collection includes a number of items on related subjects rather than on witchcraft as such. They include the undated 8th edition of Daldiamus Artemiorus's *The interpretation of dreams*, which the library dates at 1673, and which is not included among the editions listed in Wing. The library also holds an undated edition of the same author's *Les ivgemens astronomiques des songes*, published in Paris, and which the library dates at 1664. All editions of this work, first published as early as 1575, appear to be rare in the UK. Less rare 17th cent items are v 1 and 3 of Balthazar Bekker's *Le monde enchanté*, published in Amsterdam in 1694, in 4 v, and also the translation of v 1, the only volume to be published in English, in 1695 as *The world bewitch'd* (Wing B1781). Another less rare 17th cent item which is contained in the library's general collection of book rarities is *Scot's discovery of witchcraft*, (Wing 5943). In addition to books, there are a few pamphlets, some newspaper cuttings, and several sales catalogues, both British and foreign, which were published in the later 19th and early 20th cent.

Listed in the general cats in the Catalogue Hall.

Tract Collection Most of the older tracts belong to a series of political and commercial items which were collected in the mid 18th cent by a Danish merchant in London, Mr Nicholas Magens, whose family continued to add to them. They were purchased by the library in 1852; and 13 other collections were acquired during the next couple of years or so. One of these which also contains much older material was that collected in the first half of the 18th cent by John Perceval, Earl of Egmont

(1683–1748), who was one of the founders of the Colony of Georgia. Another of these collections which has particular importance consists of *c*1,800 items which had been collected by Nicholas Vansittart, Lord Bexley, while Chancellor of the Exchequer, 1812–22. It includes many documents which were privately printed for the use of various Government departments, and also many which are rare on other counts. By 1855, the Tract Collection comprised over 15,000 documents, dating from 1576–1850, bound into 2,576 v. Further acquisitions in the second half of the 19th cent increased the total to *c*40,000 documents in 3,785 v, of which *c*1,800 are pre-1850.

Most of the tracts are listed in the printed author cat of 1864 and its supplement of 1879. More useful, however, is the *Index of names and subjects* published in 1881, which lists the contents of the two earlier volumes in a kind of dictionary-catalogue arrangement.

Also listed in the general pre-1980 classified cat on microfilm.

The only completely exhaustive repertory is the tract shelflist which is arranged in the same order as the tracts.

Manchester Free Library. *Third annual report*, 1855, p9-12.

Technical Library

One of the oldest subject-departments, established with stock which had been acquired by the General Reference Library since 1852. Probably 1,000 or more pre-1850 books and volumes of older periodicals. The department's stock of older books covers all fields of science and technology. The earliest books are probably most numerous in the field of botany, starting with herbals of the late 16th cent. Mostly published in England, the earliest such items (for which STC and Wing numbers are given in parenthesis) date from 1578 (6984), 1597 (11750), 1640 (19302), 1665 (L3244), 1680 (M2771), 1694 (P1021), 1696 (S3998) and 1699 (M2772). Probably rarer in the UK than any of these is Simon Paul's *Quadripartitum botanicum* of 1667, with an appendix in 1668, published at Strassburg. Probably larger in number, although in general dating only from the mid-17th cent onwards, are works in the field of the zoological sciences. The earliest of these published in England date from 1653 (H1085), 1658 (B328), 1661 (L3247), 1667 (W970), 1668 (C3688), 1675 (L947), 1677 (P2586), 1687 (W2880) and 1686 (P2588). 18th cent British books which appear to be very rare include Eleazar Albin's *A natural history of English insects*, 1720; *A natural history of Ireland*, 1726, by Gerard Boate and others; the 1761 edition of Robert Whytt's *Physiological essays*, published at Edinburgh and James Bolton's *Harmonia naturalis*, published at Halifax in two volumes, 1794–6. The very large number of older zoological works published at various continental centres include some 17th cent editions of the works of Ulysse Aldrovandus, of which the *Serpentum et draconum historiae*, published at Bologna in 1640, appears to be particularly rare in the UK. So, too, does the edition of John Johnston's *Historiae naturalis* published at Frankfurt, 1650–3. The numerous 18th cent zoological works published on the continent include a few by Marie Sybille de Merian, of which the rarest in the UK appears to be the third edition revised by Pierre Joseph Buc'hoz, of *Histoire des insectes de Surinam et de l'Europe*, published in Paris in 1771. Larger works include the 15 v published 1749–67 of Buffon's *Histoire naturelle*. There are also many files of older periodicals, including, for instance, *Curtis's Botanical Magazine* from its inception in 1787. There is also a complete collection of the publication of the British Patent Office since its inception in 1852, including the retrospective abridgments covering back to 1617.

Stock recorded in the general reference cats in the adjoining Catalogue Hall; on cards except for the pre-1950 subject cat which is on microfilm.

Printed cat for holdings on printing, published in two parts, 1961–3, and arranged by Dewey.

Chetham's Library, Long Millgate, Manchester M3 1SB. Tel (061) 834 7961. Open Mon-Fri 9.30 am-12.30 pm, 1.30-5 pm. No restrictions of access to bona fide researchers, but advance notice is advisable. Staff will undertake research at a nominal charge (£5 per day in 1982). Photocopies can be supplied.

The library has operated continuously since 1655, having been founded as a chained library initially, under the terms of the will of Humphrey Chetham (1580–1653), a prosperous Manchester merchant and landowner whereby £1,000 and the residue of his estate was bequeathed for the purchase of books and other necessary expenses, together with a sufficient sum of money for the acquisition of the 15th cent building which had initially been the home of the Lords of the Manor of Manchester, and later became the College House for the Warden and clergy of the Collegiate Church, now Manchester Cathedral. The building was acquired early in 1654 and housed, in addition to the library, a Blue Coat School, now Chetham's School of Music, which was also founded under the terms of Chetham's will, and which has since largely expanded into an adjacent later building. Most of the library's older stock was acquired over the years, starting in 1655, as a contemporary working collection available to all scholars. For the first few years the stock was almost wholly theological, but as early as 1663 the subject coverage was extended (and again in the mid-1680s) to cover virtually the whole range of knowledge and, to some extent, belle-lettres, particularly the ancient classics. An article on the library's book purchases 1655–85 is due to appear in 1984 in the John Rylands Library Bulletin of the University of Manchester. (For the nature of early acquisitions, see first two vols of the printed cat published 1791; Supplementary v III, covering acquisitions 1791–1825; Supplementary v IV covering acquisitions 1826–61.)

The collections expanded considerably from the mid-19th cent. It was recorded that the number of books grew from 19,000 in 1845 to 49,000 in the next 30 years, though it seems certain that these figures refer to the number of volumes rather than of editions, which probably numbered little more than half the figures quoted, thus constituting an increase from *c*10,000 editions to *c*25,000. (This would tally with J O Halliwell's estimate of *c*8,000 printed books in 1842.) This growth was aided by a substantial increase in the number of donations, which previously had been almost negligible in quantity (though not, in some instances, in quality, it having been recorded that only 450 books (=volumes?) were donated up to 1842. Thereafter, donations, including much old and rare material, mainly printed, but also including many ms items, largely of local and/or historical interest, became a significant source of acquisitions and largely remained so up to the 1939–45 War. Outstanding among the collections donated in the mid-19th cent was that of over 3,000 broadside items, mainly of the 17th and 18th cent, which was presented in 1850 by J O Halliwell (later Halliwell-Phillips). A printed cat was published in 1851.

The other major donation of the 19th cent was the library of John Byrom (1692–1763), the poet and shorthand teacher, which was presented in 1870 by his descendants. An author cat of the collection which had been published in 1848 indicates that, while most of the *c*3,000 printed books and the many shorter items such as tracts and sermons date mainly from the 17th and early 18th cent, there are also many from the 16th, including the early years of the century, and also a few incunabula. The collection is particularly strong, not only in shorthand and theology, but also in medicine. The contents of the Byrom collection are included among the 15,000 or so editions added to the library from 1863–81 which are listed in the supplementary v VI of the printed cat published in 1883. Although it is not obvious from the supplementary cats of 1883, 1897 and 1907, the policy of covering the whole range of scholarly literature was increasingly abandoned after the middle of the 19th cent because of the inadequacy of the available funds. Moreover, by this time the municipal Manchester Free Library, established in 1851, was providing a general service to the public. Chetham's therefore concentrated on the arts, specializing particularly in British history and topography. Among the many donations in the field of British history, both ms and printed, outstanding is the John Radcliffe collection of 1,000 or so printed books. John Radcliffe (1845–1911), the son of a successful Lancashire manufacturer, was able to retire from business in 1872 in order to devote himself to antiquarian studies, in process of which he built up his collection of mainly old books. Particularly strong in genealogy and heraldry, nearly all of the material is pre-1851, with possibly as much as a half being pre-1800, and including material dating as far back as the late 16th cent. The collection was bequeathed to Chetham's in 1918 by John Radcliffe's son, James (1891–1918), following his death in action at Ypres. An author cat was published in 1937.

An important acquisition of more local interest was that in 1937 of the *c*3,500 v mostly of the 18th and 19th cent, in the collection of William Asheton Tonge (1860–1936) of the Old Rectory, Warburton, Cheshire. While the collection included several hundred 18th cent sermons and *c*300 v of English poetry, and also many works on genealogy and heraldry, the emphasis was on the topography, archaeology and antiquities of Lancashire, Cheshire and Yorkshire. There was also much material of biographical value, including many volumes of local biography *c*70 18th and 19th cent directories of Lancashire and Yorkshire, and 34 v of ms extracts from parish registers concerned with the Tonge and related families. Since *c*1950, the acquisitions policy of the library has narrowed from the history and topography of Great Britain to that of North-West England. Very little older material is now being acquired, either by purchase or donation.

In February 1984 the library acquired, on indefinite loan, the 17th cent chained library of the parish church of St James, Gorton, now in Manchester. The 51 works, which virtually represent the original collection purchased in 1657-8, are chained in one of the two remaining bookchests (which bear the inscription 'The gift of Humphrey Chetham Esquire 1655') out of the five which housed the church libraries which were created as a result of bequests from Chetham's estate. The works, which are all of a religious nature and reflect Chetham's Puritan beliefs, all date from 1610–56, apart from *The Commonplaces of Peter Martyr (Anglerius)... Translated and partlie gathered by...Anthonie Marten*, published in 1583, and not apparently listed in STC. There are typescript lists for the contents of each of the four shelves in the bookcase. The bindings, which appear to be original, are in a remarkably good state of preservation.

Printed Books Pre-1850 printed material includes *c*30,000 books in *c*60,000 v, *c*4,000 tracts, and more than 3,000 broadside items; also *c*600 mss. The *c*30,000 printed editions include *c*120 incunabula, of which 30 or more were printed pre-1480, the earliest being the 1468 *Lactantius* of Sweynheym and Pannartz. Of the library's four incunabula published in England, the earliest is the very rare edition of Aristotle's *Ethics* which was the second book printed, anonymously, by Theodoric Rood at Oxford in 1479 (STC 752). The other three are Wynkyn's 1495 edition of Higden's *Polychronicon* (STC 13439) and the two legal works printed for Pynson by Tailleur at Rouen in or about 1490 (STC 15721, 23238). There are also a few early 16th cent books from Wynkyn, and one or two from Peter Treveris in the 1520s. Among a few STC items which are not recorded by Ramage is a Wynkyn of 1526 (STC 17532). According to Ramage, the library possesses 1,030 STC items altogether, including tracts and ballad sheets as well as books.

The library is rich in books of the 16th and 17th cent, as well as the 18th and early 19th cent. Virtually the whole range of subjects studied in these periods is covered, though the sale of *c*400 v in November 1980 very seriously depleted the fine collection of large illustrated volumes of the 16th-19th cent in the fields of geography, topography, travel, botany and zoology. The library remains singularly strong in religion, law and English history, with its greatest strength in the history and topography of Lancashire and Cheshire. It also possesses one of the finest collections in Britain in the field of shorthand. John O'Donnell in his *British shorthand libraries*, 1906, estimated the collection to contain *c*360 printed books and *c*40 mss. It is based mainly on the 2 collections respectively of the poet John Byrom (1692–1763) which was donated by his descendants in 1870, and of John Harland of the *Manchester Guardian*, acquired on his death in 1868. The collection is notable as compared with larger ones, for the number of very rare and, in some cases, possibly unique editions of the 17th cent or earlier, of which O'Donnell (p122, 124) gives some impression. They include the earliest recorded editions of Peter Bales' *The writing schoolmaster*, 1590 (STC 1312), John Farthing's *Shorthand writing shortened*, 1654 (Wing F532), Jeremiah Rich's *The pen's dexterity*, 1659 (R1346) and Thomas Shelton's *A tutor to tachygraphy*, 1642 (S3087). An undated edition of Shelton's *Tachygraphy*, 'printed and are to be sold by the booksellers of London and Westminster', has been dated by the library as 1642, whereas, according to Westby-Gibson's bibliography of 1887, the imprints of all editions printed before *c*1646 named specific publishers. This edition could therefore be the one described by Westby-Gibson as 'a late and cheap bookseller's venture' of *c*1646. Apparently a 16mo, it would therefore not appear to be the undated octavo edition which Wing (S3079) estimates as being of 1646. There is also the very rare undated edition of William Hopkins' *The flying pen-man*, 'printed for Samuel Lee', for which Wing (H2751a), which does not record the Chetham's copy, gives the date as 1670, possibly derived from Westby-Gibson, whereas according to Henry Plomer, Lee was not active until 1677, in which case the edition dated 1674, 'printed for the author' (H2752), also in the collection, would precede it.

Rare 17th cent reprints include the second edition, 1627, of Edmond Willis' *An abbreviation of writing by character* (STC 25742), the 1668 edition of Theophilus Metcalfe's *A school-master to radio-stenography* (M1924) and the 1669 edition of his *Short-writing* (M1931). Very rare editions of John Willis' works include an incomplete copy of *The art of stenographie, teaching by plaine and certaine rules*, which is thought to belong to one of the 1602 issues (STC 25744a); also the only copy recorded, in STC (25744a.5) of the 1617 edition of *The art of stenographie, or short writing*. It is also the earliest edition recorded, in spite of being designated as the fifth edition which, as Westby-Gibson suggests, is presumably because the numbering of editions is continued from Willis's earlier book, aforementioned, which, however, constitutes a quite different presentation of the subject. The collection also contains the 1644 edition, designated as the 13th (W2809) which, like all the early reprints, is very rare.

The collection also contains large numbers of books, many of them very rare, on cryptography, spelling reform, universal languages etc. A list of Harland's collection was published in the *Phonetic Journal* in 1859, but it is incomplete, having been compiled some years earlier. Byrom's collection is included with the other items in his library in the author catalogue published in 1848. Entries for the Chetham's shorthand collection as a whole are included in the supplementary vol VI of the library's general printed cat, published in 1883. None of these listings is adequate for identifying some of the undated 17th cent editions, not having had the benefit of the availability of Westby-Gibson's bibliography, which was not published until 1887, and which can assist in solving some of the problems. Also, O'Donnell's book can help in discovering editions which are not included in the listings by the library and its donors

Tracts There are *c*4,000 or more separate pre-1851 tracts, bound into volumes, apart from many volumes of reprinted collections. The great majority of the original items are of the 17th and 18th cent. A few date from the reigns of Elizabeth I and James I. Possibly *c*200 date from the Civil War and Commonwealth period; many of them describe military sieges etc, particularly in Manchester and elsewhere in Lancashire and Cheshire. The several hundred items from the later 17th cent are predominantly religious and include *c*500 concerned with the 'Popish controversy', published mainly in the 1680s. Although they are noted in v 1 (1791) of the printed catalogue, they were not listed individually until v IV (1862), in two sequences, following the publication of a printed catalogue of the collection in 1859–65. The latter, which is annotated, follows the systematic arrangement by areas of controversy which is used in Francis Peck's *Catalogue of discourses on popery*. . ., published in 1735. Chetham's did not have copies in 1865, some of which were subsequently acquired. It also lists a number of items which are not included in Peck. Many subject areas are represented by tracts of the late 17th and 18th cent; not only religion, politics etc, but also science and, particularly, medicine, of which there are more than 80 v, including more than 20 v of medical tracts published abroad in various European cities, eg Uppsala and Lyon. Only a selection of the medical tracts are listed in the printed catalogue (v III), but there is a fuller, albeit still incomplete, listing in a special ms catalogue. From the late 18th cent onwards the emphasis is on religion, politics and commerce.

Manuscripts Some indication of the scope of the library's manuscript holdings and some reference to the more important collections and individual volumes is given in the article by Hilda Lofthouse in the Winter 1956 issue of the *Manchester Review*, p325-7.

Broadsides The collection consists mainly of a bequest of over 3,000 items, mainly of the 17th and 18th cent, by J O Halliwell in 1850. Bound in 32 v, the arrangement is, with few exceptions, very unsystematic. Analysis of the collection is thus difficult, particularly as the catalogue of the collection, published in 1851, follows the arrangement of the bound volumes. The preface to the catalogue provides some analysis, as also, to some extent, does the entry, no 9745, in v IV of the library catalogue. A large part of the collection consists of official proclamations, the earliest dating from the time of Charles I, but most from the reigns of Charles II, James II and William III. Together with many less official posters, eg speeches, they cover a very wide range of political, religious and legal issues of the 17th and 18th cent. There are also large numbers of posters concerned with various aspects of trade and commerce. There are also many song-sheets of the, mainly later, 18th cent, as well as some black-letter ballads, which include 2 items, dating from 1570 and 1571, for which neither STC nor Ramage give any other location, viz STC 17495 and STC 5104. The STC entry for the latter incidentally refers to the nun-author of this religious ballad somewhat erroneously as 'a madcap virgine', whereas in ballad-sheet she is 'a modest virgine'. The earliest item in the collection is an indulgence of 1520 which is credited to Wynkyn de Worde in the printed catalogue of the collection, published in 1851. The text, which is preceded by a small woodcut of St George and the dragon, commences 'Unto all maner and singuler christen people beholdynge or herynge these present letters'. It may, therefore, be STC 14077c.72, attributed to Richard Pynson.

Other material In addition to the categories already mentioned, the library contains a large quantity of other materials, mainly of local historical interest—maps, directories, publications of local societies, early local newspapers, including a complete file of the *Manchester Mercury*, 1752–1825, newspaper cuttings, prints and photographs.

The contents, arrangement etc of the printed cats listed here are, in the main, described above.

General cat of the library: *Bibliotheca Chethamensis . . . catalogus*. Manchester 1791–1883. 6 v (title varies between volumes); continued by card cats of post-1881 accessions in two sequences, viz author and alphabetical subject.

Catalogue of the library of . . . John Byrom, compiled by B R Wheatley. London, 1848 (privately printed).

Catalogue of proclamations, broadsides, ballads and poems, presented . . . by James O Halliwell. London, 1851 (privately printed in a limited edition of 100 copies).

Catalogue of the collection of tracts for and against popery published in or about the reign of James II, ed by Thomas Jones. Manchester, 1859–65. 2 v. *Chetham Society Publications*, original ser nos 48, 64.

Catalogue of the John Radcliffe Collection, compiled by C T E Phillips. Manchester, 1937.

Charles T E Phillips, 'Humphrey Chetham and his library', in *Manchester Review*, v 3, Winter 1944/5, p280-93. (The life of Sir Humphrey Chetham, his foundation of the library, and its subsequent administration and growth up to the early 1900s.)

Hilda Lofthouse, 'Chetham's Library' in *The Book Collector*, (Winter 1956), p323-30. (Mainly surveys the scope of the stock of the library.)

The book stock is arranged in a multiplicity of classified sequences; in the case of most of the older stock by a system based on that devised for Cambridge University Library by Conyers Middleton in the 18th cent; and in the case of accessions since 1940 by Dewey. These sequences are not paralleled in the various card subject cat which in general are arranged by alphabetical subject.

Since 1972, and particularly between Oct 1980 and Dec 1981, in order to finance its current operations, the library has been obliged to sell more than 400 of its most financially valuable works, comprising mainly large illustrated books, with the emphasis on botany, zoology and topography, amounting to *c*1,000 v. On 26 June 1972, 6 notable illustrated ornithological works, totalling 20 v were auctioned by Sotheby's (reported in *The Times*, 27 June 1972). In Oct 1980 the earliest of the 5 known collections of John Abbot's bird drawings, comprising 153 water-colours of the birds of Georgia in 4 v were sold in New York by Christie's to Quaritch for nearly £25,000 (reported in the *Daily Telegraph* 20 Oct 1980). A succession of Christie's sales in London from Oct 1980 onwards included one or more Chetham's items, and a sale on 26-27 Nov was concerned solely with Chetham's books, of which *c*400 were sold. On 20 Nov 1980 6 works (lots 283-7) realized a total of £32,250 (reported in the *Daily Telegraph* 21 Nov 1980). For reports on other sales, see *Daily Telegraph* 27 Nov, 1 Dec (1980), 24 Feb (1981).

Manchester Grammar School, Manchester M13 0XT. Tel (061) 224 7201. Open (Term) 9.45 am-3.45 pm; other times on request to the librarian-curator. Photocopying facilities.

The School was founded in 1515 and the library, which contains *c*500 v pre-1851, began probably in the 1640s with a donation of an unknown number of books. The collection now contains *c*250 v 1801–50, and *c*250 v are pre-1801. The latter represent *c*165 editions, of which 2 are Italian incunabula of 1494, and a further 20 v, nearly all continental, date from the 16th cent. There are *c*55 v of the 17th cent and 88 v of the 18th cent. Greek and Latin classics form the largest subject category, with theology the second largest, followed by history and topography. *c*20 v from the library were given to the John Rylands Library in 1950.

There is a computer print-out of pre-1801 books, arranged by date of publication, but not giving details of publisher or place of publication.

There is as yet no listing of 1801–50 material.

Author and Dewey card cats of the library's pre-1901 books are in the early stages of compilation and are unlikely to be completed before 1987.

Manchester Polytechnic, All Saints Building, Oxford Road, Manchester M15 6BH. Tel (061) 228 6171. Open (Term) Mon-Fri 9 am-9 pm; (Vacation) 9 am-5 pm. Admission by written application to the librarian. Photocopying facilities; typing carrel available.

Although the Polytechnic was only established in the 1960s, one of its constituents, the Manchester Regional College of Art, now the Faculty of Art and Design had a library since 1845. It contained many older books in all fields of art and design, and included many folio architectural works of the late-18th and early-19th cent, which were richly augmented in the 1960s by the donation of the rare book collection of the Manchester Society of Architects. The College of Art Library also contained many private press books and other examples of fine printing which have been rigorously augmented to build up a special *Book Design Collection* which covers all physical aspects of British book production from the early 19th cent onwards.

In 1977 the Didsbury College of Education was absorbed into the Polytechnic and now houses the Department of Education. Its library contains the *Morten-Dandy Collection* of children's books and periodicals, textbooks and books on education, all mainly 19th cent, though covering up to 1949. It is based on an initial bequest by Miss Madge Dandy in 1968 of *c*400 books which were supplemented in 1973 by 120 books and a collection of 19th cent children's exercise books which were donated by a Didsbury bookseller, who has continued to donate to the collection. Other gifts and purchases have increased the collection to more than 1,500 v, including 20th cent items. The Polytechnic central library has also, since 1972, built up a special collection of more than 2,000 children's books, mostly of the 20th cent, but including many from the later-19th cent. The Department of Library and Information Studies also holds a considerable number of children's books, including several hundred from the 19th cent.

The collection of *c*1,350 folio volumes, with a strong bias towards architecture, dates mainly from the 19th cent. Earlier items include Basilii Besleri's *Hortus eystettensis* (Nuremberg, 1613), G B Falda's *Le fontane di Roma* (Rome 1645), Andrea Palladio's *Le fabbriche e i disegni* (Vicenza, 1776) and Stuart and Revett's *Antiquities of Athens* (London, 1762–1816). There is also an almost complete set of Piranesi engravings, comprising *c*33 v. For other 18th cent items, see 'Palladianism and its sources: an exhibition from the Manchester Society of Architects Collection', (1978).

The 4,000 v in the *Book Design Collection*, while they include much 20th cent material, cover British publications from the early 19th cent onwards, with examples of the work of Bulmer, Bensley and Pickering, among others.

Private presses represented include Kelmscott, the Vale, Golden Cockerel and Nonesuch. Less rare 20th cent material in the *Book Design Collection* are books illustrated by certain artists, notably Agnes Miller Parker, Claire Leighton, Herbert Railton and Barnett Freedman. The library also has a Barnett Freedman Archive, whose contents include mss, drawings, correspondence, press-cuttings, books illustrated by Freedman, and jackets and other material designed by him. The material was mainly, if not wholly, collected by Charles Aukin, Freedman's solicitor and friend until the artist's death in 1958. Aukin gave his collection to Freedman's family who, in turn, donated it to the Polytechnic in 1980–1. A manuscript catalogue of the archive was compiled in 1981.

The various collections of children's books in the Polytechnic Central and Disbury Libraries, for which a joint catalogue is projected, and in the Department of Library and Information Studies, include more than 2,000 v dating from the 19th cent.

A general cat on microfiche includes added entries for the *Book Design Collection* under presses, printers, illustrators etc.

The Nonesuch Press holdings are listed in Ian Rogerson, *Sir Frances Maynell and the Nonesuch Press*, Manchester Polytechnic (1979).

W H Shercliff, *The Morten-Dandy Collection of older children's books, textbooks and books on education*, Manchester Polytechnic (1978).

The Portico Library, 57 Mosley Street, Manchester M2 3HY. Tel (061) 236 6785. Open Mon-Fri 9.30 am-4.30 pm. Admission by written application, including two academic references.

Permanent Collection The Portico, planned as early as 1796 by two Manchester businessmen in emulation of the Lyceum Library at Liverpool, was opened in 1806 as a proprietary subscription library for professional and business men in one of the first Greek Revival buildings in England, designed by Thomas Harrison. The first secretary was Peter Mark Roget, who probably carried out his earliest work on thesauri in the library. Other early members included John Dalton and a youthful Robert Peel. The book stock grew rapidly, though later in the century there was some borrowing from Mudie's circulating library. In 1905 the stock was estimated at more than 60,000 v. Thereafter, as membership declined, so too did accessions until they virtually ceased in the 1930s. Moreover, in the 1920s the stock was considerably reduced by the sale of possibly as many as 20,000 v when (to alleviate its financial problems) the library was obliged to lease the ground floor of the building to a bank, and the bookstock thus had to be confined to the first floor. The library, however, continues to function largely in its traditional form, and while this means that its purchases are mainly of current material—newspapers, periodicals and books, which are eventually discarded,—additions, including some older material, are made to certain areas of the permanent stock in order to cater for researchers. Much of the older stock had deteriorated physically but, with the aid of grants, a systematic programme of conservation was instituted in 1983, including a limited amount of repair and rebinding.

The permanent stock comprises *c*30,000 v, mostly of the 18th and 19th cent, but including at least 28 of the 17th and 3 of the 16th cent. There are *c*7 STC and *c*18 Wing items. Of the oldest items known to be in the library, the earliest Continental books are the 1557 Basle edition of John Bale's *Scriptorum illustrium majoris Brytanniae... catalogus*; the 1574 Paris edition of Hector Boethius' *Scotorum historiae*, and the 1601 Frankfurt edition of the so-called Matthew of Westminster's *Flores historiarum*.

The pre-1700 material consists mainly of substantial works on British history—general and ecclesiastical. The 18th and 19th cent collection is strong on architecture, and includes Wenver's *Ancient funerall monuments*, 1631; Leycester's *Historical antiquities*, 1672; and Freart de Chambray's *A parallel of the ancient architecture with the modern*, 1664. 19th cent British topography and local history, biography, literature (including many first and early editions of 19th cent writers) are well represented. The library is in the process of creating a *Collection of North West Fiction* comprising novels by local authors, or published locally, or set against a local background. Accessions to the permanent collection are restricted to those categories of material, namely: 19th and early 20th cent fiction; the North West Fiction Collection; non-fiction relating to Manchester and its environs.

Items disposed of in the 1920s included the important 18th cent Adlington Pamphlets which were sold to John Rylands Library in 1927.

A series of printed cats were produced up to 1895, and continued by a card cat. All these are misleading as they still contain entries for the 20,000 or so volumes sold. A programme of re-cataloguing based on a modified AACR2 was instituted in 1980 and aided in 1983 by a grant from the British Library.

Tinsley Pratt, *The Portico Library*, Manchester, 1922.

R Horsfield, 'The Portico Library, Manchester', in *Manchester Review* v 12, no 1, 1971, p15-48.

S Fearnley, 'Trio' in *Lancashire Life* v 24, no 2 (Feb) 1976, p36-9.

John Rylands University Library of Manchester, Oxford Road, Manchester M13 9PP. Tel (061) 273 3333. Open Mon-Fri 10 am-5.30 pm; Sat 10 am-1 pm. A reader's ticket is required which can be obtained by producing proof of identity and academic status, normally in advance. Full photographic service.

Note It should be emphasized that the rare book collections are to be found in the Deansgate Building in the city centre and not in the Main University Library in Oxford Road.

The John Rylands University Library of Manchester was created in 1972 by the merger of the library of the University of Manchester and the John Rylands Library, a previously independent library which had existed since 1900. The present library is the largest and most comprehensive university library in Great Britain outside Oxford and Cambridge. It contains well over three million volumes in addition to some 20,000 mss and hundreds of thousands of archival items. There are *c*3,500 incunabula; *c*8,000 STC; and *c*19,500 Wing items.

Before the merger each library can point to a long list of special collections, but there is in each case one which bibliographically can claim prominence: that which came to the University in 1901 on the death of Chancellor Christie, and the Althorp Library purchased by Mrs Rylands in 1892. Until the merger the former remained the outstanding University collection in this field. Formed mainly to illustrate the Renaissance, 'especially the classical Renaissance of Italy and France', it contains over 200 incunabula, and is rich in literary and bibliographical materials, particularly of the 16th cent. Nearly every Greek *editio princeps* is represented, as are the works of other printers whose Greek types and productions are of particular interest to scholars, and there are several Latin first editions. Of editions, translations and commentaries of Horace, for example, there are 798 beginning with the Milan edition of 1474, and nearly 100 v of Latin classics printed by Gryphius between 1533 and 1546. Christie selected some dozen scholars of the period on whom to specialize, and of 6 of these, Dolet, Giulio Camillo, Ramus, Sturm, Postel and Scioppius, he claimed the most complete collection in Europe. His Aldines included 'every book of interest and merit' associated with the name save 4, as well as over 50 of the counterfeits, and many of his volumes are from well-known English and continental libraries. With the merger, his books came to join and supplement another outstanding bibliographical collection, the Althorp Library of the 2nd Earl Spencer (*d*1834).

The Althorp Library numbers over 40,000 v and itself contains the famous libraries of Count Reviczky, Stanesby Alchorne and the Duke of Cassano-Serra. It brought to Manchester one of the most important single collections illustrating the origin and development of Western printing ever formed, as well as many superb bindings. Included are a rare 15th cent printer's block, the St Christopher wood-cut of 1423 (apparently the earliest piece of European printing with an undisputed date), 15 block-books, and over 3,000 incunabula, *c*two-thirds pre-1480. Of the earliest type-printed documents to which a place or date can be assigned there are the 'Letters of Indulgence' of Pope Nicolas V, the 36-line and 42-line Bibles, the first 3 Mainz *Psalters*, and, in all, *c*50 productions of the Mainz press or presses associated with Gutenberg, Fust and Schoeffer, several the only recorded copies. Examples of the work of well over 100 15th cent German presses occur. The full development of the new art took place, of course, in Italy, the first printers there being the migrant Germans Sweynheym and Pannartz. Of the 50 works they printed at Subiaco and Rome, enumerated in their 1472 cat, the Library has all save 2, and 1 of these has apparently not survived. The early presses at Venice, Naples, Milan and Florence and in other Italian cities are also strongly represented, in many cases by the first works produced there, as are those of Basle, Paris, Lyons and other centres of printing in France, Holland and Belgium. There are over 60 examples from Caxton's press (36 perfect and several the only copies known) and Wynkyn de Worde, Lettou, Machlinia, Pynson, Julian Notary and the schoolmaster printer of St Albans are all well represented among the productions of English presses. Reference has been made to the Christie Aldines. The Spencer Aldines number over 800 v, many printed on vellum; with them are over 100 of the forgeries against which Aldus so bitterly complained.

The Althorp Library also includes a valuable Bible collection. The Latin Vulgate was, of course, the earliest printed Bible, and of this there are over 80 of the pre-1500 editions, together with the most important of those of the 16th and later centuries, the 4 great Polyglots, the 6 editions of the Erasmian New Testament of 1516–42, and the first editions in many European and other languages. In all, copies of the Bible occur in upwards of 400 languages and dialects. Of each of the 50 principal Greek and Latin writers, the Library has the first printed edition; in the case of Cicero, Virgil and Horace, there are, respectively, no less than 64, 17 and 8 editions printed pre-1480. Also included is the only known copy of the *Batrachomyomachia* of 1474, the first printed Greek classic. The later presses are also present, such as Bodoni, Didot, Baskerville and, of course, Aldine, as are the modern critical editions. In English literature occur the first 4 Shakespeare folios (1623, 1632, 1664, 1685), the even more important 1609 *Sonnets*, and Steevens's own copy of the plays he edited with Johnson in 1793, enriched by the insertion of some thousands of engravings, many of extreme rarity. Chaucer is represented by all the earliest editions, beginning with *The Canterbury Tales* printed by Caxton in 1478 and 1483, and most others of the English classics are to be found in the original editions, from the 15th cent to modern times. These include, to cite only some of the earlier examples, Spenser's rare *Amoretti and Epithalamion* of 1595, 7 editions of *Paradise Lost* between 1667 and 1669, and the first editions of *The Compleat Angler* and of Bunyan's works, among them his first published book, *Some Gospel-Truths Opened*, 1656. Among Italian classics may be mentioned the 3 earliest editions of the *Divina Commedia* (1472), the only known perfect copy of the Valdarfer *Decamerone* (1471), the rare Petrarch printed by Laver of Rome in 1471, and 25 editions of the *Orlando Furioso* before 1585, including the first (1516) and the Venetian editions (1527, 1530). The Dante collection alone numbers over 6,000 v.

Many such specialist groupings occur, adding considerably to other information provided by the Library in a wide range of subjects. Among the more substantial, with their main themes, are those of Professor W Ll Bullock (Italian 16th cent literature), Dr Moses Gaster (Jewish studies), Bishop Prince Lee (Biblical literature, theology and history), and E Kenneth Brown (British railways, mainly early 19th cent (pre-1848) railway acts and maps). The nucleus of the French Revolutionary and Napoleonic Collection, perhaps the most notable of its kind outside France, was a gift of the 27th Earl of Crawford, and large and significant additions were made to it by his son. The 28th Earl also deposited in the Library *c*3,000 Civil War newsbooks and valuable collections of Royal Proclamations, Church Briefs, Broadsides, English Ballads, and English Pamphlets and Tracts. The Library's pamphlet collection, itself an extensive one, owes much to such additions. Mrs Ernest Hartland of Chepstow was the donor of 2,000 Bibles as well as 1,500 other volumes, among them 32 incunabula; and a large anti-slavery collection of books, pamphlets and periodicals came from the executors of the Sheffield MP Mr H G Wilson. Dr Lloyd Roberts' bequest numbered amongst its 5,000 v many fine bindings and associated copies, and a collection of editions of the *Religio Medici*. Institutions and societies, as well as individuals, have made their contributions, and here may be mentioned the Goethe collection from the Manchester Goethe Society, the libraries of the Manchester Geographical Society (some 4,500 books and over 3,000 maps) and the Unitarian College, the Raffles Collection of theological books from the Congregational College, the Morley Library of Ashburne Hall, and the William Temple College Library. The list could be extended even for larger groupings but must close with a reference to the Methodist Archives, an unrivalled source for the study of Methodism, with its 26,000 books, including every edition of John Wesley's works listed in Green's *Bibliography* and the personal libraries of Charles Wesley and John Fletcher, and over 6,000 pamphlets.

Resources in science and medicine are no less strong than those in the humanities. There is, of course, close co-operation between the three, and many of the collections mentioned above themselves contain scientific and medical items, not least among the incunabula and the rare and early printed books. On the science side, the more particular accessions include the library of Manchester Museum, important both in itself and as providing a nucleus around which additions could gather. The J R Partington bequest of over 1,500 v has added considerably to the materials available for the history of science, and particularly of chemistry.

The Medical Library, the largest in the provinces, belonged originally to the Manchester Medical Society, and acted as joint library for both Society and University until October 1930, when the University formally took charge of it. Although supplemented as regards its earlier holdings by other University collections, the Medical Library also has many rarities of its own, including incunabula, first editions of the classical writers in this field and of classical English medical books, and many pre-1600 works from foreign presses. It, too, has had many benefactors, personal and institutional, among them Mrs Rylands, who gave some 200 v from the Althorp collection in 1894, Dr Thomas Windsor, and the Macclesfield and Bolton Infirmaries, who both presented their books. Another specialist aspect was greatly strengthened in 1934, on the centenary of the founding of the Manchester Medical Society, when Dr E B Leech presented his large collection of books, pamphlets and other materials relating to the history of medicine in Manchester.

Catalogue of the printed books in the John Rylands Library Manchester, 1899. 3 v. Contains details of the Spencer Collection as well as the basic information on the core of the library's rare books collections.

English incunabula in the John Rylands Library: a catalogue of books printed in England and of English books printed abroad between the years 1475 and 1500: with chronological index, index of printers and stationers, subject index and... facsimiles. Manchester (Aberdeen printed), 1930.

Catalogue of books in the John Rylands Library Manchester printed in England, Scotland and Ireland, and of books in English printed abroad to the end of the year 1640. Manchester, Cornish, 1895.

Woodcuts of the fifteenth century in the John Rylands Library, Manchester. Reproduced in facsimile with an introduction and notes by Campbell Dodgson... (John Rylands Facsimiles 4. Manchester, 1915).

Catalogue of medical books in Manchester University Library, 1480–1700. Compiled by Ethel M Parkinson, assisted by Audrey E Lumb, Manchester: Manchester University Press, 1972. (Bibliographical Ser.3.)

Catalogue of the Christie collection: comprising the printed books and manuscripts bequeathed to the library of the University of Manchester by... Richard Copley Christie... Compiled under the direction of Charles W E Leigh... (with portrait). (Publications of the University of Manchester Bibliographical Soc.) Manchester, 1915.

Catalogue of valuable books... etc, including... H von Holtorp's... typographical and xylographical collections ... which will be sold by auction, by... Sotheby, Wilkinson and Hodge... on... 27th day of March, 1906, and four following days... (London, 1906). The pages dealing with von Holtorp's collections only. The collections are now preserved in the John Rylands Library.

The English Bible in the John Rylands Library, 1525–1640. With... facsimiles and... engravings (by R Lovett) (Manchester). Printed for private circulation, 1899.

The John Rylands Library Dante Collection... Reprinted from the *Bulletin of the John Rylands Library* ... 1961... Manchester, 1961.

Journaux et publications periodiques de la revolution française, le premier empire et la restauration (preserved in the Bibliotheca Lindesiana in the possession of the Earl of Crawford. A catalogue). 1911. The collection is now preserved in the John Rylands Library.

French revolutionary collection in the John Rylands Library: a brief survey by A Goodwin. (Reprinted from the *Bulletin of the John Rylands Library*, v 42, no 1, Sept 1959). Manchester, 1959.

The *Bulletin of the John Rylands (University) Library (of Manchester)* is the most important of the Library's publications. The first section of each issue 'Notes and News' normally contains details of each important collection as soon as it has been acquired. Indexes to the *Bulletin* for v 1–25, 26–50 and 51–60 have so far been published.

The John Rylands Library, Manchester, 1899–1924: A record of its history with brief descriptions of the building and its contents. Illustrated with... views and facsimiles. By the librarian, Henry Guppy. Manchester (Aberdeen printed), 1924.

The John Rylands Library, Manchester: 1899–1935. A brief record of its history with descriptions of the buildings and its contents. Illustrated with 60 views and facsimiles. By the librarian, Henry Guppy. Manchester (Aberdeen printed), 1935.

The John Rylands University Library of Manchester (Printed by Elliott Brothers and Yeoman Ltd, Speke, Liverpool, 1982 (pamphlet).

Royal Northern College of Music, 124 Oxford Road, Manchester M13 9RD. Tel (061) 273 6283. Open Mon-Fri (Term) 9 am-5.30 pm; Sat 1 pm; (Vacation) 9.30 am-5 pm. No restrictions on use for reference. Material may also be borrowed at the discretion of the librarian.

Special Collections Formed initially from the holdings of the Royal Manchester College of Music (founded 1893) and of the Northern School of Music (founded 1920) on their amalgamation to form the RNCM in 1972. The Royal Manchester College had received some of its material from the family of Gustav Behrens, who was a member of its council from its inception in 1893 until 1934. Another collection was received from Chester Public Library and may have belonged previously to the Westminster estates. There are *c*1,800 items of printed music, *c*200 books on music and *c*60 music manuscripts. The value of most of the printed items lies in either their associations, in the ms additions which they contain or, in the case of a large collection of scores of Scandinavian music, in their scarcity in the UK. Of the printed music collection of *c*300 items, British and foreign, almost all are pre-1851 and 154 pre-1801. The College's holdings of the latter are not recorded in BUCEM. Of some items in the collection, the RNCM is only aware of one other location. The large quantity of chamber and vocal music includes several rare printings by Preston and Bremner. Other rare items include the first edition printed in England of Corelli's opus 6 *Concerti Grossi* (Walsh and Hare, 1715), complete sets of John Stafford Smith's *Musica antiqua* (Preston, 1812) and Thomas Moore's *Irish melodies* (Power, 1824–34). There is a representative collection of early 19th cent piano music in which Ignaz Moscheles (1794–1870) is particularly well represented. There is also one of the few known copies of the 'complete' *Diabelli Variations* (Vienna, 1824). The post-1850 material in the archive consists either of first editions or of scores which have important markings or autographs, including those of Brahms, Joachim, Elgar and Charles Halle.

Of the *c*600 ms items, 50 are autograph and holograph copies of the compositions, including several which have not been published, of Alan Rawsthorne (1905–71), who had been a student at the Royal Manchester College. Others include the autograph ms of Delius's *First sonata for violin and piano*, which was thought to be lost until it was found at the RNCM in December 1980, in company with less important sketches for other works by Delius, some of which are not in the composer's hand.

Special collections include *Dame Eva Turner Collection*: 1,257 items, mostly vocal scores of operas, cantatas, and musical comedies, and sheet songs, donated by Dame Eva. Its main value lies in the ms annotations and inscriptions in a large proportion of the scores. *(Jascha) Horenstein Collection: c*185 books bequeathed to the library on the death of the conductor in 1973, the contents being chiefly of interest as having been his personal library. *Hansen Collection*: copies of 20th cent music donated by the Copenhagen publishing house of Wilhelm Hansen, arising from the close links between the RNCM and the Royal Danish Academy of Music. An initial donation of 521 items was made in 1981, with an undertaking to supplement it. Its value lies in its constituting an archive in the UK of 20th cent Scandinavian music.

The Hansen and Horenstein material is entered in the general card cats.

Archive printed music and the Rawsthorne mss are listed in a separate, incomplete card cat.

Card index of the Eva Turner Collection.

A printed cat of all the library's holdings is planned for some time in the future.

University of Manchester Institute of Science and Technology, Sackville Street, Manchester M60 1QD. Tel (061) 236 3311 Ext 2877. Open (Summer Term) Mon-Fri 9 am-9 pm; Sat 9 am-5 pm (12 noon other terms and vacations). Closed between Christmas Day and New Year's Day, and on all Bank Holidays other than Spring Bank Holiday. Admission by written application to the librarian. Copiers; microform readers available.

Joule Collection (other rare material in General Collection, never separately identified). The personal library of James Prescott Joule (1818–89), physicist, containing *c*250 v. *c*1,500 other pre-1851 books in general collection. The Joule Collection includes one of his notebooks, while some of his books have ms annotations.

General Collection includes late 18th and early 19th cent books on scientific and technical subjects.

No separate cat.

Card cat to whole library.

Note Most of the original collection of the Manchester Mechanics' Institution has been discarded. No information on date or method of discard.

Working Class Movement Library, 111 Kings Road, Old Trafford, Manchester M16 9NU. Tel (061) 881 9269. Open Mon-Fri 9 am-5 pm by appointment with the Curators. A singularly detailed knowledge of the stock is available to researchers.

Working Class Movement Library The collection was mainly built up after the Frows's marriage in 1953 by the systematic expansion of their joint collection of 3,000 books on the working class movement and other aspects of sociology. Both had long been active trade unionists. Mr Frow, a toolmaker who had experienced lengthy periods of unemployment, finished his working life as the full-time secretary of the Manchester District of the Amalgamated Union of Engineering Workers from 1961 to 1971. Mrs Frow was active in the National Union of Teachers before her retirement as deputy head of a Manchester comprehensive school in 1979. In order to acquire older publications the Frows spent their summer holidays scouring second-hand bookshops throughout Britain. Although the collection, including the more recent material, had grown by 1982 to comprise *c*10,000 books and *c*15,000 pamphlets, in addition to other kinds of material, it is still housed in their semi-detached home, where it occupies part of every fair-sized room and passage-way. In 1969 the Frows transferred ownership to a charitable trust, at which time the present name of the collection was adopted. The Frows continue, as at 1983, to be responsible for the curatorship and financial management of the collection.

There are *c*1,500 items which qualify as rare. Subjects covered relate to social conditions and developments from the 1760s onwards. In addition to books, pamphlets and periodicals, other material includes posters, handbills for lectures at mechanics institutes, photographs, prints, Radical cartoons and trade union and suffragette badges. Printed material covers economic, political and social history, including Poor Laws, housing conditions, child labour, juvenile delinquency, the early Radical Movement 1770–1850, trade unionism, the Women's Movement, political poetry, political trials, biography and autobiography related to the labour movement. The library's strongest asset is probably its collection of trade union records, some of which may well be unique copies. Rare early items include pamphlets of trade union rules published in 1807, 1816 and 1823. There are, in particular, large numbers of the records of trade union organizations in the Manchester area, largely as a result of numerous deposits which were made in consequence of a special project which, on Mr Frow's initiative, was carried out in 1976 by the Manchester Studies Unit of Manchester Polytechnic.

Name and classified (modified Dewey) cats on cards, with pamphlets and ephemera in a separate sequence from books.

Geraldine M Knight, 'The Working Class Movement Library', (thesis submitted to Loughborough University of Technology), 1983, 58pp. (Examines especially the library's holdings of trade union records and material relating to the Peterloo Massacre of 1819, the General Strike of 1926 and the Spanish Civil War. Also relates the library's holdings in general to those in other collections in its field of coverage.)

Christopher Cook, *Sources in British political history*, 1975, v 1, p160.

E and R Frow, 'Travels with a caravan', *Journ of Socialist Historians*: history workshop 2, Autumn 1976, p177.

Joyce Marlowe, 'Labour of love', in *Observer Colour Magazine*, 25 March 1979, p64, 66.

Brian Hope, 'The house of 10,000 books' in *Manchester Evening News*, 18 March, 1976.

Rochdale

Rochdale Public Libraries, Area Central Library, The Esplanade, Rochdale, Lancashire OL16 1AQ. Tel (0706) 47474 (49116 for evening and Sat). Rochdale Central: Open Mon, Tues, Thurs, Fri 9.30 am-8 pm; Wed 5 pm; Sat 4 pm. Except for the collection of Early Printed Books to 1640 there are no formalities for admission, but because the general and local material is dispersed at different locations, it may be advisable to contact the Local Studies Librarian in advance. Photocopying facilities; micro-readers.

General and Local Collections These are distributed among the libraries of the three local authorities which were amalgamated in 1974, viz Rochdale (established 1872), Heywood (1874) and Middleton (1889). They exclude material published up to 1640, which constitutes one of the three special collections housed at Rochdale Central Library. Sources of the stock in general include donations early in the present cent by Lieut-Col Henry Fishwick (1835–1914), Richard T Heape (1847–1917) and Col Sir Clement Royds, MP (1842–1916).

The total number of books of the period 1641–1850 which have been identified in the general and local collections at Rochdale, Heywood and Middleton is 773, but there could be more. (This is additional to the 600 or so books of this period which are contained in two of the special collections, and the 106 pre-1641 books.) There are *c*21 Wing items; 103 ESTC and 649 1801–50. Many of these works relate to Lancashire. Items which are thought to be particularly rare include *Latham Spaw in Lancashire: with some remarkable cases and cures effected by it*, published by Robert Clavel in 1670 (Wing 1769). Also *Bailey's Northern directory...for the year 1781* printed by William Ashton at Warrington. The local collection at Rochdale includes many posters of various kinds, of which *c*300 are pre-1851, with a small proportion dating from the 18th cent. *c*One-half of them are concerned with political or religious matters or with local trade disputes, and date mostly from 1800–50. The other half consists of theatre bills, including a number from the second half of the 18th cent. Until fairly recently the poster collections in general were filed somewhat unsystematically in various forms—scrapbooks, a broadsheets file and cardboard boxes. A programme of conservation and systematization is now (1982) well under way, but much still remains to be done. The theatre bills have, however, been listed.

Post-1640 bookstock is only included in the general cats of the three area libraries, which only list their own stock on microfiche for the general reference departments, and on cards for the local studies collections.

Note An estimated 3–4,000 old, though not necessarily rare, volumes were transferred to the National Central Library in the 1960s; they consisted mainly of runs of periodicals, and there were also some encyclopaedias, yearbooks and other reference works.

Early printed books (to 1640) The collection consists of 106 v, mainly continental up to *c*1580, and mainly English thereafter. They include 19 incunabula (all continental); 45 1501–1600; *c*43 Wing items. A feature of the continental books is the large proportion which are illustrated, starting with Erhard Ratdolt's 1484 edition of *Fascisculus temporum* and Sebastian Brant's 1502 edition of *Virgil*. The subject-emphasis of the continental books is on religion and the Latin classics. The earliest English books date from 1542, 1547, 1578, after which most of the books up to 1640 are English. They number *c*43, with the emphasis strongly on religion, followed by law, with a few on history or geography. The Rochdale holdings are not recorded in Ramage. They include one work which is not, apparently, listed in STC—*Catalogue of the Dukes, Earles and Palatines of Lancaster*, an illustrated folio which was anonymously printed in London in 1610. There is also an edition of John Speed's *Theatre of the Empire of Great Britain*, printed in London for Thomas Bassett and Richard Chiswell (neither of whom are recorded in Morrison) in 1610, which pre-dates the earliest edition recorded in STC, that printed in 1611 for J Sudbury and G Humble (STC 23041).

'Chronological list of early printed books (to 1640) in the Reference Department' 1962. 14p. (stencilled). (Information for each entry includes imprint, format and library call number.) Photocopies can be supplied at cost.

Tim Bobbin Collection An initial donation by Lieut-Col Henry Fishwick (1835–1914), a noted antiquary, local historian and author, who was an authority on Tim Bobbin, was augmented over the years by the library. Containing 123 v, it constitutes an exhaustive collection of the various editions of the works of John Collier (1708–86), the satirist and pioneer of writing in the Lancashire dialect, who lived at Milnrow, near Rochdale. Included are the first, (or first known) editions of *A view of the Lancashire dialect* (1746); *Tim Bobbin's Toy Shop* (1763) and *Curious remarks on the history of Manchester* (1771); also the very rare earliest extant edition of *Human passions delineated* (1773)—it is thought likely that there was a small edition published at Rochdale in 1772, but no copies are recorded. One title, *More fruits from the same pannier* (1773) is not recorded in *Eighteenth century British books.*

Older material is still being purchased when it becomes available.

Listed in the general card cat of the Rochdale Local Studies Collection.

(John) Bright Bookcase Consists of the greater part of a collection of *c*1,200 v which were purchased by public subscription in 1847 for the Rochdale MP, John Bright, consequent upon his successful campaign for the repeal of the Corn Laws in 1846. The bookcase was presented to Rochdale PL in 1925 by John Bright's daughter-in-law. There are *c*507 works in 1,108 v (of which 9 were missing in 1982). The 1,099 v which are to hand at present (1982) include 15 Wing items; 36 ESTC and 1,048 of the period 1801–50. Subjects covered are mainly history, topography and religion.

A typescript 20-page author list was produced in 1982; photocopies can be supplied.

As the collection is not listed in any of the library's general cats, its contents are nowhere indexed by subject. It is proposd to rectify this by *c*1988.

Salford

Pendlebury Arts Centre, Bolton Road, Pendlebury M27 2QT. Tel (061) 794 3156; and Broughton District Library, 400-4 Bury New Road, Salford M7 0EA. Tel (061) 792 6640. Open (Broughton District Library) Mon, Wed, Fri 9 am-7 pm, Tues 9 am-5 pm, Thurs and Sat 9 am-1 pm. Admission on written application to the Cultural Services Manager. Photocopier at Broughton District Library.

The Ghosh Collection Bequeathed to the City of Salford by Dr J Ghosh in 1949, the collection contains *c*100 v which come within the scope of the Directory. It is a personal library covering a wide variety of subjects, including literature, history and many general subjects. It includes a first edition of *Encyclopaedia Britannia,* Plinius Secundus *Historia naturale* (Venice 1481), *Aristotle's Philosophy* (Basle, 1538), Sir Walter Scott's *Provincial antiquities and picturesque scenery of Scotland,* 1826, an edition of Fletcher and Beaumont 1750, Frances Burney's *Cecilia* 1783, Mrs Inchbald's *The British theatre* 25 v, 1808, Howard's *State of the prisons in England and Wales. . . ,* 1777, etc.

Card cat.

Salford City Libraries, Walkden District Library, Memorial Road, Walkden, Worsley M28 5AQ. Tel (061) 790 4579. Open Mon-Fri 9 am-7 pm, Sat 9 am-1 pm. Admission on written application to the Cultural Manager. Photocopier.

Boothstown Botanical and Gardeners' Society Library The Society was founded in 1834 and was one of a number of botanical societies which flourished in the North West. Eventually the collection of books became an embarrassment and they were passed to the keeping of Lancashire County Library, and then to Salford City Libraries when Boothstown became part of the City. The collection consists of *c*100 works in 150 v on botanical, horticultural and gardening subjects, mainly 19th cent, but including a number of 18th cent items, the earliest of which is *Dictionaire Oeconomique: or the family dictionary* by R Bradley, 1705. There is a run of the *Horticultural Cabinet and florists' magazine* (1834–58) and the *Gardeners' magazine* (1828–34).

Card cat.

Salford City Libraries, Salford Central Area Library, Peel Park, Salford M5 4WU. Tel (061) 736 3353/4246. Open Mon, Tues, Wed, Fri 9 am-7 pm, Thurs 9 am-5 pm, Sat 9 am-1 pm. Admission to non-members by written application to the Cultural Services Manager. Microfilm readers, photocopier.

Cowan Collection Bequeathed to Salford by the Rev John Cowan, a former member of staff who died in 1969. It contains 19 v of 17th cent theological works.

Card cat.

Davies Collection Bequeathed to Salford during the 19th cent by Rev John Davies, it contains 282 v of printed books and pamphlets, many of local (ie Salford and Manchester) or Lancashire interest. Also included are items of general, literary, historical nature and curiosities such as the Goldsmith's diary.

Card cat.

Trinity Collection Passed to Salford from Trinity Church, Salford, in late 19th cent. It contains 70 v of theological works, mainly of the 17th and 18th cent, but also including Thomas Rogers, *The English Creede,* 1578, and Georgius Agricola, *De re metallica,* libri xii, 1556.

Card cat.

Section of Salford City Libraries general reserve stock The collection forms part of the original public library stock and many items were donated during the years following the establishment of the public library in 1849. It consists of several hundred v. (*NB* Impossible to be more specific at this stage because they are to be found throughout the reserve stock.) The collection is a general one and includes early travel and topographical books, some outstanding natural history books with coloured plates, history, literature, eg Maund's *Botanic Garden,* 11 v (1825); Sowerby's *English Botany,* 36 v (1790–1820); Shaw and Nodder's *Naturalists Miscellany,* 24 v (1789–1813); C J L Bonaparte, *Iconografia della fauna Italia. . . ,* 3 v (1832–41) and *Illustrations of the ornithology of Alexander Wilson* (1831); Andrew Smith, *Illustrations of the zoology of South Africa,* 3 v (1838); John Edwards's *British herbal* (1770); Sir William

Jardine's *Naturalist's Library*, 40 v (1833–44), and several Thomas Pennant titles.

Card cat.

The Library, University of Salford, Salford M5 4WT. Tel (061) 736 5843. Open Mon-Fri 9 am-9 pm; Sat 9 am-12 noon during term; 9 am-5 pm during vacation. Open to non-members by written application.

Badnall Papers Collection of letters and other manuscripts, oaths, bills, etc relating to Badnall's invention of an 'undulating railway', amounting to 43 documents.

Separate card cat (in Secure Room).

Walter Greenwood Collection Acquired by purchase from Greenwood's estate; since added to by the library, mainly by purchase. It contains 146 books belonging to Walter Greenwood, also first editions, translations etc of his works; 73 ms and typescript drafts of plays, film and TV scripts, novels and short stories; 2 files of letters; 5 files of press cuttings and photographs.

Partly completed card cat; the printed books are recorded in the Main Library cat.

Salford Technical and Engineering Association documents First deposited by the Association in 1974, the documents, numbering 383 items, relate to the development of technical education in Salford, from the foundation of the Association in 1891 to date—letters, certificates, syllabuses, lecture texts, photographs, etc.

Printed cat, updated by ms cards. 2nd ed of printed cat in preparation.

Special Collection Built up by the library from its foundation as part of the Royal Technical Institute (1896) to its present University status. It includes books donated by Lionel M Angus-Butterworth and deposited from the Thomas Hope Floyd Collection. There are 720 v; 1 ms novel; 1 ms collection of letters (*NB* this includes 1850–1900 material). The content is varied and includes ms of Robert Robert's novel 'a ragged schooling'; Joyce Knowlson theatre papers—records of performances at Salford theatres and music halls 1868–1910; Dockray papers—correspondence of Robert Dockray, largely on railways (39 letters).

Special Collection books are included in the main library cat.

Dockray papers have been calendared in ms.

Willink Papers Acquired by purchase from Mrs F A Willink in 1975, they comprise *c*114 items, including documents of Birmingham Canal Navigations, comprising maps, reports and accounts, and miscellaneous papers and correspondence, 1847–1948.

List of documents.

Stalybridge

Tameside Metropolitan Borough. Local Studies Library, Stalybridge Library, Trinity Street, Stalybridge, Cheshire SK15 2BN. Tel (061) 338 3831. Open Mon-Fri 9 am-8 pm; Sat 9 am-4 pm. Photocopying facilities.

Tameside Metropolitan Borough comprises a number of small formerly separate local authorities on the eastern outskirts of Manchester, whose local collections were brought together in 1976, the largest being those at Stalybridge and Ashton-under-Lyne, where the administrative centre of the new authority is located, including the Libraries and Arts Department.

Pre-1851 material comprises more than 400 books, tracts and volumes of serials and *c*40 maps, out of a total departmental collection of over 7,000 v and *c*900 maps.

In addition to material which has a local connection, the collection contains a number of works of a more general nature, including the earliest items, published in 1645 (Wing E118), 1650 (E123) and 1673 (L964). The earliest material of local interest consists of two small-scale maps of Cheshire, dated 1693 (Blome) and 1695 (Morden) and a book of 1700 (L975). While there are a number of items from the early 18th cent, most of the pre-1851 material dates from the 1770s onwards. Some of the books published in the first half of the 19th cent are on non-local subjects but were either written by local authors or were issued by local publishers. Material of purely local interest covers history of localities and families, antiquities, topography, geology, natural history, verse, writings in dialect, folklore, religion (including the Christian Israelite Movement Church, which was based in Ashton), institutions and societies, social and economic conditions, and politics. Many of the more topical items in particular were published locally in Manchester, Stalybridge or Ashton.

Typescript lists of pre-1851 items: books in two parallel alphabetical sequences, 14pp and 19pp; maps 4pp. Copies of these can be supplied.

Wigan

Wigan College of Technology, Parsons Walk, Wigan. Tel (0942) 41711. Open Mon-Thurs 9 am-9 pm, Fri 9 am-5 pm. Open to the public for reference use. Microfilm reader and photocopying facilities.

Manchester Geological Society Donated by Manchester Geological Society to the College in 1949, comprising 62 v pre-1840 on mining geology and related subjects.

Printed list available: 'A bibliography of books in the College Library on geology, mining and related subjects'. The Library, Wigan College of Technology.

Wigan Library, Rodney Street, Wigan WN1 1DQ. Tel (0942) 41387. Open Mon, Tues, Thurs, Fri 9.30 am-7 pm; Wed 9.30 am-1 pm; Sat 10 am-3.30 pm. Admission unrestricted. Photocopying facilities.

Rare book collections Collections of rare books were built up from the inception of the Wigan Public Library in

1878 by Henry Tennyson Folkard, the first librarian, up to 1916. Folkard was aided by fellow-bibliophiles, either by financial donations (notably £12,000 from Dr Joseph Taylor Winnard), or (as in the case of James Ludovic Lindsay (1847–1913), astronomer and MP for Wigan 1874–80—later Earl of Crawford and Balcarres of Haigh Hall), by donations of books which included, *inter alia*, some ms books and important collections of 16th-17th cent topographical works by Theodore de Bry; early Lancashire printing and freemasonry. The policy of acquiring rare books was continued for some time after Folkard's death in 1916, mainly by another bibliophile Borough Librarian, Arthur John Hawkes, from 1919.

The collection comprises over 4,000 pre-1800 works, including 80 incunabula (all continental) and 280 pre-1641 British books. The earliest datable work is Rodericus Zamorensis's *Compendiosa historia Hispanica*, printed in Rome by Ulrich Han, 1470. There are many other editions, both Italian and German, from the early, mid- and late-1470s, as well as from the 1480 and 1490s. Although most continental countries are represented, editions from a wide variety of centres in Italy predominate, with many also from Germany. A few of the items have not been traced in the British Library catalogue of incunabula. There is a carefully-compiled up-to-date 6-page typescript author list of the collection, which gives full imprints and also the Goff, *Gezamtkatalog* and BL incunabula catalogue numbers. There is a valuable collection of 60 v, mainly topographical works on India and America by Theodore de Bry, published at Frankfurt 1590–1633.

Of the 280 STC items, 40 are pre-1600, with the earliest dating from 1543 (STC 5170a). While the subject emphasis is on religion, including some Catholic books printed, probably, at Birchley Hall, near Wigan, in 1608 and 1620 (as well as St Omer, Douai, Louvain etc), the subject-scope of the STC books is quite varied. They include a few works on ancient Rome and also a few plays by lesser-known English writers. Among the rarer STC items are STC 1178, 2186, 3590, 5170a, 10645, 16683, 16990, 17918, 20529, 22507 and 25142. The library's holdings are listed in Ramage and in the 2nd ed of STC. All but four of them are listed in a 5-page typescript author-list which, while excluding imprints, other than dates, gives STC numbers. The 4 STC books which are not included in this list (STC 16990, 19292, 2186 and 5170a) are among a separately-shelved collection of 48 books which is labelled 'early printing and manuscripts' which also includes 14 Wing-period items; 14 continental books of the 16th cent; 2 of the 17th and 1 of the 18th cent; 6 European ms books of the 13th-16th cent, and a Persian ms; and 6 British editions dating from 1705 to 1926. They are listed in one sequence by author in a 4-page typescript. The reason for separating this material as a special collection is no longer known. Some of the earlier items may well be quite rare, as are the 4 STC items, which are the only ones in this collection which have been checked for rarity in bibliographies. Other rare items may well include a chapbook, *The murthers reward*, undated, but bearing the publisher's imprint of W Thackeray and T Passinger, which, according to Cyprian Blagden (in *Studies in Bibliography*, v 6, 1953, p172-3) was only used from late 1686 to early 1688, when Passinger died. This item is not included in the undated list (reproduced in Blagden's article) of chapbooks, ballad-sheets etc which Thackeray issued in, according to Blagden (*op cit*, p173), 1689.

In addition to the very early material, the general stock of the library contains over 3,600 British and foreign books which were published pre-1800. Although they are shelved as a separate collection from the post-1800 stock, they have not, as at 1983, been analyzed by period. Thus it has not been established how many are of the Wing period, nor is the number of works dating from the first half of the 19th cent known.

Material from the 18th and early 19th cent constitutes most of the items in a collection of early Lancashire printing. The library's holdings of the pre-1801 material in this collection are recorded in *Lancashire printed books: a bibliography of all the books printed in Lancashire down to the year 1800, based upon an exhibition...in the Wigan Reference Library, during May, 1925*, compiled and edited by the Borough Librarian, Arthur John Hawkes and published in 1925. A collection of books by Wigan authors, or printed in Wigan, includes *c*500 v published before 1900. A collection of books on freemasonry comprises over 500 works dating from the late 18th to the early 20th cent. A fair number of French publications includes the 61-volume Paris edition of 1863 of the 17th cent work, *Acta sanctorum* by Bollandus and Henschenius.

In addition to the typescript lists of the very early material, already referred to (and available at 10p per page, in 1983), the principal record of the rare bookstock is the printed dictionary cat published 1890–1918 in 13 v. Now out of print, it is in any case very misleading in that it includes entries for most of the *c*30,000* items which were sold in 1978–83, and also for most of the 20,000 items which it is proposed to sell. Much rare material is also recorded in the complementary dictionary card cat which was also started in 1890. In 1974 it was superseded for new accessions by name and classified cats, simultaneously with a changeover to the Dewey classification scheme from Library of Congress. It is proposed eventually to reclassify the whole stock and to transfer the entries to the new cat but, as at 1983, this has only extended to post-1960 material and to post-1800 English history and topography.

*These were post-1800 works, including many pre-1850 items, of which 1,500 v were on fine art, and acquired in the 19th cent; others were private press books. *c*60 per cent of the books were sold to the antiquarian book trade, and *c*30 per cent to the British Library.

Merseyside

Liverpool

The Athenaeum, Church Alley, Liverpool L1 3DD. Tel (051) 709 0418. Open 12 noon-3 pm. Library assistants in attendance Tues-Thurs. Admission restricted to proprietors, but bona fide research workers may be admitted to use the library on written application to the Chairman of the Library Sub-committee. No photocopying or microfilming available.

The Athenaeum Library, Liverpool A Literary and Scientific Institution founded in 1797 to provide a newsroom and a library. The books number *c*60,000 v, which include 36 incunabula. No figures available for post-1500 works. Special collections include: (those marked * are kept as units, the others are in a Dewey classified sequence).

**Norris books* 15 v, mainly legal, incunabula, and early 16th cent, acquired by Sir William Norris after the capture of Edinburgh in 1543. Some vols have inscriptions relating to two successive Abbots of Cambuskenneth and perhaps were looted from the Abbots' official residence in the Lawnmarket. Acquired by the Athenaeum after Speke Hall handed over to the National Trust in 1943.

Eshelby Collection *c*800 v on Yorkshire history, topography, genealogy and archaeology presented by Mrs Eshelby in 1905. Mainly post-1850.

Teignmouth Bibles Lord Teignmouth (1751–1834), first President of the British and Foreign Bible Society, presented a collection of Bibles in various languages in 1822 (some additions have been made).

Stewart Brown Collection Liverpool, Lancashire and Cheshire: mss and printed books, mainly post-1850.

**South American Collection* Mainly Indian dialect grammars compiled by Jesuit and other missionaries in South America, acquired 1834–45 via G P Parry of Buenos Aires. *c*40 v, 17th cent and earlier.

**Blanco White Collection* Bequeathed by Blanco White (1775–1841) to John Hamilton Thom, a past President of the Athenaeum, who presented them to the library. *c*200 v all pre-1850, mainly in Spanish.

Genealogical Collection, including heraldry, sets of church registers, peerages, family history, etc. Presented by J Paul Rylands, W Harry Rylands and Frank C Beazley. Mainly post-1800.

Gladstone Collection Bequeathed by Robert Gladstone (1866–1940): general works, but strong in 17th cent law books, deeds, local history, manuscript material. Card cat in progress.

**Roscoe Collection* Books and manuscripts purchased back from the Roscoe sale in 1816 and donated by his friends in 1817: Renaissance Italian and English mss; some mss of Roscoe's own poems and letters; incunabula, 16th-18th cent books, mainly Italian, and finely bound (Liverpool binders) copies of Roscoe's own books.

Ms cat.

**Pamphlets* 142 bound vols and 98 boxes of pamphlets, a general collection, but with a substantial number of local items (many pre-1850). Separate card cat.

**Jackson Collection* 60 v of pamphlets: sociology, economics, trade, tariffs, etc, presented by J Hampden Jackson in 1914. Separate card cat.

**Playbills* 22 v of Liverpool playbills, 1773–1830 (used extensively by R J Broadbent in his *History of the Liverpool stage*, 1908).

Local Collection Liverpool, Lancashire and Cheshire: books, maps, plans, drawings, portraits and news-cuttings relating to local people. 2,000 items. Card indices.

Published cats: 1802, 1820, 1864, Suppl 1875, Suppl 1892.

History of the Athenaeum, Liverpool, 1798–1898, compiled by G T Shaw, revised by W F Wilson. Liverpool, The Athenaeum, 1898.

F G Blair, *The Athenaeum Library, Liverpool*. Liverpool, Eaton Press, 1947.

F Harlan Taylor, *Liverpool and the Athenaeum*, Liverpool, The Athenaeum, 1965.

Crosby Hall Library, c/o Curator of Special Collections, Sydney Jones Library, University of Liverpool, P O Box 123, Liverpool L69 3DA. Tel (051) 709 6022 Ext 3128. Open to bona fide research workers by appointment via Liverpool University Library only. Research facilities as those of Liverpool University Library (photography, photocopying, etc) by appointment.

Crosby Hall Library The library was formed mainly during the lifetime of William Blundell who succeeded to Crosby in 1795 and died 1854. The library room, with its furnishings and fittings, dates from 1815. There are *c*2,600 v, principally historical and literary sets published between *c*1780 and *c*1820, mainly in English and French. No incunabula; some 16th cent classical texts; 16th and 17th cent theology; 17th and 18th cent classics (including four printed by Baskerville); travel and topography. Exceptional items: Moses Pitt, *The English atlas*, 1680 (LP copy) and Ackermann's *Oxford*, 1814 and *Cambridge*, 1815 (LP copies with portraits of the founders and in contemporary red morocco).

The library is illustrated in *Country Heritage: the stately homes of the North West Counties and North Wales*. Liverpool Daily Post, 1951.

Liverpool Cathedral, St James' Mount, Liverpool L1 7AZ. Tel (051) 709 6271. Open Wed and Fri 11 am-12.30 pm; other times by appointment. Admission by postal application to the Librarian. No lending of pre-1851 books; photocopying orders sent out.

The Radcliffe Library Founded by Sir Frederick Radcliffe (1861–1952) in 1932, the library includes the liturgical books of Christopher Wordsworth (1848–1938), Chancellor of Salisbury Cathedral (purchased 1938) and other scarce early printed works, which together total *c*1,000 items. There are 27 incunabula; 189 16th cent; 408 17th cent; over 126 18th cent items, and *c*150 items of the period 1801–50. Subject content strong in liturgy, good holdings of theology, Latin classics, early herbals, history and a few English literary works. Also *c*98 v of private press books, and limited editions, eg Kelmscott, Gregynog, Golden Cockerel, etc). The library also contains *c*35 mediaeval/Renaissance mss (plus fragments and framed leaves) seen by N R Ker, mainly liturgical, with some music; a Book of Hours belonging to Elizabeth of York; the Shepton Beauchamp Missal, late 14th cent; and 12 17th and 18th cent mss.

D F Cook, *Short title catalogue of books printed before 1801*, Liverpool (Cathedral) 1968 (includes full references, notes on outstanding bindings, provenances etc). Some 18th cent books not included in the cat.

Card cat of modern working library.

Review of the published cat by Paul Morgan in *The Library*, 5th ser 24, 1969, p163-4.

Liverpool City Libraries, William Brown Street, Liverpool L3 8EW. Tel (051) 207 2147. Open Mon-Fri 9 am-9 pm, Sat 9 am-5 pm. Closed Sundays and Bank Holidays. Admission unrestricted. Photocopying services available; extensive reference collection of catalogues and bibliographies.

Rare Book Collection Books have been acquired by purchase, donation, bequest and exchange since the libraries were established in 1850. Appropriate additions are made as part of a continuing acquisitions policy. The collection is made up of *c*6,000 v which include 14 medieval manuscripts (noted by Ker), 22 incunabula, *c*850 STC and *c*1,000 Wing books, modern presses and modern fine bindings, many colourplate natural history books, including Audubon, *Birds of America*; also *c*4,000 autograph letters and *c*40,000 bookplates.

There are no separate cats; printed and sheaf cats of the main reference collections available.

Liverpool Public Library: catalogue of books received. Parts I-III 1850–1891 (op) (and includes some rare books destroyed by enemy action 1939–45).

Hornby Library Open Mon-Sat 9 am-5 pm; others times by appointment.

The private collection of Hugh Frederick Hornby (? –1899), merchant of Liverpool, bequeathed on his death to the City of Liverpool, and staffed and maintained by the Liverpool City Libraries. It comprises *c*7,800 v, 8,000 prints and 4,000 autograph letters, and includes three incunabula, 18th and 19th cent first editions, English and Foreign illustrated books; strong collections of works of Thomas Bewick, George Cruikshank and others, Kelmscott Press, and Extra-illustrated books. Prints include works of Dürer, Rembrandt, Nanteuil, Hollar, Palmer, Meryon, and Turner's *Liber Studiorum*.

Printed cat of books only. Author entry with index of artists. Sheaf cats of prints, autograph letters and engraved portraits.

Liverpool Public Library: catalogue of Art Library of Hugh Frederick Hornby, 1916. (In print, £5).

Liverpool Record Office and Local History Department

Local History Collection Open Mon-Fri 9 am-9 pm, Sat 9 am-5 pm. Continuously acquired since opening of library in 1852. It consists of *c*2,000 rare printed items of local history material, special collection of locally printed items, mss of works of a number of authors with local connections, eg Hanley, Monsariat; a collection of local maps from the 17th cent onwards.

The Music Library Contains *c*500 early editions, mss and first editions including: 1. Carl Rosa Opera Company Library (donated in 1965) of music scores and orchestral parts (in mss) and vocal scores belonging to the former Carl Rosa Opera Company; 2. Alfred Booth Collection of Catholic liturgical material (part destroyed during 1939–45 war); 3. Earl of Sefton Collection of early piano music, especially early English editions of Haydn and Playl; 4. William Faulkes Collection of his manuscript compositions, mainly chamber works.

1954 cat; supplement in progress.

Liverpool Medical Institution, 114 Mount Pleasant, Liverpool L3 5SR. Open Mon-Fri 9.30 am-6 pm; Sat 9.30 am-12.30 pm. Open to subscribers and to bona fide research workers. Photocopying.

Liverpool Medical Institution Library The Liverpool Medical Library was started in 1779 and housed at various addresses until 1837 when the Liverpool Medical Institution was opened at the above address. An extension was opened in 1966. The collection comprises *c*40,000 v and 200 current journals. The main subject fields are medicine and anatomy, and include 65 mss, 34 STC, 97 Wing, 38 16th cent continental and 185 17th cent continental works; 1,875 English for 1801–50 period, and 2,890 English for 1851–1900 period; 1,049 19th cent continental works.

Catalogue of the books in the Liverpool Medical Institution Library to the end of the nineteenth century. Liverpool Medical Institution, 1968.

John A Shepherd, *A history of the Liverpool Medical Institution*, Liverpool Medical Institution, 1979 (contains a history of the library, and details of its published cats and references).

Liverpool University Library, Sydney Jones Library, University of Liverpool, P O Box 123, Liverpool L69 3DA. Tel (051) 709 6022. Open Mon-Fri (term) 9 am-9.30 pm; (vacation) 9 am-5 pm; Sat 9 am-1 pm. Special Collections Dept: Mon-Fri 9 am-1 pm and 2-5 pm. Admission by introductory letter to all bona fide research workers. Photocopying; photographic service (microfilming only by arrangement with a commercial firm); microform readers.

Liverpool University Library Special Collections The collections (including those in Departmental libraries) comprise *c*14,500 books, and these include: 240 incunabula (a further 29 being on deposit); *c*1,200 STC; *c*5,000 Wing, and 7,800 18th cent English works. For the purposes of the Directory, some very small collections have been omitted, and only the larger and more relevant collections have been noted. They are as follows:

Fraser A collection of over 2,300 books and pamphlets made by John Fraser (1836–1902), advertising manager of the Liverpool tobacco firm of Cope Brothers & Co Ltd. *c*900 items (17th-20th cent) relate to tobacco, and other major subjects represented are art, English literature, Scottish books, positivism, secularism and phrenology. The collection also includes mss and ALs of James Thomson ('B V'), Richard Le Galliene and others, and posters and other material advertising Cope Brothers' products.

Knowsley A collection of books and pamphlets purchased from the Earl of Derby's library at Knowsley Hall. It contains *c*800 books published in England before 1801; *c*2,000 English pamphlets of the 18th and 19th cent, and 1,500 of the period 1830–65. It also contains *c*550 pre-1801 books (mainly Latin, French, Italian) published on the Continent.

Noble A collection of *c*2,000 finely printed and private press books of the late 19th and early 20th cent (*see A catalogue of the books collected by the late William Noble*, 1913).

Peers A miscellaneous collection of books (*c*460), newspapers, pamphlets (*c*170), newscuttings and other printed material, mainly on the Spanish Civil War (1936–9). Originally collected by Prof Edgar Allison Peers, the collection is being 'added to'.

Rylands A general collection of *c*2,700 books (including 77 incunabula) and pamphlets bequeathed by Thomas Glazebrook Rylands. The collection covers the history of Lancashire and Cheshire, and early cartography. (*See A catalogue of books, printed and in manuscript, bequeathed by T G Rylands*. Compiled by John Sampson, 1900.)

Scott Macfie *c*1,600 books, pamphlets, mss, broadsides, drawings, prints, photographs, newscuttings, sheet music, records, tapes on Romany and Gypsy lore. Collected by R A Scott Macfie, and given by his sister to the Gypsy Lore Society, it was later presented by the Society to the University Library. (*A catalogue of the Gypsy books collected by R A Macfie*. Compiled by Dora E Yates, 1936.)

A guide to Special Collections (1978). Free on request.

D I Masson, *Handlist of incunabula in the University Library Liverpool*. Privately printed, Liverpool, 1949; First supplement, 1955.

John Sampson, *A handlist of the books of the Literary & Philosophical Society of Liverpool*. Liverpool, Marples, 1899.

——*In memoriam Thomas Glazebrook Rylands: a catalogue of the books...bequeathed...to the library of University College Liverpool*. Liverpool, University Press, 1900. (op)

——*Handlist of books and pamphlets of the Liverpool Royal Institution kept at the Tate Library, University College, Liverpool*. Liverpool, Marples, 1895; additional list, 1896.

In memoriam William Noble...a catalogue of the books bequeathed by him to the University Library. Liverpool, University Press, 1913.

In memoriam John Hamilton Thom: list of books bequeathed...to the Tate Library of the University College, Liverpool, with separate index of the books once belonging to the late Rev Joseph Blanco White. Liverpool, S Hill, 1895. (op)

University of Liverpool, School of Education Library, Abercromby House, 22 Abercromby Square, P O Box 147, Liverpool L69 3BX. Tel (051) 709 7312. Open, Term: Mon-Thurs 9 am-7 pm, Fri 9 am-5.30 pm; Vacation: Mon-Fri 9 am-5.30 pm; Sat 9 am-12 noon. Admission to bona fide research workers only. Photocopying; microform reader/printer; photographic services available.

School of Education Library – Special Collections The collections have developed with the growth and expansion of the University, and now total *c*7,000 v. They include: (a) *c*1,500 titles of 19th cent children's books by such writers as R M Ballantyne; Mrs Frances Hodgson Burnett; Mrs Lucy Littleton Cameron; Charlotte Elizabeth (ie Charlotte Elizabeth Phelan); G Manville Fenn; G A Henty; Mrs Barbara Hofland; W H G Kingston; Mrs Emma Marshall; L T Meade; Mrs M L Molesworth; Mrs Mary Martha Sherwood; Gordon Stables; Hesba Stretton (ie Sarah Smith); A L O E (ie

Charlotte Maria Tucker); Mrs Sarah Trimmer; Mrs Priscilla Wakefield; Mrs O F Walton and Charlotte Yonge; (b) Over 19 Victorian children's periodicals; (c) A collection of pre-1914 school textbooks; (d) A small collection of ms exercise books; (e) Illustrated children's books, especially the Oldham Collection (*c*1,000 items purchased from Mr and Mrs S Oldham, Oxton, Merseyside in 1972/3).

J E Vaughan, 'The Liverpool collection of early children's books', *The School Librarian*, 28, ii, June 1980.

Norfolk

Blickling

Blickling Hall (National Trust), Blickling, Norwich NR11 6NF. Open strictly by special prior arrangement only. Application to be made in writing to the Libraries Adviser, National Trust, 42 Queen's Gate, London SW1. No research facilities.

The library is mainly the collection of Sir Richard Ellys (*c*1688–1742), formed in the early 18th cent, but other family books subsequently added. Contains *c*12,000 v, including 90 incunabula, many early 16th cent works printed in Italy; large collection of 17th and 18th cent pamphlets with strong emphasis on classics, theology, French and non-English works generally; some fine atlases.

Card author cat and shelflist available. A copy of the card cat may be seen more conveniently in the Library of the University of East Anglia.

Partial dispersal of the library occurred *c*1930.

Blickling Hall, Norfolk, National Trust, 1980.

Felbrigg

Felbrigg Hall (National Trust), Felbrigg, Nr Cromer, Norfolk. Admission for bona fide research work by special arrangement following an application in writing to the Libraries Adviser, National Trust, 42 Queen's Gate, London SW1.

The Library was brought together mainly in the 18th cent by the Wyndham family, and added to by the late owner, R Ketton-Cromer. It contains *c*6,000 v, mainly Wing and later, and is strong in the subject areas of the classics and local topography. The collection is added to regularly, and no disposal of stock has occurred since the mid-19th cent.

Author card cat.

Holt

Gresham's School Foundation Library, Gresham's School, Holt, Norfolk NR25 6EA. Tel (026 371) 3271. Admission to students with an interest in the Library's contents on written application to the librarian. Photocopying facilities.

Foundation Library Nine books were bequeathed by Thomas Tallis, Master of Gresham's School 1605–40; seven still survive. Dates of subsequent accessions before 1729 are known, but in that year the new Master, John Holmes (Master 1729–60), persuaded the Fishmongers' Company to provide 'a valuable and useful Library of the best Latin and Greek authors now used in the most celebrated schools in England with a pair of globes'. The books cost £87.8.4., including £14.14.0. binding. The Foundation Library was rebound by Grey of Cambridge in 1962–3 when it was moved to its present location in the modern library block. It contains principally Greek and Latin classics in 16th-18th cent eds. Masters John Holmes (1729–60), John Knox (1760) and C J Howson (1900–19) gave some of their own works. The library has some correspondence relating to the production of the second ed of the *Public School Hymn Book* (1949).

P J Lee, *Gresham's School. A catalogue of the foundation library (with notes and an historical introduction)*. Holt, 1965.

King's Lynn

King's Lynn Public Library, London Road, King's Lynn, Norfolk. Tel (0553) 2568. Open daily 9 am-5 pm. Admission free. Photocopying.

St Margaret's Church Library Founded 1619 at St Nicholas Chapel and transferred, with new accessions, *c*1631 to St Margaret's Church. Augmented by various other collections, including the medical books of Robert Barker, a local doctor (1720), and a general collection (430 v) of John Home, Master of the Grammar School *c*1750. The library was restored 1970–75, and is now in the King's Lynn Central Library. Mainly theological, including at least three incunabula. A detailed list was compiled by Father George Wrigglesworth in 1890, but not all the books listed still survive.

Card cat (computer cat in progress).

Raymond Wilson, *A History of King's Lynn Libraries 1797–1905*, 1970 (LA Fellowship thesis).

Norwich

Bishop of Norwich's Committee for Books and Documents, c/o Norfolk Record Office, Bethel Street, Norwich. Tel (0603) 611277. Admission by arrangement with the Secretary for Books of the Committee. Pre-1700 books are available through the Reference Library, Norwich Central Library, and by arrangement with the Secretary for Books during normal library opening hours. Post-1700 books are stored in the County Library HQ at County Hall, Norwich, and may be consulted by arrangement as above.

Printed materials on deposit from Norfolk parish churches Care of documents having been formally taken over by the Norfolk Record Office in 1978, the Committee decided to offer a deposit service for printed books which are at risk in unused churches. To date (1982) *c*2,000 v have been deposited, as well as large collections of sheet music, service sheets, and a few posters. The major part of the collection is liturgical—Bibles, Prayer Books, hymn books and sheets, and music. There have been parish library deposits from two parishes to date, consisting mainly of 19th-20th cent works, some theological and some in the manner of 'improving tracts'. No incunabula have been found to date, although there are *c*50 STC/Wing items, some in remarkably good condition.

Card cat is maintained by the Secretary for Books and her assistants, from which copies of receipt lists are compiled and sent to the relevant parish and the county libraries.

John Innes Institute, Colney Lane, Norwich NR4 7UH. Tel (0603) 52571. Open Mon-Fri 9 am-5.50 pm. Admission by application to the librarian. Study rooms, photocopier, photographic department, biographical works on the books in the collection.

The John Innes special collection of rare botanical books Collected by William Bateson (1861–1926), pioneer geneticist and first Director of the John Innes Institute 1911–26. It contains 900 v covering the history of genetics from its origins to date. The rare book collection covers completely the new science of Genetics. In addition the collection contains many of the major botanical works from 1536—including 16th cent herbals, hand-coloured classics of Redouté, Sibthorpe, Curtis, Ehret, Trew, etc. It also contains *Gregor Mendel's* original papers and it can be said to cover the art of botanical illustration from the first printed woodblock herbals to date. About 1950 many of the non-botanical books were sold to Wm Dawson, but no details exist of the books sold.

Card cat.

Elizabeth Atchison, *The John Innes Special Collection: a catalogue of selected books from the library of the John Innes Institute*, 1978.

Norfolk County Library, Central Library, Bethel Street, Norwich NR2 1NJ. Tel (0603) 22233 Ext 644. Open Mon-Sat 9 am-5 pm (except public holidays). Admission by written application. Microfilm reader, photocopying, photo reproduction by prior arrangement.

The City Library Founded 1608 by the Norwich Municipal Assembly as a library for visiting preachers. Increased mainly by gifts to *c*5,000 v, and occupied various homes including the recently defunct Norfolk and Norwich Subscription Library before its return to the new Free Library in 1862. It includes 8 early mss, 28 incunabula and numerous Wing and STC items. Wynkyn de Worde, Anton Kobinger, the Schoolmaster printer, Richard Pynson, Johann Froben, Julian Notary, John Day, Richard Tottell, Christopher Barker, the Estiennes, Elzevirs, Grypheus and Christopher Plantin are represented. Divinity, history, geography, travel and law are all well represented.

Catalogus Librorum in Bibliotheca Norwicean, 1883.

Modern card cat.

G A Stephen, *Three centuries of a city library*, 1917. (op)

Colman Library Collected by Jeremiah James Colman (1830–98), the Norwich industrialist and Liberal MP, and his son Russell James Colman (1861–1946), who purchased at auction complete antiquarian collections beginning (1878) with that of William Enfield (1741–97). Housed successively at Carrow House and Carrow Abbey, Norwich (decorative bookcases *in situ* at Carrow Abbey (1977), Crown Point House, Norwich City Hall (1955) and since 1963, present separate location. The library, which consists of *c*10,000 v was presented to the City of Norwich in 1955. It is confined mainly to items with a Norfolk connotation, and is strongest in religion, politics, sociology and topography. Made-up vols include proceedings of Norfolk and Norwich organizations covering full 19th cent. Non-book materials include maps, prints, photographs, ephemera. The associated ms material is normally produced in the adjoining Norfolk Record Office (qv).

Individual rare books include early Norwich printing (Anthony de Solemne, the pioneer newspapers *Norwich Post, Norwich Postman*); rare works by the philosopher Sir Thomas Browne (1605–82); the landscape gardener Humphrey Repton (1752–1818); books by and on the Norwich School of painting (original prints are in the Norwich Castle Museum); and the naturalistic photographer Peter Henry Emerson (1856–1936). Twenty items relate to the Brownists (nonconformist sect). Francis Blomefield's *Norfolk* (5 v, 1739–75), grangerized by J T Todd (1839–1916) to 24 v is in the Castle Museum Norwich.

Interleaved updated cats (*Bibliotheca Norfolciensis*) disclose few additions after 1930. Card cat showing relativity to Rye Library (qv) being built up.

John Quinton (compiler) *Bibliotheca Norfolciensis*, 1896. (op)

P Hepworth, 'The Colman Library, Norwich' in *East Anglian Magazine* 14 (1955), p242-9. (op)

Rye Library The Norwich Public Libraries' local collection was started in 1880 from the proceeds of library fines. Greatest impetus to the collection was given by Walter Rye (1843–1929), a local antiquary, after whom the collection was named (1963); his contributions are listed in G A Stephen, *Walter Rye: memoir bibliography and catalogue*, 1929 (op). The Rye Library of c50,000 v is stronger in Norfolk and East Anglian topography and biography than the Colman Library, and updates the Colman material on local organizations and ephemera. It is, in fact, the current County Local Studies Library, continually being added to in all fields. Current acquisitions aim at complete coverage (E Darroch and B Taylor's *Bibliography of Norfolk history* 1975, states 'most books and pamphlets...in the Colman and Rye collections'). The library also include prints (topographical and portraits), local map sheets, cuttings (arranged by places, persons, subjects), local broadsides, posters, theatre bills. The introduction to P Hepworth, *Victorian and Edwardian Norfolk from old photographs* (revised 1974), refers to all significant photographic material held at Norwich.

Computer printout cat being built up.

P Hepworth and M Alexander, *Norwich Public Libraries, Norfolk and Norwich Record Office*, 1964. Norfolk County Libraries.

Shipdham Library The Shipdham Rectorial Library was founded by the Rev Thomas Townshend, a member of the Townshend family of Raynham Hall, Norfolk, Rector of Shipdham, Norfolk (1707–54), and was placed in a small room over the church porch. On his death at Mattishall, in 1764, Townshend left the library to his nephew and successor, the Rev Colby Bullock, and 'to his successors for ever'. The bibliographer W Blades visited Shipdham in 1861, and found the library intact but dirty (*Notes and Queries* 2nd ser 12, p469, 1861). In 1928 a faculty for the sale of the library, still in its original location, was granted; after delays in 1942 and 1950, well documented in the local press, it was auctioned in 220 lots on March 29, 1951. Attempts to sell it privately to Cambridge University Library, Norwich Cathedral Library and Norwich City Library failed. The sale realized over £7,000, some books being acquired by the Folger Library, Washington, DC, and others by the Huntingdon Library, San Marino, California. The unsold ones were housed temporarily in the Norwich Museums, and are now in the Norwich Cathedral Library, augmented by some 30 others bought at the sale by an Essex man, H Crawshay Frost, and subsequently presented. In 1927 J E Hodgson stated (*Eastern Daily Press* 9.11.27) 'the Library comprises...rather less than 1,100 volumes, including a collection of tracts on miscellaneous subjects bound in nearly 80 v...comprising ...four to ten or twelve separate tracts'. The number now remaining at the Central Library, Norwich, is about 550, including bound-up pamphlets. In 1927 also, J E Hodgson (*op cit*) stated the works to be generally classical or theological of the 16th or 17th cent, mostly in contemporary calf bindings. A 13th cent English psalter written for the monastery of Campsea Ash, Suffolk, is mentioned. Two mss are recorded (Parochial Libraries, below), Add mss 7220, 7221, as in Cambridge Univ Library. Individual books mentioned by Hodgson include *The Royal Book, or Book for a King* (printed Pynson, 1507), the first ed of Milton, *Lycidas* (Cambridge, 1638), and *Mynde of the Godly John Calvin* (Oswen, Ipswich, 1548). Early Americana are believed to have been acquired by the Folger Library, the earliest being Lewis Hughes, *A Letter into England from the Summer Islands (1615)*.

The books at Norwich Central Library are being cat on cards.

J E Hodgson, 'Shipdham Rectorial Library' in *Eastern Daily Press*, Nov 1927. (op)

Hodgson and Co auctioneers, *A catalogue...including the Shipdham Church Library...sold...*April 27, 1950 (no 8, 1949–50); March 29, 1951 (no 6, 1950–51). (op)

Central Council for the Care of Churches, *The Parochial Libraries of the Church of England*, 1959. (op)

Norfolk Museums Service (Headquarters), Castle Museum, Norwich NR1 3JU. Tel (0603) 22233 Ext 631. Open Mon-Fri 9 am-5 pm. Admission by appointment on written application giving details of specific requirements. Photocopying (except at Thetford) facilities.

Castle Museum Collections The collections stem from many sources. The Norwich collections in all departments were housed in the Castle Museum, a former prison, from 1894 until branch museums began to be formed in the 1920s. Much of the printed and archival material in the art department accompanied portrait and picture bequests, notably that of the Colman family in 1899 and 1946. Material in the archaeology and natural history departments dates back to the origins of the Norwich Museum in 1826, and additions have continued since. The collections at Norwich now comprise the *Norwich Castle Museum of art, archaeology and natural history*; the *Strangers' Hall Museum of domestic life* (qv); the *Bridewell Museum of local industries* and the *St Peter Hungate Church museum* (qv). Since 1974 the *Ancient House Museum at Thetford*; the *Lynn Museum* and the *Lynn Museum of Social History* at King's Lynn (qv); the *Norfolk Rural Life Museum* at Gresenhall; the *Maritime Museum for East Anglia*; the *Elizabethan House Museum* and the *Tolhouse Museum* at Great Yarmouth, along with the *Shirehall Museum* at Walsingham, have joined the Norfolk Museums.

The art section includes limited 19th-20th cent eds; Tom Blomefield (grangerized ed of F J Blomefield, *Norfolk*). The archaeology section includes local drawings, letters, field notebooks, numerous charts; early printed Norfolk maps; few pre-1850 books include Sir Richard Colt's *Wiltshire* (1812–19); C Roach-Smith's *Collectanea antiqua* (1848–51) and James Conder *Arrangement of provincial coins tokens and medals*. It also include Robert Fitch (1802–93) misc antiquarian collection. The natural history section houses the Norfolk and Norwich Naturalists Society's (founded 1868) collections, with some 150 pre-1850 books which include editions of W Curtis *Flora Londinensis* and *Entomology*;

Philip Miller's *Gardeners' dictionary* (1732); John Gould *Birds of Australia* and *Birds of the Himalayan mountains*; 1st and 2nd eds of James Sowerby's *English Botany* and several scarce illustrated works by the local W J Hooker (1785–1865) and John Lindley (1799–1865).

Card cat. Descriptive lists (incomplete).

P Hepworth, 'Supplementing Blomefield' in *Norfolk Archaeology* 31, 1957, p427-34.

T Chubb and G A Stephen, *Norfolk maps and Norwich plans*, 1928 (op).

Strangers Hall Museum Collection (Charing Cross, Norwich. Tel (0603) 22233 Ext 645).
This consists of several hundred v mainly 19th cent topography, devotional works and literature; 15 mss (1762–1905); and 27 printed (1710–1851) cookery books. Over 100 pre-1851 childrens' books. Randolph Caldecott, Walter Crane and Kate Greenaway are represented among later books.

St Peter Hungate Church Museum Collection (Prince's Street, Norwich. Tel (0603) 22223 Ext 703).
There are *c*50 v of Bibles, liturgies, commentaries, etc which include a number of STC and Wing items, and examples of illumination and fine-binding. A significant part comprises 10 v bequeathed by Col R E Patteson, Beeston St Andrew, Norfolk, which include *inter alia*: late 15th cent Book of Hours (Flemish); 13th cent metrical version of Bible known as *Aurora*; 15th cent (with 2 13th cent illuminations) liturgical psalter and breviary; 15th cent processional with music; early 14th cent Book of Hours, E Anglian; 15th cent *Libellus qui dicitur*; 3 tracts by Wycliffe *c*1324—84 bound together with name 'Robert Cotton'; Religious tracts—St Jerome on Virginity; On the Seven deadly sins; On the Pater Noster (bookplate Wm Cecil, 1570–1640).

Card cat.

See H C Beeching in *Norfolk Archaeology*, XIX (1917), p67-116.

Maritime Museum Reference Library (Marine Parade, Great Yarmouth. Tel (0493) 2267).
The Library has *c*1,500 v, specializing in maritime history. The miscellaneous material in the Capt Hamilton Collection and the World Ship Society Collection is of most interest.

Part card cat.

King's Lynn Museum Library (Market Street, King's Lynn. Tel (0553) 5001).
The Library contains *c*200 v; *c*5,000 posters; *c*7,000 engineering and fairground drawings. Included are some STC and Wing items; 17th-19th cent political, theatrical and social posters; 19th cent engineering and fairground drawings from local firms.

Norfolk Record Office, Central Library, Bethel Street, Norwich NR2 1NY. Tel (0603) 22233 Ext 599. Open Mon-Fri 9 am-5 pm; Sat 9 am-12 noon. Advance appointment for admission appreciated. Xerox copying/microfilming by arrangement.

Dr Tanner's Law Library Thomas Tanner (1674–1735) became private chaplain to John Moore, Bishop of Norwich 1691–1707, whose daughter he married in 1701. He became Chancellor of the Diocese 1700/1; his Norfolk associations ceased on his elevation to the Bishopric of St Asaph, 1731/2. The library consists of 41 v of works on jurisprudence, of dates 1505–1733, but mostly 16th cent material.

Cat in cyclostyled list of Norwich Diocesan Archives by T F Barton, 1963.

Background reference DNB.

Shotesham Collection The collection has survived with the family papers of the Fellowes family of Shotesham, Norfolk, and deposited through the Norfolk Record Society in the Norwich Public Libraries (*c*1950); transferred in 1963 to the Norfolk Record Office (built that year in the basement of the new Norwich Central Library). It consists of *c*100 items, political pamphlets, sermons, etc, ranging from 1674–1824.

Cat of whole collection in progress; will be reproduced xerographically by National Register of Archives.

E H Fellowes, *The family and descendants of William Fellowes of Eggesford*, 1910. (op)

A Batty Shaw, 'William Fellowes, man of Shotesham' in *Norfolk Archaeology* 35, 1972, p183-91.

Norwich Cathedral, Dean and Chapter Library, The Cathedral, Norwich NR1 9EG. Tel (0603) 20715 (Cathedral Office). Open by arrangement on written application stating specific purpose to the Canon Librarian. In appropriate circumstances photocopying may be arranged on advance payment through other local libraries or through the Norfolk County Record Office which holds the Cathedral archives.

The Dean and Chapter Library Founded by Bishop Herbert de Losinga (1094–1119), the library probably contained *c*1,300 v when dispersed at the Reformation. It was revived at the end of the 17th cent in the time of Hemphrey Prideaux (Prebendary, subsequently Dean). Principal benefactors were Nicholas Penny (1674–1745), Prebendary of the Cathedral (1722–45) and Frank Sayers (1763–1817), Norwich poet, critic and antiquary. Books of Norfolk and Norwich Clerical Society were acquired *c*1890. Later substantial bequests came from Dean Edward Meyrick Coulburn (1866–89) and Dean Henry Charles Beeching (1911–19). Comparatively few accessions since 1930, though books of local interest have been added by donation. Recent theology is collected in a separate library at Centre 71, The Close. The Library contains *c*8,000 titles (including multi-v and multi-titled v). Theology predominates, but history, topography, the Classics, heraldry and law are well represented. There are early Chaldaic, Hebrew and Greek dictionaries, some natural history, six medieval mss, including two from the pre-Reformation library, as well as an illuminated ms 'Domesday' parochial survey of the 15th cent. (The mss are deposited in the Norfolk Record Office.) The presses of Wynkyn de Worde, Richard Pynson and John Day (*Testimonie of Antiquitie* 1567, A S types), and 18th cent Norwich presses are represented, and also early European presses. There are *c*800 pamphlets on theology and politics of the period *c*1625–1750. The collection includes 7 incunabula; *c*170 STC; *c*1,100 Wing; *c*630 foreign printed to 1700; total (titles) pre-1851 *c*6,500. Ker records (mostly at Cambridge) 121 from the Norwich Benedictine monastery.

Cat ms *c*1775 and *c*1890; printed 1819, 1836. Also cat of Norfolk and Norwich Clerical Society, printed 1838; ms card cat *c*1930 under continuous revision since 1961. Cat of pamphlets in preparation 1977.

Beriah Botfield, *English Cathedral Libraries* (1849), p330-47. (op)

H C Beeching, 'The Library of the Cathedral Church of Norwich, with Appendix of Priory mss now in English Libraries' (by M R James) in *Norfolk Archaeology* XIX (1917), p67-116. (op)

G A Stephen, 'The Cathedral Library' in his *Norfolk Bibliography* (1921), p23-5. (op)

P Hepworth, 'The Dean and Chapter's Library, Norwich' in *East Anglian Magazine*, v 14, no 12 (1955), p680-6. (op)

N R Ker, 'Medieval manuscripts from Norwich Cathedral Priory' in *Trans Camb Bib Soc* 1 (1950), p1-28. (op)

——(ed) *Medieval Libraries of Great Britain* (1964), p135-9. (op)

University of East Anglia Library, Norwich NR4 7TJ. Tel (0603) 56161. Open (Term) Mon-Fri 9 am-10 pm; Sat 9 am-5 pm; Sun 2-7 pm; (Vacation) Mon-Fri 9 am-6 pm; Sat and Sun closed.

Abbott Collection A bequest to UEA Library by Professor Claude Colleer Abbott of the University of Durham on his death in 1971. The collection consists of *c*1,000 items (mostly books; some pamphlets), and represents about one-fifth of the total bequest, the rest having been dispersed among the Library's stock. Special strengths include the 18th cent writers (especially Johnson and Boswell), the pre-Raphaelites, Gerard Manley Hopkins and his circle; 20th cent writers (including many with whom Professor Abbott was personally acquainted, especially Gordon Bottomley), and a miscellaneous selection of Private Press books. It is a collection of fine or rare editions of English literature.

All items are included in the Library's card cat, and there is a separate card cat by author.

There is no cat in book form.

Gordon Bottomley and his circle, (Catalogue of an exhibition, Dec 1974) UEA Library, 1974.

Illustrated Books Collection The collection has been built up over the years by purchase and donation; it includes relevant items from the Claude Abbott bequest, and totals *c*600 v. While it contains a representative group of facsimiles of illustrated manuscripts, the collection is basically one of original illustrated and designed books. It is strongest in 19th cent publications, but ranges from the 1611 English edition of Serlio, to examples of recent artists' bookworks.

Card cat.

Military History Collection The works in this collection were originally the property of Capt Charles Broke, RE (*c*1815–55), and passed by marriage to the De Saumarez family. They were donated to UEA in 1964; *c*150 books, pamphlets and 200 maps. The collection comprises mainly English and continental publications from the period of the Revolutionary and Napoleonic Wars. It includes campaign histories, manuals on drill, tactics, military engineering etc and a considerable number of maps and town plans of the period.

Card cat.

Ketton-Cremer Collection The working collection of the Norfolk scholar, R W Ketton-Cremer, bequeathed to the Library in 1969, and covering all aspects of Norfolk history, *c*1,000 v. Includes poll books, pamphlets, and other scarce research material.

Card cat.

Norfolk and Norwich Law Society Library *c*150 v of older law material, including law reports of the 17th-19th cent, purchased from the Society in 1977.

Card cat.

Note All the collections contain a small number of STC or Wing items. Precise numbers not known.

The Sainsbury Centre for Visual Arts, University of East Anglia, Norwich. Tel (0603) 56161. Open weekdays (except Mon) 12 noon-5 pm. Admission to Reference Library only by enquiry by letter to the Keeper, stating bona fides. Photocopying by arrangement.

D L Munby Collection Given by the family of Denys L Munby, Reader in Economics and Organisation of Transport, Oxford University (1919–1976), the collection totals 2,800 v and numerous pamphlets (catalogues of exhibitions) on art and architecture covering Western Europe and North and South America, mostly relating to Munby's own travels (mid-1950s to mid-1970s). Particularly strong in individual exhibition catalogues. Numerous items not in main University Library. Other items bequeathed by Ioan Evans (1893–1977).

Slip cat under reorganization.

St Peter Mancroft Church, Bethel Street, Norwich. Custodian The Vicar, the Vicarage, 37 Unthank Road, Norwich. Enquiries for admission may be referred to the Central Public Library, Norwich.

The St Peter Mancroft Parochial Library A small library containing some 16 v, 5 of which were presented by Thomas Temson (1636–1715), minister of the church 1674–6, later Archbishop of Canterbury. Most volumes are theological (17th cent) but the 12th cent mss of the Pauline Epistles is described as 'the most important book in Norfolk'. Although it has been at Mancroft for 300 years, it is believed to originate in Durham.

N R Ker, *Medieval Libraries of Great Britain*, 2nd ed 1964.

Central Council for the Care of Churches, *Parochial Libraries*, 1959.

Swaffham

Church of St Peter and St Paul, Swaffham, Norfolk. Admission on application to the Vicar.

Swaffham Church Library Presented by members of the family of Sir Henry Spelman (1560–1641), an antiquary who founded a short-lived lectureship in Anglo-Saxon at Cambridge. Books came to Swaffham in 1684, and now total *c*400 v, mainly on divinity and topography, including early Bibles; Holenshed's *Chronicle* (1577); legal and geographical works; *Common Prayer* (printed by John Sturt), 1717. The mss collection includes a *Book of Hours* (*c*1420), and the ms known as the 'Black Book of Swaffham' given by John Botright, Rector of Swaffham 1435–74.

W B Rix, The *Pride of Swaffham* (1954). (op)

Thetford

Norfolk County Branch Library, Raymond Street, Thetford, Norfolk IP24 2EA. Tel (0842) 2048. Open Mon, Thurs 10 am-5 pm; Tues, Fri 10 am-8 pm; Wed, Sat 10 am-1 pm. Admission to Deposit Collection upon identification.

Thomas Paine Collection The executors of Ambrose C Barker passed this collection to the Borough Council of Thetford in October 1963, and from then onwards it has been administered by the County Branch Librarian. It consists of over 500 v listed in *An analytical catalogue of the Ambrose G Barker Thomas Paine Collection* (Norfolk County Library, 1970). Aims to provide all works by, or concerning, Paine; revised edition in progress. Thomas Paine Society of GB has deposited several hundred items on permanent loan. It also contains numerous items of an ephemeral nature, viz press cuttings, programmes, tokens, Paine's marriage banns (1759), etc.

Printed analytical cat.

Staniforth Collection Bequeathed to Borough of Thetford in 1947 by George Wild Staniforth of King's House, Thetford, together with the property. Originally *c*13,000 v, it is now reduced to *c*8,500. Some of the discarded material is held at the Norwich Reference Library. Very strong in travel, natural history, folklore, English literature, Egyptology, church history, big-game hunting. Several hundred novels of late 19th cent. Numerous items on history and travel of Northern England.

Classified card cat.

New Reading in Norwich, Aug 1974 (short article).

Wells-on-Sea

Holkham Hall Library, Wells-on-Sea, Norfolk. Admission strictly by appointment with the librarian, c/o Bodleian Library, Oxford. (The private house, the staterooms but not the library are open to the public.) Admission granted for research on original materials not available elsewhere, or not reproduced photographically.

The Library of the Earls of Leicester (at present of Viscount Coke) The library of Chief Justice Coke (1552–1634) and his heir Thomas Coke (1697–1759) with the agricultural and estate letter books (from 1816) of 'Coke of Norfolk'. The Chief Justice's (T W Coke, 1754–1842) library was greater, in its day, than that of Cambridge University. Thomas Coke's purchases on the Grand Tour concentrated on mss from Lyons, Naples, Padua and Venice, and the Palladian house he had built was designed to house his treasures (started 1734). The 2nd Earl sold some books and bought some rarities. Through W Roscoe, T W Coke bought treasures, of which only Virgil remains. The collection contains *c*20,000 v, arranged in 12 places throughout the Hall. Only the books in the Tribune can be seen on open days by the public. Subjects covered are antiquities, classics, architecture, Latin, French and Italian; Civil War and Commonwealth tracts. The books in the Long Library are part of the interior decoration bound by Robiquet for the 1st Earl. There is detailed medieval documentation of the estate, building and domestic accounts. Incunabula include Gutenberg's *Catholicon* and Subiaco *Lactantius*. It may be said that it is the greatest privately owned ancient library in England still largely in the house of the family which has owned it since the late 16th cent. For a note of the partial dispersal of the printed books, see *A Catalogue of the Library of Sir Edward Coke*, edited by W O Hassall, with a preface by Samuel E Thorne (Yale Law Library Publication, no 12, Oct 1950) distinguishing by asterisks books remaining at Holkham; lists Hatton books in Italian now in Bodleian Library placed next each other; indicates Coke's ms annotations in printed law books, deposited first in East Anglia University Library and now in the Inner Temple.

There is an inventory of printed books in 2 folio v and a card index of incunabula and other books in the Classical Library. For mss *see* Seymour De Ricci, *Handlist of Manuscripts in the Library of the Earl of Leicester at Holkham Hall abstracted from the catalogues of William Roscoe and Frederic Madden and annotated by Seymour De Ricci*, Bibliographical Society, 1932. Roscoe and Madden's 8 v catalogue ms 770 is available on microfilm, E P Productions, East Ardsley, Wakefield, Yorks.

C W James, 'Some Notes on the Library of Printed

Books at Holkham', *The Library*, XI, (1930–1), p435-60.

——'Some Notes on the Manuscript Library at Holkham', *The Library* II (1921–2), p213-37.

W Roscoe, 'Some Account of the Manuscript Library at Holkham in Norfolk, belonging to T W Coke Esq', in *Trans Roy Soc Lit*, II (1834), p352-79.

Beriah Botfield, 'The Holkham Library', in *Miscellanies of the Philobiblon Soc*, VI.4 (1860–1), p72-85.

H Delahaye, 'Catalogus codicum hagiographicorum Graecorum Bibliothecae Comitis de Leicester Holkhamiae in Anglia', in *Analecta Bollandiana*, XXV (1906), p451-77.

Valdo Vinay, 'Domenico Antonio Ferrari, bibliofilo napoletano in Inghilterra nella metà del xvii secolo', *Studi di letteratura storia e filosofia in onore di Bruno Revel*, Florence 1965. (Dr Ferrari, a Neapolitan Protestant, was first librarian at Holkham and left his own learned library to his patron.)

John Mitchell, 'Trevisan and Soranzo', *Bodleian Library Record*, VIII, no 3 (on a library much of which is at Bodley and some at Holkham), 1969.

W O Hassall, 'Portrait of bibliophile II: Thomas Coke, Earl of Leicester 1679–1759', *The Book Collector*, 8, no 3, 1959, p249-61.

Northamptonshire

Finedon

Finedon Church Library, Church of St Mary the Virgin, Finedon, Northants. Tel (0933) 680747. Admission strictly by application in writing to the Librarian.

The library was founded by Sir John English Dolben in 1788, and includes some later additions. The printed books total *c*885 v, with four incunabula and 18 STC items. Subject coverage is mostly theological. Books missing after 1824 are listed in the catalogue.

Typewritten cat (copy in Cambridge University Library).

R Underwood, *The pageant of Finedon* (1942), p36-40.

J L H Bailey, *Finedon otherwise Thingdon*, 1975.

King's Cliffe

King's Cliffe Library, Library House, Bridge Street, King's Cliffe, Peterborough. Tel (078 087) 675. Admission by application in writing to the Librarian.

The library was founded by William Law in 1752, with few later additions. It contains *c*500 works, mainly 18th cent theological, including a notable collection of late 17th and early 18th cent French and German theology, and a good collection of William Law's works and some books owned by him. A number of duplicates disposed of in 1885 are noted in printed cat.

A catalogue of the library at King's Cliffe, Northamptonshire, founded by William Law, 1752–1927, 1927.

Stephen Hobhouse, *Selected mystical writings of William Law*, 1938.

Northampton

Northamptonshire Libraries, Central Library, Abington Street, Northampton NN1 2BA. Tel (0604) 33628. Open Mon, Wed, Fri 9 am-8 pm, Tues, Thurs 9 am-5 pm; Sat 9 am-4 pm. Admission by appointment desirable. Photocopying; microfilm reader/printer available.

John Clare Collection The collection of the 19th cent poet's works grew up from a series of purchases beginning with that of Clare's own library by John Taylor of Northampton. In 1920 the Stewart Beathe Collection containing many Clare items was also purchased. The catalogue and supplement list 415 items, some of which are substantial collections of letters etc. There is also a large collection of books on Clare; mss letters and other memoranda by Clare. 15 v from Clare's library were sold by the Public Libraries Committee in 1902.

Catalogue of the John Clare Collection in the Northampton Public Library, Northampton, 1965. *Supplement*, 1971.

Lamport Hall Library, Lamport Hall, Northampton. Tel (060 128) 272. Open Sunday afternoons Easter to September. Admission by prior arrangement with the Administrator, Lamport Hall Trust.

Lamport Hall Library The private collection of the Isham family, 1560–1976, now the property of the Lamport Hall Preservation Trust. Its stock totals *c*3,000 v, and includes 2 incunabula; *c*150 STC; and *c*750 Wing items. The subject areas are mainly theology, classics, topography, many 17th cent French and Italian books purchased by Sir Thomas Isham, 3rd Bart on the Grand Tour 1680, and some privately lithographed verse by Sir Charles Isham, 10th Bart. A fine specimen of a 17th and 18th cent Tory squire's library to which little has been added after 1737.

Card cat (by H A N Hallam) 1960s, superseding ms cat by Mr Edmonds of Sotheran, *c*1880.

H A N Hallam, 'Lamport Hall revisited' in *Book Collector* 1967.

Northamptonshire Record Office, Delapre Abbey, London Road, Northampton NN5 9AW. Open Mon, Tues, Wed, Fri 9.15 am-4.45 pm, Thurs 9.15 am-7.45 pm; Sat 9 am-12.15 pm. Open to members of the public. Catalogues and indexes of records. Xerox and photostats can be made. Small reference library.

The Record Office Library includes the following collections: (a) The Library of Guilsborough Grammar School made up of 533 v, mostly given by Edmund Batemen (*d*1742), but includes other donations. There are some 16th cent items, but mostly 17th cent British and foreign books covering the classics and theology; (b) Two small collections deposited by two local legal firms consisting of 100+ v, 17th-19th cent British legal works, and *c*25 17th cent Law Reports; (c) The Library of Northamptonshire Antiquarian Society (now defunct) consisting of *c*600 v, mainly 19th cent and later antiquarian and ecclesiastical works.

Typed cat lists.

Nottinghamshire

Nottingham

The Boots Company Ltd, Industrial Division, Research Library, Pennyfoot Street, Nottingham NG2 3AA. Tel (0602) 56255 Ext 310. Open Mon-Fri 9 am-4 pm. Admission on written application to Chief Research Librarian. Photocopier; microfiche reader. Access to photographic reproduction facilities.

Company archives Collecting began *c*1950, although the business was begun in 1877. The collection includes 29 v of five works published by Boots (early 20th cent); 11 ms v (recipes, order books, branch wages, product labels, 1890–1940); *c*1,000 photographs (shops, offices, factories, products, people connected with the company, 1890 to date); 'Thurgarton (Notts) archaeological investigations (1949–52)'; 15 v (typed reports, photographs, maps); 50 postcards.

Card index to photographs only.

Nottingham City Museums. Nottingham Natural History Museum, Wollaton Hall, Wollaton Park, Nottingham NG8 2AE. Open Mon-Fri 10 am-4 pm. Admission by written application to Curator. Access to photocopier at Castle Museum, Nottingham.

The Museum Library was transferred from University College, Nottingham in 1926, most of the rare books being acquired by John Wesley Carr (1862–1939), Director of the Museum and Professor of Biology at the College. The collection of rare books contains 30-40 titles in 40-50 v relating to natural history (especially British) and include Godfrey Howitt and William Valentine, *Muscologia Nottinghamiensis*, Fasc 1 only (1833) extra-illustrated with specimens, and Thomas Jowett, 'Collections for a flora Nottinghamiensis' 1822 (ms v). 1 Wing item.

Author cat on cards (discontinued in early 1960s).

Nottingham City Museums, Newstead Abbey, Linby, Nottingham NG15 8GE. Tel (062 34) 3557. Admission by written application to the Curator. Access to photocopier at Castle Museum, Nottingham.

Newstead Abbey Collection, including the Roe-Byron Collection The Roe-Byron Collection, accumulated by Herbert Charles Roe (1873–1923) was bequeathed to the City of Nottingham, and placed in the Abbey in 1937. The nucleus of the general Abbey collection was gathered by the Fraser family, the last private occupants, and was presented by them in 1931, and has been added to subsequently by gift and purchase. Both Collections contain literary and biographical material. They consist of *c*270 works which relate to George Gordon Noel, 6th Baron Byron (1788–1824), his works, life and circle, and to Newstead Abbey and its previous owners. 1 Wing item.

There are also 183 mss, of which 59 are literary; *c*200 illustrative items, mostly printed or engraved.

Printed cat of the Roe-Byron Collection, 1937.

Card cat of printed and ms material on George Gordon Noel, 6th Baron Byron (1788–1824) and the Byron family.

Nottinghamshire County Library, Central Library, Angel Row, Nottingham NG1 6HP. Tel (0602) 412121. Open Mon-Fri 9.30 am-8 pm; Sat 9 am-1 pm. Study accommodation; photocopier; microfilm/fiche readers; microfilm reader/printer.

Arts Library - Rare Books Collection Nottingham City Library, established 1868, and became part of Nottinghamshire County Library 1974. The collection totals *c*2,500 v, and contains all pre-1800 titles (excluding those in the Local Studies Library, but including a few books on science and technology). Main subject areas are 17th and 18th cent county histories; 18th cent travel (especially Asia and Africa). There are *c*150 STC and *c*200 Wing; and *c*50 pre-1701 continental items.

Card cat author and classified.

Local Studies Library Local history collecting began in 1868 with the foundation of the Nottingham Public Libraries, which became part of Nottinghamshire County in 1974. Present stock totals over 50,000 v, and constitutes a comprehensive collection of printed material on Nottinghamshire, local printing, and books by local authors. It includes 7 STC and *c*100 Wing items. Specialist collections are: Local printing (*c*1,657 items); D H Lawrence (*c*4,000 items); Robin Hood (800 items); Byron (*c*1,500 items). William and Mary Howitt (376 items) and Henry Kirke White (202 items) are strongly represented. Other rarities include literary mss by Cecil Roberts and Stanley Middleton. The parish library of Elston (Notts) collected in the early 18th cent, and consisting of 24 works in 24 v was deposited with the former County Library in 1950 (mainly on theology); two-thirds printed on the Continent 1593—1634, but include 3 STC; and 2 Wing items.

Card and microfiche author and classified cat.

D H Lawrence: a finding list.

S Cooke and S Best, *In print I found it...*, Nottingham, 1976.

Nottinghamshire Record Office, County House, High Pavement, Nottingham NG1 1HR. Tel (0602) 54524. Open Mon 9 am-4.45 pm, Tues 9 am-7.15 pm, Wed, Thurs 9 am-4.45 pm, Fri 9 am-4.15 pm. 1st and 3rd Sat of each month, 9.30 am-12.45 pm. Admission unrestricted. Microfilm reader/printer, photocopier, ultraviolet lamp available.

Belper Library The Nottinghamshire part of the library of books, prints and maps relating to Derbyshire and Nottinghamshire, built up by the Hon Frederick Strutt (1843—1909), was presented to Nottinghamshire County Council in 1912 by his brother Henry Strutt, 2nd Baron Belper (1840—1914). A few gifts were received between 1912 and the publication of the catalogue in 1915, since when it has been added to as a working library. The Belper Library consists almost exclusively of books on Nottinghamshire, or by Nottinghamshire authors, together with a few general antiquarian works. It includes 2 STC; 40 Wing and *c*540 pre-1851 works. About 30 titles have been transferred to the Humanities Library, County Library, Angel Row, Nottingham, all being in the printed catalogue and indicated in a marked copy available at the Record Office.

Printed cat (by Richard W Goulding), 1915, with typed supplement *c*1937.

A card cat of new accessions was begun *c*1950. The additions of the intervening period are not catalogued, but are not likely to include a significant amount of rare material.

Printed material in record collections Accumulated as part of various record collections since the establishment of the Office in 1949, the collection totals *c*240 items–Acts of Parliament, mostly Nottinghamshire and neighbouring counties (including many canal, enclosure, municipal, private, turnpike road), chiefly 18th and 19th cent.

Card cat.

Nottingham Subscription Library Ltd, Angel Row, Nottingham. Tel (0602) 43134. Open Mon-Fri 9.30 am-5 pm. Open to members and bona fide scholars on application. No research facilities.

A proprietary library was founded in 1816, and incorporated as a limited company in 1926. The library (which is often known as Bromley House Library) now totals *c*30,000 v in a general library, with older books on all subjects, but mainly on the humanities. Items of exceptional rarity are the Sherwood Forest Book (ms, 17th-18th cent) and the ms of G C Deering's *Nottinghamia vetus et nova* (published 1751). Special collections include the *James Ward* collection of books on Nottinghamshire (over 300 works, including many by local authors and locally printed) and a selection of *c*200 works from the library of *Philip James Bailey* (1816—1902).

Dictionary cat on cards.

Printed complete cats and supplements (S) 1819, 1925 (S), 1826 (S), 1829, 1835, 1841, 1847, 1857 (A), 1864, 1866 (S), 1881, 1887 (S), 1895 (S).

James Ward, *A descriptive catalogue of books relating to Nottinghamshire in the library of James Ward*. Nottingham, 1892.

John Russell, *A history of the Nottingham Subscription Library, Nottingham*, 1916. (op)

St Hugh's College, Tollerton, Tollerton Hall, Nottingham NG12 4FZ. Tel (060 77) 2334. Open by arrangement on application in writing to the Librarian.

Upper Library The College (a Roman Catholic boys' school) was opened in 1948, and had a library from the start. Acquisition of older material has not been systematic. It contains *c*150 v (*c*100 works) on Christian theology, and includes 1 French-printed 17th cent; 16 English Roman Catholic devotional books pre-1851; 1 ms (Dutch gradual, 15th cent).

St John's College, Bramcote, Nottingham NG9 3DS. Tel (0602) 251114 Ext 29. Open Mon-Fri 9 am-5 pm. Admission by arrangement with the Librarian. Photocopier available.

The College has had a library since it was opened, as the London College of Divinity, in 1863 (the oldest Evangelical theological college in the Church of England). Few rare books remain, many having been lost by fire and/or water in 1946, and extensive sales having taken place in the 1950s and 1960s. (The books sold appeared in Blackwell's theology cats.) The present collection totals 160-200 (*c*300 v) of works on theology and church history. There are 5 STC and 6 Wing items.

Card cat to the general collection, including some of the earlier books. Many of the earlier books are uncat.

Trent Polytechnic School of Art and Design, Trent Polytechnic Central Library, Dryden Street, Nottingham. Tel (0602) 48248 Ext 2199. Open Term: Mon-Fri 8.30 am-9 pm, Sat 8.30 am-5 pm; Vacation: Mon-Fri only 8.30 am-5 pm. Admission to members of Trent Polytechnic; to others on written application to School Librarian. Microform readers, photocopier, photographic and slide-making facilities.

The School was opened in 1843 as the Government School of Design, and immediately began to acquire books, although it was during the principalship of Joseph Harrison (1888–1923) that major purchases of rare and valuable material were made. The collection consists of *c*3,000 titles, of which 300 or 400 are pre-1851. They relate to art and design, especially strong in lace, including *c*200 drafts (with samples); 30 books of machine-made lace samples (Nottingham); 10 sample books of unknown origin (all 19th or early 20th cent) and 1 ms v of lace designs (19th cent). The lace material relates mostly to the Levers branch of the industry. Ms sketch-book of continental domestic and ecclesiastical architecture, compiled 1849–50 by S Salter. Architectural books were transferred to the University of Nottingham Library with the transfer of the School of Architecture to the University in 1964.

General card cat of the school library only.

University of Nottingham Library, University Park, Nottingham NG7 2RD. Tel (0602) 56101. Dept of Special Collections open Mon-Fri 9 am-5 pm. Admission to any registered user of the University Library; others on application to the University Librarian. Microform readers. Photocopying, photography, microfilming facilities.

The Special Collection Until 1928 University College, Nottingham, shared a common library with the City. In that year a separate library was started for the college (now the University of Nottingham), and Special Collections have been built up by gift, purchase and transfer from the library's general stock since then. They total *c*1,100 works in *c*1,400 v, and include the University Library's general stock of rare books in the humanities and social sciences, and all books printed before 1701. The best represented subjects are English literature and theology (in English), classics, English history and fine art. Among finely printed books are: Baskerville 6; Kelmscott 7. Among individual items are a ms 'index of all ye plays printed in ye English language to 1747' (174?–?), by (?) Wincup; *A catalogue of the library of the Rt Hon Lord Foley, Witley Court, Worcestershire* (London, 1813), with ms additions to 1869; 2 albums containing over 300 18th and 19th cent broadside ballads (40 printed at Nottingham); 1 album of proofs and originals of drawings by Kate (Catherine) Greenaway; 24 limited editions (*c*200 copies); *c*50 pre-1701 works from the library of Robert Walter Shirley, 12th Earl Ferrers; 8 incunabula; 80 STC; 320 Wing; 290 16th-17th cent foreign books. These numbers (except incunabula) can be expected to increase as older books are identified in the general stock and transferred to Special Collections.

Shelflist. Author cards in library's main cat.

W A Briggs Collection of Early Educational Literature Given with an endowment in 1950 by Dr William Gerald Briggs, and added to considerably since then by Dr Briggs, and by purchase. The Collection includes 1,120 printed works; 24 educational games and 200 mss. It is basically a collection of educational books for children, published before 1851, the great majority in English and published in Great Britain; about two-thirds dating from 1801–50. All subjects are covered, and there are 200 works of improving literature. There are 12 STC; 60 Wing items and 6 16th-17th cent foreign books. The mss include 50 exercise and school workbooks (1789–1875); 100 school bills (tuition and tradesmen's) (1744–1877); 4 schoolboys' letters home (1810–31); 5 Greek verb 'trees' (1847); account book for Radbourn and Mugginton Charity Schools (both Derbyshire) 1748–64. Derbyshire is well represented among the ms items generally.

Duplicated *Handlist* (1970) kept up to date by name cat on cards. Subject approach is available through the shelflist only. Author cards in general library cat.

Cambridge Drama Collection Presented to the library in 1960 by Cambridge City Libraries, to which the original collection had been given by Henry Thomas Hall in the late 19th cent. Some of the books had previously belonged to the Cambridge Garrick Club. The library has added to the collection by purchase and transfer from its general stock. It contains *c*600 v and *c*40 pamphlets, numbering *c*1,200 items in all. *c*80 items are post-1851. Subjects covered include English plays (including editions and adaptations of plays by earlier authors and translations, and the British theatre (both 1750–1850); histories of the stage and of individual theatres; lives of actors; controversial literature, but not the study of the drama as a literary form. The bulk of the collection consists of over 1,000 separately printed plays or collections published as such, all pre-1851, with *c*160 items on the theatre, of which about half are post-1850. Items in the original gift falling outside the period 1750–1850 have been added to the general library stock.

Author card cat; Cambridge Free Library, *Catalogue of the books in the Cambridge Free Library reference department*, 4 pts, 1874–99.

Cambridge Shakespeare Collection Presented to the library in 1960 by Cambridge City Libraries, to which the original collection had been given by Henry Thomas Hall in the late 19th cent. It contains 177 works in *c*1,400 v of which 99 works, in *c*900 v, are pre-1851. The original collection consisted of complete editions of Shakespeare, together with works on his life and art. The latter have been added to the general stock of the library, so that the collection now consists of complete editions (single and multi-volume), published between 1709 and 1893. No incunabula, STC, Wing, foreign, pre-1701.

Typed handlist; Cambridge Free Library, *Catalogue of the books in the Cambridge Free Library reference department*, 4 pts 1874–99.

William Jaggard, *Shakespeare bibliography* (Stratford-upon-Avon, 1911) gives Cambridge Public Library locations. Some of these items are now in the Cambridge Shakespeare Collection, others in the general stock of the University Library.

East Midlands Collection Built up by the library since *c*1928. The East Midlands (mainly Nottinghamshire) section of the Thoroton Society Library accepted on deposit 1981. There are *c*8,000 works (including pamphlets), of which *c*250 are pre-1801, and an estimated 800 between 1801 and 1850; they cover various aspects of the East Midlands (the historic counties of Derbyshire, Leicestershire, Lincolnshire, Nottinghamshire and Rutland) with an historical bias. Most of the pre-1851 books were printed in Nottingham and elsewhere in the region, including 20 chapbooks. The collection also includes 110 literary and other works by Mary and William Howitt (over half probably being first editions); 20 limited editions (200 copies or fewer); 10 works with annotations by the author (or another scholar); 56 known works having subscription lists; 2 books of photographs of Welbeck Abbey in 1882; 6 albums of Derbyshire geological photographs by H H Arnold-Forster; 300 aerial photographs of the East Midlands (from the Cambridge University Collection); and an album of 80 broadsides relating to Nottinghamshire trials 1759–1862. There are 1 STC and 55 Wing items.

Name and subject card cats; the name cards are also in the library's general cat.

61 pre-1815 Nottinghamshire-printed items, not on local subjects or by local authors, are listed in S Cooke and S Best, *In print I found it* (Nottingham, 1976).

Michael Brook, 'The East Midlands Collection of Nottingham University Library, with notes on local material in some other special collections', *Bull Local Hist: East Midland Region*, 10 (1975), p9-12.

French Revolution Collection The collection consists mainly of duplicates from the Bibliotheca Lindesiana, collected by James Ludovic Lindsay, 26th Earl of Crawford and 9th Earl of Balcarres, and were purchased from the John Rylands Library, Manchester, between 1928 and 1933. It contains *c*900 works and *c*250 periodicals relating to the French Revolution and First Empire (of which three-quarters relate to the Revolutionary period). Almost everything is printed before 1900. *c*400 pre-1851 works printed on the Continent (mostly in France), 40 in England; *c*200 periodical titles (all printed in France), usually incomplete, published 1788–1800; and *c*40 (many represented by single numbers) published during the Revolution of 1848.

Typescript cat (1937) and supplement (1971), which includes a finding list of serials.

Author and (for serials) title cards in the general card cat of the library. Subject approach provided by the shelflist and the library's classified card cat.

'University of Nottingham Library', *The Library* (1950), p18-19.

D H Lawrence Collection Lawrence material was originally treated as part of the East Midlands Collection, from which it was removed to form a separate collection in the early 1950s. It has been built up by the library, although there have been some gifts. It comprises *c*350 v and *c*70 pamphlets by and about David Herbert Lawrence, including *c*50 first editions of works by Lawrence; 2 scrapbooks; 1 box of ephemera; 1 box of photographic blocks for *Lawrence in love. Letters to Louie Burrows*, ed J T Boulton (Nottingham 1968); portrait of Lawrence by Edmond X Kapp (1923). The Department of Manuscripts of the University Library holds letters, literary manuscripts and paintings by Lawrence. *See* University of Nottingham Manuscripts Department: *D H Lawrence Collection Catalogue* (1979).

Author cat on cards. *See also* Sheila M Cooke, *D H Lawrence: a finding list.*

A catalogue of printed material in the County and University Libraries of Nottingham, 2nd ed (West Bridgford?), 1980.

Coventry Patmore Collection Built up by the library during the 1930s, the collection totals 102 v, containing 63 works consisting mainly of works by Coventry Patmore (1823–96), including 18 first editions, and a copy of *The angel in the house* (4th ed 1866) with corrections by the author, together with five works by the poet's father, Peter George Patmore (1786–1855). There is a Coventry Patmore Collection in the Manuscripts Department of the library.

The Patmore section of the main library cat forms the cat. There is also a shelflist.

University of Nottingham Library. *The Library* (1950), p18.

Woodward Collection This collection of *c*240 works in *c*290 v and *c*40 pamphlets was brought together by Parker Woodward, a Nottingham solicitor and Baconian, and was presented to the library by his son Wilfrid Owen Woodward in 1945, with a smaller supplementary gift in 1978. It is devoted to Francis Bacon, 1st Viscount St Albans, and particularly to the claim that he wrote the plays commonly attributed to Shakespeare. It consists mostly of controversial literature published in the late 19th and early 20th cent (much of it probably rare), but it also contains 17 pre-1851 titles, including 1 STC and 2 Wing items. There are 4 limited editions and 8 works by Parker Woodward, including 1 of the 2 surviving copies of *Sir Francis Bacon. . . essay by Parker Woodward towards a more correct biography* (Leicester 1920); also 1 scrapbook of newspaper cuttings (1901–11) and 1 scrapbook containing leaflets and 3 letters to Parker Woodward (1894–1927).

No separate cat. Author cards are in the general library cat and there is a shelflist of the collection.

Law Library Special Collection The Law Library was founded in 1950, and most of the books in the collection were added in the mid-1950s, mostly by donation, but to some extent by purchase (with funds granted by the Hind Trust). It contains *c*300 works (of which *c*250 are pre-1851) in *c*530 v. The collection is the general stock of rare books in the Law Library (mostly in English and on English Law), and contains 24 STC; 39 Wing; 3 foreign pre-1700 items.

Duplicated author checklist. Author cards in Law Library and University Library cat.

Medical Library Rare Book Collection (located at Queen's Medical Centre, Clifton Boulevard, Nottingham NG7 2UH. Tel (0602) 700111 Ext 3644. Open Mon-Fri 9 am-7 pm, Sat 9 am-12.30 pm. Admission to non-registered users on application to the Medical Librarian). The Medical Library was set up in 1968. The Rare Book Collection has been accumulated since 1972 by transfer from the stock of the Science Library, and comprises 32 pre-1850 medical titles in 35 v, including T Paytherus, *A comparative statement of facts and observations relative to the cow-pox* (1800) which is the only evidence of the existence of the Medical Book Society of Newark, Southwell, and the Neighbourhood, founded 1795, and including a list of members.

Shelflist. Author and subject cards in Medical Library cat.

J B Cochrane, *Nottingham Medico-Chirurgical Society* (Nottingham, 1978) especially p12-18, 37-40, 65-6, 80-3.

Nottingham Medico-Chirurgical Society Library (located at Queen's Medical Centre under Medical Library) The Society was founded as the Medical Book Society before 1815, and continued to add to the library until the early 20th cent. The Society still exists, but the contents of the library were bought by the University in 1971 with funds provided by Mrs Miriam Kaplowitch. It contains *c*800 works in *c*1,000 v, and 30 titles of journals in *c*600 v, all relating to medicine, especially works published 1800–60 (almost all in English). More than half the stock is pre-1851.

Printed 1831 (author, bound with rules of Society), ms 1838 (author), printed 1888 (author and subject), typescript v 1955 (shelflist), card 1972 (author and subject).

Music Library (located at Beeston Lane, University Park) Accumulated in University Library, from which it was transferred when the Music Library was set up in 1956. It contains *c*200 works in *c*160 v consisting of 18th and 19th cent scores by contemporary British and foreign composers, half printed in England and half on the Continent.

Author and classified subject cat.

School of Agriculture Rare Book Collection (located at Sutton Bonnington, Loughborough, Leicestershire LE12 5RD). Tel (050 97) 2386 Ext 33. Open Term: Mon-Fri 9 am-10 pm. Vacation: same, but some limitation of hours in summer (write or telephone for information). Admission on application to the School of Agriculture Librarian. The School was opened in 1895 as the Midland Dairy Institute. It was known as the Midland Agricultural College from 1905–47, when it became part of the University College, Nottingham. The library was started in 1908, most of the Rare Book Collection being accumulated during the 1930s and 1940s, by purchase, but some by gifts and transfers from the general stock. The collection of rare books totals *c*260 works in *c*340 v and 10 periodical sets, of which *c*230 works and 8 periodical sets are pre-1851. They are British publications on agriculture and horticulture, including 88 Board of Agriculture Reports, 1793–7, and include 6 STC and 9 Wing items.

Author cat on cards; also available as typed list. Subject approach via shelflist of the collection.

Science Library Rare Book Collection Tel (0602) 56101 Ext 2571. Open Term: 9 am-10 pm; Vacation: 9 am-5 pm; Sat 9 am-12.30 pm (closed in August). Admission to any registered user of the University Library; others on application to the Science Librarian. Begun *c*1928 and added to by gift, purchase and transfer from general stock, it now totals *c*325 works in *c*375 v. There are *c*50 pre-1701 items in this somewhat fortuitously assembled collection of books in the field of science and technology, including 7 STC; 25 Wing; and 18 foreign pre-1700 items. Of the early printed books, the main interest lies in a group of herbals and pharmacopoeias.

Author and subject cards in general cat of Science Library and University Library. Shelflist.

Porter Collection The collection was built up by Sydney Porter, a Derbyshire ornithologist, and bequeathed by him at his death in 1958. It comprises *c*900 v, containing *c*750 works, of which *c*20 are pre-1851, and *c*50 other works, chiefly of late 19th cent are also rare. The subject covered is ornithology.

Typed author handlist of original collection (1958), author and subject cards in general cat of Science Library and University Library. Shelflist, subject index (on cards).

Oakham Parish Library A theological library presented to Oakham (Rutland, now Leicestershire) Parish Church in 1616 by Lady Anne Harington, together with a few later additions. Deposited on indefinite loan 1981. It contains *c*90 works on theology, church history, canon law, and includes 4 incunabula; 66 17th and 18th cent titles (almost all continental, mostly Swiss, German and French printing). There has been a partial dispersal of stock before transfer from Oakham.

Author and subject card cats.

Typed author cat by Anne L Herbert, 1978 (special study for MA in Librarianship, Univ of Sheffield).

Ms cat arranged by title, probably early 20th cent.

A private library A country house library, built up chiefly between 1685 and 1814, but depleted by sales. Admission by written application to the Librarian, University Library, University Park, Nottingham NG7 2RD.

The library contains c5,000 v, of which c3,000 are pre-1851. Principal subjects covered are history, classics, and travel (mostly 18th and 19th cent). There are no incunabula, but there are French and Italian books of the 16th-18th cent (mainly the latter) and some STC and Wing items. There are c120 bound volumes of political and other pamphlets, 1700–1810.

A private library Admission by written application to the Librarian, University Library, University Park, Nottingham NG7 2RD.

A family library to replace an original collection almost completely destroyed by fire in 1745. The replacement probably began c1760, but was slow until c1870. Little has been added in the 20th cent. It contains c3,800 v, c1,200 titles. Principal subjects are English and French literature and history, and the classics. There are 1 STC; 14 Wing; and 11 pre-1701 foreign.

Shelflist, 1946.

Detailed cat in course of preparation.

Note Lincoln Cathedral Library is at present temporarily housed in Nottingham University. Enquiries about access should be referred to either the University Librarian at Nottingham or the Cathedral Library at Lincoln. Meanwhile researchers are referred to: Clive Hurst, *Catalogue of Wren Library of Lincoln Cathedral: Books printed before 1801.* Cambridge University Press, 1982. (Editor)

(Loughborough)

Co-operative College, Stanford Hall, Loughborough, Leicestershire. Tel (050 982) 2333. Open Mon-Fri 9 am-5 pm; other times by arrangement. Admission preferably by written or telephone appointment. Photocopier available.

Robert Owen Collection The College and library were founded in 1919, in Manchester, and moved to Stanford Hall 1946, when the library was split, part of it remaining in Manchester as the library of the Co-operative Union. There are c150 pre-1851 v (80-90 works). In the general stock, outside the Robert Owen Collection, are over 300 socialist pamphlets (late 19th and early 20th cent) including 47 Clarion and 45 ILP titles (bound in 6 v). The material deals mainly with the Co-operative movement in England, especially works of Robert Owen and early co-operative periodicals. Also 6 ft of mss research material on co-operative history, gathered by Thomas William Mercer (1884–1947), author and journalist.

Author and classified cat on cards.

Mansfield

Queen Elizabeth's School for Boys, Mansfield, 150 Chesterfield Road South, Mansfield, Nottinghamshire. Tel (0623) 23559. Open by prior arrangement between 9 am and 3.30 pm. Admission by written application. Photocopier available.

The school's collection of rare books has been built up over a long period through donations and purchases. It includes c70 works, mostly pre-1800, 4 STC, 4 Wing and 20 pre-1701 foreign imprints (8 Basle). There is no catalogue. A provisional list is provided in: Leslie Brettle, *A history of Queen Elizabeth's Grammar School for Boys*, Mansfield (Mansfield, 1971), p90-1. Some time before 1833, 130 v (forming the then school library) were removed to Mansfield Vicarage. The relationship between the present library and the 130 v collection is not known as there is no catalogue of the earlier library.

Newark

Church of St Mary Magdalene, Newark, Nottinghamshire. Open by arrangement. Bona fide research workers and students admitted on written application to the Librarian.

Newark Parish Church Library Bequeathed to the Mayor, Aldermen and Vicar of Newark by the will of Thomas White (1628–98), Bishop of Peterborough, the library contains 1,256 v, with some ms material, covering an extensive subject range, including theology, history, geography, medicine, classics. 117 v printed pre-1600; 1,057 v printed 1601–1700. Of these, 707 were printed in Britain, 467 on the Continent. No precise count of Wing/STC available.

Card and typescript author cats compiled since 1950.

Printed cat 1854.

John Morley, 'Libraries of Newark-on-Trent, 1698–1960', (FLA thesis, 1969), p9-24, 283-5.

Newark District Council Museum, Appletongate, Newark, Nottinghamshire NG24 1GY. Tel (0636) 702358. Open Mon-Wed, Fri-Sat 10 am-1 pm, 2-5 pm, Thurs 10 am-1 pm. Admission preferably by written permission. Microfilm reader and photocopying facilities available.

The museum was opened in 1912 and printed material began to be collected in 1928 with the gift of William Bradley's collection of Newark material by his widow. Since then there have been some additions of rare material by donation and purchase. The library now comprises c250 titles, including broadsides, maps and prints relating mainly to Newark and district, including Newark printing. Author and subject catalogues of the whole printed collection available on cards. A ms catalogue of William Bradley's collection maintained to the year of his death (1927). Thomas Mathews Blagg, *Newark as a publishing town* (Newark, privately printed, 1898) probably offers a guide to the collection.

Newstead Abbey

see under Nottingham City Museums.

Oakham Parish Library

see under University of Nottingham Library.

Southwell

Southwell Minster, Southwell, Nottinghamshire. No telephone. Admission by arrangement in writing to bona fide scholars.

Minster Library The main period of book buying for the library was *c*1670–*c*1830. Later additions were mostly gifts. It contains *c*1,200 works in the pre-1830 collection, whose main subject emphases are: Bibles; Greek and Latin classics (mainly in 16th cent continental editions); 'Popery' pamphlets of the 1680s; English literature and history; theology. There are 79 STC, 259 Wing, 118 pre-1600 continental and 142 1600–1700 continental items.

Author, on cards, giving STC, Wing, and Adams references.

18th cent ms cats.

Upton

British Horological Institute Ltd, Upton Hall, Upton, Newark, Nottinghamshire. Tel (0636) 813795. Open Mon-Fri 9 am-1 pm, 2-5 pm. Admission on written application. Photocopier available.

British Horological Institute Library Institute and Library were founded in 1858, and moved from London to Upton in 1972. Built up largely by gift from members, the library contains *c*3,000 v relating to Horology, and includes mss; archives of the Institute, 1858 to date; and workbooks of Benjamin Vulliamy (1755–1820), of London.

Author and classified cat on cards.

Oxfordshire

Abingdon

Abingdon School, Park Crescent, Abingdon, Oxon OX14 1DE. Tel (0235) 21563. Open during school term only to bona fide scholars upon written application. Xerox facilities.

The school was founded in 1563, and moved to its present premises in 1870. Rare books contained in the school library were given by: (a) former pupils, many in the 18th cent which still bear elaborate inscriptions recording the donor's name and the date; (b) French prisoners of war confined at Abingdon during the Seven Years War, 1756–63, and bearing interesting inscriptions. They comprise *c*110 items, of which 3 are 16th cent, 43 17th cent, 50 18th cent, and 14 19th cent books. The classics are well represented, and also many editions of the works of Thomas Godwyn, Headmaster of the School (*d*1642); works by Peter Heylyn, Chaplain to Charles I, who lived in Lacies Court (now the Headmaster's house) during the Cromwellian period, but no known connection with the School.

Separate handlist of rare books; includes notes of provenance.

Radley College, Radley, Abingdon, Oxon OX14 3Q. Tel (0235) 20294. Open by appointment, during term time only, to bona fide scholars, upon written application. Xerox facilities.

The Wilson Library The College was founded in 1847 and rare books have been donated to the library since then by various benefactors. The library's stock totals *c*14,000 v, of which *c*500 are rare. These include very few 16th and 17th cent items; a collection of Italian imprints; classics; Foulis press of the 18th cent; an incomplete set of 'Cheap Edition' of Dickens, 1847–52, boxed in original parts; plate books, especially ornithology and topography, of the 19th cent, and fine private press folios of the 20th cent. Mss collection includes a fine illuminated folio MS Antiphonal *c*1500, possibly Flemish (cf also printed Roman Psalter by Plantin, 1717, and Antiphonal by Plantin, 1773).

Card cat of working collection; no cat of older books.

Banbury

Banbury Parish Church (Library). Enquiries to the Vicar, St Mary's House, 89 Oxford Road, Banbury, Oxon. Tel (0295) 2370. Open by arrangement.

The Parish Library St Mary's Church was rebuilt after a fire in the 19th cent. At that time the residue of the library was donated to the Public Library. At the time of county amalgamation, it was proposed to dispose of this collection, but the Vicar asked for its return. It is made up of 13 v, including 5 STC, 3 Wing, and a short run of the 19th cent Parish Magazine. Mainly religious in subject content, the books include a rather battered 'treacle' Bible and two of Wm Whateley's works (he was Vicar of Banbury). The run of bound parish magazines would be of value to local historians. Many of the books are in poor condition. About half of the collection is equipped with descriptive cards from an exhibition.

Bloxham School, Banbury, Oxon. OX15 4PE. Tel (0295) 720206. Open by arrangement to bona fide scholars. Xerox facilities.

Bloxham School Library The school is a 19th cent foundation, and the rare books have been given by various donors since then. Numbering *c*190 v, they include 2 STC, 2 Wing, 10 18th cent (largely theological), *c*70 19th cent v in classics, literature, history, plus Dodsley's *Annual Register* 1758–1863. The library also includes the Liddon Bequest (of Henry Parry Liddon) of largely 1890s theological material relating to the Oxford Movement, and patristic literature; *c*200 v.

Cat; list in Librarian's keeping.

Broughton Castle, Banbury, Oxon OX15 5EB. Tel (0295) 62624. Open by arrangement to bona fide scholars on written application to Lord Saye and Sele.

The library, comprising the Twistleton-Wykeham-Fiennes family books, probably collected since the sale of 1837, and books of Sir G E Hammond and family, contains *c*3,000 v relating to the classics, theology, children's books, travel and topography, and general works, mainly late-18th and early-19th cent. Civil War pamphlets by Nathaniel Fiennes (1608?–69), and a ms diary of Celia Fiennes (1662–1741).

It seems that all books previously in the Castle were sold in 1837, but no sale cat can be traced.

Begbroke

Priory of the Friars Servants of Mary, St Philip's Priory, 2 Spring Hill Road, Begbroke, Oxon. Tel (086 75) 2149. Admission to bona fide scholars by prior arrangement. Xerox facilities.

The Library of the Priory of the Friars Servants of Mary The Order was founded in 1233, but did not come to England until the 19th cent when books were brought from the Italian priories of the Order at Bologna and Venice, but more especially from Florence. St Philip's Priory was founded in 1890. Many of the books still bear the early Italian bookplates and bookstamps. In the last 15 years, older books from the priories at Bognor and London have been gathered together at St Philip's as well. The Collection, which consists of *c*7,000 v, includes 120 v from 17th and 18th cent; approx 500 v rare modern Servite material. The main subject field covers the history of the Order of the Friars Servants of Mary; some early Servite theology; a few early Servite liturgical books. Many of the books have Italian imprints. Special collection of more recent Servite material, both historical and modern, up to 1967/8. All books are owned in common by Servite priories throughout the Order, and therefore may be transferred to other priories from time to time. Among the English priories, St Philip's is the main centre for historical research. Several hundred vols deposited with Heythrop College, then in Oxford, in late 1960s; Heythrop College subsequently moved to London in 1969 (qv). No list of these either at St Philip's or Heythrop, but comprised 16th-18th cent printed books of non-Servite interest. During the Napoleonic Wars many books from the Italian Servite priories were dispersed, and now are sometimes met with on the book market, recognizable by their Italian bookplates. These are purchased when funds are available.

Card cat of modern collection available, but does not appear to include entries for older books.

Studi Storici (Rome, 1933–).

Marianum (Rome, 1939–). Both periodicals are likely to contain general articles on Servite books and libraries.

Cuddesdon

Ripon College, Cuddesdon, Oxford OX9 9EX. Tel (0865) 774427. Open 9 am-5.45 pm weekdays only. Admission on personal application to the Principal. Xeroxing facilities.

Cuddesdon Theological College and Ripon Hall, Oxford, merged in 1975. Cuddesdon was founded in 1845 and Ripon Hall in 1897 in Ripon, moving to Oxford in 1919. The older books are made up of *c*75 titles, many of them multi-volume folios, plus bound v of tracts relating to liturgy, patristics, biblical commentaries, mainly of the 17th and 18th cent; bound v of tracts 18th and early 19th cent many liturgical.

Card cat (author and subject) includes entries for the older books.

Also separate list of pre-1800 books.

Enstone

The Ditchley Foundation, Ditchley Park, Enstone, Oxon. OX7 4ER. Tel (060 872) 346. Open by appointment to bona fide students. Xerox facilities.

The Ditchley Library The present collection at Ditchley has been formed since the present owner, Mr H D H Wills, bought the house in 1958. It includes 298 v pre-1850, with 1 STC; 55 18th cent v; 242 items dated 1800–50, mainly literary, with emphasis on Scott. It also includes typescripts of Dillon family letters (1762–1871).

The 18th cent Dillon/Lee family library was still at Ditchley in 1933 when Mr Ronald Tree bought the house. It subsequently moved with Mrs Tree (now Mrs Nancy Lancaster) to Haseley Court, Little Haseley, Oxon, and thence to Stratford Hall Plantation, Stratford, Virginia, USA (the home of the Lee family of Virginia, said to be related to the Lee family of Ditchley) to which the library was presented by Mrs Lancaster in September 1971. It consisted of *c*3,000 v covering history, religion, medicine, travel, classical translations, English and French literature, law, military history—all mainly of the 17th and 18th cent.

No cat of pre-1850 books, only of modern collection.

Henley-on-Thames

Divine Mercy College of the Marian Fathers, Fawley Court, Henley-on-Thames, Oxon. RG9 3AE. Tel (04912) 4917. Open Wed 2-5 pm, by appointment with the Curator.

Fawley Court Museum and Library The library contains *c*12,000 v of historic value, dating from the 15th-19th cent, including Bibles, theological works, poetry, history, travel, politics etc in Latin, Polish, English, French and German. The library is particularly strong in early Polish printing.

Register of holdings available.

Kelmscott

Kelmscott Manor, Kelmscott, Oxon. Tel (0367) 52486. Admission to bona fide scholars strictly by written application to the Curator, Kelmscott Manor.

Kelmscott Manor Library The library comprises (a) the Morris Collection of *c*168 books owned by William Morris and other members of his family and circle, including books printed by him at the Kelmscott Press, Hammersmith (Morris lived at Kelmscott Manor 1871–96), and (b) the bequest of Prof Ney Lannes McMinn of Northwestern University of 175 books by and about Morris and his circle. The Morris Collection includes very many books with inscriptions from Morris to his daughter May; also a Doves Press Bible and three Ashendene Press items, including Malory's *Morte d'Arthur* presented to May Morris by St John Hunt. Many books have interesting inscriptions, eg from Morris to his wife Jane, and daughter May; from D G Rossetti to Jane Morris; from Swinburne to Morris (good collection of Swinburne first editions); other books bear the autograph of William Morris while at Exeter College, Oxford, and of Jane Morris while living at Kelmscott Manor. The Collection also includes works of William Morris not published by the Kelmscott Press, including a collection of rare 1d and 2d pamphlets by Morris, distributed after lectures and early printed books, evidently used by Morris as inspiration for his own book designs.

There are 4 incunabula; 7 16th cent items (including a copy of the writing book, *Il modo de temperare le penze con le varie sorti de littere* (Venice, 1523, by Vicentino); 3 17th cent items (including an edition of Burton's *Anatomy of Melancholy*, 6th ed 1651, with small pen and ink drawing of Jane Morris by D G Rossetti, done in lieu of presentation inscription to her from the artist).

The mss include (a) two illuminated mss by William Morris of parts of the Heimskringla; (b) Ms translation by William Morris of Lancelot du Lake (3 v), and an unfinished copy of same; (c) unfinished ms by William Morris of 'The King's Son and the Carle's son'.

Non-book items include a collection of trial pages printed at Kelmscott Press.

Series of woodcut blocks of Cupid and Psyche, designed by Sir Edward Burne-Jones and cut by William Morris and others, for a projected illustrated edition of *The Earthly Paradise*, not published until 1974 (ed Dufty). Possibly the only surviving examples of Troy, Chaucer and Goden types, but to Morris's designs for use at the Kelmscott Press.

Note: The incunabula section is in the custody of the Librarian, Society of Antiquaries, Burlington House, London W1.

Morris sold some of his books in 1875 but no cat can be traced. For the sale of books after his death, see Sotheby's Catalogue 5th Dec 1898.

Sheaf cat: two copies, one at Kelmscott Manor and one in possession of the Librarian at Burlington House, London W1.

William Morris and Kelmscott. The Design Council, 1981.

Oxford

The entries on the Oxford libraries outside the Bodleian rest heavily on Paul Morgan's *Oxford libraries outside the Bodleian: a guide*, 2nd edition, Oxford, Bodleian Library, 1980, to which researchers are referred. Attention is drawn to Morgan's warning that most of these libraries are independently owned collections maintained primarily for the use of their own members, and that others wishing to use them should first obtain permission, in writing, from the librarian concerned.

The College libraries were, in the main, assembled as working collections by former scholars and teachers, with the addition of benefactions and bequests. They contain substantial collections of books from the 15th cent onwards, the standard works and the best editions of each age in the Greek and Latin classics, theology, medicine, law and so on. Nearly all College libraries, especially the older ones, and those with denominational affiliations, have pamphlet collections concerned with the many 19th cent theological controversies. Some College libraries are older than the Bodleian, and are therefore likely to possess, through acquisition upon, or soon after, publication, books not in the Bodleian. In fact, all College libraries own such books, either through retrospective purchase or by gift. Because the Bodleian has enjoyed the privilege of copyright deposit for English books from early in its history, the likelihood that College libraries will have books not in the Bodleian is greater in the sphere of foreign books. College libraries also contain more specialized collections of books, many the result of benefactions or bequests.

The University libraries, faculty and departmental, are mainly specialist collections. Those that contain the highest number of pre-1850 books include the Ashmolean Museum Library, the English Faculty Library, the Museum of the History of Science, and the Taylor Institution Library.

It has been estimated that there are 490,000 copies of pre-1801 books, possibly representing 353,000 works, in Oxford libraries outside the Bodleian (See J W Jolliffe, *Computers and early books: report of the LOC project investigating means of compiling a machine-readable catalogue of pre-1801 books in Oxford, Cambridge and the British Museum*, London, 1974).

College Libraries

N R Ker, 'Oxford College libraries in the sixteenth century', *Bodleian Library Record* 6 (1959), p459-515.

Oxford College libraries in 1556, guide to an exhibition, Oxford, Bodleian Library, 1956.

Science Libraries and Books

D F Shaw, *Oxford University Science Libraries, a Guide*, Oxford, Bodleian Library, 1981.

R T Gunther, *Oxford and the History of Science, with an appendix on scientific collections in College Libraries*, (1934), p38-49. Reprinted in his *Early Science in Oxford*, xi (1937), p325-36.

Incunabula

D E Rhodes, *A catalogue of incunabula in all the libraries of Oxford University outside the Bodleian*, Oxford, 1982. A union catalogue of 2,585 copies of 1847 editions of incunabula.

Early Printed Books to 1640

The Inter-Collegiate Catalogue, covering books printed before 1641, and including brief entries for incunabula, available for consultation at the Bodleian is in two sequences: (i) Books printed or published outside Britain and not in English; (ii) Books printed or published in Britain and books in English printed abroad: includes over 21,600 items. There are also available typescript lists (i) of pre-1640 foreign books in Oxford libraries outside the Bodleian (though this is imperfect and incomplete), and (ii) of all those holdings in Oxford libraries outside the Bodleian, of works covered by v 2 of the revised *Short-title catalogue...1475–1640* (1976), keyed to the new STC numbers.

English books 1641–1700

The location in certain College libraries given by Donald Wing in his *Short-title catalogue...1641–1700* (1945–51) must be treated with caution, since they were, to a large extent, based on obsolete printed catalogues.

Bindings

Fine bindings 1500–1700 from Oxford libraries, catalogue of an exhibition. Oxford, Bodleian Library, 1968.

All Souls College, Codrington Library, Oxford OX1 4AL. Tel (0865) 722251. Open Mon-Fri (Term) 9.30 am-6.30 pm; Sat 9.30 am-12.30 pm, (Vacation) 9.30 am-4.30 pm. Closed during the months of August and September. Admission to undergraduate and graduate students of the University of Oxford on recommendation of tutors, supervisors, or heads of colleges; to others on written application, subject to approval by the Librarian. Xeroxing; microfilm (photography and reading); microfiche (reading).

The library was established in 1438. It received a bequest of *c*10,000 v from Christopher Codrington (1668–1710), and systematic collection began towards the middle of the 18th cent. Of its total of 110,000 v, *c*50,000 v are pre-1851 and include 380 incunabula (some being rare legal texts) and 950 STC items. The collection is strong in Continental printing of the 16th and 17th cent, Spanish literature of the 17th and 18th cent is also well represented. The subject areas of special collection are law, British and French military, and ecclesiastical history. There was a bias towards law when books were purchased in the 1540s. The predominant interests of the library bequeathed by Christopher Codrington were law and history, but also included were 16th and 17th cent foreign printed books. From the mid-19th cent purchases have been largely restricted to law and history, together with political science and economics.

Other benefactions include: A collection bequeathed by J A Doyle (1844–1907), a former fellow and librarian, especially strong in Americana and British Colonial history; 300 v of military history from his own collection were given in memory of Sir Foster H E Cunliffe, Bart, killed in action in 1916; *c*1,600 v on the French Revolution and the Napoleonic period were given by Colonel Ramsay Phipps in 1920; Dudley Digges (1613–43) left a general library of over 1,300 v, including English and European literary works; Ralph Freman, a fellow, bequeathed in 1774, a large general library, comprising books owned by his father, another Ralph (*d*1746), Sir Thomas Brograve and Thomas Leigh (*d*1686) of Bishop's Stortford, and particularly interesting for English and Italian literature of the 17th and 18th cent, and 16th and 17th cent pamphlets; Spanish literature of the 17th and 18th cent was given in 1834 by Peter Frye Hony (*d*1876); collection of *c*150 books and pamphlets dealing with the question of the authorship of the *Letters of Junius*, presented by F F Urquhart (1868–1934) in 1931 (many had been owned by his mother's relative, Chichester Fortescue, 1st Baron Carlingford (1823–98); 60 v of early editions of the works of the late 18th cent writers Richard Graves, William Shenstone and William Somervile, given in 1931 by Sir Charles Oman (they had been bequeathed to him by W H Hutton (1860–1930)).

Though there is no alumnus collection as such, the library is rich in the writings of members of the College, and in fine bindings, especially French and Italian examples of the 16th and 17th cent. There is also a quantity of English newspapers of the first half of the 18th cent.

Author cat on cards.

Printed author cat covering letters A-C started 1911, stopped 1917, published 1923 as *Catalogue of the books contained in the Codrington Library*, v 1: A-C.

Earlier cats survive.

Catalogue of Canon and Civil law, made by G Hawke of Wadham in 1893 is kept in the Library.

E Craster (Sir), *The history of All Souls College Library*, ed E F Jacobs, London, 1971.

Dispersal of stock In 1926 *c*1,200 v of early science and theology, and in 1927 items of 18th cent theology were given to the Brotherton Library, University of Leeds. In 1926 400 v, together with Oriental books and the Bible Clerk's small library, and in 1927 items of 18th cent theology were transferred to the Bodleian. Sets of law reports, together with the section on Roman-Dutch law, given to the Bodleian at various times.

Ashmolean Museum, Beaumont Street, Oxford OX1 2PH. Tel (0865) 512651. Open Mon-Fri (Full term) 9 am-7 pm, (Vacations) 9 am-5 pm; Sat 9 am-1 pm. Admission by membership of Oxford University, or introduction by senior member of the same. Microfilm reader. Photocopier (operated by staff only).

Ashmolean Museum of Art and Archaeology Library The library, as it now exists, is a 19th cent creation that has grown proportionately with the development of classical, archaeological and fine art studies within the University. Its nucleus was formed by bringing together, in 1901, the Eldon (Art) Library, established 1873, the Archaeological (Classical) Library, established 1888, and the books of the Museum, founded in 1677, not transferred to the Bodleian. Its original function was to provide a working collection for the Museum staff, but it has come to serve also as a faculty library in the fields of Near Eastern, classical and European archaeology, classical history and literature, as well as an important library for research. The stock totals *c*150,000 with 1 incunabulum and 20 STC books. The present parts of the library give a picture of the subjects covered: the departments of Western Art, Eastern Art, and Antiquities; the libraries of Classical Archaeology, of Classical literature, or European Archaeology and of the Heberden Coin Room; the Haverfield library of Ancient History; the Griffith Institute Library (for Near Eastern Archaeology and Egyptology); and the Grenfell and Hunt Papyrological Library. Donors of special collections have included the following:

C D E Fortnum (1822–99), art books; F P Barnard (1854–1931), numismatics; E T Leeds (1877–1955), British archaeology; Gilbert Murray (1866–1957), classical literature; Margaret Venables Taylor (*d*1965), Roman archaeology; E O James (1888–1972), a general archaeological library; F L Griffith (1862–1934) and Nora C C Griffith (*d*1965), whose books form the basis of the Egyptological Library in the Griffith Institute, opened 1939; B P Grenfell (1869–1926) and A S Hunt (1871–1934) whose books are the foundation of the Papyrological Library named after them; the library of the Oxford Architectural and Historical Society is useful for English topographical works and is particularly strong in early 19th cent works on Oxford city and university; that part of the library of Frederick William Hope (1797–1862), not concerned with entomology, contains a fair collection of 18th and 19th cent travel and European guidebooks, many of an ephemeral nature, also volumes from which he had removed the illustrations for his print collection, and a group of biographical works of the 17th-19th cent for use with his portraits. There is a collection of editions of, and works relating to, John Ruskin (1819–1900), gathered by Sir Edward Tyas Cook and Alexander Wedderburn when preparing their edition of his works, published 1903–12.

The Dept of Western Art has several remarkable collections of prints: (i) the collection of *Frederick William Hope* (1797–1862), classified by subject and partially indexed, containing *c*140,000 portraits, 70,000 topographical, and more than 20,000 natural history engravings; (ii) the collection of more than 19,000 prints (of which 15,000 are portraits of historical personages of the 17th cent, the remainder chiefly topographical) which had been formed as extra illustrations to Edward Hyde, 1st Earl of Clarendon's *History of the Rebellion* (1702–4), and *Life of Clarendon* (1759) and Bishop Gilbert Burnet's *History of his own times* (1722–34), and presented to the Bodleian by Mrs C Sutherland in 1837. (See Bodleian Library: Sutherland Collection.) Transferred to Ashmolean 1951. Mrs C Sutherland *Catalogue of the Sutherland Collection*, Oxford, 1837. *Supplement* 1838. 'The transfer of the Sutherland Collection of prints and drawings', *BLR* 3 (1951) p115-16. (iii) the collection of Francis Douce (1757–1834), rich on the German Renaissance period. J G Mann, 'Francis Douce as a collector', *BQR* vii, no 81 (1934), p360-5 (see also entry for Douce under Bodleian Library).

A central card cat covers all holdings except for a portion of the Dept of Eastern Art, and including the library of the Dept of the History of Art.

Subsidiary cats for the Grenfell and Hunt Papyrological Library, the Griffith Institute, the Heberden Coin Room and the Dept of Western Art.

Balliol College, Oxford OX1 3BJ. Tel (0865) 249601. Admission by appointment. Microfilm reader available.

Balliol College Library has a collection of *c*70,000 v, including 58 incunabula; 1,223 STC and *c*3,500 Wing items. It includes a small number of early scientific and medical works, a large number of bound volumes of medical tracts of the late 17th cent, and some scarce early editions of Bibles and Prayer Books. Major benefactions have included the following:

Over 2,000 v received in 1677 from Sir Thomas Wendy (1613–73); the scholar's working library, with an appendage of tract volumes on all kinds of topics, bequeathed by Nicholas Crouch (fellow 1641–89)—Crouch noted on fly-leaves the prices paid and the cost of binding; an academic collection left by Roger Mander, Master 1687–1704; books formerly owned by Nathaniel Crynes (*d*1745), probably duplicates from the bequests to the Bodleian and St John's College; the extensive library, containing many early printed books on a wide range of subjects, left by George Coningesby (1693–1766), a Herefordshire clergyman with bibliophilic tastes; some of the English theological books collected by H H Norris (*d*1853) and given by Henry Norris in 1863 (many of Norris's books were among those alienated in 1928); the remnant of the library of New Inn Hall, mainly 18th cent English law books, taken over in 1887; the books of Arnold Toynbee (1852–83), the pioneer economic historian; the classical working collection, including numerous presentation copies, bequeathed by Benjamin Jowett, Master 1870–93; the library of Italian literature and history of Paget Toynbee (1855–1932) was divided between the Bodleian and Balliol; a collection of editions of E Fitzgerald's translation of the *Rubaiyat of Omar Khayyam*, once owned by F York Powell (1850–1904); a small collection of books connected with the Salvation Army (provenance unknown); a collection of the works of Robert Browning, and small collections of A H Clough, Matthew Arnold and A C Swinburne; among the books and pamphlets bequeathed by Sir Robert C K Ensor (1877–1958) there is a small collection relating to Trade Unions and the early Labour Movement.

More than 3,000 theological works, printed post 1600, were put out in 1928, of which *c*1,000 went to the Bodleian; a few were given to other institutions, and the remainder sold.

Guardbook cat, with card cat of additions 1963–

Separate guardbook cat of tracts and pamphlets.

Earlier cats survive.

Catalogue of the printed books in Balliol College Library (1871): numerous items in it were included in the 1928 sale.

Blackfriars, 64 St Giles, Oxford. Tel (0865) 57607. Open 9 am-5.30 pm. Admission on application to the Librarian.

Blackfriars (Priory of the Holy Ghost Order of Preachers) Library The library contains 28 incunabula; 35 STC books; 230 pre-1641 foreign books; 54 Wing books; nearly 350 books printed pre-1700. It specializes in works on theology and philosophy rather than ecclesiastical history, with an emphasis on the Dominican Order. St Thomas Aquinas, and members of the Order, such as Leonardus de Utino, Meister Eckhart, Robert Holcot and Luis of Granada, are well represented. Many of these older volumes were formerly at smaller Dominican houses. Some groups of books of literary interest include presentation copies to himself from other contemporary writers, and some editions of William Beckford, bequeathed by André Raffalovich (1864–1934); items printed at the St Dominic's Press, Ditchling, Sussex, together with a few specimens from other private presses and of English literature of the 1920s, given by Michael Gerveys Sewell.

Cat on cards.

Bodleian Library, Oxford OX1 3BG. Tel (0865) 244675. Most reading rooms are open Mon-Fri (Term) 9 am-10 pm, (Vacation) 9 am-7 pm; Sat 9 am-1 pm. The library is closed from Good Friday to Easter Monday inclusive; for the week beginning the last Monday in August; and from Christmas Eve until 1 January inclusive. Admission to members of Oxford University, and to other bona fide scholars on production of a suitable letter of recommendation and proof of identity. The Curators of the library may make a charge for non-members of Oxford University. All books must be read in the library (except for certain dependent library lending collections). Books printed pre-1641 and most mss must be read in Duke Humfrey's Library. Blind students' reading room; collator (Hinman) and comparator (Lindstrom); infra-red light source; ultra-violet light source; inter-library loans; microform readers; photocopying (quick copy xerox service); photography (including beta-radiography of watermarks) subject to copyright regulations and certain other conditions. (A charge is made for these services.) Typing room.

The Bodleian is the library of Oxford University and, in Britain, is second in size only to the British Library, having a stock of 4.5 million volumes. It is named after Sir Thomas Bodley (1545–1613), scholar and diplomat, who re-endowed the library on the site of an earlier foundation. It is a library of deposit under the Copyright Act, a privilege which originated in the agreement made by Sir Thomas Bodley with the Company of Stationers in 1611 that the Company would grant the library a perfect copy of every book printed by their members on certain conditions. But the Company was not always willing or able to compel its members strictly to observe the agreement with Sir Thomas Bodley. Further, Sir Thomas Bodley and the early librarians were selective: they favoured books in learned languages and, for instance, few of the early editions of Jacobean dramatists nor much early English literature was accepted—the library had to wait for such collections as those of Robert Burton, Edmund Malone, Elias Ashmole and Anthony Wood to make it important in these fields.

The first statutory obligation upon the Company to deliver to the library a copy of each book printed by its members was imposed by the Press Licencing Act of 1622 for two years, and then renewed from time to time until the Act lapsed in 1695. It was the first Copyright Act, passed in 1710, that required the depositing of copies at certain libraries, including the Bodleian, of all works entered at Stationers' Hall. The 1710 Act did little, however, to alter the Company's token co-operation, and the claiming of copies by the library was erratic, with no certain knowledge of what was due. It was not until after the Copyright Act of 1814 recognized the right of privileged libraries to every publication, whether entered at Stationers' Hall or not, that the library began to reap the full benefit of the copyright privilege, and the number of books received by copyright deposit increased steadily from then onwards. (*See* J P Chalmers, 'Bodleian deposit survivors of the first sixteen years of the Copyright Act of Queen Anne, April 10 1710 to March 25 1726'. Oxford, 1974. (B Litt thesis).

In purchasing arrears of English and of foreign literature, Sir Thomas Bodley selected many of the books purchased in his lifetime: he endeavoured to provide the means for the profitable study of every branch of knowledge then recognized but he favoured books in learned languages and he preferred folios to small books. In the late 17th and in the 18th cent the income from the original Bodleian endowment, which had been intended to include book purchases, became inadequate and began to be consumed by general running costs. It was only after 1780 that a substantial and growing income became available for purchases. (*See* I G Philip, 'The background to Bodleian purchases of incunabula at the Pinelli and Crevenna sales, 1789–90'. *Trans Cambridge Bib Soc*, 7 (1974), p369-75. This led to the publication of an annual printed list of purchases: *A catalogue of books purchased for the Bodleian Library...1780 (−1861).* (With) *Donations to the library...1796 (−1861).* Purchasing increased during the first half of the 19th cent but began to decline after 1860, during a period of financial stringency lasting some 80 years.

Sir Thomas Bodley realized the importance of attracting benefactions, and the library has been rewarded with a stream of donations etc, the major part of which now form separate collections within the library. From 1796 to 1861 a printed list of donations appeared with the printed list of purchases (see above). This was followed by the annual list, *Donations to the Bodleian Library...1862 (−1885).* During the 20th cent the Friends of the Bodleian and Bodley's American Friends have been the source of many gifts to the library.

W D Macray, *Annals of the Bodleian Library, Oxford.* Oxford, 1890.

Sir E Craster, *History of the Bodleian Library, 1845–1945.* Oxford, 1952.

General catalogues of printed books

T James, *Catalogus Librorum Bibliothecae publicae quam...Thomas Bodleius...in Academia Oxoniensi nuper instituit.* Oxoniae, 1605. Includes both printed books and mss arranged as they were shelved according to the four faculties, with an author index.

——*Catalogus universalis librorum in Bibliotheca Bodleiana.* Oxoniae, 1620. Adopts the alphabetical arrangement.

T Hyde, *Catalogus impressorum librorum Bibliothecae Bodleianae.* Oxonii, 1674. (See H Carter, *A history of the Oxford University Press*, v 1 (1975), p76-7).

Catalogus impressorum librorum Bibliothecae Bodleianae. Oxonii, 1738. 2 v. (See H Carter, *loc cit*, p294-6).

Catalogus librorum impressorum Bibliothecae Bodleianae. 3 v, 1843. Excludes the Gough and Douce collections, and the collections of dissertations and of Hebrew books, of which special cats were in print.

Catalogus...librorum quibus aucta est Bibliotheca... MD CCCXXXV-MD CCCXLVII.

References

G Wheeler, *The earliest catalogues of the Bodleian Library.* Oxford, 1928.

'Bodleian catalogues of the 17th Century', *BQR* (1915), p228-32.

Books in the collections are catalogued in the Library's current General Catalogue of Printed Books, which is an author cat, and which is in two sections: one listing books published up to 1919, the other listing those published from 1920 onwards. There is no subject cat.

Special catalogues and guides

Almanacs

F J King, *A check list of almanacs, chiefly before 1801, in the Bodleian Library* Oxford, 1974. (Reproduced from computer print-out with ms additions.) Sets out in detail holdings of almanacs (ie calendars or calendars containing also prognostications), for the most part in series, of date prior to 1801. A conspectus of the shelfmarks of all copies in the collections of Ashmole, Douce, Rawlinson and Wood, the principal sources of the Library's almanacs.

Almanacs 1695–1705 (shelfmarked 8°C52-62 Jur). (Ms, shelfmarked R.6.222).

Combined index of almanacs in Ashmole, Douce, Jur, Linc, Rawlinson and Wood collections (alphabetical with date and collection symbol): *with an index of years (1569–1771).* (Bodleian shelfmark R.6.225).

Incunabula (the Bodleian has a total of 6,500).

L A Sheppard, *Catalogue of the 15th century books in the Bodleian Library.* Xeroxes of ms entries. With Proctor concordance to Sheppard slips.

[*With*] J W Jolliffe, Index of authors, anonymous books, commentators, editors, translators, printers, publishers, anonymous presses and places of printing in L A Sheppard's *loc cit*. [Xeroxes of ms entries. Bodleian shelfmark *25843 b.3,3** = R.5.101.Oxf.2,2*']

Bodleian incunabula. Conspectus of shelfmarks. Compiled by F O Underhill. 1915. [Ms Bodleian shelfmark R.5.101.Oxf.1.]

Newspapers and Periodicals

The Bodleian derives its early English newspapers and periodicals in the main from the collections formed by John Nichols and F W Hope. For the 17th cent it has newspapers preserved by Anthony Wood and Elias Ashmole. It is especially rich in early newspapers and corantos, Civil War periodicals, London newspapers from 1672–1737, and literary periodicals of the 18th cent.

R T Milford and D M Sutherland, *A catalogue of English newspapers and periodicals in the Bodleian Library, 1622–1800.* Oxford. Oxford Bib Soc, 1936. (With printed Bodleian Shelfmarks. Bodleian copy shelfmarked 2590d.Ox.le.5 = B.1.1202 is annotated with additions.)

Bodleian holdings are also shown in the *British Union-Catalogue of Periodicals, a record of the periodicals of the world, from the 17th century to the present day, in British libraries.* 5 v and Supplement. London, 1955–62.

Oxfordshire bibliography and Oxford printing

E H Cordeaux and D H Merry, A bibliography of printed works relating to Oxfordshire, excluding the University and City of Oxford. Oxfordshire Hist Soc new ser v 11. Oxford, 1955.

——Supplementary volumes. Ibid. v 28, Oxford 1981.

——*A bibliography of printed works relating to the University of Oxford.* Oxford, 1968.

——*A bibliography of printed works relating to the City of Oxford.* Oxfordshire Hist Soc new ser v 25. Oxford 1976.

The above three bibliographies include Bodleian shelfmarks.

F Madan, *The early Oxford press: a bibliography of printing and publishing at Oxford, '1468'–1640.* Oxford, 1895.

——v 2 [entitled] *Oxford books: a bibliography of printed works relating to the University and City of Oxford or printed or published there. Oxford literature 1450–1640, and 1641–1650.* Oxford, 1912.

——v 3 *1651–1680.* Oxford, 1931.

Bindings

W Salt Brassington, *Historic bindings in the Bodleian Library*, 1891.

S Gibson, *Some notable Bodleian bindings*, 1901–4.

——*Early Oxford bindings*, 1903.

[I G Philip], *Gold tooled bookbindings.* (Bodleian picture books, no 2). Oxford, 1951.

N R Ker, *Fragments of medieval manuscripts used in pastedowns in Oxford bindings, with a survey of Oxford binding c1515–1620.* Oxford, 1954.

Fine bindings 1500–1700 from Oxford libraries, catalogue of an exhibition. Oxford, 1968.

[G G Barber], *Textile and embroidered bindings.* (Bodleian picture books, special series, no 2). Oxford, 1971.

The Bodleian Library's printed rare book collections, listed below, bear shelfmarks (often abbreviated) which are of several types, namely: (a) Names of former owners or libraries whose books have been acquired and are still kept together as separate collections, eg Bliss, Broxbourne, Douce, Holkham, Selden; (b) Descriptions of categories of books grouped by subject matter, eg Art [Arts/Artes], Bib. [Bible Collection], Med. [Medicine], Tr Luth [Tractati Lutherani]; (c) Groups having a common origin: eg Don. [Donations], Diss. [Dissertations], Inc. [Incunabula], Kelmscott Press, Lib. Polen [Libri Polonici], Tauchnitz; (d) Groups described by locations in which they are (or were formerly) kept: eg Arch. [Archiva or Archives cupboard], Auct. [Auctarium].

In describing the collections which follow, use has been made of the following references: *BLR: Bodleian Library Record*, 1938 to date; *BQR: Bodleian Quarterly Record*, Vols 1-8, 1914–38; Craster: Sir E Craster, *History of the Bodleian Library, 1845–1945.* Oxford, 1952; Macray: W D Macray, *Annals of the Bodleian Library, Oxford.* 2nd ed Oxford, 1890; Use has also been made of G W Wheeler, 'Bodleian pressmarks in relation to classification', *BQR* 1 (1916) 280-292; 311-22.

A Department of Printed Books (Western)

The rare book collections and special collections include the following:

Percy Stafford Allen (1869–1933), Erasmus scholar, President of Corpus Christi College (1924), and Mrs H M Allen, his widow. Bequeathed by Mrs Allen in accordance with the wishes of her husband, in 1953. A collection comprising original editions of the works of Erasmus, and a comprehensive working library of *c*2,000 items relating to Erasmus, built up by the Allens in the course of editing the *Opus epistolarum.* The books date from the 16th-20th cent, with a wide variety of places of publication, and include a collection of offprints and pamphlets.

'The Allen bequest', *BLR* 4 (1953), p178-9.

ALM. [*Almanac*] A collection of almanacs, shelved in chronological sequence. *c*250 v of all dates, some containing several almanacs.

ANTIQ. [*Antiquiora*] A shelfmark used between 1883 and 1936 for antiquarian accessions, with subdivision by size, place of printing and date. *c*4,000 v of the 16th-18th cent.

ARCH. [*Archiva/Archives*] Certain categories of books of all periods which, on account of their rarity, value, very small size etc, would be unsuitably placed in the current classification. Sections include: over 800 specially valuable books printed in England or printed in English abroad; over 250 foreign books; over 200 fine examples of modern (including 18th cent) printing, and books printed in very limited editions; *c*150 books judged to be pornographic but possessing literary merit; *c*150 examples of early English printing; over 40 examples of important association copies and books with ms notes.

ARCH.ANTIQ. 250 books of the 18th and 19th cent.

ARCH.JUR. [*Archiva Jurisprudentia*] 280 v of the 16th-18th cent, including editions of Horace.

ARCH.NAT.HIST. *c*370 works of natural history of the 18th and 19th cent.

ARCH.NUM. Over 1,200 works on numismatics, mainly 18th and 19th cent.

ARCH.SELD. c180 works of the 17th-19th cent, and including Spanish books.

ARCH.SIGMA 270 works, mainly Spanish, of the 16th-18th cent.

ART. [*Artes/Arts*] One part of the original Bodleian four-part classification by faculty or subject. Any books which did not come under Theol. Med. or Jur. were considered to be Arts, including mathematics, history, philosophy and literature. In use in various forms 1602–1789, and less frequently until c1840. In later years the distribution by faculty began to be disregarded and books were added where there was space on the shelves. Over 8,000 v of the 16th-early 19th cent.

ARTS Over 500 folios and large quartos on arts subjects received among the new books between 1861 and 1883.

A S. (an arbitrary symbol, formed by analogy with B S.) Used between 1805 and 1820 as a shelfmark for the smaller volumes in quarto. 540 v, some containing several works, of the late-18th and early-19th cent, English and foreign, and on all subjects.

Elias Ashmole (1617–92), antiquary, founder of the Ashmolean Museum, to which he presented his collections in 1677. The Visitors of the Ashmolean offered all the mss and printed books to the Bodleian in 1858, where they arrived in 1860. The Ashmole collection is in two sequences [MS.] Ashmole 1-1836, containing c1,100 printed books as well as mss, and Ashmole A-H, consisting of 350 printed books. Ashmole 1549–1836 and Ashmole A-H are accessions to Ashmole's original collection from the libraries of John Aubrey (1626–97), Edward Lhuyd (1660–1709), and Martin Lister (1638–1712), and from the University chemical library founded in 1683. Most of Lister's books are in the Bodleian collection shelfmarked 'Lister' (qv). The printed books fall into two main categories: (a) a collection of contemporary pamphlets, dealing in the main with English political and theological controversy, including Civil War tracts, poems, sermons, newspapers and book catalogues, all collected by Ashmole between 1679 and 1690; (b) a library of astrology, astronomy and kindred topics, including prognostications, ephemerides or astronomical calendars, and a set of almanacs for the years 1571–1690 which, in part duplicates, in part supplements, the more extensive collection of almanacs acquired by gift from Richard Rawlinson, extending from 1607–1747. c146 of Ashmole's volumes contain the signature of William Lilly (Merlinus Anglicanus, 1602–81).

R T Gunther, 'The Ashmole printed books', *BQR* 6 (1930), p193-5.

——'The Chemical Library of the University', *Ibid* p201-3.

——'The Library of John Aubrey, FRS', *Ibid* (1931), p230-6.

R W Hunt, 'The cataloguing of Ashmolean collections of books and manuscripts', *BLR* 4 (1952), p161-70.

Sir E Craster, *History of the Bodleian Library 1845–1945*, Oxford, Clarendon Press, 1952, p65-8.

B F Roberts, 'Edward Lhuyd's collection of printed books', *BLR* 10 (1979), p112-27.

Index to the English almanacs in the Ashmolean collection (with) Ashmole almanacs (handlist). (MS Bodleian shelfmark R.6.220).

AUCT. [*Auctarium, a room formerly the Anatomy School, now the South West room of the Lower Reading Room*] A shelfmark denoting c5,000 v (including early Bibles, *editiones principes*, and other 15th cent editions of the classics, Aldines, and texts of classical authors annotated with scholia and marginalia), either removed from the older collections at the end of the 18th or the beginning of the 19th cent, or added to the Library between then and 1940(?), and placed in the Auctarium.

Bible Collection Editions of the Bible, the Old Testament, the New Testament, the Apocrypha, the Psalms and the Book of Common Prayer, including pre-1850 editions, in all languages, acquired since 1883. Sections sub-divided by language and, in some cases, date. Estimated at over 7,000 v.

Thomas Barlow (1607–91), Bodley's Librarian (1642–60), Provost of the Queen's College (1657), Lady Margaret Professor of Divinity (1660), Bishop of Lincoln (1675), bequeathed those books in his library not already in the Bodleian (others went to the Queen's College). The quarto and octavo printed books, particularly rich in tracts and pamphlets of the reign of Charles I and of the Civil Wars and Interregnum and in early theology, are kept under the shelfmark *Linc.* [Lincolniensis]. (Some later volumes, not Barlow's, have been added to *Linc*, particularly during the 18th cent making a total of c6,000 v.) The folio volumes from Barlow's library, not numerous, are dispersed amongst other folio volumes.

Macray 157-9.

William John Birkbeck (1859–1916), theologian and liturgical scholar, who worked for the union of the Anglican and Orthodox Churches. Bequeathed to Magdalen College, and deposited in the Bodleian in 1920, c300 historical and theological works, mostly of the 19th cent in Slavonic languages.

Craster, 283.

Philip Bliss (1787–1857), antiquary, Sub-librarian, Bodleian Library (1822–8), University Registrar (1824–53), Keeper of the University Archives (1826–57), Principal of St Mary Hall (1848–57). Bliss bequeathed to the Bodleian his copy of Wood's *Athenae Oxoniensis*, with many ms additions, but preferred that his library should be sold at auction. At the sale in 1858 the Library bought 745 v of the 16th-19th cent, including books printed at Oxford, books printed in London in the three years preceding the Great Fire, works relating to the plague, works relating to the Quakers, works illustrative of Oxford and Oxfordshire, editions of and commentaries on the Psalms, works of royal and noble authors, works of the 16th and 17th cent poets, and works illustrative of the characters of men in their various occupations. Bliss entered on the fly-leaf the source of his copy, and frequently added bibliographical notes. The miscellaneous antiquarian collections and bibliographical memoranda which Bliss left behind in the University Archives were transferred to the Bodleian in 1933.

Catalogue of... the... library formed by the late Rev Philip Bliss... which will be sold by auction... by Messrs S Leigh Sotheby and John Wilkinson 28 June (9 Aug) 1858. London, 1858.

Macray, 367-8.

Craster, 64, 71.

S Gibson and C J Hindle, 'Philip Bliss (1787–1857) editor and bibliographer. Bliss's library', *Oxford Biblio Soc Proc and Papers*, 3 (1933).

Sir George Bowyer 7th Bart (1811–83), lawyer, presented during the years 1838–43, 78 printed volumes and 4 mss of the statutes of Italian cities, chiefly of the 17th and 18th cent. He had, in 1838, published his *Dissertation on the statutes of the cities of Italy.*

Macray, 338.

BS. [*Bibliotheca Seldeniana*] The second general collection in the history of the Library (after the division by the four faculties), started *c*1668 and added to up to *c*1840. At first it was used for previously un-shelfmarked additions made during 1650–68, the folios being unclassified, the other sizes divided by the four faculty subdivisions (arts, jurisprudence, medicine, theology). During the period 1789–1823 the subdivision by faculties was abandoned. From 1805–20, while BS. was used for the larger of the volumes in quarto, the shelfmark AS. (qv) was used for the smaller volumes in quarto. In the 1830s there was a revival of the classified BS. sequence. The collection comprises over 16,000 v of the 16th-19th cent.

Broxbourne A collection presented in 1978 through the Friends of the National Libraries by Mr John Ehrman in memory of his father, Albert Ehrman, who made the collection. It contains over 4,000 items, and includes over 100 mss, and of the printed books, 140 are incunabula (including many rare or unique single sheets); 104 are STC items; 664 were printed in the 16th cent and 422 in the 17th cent. The collection divides into three sections: (a) *c*2,000 examples of bindings from the 12th-20th cent, and from many countries. There is an especially strong group of blind-stamped 16th cent specimens, and examples of the work of some of the finest contemporary British and French binders. Described as one of the three great English 20th cent collections of bookbindings by Mr H M Nixon who, in his *Broxbourne Library: styles and designs of bookbindings from the twelfth to the twentieth century*, London, 1956, describes a representative selection of the most notable examples from each century; (b) The remarkable collection of book sale catalogues and material for book trade history used for, and listed in, G Pollard and A Ehrman, *The distribution of books by Catalogue to 1800*, Roxburghe Club, 1965. 347 items are there described, and there are *c*50 additions. They include the catalogues of printers, publishers, booksellers, auctioneers and libraries. Most of the countries of Europe are represented, and a wide range of book trade practices are illustrated; (c) A binding and printing history reference collection.

Author cat on cards, a shelflist and guide to the arrangement of the collection, with indexes of provenances and of types of bindings by country and by binder.

The type specimens and related material, comprising books of typographical importance, excellence or curiosity, and works of reference, previously part of the Broxbourne Library, are now in Cambridge University Library.

'The Broxbourne Library', *BLR* 10 (1979), p78-80.

University of Oxford, *Annual Report of the Curators of the Bodleian Library for 1977–78*, Supplement no 3 to the *University Gazette*, June 1979, p41-2.

Thomas Ryburn Buchanan, PC, MP (1846–1911), Fellow of All Souls and Librarian, Codrington Library. His widow allowed the Bodleian and All Souls to make their selection from his library. The collection of *c*500 printed books, ranging in date from the 15th-20th cent, received by the Bodleian in 1941, is notable for its specimens of fine printing and its fine bindings. The bindings are chiefly Scottish and European of the 16th-19th cent, including many plain morocco bindings bearing the arms of J A de Thou, and books from the Seillère collection finely bound in red morocco by modern French binders.

Craster, p286-7.

S Gibson, 'Bookbindings in the Buchanan collection', *BLR* 2 (1941), p6-12.

M J Sommerlad, *Scottish 'wheel' and 'herring-bone' bindings in the Bodleian Library*, Oxford Biblio Soc Occasional Publication no 1, Oxford, 1967.

Fine bindings 1500–1700 from Oxford libraries, catalogue of an exhibition. Bodleian Library, Oxford, 1968.

Robert Burton (1577–1640), Student of Christ Church (1599), author of *The Anatomy of Melancholy* (1621), bequeathed his books to the Bodleian, duplicates of books already there to be passed on to Christ Church. 581 books were selected for the Bodleian, including some theology, but also works by most of the great names of Elizabethan literature (including Shakespeare), pamphlets, jest-books, newsbooks, ie just those sort of books which Sir Thomas Bodley had rejected. The majority of the books are still in the Library, chiefly in the classes shelfmarked 4° Art., Th., and Art.BS., but a number of plays, duplicated when the Malorie collection was received in 1821, were sold in the Bodleian duplicate sale of 1862.

Macray 90-2.

Sir W Osler, 'The Library of Robert Burton', *Oxford Biblio Soc Proc and Papers* 1 (1926), p182-90.

'Two lists of Burton's books, ed by S Gibson and F R D Needham', *Ibid* p222-46. (Copy in the Bodleian annotated with Bodleian shelfmarks.)

The Bodleian Library in the seventeenth century: guide to an exhibition, Oxford, Bodleian Library, 1951, p16, 41.

Ingram Bywater (1840–1914), Fellow of Exeter College, Sub-Librarian, Bodleian Library 1879, Regius Professor of Greek 1893–1908, bequeathed *c*4,000 v, listed in the privately printed *Elenchus vetustiorum apud*** [*I Bywater*] *hospitantium* 1911 and in an interleaved copy of acquisitions to his library from 1911 to his death. Bywater chose his books to illustrate the history of classical learning from Bessarion down to the immediate successors of Scaliger and Casaubon, and insisted on fine condition. The collection contains the names of the great, and many of the obscurer, European humanists of the 16th and early-17th cent. Aristotle and his commentators are well represented. *c*50 books have ms marginalia by scholars, near 200 are autographed, and *c*50 bear the arms of De Thou on their bindings. Most of the books are pre-1650, including *c*150 incunabula, and over 1,100 books were printed in the first half of the 16th cent, a third of these by Paris presses.

Craster 281-2.

'The Bywater Collection', *BQR* (1915), 80-1.

W W Jackson, *Ingram Bywater, the memoir of an Oxford Scholar, 1840–1914*, Oxford, 1917.

CAPS. A shelfmark used in the period 1860–83 for antiquarian accessions of folios and large quartos. 550 v of the 16th-19th cent.

John Waynflete Carter (1905–75) The collection purchased in 1957 from John Carter and added to from time to time, consists of over 350 v ranging in date from 1702 to the present day, and illustrates the history of publishers' binding during the 19th cent. Most of the books are bound in cloth, though others are bound in silk, plush, wood and even metal, some of the gift-book type being elaborate and ornate.

Card cat under author, with descriptions of the bindings, an index of the binders' names (when known), and a selective subject index. Mr Carter later presented the file of his rubbings and notes compiled in the preparation of his books *Binding variants in English publishing 1820–1900* (1932) and *More binding variants* (1938).

'The Carter collection of publishers' bindings', *BLR* 8 (1967), 5-6.

Arthur Joyce Lunel Cary (1888–1957), novelist. Cary's library of over 2,000 printed books and mss was presented to the Bodleian through Bodley's American Friends in 1957 by James Marshall Osborn. The printed books comprise works by Cary, including articles, short stories etc in periodicals, translations and proofs; works or items about Cary; books presented by their authors to Cary; books (some presented) annotated by Cary; the residue of Cary's library, eg books on Africa, India etc; works of English literature; works of foreign literature; works on art; works on history etc. Books added or published after the date of the original collection are shelfmarked *Cary adds.*

D G Neill, 'The Joyce Cary collection at the Bodleian Library', *Books* no 321 (Jan-Feb 1959), p7-11.

Clarendon Press A collection of *c*2,000 v consisting of: (a) Books published by the Clarendon Press from 1720–1892, arranged according to subject (theology, medicine, arts and trades, mathematics and physics, law, history, Greek prose, Greek verse, Greek commentaries, Latin prose, Latin verse, Latin commentaries, philology), shelfmarked *Clar.Press la.1-66c.10;* (b) 200 books of the 16th-19th cent chiefly texts of the classics and of the Fathers, and including Septuagint and Greek patristic texts from the library of Dr Robert Holmes (*d*1805), deposited in the Bodleian by the Delegates of the University Press in 1885 and presented outright in 1922. Shelfmarked *Clar.Press b.1-e.123.* The strength of the early 19th cent section lies in the classical texts with ms editorial annotations; (c) *c*1,000 Clarendon Press file copies (for the use of the Secretary to the Delegates) of books printed from 1830–20th cent, and mostly bound at the time in original boards or cloth bindings, deposited on permanent loan in the Bodleian by the University Press. (Not yet catalogued and shelfmarked.)

Nathaniel Crynes (1688–1745), Fellow of St John's College and Superior Bedel of Arts (1716), bequeathed to the Bodleian all such books out of his own collections as the Library did not already possess. 968 v in octavo and smaller sizes, with a few quartos, dating from the 16th-18th cent, many very rare, were kept by the Bodleian. The rest of his books went to St John's College and Balliol College.

Macray 220.

George Nathaniel, Marquess Curzon of Kedleston (1859–1925) A collection of *c*330 works on Napoleon bequeathed by Lord Curzon, originally brought together by A M Broadley, bought at the sale of his books in 1916 and added to by Lord Curzon. It relates in the main to Napoleon's captivity on St Helena, but also includes sets of *The Life of Napoleon I* by J Holland Rose and *The last phase* by the Earl of Rosebery, extra-illustrated by A M Broadley, 1905, and of A M Broadley's *Napoleon in caricature 1795–1821,* 1911, extra-illustrated by A Brewis, grangerized into 39 folio volumes, illustrated by the addition of thousands of portraits, views, contemporary caricatures, broadsides, autograph letters and original drawings.

J M Thompson, *Curzon collection: index to autographs and portraits*, 1928. (Typescript, Bodleian shelfmark *MS. Curzon d.3=R.6.85*)

Craster 284.

A catalogue of the...collection of Napoleonic books, autographs and engravings formed by the late A M Broadley...sold by auction by Messrs Hodgson & Co., 7-8 December, 1916.

△ [*DELTA*] A collection of over 5,000 v of the 16th-19th cent, the various sections being used for both English and foreign books in quarto between 1824 and 1861, for folio volumes between 1840 and 1861, and for older books in folio and large quarto between 1861 and 1883.

Denyer A collection of 21 English 16th cent Bibles including Coverdale, Cranmer, Tyndale and Grafton, and of 21 English theological works, nearly all printed before 1600. Bequeathed in 1825 by Mrs Eliza D Denyer, widow of John Denyer (*d*1806).

Macray 315.

DISS. [*Dissertations*] 43,400 German, Dutch and Scandinavian academic dissertations of the 17th, 18th and early-19th cent, including many subjects in Roman and German law, theology and history, bought in 1827.

Catalogus dissertationum academicarum quibus nuper aucta est Bibliotheca Bodleiana MD CCCXXXII. Oxonii, 1834. (Bodleian copy, shelfmark *2590b.Oxf. lc.27=R.6, 202*, annotated with Bodleian shelfmarks.) 10,000 further dissertations on a wide range of subjects, including Edinburgh medical dissertations of the 18th and early 19th cent and dissertations of the end of the 19th cent, were added in later years.

Macray 317.

Dobell 450 v acquired in 1972, being the collections of Bertram Dobell and his sons P J and A E Dobell, booksellers and publishers of Tunbridge Wells and London, largely works written or published by them, including proofs, trial copies etc, dating from 1885 up to the 1930s, sets of their catalogues, 1876–1916, copies of books presented to them up to 1957, and books with ms notes by them.

DON. [*Donations*] Books presented to the Library from 1925–82, either through the Friends of the Bodleian or Bodley's American Friends or, less frequently, direct. Over 2,000 v of all periods.

From 1975, pre-1850 gifts through FOB and BAF have been classified into VET (qv).

Francis Douce (1757–1834) antiquary, Keeper of Manuscripts at the British Museum. Bequeathed 17,000 v of printed books of all periods, including over 300 incunabula (largely romanas, histories and liturgical books) and including 15 items printed by Caxton; block books and books printed on vellum; Bibles, Horae, Primers, Books of Common Prayer, Psalters; early-printed editions of Medieval romances, and editions of the popularized versions of the 16th and 17th cent; editions of novels and tales, including editions of works of lighter French fiction, original and translated, of the 17th and 18th cent, amorous and facetious tales and 'contes galantes'; original and early editions of 17th and 18th cent English drama (foreign drama is less well represented); a collection of poems, songs and ballads, including a remarkable collection of broadside ballads of the second half of the 17th, of the 18th and early 19th cent; chapbooks and children's books of the 18th and early 19th cent; almanacs and prognostications covering the period 1674–1771 (supplementing the Rawlinson and Ashmole collections), with some from earlier years; fragments of works by early English printers; volumes especially noteworthy as examples of the engraver's art; sale catalogues, with notes of his purchases and the prices he paid; books in fine bindings, especially French bindings; bindings (loose covers, mainly 16th cent blind-stamped and gold-tooled).

Douce's collection is strong in history, biography, antiquities, manners, customs, the fine arts, travel, archaeology, witchcraft, and the 'Dance of Death', and in foreign books.

In addition to the printed books, Douce's bequest included nearly 400 mss, woodblocks, prints, drawings, coins, playing cards. Most of the prints, the drawings and the coins are now in the Ashmolean Museum; only those prints belonging to, or closely connected with books as distinct from pure art, were retained in the Bodleian.

The Library now also preserves Douce's correspondence and a series of notebooks kept by him for most of the later half of his collecting life.

The shelfmark *Douce Adds.* was in use *c*1834–80, largely for retrospective accessions of children's books, chapbooks and similar ephemeral literature and include some specimens of early printing, and some material from Douce's own collections, including Douce's albums of early printed initials, devices and title-pages, many removed from his own books. There is a total of 333 v representing a larger number of bibliographical items, of the 18th and 19th cent.

Catalogue of the printed books and manuscripts bequeathed by Francis Douce, Esq to the Bodleian Library. Oxford, 1840. (Bodleian copies shelfmarked *2590 b.Oxf.1.4.=R.6.92 and 2590 b.Oxf.1.3=X.1.28* are annotated in ms with the shelfmarks of the printed books.)

J O Halliwell-Phillipps. *A hand-list of the early English literature preserved in the Douce collection in the Bodleian Library, selected from the printed catalogue of that collection.* 1860.

A C Madan, *A catalogue of the collection of engravings &c in portfolios bequeathed by Francis Douce in 1835 and not transferred to the Ashmolean Museum as of special artistic value.* (In MS. Bodleian shelfmark *R.6.260*).

G R Scott, *A catalogue of the collection of engravings &c in portfolios bequeathed by Francis Douce in 1835 and received back from the Ashmolean Museum, in which they had been deposited for about 45 years, in 1915.* (In MS. Bodleian shelfmark *R.6.260.*)

Handlist of the octavo English almanacks in the Douce collection. (In MS Bodleian shelfmark *R.6.221.*)

Macray 326-9.

Craster 15-16.

'Francis Douce 1757–1834', *BQR* 7 (1934), 359-84.

'Children's games: an exhibition [of engravings from the Douce collection]', *BLR* (1940), 182-7.

A N L Munby, *Connoisseurs and Medieval Miniatures, 1750–1850*, Oxford, 1972.

Dunston Collection In 1981 Miss Emma Frederica Isabella Dunston, of Burltons, Donhead St Mary, Wiltshire, the last surviving member of an extraordinary family of book collectors, botanists, mycologists and photographers, bequeathed her books to the University of Oxford, which had been *alma mater* to her father and brothers. Those books which the Bodleian has taken represent the width and richness of the whole collection: literature, botany, history, travel, religion, biography, children's books etc. The collection will be treated as a 'reserve' collection of English literature (the field in which it is richest), although it contains much else of interest. F W Dunston's interest in his ancestor William Roscoe (1753–1831) and the Roscoe family is an important component in the collection.

Judge Robert Paul Eckert (*d*1966), biographer and bibliographer of the Oxford poet Philip Edward Thomas (1878–1917), bequeathed 190 works previously owned by Thomas or written by or about Thomas.

Edward Thomas, 1878–1917, an exhibition, Oxford 1968.

'Edward Thomas exhibition', *BLR* 8 (1969), 120-1.

FACS. [*Facsimiles*] Over 400 photographic reproductions of works of all periods, but mainly early printed books. (Published facsimiles are now classified as contemporary books according to the current classification.)

Frederic Sutherland Ferguson (1878–1967), bibliographer, and Director of Bernard Quaritch Ltd. A collection of 220 Scottish books, mainly of the 17th cent, some of the 16th cent, bequeathed in 1967. The Bodleian was given second choice after the National Library of Scotland.

Sir Charles Harding Firth (1857–1936), Fellow of All Souls (1902), Regius Professor of Modern History (1904), the editor of Clarendon. Part of his library donated by his widow. The 380 v of printed material include 24 v of printed portraits and caricatures illustrative of English history from *c*1603–*c*1830, the main series arranged chronologically; *c*20 v of broadside poems and ballads of the second half of the 17th, the 18th and early 19th cent, largely arranged by subject, including those on political, naval and military topics (Bodley also has Firth's ms and typewritten transcripts and notes); 4 v of proclamations and other broadsides of the 17th and 18th cent; *c*100 v of miscellaneous literature, including chap-books, song garlands, and other popular literature of the 18th and early 19th cent; poetical pamphlets of the second half of the 17th and the 18th cent; 84 v of political tracts, mostly of the latter half of the 17th cent; mid-17th cent newspapers and newsbooks. The remainder of Firth's collections are at Worcester College, Oxford, and the University of Sheffield.

Craster 279-80, 314.

'Lady Firth's donation', *BQR* 8 (1936), 208-9.

Strickland Gibson (1877–1958), Keeper of Printed Books, Bodleian Library (1942). A collection of over 400 items presented by him (and added to since then) to provide illustrative material for the study of every stage of the process of making a printed book, for use in his course on bibliography. Though chiefly intended for the study of English books printed on a hand-press, it contains some examples of the work of a number of European printers before 1500, with a few examples of the work of modern presses, and a small collection on typography. Included are specimens of printer's copy, of proof sheets, of methods of imposition, of cancels etc and samples of all kinds of wrappers and bindings. More than half of the printed volumes consist of Gibson's own collection of bindings. There are few rare books, but some volumes are of interest for their inscriptions or annotations, or because of their provenance.

Alphabetical subject index on cards.

'The Gibson donation', *BLR* 4 (1953), p179.

H J Davis, 'The Strickland Gibson collection', *BLR* 6 (1961), p645-54.

Mrs E G V Gilliat (a cousin of the Sitwells) 55 v, being works of the Sitwells, chiefly Edith, but also Osbert and Sacheverell, mainly presentation copies.

William Ewart Gladstone (1809–98), statesman and author. 256 pamphlets on Homeric subjects, mainly 19th cent from his library, presented in 1923 by Henry N Gladstone. The rest of his library is at St Deiniol's Hawarden (qv).

Craster p281.

Rev Charles Godwyn (1700?–70), Fellow of Balliol The collection he bequeathed consists chiefly of works in English and general history, civil and ecclesiastical, published in the 18th cent, and includes the later Benedictine editions of the Fathers. The books, *c*1,600 in number, are shelfmarked *Godw*, and the tracts or pamphlets, mainly theological and literary, *G.Pamph* [Godwyn pamphlets]. To the series *G.Pamph* the Bodleian has added: (a) *c*300 tracts in 41 v (*G.Pamph 276-316*) relating to American affairs and the War of Independence, a collection formed by the Rev Jonathan Boucher and bought by the Bodleian in 1836; (b) A series of pamphlets in 75 v (*G.Pamph 327-402*), chiefly relating to Irish history and to literary matters, from the library of Edmond Malone and bought by the Bodleian in 1838. Many volumes uniformly bound in half calf, with 'E M' in an interleaved monogram on the spine; (c) Pamphlets mainly of the 17th-19th cent on all subjects, making a total of over 2,900 v, and *c*38,000 separate works.

Godwyn pamphlets: complete index (MS Bodleian shelfmark R.6.204).

Macray p263-4; 308; 331.

Richard Gough (1735–1809), antiquary, bibliographer, topographer, Director of the Society of Antiquaries (1771–97), bequeathed to the Bodleian upwards of 3,700 v, many annotated by him and with printed insertions, comprising: (a) all his topographical collections of maps, topographical prints, drawings etc arranged under the names of the counties of the British Isles (shelfmarked *Gough maps 1-260*) and over 2,500 printed books arranged under the headings of General topography, Ecclesiastical topography, Natural history, and the counties of England, Wales, Scotland and Ireland. They are mostly 18th cent, but include some of the 16th, 17th and early 19th cent. Included are his interleaved copies of his *British topography* (the 1780 edition, comprising his collections for a third edition), of his Sepulchral monuments of Great Britain (1786–96), and of his edition of Camden's *Britannia* (1789). *c*250 book prospectuses printed pre-1801, many for antiquarian and topographical works, are to be found, some pasted into the volumes to which they relate, some in his working notes and manuscript collections, many in his collection for a third edition of his British topography; (b) 227 printed volumes connected with Anglo-Saxon literature and that of the Scandinavian races generally, mainly of the 18th cent; (c) Over 200 printed service books of the English church before the Reformation, (many of Sarum or York use) including Missals, Breviaries, Manuals, Hours, Graduals, Psalters, Processionals, Hymns, Primers, and a few manuscripts, chiefly *Horae*; (d) 16 large folio volumes of coloured drawings of monuments in the Churches of France, (detached from a large collection of drawings of royal and other monuments and tombs made by Francis Roger de Gaignières); (e) 400 copper plates, used mainly for his *Sepulchral monuments of Great Britain*; (f) Mss, including much unpublished topographical material by Gough himself, and his diary for 1747–51 and 1755–73.

[B Bandinel], *A catalogue of the books, relating to British topography and Saxon and northern literature, bequeathed to the Bodleian Library in the year MDCCCIX by Richard Gough*, Oxford, 1814.

Summary list of Gough prints and drawings (ie Gough maps)... Miscellaneous prints in certain volumes in Gough General topography and Gough maps (in MS Bodleian shelfmark R.6.262).

Macray, p285-90.

Craster, p79.

Sir George Fordham, 'Richard Gough, an address, 5 August 1926', *BQR* 5 (1926), p69-71.

R P Doig, 'A bibliographical study of Gough's *British topography* (Printed from *Edinburgh Bib Soc Trans* iv, 1963). Edinburgh, 1963.

J P Feather, *Book prospectuses before 1801 in the Gough collection, Bodleian Library, Oxford, a catalogue with microfiches.* Oxford. Oxford Microform Pub, 1980.

Note: The shelfmark *G.A.* [Gough Additions] has been in use since 1860 for current and antiquarian accessions of works on British topography, rivers, roads and railways. Since 1937 such accessions published in the period 1501–1800, and since 1974, such accessions published in the period 1501–1850, have been placed in the *Vet.* classification.

Thomas William Hanson, father of Laurence William Hanson, Keeper of Printed Books Bodleian Library, 1948–66, collected material relating to the seven members of the Edwards family, booksellers, bookbinders, and coll-ectors of Halifax and London, including William (1723–1808), James (1756–1816), Richard (1768–1827), and Thomas (1762–1834). Their specialities were a process for rendering scraped vellum transparent and painting or drawing designs on the underside, the Etruscan style of decorating calf, and fore-edge painting. The collection was purchased by the Bodleian in 1966, after a subscription by the Friends of the Bodleian, in memory of L W Hanson. It consists of primary material (their publications, catalogues, bindings, fore-edge paintings) and of secondary material.

T W Hanson, 'Edwards of Halifax, a family of booksellers, collectors and bookbinders', *Papers, Reports etc read before the Halifax Antiq Soc*, 1912, p141-200.

Walter N H Harding (1883–1973), born in London and retained British nationality, but lived in Chicago and pursued a career as a music-hall pianist and cinema organist. Songbooks were the central theme of his collecting, including music and ballad operas, but it extended into the fields of English and French poetry, poetical miscellanies, and English drama. His collections were bequeathed to the Bodleian, where they arrived in 1975. They will take many years to catalogue fully. They include: (a) Music, (*c*100,000 items) in seven main categories: English secular song (including folksong and ballads) from 1650, English opera (including libretti), French songs from 1700, French opera libretti *c*1680–1800, French opera full scores *c*1680–1820, French, German and Italian opera vocal scores *c*1800–50, American songs (70-80,000) from *c*1800; (b) Chapbooks in verse and prose, mainly English, but some French, German and Italian, English songsters, garlands or collections of songs, Cheap Repository Tracts, children's chapbooks, juvenile drama etc, *c*1,000 v of the 17th-19th cent, including many provincial imprints; (c) English songbooks and poetry, including the works of minor poets, poetical miscellanies, anthologies and collections of poetry 17th-19th cent (*c*4-5,000 v). Harding bought songbooks etc from the collections of W W Robinson of Oxford, J W Ebsworth (some presented to him by William C Chappell), W A Barrett, Thorn-Drury, and Sir John Stainer (the most extensive collection of such material formed in England, bought *en bloc*); (d) English plays (many, but not all, containing songs), 17th-19th cent, one-tenth estimated to be pre-1700. Estimated over 3,000 v (over 4,000 cards in the indexes, some cards analysing collections of plays); (e) English jestbooks, 18th and 19th cent (*c*300 v); (f) French songbooks, 18th and 19th cent (*c*2,000 v), includes the Henri Bachimont collection of 800 v (1790–1880), bought in 1927. A representative collection from 1700 onwards. There are also French chapbooks, jestbooks and plays; (g) Transcripts of songs and ballads in other collections (eg Madden Collection, Cambridge University Library; Samuel Pepys Collection, Pepysian Library, Magdalene College, Cambridge; and Narcissus Luttrell Collection, British Library); (h) Street ballads and broadsides (*c*15,000), many 18th and 19th cent, include the song type and lamplighter and Newsmen's poems, but also murder sheets, election sheets, etc; (i) American and English comic valentines; (j) Miscellaneous literature, periodicals, African travel; (k) American book auction catalogues.

Indexes First-line analytical index to English songbooks (both with and without music) *c*1600–1850.

Title index to chapbooks: on cards.

Author or title index to English poetry: on cards.

Title and author index to English plays: on cards.

Several typescript lists compiled at various dates.

W N H Harding, 'British song books and kindred subjects' (Contemporary collectors, 33), *Book Collector* 11 (1962), p448-59.

Sir John Stainer, *Catalogue of English song books, forming a portion of the library of Sir John Stainer, with appendices of foreign song books, collections of carols, books on bells.* London, 1891.

C L Day and E B Murrie, *English song books 1651–1702, a bibliography*. London. Bib Soc, 1940. Indicating locations in the Harding collection.

'Miscellanies, anthologies and collections of poetry: Poetical miscellanies, song books and verse collections of multiple authorship', *New Cambridge Bib of English Literature*, v 2: 1660–1800, 1971, col 327-430; cites Harding and Stainer copies when not found in the British Library or the Bodleian and not recorded in Wing's *Short title catalogue 1641–1700*, Case's *Bibliography of English poetical miscellanies 1521–1750*, or Day and Murrie's *English song books 1651–1702.*

D F Foxon, *English verse 1701–1750*, 2 v. London, Cambridge University Press, 1975. (With locations in the Harding collection.)

History A collection of *c*500 folios and large quartos on historical and geographical subjects received among the new books between 1861 and 1883.

Holkham Collection Purchased in 1953 from the family library of the Earl of Leicester at Holkham Hall, Norfolk, the collection consists of more than 800 works, broadly representative of the Holkham Library as a whole, including an element of the law library of the early generations of the family, books belonging to Chief Justice Sir Edward Coke (1552–1634), English literature and plays gathered by the 18th cent members of the family, classical and other incunabula, and English and Italian literature collected by Thomas William Coke, first Earl of Leicester (1752–1842). It divides into four main categories: 35 incunabula, many very rare, including editions of the Classics; 33 books printed in the United Kingdom up to 1640 (STC), including 5 in Italian and 3 English Bibles; 30 uniformly bound volumes in quarto, the collection of English Restoration plays put together by Edward Coke and his wife, Cary, the parents of the First Earl, consisting of 317 items, 305 of them plays, all but 15 of them printed between 1663 and 1700, the rest not later than 1705; *c*500 Italian works, printed pre-1601, in the main from two sources: (i) more than 150 from the library of Chief Justice Sir Edward Coke (1552–1634), and of these two-thirds are books owned by Sir Christopher Hatton (1540–91), and (ii) the more numerous books bought by the Third Earl. The Italian portion of the collection contains few imprints pre-1525, and few exceptional rarities. It is broadly representative of the Italian books being printed throughout the major portion of that country, when Italy's cultural pre-eminence was still unrivalled, and includes works, original or translated in the fields of theology, philosophy, law, politics, history, travel, biography, antiquities, medicine, agriculture, music, painting and architecture, as well as poetry, drama, letters, dialogues and literary criticism. Bindings on the Holkham collection books are representative of the library and its various owners, eg Elizabethan bindings are richly represented among the Hatton books, the splendour of 18th cent bindings is shown on the First Earl's books.

Dr D M Rogers, 'The Holkham collection', *BLR* 4 (1953), 255-67.

Frederick William Hope (1797–1862) presented in 1862 to the Bodleian a collection of newspapers and periodical essays collected by his father, John Thomas Hope. They number 1,300 items and *c*760 works, and date from the 17th-19th cent, the majority being 18th cent.

J H Burn, *Catalogue of a collection of early newspapers and essayists, formed by the late John Thomas Hope, Esq, and with [omissions and additions] presented to the Bodleian Library by Frederick William Hope*. Oxford, 1865. The cat presents a chronological arrangement from 1640–1840, with some undated volumes. [Bodleian copy shelfmarked *2590 d.Oxf.1c.10=R.6.206* annotated with Bodleian shelfmarks.]

Craster, p77.

Imprint Society Over 50 publications of the Imprint Society, Barre, Mass, from 1969. Bought from the funds of Bodley's American Friends.

INC. [Incunabula] *c*530 15th cent v acquired since 1937. Shelved by size, place and date of publication.

Professor Friedrich Christian W Jacobs (1764–1847), classical scholar, editor of the *Anthologia Graeca*. At the sale of his library in 1849, the Bodleian bought 300 foreign dissertations on classical subjects, dating from the 18th and the first half of the 19th cent.

A catalogue of the books purchased for the Bodleian Library... during the year ending November 8, 1849: p57-68 'Books purchased from the library of Professor Jacobs, editor of the Anthologia Graeca' &c.

Frederic Jessel (*d*1934), author of *A bibliography of works in English on playing cards and gaming...* (1905), bequeathed, in 1934, to the Bodleian *c*3,400 v relating to the history and use of playing cards, card games, games of chance, gaming at casinos, fortune-telling by cards, and card-tricks. They include satires and tracts on the social aspects of gaming; novels, poems and plays in which card-playing figures; Acts of Parliament directed towards the control of gaming and lotteries, extracts from periodicals, newspaper cuttings, packs of cards etc. They range in date from the 16th-20th cent. There are some practically complete sets of editions of some of the most important works on the subject, both English and foreign. The collection also includes a few packs of cards.

'The Jessel bequest', *BQR* 7 (1934), p520.

'The Jessel collection', *BLR* 1 (1939), p116-18.

Craster, p278.

John de Monins Johnson (1882–1955), Printer to the University of Oxford, 1925–46. A collection mainly of printed ephemera, or non-book printed materials, but including books and pamphlets, chiefly English, formed by John Johnson at the University Press, where it was known as the Constance Meade Collection, and transferred to the Bodleian Library in 1968, where it is known as the John Johnson Collection. Johnson made 1939 the *terminus ad quem* of the collection. He restricted his collecting of post-1939 material, but he continued to collect current material in some areas until his death in 1955, and later material has been added since the collection came to the Bodleian.

Constance Meade, the great-granddaughter of Bishop Percy of Dromore, donated to Johnson's collection in 1930 the printed ephemera which had passed into the Meade family with the residue of Bishop Percy's books and papers. During the period when the Bodleian's attitude to ephemera was antipathetic, Strickland Gibson steered material eliminated from the library into Johnson's collection (including almanacs, booksellers' and publishers' lists, books for young children). Johnson also acquired material originally collected by W D Macray (1826–1916), Robert Proctor (1868–1903), and E W B Nicholson (1849–1912). Other specialized sections of the collections include: the Edward Heron-Allen (1861–1943) collection of watchpapers; the E Maude Hayter collection of valentines and Christmas cards, in addition to Andrew White Tuer's collection; the Sir John Evans (1823–1908) collection of banknotes and paper money; the M L Horn (1889–1953) collection of cigarette cards; the F A Bellamy and H F N Jourdain collection of postage stamps, postal stationery and material relating to the Post Office. The printed books in the collection are estimated to number *c*5,000 v, including almanacs, auction catalogues, novels, periodicals, plays and sermons, dating from the 17th-20th cent.

A collection of writing masters copy books (shelfmarked *Johnson penmen 1-386*), both English and foreign (France, Germany, Italy, Spain and the US being the other countries represented), dating from the 16th-20th cent was built up for Johnson by Graham Pollard. The ephemera collection also includes single sheets by, or relating to, writing masters, chiefly English of the 18th cent, and a small collection of engraved writing blanks, English of the 18th and early 19th cent.

Guard books contain *c*440 book prospectuses covering the period *c*1680–1800; 17th and 18th cent single sheet proclamations; and single sheet items of the periods covered by STC and Wing.

The collection of ephemera is largely arranged by subject, in some cases by form of material, and the following are some of the sections: material on the history of book production and the book trade, including 18th cent catalogues of the sales of copies or shares in copies, ie booksellers trade sale catalogues, thought to have been those belonging to the firm of Rivington; booksale and booksellers' catalogues; catalogues and labels of circulating and subscription libraries of the 18th and 19th cent; bookplates (one of the largest institutional collections); material relating to private presses, including the Chiswick Press; early news-books and newspapers; prospectuses; playbills and programmes for popular entertainments; broadsides, including ballads; passports; chapbooks and songbooks; Oxford material, including Oxford and University societies; Christmas cards; material on authors such as Dickens; on elections; taxation; religion; education; the armed forces; trade and finance; agriculture; food and drink; dress; transport; games and pastimes; sport etc.

A typed subject guide to the whole collection is available, together with a printed list of main subject headings. There are in addition detailed indexes to various parts of the collection.

[M L Turner], *The John Johnson collection, catalogue of an exhibition*, Oxford, Bodleian Library, 1971.

J P Feather, *Book prospectuses before 1801 in the John Johnson collection, a catalogue with microfiches*, Oxford Microform Publ for the Bodleian Library, 1976.

J H Wiener, *A descriptive finding list of unstamped British periodicals 1830–1836*, London Bibl Soc 1970. [With locations in the John Johnson collection.]

Dickens playbills in the Bodleian Library, ed by C Hurst. Oxford Microform Publ, 1981. [9 fiches with letterpress booklet.]

The Warwick guide to labour periodicals, 1790–1970: a checklist, arranged and compiled by R Harrison [and others]. Hassocks, Harvester Press, 1977. With locations in the Bodleian and the John Johnson collection.

Juel-Jensen Drayton Collection Presented by Dr B E Juel-Jensen in 1977. *c*340 editions of works by and about Michael Drayton the poet (1563–1631). Includes *c*80 STC items and over 150 works printed pre-1700. The collection comprises works by Drayton, including rare early editions of the individual works as published, collected poems and works, volumes containing selections, translations, works with dedicatory and other verse by him, and later editions. Many works are present in multiple copies, collected because each copy may be of bibliographical interest, representing different issues or, in their various combinations of uncorrected and corrected sheets, different states, or because each copy reflects the taste and period of the original collector. The collection also includes photocopies of books not otherwise represented, and bibliographical, biographical and critical works on Drayton.

The Bodleian's collection of this poet is now at least equal in quality, and certainly superior in number, to those of the British Library and the Huntington Library.

Dr B E Juel-Jensen, *'Polyolbion, Poems lyrick and pastoral, Poems 1619, The owle,* and a few other books by Michael Drayton'. *The Library* 5th ser, 8 (1953), p145-62.

——'A Drayton collection', *Book Collector* 4 (1955), p133-43.

——'Bibliography of the early editions of the writings of Michael Drayton', *The works of Michael Drayton, edited by J W Hebel (K Tillotson and B Newdigate)*, Corrected ed, Oxford, 1961, v 5, p265-306.

'The Juel-Jensen gift of books by Michael Drayton', *BLR* 10 (1978, p1-2).

JUR. [*Jurisprudentia*] One part of the original Bodleian four-part classification by faculty or subject in use in various forms over the period 1602–1789, and less frequently until *c*1840, though by the early 18th cent *Jur.* was already being used for books not on legal subjects, as other shelves filled up. The collection comprises over 8,000 v of the 16th-19th cent. Part of the collection is now shelved at the Law Library.

Kelmscott Press Collection 60 items, mainly works, including proofs, printed at the Press by William Morris (1834–96), brought together as a collection from copies in the general classification.

Sǿren Aubye Kierkegaard (1813–55), Danish philosopher and theologian. *c*80 works of the 19th and 20th cent in 62 v, by and about Kierkegaard. Purchased in 1981.

Robert Warden Lee (1868–1958), Rhodes Professor of Roman-Dutch law, and Fellow of All Souls (1921–56) presented in 1949. 160 works, dating from the 17th-20th cent relating mainly to Dutch law and history.

Libri Hungarici A collection purchased in 1815 from an unknown German dealer. 416 v, mostly dating from the period 1700–1830, on the history, civil and ecclesiastical, and topography of Hungary and South Eastern Europe. Includes some large volumes of 17th cent Protestant theology. Few items are genuinely rare, and these tend to be the less distinguished pieces.

Bibliotheca Hungarica. Kirchen- und Profan-Geschichte, Verfassung, Jurisprudenz, Literarhistorie, Geographie und Topographie von Ungarn, Siebenbürgen, Croatien, Dalmatien und den unteren Donauländern. [Bodleian *shelfmark 2590 e.Oxf.lc.17=R.6.238*: a section of a bookseller's catalogue.]

J R W Evans, 'Hungarica in the Bodleian: a historical sketch', *BLR* 9 (1978), p338, 342-3.

Macray, p353.

Craster, p76.

Libri Polonici A collection of 1,675 v in both Polish and Latin, dating from the 16th-19th cent. Bought in 1850 from the library of Jósef Andrzej Lukaszewicz, the Polish Protestant writer. Includes works printed in Polish in the 16th cent, particularly books printed at Cracow, Polish translations of the Bible, and numerous editions of the poems of the Polish 17th cent author Maciej Kazimierz Sarbiewski.

Macray, p353.

Craster, p76.

'The Polish exhibition at the Bodleian', *Oxford Magazine* lxii (27 January 1944), p127.

Limited Editions Club A collection of over 500 publications of the Limited Editions Club, New York, from 1929, bought from the funds of Bodley's American Friends.

Martin Lister (1638?–1712), physician and zoologist. *c*1,260 v dating from the 16th-18th cent, but mainly 17th cent on medicine, anatomy, natural philosophy, botany, and voyages and travels, bequeathed to the Ashmolean Museum, but transferred to the Bodleian in 1860. A small number of Lister's books are in the collection shelfmarked *Ashmole A-H* (qv).

R T Gunther, 'The Ashmole printed books', *BQR* 6 (1930), p193-5.

Macray, p366.

Craster, p65.

John Locke (1632–1704), philosopher. From 1691 Locke lived with the Masham family at Oates, Essex. On his death he left all his mss and his interleaved books, and one 'Moiety' of the rest of his books to his cousin Peter King, later Lord King (1669–1734). The papers and correspondence remained in the possession of Lord King's descendants, who later became the Earls of Lovelace, until 1947, when most were bought by the Bodleian. In 1951 the remainder of the King moiety of Locke's library was discovered at Ben Damph Forest, a seat of the Earl of Lovelace, and were later bought by Mr Paul Mellon who presented them to the Bodleian, transferring them there in 1978, plus a number of other books from Locke's library which he had in the meantime bought. The Bodleian now holds in its Locke Room, in addition to the mss purchased in 1947 and mss given by Mr Mellon, all the books with the location 'Oak Spring' in Harrison and Laslett's *The Library of John Locke* and other printed volumes from Locke's library, a total of over 800 printed volumes. Volumes from other Bodleian collections known to have belonged to Locke, and some which belonged to the other 'moiety' of Locke's library (left to Frances Cudworth Masham and subsequently dispersed) have been integrated with Mr Mellon's gift.

P Long, *A summary catalogue of the Lovelace collection of the papers of John Locke in the Bodleian Library*, Oxford Bib Soc publications, new ser v 8, Oxford, 1959.

——'The Mellon donation of additional manuscripts of John Locke from the Lovelace collection', *BLR* 7 (1964), p185-93.

'Gifts from Mr Paul Mellon and Dr E S de Beer', *Ibid* 6 (1960), p575-6.

University of Oxford, *Annual Report of the Curators of the Bodleian Library for 1977–1978* (June 1979), p42-3.

R J Roberts, 'The John Locke Room in the Bodleian Library, Oxford', *The Locke newsletter* no 9 (1978).

[Books donated from the Locke collection donated to the Bodleian Library by Mr Paul Mellon and published in the period covered by Wing's *Short-title catalogue 1641–1700*], *BLR* 10 (May 1982), p376-82.

P Laslett, 'Lord Masham's library at Oates', *TLS* 15 August 1952, p533.

J Harrison and P Laslett, 'The library of John Locke', *Ibid* 27 December 1957, p792.

'John Locke's books and papers for his own university', *Ibid* 11 March 1960, p168.

J Harrison and P Laslett, *The library of John Locke*, Oxford Bib Soc Pubn, new ser v 13, Oxford 1965; 2nd edition, Oxford 1971.

Rev Robert James McGhee (1789–1872), Roman Catholic priest, presented 32 v of Roman Catholic theology, ranging in date from 1770–1850, but mostly of the first half of the 19th cent. Includes editions of the Douay and Rheims versions of the Bible, of some Irish diocesan statutes, of Bailly's *Theologia moralis* and Delahogue's dogmatic treatises and various Irish polemical pamphlets, some by the donor.

R J McGhee, *The Church of Rome: her present moral theology, scriptural instruction and canon law, a report on the books and documents on the Papacy deposited in the University Library, Cambridge, the Bodleian Library, Oxford, and the library of Trinity College, Dublin, AD 1840*. London, 1853. A list of the volumes is printed pxiv-xxiii.

Macray, p340.

Edmond Malone (1741–1812), Shakespearian scholar, bequeathed his library to his brother, Lord Sunderlin, who presented to the Bodleian 770 v containing *c*3,000 items, the rest of the library being sold in 1818. The collection is chiefly of Elizabethan, Jacobean and Caroline literature, particularly drama, but it also contains some Restoration drama and Dryden. Malone's collection of the early editions of Shakespeare's plays and poems in seven quarto volumes (*Malone 32-8*, kept as *Arch.G.d.39-45*) represented in Malone's time the most complete collection of early editions ever made. Included in the Malone collection are almost 1,000 printed plays given him by George Steevens (1736–1800) and augmented by Malone in two series: (i) *Malone 39-128*, containing late-17th and early-18th cent editions, (ii) *Malone 158-234*, most of which are Caroline, though a few are Elizabethan and others are dated after 1660: Shakespeare is largely absent. Included also is Malone's own copy of his Shakespeare of 1790 (*Malone 1046-57*), heavily annotated for the second edition he did not live to publish. Malone's books were working copies, which he annotated: the pages of his Shakespeare quartos were inlaid within large margins. Bound volumes of plays were split up at the suggestion of F P Wilson. The Bodleian has also acquired some of Malone's other printed books (see Godwyn), and some of his ms collections.

Catalogue of early English poetry and other miscellaneous works illustrating the British drama, collected by E Malone, and now preserved in the Bodleian Library, Oxford, 1836. [Bodleian copy shelfmarked *2590 d.Oxf.1.43=R.6.100* annotated with shelfmarks in ms].

J O Halliwell-Phillipps, *A handlist of the early English literature preserved in the Malone collection in the Bodleian Library, selected from the printed catalogue of that collection*, 1860.

Macray, p306-8.

L W Hanson, 'The Shakespeare collection in the Bodleian Library, Oxford', *Shakespeare Survey* 4 (1951), p78-95.

William Shakespeare, 1564–1964, a catalogue of the quatercentenary exhibition in the Divinity School, Oxford. Oxford, Bodleian Library, 1964.

J M Osborn, 'Edmund Malone: scholar-collector', *The Library*, 5th ser, 19 (1964), p11-37.

C J Stratman, 'A survey of the Bodleian Library's holdings in the field of English printed tragedy', *BLR* 7 (1964), p133-43.

Bodleian accessions of English drama from *c*1860–83 were added to the Malone collection.

Percy Manning, (*d*1917) bequeathed *c*500 books, mainly of the 19th and early-20th cent, on the city, county and university of Oxford and its neighbouring areas.

Craster, 313.

Mansfield College Collection Purchased from Mansfield College, Oxford, in 1965, it contains over 500 bound v, comprising many more items, mainly theological of Congregational Church interest. Included are 140 bound volumes of pamphlets, mostly Dutch and German, of the 19th and early-20th cent, volumes of sermons and tracts, especially provincial tracts, English and foreign books of the 17th-20th cent, and a few early printed books. Many volumes bear the bookplates of former owners, including Spring Hill College, Birmingham (the former name of Mansfield College); in 1872 Thomas Smith James (1809–74), son of John Angell James (1785–1859), presented to Spring Hill College over 600 v, many formerly owned by his father.

P Morgan, *Oxford libraries outside the Bodleian*, 2nd edition, Oxford, 1920, p82.

Thomas Marshall (1621–85), Rector of Lincoln College (1672), Dean of Gloucester (1681), bequeathed to the Bodleian his mss, and such of his printed books as were not already in the library. The printed books include contemporary Protestant theology (English and Continental), and works on Anglo-Saxon and Middle Eastern languages, reflecting his exile in the Netherlands during the Commonwealth, and an interest in linguistics and philology. There are now *c*900 printed volumes in the collection, some of these being additions to the Marshall bequest. Lincoln College, Oxford (qv) also received books from Marshall.

Macray, p154.

Robert Mason (*d*1841), DD, of The Queen's College, bequeathed to the Bodleian the sum of £36,000, used for the purchase of *c*8,000 v of the 16th-19th cent, including plate books, editions de luxe, and works of some degree of value or rarity in various languages.

Macray, p342.

Craster, p17, 35.

Mathematics A collection of 60 folios and large quartos on mathematical and technical subjects received among the new books between 1861 and 1883.

Mather A collection assembled by H O Coxe when Bodley's Librarian, partly from books already in the library, partly from special purchases. Over 170 works of the 17th-19th cent, mostly Boston imprints, being works by, or on, Cotton Mather (1663–1728) and Increase Mather (1639–1723), New England divines, and other members of the Mather family.

Macray, p383.

Craster, p77.

MED. [*Medicina*] One part of the original Bodleian four-part classification by faculty, or subject, in use in various forms over the period 1602–1789 and less frequently until *c*1840. In the later years the distinction by faculty began to be disregarded, and books were added where there was space on the shelves. The collection comprises over 2,700 v of the 16th-19th cent.

Medicine A collection of *c*30 folios and large quartos on medical subjects among the new books received between 1861 and 1883.

Meerman John Meerman, the only son of Gerard, the author of *Origines typographicae* (1765), had inherited his father's library in 1771. *c*1,500 v were bought at the sale of the library at The Hague in 1824, including works of foreign history and law, and some classics, dating from the 16th-19th cent.

Bibliotheca Meermanniana; sive Catalogus librorum impressorum et codicum manuscriptorum...quos... collegerunt...Gerardus & Joannes Meerman; morte dereliquit Joannes Meerman...quorum publica fiet auctio...MDCCCXXIV 4 tom. Hague Comitum, 1824.

A catalogue of books purchased for the Bodleian Library during the year ending November 8, 1824. [With] *A catalogue of books purchased for the Bodleian Library at the sale of M Meerman at The Hague, June 8-July 4, 1824, with a statement of the expenses attending the purchase.*

[*Mexican pamphlets: 41 v shelfmarked 233 f.101-140 and 274 b.18*] Collected during 1861 by Henry Ward Poole (1825–90) in Mexico City: he sold to Henry Stevens, the bookdealer, who sold to the Bodleian in 1870. 1,446 separate pamphlets, excluding duplicates and triplicates and several runs of periodicals, printed in the period 1784–1841, mainly in Mexico City. 945 pamphlets out of the 1,446 relate to the years 1820–7, the period during which Mexico attained independence and abolished censorship of the press; 444 pamphlets date from 1820. The main set of volumes at *233 f.101-140* divide into three sections: the first 6 v containing *c*340 pamphlets, were almost all printed in 1820; the next 18 v date from the period 1820–7. Poole made detailed pencil annotations on the pamphlets, particularly in the last 8 v of this main set.

A R Bonner, 'Mexican pamphlets in the Bodleian Library', *BLR* 8 (1970), p205-13.

C Steele and M P Costeloe, *Independent Mexico: a collection of Mexican pamphlets in the Bodleian Library.* London, Mansell, 1973.

Mill House Press Collection *c*50 books etc printed at the Mill House Press, Stanford Dingley, Reading, Berkshire, 1926–71, given by Robert Gathorne-Hardy (1902–73) in memory of Kyrle Leng (1900–58). Some have ms notes, some are Kyrle Leng's copies, some are special copies.

David Binning Monro (1836–1905), fellow (1859) and Provost (1882) of Oriel College. Over 1,000 v on Homeric studies, mainly 19th cent, were purchased by subscription from his library in memory of him by a number of his friends and presented to the Bodleian. He had left to Oriel College *c*1,000 v on comparative philology and mythology, and most of these are now on permanent loan to the library of the Taylor Institution, Oxford (qv).

Craster, p182.

J C Wilson, *David Binning Monro: a short memoir,* Oxford, 1907, p14.

Captain Montagu Montagu, RN (*d*1863) bequeathed to the Bodleian *c*700 v in various branches of literature, dating from 16th-19th cent, including 90 editions and versions of the Psalter, with works on Psalmody, editions of Anacreon, Horace, Juvenal, Phaedrus, Petrarch, Boileau and La Fontaine, and topographical and biographical works grangerized with additional engravings.

List of manuscripts...illustrated and other books, etc, the bequest of the late Captain Montagu Montagu to the Bodleian Library. Oxford, 1864. [Bodleian copy shelfmarked *2590 e.Oxf.1.50=R.6.208* annotated with Bodleian shelfmarks.]

Macray, p377-8.

Conte Alessandro Mortara The Bodleian bought from him in 1852 1,400 v dating from 16th-19th cent, rich in rare 16th cent editions of Italian authors, and including early editions of Ariosto, Boccaccio, Dante and Tasso.

A Mortara, *Biblioteca Italica ossio Catalogo de' testi a stampa citati nel Vocabolario degli Accademici della Crusca e di altri libri italiani pregevoli e rari già posseduti dal C A M ed ora passati in proprietà della Biblioteca Bodleiana*, Oxford, 1852.

Macray, p357.

Craster, p75-6.

Colonel William E Moss (1875–1953) made donations to the Bodleian during his lifetime. On his death in 1953 his widow presented a collection of books and papers on bookbinding and on William Blake. Included are photographs and rubbings of, and offprints, cuttings and notes, on Renaissance bindings, especially bindings for Grolier, Maioli, Thomas Wotton, Archbishop Parker and Robert Dudley, Earl of Leicester, and also on Mearne type and Elkanah Settle bindings.

'Elkanah Settle', *BLR* 2 (1944), p92-3.

S Gibson 'Colonel William E Moss' [with] 'The Moss donation [a list]', *BLR* 5 (1955), p156-66.

Harold James R Murray (*d*1955), author of *History of chess* (1913), bequeathed in 1935, *c*240 items of 16th-20th cent, but mostly 19th and 20th cent, being books on chess, plus newspaper cuttings, book catalogues, prospectuses of books etc.

MUS.BIBL. [*Museum Bibliographicum*].

MUS.BIBL.II *c*120 v, being editions of works by Thomas Hearne (1678–1735), historical antiquary, bought together from existing collections and added to.

MUS.BIBL.III Over 800 v, representing many more items. Auction, booksellers' and library catalogues of 17th-19th cent brought together from *c*1860, some from existing collections, while others were current catalogues of the period and others were purchased.

D M Rogers, 'Book auction sale catalogues', *BLR* 10 (1981), p269-70.

List of catalogues of English book sales, 1676–1900, now in the British Museum (1915), arranged chronologically, with index of owners: Bodleian Library has xeroxes of A N L Munby's interleaved copy annotated with additions and Bodleian Library's shelfmarks.

A N L Munby and L Coral, *British book sale catalogues 1676–1800: a union list*. London, Mansell, 1977. [With locations in the Bodleian.]

N.N. [Nichols Newspapers] Formed by John Nichols (1745–1820), printer, publisher and author of the *Literary anecdotes*, and purchased by the Bodleian in 1865 from John Bowyer Nichols (1779–1863), his son. *c*1,100 items, more or less complete sets, in chronological order of issue, of London newspapers from 1672–1737.

Craster, p77.

A catalogue of newspapers, political papers, trials &c the property of the late John Nichols, FSA: folios 6-133. [*Bodleian MS.Eng.misc.c.138* = *R.6.210.*]

PAMPH. [Bartholomew Pamphlets] Humphrey Bartholomew, of University College, presented to the Radcliffe Library in 1749 *c*50,000 English pamphlets of the period 1603–1740, including Civil War pamphlets, bound chronologically in 410 v. They were transferred to the Bodleian in *c*1861 and shelfmarked *Pamph.*

'Pamphlets index' [MS Bodleian shelfmark *R.6.200.*]

Thomas Percy (1729–1811) Bishop of Dromore, antiquary, editor of the *Reliques of ancient English poetry*, and a member of the Johnson circle. A collection of *c*120 v, mainly literary and of 17th-19th cent, which his daughters kept on his death, were presented to the Bodleian in 1933 by his great-granddaughter, Miss Constance Meade, and were augmented by other books and mss associated with him. They include annotated copies of Goldsmith, Johnson and other 18th cent authors; a set of *The Rambler* (1756) with ms notes by Percy, and of *The Idler* (1761) with ms notes by Percy and Johnson, and works edited and translated by Percy. The printed ephemera, which had passed into the Meade family with the residue of Bishop Percy's books and papers, was given in 1930 to John Johnson's collection of printed ephemera at the University Press, and is now part of the John Johnson collection at the Bodleian.

D Nicol Smith, 'The contributors to *The Rambler* and *The Idler*', *BQR* 7 (1934), p508-9.

——'The Constance Mead collection and the University Press Museum', *BLR* 6 (1958), p427-33.

The Library of Thomas Percy (1729–1811), Bishop of Dromore...removed to Caledon House, Co Tyrone, in 1812 and now sold...by auction by Sotheby & Co, 23 June, 1969.

Frank Pettingell (1891–1966), stage and screen actor. A collection of 800 v of 19th cent 'penny-dreadful' publications, many published in parts, purchased by the Bodleian in 1966 from his widow. Of greatest value for the study of the prolific, but less well-known, popular writers of the period, and a valuable supplement to the Library's holdings received by copyright, for the copyright system failed to bring in many of these very cheap and ephemeral but, for the social historian, very significant, printed pieces.

Ms handlist/catalogue.

University of Oxford. *Annual Report of the Curators of the Bodleian Library for 1966–7.*

Louis James, *Fiction for the working man 1830–1850*, London, 1963. Appendix III (p184-94): Checklist of penny-issue novels not listed in Montague Summers's *Gothic Bibliography*; includes Pettingell locations.

Physics A collection of 170 folios and large quartos on physics and other scientific subjects received among the new books between 1861 and 1883.

Poetry A collection of 70 folios and large quartos of verse received among the new books between 1861 and 1883.

Professor Baden Powell (1796–1860), Savilian Professor of Geometry (1827). 170 v from his library presented in 1970 by his grandson, D F W Baden Powell, including some science, some theology, 17th and 18th cent editions of the classics, and works on education, including a collection of papers on the University syllabuses annotated by him.

'The Baden Powell Library', *BLR* 8 (1970), p172.

[*Printer's Library*] Deposited on permanent loan in the Bodleian by the Printer to the University. A collection, begun by John Johnson while he was Printer to the University, of *c*2,000 books printed in Oxford from 1585 to the 20th cent, including some items formerly owned by Falconer Madan (1851–1935), the historian of Oxford printing. Includes a few large quarto and folio finely bound Bibles and Books of Common Prayer. Arranged by size and by date.

Separate slip cats by author, printer and date.

Card index of names of former owners, bookplates, etc.

RADCL. [Radcliffe] The Radcliffe collection had formed part of the Radcliffe Library and was handed over to the Bodleian by the Radcliffe Trustees in 1893. It comprises 780 v, being non-scientific works of 16th-18th cent, and including books on architecture, classics, history, literature and theology. Included are books bequeathed to the Radcliffe Library by James Gibbs

(1682–1754), the architect of the building, Richard Frewin (1681?–1761), Charles Viner (1678–1756) and other benefactors. Other non-scientific works not wanted by the Bodleian were sold in 1894.

Bibliotheca Radcliviana, 1749–1949, Catalogue of an exhibition. Oxford, 1949.

Richard Rawlinson (1690–1755), non-juror, antiquary and collector, had formed a foreign, classical and English library, and bought a large proportion of the Oriental volumes at the sale of his brother's library in 1726. He had been a considerable benefactor during his lifetime: some hundreds of books in the shelfmark *Jur* and elsewhere were given by him. A series of almanacs in 175 v, ranging in date from 1606–1747, were sent to the library in 1752–55, and are shelfmarked *Rawlinson Almanacs*: other almanacs have been added to the collection. He bequeathed to the Bodleian his large collection of mss, among which are bound sheets and book prospectuses; those printed books containing ms notes. *c*1,800 v in quarto and smaller sizes are shelfmarked *Rawlinson*. They date from 16th-18th cent and include theology, contemporary politics, history and antiquities, topography and early English literature. A volume containing a collection of the broadside proclamations issued during the reign of Elizabeth I is now kept as *Arch.G.c.6*.

Rawlinson's books include some owned by Thomas Hearne (1678–1735): Hearne bequeathed all his mss and books with ms notes, to William Bedford, from whose widow Rawlinson bought them. Some of the Rawlinson printed books appear to have been disposed of in sales of Bodleian duplicates.

Rawlinson almanacks, with index [Ms Bodleian shelfmark *R.6.223*].

Index to the Rawlinson copperplates [Bodleian *Ms.Top.Oxon d.276=R.6.236*].

Macray, p231-5.

B J Enright, 'Rawlinson and the chandlers', *BLR* 4 (1953), p216-7.

REC. [Recentiores] A collection of 100 books published after 1850 which would be unsuitably placed dispersed through the current classification for modern books, eg books having dust jackets before the period when these were preserved generally, proof copies, series.

Stephen Peter Rigaud (1774–1839), mathematical historian and astronomer, Fellow of Exeter College (1794–1810, Savilian Professor of Geometry (1810–27), Savilian Professor of Astronomy and Radcliffe Observer (1827–39). When his large library, chiefly of 18th cent writers, was sold in 1839, his books on astronomy, mathematics, and physics were purchased by the Radcliffe Trustees for the Observatory. In 1935, 840 books, not then in the Bodleian, were presented to the library and the rest sold.

Catalogue of the theological, classical and miscellaneous library of Stephen Peter Rigaud...which will be sold by auction by Mr Evans. London, 1839.

Craster, p185-6.

Robert Ross Memorial Collection Brought together by Walter Edwin Ledger (*d*1931), Wilde's bibliographer, and named after Robert Baldwin Ross (1869–1918), Wilde's friend and literary executor. Presented to University College, Oxford, by Donald C L Cree, Ledger's friend and executor, and an alumnus of the College, and deposited in the Bodleian. *c*1,000 works being editions and translations of the works of Oscar Wilde (1856–1900), works on Wilde, works illustrating literary movements in England in the 1890s, including periodicals, sale and booksellers' catalogues and newspaper cuttings.

Roxburghe Club A collection of 230 publications of the Roxburghe Club from 1814.

(N) Barker, *The publications of the Roxburghe Club 1814–1962, an essay with a bibliographical table.* Cambridge, Roxburghe Club, 1964.

James St Amand (1687–1754), antiquary, bequeathed his books to the Bodleian (those not wanted were to go to Lincoln College). The 600 books taken by the Bodleian consist chiefly of contemporary editions of the classics and of the writings of modern Latin scholars (many had formerly belonged to Arthur Charlett, 1655–1722, Master of University College, 1692).

Macray, p252-4.

Sir Henry Savile (1549–1622), Warden of Merton College (1585–1622), Provost of Eton (1596), founded lectureships in mathematics, one in astronomy, the other in geometry, in the University of Oxford. To each he attached a library, drawn from his own collections, covering the whole field of mathematics, and including the allied subjects of optics, harmonics, mechanics, cosmography, and the applied sciences of surveying, navigation and fortification, and a quantity of fine printed books, chiefly of the 16th cent. Nearly all of the Savilian professors added to the library: Sir Christopher Wren, holder of the Chair of Astronomy (1661–1773) left his astronomy and geometry books to the library when he retired from the Chair; and John Wallis, holder of the Chair of Geometry (1649–1704), gave some books during his lifetime, but many more were presented after his death by his son. Thus, the Savilian Library is a very complete collection of mathematical works up to the end of the 17th cent, and contains some 18th and 19th cent items. It was handed over to the Bodleian in 1884. The Wren and Wallis books are shelfmarked *Savile A-H* and *K-M*; Savile's original donations are in *Savile N-Z, Aa* and *Bb*. The collection totals *c*1,180 v.

Craster, p183-6.

C J Scriba, *Studien zur Mathematik des John Wallis (1616–1703): Winkelteilungen, Kombinationslehre und Zahlentheoretische Probleme im Anhang die Bücher und Handschriften von Wallis in der Bodleian Library zu Oxford*, Wiesbaden, 1966. p112-42: *Anhang die Bücher und Handschriften von John Wallis mit einem Überblick über die Geschichte der Savile Collection (jetzt Teil der Bodleian Library in Oxford).* [Bodleian copy shelfmarked *R.6.108m*.]

John Selden (1584–1654), lawyer, antiquary and Orientalist, bequeathed to the University of Oxford his Oriental and Greek mss, together with some Latin mss, and such of his Talmudical and Rabbinical books not already in the Bodleian. *c*8,000 v of his were presented by his executors in 1659. Selden's was the greatest single collection received in the 17th cent. It was placed in the west wing of Duke Humfrey's Library, which became known as Selden End, and the books were subdivided by the four faculty subdivisions (theology, jurisprudence, medicine, and arts). The collection is rich in books that once belonged to famous owners, or that were given to him, many as author's presentation copies. Among the printed books many European languages are represented as well as Oriental languages. Much of the collection comprises 16th and 17th cent works in classical and foreign languages. Though he owned few literary texts in English, some of these are of special interest. He was one of the earliest collectors of Caxtons, and the 13 he owned (all but one in English) were the first that came into the Bodleian. Other subjects represented are medicine, science, theology, history, law and Hebrew literature. Some duplicates were disposed of when the collection first came to the library, some to Gloucester Cathedral library. Some additions, which were not Selden's own books, were made to the Selden collection during the 18th and 19th cent.

J Sparrow, 'The earlier owners of books in John Selden's library', *BQR* 6 (1931), p263-71.

Dr D M Barratt, 'The library of John Selden and its later history', *BLR* 3 (1951), p128-42.

The Bodleian Library in the seventeenth century, guide to an exhibition. Oxford, 1951, p43-7.

Macray, p110-23.

Sermons A collection of 570 English sermons of 17th-19th cent, bound in 26 v, purchased in 1850.

Macray, p354.

William Sherard (1659–1728), botanist and founder of the Chair of Botany, one of the benefactors of this collection now named after him and deposited in the Bodleian by the Department of Botany in 1960. It consists of 750 printed books, spanning four centuries (15th-18th), but mostly printed pre-1750, nearly half in the last 50 years of the 17th cent. It includes editions of all the major pre-Linnean botanical classics and catalogues of foreign botanical gardens, from the libraries of Jacob Bobart (1641–1719), William Sherard, John Sibthorp (1758–96), George Williams (1762–1834), S H Vines (1849–1934), G C Druce (1850–1931), and J B Davy (1870–1940). The books were essentially the working libraries of the donors, reflecting both their interests and, in the presentation copies, their connections with international botanical circles. There are also *c*480 ms volumes, consisting mainly of papers connected with the benefactors of the collection.

'Books and manuscripts from the Department of Botany', *BLR* 6 (1960), p581-3.

Shrivenham Collection Presented in 1945 by Shrivenham American University, the temporary American servicemen's University. A miscellaneous collection of over 400 textbooks of the 1930s and 1940s, including books on science, engineering, geography, American history and literature.

Bertram Shuttleworth Presented in 1934, 378 v including editions of Richard Brinsley Sheridan's plays, music for the plays and the songs in them, translations, and works on Sheridan, being editions and works not already in the Bodleian.

'Gift from Mr Bertram Shuttleworth', *BLR* 6 (1958), p393.

ϟ [Sigma] A collection of over 2,600 v of 16th-19th cent added to the library, and shelved in Selden End and the Selden Galleries, between 1826 and 1850.

SLAV. [Slavonic] A collection of 190 Slavonic books and books on Eastern Europe (19th cent).

George Smith (1871–1963), of Great Bedwyn, presented to the Bodleian his collection of early newsbooks, corantos and newspapers. The collection extends over the 16th-20th cent, and includes rare 16th and 17th cent newsbooks (including Civil War items), mainly English, though some items are foreign; 18th cent local newspapers; proclamations; and broadsides.

'George Smith donation', *BLR* (1953), p290.

Sutherland Collection In 1795 Alexander Hendras Sutherland started to grangerize Edward Hyde, First Earl of Clarendon's *History of the Rebellion* (1702–4) and *Life of Clarendon* (1759), and Bishop Gilbert Burnet's *History of his own times* (1722–34), with portraits of every person and place mentioned in the text or connected with the subject matter, and on his death (1820) the work was taken up by his widow. These grangerized copies, including both letterpress and engraved material, were presented by Mrs Sutherland to the Bodleian in 1837, but were transferred to the Ashmolean Museum (qv) in 1951. Mrs Sutherland also presented to the Bodleian 35 illustrated biographical and historical works, many also enriched with additional engravings, and these remain in the Bodleian, shelfmarked *Sutherland*.

Mrs C Sutherland, *Catalogue of the Sutherland Collection*, Oxford, 1837.

Supplement, 1838.

A catalogue of books purchased for the Bodleian... 1843 [With] List of works presented to the library by Mrs Sutherland. Oxford, (1843?).

'The transfer of the Sutherland Collection of prints and drawings', *BLR* 3 (1951), p115-16.

Macray, p331-5.

Craster, p113, 314.

Thomas Tanner (1674–1735), Fellow of All Souls (1696), Canon of Christ Church (1724), Bishop of St Asaph (1732–5), antiquary and ecclesiastical historian, bequeathed to the Bodleian his mss and such printed books, not already in the library, as the library should think fit to accept. The printed books, *c*960 in number, date from 15th-18th cent, but are mainly 16th and 17th cent. They include many early and important books, such as works printed by Caxton, and theological works by the Reformers and their opponents, many being scarce tracts in the vernacular.

Macray, p209-12.

Tauchnitz The collection of British authors, subsequently of British and American authors (though from the first American authors were included) was launched by Bernhard Tauchnitz jun. in Leipzig in 1841. Its aim was the publication, by special arrangement with the author or his representative, of favourite works by well-known authors, mainly for continental circulation, and as far as possible simultaneously with their appearance in England or America. The Tauchnitz text sometimes represented an earlier stage of the author's text than in the English edition. The greater part of the series was devoted to fiction, but it also contained a large number of works of history, biography, science, philosophy etc. By the end of the Second World War the series comprised almost 5,500 v, issued in over 4,000,000 copies. In 1980 the Bodleian's holdings of the series were gathered together as a collection, arranged by Tauchnitz no, and at the end of 1982 totalled *c*1,300 v. It is the library's intention to add to them.

The library holds a series of catalogues of the Tauchnitz edition, published by the firm over the period 1907—37.

'The Tauchnitz edition', *BLR* 10 (1981), p210-11.

TH. [*Theologia*] One part of the original Bodleian four-part classification by faculty or subject, in use in various forms over the period 1602—1789, and less frequently until about 1840. In the later years the distinction by faculty began to be disregarded and books were added where there was space on the shelves. The collection comprises *c*11,000 v of 16th-19th cent.

THEOL. [*Theology*] *c*30 folios and large quartos on theological subjects received among the new books between 1861 and 1883.

Ⓗ [*Theta*] Shelfmark used between 1840 and 1861 for multi-volume sets in quarto and octavo, between 1845 and 1861 for older books in folio, and between 1923 and 1936 for retrospective purchases of 18th and 19th cent English books. Over 5,500 v.

George Thorn-Drury, literary scholar, editor of the poets Randolph and Waller, and a specialist in the minor poets of the Restoration period. A collection of *c*70 v of late 17th cent English poetical texts and also works of reference, all heavily annotated by him, many grangerized and indexed, preserving intact the unpublished portion of Thorn-Drury's life's work, providing a mine of bibliographical information on the poetical writers of the Restoration and on those of an earlier and of a slightly later age. Purchased by the Friends of the Bodleian in 1931, with additions acquired later.

Craster, p277.

Paget Jackson Toynbee (1855—1932), Dante scholar, made donations to the Bodleian in 1912, 1913, 1916, 1917 and 1923. The 1912 donation, *c*360 works, includes numerous editions of the works of Boccaccio, mainly printed at Florence or Venice in 16th cent, and of Petrarch; works printed at Strawberry Hill; works from the library of Horace Walpole, 4th Earl of Orford, and works on Walpole and the Strawberry Hill Press. The 1913 donation consists of *c*375 v, largely Italian translations of the classics, 16th-19th cent, with many Aldine, Elzevier and Giunta editions. The 1916 donation consists of *c*350 v, mainly editions of Dante, 16th-19th cent. The 1917 donation is of 700 v of Dante editions, translations and commentaries, many of 19th and 20th cent. The 1923 donation is of *c*600 v of general Italian literature of 16th-20th cent. He bequeathed the remaining part of his library, expressing the wish that all his books relating to Dante should be included in the selection made from it: *c*1,300 v were selected.

'Chief accessions of printed books', *BQR* 2 (1918), p204.

'The Toynbee collection', *Ibid*, 4 (1923), p74-5.

Craster, p282.

Tractati Lutherani A collection of 538 v. Those numbered 1-126 consist of two series, each arranged chronologically: 84 v containing *c*1,670 Latin and German tracts by the German Reformers, 1518—50, including 640 by Luther, and a further collection of tracts, ranging in date from 1498—1629. To these two series have been added (vols numbered 127-538) works, mainly of 16th cent, but also some of 17th-19th cent, including editions of Luther's works.

Some account of Dr May's of Augsburg collection of tracts on the Reformation. [With catalogue, Ms. Bodleian shelfmark *R.6.212*].

M A Pegg, *A catalogue of German Reformation pamphlets, 1516—1546, in the libraries of Great Britain and Ireland.* (Bibliotheca bibliographica Aureliana, 45.) [With location in the Bodleian.] Baden Baden, 1973.

Trades A collection of 40 folios and large quartos on commercial and practical subjects received among the new books between 1861 and 1883.

Trinity College Collection Collected by Sir Charles Edward H Chadwyck-Healey, Bart (1845—1919), presented to Trinity College during World War II, and now deposited in the Bodleian. It contains over 80 editions of the Bible, mostly English of 16th and 17th cent, ranging from Coverdale of 1535 to the Doves Press edition of 1903, and including interesting association copies.

P Morgan, *Oxford libraries outside the Bodleian*, 2nd ed, Oxford, 1980, p142.

University College A collection of over 100 early printed and scarce works of 15th-17th cent presented to the Bodleian between 1923 and 1935 by the Master and Fellows of University College. Shelfmarked *Univ Coll*; a number of volumes on various subjects, discarded by

University College, are awaiting incorporation with the above (these comprise items apparently not in the Bodleian, and authors' presentation copies to the College and association copies); a collection of English 17th cent theological works, deposited in the Bodleian by University College, and shelfmarked *Univ II*. Entered in the Bodleian's Intercollegiate Catalogue of STC and Wing books only.

VET. [Vetera/Veteriora] Shelfmark used since 1937 for antiquarian accessions of the period 1501—1800 (since 1974, 1501—1850). Subdivided by country of printing (Great Britain and Ireland; Netherlands and Belgium; Denmark, Norway, Sweden and Iceland; Germany, Austria and Switzerland; France; Italy; Spain and Portugal; Russia, Poland and Hungary; Rest of Europe; North America; Rest of the world) and by period of printing (the period subdivisions being 1501—1600; 1601—40; 1541—1700; 1701—50; 1751—1800; 1801—50). The collection is estimated to include over 35,000 editions.

Sir Hugh Seymour Walpole (1884—1941), novelist, formed, and bequeathed to the Bodleian, a collection of printed books and mss containing over 1,300 v, mainly first editions, of the works of English writers of fiction, poetry and belles lettres published in the 1890s, and including a few books published a little before and after the 1890s in order to give a complete survey of the works of authors whose most characteristic work fell within that period. While most of the books concern the coteries of second rank writers, notably that which came to centre on the *Yellow Book*, there are fine copies of first editions of the more important writers such as Hardy and Kipling. The collection includes copies autographed by their authors, or having some association with the leading literary figures of the time. Many have notes by Walpole. The mss include autograph letters, the bulk of the ms material concerning three authors, William Watson, Stephen Phillips and Frederick Rolfe, Baron Corvo.

'Sir Hugh Walpole's "Nineties" collection', *BLR* 2 (1942), p40-1.

Craster, p279.

Anthony Wood (1632—95), antiquary and historian. In 1695 Wood's mss, and such of his printed books and pamphlets as were not already in that institution were deposited in the library of the Ashmolean Museum, and were transferred to the Bodleian in 1860. There are *c*960 printed volumes, representing a far greater number of printed pieces, mainly of 17th cent, strong in books printed at Oxford, or written by Oxford men, and in ephemeral and vernacular items not collected by the Bodleian in the 17th cent. Included are: a series of almanacs dated 1629—95, the interleaved volumes 1657—95 with Wood's diaries written in them; newspapers and literary periodicals; pamphlets, mainly concerned with contemporary English and Irish history, also many Oxford pamphlets (1572—1691); chapbooks, ballads and poems; book catalogues and book prospectuses.

Index to Wood's almanacs and diaries (alphabetical by author/title): (Bodleian shelfmark *R.6.224*).

Andrew Clark, 'The Wood collection of manuscripts and printed books, *The life and times of Anthony Wood, described by himself, collected from his diaries'* [&c], Oxford Hist Soc, v 19, i (1891), p6-21.

Craster, p68-9, 77.

R T Gunther, 'The Ashmole printed books', *BQR* 6 (1930), p193-5.

[Yearbooks] A collection of octavo volumes added in the years 1824—50, the shelfmark being the last two numerals of the year separated by a stop from a running number, the books in each year having been arranged in alphabetical order of author or title. Over 32,000 v 1824—49, the 2,000 v in 1850 having been moved to the current classification. Books on all subjects, including fiction. No serials.

Unnamed Collection A one and two-figure classification scheme, running from 1 through 20, 30 etc to 90, was in use 1861—83 to classify older books purchased in octavo and small quarto into 10 subdivisions, including: theology (over 1,300 v), medicine (58 v), arts and trades (39 v), law (260 v), now housed at Law Library, mathematics and physics (55 v), history (over 700 v), literature (270 v), poetry (190 v), and philology (180 v). Books of 16th-19th cent.

B **Department of Oriental Books**

Backhouse Collection Made by Sir Edmund Backhouse in Peking at the turn of the century, and donated to the Bodleian Library in stages between 1913 and 1922, the collection contains *c*850 items, mostly printed books, of which *c*120 are Ming editions. There are 20 mss, and 76 items of calligraphy and painting. The collection is closed.

A catalogue of the old Chinese books in the Bodleian Library, vol 1 *The Backhouse Collection* by David Helliwell. Bodleian Library, Oxford, 1983.

Hugh Trevor-Roper, *A hidden life, the enigma of Sir Edmund Backhouse*. London, 1976. (Two chapters of this biography deal with the donation of the collection to the library. There is no reliable account of the contents of the collection.)

Oppenheimer Collection Formed by David Oppenheimer, born Worms 1667, became Chief Rabbi at Prague, died there 1735. His library of Hebrew printed books and mss passed to a son and afterwards to Isaak Berend Salomon at Hamburg. Purchased by the Bodleian Library 1829, it contains *c*4,350 v covering the entire range of Hebrew literature from the Bible up to early 18th cent. Particularly strong in Bible editions with commentaries, rabbinics, service-books. *c*60 Hebrew incunabula. Includes *c*70 per cent of all products of the first century of Yiddish printing, say from the 1530s to 1650. A set of the first edition of the Talmud printed by Daniel Bomberg in Venice, and a complete Talmud on vellum in 24 v (Berlin and Frankfurt a O, 1715—21).

Collectio Davidis, compiled by I Metz, provided with a

Latin translation by E Emden. (Hamburg, 1826).

Referred to in all the major Jewish encyclopaedias. Innumerable other references.

Sinica Collection Recently formed, to include all books in Chinese acquired from 17th-19th cent, as well as modern acquisitions of rare books, including miscellaneous acquisitions of 17th and 18th cent, and the collections of Edwin Evans, acquired in 1856, and Alexander Wylie, purchased 1882. There are *c*2,500 items, mostly printed books, including *c*100 Ming editions and a collection of *c*900 19th cent Protestant missionary publications. There are a few unique copies of late Ming commercial editions. The collection is added to from either discoveries of rare books in the modern Chinese collection, or from occasional purchases.

There is no cat, but it is intended to publish the collection in stages.

Wardrop Collection Formed by Sir Oliver Wardrop (1864–1948) and his sister Marjory (1869–1909). Following his sister's death, Sir Oliver, who was already concerned with the creation at Oxford University of a fund for the encouragement of Georgian studies presented the entire collection to the Bodleian. In subsequent years the collection was augmented by further books and mss acquired by Sir Oliver or through the Wardrop Fund. The collection was kept separate from the library's existing 'Georgica' collection, which also continued to grow. The collection consists of 1,454 items, of which 215 are periodicals and 73 are series. Included are 74 mss in the category of texts and collections of Georgian literature. It contains mss of the following nature: (i) the aforementioned texts and collections of Georgian books; (ii) papers relating to these; (iii) the correspondence and other papers of Sir Oliver and Marjory Wardrop either in Georgian or relating to Georgia. The earliest ms item is an 8th cent palimpsest. The 11th cent Menologion is the earliest complete ms. Rustaveli's epic *The man in the panther skin* appears in the collection in the printed edition published by King Vahtang in 1712 and also in the form of two illuminated mss, both believed to be of the 17th cent.

Barrett (David). *Catalogue of the Wardrop collection and of other Georgian books and manuscripts in the Bodleian Library*. (Oxford, 1973.)

The introduction to the above cat. Also, D M Lang: 'Georgian studies in Oxford' in *Oxford Slavonic papers*, 6, 1955.

With the publication of the Barrett *Catalogue* the collection was closed, and all further accessions, whatever their origins, were added to 'Georgica'.

C Law Library

The library contains the following collections:

(i) *Charles Viner* (1678–1756), jurist, founder of the Vinerian Professorship, compiler of *Abridgment of law and equity* (23 v, 1742–53). His working library, mainly of legal works, bequeathed to the Radcliffe Library, incorporated into the Bodleian in 1860, and now housed in the Bodleian Law Library. The library, taken over from the Radcliffe Library, consisted of 542 printed volumes and 38 mss. The mss are now housed in the Bodleian. 61 printed volumes were subsequently withdrawn from the collection as having been incorrectly included. 97 v are duplicate copies of Viner's *Abridgment*. The majority of the works are of 17th and first half of 18th cent, with some 16th cent works. Many volumes carry Viner's signature and annotations in his hand.

(ii) *Class 35* (Law) of the one- and two-figure classification scheme in use in the Bodleian from 1861–83, mainly to classify older books purchased in octavo and small quarto. Now housed in the Bodleian Law Library, with the original shelfmarks. Over 260 v, some containing several titles, dating from the 16th-19th cent.

(iii) *Over 1,600 books* originally shelfmarked *Jur* (one part of the original Bodleian classification by faculty) are now shelved in the Bodleian Law Library, though no longer by the original shelfmark. Mainly books printed after 1800, though there are some of 16th-18th cent.

D Radcliffe Science Library

The scientific, medical and mathematics library of the University, and a dependent library of the Bodleian. Began its existence as the Radcliffe Library, housed in the Radcliffe Camera (1749–1860). The Radcliffe Trustees in 1927 presented the Radcliffe Library to the University. (The Trustees had in 1893 handed over to the Bodleian those books on non-scientific subjects which the Bodleian cared to take, and sold non-scientific works not wanted by the Bodleian.)

The Rare Book Collection in the library comprises the *Committee Room* and the *Rare Book Room Collections*, both of Radcliffe Library origin. The part of the Committee Room Collection, shelfmarked *CR.A-CR.M*, consists of over 250 works on botany and natural history, including platebooks, English and foreign, mostly dating from the 18th and 19th cent, with some of the 17th and 20th cent. The part of the Committee Room Collection shelfmarked *CR.N-CR.S* consists of over 800 works printed pre-1850, English and foreign, on the natural sciences and medicine, taken out of the stack in the late 1970s (though the stack still contains many pre-1850 volumes). Some of these are of Bodleian (as opposed to Radcliffe Library) origin.

The Rare Book Room Collection, shelfmarked *RR*, consists of over 620 titles of the 15th-20th cent, English and foreign, mainly on the natural sciences and medicine. Some of these were bequeathed to the Radcliffe Library by James Gibbs (1682–1754) and Richard Frewin (1681?–1761).

All the titles in the Rare Book Collection are entered in the main Radcliffe Science Library cat. The minority of Bodleian origin are entered also in the Bodleian General Cat of Printed Books; those of Radcliffe origin are entered in the Bodleian's revised pre-1920 cat.

Sir Henry Wentworth Acland (1815–1900), physician, Fellow of All Souls (1840), Radcliffe Librarian (1851), Regius Professor of Medicine (1858), presented to the Radcliffe Library 40 v containing *c*640 pamphlets, published between *c*1830 and 1900, mainly in the English language, on medical subjects. Arranged by subject. Each volume includes a list of contents.

No handlist.

Catalogued in the Radcliffe Science Library cat and in the Bodleian's Revised pre-1920 cat.

E Rhodes House Library

This is a dependent library of the Bodleian specializing in the history and current affairs—political, economic and social—of the British Commonwealth and former British colonial territories, of the United States of America, and of the sub-Saharan Africa, including the offshore islands. Its scope includes Sri Lanka. (It does not cover creative literature, or scientific, linguistic and philological works, which will be found in other parts of the Bodleian.) The total stock exceeds 300,000 v. Books dealing with the Library's territories and published after 1760 have been transferred from the Bodleian to Rhodes House library. Purchases are made to fill gaps in the older collections.

Sir Hannibal Publius Scicluna (1880–1981), holder of many offices in the civil and academic administration of Malta (not least the librarianship of the Royal Malta Library), presented in 1937 to the Rhodes Trustees for housing in Rhodes House Library, his collection of Melitensia. It was described then as containing 'some 1,200 works on the history of the Order of St John of Jerusalem and on the history of these islands', including the most important works on the local archaeology, natural history, folklore, language, genealogy and travel, and the best such collection after that belonging to the Royal Malta Library. Sir Hannibal continued to donate books to the end of his life, and Lady Scicluna, who died in 1977, left the library and a sum of money to develop the collection by appropriate purchases. The collection now numbers over 2,200 v, dating from the 16th-20th cent. Plans are being made to ensure that the collection is developed in the way the original benefactor would have wished.

Cat by author on cards.

Most books have entries in the cat of Rhodes House Library.

'Sir Hannibal Scicluna', *BLR* 11 (1982), p2-3.

F Private Collections

Not in Bodleian but application (stating reasons) from bona fide researchers for further information or access to the following private collections should be made initially to the Librarian, Bodleian Library, Oxford OX1 3BG.

I A collection made up of *c*300 v with 1 STC and 6 Wing items. It covers 18th cent philosophy, law, theology and husbandry; 19th cent hunting, racing etc, including the *Racing Calendar* 1774–1899. A number of the books bear the bookplates and ownership inscriptions of members of the Chauncy and Carter families, early owners of Edgcote.

II A collection formed by Charles Eyston (1667–1721), antiquary and friend of Thomas Hearne, and added to by subsequent members of the Eyston family. It includes *c*2,500 items with a few incunabula, but is mainly 17th cent. Strong Catholic emphasis: doctrinal, theological, liturgical, political, historical. (Access to this collection is through Dr D M Rogers, Bodleian Library, Oxford.)

Botany School, University of Oxford, South Parks Road, Oxford OX1 3RA. Tel (0865) 53391. Open, Term: 9 am-7 pm; Vacation: 9 am-5.30 pm. Admission by application to the Librarian. Photocopying, microfiche reader, inter-library loans, author/subject catalogues.

Sherard Collection Now deposited in the Bodleian Library, Oxford (qv); remaining in the Department Library are a few early books and a collection of *c*15,000 reprints, many pre-1850. The history of the Department of Botany is closely linked to that of the Botanic Garden, founded by Henry Denvers, first Earl of Danby, in 1621. Over the years a large collection of mss and printed books has been built up. Total stock of the Library is *c*27,500, with 25 STC items.

Card cat.

Brasenose College Library, Radcliffe Square, Oxford. Tel (0865) 248641 Ext 27. Open to non-members of the College, Mon-Fri 9.30 am-12.45 pm, 2.15-5.30 pm. Visiting scholars who require to consult rare books or documents are admitted by arrangement with the Librarian.

Brasenose College Library The library contains *c*40,000 v, with 83 incunabula; and 753 STC books; and a total of *c*3,000 pre-1641 books. The printed book collections have been built up over the centuries by numerous gifts and bequests from members and a certain amount of steady purchasing from the 17th cent onwards. The printed books given by the founders (William Smyth, *d*1514, Bishop of Lincoln, and Sir Richard Sutton, *d*1524) and others in the first half of the 16th cent were neither so numerous nor impressive as those acquired by other colleges, and the definite identification of books now on the shelves with recorded donors can only be assumed in many cases. The collections include: *c*30 v of the latest editions of the Fathers of the Church, acquired possibly by purchase in the mid-16th cent; *c*500 v, nearly all 16th and 17th cent theological works, presented by Henry Mason (*d*1647), and three smaller collections of similar content received from Edmund Leigh, fellow 1611–41, William Hutchings, Vice-Principal 1642–7, and Samuel Radcliffe (*d*1648), Principal 1614–48; a remarkable library, rich in 18th cent theological, philosophical and classical works, bequeathed by Francis Yarborough, Principal 1745–70, much of the classical literature annotated by a former owner, Christopher Wasse (*d*1690) of Queens' College, Cambridge; books bequeathed by Ralph Cawley, Principal 1770–7, and John Holmes (*d*1795), a Fellow; a collection of 19th cent theology, classics and pamphlets bequeathed by Albert Watson (1829–1904), Principal 1886–9; a collection, strong in Roman history, given by the widow of H F Pelham (1847–1907), Camden Professor of Ancient History; a collection of law books left by W T S Stallybrass (1883–1948), Principal 1936–48; some 18th cent natural history books, given by S P Duval in 1942; a collection of published works of members of the College, based on the collection made by W E Buckley (1818–92), purchased after his death, and actively maintained.

Cat on cards.

Earlier cats survive.

Separate card cat of books printed before 1641.

W E Buckley's own cat of Brasenose authors, continued until *c*1958.

Slips for all books and many fragments printed before 1601, written by Robert Proctor (1868–1903), the incunabulist, and arranged by place and printer in three sequences.

R W Jeffery, (A survey of the rarer early printed books), *The Brazen nose* v (1933) p314-27.

Campion Hall, Oxford OX1 1QS. Tel (0865) 240861. Admission by application to the Librarian.

Campion Hall is a private hall for members of the Society of Jesus established in 1896. It contains, besides a working library, a small collection of older printed books, including *c*200 books printed before 1800, mainly of a theological or classical nature, together with Catholic polemics. St Edmund Campion is represented in several early and scarce editions. The library contains 3 incunabula; 7 STC books; 39 pre-1641 foreign books and 29 Wing books.

Centre for Medieval and Renaissance Studies, St Michael's Hall, Shoe Lane, Oxford OX1 2DP. Tel (0865) 241071. Admission on written permission from the Librarian or from the Principal. Microform reader; photocopying machine; slide projector available.

The original working library was supplied by the founder, Dr J E Feneley in 1975. The library is increased annually by purchase and benefaction. The library is rebuilding, and has a stock of *c*20,000 v.

The Rare Book Collection is based on the gift of books in 1979 from the Society of St John the Evangelist, Marston Street, Oxford (known as the Cowley Fathers), mainly theological, liturgical, philosophical and historical, including 1 incunabulum; 56 pre-1640 foreign books, some not represented elsewhere in Oxford; 15 Wing books; and a substantial number of 17th and 18th cent books printed in England and on the Continent, many with interesting provenances (eg Continental monasteries and convents).

The Thornton-Jones Library, presented by Alun Thornton-Jones in 1981. It includes books printed in England and on the Continent pre-1700; 18th cent English and continental books, mainly in the classics; some first editions of 20th cent English literature, and books with fine bindings.

The Geraldine Norman Collection of art catalogues given in 1981. *c*10,000 are catalogues produced by the major auction houses in England, Europe and America from 1968 to the present. Being added to.

Card cat.

Published cat is in preparation for 1984.

Christ Church Library, Christ Church, Oxford. Tel (0865) 243957. Open to bona fide scholars by prior written application.

Christ Church Library Total stock *c*130,000, including 96 incunabula and 2,750 STC books. The library is the largest for research material in Oxford outside the Bodleian. It contains older works on practically all subjects, but is particularly rich in music, theology, classics, travel, numismatics, early science and medicine, and Hebrew studies. The large pamphlet collection has many rare items, especially of the 17th and 18th cent, but also some of the 16th cent. The number of printed plays and poetry is considerable.

The rare book collections include: 500 v on many subjects, including rare ephemeral publications, bequeathed by Robert Burton (1577–1640) (author of the *Anatomy of Melancholy* and Librarian from 1620), after the Bodleian had had first choice; Otho Nicholson in 1614 made the first substantial benefaction (£100), spent mainly on theology; as with some other sections of the library which bear the names of individual donors, shelves headed 'Nicholson' contain later books. A collection of books in Hebrew, strong in grammars and dictionaries, has been built up since 1682 with an annuity (originally £5) left by John Morris, Regius Professor of Hebrew (1626–48), who left his books as the basis of the collection; the collection reflects the purchasing policies of successive Regius Professors of Hebrew.

Henry Aldrich, Dean (1689–1710) bequeathed *c*3,000 theological, classical, mathematical, architectural and travel books, with some drama and poetry, a collection of Quaker, Civil War and Commonwealth tracts (including newspapers) bought from Francis Bugg, 8,000 pieces of 16th and 17th cent music by English and foreign composers, and over 2,000 engravings, European and English (housed in Christ Church Picture Gallery). Aldrich expressed the wish that his nephew, Charles, should be given any duplicates, a term loosely interpreted at the time. Charles was Rector of Henley-on-Thames from 1709 till his death in 1737, leaving his books to found a parochial library from which a number of books were brought to Christ Church on permanent loan in 1909, and a few more were transferred in 1942. (The residue was deposited in Reading University Library in 1957.)

In 1722, Lewis Atterbury, brother of Francis (Dean 1711–13), gave between 3,000 and 4,000 pamphlets, ranging from the early-17th cent to contemporary publications; William Stratford (1672–1729), a Canon, left a varied collection of 2,000 v, including books on mathematics, natural science, theology, philosophy, law, history and literature, as well as some 16th cent English books; Charles Boyle, Fourth Earl of Orrery (1676–1731) left a general library of 2,500 v, including many medical and scientific works in both English and French; William Wake, Archbishop of Canterbury (1657–1737) bequeathed, in addition to papers and manuscripts, *c*5,000 printed books, strong in theology, including many early printed books, finely bound large paper and presentation copies from authors, European as well as English (they are shelved according to the shelfmarks assigned by Wake himself). The Library has acquired by gift and purchase, and holds on deposit from the Dodgson and Liddell families, copies of rare pamphlets by C L Dodgson (1832–98) ('Lewis Carroll') and of numerous translations of Carroll's 'Alice' works; Frederick York Powell (1850–1904) bequeathed *c*800 v of Icelandic and Scandinavian literature, many given to him by Gudbrandr Vigfusson (1828–89). The early Bibles and more valuable printed works remain in Christ Church, the other volumes have been deposited in the English Faculty Library in Oxford. The widow of W G Rutherford (1853–1907), Headmaster of Westminster School, presented in 1908 *c*500 v on classical literature, strong in editions of, and works on Aristophanes; Henry Julian White (1859–1934, Dean from 1920) left his working library (including books bequeathed to him by John Wordsworth, Bishop of Salisbury, in 1911) and papers which he had used for his edition of the Vulgate. The widow of Kenneth Gibbs (1856–1935), Archdeacon of St Albans, presented in 1946 a collection of liturgical texts, including many early editions, and especially Books of Common Prayer, with many drafts and papers connected with Prayer Book revision in the 1920s. In 1946 Christ Church took over the care and maintenance of the separate library bequeathed by Richard Allestree in 1681 for the use of the Regius Professor of Divinity: it has a bias towards theology, but includes books on classics, science, medicine, mathematics and patristics, 138 books were formerly owned by Allestree's friend Henry Hammond (1605–60); Francis Bridgford Brady presented in 1977 English plays and theatrical ephemera, especially engraved portraits of performers and playbills of 18th-20th cent, and also a collection of mainly 19th cent Japanese theatrical prints, some of which have been presented to the Ashmolean Museum.

The Parochial Library of Wotton-under-Edge, Gloucestershire, is deposited. John Okes (*d*1710) left it to his native place. It contains *c*300 v, chiefly 17th cent theology, and with a bias towards Oriental studies. Many of the books bear the names of members of the Cholmondely family, patron of Okes's living at Whitegate, Cheshire. Some contain prices.

Ms author cat of printed books.

Ms card cat of pamphlets of the Allestree library and of the Wotton-under-Edge library.

Typed card cat of the Brady Collection.

A Hiff, *Catalogue of the printed music prior to 1801 now in the Library of Christ Church, Oxford* (1919): annotated copy. These items are also included in E B Schnapper, *The British Union Catalogue of early music printed before 1801* (1957).

A E Cowley (Sir), *A concise catalogue of the Hebrew printed books in the Bodleian Library* (1929), annotated with relevant holdings.

W G Hiscock, *The Christ Church supplement to Wing's Short-title catalogue 1641–1700* (1956).

——*The Christ Church holdings in Wing's Short-title catalogue 1641–1700 of which less than five copies are recorded in the United Kingdom* (1956) (Typescript).

Earlier cats survive, including separate cats of the Aldrich, Stratford, Orrery and Wake benefactions, and lists of music in the Aldrich bequest made by Charles Burney and William Boyce *c*1778.

W G Hiscock, *A Christ Church miscellany* (Oxford, 1946).

H R Trevor-Roper, *Christ Church, Oxford: the portrait of a College*, 2nd ed 1973, p21-4.

W Osler (Sir), 'The library of Robert Burton', *Oxford Bibliographical Soc Proceedings and Papers* I (1926), p182-90.

'Two lists of Burton's books, ed by S Gibson and F R P Needham', *Ibid*, p222-246.

The catalogue of the Old Library at Henley-on-Thames..., London, 1852. A list of 'Books retained by Christ Church, 1909' is in Reading University Library.

M Chichester, 'Later development of the Christ Church Library, Oxford', *Library History*, vol 5, no 4 (1980), p109-17.

Commonwealth Forestry Institute, South Parks Road, Oxford OX1 3RB. Tel (0865) 511431 Ext 254. Open (Term) Mon-Fri 9 am-7 pm; Sat 9 am-12 noon. (Vacation) Mon-Fri only 9 am-1 pm, 2.15-5 pm. Admission to all by prior appointment. Reference only; microform reader/printer; photocopying facilities.

Schlich Collection The library of the first Oxford Professor of Forestry, Sir William Schlich (1840–1925) formed the basis of the present Forestry Library. Items bearing Schlich's autograph were removed from the general collection to form this special collection, which totals *c*500 bound v. They include 19th cent German Forestry Journals; a few 17th and 18th cent printed books; 7 Wing items; early 20th cent general forestry textbooks and journals. The books in the main library total *c*19,200, many of which are rare in the sense that they are difficult to obtain.

Included in the main library card cat. No separate lists.

E F Hemmings, 'The Forest Library at Oxford', *Proc British Soc for Inter Bibl* viii (1946), p56-63.

——'The Forestry Library', *Oxford Univ Lib Bull* no 6 (1977), p4-6.

List of Periodicals and Serials in the Forestry Library, 3rd ed (1968).

Corpus Christi College, Merton Street, Oxford OX1 1JF. Tel (0865) 249431. Open Mon-Fri 9 am-5 pm (for visitors). Admission by application (preferably written) only. Xerox (but most probably *not* for early books); ultraviolet magnifier; microfilm reader.

Corpus Christi College Library Stock totals *c*60,000, including 15,000 early printed books; 260 incunabula and 1,931 STC items. The rare book collections include printed books dealing with contemporary classical and theological studies given by the founder, Richard Foxe (1448?–1528), a statesman cleric, and by John Claimond (1457?–1537), the first President; books reflecting an interest in the Protestant theology of the time bequeathed by Thomas Greneway (*d*1571), the fifth President; more than 100 books, mostly Biblical, and including a few botanical, scientific and geographical works, left by John Rainolds (1549–1607), President 1598–1607; *c*750 items on all subjects, but including ephemeral English printed works concerned with astrology, farriery, medicine and the light reading of the time, and books on antiquarian matters and Greek studies, bequeathed by Brian Twyne (*c*1580–1644), Reader in Greek at Corpus and the first Keeper of the University Archives; Civil War and other 17th cent tracts in the bequests of Richard Samwayes (*c*1625–69), fellow, and John Rosewell (*d*1684), Headmaster of Eton; medical books bequeathed by William Creed (*d*1711); ephemeral pamphlets and theology left by Thomas Turner (1645–1714), President 1688–1714; scientific books given in 1719 by Cuthbert Ellison; a collection on Italian history and topography, including 30 v of sketches and drawings, formed by Henry Hare, third Baron Coleraine (1693–1749) and his father; part of the historical library formed by Robert Laing (later Cuthbert Shields) (*d*1908), a fellow; the philosophical collection of Shadworth Hodgson (1832–1912), a fellow; many of the books, chiefly of historical interest, of Charles Plummer (1851–1928); a select collection of works on the Peninsular War in a bequest from Askell Benton (1880–1918); a group of early editions of works by Erasmus, formerly owned by the editor of his letters, P S Allen (1869–1933), President 1924–33; the library for the special use of holders of the Corpus Professorship of Latin bequeathed by John Conington (1825–69) and deposited in 1957; a small collection of works by *alumni*, which is being added to; printed fragments removed from bindings and arranged in albums by R G C Proctor and J G Milne in the 1890s.

Cat on cards.

Earlier cats and shelflists survive.

Some indices of former owners and bindings made by J G Milne.

J R Liddell, *The library of Corpus Christi College, 1517–1617* (B Litt thesis, Oxford, 1933).

——'The library of Corpus Christi College, Oxford, in the sixteenth century', *The Library*, 4th ser, XVIII (1938), p385-416.

J G Milne, *The early history of Corpus Christi College, Oxford* (Oxford 1946). Chap 4 'The Library', p37-53, mentions some of the outstanding books and the donors.

R F Ovenell, 'Brian Twyne's library', *Oxford Bibliographical Soc Publications* new ser IV (1952), p1-42.

R Steele, *A bibliography of the Royal proclamations of the Tudor and Stuart sovereigns, 1485–1714*. 2 v, Oxford, 1910 (with locations in Corpus Christi College Library).

Department of Agricultural Science, Parks Road, Oxford OX1 3PF. Tel (0865) 57245. Open (Term) 9 am-1 pm, 2-6.30 pm; (Vacation) 9 am-1 pm, 2.30-5.30 pm. Admission by arrangement on written application to Head of Department.

The Department's library includes *c*150 v, pre-1851 of miscellaneous works on agriculture, including sets of 19th cent periodicals and official reports, mainly of British interest. They include 2 STC; 11 pre-1641 foreign books and 9 Wing items. The collection also includes volumes from the library of John Sibthorp (1758–96).

Department of the History of Art, 35 Beaumont Street, Oxford. Tel (0865) 57262. Open 9.30 am-1 pm, 2-5 pm. Researchers are advised to use the library out of Term, and should apply, in writing, to the Librarian. No lending; restricted photo-photocopying facilities.

The library was established in 1955 and now contains *c*400 rare books; 200 are pre-1700, printed chiefly in Italy. Smaller books of 18th and 19th cent items. Several were formerly owned by Sir William Stirling Maxwell (1818–78). The library includes a remarkable collection of French Salons Criticism of the 18th and 19th cent. There are 1 STC; 121 pre-1641 foreign books and 10 Wing items.

Card cat, of which a duplicate is kept in the Western Art Library Ashmolean Museum.

Entries are also incorporated into the Main Library cat of the Ashmolean Museum.

Edward Grey Institute of Field Ornithology, Zoology Department, Oxford University, South Parks Road, Oxford. Tel (0865) 56789 Ext 549. Open weekdays, 9.30 am-1 pm, 2.15-6 pm. Admission to members of Oxford University,

British Ornithologists Union; others by prior arrangement with the Librarian. Reference only. Photocopying facilities available.

Alexander Library The Institute was set up by the British Trust for Ornithology, and received University status some years later, in 1938. The library was founded on the personal collection of W B Alexander (1885–1965), the Institute's first director, and in his retirement, its librarian. It has been added to consistently ever since. It now forms the finest collection of books on birds, certainly in Europe at least. It contains *c*10,000 v (including journals), of which *c*600 are scarce, of these 256 were published before 1851, and include 1 STC; 6 pre-1641 foreign books and 17 Wing items. The entire collection relates to ornithology.

Author cat.

English Faculty Library, St Cross Building, Manor Road, Oxford OX1 3UQ. Tel (0865) 249631. Open to members of the University reading (or teaching) for an Oxford degree in English. Others may be admitted at the discretion of the Library Committee, on written application to the Librarian in advance, giving their credentials and special reasons for wishing to use the Faculty Library. There are some old-style microfilm readers and a photocopier which is not suitable for making copies from early printed books.

General All rare books are on closed access, and nearly all in one classified sequence. None can normally be borrowed. Rare books and other special material have been added more or less steadily by purchase, gift or bequest ever since the foundation of the library in 1914, but it is now largely dependent on benefactions for additional rariora.

Two notable early accessions were the libraries of Professor A S Napier (1853–1916) and Professor Sir Walter Raleigh (1861–1922), both collections being bought to commemorate their former owners. The Napier Library was mainly concerned with Anglo-Saxon and Germanic philology, and included many late 19th cent German dissertations and offprints (kept together as a collection), some 16th, 17th and 18th cent works on Anglo-Saxon (eg Napier's annotated copy of Hickes's 'Thesaurus', 1703–5), and an archive of miscellaneous letters and papers (handlisted) concerning Napier's own work on English language, his appointment to the Merton Professorship, and the early days of the English School at Oxford.

Early printed books from Raleigh's library formed the foundation of the English Library's holdings of English literary authors in contemporary and early editions. Some discriminating purchases of 17th and 18th cent books, made mainly in the 1920s, strengthened this collection. Brief lists of books presented to the library can be found in an 'Album Benefactorum' for 1914–33 and some later records of accessions.

Donors include the following: Prof N H K A Coghill (1899–1980) who, with his brother Sir Patrick Coghill, presented in 1970 a nearly complete set of first editions of the works of 'Somerville and Ross', many of them association copies: Sir W A Craigie (1867–1957); Professor H J Davis. (1893–1967) who gave and bequeathed many books from his Swift collection, and whose working papers (mainly correspondence and notes relating to lectures and publications) are divided between the English and the Bodleian Libraries; Dr P Simpson (1865–1962), librarian 1914–34, who donated many books from his own collection, including editions of Ben Jonson's works. A small collection of working copies of books of early English and Celtic interest from the library of Prof J R R Tolkien (1892–1973), presented by his son Christopher, is housed separately from the general stock of rariora.

There are *c*7,000 v in 'General Stock' sequence of rariora. The collection is strong in editions of 17th and 18th cent English literary authors, eg Burton, Dryden, Jonson, Milton, Pope and Swift. There are over 250 STC items and over 50 18th cent journals in runs of varying length.

Card cat entries, and classified shelflists (available on application). Separate handlist for Napier archive.

J Harker, 'The historical development of the English Faculty Library', Oxford Ealing College of Higher Education (1980).

Vigfússon-York Powell collection of Icelandic and Scandinavian works The joint library of two great scholars, Dr Guodbrandr Vigfússon (1828–89) and Prof F York Powell (1850–1904), bequeathed by York Powell to Christ Church, and deposited by the college in the English Library on loan in 1957. It contains over 1,000 v and 370 pamphlets. Strong in printed editions of Icelandic sagas, with a number of early imprints. Many of the books have been extensively annotated by their two previous owners. The early Bibles and more valuable printed works and manuscripts are in Christ Church Library.

Card cat which is incorporated in the cat of the books in the Icelandic Seminar Room and Library (the Turville-Petre Room).

Handlist compiled by C Phillips in 1978.

W P Ker (1855–1923) collection of Scandinavian books Bequeathed to All Souls College in 1923, placed on deposit in the Library of the Taylor Institution in 1953, transferred on similar terms to the English Library in 1977. The collection contains over 500 items, including a small number of books published pre-1851, not separated from the rest of the collection; also a box of 51 ephemera not yet catalogued.

Separate card cat, plus handlist and shelflist (based on card cat).

Turville-Petre Library Professor E O G Turville-Petre's (1908–78) own collection of books on Icelandic and closely related subjects, bequeathed to the University, and placed in the English Library in 1981. It contains *c*2,000 v and *c*600 pamphlets, mainly working copies of post-1850 books, but also some earlier material, including 1775 *Sagan af Gunnlaugi Ormstungu* from the library of William Morris.

Not yet cat.

Meyerstein Collection Assembled by the literary executors of E H W Mayerstein (1889–1952), poet, novelist, biographer of Chatterton, and former member of Magdalen College, and deposited in the English Library as a memorial to him. There are 40 boxes of papers and a nearly-complete collection of Meyerstein's published writings, some of them in multiple copies. Besides the printed works, there are mss and typescripts (top copies or carbons) of published or unpublished, proofs, copies of letters, collections of family photographs, portraits (originals and copies), and other memorabilia.

Separate handlist, compiled in 1976.

Owen Collection The personal library of Wilfred Owen (1893–1918). Some of his mss and other possessions, family relics and related material, were preserved by Wilfred's mother, Susan Owen and his brother Harold Owen (1897–1971), who added further papers, many press-cuttings and correspondence about Wilfred's and his own writings. This archive was presented to the University for the English Library by Harold's widow, Mrs Phyllis Owen, in 1975. Further mss, including 29 letters and postcards, 5 drafts of poems and many transcripts, were presented in 1978 by Mr E L Gunston, Wilfred's cousin.

Wilfred Owen's library contains over 300 books, many of them annotated, and a nearly complete run of *The Hydra*, nos 1-(NS)9 (1917–8). When all the mss concerned have been deposited in the English Library, there will be over 400 sheets of holograph verse and prose, plus letters and cards written by, and to, Wilfred, and later letters from members of his circle or editors, eg Siegfried Sassoon (1886–1967), Edmund Blunden (1896–1974) to Susan and Harold Owen. Press cuttings and other miscellaneous papers relating to the Owen family occupy over 30 boxes.

Handlist, not fully compiled yet.

J Stallworthy, *Wilfred Owen*, OUP, 1974, p308-23.

D Hibberd, 'Wilfred Owen's Library: some additional items', *Notes and Queries*, NS 24 (1977), p447-8.

Exeter College, Oxford OX1 3DP. Tel (0865) 244681. Open weekdays 9 am-5 pm. Admission by written application to the Librarian. Photocopying facilities.

The College Library contains *c*61,000 v, including 79 incunabula, 759 STC items and *c*3,000 Wing titles. The rare books collections include: a few medical works left by John Dotyn, a Somerset clergyman, in 1561; a set of the Latin Fathers given by Sir William Petre, statesman and ambassador, in 1567; the library, covering a wide range of interests beyond theology, left by Samuel Conant in 1719; the bequest, strong in classical authors, of Edward Richards, 1729; the extensive and miscellaneous bequest of Joseph Sandford, 1774; the notable collection of Hebrew, Talmudic and early Christian literature, with relevant secondary works of Alfred Edersheim (1825–89), presented by his widow, the Hebrew section is on permanent loan in the Library of the Oriental Institute (shelflist available); books printed or published in Britain pre-1641 are shelved in a separate sequence arranged by the STC number of the first item in each volume. Books printed abroad pre-1601 are arranged by place of printing.

Cat on cards in two sequences: for books on open shelves, and for books in stack.

Separate shelflist of Edersheim collections.

Earlier cats survive.

C W Boase, *Registrum Colleii Exoniensis. Register of Exeter College, Oxford...*, New ed (Oxford Historical Society, xxvii), 1894, ppclxv-clxix.

Greyfriars, Iffley Road, Oxford OX4 1SB. Tel (0865) 243694. Admission by prior written application to the Librarian.

Greyfriars library includes (a) a small specialist library, chiefly concerned with Franciscan history and thought, based on the collection of A G Little (1863–1945), the historian of the Franciscan Order in Britain, given by his widow in 1949. It includes nearly 100 items printed pre-1700, among which are several rare editions of Franciscan devotional works; (b) an extensive range of Catholic pamphlets, mainly concerned with educational and sociological questions in the early years of the 20th cent, given by L A St L Toke (1871–1944); (c) a collection of books on Egyptian, Syrian and Coptic thought and belief, presented by S W Allen (1844–1908), Bishop of Shrewsbury.

The library has 11 STC books; 57 pre-1641 foreign books; and 12 Wing items.

Hertford College, Catte Street, Oxford. Tel (0865) 24134. This library is not open to the general public; those wishing to consult books should apply to the Librarian, preferably during the University term. The Library is closed at Christmas and Easter, and from the second week of July until the third week of September. If the Librarian is available, he will entertain applications between the dates mentioned, but no service can normally be guaranteed.

The present College is the heir of older foundations: Hart Hall, later the first Hertford College, and Magdalen Hall, and the older books belonging to the College today reflects this. Magdalen Hall books seem to outnumber those from other sources. The bulk of the library consists of the usual theological and classical material common to other colleges, though natural science is also well represented, and there is a fair number of 17th and 18th cent works on economics and geography.

The present stock totals *c*12,000 v, including 5 incunabula; 192 STC; and *c*750 Wing items. The main rare book collections include: 200 v, mainly on medicine and surgery, given by Samuel Thurnor in 1691 to Magdalen Hall; much of the library of John Cale, of Barming, Kent, bequeathed to the first Hertford College in 1777; a number of books of Oriental interest presented by J D Macbride, Principal of Magdalen Hall 1813–68, and Professor of Arabic; many contemporary works bequeathed by Edward Phillips in 1855; 44 broadsides and proclamations ranging from the reign of Charles I to Queen Anne, presented by F D S Darwin in 1934.

Cat on cards.

Earlier cats survive.

Typescript cat of books printed pre-1800.

Catalogus librorum in Bibliotheca Aulae Magdalenae, Oxford, 1661.

Catalogue of books in the Library of Hertford College printed in the fifteenth and sixteenth centuries, 1910.

Project Loc: Catalogue of pre-1801 books in the Library of Hertford College, Oxford, excluding those formerly deposited in the Printer's Library at OUP and now returned to the College (computer print-out available on application at the Bodleian).

W H Allnutt, *Catalogue* (rectior, shelflist) *of books in the Library of Hertford College*, 1888.

S G Hamilton, *Hertford College* (Univ of Oxford College histories, 1903), p157-60.

——'College Library', in *Hertford College Magazine* 6 (Dec 1912), p160-3.

C A J A(rmstrong), 'The College Library', *Ibid* 60 (1973), p820-1.

Sir C H Firth, 'Notes on Mr Darwin's collection of broadsides', *Ibid* 23 (May 1934), p118-9.

Hope Entomological Collections, University Museum, Parks Road, Oxford OX1 3PW. Tel (0865) 57467 Ext 574. Open Mon-Fri 9 am-12 pm, 2-5 pm. Admission by application, in writing, to the Librarian. Photocopying facilities.

Hope Department of Entomology Library A specialist collection on entomology, with an emphasis on taxonomic works; also a number on general natural history. It contains *c*12,000 v and periodicals, plus 1,353 boxes of catalogued pamphlets, dating from the 16th cent onwards. Older books are shelved as part of the general collection, and it is not possible to estimate the number of these in total. There are 6 STC; 5 pre-1641 foreign; and 19 Wing books. The library is based on the libraries of the Rev F W Hope (1797–1862) and of the first Hope Professor J O Westwood (1805–93). It includes the collection on *arachnida* of Octavius Pickard-Cambridge (1828–1917), of which there is a printed catalogue (*Catalogue of the arachnological library bequeathed to the University of Oxford by the Rev Octavius Pickard-Cambridge*, MA, FRS. Compiled by A W Pickard-Cambridge, Oxford, 1926.) Selected works on entomology, with an emphasis on *Lepidoptera* are being added from the library of Dr Lionel G Higgins. Works on spiritualism and other subjects from the library of Alfred Rusel Wallace (1823–1913) are also shelved here: other works from Wallace's library, including some on Botany, Evolution and Travel, are in the library of the Linnean Society of London (see *Proceedings of the Linnean Soc of London*, v 127, 1915, p37, 62-70).

Separate author and subject cat. Subject cat discontinued *c*1970, except for books and major revisions.

Institute of Agricultural Economics, University of Oxford, Dartington House, Little Clarendon Street, Oxford OX1 2HP. Tel (0865) 52921. Open (Term) Mon-Fri 9 am-5.30 pm; (Vacation) Mon-Fri 9 am-1 pm, 2.15-5.30 pm. Admission by arrangement on written application. Microform readers and photocopying facilities.

Special Collection Built up during the 1920s and 1930s under the direction of the Institute's first Director, Dr C S Orwin, the collection comprises *c*600 books and pamphlets on agricultural topics published from mid-18th cent to late 19th cent. There is a complete collection of the Board of Agriculture's 18th and early 19th cent county surveys, and many of the works of Arthur Young (1741–1820) and his contemporaries.

Jesus College, Oxford. Tel (0865) 249511. Admission by prior written application to the Librarian.

The library's stock totals 25,000 v, including 44 incunabula and 789 STC books. The bulk of the older books are in the Fellows' Library. The collection is strong in classics, theology, law, medicine and linguistics, and includes the following: *c*100 v, mainly law left by Griffith Powell, Principal 1613 till his death in 1620; a number of volumes, chiefly classics and theology, given by Lewis Roberts (1596–1640) not long before he died; *c*900 v, including Latin, Greek, English, French, Spanish and Italian books, ranging in subject matter from mathematics, medicine and music, to the physical sciences, history, theology and law, bequeathed by Edward, 1st Baron Herbert of Cherbury, on his death in 1648; a scholar's library of *c*600 v, chiefly classics and theology, given in 1649 by Francis Mansell (1579–1665); the library, with an emphasis on maritime law and works on Continental (Roman) law, bequeathed by Sir Leoline Jenkins (1625–85); the library, including classics and theology, but also tracts relating to the controversies of his own time and works relating to Socinianism, left by Jonathan Edwards, Principal 1688–1712; a library of scientific and medical works dating from the 16th cent to his own day, left by Griffith Davies (*d*1724)—the library is especially strong in the works of Robert Boyle; a collection of politico-religious pamphlets of the 17th cent, in particular, from the time of James II, given in 1724 by William Parry, a fellow; the general library, interesting for the contemporary printed items, including some literature and science, of Henry Fisher (*d*1761), University Registrar; an *alumnus* collection, including the works of J R Green (1837–83), the historian; a collection of Celtic books, including many left by Charles Plummer (*d*1927) —this is being kept as a separate collection in charge of the Jesus Professor of Celtic, and is being added to.

Duplicate volumes from the library were sold during the period 1688–1712.

Card cat.

Separate cats of the Celtic books, of the *alumnus* collection, and of signatures noticed in the printed books.

Earlier inventories and shelflists have survived.

There are interleaved annotated Bodleian printed cats of 1674, 1738 and 1843, but all are imperfect.

C J Fordyce and Sir T M Knox, 'The Library of Jesus College, Oxford, with an appendix on the books bequeathed thereto by Lord Herbert of Cherbury', *Oxford Bibliographical Soc Proc and Papers*, 5 (1937), p49-115.

Keble College, Oxford. Tel (0865) 59201. Not open to the public; for scholars, 9 am-4 pm. Admission to bona fide scholars with letters of recommendation, proof of identity, and by appointment only. Photocopying facilities available provided it is not too extensive.

General Collection Dates from the opening of the College in 1870. It totals *c*47,000 v including special collections of 85 medieval mss. (M B Parkes, *Catalogue of Medieval Manuscripts of Keble College*, 1979); 99 Incunabula; 220 STC books and uncounted numbers in Wing. Most Honours Schools subjects are covered in varying degrees, with particularly extensive law, classics and 19th cent theology libraries.

Card index.

Special collections are identified as follows:

John Keble (1792–1866) A leading Tractarian with Newman and Pusey, and in whose name the College was founded. His library (*c*1,600 v), mainly 19th cent theology and poetry, including presentation copies, his books in ms, most of his letters to, and from, leading church dignitaries and scholars of the 19th cent. Donated by his brother Thomas.

Sir Thomas Brooke, antiquary and industrialist (1830–1908). His superb collection of medieval mss, incunabula and early printed books—many in fine bindings (*c*300 v)—were given by his brother the Rev Charles Edward Brooke in 1911.

Separate sheaf cats of the Brooke bequest.

Port Royal An extensive collection of Jansenist literature given by the Rev Henry T Morgan in 1902.

Henry Parry Liddon, Canon of St Paul's (1829–90). Some of his private papers and a large part of his library, including 26 mss, and several rare books. Bequeathed in 1890.

Dr J E Millard (1824–94), Headmaster of Magdalen College School, Oxford. A small but choice collection given in 1894, including some incunabula, early service books and specimens of the work of fine printers such as Bodoni.

William Hatchett-Jackson A small but fine collection of classics—both incunabula and 16th cent editions formed by William Jackson. Given by his son, William Hatchett Jackson (1849–1924) (a former tutor of the College), in 1893.

A catalogue of the manuscripts and printed books collected by Sir Thomas Brooke and preserved at Armitage Bridge House, Near Huddersfield, 2 v, London 1891.

Catalogue of the Port-Royal Collection in the Library of Keble College, Oxford, 1905.

Lady Margaret Hall Library, Norham Gardens, Oxford OX2 6QA. Tel (0865) 54353. Open Mon-Fri 9 am-5 pm to serious scholars, preferably with a letter of recommendation if from another University. Also advisable to enquire by telephone before coming. Outsiders are preferred during vacation.

The library is primarily a working collection, and the printed books are of a rather miscellaneous character. The total stock amounts to 42,000 v. The rare books total *c*800 v, and include 1 incunabulum, 53 STC and 93 Wing items, while the pre-1641 foreign books number 68.

The rare books collections include many of his own writings given by John Ruskin in 1884; some early editions of Dante bequeathed by Lucy Ethel Willcock in 1919, supplemented by George Musgrave's comprehensive collection of Dante literature in 1932; some Spanish and Catalan books left by Suzette M Taylor in 1920; *c*350 v of English, French and Italian books, 16th-18th cent, and some Nonesuch Press editions, bequeathed in 1931 by Edward Hugh Norris Wilde, husband of a Classics don; some early editions and works concerned with 15th cent French poetry given by Dr Kathleen Chesney; 17th cent English tracts presented by Dr C V Wedgwood and Miss Mary Coate; 100 v from the library of Harold J Laski (*d*1950), the political economist; works on Buddhism formerly owned by J G Jennings (1866–1941); an almost complete set of the writings of Charlotte M Yonge presented in 1955 by Mrs C S Orwin; recently supplemented from the collection of Mrs M Dunlop; a collection of works concerned with William Blake, formed by Professor Mary Barber; a collection of 17th and 18th cent books, some about the Civil Wars, bequeathed by Dr K M Briggs.

Card cat.

There is a separate cat of the rare books and all rare items are also included in the main cat.

Lincoln College Library, Turl Street, Oxford. Tel (0865) 722741. The Senior Library is open by arrangement to non-members on written application to the Librarian. Microfilm reader available.

Lincoln College Library The stock totals 25,000 v, including the Senior Library of *c*7,000 v which includes 48 incunabula (10 of which were given by Edmund Audley, Bishop of Salisbury in 1518), and 629 STC books. The subject coverage is wide, but there is a special emphasis on classics and theology. The classics include 556 v, predominantly classical from James St Amand (*d*1754). The theology includes 105 v, almost all Biblical, rabbinic or patristic, given by Richard Kilbye, Rector 1590–1620, and books on the Septuagint given by Edward William Grinfield (1785–1864). Other important collections include:

Gilbert Watts, a fellow, bequeathed in 1657 143 v including classical and philosophical works, and natural philosophy; Thomas Marshall (1621–85) bequeathed (i) 1,040 v, the majority linguistic, oriental and theological, but also some literary, topographical, political and scientific works, (ii) 77 v of tracts, comprising nearly 2,000 items, the majority relating to the religious and political events of the Great Rebellion and printed 1640–9, others concerned with English and European history of the pre-war period, some dating from the reigns of Elizabeth I and James I, some polemic tracts on Anglo-Spanish relations and on English colonization, others include specimens of contemporary literature, poetry and popular scientific or medical works; small collection of political and religious tracts of the late 17th and first half of the 18th cent on the religious troubles of James II's reign, on non-jurors, on Arthur Bury's case and the controversies surrounding Sacheverell and Hoadley; William Vesey (*d*1755) bequeathed 200 v, including at least 7 v of late 17th and early 18th cent plays of considerable rarity; Lincoln's holdings (of 500 different plays rich in items 1680–1740) are shown in C J Stratman, *Bibliography of English printed tragedy 1565–1900*, 1960; Mrs May Hall in 1952 gave a collection of works by, or on, John Wesley and relating to the early history of Wesleyan Methodism made by the Rev Albert F Hall, including some early editions and rare tracts. (Holdings are shown in Frank Baker, *A union catalogue of the publications of John and Charles Wesley*, 1966); Donald Nicholas (*d*1973) bequeathed 50 books which represented his attempt to bring together the (400 strong) library of his ancestor, Sir Edward Nicholas, Secretary of State 1641–9; there is also a small collection of works by, or about, former members of the College.

Card cat.

Earlier cats survive.

Separate list of St Amand's books dated 1754.

V H H Green, *The Commonwealth of Lincoln College*, Oxford, 1979, Appendix 7 (ii), The College Library, p670-84.

Magdalen College, High Street, Oxford OX1 4AU. Tel (0865) 241781. Open 9 am-4.30 pm (not at weekends); admission by previous appointment only. Limited xerox copying facilities.

Provision was made for a library from the foundation of the College in 1458. It contains the usual relics of older curricula, but the holdings also reflect an interest in botany (the College is a neighbour of the Botanic Garden). It now contains *c*50,000 v, including 139 incunabula and 577 STC items. Notable contents include:

Large folio volumes of the Fathers, theology and classics printed on the Continent, especially Basle, in the 16th cent; much Protestant theology, purchased in the latter part of the 16th cent, including the library of John Jewel, Bishop of Salisbury in 1572; 74 folio works bound in 30 v from the library of Nicholas Gibbard, an Oxford physician, bequeathed in 1608; many Continental printed books on a wide variety of topics collected by Sir Nicholas Throckmorton, the Elizabethan diplomat, and by Sir Arthur, his son, given by Sir Arthur in 1626. Sir Nicholas was interested in politics and religion, Sir Arthur in literature, voyages, the military arts, natural sciences, and things Italian generally; 239 printed books in 134 v and some mss, mostly concerned with botany, bequeathed in 1664 by John Goodyear (1592–1664), Goodyear noted on the fly-leaves the prices paid for the books and for binding, with dates; Italian and French printed books on several subjects bequeathed in 1699 by John Fitzwilliam, a non-juror and fellow 1661–70; numerous tracts relating to the theological controversies of the late 17th cent presented in the early years of the 18th cent by Edward Maynard (1674–1740); early printed and later Swedish liturgical and homilectical works presented at some time in the 19th cent; tracts on 19th cent religious controversies given by John Rigaud (1821–88); the books of C G B Daubeny (1795–1867), Professor of Chemistry 1822–55, reflecting interests in pure science, botany, geology (especially volcanoes) and rural economy; part of the library of mathematical books formed by H T Gerrans, presented in 1924 for the use of the Waynflete Professor of Pure Mathematics and accredited students from outside the College (though much of this collection is now in the Mathematics Institute); 200 v of 18th cent French literature and history, given by P H B O Smithers in 1948; a few original editions of Elizabethan and Jacobean plays given by the writer E H W Meyerstein (1889–1952); a comprehensive collection of bookplates engraved by C W Sherborn (1831–1912), bequeathed by Lt Col R H R Brocklebank; the library, mainly concerned with fine art, of T S R Boase (1898–1974); a collection of works written or edited by *alumni*, begun by J R Bloxam, Librarian and Fellow (1836–63) and still actively maintained, all periods are well represented, from Colet and Lily in the 16th cent through William Camden, James Mabbe, Addison, Routh, Charles Reade, J A Symonds and the Duke of Windsor to the present day.

Author cat on cards and paste-in slips.

Separate typescript cat of the pre-1641 books.

Earlier cats have survived.

E M Macfarlane, *Catalogus librorum impressorum Bibliothecae...Collegii B Mariae Magdalenae in Academia Oxoniensi* 3 v 1860–2.

'Magdalen College Library (with a) list of books printed before 1641...not in the Bodleian Library', *Oxford Bibliographical Soc Proc and Papers*, ii (1929), p145-200.

W A B Coolidge, 'The Library of Magdalen College, Oxford', *Notes and Queries* 6th series, vii (1883), 421-3, 441-3.

(G R Driver *et al*) 'Magdalen College Library', *Oxford Bibliographical Soc Proc and Papers*, ii (1929), 144-9.

R T Gunther, 'The circulating library of a brotherhood of reformers of the sixteenth century at Magdalen College, Oxford', *Notes and Queries*, 13th series i (1923), 483-4.

——'The row of books of Nicholas Gibbard of Oxford', *Annals of medical history*, iii (1921), p324-6.

——'Goodyear's Library', in his *Early British botanists* (1922), p197-232.

——*The Daubeny Laboratory Register 1916–1923*, iii (1924), p382-8 (for an account of the scientific collections in the College and their donors).

W D Macray, *A register of the members of St Mary Magdalen College, Oxford*. ns v 2 (1897), p218-23: 'Notes of books in the Library bearing memoranda of ownership and donorship', v 3 (1901, p195-6. 'Placards printed by Wynkyn de Worde').

Magdalen College School, Cowley Place, Oxford. Tel (0865) 242191. Open (in term) 9 am-4 pm. Admission by written application. Photocopying available.

Old Waynfletes' Collection, incorporating 'Millard's Gift' Originally a small private library of works from the 16th to 19th cent written by former masters and pupils, collected by Dr James Elwin Millard (Master of the School, 1846–64) and presented by him to the School in 1870. Since then further works by masters and *alumni* have been added. The collection contains important works by authors such as William Camden, Daniel Featley, John Harmer, Laurence Humphrey, Edward Lister, Thos Pierce, Thos Sherley, Thos Smith (17th cent), J H Todd (on Milton), John Stanbridge and Robert Whittinton. There are *c*70 pre-1851 books which include 22 STC items.

Cat may be seen at the School on written application.

Manchester College Oxford, Mansfield Road, Oxford OX1 3TD. Tel (0865) 241514-241515. Open (Term) Mon-Fri 10 am-4 pm; (Vacation) by appointment only. Admission on written application; references required. Photocopying (limited service; pre-1801 publication not usually photocopied), microfilms supplied.

The Library dates from the foundation of Warrington Academy in 1757, when students all paid a compulsory library fee. This collection of books passed to Manchester Academy in 1786 (later Manchester New College) and was augmented by the libraries of the Academies at Exeter and Taunton. The College moved to London in 1853 and to Oxford in 1889, when the name changed to Manchester College Oxford. The curricula of the Dissenting Academies were designed to provide education for Protestant non-conformists who could not take degrees at Oxford and Cambridge, and who were excluded from some professions and public offices. The students therefore read subjects which prepared them for careers in the non-conformist ministry, medicine, the law, finance, commerce and industry.

The library now contains over 60,000 books, of which *c*25,000 are pre-1851. Bequests include the personal libraries of Principals Charles Wellbeloved (1769–1858), John James Tayler (1797–1869), James Martineau (1805–1900) and J Estlin Carpenter (1844–1927); and the private libraries of Benjamin Grosvenor (1676–1758), Samuel Stubbs (1715–53) are among those donated to the College. The libraries of several Unitarian Chapels have also passed to the College. There are 3 incunabula; 484 STC books among over 1,000 printed in the period 1500–1640; 4,000 printed 1640–1700 (English and foreign); and 6,000 printed 1700–1800. The subject coverage is predominantly theological and philosophical, but almost all major writers of the Enlightenment in Western Europe are represented. French influence predominates the pre-1800 works, and German scholarship in the 19th cent works. There are 11,000 tracts bound in 800 v, particularly strong for 17th and 18th cent dissent and politics, and 19th cent Unitarianism.

Special collections include the *Library of Comparative Religion* which is based on the collection of Principal J Estlin Carpenter, and consists of *c*10,000 books, of which *c*3,000 are pre-1851, and relate to 18th and 19th cent religion, mythology, anthropology, etc; *Socinian literature; Unitarian literature; Hymn Books and liturgical books; Hungarian works* (mainly 19th cent theology); Periodicals and serials, especially late 18th and early 19th cent.

Author cat (sheaf).

Subject cat of books in the main reading room (sheaf).

Two cats of pamphlets: (a) entries, written mostly in the 1880s, pasted into four guardbooks, the first two arranged A-Z by known authors, the other two with anonymous works arranged by subject; (b) A sheaf cat begun in the 1930s of the first two volumes of (a) but omitting shelfmarks.

Cat of the Carpenter Library of Comparative Religion, in two parts: author and classified by subject (sheaf).

Index to Obituary Notices and Biographical articles in *The Christian Reformer 1815–1887; The Monthly Repository 1806–1837; The Inquirer, 1842–* and some minor dissenting periodicals; sheaf cat, two sequences: 1790–1899, 1900–; both sequences in alphabetical order of subjects.

Mansfield College, Mansfield Road, Oxford. Tel (0865) 249175. Admission on application, in writing, to the Librarian.

Mansfield College Library has its origins in Spring Hill College, founded in Birmingham in 1838 for the training of Congregational ministers. It was transferred to Oxford in 1886, and its objects were broadened to train ministers of any dissenting denomination and to provide a Free Church faculty in theology. Its total stock of *c*30,000 v includes 88 STC books. The library is primarily a working collection, but it contains material for the study of Congregational history, especially accounts of local churches (about 250 in number) and early ordination sermons, and a small number of books from the 16th to 18th cent. It includes the following (shelved according to subject matter, but with bookplates showing donor): the residue of over 600 v concerned with the classics, classical antiquity, history, literature, philosophy and theology, presented by Thomas Smith James (1809–74), son of John Angell James (1785–1859); *c*400 v on theology and philology, presented by W Froggatt in 1881; books dealing with early church history, and 19th cent theological works, given by J B Paton (1830–1911); a collection of 17th cent Bibles and theological works given in 1909 by J L Cherry; *c*1,000 books, formerly part of Spring Hill College, Birmingham (kept together). All books relating to the College's distinctive inheritance are retained—Congregational, Dissenting, Evangelical.

Author and title cat on cards.

Wall slip index of books kept in each bay.

Earlier cats survive.

Mansfield College, Oxford. Paton Library for the use of ministers and students, especially of the Free Churches in England and Wales. Catalogue and rules 1909.

Note Duplicates and surplus books discarded between 1917 and 1920. In recent years a considerable quantity of the older or lesser-used material has been dispersed, some of the rarer items to the Bodleian. *c*200 v of palaeographical works presented by Canon W Sanday of Christ Church in 1919 have been sold.

Merton College Library, Merton College, Oxford. Tel (0865) 249651. Open Mon-Fri 9.30 am-1 pm, 2-4.30 pm. Closed in August. Admission on written application to the Librarian stating the author and title of book not available in the national collection.

The present library, built between 1373 and 1378, is one of the oldest surviving buildings designed for housing books in England. The printed book collections are strong in 16th cent medicine and law, and tracts of the 16th-18th cent, but weak in the *editiones principes* of the classics. The library did not begin purchasing printed books on any scale until the 1540s when a large number of standard works in all subjects taught, except law, was purchased. The 1556 catalogue prepared for the *Marian Commissioners* shows just under 200 items. The present stock totals 65,000 v, of which 10,000 v may be described as rare, and include 112 incunabula and 527 STC books. The major acquisitions of rare collections include 54 v bequeathed in 1583 by William Marshall, a fellow with Roman Catholic sympathies and an interest in the medieval schoolmen; 100 v bequeathed by James Leeche (*d*1589), a former fellow, includng law books; *c*150 of the law books of John Betts of Trinity Hall, Cambridge, purchased in 1599; a collection of mainly 16th cent medical works, including gifts and bequests from Robert Barnes (*d*1604) and Roger Gifford (*d*1597), fellows and lecturers in medicine; the gift of the library of Theodore Gulston (*d*1632) a physician and fellow, by his widow; over 600 printed books bequeathed by Griffin Higgs (1589–1659), who had been chaplain to Elizabeth of Bohemia during her exile in the Netherlands, including a series of marked and annotated auction sale catalogues, many unique (cat in preparation); the extensive library, covering many subjects other than medicine, of Sir Thomas Clayton, Regius Professor of Medicine, and Warden 1661–93; 30 v of tracts concerned with the Bangorian and other controversies of the time, bequeathed by Thomas Herne (*d*1722); over 800 v of a miscellaneous nature bequeathed by Henry Kent, a commoner, in 1737; the printed books of F H Bradley (1846–1924), the philosopher, forming the basis of the Bradley Memorial Library of Philosophy (handlist available); early editions of works by Sir Max Beerbohm (1872–1956) on alumnus, kept with his mss and drawings in the Beerbohm Room (provisional cat available); the Warden's library, a small collection of printed books, the majority 18th cent, strong in classical authors and British topography (separate typescript cat).

Card cat.

Interleaved copies of the Bodleian cats of 1674 and 1843.

Catalogue of the printed books in the library of Merton College, Oxford, 1880 to which supplements were issued in 1883, 1890 and 1899.

P S Morrish, 'A collection of seventeenth century book sale catalogues', *Quaerendo* 1 (1971), p35-45.

G Pollard and A Ehrman, *The distribution of books by catalogue. . . to A D 1800*, Roxburghe Club, 1965, p222-5. ('Auction sale catalogues in Holland to 1700').

Museum of the History of Science, Old Ashmolean Building, Broad Street, Oxford OX1 3AZ. Tel (0865) 243997. Open Mon-Fri 10.30 am-1 pm, 2.30-4 pm. Admission by arrangement with the librarian; prior notice of visits is helpful. Photocopying service; microform reader; restricted lending of some modern works to members of the University.

General Collection Built up around the founder's library (the Lewis Evans collection) since the foundation of the Museum in 1924, by purchase, gift and deposit. Much early material was acquired through the efforts of the first Curator, R T Gunther (1869–1940). Many small, or part, collections of books and mss have subsequently been acquired and incorporated into the general stock, eg the personal library of S P Rigaud (1774–1839) from the Radcliffe observatory, and R T Gunther's personal library. The library as a whole contains *c*12,000 v (including the Lewis Evans and Royal Microscopical Society collections, see below), which do not include mss, the iconographic and printed ephemera collection or the offprint collection. Subject matter is almost exclusively history of science and early scientific books, with special emphasis on scientific instruments and artefacts (such as are contained in the Museum collections). The general collection is also strong in the areas of early medical books (British and foreign, many 17th cent). There is 1 incunabulum in the general collection and 58 STC books (according to Morgan) in the library as a whole, though this is probably an underestimate. Also some individual books of great rarity.

Card index cat of the whole library; some specialized handlists available for internal use.

Until recently, printed *Annual Reports*, at first separately and later in the *University Gazette*, mentioned Library accessions.

A E Gunther, *Early Science in Oxford*, v XV—'Robert A Gunther: a pioneer in the history of science, 1869–1940', 1967.

R T Gunther, *Oxford and the History of Science*, inaugural lecture, Oxford, 1934, especially p14-17.

Lewis Evans Collection The personal library of Lewis Evans (1853–1930) acquired mainly by purchase in the late 19th and early 20th cent, and consisting of works relating to his collection of scientific instruments (mainly sundials). The latter formed the foundation of the Museum's collections in 1924; the printed books are preserved undisturbed as the founder's library, and amount to 1,007 v, plus 120 v and two bundles of mss. Printed material consist chiefly of early works of scientific instruments and associated techniques, especially sundials and astrolabes. Over 80 per cent of the collection is made up of works printed before 1851, and there are many British, and especially foreign works of the 16th and 17th cent. There are three incunabula (STC and Wing items not known), and many individual books of great rarity. The mss date from the 17th to the early 20th cent and relate to the same subjects.

Cat included in the main card index cat of the library.

Short-title handlist available for internal use.

Original card cat written by Lewis Evans still kept.

Royal Microscopical Society Collection In its present form, the collection consists exclusively of pre-1851 books, purchased from the Royal Microscopical Society in 1970, and preserved undisturbed as the core of the Royal Microscopical Society's now dispersed library. This core was built up in the mid-19th cent by the Microscopical Society of London which became the Royal Microscopical Society. It contains 218 v, including British and foreign books from the 17th cent to 1850 on microscopy and related subjects (which embrace general optics, and aspects of biology and natural history affected by the microscope). There are no incunabula (STC and Wing items not known).

Cat included in the main card index cat of the Library.

Handlist available for internal use.

Many of these books appear in *Catalogue of the Books in the Library of the Microscopical Society of London* (London: J E Adlard, 1859).

New College, Oxford. Tel (0865) 248451. Admission by prior written application to the Librarian.

New College Library's stock totals *c*90,000 v, including 332 incunabula and 556 STC books. The printed books purchased, or given, since the early days of printing have survived in large numbers, particularly in law, theology, the classics and early medicine and science. Notable among the rare book collections are: 25 printed books bequeathed by Cardinal Pole (*d*1558), Cardinal Archbishop of Canterbury (see A B Emden, *Opus epistolarum Des Erasmi Roterodami recognitum per P S Allen*, xi (1947), Appendix xxviii, p379-83); 30 v bequeathed by Thomas Martin (*d*1584), including French translations of Thucydides, Livy and Aristotle; medical and scientific books, among others, bequeathed by Walter Bailey (*d*1592), Regius Professor of Medicine; *c*400 medical books given in 1617 by Thomas Hopper (*d*1624); *c*500 v, mainly contemporary theology, given in 1617 by Arthur Lake, Warden 1613–16; a general scholarly library of *c*170 items bequeathed by Robert Pinke, Warden 1617–47; a general collection of *c*600 v bequeathed by Michael Woodward, Warden, in 1675; numerous tracts and works by Robert Boyle (1627–91), included in the benefaction by Martin Wall (1747–1824), Litchfield Professor of Clinical Medicine; the bequest of E C Wickham (1834–1910), Dean of Lincoln Cathedral, strong in classical literature; 20 bound v of pamphlets bequeathed by H B George (1858–1910), the historian; the collection of works on the history of universities of Hastings Rashdall (*d*1924) given by his widow; the printed papers collected by the sixth Earl of Donoughmore while Chairman of the Committee of Privileges of the House of Lords, 1911–31, many with his marginal notes, being of genealogical interest; a collection on the history of Eastern Europe, especially Czechoslovakia in the 20th cent, including a large number of pamphlets, presented by R W Seton-Watson in 1949; many first editions and presentation copies of 20th cent German literature, the bequest of H F Garten.

Card cat.

Earlier cats have survived, including annotated Bodleian cats of 1738 and 1843.

Nuffield College, Oxford. Tel (0865) 248014. Open Mon-Fri 9.30 am-1 pm, 2-6 pm; Sat 9.30 am-1 pm. Readers are normally graduates; undergraduates should have a letter from their Tutor. Photocopying; microfiche and microfilm readers.

G D H Cole Collection Donated by G D H Cole (1889–1959), the collection contains *c*3,000 v, including 4 STC items. Subjects covered are political economy and philosophy, 18th and 19th cent, including works by William Cobbett (1762–1835) and by Robert Owen (1771–1838). Cole also collected a large number of Cobbett mss. There is a collection (*c*100-150 items) of travel books about Great Britain, 18th and early 19th cent, and a collection of books by William Morris (1834–96).

Card index.

Cobbett holdings are marked with an asterisk in M L Pearl, *William Cobbett: a bibliographical account of his life and times* (1953).

Oriel College, Oxford OX1 4EW. Tel (0865) 721752. Admission by prior arrangements by writing to the Librarian.

Oriel College Library contains *c*37,000 v, of which 20,000 v belong to the older collections, and include 34 incunabula and 517 STC books. The older collection includes the following:

Early medical books, some the gift in 1595 of Thomas Cogan, physician; a larger collection of medical and botanical books was bequeathed by John Jackman in 1600; further medical and scientific works were given by John Sanders, Provost 1644–53; many medical books were included in the bequest of Samuel Desmaitres (*d*1686); a general collection of books bequeathed by George Royse, Provost 1691–1708; the collection of books of Edward, 5th Baron Leigh (1742–86), at Stoneleigh Abbey, Warwickshire, ranging from the classics, history, law, and the natural sciences, to music and the fine arts, and including large illustrated volumes, and some books belonging to the antiquary A C Ducarel (1713–85) (this collection gave the library a country-house flavour, and immediately doubled its size); *c*1,000 v, mostly theological, and including many presentation copies from authors, and pamphlets on the Oxford controversies 1830–78, given by the widow of Edward Hawkins (1789–1882); historical and theological books, strong in German publications and works on Dante, given by the widow of R W Church (1815–90), Dean of St Paul's; part of a collection of more than 1,000 v relating to comparative philology and mythology, bequeathed by D B Monro (1836–1905) (most of the Monro collection is on permanent loan to the Taylor Institution Oxford); *c*1,000 works on comparative philology and mythology acquired after 1870 under a plan that college libraries should specialize in different subjects; 200 v selected in the early 1920s from the parochial library at Tortworth, Gloucestershire, founded on the collection of Henry Brooks (or Brooke, *d*1757), afterwards augmented by those of John Bosworth; some 18th cent English literature from H M Margoliouth (1887–1959); some 18th cent classical and English literature from E R Marshall in 1968; many modern private press books and early 19th cent colour-plate and travel books bequeathed by S N Furness (1902–74); a collection of early editions of, and later works about, Aristotle, bequeathed by Sir David Ross (1877–1971); an extensive collection of works written by and relating to, Oriel *alumni*, including the main figures of the Tractarian movement.

Card cat.

Separate shelflists for the Senior and Junior Libraries, and for the alumnus collection.

Typescript cat for books printed pre-1641.

A catalogue of the books in the library of Oriel College connected with the studies of comparative philology and comparative mythology, 1880, *Addenda* 1885, 1891, 1903.

Some earlier cats have survived.

Oxford Polytechnic, Headington, Oxford OX3 0BP. Tel (0865) 64777. Open (Term) Mon-Fri 9 am-10 pm; Sat 9 am-1 pm; (Vacations) Mon-Fri 9 am-5.15 pm. Admission by application to the Librarian. Photocopying facilities; private study carrels.

John Fuller Collection Professor John Fuller, a former Head of the Department of Catering Management at Oxford, and at the University of Surrey, built up the collection over many years. It was acquired by the Polytechnic in 1980. It totals *c*6,100 v which include general works (including antiquarian works in English and other languages, food technology, etc); international, British and regional food preparation (including professional food preparation and production techniques); catering industry (management, marketing and planning); beverages (mainly alcoholic, including antiquarian and scientific works); food service and biographies. There are 10 mss (mostly 19th cent recipe books), 4 STC books and 2 Wing books.

Card cat, at present arranged by Prof Fuller's classification system.

Oxford University Press, Printing Division, Walton Street, Oxford OX2 6AB. Tel (0865) 512201. Admission by written application in advance to the Printer to the University.

The Printing Division Library is divided as follows:

Bible Library A collection of early printed English Bibles, as well as current Oxford printed Bibles and Prayer Books.

Title and chronological card indexes.

Typographical and Reference Library Contains *c*1,800 v, including modern works on the history of printing, type-design and type-founding, and the history of the University of Oxford and the University Press; a selection of early printed and more recent books of interest as examples of printing (including *c*70 STC books and a small number of books from Continental presses) used as models for type-design; *c*400 type specimens, the majority being recent and either English or Scottish; 68 pre-1850; 16 unique and 8 unrecorded.

Author and classified cats, and card indexes of provanances and of printers and other craftsmen.

J S G Simmons, 'Specimens of printing types before 1850 in the Typographical Library of the University Press, Oxford', *Book Collector* viii (1959), p397-410. Cat, alphabetical by name of founder or printer, and a chronological table (1695–1849).

Pembroke College, Oxford OX1 1DW. Tel (0865) 242271 Ext 61. Open for non-members of the College daily 9 am-5 pm. Admission strictly by prior arrangement.

Pembroke College Library's stock totals *c*30,000 v, with 103 incunabula; and 197 STC books. The more notable rare collections include:

A collection of 16th and 17th cent printed books, chiefly of theological interest, deriving mainly from the bequest of John Hall (1633–1710), Bishop of Bristol; a small family library of the late 17th and 18th cent, bequeathed by Francis Wightwick (*d*1776) of Wombridge, Berks; a collection of books connected with Aristotle (particularly his Nichomachean Ethics) formed by H W Chandler (1827–89), Waynflete Professor of Moral and Metaphysical philosophy (it includes early editions of Aristotle and other philosophers, many in interesting bindings); a small collection of 18th cent English literature, given by George Birkbeck Hill (1835–1903), the editor of Boswell and Johnson; a Samuel Johnson collection (books and mss).

Author cat on cards in two sections (for books printed pre-1800 and for later works) but excluding the Chandler, Hall and Wightwick (or Wombridge) collections which have separate card cats.

Catalogue of the Aristotelian and philosophical portions of the library of the late Henry William Chandler (1891), one copy of which has ms additions.

The 18th cent cats, beginning in 1733, have survived.

The Philosophy Library, University of Oxford, 10 Merton Street, Oxford. Tel (0865) 243995. Open Mon-Fri 9.30 am-5.30 pm (closed August). Admission to members of the University and bona fide research workers with a letter of recommendation to the Librarian. The collection is for use in the library only; no borrowing or photocopying allowed.

Fowler Collection Bequeathed in 1904 to the Wykeham Professor of Logic by Dr Thomas Fowler (1831–1904), President of Corpus Christi College. The collection amounts to 729 v on philosophy and logic, especially works of, or on, Aristotle and Bacon, including several early editions. There are 3 incunabula and 26 STC books.

Catalogue of books bequeathed by Thomas Fowler, DD, to the Wykeham Chair of Logic (1906).

Pitt Rivers Museum and Dept of Ethnology and Prehistory, University of Oxford, Parks Road, Oxford OX1 3PP. Tel (0865) 512541. Open (Term) Mon-Fri 9 am-12.30 pm, 2-5 pm; (Vacation) 9 am-12.30 pm, 2-4 pm. By appointment only throughout August. Closed 10 days over Christmas and Easter. Open to senior members and research students of the University of Oxford; undergraduate students taught in Dept of Ethnology and Prehistory; others at the discretion of the Librarian. Photocopying facilities and microfiche reader.

Balfour Library The library is named after Henry Balfour (1863–1939), first Curator of the Museum, who left his personal library of over 10,000 v and pamphlets to the Museum on his death in 1939. This collection forms the core of the library which now has the dual function of the research library of Pitt Rivers Museum and of the teaching and research library of the Dept of Ethnology and Prehistory. The subject coverage is ethnology, anthropology, prehistoric archaeology, religion, music, travels, and pre-industrial technology/material culture. The library's current stock totals *c*25,000 v plus periodicals, pamphlets, archives and photographs. *c*2,000 v published pre-1851 are in the collection, particularly travels and voyages (mainly 1750–1850). The collection also contains *c*2-300 limited editions and locally printed material, most of which pre-dates 1930. Most of these volumes come from the collections of Henry Balfour, H G Beasley, Capt Robert Powley Wild, and Sir Edward Burnet Tylor. Rare book holdings are integrated with the general library catalogue and are not kept as a separate collection.

Card cat.

Dr Pusey Memorial Library, Pusey House, St Giles, Oxford OX1 3LZ. Tel (0865) 59519. Open Mon-Fri 9 am-5 pm; Sat 9 am-1 pm (term time). Admission to members of the University of Oxford, or letter of recommendation. Application to Theology Faculty Librarian for printed books, and Pusey Librarian for pamphlets. Photocopying facilities.

Pusey House was founded in 1884 to commemorate the work of Edward Bouverie Pusey (1800–82), especially his contribution to the revival of English Church life in the 19th cent. Its stock totals 60,000 v, including 5 incunabula; 98 STC items; *c*5,000 pre-1850 books. The library's strength lies in its collection of theological pamphlets and 19th cent books. It includes E B Pusey's own books which reflect his part in the 19th cent Anglican Church history and his interest in Hebrew studies; a general collection of books received in 1887 from *Charles Jacomb*; a group of early Sarum missals and early liturgies given by *H P Liddon* (1829–90); many early printed theological books bequeathed by *C C Balston* of Corpus Christi College; works on canon law bequeathed in 1930 by *Cuthbert Hamilton Turner*, sometime Ireland's Professor of Exegesis of Holy Scripture; a general collection, with a bias towards ecclesiastical law, belonging to *Walter George Frank Phillimore*, 1st Baron (1845–1929), presented in 1935; A large and wide-ranging library of printed books bequeathed by *Darwell Stone*, Principal 1909–34, reflecting his interests in all the theological questions of the day, in the Fathers of the Church and in the lexicon of Patristic Greek later published in 1961–68 under the editorship of G W H Lampe.

Pamphlets from those in sympathy with the Tractarian Movement include 2,500 pamphlets, especially strong in Oxford subjects, from Archdeacon G A Denison (1805–96); 2,000 pamphlets, largely concerned with controversial matters, but also on art, literature, Darwinism and science in general, philology, and including 7 v of booksellers' catalogues from R W Church (1804–71); smaller groups from William Ince (1825–1910), Regius Professor of Divinity, Thomas Keble (1826–1903), nephew of John, and Richard Jenkyns (1782–1854), Master of Balliol.

Two large groups of pamphlets formed by men with the opposite viewpoint, ie 1,400 pamphlets, mostly connected with Oxford controversies, from W Hayward Cox (1804–71), Vice-Principal of St Mary Hall; and 1,900 pamphlets concentrating on fringe matters such as religious controversies in the British colonies, from A J Stephens, QC (1808–80).

In addition there are: *c*1,000 pamphlets, bearing on the English Church Union, reunion and European affairs, from the 2nd Viscount Halifax (1839–1934); *c*800 pamphlets, chiefly concerned with social work and church life in London parishes between 1855 and 1909, from Edward Mason Ingram; 3,000 pamphlets, dealing with most theological topics, and strong in tracts of parochial interest, from the Church House and the English Church Union libraries.

A collection of under 1,000 European books, mainly French and German, chiefly 18th and early 19th cent, the core of the collection formed by Dr Pusey, and added to from Church Union books.

Card cat (by author) of most printed books (post-1850).

Card cat of the antiquarian printed books is superseding a ms ledger one.

Card cat of the pamphlets by author, title and subject; a handlist contains notes of replies, sequels and other editions.

J A Fenwick, *Nineteenth century pamphlets at Pusey House: an introduction by Father Hugh*. London, 1961 (op).

The Queen's College, High Street, Oxford OX1 4AW. Tel (0865) 248411 Ext 46. Open (Term) Mon-Fri 9 am-10 pm; Sat 9 am-1 pm; (Vacation) Mon-Fri 9.30 am-1 pm, 2.30-5 pm; Sat 9.30 am-1 pm. Admission for accredited scholars to consult material not available elsewhere by appointment. Some photocopying, microfilming and photography through the Bodleian.

The Queen's College Library The printed books collection is one of the richest and largest to be found among the Oxford Colleges, in spite of the fact that almost all the older books had vanished by 1555 from the depredations of John Bale and others. The stock totals 130,000 v, including 286 incunabula and 2,552 STC books. The earliest notable group of books remaining is that of *c*80 v of theology bequeathed by Edmund Grindal (1519?–83), Archbishop of Canterbury; other note-worthy groups include books given or bequeathed in the 16th and 17th cent by such men as John Rainolds (1549–1607); Henry Cuffe (1563–1601); Gerard Langbaine, Provost 1646–58; and Robert Nicholas (1595–1667); the remaining part of the extensive library, not wanted by the Bodleian, of Thomas Barlow (1607–91), strong in theology, church history, ecclesiastical law and 16th and 17th cent tracts; the bequest of Sir Joseph Williamson (1633–1701), in which law, history and science were well represented, and including sets of English, French and Dutch proclamations and the *London Gazette* 1665–88; the library, mainly medical and scientific, of Sir John Floyer (1649–1734), and a collection, strong in alchemical and chemical works besides medical ones, made by Theophilus Metcalfe (1690–1757),—R T Gunther thought that these two collections included most of the 16th and 17th cent writers on medicine; books purchased from the £30,000 received in 1841 under the will of Robert Mason, an *alumnus*, including Shakespeare folios, an almost complete set of Aldines, and many colour-plate works on natural history (the Librarian aimed not only at making the holdings of standard academic works as complete as possible, but also at assembling a representative selection of rare and valuable books); a collection of theological pamphlets and offprints, mainly contemporary in date with him, left by William Sanday (1843–1920), Lady Margaret Professor of Divinity and Canon of Christ Church 1895–1919; some incunabula, and a group of books on Chinese and Japanese art bequeathed by A H Sayce (1845–1933), Professor of Assyriology; deluxe and Continental editions of the works of Louis Golding (1895–1958) left by the writer himself.

Note: In 1938 a large number of books, chiefly on bibliography and travel, were sold, and any gifts were depleted.

Cat on cards.

Earlier cats survive.

Regent's Park College, Pusey Street, Oxford. Tel (0865) 59887. Open to scholars on prior written application to the Librarian.

Regent's Park College Library Regent's Park College was first established at Stepney in 1810 to train ministers for the Baptist Churches; from 1856 in Regent's Park, London, and transferred to Oxford 1927–40. Incorporated as Permanent Private Hall of University of Oxford 1957. Its stock totals 15,000, including 385 STC books. The rare books collections are as follows:

The Angus Library, based on the material gathered by Joseph Angus (1816–1902), Principal 1849–93, and added to since then, including extensive collections of the writings of Baptist authors, particularly good for 17th cent authors, locally printed Baptist writings and histories of all periods, and including a series of editions of John Bunyan. *c*13,000 books; 20,000 titles.

A small collection of grammars, dictionaries and Bible translations in various Indian languages prepared by William Carey (1761–1834), the first Baptist missionary to India, founder of the Serampore Mission and Press.

Two Baptist church libraries are on deposit:
(i) The library of the Baptist Church at Bourton-on-the-Water, Gloucestershire, consisting basically of the books of Benjamin Beddome (1717–95), the hymn writer, minister there 1740–89, with some additions, including many theological works of the 17th and 18th cents.
(ii) The library of the Baptist Church at Abingdon, Oxon, has many 18th cent theological and patristic works collected by Harding Tomkins of Hackney, and his son-in-law, William Tomkins of Abingdon, presented in 1755, supplemented by a legacy of 1778.

Cat on cards.

Catalogue of the books, pamphlets and manuscripts in the Angus Library at Regent's Park College, London, 1908. Card cat in the Library.

W T Whitley, *A Baptist bibliography 1526–1776 (1777–1837)*. 2 vols 1916-22. (With locations in the Angus Library).

E C Starr, ed, *A Baptist bibliography*, 25 vols 1947–76. (With locations in the Angus Library).

Note: The library of the Baptist Church at Broughton, Hants, was sold by auction in 1976.

*c*450 items, including early printed books and works on Baptist history were sold in 1981 (*see* R A Gilbert, Books and Clifton Books, Westcliff-on-Sea, Cat Baptist /81).

St Anne's College, Oxford OX2 6HS. Tel (0865) 57417. Open Mon-Fri 9 am-5 pm. Admission by application, in writing to the Librarian. Xerox, typewriter, microfilm readers, microcomputer.

The library's stock totals *c*70,000 v, with 6 incunabula; 56 STC; 28 Wing books; and 26 pre-1641 foreign books. The library is composed of two libraries—for many years administratively and financially separate:

The Nettleship Library Originally an intercollegiate women's library, founded in 1895 as a result of a gift from the widow of Henry Nettleship (1829–93), Corpus Professor of Latin, of part of his collection of classical books. Ceded to St Anne's by the other women's colleges of Oxford University in 1934. Now forms the basis of the main undergraduate working library.

The Geldart Law Library In 1922 Mrs Emily Geldart gave the law books of her late husband, William Martin Geldart (1870–1922), Vinerian Professor of Law 1909–22, as the nucleus for an intercollegiate women's law library. Ceded to St Anne's by the other women's colleges in 1978. Now the College Law Library.

St Anne's College Library is primarily a working collection, but includes a number of older and rarer books acquired either by gift or bequest, and these include:

(i) *Marianne Cecile Gabrielle Hugon* (1881–1952) bequeathed a collection concerned with European literature, including some older books, and a collection of children's books.

(ii) *Claude Jenkins* (1877–1959), Canon of Christ Church and Professor of Ecclesiastical History, bequeathed *c*7,000 v, including some early printed books, bibliography and much theology and ecclesiastical history.

(iii) *Hon Eleonor Plumer* (1885–1967) Principal of St Anne's College 1940–53, bequeathed a collection of books on art and archaeology, some rare.

(iv) *Phyllis Margaret Handover* (1923–74) left her library, strong in works on typography and book design (including some formerly owned and annotated by Stanley Morison), together with a collection of English children's books and some early Bibles.

Card cat.

St Edmund Hall, Queen's Lane, Oxford OX1 4AR. Tel (0865) 245511 Ext 48. Admission by prior written application to the Librarian.

St Edmund Hall Library was begun by Thomas Tullie, Principal 1658–76. By the mid-19th cent, as a result of donations, there must have been a small general library with an emphasis on theology, suitable for the training and reading of Anglican clergymen. During the 20th cent this emphasis has shifted, so far as the older books are concerned, to works written by, about, or formerly owned by Aularians, or having something to do with Hall's history. This *alumnus* collection includes good sequences of editions of the poets John Oldham (1653–83) and Sir Richard Blackmore (*d*1729), and an almost complete collection of Thomas Hearne's works, and several volumes from his own library. The present stock totals: Old Library, *c*4,300 v; Working Library, *c*35,000, including 3 incunabula and 150 STC. Most books post-1900 are now housed in the library of the converted church of St Peter-in-the-East, which includes the following special collections:

Emden Collection Books on naval history, espionage and intelligence, mainly to do with the First and Second World Wars.

Risborough Collection Books and pamphlets on the Labour Movement and industrial relations; at present uncat.

St Peter-in-the-East Parish Library Eleven out of the 200 or so volumes have been recovered and added to the Hall's books.

Card cat, with separate sequences for books housed in St Peter-in-the-East, and for those in the original library building.

A B Emden, *An account of the chapel and library building of St Edmund Hall*, Oxford 1932, p27-33.

St Hilda's College, Cowley Place, Oxford OX4 1DY. Tel (0865) 241821. Admission on application, in writing, to the Librarian. Research facilities at discretion of Librarian; photocopying.

St Hilda's College Library A working library for graduates and undergraduate members of the College, built up since the College was founded in 1893, and enriched by gift and bequest. It contains *c*50,000 items (including *c*750 pamphlets). Included are *c*30 books on the history of Marie Antoinette; *c*300 on Scottish matters; a small collection of various older printed books, including 16th and 17th cent Italian and a few 16th-18th cent English and French books. There are 23 STC; 33 Wing; 31 pre-1641 foreign books.

Card cat and handlists.

St Hugh's College, Oxford OX2 6LE. Tel (0865) 57341. Admission by prior arrangement with the Librarian.

St Hugh's College Library contains *c*50,000 v, including 26 incunabula; 40 STC books; 65 pre-1641 foreign books and 47 Wing items. Notable collections include:

Several 15th and 16th cent Italian books among those bequeathed in 1926 by Mary, daughter of R W Church, Dean of St Paul's; most had been owned by her father; the library, especially strong in 18th cent French literature and history, of Eleonor Frances Jourdain, Principal 1915–24; Early English printed books, mainly Bibles and theology, left by Canon B H Streeter (1874–1937), Provost of Queen's; Mary du Caurroy (1865–1937), wife of the 11th Duke of Bedford. Her library reflecting her great interest in ornithology, natural history and the fine arts, including numerous large paper copies, limited or specially illustrated editions, mostly published during her lifetime, and all in fine bindings of the period; Cecilia Ady, the historian, bequeathed, in 1958, *c*400 v, chiefly concerned with Italian history and art, including some early printed books; in 1962 Miss E E S Proctor, Principal, gave a collection of historical works, including several 17th cent items, and further items were bequeathed in 1981; some English literature formerly owned and heavily annotated by Edith Seaton (Fellow 1926–52) was given in 1972.

Name cat on cards.

Separate card cat of the Jourdain bequest.

St John's College, Oxford OX1 3JP. Tel (0865) 247671. Admission by prior written application to the Librarian.

The strength of the library lies in its holdings of books on medicine and the natural sciences, but it is also important for its orientalia and liturgical works and its scarce tracts. The theology, classics and law elements necessary for past curricula are mostly still present. It is also rich in the writings of former members. Its stock totals *c*60,000 v, including 145 incunabula and 1,077 STC books. Notable contents include:

155 v given in 1555 by Sir Thomas White, the founder and his friends. Other early donors were Henry Cole (*c*1500–80), Dean of St Paul's; Gabriel Dunne (*c*1558), Canon of St Paul's; and Thomas Paynell (*d*1564), Canon of Merton Abbey, all of whom had Roman Catholic sympathies. The gifts of Cole and Dunne were strong in books in Greek—the Fathers, Homer, Plato, Aristotle, etc; about two-thirds of their gifts have been retained. Over 100 of Paynell's books survive, covering law, theology, philosophy, grammar and patristics. 80 v of Protestant theology given *c*1600 by two London mercers, Robert Lee and Laurence Holiday; 30 v of historical works, some in Italian, given by Sir Thomas Ducket in 1600; 800 books, mainly of medical interest, but also including law books and scholastic commentaries, given by Sir William Paddy (1554–1635), physician to James I and an alumnus, between 1600 and his death; nearly 200 books, chiefly the Fathers of the Church, given between 1598 and 1605 by Sir Thomas Tresham (*d*1605), a Recusant; Orientalia given between 1620 and 1642 by William Laud (1573–1645), President 1611–21; the library of Archbishop Juxon (1582–1663), President 1621–33, (mostly theological and historical in character), given by his son Sir William Juxon in 1664; a very general collection bequeathed by Charles Perrott (*d*1686), a lawyer; 200 v, over half medical and the others concerned with antiquities, travel and the classics, bequeathed by William Brewster (1665–1715), a physician of Hereford; over 1,500 v covering many subjects, and including many rare books (eg 11 Caxtons), bequeathed by Nathaniel Crynes (1688–1745), physician and book-collector; a general library, strong in Italian literature of the 17th and 18th cent, bequeathed by Daniel Lombard (1678–1748), and strengthened by a bequest of Italian literature and books written in English on Italy by Lacy C Collison-Morley (1875–1958); a general library, strong in early medical works and the literature of spas given by John Merrick (1705–64?), a physician; the general library, useful for works on 17th cent history and for English literature from the 17th to the 19th cent, bequeathed by W H Hutton (1860–1930); a group of classical books formerly owned by A E Housman (1859–1936), some with marginalia.

Current author cat on cards divided into two parts; books printed before 1643, and books printed 1643 to date.

Earlier cats have survived, including Bodleian cats of 1674 and 1843.

C B Chapman, 'A comment on the holdings in old medicine and science in St John's College Library', *American Oxonian*, li (1964), p116-23.

J F Fuggles, 'The Library of St John's College, Oxford, 1555–1660', in *Library Assoc Rare Books Group Newsletter* no 13 (1979), p5-11.

——'William Laud and the Library of St John's College, Oxford', *The Book Collector*, 30 (1981), p19-38.

——'A history of the library of St John's College, Oxford, from the foundation of the College to 1660'. (Univ of Oxford B Litt thesis, 1975).

Somerville College, Oxford. Tel (0865) 57595. Open (for non-members of the College) Mon-Fri 9 am-5 pm. Admission to bona fide scholars by prior arrangement with the Librarian. Microfilm reader; xeroxing facilities.

Somerville College Library contains *c*85,000 v, including 32 STC books. The rare books collections include:

500 items from the library of Mark Pattison (1813–84), selected by his widow and Ingram Bywater; the library of John Stuart Mill (1806–73) of *c*2,000 v, varying from Aldines to the writings of Mill himself, with Mill's annotations and notes, presented in 1905 by Miss Helen Taylor (his step-daughter) (separate cat); a large number of the printed books of Amelia B Edwards (1831–92), novelist and the first secretary of the Egypt Exploration Fund came with her papers in 1907—wide-ranging in subject (separate cat); part of the library of Sir William Bousfield (1842–1910) who had been concerned with education and social work in London, received in 1920; *c*300 books formerly owned by A V Dicey (1834–1922), the legal historian; the historical library of Maude Violet Clarke (*d*1935), including books printed in the early 17th cent and scarce monographs; a selection of works on diplomatic history from the collection of David Morier (1784–1807) and Sir Robert Morier (1826–93), presented in 1955 by the Hon Mrs Cunnack; the books and pamphlets of Percy Withers (1867–1945), including many inscribed by their authors, presented by his daughters Miss Monica Withers and Mrs Audrey Kennett in 1976, together with a large literary correspondence (separate cat); a collection of works of Robert Bridges presented in 1954 by Helen Darbishire (1881–1961) and Principal 1931–45, and a collection of early editions of Milton, bequeathed in 1961.

Author cat on cards.

Separate card cats of John Stuart Mills library, Amelia Edwards's Library, and the Percy Withers collection.

Taylor Institution Library, St Giles', Oxford OX1 3NA. Tel (0865) 53152. Open Mon-Fri 1 Oct-30 June 9 am-7 pm, Sat 9 am-1 pm; 1 July-30 Sept 10 am-1 pm, 2-5 pm, Sat 10 am-1 pm. Closed Sundays, Christmas to New Year, and week beginning with August Bank Holiday. Admission to members of University of Oxford on registration; others engaged on appropriate research on application. Reading rooms, loan services, microform readers, photocopying facilities.

Taylor Institution Library The Taylor Institution is the centre for the teaching of modern European languages (except English) in Oxford. Its library, established in 1847, now claims to be the largest separate collection of its kind in Britain. Its stock totals 250,000 v, including 56 incunabula, mainly in the vernacular, and 52 STC books, *c*1,300 16th cent books, *c*2,600 17th cent and *c*8,500 18th cent books. After its establishment, the Bodleian considered itself relieved of any obligation to acquire modern European literature, but the Bodleian's large collections of older mss and printed books mean that research in most literary subjects, especially if concerned with the period before 1800, involves the use of both libraries. The Taylor Institution Library is rich in research material connected with all the languages and literatures of Continental Europe, especially those studied at Oxford. It contains the chief literary and philological works in the principal European languages, a large number of periodicals, and a substantial supporting collection of foreign historical, philosophical and topographical works and linguistic atlases. Its special collections of older books include the following:

Sir Robert Taylor (1714–88), the founder, left his own copies of the great architectural publications of his own day (see D J Gilson, *Books from the library of Sir Robert Taylor in the Library of the Taylor Institution: a checklist* 1973); Robert Finch (1783–1830) bequeathed his large general library to the University (see *A catalogue of the books in the Finch collection*, Oxford, 1874). In 1921 the books were divided among the Bodleian, the Taylor Institution and the Ashmolean Museum. The Taylor Institution Library contains many literary and linguistic works of the 16th-18th cent from this source; the Misses Esther Catherine, Susan Mary and Josephine Fry, in 1955, gave books from their family library, including just under 100 v of herbals and botanical works, over 70 of which were printed before 1800 (see D J Gilson, 'Herbals in the Fry collection in the Taylor Institution', *The Book Collector*, 22 Spring 1973, p44-62.

The major European languages and literatures are represented in the following collections:

French The library is strong in works of French literature, history and culture, notably of the 17th and 18th cent, and there are also a good number of earlier printed books. Notable are over 1,000 v formerly owned by Gustave Rudler (1872–1957), Professor of French Literature, including rare 18th cent editions, Benjamin Constant material, and autographed works by 20th cent authors, and the collection of Voltaire and Voltairiana given by Dr Theodore Besterman (*d*1976), who defrayed much of the cost of the establishment of the Voltaire Room, to act as a centre for the study of Voltaire and of the Enlightenment in general.

German The collection of German literature, philology and history is no less remarkable than the French. Notable are *c*350 tracts and *Flugschriften* by Luther, Melancthon, Zwingli, Erasmus, and others, and gifts from H G Fiedler (1862–1945), Professor of German 1907–37, and his daughter, including 2,500 literary, philological and historical works (see *Catalogue of the Fiedler collection: manuscript material and books up to and including 1850*, 1962).

Italian The Finch Library was rich in works of Italian literature. Edward Moore (1864–1916) bequeathed to The Queen's College nearly 900 v of editions of Dante and related works, now deposited in the Taylor Institution; Paget Toynbee, the Dante scholar, gave a collection in 1909.

Spanish and Portuguese Miss W M Martin, in 1895, bequeathed *c*1,000 Spanish and Portuguese books, including early editions of Cervantes, Calderon and Lope de Vega, also some historical works. St John's College has placed on loan the greater part of the collection left by H Butler Clarke (1863–1904), including Latin, Arabic and Spanish books concerned with the study of Spanish Civilization before the re-discovery of America, and also literary works (see F de Arteaga y Pereira, *A catalogue of the portion of the library of H Butler Clarke, now in the library of St John's College*, 1906). Some 16th cent Portuguese books were purchased from the library of Fernando de Arteaga y Pereira in 1935.

Modern Greek R M Dawkins (1871–1955), Bywater and Sotheby Professor of Byzantine and Modern Greek, left his remarkable collection of works in the literature and history of modern Greece, Albania and Byzantium to Exeter College, now deposited in the Taylor Institution—*c*2,000 books and a large number of pamphlets.

Separate card cat.

Slavonic W R Morfill (1834–1909), Professor of Russian, left his Slavonic library to The Queen's College, now deposited in the Taylorian: a wide-ranging collection of nearly 4,000 v, strong in folk literature and the Russian Symbolist movement. Nevill Forbes (1883–1929), Morfill's successor, left 2,600 v of Slavonic interest (see J S G Simmons, 'Slavica Tayloriana Oxoniensia', *Cahiers du monde Russe et Sovietique*, x (1969), p536-45.

Ms cat of the W R Morfill collection.

There are smaller holdings in Afrikaans, Albanian (including the collection of Mrs M M Hasluck), Basque (including a collection presented by E S Dodgson), Celtic, Dutch, etc.

All dictionaries published before 1800, except for a few major works already on open shelves or those kept in the Slavonic Dept are grouped together in one room in chronological order.

Author cat with a few subject headings available.

Chronological index for works printed before 1800.

Card indexes of selected fine bindings and of some provenances.

Chronological card index of 56 incunabula.

Cat of the collection of dictionaries published pre-1800, by authors, and also by language chronologically: to be enriched by cards to cover the Bodleian and the major College holdings.

Catalogue of the library of the Taylor Institution, Oxford, 1861; *Addenda* 1879/80-82/3; Additions 1883/4-1919/20.

Trinity College Library, Oxford. Tel (0865) 241801. Open to bona fide scholars on written application in advance.

Trinity College Library Among the most notable collections in the library are: the gift of Sir Thomas Pope (the founder) of printed books, mainly 16th cent theological works, some of which were acquired from Greenwich and Hampton Court Palaces, and finely bound; the books, strong in British topography, bequeathed by John Skinner of Camerton (1750–1823); the extensive library, including topography, linguistics, history and theology left by James Ingram, President, in 1850; a small collection of 17th and 18th cent works by or about non-jurors given by W J Copeland (1805–85) in 1847; a collection of Icelandic books bequeathed by Eric Rücker Eddison in 1945; early editions of Walter Savage Landor (1775–1864) presented by C H Wilkinson (1888–1960); a general library built up over three generations, of *c*25,000 items bequeathed by John Raymond Danson (1893–1977), including books on literature, military history, heraldry, travels and India. The illustrated books are especially fine, and there is a remarkable collection of pornography. There are 40 incunabula and 308 STC books.

Some of the older volumes were sold or thrown away during the late 18th and early 19th cent. In 1807 books presented in the 16th and 17th cent were discovered, greatly decayed, and only some fragments survive.

The current cat has been in use since 1860.

Earlier cats survive.

Separate cat of James Ingram's books.

Separate card cat of the New Library for undergraduates.

Catalogue of books in the New Library, 1891. With supplements covering additions 1891–2, 1898–9, and 1899–1901.

University College, High Street, Oxford OX1 4BH. Tel (0865) 241661 Ext 261. Open 8.30 am-2 pm in term; restricted opening in vacation. Admission to members of the College only; others by appointment in writing.

The University College Library still contains a fair number of early printed works, though perhaps little that is outstanding or not available in other Oxford libraries.

It is fairly strong in theology and classics, and also scientific works. A considerable number of 17th cent pamphlets were deposited in the Bodleian after 1915; also classical texts were sent to the University of Louvain after the First World War. Some discarding between 1923 and 1935 from all parts of the library occurred, and many early printed and scarce works were deposited in the Bodleian (where they are kept as a separate collection, named after the College), and the older theological section was later deposited in the Bodleian. *c*350 titles of early scientific works have been put on permanent loan in the Museum of the History of Science. Also the Robert Ross Collection of editions and translations of Oscar Wilde, together with works illustrating literary movements in England in the 1890s, gathered by W E Ledger and presented to the College in 1930 by D C L Cree, have been deposited in the Bodleian (qv). The present stock totals *c*40,000 v, with 3 incunabula and 427 STC books. The rare books collections include:

A small *alumnus* collection, but not actively maintained; part of the library of William Holcott (*d*1575), a Berkshire squire who returned to the College from time to time to pursue his theological studies; a collection of 16th cent theological works left by John Reiner (*d*1613); more general collections bequeathed by William Pindar (*d*1678) and John Ledgard (*d*1683); liturgical and controversial books given by Obadiah Walker (*d*1699), Master 1679–89, a Roman Catholic convert; a collection of books relative to his writings on husbandry bequeathed by Timothy Nourse (*d*1699); a collection, chiefly 17th cent theology, bequeathed by Thomas Hudson (*d*1719), a former Fellow and later Bodley's Librarian; the residue of a good general collection, strong in theology, left by John Browne, Master 1745–64, still shelved in the Master's Lodging (separate cat available); theological books given by F C Plumptre, Master 1836–70 in 1861; anthropological and historical books from the library of E J Payne, received in 1904; 21 sets of works published by the Nonesuch Press, mostly bequeathed by Sir Alleyne Percival Boxall, Bart, in 1945, with a few left by Oliver Bell in 1952; a library of late 19th and 20th cent English, French and German literature, and books on fine arts, bequeathed by E A Alport (*d*1972) and to be kept separate (other gifts are shelved as part of the general collections).

Cat on cards.

Separate cat of the Browne Library.

Cats of the books on deposit in the Bodleian and the Museum of the History of Science.

Earlier cats survive.

Wadham College, Oxford. Tel (0865) 242564 Ext 97. Open 9 am-4 pm (for visiting scholars) after written application to the Librarian. (Locked) carrels for research scholars. Coin-operated Xerox machine.

Wadham College Library The College Library includes 53 incunabula and 690 STC books. In addition to the usual emphasis on theology and classics, several large gifts from the 18th cent onwards make this library important in the fields of English literature and Spanish studies, and the close connection of the College with the early days of the Royal Society makes it strong in the history of the natural sciences.

The rare book and special collections include:

The library of Philip Bisse (*c*1541–1613), Archdeacon of Taunton, consisting chiefly of Continental printed theology, with a few other subjects such as classics sparsely represented—estimated to be *c*2,000 v; Theological books left by Gilbert Drake, a fellow, in 1629; Medical books ranging from 1530 to 1617 left by John Goodrich, a fellow, in 1651; many books from all periods printed in Spain, chiefly of historical and theological interest, which belonged to Sir William Godolphin (1634?–96), Ambassador in Madrid 1671–78, bequeathed by a relative, Charles Godolphin (*c*1650–1720); a varied collection, strong in European literature and reflecting an interest in many subjects, bequeathed by Alexander Thistlethwayte (1718–71) an *alumnus*; over 4,000 v, including English literature (plays and works by Elizabethan and Jacobean writers), European literature and botany, left by Richard Warner (*d*1775) of Woodford Row, Essex, author of *Plantae Woodforienses*; the books, strong in 18th cent works, especially theology, left by Samuel Bush (*d*1783), Vicar of Wadhurst, Sussex; the printed books relating to the history and contemporary struggles of church reform in Spain, and including many editions of Juande Valdes (*c*1500–41), and 19th cent works left by Benjamin Barron Wiffen (1796–1867), a Quaker; original editions of the Elizabethan Homilies left by John Griffiths (1806–85), Warden 1871–88, a fellow; a collection of works by *alumni* left by R B Gardiner in the early 1900s; a large collection of editions of Aristophanes, together with the rest of the library, strong in classical subjects and including a few early editions of Jane Austen, Benjamin Disraeli and other early 19th cent novelists, of Benjamin Bickley Rogers (1828–1919), a fellow 1852–61; the miscellaneous books, with an emphasis on classics, of F W Hirst (1873–1953); the library reflecting wide-ranging interests in Greek (especially Pinder), Russian, Oriental and English literature, of Sir Maurice Bowra (1898–1971), with many presentation copies; Armenian early printed books donated by Dr Caro Minasian of Isfahan, Iran.

New cat on cards.

Earlier cats survive.

H A Wheeler, *A short catalogue of books printed in English, and English books printed abroad before 1641 in the library of Wadham College, Oxford*, 1929: omits all relevant items in the Wiffen collection and some other groups, but gives full descriptions with details of imperfections.

Manuscript catalogue of the Wiffen collection of printed books, and a chronological list of items printed before 1526 and 1699, both completed in 1881 by George Parker of the Bodleian.

E Boehmer, *Bibliotheca Wiffeniana: Spanish reformers of two centuries from 1520, their lives and writings*. 3 vols, 1874–1904: indicates books now in Wadham.

A descriptive catalogue of the Godolphin collection, and an historical introduction was started, but not finished, by William Greve Caldwell (*d*1972): copies in the Bodleian, Wadham and Worcester College libraries.

Sir Thomas G Jackson, *Wadham College, Oxford*, Oxford 1893, gives a very general survey describing the principal donors (193-97). E Gordon Duff (198-200) concentrated on the incunabula and the 16th cent books.

Duplicates were sold in 1736 and 1788.

Worcester College Library, Worcester College, Oxford. Tel (0865) 247251. Open weekdays 10 am-6 pm. Admission by appointment. Photography at the discretion of the Librarian is arranged through the Bodleian.

Though founded in 1714, Worcester College Library contains several hundred volumes from Gloucester Hall, the post-Reformation foundation, including a group of about 40, mostly mathematical, owned and annotated by John Aubrey, the antiquary. The library holds 175,000 v, including 29 incunabula; and 1,660 STC books. The more notable collections include:

A general library of over 400 items given by Samuel Cooke in 1714; a remarkable collection of 17th cent pamphlets and Civil War tracts, many of Scottish interest, collected by Sir William Clarke (1623?–66), of old English plays and literature, and of books on architecture, some once belonging to Inigo Jones, all bequeathed by George Clarke (1661–1736), politician and Fellow of All Souls; (*Note* In addition to Inigo Jones's books, the library holds about half of his architectural drawings to survive); the remarkable library bequeathed by William Gower, Provost 1736–77, including the standard works and texts of the time, but notable for its Spanish printed books of the 16th and 17th cent, some formerly owned by Sir William Godolphin (1634?–96), sometime Ambassador in Spain, and for its collection of early English plays (duplicates from this collection were sold, probably at the time of receipt); the collections, covering all subjects and periods, bequeathed by H A Pottinger (1824–1911), College Librarian, including a large number of 19th cent tracts and ephemera; a small group of late 17th and early 18th cent tracts and books, and a working library bequeathed by Sir Charles Firth (1857–1936); a select collection of English literature of the late 17th cent bequeathed by C H Wilkinson (1888–1960), College Librarian, to which have been added some judicious purchases from the sale of his books (Sotheby's 24-25 Oct 1960, 27-29 Mar, 26-27 June 1961); a collection of modern private press books and a comprehensive set of the products of the press maintained, for many years within the College, by C H O Daniel, Provost 1903–1919; The parochial library of Denchworth, Berks (founded 1693) of *c*150 v, mainly of theological interest, has been deposited; the library contains *c*1,200 plays printed before 1750, and interesting bindings and book-sale catalogues.

Author cat in the form of ledgers with ms entries, dating from the late 19th cent.

Ms cat of the Pottinger collection.

Chronological list of pamphlets up to 1900, arranged by year of publication, and including Pottinger's tracts.

A catalogue of the books relating to classical archaeology and ancient history in the Library of Worcester College, 1878. Additions 1878/9-1879/80.

A handlist of English plays and masques printed before 1750 in... Worcester College, Oxford. 1929. *Plays added up to March 1948, including some previously omitted*. (1948).

Relevant holdings are also shown in Sir W W Greg, *A bibliography of the English printed drama to the Restoration*. 4 v. Bibliographical Soc Illus Monographs, no xxiv, 1939–59.

List of bookplates and list of signatures of former owners, made by E M Girling, 1900–01, but incomplete.

C H Wilkinson, 'Worcester College Library', *Oxford Bibl Soc Proc and Papers* i (1927), p263-320.

Woodstock

Blenheim Palace, Woodstock, Oxford OX7 1PX. Tel (0993) 811325. Open by arrangement to bona fide scholars on written application.

Blenheim Palace Library The library is based upon the collection made by Stuart J Reid for the 9th Duke of Marlborough in the years 1897–1900. (The Sunderland Library, collected by Charles Spencer, 3rd Earl of Sunderland, 1674–1722, and formerly housed at Blenheim, was dispersed and sold by Puttick and Simpson in 1881–3. (See Sale Catalogue, *Bibliotheca Sunderlandiana* London, 1881–3).) The present collection consists of 10,000 v, and includes a number of rare volumes of the 18th cent relating to the military exploits of John, Duke, and the career of Sarah, Duchess of Marlborough, during the reign of Queen Anne; these number *c*225 v, plus much related 19th cent material, in the fields of military and naval history, biography, and legal and political history. The majority of the remaining volumes dates from the second half of the 19th cent and the first decade of the 20th; there is much fine natural history (especially horticulture), agriculture and forestry, science, literature, including 1st editions of Conrad, Wells, and Bennett, and a section of French literature, art and architecture, music, including 92 organ rolls, classics, theology, travel and topography, hunting, shooting, fishing etc. Most have been finely rebound in leather. Books by and about Sir Winston Churchill are added as regular policy.

(a) Alphabetical list of the books in the Long Library...(see below) giving full author, title, imprint, format, but no locations.

(b) Classified catalogue, 8 vols.

(c) One-volume looseleaf classified catalogue, incorporating recent accessions; gives author and short title only, plus current locations. If (a) and (b) are used in tandem, most items can be identified and located without difficulty.

(d) MS inventory of the Sunderland Library, made 1817–20, 94 vols.

Michael Kerney, 'Charles Spencer, Third Earl of Sunderland, 1675 (*sic*)–1722' in (Bernard Quaritch ed) *Contributions towards a Dictionary of English Book-Collectors*, London, 1892–1921, pt II.

A L Rowse, *The Later Churchills* (London 1958), pp6-7, 240-1.

Seymour de Ricci, *English Collectors of Books and Manuscripts (1530–1930) and their Marks of Ownership* (Cambridge, 1930), p33-43.

See also the printed catalogue of the Sunderland Library, *Catalogue of the Books in the Library at Blenheim Palace, collected by Charles, Third Earl of Sunderland* (Oxford, 1872) and the sale catalogue.

Alphabetical list of the books in the Long Library— Blenheim. Collected by Stuart J Reid, TS, p1.

Archives now mainly in the British Library; some estate papers remaining at Blenheim.

Salop

Shrewsbury

Shrewsbury School, The Schools, Shrewsbury, Shropshire. Tel (0743) 62926. The Taylor (ancient) Library is open by arrangement on written application.

Shrewsbury School Library Basically a 17th-18th cent county grammar school library, the collection dates from 1606, with acquisitions by purchase, donation and bequest. Its stock, mostly pre-1760, totals *c*7,000 v, including 76 incunabula and probably several hundred STC items. The subject coverage is wide, and not confined to the narrow interests of the 17th cent grammar school. The 20th cent collections have been formed of Shropshire local history, including 18th and 19th cent ephemera. The collection also includes the books of two 17th cent Shrewsbury doctors, Dr Andrew Griffiths (*d*1688) and Dr Edward Phillips (*d*1713) in addition to the extensive library of the 18th cent classical scholar Dr John Taylor (1704–66) who bequeathed the major part of his library (*c*3,000 v) to the school in 1766. The strength of his library lay in editions of Demosthenes, Roman coins and inscriptions, and English topography.

The library has a fine collection of English blind-stamped bindings of the 15th-17th cent, as well as other bindings. Originally a chained library; the chains were removed in 1736, while the present furniture, much reconstructed, dates essentially from 1829. The detailed library archives document the growth and arrangement of the library, and include Accession Registers 1606–*c*1800, borrowing registers 1736–1826, and shelf and other catalogues of 1613, *c*1640, 1664, 1736, 1788, and *c*1805—the last is still in use.

J B Oldham, *Shrewsbury School Library Bindings*, OUP, 1943.

——'Shrewsbury School Library: its earlier history and organisation', *The Library* (1935), p49-60.

——'Shrewsbury School Library', *The Library* (1959), p81-99.

——'Shrewsbury School Library: its history and contents', *Trans Shropshire Arch Soc* LI, (1941), p53-81.

P Kaufman, 'The Loan records of Shrewsbury School', *The Library* 5th ser, v XXII, p252-6.

Shropshire County Library, Column House, 7 London Road, Shrewsbury SY2 6NW. Tel (0743) 52561. Telex 35187. Open Mon-Thurs 9 am-5 pm, Fri 9 am-4 pm. Admission to the collections is strictly on application from bona fide researchers to the County Librarian, and use of the collection is under supervision only. Photocopying facilities.

The Shropshire Parochial Libraries Collection Contains the books from 8 (including one Bray) of some 11 surviving parochial libraries of Shropshire which have been placed on deposit under the care of the County Library. Another library—the Prees Parochial Library—is housed in the Shropshire County Record Office, while the other two are still in their respective Parish Churches, St Luke at Hodnet and St Peter at More. The eight libraries which comprise this collection are:

Atcham (St Eata's) *c*200 v mainly of the 16th and 17th cent, and include a chained copy of the 1609 ed of Jewel's *Works*.

Card cat.

Bridgnorth (St Leonard's) *c*5,000 v, mainly of the 18th cent.

Card cat.

Chirbury (St Michael's) Probably one of the oldest of the Shropshire parochial libraries. It was bequeathed in 1677 by Edward Lewis, Vicar, for 'the use of the Schoolmaster or any other of his parishioners who shall desire to read them'. Many of the surviving 250 v still carry their original chains.

Card cat.

Preston Gubbals (St Martin's) 100 v, mainly 18th cent divinity.
Card cat.

Tong (St Bartholomew's) A library created by Gervase Pierrepont (later Lord Pierrepont) of Tong Castle in 1697 'for the use of the minister and his successors'. It was originally housed in the castle and not in the church. There are *c*1,000 v forming 'an impressive collection' of folios bound in leather or vellum, as well as many smaller works.
Card cat.

Wentnor (St Michael's) The books were in most part bequeathed by Edward Rogers, Rector of Mindtown, in 1788. The collection now totals 150 v, including a number of service-books and a work by Jewel.
Card cat.

Whitchurch (St Alkmund's) A library founded by a collection of 2,250 v belonging to Clement Sankey, a former rector, bought by Jane, Dowager Countess of Bridgwater, and in 1717 presented to the church. In 1849 there were 3,007 v in all, including 834 folios. *c*3,000 v still survive, and include a chained copy of the 1566 ed of Fox's *Book of Martyrs.*
Card cat.

Dudleston (Bray Library) Established in 1712, *c*200 v have survived. The original packing case/bookcase in which the books were sent to Dudleston also survive.
Card cat.
Catalogue of books from Parochial Libraries in Shropshire. . ., Mansell, London, 1971. (*Note*: The books are listed alphabetically by author and title. A code letter is used indicating the particular library to which the copy belongs.)

Somerset

Stratton-on-the-Fosse

Downside Abbey, Stratton-on-the-Fosse, Nr Bath, Somerset BA3 4RG. Tel (0761) 232513. Open daily 9 am-5 pm only to *bona fide* students who could not normally consult the books they require elsewhere. Application by letter to the Librarian. No lending or photocopying facilities.

Downside Abbey Library Founded 1814 at Downside, at Douai in Flanders 1607–1795, at Acton Burnell in Shropshire 1795–1814, but few books and archives remain from pre-1814. Contains over 70,000 works, being the major library of the English Benedictine Congregation relating to Catholic theological, liturgical and mystical literature, recorded in STC and Wing, the individual subcollections being as follows:

English Catholic authors Printed books in any language by English Catholic authors, editors or translators, 1540–1829, the earlier works printed illegally or smuggled into the country. Includes a number of anti-Catholic tracts of historical importance. (1,500 works).

Minor ascetical works By Benedictine authors, including many by 'Maurists', printed before 1800. With a few books of Emblems. (200 works).

Religious orders Rules Constitutions and Documents concerning religious orders, with a few controversies between orders. The original tracts are here included, not modern accounts. Commentaries on the Rule of St Benedict are also included. (200 works).

Periodicals The main monastic periodicals of Britain, France and Germany, including complete runs of *Catholic Directory* and *The Tablet*. Many minor 19th cent Catholic periodicals, many short-lived titles.

Tracts and pamphlets About 1,300 bound v containing some 12,000 tracts and pamphlets mainly religious and dating from the 17th cent.

Canon Law A collection dating from the 16th cent onwards. Has the commoner works but many are rare and the collection possibly unique. (2,000 works).

Theology Printed books from the 16th cent onwards. (7,000 works).

Hagiography Lives of the Saints from the 16th cent onwards. (3,000 works).

Thomas à Kempis A special collection on him and the authorship of the *Imitation of Christ*, dating from the 16th cent onwards. (200 works).

Mystical works A collection of works of Christian prayer dating from the 16th cent. (1,000 works).

Patristics A collection of the Fathers of the Church and commentaries on patristics generally, including nearly all the early folio printed editions. Includes Migne, the *Vienna Corpus*, the *Corpus Christianorum*, and *Sources Chrétiennes*. (10,000 works).

Monastic history Includes all Western Europe and a certain amount on the Eastern Church. (5,000 works).

Liturgy Liturgical texts of Western Europe dating from the 16th cent onwards. (2,500 works).

Bishop Library The complete collection of Edmund Bishop concerned chiefly with liturgy, monastic history, and inventories. A detailed account can be found in the biography of Bishop by Donald Atwater, including a bibliography of Bishop's own writings. (7,000 works).

Tolhurst Collection A unique and possibly complete collection of photostats of every page of every office book of the mediaeval English monasteries that still survives. Made by John Tolhurst.

Postcards Two collections. The first of some 12-14,000 cards collected by J Tolhurst and concerned with mediaeval and Gothic buildings throughout Western Europe. The second, some 12,000 cards, mainly ecclesiastical, arranged by subject, collected by Dom Bede Camm.

Street

Street Library, 1 Leigh Road, Street, Somerset BA16 0HA. Tel (0458) 42032. Open Mon, Tues, Thurs 10 am-5 pm, Fri 10 am-7.30 pm; Sat 9.30 am-4 pm. Admission by appointment preferred. Study area in Public Lending Library. Photocopier available.

Housman Collection Accumulated by Roger and Sarah Clark, close friends of Laurence and Clemence Housman, in Street. The correspondence between the two families dates from 1908. Collection presented by the Clark family to Street Library in 1967. It comprises 16 drawings, 200 letters, 150 books by, or including writing or illustrations by Laurence Housman; 22 letters, 3 novels and 1 short story by Clemence Housman.

Bound folders: Drawings and letters, original and unpublished MSS (some still found in books). A number of autograph letters and poems in the hands of Max Beerbohm, Laurence Binyon, John Masefield, G K Chesterton, Sir Arthur Quiller-Couch, Bernard Shaw, E H Shepard. Sir Charles Trevelyan, Oscar Wilde and A E Housman.

Cat prepared by Ivor Kemp, 1967. Supplement 1974.

Taunton

Somerset Archaeological and Natural History Society, The Castle, Castle Green, Taunton, Somerset TA1 4AD. Tel (0823) 88871. Open Tues-Fri 9.30 am-12.30 pm, 2-4.45 pm; Sat 9.30 am-12.30 pm, 2-4 pm. Only members admitted to the shelves, but books available for consultation by the public in Somerset County Council's Local History Library (qv) at the same address. Loans to members only. Access to photocopying facilities.

Somerset Archaeological and Natural History Society Library The library has been built up by purchase, gift and exchange since the Society's formation in 1849. It contains *c*20,000 books, the major collection of material relating to the history, archaeology, natural history, genealogy and literature of the ancient County of Somerset. The Tite Collection of Somerset books (*c*4,000) contains a good proportion of general works, sermons etc by Somerset authors. There are 55 STC and 385 Wing items (including 45 Civil War Tracts).

Worthy of note are the Piggott and Braikenridge Collections of Somerset drawings—*c*2,000 items.

Card dictionary cat to general collection.

Bound typescript dictionary cat to the Tite Collection.

Neil Ker, 'Four medieval manuscripts in the Taunton Castle Museum', *Proceedings Somerset Arch and Nat Hist Soc*, 96 (1951), p224-28.

Somerset County Council, Local History Library, The Castle, Castle Green, Taunton TA1 4AD. Tel (0823) 88871. Open to public for reference only Tues-Fri 9.30 am-12.30 pm, 2-5.30 pm; Sat 9.30 am-12.30 pm, 2-4 pm. Microfilm reader, photographing facilities, loans to other libraries for reference only.

Local History Collection Separated from Somerset County Library's general reference collection in January 1973, with minor additions from the former Bridgwater, Taunton and Yeovil Borough Libraries' collections after April 1974. Estimated 5,000 books, pamphlets and bound periodical volumes, 560 reels of microfilmed newspapers and theses cover the history, antiquities and literature of the pre-1974 county of Somerset, but with relatively little on the former county borough of Bath. Includes approximately 12 books published 1500–1640, and 45 published 1641–1700. Authors of these include Joseph Alleine, Richard Bernard, Thomas Coryate, Samuel Cradock, William Prynne and Francis Roberts. The collection is added to regularly.

Public access to the Somerset Archaeological and Natural History Society's library (qv) is provided through this library.

Wells

Wells Cathedral, Somerset. The Library is available to bona fide research students on written application to the Chancellor. Research facilities and services.

Wells Cathedral Library The library existed in the 13th cent, but moved to its present location in 1424, dispersed under Commonwealth, re-established and refurbished 1660–70, extended in 1885, and Annexe provided in 1972. The library is now basically a working library and muniments depository for the Dean and Chapter. There are *c*5,000 books (excluding muniments), of which *c*250 are chained. These include 8 incunabula and 70 books printed pre-1550. The Bath Abbey Collection is deposited at Wells for safe keeping, and contains mainly early medical and scientific books.

Wells Cathedral Library, Friends of Wells Cathedral, 1974 (pamph).

Sir Robert Birley, *The Cathedral Library (in) Wells Cathedral: a history*, ed by L S Colchester. Open Books, 1982, p204-11.

Staffordshire

Keele

University Library, Keele, Staffs ST5 5BG. Tel (0782) 621111. Open Mon-Fri 9.30 am-10 pm (Term), 9.30 am-5 pm (Vacation), but access to special collections only before 5 pm. Non-members should write to the Librarian before visiting. Microform readers; photocopying and photographic facilities.

General Reserve Collection 14,000 items (books, pamphlets, periodicals) for the most part printed before 1830; *c*2,000 STC and Wing books. Bulk of collection from the library of Charles Sarolea (1870–1953) Professor of French at Edinburgh, and Belgian Consul; greatest strengths reflect his interests in history, travel, divinity, languages, especially French.

All material listed in library's main cat.

Supplementary cat of pre-1700 imprints.

Turner Collection of the History of Mathematics, the gift of Charles W Turner (*d*1973) in 1968. 1,400 v from late 15th to mid-19th cent; 16 incunabula. Unusually complete set of early editions of Euclid; and of Sir Isaac Newton, including 8 v from his private library, one (Boyle's *Medicina hydrostatica*, 1690) with his autograph notes and corrections; also ms draft of the last two paragraphs of his *Lectiones opticae* concerning the formation of the rainbow (item 301 in Portsmouth sale, 1936).

S Shapin and S Hill, 'Turner collection of the history of mathematics', *British Journ Hist Sci*, 6 (1973).

S Hill, *Catalogue of the Turner Collection of the history of mathematics*, Keele, 1982.

The mss collections include:

Arnold Bennett mss, accumulated from different sources. *c*1,000 items, mainly letters (some still sealed and not available for consultation), but including the mss of Bennett's *Journal*, v 6, *Amateur at the opera*, *Jock at a venture*, *Lilian*, *Reviewers*, *Schooldays in the Five Towns*.

Classified handlist available in the library.

Raymond Richards (1906–78) Collection of miscellaneous historical mss, purchased in 1957 (had earlier been on deposit in John Rylands Library). *c*6,000 documents dating from early 12th cent (charter of King Stephen) to 19th cent. 120 political cartoons, some by John Doyle.

Handlist available in the library.

Wedgwood accumulation, deposited by Messrs J Wedgewood and Sons Ltd of Barlaston, Stoke-on-Trent, whose permission is required for publication or reproduction, relates to Wedgwood family and business interests. As well as correspondence with business partners, there is correspondence with contemporaries of note. The most important material (W Wordsworth, S T Coleridge, Mrs Gaskell, Harriet Martineau, Maria Edgeworth, T Carlyle, Darwin family, Sir Joseph Banks, J Priestley, George Stubbs, Joseph Wright) has been published.

Smaller ms collections include the papers of A D Lindsay (1879–1952), 1st Baron Lindsay of Birker, and first Principal of the University College of North Staffordshire (*c*1,500 items); and some working papers of Karl Mannheim (1893–1947), German sociologist (*c*500 items).

Lichfield

Lichfield Cathedral Library, The Cathedral, Lichfield, Staffs. (No tel). Access by arrangement, in writing, to bona fide research workers providing a letter of introduction; application to be made to the Hon Librarian or Consultant Librarian, Main Library, University of Birmingham, P O Box 363, Birmingham B15 2TT. Microfilming and photocopying by special permission of the Dean and Chapter; application *must* be made in writing.

The library is basically that of the Dean and Chapter of Lichfield as re-founded after the Restoration through the initial gift of William, 2nd Duke of Somerset, and since augmented by gift and purchase. Content almost entirely theological, but with some 18th and 19th cent literature. 14 medieval mss (including St Chad's Gospels, 8th cent, Chaucer's *Canterbury Tales*, Wycliffite New Testament (*c*1410)) and 80 other mss, particularly Cathedral history. Printed books: *c*8,000 v, including 8 incunabula, 3,000 v pre-1700; 3,600 v 18th and 19th cent theology. Dean H E Savage (1854–1939) papers, *c*1,200 items.

A Catalogue of the printed books and manuscripts in the Library of the Cathedral Church of Lichfield (and) *Supplement*. London, H Sotheran, 1888, 1911.

B S Benedikz, *Lichfield Cathedral Library. A Catalogue of the...Manuscripts. Revised version*. Birmingham, 1978.

——*Lichfield Cathedral Library. A Handlist of the Papers of the Very Rev H E Savage*. Birmingham, 1977.

——'The Cathedral Library', *Ann Rept of the Friends of Lichfield Cathedral*, 39 (1976), p8-12.

Stafford

William Salt Library, Eastgate Street, Stafford. Tel (0785) 52276. Open Tues-Thurs 9.30 am-12.45 pm, 1.45-5 pm, Fri 9.30 am-12.15 pm, 1.45-4.30 pm; Sat 9.30 am-1 pm. Please ring the bell. Photocopying and photostat facilities by arrangement with the County Record Office.

General Collection Contains *c*12-15,000 printed books whose subject matter is mainly Staffordshire topography, genealogy and history; early editions of books by

Staffordshire authors or those with Staffordshire connections; Staffordshire periodicals; maps of Staffordshire dating from the 16th cent; ephemera; and the notes of local antiquaries. There are also *c*1,000 ft of shelving of mss, covering all dates from Anglo-Saxon charters to 20th cent notebooks, and all subjects with a local connection, and includes parish register transcripts.

Card cat.

William Salt (1808–63) A banker who drew on his family's and, later, his own wealth to indulge his interest in Staffordshire and its history by purchasing relevant material on a large scale. In 1868, five years after his death, his widow put his collection up for auction. She was persuaded to offer it to the county, and it subsequently formed the basis of the William Salt Library, opened in 1872. It consists of more than 4,000 v and mss, including *c*20 incunabula and *c*100 Wing and STC items. Particular strengths are Civil War letters and tracts, both originals and transcripts, and proclamations.

Printed cat originally produced for auction, 1868.

Pamphlet Collection Several thousand pamphlets dating from the 18th cent to the present day and arranged topographically and by subject.

Card cat.

Picture Collection Includes more than 3,000 Staffordshire views commissioned or collected and assembled by William Salt, mostly early 19th cent; also collections of sketches and watercolours by local artists, and a collection of 18th and 19th cent cartoons and caricatures. There is also a collection of photographs and postcards arranged topographically.

Card cat

Gerald P Mander, 'Descriptive catalogue of the... Staffordshire Views Collection', *Collections for a history of Staffordshire*, Staffordshire Record Society, 1942–3. (op)

Suffolk

Aldeburgh

Britten-Pears Library, The Red House, Aldeburgh, Suffolk IP15 1PZ. Tel (072 885) 2615. The library is open to scholars and research students by appointment only on written application to the Librarian.

The Britten-Pears Library Over the years Benjamin Britten and Peter Pears built up a collection of books and music which reflects the interest and activities of both the composer and the singer. The library contains principally: (a) A comprehensive collection of English songs from the 16th cent to the present day; (b) Literature relating to English song and singers; (c) A general collection of music, including a number of collected editions; (d) A general collection of books on poetry, drama and other subjects, including source material for the study of Britten's works; (e) A large collection of ms material, including major works by Britten and Holst; conducting scores annotated by Britten.

Card cat of music scores and literature.

Title and analytical song indexes.

The Britten-Pears Library. Aldeburgh, Suffolk. (pamphlet)

Bury St Edmunds

Ickworth House, Ickworth Rotunda, Horringer, Bury St Edmunds, Suffolk IP29 5QE. Tel (028 488) 270. Admission by written application to the Libraries Adviser, National Trust, 42 Queen Anne's Gate, London SW1.

Hervey/Bristol Family Collection In 1658 (after their marriage), Sir Thomas and Lady Isabella Hervey began the library which was continually added to by their relatives and descendants of the families Hervey and (Earls of) Bristol throughout the 17th and 18th cent. Since the house was completed (1830) the books have remained in shelves in corridors and various parts of the building. It became National Trust property in 1956. The library contains *c*7,000 v, including *c*50 v of pamphlets, covering British political and parliamentary history, astronomy, fine art and architecture, drama, agriculture and horticulture, law and topography. There are *c*100 Wing items; *c*150 18th cent English imprints and *c*75 18th cent foreign (mainly French) items.

Typed card index filed in study in three sequences: author, subject, title.

Ms file of ownership, inscriptions etc.

St Edmundsbury Cathedral, The Cathedral Church of St James, Bury St Edmunds, Suffolk. Admission by written or personal application to the Provost.

St James Parish Library The library began in 1595 with gifts of books by Samuel Aylmer (Mowden Hall, Essex) and other local laymen and clergy. By 1599, 200 v were listed which were added to by gifts until 1764. The library was removed to the Guildhall (1846–65) to form part of Bury and Suffolk Library. In 1960 volumes were 'rescued' from the vestry of St James (now a Cathedral church) and filled part of a newly built library room. The collection contains 480 v, including 5 incunabula; 45 STC and 53 Wing items. There are also 7 ms music compositions, autographed organ pieces, by William 'Vayland' Jones.

Card shelf-index.

Suffolk Parochial Libraries—a catalogue. Mansell, 1977.

F K Eagle, *Catalogue of the library of St James Church. . .*, Bury, 1847.

J A Fitch, 'Some ancient Suffolk parochial libraries'. *Suffolk Inst of Arch Proceedings*, XXX (1965), p44-87.

The following parochial libraries are on permanent loan to the Cathedral:

Assington Parish Library Founded in 1690 under the terms of the will of the Rev Thomas Alston, incumbent, who listed nearly 300 titles in his parish notebook (now in Suffolk Record Office, Bury Branch). The books were housed in the Rectory. There are now 350 v (*c*500 items), *c*190 identifiable as being Thomas Alston's—many of which are annotated. They include 1 incunabulum; 220 STC and 180 Wing items; and 20 17th cent foreign imprints.

Suffolk Parochial Libraries catalogue. Mansell, 1977.

J A Fitch, *op cit.* p55-8.

Beccles Parish Library Begun *c*1707 by the Rev Thomas Armstrong (Rector 1671–1715), by donations from local gentry and learned clerics, the library was deposited with Beccles first Public Library in 1840 where it remained for *c*30 years. In 1962 what remained were 'rescued' from a damp vestry, repaired by East Suffolk Record Office and rehoused in the Cathedral in 1964. There are *c*150 v on theology and the classics. These include 1 incunabulum; 8 STC and 30 Wing items; 12 16th cent and 33 17th cent Continental Latin works.

Printed cat of 1846 in *Suffolk Parochial Libraries Catalogue*, Mansell, 1977.

J A Fitch, *op cit.* p44-82.

Coddenham Parish Library Originated in 1739 from a bequest of the French (Huguenot) Vicar Baltazar Gardemau to which the Bacon family added 12 v. There are *c*365 v (400 items), nearly 50 being French publications; *c*100 contemporary pamphlets (1685–87), bound as 'controversial tracts'. There are 3 STC and 175 Wing items.

Suffolk Parochial Libraries catalogue, Mansell, 1977.

J A Fitch, *op cit.* p77-83.

——'Baltazar Gardemau: a Huguenot squarson and his library', *Huguenot Soc of London Proc*, v 31 (3), p241-72.

Lawshall Parish Library Begun in 1704 from a bequest of the Rector (1681–1704), the Rev Stephen Camborne, which included some of his father's (Rev Thomas Camborne, Rector of Campsea Ashe) library. There were a few 19th cent additions. The collection totals 136 items (127 of which are signed by Stephen Camborne) which include 4 STC and 63 Wing items. They cover theology, classics (mainly 17th cent Continental imprints) in Latin and Greek.

Ms cat in Suffolk Record Office, Ipswich, dated 1709.

Suffolk Parochial Libraries: a catalogue, Mansell, 1977.

J A Fitch, *op cit.* p44-87.

Suffolk Record Office, Bury Branch, School Hall Street, Bury St Edmunds, Suffolk. Tel (0284) 63141 Ext 384 or 388. Open Mon-Thurs 9 am-5.15 pm, Fri 9 am-4.15 pm; Sat 9 am-1 pm, 2-5 pm. Research facilities and services as available to Record Office researchers.

Cullum Library The Cullum family collection from Hardwick House, Bury, was acquired between 1656 and 1922; a bequest to the Borough of Bury St Edmunds by Sir G Milner Gibson Cullum in 1922 of 'English non-fiction', while foreign language items were left to Trinity College, Cambridge (*c*1,500), and fiction to a surviving relative. The collection of *c*4,200 v (of which 3,000 v are shelved with local history) was absorbed into the Borough Library reference collection in 1963, and County Library in 1974 (now in the same building and administered by the Suffolk Record Office). Main subject areas are natural history, genealogy, history, travel, biography, East Anglian and local history and topography. The collection includes *c*100 STC titles (11751 and 11752, the latter hand-coloured); *c*500 Wing items. About 25 pre-1800 items have interesting armorial binding or provenance. Most items are leather bound with family crest, and these have bookplates and notes in ms of original owner, purchase details etc. The Record Office holds the Cullum family papers, diaries and letters. Many books are listed in the sale contents of Hardwick House in 1924.

F C Brooke, 'The catalogue of books, mss and paintings at Hardwick House' (1844); typescript list *c*1922; current card cat of non-historical material.

L J Redstone, 'Hardwick House', *Proc Suffolk Inst Arch*, XIV, 1912.

Philip Hepworth, 'The Cullum Library', *East Anglian Magazine*, April 1955.

Local History Collection Formed in 1974, the Suffolk Inst of Arch and Cullum collections, Borough and County Reference Libraries and Moyses Hall Collection. In 1854 a library was formed by the newly-established Suffolk Inst of Arch and Nat Hist, and housed in the Athenaeum, and later moved to Moyses Hall Museum. In 1961 some non-local items were sold, and the collection was moved to the County Library. It contained 120 items, of which *c*50 are pre-1851, and the 'Raven' pamphlet collection (26 v) of the late 18th and early 19th cent, early works on East Anglian biography (17th cent onwards), and topographers.

Card cat; catalogues included in Appendices to the *Proc Suffolk Inst Arch*, especially 1856 and 1891.

A V Steward, 'A Suffolk bibliography', *Suffolk Records Society*, July 1979.

Ipswich

Ipswich Central Library (Suffolk County Library), Northgate Street, Ipswich IP1 3DE. Tel (0473) 214370 and 53561. Open Mon-Thurs 9.30 am-6 pm, Fri 9.30 am-8 pm; Sat 9.30 am-5 pm. Admission by personal or written application. Research facilities are available from Reference Library (upstairs).

Ipswich Old Town Library Initially a 1599 bequest by William Smart (Portman, ie Alderman of Ipswich) of some 20 v which, in 1615, with other donations, was formed into the Town Library. By 1799 there were some 800 v listed. It now consists of *c*700 works relating to local history and topography, theology, natural history: there are 2 incunabula; 59 STC and 71 Wing items. Also 8 mss probably from the Abbey, Bury St Edmunds.

Ms list of benefactors begun 1615 and continued to 1759.

Ms sheaf cat (1920s) kept in Reference Library.

A numerical catalogue..., prepared by Rev John King. Burrell, Ipswich, 1799.

M R James, 'Description of the ancient mss in Ipswich Public Library', *Suffolk Inst of Arch Proceedings*, XXII (1) 1934.

J A Fitch, 'Some early parish libraries', *op cit* XXX (1965).

H R Hammelmann, 'An ancient public library', *TLS* 18 Aug 1950.

Newmarket

Newmarket County Branch Library, 1A The Rookery, Newmarket, Suffolk. Tel (0683) 61216/7. Closed Mon. Open Tues and Fri 9 am-7.30 pm, Wed 9 am-1 pm; Sat 9 am-5 pm.

Racing Collection Built up by purchase and gift from 1973 onwards as a special collection. Since September 1976 it has been made available to the public in the new library building. It contains *c*750 v, and covers the subject areas of flat-racing history and biographies; steeplechasing; study and anatomy of the horse; sporting memoirs and periodicals—mostly 19th or 20th cent, but includes several rare 18th cent items.

Author (main entries) card index (giving purchase prices).

Classified index.

The Jockey Club, Newmarket, Suffolk CB8 8JL. Tel (0638) 4151. Admission by special arrangement on written application to the Agent.

Jockey Club Room's Library Collected over the years (since the 19th cent) by donations, the library contains *c*500 v, of which *c*300 are racing calendars or similar serials publications. The remaining 200 v consist mainly of sporting memoirs of the late 19th and 20th cent with notable exceptions, eg Sam Chifney, *Genius genuine* (1791); James and Henry Roberts, *The sportsman's companion or portraitures...of the most eminent race horses*, J Barker (1760); Charles Hunt, *Portraits of winning horses*, Rock and Payne (1849).

Mss collection includes autograph set of five notebooks; betting books of John Gully (1810–24).

Typescript alphabetical list of authors and titles.

Sudbury

Sudbury Preparative Meeting (The Society of Friends), Friends Meeting House, Friars Street, Sudbury, Suffolk. Tel (0787) 73353. Open by arrangement with the librarian.

Bury Monthly Meeting Library Set up for the Bury St Edmunds Meeting, from 1780. Moved to Sudbury 1843, the library contains *c*120 v, 12 of which are of collected tracts, 1771–1812 (4-5 in each v). They relate to Quaker literature and memoirs of the late 18th and early 19th cent; 6 items are pre-1753. Many provincial publications included in the collection. Another 100 items relate to late 19th cent Sunday School and temperance material.

A catalogue of the books of Bury Monthly Meeting Library. Wright, Sudbury, 1847.

Woodbridge

Woodbridge Parish Library, St Mary's Church, Woodbridge, Suffolk. Tel (039 43) 2155. Admission on application to the incumbent, The Rectory, 100 Seekford Street, Woodbridge.

Woodbridge Parish Library The library originated from a bequest in 1773 under the will of the Rev Thomas Hewett, MA, Rector of Bucklesham, and kept in the vestry in original leather binding. It contains *c*180 v (150 items) mainly on theology, history, medicine and astronomy, and these include 11 STC and 50 Wing items; 15 Latin works of the 17th cent, and 10 Latin works of the 18th cent. T Hewett's autograph signature and annotations in most volumes.

Ms cat (by V B Redstone), 1936.

Suffolk Parochial Libraries: a catalogue, Mansell, 1977.

J A Fitch, *op cit*. p44-87.

Surrey

Camberley

Royal Military Academy, Sandhurst, Camberley, Surrey. (The College is in Berkshire, but is entered from Surrey.) Tel (0276) 63344 Ext 367. Open Mon, Tues, Thurs 8.30 am-12.30 pm, 1.30-7 pm, Wed, Fri 8.30 am-12.30 pm, 1.30-5 pm. Admission to members of the Academy; others strictly by appointment. Photocopier available.

The College was founded in 1801, and the book collection of *c*90,000 v has been acquired by gift and purchase. There are special collections of early books on fortification, campaigns, regimental histories; Army lists from 1772; 18 v of 18th cent pamphlets.

Sheaf author and subject cats.

Staff College, Camberley, Surrey. Tel (0276) 63344 Ext 692. Open Mon-Thurs 8.30 am-5 pm, Fri 8.30 am-4.30 pm. Admission to members of the College; others strictly by appointment. Photocopier available.

The College was founded in 1820 and moved to Camberley in 1860. Acquisitions of older printed material was largely by individual donations. The library contains *c*50,000 v, of which *c*900 v are pre-1851, and mostly early 19th cent. Subject areas are mainly military science, campaign histories, regimental histories. The collection includes R Valturius *De re militari* (Paris, 1532); N Machiavelli *Opere* ('1550', ie 1610-45); L Rusius *Hippiatria* (Paris, 1531); F Vegatius Renatus *De militari libri quatuor* (Paris, 1532); and A Durer *De urbibus* (Paris, 1535).

Older books not yet cat.

Chertsey

Chertsey Museum (Runnymede Borough Council), The Cedars, Windsor Street, Chertsey, Surrey KT16 8AT. Tel (09328) 65764. Open Tues, Thurs 2-4.30 pm, Wed, Fri, Sat 10 am-1 pm, 2-4.30 pm. Exhibition galleries open free to public; printed material available for reference on prior application to the Curator. Photocopying facilities available.

The Museum was founded in 1972 and acquisitions have been acquired by donation and permanent loan. The library contains *c*12 pre-1851 works, including 1 Wing (A1128), 200 locally printed programmes, and other ephemera.

Effingham

Effingham Parish Church, c/o The Vicar, St Laurence Vicarage, Lower Road, Effingham, Surrey KT24 5JR. Tel (0372) 58314. Open by appointment.

Only two books survive of the library of the Rev John Miller who died as Vicar of Effingham in 1724. Two sermons of Bishop Browning, 1664; certificate for the King's Evil, 1684. Earliest seed catalogue (deposited at Guildford Muniment Room); Miller's ms diary as regimental chaplain to the New York Garrison in the 1650s (also deposited at Guildford Muniment Room). Little Bookham (same incumbent) Church has a Vulgate Bible, Lyons, 1675.

Miller's ms cat deposited at Guildford Muniment Room.

Egham

Royal Holloway College, Main Library, Founder's Building, Egham Hill, Egham, Surrey TW20 0EX. Tel (0784) 34455. Open Mon-Fri (Term) 9 am-9 pm, (Vacation) 9 am-5 pm; Sat (term only) 9 am-1 pm, Sun (term only) 2-6 pm to members of the College; to others at the discretion of the Librarian after written application in advance. Photocopying.

The College was founded as a women's college in 1886 from an endowment in memory of his wife by Thomas Holloway (1800—83), who had made his fortune from the manufacture of Holloway's pills. In 1900 it became a school of the University of London, and it is now co-educational. The library represents the subjects taught, which are more in the humanities than in the sciences.

Rare Book Collection consists of 560 v, including 262 pre-1851 items (12 STC, 26 Wing). English literature, including first and limited editions; 28 (chiefly first) editions by or about T E Lawrence (1888—1935) donated by Miss K W Elliott in 1968. Subjects covered include French literature, classics, history, music and other subjects in the humanities. Also 50 v science (chiefly botany).

Classified sheaf cat.

Farnham

Farnham Museum (Waverley District Council), Willmer House, West Street, Farnham, Surrey. Tel (0252) 715094. Open Tues-Sat 11 am-1 pm, 2-5 pm; also Wed (May-Sept) 7-9 pm. Exhibition galleries open to public, but access to printed material is by appointment. Photocopier available.

The total book collection amounts to *c*2,000 v, of which *c*90 are pre-1851, and include 13 STC and 2 Wing items; 14 18th cent v; also Norden's map of Surrey 1604, 1607; maps of Farnham 1839, 1840; a collection of 13 contemporary eds of William Cobbett, including his Preston election address for 1827; specimens of early Farnham printing, 1815 onwards; Farnham almanacks and directories, 1837–1909, and local property sale catalogues from 1856.

Forestry Commission Library, Alice Holt Lodge, Wrecclesham, Farnham, Surrey GU10 4LH. Open Mon-Fri 10 am-4.30 pm. Admission to staff and others interested, preferably by appointment. Photocopying, microfilm reader available.

Central Library of the Commission The collection contains *c*8,000 v, of which 50 are pre-1851 (including 2 Wing items), and contains the most significant works on forestry published before 1851; Board of Agriculture reports; 20 v New Forest Acts, 1695–1849.

Published classified cat, 1977.

West Surrey College of Art and Design, Falkner Road, The Hart, Farnham, Surrey GU9 7DS. Tel (0252) 722441 Ext 263. Open (Term) Mon-Fri 9 am-10 pm; Sat 9 am-12.30 pm. (Vacation) Mon-Fri 9 am-5 pm. Admission to members of the College; others by appointment. Photocopier, microfilm reader-printer available.

Rare Books Collection Of a total stock of 42,000 v, *c*300 v are rare, and were donated by Bishop Macmillan of Guildford, Canon Crum, *c*1950. They include two 18th cent legal works; a small collection of books on architecture; a comprehensive collection of 19th cent editions of Ruskin; 1910 limited edition of William Morris works.

Card cat.

Forthcoming cat of William Morris exhibition, 1981.

Godalming

Charterhouse School, Godalming, Surrey GU7 2DX. Tel (04868) 6226. Admission by appointment during school terms.

Daniel Wray Collection The library of Daniel Wray (18th cent antiquary, and educated at Charterhouse) was left to the school by his widow, but many books were sold during the late 19th cent and in the 1920s. The collection contains 3,000 v which include three incunabula, numerous foreign 16th cent works by old Carthusians, including a ms of Thackeray's *The Newcomes*; school scrapbooks and ephemera.

A catalogue of the library of Daniel Wray...given by his widow...for the use of the Charterhouse in the year 1785. London, 1790. (Revised, but not published, 1939.)

Exhibition of books in library, 8th July 1971 by R Birley (5 page typescript listing 63 of the library's outstanding volumes).

Guildford

The Guildford Institute, Ward Street, Guildford, Surrey GU1 4LH. Tel (0483) 62142. Open Mon-Fri 10 am-3 pm; Sat 11 am-1 pm (subject to variation). Admission by subscription, £2 per annum, and research facilities afforded at the discretion of the Librarian, preferably by appointment. (Archives of GI (minutes, correspondence etc local history) are the main fields of research.)

The Guildford Institute was founded on 11 March 1834 by a group of prominent citizens 'for the promotion of useful knowledge among the working classes'. A part of the Mechanics Institute, it changed its name and form several times over the next few decades, but by the 1870s it emerged as Guildford's major cultural and educational organization. It holds *c*5,000 pre-1900 v, covering local history, natural history, Victorian scrapbooks, playbills (from 1822) of the Guildford Theatre (bound in 2 v), and of the Theatre Royal and Borough Halls (loose).

Ms cat.

Guildford Muniment Room (Part of Surrey Record Office), Castle Arch, Guildford, Surrey GU1 3SX. Tel (0483) 573942. Open Tues-Fri 9.30 am-12.30 pm, 1.45-4.45 pm; Sat 9.30 am-12.30 pm (1st and 3rd in month by appointment only). Free to public by appointment. Photocopying facilities subject to conservation safeguards.

There is no collection of books as such, but a few rare printed books and pamphlets contained in groups of family papers etc deposited, and include *Parlyament of devylles* (W de Worde, 1509) (STC 19305); G Eglisham, *Forerunner of revenge*, Frankfurt 1626 (STC 7548); *Weights and measures collected for the benefit of youth in all schools, but especially in Guildford* (1677); 7 Civil War pamphlets, and miscellaneous 18th cent pamphlets collected by William Bray.

Hospital of the Blessed Trinity, High Street, Guildford, Surrey GU1 3AJ. Open by appointment only.

The Hospital, founded in 1619, has a collection of works (10 v) by and about George Abbot, the founder, and his brother Robert, respectively Archbishop of Canterbury and Bishop of Salisbury. There are 6 STC items by George and Robert Abbot; 2 18th cent prayer books.

George Abbot holdings are described in R A Christopher's *George Abbot...bibliography* (Charlottesville, 1966).

Royal Grammar School of King Edward VI, High Street, Guildford, Surrey. Tel (0483) 502424. Admission by appointment.

Chained Library A library existed before 1573, but there is no trace of its stock or extent. The library contains 86 Latin v from a bequest of Bishop Parkhurst of Norwich, 1573, and subsequent gifts, especially *c*1650 until 1800. It was in decline 1800–90, when it was rehoused and refurbished and catalogued; restored to its original room 1953. Its holdings total 452 works in 484 v relating to the church fathers, Geneva theology, sermons, early school textbooks. There are 4 incunabula plus a fragment and others in pastedowns; 31 STC and 72 Wing items; editions from Estienne and Froben presses. 87 v pre-1644 are now chained: these include most of the Parkhurst bequest, but some volumes may have been rechained without historical warrant. It is the fifth largest chained library in England, and one of only two in schools; it has a claim to being one of the earliest town libraries.

G Woodward and R A Christophers, *The Chained Library of the Royal Grammar School Guildford: Catalogue*. Guildford, The School, 1972.

Introduction to catalogue also in *The Book Collector* 22 (1) (Spring 1973), p17-34.

H A Powell, *A catalogue of the old library of the Guildford Grammar School*. Guildford, 1900 (op).

G C Williamson, *The Royal Grammar School of King Edward VI at Guildford*. London, Bell, 1929 (op).

D M Sturley, *The Royal Grammar School Guildford*. Guildford, The School, 1979.

St John's Seminary, Wonersh, Guildford, Surrey GU5 0QX. Tel (0483) 892217. Open by arrangement. Photocopier available.

The College, founded in 1891 as a seminary for training for the Roman Catholic priesthood. The library has been acquired mostly by legacy and donation. Of *c*14,000 v, *c*1,000 are pre-1800, consisting mostly of continental Catholic theology, also legal, patristic works. Included is the Gaisford Collection, on loan from the trustees of Thomas Gaisford of Christ Church, Oxford. Probably only 3 v are pre-1600, including the 1603 ed of St Thomas Aquinas from the Jesuit house at Ingolstadt.

Card cat.

Surrey Archaeological Society, Castle Arch, Guildford, Surrey GU1 3SX. Tel (0483) 32454. Open Mon-Sat 9 am-5 pm (Staffed 9.30 am-1 pm only: times are subject to alteration; enquire before visiting). Admission to members of the Society; others by appointment only. Limited photocopying, microfiche reader available.

The Society was founded in 1857, and its rare books collection has been acquired by donation from members. The library contains *c*8,000 v, also maps, pamphlets, ephemera, illustrations. There are 3 STC and 10 Wing items included in *c*100 pre-1851 v which cover all topics concerning Surrey: many ephemera, drawings etc in research collections; and sale catalogues, Guildford directories from 1838; poll books; county histories, and a unique copy of v 1-3 of *Surrey Advertiser* (1864–66).

Currently author and subject card cat of books.

Card cat of maps.

Book cat of sale cats and research material.

Printed cat issued 1906 (op).

Brief history in *Surrey Archaeological Collections*, v 53 (1957), p46-60.

Surrey County Library, Local Studies Library, Branch Library, North Street, Guildford, Surrey GU1 4AL. Tel (0483) 34054. Open Mon and Fri 10 am-8 pm, Tues, Thurs 10 am-5 pm, Wed 10 am-1.30 pm; Sat 9.30 am-4 pm. Admission on application to the Librarian during the above times. Study room, microfilm reader available.

Local Studies Library The library is an amalgamation of Guildford Library's local collection (including that of G C Williamson and Mrs A J B Green), Surrey County Library's HQ collection, the George Underwood collection (acquired 1978) and material from other Surrey libraries. The library was started on 1 March 1981, and is therefore in the early stages of redevelopment and arrangement. Other branch libraries include local and ephemeral material, but application for admission must initially be made to Guildford. Exceptionally the Bourne Hall Library, Spring Street, Ewell, Epsom (Tel (01) 394 0951, opening hours as Guildford) houses the Epsom and Ewell Local History collection. Total stock amounts to several thousand books. The Guildford library has 2 STC; 1 Wing v; 26 18th cent, and 33 1801–50. Subjects include Surrey histories, works by local authors, pamphlets, ephemera etc, local meteorology, flora and fauna, folklore. Maps, postcards, directories and poll books. Ewell library has 2 Wing items; Epsom race cards 1835– ; sale particulars 1819– .

Published cats: *Epsom and Ewell past and present*, 1970.

Guildford Public Library, Reference Department. *Catalogue of works in the library relating to the county of Surrey*, 1957. Supplement, 1968.

United Society for Christian Literature, Lutterworth Press, Luke House, Farnham Road, Guildford, Surrey GU1 4XD. Tel (0483) 77536. Telex 858623. Enquiries to the General Secretary. Admission by appointment only. Photocopying facilities.

File copies of publications The Religious Tract Society was founded in 1799, and became the United Society for Christian Literature in 1935. Originally it published only tracts and handbills, numbering at least 1,527, but developed into a book and periodical publisher, being especially associated with Bunyan's *Pilgrim's Progress*, of which it has published editions in 159 languages and dialects. Most of the Society's historic collections of its publications were destroyed by bombing of its then headquarters in London in 1941, although the volumes now remaining at Guildford constitute a representative collection of publications. They consist of *c*250 v, including *c*750 tracts, etc and contain a selection of RTS tracts (from no 9 onwards), handbills (1-117), Tracts published by Joseph Masters, Whittemore, SPCK, 20 v of 'Reward', *c*1810, and other reward books. Contemporary bound volumes of *Boy's Own* paper, *Sunday at Home*, *Leisure Hour* and *Pilgrim's Progress* in 32 foreign editions.

The Society's archives are to be deposited with the School of Oriental and African Studies, and will contain a small selection of copies of tracts, etc.

Card cat.

Reigate

Cranston Library, St Mary's Parish Church, Reigate, Surrey. Admission on application to the Secretary to the Trustees.

Founded in 1701 by the Rev Andrew Cranston, Vicar of Reigate (1697—1708), as a library for the clergy of the Archdeaconry of Ewell, and the parishioners of Reigate. Most of the books were acquired in the early 18th cent when it functioned as a public library. It was revived and added to by the Rev J N Harrison, Vicar of Reigate 1847—1901. It is now established as a registered charity with a board of trustees, including a representative of Surrey County Library. It contains *c*2,500 v, mostly late 17th-18th cent works, but includes three incunabula and some mss. The subject field is principally theology and contemporary controversial works, also travel, medicine, astronomy, mathematics, science, ecclesiastical history and Quakerism. Special press include Elsevir, Estienne family, Froben, Plantin/Moretus, Blaeu, Gryphius, Aldus. Presentation copies of Granville Sharp's anti-slavery works.

Bibliotheca Reigatiana, 1893. (op)

Revised cat in 48X microfiche, including subject printer and donor index.

D M Williams, 'English parochial libraries', *Antiquarian book monthly review*, Nov 1978, p138-47.

Holmesdale Natural History Club, The Museum, Croydon Road, Reigate, Surrey. Open by appointment to accredited enquirers.

The Club, founded in 1857, acts as a focus for natural history, archaeological and local history work in Reigate and district. It includes the library of Reigate Mechanics Institute, largely acquired by local donation. Its books total *c*600 v, and includes 1 STC (14269); 1 Wing; 9 18th cent; 70 pre-1851 v; early works relate mostly to flora and fauna, particularly local, including G Luxford *Flora of Reigate*, 1838, also Cuvier's *Regne animal* (incomplete set of plates), T Moore, *Ferns of Great Britain and Ireland*, 1855, nature printed.

Card cat.

Thames Ditton

Milk Marketing Board, Thames Ditton, Surrey KT7 0EL. Tel (01) 398 4101 Ext 204. Open Mon-Fri 9 am-5.30 pm. Admission at Librarian's discretion to non-Milk Marketing Board enquirers.

Hammond collection on milk Collected by Sir John Hammond, a pioneer in development of artificial insemination, it includes a total of 71 v (2,400 papers) on all aspects of meat and milk, the latter donated to the Milk Marketing Board by Hammond shortly before his death in 1964. The Collection is strong in official publications from Czechoslovakia, Scandinavia, Germany, Belgium, New Zealand, United States.

Sussex

Arundel

Arundel Castle Library, Arundel Castle, Sussex. Tel (0243) 83490. The library is not 'open' in the usual sense of the term. Facilities for the examination of a particular book or books are only provided in exceptional circumstances; all applicants must supply bona fide references in advance of a visit.

The Library of His Grace the Duke of Norfolk A private library begun by Edward, 9th Duke of Norfolk (*d*1777), extensively added to by Bernard Edward, 12th Duke (*d*1842) and Henry, 15th Duke (*d*1917), and now consists of *c*12,000 v. It is rich in topography, heraldry, architecture, horticulture, travel, natural history, classics, Bibles, Catholicism (including over 50 v of 17th cent pamphlets entitled 'Popery Pro and Con'), books with fine coloured plates. A quantity of incunabula, not counted, but fairly extensive. In brief, it may be said that the Collection comprises the best of everything that may be expected in a private library of this size and distinction. There is an important collection of illuminated and other mss which, although forming part of the library, are kept in a strongroom.

Bognor Regis

West Sussex Institute of Higher Education, Bognor Regis College, Bognor Regis, West Sussex PO21 1HR. Tel (024 33) 5581. Open (Term) Mon-Fri 9 am-9 pm; Sat 9 am-12 noon; (Vacation) Mon-Fri 9 am-5.30 pm. Admission to non-members by advance arrangement with the Librarian. Photocopying and photographic work by arrangement. Collection for reference use only.

The Gerard Young Collection Gerard Young (1912–72), journalist and author with a lifelong enthusiasm for local history, assembled this collection of books and other materials on Bognor Regis and West Sussex. His executors presented this material to Bognor Regis College Library to form the Gerard Young Collection. It contains *c*1,000 books (few 'rare') and several thousand photographs, postcards, cuttings and other ephemera. All material relates to the history of Bognor Regis, its immediate neighbourhood, and—more patchily—West Sussex as a whole. There are a few pre-1851 items among the books, eg William Hayley's *Poems and plays* (6 v 1788), Parry's *Historical and descriptive account of the coast of Sussex* (1833), Horsfield's *History, antiquities and topography of the county of Sussex* (2 v, 1835). The non-book section (photographs, postcards, slides, cuttings, plans etc) because of its ephemeral nature, contains more than may be easily found elsewhere.

The books are classified by the scheme in Hobbs' *Local history and the library*, and recorded in a dictionary catalogue. The non-book material is grouped in broad categories, and not yet indexed in full detail.

K G Leslie and T J McCann, *Local history in West Sussex: a guide to sources*. 2nd ed, Chichester: West Sussex County Council, 1975, p59.

Brighton

Booth Museum of Natural History, 194 Dyke Road, Brighton BN1 5AA. Tel (0273) 552586 or 603005 Ext 64. Open Mon-Fri 10 am-5 pm. Admission on request during opening hours. Photocopier and microfiche reader available.

Booth Museum Library The principal collection of books was donated by the widow of E T Booth (the donor of the museum specimens to Brighton Corporation) at the end of the 19th cent. The whole collection consists of *c*2,000 v with few pre-1851, some 10 or 12 monographs covering all areas of natural history, with strong emphasis on entomology. No additions are being made to the rare books. An out-of-date card index available, but a computerized catalogue of exhibits and books is being compiled.

Brighton and Sussex Medico-Chirurgical Society, Sussex Postgraduate Medical Centre, Elm Grove, Brighton BN2 3EW. Tel (0273) 605650. Open 9 am-6 pm. Admission by arrangement. Lending to members. Photocopier available.

Brighton and Sussex Medico-Chirurgical Library The Society was founded in 1847 'to form a library, and to meet periodically . . .'. It contains *c*200 monographs in total collection: *c*12 pre-1851 items; *c*800 v of periodicals. All medical topics. The Postgraduate Medical Centre Library has, in effect, replaced this library.

Rudimentary author/title cat.

Brighton College, Eastern Road, Brighton BN2 2AL. Tel (0273) 606033. Open 9 am-6 pm. Admission by written application to the Librarian and Archivist. Photocopier available in the College.

The College was founded in 1847 and the collection was built up by purchase and gifts from old boys etc. It contains *c*400 v, mainly 19th cent, some 18th cent, a few earlier (1 STC, 1 Wing). Classical literature, geography and travel, English literature, theology well represented.

Cat in preparation.

Brighton Reference Library, Brighton Public Library, Church Street, Brighton BN1 1VE. Tel (0273) 691195/601197. Telex 87167. Open Mon 11 am-7 pm, Tues-Fri 10 am-7 pm; Sat 10 am-4 pm. Access to rare books and incunabula by appointment (24 hours notice necessary). Photocopier; reader/printer.

Brighton Reference Library General Collection Began in 1866 with the gift of *c*20,000 books from the Brighton Library and Scientific Society to Brighton Corporation. It contains *c*140,000 v, of which *c*25,000 are pre-1851 which include 7 incunabula. Strong in books on bibliography, early printed books, costume, manners and customs. There are *inter alia c*500 pre-1851 theatre programmes and bills.

Bloomfield Collection Bequeathed in 1917 by L L Bloomfield, a bibliophile who had collected *c*1870–1917. A collection of 13,255 v of which *c*9,000 v are pre-1851. The latter include 26 incunabula (including 1 Caxton); *c*7,000 STC and Wing items; *c*2,000 books with coloured plates or steel engravings of the period *c*1760–1830; *c*40 mss of various dates, all good items; 10 being medieval illuminated mss (Book of Hours, etc). The collection is strong in bibliography (both historical and descriptive), history, travel and topography, costume, religion and early Bibles, engravings and books on fine arts.

Card cat integrated with Reference Library cat. Dewey/author.

Catalogue of Ms and Printed Books before 1500, (Brighton 1962) consists mainly of Bloomfield material.

Clericetti Collection The library of Count Carlo Angiolini Clericetti, bequeathed in 1888 in gratitude to

Brighton for giving him shelter when a refugee from the troubles in Italy in the late 1840s. It contains 570 v, mainly pre-1851, and includes original editions or translations of celebrated Italian writers and many editions of Machievelli's works etc.

Cat in main Reference Library Collection. Dewey Decimal/author.

Cobden Collection Part of the personal library of Richard Cobden, presented by Henry Willett in 1873. It consists of *c*3,000 pamphlets and *c*100 books. The pamphlets are very important and rare, mainly early 19th cent and mostly in French and English. Many of the books are fellow authors' complimentary copies to Cobden. Main subjects covered are economics, politics, agriculture.

Catalogued in main Reference Library Collection. Dewey Decimal/author.

Elliott Collection Property of the Rev Henry Venn Elliott, bequeathed in 1871. It represents a clergyman's working library and contains *c*3,000 v, including works on dogma and theology, 18th cent Greek and Latin texts and works of early Christian Fathers (Origen etc in both English and the original).

Cat in main Reference Library collection. Dewey Decimal/author.

Local Studies Collection, Brighton Reference Library A general collection of *c*13,000 v containing *c*500 pre-1851 topographical books or directories; *c*2,000 (out of 10,000) pre-1851 topographical, biographical or historical pamphlets relating to Sussex; *c*250 annual volumes (five titles) of Sussex newspapers 1749–1851; 3,000 local engravings, mainly topographical or biographical; *c*200 pre-1851 local theatre bills.

In General Author Catalogue for Reference Library.

In separate Sussex Collection card cat (Dictionary subject and author).

Long Collection The library of Professor George Long, Classical Lecturer at Brighton College 1849–71. Presented in 1878, it contains *c*3,000 v mainly Greek and Latin texts (many 18th cent, some 16th and 17th cent material) and commentaries.

Cat in main Reference Library collection. Dewey Decimal/author.

Mathews Collection The library of Henry John Mathews, an oriental scholar and Chairman of the Library Committee. It contains *c*3,500 v covering mainly religious texts (in Coptic, Samaritan, Syriac, Aramaic, Babylonian, Arabic); dictionaries (some very early, including German/Oriental from Göttingen, Leipzig, etc); commentaries. Of the 100 Arabic items, most are 19th cent but few are 16th and 17th cent.

Cat in main Reference Library collection. Dewey Decimal/author.

Phillipps Collection This constitutes half the library of J O Halliwell-Phillipps, the Shakespearean scholar and son-in-law of Sir Thomas Phillipps (1792–1872) of Middle-Hill. It contains *c*1,000 v and many rare items of Shakespeariana.

Cat in main Reference Library collection. Dewey Decimal/author.

Preston Manor, Preston Park, Brighton BN1 6SD. Tel (0273) 552101. Open Wed to Sat 10 am-5 pm; Sun 2-5 pm. Admission free to users of the library, but books may be consulted only in the presence of the Keeper. Microfiche/microfilm reader available.

Thomas-Stanford Collection The collection of Sir Thomas-Stanford, who willed the Manor and adjoining land to Brighton Corporation in 1925. It consists of *c*500 printed works about Sussex or by Sussex-born authors, notably Thomas Paine and John Seldon, and includes some first editions (eg Belloc). The collection also includes *c*2,000 documents of local interest; autograph letters; Civil War musters; documents relating to the Stanford estates in Brighton and Hove, and the Kipling collection. Checklist of Seldon collection available, and a 'primitive card index' and list of Mss, both of which are being revised.

See *Bulletin of the Friends of the University of Sussex Library* (No 1), Summer 1974.

University of Sussex Library, Brighton BN1 9QL. Tel (0273) 606755. Open (Term) Mon-Thurs 9 am-9.45 pm; Fri 9 am-7.30 pm; Sat 10 am-6 pm; Sun 2-7.30 pm. (Vacation) Mon-Fri 9 am-5.30 pm. Admission on written application. Photocopying; microfilm readers.

Commune Collection Original collection purchased in 1968 from the booksellers Martinus Nijoff. It comprises *c*1,000 v, *c*280 newspapers and periodicals, *c*100 posters, *c*700 cartoons, caricatures, etc, all relating to the Paris Commune of 1871.

The Paris Commune, 1871. Inventory of the collection in the University of Sussex Library. Introduction by Eugene W Schulkird, Brighton, University of Sussex Library, 1975.

Hogarth Press Collection Part of the Leonard Woolf estate presented to the University of Sussex Library by Mrs T Parsons, consisting of *c*620 v, being mainly Leonard Woolf's file copies of the Hogarth Press List, including Virginia Woolf titles. (A useful Virginia and Leonard Woolf research source in conjunction with the Monks House and Leonard Woolf papers.)

Card cat.

Travers Collection Private collection of the collector, Michael Travers, given to the University of Sussex Library, 1978. It consists of 325 v, including 16 incunabula, 178 STC, 26 Wing, 25 ESTC.

Handlist only. Specialist cataloguing of collection in the offing.

Mss Collection Includes several important accessions of personal papers of distinguished authors and litterateurs, eg (a) *Stamp Papers* (Sir Laurence Dudley Stamp, CBE, 1898–1966)—mainly geographical papers, especially land use; Land Use Survey: Royal Commission on Common Land; affairs of FAO and UNESCO; (b) *'Mark Rutherford' Letters* (ie William Hale White, 1831–1913), novelist, critic, scholar, journalist; (c) *Kingsley Martin Papers* (Kingsley Martin, 1897–1969), editor *New Statesman and Nation*, 1931–60; (d) *Leonard Woolf Papers*, literary, political, domestic and personal affairs; (e) *Monk House Papers*, literary papers and correspondence of Viriginia Woolf; (f) *Kipling Papers—Wimpole Archive*, letters, verses, etc of Rudyard Kipling and of his father John Lockwood Kipling; (g) *Gregory Papers*, autograph, typescript and printed papers, correspondence, diaries etc of Sir Richard Gregory (1864–1952); (h) *Kenneth Allsop Papers*, papers relating to the books *Adventure lit their star* (1949), *The angry decade: a story of the cultural revolt of the 1950s* (1958), etc; autograph and printed papers, notes and drafts; (i) *Rosey Pool Papers*, the papers of Dr Rosey Eva Pool (1905–71) comprising American negro literature, especially verse and drama, including Owen Dodson, Chester Himes, Langston Hughes and others.

Chichester

Chichester Cathedral Library, Chichester Cathedral, Sussex. Tel (0243) 83490. Open by arrangement following application in writing. No research facilities, but the Librarian is willing to try and organize photocopies through other organizations if all charges (including travelling) are paid by the applicant. Facilities for long-term examination of a rare book can be made if the Dean and Chapter agree that such an application is beneficial to academic research.

The Library of the Dean and Chapter of Chichester Cathedral The library dates from very early times, but the original holdings were dispersed at the time of the Civil War. The library was re-founded by Henry King, Bishop of Chichester 1642–69, and has been added to by numerous gifts, especially in the 18th, 19th and early 20th cent. It contains *c*5,000 v, containing some 6,000 works.

The library's principal holdings concern theology, biography, topography and history; a good collection of psalmody, hymnody and liturgy; a few items from the library of John Donne; a copy of the *Treatise concerning the fruitful sayings of David*, printed by Wynkyn de Worde, 1508; Sir Christopher Hatton's copy of Chaucer; the works of Sir Thomas More, 1523; some good examples of books printed on the Continent, including the *Moralia of St Gregory* (Paris, 1495); the works of St John Chrysostom printed at Eton, 1613; Solinus *Polyhistor* (1520); Hermann Von Wied, *Nostra*, which belonged to Thomas Cranmer; a notable collection of 19th cent pamphlets bound in vols; a few mss described in N R Ker *Medieval manuscripts in British libraries*, 2 (1977), p390-5.

Cat printed in 1871, but now obsolete. Modern card cat, except for contents of bound vols of pamphlets.

F W Steer, *Chichester Cathedral Library* (1964) [op]

The Theological College, Westgate, Chichester, West Sussex. Tel (0243) 83369. Open seven days 8.30 am-9.30 pm; in vacation by arrangement. Free admission to members of the College; to bona fide students by arrangement.

College Library Built up by gift and purchase from the foundation of the College in 1849, it contains 15,000 v, of which 220 are 16th, 17th and 18th cent items. Some items before 1851 may be in main catalogue, but are generally uncatalogued.

West Sussex County Library, Tower Street, Chichester, West Sussex PO10 1QJ. Tel (0243) 86563. Open Mon-Fri 9.30 am-7.30 pm; Sat 9.30 am-5 pm. Admission free. Microfilm and fiche reader facilities.

Local Studies Collection The collection, which relates to the history of Sussex, has been continuously built up since 1926, and comprises 4,000 printed books; over 1,000 photos; 2,000 postcard views; 300 maps (modern); local newspapers on microfilm. It also includes E Dudley Juvenile researches, published locally 1829; old Guide Books on Sussex (1790–1840) and some privately printed and published material, eg Pear Tree Press and Vine Press (local).

Author card cat. Later items added since 1976 on computer cat for Local Studies Collection.

West Sussex Record Office, County Hall, Chichester, West Sussex PO19 1RN. Tel (0243) 85100. Open Mon-Fri 9.15 am-12.30 pm, 1.30-5 pm. Admission to bona fide students by prior arrangement. Xerox copying, microfilm/fiche, ultraviolet lamp available.

Record Office Library Maintained to serve the needs of staff and researchers, the library holds *c*3,000 v which include *c*300 v of early Chichester printing, some of which are contained in the *Crookshank and Fuller Collection of Sussex books*. Part of the Mitford library also housed here, containing 19th cent religious works and children's books.

Union cat of all materials, author, subject, etc. Handlists available on application.

The Crookshank Collection [of books] ed by Francis W Steer, 1960.

The Mitford Archives, ed by Francis W Steer, Vol 1 1961, Vol II 1970.

Hailsham

Royal Greenwich Observatory, Herstmonceux Castle, Hailsham, Sussex BN27 1RP. Tel (031181) 3171. Open 9 am-5 pm. Admission by arrangement and appointment in writing to the Librarian. Microfiche reader, microfiche reader/printer, microfilm reader/printer. Xerox copying.

Royal Greenwich Observatory Library and Archives. Rare Books Collection Accrued collections of Astronomers Royal (current acquisition by gift only), consisting of *c*400 v of the period 1492–1837, covering astronomy and the history of science. There is a complete set of *Philosophical Transactions of the Royal Society* in original printing and bindings. Mss include Archives of the Astronomers Royal and the Royal Greenwich Observatory, 1675 to date; Board of Longitude papers, including the log books of The Adventure, the log book of The Resolution, Captain Cook's *Journal* for 1776. STC and Wing items not quantified, but several expected to be present. The library is also in charge of the collection of H M Nautical Almanac Office, containing nautical almanacs and ephemerides, British and foreign from 1767 to date.

Basic card file.

State Librarian, 27 (1), March 1979.

Hastings

Hastings Museum and Art Gallery, John's Place, Cambridge Road, Hastings TN34 1ET. Tel (0424) 435952. Open Mon-Sat 10 am-1 pm, 2-5 pm; Sun 3-5 pm. Admission free. Books in the collection may be consulted on the spot by genuine researchers. No loans.

Markwick Library The library of William Markwick, later known as Eversfield (*d*1813). He lived in Catsfield, and his *Calendar and observations* or *Naturalists' calendar* are appended to some editions of Gilbert White's *Selborne*. The collection was presented to the Museum in 1925 by Miss Bethune, a descendant of the Markwicks. The library consists of 250 v and 46 v of bound manuscripts. These belong to the Hastings and St Leonards Natural History Society, and have been deposited with the Museum. The main subjects covered are natural history/farming (titles by Bauhin, Blackstone, Walter Charleton, Dodoens, George Edwards, John Evelyn, John Reinhold Foster, Van Leeuwenhoeck, Linnaeus, Lister, Pallas, Thomas Pennant, Robert Plot, Pontoppidan, John Ray, Van Rheede, Rondelet, William Smellie, Tull and others), and travel/topography with a few literary and historical volumes. The books are mainly 18th cent with 11 from the early 1800s. In addition there are 4 STC, 20 Wing, and *c*8 17th cent titles printed abroad (eg Amsterdam, Basle, Leyden, Rotterdam). The ms volumes mainly contain William Markwick's notes and extracts made in the course of his reading. There are volumes of flower illustrations and his natural history diary; a catalogue of birds; notes on British ornithology and zoology and related subjects.

List in manuscript.

Horsham

Horsham Museum, Causeway House, Horsham, West Sussex. Tel (0403) 4959. Open Tues-Fri 1-5 pm; Sat 10 am-5 pm or by arrangement. Free admission to members of Horsham Museum Society; others by arrangement.

Horsham Museum Library Collected by members since 1893, the library holds *c*2,000 documents in Albery mss (the *Sussex Archaeological Collections*, v 69, p117 describes many of the Albery mss), some mss maps of local estates and printed material on Sussex parliamentary history, particularly Horsham, and history of the Borough. Few copies of early Horsham newspapers (from 1840 to end of 19th cent) and local directories from 1844. *c*1,000 photographs.

Manuscripts in process of being catalogued; books etc on cards.

Hove

Library of the Gospel Standard Baptists, (91 Buckingham Road, Brighton), c/o 6 Tredcroft Road, Hove BN3 6UH. Tel (0273) 555839. Admission by appointment. Access to photocopier. Postal loan facilities.

The library was founded in 1946, mainly by gifts, and kept up to date by gift and purchase of mainly older material, but some contemporary material. It contains *c*3,000-4,000 titles in 4,000-5,000 v (including duplicates, of which *c*800 v (600 titles) are pre-1851. STC and Wing items number 60-80. Subjects covered include the Bible, texts, commentaries etc, Christian biographies, letters, writings, sermons, Church histories, theological lectures and writings, usually in accordance with the doctrines of the denomination.

Cat printed 1952, supplement 1977, annual list of accessions.

(The printed lists are by subject and by author/title.)

Card index being compiled of biographical references to GS Baptists in *c*6 prominent GSB journals, mainly *Gospel Standard*.

Sussex County Cricket Club, County Ground, Eaton Road, Hove BN3 3AN. Tel (0273) 71549. Open to members only during lunch interval on County Championship Day.

Sussex County Cricket Club Library Established *c*1950, and built up piecemeal since, the library now has *c*900 v, of which only a few are pre-1851. A number of late 18th and early 19th cent works include *New articles on the game of cricket*, 1775, *Young cricketer's tutor* by J Nyren, 1833, and *Cricketer's Manual* by 'Bat', 1851.

Typed list, title order.

Lewes

Lewes Area Library, Albion Street, Lewes, Sussex. Tel (0796 16) 4232. Open Mon-Fri 9.30 am-7 pm; Sat 9.30 am-5 pm. Admission free; reference on demand.

Residue of Lewes Book Society Library The small residue of the books of the Lewes Book Society which was in operation at the turn of the 18th-19th cent. Numbering *c*300 v, they are mainly dated late-18th—early-19th cent and consist of chiefly standard works of English literature, eg Johnson's *Lives of Poets*, Paine's *Rights of Man*.

In Lewes Library general catalogue.

Sussex Archaeological Society, Barbican House, Lewes, East Sussex. Tel (079 16) 4379. Open primarily for members of the Sussex Archaeological Society; by application in writing to non-members. Limited photocopying facilities.

Sussex Archaeological Society Library The Society was founded in 1846 and provision for books was made in the Rules (see *Sussex Archaeological Collections*, v 85, 1946, p77-92). The library contains *c*11,000 v, of which *c*1,020 are pre-1851. There are 5 STC and 16 Wing items. Subjects covered include archaeology and local history and topography of Sussex, with some theology and literature. Mss include numerous notebooks compiled by local antiquarians and historians (including Walter Budgen, T Woollgar, E Dunkin and John Elliot).

Card index of Sussex clergy.

Card index. Also published in *Sussex Archaeological Collections*, v 36, 1888, p193-238, with additions in v 38, 1892, pxxvi-xxix. Further additions regularly listed in SAC volumes.

E H W Dunkin, 'A calendar of the deeds and other documents in the possession of the Sussex Archaeological Society', *SAC*, v 37, 1880, p39-110. Continued in v 38, 1892, p137-40.

Thomas Sutton, 'The Library and Museums', *SAC*, v 85, 1946, p77-112.

L F Salzman, 'A history of the Sussex Archaeological Society', *SAC*, v 85, 1946, p4-76.

Old Heathfield

All Saints Church, The Vicarage, Old Heathfield, Heathfield, East Sussex TN21 9AB. Tel (043 52) 2457. The collection can be made available to scholars on request.

The Library of All Saints Church, Old Heathfield Begun in 1645 by the Rev William Wilkin whose son, Richard, was an associate of Jacob Tonson, the Fleet Street publisher. The collection consists of 104 works in 123 v, all ESTC items, excepting *c*13 Wing. They are works of religious controversy and classical scholarship.

Rough list made on survey visit.

Petworth

Petworth House, Petworth Park, Petworth, West Sussex. Admission to bona fide research workers only on application by letter to Lord Egremont.

The Library of Lord Egremont Collected by the family from the 15th cent, originally by the Percys, Earls of Northumberland. The 9th Earl (1564—1632) bound many of the items uniformly in white limp vellum with arms in gold. The collection has not been added to since the end of the 19th cent. The library consists of *c*11,500 v housed in the White Library and the Old Library. It is a gentleman's library covering literature, history, fine art, etc, especially of the 18th cent; strong in classics and French literature and greatly representative of the 16th and 17th cent Continental printing (Plantin, Elzevir, etc). It also includes a ms copy of Chaucer's *Canterbury Tales*, illuminated on vellum *c*1425—50, and known to have been owned by the Earl of Northumberland before 1489; two 17th cent pamphlets with covers of ms leaves, and 12 other 17th cent pamphlets in original condition. Book restoration and repair work is under expert supervision.

Two ms v of cat 1876, which also contain items sold in 1927.

Shoreham-by-Sea

Lancing College, West Sussex BN15 0RW. Tel (079 17) 2213. Open 9 am-10 pm. Public admitted on application. Xerox copier in the school.

The College was founded in 1848. There were originally two libraries established, the Boys' and the Fellows' libraries, but they were later amalgamated, and the collection has grown with purchases, donations and bequests (eg Beeding Priory). Stock totals *c*17,000-18,000 v, of which 200-300 are pre-1851. Main strength is in the classics, 17th and 18th cent texts, and theology, especially 16th-17th cent editions of the Early Fathers.

Card cat author, title, shelf list.

Worthing

Worthing Library, Richmond Road, Worthing, West Sussex BN11 1HD. Tel (0903) 206961. Open Mon-Fri 9.30 am-7.30 pm; Sat 9.30 am-5 pm. Admission free. Microfilm reader.

The rare book collection has been progressively built up since 1908, mainly by donation. It contains *c*1,600 v, including *c*600 Sussex items and 50 private press books. The collection is general in character, but has a notable section of finely illustrated botanical books including a long run of Curtis, and *Botanical Cabinet*, Blackwell's *Herbal* and F Kranzlin's *Zenia Orchidacae* (Leipzig, 1900). The Sussex books include many early guides, sermons and pamphlets, and a Selden collection of *c*40 v (mostly first or early eds). The Private Press Collection includes material from North Sussex (Pear Tree, Vine, Dominic etc) and other presses. Appended to the Sussex Collection are extensive collections of local prints, photographs and maps.

Note: Much of the collection is in reserve—notice of use would therefore be helpful.

Typed author lists plus card cat for Sussex Collection will be put into the computer cat in the fairly near future.

Warwickshire

Nuneaton

Nuneaton Library (Warwickshire County Library), Church Street, Nuneaton. Tel (0682) 384027. Open Mon-Fri 9 am-6 pm; Sat 9 am-4 pm. Admission free. Study area. Photocopying facilities for page extracts. Reference only.

George Eliot Collection Collecting started 1952 and became available to the public in October 1962. There are 750 v, including 50 first fine editions; 15 mss and letters; 2,000 pamphlets, including George Eliot notebooks, 13 letters, George Eliot copy of 'Cicero', collection of contemporary reviews, collection of pamphlets, scrapbooks.

Card/dictionary cat.

Rugby

Institution of Chemical Engineers, George E Davis Building, 165-171 Railway Terrace, Rugby CV21 3HQ. Tel (0788) 78214. Open Mon-Fri 9 am-5 pm to bona fide visitors. No research facilities.

Eight titles, consisting of dictionaries of chemistry 1808–46 (Nicholson, Brande, Parkes and Ure), Cavendish Society Chemical Report 1848, and Wilson's life of Cavendish 1851. 21 titles (all post-1851) connected with George E Davis, and ms copies of his letters to his parents 1870s.

UDC cat.

Stratford-upon-Avon

The Shakespeare Centre Library, The Shakespeare Birthplace Trust, Henley Street, Stratford-upon-Avon, CV37 6QW. Tel (0789) 4016. Open Mon-Fri 10 am-5 pm; Sat 9.30 am-12.30 pm. Admission by Reader's Ticket available on application to the Director, or in person at the Library. Reference library only. Photocopy available (at discretion of the librarian). Photograph reproduction by special arrangement. Microfilm reader, tape recorder and gramophone record player available for use with collection items.

The Shakespeare Centre Library The Shakespeare Birthplace Trust Library founded in 1862; first librarian appointed in 1873. The Shakespeare Memorial Library was founded in 1880. In 1947 the two came under the supervision of the Director of the Birthplace Trust, and in 1964 they were amalgamated in the Shakespeare Centre Library. The library contains *c*30,000 items, including printed books, pamphlets, manuscripts and engravings, but excluding the Shakespeare Birthplace Trust Records Office Collections (for details see (h) below). Of these 30,000, about one-third are 'rare' items, and include 1 incunabulum; 262 STC; and 339 Wing items. Subject areas covered are Shakespeare's life, work and times; criticism; theatre, history (especially of Shakespeare and Elizabethan drama); topography of Warwickshire; aspects of Elizabethan and Jacobean life (eg forest crafts and hunting, medicine, gardens, etc); archive collections of Royal Shakespeare Theatre.

Card cat for book collections—author/title; also classified cat (Library's own classification scheme). Additional indexes for STC books (including printers pre-1640) and Indexes to the special collections listed below.

English books 1529–1640 with STC Reference. Shakespeare's Birthplace Library, 1955. [op]

In Honour of Shakespeare, Levi Fox, Jarrold, Norwich, 1972 (describes the work of the Shakespeare Birthplace Trust, including the library and some of its special items).

The following separate collections are incorporated in the Centre Library:

(a) *Early printed books, before 1700* Collection gathered by Shakespeare's Birthplace Library and Shakespeare Memorial Library from 1860s and 1880s onwards. Donors include James Orchard Halliwell-Phillipps, Sir Sidney Lee, Charles Edward Flower, etc. It includes 1 incunabulum (*Herodiani historiae de Imperio post Marcum*. Bononiae, Bazalerius de Bazaleriis, 1493); 262 STC items, including Shakespeare 'First Folio', 1623, (Lee census copies xvii, cxlii and cviii); 2nd Folio (STC 22,

274a); Quartos (STC 22,293; 22,295; 22,297; 22,300 and 22,303); *Grete Herbal*; Jonson *Works*; Laneham *Letter*; Montaigne *Essayes*; Plutarch *History*; Stubbes *Anatomy of abuses*; Taylor *Works*; Withals *Dictionary*; 339 Wing items, including Shakespeare '3rd Folio'; and '4th Folio'; works by Dryden, Aphra Behn etc.

(b) *Halliwell-Phillipps Notebooks* A collection of 128 bound notebooks prepared by James Orchard Halliwell-Phillipps when editing Shakespeare's *Works*. One to four volumes on each play, containing ms notes and clippings from a variety of printed works, including books printed before 1700.

(c) *Royal Shakespeare Theatre Archives* Collection begun after the foundation of the Shakespeare Memorial committee in 1875; continued and expanded as Royal Shakespeare Company collections after this received its charter in 1961. *c*1,000 v; approx 50 boxes (various sizes) and *c*6,000 loose photographs; *c*200 costume designs etc. These cover prompt copies of productions at Stratford-upon-Avon Shakespeare Memorial Theatre (including Benson Company) from 1880s; prompt copies (also some stage manager's scripts) of Royal Shakespeare Company productions (Shakespeare and non-Shakespearian) in Stratford-upon-Avon, London and on tour 1961 onwards. *c*90 scrapbooks of newscuttings from 1873 to present; programmes; production photographs and miscellaneous ephemera relating to Shakespeare Memorial and Royal Shakespeare Theatres from 1879 to present day.

Books catalogued in main library cat; separate indexes for photograph files, programme collection and handlist for original costume designs.

(d) *The Beisley Collection* Collection of Sidney Beisley, Esq, bequeathed to the Shakespeare Birthplace Trust by his widow of Laurie Park, Sydenham, in January 1886. It contains 600 works which include 144 items from STC and Wing periods. (These are included in the total given for the library.) Subjects covered are English literature, 18th-19th cent botany, 18th-19th cent philosophy and theology.

Temporary slip cat. Card cat for pre-1700 items, in process of completing cataloguing in full.

(e) *A H Bullen Collection* Collection formed in 1960 in memory of A H Bullen, founder of the Shakespeare Head Press. Donated to the Shakespeare Birthplace Library by F C Owlett, Esq, of Holland Park, London, on behalf of the Bullen Memorial Fund in 1961. It contains 29 v connected with A H Bullen's work with the Shakespeare Head Press in Stratford-upon-Avon. In addition to these the library has *c*90 items printed by the Shakespeare Head Press in Stratford-upon-Avon, and in Oxford, and the 'Stratford Town Shakespeare' 1904–7.

All items catalogued in main library cat. Separate handlist to the collection also available.

(f) *Bram Stoker Collection* Formed by Bram Stoker, Manager of the Lyceum Theatre, London, and working with Sir Henry Irving 1878–95; sold at Sotheby's March 12th 1920; purchased by Dobell on behalf of an anonymous purchaser who presented the collection to the Shakespeare Memorial Theatre in April 1920. It consists of 77 archive boxes (various sizes) containing all varieties of theatre ephemera relating to the careers of Sir Henry Irving and Ellen Terry, and the theatres with which Stoker was connected.

Cat listed in Stoker Collection handlist, and detailed list in each box.

(g) *Playbill Collection* Accumulated in Shakespeare Memorial Library from 1880 onwards, and includes *c*6,000 playbills (some bound into 31 albums); earliest playbill is from 1752. Collection strengths are in early to mid-19th cent London Shakespeare playbills (Covent Garden, Drury Lane, etc).

Card index for staff use only.

(h) *The Shakespeare Birthplace Trust Records Office* Until 1964 the Shakespeare Birthplace Library incorporated the local history and mss collections of the Shakespeare Birthplace Trust. When the Shakespeare Centre Library was opened in 1964 these collections were not transferred and became the nucleus of the Shakespeare Birthplace Trust Records Office. The Records Office as such is not within the scope of the present survey, but the printed books and pamphlets in this department are regarded as part of the library and are processed by them. The library contains *c*5,000 books and 3,000 pamphlets, of which about 500 books and 1,000 pamphlets might be considered 'rare'. Subjects covered are topography of Warwickshire, especially the Stratford-upon-Avon district, including archaeology and antiquities of local interest, biography of local families, etc.

Books and pamphlets are all catalogued in the main Shakespeare Centre Library cat, with a duplicate card cat in the Records Office Reading Room.

Stratford-upon-Avon Public Library, Henley Street, Stratford-upon-Avon. Tel (0789) 2209. Open Mon, Fri 9.30 am-7 pm, Tues, Wed 9.30 am-5.30 pm, Thurs 9.30 am-1 pm; Sat 9.30 am-4 pm. Admission free. Photocopy.

Part of Reference Library stock 35 STC and Wing items, including works by Fuller, Bacon, Bartholin, Boyle, Dugdale (Warks), Thoroton (Notts), Wright (Rutland), Derham's *Hydrologia Philosophia* (Ilmington), and Yarranton's *England's Improvements*. 18th and early 19th cent county histories of Glos, Northants, Worcs and Staffs, the Warwickshire section of 1792 *Universal British Directory*, Fisher's reproductions of Guild Chapel frescoes (1838), *Annals of Shakespeare's School* (MS) by Savage, 1952. Two large fo v of Hogarth's etchings ed by John Nichols [nd] with inserted plates. Bell's *British Drama* 1791–5, Inchbald's *British Theatre* 1806–9, and a *Collection of farces* 1809– all incomplete. Periodicals: *Archaeologia* V 1-77, 1770–1927, *Le Gazette* 1711–12 (incomplete), *Gentleman's Magazine* 1762–6, 1788–1825,

London Magazine 1760–2, *Weekly Worcester Journal* 1745–8.

Author and classified cats.

Warwick

Charlecote Park, Warwick (National Trust). Tel (0789) 840277. Admission by appointment with the Libraries Adviser, 42 Queen Anne's Gate, London SW1H 9AS.

Lucy family library Dates from early 16th cent. Contained *c*1,400 v in 1681. Substantial additions came (a) in 1697 when George Lucy married Mary Bohum who brought the books of her father, John Bohum of Finham; (b) in 1786 when a cousin, John Hammond, inherited Charlecote and brought with him the books of his father John Hammond, Rector of Tolland in Somerset; (c) in the early 19th cent when the present library was built. Presented to the National Trust in 1945 by Sir Montgomerie Fairfax-Lucy. It contains *c*3,800 v (4 mss, 5 incunabula). Strong in 16th and 17th cent theology and classics. Ms (*c*1525) of Machiavelli's *Il principe* in fine contemporary Italian binding (article by J H Whitfield in his *Discourses on Machiavelli*, Heffer, 1969, and a facsimile edition with an essay by J H Whitfield published by S R Publishers, 1969).

Alphabetical author card index. Typescript copy of 1681 cat (original now destroyed).

H R T Summerson, *The Lucys of Charlecote and their library*. 1978?

The County Museum, Warwick. Tel (0926) 43431. Open Mon-Sat 10 am-5.30 pm. Limited access on written application.

Started in 1834 as library of Warwick and Leamington Phrenological Society; absorbed in 1836 by Warwickshire Natural History and Archaeological Society which became moribund about 1900, and defunct in the late 1920s. Some books, mainly of local interest, went to the Warwick County Record Office. *c*1,000 titles, about half pre-1851. Mainly history (7 STC, 54 Wing) with emphasis on late 17th cent, eg 39 Popish plot pamphlets; geology, especially fossils; natural history, including a good collection of local flora.

Author card cat.

Warwick County Record Office, Priory Park, Cape Road, Warwick. Tel (0926) 43431 Ext 2506-8. Open Mon-Thurs 9 am-1 pm, 2-5.30 pm, Fri 9 am-1 pm, 2-5 pm; Sat 9 am-12.30 pm. Free access. Microfilm and microfiche readers, photocopying and microfilming.

The library started when the Record Office opened in 1932 with a number of books from the Warwickshire Natural History and Archaeological Society (see also under Warwickshire Museum) and from the County Education Office Library. Mostly added to by purchase. It contains *c*8,500 v (*c*400 pre-1851; *c*20 STC; *c*50 Wing). Aims to include a copy of every book relating to the county, and is the largest ever collection in the county. Complete sets of *Warwick Advertiser* from 1806 and *Leamington Courier* from 1828.

Card indexes: author, topographical (for Warwickshire) and subject.

An index of Warwickshire books not in the library is also being compiled.

West Midlands

Birmingham

Birmingham Public Libraries, Central Library, Birmingham B3 3HQ. Tel (021) 235 4511. Open Mon, Fri 9 am-6 pm, Tues, Wed, Thurs 9 am-8 pm; Sat 9 am-5 pm. Admission unrestricted. Reference facilities only. Carrels; photocopiers (subject to librarian's discretion). Enquiry service: written and telephone enquiries welcomed.

The following collections are all in the Language and Literature Department, unless otherwise stated.

Shakespeare Library Founded by the local Shakespeare club in April 1864 to celebrate the tercentenary of Shakespeare's birth, it contains *c*37,000 items, with translations in 90 languages, and include two copies of each of the four early folio editions and some of the quartos, including the Pavier quartos. A copy of the collected edition of the poems of 1640 (imperfect). A unique possession of the library is the more complete of the two known copies of Theobald's first Dublin edition of 1739. The library has over 800 19th cent editions of the complete works, ranging from those edited by Charles Knight to curiosities like the *Penny Shakespeare*. The 86 language sections range from Abkhazian to Zulu. The library possesses a Czech translation of *Macbeth* of 1786, and an early translation of *Julius Caesar* into Italian.

A Shakespeare Bibliography: the Catalogue of the Birmingham Shakespeare Library, Birmingham Public Libraries, v 1-7. London, Mansell, 1971. (Updated by additions to the BLCMP in microfiche cat.)

Shakespeare Memorial Library, Birmingham. Materials

for a history; collection of circulars, illustrations, newscuttings. 1861.

The Shakespeare Library (a brief description). Descriptive booklet available from Birmingham Public Libraries constantly updated.

For further references see the published cat above.

War Poetry Collection The original collection was presented anonymously to the library by William John Cross of Rubery, in memory of William John Billington, 2/24 London Regiment (Queen's) who was killed in action in Palestine in 1918. It contains *c*2,480 books and pamphlets, mainly first editions, some rare items relating mainly to First and Second World Wars, but also earlier or later material. Contains many examples of War poetry by members of the British and Allied Nations of the First World War in English, French, Italian and other languages. Works of great poets such as Binyon, Bridges, Brooke, Gibson, Graves, Hardy, Masefield and Sassoon stand side by side with the poetry of ordinary soldiers and civilians inspired by patriotism, horror and grief.

Printed cat 1921.

Supplementary entries on card index by author and title, together with subject index.

Open Access, p10-12, July 1964.

Parker Collection of Early Children's Books This collection was given to the library in 1956 by Mr and Mrs J F Parker of Tickenhill Folk Museum, Bewdley. It includes Mrs M Berkeley's collection of over 4,600 v of pre-1830 children's books, and *c*90 Georgian and Victorian educational games. The collection covers the period from 1538 to the present day. It contains a few Puritan exemplary stories and many chapbooks and early 19th cent moral stories. There are several works published by John Newbery, and a large number of miniature books; a large number of picture books, many by well known illustrators such as Kate Greenaway, and several moveable and toy books. There are 25 pre-1700 books, and 210 1701–1800 books.

Card index, with recent acquisitions on microfilm cassette.

F C Morgan (ed), *Children's books published before 1830 exhibited at Malvern Public Library in 1911.* Hereford, 1976. (op)

N Rathbone, 'The Parker collection of early children's books'. *Open Access* v 24, no 2, March 1981, p8.

——'Mirth without mischief: an introduction to the Parker collection of early children's books and games'. *West Midland Branch of the Library Association Occasional Pamphlet*, No 2, 1982.

B Staples, 'The Parker Collection'. *Open Access*, v 9, no 1, Oct 1962, p1-3; v 9, no 2, Jan 1963, p1-4.

Joseph Priestley Collection *c*580 items, many original editions, and *c*80 books relating to Priestley; newscuttings.

No published cat.

Entries included in Local Studies Departmental cat.

Cervantes Collection First books were donated by William Bragge of Birmingham in 1873, and now totals *c*1,200 v, including the first complete English edition, (Pt 1 and 2) of *Don Quixote*, 1620, one of the few books to survive the fire which destroyed the library in 1879, and many other early editions. There are 25 pre-1701 books, and 24 early editions in various languages.

Card index, with recent acquisitions on microfilm cassette.

Descriptive booklet available from Birmingham Public Libraries.

Johnson Collection Founded by the City (*c*1900) to celebrate Samuel Johnson's association with Birmingham where he stayed between 1732 and 1734, and began his professional career with some contributions to the *Birmingham Journal*. A very comprehensive collection, and contains *c*1,800 works of criticism and editions of Johnson's work, many first and early editions and some scarce foreign ones, including several pirated Dublin editions. Also contains much interesting Johnsoniana, including early editions of Mrs Piozzi's anecdotes, and Boswell's *Life of Johnson.*

Author index of cards, and most recently acquired material on microfilm.

Exhibition cats.

Dr Samuel Johnson, 1709–1784: celebrations in Birmingham. Birmingham Public Libraries, 1959. (op)

The Highland Tour: Johnson and Boswell in Scotland. Ibid 1978. (op)

Descriptive booklet available from Birmingham Public Libraries.

Milton Collection A collection of 1,400 v, including a gift of some 160 v of editions of Milton's works and Miltoniana, made by Frank Wright (1853–1922), a member of the Free Library Building Sub-committee in 1882. The collection includes 54 pre-1701 books; 45 first and early editions; 9 early Miltoniana; illustrated and private press edition.

Card index with recent acquisitions on microfilm cassette.

Descriptive booklet available from Birmingham Public Libraries.

Milton Illustrated: visions of Paradise. 1978. (op) (exhibition cat).

W R Parker, *Milton: a biography*. 2 v, Oxford, 1968. (op)

Early and Fine Printing Collection (including the Baskerville and King's Norton and Sheldon Parochial Libraries). Since its early days, the Reference Library has built up a large collection of books printed before 1701 and of finely printed and illustrated books of later date. It has acquired by gift the parish libraries of King's Norton (originally the library of the Rev Thomas Hall, 1610–65, containing *c*700 items) and of Sheldon (originally the personal library of Dr Thomas Bray, 1656–1730 containing 371 items). The collection totals 11,726 v which include 128 incunabula; 7,724 books and pamphlets printed from 1501–1700; 1,987 finely printed books; 378 fine bindings; and 1,135 finely illustrated books. There is an almost complete collection of books printed by John Baskerville, and a good representative collection of books printed by the Kelmscott Press and later members of the private press movement, to which contemporary examples from the work of modern private presses are added each year.

Card index, with recent acquisitions on microfilm cassette.

W Salt Brassington, *Report upon the King's Norton Parish Library*, 1893.

——'Thomas Hall and the library founded by him at King's Norton'. *Library Chronicle*, 5, 1888, p61-71.

Audrey H Higgs, 'Two parish libraries and their founders. (1) Thomas Hall Library'. *Open Access*, XVI, New Series no 3, Spring 1968, p2-4.

F S Stych, 'The Thomas Bray Library from Sheldon in the Birmingham Reference Library', *Ibid* XII, no 2, January 1964, p1-4.

The Library, The University of Birmingham, PO Box 363, Birmingham B15 2TT. Tel (021) 472 1301 Ext 2439. Open, Special Collections, Barnes Medical Library, and Music Library, Mon-Fri 9 am-5 pm. Admission to all bona fide research workers on application to the University Librarian. Photocopying services (xerox, microfilm) at the discretion of the University Librarian.

A The Main Library Special Collections

These have been acquired by gift, deposit or purchase since 1825 (Queen's College Medical School); 1880 (Mason College of Science); and 1900 (University of Birmingham). They comprise (i) *c*60,000 v of printed books which include 65 incunabula; *c*2,000 STC; and *c*3,500 Wing items; *c*10,000 v of early Italian printing; (ii) *c*30 medieval mss and 300,000 modern ms items; (iii) *c*2,000 early printed books of medical interest (1500–1800) in the Barnes Medical Library Special Collection; (iv) 470 music mss (medieval to present day) and 750 early printed music books and scores (17th-18th cent) in the Music Library Special Collection.

B Principal Special Collection

Printed Books (i) *Selborne Library* comprising *c*13,000 v of rare printed books 15th-20th cent, special strength in *c*3,000 v of pre-1800 scientific and early printed books; also *c*1,000 ms items, mostly 18th-20th cent letters from notable persons; (ii) *The Wedgewood Collection*, comprising early books on languages (almost all non-English) given to Mason College in 1889; (iii) *The Parish Library of St Mary's Warwick* (deposited 1959, purchased 1980–1), comprising *c*2,000 v of pre-1850 theology, classics and general literature; (iv) *The Thomas Wigan Library, Bewdley* (deposited by the trustees in 1950), consisting of *c*3,200 printed v on pre-1800 general literature; (v) *The Shaw Library, Bengeworth* (deposited 1964) of *c*1,000 v of pre-1860 theological works.

Cat: All printed books are recorded in the University Library's microfiche cats; (a) items acquired pre-1971; (b) items acquired post-1971.

H B Evans, *The library over a hundred years (1880–1980)*, Birmingham University Library, 1981.

I Fenlon, *Catalogue of printed music and music mss before 1801 in the Music Library of the University of Birmingham*, London, Mansell, 1976.

C Manuscript Collection

(i) *Chamberlain Family Archive* (given in 1975) comprising *c*130,000 letters, memoranda etc; (ii) *The Avon Papers* (given in 1977) of *c*30,000 ms items relating to the personal and official career of Sir Anthony Eden, 1st Earl of Avon; (iii) *The Church Missionary Society Archive* (in process of deposit) of *c*100,000 items relating to CMS missions 1979; (iv) *The Francis Brett Young* papers (given 1971) of *c*6,000 items relating to Francis and Jessica Brett Young; (v) *Business Archives* of *c*15,000 items relating to various 19th cent Birmingham firms (deposited papers); (vi) *The Jerningham Letters* (purchased 1967) consisting of *c*1,600 letters relating to Recusant family life *c*1780–1815; (vii) *A Galsworthy Archive of c*3,000 small printed and ms items relating to John and Ada Galsworthy.

Ms items are catalogued by handlists of individual collections, and by card cat of individual items (both available in the Library).

D W Evans, *Catalogue of the Cadbury papers*, Birmingham University Library, 1973.

B S Benedikz, *Guide to the Chamberlain papers*, Ibid, 1978.

——*Handlist of the Galsworthy papers... bequeathed by Mr R H Sauter*. Ibid, 1978.

——*Handlist of the papers of Sir Oliver Lodge*, Ibid, 1979.

Coventry

University of Warwick Library, Coventry CV4 7AL. Tel (0203) 24011. Open Mon-Thurs 9 am-1 pm, 1.30-5 pm, Fri 9 am-1 pm, 1.30-4 pm. Books are available for use by undergraduates and researchers (including visitors to the University) in the (supervised) search room of the Modern Records Centre (the University Library Archives Department) on request to the staff of the Humanities Division of the Library. Photocopying service available, subject to approval of the Humanities Division staff.

University of Warwick Library Special Collections The Special Collections contain all books published before 1830 acquired by the library since the University was opened in 1964, together with items of particular rarity or value. They contain over 2,500 v and the major collection of importance consisting of 4,000 18th and 19th cent French plays published in pamphlet form (the Marandet Collection). There are also books from the collections of the Howard League for Penal Reform and of Edward Hutton, among others, and a small collection of contemporary American poetry and little magazines. There is a small number (*c*60) of 16th, 17th and 18th cent books printed in Italy on literature, history and religion (mainly from the Hutton Library), and a slightly smaller number of 17th and early 18th cent works on English political and ecclesiastical history. The only book believed to be unique is Francesco Suriano, *Sermo egregius de indulgentiae Sancte Marie de Angelis apud Assisium* (1526?) (from the collection of Edward Hutton).

Guide to the Marandet Collection of French plays, by Jean Emelina and Peter Larkin (University of Warwick Library occasional publications, 6), 1979.

Selly Oak

Selly Oak Colleges Library, Selly Oak Colleges, Birmingham B29 6LE. Tel (021) 472 4231. Open Mon-Fri 9 am-1 pm, 2-5.30 pm. Admission free to all bona fide scholars and students. Photocopier, microfilm and microfiche readers. Inter-library loan services.

Selly Oak Colleges Library Rare Books Collection Given over the years by Edward Cadbury (founder of the library), Dr Rendel Harris, and scholar friends and collectors. The books were all brought together into one room in 1974 and shelved by date order. It contains *c*2,840 printed books dating from 1475–1850 and 9 incunabula; 68 STC and 165 Wing items. Strong on Puritan pamphlets, the early Jesuit missions, early children's literature, some very old herbals. Cards being examined for incorporation in the ESTC.

Handlist arranged by author, with chronological and subject index.

Available on microfiche (three fiche in set).

Wootton Wawen

St Peter's Church, Wootton Wawen, Warks. The Vicarage, Wootton Wawen, Solihull, West Midlands. Tel (056 42) 2659. Admission by written application to the Vicar.

Wootton Wawen Parish Library Given by the Rev George Dunscombe, vicar during the Commonwealth period. It contains 9 v—a characteristically small parish collection, still chained. Includes volume of 13 'fast sermons' of 1642, works by Jewell and Andrewes and Calvin's *Institutes*.

Notes & Queries. VIII, 1877, p325-6. (op)

W Cooper, *Wootton Wawen*, p102-3. (op)

Yorkshire, Derbyshire

Barnsley

Barnsley Central Library, Shambles Street, Barnsley S70 2JF. Tel (0226) 83241. Open Mon-Fri 9.30 am-8 pm; Sat 9.30 am-5 pm. Local Studies: Mon-Fri 9.30 am-1 pm, 2-6 pm; Sat 9.30 am-1 pm, 2-5 pm. Copying in main library. Separate local studies room with micro-reader.

No separate rare book collections, but items acquired over a number of years mainly included in stock of local studies department. The number of pre-1900 books, and pamphlets (excluding Barnsley printed books), totals *c*600; pre-1900 Barnsley printed books and pamphlets total *c*300.

Frank J Taylor, *Bibliographical list of books, pamphlets and articles connected with Barnsley...*, Barnsley, Public Library Committee, 1916.

Boston Spa

The British Library Lending Division, Boston Spa, Wetherby LS23 7BQ. Tel (0937) 843434. Although primarily a postal lending library, loans being negotiated through the applicant's own library, a reading room is available for casual visitors between 8.30 am and 5 pm Mon-Fri. Photocopying facilities available.

Pre-1801 Collection Currently about 7,000 v on a wide range of subjects, acquired by purchase or donation.

Edward Tottenham Collection A collection of about 700 v of 18th and early 19th cent theology, originally given by Edward Tottenham to Bath Public Library and subsequently transferred to the National Central Library in 1963, and thence to BLLD.

Dr Maurice Ernest Collection *c*1,000 v on longevity and old age, some published pre-1851, collected by Dr Maurice Ernest and placed in the National Central Library; subsequently transferred to BLLD.

All monographs are catalogued.

Bradford

Bolling Hall Museum, Bolling Hall Road, Bradford BD4 7LP. Tel (0274) 23057. Open Mon-Fri 10 am-5 pm; admission by prior appointment with the Curator. There are no copying or other research facilities for bibliographical study. A brief handlist of the books is available.

Bolling Hall is a 17th cent house used as a museum by Bradford Museums Service; it has about 1,000 older printed books which used to 'furnish' some fine 18th cent bookcases. It is a miscellaneous collection of mainly 18th cent and earlier printed books, many originating from the collecting of W Danby, who lived locally *c*1740–*c*1808. There are 4 v printed in the 16th cent, including a copy of the *Bishops' Bible*; about 50 v of the 17th cent are mainly classical texts; the remaining v of the 18th and early 19th cent are on a variety of subjects but mainly literature, history, topography and theology.

Bradford Cathedral Chapter Library, The Cathedral, Bradford BD1 4EG. No telephone.

The library was formed in 1979 primarily for the use of the clergy of the diocese, and contains mainly modern works in theology and local history, but also preserves the residue of several parish libraries: (a) *Dent parish library*: 10 v, mostly 18th cent theology; (b) *Kildwick parish library*: *c*52 titles in 57 v, mainly theological, 16th and 17th cent, many the gift of the Currer family of Kildwick parish church, especially from Henry Currer (1651–1722) and Haworth Currer (1690–1744); (c) *Pudsey parish library*: 4 titles in 6 v, early 19th cent theology.

Applications to consult older material should be made in writing as far in advance as possible. There are no photocopying facilities.

Classified cat (Dewey) and author index, and lists of contents of the parish libraries.

Bradford Central Public Library, Prince's Way, Bradford BD1 1NN. Tel (0274) 33081. Open Mon-Fri 9 am-9 pm; Sat 9 am-5 pm. Photocopying facilities.

The library includes:

Dickons Collection *c*420 v (collected by J N Dickons and acquired by the library in 1912 for a nominal sum, under the provisions of his will) on religion and local history, principally Yorkshire.

Federer Collection *c*9,000 v collected by C A Federer and acquired by Bradford Public Library in 1908, comprising books by Yorkshire authors, books on Yorkshire and books printed in Yorkshire. The towns of Bradford, Leeds, Hull, York and Whitby are especially well represented.

Lees Botanical Collection *c*530 v and pamphlets collected by Dr F Arnold Lees and acquired by the library in 1905, mainly devoted to geo-botany and regional flora.

There are author and subject cats.

Bradford Public Library. *Catalogue of the books and pamphlets relating to Yorkshire* (Bradford, 1892).

——*Catalogue of the Lees Collection in the Reference Library* (Bradford, 1909).

Castleton

Castleton Parish Library, St Edmund's Parish Church, Castleton, Derbyshire. Tel (0433) 20534. Enquiries to the Vicar. Consultation only.

The Farran Library A collection made, and bequeathed to the church by a former incumbent, the Rev Frederic Farran, 1780–1817. It comprises 740 v (880 items); 30 v of pamphlets, sermons, etc bound together. The collection consists mainly of 18th cent theological works, with *c*70 of the 17th cent; 105 STC and Wing items.

Partial contemporary ms cat.

E D Mackerness, 'The Castleton Parish Library', *J Derbyshire Arch and Nat Hist Soc*, 58, p38-48.

J E Friedman, *Name Catalogue*..., Postgrad School of Lib and Inf Science, Sheffield, 1978.

Doncaster

Campsall Church (S Mary Magdalene), Campsall Vicarage, Doncaster, Yorks. (Nr Askern 7 miles NW of Doncaster). Tel (0302) 700286 (The Vicarage). Admission by prior arrangement with the Vicar.

The library was made up by a previous incumbent early in the 18th cent. It contains 143 items, mainly 17th and 18th cent, including Bibles and commentaries; prayer books; theology.

A list (in Sheffield City Libraries Local History Collection) drafted in 1959, in the course of one visit to Campsall Church.

'A catalogue compiled by Michael Gallico in 1980' (in partial fulfilment of the requirements for MA (Lib) Univ of Sheffield).

Halifax

Central Public Library, Lister Lane, Halifax HX1 5LA. Tel (0422) 65105. Open Mon, Tues, Thurs and Fri 10 am-8 pm, Wed 10 am-12 noon; Sat 10 am-5 pm. There are author and other catalogues, and photocopying facilities. The following collections may be viewed by application to the Librarian.

Edwards Bindings 17 examples of books bound by the firm of Halifax binders, Edwards, including examples of Etruscan calf binding, transparent vellum binding with decoration under, morocco binding and 3 v with fore-edge painting.

Milner Collection 706 v (124 pre-1850) published by the local firm of William Milner (1834–51)—later Milner and

Sowerby, Milner & Co, Milner & Co Ltd—mainly cheap editions of English and American classics (some pirated), religious, moral and educational works, acquired by purchase and by donation from various sources, especially the collection of Joseph Horsfall Turner (1845–1915).

Lister Collection A small collection of 16 miscellaneous early-printed books (including five incunabula) and two 15th cent Dutch mss, collected by John Lister (1847–1933) antiquary, of Shibden Hall.

D Bridge, 'William Milner: printer and bookseller', in *Trans Halifax Antiquarian Society* (1969), p75-83.

T W Hanson, 'Edwards of Halifax', *Ibid* (1912), p141-200.

(*Note*. Non-local literature on Edwards has been ignored; neither of the works cited above are exclusively or even explicitly based on the collections at Halifax, but are obviously related to them.)

Haworth

Haworth Parsonage Brontë Museum, Haworth, Keighley BD22 2DR. Tel (0535) 42323. Open Mon-Fri 11 am-6 pm (5 pm in winter). Bona fide students who are not members of the Brontë Society may be admitted to the library upon making written application, in advance, stating the nature of their research. Photocopying facilities available, and the collection is fully catalogued.

The collection has grown by purchase, gift and permanent loan since the foundation of the Brontë Society in 1893, and has been greatly extended since 1928 when Haworth Parsonage became the Brontë Museum. It contains the following collections:

Brontë Society Collection Over 130 books once belonging to the Brontë family; first and early editions of works by the family; books, pamphlets and offprints about the family; 204 mss of Charlotte, Branwell, Emily and Anne; 60 letters chiefly to and from Charlotte, and numerous sketches, drawings and paintings by members of the family.

The Bonnell Collection 23 books owned by the family; 78 mss by various members of the family and other items of Brontëana, collected by Henry Houston Bonnell of Philadelphia and presented to the Society on his death in 1928.

Brontë Society. *Transactions* I-, (1898). (Latterly, these have contained an annual report on the library with notes and lists of recent accessions.)

Brontë Society. *Catalogue of the Bonnell Collection in the Brontë Parsonage Museum* (Haworth, 1932).

Brontë Society. *Opening of the Old Parsonage, Haworth, as a museum and library*. (Shipley, 1928).

J A Symington. *Catalogue of the museum & library of the Brontë Society*. (Haworth, 1927).

Huddersfield

Huddersfield Polytechnic, Queensgate, Huddersfield HD1 3DH. Tel (0484) 22288. Hours of opening vary, but generally Mon-Fri 9 am-5 pm. Non-members wishing to consult the rare book collection should write to the Librarian in advance. Photocopying facilities available.

The library began in 1841 with donations to the Huddersfield Young Men's Improvement Society; the one-time Mechanics' Institute was eventually designated a polytechnic in 1970. It contains a small rare books collection of about 600 v covering classics of science and technology, and copies of principal historical and literary publications, both English and foreign, mainly of the period 1800–50; 2 Wing items.

Huddersfield Technical School (afterwards Technical College) *Catalogue of the library* (Huddersfield, 1885–7). 2nd ed, Huddersfield, 1899.

M Tylecote. *The Mechanics' Institutes of Lancashire and Yorkshire before 1851* (Manchester, 1957), p190 *et seq*.

Kirklees Libraries and Museums Service, Local Studies and Archives Department, Princess Alexandra Walk, Huddersfield HD1 2SU. Tel (0484) 21356. Open Mon-Fri 9 am-8.30 pm; Sat 9 am-4 pm. Microfilming, photocopying and ultraviolet lamp facilities available.

Local Studies Collection Comprises the private collection of the local antiquary, G W Tomlinson (1837–97) and items acquired directly by the library, and includes a wide range of material on Huddersfield, Dewsbury and district—books, pamphlets, handbills and other ephemera, directories, sermons, poll-books and examples of local printing.

Tolson Memorial Museum Collection Some 204 v of juvenilia, theatre bills and other handbills, atlases, locally printed material and works on local history (kept at Tolson Memorial Museum, Wakefield Road, Huddersfield; Tel (0484) 30591).

Other Collections Smaller collections of older books, mainly on local history, are kept in other constituent libraries at Dewsbury, Batley and Heckmondwike, and in other constituent museums at Wilton Park (Batley), Red House (Gomersal) and Oakwell Hall (Birstall).

Local history collection is catalogued by author, subject and place; there is also a card index under printer, place and date for locally printed items.

Leeds

Central Public Library, Calverley Street, Leeds LS1 3AB. Tel (0532) 462016 (Reference Department). Opening hours vary, but generally Mon-Fri 9 am-5 pm; Sat 9 am-4 pm. Facilities for microfilming, photocopying and conventional photography.

English books 1640–49 c300 v printed in the decade 1640–49, originally only a collection of English Civil War tracts, but subsequently added to under the Background scheme.

Gascoigne Collection Over 3,000 items of naval and military science and history assembled by Col F T Gascoigne of Lotherton Hall and presented to the city, with Lotherton Hall, in 1968. The collection includes military science, army lists and regulations, histories of wars and campaigns, regimental histories, biographies, books of travel and non-warlike expeditions by military and naval men, and some fiction with a military or naval background.

Gott bequest A small collection of about 160 v on early gardening and botany from Mrs Beryl Gott, received in 1941.

Local History Collection c40,000 items (proportion pre-1851 not known), printed books, maps, directories, prints and ephemera on Leeds and district, and on Yorkshire generally. A separate catalogue of prints is maintained, arranged topographically.

Porton Collection c3,000 items of Hebraica and Judaica comprising the library of Rabbi Moses Abrahams (*d*1919) and the Hebrew books from the former Hebrew Literary Society of Leeds, presented to the Public Library and accommodated in a specially furnished room in 1938.

Main collections are included in a dictionary cat, and there are also various subsidiary cats.

Leeds Incorporated Law Society, 1 Albion Place, Leeds LS1 6JL. A private subscription library for solicitors practising in Leeds and district, founded c1831 and occupying its present site since 1920. Non-members may be admitted upon written application, stating the nature of their proposed research, being made to the Librarian; normally non-members are not admitted to pursue legal research. No research equipment.

The library consists principally of legal report literature, including a nearly full set of the private reports, in original editions; long runs of legal journals, including *Law Journal* from 1832; some treatises.

A handlist is available.

The Leeds Library, 18 Commercial Street, Leeds LS1 6AL. Tel (0532) 453071. Non-members with research interests which cannot be readily satisfied elsewhere may be allowed reference facilities upon making written application in advance, stating their needs. There are no photocopying or other research facilities.

Founded in 1768, this is the oldest English private subscription library still in operation. The present stock of c115,000 v was acquired by purchase and by gift. It comprises a general collection in the humanities, with some early science. Special features include: English Civil War tracts and Popish Plot tracts (17th cent); an extensive collection of 'three-decker' English novels of the earlier 19th cent; 19th cent juvenilia; long and almost unbroken runs of many general and literary periodicals (eg *Annual Register, Athenaeum, Blackwood's, Cornhill, Gentleman's, Note & Queries* and *Punch*); *Army* and *Navy lists* to 1914; *British Museum library catalogue* (1813–19), 7 v, and Thomas Wilson collection of Yorkshire and Lancashire pedigrees.

The library has an author cat.

Leeds Library, *Catalogue of the Leeds Library* (Leeds, 1889; supplements, 1890–1937).

F Beckwith, *The Leeds Library 1768–1968*, Leeds, priv prin, 1968.

Leeds Parish Church (Music Library), Kirkgate, Leeds 2. Scholars wishing to view the collection of older music in the Wesley Room should make an appointment with the Master of the Music in writing, well in advance, stating the nature of their research. There are no research facilities.

The library consists of a collection of over 100 v of predominantly church music, acquired by purchase and subscription, mostly mid-18th to mid-19th cent, including services, part-books, anthems and oratorio scores for piano and voices; some ms scores by S S Wesley and E C Bairstow; privately printed collection of S S Wesley's anthems, c1840.

Leeds (Roman Catholic) Diocesan Library, Curia House, 13 North Grange Road, Leeds LS6 2BR. Access by appointment; applications should be made in writing, stating the nature of the applicant's research. There is no research apparatus.

The library is what remains of the library of the Leeds Diocesan Seminary (1878–1939), most of which was sold in 1951. That library had developed out of the libraries of the Vicars Apostolic of the Northern District (1688–1840) and of the Bishops of Beverley (1840–78). Some other books from these sources have migrated to Ushaw. There are c1,000 v, mainly of Catholic theology, apologetic and history, many printed in the 16th and 17th cent, including several dozen STC/Wing items, pamphlets on the siege of Londonderry (1689 and 1690); 11 bound v of 19th cent pamphlets on social, religious and political affairs, and a complete run of the *Catholic Directory* (formerly *Laity's Directory*) from 1803.

Temple Newsam House, Leeds LS15 0AE. Tel (0532) 647321. The House is principally a museum, open to the general public; the library collections are available freely to research students Tues-Fri 10 am-5 pm, upon written application being made in advance.

The library's holdings number *c*10,000 items which include:

Pratt Collection *c*350 furniture trade catalogues, mostly English, of the Victorian and Edwardian period, many being apparently unique surviving copies, the gift of C B Pratt, Esq, of Bradford.

Temple Newsam Library A miscellaneous collection of *c*1,000 printed books of the 17th cent onwards, being the remains of the accumulated library of the Irwin family, acquired with the house by Leeds Corporation in 1922. A handlist of authors and titles is kept in Leeds Central Public Library (reference department). A similar, but smaller, collection is kept at Lotherton Hall (Aberford, Leeds, LS25 3EB).

C G Gilbert, 'Check-list of the Pratt Collection', in *Furniture at Temple Newsam and Lotherton Hall*. [1978].

C Ramsay, 'The Formation of the eighteenth century library (a bibliographical account)', *Leeds Arts Calendar*, no 76 (1975), p5-9.

Thoresby Society Library, 23 Clarendon Road, Leeds LS2 9NZ.

The Society was founded in 1889 to encourage the study of the history of Leeds, and maintains a library, mostly assembled by gift, of *c*4,000 v of printed books besides pamphlets, lantern slides, maps, plans and other material. Non-members wishing to use the library should seek permission from the librarian in writing. Photocopying facilities provided by the Yorkshire Archaeological Society on the same premises. The library contains mss and printed books relating to Leeds and district, principally post-1700, including sermons, street directories and some items from the library of Ralph Thoresby (1658–1725), the antiquary, after whom the Society is named.

Author cat.

K J Bonser and H Nichols, *Printed maps and plans of Leeds, 1711–1900* (Thoresby Soc, publn v 47, 1960).

G E Kirk, 'The Library of the Thoresby Society', in *Thoresby Soc Publications*, v 41 (1954), p259-74.

Trinity and All Saints' College, Brownberrie Lane, Horsforth, Leeds LS18 5HD. Tel (0532) 584341. Open generally Mon-Fri 9.15 am-5 pm. Photocopying facilities.

The College was founded in 1966 as a college of education, and has since become a college of higher education. Its library contains a local history collection with older material as a basis for teaching in local studies, and includes *c*50 pre-1851 items.

Author and classified cats.

University of Leeds Library, Leeds LS2 9JT. Tel (0532) 31751 (general enquiries Ext 6551; for particular departments, see below). Opening hours vary but non-members should confine their visits ordinarily to Mon-Fri 9 am-5 pm. Non-members may be allowed to use the collections for reference purposes upon making written application in advance to the Librarian; persons wishing to use the Brotherton Collection must normally furnish a suitable recommendation from somebody in a recognized position have personal knowledge of the applicant. Photocopying and other research facilities are available. The total stock of printed books and pamphlets numbers *c*1,380,000 items.

Author and subject cats.

A **Brotherton Collection** (also open Saturday mornings 9 am-1 pm; 12.30 in long vacation), but closed Mon-Fri 1-2.15 pm. Tel Ext 6552.

This rare book collection has been developed from the private library of Edward Allen Brotherton, Baron Brotherton of Wakefield (1856–1930), which was presented to the University in 1935 in accordance with his known wishes. It is supported by an endowment from Lord Brotherton and by further funds given by his niece-in-law, Mrs Dorothy Una McGrigor Phillips (Dorothy Una Ratcliffe), and others. The present stock comprises *c*50,000 printed books and pamphlets, *c*43,000 letters and *c*8,000 other mss and deeds. The Brotherton Collection includes the following:

(i) 252 incunabula, including the unique copy of Laurentius Gulielmus, *Epitome margaritae eloquentiae*, printed by Caxton *c*1480 and formerly in Ripon Cathedral Library.

(ii) *English literature, 1600–1750*: this is the main field of current acquisition and now contains some 6,500 items. It is especially strong in drama and poetry, and includes numerous items by Beaumont, Mrs Aphra Behn, Mrs Susannah Centlivre, Congreve, Crowne, Dryden, Durfey, Fielding, Fletcher, Gay, the Killigrews, Lee, Otway, Pope, Prior, Shadwell, Shirley, Swift, Vanbrugh and Wycherley. There are numerous verse miscellanies and broadsides. It is supported by background material including English science and travel books of the same period, some 700 Civil War and Commonwealth tracts, and about 300 political tracts from 1660 to the early 18th cent.

(iii) *English literature 1750–1900*: some 4,000 printed books, literary mss and letters. Writers include: Dr Thomas Arnold of Rugby, Borrow, the Brontës, the Brownings, Byron, Crabbe, Dickens, H A Jones, the Rossettis, G A Sala, Scott, Swinburne and Tennyson. The Arnold collection includes diaries and correspondence. The Brontë material includes manuscripts and letters and a major collection of the writings and mss of Patrick Branwell Brontë; also 12 v of letters of Mrs Gaskell. The Swinburne collection comprises a virtually complete set of the important printed editions and a considerable number of mss and letters.

(iv) *Novello Cowden Clarke Collection*: consists of c1,100 printed volumes and numerous mss, albums and sketch books, also music. This material relates to the family of Vincent Novello (1781–1861) and especially to Charles and Mary Cowden Clarke (née Novello) and was presented mainly in 1954 by Donna Nerina Medici di Marignano Gigliucci and the Contessa Bona Gigliucci, great-grand-daughters of Vincent Novello. It also includes printed works by Keats, Byron, Tennyson and Dickens, and letters from many 19th cent writers including Dickens and Leigh Hunt. The diaries of Vincent and Mary Novello record their visit in 1829 to Mozart's widow and sister.

(v) *Gosse correspondence*: Sir Edmund Gosse's voluminous correspondence was acquired after his death in 1928 and further material, including pocket diaries for 1877 and 1928, was added after 1945 by his son, Dr Philip Gosse. His correspondents include more than 1,000 literary and political figures of the late 19th and early 20th cent.

(vi) *Yorkshire collection*: some 2,600 v and numerous pamphlets including the collection assembled by W T Freemantle in connection with his bibliographical researches (especially strong on Sheffield, Rotherham and South Yorkshire generally); also the antiquarian papers of the Rev Carus Vale Collier, deeds of Marrick Priory, and Civil War tracts relating to Yorkshire.

(vii) *Fine bindings*: as well as many examples scattered throughout the Brotherton Collection, there are some 120 examples of early printed books bound in antique styles by Riviere for Lord Howard de Walden.

(viii) *Miscellaneous Collections*: a small collection of English printed books 1501–1600; a travelling library of 43 miniature volumes printed in Holland and housed in a special box (c1617), probably once belonging to Sir Julius Caesar (1558–1636), Master of the Rolls; about 650 miscellaneous foreign printed books of 16th-18th cent; over 550 tracts relating to the Brabant revolution, 1789–90; papers of Chevalier d'Eon; letters from Juliette Drouet to Victor Hugo, and from Alfred de Vigny and others to Sutton Sharpe; over 4,000 items of music, many from the collection of W T Freemantle, also numerous 18th cent scores, especially by Corelli; some 100 v by Charles Dibdin; many printed volumes of Mendelssohn's music and 70 letters from him; works by Sterndale Bennett and S C Foster; correspondence of C K Shorter (Brontë and Gaskell connections); papers of Edward Clodd; papers of Bram Stoker, mostly connected with the theatre; and the Romany Collection, one of the two major British collections on the gypsies, presented by Mrs McGrigor Phillips in 1950 and specially endowed to permit its development.

The Brotherton Collection also contains a number of important modern and contemporary literary collections which fall well beyond the chronological limit of this survey.

B **Special Collections**

(Tel Ext 7278). This department contains most of the other mss and older printed books, mainly pre-1851, acquired by gift or purchase since the foundation of the Yorkshire College in 1874, with the exception of certain further collections mentioned separately below. The following are especially notable:

(i) *Anglo-French Collection*: more than 5,000 v, mainly French translations of British writers, but also French works on Great Britain, published before 1805.

(ii) *Cookery Collections*: more than 2,200 v on cookery and domestic management from the 16th cent onwards, based on the collections presented respectively by Mrs Blance Leigh in 1939 and Mr John F Preston in 1962.

(iii) *Early science*: over 3,200 scientific works, mainly pre-1800, including those presented by All Souls College, Oxford, in 1926 and others from the library of Alfred Chaston Chapman, FRS, presented by his widow in 1939, and especially strong in early scientific periodicals.

(iv) *French, Barbier, Buckmaster and Early French Collections*: more than 5,000 v, and especially strong in 18th cent French literature (mainly acquired from the collection of Mr C A Buckmaster in 1950) and on provincial and dialect lexicography (the collection of Prof Paul Barbier who died in 1947).

(v) *German and Anglo-German Collections*: c2,000 v especially representing late 17th and 18th cent German literature and literary periodicals; also a good collection of first editions of 19th and 20th cent German writers, mainly from the bequest of Dr Hans Rosenbusch (1883–1966). The Anglo-German collection comprises German translations of English works, mostly published in the 18th cent.

(vi) *Cecil Roth and Travers Herford Collections*: c1,000 v of Judaica, including older printed books and mss (c300) from the library of Dr Cecil Roth (1899–1970), acquired anonymously for the Brotherton Library in 1961, mainly on the post-Biblical history of the Jews in England and Europe; also the mainly liturgical and scriptural collection of the Rev Travers Herford, deposited on permanent loan by the Unitarian College, Manchester.

(vii) *Theology*: over 3,500 v, including those presented by All Souls College, Oxford, in 1929 and other older material from the Holden Library of the diocese of Ripon; includes some 17th cent Socinian literature.

(viii) *Whitaker Collection*: some 500 atlases and road-books, principally of England and Wales, presented by Dr Harold Whitaker in 1939.

(ix) *Leeds Friends' Old Library*: c1,200 titles, in somewhat fewer volumes, rich in Quaker devotional and historical literature, formerly in the circulating library of the Carlton Hill Preparative Meeting of the Society of Friends, in Leeds, deposited in 1976 and since gifted; also some similar material from other meetings in Yorkshire.

(x) *National Collection of Greek and Latin school textbooks*: about 6,000 v of Greek and Latin textbooks used in British schools since *c*1800; also some material on the methodology of classics teaching and on the historical and cultural background to Greek and Latin literature. The collection began as a private venture by Mr W B Thompson in the 1950s and was transferred to the Library in 1979.

(xi) *'Background' Collection*: under the Background Scheme the library collects British publications issued in the period 1710–19.

C **Icelandic Collection**

(Tel Ext 300). This collection, to which items are still being added, not least by gift from Iceland, was originally the private library of Mr B T Melsted (1860–1929), an Icelandic historian and author; it was acquired for the University through the good offices of Sir Edwin Airey in 1929. The present stock numbers *c*13,000 items and includes more than 100 Icelandic books printed before 1800, a substantial run of the proceedings of the Icelandic parliament from 1696 (some in manuscript), a copy of *Jónsbok* (1580), and much other material including small sections devoted to other Scandinavian countries and to the Faroe, Orkney and Shetland islands and to Greenland.

D **Medical Library: Historical Collection**

(Tel Ext 7597). This collection of *c*1,300 v contains many important early medical works and others of lesser significance, but which represent a working medical library of the late 18th cent. It comprises the older books from the Leeds Medical School (founded in 1831) which included books presented by Dr Hunter in 1834, and from the library of the Leeds General Infirmary (founded in 1767) which had been given to the School in 1865.

J S Andrews, 'The University's Romany Collection', *University of Leeds Review*, vi (1958), p51-60.

Encyclopaedia of library and information science, ed A Kent and H Lancour, v iii (1970), p359-67 (The Brotherton Collection by B S Page and D I Masson); xiv (1975), p130-40 (Leeds University Library, by D Cox).

D I Masson, 'The Brotherton College of rare books and manuscripts', *University of Leeds Review*, xxi (1978), p135-54.

P S Morrish, 'The Brotherton Library, its Judaica and Cecil Roth', in *University of Leeds Review*, v 23 (1980), p218-33.

R Offor, 'A Collection of books in the library of the University of Leeds...translations from English into French (and) written in French on Great Britain and British affairs', *Proc Leeds Phil and Lit Soc, historical and literary section*, i (1925–8), p292-8; ii (1928–32), p109-123 and 361-76; iv (1936–8), p55-76; v (1938–43), p277-93 and 403-11; vi (1944–52), p111-24, 196-215, 283-312.

——*A descriptive guide to the libraries of the University of Leeds* (Leeds, 1947).

——*Supplement* (Leeds, 1949).

C Roth, 'Catalogue of manuscripts in the Roth Collection', *Alexander Marx jubilee volume, English section* (New York, 1950), p503-35 [reprinted with addenda in: C Roth, *Studies in books and booklore* (Farnborough, 1972), p255-87].

J A Symington, *The Brotherton Library* [ie Collection]; *a catalogue of ancient manuscripts and early printed books* (Leeds, 1931).

W B Thompson and J D Ridge, *Catalogue of the National Collection of Greek and Latin school text-books* (Leeds, 1970–4). 2 v.

University of Leeds. Libraries. *Annual report of the Librarian* (Leeds, 1949–). [Previous reports may be found in the annual report of the University.]

——*Annual report of the Brotherton Collection Committee* (Leeds, 1936–).

——*Catalogue of the Icelandic Collection* (Leeds, 1978).

——*Catalogue of the Romany Collection formed by D U McGrigor Phillips and presented to the University of Leeds* (Edinburgh, 1962).

——*Catalogue of the Gosse correspondence in the Brotherton Collection* (Leeds, 1950).

——*German literature printed in the 17th and 18th centuries:a catalogue of the Library's collection* (Leeds, 1973).

——*Supplement* (Leeds, 1976).

——*Leeds Friends' Old Library: an alphabetical checklist* (Leeds, 1978).

H Whitaker, *The Harold Whitaker Collection of county atlases, road-books and maps presented to the University of Leeds* (Leeds, 1947).

P B Wood and J V Golinski, 'Collections VIII. Library and archive resources in the history of science and medicine at the University of Leeds', in *British Jnl for the History of Science*, v 14 (1981), p263-81.

Yorkshire Archaeological Society Library, Claremont, 23 Clarendon Road, Leeds LS2 9NZ. Tel (0532) 457910. Non-members wishing to use the library should seek permission from the librarian in writing in advance. Photocopying facilities.

The Society was founded in Huddersfield in 1863, and moved to Leeds in 1896; it occupied its present premises in 1968. The library contains *c*25,000 items, exclusive of the collection of mss, mostly given or bequeathed, and amongst the more important donations are those by Miss M E Turner of her own and her uncle's topographical collections in 1867, and by Sir Thomas Brooke, Bart, in 1907. The most important works relate to the history and archaeology of Yorkshire; northern religious tracts and sermons of the 18th and 19th cent; some English Civil War tracts; and antiquarians' bookplates. There are *c*200 STC/Wing items.

The library has a dictionary cat.

G E Kirk, *Catalogue of maps and plans in the library of the Yorkshire Archaeological Society*. (Leeds, 1937).

——*Catalogue of printed books and pamphlets in the library of the Yorkshire Archaeological Society*. (Wakefield, 1935–6).

W T Lancaster, *Catalogue of the manuscripts in the library of the Yorkshire Archaeological Society*. (Leeds, 1912).

J W Walker, *The History of the Yorkshire Archaeological Society*. (Leeds, 1947).

Pontefract

Ackworth School Library, Pontefract Road, Ackworth, Pontefract WF7 7LT. Ackworth School is an independent Quaker school and its library is only available to members of the public upon written application to the Headmaster, stating the nature of the applicant's research.

The school was established in 1779, and many of the books in the library are gifts from former pupils. The library has a special rare book collection containing *c*100 v (7 STC and 10 Wing), the majority of which have a Quaker interest and many have interesting provenances; there are a number of works by the Fothergills, including Dr John Fothergill's *Works* (1784), presented by its editor J C Lettsome. There is a volume of *Psalms, hymns and anthems for the use of children of the Hospital* (York, 1767) from the Foundling Hospital period of the school's premises. Bibles include: *Great Bible* (1539), *Bishops' Bible* (3rd ed, 1572), *Breeches Bible* (1596), *Douai Bible* (1610), *Vulgate* (1679) and Purver's *Bible* (1764).

Ackworth School, *Catalogue of the library of Ackworth School*. (York, 1848).

——*Catalogues of the Centre, West Wing, and Classical Libraries at Ackworth School*. (York, 1850).

E Vipont, *Ackworth School*. (London, 1959).

Ripon

Cathedral Church of St Peter and St Wilfrid, Ripon, North Yorkshire. Admission by written application to the Canon Librarian. Tel (0765) 2658. Photocopying etc by arrangement with the Brotherton Library, University of Leeds, Leeds LS2 9JT, upon application to the Canon Librarian.

Ripon Cathedral Library Originated by a bequest of Anthony Higgin (Dean of Ripon 1608–24) of all his books to the Collegiate Church of Ripon; supplemented by purchases and individual gifts during succeeding years, and by the bequest of the Rev Edward Feilde's library in 1868. Dean Higgin's library, of which *c*1,250 v survive, was primarily a theological collection, containing editions of the Bible, commentaries, sermons, works of the Fathers of the Church, controversial works of the 16th cent etc. Classical authors are also well represented, particularly Cicero's rhetorical works; there are many books on Greek and Latin grammar, and a number on Hebrew grammar; *c*20 medical works; a few volumes on astronomy and geography; and *c*15 law books, with a number of general chronicles and histories.

A few additions were made between 1624 and the beginning of the 18th cent. *c*50 copies remain of the Brief of Charles II, issued in 1661, authorizing the collection of funds towards the repair of the Minster after the damage caused in the Civil Wars and from the fall of the central spire in 1660. Additions were made during the 18th cent, mainly by gift. Purchases began to be made in the second part of the 19th cent, mainly in the field of English church history. Copies of such standard works as Dugdale's *Monasticon* (1846) were added during this period; the bequest of the Rev Edward Feilde of Harrogate included works on theology, commentaries, and books on history and travel.

An interesting 18th cent gift to the Library is a small carved oak bookcase containing a Bible (1716–17) and Prayer Book (1717) presented (on 25 December 1779) by Sir Fletcher Norton (afterwards Lord Grantley) of Grantley Hall near Ripon, Speaker of the House of Commons.

The stock totals *c*4,000 v (4,200 works), and includes 55 incunabula; 215 STC and 110 Wing items; 970 foreign books, 1501–1600; and 160 foreign books of 1601–1700.

Card cat (dictionary form) compiled 1952–3.

Ms cat in 2 v, by Rev J T Fowler, 1873.

B Botfield, *Notes on the cathedral libraries of England* (1849), p384.

J T Fowler, 'Ripon Minster Library and its founder', *Yorks Arch Journal* II (1873), p371-402.

A T Waugh, *The Library of Ripon Minster*. (Printed as Appendix I in Lucius Smith's *The story of Ripon Minster*, 1914.)

'The Library Catalogue of Anthony Higgin, Dean of Ripon (1608–1624)', ed by J E Mortimer in *Proc Leeds Philosophical and Literary Society*, Literary and Historical Section, v X, pt 1 (June 1962).

Rotherham

The Brian O'Malley Central Library and Arts Centre, Walker Place, Rotherham S64 1JH. Tel (0709) 2121. Open Mon-Fri 10 am-8 pm; Sat 9 am-5 pm. Copying and microfilm reader available.

The Collection was founded by Mrs Frances Mansel in 1728; a collection, chiefly of theological works, to the amount of £100,000, for the use of the clergy and parishioners of Rotherham. Offered to Rotherham Public Library by the Vicar and Church Wardens, 1893 (204 v at that time). One case of books was saved after a fire at the Public Library in 1925. The collection now comprises 44 items, mainly 18th cent theological works—English imprints.

Checklist compiled by Mrs F V Crowden, April 1978.

Sandbeck Park, Maltby, Rotherham, Yorkshire. Tel (0302) 742210. Admission by appointment for bona fide research workers.

The Library, which is owned by the Earl of Scarborough, was collected mainly between 1840 and 1870, replacing the previous collections which had been sold. It consists of *c*3,000 v, mainly 18th and early 19th cent works on topography, history, local history, literature, sport (especially racing), natural history (mainly botany), with some printed music.

Lumley, John, *Baron* (1534?–1609). *The Lumley Library: the Catalogue of 1609*, edited by Sears Jayne and Francis R Johnson, London, British Museum, 1956.

Sheffield

Ecclesfield Parish Church, Ecclesfield, Sheffield. Tel (0742) 467569. Admission is by arrangement with the Vicar.

Ecclesfield Parish Library Now only the remains of a chained library and comprising four v (in two), including items by Dionysius and Lira, referred to in W Blades, *Books in chains*. . . , London, 1892, p45.

Central Council for the Care of the Churches. Parish Libraries of the Church of England. . . , 1959, p78.

The Gatty Collection Built up on account of the Rev R Mayland's personal interest in the Gatty family and their writings, especially children's literature of the Victorian period. With the exception of three works, it is a complete collection, including many first editions, paperbacks, small pocket editions, collected works and illustrated editions (pre-Raphaelite School). The subject content, although fictional, is based on Vicarage, Vicarage Garden, Church and Village life.

Checklist, but a cat of the collection available at Sheffield University. (1981)

Ruskin Museum of the Guild of St George. The collection is now in the care of the Graves Art Gallery, Surrey Street, Sheffield S1 1XZ. Tel (0742) 734781. Due to open Spring 1985. Enquiries to the Director.

Ruskin Museum Library The Museum dates from the foundation of the Guild of St George by John Ruskin in 1878. Some proportion of the contents from Ruskin himself. Opened first at Walkley, Sheffield, moved to Meersbrook Park 1890. The Leplay House Library was incorporated in the 1940s. After 1950 when the Museum was closed, items from it were exhibited at the Sheffield Art Gallery until the complete collection was moved to Reading in 1963. It comprises a library and print room with adjacent exhibition area, and includes *c*2,500 printed books; 400 watercolours; drawings and oil paintings; engravings, lithographs and photographs; 7,000 hand-coloured bird prints, a substantial number by John Gould. Illuminated manuscripts and autograph letters are held in the University Library's manuscript collection (qv). The bulk of the collection is concerned with art and architectural history, natural history and Ruskin studies. Unknown number of pre-1851 items include a small number of early books, among them Holbein's 'Dance of death' (Lyons 1538), *Die Gantze Bibel* (Zürich, Froschouer 1540) and Chaucer's *Workes* (1542). There are also some Kelmscott and Doves Press books, and a binding by T J Cobden-Sanderson on Ruskin's *Untothis last*.

Inventory of the Ruskin collection, being the property of the Guild of St George, Sheffield City Art Galleries (1954); also separate detailed catalogues of the original works of art, bird prints, and minerals, are with the collection; various card indexes in the library room, and copies of the Guild's early printed handbooks and catalogues.

William White. *The principles of art as illustrated by examples in the Ruskin Museum at Sheffield* (1895).

John Ruskin, *The works of John Ruskin*, v 30: The Guild and Museum of St George: reports, catalogues and other papers (1907).

A Finn. (Carruthers) 'Ruskin's Museum of the Guild of St George' (*Southern Arts* May 1973, p11).

Sheffield City Libraries, Surrey Street, Sheffield S1 1XZ. Tel (0742) 734711/3. Open Mon-Fri 9 am-9 pm (Reference); Sat 9 am-4.30 pm (Reference).

Central Library

Miscellaneous small collections—Arts and Humanities Division Founded in 1856, the rare books include 75 titles (100 v); private press collection, 720 v representing 280 presses; *Whitworth* bequest of prospectuses on, and books about, organs; *Bayreuth Collection* on Wagner (of T Walter Hall); *Quaker* pamphlets; *Evans Collection of pamphlets on socialism; Sheffield Philatelic Society Library* on loan deposit; special collection on silver and glass. On deposit are the *Bradfield, Norton, Tankersley* and *Worsborough* libraries (See separate entries).

Author and classified with subject index.

E C Gilberthorpe, 'Sheffield City Libraries private press books'. *Book Auction Records Quarterly*, 1977, 74 (2) 5.

Bradfield Parish Library: The Turie Library The library constituted the remainder of a collection of books bequeathed by the Rev Robert Turie (Vicar of Eccleshall) to Bradfield Chapelry in 1970. Originally 225 v, a catalogue printed by J Eastwood in 1859 contains 149 titles only. The present collection totals 39 v (1600–1764 imprints) of classics and theological works. These include 5 STC and 22 Wing items.

Checklist compiled by Richard Turner, Nov 1977.

Cat compiled by S Boorman and J Ewbank, 1980.

John C Wilson, *Bradfield Churchwarden and Feoffee* The Parish Church of St Nicholas, Bradfield. . . Sheffield: Gaion and King (*c*1970).

Norton Parish Library Most of the books in the library were bequeathed by Cavendish Nevile, Rector 1710–49 (*d*1749) and bear his bookplate. There are 447 items in all: *c*38 being Bibles and Commentaries, the remainder mainly classics and theology (1512–1831 French, German, Swiss and Dutch imprints). There are 12 STC and 175 Wing items.

Items other than Bibles and Commentaries arranged in chronological order of imprint.

Cat by Roger C Norris: a study submitted in partial fulfilment of the requirements for the postgraduate diploma in librarianship at the University of Sheffield, 1965.

Central Council for the Care of Churches.

The parochial libraries of the Church of England, London, Faith Press, 1959, p93.

Tankersley Parish Library Books bequeathed by Robert Booth (1615) to John Nevinson, Rector (*d*1634); 32 items recovered in 1947 from the cockloft of Worsborough vicarage. There are 41 items covering classics, early medicine and theology; 34 are 16th cent French, Italian, Swiss and German imprints, the remainder are English; 1 Wing; others are 18th cent.

1963, bound with Worsborough Grammar School collection cat (qv).

Central Council for the Care of Churches.

The parochial libraries of the Church of England, London, Faith Press, 1959, p101.

Worsborough Grammar School Library Originally it comprised *c*580 v, many of them bequests made in the 17th and 18th cent. They were in the keeping of the Vicar of Worsborough until 1959, then deposited in Sheffield Central Library. The collection now totals 556 items, covering classical texts and grammars, theology, a few early medical works; 32 are undated or incomplete items, without means of dating. 44 books dated 1500–50 bear French, Swiss, German and Italian imprints; there are 40 STC and 90 Wing items.

Temporary cat (compiled from National Register of Archives, 1966, and including Tankersley Parish Library (qv), deposited in Sheffield Central Library.

Bibliographic cat of the 105 v numbered W33-W138, compiled in 1975 by Susan Costin, in partial fulfilment of the requirements for MA (Lib), University of Sheffield.

Local Studies Library (Tel 734753/734756)

Carpenter Collection The Library of Edward Carpenter, socialist and poet (1844–1929), presented by his executors in 1934. *c*800 v, including bound v of pamphlets. Editions of author's works, including translations; works on allied subjects, including socialism, oriental religion and philosophy, penal reform, sexual ethics, mostly Victorian or Edwardian. Anarchist and socialist periodicals and ephemera, some foreign. Correspondence (in Archives Division). Newspaper cuttings, photographs and personalia.

Sheffield City Libraries. *A bibliography of Edward Carpenter* (printed), 1949.

——*A catalogue of the portion of Edward Carpenter's library not in the. . . Sheffield City Libraries* (unpublished typescript), 1963.

All cat in the main cat of the Arts and Humanities Library.

Sheffield Collection Built up since 1856 as a result of purchase, gift and bequest. Local material, including mss was separated from general reference material in 1934. Ms material is now the responsibility of the Archives Division. Printed material, current and retrospective, is still acquired. It would be very difficult to estimate the proportion of 'rare' items. Material relating to Sheffield and the immediate surrounding area includes items printed in Sheffield before 1840, and written by authors born in Sheffield or resident there at the time of writing. Printed ephemera, broadsides, theatre bills, trade cats, mostly silver-plated ware and edge tools.

Dictionary cat on card. Author and subject in one sequence.

Jackson Collection Collected by three generations of the Jackson family of Sheffield, and presented by the executors of Arthur Jackson (1844–95) in 1914. It is made up of *c*300 books and bound v of pamphlets, and many v of mss pedigrees, charters, deeds, ephemera etc, most of it probably 'rare', and includes 18th and early 19th cent books and pamphlets of local interest, including sermons, tracts on town improvements and topical items. Deeds and Charters, mainly local 14th-18th cent; pedigrees and notebooks compiled by William Swift (1818–74), the Sheffield genealogist. Papers and notebooks of Joseph Hunter (1783–1861), the historian of South Yorkshire; 18th and early 19th cent ephemera, mainly locally; 18th and early 19th cent local newspapers.

T W Hall and A H Thomas, *Descriptive catalogue of the. . . Jackson Collection*, 1914. Excludes most printed items, which are entered in the general Sheffield Collection cat.

Sheffield City Polytechnic, Faculty of Art and Design, Psalter Lane, Sheffield S11 8UZ. Tel (0742) 56101 Ext 30. Open Mon-Fri (Term) 9 am-8.30 pm (Friday 5 pm); (Vacation) 9 am-5 pm. Admission by written application to the Librarian. Xerox copying facilities.

Faculty of Art and Design Library Special Collection The School of Design was opened in 1843 and the library was established in 1847. Books were acquired by purchase and gift, and were intended to support the courses provided in the mid-19th cent. The collection, which is still being added to, consists of *c*850 items of which 100 are pre-1851, and includes 18th and early 19th cent works on perspective and ancient architecture, and portfolios of the work of important artists and designers of the time.

Author and classified subject cats available.

S Pickering, *Sheffield City Polytechnic Faculty of Art and Design Library. The Special Collection: a selective catalogue.*

University of Sheffield, Western Bank, Sheffield S10 2TN. Tel (0742) 78555 Ext 333. Open (Term) Mon-Fri 9 am-9.30 pm; Sat 9 am-1 pm; (Vacation) Mon-Fri 9 am-5 pm (Easter vac 9.30 am); Sat 9 am-12.30 pm. Admission free to members of the University; others by arrangement with the Librarian. Microfilm readers, Xerox copying, photographic service.

Sheffield University Library Rare Book Collection The Medical School was founded in 1828; Firth College was founded in 1879, and in 1905 the University Charter was granted. The collection contains 2,161 items (estimated *c*10,000 other pre-1851 items are dispersed throughout the general collection) on a wide subject range. Particular strength lies in 18th cent medical works and in 17th cent tracts and other material bequeathed by Charles Harding Firth. There is a small collection of private press books; a collection of ballads, and Restoration drama is well represented. The collection includes 13 incunabula and 449 STC items.

Alphabetical author and subject cats.

Wakefield

HM Prison Service Staff College Library, Love Lane, Wakefield WF2 9AQ. Tel (0924) 71291 Ext 47. All enquiries should be sent in writing to the Librarian; the library is not normally open to the public.

The library includes a historical reference collection of *c*200 older volumes on penology and prisons, both official publications and treatises, and some related ephemera, mostly since 1800. A duplicated handlist is available.

Queen Elizabeth Grammar School Library, Northgate, Wakefield WF1 3QX. Access to the Foundation Library may be granted upon prior application to the Headmaster in writing, stating the nature of the applicant's research.

The school library was founded early in the 17th cent and was greatly extended in the early 18th cent by the Rev Thomas Clarke, Headmaster; it appears originally to have been open to the inhabitants of Wakefield. Many of the books are the gift of former pupils. It contains *c*100 v of the 17th and 18th cent, including Isaac Newton's *Geographia Generalis* (1672); Horace, *Carmina* (1670), given to the school by Richard Bentley, former pupil, with his inscription and probably a copy he used in school; Bentley's edition of Horace (1711) and various other items of Bentleiana. There are 7 STC/Wing items.

M H Peacock, *History of the free grammar school of Queen Elizabeth at Wakefield.* Wakefield, 1892, p166-72.

York

University of York, J B Morrell Library, Heslington, York YO1 5DD. Tel (0904) 59861. Telex 57933 YORKUL. Open (Term) Mon-Fri 9 am-10 pm, (Vacation) 9 am-9 pm (July-August 5.15 pm). Photocopier, microform camera, microfilm reader.

The University, founded in 1961, appointed its librarian in 1962 and the library was opened to students in 1963. The library's stock totals *c*250,000 printed books, which include the following special collections:

A **Special Collections Room**

Dyson Collection A collection of *c*1,500 v, nearly all first editions, and finely bound, of 17th, 18th and early 19th cent literature which originally formed part of the library of H V Dyson, Emeritus Fellow of Merton College, Oxford, from whom it was purchased in 1963. Mainly poetry, a little drama and critical prose (but no fiction), the principal authors represented are Dryden, Pope and the Romantic poets. Its treasures include the first subscription edition of James Thomson's *The Seasons*, 1730, with illustrations by the architect William Kent; the third edition of Samuel Richardson's *Letters written to and for particular friends*, 1746; and the first edition of John Keat's *Endymion*, 1818. The collection is slowly expanding.

No separate cat of the Dyson Collection, and books in it may be found from the main author and classified cats.

Eliot Collection A slowly-growing collection of first editions of 20th cent English literature. Its nucleus was a small number of books by and about T S Eliot, donated in 1972 by the library of King's College, Cambridge. They came from a bequest to King's College by Eliot's friend John Hayward, and consisted of those books in the Hayward Collection which King's College already owned. The collection has since been expanded, both by the acquisition of new books by gift and purchase, and by transferring to it books previously on the open shelves. It now covers such authors as W B Yeats, Robert Graves, D H Lawrence and Aldous Huxley, and will continue to grow.

No separate cat of this collection; books may be found through the main author and classified cats.

Kennet Collection One of the most interesting and valuable collections lent to the library by Lord Kennet (Wayland Young), author and former Parliamentary Secretary to the Ministry of Housing and Local Government. These books, mainly collected by his father, the first Baron Kennet, include two medieval illuminated mss, several incunabula, among them the first collected edition of Homer printed in Florence in 1488; and the first editions of such works as Sir Isaac Newton's *Principia mathematica*, 1687; David Hume's *Treatise of human nature*, 1739; and James Boswell's *Life of Samuel Johnson*, 1791. These books can be consulted only under supervision.

A separate cat of the collection is kept in the Special Collections Room.

Kennet Spinoza Collection A small collection of books by and about the philosopher Benedict Spinoza loaned by Lord Kennet.

A separate cat of these books is kept with the cat of the Kennet Collection.

S C Section The rest of the Special Collections room is filled by what are known as S.C. books. These are miscellaneous books considered unsuitable, for a variety of reasons, to be placed on the open shelves, but not fitting appropriately into any of the special collections. They are indicated on catalogue cards by the letters S C in front of the classmark. They include books published pre-1700; books with special bindings or illustrations, the only books in the library with a fore-edge painting (an historical essay on the Magna Carta, by Richard Thompson, 1829); books specially connected with York and the University; and a complete set of the Trianon Press facsimiles of the works of William Blake. There are also a number of association copies—books belonging to, and inscribed by, famous people. Among them are books presented to Lord Attlee by Nehru, Beneš and the Webbs; a proof copy of the Beveridge Report, annotated by its author; and several books autographed by Henry Moor, and given to him to the library.

B **Halifax Room**

Halifax Collection A part of the library of Halifax Parish Church, deposited here on permanent loan in 1966. The library was founded by Robert Clay, Vicar of Halifax 1624–8, who presented some of his own books, and solicited gifts from other people. Over the next 200 years many other books were added, notably a large collection belonging to Simon Sterne, son of Richard Sterne, Archbishop of York 1664–83, which included some of his father's books. Not all of the earlier books survive, but the collection contains *c*260 works, all pre-1700, including some incunabula, and many inscribed by the original owners. Although most of them are theological, there are also some works of classical literature; a copy of the 1695 edition of William Camden's *Britannia;* and some scientific and medical books, including the first Latin edition of Galileo's *Systema cosmicum,* 1635; and the first edition, 1624, of *Arithmetica logarithmica,* by Henry Briggs, first Savilian Professor of Geometry at Oxford, who presented it to the Halifax library in 1627, bound at the end of a volume of J A de Thou's *Historia sui temporis.*

A separate cat of the collection is kept in the room.

Milnes-Walker Collection Consists of early medical books from the Old Medical Library at Wakefield. They were donated in 1968 by Robert Milnes-Walker, Professor Emeritus of Surgery in the University of Bristol.

A separate cat of the collection is kept in the room.

Slaithwaite Collection The parish library of the church of Slaithwaite, near Huddersfield. This is a somewhat smaller and later collection, having been founded by the Rev Robert Meeke, Vicar from 1685 until his death in 1724, who, in his will, provided that part of this own library should be kept for the use of his successors. It was placed in the library on permanent loan in 1967. It consists mainly of 17th and 18th cent theology, with a few rather surprising exceptions, such as 17th cent edition of the *Gesta Romanorum,* and a (mutilated) copy of J H Van Linschoten's *Navigatio ac itinerarium...in orientalem,* 1599. There are also some mss of local interest.

A separate cat of the collection is kept in the room.

C **Mirfield Room**

The books in this collection are mainly pre-1800, and formed part of the library of the Community of the Resurrection, West Yorkshire. This Anglican religious community for men was founded in Oxford in 1892, and moved to Mirfield in 1898. The library was built up mainly by gifts of books from members and friends, and contains much valuable early material. All the pre-1800 books, plus a few sets of the publications of historical record societies, such as the Royal Historical Society and the Surtees Society, were deposited here on permanent loan in 1973. The collection includes several incunabula, including an edition of St Augustine's *De civitate Dei,* printed by Nicolas Jenson in Venice, 1475. Although the books are predominantly theological, there are many other items—for example, the first collected edition of the works of Sir Philip Sidney, 1598; the second edition of Thomas Hobbes's *Leviathan,* 1651; the first edition of *A journey to the western islands of Scotland,* by Samuel Johnson, 1775. There are also a few mss and some interesting early music books.

The arrangement of books on the shelves differs from that in other collections, being chronological, by date of publication (the arrangement used in the original library at Mirfield). There are two sequences—large (quarto) books on the shelves round the walls, and other books in the free-standing bookcases in the centre of the room.

A ms cat, compiled at Mirfield, is kept with the collection, but as this is incomplete, and somewhat inaccurate, the books are gradually being recatalogued. Cards for those which have been recatalogued are filed in the author and classified cats, and there is also a card cat in the room.

D **Milner-White Collection**

The Very Rev Eric Milner-White, Dean of York from 1941 until his death in 1963, was a member of the University Promotion Committee, which was responsible for the original organization and planning of the University of York. One of his many interests was book-collecting, and he formed a fine collection of English detective fiction, which came to the J B Morrell Library after his death. It contains *c*800 v, mainly first editions of works published in the first half of this century. There are virtually complete sets of the works of such authors as H C Bailey, Nicholas Blake and Dorothy Sayers, with a few earlier books of interest such as Fergus Hume's *The mystery of a hansom cab, 1888*. The collection is housed in a private office, and books from it may not be borrowed, but they may be read in the library.

Cards in author cat.

Separate cat which may be consulted by applying to the Enquiry Desk.

E **Peggy Janiurek Collection**

A representative collection of children's literature, assembled originally in collaboration with the University's Department of Education, and named in memory of a former student. It is to be found beside the education section (K) on the top floor of the library. The books are arranged alphabetically by author. A few volumes are added to it every year.

No separate cat but cards for the books appear in the main author cat.

F **Wormald Collection**

The Wormald Collection is housed at King's Manor, in a room adjacent to the library of the Institute of Advanced Architectural Studies, and readers may obtain access to it by applying to the Institute's Librarian. It was formerly the library of the late Francis Wormald, President of the Society of Antiquaries of London, and Director of the Institute of Historical Research, and was given to the University of York by his widow in 1972. It consists mainly of books on medieval history and literature, and on the history of art.

Cards in the public cats of the J B Morrell Library, and in a separate cat at King's Manor.

York Minster Library, Dean's Park, York YO1 2JD. Tel (0904) 25308. Open Mon-Fri 9 am-5 pm. Admission unrestricted. Photocopying facilities; microfiche reader; ultraviolet light.

Established *c*750 AD, the library was destroyed in 866 AD, and throughout a great part of the Middle Ages there was no cathedral library, as Minster clergy had their own books, and several made bequests to the Universities of Oxford and Cambridge. The library was re-founded in 1414 by a bequest of 40 v from the Treasurer, John Newton, and housed in a building specially erected 1418–21 by the Minster. The library has had a continuous history since then, and with the gift in 1628 of Archbishop Tobie Mathew's collection of 3,000 v, it became at once one of the largest cathedral libraries in the land. Today it is the largest cathedral library in the country, with a collection of *c*80,000 v, of which *c*20,000 are early printed books, including 80 incunabula; 80 medieval mss; 400 post-medieval mss; and 200 music mss. Its special collections include (a) Liturgy printed books and medieval mss, particularly of the use of York, which came partly from the Rev Marmaduke Fothergill, DD (*d*1731) and Canon T B Simmons (*d*1884); (b) Yorkshire local history collection, mostly from the Edward Hailstone (*d*1890) collection, now totalling 15,000 printed books, plus *c*10,000 mss (archives, antiquarian notes etc). The more comprehensive collection of earlier material for Yorkshire local history in general incorporates York and Yorkshire printing and publishing, Civil War tracts (*c*2,000 items) many relating to York and Yorkshire; (c) The parish library collections include: Stainton in Cleveland (*c*300 v); Hackness (*c*112 v); East Harbery (*c*300 v); (d) A collection of 500 printed items, including most of the predominantly ecclesiastical, and the Minster repertoire from *c*1600 to the present day, and compositions by Minster organists; rare printed music by William Byrd and printed and mss music by Purcell. Also the Gostling mss of English church music composed in the Restoration period (8 v), and the Dunnington-Jefferson ms of church music, probably written in Durham, 1640.

Cat of mss music, by David Griffiths, published 1981.

Cat of printed music, by David Griffiths, published 1971.

C B L Barr, 'The Minster Library' in G E Aylmer and R Cant (eds) *A history of York Minster*, Oxford 1977, Chap XI, p487-539.

E Anne Read, *A checklist of books, catalogues and periodical articles relating to the Cathedral libraries of England*. Oxford Biblio Soc, Occasional Publications no 6, 1970, p51-3; Supplement, 'Cathedral libraries: a supplementary check list', *Library History*, vol 9, no 5 (Spring 1978), p156-7.

NORTHERN IRELAND

Co. Armagh

Armagh

Armagh County Museum, The Mall East, Armagh, Co Armagh. Tel (0861) 523070. Open Mon-Sat 10 am-1 pm, 2-5 pm. Admission on application to the Curator. Xerox copying and photographic service available.

Reference Library The Museum was opened in 1937 by Armagh County Council, the foundation collections being the old museum of the Armagh Natural History and Philosophical Society. The Society had been established in 1839, and also had a library and reading-room, but this was dispersed in 1955. The present Reference Library of the Museum was assembled from 1935 onwards by the first Curator, T G F Paterson. The Museum is now a branch of the Ulster Museum in Belfast.

Of a total of *c*4,000 v, *c*550 are pre-1851, which include 4 STC and 18 Wing items. The library contains printed books, manuscripts, typescripts relating to Co Armagh, including many books from the library of the Blacker family (occupants of Carrickblacker House, Portadown, Co Armagh since 1692); the Irish genealogical and historical collection of A G Sloan from Ballyworkan House, Co Armagh; the library of T G F Paterson which has particularly good collections of the works of the minor 19th cent local and 'weaver' poets of Ulster, and of George Russell ('AE'). Individual books of importance include all the author's own copies of political discourses of George Ensor (*d*1845) of Ardress, Co Armagh; George Bickham's *Universal Penman*, 1743; first edition of Handel's *Tamerlane* (1725).

Alphabetical author and title card cat.

D R M Weatherup, 'Armagh County Museum—the reference library', *Irish booklore*, 2 (1972), p44-53.

Armagh Observatory, College Hill, Armagh, Co Armagh BT61 9DG. Tel (0861) 522928. Open by prior arrangement with the Administrative Officer. Xerox copying facilities.

The Observatory was founded in 1790 by the Archbishop of Armagh, Richard Robinson, Baron Rokeby. Many of the earlier books in the library were collected by Thomas Romney Robinson, FRS, the astronomer-in-charge, from 1823 until his death in 1882. The library totals *c*5,000 almost entirely modern works, but there are *c*180 pre-1851 works, principally of the 18th cent and these include a small collection of particularly valuable astronomical books housed in the Director's office, including Aldus: *Astronomici veteres* (2 v, Venice, 1499); Kepler: *Tabulae Rudolphinae*, 1627; Hevelius: *Selenographia*, 1647; the first collected edition of Galileo, 1656; Lubienitz: *Theatrum cometicum*, 1668; Euler: *Theoria motuum planetarum et cometarum*, 1744.

Alphabetical author and classified (UDC) card cats.

Patrick Moore, *Armagh Observatory, 1790–1967*. Armagh, The Observatory, 1967, *passim*.

Public Library of Armagh, Abbey Street, Armagh, Co Armagh. Tel (0861) 523142. Open Mon-Fri 11 am-1 pm, 2-4 pm. Admission unrestricted. Photocopies can be made locally.

Founded in 1771 by the Archbishop of Armagh, Richard Robinson, Baron Rokeby, the foundation collection of *c*8,000 v being Robinson's own personal library (there is a ms cat). Other frequently occurring provenances are Edward Conway, 2nd Viscount Killultagh (*d*1655, 60 v); J E Jackson, Dean of Armagh (*d*1841, 300 v); H B Swanzy, Dean of Dromore (*d*1932, 460 v), principally genealogical and Irish newspapers; R G S King, Dean of Derry (*d*1958, early English Bibles and Greek Testaments).

There are *c*40,000 v, of which *c*12,000 are pre-1851, and include 4 incunabula; *c*350 STC; and *c*2,150 Wing items. Although this is technically *not* a cathedral or diocesan library, the theological section is extensive, especially in the area of Biblical criticism. However, the largest section is devoted to history, with an emphasis on Ireland and Britain (there are particularly good holdings of pamphlets dealing with the Union). There are many pre-1701 books of travel and geographical description. Notable titles in all areas include Gerson: *De praeceptis decalogi*, Strasburg, 1488; Seneca: *Tragoediae*, Venice, 1493; Richard Fitz Ralph: *Defensiones curatorum*, 1496; T Coryate: *Coryats crudites*, 1611; Samuel Purchas: *...Purchas his pilgrimes*, 1625–26; John Colgan: *Acta sanctorum...Hiberniae*, 1645; Jeremiah Rich's shorthand New Testament of 1659; some very fine volumes of Hogarth and Piranesi prints; and Swift's *Gulliver's* *travels*, 1726, with emendations in his own hand. The 18th cent is strongly represented throughout the library.

(a) Catalogus librorum impressorum. 1867. 2 v in 4 (1300 p in ms compiled by William Reeves).

(b) *List of books selected from the catalogue*, Belfast, Baird, 1892. 67 p (op).

(c) Catalogue of the books in the Keeper's Room. 1924 (-1930) 248 p (in ms compiled by J Dean).

(d) Catalogue of mezzotints mounted and unmounted in the collection given by Richard Robinson, 1924. 333 leaves (typescript, compiled by F M Hobson).

(e) Alphabetical author and subject card cats for acquisitions subsequent to (a) and (c) above.

W Reeves, *A memoir of the Public Library of Armagh*, Chiswick Press, 1886, 15 p (op) (also appeared in *Trans and Proc of the Library Assoc... 7th annual meeting... Dublin... 1884*, 1890, p31-44).

J Dean, 'Sketches of Primate Robinson, his library and Armagh history', *Armagh Guardian*, 30 May 1930.

Maura Tallon, *Church of Ireland diocesan libraries*, Dublin 1959, p5-6 (op).

G O Simms, 'The founder of Armagh's Public Library: some sidelights on Primate Robinson, Baron Rokeby of Armagh', *Long Room*, 5 (1972), p17-20.

D R M Weatherup, 'The Armagh Public Library, 1771—1971', *Irish Booklore*, 2 (1975), p268-99.

G McKelvie, 'Early English books in Armagh Public Library: a short-title catalogue of books printed before 1641', *Ibid* 3 (1977), p91-103.

——'An unrecorded book from Ben Johnson's library (in Armagh Public Library)', *Ibid*, p124-6.

Belfast

Belfast

Belfast Harbour Commissioners, Harbour Office, Corporation Square, Belfast BT1 3AL. Tel (0232) 234422. Not open to the public. Admission by prior arrangement with the Senior Administrative Officer. Xerox copying.

The Commissioners were established in 1847, but an earlier body for the improvement of the harbour had existed since 1785. The library was set up in 1854 and is very largely an accumulation of gifts from individual Commissioners. It contains *c*2,000 v, of which 484 are pre-1851, and include 4 Wing items.

The bulk of the pre-1851 material is made up of late 18th and early 19th cent pamphlets on trade, customs, tariffs, transport and economic conditions, with a natural emphasis on Ireland. Standard works on Irish history and politics are well represented, including a complete set of the Royal Dublin Society's statistical surveys of counties. The largest section, on harbours, contains many of the Commissioners' business papers in manuscript, but also in the form of rare ephemeral printed documents.

A comparison of the typescript cat of 1923 with the present alphabetical name and subject card cats of 1979 indicates that much of value has been removed from the library during the last 50 years or so.

Central Library (Belfast Education and Library Board), Royal Avenue, Belfast BT1. Tel (0232) 243233. Telex 747359. Open Mon, Thurs 9.30 am-8 pm, Tues, Wed, Fri 9.30 am-5.30 pm; Sat 9.30 am-1 pm. Consultation of special collections material by prior arrangement; use of Irish collection on application. Occasional inter-library loans to other institutions. All varieties of microform reader, including reader/printer; copying available as microfilm or xerox.

Belfast first adopted the Public Libraries Acts in 1882, and the Central Library was opened six years later, in 1888. The present special collections fall into two groups: the Irish Library, and a general 'fine books' collection. The Irish Library owes much of its size and quality to two substantial private collections, that of Francis Joseph Bigger (*d*1926), *c*3,000 v presented by his brother in 1927, and the bequest of John Smyth Crone (*d*1945). Many of the early printed books in the general collection were given by Canon John Grainger shortly before he died in 1891.

The Irish Library contains 57,000 v (plus pamphlets and ephemera) of which *c*8,000 are pre-1851, and with its many duplicate and multiple copies, is the largest in Northern Ireland, being particularly strong in 19th cent material. Among the more notable holdings are over 800 pre-1851 Belfast printed books; over 400 printed maps of Ireland (both general and local) up to the early 19th cent; complete author collections for Forrest Reid (including substantial manuscripts) and Amanda McKittrick Ros (including all her literary papers); and a representative selection of Marcus Ward bindings.

The Fine Book Collection of *c*4,000 v contains 10 incunabula, 313 English books printed before 1701 (with a good group of Popish plot pamphlets), and long runs of private press publications (especially Nonesuch and Golden Cockerel; The Cuala Press books are complete). However, over the last 20 years or so a special emphasis has been placed on building up a very large collection of the great colour-plate books of topography and natural history of the first half of the 19th cent: the holdings of John Gould and D G Elliot are now all but complete, and of Thomas and William Daniell and Rudolph Ackermann, extensive.

a Irish Library

Finding list of books added to the stock of the Irish and local history collection before 1956, Belfast, 1964. 2 v (Duplicated typescript). Author and subject sections; includes the Crone collection, but excludes pamphlets, serials and government publications.

Catalogue of books and bound mss of the Irish historical, archaeological and antiquarian library of the late Francis Joseph Bigger. Belfast, J Adams, 1930, p303. Author and subject dictionary arrangement.

Alphabetical author and subject card cats.

Irish antiquarian maps, (Belfast), Belfast City Libraries (*c*1965) (Typescript).

b General

Catalogue of the Reference Department. Compiled by G H Elliott, Belfast, Ward, 1896, p8, 480.

Finding list of books added to the stock of the reference libraries before 1956. Section 1: Main author and title entries. Belfast, 1964, p918, 932. (Duplicated typescript).

Alphabetical author, and subject card cats.

Guide to the Irish and Local Studies Department at the Central Library, Belfast (Belfast), Belfast Educ and Library Board, 1979, (3) 18 leaves (Duplicated typescript).

Hilary Frazer: Local history collections in Belfast (unpublished thesis, MA (Library and Information Studies), Univ London, 1976), p48-61. Chap 4: 'Belfast Education and Library Board, Central Library'.

Diocesan Library of Down and Dromore and Connor, Church of Ireland Diocesan Office, 12 Talbot Street, Belfast BT1. Tel (0232) 22268. Open by arrangement with the Librarian.

The library is presently administered as a theological studies library for the clergy and laity of the separate dioceses of Connor and Down and Dromore; others are admitted on application. Xerox copying available in Diocesan Office.

The library was established in 1854 and first housed in the old Clerical Rooms, Arthur Street, Belfast. Later transferred to the Diocesan Office, Clarence Place, Belfast, and now has accommodation in the crypt of St Anne's Cathedral adjoining the present Diocesan Offices in Talbot Street. The collection of Charles Parsons Reichel, Bishop of Meath (1894) was presented *c*1895. The library contains 2,500 titles in *c*3,500 v plus *c*750 pamphlets. *c*600 titles are pre-1851 and include 1 incunabulum; 8 STC; 40 Wing items; and 15 Continental pre-1701. Main subjects covered are theology, ecclesiastical history and law, general and Irish history and biography.

Catalogue of books in the diocesan collection: and of the books in the Bishop Reichel Memorial Library; with a descriptive catalogue (by J R Garstin) of the mss in Bishop Reeves' Collection, Belfast, Carswell, 1899. 110 p (op).

Alphabetical author card cat (as yet incomplete).

Maura Tallon, *Church of Ireland diocesan libraries.* Dublin, Lib Assoc of Ireland, 1959, p12-14 (op).

Linen Hall Library, 17 Donegall Square North, Belfast BT1. Tel (0232) 221707. Open Mon-Fri 9.30 am-6 pm; Sat 9.30 am-4 pm to members only, but bona fide students and researchers may have access to reference facilities on application. Microfilm reader/printer; xerox copying.

Founded 1788 as the Belfast Reading Society, and renamed the Belfast Society for Promoting Knowledge in 1792, this private subscription library takes its more customary, though unofficial, name from Belfast's old White Linen Hall where its rooms were situated from 1802 until 1896 before moving to its present premises. Its stock totals *c*150,000 v, of which *c*48,000 v are in the special collections or are pre-1851. The library's general strength lies in the areas of history, genealogy, biography and travel, but its principal special collections are (a) the Gibson Collection; (b) the pre-1701 early printed book collection; (c) the McCready Collection; and (d) the very important and extensive Irish Collections.

General catalogue (compiled by G Smith) (and Supplements), Belfast, 1896–1908.

Earlier cats and supplements were published in 1793, 1795, 1806, 1808–11, 1814–18, 1819–22, 1825–29, 1836–41, 1843, 1851–58, 1862–67, 1877–78, 1883–90.

Catalogue of books in the foreign literature section. London, Spottiswoode, 1914. 5, 66p. (This section was largely dispersed by sale to the members in 1982.)

Card cat, author and subject (dictionary).

J Anderson, *History of the Belfast Library and Society for Promoting Knowledge, commonly known as the Linen Hall Library*. Belfast, McCaw, Stevenson and Orr, 1888. 128p (op).

J M D Crossey, 'The Linen Hall Library', *An leabharlann*, 15, 1957, p61-7.

J Magee, *The Linen Hall Library and the cultural life of Georgian Belfast*, (Armagh), Library Assoc Northern Ireland Branch, 1982, 20p.

Gibson Collection Purchased for a nominal sum in 1901 from Andrew Gibson of Belfast, it contains 2,000 v which are representative of the 19th cent publishing boom in Burns, especially in the provinces, but also including the principal 18th cent editions, with the exception of Kilmarnock.

The Gibson collection of Burns and Burnsiana: an exhibition held in the Linen Hall Library. (Belfast, 1972), 24 leaves (duplicated typescript).

Early Printed Books A large number of the items in this section came from the collections of Lavens M Ewart (*d*1898) of Belfast and R R Belshaw (*d*1914) of Dublin.

There are *c*3,000 titles which include 469 STC (almost entirely sermons and religious controversy, with several titles being heraldry and classics); 2,320 Wing (including a very large number of sermons, but Commonwealth and Restoration pamphlets on Ireland are well represented).

McCready Collection Donated in 1982 by William McCready of Jordanstown, Co Antrim, the collection contains *c*750 v made up of limited editions autographed by English authors of the 1920s and 1930s (eg Edmund Blunden, G K Chesterton, Walter De La Mare, Forrest Reid, Siegfried Sassoon, Bernard Shaw, H G Wells); and private press books, especially Cuala, Golden Cockerel and Nonesuch.

Irish Collections *c*43,000 v (plus pamphlets and ephemera). Whilst the Irish collections as a whole are comprehensive on all topics (with notably good 18th cent holdings), individual subject strengths stem from particular provenances: history and genealogy from Lavens M Ewart, R R Belshaw, Robert S Lepper (*d*1953) and R W H Blackwood (*d*1961); education, social science and books in Irish from J J Campbell (*d*1981); West Ulster from A A Campbell (*d*1959); rural weaver and artisan poetry of Ulster in the late 18th and early 19th cent and more recent Ulster poetry, donated by David Kennedy in 1926.

There are three more substantial sub-sections: (i) the political periodicals and ephemera issued during the current Northern Ireland 'troubles' since 1968 and methodically collected by the Library (150 box files); (ii) the long and early runs (*c*1,700 v) of local newspapers, including the *Belfast news letter* since its commencement in 1737, and perhaps the longest available runs of the *Down Recorder* and the *Lisburn Standard*; and (iii) Ulster local printing (7,500 items) including the Belfast printed book collection commenced by the Library in 1871 and greatly augmented by the Lavens M Ewart collection bequeathed in 1898. (An interleaved copy of J Anderson's *Catalogue of early Belfast printed books, 1694–1830*, 3rd ed, 1890–1902 is kept marked up by the Library as a supplement of newly reported titles.)

Catalogue of...the Irish section. Belfast, MacBride, 1917, 6, 268p. (Compiled by F J P Burgoyne.)

Author and subject dictionary card supplement available.

Chronological ledger cat in manuscript of Ulster printed book collection.

'Northern Ireland political literature, 1968–1970: a catalogue of the collection in the Linen Hall Library', *Irish Booklore*, 1, 1917, p44-82. (A-I only, compiled by J W Gracey and Paula Howard; no more published.)

Northern Ireland political literature, 1968–1975; edited from the collection in the Linen Hall Library, Belfast. Dublin, Irish Microforms, 1973–76. 222 microfiches.

Hilary Frazer, Local history collections in Belfast (*unpublished thesis*, MA (Library and Information Studies), Univ London 1976), p34-47. Chap 3, 'The Linen Hall Library.

Presbyterian Historical Society of Ireland, Church House, Fisherwick Place, Belfast BT1 6DW. Tel (0232) 23936. Open Mon-Fri 10 am-12.30 pm, and by application. Open to non-members by application to the Librarian. Xerox copying available.

The Society was founded in 1907. Its library contains 2,200 v, of which, especially those dealing with Irish history, were presented by Robert McCahan of Ballycastle, Co Antrim (*d*1942). There are *c*550 pre-1851 items which include 24 STC; 82 Wing, principally relating to Calvinist, and Puritan controversy; a small collection of 16th and 17th cent Bibles, including the Edinburgh Bassandyne Bible of 1576–9. It contains strong holdings of congregational histories and of biographies of ministers.

Alphabetical author card cat.

Aiken McClelland, 'Treasures of the Society's room and museum', *Bull Presbyterian Hist Soc Ireland*, Dec 1970, p12-13.

Public Record Office of Northern Ireland, 66 Balmoral Avenue, Belfast BT9 6NY. Tel (0232) 661621. Open Mon-Fri 9.30 am-4.45 pm. Admission on completion of application form. All varieties of microform reader, including reader/printer; copying available as photographic prints, microfilm or xerox.

The Record Office was set up in 1923, but much material relating to the geographical area of Northern Ireland from before that date is now to be found there. The content of the Record Office falls outside the scope of the Directory, apart from maps, broadsides, Acts, proclamations, prints, and other ephemeral printed items contained in manuscript groups.

Beck Irish reference collection A collection of *c*10,000 items such as town directories, professional and commercial lists, army and navy lists, local Acts, and newspapers, with an extensive, though less representative, collection of secondary material on Ireland as a whole. There are *c*30 pre-1831 printed maps of Ireland or parts of Ireland. Subject index entries for important printed pieces are made in the general card indexes to the manuscript collections.

Alphabetical author and title card cat.

General maps of Ireland and Ulster c1538–c1830. (How to use the Record Office, Leaflet 18, Belfast, nd, 15pp.) There are seven other similar leaflets for Belfast and the counties of Northern Ireland, but they contain little printed material.

Hilary Frazer: *op cit* Chap 2, p17-33, 'The Public Record Office of Northern Ireland'.

The Queen's University of Belfast, University Road, Belfast BT7 1NN. Tel (0232) 245133. Telex 74487. Open (Special Collections) Mon-Fri 9 am-

5.30 pm. Admission to members of the University; others, with letter of introduction, by prior application, or on presentation of acceptable identification. All varieties of microform reader, including reader/printer; copying available as photographic prints, slides or xerox. Loans of special collections material to other institutions would be considered.

Three separate Queen's Colleges, in Belfast, Cork and Galway, were founded in 1845, and opened in 1849. All three became constituent colleges of the Queen's University in Ireland which was established in 1850. On the creation of the Royal University of Ireland in 1880 the Queen's University in Ireland was dissolved, and its former colleges joined other existing university colleges in Ireland in a relationship external to the new university, which was in effect merely an examining body. In 1908 the Royal University was in its turn dissolved upon the establishment of a new federal National University of Ireland with its seat in Dublin; Queen's College, Belfast, was at the same time elevated to full independent university status.

The Special Collections contain *c*45,000 v which include 20 incunabula; 267 STC and 1,430 Wing items. They fall into three groups: (a) three period divisions—early printed books, 18th cent books and 19th cent and modern books; (b) three libraries—the Antrim Presbytery Library, the Thomas Percy Library, and books from the Library of Adam Smith; (c) four subject collections—the Hibernia collections, the MacDouall collection of early 19th cent philology, the early economics collection, and the medical collection.

Catalogue of books in the library of Queen's College, Belfast. Belfast, Mayne and Boyd, 1897, 975pp. (Compiled by J W Morgan.)

Earlier sectional and general cats, with supplements, were published in 1849, 1856–8, 1859–78, and 1887.

Alphabetical name and classified subject card cats.

As yet incomplete card indexes to special collections, for printers arranged by place; imprints arranged chronologically; and provenances.

H Heaney, 'Special collections in the University Library', *Queen's Univ Assoc Annual Record*, 1973, p71-8; illus.

Early printed books before 1701 A collection of 2,043 v (plus other early printing in, for example, the Antrim Presbytery Library, the Thomas Percy Library, the Medical Collection). This is an accumulation of gifts and purchases since the setting up of the Library in 1849. Two of the most frequent provenances are R G S King (*d*1958), Dean of Derry, who presented two groups of books, many of them of Irish interest, in 1946 and 1948; and R M Henry (*d*1950), Professor of Latin at Queen's until 1938, and then Professor of Humanity at St Andrews, whose classical library was purchased in 1951. The Library's period under the British Library's (formerly the Joint Standing Committee's) Background Materials Scheme is 1650–9; until 1961 it was 1625–34.

Eighteenth-century books The bulk of the Library's 18th cent material is still in the open stacks. However, a new special collection has just been instituted, and it is hoped in the course of 1984 to retrieve the scattered holdings, when new extended accommodation has become available for Special Collections. The extent of such a collection is, as yet, unknown, but the 18th cent is already well represented in some of the other special collections, such as the Antrim Presbytery Library, the Thomas Percy Library, and the Foster pamphlets in the Hibernica Collections. One particular strength will be the Allan Ramsay titles collected by Andrew Gibson of Belfast.

Nineteenth-century and modern books A miscellaneous collection of valuable, limited, fine, or rare items, including a representative selection from all the major private presses (with extensive holdings of the Cuala Press). Much of the Victorian fiction (G P R James, Mayne Reid and Fenimore Cooper) came from the library of John Nesbitt (*d*1946) of Belfast; and the poetry from W B Morton (*d*1949), Professor of Physics at Queen's.

Antrim Presbytery Library Started as 'The Belfast Library' *c*1765 by the Rev James Mackay, minister of First Rosemary Street, the collection was subsequently (from 1783) accommodated in the vestries of the adjoining First and Second Belfast churches. About 1790 it was moved to Belfast Academy, of which Dr William Bruce, minister of the First Belfast, was also Principal. Following a brief stay for a few months in the Linen Hall in 1823, the library was transferred to the house in Donegall Place of Rev William Bruce, the elder Bruce's son, assistant minister at First Belfast, and Professor of Classics and Hebrew at the Belfast Academical Institution. Six years later, the books were reteurned once more to the vestry of Second Belfast. The Presbytery of Antrim and the Northern Presbytery of Antrim deposited what had come to be known as 'The Antrim Library' at Queen's College in 1873. The library holds 1,948 v (*c*2,030 items), almost all pre-1800. In addition to theology, the Classics, civil and ecclesiastical history and politics are well represented. It was the first corporate collection in Belfast, and seems to have been intended more for the town's intellectuals in general than for its ministers.

Catalogue of books in the Antrim Library, now deposited in Queen's College, Belfast. Belfast, Mayne, 1874, 66p. (Earlier cats were published in 1796 and 1851.)

Typescript ledger shelflist.

R Allen, *The Presbyterian College 1853–1953*, Belfast, Maullan, 1954, p276-8.

Thomas Percy Library Most of the surviving personal collection of Thomas Percy (1729–1811), Bishop of Dromore, and editor of *The reliques of ancient English poetry*. During his lifetime Percy had sold his Spanish books of chivalry to Louis Dutens, and in 1780 many of his early romances were destroyed in a fire at Northumberland House in London. After his death, his library at Dromore was purchased in 1812 by the Earl of Caledon, with the exception of some volumes retained by his daughters, 120 of which were presented to the Bodleian in 1932 by Miss Constance Meade, Percy's great granddaughter. Dr A S W Rosenbach, the New York book dealer, bought a small number of early English literature high spots from the Percy books at Caledon House, Co Tyrone, in 1928. The remainder of the Caledon Percy collection was purchased by Queen's University at Sotheby's in 1969. The library contains 741 v and 1,225 pamphlets. Its particular emphases are English literature (especially 16th and 17th cent verse, Shakespearean controversies, ballad poetry); Gaelic and northern poetry and antiquities; popular metrical and prose romances of Europe. As a member of 'The Club', Percy owned association or presentation copies from Samuel Johnson, Oliver Goldsmith, Edmond Malone, George Steevens, etc. He annotated his books extensively, one of the most interesting of which is a copy of the third edition (1775) of his own *Reliques* enlarged and amended in preparation for a new edition. A unique item in the library is the earliest known English *Gesta Romanorum*, printed by Wynkyn de Worde in ?1502 (STC 21286.2).

Books removed from (and books added to the library at) Dromore House, since the Catalogue was made in 1802. 4p (Manuscript list; paper watermarked 1810.)

Books at Dromore House, 37p (Manuscript cat; paper watermarked 1808) but probably compiled 1812.

Pamphlets, [at Dromore House], 33p. Ms cat...1812?

The library of Thomas Percy...now sold...by Sotheby and Co...23rd June, 1969, (London), Sotheby, 1969. 54p; illus (Covers only about one-third of the collection).

R Leslie, 'The Percy Library', *The Book-collector's quarterly*, 14 (1934), p11-24.

Adam Smith Library A section of 223 v (mostly classics) of the surviving personal collection of Adam Smith (1723–90), the philosopher and economic theorist and another member of 'The Club'. The remainder of his library is now divided between New College Edinburgh and the Imperial University of Tokyo. The provenance of the Queen's portion is via Smith's cousin, David Douglas, Lord Reston (*d*1819); Douglas's daughter, Mrs W B Cunningham, and Mrs Cunningham's son, R O Cunningham, Professor of Natural History and Geology at Queen's College, who presented the books in 1887.

A cat of books belonging to Adam Smith Esq 1781. (Ms now in possession of Imperial University of Tokyo, and published in T Yanaihara: *A full and detailed catalogue of books which belonged to Adam Smith now in the possession of the...University of Tokyo*. New York, Kelley, 1966, p71-126.)

J Bonar, *A catalogue of the library of Adam Smith...2nd ed*. London, Macmillan, 1932. xxiv, 218p; illus.

H Mizuta, *Adam Smith's library: a supplement to Bonar's catalogue with a checklist of the whole library*. Cambridge Univ Press, 1967, xix, 153p.

(Queen's portion). Manuscript alphabetical author cat, 1887.

Typescript ledger shelflist, *c*1910.

Hibernica Collections Although the University Library had since its inception in 1849 naturally accumulated much relating to Ireland, it was only in 1929, following a specific donation of 1,000 v by R M Henry (*d*1950), then Professor of Latin at Queen's, that a special collection was set up. This was subsequently added to by Professor Henry in 1939, when he had left Queen's to become Professor of Humanity at St Andrews, and by transfers from his residual library, which was purchased by the University after his death. The collection was at first known as the Henry Collection, but with the addition of the many other collections detailed below, the name has been changed to the present form. It now totals 22,000 v (plus pamphlets).

The principal emphasis of R M Henry's original donation was Irish history and politics, but further areas and strengths have since been based on acquisitions of material on Irish (and English) politics and economics, mainly the period 1749–1814. For example, the pamphlet collection made by John Foster, Baron Oriel (*d*1828), last Speaker of the Irish House of Commons (2,200 items, 1686–1814, in 287 v purchased in 1942 from his descendant, Viscount Massareene, of Antrim); local history (especially Co Tyrone), and Anglo-Irish literature—the library of J J Marshall (*d c*1950), purchased in the 1950s; literature in Irish, and Celtic philology—the library of Professor T F O'Rahilly (*d*1953) of Dublin, purchased in the 1950s; foreign books relating to Ireland, and books by Irishmen printed abroad, pre-1701—117 v from a large general collection on Ireland purchased in 1960 from Dr Samuel Simms (*d*1967) of Belfast.

Catalogue of the Antrim Castle Library. Belfast, Ward, 1863, 2, 42p. (Contains the Foster pamphlets.)

Foster pamphlets. Typescript chronological list, with author index. 19, 146 leaves.

Hilary Frazer, Local history collections in Belfast (*unpublished thesis*, MA (Library and Information Studies), Univ London, 1976), p78-88 (Chap 7, 'The Queen's University of Belfast').

S Simms, 'List of Irish books printed abroad, lent by Dr Samuel Simms', *Belfast Municipal Museum and Art Gallery. Quarterly Notes*, 52, 1934, p1-7. (Cat of an exhibition of 51 items, 1494–1931, at the Belfast Municipal Museum).

MacDouall Collection In 1879 friends and former pupils of Charles MacDouall (*d*1883), first Professor of Latin and second Professor of Greek at Queen's College, presented a selection purchased from his personal library. It contains 1,089 v, covering Classical, Eastern and Middle Eastern languages, and comparative philology, principally of the first half of the 19th cent.

Early Economics Collection A collection of 227 v assembled since 1966 by transfers from the open stacks and by purchase of the Classics of economic theory from the 1680s to the 1880s, though mainly of the late 18th and early 19th cent.

Medical Collection (housed at the Queen's University Medical Library, Institute of Clinical Science, Royal

Victoria Hospital, Grosvenor Road, Belfast BT12 6BJ). The origin of the main part of the University's historical medical collections lies in two principal sources. The Belfast Medical Society, founded in 1806 had established a lending library for its members in 1826. In 1862 the Society merged with the Belfast Clinical and Pathological Society to form the Ulster Medical Society. The Ulster Medical Society's 16th, 17th and 18th cent books were presented to Queen's University in 1915 and 1916. The second major collection to be acquired was the distinguished library (3,600 v) of early medical works and medical history belonging to Dr Samuel Simms (*d*1967) of Belfast. This was purchased in two instalments, in 1962 and 1968. The collection contains 8,500 v pre-1851.

Catalogue of the Belfast Medical Library... Belfast, Advertiser Office, 1859. 8, 8, p11-92.

Manuscript cat and index of works presented by the Ulster Medical Society, 1915.

Queen's University Medical Library. (Interim) short-title list of...Samuel Simms Collection. 1965–72. 2 v (Duplicated typescript).

Stranmillis College, Stranmillis Road, Belfast BT9 5DY. Tel (0232) 665271 Ext 309. Open (Term) Mon-Fri 9 am-10 pm; Sat 9.30 am-12.30 pm; (Vacation) Mon-Fri 9 am-5 pm. Members of the public may make consultation for research and study at the discretion of the Librarian. All varieties of microform reader, including reader/printer; copying available as photographic prints, slides or xerox.

This teachers' training college was founded in 1922, but the present library was established only in 1951. Separately shelved among the extensive collections of modern books on education are 223 pre-1931 Irish school and college textbooks and readers, of which 134 fall within the period 1769–1899.

Alphabetical author and classified card cats with subject index.

Ulster Museum, Botanic Gardens, Stranmillis Road, Belfast BT9 5AB. Tel (0232) 668251. Open Mon-Thurs 10 am-12.30 pm, 2-5.15 pm. Admission by prior application. Copying available as photographic prints, slides or xerox; microfiche reader.

Belfast's first museum was built by Belfast Natural History and Philosophical Society (founded 1821) in 1831. The Society's collections of museum objects and specimens were transferred into the keeping of the City of Belfast Museum and Art Gallery (founded 1888) in 1910; following the opening of the Belfast Museum and Art Gallery's new building at Stranmillis in 1929, the Society's Library was divided between the Museum (monographs) and Queen's University, Belfast (periodicals). In 1962 the Museum ceased to be the responsibility of Belfast Corporation, and became the Ulster Museum. Since about 1980, the Museum's library is no longer centralized, but has been subdivided between the various curatorial departments.

There are *c*20,000 v, principally museology, botany, zoology, geology, archaeology, art, Irish local history and numismatics. *c*3,000 v pre-1851, *c*3 16th cent, 20 17th cent (of which 3 are STC and 6 Wing); 175 18th cent titles; there are 180 maps of Ireland, its districts and towns for the period 1572–1850. There is a good collection of early Belfast printing (*c*230 v up to 1850). The Calwell collection of Dublin and Belfast pamphlets is particularly strong for the 1790s. One of the most outstanding resources of the Local History Department of the Museum is the large collection of photographs of Ireland taken *c*1880–1935 by R J Welch, a Belfast photographer.

Alphabetical author/title and classified card cats. There is no subject index to the classified cat.

Catalogue of books in the library of the Natural History and Philosophical Society. Belfast, Mayne and Boyd, 1892, p39. (Earlier cats were published in 1847 and 1874.)

A list of the photographs in the R J Welch Collection in the Ulster Museum. v 1: *Topography and History* (Belfast), Ulster Museum, 1979, p110.

Hilary Frazer: Local History Collections in Belfast (unpublished thesis, MA (Library and Information Studies), Univ London 1976), p62-9. Chap 5: 'The Ulster Museum'.

Union Theological College (Gamble Library), Botanic Avenue, Belfast BT7. Tel (0232) 25374. Open Mon-Fri 10 am-12.45 pm, 2-4 pm. Admission by prior application.

The college was founded in 1853 by the General Assembly of the Presbyterian Church in Ireland, and was known variously as Assembly's College or the Presbyterian College until 1971 when the present name marked amalgamation with Magee Theological College which transferred from Londonderry. The library of the Presbyterian Assembly actually predated the college, and was formed from 1845 onwards. Other foundation collections were the class libraries for divinity students formed in the early 19th cent at the Belfast Academical Institution. Over 600 v containing much of the better early material in the library's current holdings of Irish civil and ecclesiastical history were purchased from the estate of Rev James Seaton Reid (*d*1851). In 1886 *c*6,000 v from the library of W Fleming Stevenson were presented by his widow and relatives. The bulk of the Magee College pamphlet collection was removed from Londonderry to Belfast in 1977.

There are *c*50,000 v with a predominantly theological subject content, being particularly strong in the history of Puritanism and Presbyterianism; 117 STC; 500 Wing items, again almost exclusively Protestant theology, but with a little Irish history; the 211 pre-1701 foreign books include *c*20 16th cent printings of Erasmus, Luther, Melanchthon, Calvin, Beza, and Cocklaeus. There is a small collection of 17th and 18th cent books by, and on, the Jesuits (mostly in French). Amongst the many versions and editions of the Bible, those of special interest are the Bassandyne Bible (Edinburgh 1576–9) and the Hutter Hebrew Bible (Hamburg, 1587–8).

Catalogue of books in the Fleming Stevenson Memorial Library, Belfast, 1887. 240p. The Appendix analyses over 200 v of principally 19th cent pamphlets.

Catalogue of... theology and general literature. Belfast, 1912. 100p. (Compiled by J W Kernohan. An earlier general cat was published in 1866.) Excludes pamphlets and the Jesuit collection.

Magee University College, Londonderry: *Catalogue of pamphlet collection in the Library* (Londonderry), Jan 1971, (i), 178, 99p. (Duplicated typescript.) A small number of unbound pamphlets with pressmarks prefaced MP in this cat are still at Magee University College.

Alphabetical author and subject card cats.

R Allen, 'The College Library' in his *The Presbyterian College, Belfast, 1853–1953*. Belfast, Mullan, 1954, p275-96.

Wesley Historical Society (Irish Branch), Aldersgate House, University Road, Belfast BT7. Tel (0232) 648762. Open to non-members by application to the Archivist.

The Irish branch of the Society was founded in 1926, and the library was in the keeping of the Dublin Repository Committee until its removal in 1934 to Edgehill College in Belfast; the transfer to Aldersgate House took place in 1961. The David B Bradshaw collection was added in the late 1940s.

The library contains *c*4,000 v, and is strong in the works of John and Charles Wesley and Adam Clarke (400 of the Society's books are recorded in Frank Baker: *A union catalogue of the publications of John and Charles Wesley*, Durham, NC, Duke University Divinity School, 1966; a marked copy of Richard Green: *The works of John and Charles Wesley: a bibliography*, 1896 is kept up in the library). There are extensive runs of 18th and early 19th cent Methodist journals and *c*50 STC and Wing items.

Alphabetical name, geographical, and keyword card cats (but acquisitions after 1940 have not been entered).

Shelflist in ms of archival material (both ms and printed).

Marion Kelly, 'Wesleyana in Ireland 1967: a review of the record and work of the Irish Branch of the Wesley Historical Society', *Irish Christian Advocate*, 46 (21), 1967.

Co. Down

Cultra

Ulster Folk and Transport Museum, Cultra Manor, 153 Bangor Road, Holywood, Co Down BT18 0EU. Tel (023 17) 5411. Open Mon-Fri 9 am-5 pm. Admission by prior application. Microfilm reader; copying available as photographic prints, slides and xerox.

Established in 1958, the Ulster Folk Museum acquired its present title in 1973, when the collections of the Belfast Transport Museum (opened in 1955) were transferred to it by Belfast Corporation. The library of the Folk Museum has been methodically developed only since 1964, and contains *c*10,000 v.

Besides a good collection of local histories of Irish towns and parishes, particular strengths include 19th cent books on agriculture and horticulture, with long runs of early Irish farming journals; the collection of 19th and 20th cent novels put together by Professor K H Connell (*d*1974) as a source for Irish social history; *c*500 readers and textbooks as used in Irish schools from the 18th to the early 20th cent; 18th and 19th cent tour and travel books covering the whole of Ireland; local ballad and song sheets and chapbooks. The Museum maintains its own photographic archive of past and present local manners, customs, implements, scenes and vernacular architecture (now containing upwards of 18,000 prints) and has, in addition, the W A Green collection (3,908 photographs) of similar material of the earlier part of the 20th cent.

Alphabetical author and subject card cats.

Index to pre-1900 illustrations of Irish ethnographical interest.

Hilary Frazer, *op cit*, p70-7, Chapter 6: 'The Ulster Folk and Transport Museum'.

Strangford

Castle Ward (National Trust), Strangford, Downpatrick, Co Down, BT30 7LS. Tel (039686) 204. Application for access to the Libraries Adviser, National Trust, 42 Queen Anne's Gate, London SW1. Photocopying facilities available by arrangement with The Historic Buildings Representative, National Trust Regional Office, Rowallane, Saintfield, Ballynahinch, Co Down BT24 7LH. Tel (0238) 510721.

The library contains the books of the Ward family (from 1781 Viscounts Bangor) who first settled in the area in

1570. The present house (the third on the estate) dates from the early 1760s, and passed into the keeping of the National Trust following the death of the 6th Viscount in 1950. 188 different provenances have been noted, the most frequently occurring, other than Ward, being the families connected to the Wards by marriage, especially the Echlins of Echlinville, Kircubbin, Co Down (connected in the 1660s) and the Hamiltons of Killyleagh Castle and Bangor, Co Down (variously Viscounts Claneboye, Earls Clanbrassill and without title; connected in 1709). 109 titles have Hamilton ownership inscriptions, the earliest inscription dated 1614 and the latest 1707. There are 943 titles in 1,387 v in the main library room which include 367 pre-1701 English and foreign titles with 19 STC and 255 Wing items. The morning-room collection is principally of the second half of the 19th cent and the 20th cent. The subject coverage is typical of an 18th cent gentleman's library ranging from history (the most numerous), theology, politics, literature, geography and travel to science, agriculture and medicine. French history and literature are unusually well represented (there is a set of the Boucher illustrated Molière, 1733–4), and the many law books and collections of statutes are accounted for by the fact that Michael Ward (*d*1759) was a judge of the King's Bench in Ireland. Of particular interest are over 200 sermons for the period 1690–1710; the sets of Votes of the Irish House of Commons, 1695–9, 1723–8, and of the English House, 1689–95; and some fine early 19th cent costume plate books.

'Catalogue of Books in Castleward Library taken July 1813 by Geo Moore' in manuscript. Alphabetical by title or author.

Fully cat (including printers, provenances and chronological listing) 1974/5. Worksheets of cat available for consultation in library of Queen's University, Belfast, pending typing of cards.

The pre-1701 titles have been noted for the National Trust's union cat.

Co.Fermanagh

Florence Court see under Co.Londonderry: Moneymore.

Co.Londonderry

Coleraine

New University of Ulster, Coleraine, Co Londonderry BT52 1SA. Tel (0265) 4141. Open (Term) Mon-Fri 9 am-10 pm; Sat 9 am-1 pm; (Vacation) Mon-Fri 9.30 am-5.30 pm to members of the University; others, with letter of introduction, or by prior application. Microfilm, microcard and microfiche readers; copying available as photographic prints, slides or xerox. Loans of special collections material to other institutions would be considered.

The University was established in 1968, incorporating as a constituent college, Magee University College (founded 1865) at Londonderry. The library's principal special collections are (a) the Henry Davis collection; (b) a general pre-1801 Restricted Access collection; and (c) the pre-1801 collections at Magee University College (qv under Londonderry).

Henry Davis Collection Bequeathed in 1977 by Henry Davis, CBE, DLitt, who had acquired many of his books at the Yates Thompson, Dyson Perrins, Silvain Braunschweig and W B Dukes sales. (Davis's magnificent collection of bindings was bequeathed to the British Library.) It contains 189 items, which include 61 incunabula (half of which are in contemporary or near contemporary bindings); 17 STC and 18 Wing items. The incunabula are strong in early monuments of printing, including single leaves of the 42-line Bible and the 1460 *Catholicon*; the Fust and Schoeffer Bible of 1462; a leaf from a blockbook Donatus *Ars minor* (Ulm *c*1470); a single Caxton leaf from Chaucer's *Canterbury Tales* 1478; Ratdolt's 1482 *Euclid*; the 1486 Breydenbach, *Die heyligen reysen gen Jherusalem*; Aldus's *Hypnerotomachia Poliphili* 1499; there are also the *editiones principes* of Plato (1484–5) and Aristotle (1495–7) and of *Parzival* (1477). Notable 16th cent books include the Emperor Maximilian's *Theuerdanck* 1517, and Geoffrey Tory's *Champ fleury* 1529. There is a fourth folio Shakespeare, and among the more modern books are a Kelmscott Chaucer and a small group of five titles from the Gregynog Press.

The Henry Davis Gift: a catalogue of the principal books and manuscripts given to the New University of Ulster, Coleraine. Forthcoming. (Compiled by B Benedikz, with indexes of printers, provenances, binders and illustrators.)

H A Feisenberger: 'The Henry Davis Collection II: The

Ulster gift (contemporary collectors, 44)', *The Book Collector*, 21, 1972, p339-55; 12 plates.

Restricted Access Collection The collection contains pre-1801 imprints, either bought by, or donated to, the library since its opening in 1968. There are also a number of signed presentation copies of modern literary works. It contains *c*150 items, including 1 STC and 8 Wing items.

Author and classified subject card cats, with subject index.

Londonderry

Chapter House Library, St Columb's Cathedral, St Columb's Court, Londonderry. Open by arrangement with the Librarian. Consultation permitted on postal application to the Dean of Cathedral Vestry.

The library forms a reference collection, commenced in 1922, on the history of the cathedral and the City of Londonderry, and totals 350 v. Included are many 17th cent pamphlets on Irish affairs presented by Sir Frederick Heygate (*d*1940); that part of the Irish collection of A M Munn (*d*1937) which relates to the history of Londonderry (the remainder being in the Derry and Raphoe Diocesan Library); the City of Londonderry collection of Tenison Groves (*d*1938) (his County Londonderry collection being also in the Diocesan Library); and much from the library of Dean R G S King (*d*1958). There are 6 STC; and 136 Wing. Some of the more valuable books from the Diocesan Library are at present lodged in the Cathedral strong room.

Chapter House Library. Short title catalogue. Pt 1: Printed books and pamphlets. (Londonderry), 1939 (1), 13 leaves. Duplicated typescript (op).

Maura Tallon: *Church of Ireland diocesan libraries.* Dublin, Lib Assoc Ireland, 1959, p12 (op).

Derry and Raphoe Diocesan Library, Diocesan Office, London Street, Londonderry. Tel (0504) 62440. Open Mon-Fri 9 am-4.30 pm. Admission by prior application.

In 1690 William King, then Bishop of Derry, purchased the library of his predecessor, Ezekiel Hopkins. Before his translation to the archbishopric of Dublin in 1703, King had already given books for the use of the diocese of Derry, and he left Hopkins's books behind in Londonderry with the intention of building a diocesan library. By 1709 a catalogue had been drawn up, a librarian appointed and accommodation provided in the newly built 'Old School'. Probably the remnants of an older cathedral library, which was in existence at least as early as 1668, were transferred to the new Diocesan Library. Dr Gabriel Stokes, Fellow of Trinity College Dublin, and rector of Desart Martin, presented many volumes in the early part of the 19th cent; Major-General Sir William Clarke was another benefactor of the same period. In 1814 the books were transferred to a room in the 'New School', ie Foyle College, and there were many losses before their eventual removal in 1877 to their present quarters in the Synod Hall of the Diocesan Office. About 2,000 v were received by bequest from Rev C Seymour in 1883.

The Raphoe Diocesan Library was started in 1737 by Bishop Nicholas Forster. It was housed in the Diocesan School at Raphoe until its amalgamation with the Derry Diocesan Library in 1881. The largest part of the collection is the library of George Hall, Bishop of Dromore, received by bequest in 1811.

Other frequent provenances, besides those of the founders and benefactors, include William Harrison (*d*1593), the topographer and chronicler (over 160 v); George Downham (*d*1634), Bishop of Derry (over 100); Samuel Foley (*d*1695), Bishop of Down and Connor; and the Torrens family of Dungiven.

There are 6,500 v (*c*4,000 titles) pre-1851, but mostly 16th-18th cent. There are 5 incunabula; 190 STC and 930 Wing items. The subject field is mainly theology (especially 17th cent controversies), church history and classics. Amongst the more noteworthy items are Albertus Magnus: *Compendium theologiae veritatis* (1480); the Complutensian polyglot Bible (1522); Ortelius's *Geographia* (1584); and the first edition of Samuel Johnson's *Dictionary* (1755).

Catalogue of the books in the library of the United Dioceses of Derry and Raphoe. Londonderry, Sentinel, 1880, p43. (This was compiled by Rev W K Hobart and, in spite of its title, relates to the Derry portion of the library only. An earlier cat of the Derry Library was published in 1848.)

Catalogue of the Raphoe Diocesan Library. Dublin, J M O'Toole, 1868, p60.

Alphabetical author (or title) card cat, compiled *c*1933 by Col G V Hart according to B M rules. Nothing added since is catalogued.

Ms ledger shelflist.

A G Geoghegan, 'Communication on the library attached to Foyle College', *Journ of Kilkenny. . . Archaeological Soc*, ns 5 (1864/6), p230-4. (op)

Maura Tallon: *Church of Ireland diocesan libraries*, Dublin, Lib Assoc Ireland, 1959, p11: 'Derry and Raphoe', p19: 'Raphoe'.

'Annual report of the Library Committee' in *Report of the Diocesan Council*, 1870- .

Magee University College (New University of Ulster), Northland Road, Londonderry, Co Londonderry BT48 7JL. Tel (0504) 65621. Open (Term) Mon-Thurs 9.30 am-9 pm, Fri 9.30 am-5.30 pm; (Vacation) Mon-Fri 9.30 am-12.45 pm, 2-5 pm. Admission to members of the University; others, with letter of introduction, or by prior application. Microfilm and microfiche readers; copying available as photographic prints, slides or xerox.

The College was founded in 1865 as a liberal arts college with a theological department for the training of ministers for the Presbyterian Church in Ireland. It became part of the Royal University of Ireland from 1880 to 1909, and the arts department prepared students for the degrees of the University of Dublin from 1909 until 1968. The two departments separated in 1953 to become Magee University College and Magee Theological College. Since 1968 the University College has been a constituent college of the New University of Ulster, and in 1971 the Theological College transferred to Belfast to merge with the Presbyterian College there, the two eventually becoming Union Theological College. At present Magee University College fulfils the function of an institute of continuing education within the New University of Ulster.

The principal donors of books to the library have been the Rev Richard Dill of Dublin (over 1,200 v) and James Gibson QC, also of Dublin. The bulk of the collection of bound volumes of pamphlets was removed to Union Theological College in 1977. There are 85,000 v, of which *c*3,800 are pre-1851; 7 incunabula; 150 STC (listed in Ramage); and *c*200 Wing items; *c*1,700 of the 16th and 17th cent; and *c*2,100 v of the 18th cent.

Catalogue of the library (and)...supplement. Dublin, Thom, 1870–2, 2 v.

Catalogue of the pamphlet collection in the library (Londonderry), Jan 1971. (i) 178, 99p. (Duplicated typescript. An earlier pamphlets catalogue was published in 1887.) Only unbound pamphlets with pressmarks prefaced MP in this cat are still at Magee.

Alphabetical author and classified subject sheaf cats.

Card indexes (at present housed in the library of the New University of Ulster at Coleraine, Co Londonderry) of 17th cent printers arranged by place; 18th cent Irish printing; private press books; provenances; and illustrators.

Moneymore

Springhill (National Trust), Moneymore, Magherafelt, Co Londonderry BT45 7NQ. Tel (064874) 210. Application for access to the Libraries Adviser, National Trust, 42 Queen Anne's Gate, London SW1. Photocopying facilities available by arrangement with The Historic Buildings Representative, National Trust Regional Office, Rowallane, Saintfield, Ballynahinch, Co Down BT24 7LH, Tel (0238) 510721.

The library represents the accumulation of eight generations of the Conyngham (later Lenox-Conyngham) family who occupied the house from the 1680s until 1957. The principal collectors appear to have been William Conyngham (*d*1765) and William Lenox-Conyngham (*d*1858). 16 provenances other than Conyngham have been noted, particularly the Staples family of Lissan, Cookstown, Co Tyrone (allied by marriage to the Conynghams in 1819) and various branches of the Stewart family also of Tyrone, including the Earl of Blesington (*d*1769 and whose library was for a time at Springhill in the latter part of the 18th cent) and the Stewarts of Killymoon Castle, Cookstown. *c*1,850 v are housed in the library and drawing room, and a further *c*1,600 v are housed *pro tem* in the library of Florence Court, Co Fermanagh (another National Trust property).

There are 207 English and foreign pre-1701 titles, including 6 STC; 71 Wing items in the Springhill section; 76 pre-1701 titles in the Florence Court section. Considerable number of works on Puritan and religious controversy, but also interesting individual items such as Gerard's *Herball*, 1633; Raleigh's *Historie of the world*, 1634; Milton's *Eikonoklastes*, 1649; and Hobbe's *Leviathan*, 1651. The later 18th cent novels by minor writers are particularly noteworthy.

Alphabetical card cat by author or title (with notes on condition and provenance) for Springhill section only.

The pre-1701 titles from both Springhill and Florence Court have been noted for the National Trust's union cat.

Mina Lenox-Conyngham, *An old Ulster home*, Dundalk, Tempest, 1946 (op) *passim*.

REPUBLIC OF IRELAND

Cashel

Cashel Diocesan Library, Cashel, Co Tipperary. Tel (062) 61232. Admission by arrangement with the Dean of Cashel, The Deanery, Cashel, Co Tipperary.

Cashel Diocesan Library Established by Theophilus Bolton, Archbishop of Cashel, 1730–44, in the 1730s. His private library formed the original collection, and was bequeathed to his successors and the clergy of the diocese. Bolton's library was largely formed by his purchase in about 1734 of *c*4,000 v from the library of Archbishop William King, Archbishop of Dublin (1703–29), and contains *c*11,000 v. It is a general collection on the usual pattern of Anglican episcopal libraries, strongest in English books of the 17th cent, with the 16th cent also well represented, with an admixture of continental books. There are *c*20 incunabula and a handful of mss (these are listed in the 1973 printed cat). Little was added after 1730. Subject fields include Anglican theological scholarship, modern history and ecclesiastical law. Other subjects include mathematics, science and English literature. Some other special strengths are: English pamphlets of the 1640s and 1650s (*c*200 v); English 17th cent periodicals (43 titles. Parts are fully listed in the cat), a few very rare 17th cent Irish imprints, and Huguenot material including French academic theses. Some books were apparently lost or destroyed when the Archbishop's palace was occupied by soldiers in the 1798 rising. From 1910 to *c*1964 a selection, mainly of English and Irish books, was brought to Dublin and deposited first in Archbishop Marsh's Library, and later in the Library of the Representative Body of the Church of Ireland before being returned to Cashel. In the early 1960s a considerable number of books were sold to, among others, the Folger Library, Washington.

A Thom, *Catalogue of the library of the Dean and Chapter of Cashel*, Dublin, 1873 (op).

G K Hall, *Catalogue of the Cashel Diocesan Library*, Boston, Mass, 1973.

Maura Tallon, 'Church of Ireland diocesan libraries', *An leabharlann*, 17 (1959), 19-21.

Robert S Matteson, 'Archbishop William King's library: some discoveries and queries', *Long Room*, No 9 (1974), p7-16, facsims.

——'The early library of Archbishop William King', *The Library*, 5th ser, XXX (1975), p303-14.

Leaflet on 'Cashel—its cathedral and its library'.

Connemara

Kylemore Abbey, Connemara, Co Galway. Tel Kylemore 2. Not normally open to the public. Access by arrangement with the Librarian after prior letter of application from reader's institution.

Kylemore Abbey Library The present collection formed part of the library of the Benedictine Abbey at Ypres which was evacuated in 1914 (when part of the library was dispersed with the German invasion) and came to Kylemore in 1920. Part of the library was given to the Jesuits at Ypres. It comprises *c*1,000 v and is an ecclesiastical library with no profane literature. Almost entirely in the French language with French and Belgian printings of devotional literature, moral guidance for the young and Jesuit spirituality. Approximately two-thirds of the library is 18th cent material. Some items recorded in STC 1475–1640, 2nd ed and in Allison and Rogers, *A catalogue of Catholic Books in English. . . 1558–1640.*

Now being catalogued.

Cork

Cork City Libraries, Grand Parade, Cork, Ireland. Tel (021) 507110. Open Mon-Sat 10 am-6 pm. Admission unrestricted. Photocopying facilities, microfilm reader and reader/printer. Items lent only in very rare cases.

Cork Collection Built up by the library since 1894, a small proportion of the Collection was printed before 1851; *c*350 books, 40 maps, 30 newspaper titles, 60 prints, with 20 mss including items of Cork interest, or printed at Cork, or by Cork authors. Most of the pre-1851 items are 18th and early 19th cent, with a few from the 16th and 17th cent. The newspapers are mostly short runs or odd issues. There are 12 limited editions of the Golden Cockerel Press with engravings by Robert Gibbings. The library was destroyed by fire in 1921; the Library Report for 1924/5 refers to the loss of 14,000 v, many of them irreplaceable items of local interest. In particular a collection of 18th cent Irish newspapers sufficiently noteworthy to have been referred to in such periodicals as the *Irish Booklover*, together with all Cork daily papers 1893–1920, were destroyed.

Card cat with author and classified sequences. Separate cats for maps and newspapers.

St Fin Barre's Cathedral Library, 9 Dean Street, Cork, Ireland. Tel (021) 508006. Admission by arrangement with the Dean of Cork. No special facilities.

St Fin Barre's Cathedral Library Founded in 1720 by Bishop Browne. The private collections of Archdeacon Pomeroy (1725), Bishop Crow of Cloyne (1727), and Bishop Stopford (1805) form the bulk of the collection which consists of *c*3,000 v. The main subject areas are theology and ecclesiastical matters, but the classics, history, literature and science are also represented. Most of the books were printed in the 16th, 17th and 18th cent, chiefly in London and Dublin. There are three small collections of pamphlets dealing with: (i) The Popish plot, and religious controversy, etc of the last quarter of the 17th cent, chiefly English printing; (ii) Political and miscellaneous tracts of the early 18th cent, chiefly Dublin printing; (iii) Irish pamphlets of the last decades of the 18th cent, tithe war, economics, politics, etc.

Typescript author cat.

Maura Tallon, 'Church of Ireland diocesan libraries', *An leabharlann*, 17 (1959), 22-3.

University College, Cork, Ireland. Tel (021) 26871. Open Mon-Thurs 9 am-1 pm, 2.30-5.30 pm; Fri 9 am-1 pm, 2.30-5 pm. July-Sept 9 am-1 pm, 2.30-4.30 pm. Admission to non-members by arrangement. Microform readers and photocopying facilities.

Older Printed Books Collection Recently established by withdrawing items published before 1851 from the Library's general holdings. Most of these items were purchased between 1849 (when the College was founded) and 1900; some were received from institutions such as the Royal Cork Institution, the old Cork Public Library, and the Royal Irish Academy. It contains *c*13,000 v, including almost 2,000 v of folio and elephant size. The main subject coverage is history—Irish, English and European; philology, palaeography, literature, music, philosophy, natural sciences, and medicine are also represented. *c*70 items are from 16th cent, 1,230 17th cent, 6,500 18th cent and 5,200 19th cent.

No separate cat; some items appear in the old card cat.

Munster Printing Collection A collection of *c*1,000 items (half of which are pamphlets) built up by the Library. Many items were donated by Rev P Power, Professor of Archaeology, in 1948. These items were printed in the Province of Munster, chiefly in the Counties of Cork, Kerry and Waterford, from the late 17th cent to the present day. Major subject areas are Anglo-Irish literature, local history and politics, religious affairs, social conditions, education, and economics.

Author, title, date and subject cats.

Dublin

Augustinian House of Studies, Balleyboden, Dublin 16. Tel (0001) 908943. Open by arrangement for unrestricted research purposes. Xeroxing facilities and microfilm readers available.

Library of the Augustinian House of Studies The older books in the collection were assembled in 1958 from all Augustinian Houses in England and Ireland, and include *c*4,500 v printed pre-1850. Subject coverage with special reference to editions of Augustine from 1541 and Augustiniana, which form a special section; some philosophy, history, Irish history, classics and belles lettres; provincial archives for England and Ireland (mainly printed, though including some ms material). There are two incunabula.

Cat broadly Irish published. Older books (Augustiniana are occasionally bought).

Carmelites

I One house of the Order has a private library open by arrangement for research purposes only. Enquiries and application for admission in writing to Special Collections Librarian, Main Library, University College, Dublin, Belfield, Dublin 4.

The Carmelite Order returned to Ireland in the early 19th cent. Some books in the library were brought from abroad by members of the Order, and some were acquired subsequently. The collection contains *c*2,200 v pre-1851; STC and Wing items not estimated. Subject coverage: travel; dictionaries and grammars; some reference; history; church history; some Irish history; literature; some classics; some biography; theology; Carmelite studies. Imprints mainly continental, 18th-19th cent; some 16th-17th cent items. Some books formerly in Whitefriar Street are now in the Gort Muire House.

Author cat in book form in progress.

Typescript cat (1939) in book form lists items alphabetically within broad subject headings; probably not comprehensive.

II House of Studies, Gort Muire, Ballinteer, Dublin 16. Tel (0001) 984014. Bus route 48A. Open by arrangement for research purposes only; enquiries in writing to the Librarian.

The books in the library were transferred to Gort Muire when the House of Studies was moved there in 1943–4. Much of the collection was originally in the Whitefriar Street house (qv); there have been some additions, chiefly through donation and bequest. The Collection includes *c*300 v pre-1851, and covers Bible studies, theology, church history, Carmelite studies; some classics, literature, history.

Majority of older books uncat.

Central Catholic Library Incorporated (Leabharlann an Chreidimh), 74 Merrion Square, Dublin 2. Tel (0001) 761264. Open Mon-Sat 11 am-7.30 pm. Admission unrestricted.

Central Catholic Library The library was founded in 1922 to provide a general public reference and lending service covering all aspects of Catholicism. The older material in the Collection was acquired mostly through donations from religious houses, retired clergy, and other interested individuals. Totalling *c*60,000 v, only *c*800 items are of the 16th–mid-19th cent. Subjects covered include philosophy, theology, church history and biography, sermons, devotional literature, literature. Imprints Irish (mostly Dublin), British, and Continental (mostly French, some Italian and Spanish).

Ms sheaf cat; author entries only. No separate list of early printings.

S Brown, 'A Catholic library for Dublin', *Studies*, 11(42) June 1922, p307-12.

——*The Central Catholic Library: the first ten years of an Irish enterprise*. Dublin, Central Catholic Library Association, 1932 [op].

S O hÉideáin, 'Stair Leabharlann an Chreidimh—an chéad ceathrú céid', *Irish Ecclesiastical Record*, 5th ser, 70, (1948), p648-53.

Chester Beatty Library and Gallery of Oriental Art, 20 Shrewsbury Road, Ballsbridge, Dublin 4. Tel (0001) 692386. Open Tues-Fri 10 am-1 pm, 2.30-5.15 pm (Oct-March, 2.30-5 pm); (Closed on Tues following a Bank Holiday); Sat 2.30-5.15 pm (Oct-March, 2.30-5 pm). Admission unrestricted to exhibition rooms; researchers by written arrangement. Photocopying; library can also arrange photographer.

Printed Books The private library of Sir Alfred Chester Beatty, 1875–1968, who began to collect western rare books and illuminated mss *c*1910, and oriental mss and miniatures from *c*1913. The oriental collections and a small representative collection of western material were bequeathed to the Irish people, with provision for perpetual exhibition, in 1968. Printed books, which total *c*5,000, including 20 incunabula, were collected principally for plates and bindings. Subject coverage includes travel and topography; some architecture; literature; classics; biography and memoirs; natural history; Arabica and orientalia; costume; some religion and devotional literature. There are over 300 fine Irish, English and continental bindings (Irish bindings not in Craig).

Author cat in book form.

R J Hayes, *The Chester Beatty Library, Dublin*, Dublin, 1958.

The Manuscript Collection Manuscripts (*c*5,000) were acquired principally for their illumination and calligraphy. The collections include the following: western mss (mainly Biblical texts, commentaries, theology, liturgy, devotional literature); Greek papyri (mainly classical texts, letters, archival records); Biblical papyri; Turkish mss (chiefly poetry, history, genealogy and biography, theology, prayer and liturgy, astronomy and astrology, medicine, and archival records); Armenian mss (mainly Biblical and liturgical); Arabic mss (theology, law, geography, science, biography, some poetry and lexicography); Korans; Ethiopian and Persian collections. Oriental mss include Batak (divination, magic and medicine); Chinese jade books; Japanese mss including illuminated scrolls of the Nara school; Tibetan mss (religion, medicine, divination, music, history); Indian miniatures. Some western mss excluded from the Chester Beatty bequest, were sold by order of the executors: Sotheby 3 Dec 1968 and 24 June 1969.

Various published cats.

A J Arberry, *The Rubā'īyāt of Omar Khayyam; edited from a newly discovered manuscript dated 658 (1259–60) in the possession of A Chester Beatty Esq*, London, Emery Walker, 1949 (op).

——*A twelfth century reading list: a chapter in Arab bibliography*, London, Emery Walker, 1951. (Chester Beatty Monographs, 2).

B van Regemorter, *Some early bindings from Egypt in the Chester Beatty Library*, Dublin, Emery Walker, 1958. (Chester Beatty Monographs, 7).

——*Some Oriental bindings in the Chester Beatty Library*, Dublin, Hodges Figgis, 1961.

Chinese jade books in the Chester Beatty Library, described, and the Chinese texts translated by W Watson: the Manchu texts translated by J L Mish, Dublin, Hodges Figgis, 1963.

Church of Ireland College of Education, Upper Rathmines Road, Dublin 6. Tel (0001) 970033. Open by appointment for research workers only. Admission by letter to the Principal, with covering letter from university.

Kildare Place Collection The Church of Ireland College of Education, formerly the Church of Ireland Training College for teachers, has inherited, through a series of changes reflecting the history of Irish education through the 19th cent the small collection of books formed by the Society for the Education of the Poor in Ireland (known as the Kildare Place Society). This Society (1811–1831) received early advice and help from Joseph Lancaster, and took over in 1816 the work of The Cheap Book Society whose aim was to replace the popular chapbook literature of romances, rogues and rapparees with instructive books more suitable for youth. The Collection contains 400 v, and its chief feature is a run of the Kildare Place chapbooks, often known as the Dublin chapbooks. These were published from about 1815 to 1840, and formed a 'lending library', considered suitable for adult institutions as well as schools. The College of Education's Archives include all the Society's transactions, accounts, etc, including those records concerned with the sale and distribution of the chapbooks. Also included are a handful of the textbooks published by the Society, together with early 19th cent works on education and a few of a later date.

'The publications of the Kildare Place Society', Chap II in Pt II of H Kingsmill Moore, *An unwritten chapter in the history of education*, London, Macmillan, 1904, p214-64 [op].

Discalced Carmelites. Two houses of the Order have private libraries, open by arrangement for research purposes only. Enquiries in writing to Special Collections Librarian, Main Library, University College, Dublin, Belfield, Dublin 4.

I The Discalced Carmelites came to Ireland in the early 17th cent. The library of this house has been built up with books brought from the Continent by friars, as well as subsequent acquisition by gift and purchase. It includes the library of Edward Martyn, 1859—1924, Irish nationalist and playwright. Older books are occasionally acquired. Its holdings total 2,250 v printed pre-1850, covering theology, Bible studies, church history, Carmelite studies; some philosophy, history, travel, classics. Imprints: mainly Continental, 16th-19th cent, including Spanish and Portuguese imprints 16th-18th cent; possibly 50 18th cent British and Irish imprints, 19th cent. Irish provincial imprints. The Martyn Collection of 2,300 v includes philosophy, religion, music, literature, classics, geography and travel, history; books relating to Ireland and Anglo-Irish literature.

Author and classified card cats.

Some 800 v of the general collection are shelved in the main library, and are being sorted and catalogued.

Some 1,450 v (theology, church history, classics) are shelved separately awaiting processing.

II This library has been built up since the establishment of the house in the late 19th cent; it holds some items from the Martyn Collection described in I above. Older books are not now bought. It contains *c*725 v printed pre-1851; subject content includes theology, Bible studies, patristics, Carmelite studies, mainly in Continental printings 16th-18th cent; some history, classics, travel. There is one incunabulum.

There is one 14th cent ms (transcripts of works of early theologians).

Author card cat, partly completed.

Dublin City Libraries, Pearse Street, Dublin 2. Tel (0001) 777662. Open Mon-Sat 10 am-1 pm, 2-6 pm. Admission is unrestricted, but letter of introduction desirable. Xerox on premises; microfilm available if necessary. Basic bibliographical reference works.

Dix Collection E R McClintock Dix (1857—1936), the best known Irish bibliographer, collected both Irish printings and bindings, and made presents of these to many important Irish libraries. The Collection was not presented as a whole, but grew as Dix made his various gifts. It comprises *c*300 v and includes 17th and 18th cent works, Irish printing, Dublin and provincial provinces, some Wing items (Kilkenny, Waterford, Cork: 1640s), but the bulk of the Collection consists of 18th cent Dublin imprints.

Collection included in author card cat of special collections (available only on request).

T P Dowd, 'The Gilbert library and the Dublin city local collection', *An leabharlann*, (NS) 7, Summer 1978, p42-54.

Dublin Theatre Collection Largely presented by Seamus de Burca, director/playwright *b*1912, the collection contains over 700 items; mainly 20th cent (1905 to date and continuing) theatre programmes and playbills from the Dublin theatres: *c*350 programmes and 300 playbills. Also includes some concert programmes.

Included in author card cat of special collections under Theatre (available on request).

Gilbert Collection This represents the working collection of Sir John T Gilbert (1829—98), author of *The History of Dublin*, Dublin: 1854—9, 3 v, and editor of several documents relating to Irish history. It was purchased by Dublin City Libraries in 1900 and consists of 4,500 printed v, and 286 mss. Subjects covered include, besides the history of Dublin, Irish history in general, especially 17th and 18th cent: emphasis is on primary sources, eg excellent run of Dublin directories, 39 v of Dublin newspapers, especially early 18th cent, many are only known copies, Irish printing in general. It includes works of Irish interest printed abroad, handful of STC items, some Wing, 1 incunabulum. Mss mainly of historical interest, many being transcripts made for Gilbert (see catalogue). Fine bindings have been separated from main collection and are dealt with separately.

Catalogue of the books and manuscripts comprising the library of the late Sir John T Gilbert, Dublin, Brown and Nolan, 1918. (op)

Dewey classified card cat.

T P Dowd, 'The Gilbert Library and the Dublin city local collection', *An leabharlann*, (NS) 7, Summer 1978, p42-54.

P B Glynn, 'The Gilbert and local collection of the Dublin municipal libraries', *An leabharlann*, 10, (1952), p181-5.

Irish book bindings The majority of volumes drawn from Gilbert Collection but with addition of some volumes presented by E R McClintock Dix. The collection consists of *c*140 v, of which *c*100 items have been identified by Maurice Craig as the work of Dublin binders of the 18th cent; four of these are illustrated in Craig's *Irish bookbindings 1600—1800*, London, 1954.

Author entry only as for Gilbert and Dix Collections.

Yeats Collection Made by Colin Smythe (editor and publisher of the works of Lady Gregory), *c*1963—6.

Acquired by Dublin City Libraries 1966. It contains 537 v, which include books by Yeats, Dun Emer and Cuala press publications and printings, and books etc by Jack Yeats, titles associated with him and the Yeats family, and also the Irish literary revival. Of exceptional interest is W B Yeats, *Mosada*: a dramatic poem, Dublin: 1886. 100 copies only printed.

Collection included in author card cat of special collections available only on request.

Franciscan Fathers, Dun Mhuire, Seafield Road, Killiney, Co Dublin. Tel (0001) 852303. Open by arrangement for research purposes on provision of a letter of introduction. There is no restriction on women. In exceptional circumstances, xeroxing and microfilming can be arranged.

Franciscan Library, Killiney The nucleus of the collection is the remaining books and manuscripts of the Irish Franciscan College, St Anthony's, founded at Louvain in 1607. The collection was transferred to St Isidore's College, Rome, at the beginning of the 19th cent, and in 1872 to Dublin, with additional material belonging to St Isidore's College. It was housed in the Franciscan Library, Merchant's Quay, Dublin, until 1954 when it was moved to Killiney. Additional material has come, in part, from other Irish Franciscan houses. Of a total of *c*11,000 v (including pamphlets), about one-third to a half are pre-1850. Particular strengths are Celtic studies, ecclesiastical history (Irish and Franciscan). Also represented are history, belles-lettres, classical literature and other arts subjects. There are some 18th-19th cent Irish printed newspapers. The Collection includes *c*500 Irish printed books, and *c*6 rare Irish printed 17th cent broadsheets. There are 23 incunabula.

The manuscript collection consists principally of Franciscan archives. There are also 60 Irish language mss, mainly religious material and poetry, and including an autograph copy of the first part of the *Annals of the four masters* (17th cent); and 111 non-Irish mss, mainly religious material.

Subject cat on cards. There is a list of Irish printed books (a copy is in TCD); and a list of Irish printed books with subscribers' lists.

Canice Mooney, 'The Franciscan Library Merchants' Quay, Dublin', *An leabharlann*, VIII 2, 1942, p29-37.

——*Short guide to the material of interest for the student of Irish church history in the Franciscan Library, Killiney Co Dublin.* Killiney: Four Masters Press, 1954. (op)

Geological Survey of Ireland, 14 Hume Street, Dublin 2. Tel (0001) 753351. Library: Baggot Bridge House, Baggot Street, Dublin 2. Tel (0001) 687833. Bus routes 4, 10. Open Mon-Fri 9.15 am-5 pm. Admission for research purposes only; an appointment is essential.

Geological Survey Library The Geological Survey was established in 1845 and the library was presumably started at that time. Formerly an important part of the library were the books bequeathed by Major-General Joseph Ellison Portlock, RE, (1794–1864). It contains *c*75 items printed pre-1850 covering geology, with emphasis on palaeontological and stratigraphical works. Mss include field sheets and letter books of the Geological Survey of Ireland; palaeontological figures and geological sections of the Ordnance Survey (on which Portlock worked).

The library has been partly dispersed, but the majority of the older books in the Survey Library have been located in the Royal Dublin Society Library (qv) since the 1930s.

T E Hardman, *Catalogue of books in the Library of the Office of the Geological Survey of Ireland, Dublin, 1886.* Dublin: A Thom for HMSO, 1886.

There is a typed list of books printed pre-1900.

Grand Lodge of Freemasons of Ireland, Library, Freemasons' Hall, 17 Molesworth Street, Dublin 2. Tel (0001) 761337. Open by arrangement after written application to the Grand Secretary, stating purpose of research.

The Library of the Grand Lodge of Ireland The Grand Lodge of Ireland was instituted *c*1725, but the library was deliberately built up only in the 19th cent, and received some of its earlier books as part of the Chetwode Crawley Library in 1916. It contains *c*750–1,000 v (pre-1850), of which *c*200 are 18th cent. All books relate in some way to freemasonry, and particularly to Irish freemasonry, and are likely to be very rare. The collection is added to only when suitable material becomes available.

Author and rudimentary dictionary subject cats on cards available.

Arthur Guinness, Son and Co, St James's Gate, Dublin 8. Tel (0001) 756701 Ext 528. Open Mon-Fri 9.15 am-4 pm. Admission by appointment only. Xerox copying service available.

The library is maintained as part of the Guinness museum which houses relics of the brewery's 200 year history, as well as relics of the brewing trade in Ireland generally. It contains 36 v (printed material) which covers brewing and allied trades in Ireland, and the brewing industry generally. Mostly 18th and 19th cent English editions, which include some Irish imprints. Ms material consists of the Minute Books of the Brewers' Guild of Dublin 1759; Brewers' Corporation, 1805; Coopers' Guild of Dublin, 1765–1836. The charter of the Coopers' Guild is also in the collection.

Author card cat.

Henry S Guinness, 'Dublin trade gilds' (sic), *Jnl Roy Soc Antiquaries of Ireland*, 52, 1922, p143-63.

Historical Library of the Religious Society of Friends, 6 Eustace Street, Dublin 2. Tel (0001) 778088. Open Thurs 10 am-4 pm. Although there is no limitation of admission, a letter to the Curator is essential. Xerox only. There are no bibliographical reference works.

Historical library of the Religious Society of Friends The historical collection was brought together by a group of interested Friends in 1908. The printed collection is a minor part of the whole, the chief importance of which lies in the mss collection of Quaker archives, papers, letters etc. There are 800 printed v plus a large collection of pamphlets, mainly of Quaker interest (not limited to Ireland) of the 17th-19th cent. Wing items unspecified. Duplicate items were sold in January 1971.

Author and title cat on cards.

Olive C Goodbody, *Guide to Irish Quaker Records 1654–1800*, Dublin. Stationery Office for the Irish Manuscripts Commission, 1967. (op)

Irish Theatre Archive, Dublin City Archives, City Hall, Dublin 2. Tel (0001) 776811. Walking distance from City centre. Open Mon-Fri 10 am-12.45 pm, 2.15-5 pm. Admission unrestricted, but application in writing is advisable. Enquiries should be addressed to the City Archivist, City Hall.

The archive was begun in 1980, and contains *c*5,000 items, chiefly printed ephemera, such as playbills, programmes and newspaper cuttings relating to 20th cent theatre in Dublin.

Jesuit Fathers, Milltown Park, Dublin 14. Tel (0001) 975729. Open Mon-Fri 8 am-10 pm. Admission for research purposes on provision of a letter of introduction. Xeroxing facilities are available.

O'Brien Collection and Cox Collection The O'Brien Collection was the bequest of Judge William O'Brien (1832–99); the Cox Collection was built up by Michael Francis Cox (1852–1926), physician, and was presented to Milltown Park by his son Arthur Cox in 1961. The library includes 1–1,200 v pre-1850. Subject coverage: theology, patrology, classics (including printings by Aldus, Bodoni and Baskerville); material relating to Ireland, including early recusant literature; belles-lettres including contemporary Dryden editions. Five Irish bindings are described in Craig. There are 117 incunabula.

Author cat on cards, not complete. Recataloguing of the whole library has started, with files for Irish printing, private press books etc. However, early and notable printings are not being given priority.

Paul Grosjean and Daniel O'Connell, *A catalogue of incunabula in the library at Milltown Park, Dublin*. Dublin: at the Sign of the Three Candles, 1932. (op)

King's Inns, Henrietta Street, Dublin 1. Tel (0001) 747134. Open Mon 2-6 pm, Tues-Fri 11 am-6 pm; Sat 10 am-1 pm. Admission unrestricted to Members of the Honourable Society of King's Inns. Others by permission of the Benchers, on written application.

Library of the King's Inns The Honourable Society of King's Inns dates from 1541. It occupied its present site in 1798. The earliest evidence of a library is the purchase in 1787 of the professional portion of the library of Christopher Robinson, *c*1712–87, Judge of King's Bench. The library benefitted until 1836 by the Copyright Acts of 1801 and 1814. The collection includes *c*25,000 v printed pre-1851, mainly on Irish and international law, biography, history, natural history, topography, classics, belles-lettres, science. There are *c*600 v of Irish printed pamphlets, 17th-18th cent, *c*90 v printed Irish appeals to the British House of Lords. Incunabula, STC, Wing items not estimated. Three incunabula are listed in T K Abbott's Catalogue of 15th cent books; 3 Irish bindings are described in Craig. There are 31 v Irish language mss, including bardic verse, religious poetry and prose, history, genealogy, medicine, and Irish language and vocabulary. Other mss include the papers of John Patrick Prendergast, 1808–93, historian, and Irish appeals to the House of Lords.

Author cat in guardbook form; biography, newspapers and periodicals listed separately. Author and classified cat of law books. The mss are listed in Hayes.

A catalogue of the library belonging to the Honourable Societey of King's Inns, Dublin to Trinity Term 1801, [compiled by B T Duhigg] Dublin: by R Mercier, 1801. This records *c*2,100 titles. (Location: National Library of Ireland).

Catalogue of the books in the library of the Hon Society of the King's Inns. Dublin: for the Society by M Goodwin & Co, 1834. This records *c*5,600 v in two sections: (i) non-legal books; (ii) legal books (National Library of Ireland). This was re-issued with a supplement as *Catalogue of the books in the library of the King's Inns.* Dublin: printed for the Society, 1836 (Location: King's Inns).

Juridical catalogue. Compiled by Henry Connor. Dublin: by M H Gill, 1846. (Location: King's Inns). Listed in *A legal bibliography of the British Commonwealth of nations*. 2nd ed, compiled by W Harold Maxwell and Leslie F Maxwell, London: Sweet and Maxwell Ltd, 1955–64 (v 4) as Judicial [sic] catalogue of the library of King's Inns; not recorded elsewhere in this form.

A list of books printed in England prior to the year MDC in the library of the Hon Society of King's Inns Dublin, by James D Haig, Dublin: Hodges, Smith and Co, 1858.

T K Abbott, *Catalogue of fifteenth century books in the library of Trinity College Dublin*, and in *Marsh's Library, Dublin, with a few from other collections*. Dublin: Hodges Figgis, London, Longmans, Green, 1905. Lists three items from King's Inns. [op]

Catalogue of Irish manuscripts in King's Inn Library Dublin [by] Pádraig de Brun. Dublin: Institute for Advanced Studies, 1972.

Mary J Neylon, 'King's Inns Library, Dublin', *Law Librarian* IV (i) 1973, p3-4.

Law Library, Four Courts, Dublin 7. Open Mon-Fri 9.30 am-5 pm during Irish Law Terms. Admission unrestricted to subscribing members of the Irish Bar. Others, for research purposes: enquiries to be made, in writing, one month in advance. Very limited reading facilities. Xeroxing available. Microfiche reader/printer.

The library appears to have been founded in 1816 with the purchase of the collection of books from a bookseller who used to hire books to the Bar in the Four Courts. However, in 1922 the collection was severely damaged during the destruction of the Four Courts. The library was moved to King's Inns, then to Dublin Castle; in 1932 it moved to its present location. It received a grant to rebuild the collection and has been added to by gift and purchase. There are *c*2,950 v pre-1851; imprints, mainly British and Irish 18th-19th cent. *c*10 STC and 30 Wing items. Subjects covered include legal material—yearbooks, nominate reports, Irish, English and British statutes, textbooks, digests, law dictionaries.

Major portion of older books not catalogued.

Author card cat.

Archbishop Marsh's Library, St Patrick's Close, Dublin 8. Tel (0001) 753917. Open Mon 2-4 pm, Tues closed, Wed-Fri 10.30 am-12.30 pm, 2-4 pm. Admission unrestricted. Microfilming and xeroxing can be arranged.

The library comprises four main collections: Bishop Stillingfleet's library; Dr Bouhéreau's library; Archbishop Marsh's library; Bishop Stearne's library. It was established by Archbishop Narcissus Marsh as the first public library in Ireland. The founding collection was that of Edward Stillingfleet (1635–99), Bishop of Worcester, whose library Marsh bought in 1705. Narcissus Marsh (1638–1713), Archbishop of Dublin and later of Armagh, bequeathed his books to the library, as did Dr Elias Bouhéreau (1642–1714), the first librarian, and John Stearne (1660–1745), Bishop of Clogher. Books total 25,000. Subject coverage in all collections includes medicine, law, science, travel, navigation, mathematics, music, surveying, classical literature. A large collection of Bibles and liturgical works includes 15 editions of missals, breviaries, and books of hours of the Sarum use. These are early 16th cent printings, and many are known in only one or two copies. Bindings include English blind-stamped bindings by well-known English binders of the 16th and 17th cent; armorial bindings; continental leather and vellum bindings; some Irish bindings (7 described in Craig). Notable is the first example of gold tooling in England, on a book from the library of Henry VIII. A separate room is reserved for books and periodicals relating to Irish history, printed from 1800 to the present. There are *c*80 incunabula; 1,300 STC items; Wing items not estimated.

Note: A sale of duplicates is recorded in *Bibliotheca Marsiana: catalogue of books, the duplicate copies of the public library, Dublin, sold by auction on Wednesday May 8th, 1833, by Charles Sharpe.* Dublin, Richard Davis Webb, 1833.

Manuscript author and subject cat; typescript cat of books printed in and relating to Ireland to 1800 (compiled 1932); typescript cat of English pamphlets and anonymous works, 1641–1750.

The following cats have been published:

T K Abbott, *Catalogue of 15th century books in the library of Trinity College, Dublin, and in Marsh's Library, Dublin*. Dublin: Hodges, Figgis; London: Longmans, Green, 1905. [Repr. New York: B Franklin 1970. . .]

Newport J D White, *A catalogue of books in the French language, printed in or before AD 1715, remaining in Archbishop Marsh's Library, Dublin.* Dublin: University Press, 1918. (op)

——*A short catalogue of English books in Archbishop Marsh's Library, Dublin, printed before 1641.* Oxford, OUP for the Bibliographical Soc, 1905. (op)

Muriel McCarthy, 'Archbishop Marsh and his library', *Dublin Historical Record* XXIX, 1, 1975, p2-23.

J S G Simmons, 'On Cyrillic books in Marsh's Library', *The Irish Book* II, 1963, p37-42.

George Thomas Stokes, *Some worthies of the Irish church*. London, Hodder and Stoughton, 1900 (An account of Marsh and his library, p65-141). (op)

Newport B White, 'Manuscript and printed music in Marsh's Library' in *Music in Ireland: a symposium*, edited by Aloys Fleischmann. Cork, Cork Univ Press; Oxford: Blackwell, 1952, p319-21. (op)

Newport J D White, *An account of Archbishop Marsh's Library, with a note on autographs by Newport B White.* Dublin: Hodges, Figgis, 1926. (op)

'Swiftiana in Marsh's Library', *Hermathena*, 11, No 27 (1901), p369-81.

Dix Collection of Novels Collected by Ernest Reginald McClintock Dix (1857–1936), Irish bibliographer, and presented by him to the library, the collection contains 92 items, comprising novels printed in Ireland in the second half of the 18th cent.

Cat.

Typescript author list.

National Botanic Gardens, Glasnevin, Dublin 9. Tel (0001) 377596, 374388. Open Mon-Fri 9.15 am-1 pm, 2.15-5.30 pm (5.15 pm Fri). Admission by permission of the Director. No formal reading room. Xeroxing, microfilming, photographing can be arranged; microfiche reader available.

General Collection The National Botanic Gardens were founded by the (Royal) Dublin Society in 1796, and the library was founded at the same time. The Gardens and the Library were administered by the Dublin Society until 1877 when they became state-controlled; most of the early books were then transferred to the newly established National Library. In 1911 the bequest was made of the botanical books of William Edward Gumbleton, JP, (1840–1911), amateur horticulturist and bibliophile. The library contains *c*2,500 v pre-1850 (including the Gumbleton bequest of 110 items). The subject coverage is botanical, with special emphasis on the flora of Ireland and horticulture. Works date from the 16th-19th cent, mainly British imprints. The Gumbleton bequest of fine 19th cent illustrated works includes Sibthorp and Smith, *Flora Graeca;* Redouté's *Roses;* an annotated set of *Curtis's Botanical Magazine*. There are also *c*500 watercolour drawings of botanical subjects dating from the 1880s.

Limited author card cat. An author/title/subject cat in preparation. Typed cat of the library *c*1910, 1920 and 1930 extant. Mss holdings are to be included in the Society for the Bibliography of Natural History's projected *Natural History Manuscript Resources of the British Isles.*

Eileen McCracken, 'The origins of the library at Glasnevin Botanic Gardens', *Irish booklore* II 1 (1972), 82-8. (Some works listed in this are not now in the library.)

A cat of pre-1800 botanical books in Irish libraries, excluding Trinity College, Dublin, is in preparation by Dr E Charles Nelson. Papers on the Glasnevin collections are in preparation.

National Library of Ireland, Kildare Street, Dublin 2. Tel (0001) 765521. Walking distance from city centre. Open Mon-Thurs 10 am-9 pm, Fri 10 am-5 pm; Sat 10 am-1 pm. Admission unrestricted, on presentation of suitable introduction or identification. Photostating, photography, microfilming undertaken. Microfilm readers available.

General Collection The collection is based on the library acquired by the State from the Royal Dublin Society (qv) under the Dublin Science and Museum Act of 1877 which established the National Library. Bequests incorporated into the general collection include the *Alexander Thom* collection and the bequest of *David Comyn, 1854–1907.* Additions are regularly made to the collection, with emphasis on items of Irish interest. It totals 500,000 v including the Dix and Joly collections (qv); perhaps one-third of this total printed before 1851. The collection is particularly strong in material relating to Ireland, eg Irish history, politics, economics, labour history; pamphlets, including 60 v of 17th and early 18th cent pamphlets relating to contemporary Irish history; literature, including a collection of some 500 items by and about Jonathan Swift to 1830; broadsides and proclamations, mainly of political interest; broadside ballads. Scientific subjects and medicine are covered insofar as the RDS had a strong scientific bias; items of Irish interest in these fields are still acquired. There is a comprehensive first edition collection of modern Irish authors. There are early Irish newspapers and other serials (including newspapers from the Office of the Chief Secretary for Ireland); some 2,000 items of early printed music (see also Joly Collection). There are 20 incunabula, *c*100 18th and 19th cent Irish bindings of note, including work by George Mullen (Craig 1954 and 1976); and 20-30 non-Irish fine bindings.

Author and subject guardbook cat (now in process of transfer to cards).

Accessions to 1968.

Card cat: accessions 1968 onwards.

For printed cats to 1877 see Royal Dublin Society entry.

Supplemental catalogue of books by author, title and class, added to the National Library of Ireland. . . , Dublin: for HMSO [1880]—(a series of v, usually annual, recording acquisitions 1874–1913; title varies; *Rough list. . . , Temporary list. . . , Books added. . .*).

Some holdings listed in A Black, BUCEM, RISM, Craig 1954 and 1976.

Arundell Esdaile, *National Libraries of the World.* 2nd ed. London: Library Assoc, 1957, p128-33.

Patrick Henchy, 'The National Library of Ireland', *An leabharlann* 26 (1968), p44-9.

Dix Collection The gift in 1924 of Ernest Reginald McClintock Dix (1857–1936), Irish bibliographer. Additions are regularly made to the collection which totals 12,600 v, consisting of Irish imprints exclusively, arranged by town and date of printing.

Included in main cat.

Chronological cat in book form, divided into (i) Dublin, (ii) the provinces.

(Dix contributed a series of articles on Irish printing, based on his own collection, to the *Irish Book Lover*, and to the local provincial press.)

Joly Collection The gift in 1863, to the Royal Dublin Society, of Jasper Robert Joly (1819–92), book collector, the collection totals 23,000 v and 16,000 pamphlets. The special interest of the collection lies in material relating to the French Revolution and Napoleon; 18th cent French history and French literature also feature. The collection includes Irish history and topography, with a notable section of Irish topographical prints and drawings (the latter have been extracted from the collection and are held with the rest of the library's related holdings). There is an extensive collection of Irish trials, mainly of the 19th cent. There are some 6,000 items of pre-1800 printed music, including a high proportion of Irish printed song-sheets (*BUCEM, RISM).*

Books and pamphlets included in main cat.

Separate cat in book form of the Joly books only.

Music cat on cards.

Catalogue of engraved Irish portraits mainly in the Joly collection, and of original drawings, by Rosalind M Elmes. Dublin Stationary Office, (1937).

Catalogue of Irish topographical prints and drawings, (by) Rosalind M Elmes. New ed revised and enlarged by

Michael Hewson. Dublin: Malton Press for Nat Lib Ireland Soc, 1975.

Oireachtas (=Irish Parliament), Leinster House, Kildare Street, Dublin 2. Tel (0001) 789911. Open only by prior arrangement with the Librarian. Admission to the Library is normally restricted to members of the Oireachtas and Oireachtas officials. Members of the public can only be admitted by permission of the Ceann Chomhairle (=Speaker of the House).

Oireachtas Library The library was set up as an integral part of the Oireachtas administration, after the Anglo-Irish peace treaty of December 1921. It is primarily intended to serve the official needs of TDs (=MPs) and Senators. However, material transferred from the Irish Office in London, *c*1922, as well as some material transferred in 1923/4 from the office of the Chief Secretary for Ireland, in Dublin Castle, forms part of the collection. (Newspapers from the Chief Secretary's Office Library were placed in the National Library of Ireland.) The Irish Office material consists of 146 v of pamphlets, comprising *c*1,500 items. The precise number of volumes transferred from the Chief Secretary's Office is not known, as part of the collection was deposited in the National Library of Ireland, and the material has not been recatalogued. The material from the Irish Office and the Chief Secretary's Office covers all aspects of political affairs, but much of it relates specifically to the 'Irish Question'. Many of the Irish Office pamphlets date from the 17th-19th cent. *c*900 items have Irish 18th cent imprints.

The general collection is controlled by a classified (DDC) card cat.

There is no author cat. The only cats for the transferred material date from *before* the transfer.

Catalogue of books in the library of the Chief Secretary's Office. Dublin, HMSO, 1904. (op)

List of pamphlets in the library of the Irish Office. London, HMSO, 1913. (op)

Redemptorists House of Studies, 75 Orwell Road, Rathgar, Dublin 6. Tel (0001) 961688. Admission for research purposes by arrangement. Xeroxing can be arranged.

The library was started in 1900, to provide a working collection for theological students. Books are acquired by purchase, gift and exchange. The library includes *c*8-900 v pre-1851. Subject areas include moral theology manuals, Redemptorist literature, general theology from the 16th to 19th cent. Printings are mainly Continental. Older books are being acquired by exchange with other Irish houses of the Order, with emphasis on theology.

Cat in progress.

Representative Body of the Church of Ireland (Representative Church Body) (Library), Braemor Park, Dublin 14. Tel (0001) 979979. Open Mon-Fri 10 am-1 pm, 1.45-5 pm. Admission unrestricted; letter of introduction preferred. Xeroxing and microfilming can be arranged. A microfilm reader/printer is available.

Sir James Stephen Library (general collection) and the Watson Collection of prayer books and liturgical works The nucleus of the library is the collection of the Irish Guild of Witness, founded by Rosamund Stephen in 1918, and is named in memory of her father. It was transferred to the RCB in 1932. The Watson Collection was the gift of Edward John Macartney (sic) Watson, 1872–1947, physician, and was collected by him and his father Sir William Watson. The general collection (23,000 v) contains *c*550 items and *c*230 pamphlets pre-1850, mainly 18th-19th cent. The Watson Collection of 157 items includes *c*100 pre-1850. Subjects covered are theology, church history, Irish history, some literature and biography. There are *c*75 Irish 18th cent printings, including items from the Watson Collection.

Manuscripts include parish records; working notes and mss of Hugh Jackson Lawlor, DD; biographical succession lists of Church of Ireland clergy by the Rev J B Leslie; records of Church of Ireland societies; transcripts of archival material, eg (incomplete hearth money returns 1664–1766).

Author and subject cat on cards.

Newport Benjamin White, *The Watson Collection; prayer books and related liturgical works given by Edward John Macartney Watson... catalogue compiled by Newport B White.* Dublin: APCK, 1948. (op)

James Blennerhassett Leslie, *Catalogue of the manuscripts in possession of the Representative Church Body...*, Dublin, 1938. (op)

Royal College of Physicians of Ireland, 6 Kildare Street, Dublin 2. Tel (0001) 761041. Open Mon-Fri 10 am-1 pm, 2-5.30 pm. The library may be used only for research purposes on provision of a letter of introduction.

Sir Patrick Dun's Library (the general collection) The nucleus of the collection was the library of Sir Patrick Dun (1642–1713), physician and President of the College several times from 1681 until 1706. He bequeathed his books to the College in 1711. The original books belonging to Sir Patrick Dun cannot now be identified; it is probable that few have survived. The College subsequently added to the collection. In 1920 the library held 13,000 v and 186 v of pamphlets. The collection includes *c*250 v from the 17th cent, mainly continental printings, and *c*800 v from the 18th cent. Subjects covered are medicine and natural history.

Author cat on cards. 19th cent ms cats survive. The following cats were printed:

A catalogue of Sir Patrick Dun's Library. Dublin, 1794 (1,179 entries).

Thomas Herbert Orpen, *Catalogus librorum bibliothecae Patricii Dunn.* Dublin, 1828 (1,419 entries; supplement printed 1832 gives 325 additional entries).

T P C Kirkpatrick, 'Sir Patrick Dun's Library', *Dublin Journ of Medical Sci*, CXLIX 1920, p49-68 (reprinted *Papers of the Bibliographical Society of Ireland* I 5, 1918–20, and *Irish Book Lover* XVIII 4 1930, p105-117.

——'Dun's library in the Royal College of Physicians of Ireland', *Bulletin of the Medical Library Association* XXVI, 4, 1938.

Churchill Collection Presented to the RCPI in 1875 by Fleetwood Churchill (1808–78), obstetrician and medical writer. President of the College 1867–8. It totals 750 v, mainly on midwifery and diseases of children, printed 17th and mid-19th cent.

Author/title cat on cards.

Kirkpatrick Collection This represents the medical section of the working and collector's library of Thomas Percy Claude Kirkpatrick (1869–1954), physician, medical historian and bibliophile, Registrar of the RCPI 1903–53. It contains *c*1,200 v (and 3,000 pamphlets) and are mainly medical books, 18th-20th cent, mostly printed in Ireland.

Author and subject cats on cards.

Royal College of Surgeons in Ireland, St Stephen's Green, Dublin 2. Tel (0001) 780200. Open Mon-Fri 9 am-5.15 pm. Admission for research purposes on provision of a letter of introduction. Xerox copying facilities.

General Collection The College was chartered in 1784; books were acquired from 1788. Notable additions were: 1816—the library of the Physico-Chirurgical Society (1790–1816); 1871—the Arthur Jacob Collection, gift of Arthur Jacob (1790–1874), oculist, three times PRCSI. The library also holds books from the collection of Sir Thomas Molyneux (1661–1733), physician, PRCP 1702, 1709, 1713, 1720. The Collection contains 35,000 v including *c*100 16th cent, *c*220 17th cent items. 18th and 19th cent items have not been estimated; however, there were 14,000 books in the library in 1839. Subject coverage includes medicine, surgery, natural history. No incunabula; STC and Wing items not estimated. The library holds an early 15th cent ms of the *Practica* of John of Arderne.

Author cat on cards; cat of items of Irish interest on cards. A 19th cent ms cat survives.

Sir Charles A Cameron, *History of the Royal College of Surgeons in Ireland, and of the Irish schools of medicine*... Dublin: Fannin and Co; London: Bailliere, Tindall and Cox; Edinburgh: Maclachlan and Stewart, 1886, p267-74 (2nd ed revised and enlarged. Dublin: Fannin and Co; London: Simpkin, Marshall and Co; Edinburgh: James Thin, 1916, p316-24).

J D H Widdess, 'Medical libraries in the Republic of Ireland', *Libri*, 3 (1954), p81-7.

——'Practica magistri Johannis Arderne', *Irish Journ Medic Sci*, 6th ser No 207 (1943), p77-81.

Wheeler-Butcher Library The collection is made up of books donated by: Richard George Herbert Butcher (1819–91), surgeon; Sir William Ireland de Courcy Wheeler (1844–97) and William Ireland de Courcy Wheeler (1879–1943). There are 500 v covering medicine and surgery (18th and 19th cent printings), and 30 ms notebooks, including case-books of Butcher's.

The collection is included in the main library cat.

Royal Dublin Society, Ballsbridge, Dublin 4. Tel (0001) 690645. Bus routes 6, 6A, 7, 7A, 8, 45. Open Mon-Fri 10 am-7 pm; Sat 10 am-6 pm. Admission to non-members for research purposes only on written application. Xerox copying facilities.

The Dublin Society was founded in 1731, with the aim of 'improving husbandry, manufactures, and other useful arts'. Provision for a library was made in the same year. The Society was chartered in 1750. By 1826 there were 8,300 v in the library. In 1863 Jasper Robert Joly presented his collection to the library (see National Library of Ireland, Joly Collection). The majority of the Society's books were transferred in 1877 to the National Library of Ireland (qv). In 1889, the Society received the Tighe bequest, from the collection of Robert Tighe, and in 1905 the John Winter library bequeathed by Miss Anne Winter. The Portlock collection was transferred from the Geological Survey of Ireland during the 1930s.

The Tighe bequest (222 v) consists of pre-1800 editions of the classics, notably Horace. It includes Aldus, Dyson, Elzevir, Etienne and Baskerville printings, and some incunabula. Also some 15th and 16th cent mss. The Winter library consists mainly of literature, in early 19th cent London editions. The Portlock collection comprises mainly works on geology and natural history.

Author and subject sheaf cat of the library includes the Winter and Portlock collections.

Typed lists of the printed books and mss in the Tighe bequest.

Various early cats were printed: 1735–6, 1806, 1817, 1829.

Catalogue of the library of the Royal Dublin Society. Dublin. R Graisberry, 1839. (Reissued with supplements Dublin, M H Gill, 1850 and 1860.)

General catalogue of the library to June 1895, not including scientific periodicals and the publications of learned societies. Dublin, University Press, 1896. (Supplements issued 1900, 1905, 1910, 1915.)

Henry F Berry, *A history of the Royal Dublin Society*. London, Longmans, Green, 1915, p170-82. (Includes titles of books as they appeared in the original 1735–6 cat.)

Desmond J Clarke, 'The library of the Royal Dublin Society', *An leabharlann* 8 (1945), p135-40.

Terence de Vere White, *The story of the Royal Dublin Society*. Tralee, Kerryman Ltd, 1955, p135-40.

Royal Irish Academy, 19 Dawson Street, Dublin 2. Tel (0001) 762570, 764222. Open Mon-Fri 9.30 am-5.30 pm; Sat 9.30 am-1 pm (library closed 12.30-1.30 pm July, August, September; closed for three weeks in August). Non-members may use the library for research purposes if recommended by a member, or, if coming from overseas, at the discretion of the Librarian, and on provision of a letter of introduction or professional identification. Xeroxing facilities available; microfilming can be arranged. There is a microfilm reader, and also an ultraviolet ray lamp.

General Collection Made up by purchase and donation from the foundation of the Academy in 1785; many donations were made by founder and other members. It comprises 4,000 v pre-1851, including 2,000 v relating to Irish history, antiquarian studies, literature, travel, manners, customs. Other material includes 17th-18th cent religious books, 18th-19th cent collection of English literature, travel, description, and natural history. There are 8 incunabula; STC, Wing items not estimated. There are some maps, newspapers and journals, the latter principally the publications of academies in Britain and on the Continent of Europe, including Russia. There are continental and Irish bindings; 11 of the latter are described in Craig. Material of Irish interest is acquired on a regular basis. It is hoped to complete a collection of all works ever published by members of the Academy.

Dictionary cat on cards; maps, journals, newspapers, bindings listed separately. A ms cat of books to 1810 survives.

Catalogue of the Library, Royal Irish Academy House, Dublin. M Goodwin, 1822.

Caitlin Bonfield, *The Royal Irish Academy and its library: a brief description*, Dublin. (Dublin University Press), 1964 (2nd ed 1971) (op).

The Royal Irish Academy: a brief description. Dublin: the Academy, 1980.

C Bonfield and A Farrington, 'The library of the Royal Irish Academy', *An leabharlann*, 8(1941), p10-16.

Early scientific books and periodicals The collection includes the bequest of Dr Richard Kirwan, 1733–1812, chemist and philosopher, 2nd President of the Royal Irish Academy in 1799, and comprises *c*2,600 items, including the Kirwan Collection (1,204 items) which contain books and periodicals printed in Britain and on the Continent, 1654–1850; subjects covered are physics, chemistry, biology, mineralogy, botany, entomology and other aspects of natural history. The Kirwan Collection consists mainly of 18th cent books.

Included in the general RIA cat. There is also a typed author list of the Kirwan collection.

Haliday pamphlet and tract collections Collection of Charles Haliday (1789–1866), antiquary, public servant, philanthropist, MRIA 1847; donated by his widow in 1867. It consists of 2,209 v of pamphlets, 515 boxes of tracts (over 25,000 items). The pamphlets date from 1682–1859, the tracts from 1578–1859. Subjects covered include history, including social and economic history, political history, military history, ecclesiastical history; theology, education, literature, law, some medicine. (The tract collection was intended to accommodate the religious items, but this distinction was not rigidly observed.) The collections are mainly Irish printed, with some English and Scottish printings. STC, Wing items not estimated.

Ms cat in book form (compiled by John T Gilbert) in which items are listed by year, and within this, by subject. Recataloguing on cards is in progress. The collections are included in R D Collison Black, *A catalogue of pamphlets on economic subjects published between 1750 and 1900 and now housed in Irish libraries*. Belfast, Queen's University, 1969.

Thomas Moore's Library Part of the library of Thomas Moore, 1779–1852, poet; donated to the Royal Irish Academy in 1855 by his widow. It totals *c*2,000 items (including some volumes of pamphlets) which cover classics, belles-lettres, Irish and European history; Irish literature and archaeology; continental, British and Irish imprints, 16th-19th cent. Sales of the rest of Moore's manuscripts and books are recorded for 1853 and 1874; the catalogues are reprinted in *Sale catalogues of libraries of eminent persons*, v, IX, *Poets and men of letters*, ed Roy Park (London): Mansell with Sotheby Parke Bernet Publications, (1974), p289-498.

Author cat on cards; printed author cat in *Proceedings of the Royal Irish Academy* VI, 1853–7, App III, pxix-lx.

Manuscript Collection Built up by gift and purchase by members; purchase by the Academy; 156 Stowe mss were presented by the British Government; 227 mss were bought from Hodges Smith (publishers and booksellers). In all there are 2,500 items, including 1,431 mss in Irish. There are 30 mss pre-1600: Latin mss include the Psalter of St Columba (the Cathach), the Stowe missal, the Domnach Airgid; among the most important Irish vellums are the Book of Ballymote, the Book of Lecan, the Book of Fermoy, the Book of Hy-Many, the Leabhar Breac, the Leabhar na hUidre. Mss relating to Irish history include the Annals of the Four Masters (Michael, Conary and Cucoighriche O'Clery, and Fearfeasa O'Mulchonry), Ordnance Survey of Ireland memoirs, books of survey and distribution, Charles Gavan Duffy papers; mss relating to antiquarian studies include mss of John Windele, topographical drawings by George Petrie, William Frederick Wakeman, Gabriel Beranger and George Victor du Noyer; mss relating to natural history include Richard J Ussher's notes on birds, and papers of Alexander Goodman More and Charles Bethune Moffat; among family papers and deeds are the correspondence of James Caulfeild (sic), 1st Earl of Charlemont, correspondence of Marquis Patrice MacSwiney of Mashanglass, (*b*1871), papers of Henry Upton, and deeds of the Guild of St Anne (16th-17th cent).

Catalogue of the manuscripts in the Royal Irish Academy, fasc 1 [-28], Dublin. Royal Irish Academy,

Hodges Figgis, London: Williams and Northgate, 1926–70, with a general and first line index. There is a typescript list of non-Irish mss. Mss of Irish interest are listed in Hayes.

Caitlin Bonfield, 'Manuscript Irish music in the Library of the Royal Irish Academy', *Music in Ireland: a symposium*, ed by Aloys Fleischmann, Cork, Cork University Press. Oxford, Blackwell, 1952, p322-32.

Royal Society of Antiquaries of Ireland, 63 Merrion Square, Dublin 2. Tel (0001) 761749. Open Mon-Fri 2-5 pm. The library is open to non-members for research purposes. An appointment is advisable. Xeroxing can be arranged.

Library of the Royal Society of Antiquaries of Ireland The Society was founded in 1849 as the Kilkenny Archaeological Society. It had several changes of name and moved its headquarters to Dublin in the late 19th cent. The acquisition of books started with the founding of the Society; the Library was moved to Dublin in 1896. Notable bequests were the papers of Francis Elrington Ball, 1863–1829, historian and antiquary; and the papers of Lord Walter Fitzgerald, 1858–1923, soldier and antiquary, founder and editor of the *Co.Kildare Archaeological Society Journal.* The collection consists of *c*13,000 v, including 100 pre-1850 items. Subjects covered include archaeology, history, folklore, architecture, all with reference to Ireland; some maps and broadsides. Manuscripts include corporation books of Irish towns, especially from Co.Kilkenny; records of the Weavers' Guild of Dublin 1676–1840; archives of the RSAI from 1849 to the present (incomplete); a 13th cent illuminated Sarum missal; topographical drawings including 12 v of sketches by George Victor du Noyer and 1 v by George Miller; notebooks of Patrick Joseph O'Reilly (1854–1924), including transcripts of 1642 depositions, and 23 v of pedigrees of the O'Reilly's.

Author card cat of printed books; subject cat of books relating to Ireland. Handlist of ms. Some mss listed in Hayes.

William Cotter Stubbs, 'The Weavers' Guild, the Guild of the Blessed Virgin Mary, Dublin 1446–1840', *Journal of Roy Soc of Antiquaries of Ireland* XLIV, 1, 1919, p60-88.

Other groups of material are referred to or described in the *Journal of the Royal Society of Antiquaries of Ireland.*

St Mary's Priory, Tallaght, Co Dublin. Admission for research purposes only. Enquiries to be made in writing, in advance, to the Rev Librarian.

St Mary's Priory was established in 1855. The library was established then, and in 1866 received over 3,000 v from the Irish Dominican College of Corpo Santo, Lisbon. The collection has since been built up by purchase, donation and bequest, and includes *c*1,390 v pre-1851. Subject areas covered include philosophy, Bible studies, theology, church history, religious orders, some history, belles-lettres, classics. Books with Irish Catholic interest are being kept separately. Printings, mainly 16th-19th cent continental; some British and Irish 18th cent imprints. Many books in contemporary bindings. Two incunabula. STC and Wing items not estimated. The collection is being added to by the collection of older books from other Irish houses.

Virtually complete author cat on cards; partially complete subject cat on cards.

Dr Steevens' Hospital, Steevens' Lane, Dublin 8. Tel (0001) 772606. Open by special permission only. Admission for research purposes. Contact to be made through the Secretary, Dr Steevens' Hospital. Microfilming and xeroxing facilities can be arranged.

Dr Worth's Library Edward Worth (*c*1678–1733), physician and a founder of Dr Steevens's Hospital, bequeathed his books to the hospital in 1733 for the 'use, benefit and behoof of the physician and surgeon of the time being'. There are 4,500 v which include 21 incunabula, including 13 from the press of Aldus; STC and Wing items not estimated. Subjects covered are medicine, surgery, chemistry, botany, pure and applied mathematics, history, topography, antiquities, ancient classics, theology, some literature. The bindings on these books are superb examples of 17th cent French bookbinding, and are in mint condition. Former owners include the Baron de Longpierre, Jacques Auguste de Thou, Jean Baptist Colbert, Étienne Baluze, Jean Paul Bignon and Louis-Henri de Loménie, Comte de Brienne. Some of the books bound for the Brienne family have been attributed to the Abbé du Seuil. There is one Grolier binding, bound by Grolier's last binder. There are also a few examples of English Tudor and 18th cent Irish bindings.

There are three copies of a contemporary ms cat, one in the Worth Library, one in Marsh's Library and one in the Library of Trinity College, Dublin.

Robert Birley, 'The library of Louis-Henri de Loménie Comte de Brienne and the bindings of the Abbé du Seuil', *The Library*, ser 5, XVII, 2.

D W Cruickshank and E M Wilson, 'A Calderón collection in Dr Steevens' Hospital, Dublin', *Long Room* No 9, 1974, p17-27.

T P C Kirkpatrick, 'The Worth Library, Steevens' Hospital, Dublin', *Dublin Journal of medical science* CXLVII, 1919, p129-39 (reprinted *Papers of the Irish Bibliographical Society* I 3, 1918–20).

Muriel McCarthy, 'Dr Edward Worth's Library in Dr Stephens' [sic] Hospital', *Journal of the Irish Colleges of Physicians and Surgeons*, 6 (1977).

Trinity College Library, University of Dublin, College Street, Dublin 2. Tel (0001) 772941 Ext 1172. Open Mon-Thurs 10 am-10 pm, Fri 10 am-5 pm; Sat 10 am-1 pm. For approximately two months, mid-June—mid-August, the library closes at 5 pm, and is closed completely for the first two weeks of July. Admission by a temporary ticket which can be issued to any reader who requires material not available in the National or Dublin public libraries on presenting a letter of recommendation from a university or other recognized institution. Reference collection of books on historical and analytical bibliography, etc on open shelves in the Department's Reading Room. Microfilm and microfiche readers available. Copying by microfilm and photography. Limited photocopying service for modern books only.

General holdings up to 1850 The University of Dublin was founded in 1591 as a means of planting 'religion, civilitie and true obedience in the hearts of this people'. The power of the English crown was to be established over the whole of Ireland through the conversion of the natives to Anglican Protestantism, English law and civilization. Serious buying for the library started in 1601 and nearly 5,000 books were acquired in the next few years. The first major collection, however, came only in 1661 with the 10,000 books and mss of Archbishop James Ussher's Library. Two other minor gifts were received as named collections in the later 17th cent, those of the Countess of Bath and the law books of Sir Alexander Jerome. The present library building was begun in 1712 and finished in 1730, and its magnificent proportions generated two further major bequests in the libraries of Archbishop William Palliser (4,000 v in 1726) and Bishop Claudius Gilbert (13,000 v) ten years later. The library of Greffier Fagel, Chief Minister of Holland, (20,000 v) was purchased for the college in 1802. After the Union, the Copyright Act of 1801 allowed the library the privilege of claiming one copy of any book published in Great Britain and Ireland; during the first decades of the century accessions from this source were not great, but coverage later improved considerably. 19th and 20th cent acquisitions merged in the general collection include the Aiken Irvine Collection (largely 16th and 17th cent continental theology and literature), the late 18th and early 19th cent pamphlets relating to Ireland of Chief Justice Charles Kendal Bushe, small collections of German reformation pamphlets, English Commonwealth Tracts, Irish 19th cent street ballads, and the major part of an extensive country house library, Townley Hall, built up in the 18th cent.

The following figures are for the library's total holdings, and thus include all the collections that are separately described. They are based on sampling methods used in the LOC project, but are less reliable and must be considered merely as informed guesses, and are included here only to give some idea of the general scale of the holdings: 550 incunabula; 2,850 STC; 9,500 1501–1600 (continental); 14,000 1601–1700 (continental); 10,500 Wing; 24,000 (British and Irish); 8,500 1701–1800 (continental).

This is a general working library built up since 1600 for the scholarly purposes of a university. Bearing in mind the chief reasons for the founding of the college, and also that the collection's greatest strength lies in 17th cent material, theology, religious controversy, Biblical commentary etc are probably the subjects best represented, but it should be stressed that the subject coverage is general. Up to the end of the 19th cent amongst the least collected books were works of fiction. Current book selection aims at strengthening the holdings of books printed in Ireland and of works by Irish writers.

All special collections, as well as general holdings, are included in the general catalogues of the library:

Holdings up to Dec 1872: Catalogus librorum impressorum qui in Bibliotheca Collegii Sacrosanctae et Individuae Trinitatis...juxta Dublin, adservantur. Dublinii: e Typographeo Academico, 1864–87. 9 v (v9: Supplement) (op) (Apparently available on microfilm from piratical American firm).

Accessions 1873–1963: MS guardbook cat (microfilm copy available in Old Library Reading Room).

Accessions 1963 to date: Card cats: author and separate dictionary-type subject.

Since 1968 the following special card files have been generated for all material catalogued by the Department of Early Printed Books:

Separate author cats of special collections; Imprint date, arranged under country for all books to 1800, British books to 1900, and Irish books to present date; Imprint names, arranged under country; Separate files for information on: paper, illustrations, binding, provenance.

Catalogue of 15th century books in the library of Trinity College, Dublin, and in Marsh's Library, Dublin... by T K Abbott. Dublin: Hodges Figgis, London: Longmans, Green, 1905. (Reprinted New York: B Franklin, 1970, Burt Franklin bibliography and reference series, 360.) (NB Many printer and date attributions are now misleading.)

Catalogus librorum in Bibliothecae Collegii Sanctae et Individuae Trinitatis Reginae Elizabethae juxta Dublin. Dublinii: typis et impensis Johannis Hyde, (*c*1715?).

(Later printed cat (1864–87) is main working cat of collection—see above.)

H W Parke, *The library of Trinity College, Dublin: a historical description*. Dublin, 1959. [op] but a revision is in course of preparation.

Anthony Hobson, *Great libraries*. London: Weidenfeld and Nicolson, 1970, pp174-85.

Friends of the Library of Trinity College, Dublin: *Annual bulletin*, 1946–58, 13 numbers. (Contains brief articles and notes on current acquisitions of early printed books and on the library's history [op].)

Long Room: bulletin of the Friends of Trinity College Library, 1970– Theoretically issued twice a year, but now appears annually; latest numbered 19. A more substantial publication than the earlier *Bulletin* containing bibliographical and literary articles, including some on the library itself or on its books. Alternate issues carry lists of selected acquisitions by the Department of Early Printed Books and by the Department of Manuscripts. Later issues in print.

John Kells Ingram, *The library of Trinity College, Dublin*: an address delivered at the 7th annual meeting of the Library Association of the United Kingdom, 1884. London, 1886. [op]

Bender Collection Presented in 1932 in memory of his father by Albert Maurice Bender, a wealthy American businessman, it comprises *c*495 items, including approximately 40 broadsheets and single folds. It contains books from private presses, mainly at work during the years 1920–50, in California. Presses represented include: the Grabhorn, the John Henry Nash, the Helen Gentry, the Primavera, the Windsor and the presses of Mills College and Stanford University. Material was added from 1932–*c*54.

Catalogued in general cat.

Bibliotheca Earberiana (commonly known as the Crofton Collection) The pamphlets from the library of Christopher Henry Earbery (1764–*c*1811) of Dublin; on his death his estates went to his sisters, one of whom, Marcia Anastasia, married the Rev Henry William Crofton of Inchinappa, Co Wicklow. Presented by Miss A Crofton in 1955, the collection contains *c*2,000 items in 200 v, mostly 18th cent Dublin and London imprints with perhaps 10% from the 17th cent (Wing) and a few STC items. Subject emphasis on politics and economics, especially Irish.

Catalogued in general cat, with a separate typescript author list.

'The Crofton pamphlets' (a brief report with three facsimile title-pages), *Annual bulletin of Friends of the Library of Trinity College*, Dublin, p14-18.

Bibliotheca Quiniana (Quin Collection) The collection of Henry George Quin (1760–1805) bequeathed by him to Trinity College. Quin was a noted collector; he travelled widely on the continent and bought at auctions there as well as in Ireland and England. His purchases at the Crevenna sale earned him a present of the auctioneer's hammer which is still with the collection. It consists of 110 titles in 156 v. Originally 127 works, of which 14 were culled by Quin himself, and 3 were not present when the collection came to the library. The library is a miscellaneous but highly select collection of rare copies of early continental printings in fine bindings, chiefly consisting of works of classical and Italian literature. The books are arranged in their original bookcase in the order (chronologically by date of purchase) laid down by Quin. They include 16 incunabula and some notable bindings. Various works from Quin's general library have been added from time to time, including many of his sale catalogues (Crevenna, Gouttard, La Vallière, etc), and the second volume of his 'travelling diary' (housed in the Dept of Mss).

Catalogued in general (printed) cat.

Quin's own holograph cat, numbered in order of acquisition, with notes on prices, provenance and any outstanding features.

V M R Morrow, 'Bibliotheca Quiniana: a description of the books and bindings in the Quin Collection'. Unpublished thesis for Diploma in Librarianship, University College, London, 1970. Typescript. (A descriptive cat, in Quin's shelf order, of the bindings.)

T P C Kirkpatrick, 'Bibliotheca Quiniana', Friends of the Library of Trinity College: *Annual Bulletin*, 1946, p6-7.

Arthur Rau, 'Portrait of a bibliophile, XII: Henry George Quin, 1760–1805', *Book Collector*, 13 (1964), p449-62, illus.

Bonaparte-Wyse Collection Formerly part of the library of William Charles Bonaparte-Wyse, and acquired by Trinity College in 1942, for the French Department and deposited in the library *c*1969. It contains *c*1,250 v, and consists almost entirely of Provencal and Catalan literature of the second half of the 19th cent, mostly published in Provence. Many of the works were given to the collector by the authors, and there are 40 works written by Bonaparte-Wyse himself, with some issues of periodicals containing his contributions. (The Bonaparte-Wyse library was dispersed before this portion of it was given to the Trinity College Library.)

Catalogued in general (card) cat. Author list available in provenance file.

Lilian Mina Kelly, 'French texts in the Library of Trinity College, Dublin: the Bonaparte-Wyse Collection', *Hermathena*, 121 (1976), p117-20.

Eighteenth century drama collection Based on the general stock of the library, but very largely purchased 1964–80, with the small collection bought from J Barry Brown. It contains *c*2,100 items, of which perhaps 1,000 were printed in Ireland. Subject emphasis on editions of works by Irish authors, and Irish printed editions. There are *c*50 late 18th cent playbills for Dublin and New Ross, and some contemporary histories and memoirs. Frequent additions are made by purchase.

Catalogued in general cat; in process of recataloguing to card cat, with form entries (Irish drama, English drama etc) providing the only separate list of the collection.

Fagel Collection Five generations of the wealthy family of Fagel built up their library in Holland from the late 17th to the end of the 18th cent. During most of this time members of the family held high ministerial office in the Netherlands, and when Holland was overrun by the French in 1794–5, Henry Fagel's property was sequestrated. However, he eventually managed to get his library out of the country, and by 1798 negotiations were afoot for the purchase of the library for Trinity College. The deal was not clinched until 1802, after a sale catalogue had been published by the auctioneer John Christie. The collection comprises *c*20,000 items, and may be described as a general library with some emphasis on all aspects of history and politics (French and Dutch), and including notable collections of natural history, atlases, architectural books and maps. The languages best represented are Latin and French, but there are also considerable numbers of English language books with possibly some 1,500 18th cent titles. The collection includes five incunabula.

Catalogued in general (printed) cat.

'Catalogue of the Fagel Collection of maps, plans, etc', in *Catalogue of the manuscripts in the Library of Trinity College, Dublin*, compiled T K Abbott, Dublin: Hodges Figgis, 1900. . ., p438-529.

The original auction cat: *Bibliotheca Fageliana. A catalogue of the. . .Library of the Greffier Fagel. . . which will be sold by Mr Christie. . .March 1, 1802.* (London). Printed by Barker and Son, 1802, xii, 490p. (Copy with TCD classmarks in Department.)

R B McDowell, 'The acquisition of the Fagel Library', *Annual Bulletin of the Friends of the Library of TCD*, 2 (1947), p5-6.

Leendert Brummel, *Miscellanea Libraria*. . .,s Gravenhage: Martinus Nijhoff, 1957. (Chapter on Fagel Library), pp204-233.

J.-P Pittion, 'French texts in the library of TCD: The Fagel Collection', *Hermathena*, 121 (1976), p108-16.

Note: Not all items listed in Sale Catalogue 1802 came to TCD. Duplicates from the Library were sold in Holland in 1792. State papers from the Library were sold by auction in The Hague, 1803.

Library of the College Historical Society The collection is what remains of the library of the Society, founded 1770. It contains *c*350 v. The emphasis is on Philosophy, History and 'polite literature' as well as works relating to the operation of the Society, Auditors' speeches etc. It includes 11 Wing and over 200 18th cent items.

Catalogued in general (card) cat. Author listing in Provenance file.

The Michael Freyer Dolmen Press Collection A collection of all Dolmen Press publications and printings in various formats made by Michael Freyer from 1951 to 1973. The printing press was in operation from 1951 to 1979; the name Dolmen Press now continues as a publishing house only. The collection was purchased by Trinity College in 1979 to augment an extensive run of Dolmen Press publications already acquired both by copyright and purchase. Photocopies of some archival material (limited access) is also included. There are *c*446 items, with some proofs and complete set of ballad sheets; posters; greeting cards; postcards; prospectuses; exhibition catalogues; theatre programmes etc. Included are *c*346 Dolmen Press publications and 100 private printings. The collection contains copies of every publication in every format, with the exception of one item and a few reprints or reissues. There are several unrecorded or discarded publications. Additions will be made where possible for the years 1973–79.

Catalogued in general (card) cat. Michael Freyer's bibliography consisting of (a) publications and (b) printings in chronological order, giving bibliographical descriptions of different formats.

Dolmen XXV: an illustrated bibliography of the Dolmen Press, 1951–1976, compiled by Liam Miller. Dublin, Dolmen Press, 1976.

Michael Freyer, 'The Dolmen Press: a talk given to the Bibliographical Society of Ireland', *Private Library*, 8 (1960), p10-14.

Purser Shortt Collection Bequest of the Rev Canon John Purser Shortt, 1966. It consists of *c*900 items, including 160 pamphlets made up of Liturgies (mainly Anglican, including 240 Books of Common Prayer, with a few editions of liturgies of other churches), psalters, hymnals and other religious works. The collection contains *c*230 pre-1850 items—mainly 18th cent—one-third of which are Irish imprints; the rest mainly English with a very few continental imprints. There are some 6 18th cent Irish and English fine bindings.

Catalogued in general (card) cat. Author list available in Provenance file.

Sáirséal agus Dill Collection Presented to the library in 1969 by the Ó hÉigeartaigh family in memory of Seán Ó hÉigeartaigh, founder in 1944 of the firm of Sáirséal agus Dill, publishers of books in Irish. It contains 161 titles in 293 items. All publications of the firm of Sáirséal agus Dill; this includes all new editions, re-issues, variants (whether of text, binding or layout). The books consist chiefly of fiction, poetry, biographies, children's books and school books. All are in the Irish language.

Catalogued in general (card) cat of the Department. Author list available in Provenance file.

Note on 'The Sáirséal agus Dill collection', *Long Room*, 1 (1970), p43 (Note).

Starkey Collection Bequeathed by James Sullivan Starkey, 1959, it contains 380 items in 250 v. This is a collection of Hymnals and Psalters from the 18th and 19th cent. There are *c*314 pre-1850 items and 66 post-1850 items. The Wesleys are very well represented (47 v); there are *c*25 v of the Moravian Church and 50 other Hymnals in the German language. It includes 2 Wing items only.

Catalogued in general cat. Also separate typescript cat in Department.

Yeats Collection Private library of Elizabeth Corbet Yeats, 1868–1940, founder of the Dun Emer Press which later became the Cuala Press. The collection was bequeathed to Trinity Hall in 1940; transferred for safe keeping to TCD Library in 1968. It contains 194 books, including 29 periodicals, 90 theatre programmes, and 46 pamphlets. The collection consists of 19th and early 20th cent Anglo-Irish literature including items by W B Yeats, some annotated by him, and an almost complete collection of works printed at the Dun Emer and Cuala Press.

Catalogued in general (card) cat. Author list available in Provenance file.

University College Main Library, Belfield, Dublin 4. Tel (0001) 693244. Open (Special Collections) Mon-Fri 9.30 am-1 pm, 2.30-5.30 pm. Admission for research purposes. Enquiries about manuscripts to be made in writing. Xeroxing (undertaken when items will not be damaged); microfilm reader/printer; microfilming; photography can be arranged.

Special Collections Built up by purchase, donation and bequest since the establishment of the University College as part of the National University of Ireland in 1909. Holdings include books from the collections of former teachers in the College, and from the libraries of: Heinrich Zimmer (1851–1910); Celtic scholar Colm Ó Lochlainn (*d*1972); printer, binder and bibliophile Francis O'Kelley (*d*1950); historian and bibliophile the Right Hon Christopher Palles (1831–1920); Chief Baron of the Exchequer the Very Rev Patrick Canon Power (1862–1951); local historian the Right Hon Michael Francis Cox (1852–1924); Constantine Peter Curran.

The collection contains *c*25,000 v (including the library of the Catholic University of Ireland, qv). Subject coverage of the general collection is diverse, with no special concentration. The Zimmer library consists mainly of Celtica, and includes a section of 19th cent ephemera, principally devotional literature, folklore and language study. The Ó Lochlainn collection includes Irish printings and music printings; emphasis is on material of Irish interest and devotional literature. The collection includes 24 v of mss, mostly Irish language prose and poetry (listed in Hayes). The O'Kelley collection includes 17th-19th cent Irish printings and British printings of Irish interest, with emphasis on history, local history and history of printing, bookselling and publishing. The Chief Baron Palles library consists of legal material (and forms part of the Law and Official Publications Section of the Library). The Curran collection includes some James Joyce first editions, editions of the writers of the Irish literary revival, and mss of the literary revival and of Irish nationalism (listed in Hayes). The pamphlet collection includes 4,000 items printed before 1851, chiefly on Irish historical, political, economic and religious affairs, but including some literature. There are 3 incunabula; *c*35 STC; 200 Wing items (from all collections including the CUI Library) have been recorded. The Ó Lochlainn collection contains a group of fine bindings, of which 8 18th cent Irish bindings are listed in Craig.

Short-title cat on cards in progress; index maintained of printers and booksellers in pre-1801 imprints. Full cataloguing projected on completion of short-title listing, to include full bibliographical details, and files for subjects, printers, booksellers, chronology, provenance, etc.

Library of the Catholic University of Ireland The Catholic University of Ireland was estabished in 1854 by the Bishops of Ireland, 'to keep alive in our country the spirit of faith, while cultivating to their utmost development the several branches of knowledge'. The University did not, however, receive a charter. In 1882–3 it was put in the charge of the Jesuit Fathers, and affiliated to the Royal University of Ireland. The collection, built up during the thirty years of the Catholic University's existence, includes the libraries of the Most Rev Joseph Dixon, 1806–66, Archbishop of Armagh; the Most Rev Daniel Murray, 1768–1852, Archbishop of Dublin; the Very Rev Dr Flanagan, PP, and items from the library of Eugene O'Curry, 1796–1863, Irish scholar. The CUI Medical School formerly held the Munich medical library, a collection of 5,000 v built up over 150 years and completed by Dr Johann von Ringseis, 1785–1880, Rector of the University of Munich. The CUI library was kept in store from 1882 until 1909, when it was transferred to University College after the institution of the National University of Ireland. The collection has not been kept distinct, but volumes are identifiable by marks of ownership. Part of the collection is now in the library of St Patrick's College, Maynooth; The Munich medical library is no longer held, and its present location is not known.

The library's stock of 17,000 v covers theology, Bible studies, church history, devotional literature, mainly in continental printings 16th-18th cent; history; Irish history, archaeology and language; classics; literature; some oriental language items. There are 3 incunabula. (For STC, Wing estimates, see previous entry for Special Collections.)

The guard book cat of the CUI library is extant in three v (entries are alphabetical within broad subject divisions).

University College Dublin, Department of Irish Folklore, Belfield, Dublin 4. Tel (0001) 693244 Ext 8327. Open Mon, Tues, Thurs, Fri 2.30-5.30 pm. Closure during August. (Confirmation of opening times should be sought on applying to use the library.) Admission for research purposes on application, in writing. Reading facilities will be granted at the discretion of the Head of Department. If the material required is available elsewhere, facilities will only be granted in exceptional cases.

The Irish Folklore Institute was established in 1930; it was replaced by the Irish Folklore Commission in 1935. In 1971 the Commission became the Department of Irish Folklore, University College Dublin. The library has been built up by purchase and donation since 1930. Notable former owners include Séamus Ó Casaide, ?1878–1943 (music printing), Sir William Alexander Craigie 1867–1957, Carl Wilhelm von Sydow, 1878–1952, and Dr Francis Stephen K Bourke (*d*1959), physician and bibliophile. The library consists of 25,000 v (including journal runs), of which 6,000 v are pre-1851, including 80 v of pamphlets. The library serves as a research aid to use of the national folklore archive housed in the department. Its principal strength is in Irish folk narrative, folk life, material, economic and social tradition, folk belief and custom. It includes Celtic, European and other folklore material also. Books printed pre-1851 include Irish history, with a contemporary section on the Rising of 1789; travel and topography; Irish novels of the 19th cent; *c*50 chapbooks; some sheet music; some classical authors. There are 80 v of 18th-19th cent pamphlets of Irish interest. There are three incunabula. Wing and STC items have not been estimated. A collection of plays, poetry and literature, mainly of Irish interest, as yet uncatalogued, includes material printed pre-1851.

Author cat on cards. Some progress made on subject cat.

Note On Dublin libraries see also, *Guide to collections in Dublin libraries: printed books to 1850 and special collections*, ed by Norma R Jessop...and Christine J Nudds...Dublin, 1982. (Ed)

Kilkenny

St Canice's Library, Kilkenny, Ireland. Tel (056) 21633. Admission by arrangement with the Librarian. No special facilities.

St Canice's Library Founded in 1693 by Bishop Otway, who bequeathed his own collection to it. The most important subsequent addition was the bequest of Bishop Maurice in 1756. There are *c*3,000 v with theology and classics the chief subject areas, but many general subjects are also covered, including history, philosophy, science, and especially literature, French and Italian as well as English. The majority of the items, *c*1,700, are from the 17th cent, 900 18th cent, 300 16th cent, and 4 incunabula. The library is particularly strong in continental printing, and there are few works dating from later than the first three decades of the 18th cent.

Recent card author cat from which a typescript cat is being prepared. Manuscript author catalogue of 1895. Manuscript subject index to authors (excluding theology and classics).

Maura Tallon, 'Church of Ireland diocesan libraries', *An leabharlann*, 17 (1959), 52.

'St Canice's Library is 300 years old' (report of talk by Rev A M Jackson in 1959), *Old Kilkenny Review*, 22 (1970), p5-10; 23 (1971), p15-22.

Limerick

Limerick City Library, Pery Square, Limerick, Ireland. Tel (061) 44668. Open Mon-Wed 10 am-1 pm, 2.30-6 pm; Thurs, Fri 10 am-1 pm, 2.30-5.30 pm; Sat 10 am-1 pm. No restrictions on admission. Microform readers and photocopying facilities.

Reference and Local History Library Built up by the Library since its foundation in 1893. Many of the pre-1851 items came from an earlier bequest of books to the City of Limerick by George Geary Bennis. Material printed pre-1851 includes *c*460 books (125 of these in the Local History section), 3 local newspaper titles comprising 8 complete years, and 9 journal titles comprising 37 v. The majority of the books are on history and topography (including church history and economic history), with some on literature and the arts, including Irish music. Most are 19th cent, with some 90 from the 18th cent, and a handful of earlier items. The newspapers and journals are 19th cent. Many of the items in the Local History section were printed in Limerick.

Card cat with author and classified sequences. A short classified booklist of the Library as it was in 1940 is included in the article below.

Robert Herbert, 'The City of Limerick Public Library and Museum', *North Munster Antiquarian Journal*, 1940.

Maynooth

St Patrick's College, Maynooth, Co Kildare. Tel 286261/286101. Open Mon-Sat 9 am-9.30 pm; Sun 2-9 pm. Admission normally restricted to staff and students of the College; bona fide research workers admitted, but prior application to Deputy Librarian is imperative. Xeroxing available; microfilm reader/printer also available.

Maynooth College Library College founded in 1795 as an institution of higher education for Roman Catholics. Functioned purely as a seminary for secular clergy 1817–1968, but now admits lay students. A recognized college of the National University of Ireland. The College is a pontifical University. The Library's foundation collection was the private library, *c*3,000 v, mainly of religious material, of the first librarian, Rev Andrew Dunne. Other important acquisitions were the library of Dr Bartholomew Crotty, Bp of Cloyne, 1840; the mss of Dr John Murphy, Bp of Cork, *c*1847; the collection of classical authors presented by Edmund Burke in memory of his son, *c*1826*; the mss of Dr Laurence Renehan, 1857; part of the library of the Catholic University (including the mss of Eugene O'Curry), *c*1909; the Archives of the Irish College in Salamanca, 1953. The library contains *c*40,000 v, including *c*10,000 individual pamphlets and 200 v of mss. Main subject fields are scripture, theology, canon law, church history, philosophy, natural sciences, ancient classics. Pamphlets mainly concerned with religious affairs. Imprints are mainly continental European, and Irish. There are 50 incunabula. Much of the early printed material in original bindings; some volumes have fine ornate bindings.

*Richard Burke died, 1794, and his father Edmund in 1797. However, the Burke donation does not appear to have been recorded until 1826.

Mss comprise Irish language (Murphy, O'Curry and Renehan collections), Latin and French material, 13th-20th cent.

The printed material has an author card cat; and a separate author card cat of the pamphlet collection and of the material printed in Ireland before 1800. Mss of Irish interest are listed in Hayes.

J Healy, *Maynooth College, its centenary history*. Dublin, 1895, p645 ff. (op)

D Meehan, *Window on Maynooth*. Dublin, 1949, p123 ff. (op)

T Roche, 'Note on the Bishop Murphy mss', *Irish Book Lover*, 3, 1912, p181.

S Corkery, 'Maynooth College Library', *An leabharlann*, 14, ii, 1956, p51 ff.

Waterford

Waterford Cathedral Library. Tel (051) 74119. Admission by arrangement with the Dean of Waterford.
Note: The library is housed in the Cathedral, which is being renovated, so that in effect the books are unavailable and likely to remain so for some time.

Waterford Cathedral Library The library was formed when Charles Este, Bishop of Waterford, bequeathed his collection of books in 1745. There were subsequent additions from various benefactors. The collection totals *c*2,000 v, the main subjects being theology and law. There is an interesting collection of Bibles in several languages and special editions, and of Bible commentaries, including a series of Calvin's commentaries. Many of the books on law, both treatises and reports of cases, are from the 18th cent. There are *c*750 items from each of the 18th and 19th cent; 330 17th cent; 34 16th cent.

Typescript author cat, available in the Representative Church Body Library, Dublin.

Maura Tallon, 'Church of Ireland diocesan libraries', *An leabharlann*, 17 (1959), p55-6.

SCOTLAND

Aberdeen

Aberdeen Art Gallery and Museums. James McBey Memorial Print Room and Art Gallery, Schoolhill, Aberdeen AB9 1FQ. Tel (0224) 26333. Open to the public for reference use only on request, Mon-Fri 10 am-12 noon, 2-4 pm.

This is the working library of the Art Gallery and Museum, and has been developed since the present accommodation was provided by the widow of James McBey in 1960. It contains *c*5,000 books, 3,000 exhibition catalogues, mainly British and American, and 20,000 35 mm slides. The whole field of art is covered, with emphasis on 20th cent British work. There is a special collection of *c*200 books that belonged to James McBey (1883–1959), etcher and artist, presented in 1960 by his widow.

Card cat.

Aberdeen College of Education Library, Hilton Place, Aberdeen AB9 1FA. Tel (0224) 42341 Ext 221. Open (Term) Mon-Fri 9 am-9.30 pm; Sat 9.30 am-12.30 pm; (Vacation) Mon-Fri 9 am-5.15 pm. Reference and study facilities available to all bona fide students, teachers, research workers. Photocopier, typewriters, microform readers, bibliographical assistance.

Local History Collection Begun as a separate collection in the early 1970s, and developed rapidly during 1978–80. *c*500 items, mainly on the history of Aberdeen and Grampian Region. Only certain items in the collection are rare: *c*40 pre-1851 v; *c*250 locally printed items; a few limited editions and private press books.

Author and classified entries for all titles in Main Library cat.

Aberdeen Grammar School, Skene Street, Aberdeen AB9 1HT. Tel (0224) 22299. Open Mon-Fri 9 am-5 pm. Admission for reference only by arrangement with the Rector. Photocopying facilities.

The school dates from the 15th cent. The collection of *c*230 v printed before 1850 has been acquired mainly by donation. It includes 7 STC v and 54 foreign v of the same period; 41 Wing v and 15 v of the same period; 94 v published between 1700 and 1850. It is a general collection with emphasis on Latin language, classical and other literature, religion and education. There are also *c*20 ms v of magazines, Latin versions and account books.

Card cat.

'A short-title catalogue of books printed on the Continent of Europe, 1501–1600, in Aberdeen Grammar School', Supplement to *A short-title catalogue of books printed on the Continent of Europe, 1501–1600 in Aberdeen University Library*, compiled by H J H Drummond, Aberdeen University Studies No 156, OUP, 1979.

Aberdeen University Library, King's College, Aberdeen AB9 2UB. Tel (0224) 40241. Open Mon-Fri 9.15 am-4.45 pm to bona fide researchers. Photocopying facilities.

π *and SB Collection* King's College, founded in 1495, and Marischal College, founded in 1593, were separate and distinct universities until the 'fusion' in 1860. Each had its own library, and each attracted gifts and bequests of books over the centuries. The collection amounts to *c*50,000 v of all books, wherever printed, from 1501–1800 (and from 1501–1860 in the case of books on medicine and science). It is rich in religion, early medicine, science and classics. Pre-eminent in the collection are two copies each of the first two editions of Copernicus *De revolutionibus* (1543 and 1566) with unique annotations by Duncan Liddel, Professor of Mathematics at Helmstadt.

Sheaf binder cat available; books arranged by Dewey.

H J H Drummond, *A short-title catalogue of books printed on the continent of Europe 1501–1600 in Aberdeen University Library*, 1979.

Incunabula Collection This consists of 231 v, many associated with early teachers and benefactors of the University, including William Elphinstone, 1431–1514, Bishop of Aberdeen and founder of King's College, and Hector Boece, *c*1465–1536, first Principal of King's College.

William S Mitchell, *Catalogue of the incunabula in Aberdeen University Library*, 1968.

Bibliotheck of Kirkwall William Baikie, *c*1638–83, proprietor of the estate of Holland on Stronsay in Orkney bequeathed this collection of *c*300 v 'to the ministers of Kirkwall successivelie for a Publick Liberarie to be keept within the town of Kirkwall'. It was presented to the University Library in 1914. The books are largely theological, but many illustrate academic history at home and abroad. The collection contains several printed theses of the Aberdeen Universities which are unknown elsewhere.

J B Craven, *Descriptive catalogue of the Bibliotheck Kirkwall*, 1897.

Paul Kaufman, 'Discovering the oldest public bibliotheck in the Northern Isles', *Library Review*, 23, 1972, p285 f.

Biesenthal Collection Purchased from Biesenthal, a noted Rabbinist, in 1872 by William Robertson Smith, Prof of Oriental Languages and Exegesis of the Old Testament in the Free Church College, Aberdeen, the collection contains *c*2,000 v which represent a comprehensive selection of all that was published in Hebrew from the invention of printing to 1872 (the date of the sale of the collection).

A catalogue of the Hebrew books in the Biesenthal Collection, 1979, by D R G Beattie is available.

See also D R G Beattie 'Dr Biesenthal and the Biesenthal Collection' in *Aberdeen University Review*, 45, 1973–4, p275-80.

Chapman Collection The nucleus of this collection was acquired in 1963 from the widow of John Bisset Chapman (MA Aberdeen, 1897), Inspector of Schools in London. It consists of *c*1,000 v (to which additions are still being made) containing the first and special editions of literary authors of the first three decades of the 20th cent, eg Bates, Blunden, Coppard, De La Mare, Graves, Huxley, Powys, Sassoon, Woolf, many of which are signed or inscribed by the authors. Many private presses represented.

Sheaf binder cat.

Diocesan Library A collection of *c*3,000 v belonging to the Synod of Aberdeen and Orkney, deposited in 1926. It is strong in theological material (mostly 18th and 19th cent), and particularly rich in material relating to the Scottish Episcopal Church.

Catalogue of the Aberdeen Diocesan Library, 1871; *Aberdeen Diocesan Library Catalogue*, 1889.

Gregory Collection Consisting of *c*2,000 books, the bulk of the collection belonged to different members of the distinguished Gregory family, notably to John Gregory (1724–73), MD, FRS, Mediciner at King's College, Aberdeen, and later Prof of Medicine at Edinburgh University. Most of the books, which span the 16th to 19th cent, are on scientific and medical subjects, the remainder dealing mainly with philosophy, religion, literature and history.

Sheaf binder cat.

A full account of the Gregory family and an analysis of the collection are given in P D Lawrence, *The Gregory Family*, unpublished PhD thesis, Aberdeen, 1971.

Henderson Collection Alexander Henderson of Caskieben (*d*1863 aged 83) alumnus of Marischal College 1794–8, and MD Edinburgh 1803, bequeathed his books (*c*3,000) and a collection of objets d'art to the University of Aberdeen. The books are mainly of the period 1750–1850, and consist largely of general literature, history, travel, science and medicine.

MS shelf cat.

A brief memoir of Henderson appears in [W M Ramsay] *Descriptive notes on the classical vases in the Henderson Collection, Marischal College, Aberdeen*, 1881.

Herald Pamphlets Based on a collection belonging to the *Aberdeen Herald* newspaper office (1832–72). There are 173 v on a wide range of subjects.

Aberdeen University Library, *Catalogue of pamphlets in the King, the Thomson and the Herald collections*, 1927.

Juvenile Collection Presented to the library in 1953 by Prof A A Jack, it consists of *c*400 v, mainly English language, of the Victorian era. The following well-known authors are represented—Maria Edgworth, Juliana Horatia Ewing, Kate Greenaway, Andrew Lang, George Macdonald and Charlotte Mary Yonge.

Sheaf binder cat alphabetically by author.

King Pamphlets Collected by George King (1797–1872), bookseller and printer in Aberdeen from 1826, the collection contains *c*4,000 items (in 405 v) on miscellaneous topics, but particularly strong in theological literature of the 17th-19th cent and in local literature.

Aberdeen University Library *Catalogue of pamphlets in the King, the Thomson and Herald Collections*, 1927.

Alexander Keith, *Aberdeen University Press...from 1840 until...1963*, Aberdeen, 1963. (Chapter 2 gives an account of King.)

MacBean Collection Donated in 1918 by William M MacBean of Yonkers, New York, a native of Nairn. It contains *c*3,500 books; *c*1,000 pamphlets and sermons; *c*100 broadsides, and is one of the most extensive and important collections of Stuart and Jacobite material in the country. Additions, both antiquarian and modern, continue to be made to the collection.

Mabel D Allardice, *Aberdeen University Library MacBean Collection...*, 1949.

Meldrum House Collection Presented in 1951 by Sir Garden Duff of Hatton and Meldrum, it is a collection of *c*2,000 v which has been kept together as an example of the type of library found in large country houses in the area. It is a general collection mainly in the fields of history, literature, philosophy, religion, science and law, most of the books dating from the 18th and early 19th cent.

Sheaf binder cat.

Melvin Collection This collection of *c*7,000 v belonged to Dr James Melvin, 1795–1853, AM, Marischal College 1813, LLD, 1834, Rector of Aberdeen Grammar School, 1826–53. It is rich in editions of Latin and Greek classical writers and works relating to Latin language and literature. Medieval Latin is well represented. There is a substantial number of works on Scottish history and literature, and of theological and philosophical works of the Reformation and Pre-Reformation periods.

Ms shelf register.

David Masson, *James Melvin, Rector of the Grammar School of Aberdeen, 1895.*

Simpson Collection Bequeathed by Dr W Douglas Simpson, 1896–1968, Librarian of Aberdeen University, 1926–66, historian and archaeologist, the collection contains *c*250 books; *c*150 unbound pamphlets; *c*1,750 postcards and photographs, and *c*5,500 3½″ sq lantern slides, mainly of Scottish subjects. It represents the working collection of the owner as an authority on castellated architecture, particularly of Scotland, and contains all his own works as well as inscribed copies from scholars in the same field. Many of the books are interleaved and are extensively annotated.

Sheaf binder cat.

An outline of Dr Simpson's career is to be found in *Aberdeen University Review*, 41, 1965–6, p269-71.

Taylor Psalmody Collection The bulk of this collection was formed by William Lawrence Taylor, 1829–1910, a Peterhead bookseller, and presented to the library in 1910. Consisting of *c*1,200 v, the books span the period 1546 to the early 20th cent, and are in these sections: (a) complete versions of the Psalms, mostly metrical; (b) partial versions with Paraphrases and Hymns; (c) books relating to the Psalms.

Aberdeen University, *Catalogue of the Taylor Collection of Psalm versions*, 1922. The preface to the catalogue includes a short account of Taylor.

Theological Library Founded in 1700 for the use of divinity students of both Marischal College and King's College. A second Theological Library was formed in 1863, and the two were amalgamated in 1898. The collection contains *c*3,000 v, largely theological, with a certain amount of historical and philosophical works. The books are mainly of the 17th-19th cent.

A number of printed cats exist, the first being *Catalogue of books belonging to the Theological Library of Marischal College, Aberdeen*, 1790, and the last *Catalogue of books in the Students Theological Library*, 1901.

Accounts of the Library are given in the prefaces to the 1823 and 1901 cats, and in the *Report by the Library Committee to the University Court...*, 1897, anent theological libraries.

Thomson Pamphlets This collection of pamphlets in 343 v was formed by Alexander Thomson, laird of Banchory-Devenick, MA Marischal College 1816, LLD 1853. It was originally bequeathed to the Free Church College, but was transferred to the University Library when that College ceased to function. Thomson's interests are strongly represented in the collection, especially in the fields of sociology, education, ecclesiastical affairs and archaeology.

Aberdeen University Library, *Catalogue of pamphlets in the King, the Thomson and the Herald Collections*, 1927.

George Smeaton, *Memoir of Alexander Thomson of Banchory*, 1869.

Wilson Collection Consisting of *c*500 v, this collection was bequeathed by Robert Wilson, 1787–1871, MD, King's College, 1815. Wilson travelled widely in Europe and the East, and his collection, which has a strong Oriental flavour, consists largely of books on travel and, to a lesser extent, on history, archaeology, literature and medicine.

Sheaf binder cat.

Henry Hargreaves, 'Dr Robert Wilson', *Aberdeen University Review*, 43, 1969–70, p374-84.

Bishop's Library (augmented Chapeltown) Collection. Right Rev Mario Conti, PhL, STL, Bishop of Aberdeen, Bishop's House, 156 King's Gate, Aberdeen AB2 6BK. Tel (0224) 39154. Open by appointment (normally during working hours) to bona fide scholars. Special facilities will be sought at the University Library. Photocopier available at the Diocesan Pastoral and Catechetical Centre.

The Former Mission of Chapeltown Library, Braes of Glenlivet Collection (with additional material from other historic missions of the RC Diocese of Aberdeen) Established by Abbé Paul Macpherson (who built the church and schools, 1829–30) from books collected in Glenlivet and Enzie, with a considerable number of Scalan Seminary books (18th cent foundation). The collection consists of *c*550 v (460 works), of which *c*26 works are now part of Pluscarden Abbey and Aberdeen University Libraries. Additionally an unknown, but probably considerable, number are in Blairs College Library now deposited in NLS. A few volumes from other parishes have been incorporated in the library. *c*35-40 v (mid-late 19th cent and early 20th cent) formerly at Chapeltown, but not apparently belonging to the Mission, are also present.

The library is predominantly theological (for priests and seminarians) and classical (school texts) with school books on geography, history, French, Italian and Latin grammars, many devotional and pastoral works, catechisms, Breviaries and other liturgical works (including Jansenist). It includes fragments of three leaves of Aristotle, *De anima* (T Rood, Oxford 1481), found in a binding; 35 16th cent; 255 17th cent (4 STC and 9 Wing); 250 18th cent and 10 19th cent items. The collection is added to if books of the same period are discovered in the Diocesan repositories.

Note: A systematic programme of repair, restoration and rebinding is approaching completion (1983), but many volumes are incomplete.

A cat is in preparation giving access via author, subject, date, with provenance, available in draft typescript.

City of Aberdeen District Libraries, Central Library, Rosemount Viaduct, Aberdeen. Tel (0224) 28991. Open Mon-Fri 9 am-9 pm; Sat 9 am-5 pm. Xerox machine, microfilm readers and reader/printer available.

Local Collection Public Library Acts adopted in 1884, and since then the collection has been gradually built up. It consists of *c*11,500 books, and *c*10,600 pamphlets. The rare books case contains 33 STC; 12 Wing; 3 18th cent; *c*26 being Aberdeen printing; 2 foreign 16th cent and 6 foreign 17th cent.

Aberdeen Public Library: *Catalogue of the Local Collection to be found in the Reference Dept, Aberdeen, 1914.* Printed cat 1914; Card dictionary cat.

Cosmo Mitchell Collection Received in 1932 as a bequest under the will of the late Adam Cosmo Mitchell, former teacher of dancing. It contains 211 v; 54 pamphlets; 53 periodical parts; 36 Reports. The material relates to dancing, and includes works on ballroom, ballet, country and national dances.

Ms inventory available. All items appear in the general cat of the Central Reference Library.

Walker Music Collection Presented in 1891 by Mr James Walker, President of Aberdeen Musical Association, the collection contains 584 items, but of these, 124 non-musical items have been transferred to general reference stock. The remaining items include early musical works, some rare Scottish and local publications, eg J Cargill, *Harmonica Sacra; Aberdeen Psalmody*, 1823; *Scottish Psalter*, 1635.

Typescript inventory. All items are included in the general cat of the Central Reference Library.

Department of Agriculture and Fisheries for Scotland, Marine Laboratory Library, PO Box 101, Aberdeen AB9 8DB. Tel (0224) 876544. Open Mon-Thurs 9 am-5 pm, Fri 9 am-4.30 pm. Open for reference to bona fide enquirers. Photocopying, microfilm reader/printer, photographic unit in laboratory.

The general library has been built up by the Department from mid-19th cent, and in the 1890s a laboratory library was established by purchase and donation. The subjects covered include marine biology, oceanography, fisheries, fishery methods and gear; also early expedition literature, eg Challenger and Discovery reports.

UDC classified card cat; not all older material catalogued.

Ogilvie Collection on diatomaceae The collection was built up by Helen Ogilvie, planktonologist in the laboratory in the 1940s. It consists of *c*90 books; 130 pamphlets; and glass slides covering all periods.

Separate ms author cat in book form.

Macaulay Institute for Soil Research, Craigiebuckler, Aberdeen. Tel (0224) 38611 Ext 211. Open weekdays 8.45 am-5.15 pm. Admission for reference only to accredited visitors by prior arrangement with the Librarian. Photocopying facilities.

The Library of the Institute for Soil Research has been built up by donation since the foundation of the Institute in 1930. It consists of *c*5,000 v; *c*15,000 reports, pamphlets and scientific offprints. These include 1 STC item (not recorded); 32 18th cent and 40 post-1800 and pre-1850 items. Subjects covered include soil and plant science, geology, mineralogy, agriculture, chemistry and physics.

Main author and UDC classified card cat. Also separate typescript bibliography, classified.

'Macaulay Institute for Soil Research Library Services, Catalogue of Rare and Antiquarian Books held by the Library'. Bibliography 1, 1977.

North East Scotland Library Service, 14 Crown Terrace, Aberdeen AB9 2BH. Tel (0224) 572658. Open Mon-Fri 9.30 am-7.30 pm; Sat 9.30 am-5 pm. Anyone wishing to study the George MacDonald Collection should contact Headquarters in Aberdeen. Photocopying in Aberdeen.

George MacDonald Collection The ms material was donated to Huntly Library by descendants of George MacDonald, Lady Troup and Mr William Will, from the 1920s; the bulk (from Mr Will) in July 1940. The collection was officially opened in 1952. It contains *c*70 printed items (all post-1850) of and about George MacDonald, the novelist.

Checklist available.

Robert Gordon's Institute of Technology, Scott Sutherland School of Architecture, Garthdee Road, Aberdeen. Tel (0224) 33247. Open during term Mon-Thurs 9 am-5.30 pm, Fri 9 am-5 pm. The public is admitted for reference use on request. Microform readers and photocopying facilities.

The school was opened in 1914. Most of the rare books have been donated by local architects or purchased over the last 20 years. A few are from the Aberdeen Mechanics' Institution Library. The *c*120 v printed pre-1850 (including 1 Wing item (S811), and 1 foreign book of the 17th cent) are mainly on architecture and building, with a few on landscape gardening. There is a portfolio of photographs, plans of buildings, and cuttings of the work of Archibald Simpson, 1790–1847, architect of Aberdeen.

Card cat.

Rowett Research Institute, Bucksburn, Aberdeen AB2 9SB. Tel (0224) 712751. Open Mon-Fri 9 am-5.25 pm. Admission to research workers only. Usual inter-library loan and photocopying services. On-line searches undertaken for staff only.

Reid Library The bequest of Dr J F Tocher, and originally came from the libraries of Sir Archibald Grant of Monymusk and others. Bound v of 19th cent agricultural journals given by Mrs McLeod of Dunvegan to Dr W Douglas Simpson, and by him to the Reid Library. It contains *c*120 v on agriculture; *c*75 18th cent and *c*35 items 1800–51. Also *c*200 bound v of agricultural and scientific journals.

Author cat and list of journals by title.

Arbroath

Patrick Allan Fraser of Hospitalfield Trust, Hospitalfield House, Arbroath DD11 2NH. Tel (0241) 72333. Admission on application to Warden.

The library contains books belonging to the Parrott family of Warwickshire (related by marriage to the Frasers of Hospitalfield), those of the Frasers who lived at Hospitalfield from the 17th to 19th cent, and those of Patrick Allan who married Miss Fraser in 1843, adding her name to his. He was keenly interested in the visual arts which are well represented in the collection. It includes *c*1,500 v pre-1850, comprising *c*700 titles, of which 1 British and 3 foreign are 16th cent; 15 British and 13 foreign are 17th cent; 312 British and 74 foreign are 18th cent, and 166 British and 105 foreign are 1800–50. Foreign imprints, mainly Italian, are on the visual arts, and most of the 18th cent British titles are on literature and history. There are many 18th cent bindings with elegant gold tooling. A Plantin *Tacitus* (1585) is bound in fine contemporary German binding.

Card index cat by author and subject.

George Hay, *The book of Hospitalfield*. Privately printed 1894. [op]

Ardrossan

Cunninghame District Library, HQ, 39/41 Princes Street, Ardrossan KA22 8BT. Tel (0294) 69137/38/39. Open Mon-Fri 9 am-5 pm. Admission for reference only.

Alexander Wood Memorial Library A private collection donated to the Burgh of Ardrossan, and with reorganization in 1974 it came under the Cunninghame District. It contains *c*3,100 items (in addition to pamphlets and mss), of which *c*1,500 are pre-1851. Included are the *Burns Collection, Boswell and Johnson Collection*, and *Galt and Montgomery Collections.*

Author/title card cat.

Subject card cat.

Ayr

Burns Monument Trustees, Burns Cottage, Alloway, Ayr KA7 4PY. Tel (0292) 41215. Open 9 am-7 pm (shorter in Winter). All bona fide readers admitted on payment of a small admission charge. Prior application to the Curator is highly desirable. For research facilities and services, consult the Curator.

Burns Cottage Collection of Burnsiana In 1815 a public subscription list was opened for the purpose of erecting a monument to Robert Burns. In 1823 the Burns Monument was opened to the public, and in 1881 the Burns Cottage was bought by the Trustees. The acquisition of the collections of books and mss largely dates from the early years of the 20th cent. Major acquisitions include Colonel R J Bennett's bequest of his library of 523 v and J C Ewing's bequest of his comprehensive collection of books about Burns's life and times. The collection is estimated at 3,500 v, which include editions of the works of Burns; books about Burns; books owned by Burns, some with annotations by the poet; volumes of music from the 1720s to the 1820s; a collection of books printed by John Wilson, the Kilmarnock and Ayr printer; mss and autograph letters of Burns, and autograph letters of his friends and contemporaries.

Ms cat of the collection of books.

Burns Cottage and Burns Monument, Alloway: Catalogue of manuscripts, relics, paintings and other exhibits. . . with historical note, Ayr (*c*1980).

Kyle and Carrick District Library, Headquarters, Carnegie Library, 12 Main Street, Ayr. Tel (0292) 81511. Open Mon-Fri 9 am-7.30 pm. Prior warning of special requirements desirable. Photocopies will be provided subject to the condition of the item of which the photocopy is requested.

The Burns Collection *c*1,200 items which include 57 different editions of Burns's works.

The Local History Collection *c*7,500 v which include a collection of items from the Auchinleck Press and 18th cent Ayr printing.

Ayr Library Society Collection No figures available on the size of this collection, but the books date from 1762 when the Society was founded.

Author and subject cat.

Brodick Castle

Brodick Castle (National Trust for Scotland property), Isle of Arran. Application for information and access to the books should be made to The Curatorial Department, National Trust for Scotland, 5 Charlotte Square, Edinburgh EH2 4DU. Tel (031) 226 5922.

Brodick Castle Library The library contains, *inter alia*, some of the books from the library of William Beckford of Fonthill that came into the possession of the Douglas family when Beckford's daughter, Susan, married the 10th Duke of Hamilton, and material (including *c*75 v of sporting books and a few hundred volumes, mainly in French and German, of popular history and literature, well bound and probably intended for the use of Princess Marie of Baden, the wife of the 11th Duke), acquired in the latter half of the 19th cent before the Castle descended, in 1895, to the only child of the 12th Duke of Hamilton, who became Duchess of Montrose. The Castle and its contents have been administered by the National Trust for Scotland since 1958. There are *c*1,500 v, of which *c*1,000 are pre-1851, and include 1 STC-period and 15 Wing-period books. The pre-1851 books include *c*460 printed in Britain and 500 elsewhere. Subjects covered are mainly literature and history, with some travel and topography, but perhaps the most striking contents of the library are 30-40 v from Beckford's own collection, most of them with his notes, and some volumes and albums of prints and engravings, some coloured, relating to politics, sport, travel, architecture, social life and equestrianism. Individual works include five folio volumes of original coloured caricature drawings by Lib Prosperi of 19th cent politicians and other celebrities; A F Skjöldebrand's *Voyage pittoresque au Cap Nord* 1801–2; Willes Maddox, *View of Lansdown Tower Bath*, London 1844; Thomas Wright, *England under the House of Hanover, illustrated by scarce caricatures and satirical prints after Hogarth, Darley, Paul Sandby, Gillray, etc*, London 1848 (an extra-illustrated copy in 9 v); and George Stubbs, *The anatomy of the horse*, London, 1766.

There is a simple hand-written author cat on cards, compiled in 1966.

Brodie Castle

Brodie Castle (National Trust for Scotland property), Morayshire IV36 0TE. Application for information and access to the books should be made to the Curatorial Department, National Trust for Scotland, 5 Charlotte Square, Edinburgh EH2 4DU. Tel (031) 226 5922.

Brodie Castle Library The books have been acquired by members of the Brodie family, who have lived on the site since at least the 13th cent, the present castle dating from the 16th cent. Portions of the library were bought in bulk in the 18th and 19th cent. It contains *c*5,550 v which include *c*8 STC items, and 12 foreign items of the same period; 57 Wing items; and 20 foreign items of the same period; 916 items published in Britain between 1700 and 1850, and 56 of the same period published in Europe. The pre-1700 works are mainly in the fields of religion and history, with some law and classics. The same fields are the ones best represented in the material to 1850, with additional material from the fields of literature (English, with some continental), geography and travel, politics, philosophy, some science, medicine and art. The foreign material of the period 1700 to 1850 is largely literature, mainly French, with some Italian and classical; history, philosophy, law and medicine. There are a number of first editions from all periods. There are good runs of *c*12 18th and 19th cent periodicals. There is a large gardening collection of the late 19th and early 20th cent, and a range of Victorian literature.

Author index and partial subject index on cards, with reference to shelf location.

The collection is not catalogued and not systematically arranged.

Cupar

North East Fife District Library Service, Duncan Institute, Crossgate, Cupar, Fife. Tel (0334) 3722 Ext 33. Open Mon, Tues, Wed, Fri 10 am-7 pm, Thurs, Sat 10 am-5 pm. Admission is free to anyone wishing to carry out local history research. Separate local studies room with study desks available.

The General Collection at Cupar includes about 100 pre-1851 books, some of which probably originate from the Cupar Subscription Library (founded *c*1800), though these cannot now be identified for certain.

North East Fife Local History Collection The collection is made up of *c*2,200 v (also photographs, press cuttings, maps, newspapers) which include about 60 items of local pre-1851 printing—chiefly the Tullis Press.

Author, title and subject (Dewey) indexes are available, as well as an author cat of pre-1851 imprints in typescript and a typescript list of local photographic holdings. Regular additions are made to the collection.

Drum Castle

Drum Castle (National Trust for Scotland property), Aberdeenshire. Application for information and access to the books should be made to the Curatorial Department, National Trust for Scotland, 5 Charlotte Square, Edinburgh EH2 4DU. Tel (031) 226 5922.

Drum Castle Library Books had been gathered by members of the Irvine family resident at Drum from the 14th cent until 1976, but most were bought as a collection when the present room was fitted as a library in the mid-19th cent. There are *c*3,500 v which include *c*20 foreign items of the STC period; 7 Wing items and 50 foreign items of the Wing period; *c*850 items 1700–1850, of which *c*100 published abroad. There are many Scottish and several English provincial imprints of the 18th and 19th cent. This is a general collection, strongest in classics and religion in the STC period, adding to these history in the Wing period, with more literature (English and foreign), law and a little science in the pre-1850 period. A few rarities are included.

An author index sheaf cat in Aberdeen University Library covers about two-thirds of the collection, without reference to shelf location.

The collection is not catalogued, and is not systematically arranged.

Dunblane

Leighton Library, The Cross, Dunblane, Perthshire. (Postal and telephone enquiries to: Department of Rare Books, Stirling University Library, Stirling FK9 4LA.) Tel (0786) 3171 Ext 2230. Open by arrangement and by written application. Books brought for consultation on request to the Haldane Room, Stirling University Library.

Leighton Library (or Leightonian Library) Founded by the will of Archbishop Robert Leighton (1611–84) for the benefit of the Clergy of the Cathedral and Diocese (later the Presbytery) of Dunblane, the library was built 1686–7, opened 1688. In the mid-18th cent it became a subscription library, in addition to its original function. About 1,270 pre-1684 v from Leighton's bequest of 1,363 v are extant. In addition, many books were donated, or purchased by the Trustees, up to the middle of the 19th cent.

The collection comprises 3,300 works in 3,914 v. Mainly theological, but travel, law, philosophy, medicine, history and the classics are prominent. There is an interesting collection of early books on America, and Leighton's original bequest includes many examples of early printing in Hebrew and Greek. 15 languages are represented. There are 194 STC, 408 Wing items, and *c*900 16th-17th cent foreign books.

Card cat (copies in Leighton Library, Stirling University Library, National Library of Scotland and the British Library).

Approx 20 18th and early 19th cent books sold at Sotheby's 7 March, 1972.

W J Couper, 'Bibliotheca Leightoniana, Dunblane', *Society of Friends of Dunblane Cathedral Journal* 1(3), p10-26. Originally published Glasgow, 1917, as a privately printed monograph.

J Leighton, 'Our public libraries—no 1. The Bibliotheca Leightoniana at Dunblane, NB', *Bookplate Annual and Armorial Yearbook*, 1895, p6-13.

R Douglas, 'An account of the foundation of the Leightonian Library', *Bannatyne Miscellany III* 1855, p227-72 (Bannatyne Club vol 19B).

D Butler, *The life and letters of Robert Leighton*, London, 1903, p582-92.

E A Knox, *Robert Leighton, Archbishop of Glasgow*, London, 1930, p225-65.

Dundee

City of Dundee District Libraries, Central Library, The Wellgate, Dundee DD1 1DB. Tel (0382) 23141 Ext 318. Open Mon-Fri 9.30 am-7 pm; Sat 9.30 am-5 pm. Access to specific items from special collections at discretion of Librarian. Confirmation of identity required. Research services based in General Reference Department. Facilities include 8 Study Carrels; 10 Furniture Carrels; total of 263 seats in the Reference Departments; photocopier and microfiche readers; microfilm readers.

Antiquarian Collection Items recognized as being of particular interest but without the scope of the other special collections: mainly rare or unusual antiquarian items collected since the opening of the library in 1869. 340 works. There are 3 incunabula and 10 STC items, plus 21 mss.

Note: Identification of pre-1821 items from general library in progress (20.8.80). Estimated 3-4,000 v.

Ivory Collection Offered to the City by Sir James Ivory (1765–1842) in 1829, and added to the stock of the Dundee Public Library at the time of its opening in 1869. It contains 417 v, mainly mathematical and scientific works of the 17th, 18th and early 19th cent published in Paris, London and other European cities. The texts are in French, English and Latin.

Local History Collection (Open Mon, Tues, Fri, Sat 9.30 am-5 pm; Wed, Thurs 9.30 am-7 pm) The collection has been gradually built up since the opening of the library in 1869, and enriched by the excellent Lamb Collection in 1901. This collection of pamphlets, manuscripts, cuttings and material of all kinds was collected between *c*1867–97. It consists of 15,268 printed books relating to the history of Dundee and the lives and works of its people: also material relating to the surrounding areas; also pamphlets, newspapers, printed ephemera, posters, maps, prints, photographs and ms material. Includes local antiquarian material.

Hobbs classification scheme (with amendments) card cat. Not published.

Sturrock Collection Bequeathed by Mr George W L Sturrock, a Dundee merchant, in 1935. There are 260 v containing examples of the work of the Ashendene, Doves, Gregynog, Kelmscott and Nonesuch Presses.

The Wighton Collection Bequeathed by Mr Andrew John Wighton, a Dundee grocer and town councillor, and housed by the newly established Dundee Public Library in 1869. It consists of 620 bound v, containing about 700 items representing Mr Wighton's personal collection of national music (both vocal and instrumental) of Scotland chiefly, but also of England, Ireland and Wales. Contains printed and manuscript items obtained from sources in the United Kingdom and on the continent, including some unique items.

Typescript (bound). No published cat.

Edith B Schnapper (ed), *The British Union—Catalogue of early printed music.* [op]

Dundee University Library, Dundee DD1 4HN. Tel (0382) 23181. Telex 76293 ULDUND G. Open (Term) Mon-Fri 9 am-10 pm; Sat 9 am-12 noon; (Vacation) Mon-Fri 9 am-5 pm; Sat 9 am-12 noon. Admission on application to the Librarian for reference purposes. Full membership by subscription (£2 pa). Photographic department; self-service copying facilities; microform readers.

General collection of books printed pre-1801 This dates from the opening of the University College, Dundee 1882, and includes *c*3,000 v. It is strong in early medicine and dentistry, and includes 1 incunabulum, 146 STC, 247 Wing, and 1,041 ESTC items.

Brechin Diocesan Library Founded as a subscription library for the clergy of the Diocese of Brechin, and transferred to the University in 1962. It contains 10,500 v and relates to church history, especially the Episcopal Church in Scotland. It includes 4 incunabula, 1,718 STC, 424 Wing and 205 ESTC items.

Leng Collection Started in 1967 as a gift from Dr Janet Leng, it contains 300 v on Scottish philosophy and includes 171 ESTC items.

Thoms Collection Donated by Alexander Thoms *c*1900, it consists of 250 v on mineralogy and includes 5 ESTC items.

Printed catalogue of the Brechin Diocesan Library, 1869. Appendices 1879 and 1886.

All collections now catalogued in the general cats of the University Library.

Dunfermline

Dunfermline District Libraries, Central Library Headquarters, 1 Abbot Street, Dunfermline KY12 7NW, Fife. Tel (0383) 23551. Open Mon, Tues, Thurs, Fri 10 am-1 pm, 2-7 pm, Wed 10 am-1 pm; Sat 10 am-1 pm, 2-5 pm. Admission on application to the Librarian. Material for reference only. Extended study by prior arrangement.

George Reid Collection Presented by Mr George Reid (*fl*1900), a Dunfermline linen manufacturer, part of whose library was presented to the Victoria and Albert Museum. It is a small but outstanding collection of 36 items, including 6 medieval mss, and early printed books; strong in Horae and other devotional works. The printed books include 7 incunabula; the 2nd (1632) and 4th (1685) folios of Shakespeare; and the 1647 Beaumont and Fletcher folio.

Card cat.

The mss are all described in Ker, v 2, p477-83.

Local History Collection Based on a collection formed by Dr Erskine Beveridge (1851–1920), the bibliographer of Dunfermline and West Fife, and donated in 1931. It consists of *c*5,500 items, including printed books and pamphlets, mss, newspapers, photographs, maps and ephemera (posters and handbills) relating to the history of Dunfermline and West Fife. Additions are made as a regular policy.

Card cat.

Erskine Beveridge, *A bibliography of works relating to Dunfermline and the West of Fife* (Dunfermline, 1901) (op)

The Kingdom of Fife: a select list of books and a guide to the Local History Room, rev ed (Dunfermline District Libraries, 1976).

Murison Burns Collection Collected by John Murison (*d*1921), a native of Glasgow, purchased by the engineer Sir Alexander Gibb (whose firm constructed Rosyth Dockyard), and presented by him to the City of Dunfermline in 1921. There are *c*2,000 items including printed books and pamphlets by, and about, Robert Burns (1759–96); strong in early editions of the poet's works, including Kilmarnock 1786 (imperfect), Paisley 1801, Kirkcaldy 1802, and 17 Edinburgh editions prior to 1810. The collection is added to regularly.

Card cat.

Published cat: Nancie Campbell, *The Murison Burns Collection: a catalogue* (Dunfermline Public Libraries, 1953) (op)

Edinburgh

Advocates' Library, Parliament House, Edinburgh EH1 1RF. Tel (031) 226 5071. Open Mon-Fri 9 am-4 pm. Admission to members only. Books available to public through the National Library of Scotland (qv).

Historical Collection The library was formally opened in 1689, and the collection was built up during the 17th and 18th cent through purchase and donations, but after 1710 items were acquired by copyright. It includes a large number of works belonging to Lord George Douglas presented by his father, the first Duke of Queensbury. Original owners of works include Sir George Mackenzie, Edward Henryson, Henry Scrymgeour, and Isaac Casaubon. The collection comprises 5,250 items with emphasis on Roman Civil and Canon Law. Mss and incunabula preserved in the National Library of Scotland.

A Catalogue of the law books in the Advocates' Library. Edinburgh 1831 (Supplement 1839) (op); *Catalogue of printed books in the Library of the Faculty of Advocates*. 7 vols. Edinburgh, 1867–78 (Supplement 1879) (op); Author card index, and items also listed in the National Library of Scotland cats.

City of Edinburgh District Libraries, Central Library, George IV Bridge, Edinburgh EH1 1EG. Open Mon-Fri 9 am-9 pm; Sat 9 am-1 pm. Reference services open to all, admission to pre-1850 items subject to enquirer providing proof of identity and signing special consultations register. Photocopying at discretion of librarian-in-charge; photography can be arranged per local photographer by written application to the City Librarian; microfilming can also be arranged; reader/printer available.

Edinburgh Room The Edinburgh Room was set up as a separate department in 1932 from the existing collection of books on Edinburgh in the Reference Library and Cowan bequest, part of which contained examples of early Edinburgh (and Scottish) printing. The total stock consists of *c*31,308 items, of which *c*10,000 may be pre-1850, with *c*100 private press titles; *c*4-500 relate to Edinburgh printing pre-1700—special collection; *c*1,500 to Sir Walter Scott; *c*200 to James Boswell; *c*100 to Robert Fergusson. The A Conan Doyle (1859—1930) collection includes *c*150 (*Sherlock Holmes*) items; the R M Ballantyre (1825—94) collection *c*150 items, and the R L Stevenson (1850—94) collection *c*600 printed items plus prints, photographs, mss and drawings. The library also includes a set of early Edinburgh directories, 1773—1850 (plus 'modern' ones to 1974—5); *c*2,100 broadsides, including playbills, ballads, acts etc, and an unspecified number of newspapers and periodicals from the 17th cent. A policy of regular acquisition of books and other records about Edinburgh is followed.

Classified and author card cat, and subject sheaf index available.

N E S Armstrong, *Local Collections in Scotland*, Glasgow, 1977.

Full bibliographical details of the Stevenson cats are as follows:

Robert Louis Stevenson (1850—1894). Catalogue of the Stevenson Collection in the Edinburgh Room, Central Library, George IV Bridge, [Edin], 1950, 36pp.

Robert Louis Stevenson. Supplementary catalogue of the Stevenson Collection in the Edinburgh Room with a select list of books and manuscripts in Lady Stair's House Museum, [Edin], 1978, 40pp.

Fine Art Library Founded in 1936 as a separate unit of Edinburgh Public Libraries, Central Library, the library contains two collections worthy of note: (a) *The Boog Watson Collection* which was donated in April 1931. It is the collection of C B Boog Watson on the 'Dance of Death'. The earliest printed 'Dance of Death' is 1542, and there are 18 pre-1850 examples, as well as later 19th cent examples; (b) *The Norman Mitchell Hunter Bequest*, donated July 1944; it contains a variety of art subjects mainly dating from the late 19th cent to the early 1940s. Only four volumes are pre-1850.

Music Library The library was founded in 1934 and comprises *c*420 v and *c*100 items of sheet music, with particular emphasis on 17th, 18th and 19th cent Scottish music.

Sheaf indexes of music arranged by 'form' and author card cat available.

Reference Library The library was founded in 1892 and includes the Rosebery Pamphlets (18th and 19th cent) comprising *c*1,400 items which were bought in 1903 from the Edinburgh Select Subscription Library and collected originally by Archibald Philip Primrose, 5th Earl of Rosebery. The pamphlets cover a wide range of subjects. Research facilities include three microfilm readers (two fiche) and 'coin-op' photocopier.

Scottish Department Library Established as a separate department in 1961, the library has a total stock of 50,000 v, of which 20,000 books and pamphlets, 2,500 prints and photographs, 150 maps and 5 mss, are pre-1850. Subject strength of collection is Scottish Studies, in particular history and topography and Scottish family history which is covered by *c*1,200 v.

Dictionary card cat available. An annotated copy of H G Aldis *A list of books printed in Scotland before 1700*, Edinburgh, 1904, is kept in the Edinburgh Room where there are *c*600 Aldis items.

N E S Armstrong, *Local Collections in Scotland*, Glasgow, 1977, p15-16, 65-6.

The Commissioners of Northern Lighthouses, 84 George Street, Edinburgh 2. Tel (031) 226 7051. Admission to bona fide researchers by appointment with the Secretary during normal office hours.

Library of the Commissioners of Northern Lighthouses The Commissioners were constituted in 1786 and incorporated in 1798. The books were for the use of the Commissioners. Of *c*650 works, *c*300 are pre-1850, and most are late 18th and early 19th cent. Apart from the obvious books on lighthouses, harbours, marine engineering and associated charts, plans and tide tables, there is a very good collection of books of travel and exploration on the same period. The collection is added to from time to time.

Ms list alphabetical by author.

Printed cat of 1867.

Edinburgh University Library, George Square, Edinburgh EH8 9LJ. Tel (031) 667 1011. Open for consultation of rare books Mon-Fri 9 am-5 pm. Closed annually during the second week in August, between Christmas and New Year and on public holidays. Admission to non-members of the University by written application. Xerox and photographic copies; microfilm and microfiche reader. U/v light.

A **Special Collections Department**

A foundation gift in 1580 by Clement Little to the Town Council of Edinburgh was transferred to the Tounis College in 1584. This was increased subsequently by donation, purchase and copyright deposit (1710—1837).

The Special Collections Department administers almost all the Main Library's pre-1800 imprints which total *c*200,000 v. The subject range covers all branches of knowledge, but is strong in theology, with an important collection of German Reformation tracts, history of science, including mathematics, astronomy, geology and natural history, history of medicine (especially relating to the Edinburgh school), economics, literature, travel and history. There are 267 incunabula; no figures are available for STC and Wing items, although over 350 unique items have been recorded. Important named collections include those of Clement Little, William Drummond of Hawthornden, James Nairne, Adam Smith, Dugald Stewart and J O Halliwell-Phillipps. Others include the Blöndal collection of Icelandic literature, the Left Book Club publications, and the publications of writers associated with the Scottish literary renaissance. The collections generally include many first editions of major writers, interesting association copies and fine bindings. The major rare book collections are the subjects of separate entries (below).

Catalogue of the printed books in the library of the University of Edinburgh. 3 v (Edinburgh, 1918–23). All entries in this cat and subsequent additions to the collections are incorporated in the general cat in the library.

Separate cats of binding rubbings, provenance and printers, all of which are incomplete.

Edinburgh University Library, 1580–1980. A collection of historical essays, edited by Jean R Guild and Alexander Law (Edinburgh, 1982), includes a full bibliography.

Special collections of printed books in Edinburgh University Library. (Edinburgh, 1978).

Sale of scientific duplicates, Sotheby 22-23 March 1971, lots 349-63.

Library archives from the early 17th cent contain information on book acquisitions, especially by donation.

Clement Litil Bequest Clement Litil, or Little, an advocate and commissary of Edinburgh, left his library to the town and kirk of Edinburgh on his death in 1580. In 1584 the books were put into the custody of the Principal of the newly-founded Tounis College, and thus became the nucleus of the University Library. There are 276 v, *c*10 v of incunabula, the remainder 16th cent Continental works of theology.

Ms cat compiled in the 1580s and printed in *Miscellany of the Maitland Club*, v 1, Edinburgh 1834.

Inventory (indexed) in C P Finlayson, *Clement Litil and his Library*. Edinburgh, 1980.

Entries for the books are in the Library's main author cat.

C P Finlayson, *Clement Litil and his Library Edinburgh*, Edinburgh Biblio Soc and the Friends of Edinburgh University Library, 1980.

Drummond Collection At least a third of the large library collected by the 17th cent poet, man of letters, and former student of Edinburgh's Tounis College, William Drummond of Hawthornden, presented by Drummond in the 1620s and 1630s. It contains 700 v, mostly literature, Latin, Italian, French and Spanish, as well as English, but containing a substantial amount of philosophy, law and theology. A small number of incunabula, but over 200 STC books. Two Shakespeare quartos, *Love's Labours Lost* (1598) and *Romeo and Juliet* (1599).

Auctarium Bibliothecae Edinburgenae sive catalogus librorum quos G Drummondus ab Hawthornden Bibliothecae DDQ Anno 1627, Edinburgh 1627; reprinted 1815.

The Library of Drummond of Hawthornden, ed by R H Macdonald, Edinburgh UP, 1971, pt III.

Entries in main library author cat.

Nairne Bequest James Nairne, minister of Wemyss in Fife (1655–78) and chaplain-in-ordinary to Charles II (1675–8), left his library to the University of Edinburgh on his death in 1678. There are 1,838 items. The books are mainly theological (Church Fathers, biblical commentaries, doctrinal works, church history), but the collection includes some historical, philosophical and literary works, and works on the classics, medicine and science. Among individual works of note are Spenser's *Faerie Queene*, London 1596, and Napier of Merchiston's *Rabdologiae*, Edinburgh 1617.

Catalogus librorum quibus Bibliothecam Edinburgenae adauxit R D Jacobus Narnius. . . pastor Vaemiensis, 1678.

Entries in main library author cat.

Adam Smith Collection In the late 19th cent a descendant of Adam Smith's heir gave his share (about a third of the total) of Adam Smith's library to New College Library, Edinburgh. The books were transferred to the Main Library of the University in 1972. 32 more books from Smith's library are in the Hodgson Collection. There are *c*850 works. A general collection covering, for example, 18th cent literature, especially French, the classics, some law, history, science, political economy and contemporary affairs.

A cat, with a history, of all Smith's books was published in 1894: *A catalogue of the library of Adam Smith, ed with an introduction by James Bonar; a second edition, expanded,* was issued in 1932. A supplement and checklist was issued in 1967: *Adam Smith's Library: a supplement to Bonar's catalogue with a checklist of the whole library*, by H Mizuta.

Entries in main library author cat.

Dugald Stewart Collection In 1852 Colonel Matthew Stewart bequeathed his own books, those of his father, Dugald Stewart (1753–1828), Professor of Moral Philosophy at Edinburgh, 1785–1810, and those of his grandfather, Matthew Stewart (1717–85), Professor of Mathematics at Edinburgh, 1747–75, to the United Service Club in London. The books were transferred to Edinburgh University Library in 1910. There are *c*4,000 v. A general collection covering many topics, but particularly strong in political economy, moral philosophy and mathematics. There is a large number of presentation copies reflecting Dugald Stewart's wide circle of acquaintances and admirers, for example, from Jefferson, Byron and Maria Edgeworth. The younger Matthew Stewart added some early printed books and works on Oriental subjects. The collection includes 33 incunabula.

An author cat is available in the Special Collections Department.

The incunabula are listed in F C Nicholson 'List of fifteenth century books in the University Library Edinburgh', *Publ Edinburgh Biblio Soc*, v 9, 1913, p93-123, 185-6.

K C Crawford, 'The Dugald Stewart Collection (Edinburgh University Library)', *The Bibliotheck*, v 10, 1980, no 2, p31-4.

Halliwell-Phillipps Collection (1) James Orchard Halliwell-Phillipps (1820–89), the literary scholar, gave the bulk of this collection in 1872, and the remainder was given by him in subsequent years and under the terms of his will. There are *c*1,000 v. A mainly Shakespeare collection, including copies of nearly all the editions of Shakespeare published before 1660, either in the original or in facsimile.

Entries in main library author cat.

Halliwell-Phillipps Collection (2) In 1964 Edinburgh University Library acquired, at auction, virtually all items originally given by J O Halliwell-Phillipps to the Penzance Library in 1866. It contains 600 items. Mainly 17th and early 18th cent English drama, but there are 16th cent works and also foreign works. Dryden is the author best represented numerically, but perhaps most impressive qualitatively are first editions of John Webster and prompt copies of early editions of Webster and Congreve.

An author cat giving references to STC, Wing, etc, if applicable, is available in the Special Collections Department.

Entries in the main library author cat.

Hodgson Collection The books were collected by William Ballantyne Hodgson (1815–80), Professor of Political Economy at Edinburgh University, and were given to the Library by his widow in 1880. There are *c*1,000 v. The books are on economics, and include 32 items from Adam Smith's Library.

Entries in main library author cat.

Cameron Collection The collection was formed by Dr Alexander Cameron (1827–88), Celtic scholar and minister of the Free Church at Brodick, Isle of Arran, and was given to Edinburgh University Library by Sir William Mackinnon of Balinakill, who had purchased the collection in 1889 on Cameron's death.

Most of the books are about Celtic studies and Scottish theology, mainly 19th cent, but including numerous 18th cent and some 17th cent works.

Entries in main library author cat.

Blöndal Collection Purchased by the Library from the Icelandic scholar, Sigfús Blöndal in 1950, augmented by a small collection on Icelandic topics presented, also in 1950, by the Icelandic government. There are *c*3,000 books, pamphlets and journals in the Blöndal Collection, plus *c*250 items presented by the Icelandic government. A collection, mainly of modern books, on Icelandic studies.

Entries in main library author cat.

Separate author cat and author cat of other Icelandic material in the University Library are available in the Library's Cataloguing Department.

B **Reid Music Library**

Alison House, 12 Nicolson Square, Edinburgh EH8 9DF. Tel (031) 667 1011 Ext 4579. Open Mon-Fri 9 am-5 pm; Sat 9.30 am-12 noon in term only. Closed on public holidays and between Christmas and New Year. Admission to non-members of the University by written application. Xerox and photographic copies; microfilm and microfiche reader; access to music studios with piano and organ.

The nucleus of the library is the private collection of Gen John Reid (*d*1807). The library was begun *c*1850 as a class library, and from 1947 it has been a sectional (faculty) library of Edinburgh University Library. The collection contains *c*3,000 v and is rich in theoretical works of the 17th and 18th cent and in the first editions of printed music. (Researchers should also consult the holdings of the Special Collections Department, Main Library, which include items relevant to the history of music.)

Hans Gal, *Catalogue of manuscripts, printed music and books on music up to 1850 in the library of the Music Department at the University of Edinburgh (Reid Library)*. (Edinburgh, 1941).

Card cat in the Reid Music Library for subsequent additions.

J M Allan, 'The Reid Music Library, University of Edinburgh, its origins and friends', *Library World*, 51 (1948), p99-101.

C **Veterinary Library**

Royal (Dick) School of Veterinary Studies, Summerhall, Edinburgh EH8 1QH. Tel (031) 667 1011 Ext 5275. Open Mon-Fri 9 am-5 pm. Closed on public holidays and between Christmas and New Year. Admission to non-members of the University by written application. Xerox and photographic copies; microfiche readers, microfilm reader/printer.

Veterinary Library The collection dates from the 1820s when William Dick's private library was deposited in the College and made available to students. The Veterinary Library became part of Edinburgh University Library in 1951. There are *c*500 items, comprising mainly 19th cent veterinary works, but also including 18th cent works, chiefly on farriery, and a few items printed pre-1700. The 19th cent collections were the property of a student society, and books migrated from the original collection with changes in the administration of the society. (Researchers should also consult the holdings of the Special Collections Department, Main Library, which include items relevant to the history of veterinary science.)

Card cat in the Veterinary Library.
Incorporated into the general cat in the Main Library.

D **Divinity Section**

(New College Library), Mound Place, Edinburgh EH1 2LU. Tel (031) 225 8400. Open Mon-Fri 9 am-5 pm, except on Good Friday, the Edinburgh Spring and Autumn Monday holidays, and 25th Dec to 3rd Jan. Admission to non-members of the University by written application. Photocopier; microfilm and microfiche readers.

Founded in 1843 by the Free Church of Scotland as a college library for training ministers and for advanced research. It increased by purchase and donation, and more especially by the addition of the collections of the United Presbyterian Church College (1900); Edinburgh Theological Library, founded by Divinity students of the University in 1698 (1936); the Library of the General Assembly of the Church of Scotland (1958); and the Church of Scotland Lending Library (1972).

The collection totals *c*230,000 v, of which *c*100,000 are pre-1850 imprints and include *c*100 incunabula, and many more STC and Wing items than recorded in the bibliographies. The library is one of the chief British research collections in theological, religious, historical and other subjects. Biblical studies, Judaica, Dogmatic theology, Ecclesiastical history, Homiletics, Hymnology, Liturgy, Missions, and Patristics are well represented. The following are the principal special collections in New College Library: The James Thin Hymnology Collection of *c*7,000 items, founded *c*1880 with a gift of 2,000 items, and still being added to; the Dumfries Presbytery Library of *c*1,500 v of mainly 16th and 17th cent publications on theology, history and literature; and the Dalman-Christie Collection of 83 v of Hebrew texts of rabbinic and biblical works published pre-1800.

Author and classified cat in sheaf form, supplemented by the following printed cats:

Catalogue of the printed books and manuscripts in the Library of the New College, Edinburgh. Edinburgh, 1868.

Abridged catalogue of books in New College Library, Edinburgh, 1893.

Supplementary catalogue, Edinburgh 1906.

Catalogue of books, pamphlets and manuscripts in the Library of the General Assembly of the Church of Scotland. Edinburgh, 1907.

A catalogue of the books in the Library belonging to the Presbytery of Dumfries. Dumfries, 1784.

New College, Edinburgh, a centenary history by Hugh Watt, Edinburgh, 1946.

Collections are being added to as a regular policy while funds permit. Books and periodicals in natural science, English literature and other subjects not now covered, have been transferred to the NLS and Edinburgh University Library.

Freemasons' Hall, 96 George Street, Edinburgh EH2 3DF. Tel (031) 225 5304. Open Mon-Fri 9 am-5 pm to scholars and anyone genuinely interested in Freemasonry as a study in social behaviour or as a source for data concerning famous persons who have been freemasons, by arrangement with the Secretary.

Library of the Grand Lodge of Scotland including the Charles Morison Collection The Morison Collection began as the library of the Rite Ecossaise Philosophique, Paris, partly pillaged at the Revolution. On the extinction of the Philosophic Rite in 1826 it passed to Claude Antoine Thory, and on his death in 1827, to Dr Charles Morison who bequeathed it to Grand Lodge in 1849. The library contains *c*2,000 v in the Morison Collection, and *c*3,000 others. The contents of the Morison Collection are mainly of masonic interest, and a large number are in French. The other books, also mainly of masonic interest, are largely in English, but there are a number of foreign (including American) publications. The Morison Collection is largely 18th and 19th cent, but there is one foreign 16th cent item, some 17 foreign 17th cent, and one Wing. The general collection contains also the earliest Masonic Minute Book known, beginning 1598, the original Schaw Statutes 1599 and 2 early 17th cent mss known as the St Clair Charters.

Printed cat of 1906, which lists all the Morison books and a small proportion of the others.

Card cat of the Morison books in author cat.

Card cat of the rest of the library in author order.

Napier College of Commerce and Technology, Colinton Road, Edinburgh EH10 4DT. Tel (031) 447 7070. Open Mon-Thurs 8.45 am-9 pm, Fri 8.45 am-5 pm. Admission by letter to the Librarian indicating precise requirements. Photocopying and microform reading facilities.

Edward Clark Collection Edward Clark (1864–1926), Chairman of R & R Clark Ltd, printers, built up the collection and bequeathed the books to Heriot-Watt College in 1926; they were transferred to Napier College in 1964. The collection consists of *c*2,000 items on the history of printing; many of the 15th cent items are single leaves (eg leaf of the 42-line Gutenberg Bible, 1455).

Bernard Newdigate Collection The collection which belonged to Bernard Newdigate of the Shakespeare Head Press was acquired in 1966. It consists of *c*500 items mainly about 20th cent typography and private presses.

P J W Kirkpatrick (General Editor), *Catalogue of the Edward Clark Library, with typographical notes by Harry Carter and an essay on the printing of illustrations by Frank P Restall*, 2 vols. Edinburgh, 1976.

The cat includes the Newdigate collection of books and all additions to date.

National Library of Scotland, George IV Bridge, Edinburgh EH1 1EW. Tel (031) 226 4531. Telex 72638 NLSEDI G. Main Reading Room and South Reading Room (rare books and manuscripts) open Mon-Fri 9.30 am-8.30 pm; Sat 9.30 am-1 pm. The Library is closed on 1 and 2 January, Good Friday, one Monday in May (variable), Christmas Day and Boxing Day. Admission is for research and reference work using the Library's collections. Special conditions for admission of undergraduates. Enquiries to the Superintendent of Readers' Services. Photography, microfilming, photocopying, beta-radiography of watermarks; microform readers, microfilm reader/printer, plan variograph.

General Collection Founded in 1682 as the Library of the Faculty of Advocates, the non-legal books of which were transferred to the nation as the National Library of Scotland in 1925. The Library has held the British Copyright Privilege since 1710. *c*4,500,000 printed items. Over 20,000 manuscript v and over 15,000 charters catalogued, and an approximately equal quantity uncatalogued. The Library includes the largest number of Scottish books to be found together in one library beginning with the only known copies of the earliest Scottish printing, the Chepman and Myllar prints of 1508. As a result of copyright deposit, the collection of British books is probably more extensive than that of any UK library except the British Library and the libraries of the Universities of Oxford and Cambridge. Foreign books were acquired by the Advocates' Library over nearly 250 years, the greatest treasure being a Gutenberg Bible, and since 1925 foreign books have been acquired in large numbers by donation and purchase. There are upwards of 500 incunabula including, besides the 42-line Bible, a block book (a Biblia Pauperum) one leaf of a xylographic Donatus, and a number of only-known copies. Many of the books printed by the private presses of the late 19th and early 20th cent were deposited or presented and have been kept together. The law books that were in the Library before 1925 remained with the Faculty of Advocates but are entered in the general catalogue, and may be consulted in the Library. Law books deposited since then have been transferred to the Faculty. Scottish bookbindings are well represented, from the oldest known survivor (*c*1480) to the work of present day Scottish binders; included in the collection is a large number of distinctive Scottish bindings of the 18th cent. *c*4,500 STC; *c*15,400 Wing.

Printed catalogues of 1692, 1742–1807, and 1867–79. Catalogue 1 (entries on cards photographed on cassetted 16 mm microfilm) contains entries for all books published before 1968 that were catalogued before 1974. Catalogue 2 contains entries for all books published after 1967 and all books catalogued after 1973; entries added up to December 1977 are on cards; entries after January 1978 are on COM microfiche. Catalogues 1 and 2 include entries for the books in the general collection and most of the special collections. The mss and charters are catalogued in *Catalogue of Manuscripts acquired since 1925*. HMSO, 1938– , vols i *et seq*; the Advocates' Manuscripts are briefly described in *Summary Catalogue of the Advocates' Manuscripts*, HMSO, 1971.

W K Dickson and J M G Barclay, 'List of fifteenth century books in the Library of the Faculty of Advocates', *Publications of the Edinburgh Bibliographical Soc*, v IX (1909), p125-45.

W Beattie, 'First and second supplements to the handlist of incunabula in the National Library of Scotland', *Edinburgh Bibliographical Soc Trans*, v II (1946), p151-228, 331-44.

M A Pegg, 'Incunables in the National Library of Scotland: accessions 1946–66'. *Beitrage zur Inkunabelkunde*, dritte folge (Berlin, Akademie Verlag, 1968).

A short title catalogue of foreign books printed up to 1601, Edinburgh: National Library of Scotland, 1970.

M P Linton, 'Special catalogues in the Department of Printed Books in the National Library of Scotland', *The Bibliotheck*, v 3, no 5 (1962), p173-82.

W K Dickson, 'The Advocates' Library', *LAR*, v V, new series (1927), pp169-78.

——*The National Library of Scotland. An address given to the jubilee conference of the Library Association in Edinburgh, Sept 1927*, 1928 (op).

'The first twenty years of the National Library of Scotland, 1925–45: I Manuscripts by M R Dobie, II Printed Books by W Beattie'. *Edinburgh Bibliographical Soc Trans*, v II (1946), pp287-302.

A Esdaile, 'Edinburgh. The National Library of Scotland', *National Libraries of the World*, 2nd ed, LA, 1957. (op)

D M Lloyd, 'The libraries and museums', *The City of Edinburgh, the third statistical account*, Glasgow: Collins, 1966. (op)

Advocates Library, notable accessions up to 1925. A book of illustrations. Edinburgh: National Library of Scotland, 1965.

Notable accessions since 1925. A book of illustrations, Edinburgh: National Library of Scotland, 1965.

A guide to the National Library of Scotland, Edinburgh: National Library of Scotland, 1976.

Colin Steele, 'National Library of Scotland', *Major Libraries of the World: a selective guide*, Bowker, 1976.

'National Library of Scotland', *Encyclopaedia of library and information science*, v 27, New York: Marcel Dekker, 1979, p98-109.

Various references in *The Bibliotheck* and the *Publications* and the *Transactions* of the Edinburgh Bibliographical Society, including H G Aldis, 'List of books printed in Scotland before 1700', *Publications of the Edinburgh Bibliographical Society*, v VII (1904), photographically reprinted with additions and entries for books published in 1700 by the National Library of Scotland, 1970. (op)

Allhusen Collection Purchased in 1944 from the library of Ernest Lionel Allhusen (1875–1943) of Edinburgh, it totals 425 v of 20th cent French works and many books on fine art, but also including a few earlier books, of which 28 are pre-1850, including 4 STC and 24 Wing items.

Shelf cat.

Alva Collection The collection of James Erskine of Alva, Lord Barjarg (1732–96). Many of the books had previously belonged to his father, Charles Erskine, Lord Tinwald (1680–1783), Lord Justice Clerk, and bear his bookplate. It totals 377 v comprising 362 works; mainly law books of the 16th and 17th cent, including 36 16th cent and 169 17th cent foreign; 10 STC and 24 Wing items.

Shelf cat.

Antiquarian Collection of the Institute of Chartered Accountants of Scotland The library was founded in the 1890s by Richard Brown, CA, Edinburgh, a past-President of the Institution, and built up by him until 1918. Thereafter, accessions were mostly by donation until in 1962 purchasing was resumed. Many books were added from the Institute's libraries in Edinburgh, Glasgow and Aberdeen. The collection contains over 1,000 works, mainly on bookkeeping and accounting; law (Scots); commercial arithmetic; mathematics. Included are 2 incunabula (issues of the first edition of Pacioli, *Summa de Arithmetica*, Venice, 1494); and several STC items. Other items include J Tap: *The Path-Way to Knowledge*, London, 1613 (8 copies known); P Pourrat: *Le Bilan, ou Science des Contes doubles*, Lyon 1676. There are about 200 books published abroad, some 30 in the USA; 138 books pre-1700.

An accountant's book collection, 1494–1930; Catalogue of the antiquarian collection of the Institute of Chartered Accounts of Scotland. With an introduction by Anna B G Dunlop. 3rd ed. Edinburgh, 1976.

Antiquaries Collection Deposited by the Society of Antiquaries of Scotland in 1934 and transferred to the ownership of the NLS in 1949. It consists of *c*400 bound v, a number of pamphlets, and a miscellaneous collection of mss bound up into 319 v, together with 21 charters. It includes 7 incunabula; British and European books from the 16th-19th cent; printed legal documents and sale catalogues.

Shelf cat of printed books. The mss are described and indexed in v ii of the Library's *Catalogue of Manuscripts.*

Annual report of the American Historical Association, 1889– by donation.

Astorga Collection Forms part of the library of the Marqueses de Astorga. It was offered for sale by a London bookseller in 1825 and was bought for £3,000 by the Faculty of Advocates in 1826 on the advice of John Gibson Lockhart. The collection totals 3,617 v comprising *c*4,660 items. It is strong in law, history, theology, travel and the useful arts. Some 390 items in 405 v were printed before 1601, and there are 11 incunabula. Over 90 per cent of the material is in Spanish or printed in Spain. Shelf cat available.

J H London, 'The Astorga Collection of Spanish books in the National Library of Scotland', *Le IIIème Congrès international de bibliophilie, actes et communications*, Barcelona: Asociación de Bibliófilos de Barcelona, 1971, pp89-93.

Birkbeck Collection A selection of books from the library of J A Birkbeck, made after his death, in fulfilment of his wishes, and presented in 1971 by his widow, Mrs Flora Birkbeck and son Dr John Birkbeck. It comprises 260 v, including 35 v of pamphlets. The bulk of the collection is 20th cent dealing with printing and printing history. There are 29 pre-1850 items, including 2 foreign 16th cent. The books are accompanied by printing types and binder's tools.

Shelf cat.

Walter Blaikie Collection Collected by Dr Walter Biggar Blaikie (1847–1928) of the Edinburgh printing firm of T & A Constable, and presented by his daughters in 1928. The collection, which consists of 1,076 printed items in 756 v, 48 mss, 3 charters, and about 20 prints, relates to the history of Jacobitism. Besides historical works on the course of both risings in 1715 and 1745, it contains contemporary poems, satires and sermons, many in French; session papers and acts of parliament dealing with the trials, executions and expropriations that followed both; the pamphlet literature on James's birth, and the wider questions of allegiance and legitimacy that are raised by the risings.

Shelf cat, reproduced in *Shelf-catalogue of the Blaikie Collection of Jacobite pamphlets, broadsides and proclamations*, Boston, G K Hall & Co, 1969. (op) This cat does not include the manuscript items which are described and indexed in v i and ii of the Library's *Catalogue of Manuscripts.*

W G Blaikie Murdoch, 'A bequest of Stuart engravings to the National Library of Scotland', *Apollo*, v 13, January-June 1931, pp167-73.

Blair Collection Collected by Lady Evelyn Stewart Murray (1868–1940) and presented by the 10th Duke of Atholl in 1958. It totals 502 v, including books, pamphlets, music and periodical volumes and parts in, or relating to, all the Celtic languages, but mainly Scottish Gaelic. They are mostly 19th cent but include a few of earlier date.

Shelf cat.

Blairs College Library The library of St Mary's College, Blairs, Aberdeen, deposited in 1974 by the Trustees. It contains *c*27,000 books and pamphlets, and over 50 ms. *c*13,500 books are pre-1801 and include 17 incunabula; *c*200 STC; and 1,000 Wing items, and cover a wide range of topics, including Roman Catholic theology and related subjects, dating from the 15th cent onwards. A considerable number came from the libraries of the Scots Colleges on the Continent. Included are unique copies, eg John Weddington, *A breffe instruction and manner, howe to kepe, marchants bokes*, Antwerp, 1567; John Hamilton, *Ane godlie exhortation* ('The Two-apenny Faith') (St Andrews or Edinburgh, 1559); 'The Copland

Tracts' (London, 1522–33?). The medieval and later mss include the 'Hours of Marie de Rieux', 15th cent; Andrew Lundy's 'Primer', a Scottish liturgical ms of the late 15th or early 16th cent; and Robert Parsons, 'A Memoriall for the reformation of England', 1596.

Cat of printed books in progress. An inventory of the mss is available.

T A Cherry, 'The library of St Mary's College, Blairs', *Bull of the Assoc of British Theological and Philosophical Libraries*, new ser no 3, (June 1975), p10-13.

W S Mitchell, 'Blairs College bindings', *Aberdeen Univ Rev* vol XXXII (1949), p23-9.

The medieval manuscripts are detailed in N R Ker, *Medieval Manuscripts in British Libraries*, v 2, Oxford, 1977.

Graham Brown (Alpine) Collection Bequeathed by Professor Thomas Graham Brown (1882–1965), physiologist and editor of *The Alpine Journal*, and received on his death. The collection contains *c*10,000 items, including 1,317 printed v, 287 bound v of periodicals, 231 v of abstracts and cuttings, maps, films, prints, slides and postcards on Alpinism and mountaineering in general. Also those of his papers relating to his mountaineering activities, consisting of correspondence, diaries, notebooks and other material, together with papers relating to his editorship of the *Alpine Journal* and the authorship of his books. Professor Graham Brown provided a generous fund by which his collection is added to.

Shelf cat of the printed books; inventory of the mss.

Bute Collection Based on the collection of Lady Mary Wortley Montagu and built up by her son-in-law, the third Earl of Bute (1713–1792), the Prime Minister, and by her grandson the first Marquess of Bute (1744–1814), and later expanded by his descendants. It was bought from Major Michael Crichton Stuart in 1956. It comprises 1,266 English plays including seventeen 16th cent editions, 530 17th cent and 650 18th cent editions; 39 Shakespeare quartos—16 printed before 1623.

Shelf cat.

M P Linton, 'The Bute Collection of English plays', *Annual Report of the Friends of the National Libraries, 1956–7*, p8-10.

——'The Bute Collection of English Plays', *Stechert-Hafner Book News*, April 1958, p89-91.

——'Prompt-books in the Bute Collection of English Plays', *Theatre Notebook*, Vol XI, October 1956, p20-3.

——'National Library of Scotland and Edinburgh University Library copies of plays in Greg's *Bibliography of the English Printed Drama*', *Studies in Bibliography*, XV, 1962, p91-104.

The Shakespeare quartos are recorded (as Crichton Stuart copies) in H C Bartlett and A W Pollard, *A census of Shakespeare's plays in quarto, 1594–1709*, New Haven, Yale University Press, 1939.

Campbell Collection Bequeathed by the Gaelic scholar John Francis Campbell of Islay (1822–85) and received by the Faculty of Advocates in 1885. It consists of 270 v comprising 610 printed items, and his correspondence, notebooks and papers, bound up into 134 v. The books, pamphlets, periodical volumes and parts, offprints etc are of the late 18th and 19th cent, mainly on Highland folklore and Celtic subjects. Many are annotated by the collector.

Shelf cat of printed books. The mss are briefly described in the *Library's Summary catalogue of the Advocates' Manuscripts.*

Combe Collection Bequeathed by the Edinburgh phrenologist George Combe (1788–1858), author of *The constitution of man considered in relation to external objects*, 1828, and received by the Faculty of Advocates about 1868. The mss and charters were presented by The Combe Trustees in 1950. It includes 619 printed items in 256 v and his correspondence and papers bound up into 319 v, together with 16 charters. Mainly phrenology, including reviews of Combe's works, proof copies of articles and books, and many editions of Combe's own writings, with material published in Europe and America on phrenology, physiology and education.

Shelf cat and typescript inventory of printed books. The mss are described and indexed in vol vii (unpublished) of the Library's *Catalogue of Manuscripts.*

J E Sait, 'The Combe Collection in the National Library of Scotland', *The Bibliotheck*, v 8, nos 1-2 (1976), p53-4.

Cowan Collection Bequeathed by William Cowan (1852–1929), writer on Scottish liturgies and the maps and history of Edinburgh, and received in 1929. It contains 1,166 printed works in 1,117 v and 4 mss. Mainly liturgical works, including psalters and hymnals, and books on church ceremony, dating from the 16th-20th cent.

Shelf cat. The mss are described and listed in vol ii of the Library's *Catalogue of Manuscripts.*

W Cowan, 'A bibliography of the Book of Common Order and Psalm Book of the Church of Scotland', *Publications of the Edinburgh Bibliographical Soc*, v X (1913), p53-100. (70 works are described, 33 belonging to Cowan, and some of the others are also in the library.)

Cox Collection A collection of some 526 items in 222 v, mainly on temperance and Lord's Day observance, bequeathed by Robert Cox, WS to the Faculty of Advocates in 1872.

Crawford (Indulgences) A collection of 69 items formed by the Earls of Crawford in the 19th cent and deposited on long term loan in 1975 by the 28th Earl of Crawford. The documents include four Imperial decrees and a small number of almanacs and calendars, but most of them are Indulgences chiefly printed between 1479 and 1517.

Crawford (Luther) A collection of *c*1,500 pamphlets formed by the Earls of Crawford in the 19th cent and deposited on long term loan in 1974 by the 28th Earl of Crawford. It consists of tracts by Luther and his contemporaries covering the period from 1511 to 1598, but most of them were printed between 1516 and 1550.

J P Edmond, *Bibliotheca Lindesiana, Collations and notes, 7, catalogue of fifteen hundred tracts by Martin Luther and his contemporaries, 1511–1598*, privately printed, 1903.

M A Pegg, 'A catalogue of German Reformation pamphlets (1516–1546) in libraries of Great Britain and Ireland', *Bibliotheca Bibliographica Aureliana XLV*, Baden-Baden: Valentin Koerner, 1973.

Creswick Collection Presented in 1981 by Dr H R Creswick, Bodley's Librarian 1945–7, Librarian of Cambridge University 1949–67, the collection comprises 62 books and 6 microfilms, early editions of Mme de Sévigné's letters and associated texts.

Shelf cat.

Dieterichs Collection Part of a collection assembled by Georg Septimus Dieterichs, Count Palatine and Senator of Regensburg in the second half of the 18th cent, and purchased by the Advocates' Library in 1820 for £86. It comprises over 100,000 items, including Lutheran tracts, works by Luther, Melanchthon, and other leaders of the Reformation, most of them original editions and printed chiefly in the early part of the 16th cent; academic dissertations of the 16th to 19th cent, and miscellaneous literary material, speeches and announcements, all principally of German origin.

Shelf cat, and sheaf cat of the University theses.

Bibliotheca sive Catalogus librorum quibus utitur Georgius Septimus Dieterichs, 7 parts, Regensburg, 1760–3.

M A Pegg, *op cit.*

Lord George Douglas Collection The library of Lord George Douglas presented to the Faculty of Advocates in 1695 by his father, the 1st Duke of Queensberry, to commemmorate the death of his son in 1693. 831 items in 800 v have been identified. The major portion of the library, consisting of law books, has been retained in the Advocates' Library. European literature (more than half Italian literature or printing) of the 16th and 17th cent, mainly the latter, is well represented. Most of the books are calf-bound, and many have Queensberry armorial stamps.

Shelf cat.

Dowden Collection Brought together mainly by John Dowden (1840–1910), Bishop of Edinburgh. Nearly 1,500 items in 880 v were selected from the Bishop Dowden Memorial Library for deposit on long term loan by the Chapter of St Mary's Cathedral, Episcopal, Edinburgh, in 1954. The collection is of general ecclesiastical and theological interest: it includes a notable collection of liturgical works. The books range from five incunabula to early 20th cent publications.

Shelf cat.

Durdans Collection Selected from the Library at the Durdans, Epsom, and bequeathed by the writer and artist Lady Sybil Grant (1903–55), eldest daughter of the 5th Earl of Rosebery, and widow of Lieut-Gen Sir Charles Grant. Received by the Library in 1956. The collection contains 2,762 v of printed books and 25 v in ms. It is particularly rich in British and European history of the 18th and 19th cent; French and English literature; English topography, in particular Epsom and Surrey; dictionaries of cant, argot and proverbs; religion, including material relating to Cardinal Newman; and sport (including horse racing), equitation and veterinary science. It includes many privately printed books.

Shelf cat. The mss are described and indexed in v viii (unpublished) of the Library's *Catalogue of Manuscripts.*

Ferguson Collection Presented by the bibliographer, Dr F S Ferguson (1878–1967) in 1954. It contains 400 items in 239 v of Scottish printed books and pamphlets of the 16th, 17th and 18th cent.

Shelf cat.

W Beattie, 'For the National Library of Scotland', *Friends of the National Libraries Annual Report 1954–55* (1955), p8-10.

Glen Collection Collected by John Glen (1833–1904), compiler of *The Glen collection of Scottish dance music* (1891, 1895), and author of *Early Scottish melodies* (1900), and presented in 1927 by Lady Dorothea Ruggles-Brise, daughter of the 7th Duke of Atholl, in memory of her brother Lord George Stewart Murray. It contains 412 v (900 items, six of which are mss) which are mainly collections of Scottish songs and tunes, including music for the Highland bagpipe. There are some works on Scottish music, some books of English country dances, and English, Welsh and Irish songs.

Shelf cat of the printed books. Pre-1701 items are recorded in the *British union catalogue of early music.* The mss are described in v ii of the Library's *Catalogue of manuscripts acquired since 1925*, 1966.

Gray Collection Most of the books are from, or associated with, the library of the Rev John Gray of Haddington (1646–1717) which was bequeathed by Gray to his native town. They were deposited in the National Library of Scotland by the Town Council of Haddington and the Gray Library Committee in 1961. In 1983 the deposit was converted into a gift by East Lothian District Council. There are *c*1,500 v, including some 24 v of political and ecclesiastical pamphlets, and 39 v of mss. The bulk of the collection is 16th and 17th cent with some later material. Continental printing is very strongly represented, and the subjects covered are largely theology, and the Greek and Latin classics. The pamphlets are mostly ecclesiastical and political of the second half of the 17th cent. There are three incunabula. The mss are notes of sermons of Gray, written in his hand.

Shelf cat.

J Forbes Gray, *Catalogue of the library of John Gray, Haddington*, Haddington Town Council, 1929. (op)

Gregynog Press Books This collection of 111 items was deposited in 1978 by Mrs Mary M Noble of Edinburgh (niece of the Misses Gwendoline and Margaret Davies of

Gregynog Hall, Montgomeryshire, Wales). It includes the 42 separate works produced by the Gregynog Press between 1923 and 1940, with 69 miscellaneous items by and about the Press, mainly programmes and orders of service for festivals and conferences held at Gregynog Hall.

Thomas Jones, *A paper read to the Double Crown Club on 7th April, 1954 by Thomas Jones, CH* (with a bibliography of the 42 books printed and published). OUP, 1954.

W Ransom, 'The Gregynog Press', *Selective check lists of press books,* New York, Philip C Duschnes, 1963, p152-60.

W Ridler, 'Gregynog Press', *British modern press books,* 2nd ed, Folkestone, Dawson, 1975, p136-8.

Grindlay Collection The private library of the 18th cent Edinburgh merchant, George Grindlay, bequeathed by him in 1801 to the Royal High School, Edinburgh, where he had been a pupil. It was presented by the Royal High School in 1964 and has over 450 v covering a wide range of subjects such as agriculture, mathematics, business and travel.

Shelf cat.

Haxton Collection Collected by John Haxton of Markinch, Fife, and presented by him to the Society of Antiquaries of Scotland. Deposited by the Society in 1934 and transferred to the National Library's ownership in 1949. There are 191 works in 127 v, consisting of Bibles and parts of the Scriptures in English, nearly all of the 16th and 17th cent.

Shelf cat.

Hume Collection A collection of books and pamphlets on South America, presented by John Hume of Edinburgh in 1924, and consisting of 114 v printed between 1863 and 1920, the majority between 1880 and 1910. The subjects covered include history, language, folklore, costume, and the anthropology of Chile and Patagonia.

Shelf cat.

Inglis Collection Bequeathed in 1929 by Alexander Wood Inglis of Glencorse, Secretary of the Board of Manufactures (1854–1929), it totals 306 v containing 740 items (27 of the v are mss) relating mostly to English and Scottish music of the 18th and early 19th cent, including many single-sheet songs.

Shelf cat of the printed items. Pre-1701 items are recorded in the *British Union Catalogue of early music.* The mss are described and indexed in v ii of the Library's *Catalogue of Manuscripts.*

Jolly Collection Collected by Alexander Jolly (1756–1838), Bishop of Moray in the Episcopal Church. A large selection was deposited on long-term loan by the Theological College of the Episcopal Church of Scotland, Edinburgh in 1958. In 1970 this deposit was converted into a gift, and the remaining books from Jolly's library were added to it. It contains 2,976 v mostly on theological subjects. Apart from 2 incunabula, the books date from the 16th to 19th cent.

Shelf cat.

Keiller Collection This totals 239 works in 242 v collected by the Scottish archaeologist Alexander Keiller (1889–1955), and presented by his widow, Mrs Gabrielle Keiller, in 1966. It includes British, European and American works on witchcraft and demonology, including one incunabulum (Ulrich Molitor, *De lamiis et phitonicis mulieribus,* 1489), and numerous pamphlets and treatises of the 16th and 17th cent, as well as later material up to the middle of the 19th cent.

Shelf cat.

This collection is described (with seven illustrations) in *Edinburgh Tatler,* March, 1967.

Lauriston Castle Collection The collection was formed at his home, Lauriston Castle, by William Robert Reid (1854–1919), an Edinburgh businessman, with the help of his friend John A Fairley, author of several bibliographical papers on chapbooks. There are over 3,700 v containing over 11,000 items; including *c*500 v of chapbooks comprising over 5,500 items. The chapbooks were collected by Fairley, bought by the Reid Trustees, and added to the bequest from Mr and Mrs Reid in 1925. Books and pamphlets are mainly on Scottish literature, antiquities and topography, but with a considerable number on banking and trade.

Shelf cat reproduced in *Catalogue of the Lauriston Castle Chapbooks,* Boston: G K Hall & Co, 1964.

J A Fairley, 'Bibliography of the chapbooks attributed to Dougal Graham', *Records of the Glasgow Bibliographical Society,* v I (1914), p125-215.

——'Bibliography of Robert Fergusson', *Ibid* v III (1915), p115-55.

——'Peter Buchan, printer and ballad collector, with a bibliography', *Trans of the Buchan Field Club,* v VII (1904), p123-58.

——'Ancient Scottish tales—an unpublished collection made by Peter Buchan', *Ibid,* v IX (1909), p128-94.

——'Chapbooks and Aberdeen chapbooks', *Aberdeen book-lover,* v 2, no 2 (November 1916), p29-34.

E B Lyle, 'Song chapbooks with Irish imprints in the Lauriston Castle Collection, National Library of Scotland', *Irish Folk Music Studies* 2 (1975), p15-30.

Lloyd Collection Bequeathed by Robert Wylie Lloyd (1868–1958), a former vice-president of the Alpine Club, the collection contains *c*2,000 items, including some 1,400 printed v and 10 v of mss. The printed v, bound v of periodicals and abstracts, pamphlets and periodical parts relate to mountaineering, and mostly, but not exclusively, to Alpine matters. The majority of the books are from the second half of the 19th cent onwards, but a half-dozen or so are late 16th cent, over a dozen are 17th cent and over 100 date from the 18th cent. The books published before the middle of the 18th cent deal mainly with Switzerland's topography, institutions and history. Most of the books and journals are in English, but *c*300 are in French, well over 100 are in German, a score or so in Italian, and a few of the older books are in Latin.

Shelf cat reproduced in *Shelf-catalogue of the Lloyd Collection of Alpine Books*, Boston: G K Hall & Co, 1964. (op)

The mss are described and indexed in v iv of the Library's *Catalogue of Manuscripts*.

Books on the subject are added to the Graham Brown Collection.

Lyle Collection Some 300 books purchased with £500 donated, in 1925, by Sir Alexander Park Lyle, 1st Baronet of Glendelvine (1849–1938), Chairman of the Lyle Shipping Company. They are mainly books on ships, shipping and shipbuilding, including 62 printed before 1850.

Shelf cat.

Macadam Collection Bequeathed by Joseph Hancock Macadam, President of the Scottish Association of Master Bakers, and received in 1951. The collection consists of 2,837 items in 1,619 v, and includes works on baking and confectionary of the late 19th and early 20th cent, with a strong French and German representation.

Shelf cat.

James Ramsay MacDonald Collection Presented in 1981 by the children of the Rt Hon James Ramsay MacDonald and Margaret Ethel MacDonald, it contains over 600 books (including pamphlets and albums) remaining from the library of James Ramsay MacDonald (1866–1937), first Labour Prime Minister, including early school and student books relating to his studies at Lossiemouth and London; socialist and other books and pamphlets mainly acquired during his early years in politics; and other works, mainly of political interest, acquired throughout his life; also books on Scottish history and literature; albums containing press cuttings, letters and telegrams of condolence on the death of his wife, Margaret Ethel MacDonald (1870–1911); and some books that belonged to Mrs MacDonald and her family. Many of the books bear MacDonald's signature, and a few are annotated.

Eudo Mason Collection Formed by Professor Eudo Mason, Professor of German in the University of Edinburgh, and presented in 1969 by his executors following his expressed intention, the collection contains over 3,600 children's books and related material, including 21 items in ms, mainly of the 19th cent.

Shelf cat of the printed books.

There is an inventory of the mss.

Monro Collection A miscellaneous collection of 160 British and European books of the 17th to the early 19th cent from the library of the family of Monro of Auchinbowie, descendants of the famous Edinburgh medical family, presented in 1960 by Lt Col A G F Monro.

Shelf cat.

Hew Morrison Collection Bought in 1935 from the library of Hew Morrison, LLD (1850–1935), Edinburgh's first City Librarian, it consists of 320 v comprising works in and about the Scottish Gaelic language, books and pamphlets of the second half of the 18th and the 19th cent. All but a few are in Scottish Gaelic.

Shelf cat.

Lord Murray Collection Books from the library of Sir John Archibald Murray, Lord Murray (1779–1859), a Senator of the College of Justice, given to the Advocates' Library in 1853. They total 172 v, and are mainly on historical, economic and literary subjects, dating from the 16th to the first half of the 19th cent.

Shelf cat.

Newbattle Collection Bequeathed by Philip Henry Kerr, 11th Marquess of Lothian (1882–1940), and acquired by the library in 1950. It totals 5,158 books—the major portion of the Newbattle Abbey Library—relating to European literature and history of the 16th-18th cent. The collection is in the care of the present Marquess, but in special circumstances books from it can be consulted in the National Library upon application made well in advance.

Shelf cat.

NLS MSS 5818-27 cats of the family libraries at Newbattle and in London, 1666–1876.

NLS MS 5828. Letter and papers concerning the family libraries, 1643–1899.

Donald Drew Egbert, *The Tickhill Psalter*. New York, New York Public Library and Princeton University, 1940, p8-10, 128-30.

Newhailes Collection The library of Sir David Dalrymple, Lord Hailes (1726–92), Senator of the College of Justice, accepted by H M Government from the Trustees of the late Sir Mark Dalrymple Bt in lieu of estate duty and allocated to the National Library of Scotland in 1978. It contains *c*7,000 v and a number of pamphlets, broadsheets, prints, maps and music, together with the Newhailes papers, being the correspondence and papers of Lord Hailes and other Dalrymples of Hailes and Newhailes. Also Lord Hailes's own collection of books from the 16th-18th cent with one incunabulum. It comprises a large number of the best works, both British and foreign, in literature and most branches of knowledge; strongest in history and biography (1,789 v), literature, classical and modern (2,470 v), law, politics and economics (1,098 v) and theology (762 v); with science (269 v) and geography (174 v). 453 lots were disposed of by the family at a Sotheby sale on 24 and 25 May 1937, including 23 incunabula, some 182 STC books (of which 20 had Scottish imprints), and many 18th cent foreign books.

Cat in progress for printed books.

The mss are uncatalogued, but an inventory is available.

Newman Collection Acquired in 1973 from the estate of Professor S T M Newman (1906–71), Reid Professor of Music at Edinburgh University, 1941–70. It contains 1,150 items, including road-books, itineraries, guides, maps and atlases, mostly of the British Isles, ranging from the 16th to the 19th cent.

Shelf cat.

Oliphant Collection Presented in 1972 by Mrs Emily Valentine of Alyth, Perthshire, a descendant of Mrs Margaret Oliphant, the 19th cent novelist. The collection consists of 271 v, including 163 editions of books and pamphlets by Mrs Oliphant.

Shelf cat.

Orrock Collection 41 v deposited by the Minister and Session of Hawick Old Parish Church in 1980, the collection contains theological books from the library of the Rev Alexander Orrock (1652–1711), minister of Hawick (1691–1711). They comprise English and Continental books, mainly of the 17th cent, including 1 16th cent and 16 17th cent foreign; 2 STC; and 2 Wing, and a number of unidentified editions.

Checklist.

Ossian Collection Collected by J Norman Methven of Perth, and presented by him in 1941, it contains 252 works in 327 v. Dating from 1760 (the first edition of *Fragments of ancient poetry*), and bearing on James Macpherson's Ossianic publications, the collection includes early editions in several languages, works occasioned by the Ossianic controversy, and the widespread vogue of the theme in Europe and elsewhere, with some works of modern scholarship.

Shelf cat.

G F Black, 'Macpherson's Ossian and the Ossianic controversy, a contribution towards a bibliography', *Bulletin of the New York Public Library*, Vol XXX, (1926), I p424-39, II p508-24.

J J Dunn, 'Macpherson's Ossian and the Ossianic controversy: a supplementary bibliography', *Bulletin of the New York Public Library*, Vol LXXV (1971), p465-73.

Payne Collection Bequeathed by Mrs Susanna Shaxby Payne through the National Art Collections Fund, and received in 1959. It totals 400 books and pamphlets, including illustrated books, mainly of the early 19th cent, and also material relating to Francis Bacon, with a number of early editions of his works.

Shelf cat.

Perth Cathedral Library A selection of 75 v and *c*3,750 pamphlets purchased from the Rt Rev the Bishop of St Andrews, Dunkeld and Dunblane, and the Chapter of St Ninian's Cathedral, Perth, in 1977. The books include 18th cent Bibles and works by Erasmus, Melanchthon, George Buchanan, David Hume and John Locke; most of the pamphlets are on matters relating to ecclesiastical affairs, and in particular to the Episcopal Church in Scotland. The Bishop and Chapter deposited 84 v of liturgical works, many of the Episcopal Church in Scotland.

Shelf cat.

Pol E Collection Presented by the Polish Community in Edinburgh in 1962 to mark the Millenium of the Polish State, the collection contains 850 books and 139 pamphlets, mainly recent Polish publications, some commemorating the Polish Millenium.

Shelf cat.

Pol S Collection Presented by the Society of Writers to Her Majesty's Signet. In the 1820s the Society had received a collection of Polonica from Count Konstanty Zamoyski and other Polish exiles who had been allowed to use the Signet Library (qv), and in 1962 this collection was handed over to the National Library of Scotland. It totals 143 v of Polish books dating from the 16th to early 19th cent.

Shelf cat.

Pol T Collection Presented in 1964 by Count Jan Tarnowski, it contains 131 v of modern Polish works.

Shelf cat.

Preshome Chapel Library The library of the Chapel House at Preshome, Banffshire, deposited in 1975 by the Trustees consisting of *c*4,700 books, pamphlets and periodical parts. The main emphasis is on religious topics, but there are also works on literature, history, philosophy, economics and law. Much of the material was collected by Bishop James Kyle, Vicar-Apostolic of the Northern District of Scotland, 1828–69.

Cat in progress.

D McRoberts, 'Some sixteenth-century Scottish breviaries', *The Innes Review*, v III (1952), p33-48.

Protestant Institute Collection Selected works from the library of the Protestant Institute of Scotland, Edinburgh, deposited in 1963. The collection totals 571 items in 317 v, including 50 v of pamphlets and 2 v of mss, and relating to Roman Catholic and Protestant theology, mainly of the 17th, 18th and 19th cent, but including a few 16th cent items. The majority are British publications, but there are many continental works, and a few American.

Shelf cat of printed books.

The mss are described in v vii of the *Catalogue of manuscripts acquired since 1925*, unpublished.

Renwick Collection Some 27 books dealing mainly with 16th cent Italian and French literature relating to Spenserian studies, with one incunabulum, presented by Professor W L Renwick (1889–1970), Regius Professor of Rhetoric and English Literature at Edinburgh University.

Shelf cat.

Rosebery Collection Presented by the fifth Earl of Rosebery (1847–1929) in 1927, the collection contains *c*7,000 items in 3,000 v. Lord Rosebery's correspondence and papers, which are bound up in 216 v, were presented in 1966 by Lord Primrose, later the seventh Earl of Rosebery. It is in three sections: (a) a general section of some 700 v, including a series of broadsides and proclamations on Scottish subjects; (b) over 300 books relating to Mary Queen of Scots, which include most of the editions described in J Scott, 'A bibliography of works relating to Mary Queen of Scots, 1544–1700', *Publications of the Edinburgh Bibliographical Society*, vol II (1896), p1-96, with 20 facsimiles, and, in addition, about a dozen unknown to Scott; (c) over 2,000 single pamphlets and 120 v of pamphlets bound together covering the period of Scottish history from 1583–1903. All the volumes have the fifth Earl's bookplate and have either early bindings or good 19th cent bindings by well-known binders.

Shelf cat of the printed books.

Catalogue of the pamphlets (in ms), chronological with index.

The mss are described and indexed in vol viii (unpublished) of the Library's *Catalogue of Manuscripts*.

The Rosebery Collections: an exhibition held in the National Library of Scotland, 26 August-30 September, 1958. Edinburgh: National Library of Scotland, 1958.

The subjects are parts of the Library's general collecting interests.

Royal High School, Edinburgh, Library A collection of 233 v from the Royal High School Library, 94 of which were purchased in 1968, and a further 129 were presented by Edinburgh Public Libraries in 1973 (until 1968 formed part of the Royal High School Library).

The texts mainly are of or relate to Greek and Latin classics. Most of the works were published in the 17th, 18th and 19th cent, but the collection includes 1 15th cent, and 7 16th cent books.

Shelf cat.

School Prize Books Built around a nucleus of a small collection of school prize books presented by Messrs John Grant, booksellers, in 1964 and subsequently added to by purchase and gift, the collection at present consists of 410 items in 397 v. They are mainly, but not exclusively, prize books of Scottish schools, principally of the 19th cent. The collection is added to regularly.

Shelf cat. Sheaf cat by school.

Hugh Sharp Collection Collected by Hugh Sharp (1897–1937), jute manufacturer, Dundee, and presented in 1938, after his death, by his mother and sister. There are 889 printed works in 1,244 v (some of which contain inscriptions or manuscripts), mainly first editions of English and American classics, in unusually fine condition, many in original state.

Shelf cat of the printed books.

A selection of the inscriptions and mss are indexed in vol ii of the Library's *Catalogue of Manuscripts.*

Henderson Smith Collection It consists of some 90 v, and was bequeathed by Dr John Henderson Smith of Harpenden, and received in 1953. It comprises a large collection of bookplates, Scottish, English and colonial, mounted in 40 v, with indexes and 40 works about bookplates of heraldry.

Shelf cat.

Slip cat of the bookplates arranged alphabetically under the names of the owners, with brief descriptions of the bookplates and notes on points of special interest.

Note: There are three smaller collections of bookplates, the Culley (5 v), the Stitt (3 v), and the Lamb (23 v) which complement the Henderson Smith Collection.

Nichol Smith Collection Presented by Professor D Nichol Smith (1875–1962), formerly of the Merton Chair of English Literature, University of Oxford, mostly in 1959. The books, over 900 in number, were published in France, Britain and elsewhere in Western Europe in the 16th, 17th and 18th cent, and illustrate relations between English and French literature. There are also works by Defoe, and books in Anglo-Saxon types.

Shelf cat.

A S Bell, 'Nichol Smith Collections in Edinburgh and Oxford', *Studies in the Eighteenth Century II. Papers presented at the Second David Nichol Smith Memorial Seminar Canberra 1970*, Canberra: Australian National University Press, 1973, p397-409.

A ms of the address on David Nichol Smith given by Professor W Beattie at a private view of the David Nichol Smith Centenary exhibition, 1976, in the NLS is held by the Library's Department of Manuscripts. Acc No 6595.

Annie S Swan Collection Presented in 1973 by the Rev and Mrs E M Rule of Oyne, Aberdeenshire, it totals 60 v. There is also a collection of correspondence, mss, typescripts and other papers in six folio boxes. There are 65 works by Annie S Swan (Mrs Burnett-Smith) specially bound for the author.

Shelf cat of printed books.

The ms material is uncatalogued but there is an inventory.

Maitland Thomson Collection Presented in 1912 by John Maitland Thomson (1847–1923), Curator of the Historical Department of the Scottish Record Office (1895–1906), the collection is made up of 112 v comprising 161 works. They are mainly English plays, of which 2 are 16th cent editions, 6 are 18th cent, and the remainder 17th cent editions. There are also 3 incunabula.

Shelf cat.

Thorkelin Collection The nucleus of the Library's Scandinavian collection, *c*1,500 books, is formed from the personal library of Prof Grimur Thorkelin (1752–1829), the Icelandic philologist and antiquary, purchased by the Faculty of Advocates in 1819 from David Laing (1793–1878), then a young bookseller in Edinburgh, but later to become librarian to the Society of Writers to the Signet. Additions to the Scandinavian collection have been made from time to time by purchase and donation. The collection of *c*1,500 printed works and 96 ms v is particularly rich in early printed texts of the Icelandic sagas, and has some 16th cent Danish books. Its range includes law, medicine, history, language, folklore, topography and periodicals in editions published between 1500 and 1900.

Shelf cat of the printed books.

The mss are briefly described in the library's *Summary Catalogue of the Advocates' Manuscripts*, HMSO, 1971.

Norway in books and manuscripts, an exhibition, Edinburgh: National Library of Scotland, 1963.

Scandinavia, an exhibition, Edinburgh: Ibid, 1970.

A A Calderwood, 'Danish Libraries in Britain', *Denmark: a monthly review of Anglo-Danish relations* (June, July 1948), p8-9, 13-14.

D Wyn Evans, 'A note on the content of the Thorkelin Collection in the National Library of Scotland' and 'Inscriptions and bookplates from the Thorkelin Collection in the National Library of Scotland', *The Bibliotheck*, vol IV (1963–6), p79-80, 247-8.

Urquhart Collection Made up of books from the library of Adam Urquhart, Sheriff of Wigton, and presented to the Advocates' Library in 1913, the collection contains 154 v representing 39 Italian, French and English works, mainly of the 18th cent.

Shelf cat.

Warden Collection Presented by John Mabon Warden, Edinburgh, Vice-President of the Esperantista Akademio in 1927, the collection consists of *c*4,600 items relating to hundreds of systems of shorthand from the abbreviated writing of Cicero's freedman Tiro, to the most recent methods. There are *c*50 17th cent and 120 18th cent books, *c*500 works in foreign languages and *c*60 mss.

The collection was catalogued by Mr Warden himself, and the catalogue, partly ms, partly typescript, accompanied the collection. A continuation of his catalogue for works in and on shorthand acquired by the Library is still kept up to date.

Shelf cat of the printed books.

There is an inventory of the mss.

Weir Collection Presented by Miss Kathleen M Weir in 1970, the collection is made up of 525 items, including posters, mainly of Edinburgh theatres of 1870s to 1890s, with playbills, programmes, photographs and cuttings.

Shelf cat.

Mary Fleming, 'Old Edinburgh theatre posters', *Scotland's SMT Magazine* Dec 1950, p38-41.

Wordie Collection Presented in 1959 by Sir James Mann Wordie (1889–1962), geologist and explorer, Master of St John's College, Cambridge (1952–9), it comprises over 4,600 printed items (including journals, reports and over 2,000 pamphlets), 16 maps, and correspondence and papers chiefly concerned with the Discovery Committee, and some other mss relating to Polar exploration collected by Wordie, altogether made up into 68 v. The collection includes popular accounts, old and new, of travel in polar and sub-polar regions; technical reports of scientific expeditions; many detailed works confined to smaller areas; government publications; works on the geology of the polar regions; and on almost every aspect of polar studies. Most of the works published 1850–1940, with more recent issues of foreign scientific journals on polar studies, including *Meddelelser om Grønland*, beginning with the first v in 1879. The earliest printing is the second edition (1614) of Purchas; of *c*60 works published in the 18th cent (over 90 v), some are accounts of voyages and discoveries of an earlier age, several with interesting plates and maps. Most of the books are in English, over 400 are in German, *c*200 in Scandinavian languages, nearly 150 in French, over 60 in Dutch, *c*20 in Spanish (mostly Argentinian), and a few in other languages, including Russian, Italian, Latin, Czech, Polish and Eskimo.

Shelf cat reproduced: *Shelf-catalogue of the Wordie Collection of Polar Exploration*, Boston: G K Hall & Co, 1964. (op)

The mss are described and indexed in vol viii (unpublished) of the Library's *Catalogue of Manuscripts.*

Yule Collection Presented by Thomas Yule, WS, in 1927, it is made up of 184 v, many containing numerous pamphlets, and a collection (bequeathed in 1941) of mss bound up into 52 v, together with 61 charters. The collection relates chiefly to British trials and peerage cases from the 17th-19th cent.

Shelf cat of the printed books.

The mss and charters are described in vol ii of the Library's *Catalogue of Manuscripts.*

Private Libraries. Application (stating reasons) for further information and access to any of the books (either or both of which may be granted or refused at the owner's discretion) should be made to the Librarian, National Library of Scotland, George IV Bridge, Edinburgh EH1 1EW.

A

The library of a noble Scottish family, the collection of which commenced in the 16th cent, and now contains *c*4,000 v. There are 110 STC items; 67 Wing items; 150 16th cent and 190 17th cent foreign books. The library contains the collection of the founder (one of the leading Scottish politicians of his day) of *c*250 v, mostly on history, politics, political thought and literature in Latin, French and Italian, including writings by Machiavelli, Ariosto, Aretino and Montaigne. The remainder of the library represents a family collection built up over nearly four centuries, including works on history, biography, geneaology, heraldry, travel, vernacular (mainly English, French and Italian) literature, including drama, Greek and Latin classics, law, philosophy and natural history. There are *c*100 fine bindings, including some French, Italian and Spanish armorial bindings, and one example of the work of James Scott of Edinburgh.

Three-quarters of the books are recorded in a card cat which includes the founder's collection, of which there is also a separate list.

B

The library of a noble Scottish family, collected from the 17th cent onwards. It contains *c*3,000 v, roughly half of which are pre-1851. There are 1 incunabulum; 2 early Scottish books; and a strong Wing representation, mainly in a set of 30 v containing *c*200 late 17th cent ecclesiastical pamphlets. Although numerically the main strength is post-1700, there are many 16th and 17th cent books, including a copy of Ortelius, *Théâtre de l'univers*, 1587, and Hobbes, *Leviathian*, 1651. Subjects include history and antiquities, genealogy, travel and topography, literature (Scottish, English, Continental and classical), religion, including early editions of the Fathers, some law and natural history, and music of the 18th and 19th cent.

Cat of the present contents of the library.

C

A general library of *c*2,000 v covering travel, topography, natural history, art, antiquities, architecture, heraldry, genealogy, history, literature (Scottish, English, French and Italian), Greek and Latin classics, works on Mary Queen of Scots. There are 2 incunabula (Milan 1498 and Strassburg 1500); *c*50 STC; *c*90 Wing items; *c*100 v in French and a few in Italian dated post-1600 and pre-1701; over 30 v of mss, including 'Admission ceremonies of l'hostel Dieu de Paris' (17th cent); a commonplace book (1677); 4 French books of hours (15th cent); a number of royal letters (1491–1684) bound in a volume; a local court book (1739–44); 'A collection of countrey dances by David Yung' (1734)—obl 8° in a Scottish 18th cent 'wheel' binding of red morocco, gold-tooled.

Cat compiled in 1910.

D

The library of a noble Scottish family, the collection of which began in the 17th cent and now contains *c*2,600 works in 3,800 v (the residue of a larger library, much of which was dispersed). About one-third of the works are of vernacular literature, and 6 per cent of classical literature; 30 per cent are on history and topography; 20 per cent on science and the arts, including architecture; 13 per cent on philosophy, law and religion. The majority of the books were printed in the 16th, 17th and 18th cent, and more than half were printed on the Continent. There are *c*40 STC and 250 Wing items. The library contains a copy of *Valerii Maximi dictorum exempla*, Lugduni 1541, in a 16th cent binding bearing the stamp of the Earl of Moray, Regent of Scotland, and some of the works of the Foulis Press of Glasgow, including the folio Homer of 1756–8 and *Paradise Lost* of 1770. There are also some works on architecture, including Vitruvius, *De architectura*, Lugduni 1552, and Rusconi, *Della architettura*, Venetia, 1590.

Cat of the collection as it was in 1962, but some dispersal has taken place since then.

E

A family collection of *c*1,900 v (pre-1851) built up over several centuries. There are 4 incunabula and *c*40 foreign books printed in the 16th cent, *c*90 STC British books, and *c*130 Wing British books. The collection is a general one covering the Greek and Latin classics, history, literature, religion, sport and travel. There has been some loss by fire, and dispersal at auction during the 20th cent.

Cat with one-line entries that do not give places of publication.

Royal Botanic Garden, Inverleith Row, Edinburgh EH3 5LR. Tel (031) 552 7171 Ext 223. Open Mon-Fri 8.30 am-1 pm, 2-5 pm (Fri 4.30 pm). Visitors admitted by appointment. Xerox copies. Microfilm reader/printer, microfiche reader available.

Royal Botanic Garden Library Books belonging to successive Keepers have been available in the Botanic Garden since its foundation in 1670; some of these collections remain wholly, or in part, in the library. The expansion of the collection dates from 1889 when the Botanic Garden came under Government control. It now contains *c*25,000 v of pre-1850 imprints which primarily relate to botany and horticulture, including the catalogues of nurserymen and seed lists, but it is also rich in material relating to the history of medicine, agriculture, travel and the biography of botanists and natural historians. There is an extensive collection of cuttings from printed books of botanical illustrations. It is the foremost botanical and horticultural collection in Scotland.

Card cat (author and classified).

H R Fletcher and W H Brown, *The Royal Botanic Garden, Edinburgh 1670–1970* (Edinburgh, 1970).

Royal College of Physicians of Edinburgh, 9 Queen Street, Edinburgh EH2 1JQ. Tel (031) 225 5968. Open Mon-Fri 9 am-5 pm. Admission by introduction or application to Librarian if not a registered reader. Reference material available for use at the College or *via* inter-library loan; photocopying machine; microfilm reader; cassette/slide-tape recorder.

General Collection The library dates from the foundation of the College in 1681. Important early acquisitions included the libraries of Patrick Murray (1705), Dr John Drummond (1741), Dr Edward Wright of Kersie (1761), Dr John Clerk (purchased 1860). Large purchases were made at the sale of William Cullen's library in 1791. The collection of printed material comprises *c*30,000 pre-1851 titles (monographs, pamphlets and journals) and covers most of the subject fields of medicine, dating from Celsus, 1478. It is relatively strong in anatomy as well as zoology and topography, with some holdings of alchemical and chemical literature. Holdings of works by Scottish medical writers are comprehensive. The collection includes 20 incunabula, *c*500 pre-1600 and 70 STC items. A few pre-1851 journals (medical, scientific and general) are also included. The pre-1600 material is recorded in G D Hargreaves, *A Catalogue of medical incunabula in Edinburgh libraries*, Edinburgh, Royal Medical Society, 1976; D T Bird, *A Catalogue of 16th century printed medical books in Edinburgh libraries*, Edinburgh, Royal

College of Physicians, 1982. *A catalogue of the Library of the Royal College of Physicians of Edinburgh*, 2 v, Edinburgh 1898 (op); supplemented by card cat of pre-1900 material. *Royal College of Physicians of Edinburgh: The Library.* A leaflet available from the *Physicians of Edinburgh*, Edinburgh, 1976.

Simpson Collection The library of Sir James Young Simpson (1811–70), with additions. Donated by Sir Alexander Russell Simpson (1835–1916) in 1913. The collection contains 1,500 printed books and *c*2,000 pamphlets, chiefly obstetrical works dating from the 16th to 19th cent, and includes Harvey's *De motu cordis*, 1628.

Separate cat and index to pamphlets available.

Manuscripts (general) Archive material dates from the foundation of the College in 1681. Other manuscript material was donated or purchased chiefly during the 19th cent. The collection comprises *c*1,000 bound v besides loose papers and College archives. The mss range in date from 14th to 20th cent, and chiefly reflect the development of the Medical School in Edinburgh; they include monographs, lectures, case-books, notebooks, prescription notes, drawings and correspondence relating to many aspects of medicine. The collection also includes cash books, diaries and the minute books of several medical societies and clubs. Early mss include *Cursor mundi* 14th cent; *Judicium urinarum* 14th cent, and an alchemical roll of George Ripley, late 15th cent.

Typescript checklist available in the College Library.

Cullen Collection of MSS [William Cullen 1710–90]. Acquired by donations, principally through the agency of Dr John Thomson (1765–1846), Cullen's biographer. The collection consists of 102 v with a few loose papers which include lectures on medicine, clinical medicine, chemistry, materia medica, etc, as well as Cullen's ms annotations in two printed medical works.

Details in checklist of manuscripts.

Duncan Collection of MSS [Andrew Duncan 1744–1828]. Bequeathed by Andrew Duncan, the elder, in 1828, the collection consists of 180 v of ms material: medical and chemical monographs, lectures and notes dating chiefly before 1750, including works by B S Albinus, C Alston, J Black, F Nicholls, A Plummer, J Rutherford, A St Clair and others.

Details in checklist of manuscripts.

Simpson Collection of MSS *c*123 ms v collected by Sir James Young Simpson (1811–70) and his nephew Sir Alexander Russell Simpson (1835–1916), which include ms monographs, lectures and case notes, almost exclusively devoted to obstetrics. Some 18th cent material, but chiefly from the first half of the 19th cent. Authors included are W Brody, J Clarke, J Dickson, J Drummond, J Goodsir, A Gordon, J Hamilton (the younger), W Henderson, etc.

Details in checklist of manuscripts.

Royal College of Surgeons of Edinburgh, 18 Nicolson Street, Edinburgh EH8 9DW. Tel (031) 556 6206. Open Mon-Fri 9 am-5 pm. Admission by letter, with a reference, to the College. Early materials and mss not accessible except by the express permission of the Council of the College, and then to be examined only under the direct supervision of the Librarian. Photocopying on request; photographic facilities available.

The Library The College was founded in 1505 but the library was given to the University in the 18th cent. It was reformed after 1832 and helped by a gift in 1845 of *c*1,000 v from the daughters of John Abercrombie (1780–1844) which included three incunabula. The library consists of *c*6,000 v (books and periodicals) with special emphasis on surgery, history of medicine, medical biography, including papers of Sir J Y Simpson (1811–70) and John Struthers.

Dictionary card cat available.

Royal Medical Society, Students' Centre, Bristo Street, Edinburgh EH8 9AL. Tel (031) 667 1011 Ext 4561. Open 12 noon-5 pm. Xerox facilities.

Royal Medical Society Library The Society was established in 1734, and the library, which was developed subsequently, was largely disposed of (Sotheby's 10-11 Feb, 14-15 July, 27-28 Oct 1969, and 2-3 Feb 1970). The remaining stock contains *c*300 v (mostly pre-1851) medical books having a particular association with the Society or Edinburgh medicine, and copies of medical books unique to Edinburgh libraries.

Typewritten list by author.

James Gray, *History of the Royal Medical Society, 1737–1937*, ed by Douglas Guthrie (Edinburgh, 1952).

J J C Cormack, 'The Society's library', a dissertation read to the Royal Medical Society of Edinburgh, 28 Feb 1958.

——*Bull Med Lib Assoc*, 48 (1960), p125-41.

Helen Crawford, 'The Royal Medical Society of Edinburgh: sale of its library at Sotheby's', *Ibid* 58 (1970), p531-47.

Antonia J Bunch, *Hospital and medical libraries in Scotland: an historical and sociological study*, Glasgow (1975), p38-43.

Royal Observatory, Blackford Hill, Edinburgh EH9 3HJ. Tel (031) 667 3321. Open by arrangement with the Librarian or Crawford Librarian. Admission to researchers in the history of science, scholars and bibliographers. Microfiche readers, xerox facilities, photography by arrangement.

Crawford Library Presented to the nation in 1888 by James Ludovic Lindsay (1847–1913), 26th Earl of Crawford and 9th Earl of Balcarres, at a time when the future of the observatory was in doubt. The observatory, therefore, owes its continued existence to this priceless collection of old books and mss. The library is made up of *c*11,000 items with strong emphasis on astronomy, mathematics and physics, and includes the largest collection of cometary tracts in the world. It also includes the mathematical and scientific library of Charles Babbage, and books and mss of the French Academician Michel Chasles (1793–1880).

Catalogue of the Crawford Library of the Royal Observatory, Edinburgh, 1890. (op)

Supplement, Edinburgh 1977.

Standard re-cataloguing in progress, and all the pre-1600 items have been completed.

D A Kemp, 'The Crawford Library of the Royal Observatory, Edinburgh', *Isis* v 54, p482.

H A Bruck, *The Royal Observatory, Edinburgh, 1822–1972*, Edinburgh, 1972.

E G Forbes, 'The Crawford Collection of the Royal Observatory, Edinburgh', *Pub Roy Obs Edin*, v 9(1), p7-13.

M J Smyth and M F I Smyth, 'Cataloguing the Crawford Collection by Computer', *Ibid*, p14-19.

G P Johnston, 'The Crawford Library, Royal Observatory', in: *Lists of fifteenth century books in Edinburgh libraries (compiled) by members of the Edinburgh Bibliographical Society*. Edinburgh, The Society, 1913.

G D Hargreaves, *Catalogue of medical incunabula in Edinburgh libraries*, Edinburgh: Royal Medical Society, 1976.

G Grassi Conti, *Union catalogue of printed books of the XV and XVI centuries in astronomical European (sic) observatories*. Rome: Rome Astronomical Observatory, 1977.

Royal Scottish Museum, Chambers Street, Edinburgh EH1 1JF. Tel (031) 225 7534 Ext 271. Open Mon-Fri 10 am-12.30 pm, 2-5 pm (Fri 4.30 pm). Admission by appointment. Microfiche and microfilm readers.

Royal Scottish Museum Library The Royal Scottish Museum was founded in 1854 as the Industrial Museum of Scotland, inheriting the collection of the Natural History Museum of the University of Edinburgh. Books have been acquired by purchase and donation since the 1850s—eg the ornithological books of J A Harvie-Brown donated in 1942. The library contains *c*400 printed items and 100 v of mss notebooks (a larger collection of mss is housed in, and administered by, the Department of Natural History to whom enquiries should be made). The printed material covers natural history, geology, tours of Scotland, travel journals and voyages of exploration; the mss include geological and zoological notebooks, and collectors' field notes. Older books have been disposed of to other libraries in the Edinburgh area over the decades.

Author card cat available. UDC cat in progress. Mss not yet indexed, but lists of collections in the Department of Natural History.

The Royal Society Museum, art and ethnography, natural history, technology, geology, 1854–1954. (Edinburgh, 1954) (op)

Note: In the 1880s and 1890s, the Museum, then called the Edinburgh Museum of Science and Art, produced a series of printed cats to books in the Museum, but due to subsequent large-scale dispersal, it has not been thought useful to list them here. (Ed)

Scottish Beekeepers' Association (Moir) Library. Edinburgh Central Library, George IV Bridge, Edinburgh EH1 1EG. Tel (031) 225 5584. Open Mon-Fri 9 am-9 pm; Sat 9 am-1 pm. Admission for reference purposes to all. No pre-1850 items issued on loan. Research facilities, *see* under City of Edinburgh District Libraries, Central Library.

Moir Library John William Moir began collecting the books after 1912, and in 1939 his library, by then the nucleus of the Scottish Beekeepers' Association Library, was placed in the custody of the Edinburgh Public Library. It contains *c*337 pre-1850 items on bees and beekeeping. This is rarely added to.

Sheaf author and classified cat available; 1950 cat and 1963 Supplement. [op]

Catalogue of the Moir Library, Stirling, 1950.

Scottish Catholic Archives, Columba House, 16 Drummond Place, Edinburgh EG3 6PL. Tel (031) 556 3661. Admission on written application to the Keeper.

The core of the Scottish Catholic Archives is made up of material removed from Glasgow to Paris in 1560 by Archbishop James Beaton. Some destruction was caused by the French Revolution, but the substantial remnants of the collection were returned to Scotland, and housed in Blairs College, Aberdeen, after 1830. The collection has since been augmented by material from Scots colleges and monasteries in Scotland and abroad. The bulk of the manuscripts and some books have now been housed in Columba House, but the vast majority of printed books are deposited in the National Library of Scotland, where they are known as the Blairs Collection or Blairs College Library (qv).

The collection is made up of 78,000 ms letters and over 17,000 other miscellaneous ms items, together with *c*100 printed volumes. The subject emphasis is largely theology, history and literature. The unity of the groups of material within the collection is derived from their having been assembled by particular Scottish Catholic Institutions. Printed books include 1 incunabulum and a high proportion of foreign 16th cent items, among them missals belonging originally to pre-Reformation Scottish monastic houses. Among the mss is a Papal letter to Mary, Queen of Scots. The collection is added to as material becomes available from other Scottish Catholic institutions.

David McRoberts, 'The Scottish Catholic Archives 1560–1978', *The Innes Review*, vol 28, no 2 [Autumn 1977].

Signet Library, Parliament Square, Edinburgh EH1 1RF. Tel (031) 225 4923. Open Mon-Fri 9.30 am-4 pm. Admission to writers to the Signet only: others should apply in writing to the Librarian. No photocopying facilities.

Scottish Collection Acquisition commenced about 1770 and continued by purchase and donation until *c*1925. Occasional items added since. The collection contains *c*20,000 v of which *c*5,000 are pre-1850 and covers all Scottish subjects with emphasis on history, topography and literature; a pamphlet collection, on a wide range of subjects, of *c*3,000 items, of which *c*2,250 are pre-1850; a few mss, the most notable being Scott's *Bride of Lammermoor*.

General cat in 3 v (op) 1871–91 (includes subjects); on cards since.

G H Ballantyne, *The Signet Library and its Librarians 1722–1972*, Scottish Library Association, 1979.

Law Collection The collection which commenced in 1722 and continued to date, consists of *c*30,000 v with *c*4,500 pre-1850. It has a wide coverage of Scots Law, with smaller representation of other countries' jurisdiction.

'Catalogue of the law books in Library of the Society of Writers to HM Signet in Scotland', 1856. Later additions in general author cat (printed/cards).

G H Ballantyne, *op cit.*

Session Paper Collection The collection is made up of 700 v covering the period 1713–1820, which include collections of printed pleadings in cases decided in the Supreme Courts of Scotland and, on appeal, in the House of Lords.

The collection is fully indexed: (a) by party (ie defendant and pursuer), (b) by subject.

Fort George

Queen's Own Highlanders Regimental Museum, Fort George, by Inverness. Tel (0667) 62274. Open to researchers by appointment only. Reading room; photocopier on repayment. No loans.

The Regimental Museum, Queen's Own Highlanders, has been built up over the past 80 years by donation, purchase and publication. It contains documents, records, photographs, diaries and press-cuttings of the Seaforth, Cameron and Queen's Own Highlanders. *c*2,000 printed books of regimental and general military interest, the great part being post-1851.

Fort William

West Highland Museum, Cameron Square, Fort William PH33 6AJ. Tel (0397) 2169. Open 9.30 am-1 pm, 2-5 pm. Admission to library by appointment only.

Museum Library Built up by donations since the museum's establishment in 1922, it includes the library (mainly Gaelic) of the Rev J Walker MacIntyre of Kilmonivaig (*d*1925). It contains 2,500 v, mainly Highland material, especially Jacobite works, and includes a good Gaelic section (with a number of 19th cent periodicals such as 'An Teachdaire Gaelach'), also several 17th cent items, several hundred from the 18th cent (mainly Jacobite pamphlets and late 18th cent 'tours'), but most of the collection is 19th cent. There is a ms English-Gaelic dictionary (early 19th cent) inscribed by Donald Gregory.

Title card cat with separate Gaelic index. Cat to be made available in typescript.

Note: It is a reference collection for the museum and is not normally open to the general public.

Glasgow

The Cathedral Church of St Mary the Virgin, Great Western Road, Glasgow G20. Enquiries to the Provost, 45 Rowallan Gardens, Glasgow G11 7LH. Tel (041) 339 4956. Admission by written application to the Provost.

'The Bishop's Library' (Colloquially known as such since the collection is housed in the Bishop's vestry of the Cathedral). The library is not yet fully researched, but the major portion of the books once belonged to the family of Sir Archibald Edmonstone, Bt, of Duntreath near Stirling. There are *c*400 v, of which some 30 are bound v of pamphlets, sermons etc, *c*500 items mostly 19th cent theology with Tractarian bias. The pamphlets are mainly 18th cent political, some dealing with Irish questions, the 17th cent books include a set of the works of J Drexel. The collection includes ms sermons from the period when the Episcopal Church was proscribed (1745–58).

Typescript cat in preparation (May 1982). (Enquiries to the compiler Ms Brenda M Cook, Glasgow University Library.)

Glasgow University Library, Hillhead Street, Glasgow G12 8QE. Tel (041) 334 2122. Telex 778421. Special Collections Department Open Mon-Fri 9 am-5 pm; Sat 9 am-12.30 pm. Closed all Sats of Christmas vacation. Open to all bona fide researchers and readers, but prior application for admission to the Keeper of Special Collections is highly desirable. Reading Room accommodates approx 20 persons; xeroxing facilities (dependent on suitability of materials); microfilm and microfiche readers available; ultraviolet lamp.

Glasgow University Library: Special Collections Department Glasgow University was founded in 1451. By 1580 the library contained some 80 v. A manuscript cat of 1691 shows an increase to 3,300 v. Copyright privilege was held from 1710–1836. By 1791, the year of its first published catalogue, the library had expanded to 20,000 v. Throughout the five centuries of its existence, the library has attracted abundant gifts and bequests, particularly from the late 18th cent onwards. The library's Special Collections now total *c*150,000 printed items and *c*50,000 mss. There are *c*1,200 incunabula; *c*4,000 STC; *c*10,000 Wing items, and *c*30,000 ESTC. The following private and institutional libraries are included:

William Hunter (1718–83): 10,000 printed books and 650 mss (including medieval illuminated mss and 534 incunabula). Subject strengths are history of medicine (especially anatomy and obstetrics), history of science, travel and exploration, fine typography, numismatics, fine art and architecture.

John Ferguson (1837–1916): 7,000 printed books, 300 mss. Alchemy and early chemistry, witchcraft literature, gypsies, secret societies.

William Euing (1788–1874): 20,000 v. Bibles, music, 17th cent English literature, 18th cent fine printing, colour-plate books, Glasgow imprints.

David Murray (1842–1928): 20,000 items. History of Glasgow and West of Scotland, 19th cent ephemera, law, bookkeeping and arithmetic, early school books, history of railways and canals, catalogues of libraries and museums.

Sir William Stirling Maxwell (1818–78): 2,000 v. Emblem and device books, fête literature.

James Dean Ogilvie (1866–1949): 1,500 pamphlets, 300 books. English Civil War.

Robert Simson (1687–1768): 850 v. Mathematics and astronomy.

T K Monro (*d*1958): 280 v. Editions of Sir Thomas Browne's works.

J J Spencer: 190 items. The Darien Scheme.

Sir William Hamilton (1788–1856): 8,000 v. Philosophy and classics.

John Veitch (1829–94): 700 v. Editions of medieval scholastic philosophers.

William Gemmell (*d*1919): 76 v. Editions of the *Dance of Death.*

Charles Hepburn (1891–1971): 300 v 19th cent English literature, fine bindings.

Ludwig Blau (1861–1936): 193 v. Early Hebraica.

Robert Wylie (*d*1921): 1,000 v. History of Glasgow and West of Scotland.

Trinity College Library (deposited 1974): *c*7,000 pre-1800 books, mainly theology. Includes the private libraries of Konstantin von *Tischendorf* (biblical texts and accounts of the Holy Land), John *Eadie* (biblical texts and commentaries), James *Mearns* (hymnology).

The collection is added to as a matter of regular policy.

The Library's ms and archival collections (also housed and administered by the Special Collections Department) are extremely rich and varied, and include the following:

The correspondence of James McNeill *Whistler* (1834–1903): art history.

The papers of Dugald Sutherland *MacColl* (1859–1948): art history and literature.

The papers of William Thomson, Lord *Kelvin* (1824–1907): science and technology.

The papers of Henry George *Farmer* (1882–1965): oriental and military music.

The papers of Harold James Lean *Wright* (*b*1885): art history.

Scottish Theatre Archive.

Political caricatures of the Paris Commune and the Franco-Prussian War (*c*3,300 items).

Guardbook author cat (now on microfiche) for items processed before 1968.

Author and subject cats (in sheaf form) for items processed since 1968.

Special bibliographical indexes, eg imprints, provenances, illustrators and engravers, STC, Wing, ephemera, bindings, etc.

Archibald Arthur, *Catalogus impressorum librorum in Bibliotheca Universitatis Glasguensis, secundum literarum ordinem dispositus.* Glasguae: excudebat Andreas Foulis, 1791.

——*Catalogus impressorum librorum in Bibliotheca Universitatis Glasguensis, secundum pluteorum ordinem dispositus.* Glasguae: Ibid.

John Young and P Henderson Aitken, *A catalogue of the manuscripts in the Library of the Hunterian Museum in the University of Glasgow*. Glasgow: Maclehose, 1908.

Mungo Ferguson, *The printed books in the Library of the Hunterian Museum in the University of Glasgow: a catalogue*. Glasgow: Jackson, Wylie and Co, 1930.

Kelvin Papers: index to the manuscript collection of William Thomson, Baron Kelvin, in Glasgow University Library. Glasgow: GUL, 1977.

Whistler-MacColl-Wright: art history papers, 1850–1950, in Glasgow University Library, GUL, 1979.

Catalogue of the Ferguson Collection of books mainly relating to alchemy, chemistry, witchcraft and gipsies, in the Library of the University of Glasgow. 2 v, Glasgow: Maclehose, 1943.

The Euing Collection of English broadside ballads in the Library of the University of Glasgow. With an introduction by John Holloway. Glasgow, University of Glasgow, 1971.

The Euing Musical Library: catalogue of the musical library of the late W Euing bequeathed to Anderson's University, Glasgow. Glasgow: W M Ferguson, 1878. (NB This part of William Euing's library was transferred to Glasgow University Library in 1936, and reunited with the rest of his library.)

Catalogue of a collection of books and manuscripts (relating to the Darien Scheme) presented to the University of Glasgow by J J Spencer. Glasgow: Jackson, Wylie and Co, 1932.

Catalogue of the Wylie Collection of books (mainly relating to Glasgow) bequeathed to the University of Glasgow. Glasgow: Jackson, Wylie & Co, 1929.

Catalogue of a collection of civil and canon law books in the University of Glasgow. Glasgow: University of Glasgow, 1949.

Hester M Black and Philip Gaskell, 'Special Collections in Glasgow University Library', *The Book Collector*, v 16, 1967, p161-8.

——'The Stirling Maxwell Collection of emblem books in Glasgow University Library', *The Bibliotheck*, v 8, 1977, p156-67.

Jack Baldwin, 'Glasgow University Library's manuscripts: the non-Hunterian collections', *Ibid*, p127-55.

John Durkan, 'The early history of Glasgow University Library: 1475—1710', *Ibid*, p102-26.

James Robson, 'Catalogue of the oriental mss in the Library of the University of Glasgow', *Studia Semitica et Orientalia*, v 2, 1945, p116-37.

The Mitchell Library, North Street, Glasgow G3 7DN. Tel (041) 221 7030. Open Mon-Fri 9.30 am-9 pm; Sat 9.30 am-5 pm. Unrestricted admission during opening hours, but prior warning of special requirements appreciated. Reference only. Photocopying service available for items in the library stock, subject to their condition.

General Opened in 1877 as a general reference library by Glasgow Town Council, with funds bequeathed by Stephen Mitchell, a city manufacturer. In June 1982 the stock of Baillie's Institution Library (see below) was being acquired. The stock totals 1,000,000 v, covering all subjects; the pre-1851 items cannot be quantified. There are, however, 45 incunabula; *c*650 STC and *c*1,600 Wing items, and *c*19,000 ESTC items—scattered except for early Glasgow printing.

Catalogue of incunabula and STC books in The Mitchell Library. Glasgow, 1964.

The Mitchell Library, 1877—1977. Glasgow, 1977.

Baillie's Library Opened as a free public reference library in 1887 under the provisions of a trust deed executed by George Baillie, a Glasgow lawyer, in 1863, and incorporated into the Mitchell Library in 1982. It contains *c*20,000 v (not included in the general stock figure for The Mitchell Library) and includes 1 incunabulum; 28 STC and 136 Wing items (no figures available for corresponding foreign material) and 1,021 ESTC items. The collection is particularly strong in Scottish and Glasgow material. A large proportion of the Wing and ESTC material is Glasgow printed, and includes 308 items from the Foulis Press. The sale of 13,620 v which took place *c*1965, was of post-1800 works, and did not include Scottish books or books on art. Since the collection has only recently (June 1982) been deposited in The Mitchell Library, no full examination has been possible. Portions of the collection (over and above the 20,000 v noted above) are held on long term loan by the Universities of Glasgow, Strathclyde and Stirling. These do not contain rare books.

Guardbook cat covering the accessions of the first 20 years. Continues by card cat and various indexes.

Gaskell, *Bibliography of the Foulis Press*, 1964 (op, 2nd ed in preparation).

Early Glasgow Printing (EGP) Collection Collected as a matter of deliberate policy since the founding of the library, the collection contains *c*3,500 v all pre-1801 Glasgow printing, of which there are 3 STC and 64 Wing items. Subject content is particularly strong in the publications of R and A Foulis, most of which are listed in Philip Gaskell's *Bibliography of the Foulis Press*, 1964.

Collection entered in general cats.

Detailed slip cat arranged by printer, with author and date indexes.

Jeffrey Reference Library The library of Robert Jeffrey of Crosslee House, Renfrewshire, who spent 30 years collecting this library which he bequeathed to Glasgow on his death in 1902. He is said to have been advised in his purchases by the then Mitchell Librarian, Francis Thornton Baggett. The library contains *c*4,000 v, and is particularly strong in fine illustrated works, which include Audubon's *Birds of America*, and a set of ornithological works of Gould.

Not in general cat.

Author and shelf listing on slips.

Guardbook author cat.

Kidson Collection A collection built up by Frank Kidson of Leeds (1855—1926). Purchased in 1929, with additions in 1948—9. It comprises 9,000 items, with 1 STC; a number (unknown) of Wing items and 18th cent English folk song, folk dance, ballad and opera.

Slip cat of the whole collection available; also slip index of broadsides, and slip index of songs and music in the folios prepared by Kidson.

Kidson's own ms 'Index of Airs' (57 v).

Marked copy of BUCEM for pre-1800 material.

H G Farmer, 'The Kidson Collection', *The Consort*, July 1950. (op)

Morison Collection The library of the Rev James Morison (*d*1893) containing 7,000 v which include 6 incunabula and 62 STC items; the number of Wing items not available. It represents the working library of 19th cent clergyman, and is particularly strong in works on Pauline epistles, especially Romans.

In general cats.

Private Press Collection Begun in 1948 with the purchase of the library of Frank L Grant, of Craigellachie, which contained a large number of private press books. It now contains over 2,500 v from more than 300 different presses, including complete sets of Kelmscott and Vale presses, and almost complete Nonesuch, with substantial holdings of Golden Cockerel, Pear Tree, Essex House and Cuala presses.

Looseleaf typescript cat arranged by press, within each press by date of acquisition.

Author and shelf listings on cards.

Entries in general cat.

Scottish Poetry Collection Collected as a matter of deliberate policy since the founding of the library, the collection amounts to *c*17,100 v (including Scottish Drama, currently being identified as a separate collection) which includes the works of individual authors, collections, criticisms and biographies. The Burns Collection totals *c*3,750 v and includes the Kilmarnock Burns. STC and Wing items not quantified.

Entries in general cat.

Typescript cat (excluding Burns) produced in 1911 and updated by hand.

Printed cat of Burns Collection (interleaved copies updated).

Catalogue of Robert Burns Collection in the Mitchell Library, Glasgow, 1959.

Slains Castle Collection The library of James Drummond, Bishop of Brechin (*d*1695), and of his kinsfolk the Earls of Erroll until *c*1800. Intended for auction by the family when the estate was sold, it was purchased by the Library in 1918 before the auction could actually take place. Books total *c*3,200, which include 37 STC and 138 Wing items. Bishop Drummond's library of 436 v (some of which came from the libraries of his father, grandfather and brother, all clergymen) include much Continental printing such as by Plantin, Elsevier, Estienne and Ascensius. The collection also includes the household and estate account books of Bushey Park, home of William IV when Duke of Clarence (138 v).

Author cat on slips.

No entries in general cat.

The Auction cat, by which the books are shelved, is arranged by size within each part of the collection.

J F Kellas Johnstone, *Notes on the library of the Earls of Erroll, Slains Castle, Aberdeenshire*. Revised and reprinted from the *Aberdeen University Library Bulletin* for April 1917. (op)

Religious Society of Friends (Quakers) Glasgow Meeting, 16 Newton Terrace, Glasgow G3 7PJ. Tel (041) 221 7770. Open by prior arrangement, in writing, with the Librarian.

Library of the Religious Society of Friends, Glasgow Meeting The combined libraries of Glasgow and Kilmarnock Meetings of the Society of Friends were largely formed in the 19th cent by purchase or by gift from private collections. The collection includes 10 v 17th cent; 100 v 18th cent and 100 v 1800–50. The printed works are by and about Quakers from the 17th cent to the present day.

Author card cat and card cat in accession order.

No printed cat.

Royal College of Physicians and Surgeons of Glasgow, 242 St Vincent Street, Glasgow G2 5RJ. Tel (041) 248 5279. Open Mon-Fri 9.30 am-5.30 pm. Admission for graduate study on written application to the Librarian. Rare books and mss may only be consulted within the College Library—not available for loan. Photocopying services and microfiche reader available.

Rare Book Collection The nucleus of the library was formed at the end of the 17th cent by voluntary donations, chiefly from members of the Faculty, and also from several non-medical persons (see ms volume preserved in the library containing 'the names of such worthie persons as have gifted books to the Chirurgions' librarie in Glasgow' dated 1698. Most records of the library up to 1733 were destroyed by fire. After that year documents survive recording state and progress of the library. In 1799 the first published catalogue of the library's collections was authorized, and thereafter catalogues were published at fairly regular intervals up to the beginning of this century. The collection contains *c*3,500 pre-1851 works which include *c*200 STC and *c*700 Wing items. Subject areas confined to medicine and surgery.

The mss collection includes medical lecture notes; professional medical correspondence; minute books of medical societies and clubs; Sir William Macewen ms collection (surgery); Sir Ronald Ross ms collection (tropical medicine).

Card cat.

Author and subject cat.

Cat of mss in preparation.

Catalogue of books belonging to the Faculty of Physicians and Surgeons, Glasgow (Glasgow, 1799).

Idem, 1803 (with Appendix, 1804).

Idem, 1842.

Alphabetical cat of the library of the Faculty of Physicians and Surgeons of Glasgow. Preceded by an index of subjects by Alexander Duncan 2 v. Glasgow, 1885–1901.

Royal Faculty of Procurators, 62 St George's Place, Glasgow G2 1BT. Tel (041) 332 3593. Open Mon-Fri 9 am-5 pm. Use of library is normally restricted to members of the Royal Faculty of Procurators, Sheriffs and Advocates, and authorized persons. However, arrangements can be made with the Librarian for other bona fide researchers to be admitted.

Library of the Royal Faculty of Procurators The library was established in 1817 for 'Law Agents practising in

Glasgow'. It was first accommodated in the Lyceum Sale Rooms, Nelson Street, Glasgow, but in 1823 it moved to premises in Spreull's Land, Trongate, and in 1834 to 13 John Street. Since 1856 the library has been in the Faculty buildings at 62 St George's Place. It holds *c*1,500 v of pre-1851 imprints. The main subject strength is in legal literature, especially Scots, English and Roman law, and in cognate subjects such as history, biography, antiquities and economics. The library has a special collection (the 'Hill Collection') of works on Glasgow history, which includes manuscript and archival materials. These have been surveyed by the National Register of Archives (Scotland). The bulk of the pre-1851 imprints are 18th and early 19th cent; there are few 16th cent imprints. Non-legal material was sold in 1968 and 1969 (see auction catalogues issued by Morrison McChlery, Glasgow 8-10 May 1968, 6 June 1969).

Catalogue of books belonging to the Faculty of Procurators in Glasgow. (Glasgow, 1817) (with Appendix 1819).

Catalogue of the library of the Faculty of Procurators, Glasgow. (Glasgow, 1845).

Catalogue of the law books in the library of the Faculty of Procurators in Glasgow. (Glasgow, 1867).

Catalogue of the books in general literature in the library of the Faculty of Procurators in Glasgow. (Glasgow, 1873).

Catalogue of the books in the library of the Faculty of Procurators in Glasgow. Alphabetically arranged with index of subjects by John Muir. (Glasgow, 1903). With Supplement, 1903—22.

After 1922 the catalogue took the form of a card index, which is currently being revised. The librarian reports that 'a catalogue of the oldest books in the library will be xeroxed and circulated to interested libraries (mid-1982)'. Work on this is still in progress 4/5/82.

For cats of manuscript and archival material, *see* National Register of Archives (Scotland), *Western Survey: Royal Faculty of Procurators, George Square, Glasgow* (NRA Scot/0534).

St Peter's College, 33 Briar Road, Newlands, Glagow G43 2TV. Tel (041) 637 4093. Antiquarian material can be consulted only by prior arrangement with the Librarian. Bona fide scholars are welcome, but written application to the Librarian is necessary. Study area can be provided for consultation of rare books. Photocopying facilities available providing there is no risk of damage to the originals.

St Peter's College Museum (Rare Books Department) The collection was founded in 1874 at Partickhill, and the bulk of the present antiquarian collection was formed at that time, and subsequently augmented by gifts and bequests from various clerics. In 1892 the College moved to Bearsden and remained there until 1946 when the building was destroyed by fire. The College was rehoused at Kilmahew Castle, Cardross, and the rare books placed in store. In 1980 the College moved to its present site in Glasgow, and the rare books removed from storage and reunited with the main collection. The collection contains *c*650 v which include 3 incunabula; *c*30 v 16th cent; *c*150 v 17th cent; 240 v 18th cent and *c*220 v 1800—50. Main subject strengths are in theology, liturgy and history.

The fire of 1946 resulted in the loss of a number of volumes, and some that remain are damaged by fire. Around 1960 some 100 v were sold to raise funds. No precise details of this sale have survived, but some of the books listed by Durkan and Ross (*infra*) as being in the possession of the College are no longer there.

Incomplete author cat on cards and incomplete accessions register.

Work in progress on a revised cat.

J Durkan and A Ross, *Early Scottish Libraries*, Glasgow, J Burns, 1961 (in which the College is referred to as 'Cardross, St Peter's College).

University of Strathclyde, Andersonian Library, Curran Building, 101 St James's Road, Glasgow G4 0NS. Tel (041) 552 3701. Telex 77472. Open (Term) Mon-Fri 9 am-10 pm; Sat 9 am-12 noon; (Vacation) Mon-Fri 9 am-5 pm; Sat 9 am-12 noon. Admission to all bona fide workers on signing the visitors book. Inspection of rare book materials preferably by previous appointment. Small reading area. Photocopying facilities, microfilm readers available.

Andersonian Library The University of Strathclyde and the Andersonian Library have their origins in Anderson's Institution, which was founded in Glasgow in 1796. Anderson's Institution underwent several changes of title and constituent parts in the 19th and 20th cent; eg Anderson's University (1828) and Anderson's College (1877). Three collections form the basis of the Andersonian Library's antiquarian stock: (i) The personal library of John Anderson (1726—96), Professor of Natural Philosophy, University of Glasgow (*c*1,300 v); (ii) The library of Alexander Laing (*d*1882), Professor of Mathematics, Anderson's University (*c*500 v); (iii) The library of James Young of Kelly and Durris (1811—83) (*c*1,400 v). The main subject areas are alchemy, chemistry, mathematics. There are some STC and Wing items, and ms material.

A catalogue of books destined for the use of the Mechanics' Class, Anderson's Institution. Glasgow: W Lang, 1808.

A catalogue of the library of Anderson's University, Glasgow. Glasgow: E Khull, 1832.

A catalogue of books bequeathed to Anderson's College by Alexander Laing LLD, late Professor of Mathematics there. Glasgow: R Maclehose, 1883.

J Ferguson, *Bibliotheca chemica: a catalogue of the alchemical, chemical and pharmaceutical books in the collection of the late James Young of Kelly and Durris*. 2 v Glasgow: Maclehose, 1906.

Items not listed in the published cats are included in the author cat of the Andersonian Library.

Greenock

Inverclyde District Libraries, Watt Library, Union Street, Greenock PA16 8JH. Tel (0475) 20186. Open Mon, Thurs 2-5 pm, 6-8 pm, Tues, Fri 10 am-12.30 pm, 2-5 pm, Wed, Sat 10 am-1 pm. Unrestricted admission during opening hours. Reference only. Photocopying available for items in stock, subject to their condition.

The library includes the *Watt Scientific Library*, the *Caird Collection*, the *Greenock Library*, and the *Spence Mathematical Library*. Instituted on January 1st, 1783 as the Greenock Library. In 1816 it acquired the scientific library of James Watt, and became part of the Watt Institution. It operated as a private library until the Local Government reorganization (1974) when it became the local history department of the Inverclyde District Libraries. Of its kind it had developed by the middle of the 19th cent into a large library, which it remains—but dispersals have taken place and, at a very rough estimate, its present holdings of pre-1851 books would be unlikely to exceed 9,000 v.

Dictionary cat on cards.

Haddington

East Lothian District Library, Local History Centre, Haddington Branch Library, Newton Port, Haddington, East Lothian. Tel (062 082) 2531. Open at various times; telephone Library HQ (062 082 2370) previous to visits. Admission unrestricted for reference. Seating and table space for 12 persons only. Photocopying facilities available.

East Lothian Local History Collection Formed in 1976 from original County Library collection and that of the East Lothian Antiquarian and Field Naturalists' Society, it consists of *c*1,500 v, of which *c*300 are pre-1850. The emphasis is on the history and topography of the East Lothian District, and includes local printing, mainly Haddington and Dunbar. The collection is added to regularly.

Author/title cat.

Haddo House

Haddo House (National Trust for Scotland property), Aberdeenshire AB4 0ER. Application for information and access to the books should be made to the Curatorial Department, National Trust for Scotland, 5 Charlotte Square, Edinburgh EH2 4DU. Tel (031) 226 5922.

Haddo House Library The present library, incorporating older family books, was established by George Hamilton Gordon, 4th Earl of Aberdeen, 1784–1860, eminent scholar and statesman. It remained in the possession of the family until its transfer to the National Trust for Scotland in 1979. It contains *c*6-7,000 v reflecting the wide-ranging intellectual and antiquarian interests of the 4th Earl and his political involvement; also the periods of service in Ireland and Canada of the 7th Earl/1st Marquess.

There are at least 3 STC and 104 foreign items of the same period; 11 Wing and 187 foreign items of the same period; *c*1,900 British v of the period 1700–1850, and *c*1,500 foreign v of that period; 19th cent first editions, association copies; some British provincial press publications; and many large-format fine-editions of the late 19th and early 20th cent. The library is remarkable for the large number of fine bindings.

There is a fine ms author cat in two ledgers dated 1873, giving good bibliographical detail and shelf marks, and a less detailed inventory (shelflist) dated Aug 1894. Unfortunately the shelf sequence has been disturbed.

Also a ?mid-19th cent ms author ledger, and an early shelf list.

Note: Books are known to have been sold in 1796 and in the 1920s.

A Angus and Son, Booksellers, *A catalogue of several collections of books lately purchased, including the elegant and valuable library of the late Lord Haddo, consisting of above ten thousand volumes*; the whole forming the best collection that ever was offered for sale in this country. Aberdeen: A Angus and Son, 1796. (The Haddo books are indistinguishable.)

J F Kellas Johnstone, *Haddo House Library* (Aberdeen, 1924). (From extant correspondence it is known that not all books in this cat were sold. Some have been identified on the shelves. The correspondence also shows that other unspecified books were sold before and after the cat was produced.)

Innerpeffray

Innerpeffray Library, Innerpeffray, by Crieff, Perthshire. Tel (0764) 2819. Open Mon-Sat (Summer) 10 am-1 pm, 2-5 pm; (Winter) 10 am-1 pm. 2-4 pm (closed Thurs); Sun 2-4 pm. Admission for reference by appointment.

Innerpeffray Library Founded by the 1680 will of David Drummond, 3rd Lord Madertie 'for the benefit and encouragement of young students', it is probably the oldest free public library in Scotland. It houses *c*3,000 v, (now shelved in a building, completed in 1751, situated on the bank of the River Earn near Crieff, in Perthshire) which include *c*390 STC and 500 Wing items; 320 foreign books printed before 1701; in all *c*2,000 books printed before 1801. The earliest printed work in the collection is an imperfect copy of P Reginaldetus, *Speculm (sic) finalis retributionis*, Paris, 1502; other notable holdings are *The xiii. bukes of Eneados... Translatit... into Scottish metir, bi... G Douglas*, London 1553; David Browne, *The new* *invention, intituled, calligraphia,* ...Sainct-Andrewes 1622; *La Bible*... Sedan 1633 (the pocket Bible of James Graham, 1st Marquis of Montrose—'Great Marquis'); and *Biblia Sacra ex S Castellionis interpretatione*... Lipsiae 1738 (a copy that belonged to Thomas Carlyle). The library possesses its lending register in manuscript, dating back to 1747, the only known record of its kind surviving in Scotland from the 18th cent, according to Kaufman.

Typescript cat by W M Dickie of books printed before 1801 (1926).

Typescript cat of books printed after 1800 (1956).

Innerpeffray Library and Chapel, a historical sketch, 1916, reprinted 1955. Innerpeffray Library, Crieff, Perthshire (leaflet, 30p).

Paul Kaufman, 'A unique record of a people's reading', first published in *Libri* xiv, 3 (1964), p227-42; reprinted in *Libraries and their users, collected papers in library history*, London, Library Association, 1969, p153-62, as 'Innerpeffray: reading for all the people'.

R R Walls, 'Innerpeffray, Scotland's first public library', *Scottish Geographical Magazine*, vol lvi (May 1940), p65-9.

W M Dickie, 'Innerpeffray library', *LAR*, new ser vol vi (1928), p100-5.

J M Dallman, 'A notable Scots Library', *North Western Naturalist*, new ser vol I (June 1953), p171-3.

Lochinvar (*pseud*) 'Help for the oldest free library in Scotland', *Edinburgh Tatler*, vol 8, no 60, April 1966 (2 pages).

J Paul Rylands, 'A seventeenth century Perthshire public library and its bookplate', *Ex Libris Journal*, v VIII, 1899, p88-91.

Inverness

Highland Regional Library Service. The collections, apart from the Miller Institution and the Wick Local Collection, are in Inverness Library, Farraline Park, Inverness. Tel (0463) 236 463. Open Mon, Fri 9 am-7.30 pm; Tues, Thurs 9 am-6.30 pm, Wed, Sat 9 am-5 pm. For admission apply to the Senior Librarian (Reference).

Fraser-Mackintosh Collection The library of Charles Fraser-Mackintosh of Drummond (born Dochnalurg 1828, died Bournemouth 1901). He was a solicitor, local historian, Gaelic scholar and MP (Inverness Burghs 1874–5; Inverness County 1885–92). He served on the Crofters Commission and published several books on local history. The collection totals 5,400 v on a wide variety of topics; particularly strong in Gaelic, Scottish literature, history (especially Scottish genealogy and the Jacobites) and law. It contains several hundred pre-1800 imprints, including 2 incunabula, several dozen Elzevirs from the early 17th cent and many 18th cent Jacobite pamphlets. There are also 90 v of newspaper cuttings (1850–1900) dealing with the Inverness area.

Card cat with subject index.

Inverness Gaelic Society Library Inverness Gaelic Society was founded in 1871, and from the start built up a library concerned with, not only Gaelic writings but also with works on the Highlands in general. The Society still functions, but has deposited its library with the Regional Library Service. It contains 1,650 v and is strongest in Gaelic writing and on Highland history (principally books published 1870–1940). There are also books on, and in, the other Celtic languages. There are *c*60 v with pre-1800 imprints. Of the total of 1,650 v, *c*500 are pamphlets and unbound periodicals.

Card index.

Cat in progress.

M A MacDonald, 'History of the Gaelic Society of Inverness from 1871–1971', *Trans Gaelic Soc of Inverness*, v XLVI, 1971, p1-21.

Inverness Kirk Session Library Established in 1707 as a Presbyterial library, it was run by the Kirk Session of the Old High Church in Inverness. Initially created by donations, principally from London, it was developed by means of a book fund started by Dr James Fraser (1645–1731). It ceased to function as a library in the 1890s. It contains *c*3,385 v, covering theology and kindred subjects (especially classics and history); it also contains a variety of other works (eg some 17th cent medical works, and 19th cent editions of Shakespeare, Dryden, Pope, etc). It includes 126 items printed between 1525 and 1600, and almost 900 from the 17th cent (including over 20 v of pamphlets). There are many continental imprints, especially from Holland and Switzerland. Individual items include 16th cent editions of Calvin (some from Geneva), Walton's Polyglot Bible (1657), Pitt's Atlas (1680–2), Holinshed's Chronicles (1587) and Bedell's Irish Bible (1685).

Card cat, with subject and printer indexes. The printed cat (Inverness, 1897) is an inaccurate author/title list.

Inverness Kirk-Session records 1661–1800, ed by Alexander Mitchell, Inverness, 1902, p189-206. (op)

Inverness Reference Collection Built up by the Public Library from the foundation in 1882, it includes the library of Joseph Mitchell, the mid-19th cent builder of roads and railways in the Highlands. It contains 5,900 v made up of general late 19th and early 20th cent reference material, particularly strong on Highland history, including clan histories. There are *c*100 pre-1800 v (including an edition of Pliny, Frankfurt, 1583, Skene's *Lawes and constitutions of Scotland*, Edinburgh, 1609, and eight others before 1700). The majority of pre-1800 items are 18th cent Jacobite pamphlets. The collection as a whole contains many local imprints.

Card cat.

Inverness Working Men's Club Library The Working Men's Club was founded in 1865, and the books from its library became the property of the Town Council when the club became defunct. A number of the books have the bookplate of Sir George Stewart of Grandtully. There are 28 v of miscellaneous works, with 8 pre-1750 imprints, and 15 from 1750–1850. Items include an edition of

Thucydides (Frankfurt, 1594), Sanson's *Atlas Nouveau* (1696), Stuart's *Antiquities of Athens* (1762–1816), and Solvyns' *Les Hindous* (1808). There is also a Hindu ms dated 1872 (Ram-gitta, by Talsi Dars). The collection was originally much larger, but the fate of the other items is not known.

Card cat.

Nairn Literary Institute Library On deposit from the Nairn Literary Institute. Founded in the 19th cent and greatly augmented by a gift from William M MacBean of Yonkers, New York, a native of Nairn, (*d*1924), a Stuart and Jacobite collector whose main collection was presented to Aberdeen University Library (qv) in 1919. The Institute's own buying was the standard literature, history, economics, natural history etc of the period. The library contains *c*2,200 v and 300 pamphlets which are strong in the Jacobite material, most but not all duplicates from MacBean's collection, and local history relating mainly to Moray, Nairn and Inverness. Most of the MacBean material is 17th-19th cent, and most of the rest is 18th-20th cent.

Author/title card cat.

Library of the Miller Institution The Miller Institution was a school founded in 1862. The library, which was little used, is now housed in the local branch library, which was the original school building, Davidson's Lane, Thurso, tel (0847) 3237, and contains *c*3,000 v. Typical of a well-developed late Victorian school library, it is very strong in the Greek and Latin classics, history in general, and English literature. There is also a wide variety of other subjects, from the fine arts to technical subjects. Most are 19th cent editions, but there are over 100 pre-1800 items, mainly from the later 18th cent. Earlier items include Cicero's *Tusculan Disputations*, Milan 1494; an Aldine 8vo edition of *Aristophanes*, 1518; and the King James Bible of 1611. All the books are in excellent condition and are kept in glass-fronted bookcases.

Printed cat: *Catalogue of the library of the Miller Institution, Thurso*. Buckie: printed by W F Johnston (1934?). Very inadequate, containing minimum author/title information and no imprint or date.

Wick Local Collection (Books housed in Wick Branch Library, Sinclair Terrace, Wick. Tel (0955) 2864). Based on the collection of local historian John Mowat, it has been built up by the local library to a total of 2,300 v. It is principally a collection concerned with the north of Scotland, particularly Caithness, but also contains general works on Scottish history and good collections of local authors, especially Neil Gunn and John Horne (1861–1934). 57 v of pamphlets, late 19th cent, mainly local; 9 v of Caithness law cases from 1750 onwards, runs of the *Scots Magazine* (1739–1816), *The Northern Ensign* (1850–1922), the *John O'Groats Journal* (1846–). Very few pre-1800 imprints, but several hundred from 1800–50. Also a collection of maps of Caithness, some from the 18th cent, and several hundred photographs from the last hundred years.

Very incomplete card cat.

Volumes of pamphlets are indexed.

Kingussie

Highland Folk Museum, Kingussie, Inverness-shire. Tel (054 02) 307. Open Mon-Sat Apr-Oct 10 am-6 pm; Nov-Mar 10 am-3 pm (not Sat). Admission to books by appointment only.

Museum Library Established as 'Am Fasgadh' in 1935 by Dr I F Grant (authoress of *Highland Folk Ways*), the museum is now run by the Regional Council. The books are donations, mainly by local people. There are 250 v, covering a wide range of topics, but about half are theological (some in Gaelic). Most are 19th cent, a few earlier.

Title card cat (but compiled with no bibliographical experience or knowledge of Gaelic).

Detailed index of inscriptions.

Kirkcaldy

Kirkcaldy District Library, East Fergus Place, Kirkcaldy KY1 1XT, Fife. Tel (0592) 68386. Open Mon-Thurs and Sat 10 am-7 pm, Fri 10 am-5 pm.

The collection, not specifically named, comprises over 250 items—and includes pre-1851 printed books (chiefly post-1700), a few mss and ephemera relating to Scottish history, literature and local history, and some early editions of the works of Adam Smith.

A separate checklist (author) is available in ms. Some of the older books are included in the Fife County Library and Kirkcaldy Public Library *Check list of books on local subjects*, Kirkcaldy, 1957.

Kirkcudbright

Broughton House, High Street, Kirkcudbright. Tel (0557) 300437. Open to visitors 11 am-1 pm, 2-5 pm, but access to the library by prior arrangement with the Hon Librarian. Admission 20p, no charge after first if working with books and mss. Photocopies from local solicitor.

Hornel Library Broughton House was the home of artist E A Hornel. From *c*1918 he and Thomas Fraser, of Dalbeattie, set about forming a library as complete as possible on the area bounded by the Solway, Langholm, Carsphairn and Stranraer. The library is made up of works by, and on, local authors, Scottish ballad material, and a Burns collection reckoned as one of the best in Scotland. There are in all *c*15,000 v of which *c*100-150 are STC and Wing items, and 200 other pre-1850 v. Also included are *c*150 double folios of artists' reproductions of about 100 Japanese folio albums and 'common' block books. Mss total *c*1-1,500, most of which were collected by William Macmath (an Edinburgh antiquary, and author of *The Gordons of Craichlaw*), and include letters from Sir Walter Scott and other notables; letters from most of the 'Glasgow Boys' (artists of the 'Glasgow School of Painting' recognized as a group between 1880 and 1895) to Hornel.

Author card cat and subject cat in sheaf form for printed books.

Mss cat in sheaf form by author, subject and title.

Broughton House, illustrated souvenir, by Mrs M G Brown (Kirkcudbright) 1959, repr 1961.

Kirkwall

The Orkney Library, Laing Street, Kirkwall, Orkney. Tel (0856) 3166. Open Mon-Fri 9 am-8 pm; Sat 9 am-5 pm. Admission free to general public. Microfilm reader and photocopying facilities available.

The Rendall Collection The private library of the books on conchology bequeathed by the late Robert Rendall (*d*1967), poet, theologist and conchologist, to the Orkney Library, and consists of over 100 v and several hundred pamphlets.

No cat available at present.

The Marwick Collection The private library of the late Dr Hugh Marwick (*d*1965), Orkney scholar and specialist in place-names and the Orkney Norn language, bequeathed to the Orkney County Library in 1965. It consists of 680 v and 10 boxes of pamphlets.

Author/title card cat available.

Leadhills

Leadhills Library, Miners Reading Institute, 15 Main Street, Leadhills, Biggar, Lanarkshire NL12 6YE. Open Easter to October, Sat and Sun 11 am-4.30 pm. Admission at other times may be possible by previous appointment with the President, Leadhills, Biggar, Lanarkshire. All bona fide readers are admitted, provided that a member of the Committee is able to be in attendance. Reading facilities only.

Leadhills Library Sometimes known as the Allan Ramsay Library, and described on the notice outside the building as 'Instituted by Allan Ramsay'. Ramsay was born at Leadhills, but there is no evidence that he instituted the library. Founded in 1741 as the Leadhills Miners' Reading Society, it is, so far as is known, the oldest subscription library in the British Isles. It has *c*3,000 v, about a quarter of which are late 19th and 20th cent publications. The pre-1851 material covers religion (including volumes of sermons); science and technology, especially mining and mineralogy (including ms mining records of the 18th and 19th cent); history; 19th cent novels.

Printed cat 1893 and 1904.

No cat of present stock.

Paul Kaufman, 'The rise of community libraries in Scotland', *Papers of the Bibliographical Society of America*, v 59, 1965, p258-60.

——*Libraries and their users*, London 1969 (Chap 16: Leadhills, library of diggers).

John Crawford, 'Two miners' libraries in the '70s', *Lib Rev* v 23, 1971, p14-17.

Leadhills Library (leaflet), Leadhills 1973.

John Crawford, 'For our mutual improvement: sources of reading in 19th century Scotland', *Scotland's Magazine*, Jan 1974, p13-16.

Nos 1, 2, 3 and 5 may be out of print.

Leith Hall

Leith Hall (National Trust for Scotland property), Aberdeenshire AB5 4NQ. Application for information and access to the books should be made to the Curatorial Department, National Trust for Scotland, 5 Charlotte Square, Edinburgh EH2 4DU. Tel (031) 226 5922.

Leith Hall Library The library of the Leith, later Leith Hay, family, resident at Leith Hall from the late 16th to the mid-20th cent. It contains *c*1,300 v which include 1 STC item and 4 foreign items of the same period; 4 Wing items and 19 foreign items of the same period; *c*850 v of the period 1700–1850, of which *c*200 have foreign imprints, mainly French. A general library, strongest in the fields of English literature, history, biography, religion, travel, the classics, military history (including a ms diary), and gardening. Some fine bindings, including 2 v in the rare Aberdeen corner square style, and several items in original boards.

Typed inventory shelf list.

The library has not been catalogued, and the books are not systematically arranged.

Lerwick

Shetland Library, Lower Hillhead, Lerwick, Shetland ZE1 0EL. Tel (0595) 3868. Open Mon, Wed, Fri 10 am-1 pm, 2.30-5 pm, 6-8 pm. Tues, Sat 10 am-5 pm, Thurs 10 am-1 pm. Access on request to bona fide students for reference only. Photocopying facilities.

Gilbert Goudie and E S Reid-Tait Collections Two collections bequeathed by two Shetland antiquarian scholars in 1918 and 1960 respectively, consisting of *c*1,500 v (many containing 10 to 20 pamphlets) relating to the Northern Isles, especially Shetland, of the 18th, 19th and 20th cent, including local material printed and published in Shetland. The collections are added to regularly.

Author cat on cards.

Montrose

Angus District Libraries, Montrose Public Library, High Street, Montrose DD10 8PJ. Tel (0674) 3256. Open 10 am-5 pm.

Montrose Subscription Library and *Montrose Trades Library* *The Subscription Library* was founded in 1785, transferred to the Museum of the Natural History and Antiquarian Society about 1898; the Museum and its contents were donated by the Society to the Burgh of Montrose in 1974. The *Trades Library* started in 1819 as the Montrose Reading Society which has also been acquired by the Public Library. The combined collections total *c*4,000 works which are particularly strong in late 18th and 19th cent, travel books, but with good representation of science, philosophy and religion, history and economics.

Motherwell

Motherwell Public Library, Hamilton Road, Motherwell. Tel (0698) 51311. Open Mon, Tues, Thurs, Fri 9 am-7 pm, Wed 9 am-12 noon; Sat 9 am-5 pm. Access to the Hamilton Collection for reference only. Photocopying of items subject to their condition.

Lord Hamilton of Dalzell Collection Originally the private library of the Lord Hamilton of Dalzell, it was bequeathed to Motherwell library on the death of Lord Gavin George Hamilton in 1952. It contains *c*3,000 books (plus mss) covering many subjects, and reflecting the interests of the Hamilton family. There are *c*100 books printed 1542–1642, and a large number of the period 1643–1851. Many important items were sold by the Hamilton family before the collection was acquired by the library.

Card cat.

The Lord Hamilton of Dalzell Collection published by Burgh of Motherwell and Wishaw. (op)

Newburgh

North East Fife District Library Service, Laing Library and Museum, Main Street, Newburgh, Fife. Tel (0334) 3722. Admission by arrangement with the District Librarian. Accommodation is limited, and books are not allowed to be taken out of the Library.

Laing Free Library The library is the bequest of Dr Alexander Laing (1808–93), local antiquary, to the Burgh of Newburgh, of his personal library of *c*3,500 v of general Scottish history, Scottish family history, local history and heraldry. It includes books of the 16th-19th cent—mostly 19th cent—many 19th cent pamphlets, broadsides and press cuttings. The future of the collection is under discussion by the District Council and the Laing Library Trustees.

A printed cat is available at the District Library Headquarters.

Alexander Anderson, *The old libraries of Fife*, Kirkcaldy: Fife County Library, 1953, p17-18.

Perth

The Black Watch Regimental Museum, Balhousie Castle, Hay Street, Perth. Tel (0738) 26287. Open May-Oct 10 am-12 noon, 2-4.30 pm; Nov-Apr 3.30 pm. Admission by appointment only *per* National Register of Archives, Scottish Record Office, West Register House, Charlotte Square, Edinburgh.

The Regimental Library and Archives of the Black Watch (Royal Highland Regiment) consist of items preserved by the Regimental Depot and the various Battalions of the 42nd and 73rd Foot from the mid-18th cent, and are the private property vested in the Regimental Trustees. The library consists of *c*2,000 v, and constitutes the fullest regimental collection in Britain.

There is no published catalogue, but the library is currently (1980) being classified according to UDC.

Perth and Kinross District Libraries, Sandeman Library, Kinnoull Street, Perth. Tel (0738) 23329. Open Mon, Tues, Thurs 9.30 am-6 pm, Fri 9.30 am-7 pm, Wed and Sat 9.30 am-1 pm. Admission by appointment with the Reference Librarian.

MacIntosh Collection MacIntosh, said to be the last non-jurying clergyman in Scotland, ended his days in Dunkeld, leaving his large library to the town where it lay neglected until the 1920s, when the Duke of Athol deposited it in the Sandeman Library. It consists of *c*1,500 books, mainly theological, with some Scottish history. Ranging from the 16th to 18th cent, *c*750 books are 18th cent.

Cat in progress.

Note: An interesting pamphlet holding seems to have been lost from the collection.

Athol Collection Formed by Lady Ruggles-Brise, daughter of the 9th Duke, it consists of *c*500 books and mss of early Scottish music. This is a major source of reference as there are several unique items. It is especially strong on early fiddle and dance music.

No cat.

Perth Imprints A collection of *c*200 books of early Perth printing, especially of the 18th cent Morison press. This collection is added to as opportunity arises.

Local History Collection A fairly comprehensive collection covering pre-1850 material.

Pluscarden

Benedictine Abbey of Our Lady and St John the Baptist and St Andrew, Pluscarden, Elgin IV30

3UA. Tel (0343) 89 257. The library is within monastic enclosures. Admission by appointment to bona fide scholars on application to the Librarian. Women cannot be admitted, but books can be fetched for them to use in the parlour. Loans only exceptionally; reading room; photographer available. Accommodation available through Guestmaster in monastery (men), in hutted hostels nearby (women); advance booking required.

Library of Pluscarden Abbey, Rare Books Section The Community was established from Prinknash 1948. Collection established from Prinknash (some vols earlier from St Wilfred's, Preston, and Holy Cross, St Helens), and other libraries, including Chapeltown and individual donors including Dr W Douglas Simpson. All pre-1801 books withdrawn from general monastic library in 1975–77 and transferred to Rare Books Section. It comprises *c*140 works (274 bound v) pre-1801 and *c*1,000 pre-1851. Predominantly theological, including Bibles, liturgies, catechisms, mission priests' manuals; hagiography, patristics; medieval, Reformation, Counter-Reformation, Jesuitical and Jansenistic works; pious and devotional literature; topographical (background to foreign missions); historical and literary, philosophical and medical, legal and architectural v; books of specifically Scottish interest. There are no incunabula; 4 STC; 5 Wing; 13 16th cent; 40 17th cent. A few recusant books and several issued by the Propaganda Office, eg for the 'S...(ie Scottish) Mission'. Other notable books include David *Veridicus Christianus*, Antwerp, 1601, with emblem-book engravings, Origen, Froben Press, Basel, 1545. An English (1583) and Norman-French (1574) edition of Littleton's *Tenures*, printed by R Tottill, London.

Cat.

Ms author cat on cards.

Catalogue of books printed before 1801 (typescript) 1977; revised and published by University Library, St Andrews, (1980) (ISBN 0 900897 03 1; price £1.50, illus from UL St Andrews).

Sabhal Mor Ostaig

Sabhal Mor Ostaig, Isle of Skye IV44 8RQ. Tel (04714) 280. Open Mon-Fri 9 am-5 pm (members); open as required on Sat. Free to members of Caidreamh an t-Sabhail, otherwise £2 per day for the first five days, thereafter £1 per day. Translation facilities available from and into Gaelic.

General Collection, including Gillis Collection (donated by Prof Gillis of Nova Scotia). Founded in the early 1970s in association with the Gaelic College, Sabhal Mor Ostaig, the collection contains *c*1,000 v which are mostly Celtic, particularly books in Scottish Gaelic, with some Irish and Welsh; specializing in works in and about Gaelic, and about the Highlands and Islands in general; also bilingualism in general; only one in ten of the books are pre-1850.

Subject and title index on cards.

Author index (strip index) being completed.

St Andrews

North East Fife District Library Service, St Andrews Branch, Church Square, St Andrews, Fife. Tel (0334) 73381. Open Mon, Tues, Wed, Fri 10 am-7 pm, Thurs, Sat 10 am-5 pm. Incorporated in public reference library. There are separate rooms with study desks, and items not on open access are available for consultation.

Hay Fleming Collection The collection was a bequest, in 1932, of the library of David Hay Fleming (1849–1941), Scottish historian and antiquary, and consists of *c*13,000 v. The books are chiefly of the 19th and early 20th cent, but include one incunabulum, many pre-1800 items and a volume bound for James Stewart (*c*1531–70), Earl of Moray ('the Regent Moray'). The collection also includes Dr Hay Fleming's personal papers, letters and notebooks. The bulk of the collection is devoted to Scottish history, both general and ecclesiastical, and is especially strong in material relating to Mary, Queen of Scots, and local history relating to Fife and St Andrews. The collection is added to regularly.

An author page cat in ms, and typed card subject index (LC classification scheme) available.

Anthony Rodden, 'The Hay Fleming Reference Library, St Andrews', *SLA News*, no 122 (July-August) 1974, p109-113.

St Andrews University Library, North Street, St Andrews KY16 9TR, Fife. Tel (0334) 76161. Open for mss and rare books service Mon-Fri 9 am-1 pm, 2-5 pm (4 pm July-Sept incl); Sat 9 am-12.15 pm. The main area of the library remains open until 10 pm Mon-Fri during term time. The entire library is closed Sat during July-Sept incl, the Christmas vacation, and all statutory holidays which fall outside University terms, and on the Lammas Holiday (2nd Wed in Aug); normally closed for one week at end of June for the statutory annual inspection of stock. Visiting readers are asked to complete a simple registration card; advance notice is appreciated, but is only essential for mss and rare book service on Sat mornings. Mss and rare books reading room equipped with microfilm reader/printer; magnification and ultraviolet lamps; xerography and photography (subject to suitable condition of original). Items from mss and rare book collections not available for loan. All mss and pre-1701 printed books, and some later printed books of especial rarity, may be consulted only in the mss and rare books reading room.

The library has grown through accumulation, by purchase and gift, of an academic institution since the 15th cent, incorporating the old libraries of St Salvator's and St Leonard's Colleges (perhaps also St Mary's College). Copyright deposit of British publications, 1710–1837. It contains *c*70,000 v of rare printed books (as defined for the Directory), over 100,000 mss, plus the library's own archives, and a photographic and print collection of *c*150,000 items. The main subject areas of the printed books collection are theology, the classics, history, English and Scottish literature (1700–1900), but philosophical, scientific and medical books are well represented. There are 150 incunabula, *c*3,500 16th cent books, over 1,000 STC and *c*2,500 Wing items, over 30,000 v pre-1801. The early printed collections are strong in early provenances (especially Scottish), including armorial bindings. (See below under individual collections for further details.) Mss etc: strong in material of local and University interest, scientific correspondence of the 19th and 20th cent, papers relating to the Roman Catholic Modernist Movement, and photographs and prints covering the whole of the British Isles. So far as funds allow, rare books are purchased in support of teaching and research, and special efforts are made to secure mss and early printed works with important St Andrews provenances or other associations that come on the market, especially those having links with our early gift collections. So far as is known, there has never been any deliberate dispersal of what is now rare book stock, but some items are known to have been accidentally lost or destroyed over the centuries.

General 'guard-book' cat of printed books to 1977 (COM 1978–).

Separate card cat of music scores. Separate sheaf cats of mss. Sheaf cat of former owners of printed books. The printed cat of 1826, which includes entries for some manuscript books, remains a useful guide to the older collections. Earlier catalogues of the library survive in ms, and an edited transcript by R V Pringle of the 1697 cat has been published (St Andrews, 1975). A separate *Catalogue of Incunabula* was published in 1956 (Supplement by R V Pringle in *The Bibliotheck*, 8, No 3, (1976), p67-70, and a separate computer-based cat of all books printed before 1601 is in preparation. See also under the individual collections and the brief guide to the mss.

Second report of the Royal Commission on Historical Manuscripts (1871), Appendix, p206-9.

St Andrews University Library: an illustrated guide, St Andrews, 1948 (2nd ed 1955). (op)

William Smith Mitchell, *A history of Scottish bookbinding 1432–1650*, Edinburgh, 1955. (op) (Makes use of some St Andrews holdings.)

G H Bushnell, 'Unfamiliar libraries III: St Andrews University Library', *The Book Collector*, 7 (1958), p128-38.

John Durkan and Anthony Ross, *Early Scottish Libraries*, Glasgow 1961. (op) (Lists pre-1560 Scottish provenances. St Andrews Supplement by John Durkan and R V Pringle in *The Bibliotheck*, 9, No 1 (1978), p13-20.)

St Andrews University Library: guide to manuscripts and University muniments (1976)—brief guide.

St Andrews University Library: introducing the rare books and special collections (1976)—brief guide.

G D Hargreaves, 'Rare books and research at St Andrews University', *Research in St Andrews*, 1 (1978), p67-73.

Special Collections

Abbot Collection A gift in 1611 of George Abbot (1562–1633), Archbishop of Canterbury, one of the 'Foundation Gifts' to the new Common Library (see Royal Collection). It comprises 14 v with the Archbishop's armorial bookstamp in gilt on the covers. Chiefly theological works, they include one incunabulum (Goff A-721), two works by Sir Thomas More (STC 18079, 18093).

Shelflist in classifed order (LC). Also contemporary ms list of the gift in its full original extent—part of the 'Foundation List' (for modern transcript, see Royal Collection).

Alchemy Collection Conditions of admission to this collection are the same as those for St Andrews University Library where items from the collection can be made available in the Department of Rare Books for consultation only, except that advance notice to the Library (Dept of Rare Books) is essential at all times.

The collection comprises *c*350 printed items and some mss which are almost entirely devoted to alchemy and older chemistry texts. The printed books are nearly all pre-1851; there is 1 incunabulum (Goff M-551) and *c*150 pre-1701 items. Especially notable for first and early editions (14) of works by Michael Maier (1568–1662).

Cat author (sheaf), of printed items available in the University Library.

Annandale Collection A gift *c*1630 of John Murray, 1st Earl of Annandale (*c*1570–1640), to St Leonard's College. It consists of 35 v with the Earl's armorial bookstamp in gilt on the covers. Chiefly theological works, including a set of the collected works of the Spanish Jesuit, Francisco de Suarez, bound in 16 v (Mainz, 1616–30).

Shelflist in classified order (LC).

Bible Collection Developed by the library during the present century from existing stock, with additional purchases from time to time. It contains *c*1,600 v including biblical texts in many languages, with the emphasis on historical items; over half are pre-1851 and *c*300 v are pre-1701.

Shelflist in classified order (LC).

On the 1581 Ostrog Bible and 1627 *Psaltir's vossledovaniem* in this collection, see R F Christian, J Sullivan and J S G Simmons, 'Early printed Russian books at St Andrews and their background', *The Bibliotheck*, 5 (1967–70), p215-31.

Additions still made to the collection from time to time.

Bonaparte Collection *c*71 v purchased 1948 bearing armorial bookplate of Francis Frederick Fox. Books in various European dialects (chiefly British and Italian, with a few Basque), mainly consisting of translations of portions of the Bible (especially Song of Solomon and St Matthew); printed in London 1857–63 for Prince Louis-Lucien Bonaparte (1813–91) in limited editions of 250 copies. Cf Albert Ehrman, 'The private press and publishing activities of Prince Louis-Lucien Bonaparte', *The Book Collector*, 9 (1960), p31-7—does not actually make use of St Andrews material.

Shelflist in classified order (LC).

Buccleuch Collection Presented to St Leonard's College, *c*1645 by Francis Scott, 2nd Earl of Buccleuch (1626–51), a student at the College *c*1640. It consists of 113 v bearing the Earl's superb large gilt armorial bookstamp (92 x 71 mm) on the covers. Mainly theological works, but books by J C and J J Scaliger well represented.

Shelflist in classified order.

Buchanan Collection Developed by the library during the present century from existing stock, with additional purchases from time to time. It contains over 250 v of works by and about George Buchanan (1506–82), with the emphasis on early and older editions; most are pre-1851, *c*150 are pre-1701. Includes a copy of the 1582 *Rerum Scoticarum historia* formerly owned by Andrew Melville (1545–*c*1622), Principal of St Mary's College, St Andrews, with annotations thought to be in his hand. Additions still made to the collection from time to time.

Shelflist in classified order (LC).

Donaldson Collection The library of Sir James Donaldson (1831–1915), Principal of the United College of St Salvator and St Leonard at St Andrews 1886–1915 was bequeathed in 1915. It contains *c*10,000 v and includes 2 incunabula (Goff P-810, P-812), 75 books of the 16th cent; *c*600 pre-1801, but mostly 19th cent books on philsophy, religion, the classics (especially) and education. Of particular interest as the integral working library of a leading Scottish academic at the turn of the century. Principal Donaldson's ms papers also held.

Shelflist in classified order (LC); also Principal Donaldson's own thematic cat in ms.

Dudley Collection Probably acquired as early as the 16th cent. It contains 4 v, 3 of which are in the armorial binding of Robert Dudley, Earl of Leicester (*c*1532–88), with his 'bear and post' stamp; the other v bears the arms of Henry VIII on the front covers. All vols have at the foot of the title-page what G H Bushnell described as 'a peculiar and not easily decipherable inscription which I read in 1926 as a cryptogram of 'Elizabeth' and 'Leicester'. 'Independently', Bushnell continues, 'in respect of other books bearing the inscription, Colonel Moss arrived at the same reading, which he published in *The Library* in Sept 1939 (p126). It is possible that these books reached the University Library from Mary (Queen of Scots)'. *Book Collector*, 7 (1958), p130.

Cat, see general notes.

Finzi Collection Purchased 1966 from the library of the English composer Gerald Finzi (1901–56). *c*700 v, chiefly instrumental and vocal works of 18th cent English composers in 18th cent printed scores, with *c*30 books (mostly 18th cent) about music; also *c*100 mss of 18th cent English music copied in the hand of Gerald Finzi and other 20th cent hands. Additions are made from time to time.

Shelflist in classified order (LC).

Annotated cat by Cedric Thorpe Davie, OBE, Emeritus Professor of Music at St Andrews, in preparation (ie in 1978).

J D Forbes Collection The library of James David Forbes (1809–68), an eminent scientist (especially in the field of glaciology) and Principal of the United College of St Salvator and St Leonard at St Andrews from 1859; presented in 1929 by his son George Forbes, FRS. It contains *c*1,250 v (excluding periodicals) including books of the 16th-19th cent, chiefly scientific, with some classics and alpine travel; the majority are pre-1851, over 500 pre-1801. Essentially a working library in the physical sciences, but a strong interest in the history of science is evident, and there are many outstanding antiquarian items such as Paccioli, *Diuina proportione* (1509) and *Summa de arithmetica* (1523); Copernicus, *De revolutionibus orbium coelestium* (1543); several Galileos, including a presentation *Difesa* (1607); Kepler, *Astronomia nova* (1609); and Newton, *Principia* (1687) and *Opticks* (1704).

Shelflist in classified order (LC).

Frank Cunningham, 'The J D Forbes Collection of mainly scientific books in St Andrews University Library', *The Bibliotheck*, vol 11 (1982), p17-20.

Hollis Collection Presented *c*1760–70 by Thomas Hollis (1720–74), the Dorset 'Lover of Liberty' and library benefactor, it contains 9 v, 18th cent English books in characteristic Hollis bindings (? 7 by Matthewman and 2 by Montagu)—Cf Howard M Nixon, 'English bookbindings: III', *The Book Collector*, 1 (1952), p183-4.

Lang Collection Developed by the library during the present century from existing stock, with additional purchases from time to time. It totals over 430 v of works by and edited by Andrew Lang (1844–1912), Scottish man of letters and student at St Andrews 1861–3; strong in his first editions. Additions are still made from time to time. There is also a strong collection of Lang material in the Dept of Mss, including over 1,000 letters and over 50 literary and miscellaneous mss and proofs.

Shelflist in classified order (LC).

MacGillivray Collection Presented in 1939 by Angus MacGillivray of MacGillivray, 28th Chief of the Clan, it contains *c*1,250 books of the 18th-20th cent in the field of Scottish history and literature, and includes books in Gaelic and many early editions of Ossian.

Shelflist in classified order (LC).

Mackay Collection Formed by the mathematician John Sturgeon Mackay (1843–1914), MA, LLD (St Andrews), FRSE (1882), mathematical master at Edinburgh Academy. It contains 52 v, and presented in his memory by his brother Robert Mackay in 1923. It contains in 52 v mathematical works of the 16th-19th cent; all but 7 items are pre-1851, 36 are pre-1801. Strong in Euclid items (19) in various languages—mostly separate editions of the *Elementa*, including the first Greek edition (Basle, 1533) and the first Arabic edition (Rome, 1594).

Shelflist in classified order (LC).

Moore Collection A bequest made in 1681 to St Salvator's College by William Moore (*c*1640–84), Archdeacon of St Andrews and former student at the College. It consists of *c*250 v of works of the 16th and 17th cent, chiefly theological.

Shelflist in classified order (LC).

Ms cat of 1744 lists the bequest in its full original extent.

W E K Rankin, 'A seventeenth century manse library', *Records of the Scottish Church History Society*, 17 (1969–71), p47-63.

Murray Collection 1670 bequest to St Leonard's College from Mungo Murray (1599–1670), Regent of St Leonard's College, later Professor of Astronomy at Gresham College and Rector of Wells. There are 48 v (so far identified as certainly originating from this bequest) of the 16th and 17th cent, chiefly theological, but including Gerard's *Herball* (1636) and Montaigne's *Essais* (1635).

Shelflist in classified order (LC).

Contemporary ms cat lists the full original extent of bequest.

John Ward, *The lives of the Professors of Gresham College*, London, 1740, p88-90.

Royal Collection An amalgamation of two gifts from the Royal House of Stewart: (a) Gift (in *c*1560) of James Stewart (*c*1531–70), Earl of Moray, Regent of Scotland, and Commendator Prior of St Andrews, to St Leonard's College, where he was a student in 1545; (b) Gift of James VI and I and his family to mark the foundation of a new Common Library for the University in 1611–12 (the 'Foundation Gift'). It contains over 200 v and there are over 50 'Regent Moray' v, mostly in his gilt armorial bindings; associated with the Regent Moray gift are 13 v owned by Robert Stewart (*c*1520–86), Bishop of Caithness, in his personal bindings, and 1 v, in the gilt armorial binding of John Stewart (*d*1563), Commendator Prior of Coldingham and half-brother of the Regent Moray. The Foundation Gift vols have on the covers a fine large gilt stamp (98 x 80 mm) based on the 15th cent seal of the University. The collection comprises books of the 16th and early 17th cent from continental presses, and the main subject areas are theology (notably the Christian Fathers) and the classics. A further volume in a John Stewart binding (non-armorial) was added by purchase in 1975 (=Durkan & Ross No 3).

Shelflist in classified order (LC).

Contemporary ms list of the Foundation Gift in its original extent—published by the library, in a revised transcript by R V Pringle, 1976.

D W Doughty, 'Notes on the Regent Moray's books and their bindings', *The Bibliotheck*, 6 (1971–3), p65-75. On the Regent Moray's non-armorial bindings and John Stewart's bindings, see D W Doughty, 'Renaissance books, bindings and owners in St Andrews and elsewhere: the humanists', *The Bibliotheck*, 7 (1974–5), p117-33.

Scot Collection Presented to St Leonard's College in 1620 and 1646 by Sir John Scot of Scotstarvit 1585–1670) and his friends, the 1620 gift for the formation of a 'class library' in the humanities (Sir John Scot had graduated from St Leonard's in 1605). It contains 64 v of continental works of the 16th and 17th cent, chiefly in the humanities (classics and history).

Shelflist in classified order (LC).

Contemporary subscription list of the donors of the 1620 gift and their donations—transcribed in the article mentioned below.

R V Pringle, 'An early humanity class library: the gift of Sir John Scot and friends to St Leonard's College (1620)', *The Bibliotheck*, 7 (1974–5), p33-54.

Shewan Collection Presented in 1936 by Dr Alexander Shewan, Indian Civil Service, and independent Homeric scholar. The collection contains *c*5,000 pamphlets (including printed dissertations, articles, notes, and reviews) uniformly bound in 250 v in the fields of Homeric studies; mostly 19th cent.

Ms index (subjects) compiled by Dr Shewan.

Simson Collection A bequest of 1770 of James Simson (1740–70), 2nd Chandos Professor of Medicine at St Andrews—his working library, including many items previously owned by his father Thomas Simson (1696–1764), the 1st Chandos Professor. It contains over 200 v of medical books of the 16th-18th cent, chiefly 18th. Includes a coloured copy of Dioscorides, *De medicinali materia*, Frankfurt, 1549.

Shelflist in classified order (LC).

Typographical Collection Developed by the library during the present century from existing stock with additional purchases from time to time. It contains *c*4,000 v representing an assembly of early printed books not in other special collections. Arranged by country and town of printing, and normally including Continental books to 1600, English and Irish books to 1640, and Scottish books to 1775 (with some later local imprints, eg St Andrews, Cupar, Perth). A collection of this size and background naturally has many outstanding features: there are 13 incunabula owned by William Schevez (*d*1497), Archbishop of St Andrews (probably among the first printed books to come to St Andrews); 13 items presented to St Leonard's College by George Buchanan; and *c*100 v from the 1657 bequest of William Guild (1586–1657), Principal of King's College, Aberdeen (including many books with important previous Scottish provenance, see Durkan & Ross). Among individual items of special note may be mentioned a copy of Gregory's 1495 *Moralia* (Goff G-431) with the earliest known dated panel-stamp (1488) on the upper cover, and the *Catechesis religionis Christianae quae in ecclesiis Palatinatus traditur*,

Edinburgh 1591 (STC 13023, Aldis 224). New acquisitions of early printed books are normally added to this collection.

Shelflist in 'typographical' order (by country and town of printing).

On the bindings of some of the Schevez incunabula, see G D Hobson, *Bindings in Cambridge libraries*, (Cambridge, 1929), p36; on Schevez and his books generally see G H Bushnell, 'Portrait of a bibliophile IV: William Schevez, Archbishop of St Andrews, d1497', *The Book Collector*, 9 (1960), p19-29. On some other books, bindings and owners, see D W Doughty, 'Renaissance books, bindings and owners in St Andrews and elsewhere: the humanists', *The Bibliotheck*, 7 (1974–5), p117-33.

Von Hügel Collection The library of Baron Friedrich von Hügel (1852–1925), Hon LLD St Andrews 1921, philosopher of religion; bequeathed to St Andrews, received in 1926. It contains *c*5,000 v, and represents a working library of mainly 19th and 20th cent works on philosophy, religion and history; related especially to mysticism and the Catholic Modernist Movement; occasional pencilled annotation in Von Hügel's hand. St Andrews also holds Von Hügel's ms papers and other mss relating to the Catholic Modernist Movement.

Shelflist in classified order (LC).

Wedderburn Collection A bequest of Sir John Wedderburn (1599–1679), Regent of St Leonard's College and physician to Charles I, made in 1679 to St Leonard's College. At present there are 136 v but others are likely to be identified and transferred from other collections. They include books of the 15th-17th cent, chiefly medical. 7 incunabula. Includes a coloured copy of Hieronymus Bock, *De stirpium nomenclaturis*, Strassburg 1552. Some of the vols considered to belong to this bequest have on the covers the three 'choughs' or 'heathcocks' armorial bookstamp (Davenport p211) of uncertain ownership.

Shelflist in classified order (LC).

Ms cat of 1678 lists the full original extent of the bequest.

On the three choughs bookstamp, see D MacArthur, 'Three Cornish choughs: an armorial bookstamp problem', *The Library World*, June 1951, p279-80.

Williams Collection *c*58 v from the library of John Williams Williams, Professor of History at St Andrews 1929–55; presented by his executors in 1958. It is devoted entirely to the *Eikon Basilike* attributed to Charles I, chiefly comprising 17th cent editions.

Shelflist in classified order (LC).

Young Collection 9 v presented *c*1611–40 by Patrick Young (1584–1652), Librarian to James VI and I and Charles I; one of the 'Foundation Gifts' to the new Common Library (see Royal Collection). It includes two incunabula (Goff D-380 and D-394 bound together) and a set of the Complutensian Polyglot Bible (1514–17).

Shelflist in classified order (LC).

Also contemporary ms list of the gift in its original extent — part of the 'Foundation List' (for modern transcript, see Royal Collection).

Special Deposited Collections

Folger Collection The property of the Folger Shakespeare Library, Washington DC, deposited in St Andrews University Library by the trustees in 1960 on indefinite loan. It is available in St Andrews University Library (Dept of Rare Books), for consultation only, on the written authority of the University Librarian, to scholars engaged in serious research. It comprises a set of the first four folios of Shakespeare's plays (1623, 1632, 1664, and 1685), that is Folger Fo 1—No 9, Fo 2—No 31, Fo 3—No 14, and Fo 4—No 11.

See Folger Shakespeare Library, *Catalog of the Shakespeare Collection*, Boston, Mass, 1972, Vol 1, p33, 39, 42, 43.

Prof A F Falconer, 'The Shakespeare Folios', *Spectrum: Student Magazine of the University of St Andrews*, Vol 1, No 4 (9 Mar 1961), p40-1.

G H Forbes Collection Chiefly the library of George Hay Forbes (1821–75), a cousin of Principal James David Forbes (see J D Forbes Collection Note). G H Forbes was an eminent liturgiologist and Rector of the Episcopal Church in Burntisland, where he ran the private Pitsligo Press for the printing of liturgical and other theological works. After his death his library passed to the trusteeship of the Episcopal Church of Scotland and was maintained, with some additions, by the Church in Edinburgh until 1969, when it was deposited by the trustees in St Andrews University Library on indefinite loan. Items can be made available, for consultation only, in St Andrews Library (Dept of Rare Books). It contains over 4,000 v, mostly pre-1851, with 4 incunabula. Theological books predominate, with the emphasis on liturgy, ecclesiastical history, and patristics—strong in 17th and 18th cent works in these fields. Also some literature (classical, Scottish novels—7 first editions of Scott, including *Waverley*), history and science. Works, and some proofs, from the Pitsligo Press.

Separate card cat (author, and Dewey classified) available.

Also author cat (Forbes's own books only) by Alan Carter, FLS Thesis, 1967.

Low Collection The library of David Low (1768–1854), Bishop of Ross, Moray and Argyle, from his house at Pittenweem, Fife ('The Priory'), where it remained after his death, in the trusteeship of the Episcopal Church of Scotland, until 1967, when it was deposited by the trustees in St Andrews University Library on indefinite loan. Items can be made available for consultation only, in St Andrews University Library (Dept of Rare Books). It consists of *c*750 v, mostly pre-1851 and mostly theological works, especially strong in works relating to the Episcopal Church of Scotland and the American Episcopal Church. Also some literature (English and classical, including a copy of the Ged stereotyped edition of Sallust, Edinburgh 1739) and history.

Separate cat in typescript, arranged under broad subject headings.

Stirling

University of Stirling Library, University of Stirling, Stirling FK9 4LA. Tel (0786) 3171. Haldane Room open Mon-Fri 9 am-5 pm (and at other times by arrangement) to all engaged in scholarly research. Readers travelling from a distance should give advance notice. The library is equipped with a Hinman Collator and other research facilities and services.

Haldane Room Collection The Haldane Room contains the University Library's collections of rare books and mss. Additions to stock are made by purchase, donation and bequest. There are *c*7,000 v. The subject range is wide: particular strengths include early editions of Scott; other Scottish writers from the 18th cent to the present; the Watson and Tait collections of early 20th cent left wing pamphlets and newspapers; the John Grierson Archive (devoted to the founder of the Film Documentary Movement); and a collection of books printed or published locally. There are 20 STC; 100 Wing; 30 foreign 16th-17th cent. The collection is added to as a matter of regular policy. Records appear in the University Library's main catalogues.

The Haldane Room, Stirling University Library, also acts as the Reading Room for the Leighton Library, Dunblane (qv).

Wanlockhead

Wanlockhead Miners' Library, Wanlockhead, By Biggar, Lanarkshire ML12 6UJ. Open to bona fide researchers and interested members of the general public. Reference service for researchers.

The miners' library was founded in 1756 by 32 men, mainly lead miners resident in Wanlockhead, as a society for purchasing books, and was controlled by lead miners throughout its existence, with office bearers and a committee. The total number of books accumulated by 1901 (a period of 145 years) was 3,116. Printed catalogues were produced at regular intervals. It was housed successively in the local school, 1756– , a cottage in 1787– , and a purpose-built library building in 1850. The library ceased to be used in 1937, but has since been restored by the Wanlockhead Museum Trust, with the help of grants from the British Library Board and the Pilgrim Trust, and re-opened on 15 July 1978.

The collection of books now totals 2,572 v, which include imprints dated from 1636 to 1920s, most falling within the 18th and 19th cent, with many theological works, including sermons and tracts (and some early editions of Wesley); a wide selection of novels and romances (including 40 v of Scott in early editions, and other early editions of Smollett, Sterne, Mrs Radcliffe etc), and a good range of periodical titles (eg *St Pauls, Edinburgh Review, North British Review*); science and technology, particularly geology and mining. Other sections include a good selection of biography, history, poetry, plays, travels etc, several local works and imprints. Stock includes donations from various sources, especially the Duke of Buccleuch, and some presentation copies. The library also houses the archives of the Scottish lead mining industry.

Card cat prepared over the winter of 1977–8. An edited typed version has been produced, one copy of which is placed in the British Library and another in the National Library of Scotland.

Library Review, v 24, no 6 (1974), p243-50.

TLS, no 3954, 6.1.78, p16-17.

Scottish Library Association News, no 139 May-June 1977, p287-91.

L A Record, Oct 1978, p518-19.

WALES

Aberystwyth

Centre for Advanced Welsh and Celtic Studies/ Canolfan Uwchefrydiau Cymreig a Cheltaidd, Old College, King Street, Aberystwyth, Dyfed SY23 2AX. Tel (0970) 3177 Ext 237. Open, on application to the Director, to researchers working on any aspect of the language, literature and history of Wales and other Celtic countries. Microfiche reader available.

The centre was established in 1978 on the basis of an appeal fund to commemorate the contributions made to the cultural life of Wales by scholars and writers associated with the University College of Wales, Aberystwyth. The library is based mainly on the personal collections of Sir J Goronwy Edwards (1891–1976) and Sir T H Parry-Williams (1887–1975), and includes books, periodicals and pamphlets relating to Welsh and Celtic studies. The *c*7,000 v, including 25 pre-1800 books (2 Wing items) are deposited in the Hugh Owen Library.

Card cat for pre-1979 holdings; post-1979 books are recorded in UCW Aberystwyth microfiche cat.

College of Librarianship, Wales, College Library, Llanbadarn Fawr, Aberystwyth, Dyfed SY23 3AS. Tel (0970) 3181. Open (Term) Mon-Fri 9 am-10 pm, Sat 10 am-4.30 pm; (Vacation) Mon-Thurs 9 am-5.30 pm, Fri 9 am-5 pm. Admission free to bona fide students. Full range of back-up services; accommodation can often be arranged.

Oliver Simon Collection Major part of the library of Oliver Simon, typographer to Curwen Press; purchased via Tony Appleton. It contains *c*700 items which include Curwen Press imprints and related material, principally 1920–56; considerable amount of press material and ephemera sent to Simon by other leading European typographers. Ms of Simon's autobiography. Full runs of Fleuron, Signature, Woodcut.

The collection is added to as opportunity offers to acquire Curwen Press imprints 1920–56, and other material relevant to the Press.

Entries in main library cat; separate (card) shelflist; handlist of original collection.

Appleton Collection of Victorian colour printing and signed bindings Purchased as a collection *c*1971 from Tony Appleton, it contains *c*450 v; approx two-thirds colour illustrated, one-third significant bindings. Most 19th cent colour printers represented; bindings include series of papier mache bindings, multiple examples of designs of John Leighton, Warren, Rogers, Owen Jones, etc.

Fully cat in loose-leaf sheet form with multiple indexes; Tony Appleton Catalogue No 7 (for original collection). [op]

Selected additions of significant works.

Whittinghams Collection Gathered by a private collector and obtained from Tony Appleton, it contains *c*500 v printed by the two Charles Whittinghams (uncle and nephew) 1798–1857, before and after Chiswick Press imprint was adopted. Most volumes in contemporary bindings; Pickering publication well represented, eg Prayer Book series.

Ms card indexes by author and chronologically.

The National Library of Wales, Aberystwyth, Dyfed SY23 3BU. Tel (0970) 3816. Telex 35165. Open Mon-Fri 9.30 am-6 pm; Sat 9.30 am-5 pm. Admission by Reader's ticket for which formal application may be made to the Librarian by persons aged 18 or over. Photocopying facilities and microfilm readers available.

The National Library of Wales, founded by Royal Charter granted in 1907, came into existence on January 1, 1909. It specializes in printed, manuscript and graphic material relating to Wales and the Celtic countries. It is maintained by an annual grant-in-aid from Her Majesty's Treasury through the Welsh Office. One of the six libraries in the British Isles (including Eire) entitled to certain privileges under the Copyright Acts. It contains over 3,000,000 printed works (books, pamphlets, journals); 4,000,000 archival documents and 40,000 v of manuscripts and 175,000 maps.

W Ll Davies, *The National Library of Wales: A Survey of its History, its Contents and its Activities*. Aberystwyth, 1937. (op)

The National Library of Wales: A Brief Summary of its History and Activities. Aberystwyth, 1974 (reissued 1981).

A Nation's Treasury: the Story of the National Library of Wales, Aberystwyth 1982.

A **Printed Books Department**

Aberdare File The printer's file of Rev Josiah Thomas Jones (1799–1873), printer of the *Aberdare Times*, and purchased in 1912. It contains *c*1,200 items, mainly ephemera, printed at Aberdare (Glamorgan) or relating to Aberdare 1835–73.

Handwritten schedule.

Anderson Collection Purchased in Nov 1981 from the executors of R A Anderson of Llantwit Major, Glamorgan. Mr Anderson formed his collection in the early years of this century, his family having links with the Donne family who owned land near Llantwit. It is made up of *c*140 works by, or relating to, John Donne. There are 24 STC and 22 Wing items; 5 Nonesuch editions, and a number of editions of Walton's *Lives*. Donne items will be added as and when they become available.

Typewritten checklist.

Ar C'halvez Collection The library of Abbé Armand Le Calvez (Armans ar C'halvez, 1921–72) priest and educationalist, of Rennes, Brittany, donated by his friend Abbé le Clerc of Lannion. It contains over 500 monographs, and a selection of literary journals. It includes works in Breton and French dealing with the language, literature and history of Brittany, with a selection of books, pamphlets on bilingualism in education in Europe. Also a collection of private papers.

Cat in preparation.

Arzel Even Collection The library of the late Jean Raymond Francois Piette (1921–71), lecturer in Breton and Cornish in the University College of Wales, Aberystwyth, and purchased from his widow. It has 500 monographs and a selection of journals. There are works in Breton and French dealing with the language, literature and history of Brittany and a selection of scientific books, mainly in French.

Cat in preparation.

Annual Report NLW 1972–3 (Aberystwyth, 1973), p28.

Barbier Collection The major part of the library of J L A Barbier (*d*1953), Professor of French at the University College of Wales, Aberystwyth, and presented by his daughters in 1954. A supplementary collection was received later from Dr Margaret Phillips. There are *c*1,500 v relating chiefly to 19th and early 20th cent French literature. Authors strongly represented include Lamartine, Gide, Proust.

Included in main cat.

Baring-Gould Ballad Collection Purchased in 1981, about half the items came originally from the collection of the Rev S Baring-Gould. Most of the remainder were collected by Mr Harvey (a well-known Edinburgh collector). There are *c*950 items in three albums. The collection covers the whole range of 19th cent ballads and street literature in English, and includes traditional ballads like 'Lord Bateman' and 'Barbara Allen', and topical ballads on wars, mining disasters, shipwrecks, floods, railways and sport. Many items of Irish interest are included.

Typed cat and first line index prepared by the bookseller.

Idris Bell Collection The working library of Sir Idris Bell (1879–1967), former Keeper of Manuscripts at the British Museum, presented to the library, in accordance with his wishes, by his family on his death in 1967. It includes *c*1,500 items of papyrological texts and studies and background material on the history and literature of Greece, Rome and hellenistic Egypt. The collection was supplemented by Principal Brinley Rees's papyrological collection purchased in 1980.

Typewritten cat.

Blondeau Collection Purchased 1982 from a bookseller, the nucleus of the collection was the library of Henri Blondeau (1841–1926), dramatist and writer of revues, operettas, vaudevilles etc, and a well-known figure in the Paris theatres from the 1860s to the First World War. It contains 2,024 items of French dramatic texts 1815–1914, mostly published in the period 1820–70. They include works by such authors as Dumas fils, Augier and Brieux, but the bulk of the material is the light comedy, melodrama and vaudeville which were typical of the July Monarchy and Second Empire. The collection includes over 200 plays by Eugene Scribe and his collaborators. Other authors which figure largely are Ancelot, Barriere, Bayard, Bourgeois Dumanoir, Feuillet, Labiche, Meilhac and Halevy and Sardou.

Booksellers' cat, with introduction by A W Raitt.

Bourdillon Collection Assembled by Francis William Bourdillon (1852–1921), poet, literary schȯlar and bibliographer, of Midhurst, Sussex, and purchased in 1922 from the trustees of his estate. It contains 150 mss and 6,178 printed v which include 66 incunabula; *c*25 STC; 50 Wing; and 180 ESTC items, together with 320 printed on the Continent in the 16th cent and 260 in the 17th or 18th cent. The collection is rich in French medieval literary texts and studies and early illustrated books. Of especial interest are its Arthurian and other romances, including 23 eds of the *Roman de la Rose* printed before 1550. Also included are several large series, eg *Soc des Anciens Textes Francais, Recueil des historiens des Croisades*, standard classical and English authors, and reference works in bibliography, art and printing history.

Ms (ledger) cat.

F W Bourdillon, *The early editions of the Roman de la Rose*, 1906.

Carmarthen Presbyterian College Collection The Presbyterian College was founded early in the 18th cent as a Protestant Dissenting Academy for the education of Nonconformist candidates for the Christian ministry. This deposited collection formed part of the College's library, and was received in 1965 after the closure of the College in 1963. It contains *c*500 v which include 1 STC; 12 Wing; 12 ESTC; 3 pre-1600 foreign imprints; 2 17th cent foreign imprints. The broad subject categories include theological, literary and historical works of the classical writers in the original language; historical, biographical and doctrinal matter relating to the Christian Church; English Bible commentaries, mainly from the 19th and early 20th cent; a small number of

Welsh books. The collection, in part, reflects the Congregational and Unitarian emphasis of the College.

The greater part of the College's library was removed after the closure in 1963 to the School of Theology, the University College of Wales, Cardiff (qv).

Castell Gorfod Collection The library of Capt James Buckley of Castell Gorfod, St Clears, Carmarthenshire, including the library collected by his maternal grandfather, Mr Joseph Joseph, FSA, of Brecon, and deposited in the National Library of Wales by Capt Buckley in 1920. It contains 1,500 items in 1,200 v, as well as *c*100 periodical titles, and includes 20 STC and 90 Wing items. Subject areas include history, genealogy and topography mainly, being particularly rich in material relating to the counties of Brecknock and Carmarthenshire, in both English and Welsh. Among the periodicals are the only recorded copies of the two issues of the *Cambrian Magazine*, Llandovery, 1773.

Ms shelflist of the library at Castell Gorfod (undated, but probably compiled in 1905?).

Card cat compiled in the library.

Children's Books, pre-1870 The collection has been built up by various donations and purchases, but centred on the donation made by C J Knight Esq in 1937. It contains *c*450 items. The pre-1870 works contain some 18th cent imprints, but the bulk of the collection covers 1810–50. The collection contains chapbooks, readers, picture books, primers, instructional works, two scrapbooks, children's games, alphabets, fiction and non-fiction. Authors include Mrs Barbauld, Maria Edgeworth, Mrs Sherwood, Jane Taylor, Mrs Trimmer, Isaac Watts.

Typewritten cat.

Card cat.

Civil War Sermons Presented by Sir Charles Thomas-Stanford 1926, the collection consists of 145 v of sermons preached before Parliament 1641–50.

Civil War Tracts Efforts have been made along the years to collect the tracts of the Civil War and Commonwealth period that relate to Wales and the Marches. Many came to the library as part of the foundation collections of Sir John Williams (qv) and J H Davies (qv), while others have been purchased. The collection now contains *c*600 items.

Catalogue of tracts of the Civil War and Commonwealth period relating to Wales and the Borders, Aberystwyth 1911.

Material acquired after 1911 in the main card cat of the library.

The Frances Power Cobbe Collection Miss Frances Power Cobbe (1822–1904) of Hengwrt, Dolgellau, Gwynedd (formerly Merionethshire) was founder and Honorary Secretary for 18 years to the Victoria Street Society for Protection of Animals from vivisection, and President from 1898–1904(?) of the British Union for Abolition of Vivisection. In 1899 she bequeathed her library to form a Public Library in Barmouth; in 1970 Barmouth Urban District Council placed the collection on permanent loan in NLW. It consists of *c*2,500 v which include theological, scientific, zoological, historical and biographical works published mainly pre-1900. Some of the books are personal gifts to Miss Cobbe from Martineau, Mill, Shaftesbury and Darwin; others reflect her interests in vivisection and the emancipation of women.

The Frances Power Cobbe bequest. Catalogue of books. Barmouth: Barmouth Library, 1904.

Howell Davies (Ruabon) Collection Purchased in 1949, the collection contains *c*1,500 v. Howell Davies was a contributor to the OED, and his collection illustrates the growth of English lexicography from the 16th-20th cent, and contains copies of most of the principal English dictionaries from Bullokar to Wylie, together with scholarly and elementary grammars, spelling books, dialect studies and Latin, Greek, Spanish, Italian, German, Dutch and polyglot dictionaries of the same period.

In Library's main cat.

Lewis Weston Dillwyn Collection The collection came to the library as a purchase from Sir C V Llewellyn, Llysdinam, in 1928, and was once part of the library of the noted botanist L W Dillwyn (1778–1855) FRS, who lived in Glamorgan. It contains *c*1,000 v illustrating the development of botany from the 16th-19th cent. There are important works by Bacon, Bauhin, Grew, Johnson, Malpighi, Linnaeus, Parkinson, Ray, etc, together with herbals by Treviris, Turner, Dodoens and others, and a representative selection of striking illustrated works such as Martyn's *Historia plantarum rariorum*, Redouté's *Les Roses*, Thornton's *Temple of flora* and Bateman's *Orchidaceae of Mexico and Guatemala.*

Cards in main cat of the library.

Dodgson Collection Assembled by the Basque scholar Edward Spencer Dodgson who donated some items to the library. After his death in 1923, the remainder of the collection was presented by his brother Campbell Dodgson, Keeper of Prints at the British Museum. It is a collection of *c*150 books and pamphlets in or about the Basque language, mainly late 19th cent publications.

Early Law Collection Built up by donations and bequests from various sources, including the collections of Sir Samuel Evans, Henry Owen (*d*1919), Rev Henry H Knight, the Hon Mrs Lawrence Brodrick, Rear Admiral R G Rowley-Conwy and A R Llewellin Taylour. It is made up of *c*120 works comprising *c*450 v and *c*150 v of statutes, and includes *c*20 STC; 40 Wing and 60 ESTC items.

The Dr Lewis Evans Collection Part of the personal library of Dr Evan Lewis Evans (1898–1978) minister of Hope Congregational Chapel, Pontarddulais, West Glamorgan (1934–67). The collection reflects his interest in the life and work of Morgan Llwyd, the Welsh Puritan, and Jacob Boehme the German mystic. It contains *c*60 books and 50 pamphlets, together with mss material. The main part of the collection consists of studies of Jacob

Boehme's life and work, published in German or English during the 19th and 20th cent. The mss material includes both MA and DTh theses and a typescript copy of a proposed publication of a third volume of Morgan Llwyd's works. (Part of Dr Evans's personal library was acquired by the Dyfed County Library, St Peter's St, Carmarthen.)

The printed books are included in the library's author cat and there is a separate schedule of the main items in the Accessions Department.

The mss are described in the library's *Annual Report* 1979–80, p48.

Maxwell Fraser Collection Bequeathed by the authoress and travel writer Maxwell Fraser (1902–80) widow of the former Archdruid of Wales, Edgar Phillips, 'Trefin' (1889–1962), the collection consists of *c*10,000 v, the majority being of the 19th and 20th cent, and are mainly topographical works, local guides, and directories. Particularly strong on coverage of Lake District and Wales, with many late 18th cent and early 19th cent guides, journals, and accounts of tours in Wales. Also a large collection of works on Poland and Sweden.

Uncat.

Gladstone Collection Presented to the National Library of Wales in 1923 by Henry Neville Gladstone of Hawarden; additional material presented in 1933. Most of the material was owned by his father, W E Gladstone (see St Deiniol's Library, Hawarden). The collection contains *c*4,000 items in 459 v (bound by the National Library in 1925), and *c*400 loose pamphlets. Pamphlets and tracts cover mostly the period 1850–90, and relate to a variety of subjects including politics, education, religion and history. They have been sorted and bound according to subject under broad headings such as 'Theology', 'History', 'Church of England', and include many ephemera, probably scarce. There are a number of items on matters with which Gladstone was involved, eg Ireland, the Eastern Question, etc.

Cat in preparation.

Annual Reports of the National Library of Wales: May 1923, p5; Oct 1925, p5; 1932–3, p48.

The Greenwell Collection The private library of George Clementson Greenwell (1821–1900), purchased in June 1973. There are *c*1,000 items in 56 v, mainly 19th cent pamphlets, tracts and offprints dealing with the mining industry in general and the coal industry in particular. They include regional surveys on mining and geology, official reports and popular accounts of collier accidents, works on trade unions, housing and labour conditions, rule books and some rare issues of the *Miners' Monthly Magazine*.

Typed card cat.

The Gregynog Collection This represents part of the private library which was at Gregynog Hall, near Newtown, Powys, and was donated to the library in 1962 by the late Miss Margaret Davies. Gregynog Hall was the home of the famous Gregynog Press, and this collection contains 282 v, mainly about printing, designing, and book production in general. It also contains the products of other private presses, eg the Dover Press *Bible* (1903–5) and the Golden Cockerel Press edition of Chaucer's *Canterbury Tales* (1929), including some important foreign presses, eg the Cranach Press edition of the *Eclogues* of Virgil (1927), and the Bremer Presse edition of Luther's *Bible* (1926–8), and some books specially bound at the Gregynog Press Bindery. Some other editions of books published by the Gregynog Press are also in this collection.

Typewritten cat available at the library.

The Gregynog Press Collection The collection was built up at the library as the books were published, with some duplicates added later. There are *c*134 v (and some ephemera). The Gregynog Press produced 42 books, a few copies of each being specially bound. The collection includes a copy of the special binding and ordinary binding of each work, with duplicates of most of the ordinary bindings. Copies of the books produced at Gregynog since the press was re-started in 1976 have been added.

Thomas Jones, *The Gregynog Press*, OUP 1954.

D A Harrop, *A history of the Gregynog Press*, PLA, 1980.

Incunabula Collection This has been built up from various donations and purchases, and now contains *c*250 v. Purchases made from the library of Francis William Bourdillon include *c*25 French romances and translations printed at Paris or Lyons. There are seven editions of the *Roman de la rose*, and rare editions of some of the Arthurian romances. The other countries of Europe are also well represented, especially Germany and Italy, and there are a few examples of early English printing.

Card cat.

Victor Scholderer, *Hand-list of incunabula in the National Library of Wales*, Aberystwyth, 1940.

——*Hand-list of incunabula in the National Library of Wales, Addenda and corrigenda*, I, Aberystwyth, 1941.

The David Jones Collection The private library of David Jones (1895–1974), artist and poet. Deposited at the library by the Trustees of his estate in 1975, and purchased by the library in 1978. There are *c*1,760 items, including 121 periodical titles—reflecting David Jones's interests—art, literature, Wales and the Celts, religion, and Roman history. Many of the books are annotated by him.

Cat available in typescript.

Llandaff Cathedral Library The more valuable and rare printed books from the Cathedral Library were deposited in NLW in 1943. These numbered *c*800 items in 200 v, mainly theological in content, with several tract volumes containing 17th and 18th cent sermons. The collection includes 1 incunabulum; 22 STC and 234 Wing items, and some 30 16th and 17th cent foreign imprints.

There is a printed cat of the library at Llandaff, *Catalogue of the Cathedral Library*, 1887 (including

Supplement, July 1902), Cardiff, William Lewis, (1887?) and (1902?).

A schedule of books removed from the Cathedral Library, Llandaff, to the National Library of Wales, 1943. (Typescript).

Maura Tallon, *Church in Wales diocesan libraries*. Athlone, 1962.

Llanfyllin Collection Originally the Llanfyllin Parish Library—a SPCK lending library of the mid-Victorian period, housed in Llanfyllin Church vestry, and given to the NLW in 1975/6. It contains 369 v covering fiction and non-fiction adult and juvenile works. Approximately a third of the collection is SPCK material, and contains works by Mrs Carey Brock, A.L.O.E, Mrs Sherwood Samuel Smiles, Charlotte M Yonge. Works date from *c*1840–90. The bindings (having originally been covered by brown paper) are generally in very good condition. The collection is not added to. Comparison of the present collection with that listed in the published catalogue of 1858 shows that only *c*60 v remain from the library that existed at that period.

Dr Henry Owen Bequest A selection from the library of the antiquary Henry Owen (1844–1919) which includes early works relating to Pembrokeshire or by Pembrokeshire authors, including editions of Phaer's translation of Virgil 1562 and 1620 and his *Regiment of Life* 1596, three of Robert Recorde's works and Wm Owen's abridgement of the statutes, 1521. The remainder of the printed books in the library were bequeathed to the town of Haverfordwest.

Cat.

Robert Owen Collection One of the most comprehensive collections of books, pamphlets, addresses, etc by and about Robert Owen (1771–1858), the Utopian socialist reformer. It has been assembled since 1912 by donation, purchase and legal deposit, and contains *c*1,150 items, mainly of the 19th cent, of which *c*350 are pre-1851. The collection is being added to as a matter of policy.

The National Library of Wales, A bibliography of Robert Owen, 2nd ed, revised and enlarged, Aberystwyth 1925.

A revised card cat is in preparation.

Morris Parry Collection Donated by the collector who was the author of a number of articles on Welsh printing at Chester. The collection contains *c*240 items, mainly works printed at Chester, mostly in the 18th and 19th cent. Most of the items relate to Wales, and about half are in Welsh.

Typewritten schedule.

A note by William Williams in *Journal of the Welsh Bibliographical Society*, v 4 (1932), p42-3.

The Bartholomew Price Collection The collection is from the library of Dr Bartholomew Price (1818–98) FRS, who was Sedleian Professor of Natural Philosophy (1853–98) at Oxford, and Master of Pembroke College from 1891. The books were donated by his son to the library in 1940. There are *c*2,000 items of representative works, mostly from the 19th cent, which illustrate the development of mathematics, and particularly that of the calculus. Contributions from most of the eminent mathematicians of the last century are included, with English and French authors represented about equally. Some volumes are in German, and the earlier volumes in Latin include a fairly complete set of Euler's works. The whole collection has been dispersed in the library's general collection.

Cards in the main cat of the library.

NLW Jnl, v 1, 1940, p147-8 (Note).

Private Press Collection Built up at the library from donations and purchases, and items deposited under the Copyright Act, the collection contains *c*1,200 v, mainly the products of British private presses. All the important presses are represented.

No separate cat. However, all the books are recorded in the library's general cat.

Quiggin Library The library of Dr E C Quiggin of Cambridge purchased with funds donated by Mr and Mrs H Gethin Lewis, Barry, 1921. A scholar's working library of *c*3,200 v, with works on all branches of Celtic literary, philological and historical studies. Duplicates of items already in NLW were distributed to Welsh University College libraries, *c*700 to Cardiff, and 500 to Swansea.

Bruce Rogers Collection Bought by the library in 1981, this collection of 211 items includes most of the books designed by Bruce Rogers, the American typographer. Many are privately printed or are limited editions. It includes a finely bound copy of the Oxford Lectern Bible, which is regarded as Bruce Rogers's masterpiece.

Typewritten cat is available at the library.

St Asaph Cathedral Library The medieval library at St Asaph perished when the cathedral was burned down by Owain Glyndwr's troops in 1402. The modern library originated with the SPCK Lending Library for the diocese, founded in 1711. Early benefactors included Bishops William Fleetwood and Thomas Tanner. Since that period there have been many benefactors. In 1970 the greater part of the collection was placed on permanent deposit at the NLW. It consists of *c*2,500 v which include some miscellany volumes of 17th and 18th cent tracts, and a small collection of 19th cent Welsh tracts. There are *c*200 STC; 900 Wing; and 20 pre-1600 Continental items.

A catalogue of printed books from the St Asaph Cathedral Library, Aberystwyth, 1979.

Typescript author cat and shelflist compiled at NLW. Copies may be consulted at NLW and St Asaph. No copies for sale.

W Morton, *A catalogue of books in the St Asaph Cathedral Library*, London, 1878.

Maura Tallon, *Church in Wales diocesan libraries*, Athlone, 1962.

Sixteenth-century books printed on the continent of Europe These have been brought together from the library's book stock to form a separate collection, and are arranged in chronological order by place of printing. The collection, which contains *c*2,500 items covering a wide subject field, represents the art of printing in all the main European centres. The F W Bourdillon collection of French medieval romances and the numerous editions of the *Roman de la rose*, a collection of a hundred or so Aldines from the collection of J Burleigh James are noteworthy features.

Card cat, with indexes to printers and publishers, place of printing, date, subject matter and provenance.

Thomas-Stanford 'Euclid' Collection Sir Charles Thomas-Stanford donated 39 v of his collection of pre-1600 editions of Euclid's *Elements* in 1927. A further 11 v were donated by him in 1928. The collection has been enlarged by the library, and now contains 271 v representing 248 editions of all works ascribed to Euclid, and published in all periods. Although the original donation contained only early editions of part, or all, of the work known as the *Elements*, subsequent additions have been made so that the present collection encompasses all of Euclid's works. These include the lesser-known *Data, Phaenomena, Optica and Catoptrica*, etc as well as the *Elements* which is present in numerous versions, editions and languages. The collection is made up of 2 incunabula; 69 items of the period 1500–99; 67 of 1600–99; 59 of 1700–99; 48 of 1800–99; 26 of 1900– .

Cards in the main cat of the library.

A separate handlist was compiled in 1975 which showed the collection at that time (a) by date, (b) in conventional uniform title sequence.

The pre-1800 editions are shelved as one rare book collection. Post-1799 editions are shelved at one location in the library's general collection.

NLW Jnl, v I, 1939, p3-8: by S Gaselee (with 'List of editions' by Wm Williams).

Early editions of Euclid's Elements by C Thomas-Stanford, London 1926 (illustrated monograph of the Bibliographical Society, 20) (op)

Storey of Plas Nantyr Collection The private library of C B C Storey, Plas Nantyr, Glyn Ceiriog, Clwyd, was acquired by the National Library on his death in 1951. It consists of 980 v and 24 periodical titles (with long runs of the majority of them), mainly about metal mining (particularly gold), forestry and estate management, as the owner ran an estate and had mining interests in South Africa. There are a few maps of S Africa. The books are 19th and early 20th cent.

Not catalogued.

Taldir Collection The library of Francois Jaffrennou (*Taldir*), Breton poet and patriot, donated by his son Gildas Jaffrennou. There are *c*200 monographs and a selection of literary journals, and works in Breton and French dealing mainly with the language, literature and history of Brittany.

Typescript cat.

Annual Report of the NLW, 1966–7 (Aberystwyth 1967), p18.

Trefeca Collection Deposited by the South Wales Methodist Association in 1920. It is part of the library of the Pre-Theological College at Trefeca, and includes the nucleus of that library, namely the private collection of Howel Harris (1714–73). It also includes the Pantycelyn collection, and a selection of the books acquired for Trefeca by the Rev Edward Matthews (1813–92) of Ewenni. It contains 1,500 v, including 50 STC and 350 Wing items. *A catalogue of the Library at Trevecka*, Trevecka, 1793, lists 674 books. These are mainly theological, with 68 items in Welsh. A noteworthy feature of this collection is that the volumes were all bound and numbered at the Trefeca bindery. Later additions to the library are more general in scope, especially after the College was founded in 1842.

There are ms cats of the various sections of the library in the Calvinistic Methodist Archive housed at NLW, and also a printed cat of the Welsh items, entitled *Cyfres (Catalogue) o'r llyfrau sydd yn bresenol* (1880) *yn y Llyfrfa Gymreig yn Athrofa Trefecca*, Llanelly, 1880.

A typed schedule of the Welsh section has been compiled at NLW, and a card cat for all pre-1701 items.

NLW Annual Report, October 1920.

Cylchgrawn Cymdeithas Hanes y Methodistiaid Calfinaidd, V, 1, p47-9.

Gareth Davies, 'Trevecka (1706–1964)', *Brycheiniog* XV (1971), p41-56.

Tŷ Coch Collection The library of the 19th cent collector Edward Humphrey Owen (1850–1904) of 'Tŷ Coch', Caernarfon, was purchased in 1910 as the third 'foundation collection'. It contains *c*3,680 v which include *c*20 16th cent, 120 17th cent, 600 18th cent, 2,800 19th cent and 130 early 20th cent items. Mainly of Welsh interest, the collection covers archaeology, history, topography, genealogy, heraldry, bibliography. Early Welsh books include the 1567 *New Testament* and the 1588 *Bible*. There are many first editions of Ruskin and Borrow; books from the Baskerville and Strawberry Hill presses; early editions of Swinburne; a fine copy of the rare first edition of Milton's 'Paradise Lost'.

Card and ledger cat.

W Ll Davies, *op cit.*

NLW *Annual Report*, 1909–10, p14-25.

United Theological College, Aberystwyth The pre-1800 items from the College were deposited in the National Library of Wales in 1982. Most of the books were transferred to Aberystwyth from the library of Bala Theological College in 1964–5. There are *c*130 items in 170 v, mostly theological, and include 10 STC; and 40 Wing items. The Welsh books include two unique pamphlets.

In NLW card cat.

UCW Collection The 'Welsh Library' at UCW, Aberystwyth, was transferred to NLW in 1909. It included the libraries of the 19th cent collectors Rev Owen Jones, Llansantffraid (*c*7,100 v) and Richard Williams, of 'Celynog', Newtown (*c*1,300 v), and *c*5,000 v collected by the College. It constitutes the second 'foundation collection' totalling c13,400 v. Strong in 19th cent Welsh theological works, 18th cent Welsh classics and collections of hymns; also history, topography, literature. It includes c30 16th cent works; c180 17th; c1,100 18th; 1,800 19th; and 220 20th cent works.

Card and ledger cat.

W Ll Davies, *op cit.*

Jnl W Bibl Soc 1 (1910), p17-20, 56-7.

'Vaynor' Collection The J H James (of Vaynor, Merthyr Tydfil) bequest came to the library in 1939. Most of the items were probably collected by James in Italy in the first two decades of this century. There are c100 v, including works on astrolabes, early astronomy, voyages of exploration (especially Christopher Columbus), cosmography of the 16th cent, and works by Galileo. The 22 cosmographical items include important works by Ptolemy, Apianus, Piccolomini, Stoeffler, Copernicus, Danti, Sacro Bosco, Clavius and others. There are also 8 separate works by Galileo (4 first editions) and 3 editions of his collected works from the 17th-19th cent. In addition, the collection contained two sets of differing editions of Ramusio's *Navigationi e Viaggi* Venice, 1554–74.

In main cat of the library.

For the Continental 16th cent imprints, additional cards are filed in the separate cats maintained for these items. (Only the early works were originally kept together, and most of these are now dispersed in the library's collection of 16th cent imprints. Books by Galileo and some others are still kept together, but all late works have been dispersed in the library's general collection.)

NLW Jnl, v 1, 1939, p157 (Note).

Griffith John Williams Collection The library of the late Professor Griffith John Williams (*d*1963), Professor of Welsh at University College Cardiff, bequeathed by his widow. It contains c5,000 monographs, and complete sets (up to the date of his death) of the more important journals relating to Welsh and Celtic studies, and a large collection of papers dealing with various aspects of Prof Williams's published work. It includes a fine collection of Welsh language books and works related to Welsh and Celtic studies with c60 17th cent imprints, and over 200 18th cent imprints.

Cat in preparation.

NLW *Annual Report*, 1978–9 (Aberystwyth 1979, p31).

Sir John Williams Collection The principal 'foundation collection' donated in 1909 by Sir John Williams (1840–1926), court physician, and collected by him at Swansea and Llanstephan. He purchased several libraries, the most valuable being the Shirburn Castle Collection (c200 v) formed by Moses Williams (1685–1742) and his father, Samuel Williams (c1660–c1722), purchased in 1899, and the largest being that of John Parry, Llanarmon (1835–97) (c4,500 v). The whole collection contains c26,360 v, including 2 incunabula; 120 16th cent items; 650 17th cent; 2,360 18th; 19,910 19th and 2,340 early 20th cent items. It has a wide subject range, but is mainly of Welsh interest. It include 19 of the 22 Welsh books published pre-1700, including the three earliest (1546–7), ie *Yn y Lhyvyr hwnn, Oll Synnwyr pen Kembero ygyd,* and Salesbury's *A dictionary in Englyshe and Welsh.* It is rich in Welsh Bibles, prayer books, hymnals, eg Bishop Morgan's Welsh *Bible* (1588), Salesbury's *New Testament* (1567), and Kyffin's *Psalms* (1603). It also includes many books printed at the early Welsh presses, including the earliest—*Y drych Cristionogawl* (The Christian mirror), probably printed in Wales in 1586–7, and *Cân o senn i'w hen feistr tobacco* (a satirical ballad concerning tobacco), 1718; unique copies of John Penry's pamphlet, *An exhortation unto the governours*, 1588, and the 1609 Paris edition of Rosier Smyth's Welsh translation of the first part of Canisius's *Opus catechisticum*; early editions of Morgan Llwyd, Robert Recorde, Henry and Thomas Vaughan, and John Owen the epigrammist, and complete set of the *Old Welsh Texts* series; most of the Kelmscott Press publications and a large Arthurian collection, including the 1488 edition of *Lancelot du lac*; ephemera; chapbooks, almanacs, ballads, Civil War tracts.

Cat card and ledger.

NLW *Annual Report*, 1900–10, p33-41.

W Ll Davies, *op cit.*

NLW Jnl v 1 (1939–40), p203-8

Rowland Williams Collection The collection was the personal library of Rowland Williams (1817–70), a classical tutor at Cambridge University, then Professor of Hebrew at St David's College, Lampeter, and finally the vicar of Broad Chalke, near Salisbury. He bequeathed his library to any 'suitable repositore' in Wales, the first option to be given to Swansea or Caernarfon, and it was the Swansea Borough Library which accepted the bequest. In 1966 part of the collection was deposited in the National Library of Wales. It contains c3,000 v, with 6 STC; 12 Wing; 19 pre-1700 foreign imprints, and 171 ESTC items. The greater part of the collection consists of theological and philosophical works, with emphasis on the works of the Early Church Fathers in the original languages, texts in Hebrew and Syriac, Bible exegesis and comparative religion, the Church of England and its doctrine, including material of the Church of England and its doctrine including material on the Welsh diocese and collections of English sermons, and early Greek philosophy. Also included are literary, historical and philosophical works of the Classical period in the original language.

Note: Welsh books contained in the original collection were retained by the Swansea Borough Library (now the headquarters of the West Glamorgan County Library), and these included early editions of the Bible and Prayer Book and other devotional works of the 16th and 17th cent.

Cat cards prepared by the Swansea Borough Library have been photocopied at the National Library, and bound in book form for the use of readers and staff.

Williams-Wynn Memorial Collection Presented in 1911 by A W Williams-Wynn as a memorial to his grandfather

C W Williams-Wynn (1795–1850), the collection comprises 103 v, principally historical works, including 16th cent editions of Mathew Paris, Holinshed, Fabian, Grafton, Froissart, Monstrelet, Polydore, Vergil and Halle, and early 19th cent works on armour and costume.

World War I Collection Most of the collection of *c*8,000 v was acquired under the legal deposit provisions of the Copyright Act, but it also contains some important French and German series and monographs (*c*700 v) received as purchases or donations, eg *La Guerre documentee; Les armees françaises dans la Grande Guerre; Kriegsalbum der Woche; Die Britischen Amtlichen Dokumente.* Also a collection of American newspaper cuttings presented by Henry Blackwell of New York. *c*300 v of German literary works of the war period were at one time shelved with this collection, but have since been transferred to the German literature collection (PT). The collection was used as source material by the Historical Section of the War Cabinet while completing the official military history of World War I in NLW between September 1941 and September 1946.

B **Manuscripts Department**

National Library of Wales mss (NLW mss) The 'additional' manuscripts collected by NLW since its foundation total 21,800 v and are primarily mss, but including a few printed books (incunabula listed by Scholderer).

J H Davies, *Catalogue of Manuscripts, v i, Additional manuscripts in the collections of Sir John Williams, Bart, GCVO* (Aberystwyth, 1921) describes mss 1-446.

Handlist of manuscripts in the National Library of Wales (Aberystwyth, 1940–) in progress; v I-IV have appeared, describes mss 447-13685.

Victor Scholderer, *Handlist of incunabula in the National Library of Wales* Aberystwyth, 1940.

——*Handlist*... Addenda and Corrigenda I, Aberystwyth 1941.

C **Prints, Drawings and Maps Department**

Collection of Atlases and Early Geographies Built up by purchase, donation and bequest, the collection contains 96 folio v (1571–1849) and *c*300 octavo and quarto v (1616–1849) which include P Aa, *Nouvel atlas* 1714, and Saxton, *Shires of England and Wales*...*corrections by P Lea*, 1749.

Card index arranged by author, date and shelf no.

Auctioneers' Sale Catalogues Built up by purchase, donations and bequest, the collection contains *c*5,000 catalogues giving particulars prepared by the auctioneers when landed property was offered for sale. Many contain lithographed maps of the properties. Mostly dated 1820–1920.

Typescript list arranged by parish.

Books of Views Collection *c*500 v built up by purchase, donation and bequest, and containing copper and steel engravings; mezzotints; etchings; aquatints; lithographs; and half-tone reproductions usually with accompanying text describing travels and topography relating mostly to Wales.

Card index.

Ephemera Collection Built up by the Department by purchase, donation and bequest, it now forms a massive collection of broadsides and single-leaf printed items reflecting the daily life of Wales in the 19th cent in ballads; advertisements for property and events; bookplates; political posters; bidding letters; paper money; greeting cards; mourning cards; picture postcards; menu cards; tickets and postage stamps etc.

Card index for some classes of material only.

Mervyn Pritchard Collection Assembled by Ivor Mervyn Pritchard (?–1948), RCA, and purchased in 1940, the collection comprises 71 v of atlases and geographies 1559–1817, including such items as Münster, *Cosmographiae* VI, 1559; Ptolemy, *Geografia*, 1561; Strabo, *Geographicarum*, 1571.

Card index.

The Library, University College of Wales, Aberystwyth, Dyfed SY23 3DZ. Tel (0970) 3111 Ext 3591. Telex 35181 ABYUCW G. Open (Term) Mon-Fri 9 am-10 pm; Sat 9 am-1 pm; (Vacation) Mon-Fri 9 am-5.30 pm; Sat Subject to variation. The library is closed for a week at Christmas and Easter, and on Bank Holidays during vacations. Members of UCW, CLW, UTCA, the WCA, and graduates of UCW may use the library and borrow books. Visiting scholars and others engaged in serious research may use the library for reference purposes only. They should supply a suitable testimonial and obtain the written permission of the librarian before they can use the library. Photocopying machines, photographic facilities and microform readers available.

Early Printed Books Collection *c*650 separate works; 93 STC and 294 Wing items. The earliest book is an Aldine edition of Perseus dated 1501. A mixed collection with a good deal of theology and classical texts, some early scientific material and 15 pamphlets relating to the Popish Plot of 1678.

UCW Library Publication No 1, *Books printed before 1701 in the library*... (1972) lists all the items in this collection at that time; there have been very few additions to it since then. (op)

Books Printed Between 1701 and 1800 Approximately 2,500 v, covering mainly theology, history, classics, English and French literature and law.

Rare Books Printed After 1800 About 5,000 v with considerable emphasis on English literature and geology. Two smaller collections within this group include:

Private press publications (British 20th cent). *c*150 v, including a set of the publications of the Gregynog Press and *Books published in Great Britain between 1857 and 1859.* (The Library's contribution to the SCONUL Background Materials Scheme.) The emphasis is on minor authors.

John Camden Hotten Collection John Camden Hotten published a wide variety of books in London between 1856 and 1873. After his death his business was acquired by Chatto and Windus. This is a small collection (*c*60 v) which has been built up since 1971, and to which additions are made as they become available.

Swinburne Collection This developed from a small number of copies of Swinburne's works given by him to George Powell of Nanteos. Since 1970 it has been increased by purchasing early and more recent finely-printed editions of Swinburne's works. It now numbers about 50 items.

George Powell Collection George Powell of Nanteos, near Aberystwyth, gave and bequeathed many books, manuscripts and *objets d'art* to the College between 1879 and 1882. Those held by the library may be summarized as follows:

Approximately 2,500 printed books, chiefly of the 19th cent. French and English literature, Icelandic and Music are particularly strongly represented; *c*1,200 articles, poems and reviews extracted from periodicals of the mid-19th cent, together with a few pamphlets, and bound up into 97 v; *c*200 mss including music mss from the 17th to mid-19th cent and many autograph letters of writers, artists and musicians of the 19th cent.

The Powell collection includes some particularly important material, *viz*:

The copy of Warburton's edition of Shakespeare (1747) used by Samuel Johnson in the preparation of his *Dictionary* and his own edition of Shakespeare.

The ms of Swinburne's 'Appeal to England' (1867).

The ms of Restif de la Bretonne's *La Généographe* (late 18th cent).

The ms of Mendelssohn's concert overture *Calm sea and prosperous voyage* (1832).

A number of the first printed editions of the Icelandic sagas.

R Brinkley, 'George Powell of Nanteos: a further appreciation', *Anglo-Welsh Review* Vol 21, No 48 (1972, p130-34; 'The Powell, Swinburne and Camden Hotten collections of the library of the University College of Wales, Aberystwyth', *Library Association (Rare Books Group) Newsletter* No 12 (September 1978), p8-12.

D J Fletcher, 'Nicolas Edmé Restif de la Bretonne: *Le Généographe*', *Studies on Voltaire and the eighteenth century*, Vol CLXX (1977), p125-234; An edition of the mss listed in the note on the Powell Collection.

D L Jones, 'George Powell—Swinburne's "friend of many a season"', *Anglo-Welsh Review* Vol 19, No 44 (1971), p75-85.

A Cuming, 'A copy of Shakespeare's works which formerly belonged to Dr Johnson', *Review of English Studies*, Vol 3 (1927), p208-12.

NB The following material from the Powell Collection has been deposited by the College Library in the National Library of Wales. It may be consulted there but may not be reproduced without the permission of the Registrar and Librarian of this College:

*c*100 letters from Swinburne to George Powell (1865–77); *c*200 letters from other correspondents to George Powell. (Correspondents include Burne-Jones, Ford Madox Brown, Sir G J Elvey, Sir George Grove, H W Longfellow, Eirikr Magnusson, Sir F A Gore Ouseley, Clara Schumann, Simeon Solomon, Sir John Stainer, J B Zwecker); transcripts of these letters by George Eyre Evans, with some additional material relating to Powell; transcripts of 23 letters written by Powell to Eirikr Magnusson between 1862 and 1877; the letters from Swinburne have been reproduced in Cecil Lang's edition of the letters of Swinburne (New Haven, 1959–62); the College Library has also deposited in the National Library of Wales a collection of papers formed by E R G Salisbury (1819–90) many of whose books are in the Salisbury Library at University College, Cardiff. They include some manuscript material on Welsh local history and a large collection of press cuttings on the history and topography of Wales and the Welsh border and contemporary political events. The conditions on which they may be used are the same as for the George Powell mss.

Rudler Collection Approximately 4,500 pamphlets and offprints, mainly of the later 19th cent, on geology and related subjects assembled by F W Rudler, Professor of Geology in this College from 1876 to 1879.

Thomas Webster MSS Letters to Thomas Webster (1773–1844) first Professor of Geology at University College London—together with a few letters from him—bequeathed to the library by Professor F W Rudler. 149 letters, mainly on geological and scientific topics—written between 1818 and 1844.

J Challinor (ed): 'Some correspondence of Thomas Webster, geologist (1773–1844)', *Annals of Science* Vol 17, No 3 (1961), p175-95; Vol 18, No 3 (1962), p147-75; Vol 19, No 1 (1963), p59-79; No 4, p285-97; Vol 20, No 1 (1964), p59-80; No 2, p143-64.

Richard Ellis MSS This material was collected by Richard Ellis (1865–1928) for his unfinished study of the antiquary Edward Lhuyd, and consists mainly of notebooks and index slips recording the contents of manuscript and printed material relating to Lhuyd. There are in addition approximately 400 letters to Ellis and five notebooks containing some unpublished poems and short stories.

A handlist of the papers has been prepared by Professor Brynley F Roberts.

Brynley F Roberts: 'Richard Ellis MA (Edward Lhuyd and the Cymmrodorion)', Cymmrodorion Society *Transactions* (1977), p133-72.

David De Lloyd MSS David De Lloyd was Professor of Music at this College from 1926 until 1948, and the mss were presented by his widow in 1969. These include full scores and orchestral parts of the operas *Gwenllian, Tirna-Nog, Hywel of Gwent* and *Pwyll a Rhiannon*; Choral works, song and dance series; Instrumental music; Drafts of his *Requiem Gymraeg*; Settings of Welsh traditional songs; Notes on Welsh folk music; Notes on musical history and theory.

Thomas Francis Roberts MSS Papers of T F Roberts, Principal of this College from 1891 to 1919, presented by his son Dr R D Roberts in 1970. They include approximately 200 letters to T F Roberts relating mainly to College and University matters; miscellanea and ephemera relating to T F Roberts.

University College of Wales MSS Chiefly early library records—stockbooks, accessions, donations, binding etc—and some manuscripts relating to the foundation of the College; minute books of a number of student societies.

J O Francis Archive Presented by his executors in 1978. Typescripts and acting copies of his plays and broadcast talks.

Note The special collections in this College library have arisen in two ways: by bequest by an individual which have been retained as a collection or eventually collected together (eg the Powell Collection, the Rudler Collection, the J O Francis Archives), and by bringing together related material from various sources (eg the pre-1701, Swinburne and Camden Hotten Collections).

There is no separate name cat of the special collections in the library, but all printed material in the Rare Book Rooms and in the Powell and Rudler Collections is included in a separate shelflist. An inventory of the manuscripts belonging to the library is being prepared.

Bangor

University College of North Wales, Bangor, Gwynedd LL57 2DG. Tel (0248) 51151. Open (Term) 9 am-10 pm (Summer 11 pm); Sat 9 am-5 pm; Sun 12 pm-5 pm. (Vacation) 9.30 am-5 pm; Sat (except Aug) 9 am-12 noon. Science Library (Term) 9 am-9 pm; Sat 9 am-12.30 pm. Vacation as above. Free admission for reference. Borrowing at Librarian's discretion on application. Photocopiers, microfilm camera and readers. Ms and research reading rooms.

Arts Library Rare Book Room The library has been built up by donations and purchases at various periods since the college was opened in 1884. There are *c*1,793 items on a variety of subjects excepting Welsh interest, and they include 1 incunabulum, 56 STC, 474 Wing, and 1,057 ESTC items.

Author, classified (in main cat). Shelflist.

Bala Theological College Library Collection of Bibles Deposited by the Bala Theological College Committee when the library was dispersed in 1964. It contains 230 v and forms an important and valuable collection of Bibles, including the Paris Polyglot Bible 1646.

Bangor Cathedral Library Deposited 1960, it consists of the diocesan library founded 1709, and the canonry library. There are *c*4,500 v, mainly on theology, history and classics, with *c*350 titles of Welsh interest, including a fine collection of prayer books. The library is particularly strong in early continental printing, and includes 4 incunabula and 1,100 pre-1700 items.

Included in main cat.

E G Jones and J R V Johnston, *Catalogue of the Bangor Cathedral Library*, Bangor 1961.

Frank Brangwyn Collection Bequeathed to UCNW Library in 1957 by the artist F Brangwyn, the collection consists of 232 v, mainly art books.

Author, classified (in main cat). Shelflist.

Lady Reichel Memorial Collection Presented to UCNW *c*1926, the collection comprises 149 titles, all music scores.

Author, classified (in main cat). Shelflist.

Owen Pritchard Collection Presented by Dr Owen Pritchard, 1920, it consists of 350 v of late 19th and early 20th cent printed books, mainly private press books, periodicals, including *The Savoy* and *The Yellow Book*.

Sir Vincent Evans, 'Books presented by Dr Owen Pritchard. . .' in B Rackham and Sir V Evans, *University College of North Wales, Bangor*.

Science Library Rare Books Collection It includes bequests and donations from the Watkin Library, the Owen Pritchard Collection, the Talfourd Jones Collection and the Mathews Collection, and contains 870 v in the Central Science Library; *c*150 v in the Dept of Agriculture; *c*100 v in the Library's 'Store' sequence. Mostly 18th and early 19th cent books on various scientific subjects. One sequence of books on algae; two mss floras. The agriculture books include most of the Board of Agriculture county surveys.

Most items are not in the Science Library union cat. A separate cat of the agriculture books is in preparation.

Welsh Library Rare Books Collection This collection includes bequests, donations and books bought from private collections. They include such collections as the Watkin Library; the library of William Prichard Williams (1848–1916) Bangor; Richard Hughes, Tŷ Hen Isaf, Llannerch-y-medd; and Henry Rees Davies (1861–1940). Mostly books in Welsh and books relating to Wales and the Celtic countries, they include a valuable collection of Welsh ballads, *Cerddi Coleg y Gogledd*—a collection based originally on the collection of 18th cent ballads purchased from D G Goodwin of Uffington, Shropshire. Goodwin purchased them from 'Myrddin Fardd' (John Jones, 1836–1921). This collection was supplemented by the collection of 19th cent ballads of Dr T R Williams of Liverpool and Aberlleiniog. Also included in an exceptionally valuable collection of Welsh periodicals and newspapers, both of this country and America.

Author cat.

Brecon

Brecon Cathedral Dean and Chapter Library, The Cathedral, Brecon, Powys. Tel (0874) 4876. Admission to bona fide researchers only, by prior application in writing to the Dean. Reading room available.

The library has been built up from 1923 by gifts and bequests. Its stock now totals *c*3,500 v and includes the following main collections:

Hermitage Day Collection *c*400 v of liturgical and theological works from the library of Hermitage Day (*d*1927), mainly of the 19th and 20th cent. The collection contains a good run of the Alcuin Club Collections.

Trotman-Dickenson Collection *c*600 v from the library of the late Lenthall Greville Dickenson, donated by his widow Mrs Trotman-Dickenson in 1932. It contains mainly 19th cent popular religious works, some annotated.

Williamson Collection *c*850 v from the library of Bishop E W Williamson (*d*1953) relating mainly to medieval history and patristics. It includes 1 incunabulum (*The New Testament*, London, 1495); 2 Wing and 2 continental works of the same period; 4 17th cent English and 17 continental works of the same period; 4 17th cent English and 17 continental works; 6 18th cent English works and 32 continental.

Cat for the library in process of revision.

Cardiff

County of South Glamorgan Libraries. County Libraries Headquarters, Central Library, The Hayes, Cardiff CF1 2QU. Tel (0222) 22116. Telex 497416. Open Mon-Fri 9.30 am-8 pm; Sat 9.30 am-5.30 pm. Admission to Reference Library is free, and by special reader's ticket (applications in advance) to postgraduate Research Reading Room (Mss). Microform readers and xerox copying facilities available.

History The library came into existence in 1861, and developed into one of the best public libraries in England and Wales. The age of the library and the overall size of its collection of books have resulted in many rare books being scattered throughout this collection, and many of them are not identifiable as separate collections within it. Those groups which are identifiable within the library's stock are listed below.

Incunabula The nucleus of this collection dates from 1902 when a group of local luminaries purchased 67 incunabula from a local dealer, W P Lindsay Jones, and presented them to the library. Subsequent additions were made, and by the end of the 1930s the collection had been brought to its present size of 179 items—the earliest item is dated 1469.

A catalogue of early printed books, Cardiff Public Libraries, 1913; A catalogue of incunabula at the Central Library, 1965—unpublished typescript.

Welsh Books Books in Welsh, or relating to Wales, have always been acquired either by purchase or gift. There will be very few Welsh books published before 1850 which are not represented in this collection which also includes early children's books in Welsh.

A catalogue of printed literature in the Welsh Department, Cardiff Free Libraries, 1898.

English (to 1700) and Foreign (to 1800) printed books Within this collection of Early English (*c*10,000 v) and foreign (*c*2,500 v) printed books which has been built up, are clearly defined subject areas, eg Civil War Tracts (*c*800 items), and 17th cent drama (*c*800 v), mainly of the Restoration period. There is some doubt as to whether or not the items in this group are comprehensively listed in STC and Wing.

Private presses/Fine bindings Built up during the first half of this century, the collection of private press books numbers 1,271 v, representing 144 private presses. Those represented by 40 or more items are: Beaumont, Doves, Essex House, Golden Cockerel, Gregynog (complete set of productions), Kelmscott, Nonesuch and St Dominic's. Fine bindings number over 300 items, and include examples of various binding styles, forms of decoration, fore-edge, pailing etc.

Nineteenth Century Drama A collection of 1,500 plays in *c*400 v of collected drama, such as British Drama, Dick's Standard Plays, the London Stage, Bell's Theatre etc.

Early Children's Books This group includes *c*700 items, of which at least 20 are in languages other than English (*see* above under *Welsh books*). The earliest item is dated 1701 (*The newest academy of complements*), and a further 11 items are dated before 1800. Kate Greenaway works and some Beatrix Potter first and signed editions are represented.

Early Atlases etc This section includes over 100 atlases, road books etc published before 1850, of which 49 are noted in Chubb: *The printed maps. . . 1579–1870.*

Manuscripts The collection of mss is treated as an integrated whole to which there is a card index and shelf-list available for reference. For descriptive purposes the mss may be divided into three categories:

Welsh Literary MSS These were acquired in the main in 1896 by purchase from the executors of the bibliophile Sir Thomas Phillipps (1792–1872) of Middle Hill, Broadway, Worcester. They comprise *c*100 v (medieval to 18th cent) mostly poetry, but include some historical and geological works. The most noteworthy item is 'Llyfr Aneurin', a text (*c*1250) of Aneurin's *Gododdin* one of the 'Four ancient books of Wales', and is commonly held to be the oldest extant Welsh literary ms. The major part of this group has been catalogued in detail in Historical Manuscripts Commission *Report of manuscripts in the Welsh language*. Vol 2, pt 1 (1902), *sub* 'Cardiff' and 'Havod'.

Non-Welsh Medieval Mss Acquired from various sources, mainly by purchase, during the 1920s. These comprise *c*50 v, of which 16 were written in England. The majority are in Latin, and some are illuminated.

N R Ker, *Medieval manuscripts in British Libraries*, Vol 2, 1977, pxx-xxi, 331-77, *sub* 'Cardiff Public Library'.

Historical Mss These comprise over 15,000 items (*c*4,300 groups) relating mainly to Wales (especially Glamorgan), and include letters, diaries, journals of tours etc. Also included are some 19th and 20th cent literary mss (eg several mss by the novelist Jack Jones).

Note: Some of the items in this collection, along with other mss not noted here, are currently (December 1979) being removed to the strongrooms of the Glamorgan Archive Service, Mid-Glamorgan County Hall, Cathays Park, Cardiff.

Mackworth Collection of Early Music This collection is the library of mss and printed music of the Neath industrialist Sir Herbert Mackworth (1739–91), and was presented in 1919 to the then Cardiff Central Library. Most of the items were acquired by Sir Herbert between 1761 and 1788. In 1916 his descendants placed the collection on the market, and it was purchased for the library by Richard Bonner Morgan, a Cardiff optician. The printed items date from the 18th cent, more especially the period 1720–75, and are strong in works by Handel and Hasse. The mss, which number about 60, include scores of Italian operas, Italian and Spanish Cantatas, and English songs. The printed music has been listed in the *British Union Catalogue of Early Music*.

Malcolm Boyd, *Catalogue of manuscript music, printed music and printed books in the Mackworth Collection at Cardiff Central Library*, 1970 (Unpublished typescript).

—— 'Music manuscripts in the Mackworth Collection at Cardiff', *Music and Letters*, Vol 54, 1973, p133-41.

Glamorgan Archive Service, County Hall, Cathays Park, Cardiff CF1 3NE. Tel (0222) 28033 Ext 282. Open Tues-Thurs 9 am-5 pm, Fri 9 am-4.30 pm.

Clerk of Peace Library The library constitutes the Clerk of Peace working collection acquired by the Record Office along with the records. It consists of *c*34 v, including 5 16th cent, 12 17th cent, and 10 18th cent items relating to legal practice.

Llandaff Cathedral Library, Llandaff, Cardiff. Admission by arrangement, after written application to the Librarian.

The library has been accumulated from the Middle Ages. It contains *c*11,000 items, mainly theological and historical in content, which include many 17th cent and early 19th cent tracts, sermons etc. The more valuable and rare printed books were deposited in the National Library of Wales (qv) in 1943. They included 1 incunabulum; 22 STC and 234 Wing items, and some 30 16th and 17th cent foreign imprints. Another section of the original library has been transferred on permanent loan to the library at Cardiff Castle. This section includes 4 v 18th cent (1717–65) and 55 v 19th cent (1804–83).

Card cat for reference.

Catalogue of the Cathedral Library, William Lewis, Cardiff, 1887 (Supplement, 1902), available in the library at Llandaff.

National Museum of Wales, Cathays Park, Cardiff CF1 3NP. Tel (0222) 26241. Open Mon-Fri 10 am-1 pm, 2-5 pm. Admission by formal application (postal or personal). Photocopying (xerox) available.

Willoughby Gardner Library This collection was bequeathed to the Museum by Dr Willoughby Gardner, Y Berlfa, Deganwy, N Wales. It consists of 330 works, including two incunabula, with main subject emphasis on natural history.

Tomlin Collection Donated by J R Le B Tomlin (*d*1954), the collection includes 2,200 bound v and over 7,000 pamphlets relating mainly to conchology.

C T and E Vachell Herbarium The collection, bequeathed by Miss Eleanor Vachell, comprises 50 books mainly on British flowering plants, including some hand-coloured by the donor.

University College Cardiff, Library, PO Box 78, Cathays Park, Cardiff CF1 1XL. Tel (0222) 44211. Open (Term) 9 am-10 pm, (Vacation) 9 am-5 pm; Sat 9 am-1 pm. Admission upon written application to the Librarian. Full microreading, photocopying and photographic facilities.

The Special Collection Basically the books of Richard Reece, FSA (1772–1850) of Cardiff, presented to the College in 1919, to which the older and more valuable books in the library's possession have been added. It contains *c*2,500 v, including a small number of mss. Reece's books reflect the interests of an early 19th cent antiquary and are strong on English history, topography and English literature. They include 14 STC and 81 Wing books. The most interesting groups are the set of Gregynog Press books, the works of William Gilpin, W H Ireland, Maggini, and modern facsimiles of William Blake. Mss associated with the Special Collection include an important group of Edward Thomas (1878–1917) letters, notebooks and press cuttings.

Separate shelflists and chronological lists on cards available. Special author cat (ms cards) of Reece's library.

The Salisbury Library The private collection of E R G Salisbury (1819–90) lawyer and bibliophile of Chester, purchased by the College in 1886 and subsequently added to by gift and purchase. It contains *c*30,000 books, periodicals and pamphlets, together with an unnumbered quantity of prints, maps, mss, miscellaneous papers, press cuttings etc. The original Salisbury Collection includes books and pamphlets in Welsh (from the 16th cent), books by Welsh authors and books relating to Wales and the border counties (especially Cheshire and Shropshire). Subsequent additions have been in these subject fields, including Celtic Studies, Irish, Breton, Gaelic, Manx and Cornish books, Arthuriana and cognate subjects. There are *c*750 STC and Wing books, and many books of exceptional rarity, including a unique copy of William Godwin's novel *Imogen* (1784) and 1508 and 1517 editions of *Historia Regum Britanniae.*

A card cat on ms cards of original Salisbury Library available.

Published reference (in Welsh); J Hubert Morgan, 'Y Salesbury', *Y Llenor* 1937, p39-51.

Tennyson Collection Collected by A C A Brett (1882–1936), Professor of English at the College (1921–36) and purchased by the College after his death in 1936. It consists of 416 items (exclusive of multiple copies of some editions), mainly first and early editions of the works of Alfred Tennyson published in his lifetime, some biographical and critical works, besides works by other members of the Tennyson family.

Sian Allsobrook and Peter Revell, *A catalogue of the Tennyson Collection in the Library of University College, Cardiff*, 1972.

Carmarthen Library Formerly of the Presbyterian College, Carmarthen, founded *c*1700 and closed 1960 when the bulk of the library was transferred to Cardiff. Only the older books remain as a separate collection. It totals *c*4,000 v, mainly pre-1750, on theology, philosophy and science, especially strong for 1650–1750. Some STC items, large number of Wing. An excellent example of an 18th cent Dissenting Academy Library.

Ms cat in book form 1840, and a rough finding-list of the present collection recently compiled on cards.

Fonmon Castle Library Fonmon Castle, Barry, Glamorgan. Fonmon Castle is the seat of Sir Hugo Boothby, Bt, but application for admission to the library must be made in the first instance to The Librarian, University College Library, PO Box 78, Cathays Park, Cardiff CF1 1XL.

Private gentleman's library accumulated by the descendants of Philip Jones (1618–74) Colonel in the Parliamentary Army, and a member of Cromwell's Second House, and their connections, especially the Seys, Valpy and Boothby families. The books number *c*1,150 published before 1900 and are strong in English and French literature of the 17th to 19th cent; they include 23 STC, 124 Wing (plus 4 not in Wing), and a 15th cent ms book of hours. A collection of pamphlets of the 17th and 18th cent relates mainly to John Wilkes.

M E Evans, *A Catalogue of the library at Fonmon Castle, Glamorgan*, Cardiff 1969.

Music Department, Robbins Landon Library, PO Box 78, University College, Cardiff CF1 1XL. Tel (0222) 44211 Ext 2522. Open to bona fide scholars on written application to Mr I Cheverton. Microfilm reader, photocopying facilities through the University Library; audio equipment.

Robbins Landon Collection A unique collection, being the personal library of Professor and Mrs Robbins Landon, and now on permanent loan to the University College, Cardiff. The collection has grown over many years in the wake of Prof Landon's extensive researches into Haydn and his world. It comprises a large number of photographic copies, original mss and printed source material relating to Joseph Haydn (1732–1809), together with a limited number of items representing some of Haydn's contemporaries. The collection is divided into the following four sections, each emphasizing its specialization; (i) microfilm and photographic copies of printed and ms source material; (ii) original printed editions; (iii) a miscellaneous collection of autographs, letters and ms copies of music; (iv) *c*200 printed books and periodicals, 1782–1810 (including *The Ladies' Magazine* and *Literary Magazine* and *British Review*), incomplete v of newspapers such as *The True Briton* (1793–5), the *Courier and Evening Gazette* (1794–5), *The Morning Star* (1791–5), also a growing collection of early recordings on disc and tape.

The collection is being augmented regularly.

Card cat in preparation.

Robbins Landon, 'Haydn: *Chronicle and Works*', 5 v, London, Thames and Hudson, 1976–80.

Haydn Year Book, v 11, 1980- University College Cardiff Press, 1980.

University of Wales Institute of Science and Technology, King Edward VII Avenue, Cathays Park, Cardiff CF1 3NU. Tel (0222) 42522 Ext 210. Open Mon-Fri 9 am-9 pm; Sat 9 am-5 pm (and weekdays in vacation). Non-members of UWIST should apply in writing. Microform readers, reader printer and photocopying facilities.

Welsh School of Architecture Collection The collection comprises books acquired by the School through purchase or donation; four items belong to the South Wales Institute of Architects; other items from the library of Robert Williams FRIBA (1848–1915) of Ystradowen, Glamorgan, on indefinite loan from the University College Cardiff Library. It contains fewer than 100 items, 18th and 19th cent which are mainly accounts and details of architecture and antiquities of various periods.

Included in general library cat.

Handlist of short titles.

Welsh Music Information Centre, PO Box 78, University College Cardiff, Cardiff CF1 1XL. Tel (0222) 44211 Ext 2150. Open Mon-Fri 9.30 am-12.30 pm; 2-5 pm by appointment with the Director. Photocopying facilities; reading and audio service.

The Welsh Music Information Centre was established in September 1983, and incorporates the Welsh Music Archive established in 1976. It is a reference and research centre, and also an information clearing house. Built up by donations, loan deposits and purchases, it contains a collection of *c*2,000 items including scores — printed, ms and photocopied — by contemporary Welsh and Welsh resident composers, and is rapidly expanding its holdings of Welsh music of more historic and social interest. It has on loan deposit the complete mss of Morfydd Llwyn Owen (1891–1918); Grace Williams (1906–77); J Morgan Nicholas (1895–1963) and J R Heath (1887–1950).

Cat in preparation.

Welsh National School of Medicine, Main Library, Heath Park, Cardiff CF4 4XN. Tel (0222) 755944 Ext 2874. Open Mon-Fri 9 am-9 pm, (9 am-7 pm July and August); Sat 9 am-12.30 pm. Admission to members only; others by application to the Librarian. Reading room for historical collection. Photocopying facilities except for books with fragile bindings.

Welsh National School of Medicine Historical Collection Acquired piecemeal by gift and purchase since the School's foundation, the collection consists of 2,000 v, of which *c*250 v comprise part of the Lloyd Roberts collection which is in the library of the Royal College of Physicians, London. The subject areas of the collection cover the whole field of medicine, but is particularly strong in obstetrics.

Author card cat.

Author annotated cat (uncompleted) covers the 610 earliest items to 1815. The collection is added to through donations only.

Carmarthen

Carmarthen Museum, Abergwili, Carmarthen, Dyfed. Tel (0267) 31691. Open 10 am-4.30 pm. Admission unrestricted. Library facilities available by appointment during Museum opening hours.

Carmarthen Museum Collection Started in 1905 by Carmarthenshire Antiquarian Society, the collection includes volumes from earlier individuals libraries, including George Eyre Evans, E V Collier, David Evans and various local dignitaries. There are altogether some 8-10,000 v which include *c*500 pre-1850 v relating to archaeology, folk life, ceramics and local printing.

Author cat.

Carmarthen Presbyterian College Library *see* University College Cardiff Library.

Cwmbran

Gwent County Library, County Hall, Croesyceiliog, Cwmbran. Tel (063 33) 67711. Hours of opening variable. Admission on production of library ticket. Microfilm reader, photocopier available.

Newport Reference and Local Collection Newport Public Library opened in 1873. It has a strong local history collection which includes works by, and about, Arthur Machen, Chartism, steel manufacturing, and a Quaker collection.

Classified, author and place cats.

Harlech

Coleg Harlech, Harlech, Gwynedd LL46 2PU. Tel (0766) 363 and 561. The library is open (term time) Mon-Thurs 9 am-9 pm, Fri 9 am-5 pm. Admission to non-members of the College by prior application to the librarian. Reading room facilities during term time; photocopier and microfiche reader.

Welsh Hymnology Collection *c*150 v from the original collections of the Rev J G Moelwyn Hughes (1866–1944) and the Rev H Elfet Lewis (1860–1953).

Cat in preparation.

Peter Stead, *Coleg Harlech — the first fifty years*, University of Wales Press, 1977.

Haverfordwest

Dyfed County Library, Dew Street, Haverfordwest, Dyfed. Tel (0437) 2070 or 4920. Open Mon, Wed, Thurs 9.30 am-5 pm, Tues, Fri 9.30 am-7 pm; Sat 9.30 am-1 pm. Photocopying facilities available.

Henry Owen Library The library was collected by the late Dr Henry Owen (*d*1919) of Poyston, near Haverfordwest, a retired solicitor. He bequeathed the library to the town of Haverfordwest on condition that suitable premises were provided and that the collection should be made available to the people of Haverfordwest. The collection consists of some 5,000 v on miscellaneous subjects, but with strong emphasis on law and local history.

Card author cat.

Hawarden

St Deiniol's Library, Hawarden, Deeside, Clwyd CH5 3DF. Tel (0244) 532350. A residential library, it is open to residents daily from 9 am-10 pm, and on weekdays from 9.30 am-7 pm to external readers. New applications should furnish a testimonial. Full board residence and guest rooms, each with study facilities.

St Deiniol's Residential Library, which is a unique academic institution, was the brilliant conception of its founder, the Rt Hon W E Gladstone who spent many happy peaceful days at Hawarden during his long years of public life. One of his ambitions was to create a foundation for the promotion of Divine learning, through the study of all branches of knowledge, especially history, theology, philosophy and literature. He set up the trust in 1896, one of his gifts being his own great library of *c*30,000 v, and by the time of his death in 1898, the library was already a reality. The present magnificent buildings were erected as a national memorial to him.

The library has now grown to over 120,000 v, *c*40,000 pamphlets, and a large collection of mss. Because of its collection, St Deiniol's is becoming increasingly popular as a centre for 19th cent studies, though the main subjects covered—history, philosophy, classics, literature—go far beyond this period. Every collection has its own card cat.

The rare book collections held at St Deiniol's may be identified as follows:

Pre-1800 Collection Gladstone's own library forms the nucleus of this collection which now totals over 8,500. These have been accounted for in the following bibliographies: *A Bibliography of Books printed before 1800*: Vol 1 *Biblical Studies and Patristics*, compiled by Gordon C Careless; 2 *Philosophy and Christian Doctrine* ; 3 *Life in the church: spirituality, homilitics* ; 4 *Liturgical Studies* ; 5 *Church History* Pt 1 (The beginnings to the Reformation); 6 *Church History* Pt 2 (The Anglican and Protestant churches in Great Britain and Ireland), compiled by Pamela Morris; 7 *European History*, compiled by G C Careless; 8 *Language and Literature* ; 9 *Miscellaneous*, including topography and Addenda to Vols 1-5.

The Stephen Glynne Collection The Glynne Library consists of books dating from the 16th to 19th cent which formerly belonged to the Glynne family of Hawarden Castle until the death of the 9th and last baronet, Sir Stephen Richard Glynne in 1874, and subsequently inherited by the Gladstone family who presented them to St Deiniol's library. The collection totals *c*1,000 items relating to patristics, theology, biblical studies, church history and Anglican controversies of the 17th and 18th cent.

A bibliography of the Glynne Library Collection of rare books dating from the 16th to 19th century at St Deiniol's Library. Compiled by Diana C MacIntyre (£1.80).

Benson Rabbinic Collection A collection of *c*70 v relating to Jewish scriptures, Rabbinic commentaries on the Old Testament, doctrine, liturgy and worship, history and culture. The collection reflects the growth of interest in Hebrew scholarship in Britain.

A bibliography of books on Judaism in the Benson Collection at St Deiniol's Library. Compiled by Pamela Morris.

French Spirituality Collection Richard Meux Benson (*b*1824) founded, in 1866, the Society of St John the Evangelist at Cowley, Oxford. The Society handed over to St Deiniol's library in 1979 its collection of French Counter-Reformation Spirituality, consisting of *c*500 works, including 9 17th cent; 99 18th cent; and 306 19th cent works. There are 43 v of the works of Bossuet, as well as an early 18th cent edition of the *Opuscules Spirituels* of Mme Guyon.

A bibliography of the 17th-20th century books on French Spirituality at St Deiniol's Library. Compiled by P Morris and A Cotterill (75p).

Gladstone and Hawarden Castle Tract Collection *c*4,000 items in 200 v.

Cat available.

St Deiniol's Pamphlet Collection A number of bibliographies relating to this collection are being produced, and will be available in 1982/3.

Lampeter

St David's University College, Lampeter, Dyfed SA48 7ED. Tel (0570) 422 351. The Old Library is open by arrangement to non-members on written application. Microform readers and photocopying facilities.

General Collection Dates from opening of the College in 1827 and houses books printed before 1850. Overall statistics, including collections below, are *c*23,000 v. These include a small collection of medieval mss (noted by Ker), 60 incunabula, *c*550 STC; 4,500 Wing; *c*1,760 foreign books of the 16th and 17th cent. The subject coverage is wide, but with special emphasis on theology and the classics. There is also a collection of early Welsh books and periodicals. Many duplicates have been disposed of.

Printed cat of 1836.

Card cat.

R C Rider, 'The library of St David's College, Lampeter', *Library Association Record*, 66 (1964), p255-8.

——'The library of St David's College (I)', *Trivium*, 1 (1966), p36-43 and 2 (1967), p152.

L J Harris and B Ll James, 'The library of St David's University College, Lampeter (Unfamiliar libraries XXI)', *Book Collector*, 26 (1977), p195-227.

D T W Price, *A history of St David's University College, Lampeter*, Vol 1 to 1898. Ch IX, p175-87. Univ of Wales Press, 1977.

Thomas Burgess (1757—1837) Bishop of St David's 1803—25, and of Salisbury 1825—37. Principal founder of St David's College 1822. His library, estimated by a contemporry at *c*10,000 v was received by bequest in 1837. Particular strengths are classics, biblical and patristic scholarship and editions of Milton. For his collection of pamphlets, see under Tract Collection below.

Thomas Phillips (1760–1851) A surgeon in the service of the East India Company in India and the Far East, he amassed a fortune which he wished to spend in the cause of Welsh education, and distributed books in large quantities. More than 22,000 v came to St David's between 1834 and 1852. Books were bought at random and are of all subjects and dates, including a small number of medieval mss and 50 incunabula. They include books from the libraries of Richard Heber, the Duke of Sussex, Sir Mark Masterman Sykes, Michael Wodhull, Robert Southey and Richard Rawlinson. For his collection of pamphlets see under Tract Collection below.

Tract Collection 11,395 separate pieces bound in 828 v and dated *c*1520–1843. There are 176 STC; 3,352 Wing; 4,477 18th cent items, 6,814 are dated between 1681 and 1720, of which 2,015 are 1709–13. 552 v (*c*9,000 pieces) were collected by the Bowdler family from 1638–1787, and almost certainly presented by Dr Thomas Bowdler, editor of the *Family Shakespeare*. The major collector was Thomas Bowdler II (1661–1738) who had a post in the Navy Office but resigned in 1689, along with Pepys, rather than take the oath of allegiance to William and Mary. It is one of the best collections of non-juring literature extant. It includes extensive collections of pamphlets of Dryden, Defoe, Locke, Swift, Pope, Gilbert Burnet, Charles Leslie, Sir Roger L'Estrange, Sacheverell, Benjamin Hoadly, Thomas and William Sherlock and William Whiston. Bowdler also acquired collections from the libraries of George Hickes and John Gauden (both with annotations in their hands) and of Francis Turner, deposed Bishop of Ely. From Thomas Burgess's library came 440 pamphlets in 51 v, mainly 18th and 19th cent sermons, religious polemics (eg Joseph Priestley) and learned controversies (eg Richard Bentley and Conyers Middleton). Thomas Phillips added 169 v, the most interesting being 14 v of 'Political tracts' dating from the 1790s. The remainder are from various sources. A number of duplicates, sold in 1885 to C H Firth, are now in Worcester College, Oxford.

A catalogue of the tract collection of St David's University College, Lampeter, Mansell, 1975.

L J Harris and B Ll James, 'The tract collection of St David's University College, Lampeter', *Trivium*, 9 (1974), 100-9.

Mold

Clwyd Library Service, Headquarters Library, County Civic Centre, Shire Hall, Mold. Tel (0352) 2121 Ext 480. Open Mon-Thurs 8.45 am-5 pm, Fri 8.45 am-4.30 pm. Reference libraries with study facilities and photocopying service.

The library has two special collections worthy of note:

The Arthurian Collection Founded in 1952, it now comprises *c*2,400 items including texts (in some 12 languages), criticisms, poetry, prose, plays, children's stories etc. The earliest book in the collection is a copy of Gildas's *De Excidio Britanniae*, 1568.

A computerized cat of the collection may be purchased.

The Welsh Bibles Collection Inherited on the reorganization from Denbighshire and Flintshire Library Services, the collection contains *c*140 Welsh Bibles, an annotated list of which is available.

Newport

Business Statistics Office Library, Cardiff Road, Newport, Gwent NPT 1XG. Tel (0633) 56111 Ext 2973. Telex 497121/2. Open for reference to members of the public, Mon-Fri 9 am-5 pm (except public holidays), but access to the Porter Collection by prior arrangement with the librarian. Photocopying facilities.

The Business Statistics Office is the principal Government agency for collecting and producing business statistics. Among the major enquiries conducted by the Office are the annual Censuses of Production, quarterly enquiries into manufacturers' sales in more than 160 industries, and annual enquiries into retailing.

The Library, as well as being the major Government enquiry point for statistical information about industry and commerce in the UK, has a similar, but wider, role for the Government Statistical Service. It can call on the combined resources of the UK Government Departments to discover whether or not statistics exist on a particular topic, and advise on sources.

Porter Collection G R Porter (1792–1852) was one of the founder members of the (Royal) Statistical Society, and supervised the establishment of the Board of Trade Statistics Division in 1834. Porter bequeathed his personal collection of monographs, reports and statistical publications to the RSS, and similar material has been added up to the 1960s. Because of lack of storage space at the RSS premises in London, a large part of the collection has been stored at the Business Statistics Office since the early 1970s. The collection contains *c*4,000 items, including *c*50 ESTC, *c*1,270 19th cent (of which *c*400 are pre-1851), and is arranged into three groups of material: (a) *Monographs and Official Reports*. These consist of British and European publications on economic, political, social and medical topics. The earliest works include Charles d'Avenant, *The political and commercial works*, Vol II; R Horsfield, 1771; William Prynne, *The legal means of political reformation*, (3rd ed), 1780; (b) *UK Statistical Material*. Mainly material dating from the second half of the 19th cent; (c) *Overseas Statistical Material* contains statistical periodicals from international organizations and 92 overseas countries. A small part of this section is to be taken over by the University of Warwick Statistics Library, and the Latin American material will possibly go to the BL Official Publication Library.

Cat of the collection is available on request.

Newtown

Robert Owen Memorial Museum, The Cross, Newtown, Powys. Tel (0686) 26220. Open (Winter) Mon-Fri 10-11.30 am, 2-3.30 pm, Sat 10-11.30 am only; (Summer, ie Easter-Sept incl) Mon-Sat 10 am-1 pm, 2-5.30 pm. Access to written and mss material to bona fide researchers only, after prior written application to the Secretary. Photocopying subject to the permission of the Museum Committee.

Robert Owen Museum Collection Robert Owen (1771–1858), the Utopian Socialist, was born at Newton, Mont, Powys, 14 May 1771, and after spending most of his life away from his native town, he returned in 1858 and died there on 17 Nov 1858. In addition to various personalia, the museum contains a small collection of *c*100 v of works by, and about, Owen, many of them first editions; *c*200 books donated by Owen himself to the library at New Lanark, which cover the subject fields of politics, religion, history and philosophy. All the books are pre-1850; *c*50 pre-1800. Also *c*100 mss, including holograph letters relating to New Harmony, and notes on spiritualism in Owen's own hand; and a diary kept by an acquaintance describing Owen's last days at Newtown.

Card cat (being revised).

Powys Library Service, Area Library, Park Lane, Newtown, Powys. Tel (0686) 26934. Open Mon, Wed, Thurs 9.30 am-5.30 pm, Tues, Fri 9.30 am-7.30 pm; Sat 9.30 am-12.30 pm. Admission to private collection by prior arrangement with the Librarian.

Gregynog Press Collection The collection contains a complete set of the 42 books printed at the Gregynog Press, Gregynog, Mont between 1923 and 1942, together with an unusually good collection of ephemeral material, including festival programmes, service sheets and personal greetings from the same press.

For a history of the press see:

Thomas Jones, *The Gregynog Press*, OUP (1954).

Dorothy A Harrop, *A history of the Gregynog Press*, PLA (1980).

——'The Gregynog Press', *Gregynog* (ed by Glyn Tegai Hughes, Prys Morgan and J Gareth Thomas). University of Wales Press, 1977, p95-118.

St Davids

St Davids Cathedral Library, St Davids, Pembrokeshire, Dyfed SA62 6RH. Open Thurs 2.30-4.30 pm by arrangement. Application should be made well in advance of proposed visit. A charge of 10p is made for each visit. No photocopying facilities.

General Collection A Cathedral Library and Scriptorium have been in existence since the founding of the present Cathedral in 1180 AD, and formed an important part of the Cathedral's teaching role when Bishop Adam Houghton with John of Gaunt founded St Mary's College adjacent to the Cathedral itself which was recently restored for use as a Cathedral hall. After the Reformation there was wanton destruction of medieval mss and books, and the library had to be virtually started again from scratch. Ker mentions 3 books only from St Davids—2 in Corpus Christi Library, Cambridge (Mss 153, 159) and 1 taken out of the library by the then Treasurer and sent to Sir John Prise in London, probably before 1540, and now in the Cotton MS Collection in the British Museum. The post-Reformation books were kept in the Canonry whence they were removed to the Chapter House in 1795 where they remained in heaps on the floor (because there were no bookshelves) until 1955. A grant was obtained from the Pilgrim Trust for the provision of bookshelves, tables and chairs. The gallery and shelves were built later in memory of Bishop Havard who died in 1956.

The present collection comprises *c*8,000 v which include a special collection of 100 v of classical literature, 20 being pre-1600. Many duplicate vols have been sold.

Author cat.

Maura Tallon, *Church in Wales Diocesan Libraries* (though not a Diocesan Library).

Swansea

Royal Institution of South Wales, Victoria Road, Swansea, West Glamorgan SA1 1SH. Open Mon-Sat 10 am-4.30 pm. Closed Sun. Admission restricted to members of the RISW and accredited researchers. Reference only. Photocopier and microfilm reader available.

RISW Library Based on the early collection acquired by George Grant Francis (1814–82) who founded the RISW in 1835, and was largely responsible for building a unique stock of rare items throughout the 19th cent. It comprises 5,000 books, 300 v periodicals, *c*3,000 pamphlets (listed and subject-indexed) relating to the history of Wales, and to Swansea in particular; early scientific works by scholars such as Lewis Weston. Strong on rare 19th cent guides and ephemeral pamphlets; a unique set of the *Cambrian* the Swansea weekly newspaper 1804–1915. Rarely added to; substantial number of non-Welsh items sold to various buyers in 1964. Catalogue of 1877 indicates the range of material disposed of.

Swansea Public Library, Alexandra Road, Swansea SA1 5DX. Tel (0792) 54065-6 (Ref Lib 55521). Open 9 am-7 pm (Thurs and Sat 5 pm). Admission unrestricted. Photocopying facilities.

The library's general stock includes 2 incunabula and 60 other works published before 1700.

Dylan Thomas Collection Commenced in 1952, it comprises some 708 books (some first editions), periodical parts and 425 newspaper cuttings, which include material by and about Dylan Thomas.

The Local Collection This collection of books, periodicals and pamphlets covers the history of Swansea, Swansea Valley and Gower. Many of the books are by local authors, and include many rare items for which there are no separate records.

Two special collections belonging to the library are on deposit at other libraries—the Rowland Williams Collection at the National Library of Wales (qv), and the Deffett Francis Collection at the Library, University College, Singleton Park Swansea (qv).

Card cat available.

Swansea University College Library, Singleton Park, Swansea SA2 8PP. Tel (0792) 25678. Open (Term) 9 am-10 pm; (Vacation) 9 am-5 pm. Admission to non-members by prior notification of visit. Open and closed carrels, micro reading room, and photocopying and microfilming facilities.

Rare Books Collection The collection has grown partly by gifts and by purchase since the foundation of the College in 1920. It consists of *c*1,550 v and 10 boxes of rare pamphlets. The printed vols include 3 incunabula; 58 v printed 1501–99; 432 v printed 1600–1700, of which 95 are listed in the STC and 188 Wing. There are 171 pre-1800 Welsh imprints, and a collection of *c*350 Welsh ballads, 12 emblem books, 64 private press productions (31 Gregynog Press and 10 Golden Cockerell Press), 36 limited editions, and many first editions.

Included in main card cat but with separate handlist.

Chronological cat of pre-1750 items.

Cat of private press publications.

Cymmrodorion Collection Books and periodicals deposited by the Honourable Society of Cymmrodorion in the City of Westminster Public Library in 1938, and later transferred to Swansea University College Library (on loan). 807 v almost all in Welsh, consisting of literary works in Welsh, Welsh language, religion, literary criticism, publications of the National Eisteddfod, and of the Hon Society of Cymmrodorion, and Welsh periodicals (transferred to NLW 23.11.82).

Printed cat.

Deffett Francis Collection John Deffett Francis (1815–1901) presented his library (of *c*600 books) to Swansea Public Library in October 1876—for reference only; he later collected more books on literature, theatre, art, topography, biography and music, to give to the Public Library—his collection eventually totalling over 7,000 v, with paintings, drawings and engravings. The collection was deposited in Swansea University College Library in September 1965.

Card cat in the Rare Books Room.

Two copies of the printed cat published in 1887.

David Salmon Collection A collection of pamphlets on education and Welsh affairs belonging to David Salmon (1852–1944), Principal of Swansea Training College, 1892–1922, and donated to the University College Library by his daughter Miss Mary Salmon. The pamphlets number *c*1,700 items in 146 v, and are mainly on education and Welsh affairs, with 11 v of Charity sermons and reports of early Charity Schools, mostly of the 18th cent. There are also articles or extracts of articles reprinted from periodicals, mainly on religion and education, and some American material, including Mr Salmon's experiences and impressions during his tour of America.

Typed list, author and title.

Ms subject/author card index.

Swansea University College (Dept of Adult and Continuing Education), South Wales Miners' Library, Maes-yr-haf, 50 Sketty Road, Swansea. Tel (0792) 298259. Open Mon-Thurs 9.15 am-12.15 pm, 1.15-4.30 pm. Admission is unrestricted, but visiting researchers are advised to phone or write in advance.

The South Wales Miners' Library was opened on 20 October 1973 as part of the celebrations marking the 75th anniversary of the founding of the South Wales Miners' Federation. It also marked the culmination of the Coalfield History Project set up in 1971 at the University College, Swansea with funds from the Social Science Research Council, and the support of the South Wales Area of the National Union of Mineworkers. The stock totals *c*26,700 v (including periodicals) representing the surviving libraries of 33 Miners' Institutes within the South Wales coalfield. There are also the personal libraries of miners' leaders and others. It should be noted that almost all the incorporated libraries and other material are on temporary or permanent loan by the NUM or by the respective local institutes and Welfare Hall Committees.

Cat.

Hywel Francis, 'The Origins of the South Wales Miners' Library' in *History Workshop: a journal of Socialist Historians*, no 2, 1976, p183-205.

Pamphlet Collection *c*10,000 items comprising pamphlets relating to left-wing movements in South Wales from *c*1900 onwards.

Author and subject cat.

Spanish Civil War Collection *c*300 items, including

personal letters from members of the International Brigade (reflecting S Wales participation), other mss, books, pamphlets, posters and journals.
Cat.

Transcript Collection c500 tape-recordings of individual interviews made during the South Wales Coalfield Project (1971–3), almost all of which have been transcribed and indexed.

Miscellaneous Collection A collection of colliery maps, price lists, pay docketts, posters, ballads, sheet-music, old newspaper cuttings etc.
Cat and index.

Photographic Collection Several hundred photographs related to the mining valleys, including photographs of miners, local politicians and miners' leaders.
Indexed.

Gwyn Thomas Library The library of Gwyn Thomas (1913–81), author and playwright, containing *c*1,300 v, of which 25 per cent are fiction, ranging from Dickens, Thackeray, Priestly, D H Lawrence and H G Wells to a few contemporary Anglo-Welsh authors, including W H Davies and Raymond Williams, with 9 of Thomas's own publications. The remainder of the collection is wide-ranging, and includes books mainly on history, travel, music, art, the sciences and politics—there are 30 publications on the Left Book Club. A few of the books are annotated.
Cat in preparation.

West Glamorgan Institute of Higher Education Library, Townhill Road, Townhill, Swansea SA2 0UT. Tel (0792) 203482 Ext 240. Open (Term) Mon-Thurs 9 am-9 pm, Fri 9 am-4.30 pm. (Vacation) 9 am-5 pm. Admission on application to Librarian. Microfiche readers, photocopier available.

Salmon Library The reference library of the Swansea College of Education includes the books purchased by Principal David Salmon (1892–1922) and donated to the Library. Of a total of *c*14,000 books, the major part is pre-1900; *c*100 books and pamphlets pre-1700; *c*1,000 books 1700–1800. Some material has disappeared over the past 50 years. The collection has not been catalogued. Books of obvious interest include Du Carge *Glossarium*, 10 v 1733; Berquin, *L'Ami de L'adolescence*; Holinshed, 2 parts of 'Chronicles' 1577, 3 v; 1 owned by Jane Austen, 2 by Cassandra Austen.
Shelflist only (incomplete).

Tenby

Tenby Museum, Castle Hill, Tenby, Pembrokeshire, Dyfed. Tel (0834) 2809. Open June/Sept Weekdays 10 am-6 pm; Sun 2-6 pm;. Oct/May Weekdays 10 am-1 pm, 2-4 pm (6 pm April and May), closed Fri afternoons. Admission to library by appointment with the Hon Librarian.

The museum was founded in July 1878, and the library has grown up by gifts of books from Dr F Dyster and others. The books now total *c*1,500, of which 25 are pre-1800 and 100 of 1801–50. Subjects covered include palaeontology, archaeology, natural history, marine and freshwater biology, fungi, conchology, zoological sciences, local guidebooks, local history, heraldry, biographies, etc.
Card index.

Trefecca

The Howel Harris Museum, Trefecca, Brecon, Powys LD3 0PP. Tel (0874) 711 241, or Coleg Trefeca 711423. Open 11 am-5 pm. Admission free. Access to bookcase by appointment. Books only loaned for perusal on premises. Overnight hospitality available at Coleg Trefeca if booked in advance.

Howel Harris Museum Library Originally part of the Trevecca Theological College Library collected by the Rev Edward Matthews (1874), but in 1906 some were removed to the Trevecca Collection at the National Library of Wales, and the remainder in 1964 when the Preparatory College was removed to Aberystwyth. The present collection comprises 24 18th cent Welsh titles dated 1713–93, 15 of which were printed at Trefecca. Subject range mainly theological.

Welshpool

Powysland Museum Library, c/o Welshpool Branch Library, Welshpool, Powys. Tel (0938) 3001. Admission by arrangement with the Librarian.

Dr J D K Lloyd Memorial Collection The collection comprises a complete and annotated set of the *Montgomeryshire Collections* bequeathed by the late Dr J D K Lloyd (1900–78), historian and editor of the *Mont Coll* for 30 years. His collection of books was sold to Blackwell's, Oxford, *c*1979.

CHANNEL ISLANDS

Alderney

Alderney Society Museum, Old School House, High Street, St Anne, Alderney. Tel (048182) 3222.

During the German occupation 1940–45 all libraries and archives on the island of Alderney were totally destroyed, except some ecclesiastical records which had been removed to Winchester. The Alderney Library was later established to provide a public library service, but it does not collect rare books. The Alderney Society has established a museum and reference library of works which relate to the Channel Islands, though as yet it has only a few rare books.

Alderney Society and Museum *Quarterly Bulletin.*

Guernsey

German Occupation Museum, Le Bourg, Forest, Guernsey. Tel (0481) 38205.

The Museum was established *c*1965 to collect and display material relating to the occupation of the island 1940–5 by the German armed forces. There is a large accumulation of printed and ms documents, of which some are on public display, and others may be seen by appointment.

(There is a much smaller collection on public display at the German Underground Hospital, St Andrew's.)

Guille-Allès Library, Market Street, St Peter Port, Guernsey. Tel (0481) 20392. Open Mon 9.10 am-5 pm, Tues, Wed and Fri 5.15 pm, Thurs 12.30 pm; Sat 5.30 pm to registered readers; visitors who wish to see rare books should write in advance to the Principal Librarian, but are warned that some may be temporarily inaccessible.

The Guille-Allès Library is owned by a trust and financed jointly by endowments and an annual grant from the States of Guernsey. Until 1981 it was a subscription library.

J Linwood Pitts, 'The story in brief of the Guilles-Allès Library' in his *Witchcraft. . .*, 1886, p33-40.

——*Guille-Allès Library and Museum: their history and formation. . .*, Guernsey, 1891; also prefixed to its *Encyclopaedic catalogue*, 1891.

B T Rowswell, 'The story of the Guille-Allès Library', *Book Auction Records* 17 (1919–20), pi-viii.

J P Warren, 'The Guilles-Allès Library and Museum', *Société Guernesiaise Trans* 16 (1959), p72-5.

M C Poinsot, 'Les deux bibliothèques de Saint Pierre-Port', *Revue d'Europe et d'Amérique* 14 (1911), p1-8.

A The Collections to 1980

The library is in the process of total reorganization. This section explains the growth and partial dispersal of the collections before that event.

Guille Library to 1881 Thomas Guille (1817–96) left Guernsey in 1832 to make his fortune in New York, where he became apprentice and then partner in the building firm of his fellow-Guernseyman Daniel Mauger. He formed a private library there, but in 1856 he donated it, with a large endowment, to the people of St Peter Port as a public lending library, originally intended to be rotated through different branches round the island. In 1869 Guille returned to Guernsey, bringing with him more books for addition to the library.

Catalogue de la Bibliothèque Guille, à l'usage des habitants des paroisses de la campagne et de St Pierre-Port. . ., Guernsey, [1856?].

Guernsey Mechanics' Institution, 1832–81 The Guernsey Mechanics' Institution, founded in 1832, built up a library of *c*3,000 v, including 18th cent works of travel, history and literature.

Classified catalogue of the books in the library of the Guernsey Mechanics' Institution, with a general index, 1852, interleaved copy with ms additions to *c*1874.

Classified addenda to the Catalogue of books in the library of the Guernsey Mechanics' Institute and Literary Society, 1866.

'The Guernsey Mechanics' Institution and the Guille-Allès Library', *Guernsey Magazine* 10 (1882), p7-8.

Société Guernesiaise 1867–1881 This society, founded in 1867, and now defunct, built up a library mainly of books of local interest. (It must not be confused with another society which now has the same name and a library, but without rare books.)

Merger of Libraries 1881–2 In 1881–2 the Guille Library moved to its present site and absorbed the libraries of the Guernsey Mechanics' Institution and the Société Guernesiaise, together with the large private library of Guille's fellow emigrant and business partner Frédéric Mansell Allès (1881–95), rich in rare books. It was then reopened as the Guille Allès Library in 1882, with over 50,000 v.

Guille-Allès Library, 1882–1981 The new library enjoyed a period of very rapid expansion until by 1910 there were over 100,000 v. In 1895 a subsidiary collection at the Guille-Allès Artisans' Institute was begun, later incorporated in the main library. After 1910 the reference collection was hardly added to, and after 1975 about a third of the books (including much of the 19th cent material and some earlier) were sold or pulped.

Guilles-Allès Library and Museum, *Encyclopaedic catalgue of the Lending Department* by A Cotgreave, 1891.

Henri Boland, *Catalogue des ouvrages à emporter de la Bibliothèque Guille-Allès à Guernsey, section françoise*, 1889.

B **The Reorganized Collections**

The library contains *c*60,000 v, of which many are not at present accessible pending reclassification and cataloguing. The former reference and lending libraries, except the segregated collections below, have been merged in a series of subject libraries; these contain much pre-1851 material (figures not available).

Card cat (author and classified) in course of compilation.

General Rare Book Collection (not expected to be catalogued or accessible until 1985). *c*1,000 v, mostly pre-1801, but including some later publications of outstanding rarity. At least six incunabula. The collection covers a wide variety of subjects. Special strengths are Oriental Bibles; natural history books with coloured plates, including the Allès copy of Audubon's *Birds of America*, New York, 1860, with many earlier botany and zoology books from 1639 onwards; and a collection of English plays 1664–1702.

Bibliothèque Française *c*1,600 v of French books, especially literature, history, art and general reference books; mainly editions published in the 19th cent (many in decorative bindings), with some of the 18th cent.

Local Studies Library At least 5,000 v. Though the greater part relates specifically to Guernsey, there are substantial collections on the other Channel Islands and on Normandy. The collection of publications of the States of Guernsey includes a complete set of the Billets d'États. Guernsey and Jersey periodicals, including many 19th cent church magazines. There are many runs (several of which are unique) of Jersey and Guernsey newspapers, especially of the early 19th cent, including the *Gazette de Guernesey* from 1791, and the *Gazette de Jersey* from 1786.

Typescript list in dictionary form, very incomplete (especially for periodicals and newspapers); to be superseded eventually by card cat.

Hauteville House, 38 Hauteville, St Peter Port, Guernsey. Tel (0481) 21911. Though the house is open to the public, the books may be examined only by appointment after written application to the Administrator.

Hauteville House was the home of Victor Hugo (1802–85), the poet and novelist, during his exile from his native France 1856–70. Here he wrote *Legende des siecles, Les travailleurs de la mer*, and part of *Les miserable.* In 1927 it was given by his family to the municipality of Paris, and it has been kept, as far as possible, in the state in which Hugo left it, but retaining the library on the top floor which had been added later. It is controlled by the Conservateur de la Maison de Victor Hugo et de Hauteville House from his office at the Maison de Victor Hugo, 6 Place des Vosges, Paris 75004 (Hugo's last home, with his later library, and a secondary collection of Hugo studies).

Victor Hugo's Library (general) There are *c*3,000 v at Hauteville House, of which more than 2,000 are Hugo's own books (with a few later additions comprising mainly editions of his works) in the 'Bibliothèque' on the second floor. They include a few books which escaped the sale of his effects in Paris in June 1852; but most were acquired during his residence in Guernsey, the greater part from local dealers, while some were obtained in London, during journeys on the Continent, or were sent as gifts. There is also a library on the third floor landing between the top of the stairs and the 'Look-out' where Hugo worked. This was added by his son François-Victor (the translator of Shakespeare) to house his own books, but now contains a mixture of Hugo's books and later accretions. Some of the books were retained by the Hugo family, and a few of the rarer items have been transferred to the Maison de Victor Hugo in Paris and the Musée de Paris. The arrangement of the books is haphazard; the chief categories are indicated below, under headings which have been chosen for convenience.

Complete cat on cards held at Maison de Victor Hugo (Paris), where there is also an obsolete list of 1928.

Victor Hugo en exil: Ville de Paris, Hauteville-House (Guernsey) juin-oct 1955 (exhibition cat in French and English).

Jean Delalande, *Victor Hugo à Hauteville House*, Paris, Albin Michel, 1947, is the only fully detailed description of the house; p102-20 and 140-5 describe the library shelf by shelf, listing the most significant books individually.

Jean-Bertrand Barrère, *Victor Hugo à l'oeuvre: le poete en exil et en voyage*, Paris, Klincksieck, 1965 (a revised version of articles in *Revue d'histoire littéraire de la France* 1946–53), includes a subject analysis of the library (p25-70), an author list (selective though that is not stated, p281-311), and the selective inventory compiled in the 1870s by Hugo's sister-in-law Julie Chenay (p311-6).

J Sergent, 'Guernesey', *Arts et métiers graphiques*, 1 juin 1935 (Victor Hugo issue), p58-66, describes and illustrates some of the rare books. The editions by Paul Berret of *Légende des siecles* (Paris 1921-5) and *Les châtiments* (Paris 1932) include lists of related books at Hauteville House.

See also Paul Stapfer, 'Victor Hugo à Guernesey', Paris 1905; N Clément-Janin, *Victor Hugo en exil* 5 éd Paris, 1922; Rene Weiss, *La maison de Victor Hugo à Guernesey*, Paris 1928; Elliott M Grant, *Victor Hugo. . . bibliography*, Chapel Hill, 1967; F Michaux, *Essais bibliographiques concernant les oeuvres des Victor*

Hugo parues pendant l'exil, Paris, 1930.

Note: The Maison de Victor Hugo in Paris has a card cat of the library there; a published *Catalogue* (par Jean Sergent), 1934; and many exhibition cats. Hugo's diary of the exile period and mss are at the Bibliothèque Nationale in Paris.

Works by Hugo The collection is by no means complete. It includes some proof copies. There are some editions published after 1870, down to *c*1910. There are also periodicals with articles on Hugo to the same date.

Guernsey imprints These are very few, because Hugo took little interest in local affairs. The most significant is Henri E Marquand's *John Brown* 1860 (see below under Periodicals; there is also his *Souvenirs des Indes occidentales* Londres 1853). There are several copies of *The contemplated infant asylum 'La Creche'* 1860, a pamphlet issued to support an appeal by Madame Hugo.

16th and 17th century editions These are relatively few, and are to be found mostly on the third floor. Some certainly did not belong to Victor, but there is a substantial group of mostly late 17th cent classical and miscellaneous works which he probably acquired for their contemporary decorative gold-tooled bindings and were intended no doubt as part of the furnishings. There is a copy of Plutarch *Vies* Lausanne 1574 which François used in preparing his edition of Shakespeare.

Dictionaries and encyclopaedias Hugo had a wide range of dictionaries, including Du Cange *Glossarium... mediae... latinitatis* 1678, given by a Guernsey man, and Moreri *Grand dictionaire* 1683. Most of the standard French dictionaries of the 18th and 19th cent are present, and several encyclopaedias including Diderot 1751–65 (first edition), and historical dictionaries, eg Bayle.

English Literature The library has English literature in the original (sometimes editions printed in France). Several of these undoubtedly belonged to Francois-Victor, including John Fox *Journal* 1594; Butler *Hudibras* 1750; and the *Vicar of Wakefield* 1800. But Victor Hugo seems to have himself acquired the works of Browning, Burns, Chatterton and other poets. The major novelists, especially Scott, Thackeray, and Dickens, he bought in French translations (as also Shakespeare).

French Literature Sets of Corneille, Madame de Sevigné, La Fontaine, Racine, and individual volumes by other classic authors, including the philosophers. The main bulk of the collection, however, is of the 19th cent (including some editions printed in the British Isles), eg Lamartine, Balzac, and many lesser known writers.

Presentation Copies Many copies (mostly paperbound) of contemporary works, inscribed for presentation to Victor Hugo. He wrote the letter 'r' on the cover or endpaper of those which he acknowledged (mainly poems and novels), though some of these are partly or wholly unopened. The vast majority, however, were unacknowledged, and consist for the most part of books in languages with which Hugo was unfamiliar, many from South America, and some Eastern Europe.

History and Politics A large section of the library, including several 18th cent sets of universal histories, standard 19th cent histories of religion, and some major works on ancient, chiefly Roman, history. Histories of several European countries and France, chiefly the Revolution, on which there is a large collection. There is also a collection on the coup of 2nd Dec 1851 and its immediate aftermath, with a scattering of works on later political events in France.

Miscellaneous Subjects There are many works on the occult, such as the *Traité du sortilège...*, Paris 1622; *Lettres cabalistiques*, La Haye 1766, tome 7, and a number of mid-19th cent works. There are also many scientific books of the 19th cent, children's books of the same period, and 18th cent editions of voyages.

Periodicals and newspapers There are unbound runs of a number of papers which Hugo received regularly, eg *Le Charivari; Le Rappel.* Bound v of *Courrier de l'Europe*, the French weekly newspaper published in London, for 1842–7 and 1851–2; and the Brussels weekly *La Lanterne* by Henri Rochefort, 1868. Among substantial runs of magazines and reviews are the *Gazette des Beaux-Arts* from its foundation in 1859, the *Revue Trimestrielle* (Brussels), and the *Revue* and *Nouvelle Revue de Paris*. There are odd numbers of papers relating to the execution of John Brown (1800–59) the American abolitionist who was captured at Harper's Ferry (together with the pamphlet on Brown by the editor of the *Gazette de Guernesey*, Henri E Marquand).

Priaulx Library, Candie Road, St Peter Port, Guernsey. Tel (0481) 21998. Open Mon-Sat 10 am-5 pm (normally closed 1-2 pm) to the public; visitors wishing to use rare books are recommended to write in advance.

Osmond de Beauvoir Priaulx (1805–91), a barrister from Guernsey, active in the Reform Club, owned Candie House but lived as a gentleman of leisure in Cavendish Square in London. In 1871 he gave Candie House to the States of Guernsey; in 1880 he endowed the library; and in 1889 it was opened to the public, as the Candie Library, with a small part of his book collection; the remainder came by his will in 1891. It is aided by the States of Guernsey, which is represented on the controlling trust. It has absorbed the library of the Grange Club.

(a) *General* The Priaulx Library is primarily a reference library in the humanities, containing over 30,000 v. Priaulx's own collection numbered *c*18,000 v, though some of these (mainly duplicates) were dispersed 1945–70. At least 3,000 are pre-1851, including several incunabula, and *c*150 pre-1701 items. Paragraphs b-k below indicate the strongest subject areas of the General Library.

G E Lee, *Catalogue of the books in the Candie Library*, Guernsey, 1895 (authors, with subject index); interleaved copy with ms additions and deletions; this is more complete for early printed books than the card cat (author/name and alphabetical subject), but neither is comprehensive.

The Priaulx Library, 1979 (leaflet).

The Star (Guernsey), 17 Jan 1891 (obit of Priaulx).

Guernsey Magazine, June 1890.

(b) *History* This is the primary emphasis of the collections, which are predominantly on British and foreign, including particularly Eastern, history. Unusual material includes a collection of caricatures of the 1870 siege of Paris.

(c) *Military history* This subject is strong as a whole. There is a fine collection of regimental histories of the British Army, including many that are privately printed and scarce, and this collection is kept up to date. There is also a major section on the Indian Army.

The *Army List* is complete from 1714 to 1839; also *Hart's Army List* from 1860.

(d) *Dictionaries* A substantial collection of monolingual and bilingual dictionaries from the 18th cent onwards, particularly strong in dictionaries of English, French, Latin and Oriental languages.

(e) *English Literature* A very extensive collection whose greatest strength is in the 19th cent, and in 19th cent editions of earlier, especially traditional literature, particularly standard sets such as the Percy Society, English Dialect Society and Shakespeare Society. Priaulx had a fine collection of Victorian fiction, including first editions, especially of Dickens (some dispersed). Scottish literature is well represented; there are some contemporary editions of Restoration and 18th cent English plays. Most to be passed on to Guille-Allès, especially modern.

(f) French Literature Not as extensive a collection as the English, but including sets of probably all the classical authors, mostly in late 18th or 19th cent editions.

(g) *Foreign Literature* Substantial sets of German authors. Some Oriental literature, including translations; chiefly from the Indian subcontinent.

(h) *Religion* Editions of the Fathers, 16th-19th cent, mostly in the original Greek and Latin, and some standard works of Christian theology and church history. Works on Oriental religions.

(i) *Folklore* A collection on folklore, the occult, and witchcraft, with special emphasis on the Channel Islands. Early editions of Agrippa von Nettesheim.

(j) *Travel and Exploration* A good general collection, mostly of 19th cent editions, but with some earlier; strong in Eastern travel, especially Jesuit exploration in China. Ptolemy's atlas of 1618.

(k) *Art* A substantial section which includes a good collection of Piranesi. Illustrated works include several of the Jorrocks books by R S Surtees.

Periodicals There are a number of runs of journals from their foundations, including the *Annual Register, Gentlemen's Magazine*, the *Illustrated London News* to 1917, and *Archaeologia* to v 41.

Channel Islands Collection c1,500 books and pamphlets, together with runs of periodicals. The greater part of the collection came from the bequest of Edith Frances Carey (1864–1935), President of the Société Guernesiaise, and author of *The Channel Islands*; her bequest was especially strong in local genealogy and heraldry (and included much ms material in that field). There are some early 19th cent Guernsey newspapers.

Separate card cat (author) and alphabetical subject (incomplete), and supplementary index for some of these.

Guernsey Bookplates Several hundred bookplates of Guernsey individuals and institutions, built around a nucleus from Edith F Carey's collection. There are some bookplates and circulation slips from local commercial circulating libraries and book clubs of the early and mid-19th cent.

Royal Court, St Peter Port, Guernsey.

The Royal Court was established in the 13th cent for the judicial and administrative control of the Bailiwick of Guernsey. The Bailiff is its President. Its deliberative and legislative assembly, called The States, has met here regularly since 1605, but administrative departments of The States are housed elsewhere.

A The Greffe

Tel (0481) 25277. Open Mon-Fri 9 am-1 pm, 2-4 pm by appointment with Her Majesty's Greffier, after written application enclosing a letter of introduction.

The Greffe is the official archive repository of the Royal Court (including The States). It also has other record office functions, being the registry of births, marriages and deaths, and a repository for private deposited papers.

List of records in the Greffe, Guernsey, London, List and Index Society, 1969–82, 3 v.

Greffe Records The official court records from 1526 (mostly ms) with some earlier documents. Also records of the occupying German Feldkommandatur 1940–5, including some printed material.

Greffe Library Official printed documents of the Court and the States, including *Actes de l'Etat* (1605–1845), 1851, 8 v, and the earlier occasional *Billets et devises; Recueil d'ordonnances de la Cour Royale* (from 1533), 1852–; *Recueil des Ordres de Conseil* (1803–1926), 1903–66.

Greffe Law Library A collection of *c*50 reference books on Guernsey law, comprising works on the customary law of Normandy, including 1574 and later editions of G Terrien *Commentaires* and the edition of the *Approbation des lois coutumes et usage de l'Ile de Guernesey*, published in 1822 by the Privy Council, giving legal sanction in Guernsey to specific sections of Terrien; and standard 18th and 19th cent Guernsey imprints such as Thomas Le Marchant, *Remarques... sur l'Approbation des lois... usitées ès jurisdictions de Guernezé*, 1826.

Deposited Collections Deposited collections of mss are numerous, and some include printed works. The papers of Georges Métivier (1789?–1881), the poet and compiler of the *Dictionnaire franco-normand* 1870, the ms of which is included, together with some printed papers, and a genealogical collection which includes printed pedigrees. Part of the collection of the family de Sausmarez, including important naval documents of the 17th cent and later (but the family library and some papers remain in their private possession at Sausmarez Manor, St Martin's). A collection deposited by B M M Gosselin-Lefebvre, mainly on the Carey family and the Fief de Blanchelande, formed by Admiral Nicholas Lefebvre (1803–84).

Pamphlet Collection A haphazard collection of *c*50 pamphlets, mostly of the late 18th and 19th cent, housed in the gallery of the main records strongroom, mostly locally printed, over half legal, with some popular accounts of criminals. They include one of the earliest specimens of Guernsey printing, *Pièces relatives au differences entre de Baillif et les jurés*, 1778.

B Royal Court Library

Tel (0481) 26161. Open Mon-Fri 9 am-1 pm, 2-4 pm by appointment with the Bailiff's Clerk after written application enclosing a letter of introduction.

The Royal Court Library is a working library for the Bailiff, the Jurats, and the Advocates of the Royal Court, and for the Deputies of the States. It is primarily a library on the law, constitution, and history of Guernsey, though other subjects are represented.

Catalogue: law and general library of the Royal Court of the Island of Guernsey, compiled by Basil T Rowswell, Guernsey, 1906; copy with ms additions which include the Ridgway collection is kept in the library.

Law and General Library This collection, housed not only in 'The Library', but also in the Bailiff's and other private offices, contains at least 5,000 v including *c*20 STC items; *c*50 Wing; *c*100 ESTC; and *c*300 pre-1801 foreign books. The Court seems to have depended on private libraries until a Bailiff, Sir Peter Stafford Carey (1803–86), who had been Prof of English Law at University College, London, allowed his private collection of law books to remain as an official library after his retirement in 1883. Since the law of Guernsey is based on Norman customary law, with accretions from certain parts of the English law, the library contains extensive collections of works on French, English and island law. English law reports are well represented from the 17th cent onwards (at least 300 v pre-1851), and there are considerable collections of older monographs on the English law of commerce, bankruptcy, and bills of exchange; maritime law; common law; criminal law; and ecclesiastical law. The French law books consist mainly of the 16th-17th cent *coutumiers* of Normandy, Brittany, and other parts of France; 18th cent general law manuals, including numerous editions of Robert Joseph Pothier (1699–1772); and the Napoleonic codes. There is an extensive collection of dictionaries, particularly law dictionaries, of all periods of French, law-French, Norman-French, and English. There are also *c*150 books and pamphlets, mostly pre-1851, on the history of Guernsey, and to a much smaller extent the other Channel Islands.

Ridgway Collection *c*300 v from the library of George John Proctor Ridgway, an advocate, probably given to the Court *c*1943, kept as a separate collection. Its main strength is in French law, especially Norman *coutumiers* and 18th cent jurists, with later codes. Also Roman law; modern English law (and Blackstone 1741); and general reference books. Also some mss on Guernsey law, and a probably unique (but imperfect) printed copy of Privy Council proceedings relative to Guernsey 1775–6. Terrien, 2nd ed 1678 and early 19th cent Guernsey law books. There are a few non-legal books, eg Nollet *Leçons de physique experimentale Paris* 1759.

C Receiver General's Office

Tel (0481) 20169. Open Mon-Fri by appointment with the Clerk to Her Majesty's Receiver General.

The Office is responsible for the collection of Crown revenues in the island, and holds the records of those Fiefs (about 70%) which are the property of the Sovereign. These include the Livres de Perquage, in ms copies and from *c*1830 to the present printed editions (usually limited to about 20 copies). The printed sets include, though incompletely, the private Fiefs also. Information on the location of copies of editions not held can be obtained from the Office.

St Saviour's Church Rectorial Library, St Saviour, Guernsey.

The library bequeathed in the mid-17th cent by Pierre Carey to the rector and his successors for ever disappeared from the church during the German occupation 1940–5.

Ms list in Priaulx Library, St Peter Port.

Jersey

Société Jersiaise, Lord Coutanche Memorial Library, 7 Pier Road, St Helier, Jersey. Open Mon-Sat 10 am-12.30 pm, 2.30-5 pm to the public, but visitors are recommended to write in advance to the Librarian.

The Society was founded in 1873 for the study of the history, language, geology, natural history, and antiquities of Jersey. The library contains books, periodicals, newspapers and documents on Jersey, the other Channel Islands, the neighbouring parts of England and France, and on Jersey families throughout the world. It incorporates the bequests of H M Godfray and Edouard Le Brun, and E T Nicolle.

Cat 1881 by E K Cable (published?).

Société Jersiaise, *Special bulletin 1873–1973*, p76-80 (see also p25-32).

ISLE OF MAN

Bishop's Court Library (now housed in St George's Church, Douglas), c/o The Rt Revd the Lord Bishop of Sodor and Man, Bishop's House, Quarterbridge Road, IOM. Te (0624) 22108. Open by arrangement with the Vicar of St George's Church, Douglas (Rev D A Willoughby, St George's Vicarage, Devonshire Road, Douglas, IOM). Tel (0624) 5430.

The library, formerly housed at Bishop's Court, Kirk Michael, was built up for the use of staff and students at the Manx Theological College, and was kept up to date until the College closed in 1937. After 1977, when the Bishop of Sodor and Man ceased to reside at Bishop's Court, the library was removed to Douglas. The collection now consists of *c*2,500 v (a significant amount of modern theological literature would appear to have been fairly recently acquired) which include *c*150 18th and early 19th cent items, mainly theology, including a substantial number of the works of Bishop Thomas Wilson, the 3 v Cruttwell Bible, 1785. Early 19th cent Anglican classics were sold to Lambeth Palace Library previous to 1977. Since 1977 a large proportion of the remaining early material has been sold.

Ms card cat.

Douglas Public Library, Ridgway Street, Douglas, Isle of Man. Tel (0624) 23021. Open Mon-Sat 9.15 am-5.30 pm. Admission for the public for reference purposes only.

Talbot Collection Donated to Douglas Corporation in 1908 by the Rev Theosophilus Talbot, the collection contains *c*1,000 v, *c*1,500 works. These include 10 STC (including 24548a) and 50 Wing (including C375, C6489, D2492, P3905, R1436) items. Late 18th and early 19th cent items include Pennant; J Maculloch's *A description of the Western Isles of Scotland including the Isle of Man*, London, 1819 3 v; Robertson's *History of Scotland*, 1791, 3 v; and Lord Teignmouth's *Sketches of the coasts and islands of Scotland and the Isle of Man*, 1836, 2 v. There is also a good copy of Owen Jones's *Grammar or ornament*, 1856.

Typed card cat. This is also available in the Manx Museum Library.

Manx Quarterly, 4 April 1908, p365; 6 May 1909, p549-52.

Manx Patriot, 19 April 1908, p30-2 (op).

King William's College, Castletown, Isle of Man. Tel (0624) 2552. Open by prior arrangement with the Librarian. Admission by courtesy of the Librarian on written application. Xeroxing facilities.

The College Library is a working library for the staff and students of the major boys' public school on the Isle of Man, founded in 1833. Unfortunately many of the rarer items were destroyed in a disastrous fire in 1844. Many donations have been received from former staff and students, including important additions from the Walker and Stenning families. The collection totals *c*200 v, containing *c*300 works, mainly Greek and Latin classics of the 18th cent (50 v), and Manx local history items. Five Wing items including Wing/D171. The local history collection comprises all the major 18th cent publications, including those by Feltham, Robertson and Train. There is also a substantial collection of railway periodicals.

Ms card cat recently started by the pupils.

The Barovian, 14, 1884 and 163, 1933. (op)

Manx Museum Library, Kingswood Grove, Douglas, Isle of Man. Tel (0624) 5522. Open Mon-Sat 10 am-5 pm. Admission to the public for reference purposes only. Xeroxing facilities only.

The Special Collections include the G W Wood, G F Clucas and W Cubbon Collections. The Manx Museum Library was established in 1922 as the Manx National Reference Library to include all published works relating to the Isle of Man, together with newspapers, maps, plans, prints and photographic collections. It houses an extensive archive collection. The library is broadly the equivalent of an English county record office. Printed books total *c*15,000 v, and include 2 STC; 25 Wing (including B2031, D1091, L380) items, and 18th and early 19th cent items. Outstanding collections of material relate to T E Brown, Hall Caine, Edward Forbes.

Card cat.

William Cubbon, *A bibliographical account of works relating to the Isle of Man*. London, OUP 1933–9, 2 v. (Annotated copy available in library).

Appendix—List of Contributors

A List of Regional Organizers

ENGLAND
Avon: John Farrell
Bedfordshire: Alan Threadgill
Berkshire: David Knott
Buckinghamshire: Mrs Katherine Swift
Cambridgeshire: David McKitterick
Cheshire: Mrs Elizabeth Rathbone
Cleveland: Dr A I Doyle
Cornwall: D Wyn Evans
Cumbria: J C Day
Derbyshire: Miss J E Friedman
Devon: D Wyn Evans
Dorset: H E Radford
Durham: Dr A I Doyle
Essex: P R Gifford
Gloucestershire: Miss E M T Markwick
Hampshire: Geoffrey Hampson
Hereford: A Shaw Wright
Humberside: Charles Brook and David Pennie
Isle of Man: Michael R Perkin
Isle of Wight: Geoffrey Hampson
Kent: Peter Richards
Lancashire: B Ashton
Leicestershire: John Feather
Lincolnshire: C Hurst
London (Greater London Area): John E C Palmer (general co-ordinator), Michael F Bywater, Leonard R Payne, Miss Mary Lloyd, Ernest Bush and others
Manchester (Greater): Arthur G Shaw
Merseyside: Michael R Perkin
Norfolk: Philip Hepworth
Northampton: R Julian Roberts
Northumberland: J C Day
Nottingham: Michael Brook
Oxford: Geoffrey Groom
Oxfordshire: Mrs Katherine Swift
Salop: J B Lawson
Somerset: C R Eastwood
Staffordshire: P G Tudor
Suffolk: Mrs A E Birkby
Surrey: Dr R A Christophers
Sussex: A Tapp
Tyne and Wear (N): J C Day
Tyne and Wear (S): Dr A I Doyle
Warwickshire: H S A Smith
West Midland Metropolitan County: Dr B S Benedikz
Wiltshire: Geoffrey Hampson
Worcestershire: A Shaw Wright
Yorkshire (N): David White
Yorkshire (S): Miss J E Friedman
Yorkshire (W): P S Morrish

IRELAND
Northern Ireland: W G Wheeler
Irish Republic: Miss Mary Pollard (general co-ordinator), Miss Norma Jessop and Miss Dilys Bateman

SCOTLAND
Borders: Douglas S Mack
Central: Douglas S Mack
Dumfries and Galloway: D Donaldson, succeeded by J Preston
Edinburgh: Murray C T Simpson
Fife: G D Hargreaves
Grampian: W R MacDonald, succeeded by Mrs M I Anderson-Smith
Highland: T M Gray and M J Cormack
Lothian (excluding Edinburgh): M A Begg
Strathclyde (including Glasgow): J Baldwin and R A Gillespie
Tayside: Dr I Forbes, succeeded by Miss C M Kinnear
Western Isles, Orkney, Shetland: Dr Robert Donaldson

WALES
Dr M I Williams

CHANNEL ISLANDS
John E C Palmer

Index

B

C

D

G

H

I

J

L

M

N

O

S

T

U

V

W

X

Y

Z